THE HISTORY OF THE BRITISH PETROLEUM COMPANY

William Knox D'Arcy c. 1901

THE HISTORY OF
THE BRITISH PETROLEUM
COMPANY

R. W. FERRIER

VOLUME 1
THE DEVELOPING YEARS 1901-1932

CAMBRIDGE UNIVERSITY PRESS

CAMBRIDGE
LONDON   NEW YORK   NEW ROCHELLE
MELBOURNE   SYDNEY

Published by the Press Syndicate of the University of Cambridge
The Pitt Building, Trumpington Street, Cambridge CB2 1RP
32 East 57th Street, New York, NY 10022, USA
296 Beaconsfield Parade, Middle Park, Melbourne 3206, Australia

© The British Petroleum Co. Ltd. 1982

First published 1982

Printed in Great Britain
at the University Press, Cambridge

Library of Congress catalogue card number: 81-18019

British Library Cataloguing in Publication Data
Ferrier, R.W.
The history of The British Petroleum Company.
Vol. 1: The developing years 1901-1932
1. British Petroleum Company—History
I. Title
338.7'6223382 HD9571.9B/
ISBN 0 521 24647 4

CONTENTS

List of tables	page xi
List of illustrations	xiv
Acknowledgements	xvii
Preface	xviii
Maps	xxvi
Note on bibliography	xxix
List of abbreviations	xxx
INTRODUCTION	1

1 THE ACQUISITION OF THE D'ARCY CONCESSION 1901   15
  1 The state of Persia in 1900   15
  2 British interest in Persia   19
  3 Early oil rights in Persia   24
  4 The D'Arcy Concession   27
    (a) Discussions in Paris and London   27
    (b) Negotiations in Tehrān   33
  5 The Contemporary significance of the D'Arcy Concession   42

2 THE FUNDING AND FINDING OF OIL 1901–8   48
  1 D'Arcy on his own 1901–5   48
    (a) Introduction   48
    (b) 'The grammar of Persian affairs' June 1901 – May 1903   50
      (i) Associates and syndicates   50
      (ii) Preparations in Persia   54
    (c) 'Every purse has a limit' May 1903 – July 1904   59
      (i) Searching for finance   59
      (ii) Drilling for oil   62
    (d) The Burmah connection   67
  2 The Concessions Syndicate Ltd 1905–9   72
    (a) Introduction   72

Contents

	(b)	The Bakhtiari Agreement: Khans and guards	74
	(c)	Payment is the crux of the matter 1906	78
	(d)	'The unsettled state of south Persia and danger to the Persian business' 1907	81
	(e)	The discovery of oil at Masjid i-Suleimān in May 1908	86

3 THE FORMATION OF THE ANGLO-PERSIAN OIL COMPANY 1909 — 89
  1 Introduction — 89
  2 Action after the discovery of oil June–November 1908 — 92
  3 The incorporation of the Company November 1908–April 1909 — 97
    (a) Negotiations between D'Arcy and Burmah — 97
    (b) The Agreement — 102
  4 The issue 'a great success' — 104

4 PROGRESS IN PERSIA 1908–14 — 114
  1 Introduction — 114
  2 G.B. Reynolds: Fields General Manager, November 1908–June 1909 — 119
    (a) Preliminary preparations — 119
    (b) Negotiations — 121
      (i) Shaykh Khaz'al — 121
      (ii) The Bakhtiari Khans — 126
  3 Managing Agents — 129
    (a) Lloyd, Scott and Co. Ltd; preparations for production, pipeline and refinery 1909–10 — 129
    (b) Strick, Scott and Co. Ltd 1911–13 — 140
      (i) The visit of Charles Greenway to Persia — 140
      (ii) Agents and managers — 145
      (iii) The refinery on the rocks — 148
  4 Workers, Customs, barges and telephones — 153

5 FUEL OIL AND THE ADMIRALTY 1912–14 — 158
  1 Introduction — 158
  2 Processes, products and markets — 160
  3 Fuel oil and diplomacy — 165
  4 The Company in deep water — 170
  5 Back on course — 175

Contents

		6	Becalmed	183
		7	In port	194

6	THE GOVERNMENT AND THE COMPANY: THE EARLY YEARS 1914–19			202
	1	Introduction		202
	2	Financial objectives and objections		210
		(a)	The early calls on government capital	210
		(b)	Interference and the refinery	214
		(c)	The acquisition of the British Petroleum Company Ltd and the financial dilemma	217
		(d)	Funds for investment	220
	3	The Government, the Company and an oil policy		235
		(a)	Introduction	235
		(b)	Amalgamation — a commercial proposition	237
		(c)	The future of oil supplies — a departmental initiative	243
		(d)	The Petroleum Executive: The Harcourt Committee — a Government policy	247

7	PERSIA — THE SCENE OF OPERATIONS 1914–18			262
	1	Introduction		262
	2	Administration		263
	3	Technical operations		270
		(a)	Production and exploration	270
		(b)	The Ābādān refinery and the war effort	274
		(c)	Geological aspects	282
	4	Marketing		285

8	MANAGEMENT AND FINANCE 1918–28			295
	1	Introduction		295
	2	Post-war developments		298
		(a)	Administration in London	298
		(b)	The managing agents in Persia	306
		(c)	Finance	309
	3	Years of crisis 1921–23		312
		(a)	Management and succession	312
		(b)	The demise of the managing agents	316
		(c)	Finance for 'a gigantic business'	319
	4	The years of improvement 1924–28		333
		(a)	The administration of Cadman	333
		(b)	A better financial footing	341
	5	Conclusion		348

Contents

9	GOVERNMENT AND CONCESSIONARY RELATIONS 1919–26	350
	1 Introduction	350
	2 Clarifying the issues 1919–20	352
	(a) The letter and the spirit of the Treasury assurances	352
	(b) Confusion over Mesopotamia	355
	3 Coming to terms with Persia	358
	(a) Negotiations in Tehrān	358
	(b) The Armitage-Smith Agreement	365
	4 Changing government relations	371
	(a) Burmah rocks the boat	371
	(b) The Government makes up its mind	378
	5 The changing situation in Persia	386
	(a) Introduction	386
	(b) The imposition of central authority	388
10	TECHNICAL ACTIVITIES: YEARS OF ENDEAVOUR AND ACHIEVEMENT 1918–32	397
	1 Introduction	397
	2 Exploration and production in Persia: years of endeavour 1918–24	402
	3 Years of accomplishment 1924–32	412
	(a) Improvements and innovation	412
	(b) Success in exploration	425
	4 The Ābādān Refinery	429
	5 The pipeline	445
	6 The dredging of the Shatt-al-'Arab	449
	7 Research	452
11	DOWNSTREAM ACTIVITIES 1919–28	461
	1 Introduction	461
	2 Consolidation	464
	3 Expansion	490
	4 Rationalisation	507
	5 Overseas markets	514
	(a) Persia	514
	(b) Iraq	520
	(c) Australia	522
	6 Shipping	525

Contents

12	THE EXPANSION OF INTERNATIONAL INTERESTS 1919—28	538
	1 Introduction	538
	2 Third parties	542
	3 A forward policy	547
	(a) Introduction	547
	(b) Albania and the Italian Government	548
	(c) South America and the Government connection	551
	(d) Arabian concessions and Government provisions	561
	4 The north Persian concession	570
	5 Mesopotamia	580
13	THE IMPORTANCE OF THE PERSIAN DIMENSION 1926—32	588
	1 Introduction	588
	2 A new direction	591
	(a) A resident director in Tehrān	591
	(b) The possibility of partnership	599
	3 Revising the Concession	603
	(a) Setting up the pieces	603
	(b) The opening gambit	607
	(c) Delayed moves	610
	(d) The middle game	612
	(e) Stalemate	616
	(f) Another game	619
	(g) Checkmate	622
	CONCLUSION	632
	APPENDICES	637
0.1	World crude oil production 1900—32 (thousands of tons)	638
1.1	The D'Arcy Concession 1901	640
3.1	Definition of financial terms and an explanation of the basis of the consolidated accounts	643
6.1	The Bradbury letter 1914	645
6.2	Members of the Harcourt Committee 1918	646
8.1	The administration of the Anglo-Persian Oil Company November 1921	647
8.2	The administration of the Anglo-Persian Oil Company December 1930	648
8.3	Anglo Persian Oil Company organisation 1930	649
8.4	Directors of the Anglo-Persian Oil Company 1909 to 1932	650
8.5	Oil company dividends on ordinary shares 1913—32	652

Contents

9.1	The Armitage-Smith Agreement 1920	653
10.1	Anglo-Persian Oil Company staff and labour in Persia 1919–27 (a) Ābādān (b) Fields (c) Ahwāz and on the pipeline	659
10.2	Schedule of test wells drilled in Persia 1901–32 (excluding drilling at Masjid i-Suleimān and Haft Kel)	660
10.3	Sunbury research staff 1917–32	662
11.1	Anglo-Persian Oil Company group sales 1920–32 – benzine	663
11.2	Anglo-Persian Oil Company group sales 1920–32 – kerosine	665
11.3	Anglo-Persian Oil Company group sales 1920–32 – fuel oil	667
11.4	Anglo-Persian Oil Company group sales 1920–32 – gas oil	669
11.5	Anglo-Persian Oil Company group volume and proportions 1920–32 – benzine	671
11.6	Anglo-Persian Oil Company group volume and proportions 1920–32 – kerosine	671
11.7	Anglo-Persian Oil Company group volume and proportions 1920–32 – fuel oil	672
11.8	Anglo-Persian Oil Company group volume and proportions 1920–32 – gas oil	672
11.9	Anglo-Persian Oil Company group refinery throughputs 1920–32 – benzine	673
11.10	Anglo-Persian Oil Company group refinery throughputs 1920–32 – kerosine	673
11.11	Anglo-Persian Oil Company group refinery throughputs 1920–32 – gas oil and fuel oil	674
11.12	United Kingdom fuel oil and coal prices 1918–32	675
11.13	World tonnage and proportion of coal and oil used in vessels (1000 tons and over) 1914–32	674
11.14	Tanker tonnage (over 1000 tons) and merchant vessels (over 100 tons) under construction 1921–32 (a) World (b) United Kingdom	676
11.15	The Anglo-Persian Oil Company group overseas refinery throughput 1924–32 (a) Courchelettes refinery (Douai) 1924–32 (b) Alwand refinery 1927–32 (c) Laverton refinery 1924–32	678
11.16	The Anglo-Persian Oil Company group United Kingdom refinery throughput 1921–32 (a) Llandarcy refinery 1921–32 (b) Grangemouth refinery 1924–32	679
11.17	United Kingdom petroleum imports 1918–32	681
11.18	London petrol prices retail per gallon (first grade) 1918–32	682
11.19	United Kingdom inland consumption of petroleum products 1900–32	683
11.20	British Tanker Company cargo movements in owned and period chartered tonnage 1921	684
11.21	British Tanker Company cargo movements in owned and period chartered tonnage 1928	685
11.22	Shipping administration of the British Tanker Company 1930	686
C.1	World energy consumption in selected countries 1925	687

Biographical details of important personalities   688
Notes   698
Index   776

TABLES

4.1	Anglo-Persian Oil Company staff and labour in Persia 1911	page 154
5.1	Statement of source and application of funds of the Anglo-Persian Oil Company group 1909–13	186
5.2	Liquidity position of the Anglo-Persian Oil Company group 1910–15	187
5.3	Statement of source and application of funds of the Anglo-Persian Oil Company group for the year ended 31 March 1913	188
5.4	Statement of source and application of funds of the Anglo-Persian Oil Company group for the year ended 31 March 1914	189
5.5	Estimated expenditure and profit in the prospectus 1909	191
5.6	Statement of source and application of funds of the Anglo-Persian Oil Company group for the year ended 31 March 1915	192
6.1	Statement of source and application of funds of the Anglo-Persian Oil Company group 1914–19	224
6.2	Issues of shares and debentures by the Anglo-Persian Oil Company group 1909–23	225
6.3	Fixed assets and depreciation of the Anglo-Persian Oil Company group 1914–19	226
6.4	Increase in fixed assets of the Anglo-Persian Oil Company group 1914–19	226
6.5	Distribution of fixed assets by activity of the Anglo-Persian Oil Company group 1909–19	227
6.6	Anglo-Persian Oil Company group financial performance 1914–19	231
6.7	Anglo-Persian Oil Company — sources of income 1915–28	233
6.8	Anglo-Persian Oil Company trading account — income from sales, volume of sales and profits on sales and services 1916–28	234
6.9	Liquidity position of the Anglo-Persian Oil Company group 1914–19	236
7.1	Anglo-Persian Oil Company production of crude oil and drilling activity 1911–19	271
7.2	Anglo-Persian Oil Company staff and labour in Persia 1910–16	276
7.3	Ābādān Refinery output of products 1912–19	278
7.4	Supplies of products to Admiralty and Mesopotamian forces 1914–20	289

List of tables

8.1	Statement of source and application of funds of the Anglo-Persian Oil Company group 1919–24	325
8.2	Ownership of ordinary shares of the Anglo-Persian Oil Company 1909–23	326
8.3	Anglo-Persian Oil Company group financial performance 1919–24	326
8.4	Fixed assets and depreciation of the Anglo-Persian Oil Company group 1919–24	328
8.5	Distribution of fixed assets by activity of the Anglo-Persian Oil Company group 1919–24	329
8.6	Increase in fixed assets of the Anglo-Persian Oil Company group 1919–24	330
8.7	Liquidity position of the Anglo-Persian Oil Company group 1920–24	334
8.8	Statement of source and application of funds of the Anglo-Persian Oil Company group 1924–28	342
8.9	Increase in fixed assets of the Anglo-Persian Oil Company group 1924–28	343
8.10	Distribution of fixed assets by activity of the Anglo-Persian Oil Company group 1924–28	344
8.11	Liquidity position of the Anglo-Persian Oil Company group 1924–28	345
8.12	Anglo-Persian Oil Company group financial performance 1924–28	347
9.1	Anglo-Persian Oil Company crude oil production and royalty statistics 1918–25	370
10.1	Anglo-Persian Oil Company staff and labour in Persia 1919–32	401
10.2	Fields production costs per ton 1920–26	415
10.3	Ābādān Refinery throughput and production 1919–32	431
10.4	Anglo-Persian Oil Company group refinery costs per ton 1923–28 (a) Ābādān (b) Llandarcy (c) Grangemouth	442
11.1	Anglo-Persian Oil Company fuel oil sales 1922–32 (a) Admiralty contract (b) Burmah Oil Company	474
11.2	British Petroleum Company fixed assets 1918–28 at historic cost	484
11.3	Anglo-Persian Oil Company group refinery availability of products 1924	491
11.4	Anglo-Persian Oil Company group estimated products demand 1924	492
11.5	British Petroleum Company motor spirit distribution costs per gallon 1924–28	504
11.6	Anglo-Persian Oil Company group forward market position from May 1927 to 1932	505
11.7	Cost of Anglo-Persian Oil Company group staffing 1918	526
11.8	Shipping movements of the British Tanker Company, main cargo routes (a) Trading pattern 1921 (b) Trading pattern 1928	528
11.9	Typical British Tanker Company running costs 1922	530

List of tables

11.10	Numbers of steam turbine and motor driven ships, and steam reciprocating vessels in three of the principal oil company tanker fleets 1931	534
11.11	Growth of the British Tanker Company fleet 1921–31 in terms of numbers of vessels and deadweight tons	536
12.1	Financial comparison of oil companies 1920 and 1927 in terms of total assets	543
12.2	Anglo-Persian Oil Company group exploration expenditure in areas 1918–28	549
12.3	Oil production in South America 1920 and 1929	552
13.1	Anglo-Persian Oil Company crude production and royalty statistics 1925 to 1931	601
13.2	Persian annual average exchange rates and parity 1900–31	611
13.3	Persian Government revenues 1923–29	617
13.4	Value of total Persian visible exports and oil exports 1913–32	629

ILLUSTRATIONS

Maps

1	Middle East 1932	*page* xxvi
2	Centres of concessionary activity 1928	xxvii
3	The Transferred territories 1914	xxviii

Figures

0.1	World crude oil production 1900–32 (millions of tons)	2
6.1	Growth of fixed assets of the Anglo-Persian Oil Company group 1909–28	228–9
10.1	Oil production, Masjid i-Suleimān	404–5
10.2	Cross-section and contour map showing oil and gas levels	411
10.3	Standard cable tool drilling rig	416
10.4	Inclined oil-gas separator 1930	421
10.5	Batch and bench stills *c.* 1912	439
10.6	Crude oil distillation	440
10.7	Fractionating tower	441
11.1a	The growth of the Anglo-Persian Oil Company group sales of main products 1920–32	467
11.1b	The volume of the Anglo-Persian Oil Company group sales of main products 1920–32	468
11.2	Sales — Det Forenede Olie Kompagni (Denmark) 1922–32	472
11.3	Sales — Norsk Braendselolje (Norway) 1922–32	473
11.4	Sales — L'Alliance Société Anonyme (Belgium) 1922–32	478
11.5	Sales — Société Générale des Huiles de Pétrole (France) 1921–32	480–1
11.6	Sales — British Petroleum Company 1922–31	486
11.7	Sales — British Petroleum Company, Ireland, 1924–31	493
11.8	Sales — Benzina Petroleum (Italy) 1925–32	495
11.9	Sales — Oestereichische Naphta Import Gesellschaft (Austria) 1924–32	496
11.10	Sales — Benzin-und Petroleum Aktien Gesellschaft (Switzerland) 1925–32	497
11.11	Sales — 'Olex' Deutsche Petroleum-Verkaufsgesellschaft MBH (Germany) 1926–32	498
11.12	Sales — Benzine en Petroleum Handel Maatschapij N.V. (Holland) 1926–32	499

List of illustrations

11.13	Sales — Svenska BP (Sweden) 1927–32	499
11.14	Sources of United Kingdom petroleum imports 1918–32 (millions of tons)	515
11.15	Sales — Anglo-Persian Oil Company in Persia 1918–32	516–17
11.16	Sales — Anglo-Persian Oil Company in Iraq 1924–32, ex Ābādān and from Khanaqin Oil Company from February 1927	521
11.17	Sales — Commonwealth Oil Refineries 1924–32	524
12.1	D'Arcy Exploration Company expenditure 1916–28	553
13.1	US average crude oil and gasoline prices 1918–32	613

Photographs

William Knox D'Arcy c.1901	ii
W.K. D'Arcy and family at Rockhampton, Queensland c.1885	30
Edouard Cotte and General Antoine Kitabgi, Tehrān 1901	32
Alfred L. Marriott 1901	34
Amīn al-Sultān c.1900	37
Baku c.1900	47
Sir Boverton Redwood c.1910	49
G.B. Reynolds, Crush and Willans c.1909	55
Chīāh Surkh no. 1 well 1903	57
C.B. Rosenplaenter 1903	63
Azīz Khān and Karim Khān, with followers 1903	66
Bakhtiari Khans with Sardār Assad centre c.1905	75
'Alī Murād Khān 1907	84
Working on the road to Masjid i-Suleimān 1907	86
The Directors of the Anglo-Persian Oil Company 1909	108–9
The Prospectus of the Anglo-Persian Oil Company 1909	111
Masjid i-Suleimān 1908	114
Masjid i-Suleimān 1909	120
The mud flats of Ābādān 1909	122
Shaykh Khaz'al centre with Hājjī Ra'īs on his left 1909	124
ss *Anatolia*, first vessel alongside Ābādān 1909	131
Sternwheeler on the River Kārūn 1910	131
Transporting pipe by jimms 1910	132
Laying the pipeline 1910	133
John Black, C.A. Walpole, N.C. Ramsay and T.L. Jacks 1910	136
Payday at Masjid i-Suleimān 1910	138
Taking tank sections to Masjid i-Suleimān 1910	138
Office of Strick, Scott and Co. Ltd, Muhammara 1912	141
Charles Greenway in Persia 1911	142
Early bench of stills, Ābādān 1913	150
Barges on the River Kārūn 1910	156
Members of the Admiralty Commission in Persia 1913	194
Evening News cartoon 18 June 1914	200
Government directors of the Anglo-Persian Oil Company 1914–32	208–9
Sir John Cadman 1918	251
The staff of Strick, Scott and Co. Ltd, Muhammara 1917	266
Fording the River Tembi, early 1920s	269
Mr Bradshaw in his 'buggy' near Masjid i-Suleimān 1908	269

List of illustrations

The mudding off of F7, Masjid i-Suleimān 1926	270
The research laboratory, Sunbury 1918 with Dr A.E. Dunstan and Dr F.B. Thole	277
An aerial view of Ābādān 1918	281
Unloading a boiler at Qishm Island 1914	283
B.F.N. Macrorie, middle centre, with his wife to his right and H.G. Busk in front 1915	283
The *British Emperor*, delivered in 1916	293
Managing Directors of the Anglo-Persian Oil Company 1919–32	300-1
Britannic House nearing completion 1924	304
Sir Arnold Wilson and Sir Percy Loraine 1924	387
Rizā Khān with his entourage and Company officials at Dar-i-Khazineh 1925	393
Head of the military guard, Masjid i-Suleimān 1924	395
Bakhtiari tribesmen in the workshops at Masjid i-Suleimān 1914	401
An outcrop of the Asmari Limestone	407
The floor of a 'standard' cable tool type percussion rig 1924	417
A rotary type rig showing turntable and stem 1924	418
Masjid i-Suleimān from the main office 1926	419
'The Golden Stairs' road to Gach Sārān 1925	423
The water pumping station at Godar Landar 1926	424
Transport at Masjid i-Suleimān 1924	425
Professor Hugo de Böckh (left) and G.M. Lees 1925	426
Young Persian apprentices at Masjid i-Suleimān 1924	433
A football match at Masjid i-Suleimān 1924	434
A regatta on the lake by the Tembi power station 1924	434
A fancy dress party at Ābādān 1924	435
Medical officers and hospital staff with Dr Young, centre left 1926	435
The ending of a shift, Ābādān 1926	444
Aerial view of Ābādān 1930	445
The pipeline on the Imām Rezā slope c. 1924	446
Turbine-driven centrifugal pump, Tembi station 1926	447
River transport and offloading facilities at Dar-i-Khazineh 1926	448
Railway marshalling yards, Dar-i-Khazineh 1926	449
Directors of Société Générale des Huiles de Pétrole and members of the Board of the Anglo-Persian Oil Company at the Wembley Exhibition 1924	479
British Petroleum Company bulk delivery vehicles, Barton depot 1926	483
Kerbside pump in France 1924	489
Pump installation in Germany 1926	490
Two BP adverts 1923	501-2
BP advert using Malcolm Campbell 1927	503
Launching of the *British Aviator*, by Lady Greenway on 20 May 1924	533
Oil rigs of the Anglo-Persian Oil Company in the Comodoro Rivadavia area, Argentina 1924	559
The Key to the Future, *New York American*, 14 November 1921	574
From left to right, A.W.M. Robertson, L. Lockhart, Mustafa Fateh and W.C. Fairley, Tehrān 1926	593
H.E. Tīmurtash, Persian Minister of Court, seventh from left, being greeted by Sir John Cadman, far right, at Waterloo Station 27 July 1928	602

ACKNOWLEDGEMENTS

Acknowledgements are made to the Chairman and Board of the British Petroleum Company for their authorisation to quote and make reference to the archives of the Company and for the use of diagrams and figures from 'Our Industry' (1977); The Keeper, Public Record Office; The Librarian, India Office Library; The Archivist, Department of Archives, French Foreign Ministry for permission to quote from government sources; Appleton-Century-Crofts Inc. for the use of a diagram from Kendall Beaton, *Enterprise in Oil, A History of Shell in the United States*; the Business History Foundation for George Sweet-Gibb and Evelyn Knowlton, *The Resurgent Years, 1911-1927*, Harper and Row (New York, 1971), for financial statistics of oil company total assets; Julian Barrier and the Oxford University Press for tables of annual average exchange rates and parity and value of total Persian visible exports and oil exports from *Economic Development in Iran 1900-1970*, (Oxford, 1971); J.G. McLean and R.W. Haigh and Harvard University Press for a diagram of US average crude oil and gasoline prices 1918-32 from *The Growth of Integrated Oil Companies* (Boston, 1954); Joel Darmstadter and Johns Hopkins Press for energy consumption statistics from *Energy in the World Economy, A Statistical Review of Trends in Output, Trade and Consumption since 1925* (Baltimore, 1971); Editor, *Petroleum Almanac* for crude oil production figures; Editor, Journal of the Royal Statistical Society for data on UK consumption of petroleum products 1900-32; Editor, Colliery Year Book and Coal Trades Directory for coal prices 1918-32; Editor, *Petroleum Times* for tanker tonnage statistics 1921-32; Editor, Oil and Petroleum Yearbook for data on dividends and shares 1913-32; Department of Energy for sources of UK petroleum imports 1918-32 from *Statistical Digest* (London, 1950); Institute of Petroleum for London petrol prices 1918-32; Lloyds Register of Shipping for statistics of world shipping tonnage and the proportion of coal and oil-fired vessels 1914-32, and those of steam turbine and motor driven ships and steam reciprocating vessels, 1931.

PREFACE

In the twentieth century the role of energy has been important in a previously unprecedented manner. Human intellect and ingenuity have produced and controlled the energies required for, and resulting from, the splitting, fusion and fissuring of the elemental structure of atoms. Improving the mobility of mankind by the utilisation of oil has revolutionised the modes of travel on land, sea and in the sky. Journeys which formerly took days of difficulty are now easily accomplished in minutes. Oil, once a substance of mystical medicinal properties and practical application in brick bonding and ship caulking, has become not only an essential fuel in the provision of energy, but has also through its chemical constituents contributed decisively to broadening the scope of the chemical industry. Synthesising processes applied to oil derivatives have resulted in changes of living styles through the use of plastics.

No less important than the technical and social aspects of the oil age has been the economic and political fallout. The possession of oil, or the lack of it, has had a significant impact upon national economies and international relations. Neglected areas that were arid deserts, have been transformed by the discovery of oil. The natural accumulation of oil, often remote from the centres of consumption, has inevitably lead to transportation movements on a vast global scale of matching products to requirements. Moreover because local sources of finance were frequently inadequate, industrial facilities unprovided and manpower unavailable, the exploitation of such oil resources was undertaken on a concessional basis. Capital demands were high, technology expensive, equipment specialised and skilled engineers and chemists in short supply, so industrial strength has tended to be concentrated in relatively few enterprises possessing the necessary funds, expertise and management. It is perhaps ironical that many of the areas in which oil has been found already felt themselves 'deprived' or 'exploited'. Thus in many cases existing national stresses and strains were exacerbated by the intrusion of foreign interests upon terms that were regarded as intrinsically unfair.

The diversity of oil discoveries, national differences and varying com-

Preface

mercial responses has resulted in distinctive patterns of corporate growth within the oil industry. If business history means more than the examination of a sequence of robots along a conveyor belt, that numbing experience of mass production so movingly portrayed in Chaplin's *Modern Times*, then it is necessary to appreciate the individual characteristics of firms as they have emerged from the interaction of events, the environment in which they have operated and the cross play of personalities which have influenced them. Only in this way is it possible to plot the trends and spot the idiosyncracies which make up the historical pattern. It is, therefore, in this spirit that the history of British Petroleum has been undertaken.

Much of the history of the oil industry has been taken with a wide angle lens. There are, indeed, many vantage points from which to survey the oil scene from the beginning of the century, ranging from technical, concessionary, geographical, social, commercial, labour relations, economic, cultural, strategic and political aspects, amongst the most prominent. There seems, however, space for the study of a particular participant in the oil industry, a close-up view of a single company whose own development may not only be interesting in itself, but may be illuminating in comparison with other companies, so contributing to an understanding of the process, pace and complexities of economic change in the twentieth century within one important industry.

Moreover, whilst recognising the growth and prominence of the Company since its formation and the significant impact upon it of the principal personalities associated with it in senior management or government circles, from foreign representatives to competing businessmen, it must be realised that from the subtle alchemy of thousands of individual relationships, a distinctive corporate identity has evolved. It is easy with hindsight to touch up an historical portrait, but this must be resisted in favour of a series of 'snaps' which more convincingly convey contemporary authenticity. The interaction of the skills, experience and temperaments of engineers and secretaries, chemists and mariners, accountants and labourers, drillers and drivers from different countries employed by the same company becomes an expression of its character. Intellectual curiosity, technical challenge, personal ambition or indifference, good luck or misfortune stimulated some and restrained others. Many were anxious for promotion, others spurned responsibility. The majority of the members of the Company were ordinary people shunning the limelight of the more obviously successful, anonymous but indispensable with a place in the corporate role of honour. Their services must not be ignored in the historical balance sheet nor neglected in favour of the more readily available quantifiable sets of accounts.

Preface

Such, therefore, is the justification for this history of British Petroleum which will comprise three volumes. The present volume generally covers the period, 1901-32, dealing with the initial concessionary situation of the Anglo-Persian Oil Company (the Company as it is consistently called in the text), from its formation in 1909 to work the concession granted by the Persian Government to W.K. D'Arcy in 1901 till the cancellation of that concession in 1932. The second volume will be concerned with the revised concessionary position, 1933-54, of the Anglo-Iranian Oil Company, the same company, having changed its name in accordance with the decrees of the Persian Government in March 1935, and to the British Petroleum Company Limited in the aftermath of the nationalisation of the oil industry by the Persian Government in 1951. The third volume will cover more recent times, 1954-73, after the Company lost its privileged concessionary position in Persia and, as British Petroleum, in an age of changing traditional oil concessionary arrangements became committed to an increasing diversification of interests.

The intention is not so much to illustrate any particular theory of economic growth or political relationships, but to place in historical context the corporate biography of one large oil company. This may perhaps disappoint particular specialists, since it is impossible to be completely comprehensive and yet detailed enough to satisfy all who might be interested. Yet, even if all the aspects that might be expected to be treated in sufficient depth were included to meet with the approval of some readers, it might disappoint others. There are, for example, those principally interested in the changing relations between the industrialised and the developing countries and for whom technical or commercial considerations are so much dross compared to refinements of political and economic affairs. They would expect the fullest possible treatment of the concessionary situation between the Company and the Persian Government.

Others more concerned with the factors stimulating or impeding economic growth as it expresses itself in the development of multinational enterprises are more interested in identifying managerial concepts, administrative practices and market forces. Others again, fascinated by the impact of technology on commercial success or failure may expect a more formal analysis of the Company's technical attainments. In volume 2, however, there will be a more detailed account of the financial affairs of the Company in relation to its revenue and expenditure, both on a functional basis and in respect of its overall trading results. Industrial relations, too, in Persia and elsewhere throughout the duration of the concessionary period to 1951 will be studied in more depth there in a separate chapter. Similarly, because of the economic situation of the period, a more comprehensive treatment of the aspects of the supply and distribution in the international

Preface

markets is also reserved for the second volume in order to relate the trading arrangements between some of the major oil companies envisaged in the Achnacarry Agreement of 1928 to counter surplus production and declining prices, the effects of the Depression Years and the revival of demand in the 1930s.

The aim has been to maintain a balance which reflects the relative importance of the main elements of the Company's development as perceived in contemporary terms by those principally involved. The historian should explain what happened in so far as the evidence permits. In this respect there has been a definite attempt to utilise as much as possible of the Company's documentation which has survived the misfortunes of time, accident or destruction. Insistence on this, however, has not been to the detriment of other original historical material, such as state papers or the press. Secondary sources, where relevant, have been consulted, but greatest emphasis has been placed on the overall importance of contemporary references. Business history has suffered from the failure to preserve internally generated archival sources, without which an incomplete picture of industry appears. It is to little purpose that businessmen complain of misrepresentation when they pay so little attention to preserving the records of their own achievements. Unfortunately the archives of the Company are by no means as complete as their importance would merit. With a due sense of responsibility the Board of BP has decided to make them available for bona fide historical research on the completion of this history.

The decision of the Chairman and Board to authorise the writing of a history of the group was taken without any strings attached. In order to safeguard the independence of the history and guarantee the integrity of the historian, no less than that of the Company, the then Chairman, Sir David Steel, appointed an Editorial Advisory Committee to help him in the choice of the historian and assist in consultation during the compilation of the history. The original Committee consisted of:

Chairman Sir David Steel, Chairman BP
      The late Sir Maurice Bridgeman, formerly Chairman BP 1962–9
      Professor Alfred D. Chandler, Jr, Straus Professor of Business History, Harvard University
      Professor D.C. Coleman, formerly Professor of Economic History, Cambridge University
      Professor P. Mathias, Chichele Professor of Economic History, Oxford University
      Lord Robbins, past President British Academy
and successive Company Secretaries, D.A.G. Sarre and J.E. Wedgbury.

Preface

It would be difficult to express with sufficient gratitude my appreciation of the interest, support, and critical advice of the members of the Editorial Advisory Committee. The scope and scale of the undertaking is vast and it would have been easy to have lost oneself, mistaking the outlines of the wood for the detail of the trees. Conflicts of interest might have occurred over the requests of the historian and the claims of confidentiality. This situation has never arisen. There have been no restrictions at all on access to papers or people, no suggestions implied or direct about the treatment of any issue in a particular manner. There has been an absolute freedom to deal with the subject matter as the historian has thought right. Whilst sincerely grateful for advice and information generously and impartially given by many, the ultimate responsibility for what has been included and the manner in which it has been expressed is that of the historian alone.

This does not imply any exclusive rights to any credits. The writing of history should bear no copyright and confer no unique distinction. In the search for understanding, historians are sustained by the faith and practices of their own profession whilst recognising the heresies of some of their companions along the way. Acknowledging influences and assistance does not imply either lack of confidence or excess of pride, but recognition of mutual interests and sympathy. Amongst those to whom I am indebted are Professor Vivian Galbraith, who once decisively entered the historical lists on my behalf, Professor Charles Wilson, who supervised an incipient interest in economic history and introduced me to BP, Dr Laurence Lockhart with whom I shared an interest in Persian history long before I knew of his connection with the Company, Professor Rose Greaves, an early guide, who stimulated a fascination for the Company's history and contributed much to it which I gratefully acknowledge and Sir Maurice Bridgeman, whose apparently imperturbable manner concealed warmth, humour and much information, which he freely communicated to me when I knew little about the oil industry.

Many members of the Company have spoken to me about the period covered in this volume of the Company's history: Lister-James conveyed to me impressions of the earlier geologists and the visit of the Admiralty Commission to Persia. M.C. Seamark, the first English driller in Persia who arrived in 1913 shared his memories; Peter Cox, geologist and later managing director of the D'Arcy Exploration Company, with friendship and understanding put the exploratory activities of the Company into perspective; J.M. Pattinson, whose experience of the Company's affairs spanned his time as engineer in Persia to being Deputy Chairman in London, has shown, with his wife Peggy, the closest interest and encouragement; Sir Harold Snow, whose personal kindness made me feel at home in a large company: Julius Edwardes was always most considerate.

Preface

Many others in the various ways, like Sir Eric Berthoud, G.W. Colvill, J.W. Dix, S.E. Evans, N.L. Falcon, Robert Gillespie, J.H. Jackson, Alec Joseph, E.R.G. Northcroft, L.A. Pym, A.W.M. Robertson, P. Saunders, S. Taylor, A.T. Wright, Hans Zollinger have helped with reminiscences, and many others whom I have met and talked with about the early history of the Company on numberless occasions. Denys Cadman spoke affectionately and objectively about his father. Lady Teresa Briscoe recalled with pleasure family reminiscences of her grandfather, W.K. D'Arcy. T.A.B. Corley at Reading University was very helpful over earlier documentation from the Burmah Oil Company archives which Sir Alastair Down, Chairman of the Burmah Oil Company, gave me permission to consult. In deference to Mr Corley, who is writing the history of Burmah, I have included only the minimal information on Burmah which is relevant.

Relations with the Persian Government are of exceptional importance in the affairs of the Company but it would be presumptuous to claim to have unravelled them completely. I hope that as a result of living three years in Persia before I became at all concerned with oil matters, I have acquired a more appreciative understanding of the Persian character than I might otherwise have possessed. Not only amongst Persian friends over many years but subsequently in conversations with scholars from different countries, the history of Persia has been a constant interest to which I have previously made a contribution in respect of its relations with European countries in the seventeenth and eighteenth centuries. It is impossible to refer to all those with whom I have discussed the Company's involvement with Persia, but I cannot omit Professor A.K.S. Lambton, who over a number of years has kindly and patiently commented on drafts of articles and shared her knowledge of Persian history, and Dr R.M. Burrell, for his unstinting and always friendly and unassuming help on many historical matters. The late Sir Roger Stevens and Sir Denis Wright, both ambassadors to Persia, brought a diplomatic dimension to my interest in Persian affairs. The late Mustafa Fateh provided a well informed Persian view of the Company and his country.

Such a historical exercise requires much supporting assistance. The Company's archivists, firstly under Anne Harper and more recently under Carl Newton and Daphne Knott, have supplied an enviable service of retrieval and referencing and brought sense into archival disorder. Andrew Harper, who acquired a wide knowledge of the early commercial and management archives, Ann Challinor, who was pertinacious in searching the Public Record Office and India Office for relevant Government papers, have since moved to other posts in the Company. Julian Bowden has become an authority on the documentation of Mesopotamia

Preface

and has displayed a skill in statistical presentation. John Hooper has shown not only the value of having a chemist as technical adviser, but as a scientist has a real flair for historical research and respect for sources. Robert Brown, for a short time has been researching into marketing activities. Ann Ewing who has just recently been researching into the British Government's interest in the oil industry has also saved me from certain stylistic pitfalls. To Dick Roberts, my first research assistant and now lecturer at Sussex University, I am indebted for much original research into the financial affairs of the Company, his painstaking investigation into depreciation, sources and application of funds, interpretation of financial schedules and his consolidation of group accounts in a manner never previously attempted, for which he is responsible. His collaboration and friendship have meant more than just his exceptional ability. His brother, David, out of fraternal solicitude and professional interest generously made more than his expertise available. Cyril Shaw has kindly made sure that financial terminology and approach have been compatible with modern Company accounting procedures and Graham Boutle and his colleagues have also helped. Edward Platt, mariner turned historian, has made an invaluable contribution to the history of the tanker company. He has been ably assisted by Keith Taggart on the economics and administration of ship operations and much encouraged by G.A.B. King, until recently managing director of the British Shipping Company (formerly British Petroleum Tanker Company Limited). Fren Förster over the years has shared my interest in the Company's history, as his own account of BP and its antecedents in Germany well shows. My wife has been very helpful in translating Persian sources.

The handling of correspondence, scheduling of meetings, filing, typing, correction of drafts, keeping track of tapes and the many other enhanced secretarial responsibilities in looking after the requirements of myself and research assistants have been admirably managed by two successive secretaries. Christine Hill, who most capably started the ball rolling, left in March 1980 for personal reasons. Since then Kay Underdown has not only mastered the intricacies of word processing, in which she is ably assisted by Jenny Tyler, but coped magnificently with schedules and deadlines. Sue Pedlar has admirably dealt with the preparation of chapters for the Cambridge University Press, attended to the checking of drafts, footnotes, tables, maps, diagrams, appendices and so forth, no less than tracking down lost references and correcting spellings that have gone astray. Audrey King was ever helpful over photographs. Michael Willis, John Daffey and Richard Clisby gave helpful advice over the technical aspects of word processing and coding. Michael Stephens and John Stillwell have seen to the maps and diagrams with care and Carol McGrail has

Preface

helped with histograms and organigrams. John Unwin of Overs Ltd. has ably seen the typescript into print. Others, including those from associated companies acknowledged but not mentioned, will, I hope obtain a personal satisfaction from recognising their varied assistance.

Dr Colin Day at the Cambridge University Press was more than helpful and considerate in the preliminary discussions over publishing. The Syndics agreed to accept the history at their own risk without any prior conditions and I have been grateful for that early mark of confidence. William Davies has more recently taken charge as editor and his cooperation has been appreciated. On the design side John Trevitt has been unsparing in his attention and I could not have wished for better professional judgement. Francis Brooke has been patient over a deadline that slipped and sub-edited with care, Lyn Chatterton has ably handled a difficult production schedule. It is a privilege to record appreciatively the informative archival assistance of the staff of the Public Records Office, the India Office Library, the National Maritime Museum, L'Archive de Ministère des Affaires Etrangères and the National Archives of the United States and to acknowledge permission to quote. I am grateful to the librarians of the Petroleum Institute, the Cambridge University Library, London University Library, the Guildhall Library, the London Library, the Institute of Historical Research, Lloyds and the many who so helpfully replied to enquiries for information.

There are two final acknowledgements. Without the personal commitment and interest of Sir David Steel, this history might never have been started or the conditions existed in which it could be successfully completed. I am sincerely grateful for his encouragement and his trust. Lastly there is a tendency for those absorbed in a challenge to lose some sense of proportion in a busy life. If I have offended in this respect, I ask the forgiveness of my family. They have certainly shared in the writing of this volume not only in my presence but perhaps more in my absence from them.

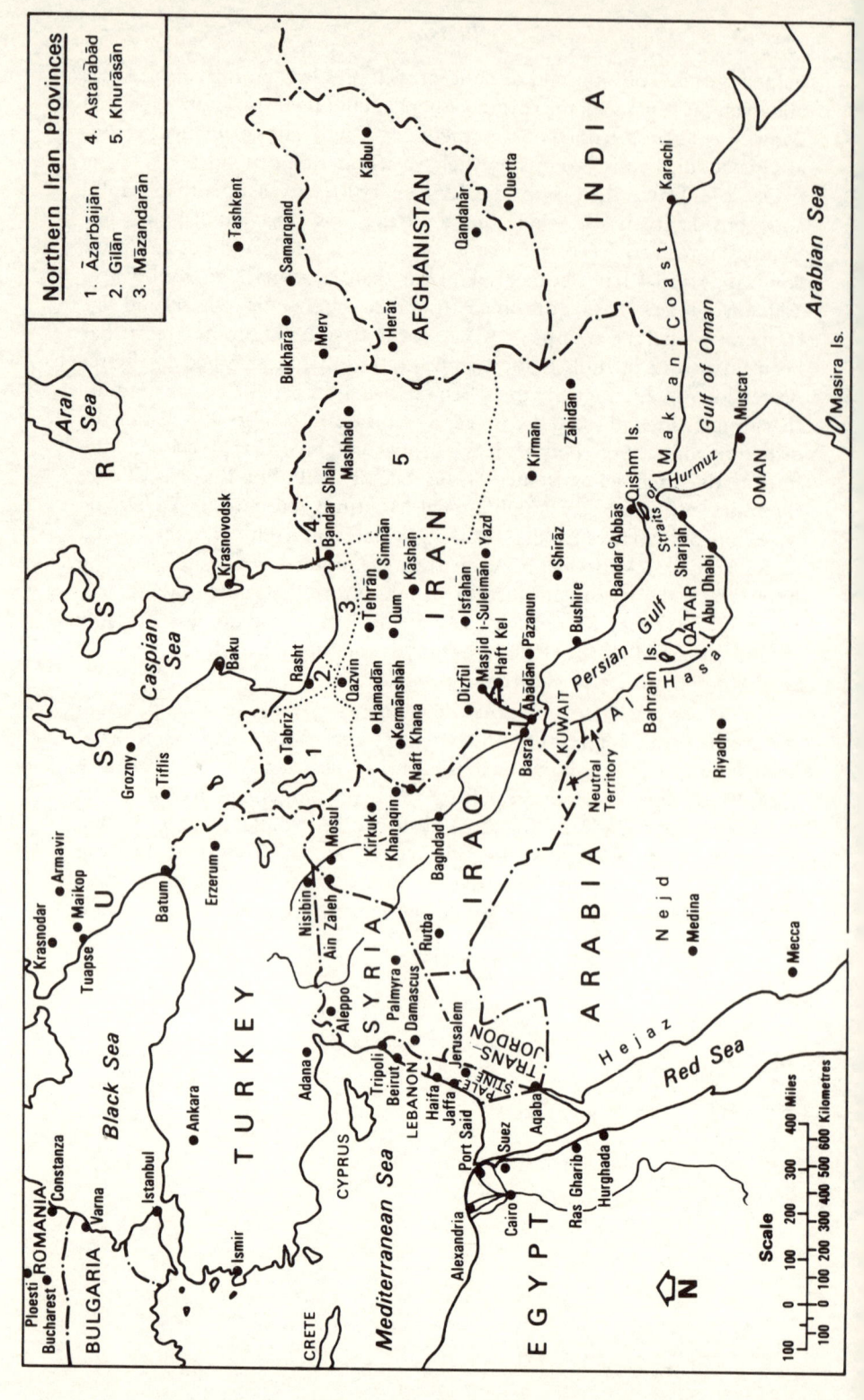

Centres of concessionary activity 1928

xxvii

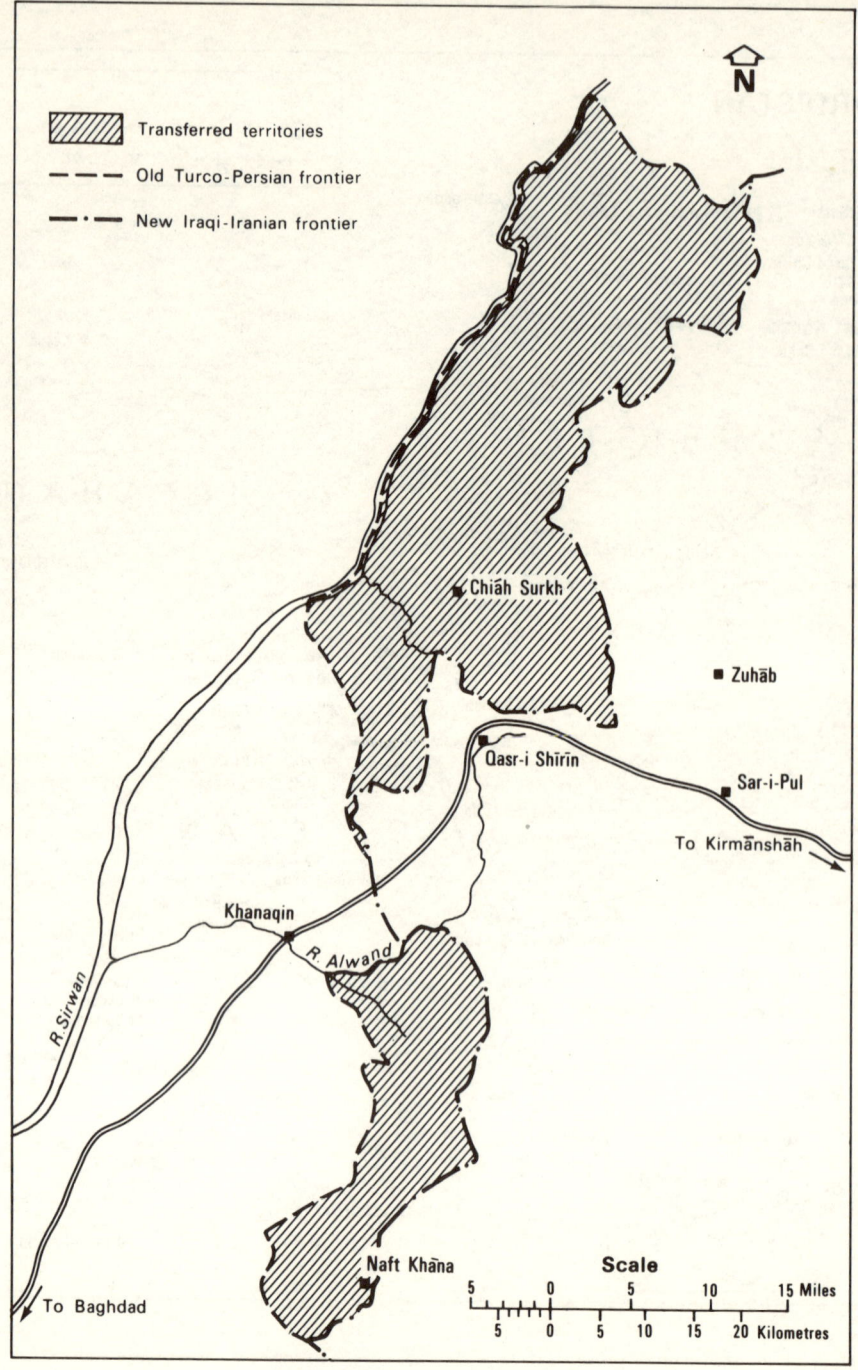

The Transferred territories 1914

NOTE ON BIBLIOGRAPHY

It has been decided to include a full bibliography in the last volume to avoid considerable duplication of references. Much emphasis has been placed upon the primary archival material. Indeed the Chairman in October 1915 had already remarked on the history of the Concession, 'which is buried in masses of correspondence'. These sources have been exhaustively used and the references are accordingly mentioned in the appropriate parts of the text. Moreover much attention has been given to the relevant documentation from government archives. The secondary literature on the oil industry is extensive. Those citations most immediately useful will be found in the notes which are correspondingly fuller than they might otherwise have been.

ABBREVIATIONS

AE	Affaires Etrangères	E&GS	Eastern and General Syndicate
AIOC	Anglo-Iranian Oil Company		
APC	Asiatic Petroleum Company	EPU	Europaïshe Petroleum Union
APOC	Anglo-Persian Oil Company	FO	Foreign Office
BOC	Burmah Oil Company	IO	India Office
BP	British Petroleum	IPC	Iraq Petroleum Company
COR	Commonwealth Oil Refineries	KOC	Khanaqin Oil Company
		PRO	Public Record Office
CSL	Concessions Syndicate Ltd	TPC	Turkish Petroleum Company
DEC	D'Arcy Exploration Company		

INTRODUCTION

The oil production of the world was dominated at the beginning of the twentieth century by Russia (51 per cent) and America (43 per cent). Kerosine for heating and illumination was the principal petroleum product (65 per cent of American refinery throughput). American wells were located in Pennsylvania, New York, Ohio, Kansas and Indiana and its industry was controlled by the Standard Oil Trust which, before its dismemberment in 1911, accounted for some 84 per cent of refinery output, 86 per cent of total exports and 85 per cent of domestic sales of oil. By 1914 over a decade after Texas and California had been discovered as major new oilfields, American oil constituted 65 per cent of world production. The Russian oil industry was principally centred in the Baku area, with Nobel interests dominant. The Baku fields peaked in 1901, but, although more oil was discovered in the Grozny and Maikop regions, the Russian share of world oil production dropped to 16.4 per cent in 1914. Generally American crude oil was light and better for benzine and kerosine, whilst that of Russia was heavy with the refining of kerosine being accompanied by much fuel oil for which uses in industrial furnaces, railways and shipping were developed.

Thus even in the opening years of this century a variation in the pattern of production is noticeable and in the market proportions of the principal producers and the companies associated with them. This is part of the dynamic of the oil industry, part of the process of almost continuous change. See Figure 0.1 and Appendix 0.1.

In 1890 as a result of the discovery of oil in Sumatra the Royal Dutch Company was formed, of which Henri Deterding, a former bank manager in Penang, became the general manager in 1900. In 1903 it was operating a refinery in Rotterdam and had established a European presence. In 1892, Marcus Samuel, engaged in a general export–import business and having connections throughout the Far East, shipped a cargo of Russian kerosine through the Suez Canal in a specially constructed tanker, the *Murex*. The following year he established the Tank Syndicate which was transformed in October 1897 into the Shell Transport and Trading Company. Mean-

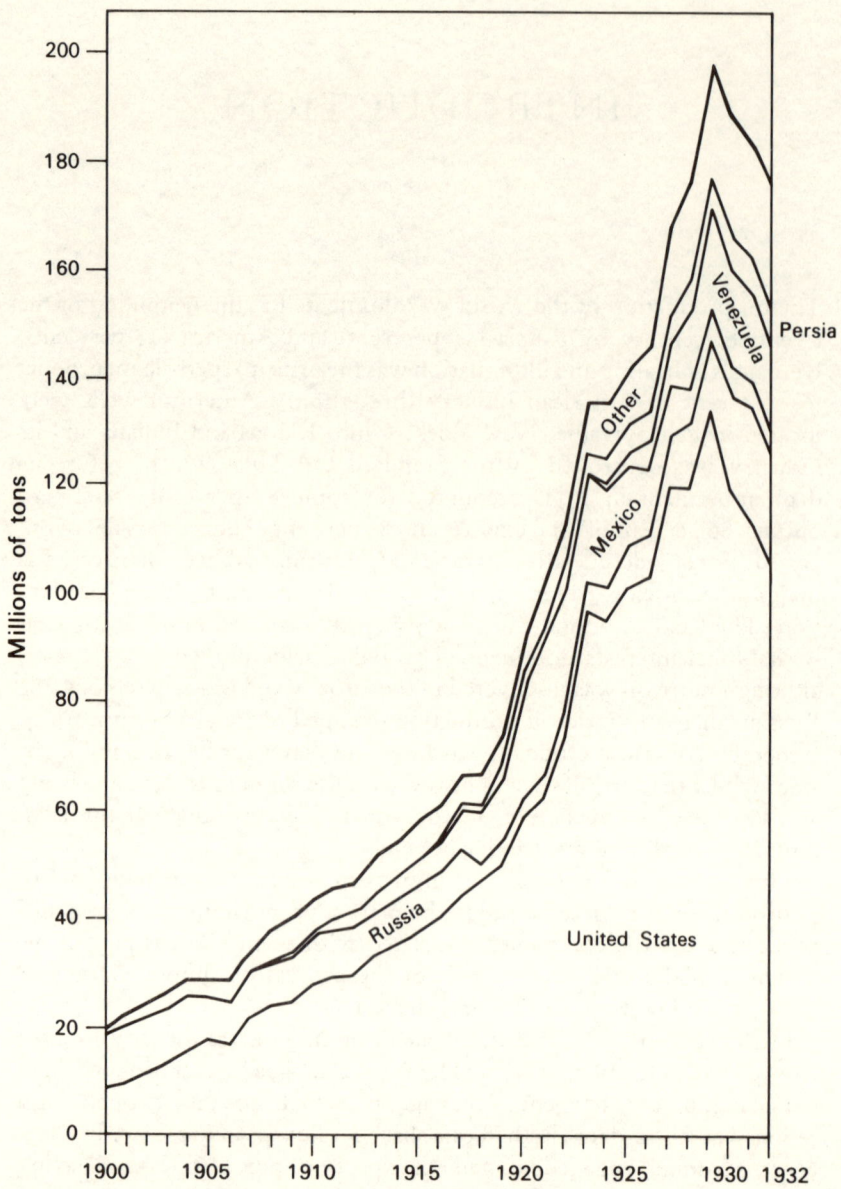

Figure 0.1 World crude oil production 1900–32 (millions of tons)
Source: *Petroleum Almanac*. Barrels converted to tons at the rate of 7.45 barrels = 1 ton.

Introduction

while Samuel had ventured into exploration and a field was discovered at Kutei in Borneo in February 1897. By 1900 the East Indies had a small share of world production (1.5 per cent) and two developing oil companies. Elsewhere in Asia, oil production in Burma was a little less than 1 per cent of the world's total but its sales of kerosine were important in the Indian market. Up to 1886 American oil exports had supplied most of that market, but at the turn of the century Russian kerosine accounted for 60 per cent of supplies there, whereas the Burma proportion was just 3 per cent, but by 1905 Burma had taken 48 per cent and in 1914 52 per cent of the market. The leading company was the Burmah Oil Company organised in 1886 by Scottish businessmen and reconstituted in 1902 under the direction of a Glasgow merchant, David Cargill. By 1914 Burma production was 2 per cent of the world total.

The only other oilfields of any importance were in Hungary and Rumania, where a small production was undertaken with American drilling equipment in the early 1880s. In 1914 production from the two areas represented some 7 per cent of world production. As in the Russian oil industry, where foreign capital represented the greater part of investment in 1914, $130 million out of $214 million, with British funds contributing $86 million (66 per cent of foreign investment or 40 per cent of total investment), so in Rumania foreign participation was considerable. Thus out of a total capital investment of 185 million French francs, Germany contributed 74 million, France 31 million, Holland 22 million, Rumania 16 million, the United States 12.5 million, Belgium 5 million, the United Kingdom 3 million and other interests 6.5 million. In Hungary the Aktiengesellschaft für Oesterreichische-Ungarische Petroleum Produkte (Olex) handled oil exports.

The extent and number of oil production areas in 1900 were limited and so too were the areas of major consumption. The United States was virtually a closed market. India absorbed a large volume of kerosine. Europe represented the largest and most profitable concentration of consumption and the scene of the most intense competition. As a result of technical innovations largely emanating from the Nobel interests in Russia and the Standard Oil group of companies in the United States, refining processes became not only more accurate in distillation and chemically more efficient, but they became continuous in operation. Pipelines were pioneered leading not only to monopolies over the distribution of products, but much cheaper transportation costs, particularly from 1881 with a six inch line from Pennsylvania to the Atlantic Coast and in 1889 with an eight inch line between the oilfields and refineries in Baku and the port of Batum on the Black Sea. Railway tanks also cheapened deliveries in bulk, but the development of marine transportation, particularly as a result of

Introduction

Nobel's pioneering work with the *Zoroaster*, commissioned in 1878, gradually transformed the market relationships, which were no longer to be confined to localised conditions, but involved a global context of supply and demand.

Economies of scale became possible with growing emphasis on efficiency of operation to maximise the return on all the constituent elements of the crude oil produced. In this respect the technical proficiency in the oil industry had already passed by 1900 from Russia to the United States, where refining processes were being improved. This shifting pattern of technical and economic factors had a major impact in the first decade of the century not only on the companies producing oil but on those marketing it, fostering a growing tendency to integrate the different operational activities within a single functional organisation. Thus Marcus Samuel, of Shell, integrated back upstream into production from his distributing base, whilst Henri Deterding in Royal Dutch integrated downstream into marketing from his production.

As this process was taking place, so the relative strengths of the companies within the different geographical regions of the oil industry were changing according to competitive pressures. This was particularly apparent in the first decade around the turn of the century. There were many trading agreements, amalgamations, mergers, associations, no less than bankruptcies and liquidations. There was a growing interest in banking circles, like the Rothschilds and Deutsche Bank to participate in oil investments, less in funding exploration than in promoting distribution. Among the most notable of these with profound commercial consequences was the creation of the Asiatic Petroleum Company in May 1902 between Royal Dutch and Shell, with the participation in June of the Rothschild interests after years of intermittent discussion and the rejection of separate offers of close cooperation by both Samuel and Deterding in December 1901 from Standard Oil. The different changing fortunes of both companies were reflected in the formal amalgamation of April 1906, in which Royal Dutch interests predominated with 60 per cent while those of Shell represented 40 per cent.

In 1894 a tentative association was formed in Russia between the major Russian oil interests, Nobels, Rothschilds and Mantashev, to cooperate in the marketing of petroleum products within certain defined geographical areas, in response to Standard Oil's aggressive marketing policy. Between 1897 and 1905 there was fierce competition and frequent 'price wars' between Shell, Royal Dutch, Standard Oil and Burmah in eastern markets of varying degrees of intensity. There was little permanency of alliances, except for mutual Shell and Royal Dutch objectives from 1902. A commercial truce was declared in 1905 with an agree-

Introduction

ment between Burmah and the Asiatic Petroleum Company to share eastern markets.

In 1906 Samuel found himself overcommitted, with the collapse of expectations in Texas and revolutionary disturbances to Russian supplies, and unable to finance his interests in the growing production from Rumania. The Deutsche Bank, to protect its European oil interests from increasing Standard Oil competition, made an alliance in July 1906 with the Nobels and Rothschilds to form a massive oil conglomerate, the Europäische Petroleum Union. This was composed of many minor European oil groupings, including that of the British Petroleum Company Ltd, which represented the Union in the United Kingdom, where it contracted to distribute refined products from Royal Dutch-Shell following their merger in 1906. Some of the principal oil companies not only became involved in marketing arrangements — more or less competitive truces — but they began to set up foreign subsidiaries for marketing, as Standard Oil had done as early as 1888 with the Anglo-American Oil Co Ltd in the United Kingdom, or for production with Romana-Americana in Rumania in 1904. Deterding too, with Royal Dutch-Shell developed a more forthright strategy by initiating marketing in the United States in 1912 and purchasing oil territories in California in 1913. With the foundation of Astra Romana in 1908, Royal Dutch-Shell possessed Rumanian production, with the acquisition of General Asphalt in 1913 it had rights to properties in Trinidad and Venezuela and by its take-over of Rothschilds' Russian concerns in 1913 it had consolidated a formidable network of world oil interests.

It is against this general historical background that William Knox D'Arcy, an Englishman, who had made a fortune from a successful Australian mining venture, was offered in 1900 the chance of acquiring an oil concession in Persia, by a cosmopolitan Persian official, General Antoine Kitabgi, through the introduction of a former British Minister in Persia, Sir Henry Drummond Wolff. D'Arcy was prepared to take the risk in floating an uncertain enterprise to explore for oil. It was simply a personal initiative for profit. It is a measure of the later fortuitous importance of D'Arcy's concession that the most machiavellian of motives have been presumed to account for his investment. In reality the skills of the geologist and driller discovered oil, not the imagination of the polemicist or the gamble of the speculator.

Persian national authority was then weak; trade was limited and resources scarcely developed. The unfortunate Qājār dynasty was declining, its administrative structure inadequate for effective government by the end of the nineteenth century. The hopes of a small but dedicated reforming movement were confused by the rival attractions of older traditional

Introduction

practices and modern secular concepts. The agony of choice was exacerbated by the presence of an alien industrialising force, representing for some an essential development of natural resources, but for others an intolerable affront to national pride. The misfortunes of earlier foreign concessionary enterprises, whatever their justification, such as the Reuter Concession, Russian, French, Belgian and Austrian propositions, for roads, railways, utilities, factories, etc., had failed to make any positive contribution to Persian economic growth.

The natural Persian temperament was more tuned to the role of the *'munshi'*, the scribe, than that of the *'muhandes'*, the engineer. The practical application of technical knowledge had little prestige in the scale of values of Persian society at the beginning of the twentieth century, when there was no real experience of industry and much distrust of its possible effects. In consequence there was little understanding of the discipline and expertise required for a complex industrial operation and little opportunity to attain the necessary technical proficiency. The majority of the workforce was recruited from the predominantly tribal area of south-west Persia. More capable workers came from elsewhere, often minority elements of the population, Armenians, Jews, Chaldeans, to live in a region which was unattractive in comparison with the capital, Tehrān, or other major cities like Tabrīz, Mashhad, Isfahān or Shīrāz, which were climatically more congenial.

The British staff recruited by the Company arrived in Persia generally on three-year contracts to do a job for which they had been previously trained. They were expatriates, whatever their length of service, living in a part of Persia which had an ancient reputation, but which had been neglected. They created their own environment with their own social conventions and amusements. Inevitably an enclave mentality developed, marked by the absence of comparable Persian company, the isolation of the region in which they lived and worked and the lack of adequate communications with the rest of the country. Yet many of the staff overcame these obstacles and established life-long friendships with Persians. Some aspired to a wide appreciation of the arts, literature and customs of Persia, and travelled in the countryside. Yet their roots never penetrated deeply into the Persian consciousness, for the Company neither operated in a developed political environment, like the United States, nor in one which then had no real national identity, like the Dutch colonies of the East Indies. When central authority in Persia was weak and local autonomy strong, the Company suffered from insecurity and uncertainty, but when the central administration was effectively controlled as under Rizā Shāh, resentment against the Company became sharper. The earlier absence of stable political institutions prejudiced attitudes and complicated

Introduction

negotiations. Persian ministries were often little more than the temporary power bases of individual ministers. Political groupings depended upon personal followings rather than ideological conviction. The activity of the Majlis, the Persian Parliament, was mostly to approve legislation, seldom to propose it.

The Persian concessionary situation, therefore, naturally exerted a profound influence upon the Company's development. Because of the involvement of the British Government in the affairs of the Company and because of the Persian image of British intervention in Persian affairs, the activities of the Company were frequently suspected by Persians. Yet, whatever the particular circumstances effecting the relations of the Persian Government with the Company, it would be unrealistic to assume that they were unique or quite unrelated to concessionary developments elsewhere. As the balance of political power was changing not only as a result of the wish for self-determination or as a result of the ideological consequences of the Russian Revolution, but also because of the gradual weakening of colonialism and the rise of nationalism, so was the concessionary basis of economic relationships being challenged. In the same way as the system of Capitulations, which had regulated European relations with the Ottoman Empire since the sixteenth century, was abolished by the Treaty of Lausanne on 24 July 1922, so there was a rejection of concessionary subservience by the newly emerging national governments. The old order was changing, prefigured not only in Mussolini's Italy and Ataturk's Turkey in the mid-twenties, but also in the Mexican oil legislation of Presidents Carranza in 1916 and Calles in 1925. The action of Riza Shāh in terminating extra-territorial rights in Persia in 1928 and in cancelling the D'Arcy Concession in 1932 are more than purely local in importance. At the same time, with the discovery of commercial quantities of oil in 1927 in Iraq and in Bahrain in 1932, the Company became involved in balancing the conflicting demands for increasing production from different countries, a concessionary juggling act.

The fascination and controversy which has accompanied concessionary affairs, however merited, has obscured the role which technology has played in the exploitation of oil. Early refining practice was based on distillation to produce kerosine. Dr James Young's British patent of 1850 was an important contribution and influential in the development of the Scottish shale oil industry. At first refining had been confined to batch processing, but from 1881 the Nobels in their refineries at Baku were continuously refining in a series of stills in which the residue, astatki (waste), was being used for heating purposes. Gradually astatki was upgraded, and as mazout (fuel oil) was used in burners as a substitute for coal in furnaces. In the latter half of the nineteenth century many chemists

Introduction

had analysed oils and their properties, but practical application was delayed. Whilst the principles of distillation and shale oil refining were well-known to Andrew Campbell, John Gillespie and Sir Boverton Redwood and the other advisers to the Company, their practical experience of Persian crude oil was negligible before the commissioning of the refinery. The refining programme was based on what was commercially desirable, rather than what was technically possible. As a result of the failure to understand the particular physical characteristics and chemical constituents of Persian crude oil, the refinery at Ābādān took nearly three times as long to come on stream as had been anticipated. This delay strained the financial resources of the Company almost to breaking point and forced it to abandon its original marketing strategy and make restrictive contracts with Royal Dutch-Shell and most importantly to seek a contractual relationship with the British Government in 1912 for the supply of fuel oil, which lead to the Government's shareholding in the Company in 1914.

The challenge to technical management which this early disaster stimulated was met by the early formation of a research organisation in 1917 and the crucial appointment of Sir John Cadman as Technical Adviser in November 1921, director, 1923, and Chairman, 1927. The technical dimension in the Company's operation was given priority. The results were remarkable. Within less than a decade the inefficient and wasteful refinery at Ābādān had been transformed into a vast complex of units capable of refining a range of products to a consistent quality economically by the most modern processes. From dependence upon a single field of unknown dimensions, yield and behaviour, which it was feared might decline like the Baku fields in 1901 or turn to water like the Mexican fields in 1920, detailed exploration and inspired interpretation of the geological and geophysical data revealed the extent of the Masjid i-Suleimān field (earlier known as the Maidan i-Naftun), and led to the discovery of the great field of Haft Kel in 1927 and the probability of other large fields at Gach Sārān, Agā Jārī and Pāzanun, which were not drilled in till the early 1940s.

It was not only that the quality of the products was improved and that the quantity of oil produced increased sufficiently to justify growing expenditure in relation to the duration of the concession, but that productive efficiency was exceptionally high owing to the scientific knowledge which had been gained of the reservoir conditions and the technical mastery by which wells were controlled. The encouragement of scientific curiosity, practical skills, careful observation and imaginative management resulted in the principles and practices of unitisation, the concept of an oilfield as a single production unit to be treated according to its own intrinsic characteristics. Development expenditure was thereby mini-

Introduction

mised, production costs reduced and the life of the field prolonged. This insistence on technical expertise and the observance of proper professional standards resulted in a tradition of the practical application of scientific principles to its operations which has kept the Company in the vanguard of the industry's exploration and production activities. The Company was able to offset its relative commercial weakness by the strength of its productive resources. The strength of its reserves position and the availability of its cheaper crude oil supplies gave it an importance and influence in international oil affairs out of all proportion to its market share. Thus, technical considerations, both negative and positive, accidental and deliberate, have exerted a decisive effect on the Company's growth.

The attitude of the British Government was important in the capital funding of the Company. Whilst the Government had no direct authority to interfere in the commercial affairs of the Company other than the prudent exercise of their responsibilities by the government directors, the commitment of government funds to satisfy the demands for increased capital raised not only questions of finance but also the nature of the Government's relationship to the Company. Was government money to be made available for operations outside of Persia? Was the Government interested in the commercial success of the Company or only in assured supplies of fuel oil for the Navy? The manner in which these matters were settled and the role of Lord Inchcape, one of the first government directors, produced compromise and flexibility which, while not directly answering the questions or ignoring the principles, provided a satisfactory result. The oil industry has always been capital intensive and the prodigious efforts of the Company in the early twenties severely strained its financial resources and precipitated a crisis in 1923.

The financial situation of the Company was influenced, apart, obviously, from its corporate performance, by the terms of the Concession which required that 16 per cent of the profits be paid to the Persian Government. The imprecision of the wording of the Concession, which could not have anticipated the subsequent expansion of the Company, was differently interpreted and caused disagreement. All efforts to find a mutually acceptable alternative basis on which to calculate royalties failed. At the heart of the controversy was the definition of profits, about which eminent accountants and counsel differed, and the substitution of the 16 per cent profit basis for a simple tonnage-based calculation. The continuing uncertainty was an accounting nightmare. It seriously exacerbated relations between the Company and the Persian Government and partly caused the cancellation of the Concession.

The Government insisted, as far as was practical, on self-financing out of retained profits, a policy that was fully observed from 1923 to 1966. So

Introduction

the Company did not need to pursue a generous dividends policy, which otherwise would have been more expected of it if it had been financed only from private capital. With the Government and Burmah dominating the ordinary share capital, there were no members of the public holding ordinary shares till 1922 to challenge this attitude which produced steady growth rather than spectacular results. The total finance employed from 1916 to 1932 increased seventeen times from £3 000 000 to £50 300 000; in the same time net income, exclusive of overseas taxation, rose from £200 000 to £5 300 000, having reached £7 500 000 in 1929. The average return on capital employed was 11.68 per cent between .1915 and 1932.

The relationship with the British Government is fundamental to any understanding of the Company's development. It is tempting with hindsight to project the image of a consistent government commitment to an oil policy based on a deliberate calculation of needs and resources and assume that the Company was cast for the leading role. There is little evidence to support such a hypothesis. There had been intermittent interest in the possibilities of oil-burning naval vessels in the first years of the century under the particular inspiration of Admiral Sir John Fisher, which was encouraged by the First Lord of the Admiralty, Lord Selborne. The Burmah Oil Company concluded a fuel oil supply contract with the Admiralty in 1905. Then enthusiasm for oil flagged and the Admiralty engineers reverted to coal-fired boilers. It was the renewed technical advocacy of Fisher and the exceptional political conviction of Churchill, which revived the idea of oil-fired engines in response to growing German naval rearmament. This view prevailed and precipitated the decision to authorise, against furious opposition, the 1912-13 naval estimates with provision for a flotilla of light fast cruisers. Such a new naval strategy depended upon a regular supply of reasonably priced fuel oil. Only the Company at that time offered to provide such a supply, although it was not intended then, or later, that there was to be any exclusivity implied in the agreement that was concluded. It was estimated that some 40 per cent of the naval needs would be covered in this respect, a volume which increased during the war.

The original arrangement with the British Government was, therefore, commercial in scope rather than strategic in intent and the government shareholding was investment protection, not an expression of political ideology. It was shrewd opportunism rather than deliberate policy, leaving many appalled at Churchill's conjuring and the mixing of his motives, which were forgotten at the outbreak of war in 1914. It was, moreover, Churchill, who, in 1924 at the prompting of Robert Waley Cohen, a director of Royal Dutch-Shell, attempted to unscramble the

Introduction

arrangement which, a decade earlier, he had believed to be so indispensable for national security.

The government shareholding was a mixed blessing for Government and Company alike. It certainly provided a supply of fuel oil to the Admiralty, which reached some 500 000 tons a year by the end of the war, and it definitely provided an assured outlet of products for the Company, without which its growth would have been seriously if not disastrously curtailed. It did not, however, advance proposals for a government oil policy, in so far as the Company was an anomaly, not a government department but neither a free enterprise corporation. Its demands for finance were embarrassing in periods of economic stringency and some of its activities were unwelcome to the British Government.

The Company too believed the Government to be less than helpful by its support for the idea of an amalgamation between Burmah and Royal Dutch-Shell to the detriment of its own position, its reluctance to authorise the purchase of a distributing organisation, the British Petroleum Company, its delayed response to capital calls, and its apparent indifference to Company activities outside Persia. This reaction, however, was probably inseparable from coming to terms with an evolving relationship, which had to reconcile the expectations of Government and the aspirations of the Company. Apart from the early protective concern over D'Arcy's exploratory endeavours in Persia, the intense diplomatic interest in the Mesopotamian Concession and the flurry of activity over the cancellation of the Concession in 1932, the Government directly intervened little more than it would have done for any comparable commercial organisation.

The Company for its part regretted that its early activities in Persia, in the absence of central authority, required the support of local consular officials, which resulted in it being unfortunately and unjustifiably identified with British Government policy. A determined effort was made after 1920 to distance the Company from the British Government, but unfortunately to little real effect in Persian minds. The Company, therefore, suffered accordingly in the fluctuating relations between the two governments. The relationship between the Company and the Government was not as simple as it has sometimes been portrayed but changed according to the circumstances of the moment. In South America, for example, the government shareholding precluded the Company from being involved in the development of the prolific fields which were discovered in the 1920s, apart from a minor interest in Argentina, as it conflicted with national mining legislation.

Since oil is an internationally traded commodity with production and consumption centres often separated by vast distances, it is not surprising that the diplomatic dimension has been important. Curzon's oft-quoted

Introduction

remark that 'the Allies floated to victory on a wave of oil' was public recognition of an obvious fact. The determination of the French Government to acquire a source of their own oil in Mesopotamia through participation in the Turkish Petroleum Company and to regulate the importation, refining and transportation of oil was confirmation of the importance of oil in national economies and represented one attitude towards it. The increasing interest in Middle East concessions shown after the First World War by some American companies and the enunciation of the 'Open Door' principle by the American State Department was another prominent example of the concern of national governments with oil.

For most of its first thirty years the Company was dominated by two successive chairmen, Charles Greenway and John Cadman, very different but complementary personalities. Greenway, managing director from 1910 and Chairman from 1914, steeped in the tradition of the managing agents working throughout the East for commission in a wide range of commodities, knew the feel of the markets, the confidence and the risk of the mercantile community through his work in the oil department of Shaw Wallace, agents of Burmah Oil Company in India. Hard-working, meticulous in detail and full of initiative, he was a resilient character, assertive, determined and persistent.

When Greenway became managing director the Company was an almost wholly owned subsidiary of the Burmah Oil Company, which controlled 97 per cent of the Company's shareholding and directed the technical and financial services of the Company from Glasgow, leaving concessionary and commercial affairs to him in London. In 1912 Greenway was obliged to conclude unfavourable contracts with Royal Dutch-Shell for ten years to preserve the independence of the Company owing to the failure of the refinery to be commissioned on time. The Company had, moreover, no financial resources to establish its own installations, depots and transportation services. As a result of these problems, the British Government was persuaded by Greenway with the agreement of Churchill to make a supply agreement with the Company for fuel oil, which the refinery could produce reasonably satisfactorily, and to take a £2 000 000 shareholding for improving the facilities of the Company to guarantee a sufficient availability of fuel oil for naval requirements and protect its investment. This in turn reduced the Burmah shareholding to a minority interest which enabled Greenway to manage the almost complete independence of the Company from its parent.

There has been a tendency to regard the Company much more as a crude oil producer, because of the extraordinary success of its production operations in Persia, and much less as a seller of petroleum products. There is much justification in this. It is also true that compared with Royal Dutch-

Introduction

Shell and Standard Oil (NJ) in particular, with their networks of global interests, the Company was initially at a disadvantage and might well have been reduced to being a mere crude oil wholesaler. Moreover the strength of the American oil industry as a whole must not be ignored even if, for much of this period, the majority of American companies mostly operated within the domestic market. Nevertheless, by any comparable standards some of the original members of the Standard Oil Trust, such as Standard Oil, New York, Standard Oil, Indiana, Atlantic Refining Company, or others like the Texas Company, Sinclair Oil Corporation, Gulf Oil Company and Tidewater Pipeline Company were formidable businesses. A number of them were getting engaged in foreign ventures in South America and the Middle East with corresponding pressures for more marketing opportunities. It is nonetheless undeniable that Greenway, in spite of the early technical and financial difficulties, never lost sight of his principal objective of eventually making the Company self-sufficient in managerial and financial terms and engaged in all aspects of the industry from exploration to marketing.

Greenway had first hand experience of the oil business. During his service with Shaw Wallace in India, 1893-1908, he had early commercial dealings with Royal Dutch and Shell Transport and Trading, particularly over the 1905 trading agreement. This left an indelible and unfavourable impression upon him and clearly influenced his attitude to his rivals for the rest of his commercial career. Greenway in 1910 was the first in the Company to recognise the growing importance of fuel oil, laying it down as a keystone in his commercial strategy because of the suitability of Persian crude oil for its production. The amount of fuel oil required by the Admiralty some 277 850 tons in 1912, was 70 per cent of its total fuel oil demand in the United Kingdom. Later supplies to it from 1914 became a crucial factor in the survival of the Company. Fuel oil afterwards not only provided the opportunity for a network of international bunkering installations along the maritime routes of the world, but also indirectly stimulated continental interest in the Company.

It was perhaps one of Greenway's greatest achievements that he was able to disengage the Company from Burmah's hold without disrupting the association, prevent the Company's absorption by Royal Dutch-Shell and preserve the independence of the Company without succumbing to government control. Viewing the Company's dismal situation in 1913 and comparing its successful position fourteen years later on his retirement is to appreciate Greenway's conduct of affairs, the impressiveness of his performance and to recognise his personal imprint. Almost a one man band at the beginning of his managerial responsibilities with a couple of London office staff and a handful in Persia, the Company having no

Introduction

pipeline, no refinery and no production, Greenway in his last years had a group of subsidiary companies providing the markets of Europe with products, refineries in England, Scotland, France and Australia, bunkering stations around the world and exploration activities in the Middle East, South America, Africa and Europe. It had not been achieved easily but the administrative structure needed to sustain the development and implementation of agreed policy had replaced individual initiatives and the inappropriate system of the managing agents in Persia.

The experience which Cadman brought to the Company was different. Cadman's training was technical not commercial. He had first proved his ability as a mining inspector in coalfields, in the Colonial Service as adviser on mineral affairs in the West Indies and as a Professor of Engineering at Birmingham University in lecturing on the importance of the practical application of scientific principles. His experience of human affairs broadened during his appointment as the head of the specially formed Petroleum Executive in the latter years of the First World War. To the detachment and impartiality of the scientist he joined the administrative discipline of the civil servant and the tact of the diplomat.

A warm approachable person, he was decisive in action. His major contributions to the Company were the recognition of the importance of properly coordinated administration based on a carefully differentiated structural organisation, the rigorous application of scientific principles to operational requirements, the definition of objectives with reference to related financial criteria, cost accounting and budgetary control, and the desirability of formulating policy by collaborative action between fully responsible managing directors reporting collectively to the Board. Beyond these practical considerations was his vision of international cooperation and understanding, his dislike of inefficiency and waste, his emphasis on research to utilise all the constituents of oil, his missionary sense of the need to conserve a primary resource of energy for the use of mankind and not squander it for the selfish advantage of a single generation.

After a precarious childhood and an unpromising adolescence, the Company grew up in the twenties to become, by 1928, one of the major international oil companies in a period of intense competition, technical change and national concern. The early stages of these developments constitute the first part of this corporate biography of BP.

I
THE ACQUISITION OF THE D'ARCY CONCESSION 1901

I THE STATE OF PERSIA IN 1900

The land of Iran has frequently resembled a crossroads of peoples on the move, or, in more settled times, a caravanserai for the exchange of goods and ideas. With the arrival of the Medes and the Persians at the end of the Second Millennium a cultural distinctiveness began to emerge. This found its earliest and most notable expression in the Achaemenian Empire, established by Cyrus the Great (559–530 B.C.), until its collapse in 323, a victim of its own decadence and the energy of Alexander the Great. Two major dynasties succeeded, the Parthians (250 B.C.–A.D. 224) and the Sasanians (A.D. 224–642), before the forces of the Prophet in 642 brought Iran within the Islamic orbit.[1] The centuries that followed were marked by an assimilation of Islamic cultural influences, a revival of the Iranian consciousness and the absorption of incursions from Central Asia, such as the Saljuqs in the beginning of the eleventh century, the hordes of Chinghiz Khān two centuries later and the raiders of Tīmūr in the latter part of the fourteenth century.[2]

In a sense modern Iran is identifiable with the founding of the Safavid dynasty in 1501, contemporary with the Mughals, Ottomans and Elizabethans. Based on Shī'ite precepts, in spiritual and secular affairs, a recognisable state was created with a centralising administration completely subservient to the Shah and his court. With Shāh 'Abbās, (1587–1629) trade was royally patronised, Armenian merchants were encouraged and commercial contacts with Europe expanded. Unfortunately the political ineptitude, persecution of minorities, court intrigue and the lack of military vigilance of later Safavid rulers resulted in an ignominious defeat in 1722 by marauding Afghans. Apart from the ephemeral glory of capturing Delhi in 1739, achieved by the military adventurer, Nādir Shāh, and the enlightened but brief rule of Karīm Khān Zand and his son Lutf 'Alī (1750–94) over the southern regions around Shīrāz, for much of the eighteenth century Iran was in a chaotic state.[3] Then in 1786 the ruthless eunuch Āqā Muhammad Khān taking Tehrān,

The acquisition of the D'Arcy Concession

seized control over the country as the leader of the Qājār northern tribal confederacy, and inaugurated a new dynasty.[4]

This extremely brief survey does not do justice to the great variety of events and influences which have interacted and shaped the chequered pattern of Iranian history, but it does perhaps indicate, and to some extent explain, the phenomenon that 'both national and individual insecurity is perhaps the dominant characteristic of modern Persian history'.[5] This was particularly true of the Qājārs, a weak dynasty in a weakened country, who in spite of surviving for over a century as rulers of Iran never fully succeeded in holding the allegiance and respect of their people. In internal affairs they adopted a conservative bureaucratic policy of minimal interference in established social and economic conditions, which caused an increasing internal stagnation. Aware of modern developments, most of the Qājār rulers generally lacked the power or the determination to reject or accept them and prevaricated by trying to ignore them. Meanwhile Fath 'Alī Shāh (1791–1834), uxorious in his pursuits and luxurious in his pleasures, deliberately revived pretensions to an earlier pre-Islamic age of imperial grandeur by imitating Achaemenian rock reliefs and patronising the arts, especially architecture and painting. The Qājārs exercised only a nominal control over the provinces apart from Āzarbāyjān, where the heir-apparent resided. This further contributed to a gradual weakening of authority in the country and revenue failed to keep pace with expenditure, straining the economy. Fath 'Alī Shāh welcomed the renewed European interest in his country occasioned by the Napoleonic Wars. Such pride, quite natural in itself, was disastrous when it coincided with attempts to recover lost territories such as Georgia without proper consideration of national resources or military capabilities, especially during the unsuccessful wars with Russia, which led to the humiliating Treaty of Turkomānchay in 1828. The memories of such defeats contributed to the latent sense of xenophobia which often arose in moments of crisis.

After the accession to power in 1848 of Nāsir al-Dīn Shāh, however, there were signs of a new vision appearing, both of the desirability of a more representative form of government and for industrial development.[6] There was a feeling that the institutions of state were inadequate and that a programme of foreign assistance was required. Between 1850 and 1860 the first Persian official newspaper appeared, published weekly, and authorised by the Prime Minister, Mīrzā Taqī Khān.[7] Under the auspices of the same minister an establishment of higher education, Dār al-Funūn, was founded in 1851, to supplement the traditional clerical training, with courses in geometry, medicine, surgery, pharmacy, mineralogy, military strategy and languages staffed by Austrian instructors. Unfortunately the minister fell from favour and was murdered and it was not until the

The acquisition of the D'Arcy Concession

appointment of Mīrzā Husayn Khān as Prime Minister in 1871 that a more serious and sustained effort to inaugurate reforms was undertaken.[8] The Prime Minister had served as ambassador in Constantinople and was acquainted with Persian reformers, including Malkam Khān Nāzim al-Dawla, whose writings, such as *Usūl-i Tamaddūn*, the Principles of Civilisation, on constitutional and administrative affairs, no less than his position as Minister in London were of fundamental importance to the movement for reform.[9]

Convinced of the appropriateness of the measures he was proposing, impatient at the delays in implementing them, Malkam Khān advocated rapid action, 'for the sake of the prosperity of Iran, it is necessary to introduce companies from abroad'. Persia could not remain in isolation, splendid or squalid, its guarantee of survival was economic not military so 'the leaders of the state must, without delay, turn over the construction of railways, the operation of mines, the establishment of a bank, and all public works and structures to foreign companies... the Government of Iran must grant as many concessions to foreign companies as possible'.[10] It was a radical and controversial programme inimical to traditional religious authority.

Many Iranians were exasperated at administrative inefficiency, military ineffectiveness and widespread corruption. Some, like the Prime Minister, were hopeful that 'men can by correct policies in time make small nations great and powerful', but he realised also that 'men can also, through negligence and indifference, obliterate a great nation'.[11] Others were more pessimistic, even fatalistic, such as Amīn al-Dawla, a later Prime Minister, who despairingly remarked in 1878 that, 'there is nothing we can do. Day by day we become more desperate... We want to become world famous for excellent outstanding deeds but we have no plan, no organisation, no money.' The reason was that, 'Alas! All were busy looking after themselves and reaching out for personal gain; yet they claimed the Shah opposed reforms. To repeat: the Shah had lost confidence in his officials and they in him.'[12] Indeed the tragedy of the modernising movement was that, far from leading to an increasingly cohesive society with commonly recognised objectives, it aggravated internal political contradictions and roused religious opposition.[13] Thus, by the time a constitution was ultimately conceded by a reluctant ailing Shah, its importance was restricted by a lack of fundamental social and economic changes or improvements in the administration of justice. Many modern ideas proved to be incompatible with the traditional forces of society. It curbed the power of the monarchy, but it was a revolution *manqué*. Iran in comparison with similar countries such as Egypt or Turkey had developed little in the course of the nineteenth century.[14]

The acquisition of the D'Arcy Concession

The limited programme of industrialisation failed to materialise through a series of misfortunes attributable to ambitious, unrealistic, ill-conceived schemes; lack of basic infrastructural support; sharp practices; resource failures and insufficient understanding. The unfortunate de Reuter Concession of 1872 and the Tobacco Régie of 1891 were the most blatant of the failures, but not necessarily the most reprehensible in the frenzied concessionary activity towards the end of the century, which responded more to the avaricious character of the royal Court than to the economic requirements of the country. Foreign investment in Iran which was insignificant in 1900 and was less than £30m in 1914, was not generally welcomed because it offended the religious susceptibilities, antagonised the merchant class and played into the hands of political opponents, who criticised its anti-national implications. It also provoked increasing distrust of the Qājār dynasty and its form of government, which was thereby further weakened at a time of the growing impact upon Iran of Anglo-Russian rivalry in Asian affairs. Professor A.K.S. Lambton, the distinguished historian of Persia, has remarked of the earlier part of the century, 'the Persian Government was not primarily interested in trade, which played little or no part in determining government policy . . . It had no specific trade policy nor did it have any consistent policy for the development of the internal resources of the country; and insecurity and maladministration militated against their development by private individuals.'[15]

This was equally true at the end of the century. Manufacturing hardly existed, whilst there was no change in the organisation of the guild system, so that artisans remained dependent on the bazaar and its association with the mosques.[16] For example, the revival of carpet-making as a form of cottage industry owed more to the initial enterprise of a Swiss firm, Ziegler and Co., than Persian appreciation of its commercial possibilities.[17] Education and social attitudes were not inclined towards an understanding of modern technical requirements and commercial practices. So, for this and other reasons, the administration of the customs services was entrusted to Belgian officials in 1898 who were considered to have no political axe to grind in the country.[18] Thus, at the opening of the twentieth century, Persia was insecure and unstable, full of opposing tensions, socially disturbed, politically troubled, economically deprived and religiously agitated.

When William Knox D'Arcy was granted his oil concession in 1901, Iran had a population of about nine million people distributed over an area of 628 000 square miles, much of it barren desert and mountainous. The climatic conditions and scenery are extraordinarily varied.[19] Agriculture and related activities occupied 90 per cent of the working population and contributed to 80–90 per cent of GNP, estimated at £70 million. Literacy

The acquisition of the D'Arcy Concession

was minimal, over 95 per cent of the population being illiterate. A quarter of the population was tribal in character and small villages predominated in the countryside. Only Tehrān, Tabrīz and Isfahān had populations of over 100 000. Communications were rudimentary with only 8 miles of railway and some 800 miles of roads, the remainder being little more than mule tracks, as there was hardly any wheeled traffic. The total government revenue for 1900–1 was estimated at approximately 67 million krans (£1.3 million), and foreign trade in 1895–6 amounted to imports of £4.86 million and exports of £2.8 million. Julian Bharier concluded in his study of Iranian economic history that, in 1900 Iran was an 'almost isolated state, barely distinguishable as an economic entity. There were signs that the economy was developing but at the turn of the century it still remained one of the most backward countries in the world'.[20]

2 BRITISH INTEREST IN PERSIA

The earliest British contacts with Iran of any importance were those made by Anthony Jenkinson on behalf of the Russia Company in 1562 at Qazvīn when he presented to Shāh Tahmāsp a letter from Queen Elizabeth I requesting permission to trade and open friendly relations. The Shah, reluctant at first to offend the Ottoman ambassador, with whom he was then negotiating, and the Armenian merchants, who virtually controlled the overland foreign trade, subsequently authorised the trade. Six trading expeditions of varying success were launched, through Russia, over the Caspian Sea and into northern Persia, principally exchanging cloth for silk. They were abandoned in 1580, following the anarchy which afflicted the country after the death of Shāh Tahmāsp.[21] Following the establishment of the Levant Company in 1581, one of their merchants, Ralph Fitch, and some companions journeyed from Aleppo to Hormuz, an island emporium at the entrance to the Persian Gulf, in 1583 to ascertain prospects for trade in that direction before being arrested by the Portuguese.[22]

The arrival in 1598 of the adventurous Sir Anthony Sherley and his brother, Robert, at the newly established capital of Shāh 'Abbās, Isfahān, seeking fame for himself and proposing a European alliance to combat the Ottomans, was a bizarre event.[23] It, nonetheless, caught the imagination of the Shah, who throughout his reign envisaged mounting a trading boycott with European assistance against his Ottoman enemies. Thus, when agents of the East India Company arrived with their first cargo of goods at the little port of Jāsk in December 1616, they were welcomed by the Shah with promises of ample returns in silk so as to divert the trade from Turkey and curb Portuguese power in the Persian Gulf based on

The acquisition of the D'Arcy Concession

Hormuz.[24] The expectations of the merchants were optimistic, for, as they picturesquely expressed it, 'we ayme not at gnatts and small flyes, but at commerce honourable and equal to two so mighty nations', but they had misgivings about the stability of the country for 'If God should call this Kinge it would bee a question whoe should suckceed'.[25]

The trade, mostly in cloth and silk, that followed in the seventeenth and early eighteenth centuries between Persia and England either sea-borne by the merchants of the East India Company or carried overland by the merchants of the Levant Company, was not spectacular or extensive. It was, nevertheless, fairly regular and contributed to some of the prosperity which marked the later Safavid period. There was little complementary political involvement. An embassy under Sir Dodmore Cotton in response to a Persian one of 1625 reached Persia in 1628 towards the end of the reign of Shāh 'Abbās but its reception was perfunctory — and it made no lasting impression.[26] Occasional royal letters were exchanged. Trade suffered in the aftermath of the Safavid collapse and a belated attempt of the Russia Company to revive its trade to northern Persia by Jonas Hanway in the 1740s was unsuccessful.[27] The unsettled conditions and general insecurity of the countryside forced the East India Company to withdraw its representation from Isfahān, Shīrāz and Kirmān and abandon in 1763 its base at Bandar 'Abbās in favour of Bushire further up the coast. By 1778 trade had almost dried up except in local commodities.

Major British interest in Iran did not arise until the nineteenth century, as a result of the threat posed to the imperial possessions in India by Napoleon's expedition to Egypt in 1798. The Governor-General of India, Lord Wellesley, fearful lest the French should instigate the Afghans under Zamān Shāh to attack British frontier posts or march further inland, sent an elaborate mission to Persia under Captain John Malcolm. In January 1801, Fath 'Alī Shāh and Malcolm concluded political and commercial treaties.[28] Inevitably the changing alliances and fortunes of the European powers had their effect on the Persian court. Fath 'Alī Shāh, who was upset because the British were not prepared to protect him from attacks by the Russians, with whom they were allied, on his Caucasian provinces, reached an agreement with Napoleon, then at the height of his power, at the Treaty of Finkenstein, May 1807. He pledged himself to declare war on the British, break off all diplomatic and commercial connections, allow French troops right of passage through the country and receive a French mission to organise his army and establish commercial relations. His purpose was to safeguard Persian territory from Russian encroachment and ensure the restoration of Georgia to Persia by Russia. Yet less than three months later Napoleon and Czar Alexander I made peace at Tilsit, after General Gardanne, the French envoy, had left for Persia, where he

The acquisition of the D'Arcy Concession

arrived in November 1807 and had the Treaty ratified. It was a pyrrhic victory for, although Gardanne was personally energetic and respected, the failure of the French to support Fath 'Alī Shāh against Russian attacks on Erivan in October 1808 was resented. So the Shah was pleased at the arrival of a British embassy despatched by the Foreign Secretary in the charge of Sir Harford Jones, with full powers to negotiate.[29] It was the first occasion since the embassy of Sir Dodmore Cotton that London had taken such an initiative and it presaged a closer interest in Persian affairs by successive British Governments. In March 1809, he concluded a further Treaty with Fath 'Alī Shāh, the provisions of which were not ratified till 1814, by which time Russia had imposed the Treaty of Gulistān in 1813, effectively advancing the Russian frontiers at the expense of Persia. The flurry of diplomatic activity had resulted in many commitments but little action. Henceforth, however, the Persian arena was seldom free of European players participating in the 'Great Game'.

Permanent British diplomatic representation in Tehrān was established. Nevertheless, although the Minister in Tehrān was nominated through the Foreign Office, there remained a division of responsibility for Persia between the Foreign Office and the Government of India, which controlled the consulates. This frequently led to different and often conflicting assessments of the internal situation in Persia and the policies to be adopted. A revival of trade took place primarily through the Persian Gulf ports from India. In the 1830s limited attempts to open up routes along the Black Sea through Trebizond into the northern part of Iran met with some success. The main channels of British trade came up from the South, especially from the 1860s with the entry into eastern service of steam-driven shipping and the later opening of the Suez Canal. 'Abbās Mīrzā, Fath 'Alī Shāh's heir-apparent, employed some British advisers and technicians, but his early death prevented this initiative from having any lasting influence. During the mid nineteenth century, apart from the unfortunate, if provoked, conduct of the Minister at the Tehrān Legation, Charles Murray and the Persian occupation of Herat during the Crimean War between Russia and Britain, which caused hostilities between Persia and Britain, 1856-7,[30] there were very few issues of specific concern, though the strategic importance of Persia was well appreciated. The consequences of the Indian Mutiny of 1857 and other considerations led to the need for improved communications. The construction took place in 1862 of a telegraphic line linking London with India through Persia. This line was augmented and improved during 1867-70 with the formation of the Indo-European Telegraph Company.[31] It considerably improved the Persian Government's communications with its provincial officials who were brought closer into touch with the capital.

The acquisition of the D'Arcy Concession

It is, however, from the 1870s that the British began again to take a serious interest in Persia apart from the remarkable studies of antiquities, archaeology and literature. This was prompted by two main causes. Firstly, the Foreign Office was perturbed at Russian advances into Central Asia to subdue the Turcoman and other tribal confederacies, which began with the capture of Tashkent in June 1865 despite assurances to the contrary given by the Russian Foreign Minister, Prince Gorshakov, to the English ambassador in Moscow, five days previously. The Foreign Secretary, Lord John Russell, hoped that 'both Powers would respect the independence of the Persian monarchy, would be careful not to encroach on the territory of Persia and not undermine the authority of the Shah'.[32] It remained a consistent objective of British policy, but it made little impression on Russian expansionism and did nothing to prevent the fall of Bukhārā, 1866, Samarqand, 1868, Krasnovodsk, 1869, Khīva, 1873 and Marv, 1884. Measures to hold Russian advances and to prevent the infringement of Persian sovereignty contained an element of bluff in so far as there was hardly any prospect of military action actually being taken because of the long land communications and difficulties in protecting areas of British interest. It was the vulnerability of India which gave rise to British concern for Persia. 'Were it not for our possessing India,' declared Lord Salisbury in 1889, 'we should trouble ourselves but little about Persia'.[33] This was the reason for preventing Persia from becoming 'an outlying Russian dependency', and why Persia was a crucial factor in Anglo-Russian diplomacy, in what became known as the 'Eastern Question'.

Force not being a credible option in the formulation of British policy towards Russia over Persia, the real alternatives were to bolster the internal stability of Persia or reach an accommodation with Russia which would include not only the territorial integrity of Persia but also guarantee the defence of India. This prompted the second major cause of interest, the furtherance of commercial relations, which accompanied the more determined diplomatic initiatives of Lord Salisbury, as Foreign Secretary, in 1888 when he appointed Sir Henry Drummond Wolff as Minister in Tehrān. Yet though to some extent this new initiative corresponded with certain Persian aspirations encouraged by Malkam Khān during his period as Persian Minister in London during the 1870s it was not necessarily endorsed by all the British trading concerns nor welcomed by an increasingly nervous and worried Shah. It certainly was not well received by the Russians. The concession-hawking in London and elsewhere by agents of the Shah, with or without his permission, the curious promotion of the Reuter Concession, irrespective of its merits or faults and its subsequent humiliating cancellation amidst a welter of diplomatic pressures, personal

The acquisition of the D'Arcy Concession

animosity, religious opposition and political opportunism was not an attractive precedent for trade promotion. The scandal of the Lottery Concession in 1889 implicating Malkam Khān, the Shah and his Ministers reflected adversely on Iranian credit rating in the international money markets.[34] Dubious and sensible concessionaires alike flocking to Tehrān were fleeced by court officials for spurious privileges. The Shah gained money but gave little in return. As Lord Salisbury came to realise,

He has a mortal dread of reform, and of all that may lead to it, and the fear lest measures for the development of his country should issue in the curtailment of his own power, stands for very much in the passive resistance which he has offered to most of our attempts to benefit his people. If he once suspects you mean to clip his wings, he will start away from you, and never let you near him again.[35]

For all his energy and panache, his self-confidence and persistence, Sir Henry Drummond Wolff was not able to get behind the reserve of Nāsir al-Dīn Shāh. He suggested the Shah should make a declaration granting civil liberties to his subjects, without the satisfaction of seeing it proclaimed before he left Tehrān, and he made no headway over the question of railway construction. He persuaded the Shah to open the River Kārūn to international shipping. He assisted the negotiations undertaken by de Reuter's son for the right to found a national bank as compensation for the abrogation in 1873 of the original Concession. This was granted and it was incorporated in London under Royal Charter in 1889 as the Imperial Bank of Persia. It became an institution of considerable importance in Iranian financial development under its able first manager, Joseph Rabino. Lord Salisbury reckoned it as a positive step in the right direction of developing local resources to arrest national decay and prevent the country being absorbed by Russia. It was, he remarked, 'a matter of capital importance to encourage the creation of commercial machinery' to achieve these ends, but he, like Lord Curzon later, was not sanguine that the prospects for strengthening Persia would come to anything, though he accepted that it was the only feasible policy to counter Russian activites, if an open collision was to be prevented.[36]

Just before Wolff returned from Tehrān following a nervous breakdown, a Major Gerald Talbot obtained a concession to control the production, marketing and exporting of all Persian tobacco. Such a monopoly, tantamount to an exclusive customs farming arrangement had been successfully implemented in Egypt and Turkey and would certainly have increased Government revenues. However, whatever its fiscal justification it conflicted with the legitimate interests of the growers and merchants and occasioned the opportunity for the religious opposition to campaign openly against the Shah and his ministers. After Russian intrigue and a series of devious manoeuvres the Shah rescinded the Concession. Compensation of £500 000 was eventually met by a loan reluctantly agreed by the Imperial Bank, thereby inaugurating the national debt.

In 1901–2, British trade with Persia was estimated at £2 759 000 (imports £2 112 000, exports £647 000), about the same as a decade previously, competing with Russian trade of £3 270 000 (imports £2 056 000, exports £1 214 000), an increase of about a third over a decade. Diplomatic activity was intense to prevent Persia falling, as I.A. Zinoviev, a former notable Russian Minister to Persia, who had served in the Legation 1856–83, said for the first time, like an overripe pear, which might have enabled the Russians to 'walk in when the time comes without striking a blow'.[37]

Life in Tehrān for the small foreign community tended to be monotonous and isolated from the rest of the country. The officials were polite but unpredictable, the court proud but petty. Few foreign merchants were free from arbitrary local obstructions or the uncertainties of local procedures. Persian society was intensely personalised and had little sense of institutionalised responsibility, so misunderstandings were frequent. For many foreign observers, Iran appeared a shadow of its former self. The contrast between the magnificent monuments of antiquity, the richness of the literary heritage and the dilapidated state of the country was noticeable. Beyond the curiosity and the fascination was the reality of much mutual incomprehension.

3 EARLY OIL RIGHTS IN PERSIA

The D'Arcy Concession was not the first sign of interest in the oil deposits of Persia, for seepages had been known and worked for centuries for caulking boats, bonding bricks, setting jewellery and in flaming missiles.[38] Travellers visiting Persia in the seventeenth century had made many references to them in the south-western districts and around Baku, then in Persian possession in the north of the country. The first serious geological reference is contained in the observations 'On the Geology of Portions of the Turco–Persian Frontier and of the Districts Adjoining' which W.K. Loftus contributed in August 1855 to the Geological Society in London.[39] Loftus had been a scientific member of the Persian–Turkish Frontier Commission of 1848 and travelled extensively over the archaeological sites in the area, noting particularly, for the first time, the oil indications in the neighbourhood of the great Parthian stone platform at Masjid i-Suleimān.[40] The de Reuter Concession, granted on 25 July 1872, had conferred on its promoters by Article 11, 'the exclusive and definite privilege to work, all over the Empire, the mines of coal, iron, copper, lead, petroleum etc.' but these lapsed with its cancellation on 10 November 1873. In 1884, the Dutch firm Hotz & Co. of Bushire obtained

The acquisition of the D'Arcy Concession

a petroleum concession for the lands around nearby Dālakī, but the small scale operations undertaken were quite unsuccessful.

Undeterred by his earlier concessionary fiasco de Reuter was granted, on 30 January 1889, a second concession for sixty years, empowering him to found a bank and develop mineral resources. The bank was duly incorporated as the Imperial Bank of Persia and the Persian Bank Mining Rights Corporation was formed to acquire, in the words of the prospectus, 'the exclusive and definite privilege of working throughout the Empire, the iron, copper and lead, mercury, coal, petroleum, manganese, borax and asbestos mines belonging to the State, and which had not been previously ceded to others'. The exploration of the concession was limited to ten years after which it lapsed if no production had been commenced. The Persian Government was entitled to 16 per cent of the net profits. The capital raised was £1 000 000 in 70 000 preferred ordinary shares of £5 each, and 130 000 ordinary shares of £5 each. The underwriters were Messrs J. Henry Schröder & Co. and D. Sassoon & Co. It was optimistically anticipated that £200 000 working capital would be sufficient to complete the operations and that the petroleum occurring at various places in Persia, notably near Shushtar and Bushire, would be so suitable that it would 'not therefore require (which the Baku petroleum does) distillation before it can be used for lamps etc.'

Indeed the example of Baku was very clearly in the minds of people at the time. Petroleum products from Russia had been appearing in Tehrān since 1876. The first American Minister to Persia (in 1883), S.G.W. Benjamin, was enthusiastic, writing about Baku in glowing terms as 'a large and rapidly growing European city, with a highly important commerce. What has done this? The answer is *petroleum*... The abundance of the petroleum is indicated by the fact that at the extensive petroleum wells, several miles north of Baku, the work is conducted at night by the aid of the flames perpetually bursting out of the earth.'[41] Lord Curzon, who travelled to Persia on his fact-finding journey via Baku, was less impressed by 'its shabby conglomeration of peoples, its oil harbour, its canopy of smoke, and its all-pervading smells'.[42] Furthermore a great number of Persian labourers worked in the Russian oil fields, much facilitated from 1890 onwards by the availability of cheap easily obtainable short-term permits. So much so, that, according to Marvin Entner in his study of Persian–Russian commercial relations, 'there were very few labourers in northern Persia who had not spent a year in Russia, and by 1910 a very substantial proportion of the common labour employed at the Baku oil fields was Persian, perhaps 20 to 30 per cent'.[43]

The Persian Bank Mining Rights Corporation was not unaware of the importance of these Russian oil fields. They recruited a British naturalised

The acquisition of the D'Arcy Concession

Armenian engineer, Mr Allahverdiantz, who had been employed as 'the manager of some oil works at Baku', according to Sir Henry Drummond Wolff who, in 1890, passed on to Lord Salisbury an optimistic report which claimed that 'the Russian oil fields are getting exhausted at the present day', whereas 'the virgin oil fields of Persia promise a good future as they may be made to engage the whole of Western markets in a short time if there be sufficient oil'.[44] Future promises were no substitute for present realities. Within a couple of years the Corporation was disheartened, admitting its 'indifferent success partly owing to natural difficulties in the severity of the winter in the north and the extreme heat in the south, partly to the backward state of the country, and the absence of communications and transport'.[45] The Chairman, Sir Lepel Griffin, also complained of the lack of support and protection from the Persian Government, without which

it is obvious that in a country like Persia, with an autocratic Government and all authority directly emanating from the Shah, no commercial enterprise of a new and strange character can be profitably carried on and it is still more certain that, if in the place of assistance and support, the Corporation meets with direct hostility, opposition and outrage from high officials of the Persian Government, its only recourse is to refuse to spend more capital on a fruitless endeavour and retire,

which the Corporation did.[46] Whilst not completely blameless over its lack of judgement, inefficiency, and false optimism it was sorely provoked by local outrages against its personnel in the four main areas where it explored for oil, Kishm Island off the northern coast of the Persian Gulf, Ram Hormuz in the south-west near Shushtar, Simnān to the east of Tehrān and Dālakī.

The Corporation detailed its charges against the Persian Government, maintaining that 'Unless compensation be awarded to the Corporation for the losses they have sustained through the obstruction of Persian officials, it is difficult to understand how any industrial undertaking in Persia can be profitably carried on.' The Foreign Office, however, was not sympathetic to those who 'went into business in Persia at their own risk and if they expected to find the same order and security which is looked for in Europe, it is their own fault if their anticipation were not realised. It ought to be made clear to them at once that no support whatever will be given to this preposterous claim.'[47] Proposals for compensation and arbitration were eventually dropped and the Corporation went into liquidation on 21 July 1901, its rights having lapsed after the ten year period of unsuccessful exploration.

Three further concessions in respect of oil rights were granted by 1900. In 1894, D.W. Torrence, an American, received a concession for the sinking of artesian wells in association with certain mineral and oil privi-

The acquisition of the D'Arcy Concession

leges for twenty-five years, but he forfeited it after a year because he did not comply with its terms. Two years later, in January 1896, the Sipahsālār Az'am, a leading politician and landowner, was granted by the Shah the right to prospect and exploit the oil resources in the province of Māzandarān. Later in 1916 the Sipahsālār Az'am disposed of his rights to a Georgian-born Persian speculator, A. Khostaria, after which they became inextricably linked with the North Persian Oil Concession in which the Company and Standard Oil were closely involved (see chapter 12). The Governor-General of Gīlān is reported to have had an oil concession to drill near the Caspian Sea in 1900, but nothing came of it.

4 THE D'ARCY CONCESSION

(a) Discussions in Paris and London

By 1900, therefore, there had been little progress in discovering oil in commercial quantities in Persia. Persian oil consumption was small and mostly confined to kerosene for lamps and cooking, but it was rising. In 1885, oil imports were valued at £2245 for Bushire and £2656 for Tabrīz.[48] Three years later they had increased to £7780 and £4600 for the same towns respectively.[49] In 1901–2 total oil imports cleared through customs were valued at £60 030 and in 1902–3 at £50 940.[50]

Already in 1888 the Political Resident in Bushire was reporting active competition between American and Russian oil firms for markets around the Persian Gulf: 'The cheapness of the Russian oil enables it to compete against superior American qualities.'[51] Serious interest in the oil possibilities of Persia was sustained by the researches and travels of M. Jacques de Morgan, who was entrusted with a scientific mission by the French Government at the invitation of the Persian Government in 1889. Between 1889 and 1891, he visited Persia and collected an encyclopaedic mass of information on its culture, geology and archaeology. He published a preliminary geological article in *Annales des Mines* in 1892[52] in which he mentioned possible oil prospects in Kurdistān. After his Persian mission, de Morgan was despatched on a similar one to Egypt for five years before returning to Persia again in 1897. Then he established the French archaeological service at Susa and constructed the Beau Geste style fort which has guarded for so many years the excavations of generations of French scholars.

The detailed volumes on his mission were published between 1894 and 1905.[53] The second volume, with his careful descriptions of oil prospects in the region around Zuhāb in the Qaṣr-i Shīrīn district of Persia, appeared in 1895. De Morgan maintained that the geology confirmed that it was an area of potential petroleum development which it would be advantageous for Persia to exploit. As the petroleum products used in China, India, Persia and Turkey either came from Baku or Pennsylvania, he suggested that the foundation of a Persian oil industry 'serait pour le gouvernement la source d'un revenu considérable sans compter les facilités qu'y trouverait l'industrie en Perse ou les combustibles et les huiles d'éclairage sont d'un prix très élevé'.[54]

He was quite convinced that the most important source of oil in the whole region lay in the oil-bearing strata, which extended from Kirkuk to the district of Pusht-i-Kuh. In particular, he singled out a site alongside a little river, locally known in Kurdish as 'Tchām-i-Tchiasorkh'.[55] When in Tehrān, de Morgan saw the principal Persian notables and officials whilst discussing his programme and in the course of his social calls met Sir Henry Drummond Wolff. De Morgan knew not only the nature of the country but the personality of its people.

Once the concessionary privileges of the Persian Bank Mining Rights Corporation had lapsed in 1898, the Persian authorities were then free to accept further offers. The experience of the Corporation however was cautionary and the glamour of Persian concessions had become less attractive. In spite of growing national expenditure, revenue was not increasing commensurately and the Persian Government was negotiating for a loan with both the Russians and the British. The extravagance of the Shah was only matched by his desperation for money. *The Statist* observed in March 1900: 'the Money markets of the world are closed to him... The reason is not far to seek. It is the old story: past breach of faith and disregard of obligations.'[56]

It was an opinion with which the Persian Prime Minister, Amīn al-Sultān would have agreed, for he confessed to the British Minister, Sir Arthur Hardinge, in 1902,

If I were Shah I should not have squandered the revenues... I should not now insist on going to Europe. But what can I do? If, in order to avoid a foreign loan I increase taxation, I shall create troubles which we have not the armed force to stamp out; if I reduce expenditure, I shall offend a host of vested interests, and if I fail to provide the Shah with money I shall lose his confidence. As regards internal reforms, ever since I resumed office three years ago, my time has been so taken up in negotiating, in the face of immense difficulties, foreign loans to meet the deficits resulting from the Shah's prodigality, that I have been unable to attend to much else.[57]

There was every incentive for Persia to offer an oil concession again as it lacked the necessary capital and technical expertise to develop an oil industry, but foreign interests were justified in their reluctance to get involved. Thus, for example, Calouste Gulbenkian, already a figure in the

The acquisition of the D'Arcy Concession

Russian oil industry and concerned in Turkish oil affairs, declined to take up a Persian oil concession.[58]

The initiative that resulted in the D'Arcy Concession came from General Antoine Kitabgi, a Persian official who, amongst other posts, had been Director-General of the Persian Customs, a lucrative and influential position. He was a very close confidant of Amīn al-Sultān, with whom he had been associated in the negotiations for the de Reuter, the Imperial Bank of Persia and the Tobacco Régie concessions and a project described by the French Minister as 'either a hare-brained scheme or a vulgar swindle', for a Banque de Perse et Afghanestan in 1885, amongst other enterprises.[59] He accompanied Nāsir al-Dīn Shāh on his European visit in 1890 in attendance on the Prime Minister. According to Sir Henry Drummond Wolff,

the Amin es-Sultan relied very much on a coadjutor of his—Kitabgi Khan—who was also of Georgian origin. He was a Roman Catholic, and married to an Armenian lady. The European element of the Persian Government was really represented by Kitabgi Khan, for he was well versed in Western matters — being able to draw up a concession and initiate commercial movements.[60]

General Kitabgi, a slim, grey-haired, mincing, dapper figure, was well connected, well travelled and well used to the wheeling and dealing of the Persian capital. In 1900 he was organising a Persian Exhibition in Paris and approaching possible concessionaires amongst French financiers. On 27 October 1900 General Kitabgi raised the question with Sir Henry Drummond Wolff in Paris, hoping that he would be able to introduce him to an English capitalist who would be interested in an oil concession. A month later Sir Henry informed Kitabgi that 'Concerning the oil, I have spoken to a capitalist of the highest order, who declares himself disposed to examine the affair, and if you so desire, I shall put him in communication with you.'[61] This was William Knox D'Arcy, introduced to Sir Henry by a mutual friend, Lord Orford.

General Kitabgi and Sir Henry Drummond Wolff, both supreme egotists, took exclusive credit for the D'Arcy Concession. Kitabgi later claimed to have been *au courant* with all contemporary events in Persia through his agents and that his timing was appropriate as 'in fact he had just obtained knowledge of the reports which had been brought forward by Mr Jacques de Morgan', irrespective of the inaccuracy of his dating, 1898.[62] Wolff, also referring to de Morgan, was no less positive and misleading, stating that 'knowing that I was largely interested in Persian matters, he mentioned the matter to me. Recognising the enormous commercial importance of the matter, I urged him to keep it confidential except so far as his employer, the French Government, was concerned, and this was done.' The reason, he alleged, was that 'in 1888 a mining

The acquisition of the D'Arcy Concession

concession had been obtained by me through the good offices of General Kitabgi Khan on behalf of Baron Julius de Reuter and his group who subsequently formed the Bank of Persia and a Company to work the mining concession'.[63] He referred to the frequent conversations he had with de Morgan and he certainly was furnished with an impressive number of reports of geological, technical and marketing importance, which have failed to survive.

Drummond Wolff was a proud, ambitious, impetuous, nervous, self-opinionated personality, who achieved much success, but admitted towards the end of his life that 'Unfortunately, what are called my declining years have not been overcrowded with enjoyment.'[64] A friend of the Prince of Wales, he had been a competent diplomat, but he suffered from a hypersensitive nature and could be furiously vindictive with those who had crossed him. Neither Kitabgi nor Wolff, unfortunately, commented on the role of Edouard Cotte, a relative of de Morgan who, as secretary to de Reuter, was an indispensable intermediary in the other principal concessional activities in which Kitabgi was involved and who brought de Morgan's reports to the attention of Kitabgi.

D'Arcy was born in 1849, the only son of an Irish solicitor who practised at Newton Abbot in Devonshire. He was educated at Westminster School. The family subsequently emigrated to Australia and settled at Rockhamp-

W.K. D'Arcy and family at Rockhampton, Queensland c.1885

The acquisition of the D'Arcy Concession

ton in Queensland where, as soon as he had qualified in law, D'Arcy joined his father's practice and soon became one of the town's leading and respected young citizens, a member of the local rowing club and the Rockhampton Jockey Club. He had an eye for a good horse as pictures of his Australian home show and he later possessed a stand at Epsom. It was in 1882 that he was approached by the brothers, Frederick, Edwin and Thomas Morgan to assist them in developing an old derelict gold mine they had acquired. Four years later a syndicate led by D'Arcy bought the mine outright and floated the Mount Morgan Mining Company with an authorised capital of a million £1 shares. After innumerable technical difficulties the mine struck gold richly and by the mid-nineties D'Arcy was a wealthy man. Rockhampton becoming too restrictive for his ambitions he returned to England as Chairman of the London Board of Mount Morgan. He gradually established himself with a town house in Grosvenor Square, a country mansion at Stanmore in Middlesex and a shooting estate at Bylaugh Park in Norfolk. On the death in 1902 of his Spanish born first wife, Elena, the mother of his five children, he married Nina Boucicault of the well-known theatrical family. His company being agreeable, his hospitality generous and his wife charming, he was very acceptable in society and had a wide range of distinguished acquaintances.

He was not, however, just content to rest on his financial laurels, but invested his money in a number of enterprises and kept in close touch with his Australian affairs. Though shrewd, he was no fly-by-night speculator. He relied on his own judgement and freely consulted his friends and his advisers. Not a city slicker, not a city gent, he kept to himself, ably served in his office by just one assistant, John Jenkin. He had no business behind him and relied upon his advisers for professional knowledge and judgement. Clearly respected by his associates, there yet remains about him the impression of a successful punter who, in spite of studying the form, still backed his hunch. Whilst he enjoyed his good fortune he was not flamboyant in displaying it, and at his shooting parties might have been mistaken for a portly poacher rather than a distinguished host. Such was William Knox D'Arcy to whose attention a Persian oil concession of unproven prospects was suddenly brought.

A month after Wolff's overtures, D'Arcy declared himself sufficiently satisfied to wish to examine the matter in more detail. Kitabgi was almost offended at such a request when there was no doubt that 'the stretch of the oil fields at Kend-i-Chirin, is a hundred times superior on the surface to the development of Bakou; in such a manner, that in taking a quarter or even less, *we are in the presence of a source of riches incalculable as to extension*, without counting the great economy on the expenses of production and transport'.[65] One wonders if D'Arcy ever recalled this fantastic hyperbole

The acquisition of the D'Arcy Concession

Edouard Cotte and General Antoine Kitabgi, Tehrān 1901

in his later dealings with the Kitabgi family or the estimate, 'the sacrifice', of the £20 000−25 000 for the expenses of the journey with a detailed ground study. The opening bids were not for the faint-hearted.

In early January 1901 Cotte visited D'Arcy in London and persuaded him to return to Paris with him and Wolff to meet Kitabgi on 8 January for the first time. Over the next two months ten more meetings were held in Paris and London often with D'Arcy's solicitors, Nicholl Manisty & Company and his geological adviser, Dr (later Sir) Boverton Redwood, the leading petroleum expert of the day, consultant to the Admiralty and the Burmah Oil Company and a kind of single-handed oil personnel agency. The terms of understanding were settled between D'Arcy and his associates, Kitabgi and Cotte on 1 March 1901 after some hard bargaining. Kitabgi received £4000 for his travelling expenses and the cost of his stay in Tehrān and an interest of seven hundredths in the concession if it was granted.[66] Cotte was given three hundredths should his services be successful. The settlement with Wolff was reached ten days later, 'one tenth part of all the profits to be derived under the said Concession or from the sale thereof'. It seems to have been the result of a reluctantly conceded compromise which the disgruntled diplomat regretted and which resulted in him becoming bitterly antagonistic towards D'Arcy. Kitabgi was also given the right to subscribe for 10 per cent of any shares offered to the

32

The acquisition of the D'Arcy Concession

public on similar terms. He agreed not to consent to any modification of the draft concession without referring to D'Arcy.[67] D'Arcy excluded the five northern provinces from the scope of his concession lest Russian interests should be antagonised. It was a wise precaution.

The arrangements were completed with the appointment of A.L. Marriott, cousin and secretary of D'Arcy's confidential adviser, G.W. Marriott, as D'Arcy's representative, 'to obtain from the Shah of Persia a concession for the oil fields believed to exist in that country'.[68] On the advice of Boverton Redwood, H.T. Burls was instructed to carry out a geological survey. Marriott and Cotte left Paris on 25 March after the departure of Kitabgi, reaching Tehrān on 16 April by way of Constantinople, Tiflis, Baku and Enzelî. Writing to Kitabgi in Paris on 7 March, D'Arcy confidently asserted that 'it is a very great *comfort to me to know my interests and those of Sir Henry are in your skilful and able hands*'.[69] Kitabgi was the pivot of the operation.

In accordance with normal practice, D'Arcy had requested diplomatic support for his application, and Marriott was furnished with a formal introduction dated 12 March 1901, and signed by Sir Martin Gosselin on behalf of the Secretary of State, Lord Lansdowne, to the Minister in Tehrān from the Foreign Office. It read simply that

this letter will be presented to you by Mr Alfred L. Marriott, who is proceding to Persia on business connected with mining. I have to request you to be good enough to afford him such assistance as he may require, and as you can properly render to him in furtherance of the object of his journey, subject to the terms of the Circular Despatch of this Series, dated 8 March 1881.[70]

(b) Negotiations in Tehrān

Kitabgi arrived in Tehrān on 10 April and called on the Minister, Sir Arthur Hardinge, whom he expected, apparently, to be fully briefed on the concessionary application and ready to use his influence on its behalf. There was a cat and mouse atmosphere about the whole negotiations for at the outset Kitabgi told the Minister that the Russians were trying to obtain permission from the Persian Government for a pipeline from Baku to southern Persia and that he had his own scheme which he hoped the Minister would support. He was reticent about the details beyond the fact that Drummond Wolff was associated with him. Hardinge thought it 'sounded rather fantastic' and took no further action.[71] Kitabgi visited his friends on his return but nothing definite was done to advance the negotiations until the arrival of Marriott. At their first meeting Marriott made it plain to Kitabgi that 'we could not expect the English Government to press

Alfred L. Marriott 1901

the matter politically' and that Kitabgi should 'commence proceedings at once'.[72]

The following day, on 17 April, Marriott called at the Legation to pay his compliments and present his letter to the Minister, but he was not in

The acquisition of the D'Arcy Concession

Tehrān and Marriott only saw him a week later. The negotiations proceeded at a leisurely pace and Kitabgi did not see the Amīn al-Sultān till 21 April, the day after strict Shī'īte religious observances celebrating the martyrdom of Husayn and Hassan in the holy month of Muharram, had begun. At this meeting the Prime Minister responded favourably but referred in his comments to the comparative influences of Russia and Great Britain on and in Persia. It was his intention to maintain a 'balance between Russian and English Governments'. It was obvious that the negotiations would be conducted in a political context.[73] The draft concession was presented and handed to the Minister for Mines, Muhandes al-Mamalek, to be translated into Persian.

The preliminaries had been completed. The first complication about the concession which presented itself was Kitabgi's opinion that it was 'dangerous to ask in Mr. D'Arcy's name and suggested asking for it in his own or some other Persian's', an idea which hardly appealed to Marriott.[74] The first meeting with the British Minister took place on 25 April and the following day Hardinge presented Marriott to the Prime Minister by whom he was courteously received and to whom he gave a letter from Wolff. It was clear, however, that little definite progress could be achieved until the month of mourning had ended. Hardinge reported to Lansdowne that he had 'introduced him [Marriott] to His Highness the Atabeg i-Azam, explaining that whilst I had no instructions to afford active support to the proposals which he and Kitabgi Khan, who is associated with him, are making, I believed from what I had heard of them that they might prove advantageous to Persia'. Marriott had made the point that 'petroleum will be found in great quantities and that an industry may be developed which will compete with that of Bakou'.[75] It was an obvious but subtle trick to play for it reflected not only the current pre-occupation with the Russian preponderance in Persian affairs but also struck a chord of historical response as Baku, previously Persian, had been annexed by Russia in 1806.

The negotiations were almost becalmed for three weeks whilst the Persian ministers were making up their minds. Marriott meantime was keeping a low profile and 'only took such steps in the matter as were absolutely necessary: ostensibly busying myself with the purchase of rugs, embroideries, etc.'[76] He was cautiously optimistic and discussed with Kitabgi some possible modifications to the concessionary draft to facilitate its acceptance more easily, such as advancing the payment of the money to the Persian Government earlier than had been proposed. In London Wolff was becoming anxious and concerned about the relationship of Amīn al-Sultān with the Shah, which he felt was deteriorating.[77] Marriott cabled on 6 May with restraint, 'We are making slow progress with business.

The acquisition of the D'Arcy Concession

Present state of affairs satisfactory, doing all possible, must act with great caution. Undue haste would be to lose the business. Please do not be impatient.'[78] The translation was taking time, having been entrusted to the son of the Minister for Foreign Affairs, Mushīr al-Dawla.

Kitabgi himself had not been idle for, according to Hardinge on 12 May, he 'has, I understand, secured in a very thorough manner the support of all the Shah's principal Ministers and courtiers, not even forgetting the personal servant who brings His Majesty his pipe and morning coffee'.[79] On the same day Kitabgi saw the Prime Minister, who had not yet read the concession text. He visited him again the next day and was told that the Minister for Mines had returned to Tehrān and more progress could be expected. Marriott, whom D'Arcy at this stage thought 'worthy of every confidence',[80] began to feel that the Persian Ministers were dragging their feet and that it was time to take up the running. Believing that 'the authorities are hesitating and want pushing', he asked Hardinge on 15 May for assistance in speaking 'energetically' to Amīn al-Sultān, who, he assumed, was procrastinating 'due to the fact that he does not know if he ought to grant this concession without first consulting the Russians'.[81] It was a dreadful predicament for the Prime Minister as he was in the midst of negotiations for a Russian loan. It was a time of decision of very great political complexity and difficulty.

Hardinge saw Amīn al-Sultān on the following day, 16 May, and pressed him to take some action. Shortly afterwards Kitabgi called on the Prime Minister officially and it was agreed that the Minister for Mines would go through the concession draft clause by clause with himself and Marriott. This took place the next day. Hardinge's intervention was important enough to indicate that whilst the British Government had no particular commitment towards the concession he, as Minister in Tehrān, was not indifferent towards its fate in the perspective of Anglo-Persian relations. He prided himself on having re-established a more friendly atmosphere between the Legation and Persian Ministers than had existed for some time and believed he was successfully countering Russian influence as officials were acting on less purely Russian lines than previously.[82]

He was unwilling to lose the advantages he had patiently gained and was prepared to use his discretion on D'Arcy's behalf, as he explained to Lansdowne on 30 May.

I was given to understand in the course of the negotiations that a word from me might considerably assist their success and I therefore took an opportunity, as an important British enterprise was at stake, of intimating to the Atabeg-i Azam my conviction that the investment of a large amount of British capital in Persia would be greatly to the advantage of that country and my hope that a concession would be

Amīn al-Sulṭān c. 1900

granted. His Highness said that he had all along been favourably disposed towards the scheme, and that I might rely on his doing his best to promote both this and all other British commercial undertakings.[83]

This was a clear statement of intent, though the Prime Minister expected better terms to be offered, a decision to proceed, but not a guarantee of

The acquisition of the D'Arcy Concession

acceptance. Yet it was sufficient to merit Marriott's clear optimism to D'Arcy on 17 May that 'very critical stage successfully passed. All is going on well and I have good hope of obtaining the concession in a week's time. Kitabgi has acted with great judgement and faithfully fulfilled all obligations.'[84]

The fencing was over. The cut and thrust of decision making followed. More explanation of the clauses of the draft concession was made to the Minister of Mines and finally on 20 May the Shah was informed and given a copy of the proposed concession. He 'refused to sign unless we paid £40 000 down and £40 000 on formation of the Company, also 16 per cent instead of 10 per cent on net profits', and went off hunting, a favourite pastime.[85] That evening Amīn al-Sultān and Kitabgi met with a number of the Ministers to discuss the situation. Marriott, examining the position, acted with determination on his own initiative 'to accept the 16 per cent if we were freed from the 5 per cent export duty', as another concession had recently been concluded on such terms.[86] He also authorised Kitabgi 'to promise his friends £5000 in advance of their shares', because, 'I considered it very necessary to act thus promptly on my own responsibility as Kitabgi had all the Ministers together discussing the affair (a chance which might not occur again) and delay might be fatal.'[87] He hoped that D'Arcy would approve his action for 'to refuse would be to lose the affair'. 'You can rely on me to make the best bargain possible', he cabled D'Arcy, who agreed, although his original instructions definitely precluded any cash down payments, and replied, 'Don't scruple if you can propose anything for facilitating affairs on my part.'[88] It seemed as if there would be no further delays, as Kitabgi told Marriott that 'the promise of the £5000 down had been of the very greatest assistance to him, and that he thought he would be able to arrange matters.'[89] On the following day there was a momentary flurry of excitement when it was revealed that the Persian Minister in London had telegraphed about another oil concession on behalf of an undisclosed rich syndicate claiming to offer higher terms, but Amīn al-Sultān remained firm in his association with Kitabgi and declined to become involved.[90] All trace of those involved in the last minute scheme seems to have disappeared.

Kitabgi's optimism was premature. On 22 May the concessionary negotiations again were stopped in their tracks, Marriott being informed that 'a difficulty had arisen, the nature of which Kitabgi had not yet found out. All he knew was that the Grand Vizier took the concession to the Shah yesterday and that the latter had not signed.'[91] Kitabgi was probably being disingenuous, as it was almost inconceivable that he was not in the confidence of the Prime Minister, but Marriott correctly surmised that Russian pressure against the concession was causing the Persian Government to hesitate. He requested authority from D'Arcy to offer a further financial inducement as a possible way out of the impasse reached, 'as if I have this authorisation I am sure that I can do the business if it is possible at all'.[92] It was a cynical but realistic assessment on a crucial day. Seeing Kitabgi in the afternoon of 23 May about the lack of progress in the stalled negotiations, he made available another £5000 if it was absolutely necessary to clinch the deal. Kitabgi returned from visiting Amīn al-Sultān in the evening 'with the news that he had the formal promise that the concession would be granted. He had found the extra £5000 most useful. It appeared that the Grand Vizier had told the Russians who tried to prevent the affair. Also from hints, I fancy the Shah wanted some ready money and stood out for some on signing the concession.'[93] The avarice of the Shah in signing the concession overcame his fears of offence to the Russians in granting it.

There was no doubt that the last anxious days turned on Russian objections and the extent to which the Persian Ministers were prepared to disregard them and maintain their balancing policy. As Marriott realised in cabling to D'Arcy on 24 May, 'Yesterday evening on account of opposition from Russian Minister there was greatest danger of losing business', but that according to Cotte, the extra consideration 'alone saved business, any delay might have been fatal'.[94] The generally accepted account of these events based on Hardinge's recollections of this phase of the negotiations in his autobiography, *A Diplomatist in the East*, is incorrect. Hardinge's memory played him false. He described how a Persian written version of the Concession was passed to the Russian Legation whilst the Oriental Secretary, Stritter, was temporarily away and that the Minister, unaware of the importance of the matter and unable to read the text, took no action, thereby giving the Persian Government enough time to sign the concession without Russian objections being raised.[95]

There is no contemporary corroboration for this imaginative tale, indeed the truth is more exciting. Amīn al-Sultān, who was well-known for his pro-Russian sympathies, was conscious that Russia did not approve of any independent Persian action and so conducted the negotiations secretly in order not to jeopardise his friendly relations with the Russian Minister, K.M. Argyropoulo. Indeed Hardinge reported at the time that,

Great secrecy was observed in preparing the necessary papers, as it was felt that if the Russian Legation got news of the project it would attempt to crush it and would almost certainly succeed in doing so. Information on the subject however reached Monsieur Argyropoulo a few days ago and the promoters of the scheme suspect that it was furnished by the Atabeg-i Azam after everything had been settled and that His Highness pleaded, in reply to the Russian Minister's remonstrances, that the Shah's promise having been given it was too late to reconsider the

The acquisition of the D'Arcy Concession

subject and strove to minimise the value of the concession. His Highness however assures me that all that passed between himself and my Russian colleague was an inquiry by the latter on or about the 24th instant respecting the truth of reports as to the projected concession which had reached him.[96]

Since a leak was obviously known to have occurred, there was no point in denying it.

The evidence from Kitabgi supports the general conclusions of Hardinge at this stage, for he stated on 24 May that there were 'substantial indications of the intrigues which surrounded the Shah in order to prevent him from signing the act of concession'.[97] Amīn al-Sultān was not exempt from the enmity which surrounded Persian courtiers. Kitabgi repeated the Minister's remarks to him, 'Do you understand what is at stake? They are capable of informing the Russians.' This apparently happened through an official in the Foreign Ministry after which Amīn al-Sultān told the Russian Minister that his apprehensions were groundless and that 'the conclusion of this affair, if it ever took place, would take many months, and that during that time, he would have plenty of leisure to inform his government and to demand instructions'.[98] Argyropoulo seemed reassured, but on 26 May probably had second thoughts and called on the Prime Minister at his home, indicating to him the need to reject the concession. Kitabgi seemed depressed at the possible consequences of this interview and though he may have exaggerated the seriousness of the situation, he asked Marriott to request the assistance of Hardinge. He felt that Argyropoulo would press the Russian Foreign Ministry at St Petersburg for precise instructions. The Russian Minister did, excusing the Prime Minister's conduct by suggesting he was, according to Russian sources, 'probably counting on eliminating the opposition, be it even indirect, of A. Hardinge to the commercial agreement with Russia (revisions of customs and tariffs) and compelling him to forgive the severity of customs regulations introduced in southern Persia'.[99]

Marriott, who was expecting the signed concession and had received D'Arcy's authorisation of £10 000 paid to the Imperial Bank for 'blue pottery and salt cellars from Kum and Resht embroidery', sent a cautiously optimistic telegram to London. Hardinge declined to intervene personally but sent 'Abbās Qulī Khān, the dragoman, to tell the Grand Vizier he hoped nothing would interfere to prevent the immediate signing of the concession which he understood had been granted'.[100] On 28 May the Concession was signed by the Shah. Marriott learnt the news at a Legation dinner party from Mushīr al-Dawla that evening. Kitabgi heard about it from Muhandes al-Mamalek. Only polite formalities remained to be exchanged. Marriot and Kitabgi called on Amīn al-Sultān on 30 May who expressed himself 'very satisfied with the concession and said he was

The acquisition of the D'Arcy Concession

sure it would be a good thing for Persia, and at the same time promote the friendship already existing between his country and England'.[101]

Muzaffar al-Dīn Shāh granted Marriott an audience on 5 June asking 'several questions about the manner in which the operations would be commenced in starting the petroleum works'.[102] Marriott returned to England on 23 June recognising that the 'highest praise is due to Kitabgi. I do not believe anyone else could have accomplished the business. M. Cotte has been of the greatest assistance throughout. The assistance from Sir A. Hardinge has been valuable.'[103] No less notable had been his own determined contribution to the negotiations and the manner in which he managed his team. Marriott received less recognition from D'Arcy than he was entitled to, probably being unfairly criticised by Wolff.

In the first flush of his success Marriott was enthusiastic, convinced that 'If the oil scheme of Mr D'Arcy succeeds, as I believe it will do with tact and good management, it should have far-reaching effects, both commercially and politically for Great Britain and cannot fail to largely increase her influence in Persia.'[104] Hardinge was much more circumspect, supposing that,

If the hopes of the concessionaires are realised, and petroleum is discovered, as their agents believe will be the case, in sufficient quantities to compete with Bakou, the concession may be fraught with important economic and indeed political results. But the soil of Persia, whether it contains oil or not, has been strewn of late years with the wrecks of so many hopeful schemes of commercial and political regeneration that it would be rash to attempt to predict the future of this latest venture.[105]

H.W. MacLean, who had been manager of the Persian Royal Mint and economic adviser to the British Government on Persian affairs, was not optimistic over trading prospects in his 1903 report on Persia, referring to enterprises which had failed to succeed in recent years because 'The great cost of installing machinery on account of the heavy freight on inland transport, the cost of fuel, the inefficiency of labour which, although cheap, is unskilled and without energy, have been the chief causes of non success.'[106]

Compared with the forward policy of Lord Salisbury towards Persia, that of the early twentieth century was essentially a holding one, though the objective was the same in 1902: 'to maintain the continued national existence and the territorial integrity of Persia and to develop her resources'.[107] 'The tendency,' it was stated in 1905, 'of British policy in Persia has been to avoid, as far as we can, any addition to our political or territorial responsibilities or any step calculated to disturb the political status quo.' As the Committee of Imperial Defence recommended in March 1905, 'It should be our object, on commercial as well as on strategic

41

grounds to maintain the *status quo* in Persia.'[108] This did not preclude defensive measures to prevent the balance tilting unfavourably against existing British interests, such as the Lansdowne Declaration of 5 May 1903 in respect of the possibility of a foreign base being erected in the Persian Gulf as 'we should certainly resist it with all means at our disposal',[109] but offensive activities were excluded. The D'Arcy Concession was not a stalking horse.

5 THE CONTEMPORARY SIGNIFICANCE OF THE D'ARCY CONCESSION

In general the terms contained provisions for a concession rather than an industry, for exploration and production rather than administration and marketing; see Appendix 1.1. The Persian Government granted to D'Arcy (Article 1) 'a special and exclusive privilege to search for and obtain, exploit, develop, render suitable for trade, carry away and sell natural gas, petroleum, asphalt and ozokerite throughout the whole extent of the Persian Empire for a term of sixty years' although D'Arcy had excluded the five northern provinces from the actual extent of his concession.[110] The first company to exploit the Concession had to be formed within two years (Article 16) and on its formation the Persian Government was to be paid £20 000 sterling in cash and £20 000 in paid-up shares, and annually and rather vaguely 'a sum equal to 16 per cent of the annual profits of any company or companies' (Article 10). The payment equalled the guarantee deposited by de Reuter in 1872. Changes from the original draft text concerned the purchase of State cultivable land 'at a reasonable price current in the province' and that of private property from the proprietors 'without their being allowed to overcharge for the use of the grounds' (Article 3) rather than being free of charge. Certain existing seepages worked privately at Shushtar, Qasr-i Shīrīn and Dālakī were included within the concessionary arrangements (Article 4).

The concessionaire was obliged to notify the Persian Government of all companies formed to exploit the Concession. The definition of the role of subsequent companies in relation to the terms of the Concession later became a matter of considerable legal dispute. The post of the Imperial Commissioner, already instituted in the Imperial Bank of Persia Concession was strengthened (Article 11) and seems to have been tailor-made for General Kitabgi, who was the appointee. He was to receive an annual salary of £1000, not £60 as first proposed, from the date of the formation of the first company, to provide all the relevant information and advice available to him, safeguard the interests of the Persian Government and be consulted by the concessionaire. Exports and imports were to be free of all taxes and duties (Article 7).

In view of experience over its unfulfilled obligations in the de Reuter, Persian Bank Mining Rights Corporation, Tobacco Régie and other concessions, the Persian Government insisted on D'Arcy bearing all the risks (Article 14). Whilst the Government pledged itself 'to take all and any necessary measures to secure the safety and the carrying out of the object of this concession... and to protect the representatives, agents and servants of the company', it was not prepared 'under any pretext whatever' to accept any liability or claims against it in these respects. There was provision for arbitration in the case of dispute. The terms seem insignificant in comparison with later practice, but it has to be remembered that the prospects were quite unpredictable, the immediate precedent very disappointing (see pp.25-6). In reality it was wild-catting on a colossal scale in a distant unsettled land. There was nothing comparable to the extent or uncertainty of D'Arcy's Concession. Dutch colonial legislation in the East Indies, under which the first discovery well was drilled on 11 July 1884 in Sumatra, was simple. The lease was competitive but conferred wide rights on the concessionaire for exploitation. In the United States between 1894 and 1904 the royalty rate was between an eighth and a sixth of production and land rights cost between $50 and $250 an acre depending upon the probability of striking oil. In the proposed 1914 concession between the Turkish Petroleum Company and Turkey, the Company was to pay an annual rental of 6 per cent of the value of land required and a royalty of 8 per cent of crude oil production. In Russia generally the Government auctioned off oil-bearing state lands in return for a lump sum payment and a low yearly rental charge. As yet D'Arcy was unaware of the magnitude of the undertaking to which he had committed himself, whilst he was congratulating Kitabgi on the tact, discretion and determination which he had displayed bringing the undertaking to such a successful conclusion.[111] He thanked Lord Lansdowne appreciatively for the introduction to Sir Arthur Hardinge and trusted that the 'enterprise will prove advantageous to British Commerce, and to the influence of this country in Persia', and asked for the Government's 'protection and countenance'.[112] Hardinge, in comparison was laconic and factual in announcing the completion of negotiations to Lansdowne.[113]

D'Arcy was, nevertheless, perceptively aware of the political realities in Persia and intended from the first, by excluding the five northernmost provinces from the Concession, that he would 'give no umbrage to Russia' and do his utmost 'to prevent any cause of complaint from Russian subjects'.[114] This was the nerve of the enterprise, for in return for renouncing the northern provinces he had safeguarded himself by the 'express

The acquisition of the D'Arcy Concession

condition that the Persian Imperial Government shall not grant to any other person the right of constructing a pipe-line to the southern rivers to the South Coast of Persia' (Article 6). Russian reaction was furious, not so much to the D'Arcy Concession as a whole but to the pipeline restriction in particular. Amīn al-Sultān was threatened that 'as long as he is in power, the repetition of anything like that, will not be forgiven by the Imperial Government'.[115] Indeed, as Kitabgi had already intimated to Hardinge, the Russians were actively considering their own plans for a pipeline to counter American competition in kerosine in the markets of the Persian Gulf and India. A detailed project was laid before Nicholas II, who approved, in August 1901, with the commendation that it 'would result in the growth of our influence in Persia and on the shore of the Indian Ocean'.[116]

Thereupon Count de Witte, the influential and aggressive Russian Finance Minister, and his Tehrān agent, E.K. Grube, opened a campaign to thwart D'Arcy's apparent veto on Russian transit pipelines, by exerting pressure on Persian negotiations for a loan by making them dependent on a solution to the pipeline issue. It was the last of a series of Russian initiatives to dominate all of Persia politically and economically, for the conditions attached to the loan were the conclusion of a new commercial treaty favourable to Russian imports and exports, the elimination of British influence from the Persian Mint and the granting of a pipeline concession to the Loan and Discount Bank which was under the supervision of the Russian Ministry of Finance. With the Russian officered Cossack Brigade, formed in 1879,[117] and a Russian imposed ban on railway construction, 1889,[118] Persian independence was as heavily compromised as its finances were in debt, some £1 216 000 according to Hardinge in November 1901.[119] In 1901–2 Persia had an adverse balance of trade, which lasted for a further seven years, and in the same year trade with Russia constituted 45 per cent of Persia's total trade, 38.0 per cent of its imports and 58.7 per cent of its exports. A decade later the comparable figures were 62.8 per cent, 58 per cent and 60 per cent respectively, whereas the British share of Persian trade dropped from under a half to less than a third.[120] 'To a remarkable extent,' stated Marvin Entner in his study of Persian–Russian trade relations, 'Persia had been drawn into Russia's economic orbit and was a functioning part of her economy.'[121] Even after the dismissal of de Witte in 1903, Count Lamsdorf, the Russian Foreign Minister, declared Russia's task as 'politically to make Persia obedient and useful; that is sufficiently strong to be a tool in our hands – economically to preserve for ourselves the major share of the Persian market for free and exclusive exploitation by Russian efforts and capital'.[122]

For the realisation of Russian objectives the D'Arcy Concession had

The acquisition of the D'Arcy Concession

become an obstacle. Russian oil exports, mostly kerosine, to Persia gradually penetrated into Northern Persia down to Qazvīn, along to Khurāsān and down to Isfahān,[123] so that in 1910–11 they amounted to 96.2 per cent of total Persian consumption.[124] As Golubev, Russian negotiator during the Russian–Persian Customs Treaty negotiations, 1901–3, wrote, 'in the interests of our exports, petroleum and petroleum products stand almost in the front rank'.[125] Russian oil production, which in 1871 had been 5.8 million gallons, was thirty years later 2965.2 million gallons of which 2817.4 million gallons came from the Baku area alone.[126] Such a production required markets, and already in the 1880s S.E. Palashkovskii, who was an extremely versatile engineer, proposed an oil pipeline to improve access to markets lying near the Indian and Pacific oceans. Russian officials were unconvinced, considering that 'the significance of the pipeline for the Russian trade had been overestimated'.[127] From 1900, however, Russian well head prices began to drop in response to increasing competition and production, and between 1900 and January 1902 they dropped dramatically from 15.7 copecks per pood to 4.6 copecks per pood.[128] No wonder the Russian reaction to the D'Arcy Concession was so hostile, for not only did it presage politically a possible resurgence in British influence, but, economically, it posed a potential threat of a new source of oil production and further competition. The Concession had become a pawn in the game of British–Russian relations on the Persian board.

In some respects, as Amīn al-Sultān probably anticipated, the D'Arcy Concession became a blessing in disguise. Hardinge, in attempting to bolster up the Prime Minister's opposition to the onerous terms of the proposed Russian loan, argued that the Concession was a

> private speculation... not actively supported by my Government in the sense of their insisting on the grant of the Concession... it gives the Persian Government a good excuse for refusing the Russian demand, on the grounds that the lawyers differ on the subject (and that these differences can only be settled by long litigation), without offending Russia by implying suspicions of her secret political designs in relation to this proposal.[129]

He later warned against the 'preposterous Concession for pipelines to the Persian Gulf, which will probably never be carried into actual effect, but will, nevertheless, afford an excuse for covering Southern Persia with surveyors, engineers and protecting detachments of Cossacks, and preparing a veiled military occupation' which would only exacerbate not relieve Persian insolvency.[130] Persisting against Russian prohibitions, the Shah's desperation for money for his European tour, and the parsimony of the British Treasury, Hardinge contended that for Persia 'at a moment when she was beginning to develop her own oil industry, it was not reasonable

The acquisition of the D'Arcy Concession

to require her to give Russian oil special facilities for competing with it'. He argued that it would serve no useful purpose for the Shah on his visit to England to be involved in more litigation over the violation of yet another concessionary agreement particularly 'when Persia was once more beginning, through Mr. D'Arcy, to get in touch with English capital'.[131]

At the beginning of 1902, particularly towards the end of January, the situation was becoming critical. De Witte, as Argyropoulo reluctantly confirmed, 'absolutely refused to afford Persia any financial assistance unless the pipe-line asked for to the Persian Gulf were conceded' alleging that as his concession was concerned 'exclusively with the export and transit of Russian oil' it did not conflict with the D'Arcy Concession which was 'a monopoly only in regard to native oil'.[132] D'Arcy, apprehensive over the threats to his Concession, offered the Persian Government on 31 January 1902 £100 000 without security if he was granted the Ahwāz Barrage Concession previously bestowed by the late Shah on his physician, Dr Tholozan, or a 'a sum of money on the security of the royalty payable by his Oil Company', some £100 000.[133] This proposal, although insufficient to cover Persia's financial requirements, probably corresponded to one of the initial objectives which Amīn al-Sultān had in mind when supporting the D'Arcy Concession, an alternative source of finance. Amīn al-Sultān had committed himself to the terms of the loan, but had not signed, as Hardinge continued his protests.

In St Petersburg on 13 February, the ambassador, Sir Charles Scott, made urgent representations to Count Lamsdorf. On 17 February, de Witte, ignoring all objections, ordered the final text of the loan agreement to be prepared. D'Arcy increased his offer to £200 000 and then £300 000, which the Amīn al-Sultān was able to brandish in his own defence. At the same time evidence that de Witte and Count Lamsdorf were in disagreement emerged from St Petersburg in a cable from the Persian Minister there on 26 February, who reported that Russia would issue the loan without the pipeline strings being attached. Personal animosities between the Russian Ministers, Persian delaying tactics and the D'Arcy offer defused the pipeline question. Persia obtained a loan. After 1902 'a year which may be said perhaps to mark the high-water mark of Russian success in the Middle East',[134] Russia for many years did not have a comparable opportunity to stymie the D'Arcy Concession, but it was only a reprieve. The Concession never escaped its political implications.

In spite of the bitter dispute over the pipeline the verdict of the Russian historian, B.V. Ananich, is exaggerated: 'By undertaking the exploitation of the oil riches of southern Iran, England dealt a serious blow to the economic interests of Russia in the Middle East and Asia.'[135] It has to be remembered that, notwithstanding all the efforts of the geologists and

The acquisition of the D'Arcy Concession

Baku c.1900

drillers, oil was not discovered in Persia till 1908. Moreover, by then internal conditions in Russia had changed as a result of its defeat by the Japanese in 1904, the outbreak of the revolutionary movements in 1905 and the rapprochement with Great Britain over Persia in 1907. Besides, Russian trade with Persia continued to outpace substantially that of the British till 1914, when it dominated two thirds of the total Persian trade compared to the British fifth. The conclusive evidence, however, with increasing competition cutting the price four-fold by 1902, is to be found in the falling oil production of Baku by half from 2817.4 million gallons in 1901 to 1419.6 million gallons in 1914.[136] This was not accompanied by any switch of British oil funds out of Russian companies for, with the growth of the more northern oilfields at Maikop, British capital constituted two thirds of the foreign capital invested in the Russian oil industry by 1917.[137] A causal relationship between the granting of the D'Arcy Concession and declining Russian oil exports or trade to the Middle Eastern area is not proven in this period. The circumstances surrounding D'Arcy's concessionary interest were too unconnected to draw a definite national inference. It was the particular political complexities of Persia which gave the Concession a potential major international significance.

2
THE FUNDING AND FINDING OF OIL 1901-8

I D'ARCY ON HIS OWN 1901-5

(a) Introduction

The granting of the D'Arcy Concession had been, primarily, a political decision accompanied by the customary haggling over terms. Its development depended on finance, technical expertise and an ability to understand the Persian environment in which it would be worked. D'Arcy was not an entrepreneur, he had no engineering experience and little knowledge of Persia. He was an investor who, after consulting his acquaintances and advisers, expected to make a profitable return on his capital by forming a company to exploit his concession. He owed his opportunity to General Kitabgi and Sir Henry Drummond Wolff and he depended upon Dr Redwood for technical advice, as the most distinguished oil technologist of his time.[1] There was no large organisation behind D'Arcy. All his business affairs were handled by his secretary, John Jenkin and later H. E. Nichols,[2] who merely added Persian correspondence to their other duties, including those of the Mount Morgan Mining Company in London. Kitabgi clearly intended to manage affairs in Persia as his own responsibility.

Such a division of responsibilities, which seemed simple, in reality became uncommonly complicated. The preparations for drilling were not easy, needing local negotiations and long haulage of equipment over difficult terrain. There were problems over labour and supplies. Wolff was uncooperative and Kitabgi, insistent upon 'the necessity of acting in Persia according to the Persian ideas and not those of the English',[3] was disregarding Redwood's advice and disagreeing with the views of Reynolds, D'Arcy's engineer. The raising of finance proved desperately more difficult than had been anticipated and within a short time it became necessary to take legal advice on the Concession owing to the imprecision of its language. The early years, then, were marked by adversity rather than success, notable more for the persistence of D'Arcy and the determination of Reynolds than for the results of their efforts.

The funding and finding of oil 1901-8

Sir Boverton Redwood c. 1910

The funding and finding of oil 1901-8

(b) 'The grammar of Persian affairs' June 1901 - May 1903

(i) Associates and syndicates

Although D'Arcy fully backed his new investment, he did not see himself as more than the person who would initially crank the engine and that once started other fare-paying passengers would come for the ride and share the pleasure. Once the Concession was signed it became imperative to put his rights on a permanent basis, and relieve himself of the total responsibility he was shouldering. In June 1901 it was proposed to form the 'Persian Petroleum Exploration Syndicate' with a capital of £300 000 in £1 shares, of which 270 000 were to be issued as fully paid to D'Arcy in consideration of his concessionary rights and privileges.[4] The remainder of the shares issued for cash would provide for the necessary preliminary expenses. Redwood estimated that plant for drilling two wells would cost £10 000 and recognised at the outset D'Arcy's desire 'to economise as much as possible'.[5] He also engaged as engineer, George Reynolds, at a salary of £1500 p.a.[6] In August D'Arcy wrote to Kitabgi about the new arrangements. Thanking him again for his part in the successful negotiations, D'Arcy admitted that he found the enterprise had expanded to such an extent that it would surpass in a short time, his individual resources.[7] He felt it was a dangerous situation, for, if his health failed, those associated with the Concession, not least the Shah, would be endangered. So he suggested forming a syndicate in advance of the first exploitation company sanctioned in the Concession which would 'entirely take over my responsibilities, leaving intact my obligations towards His Imperial Majesty'.

The proposal was easier than its accomplishment. A year later D'Arcy confided to Jenkin, 'the fact is difficulties which I did not anticipate have presented themselves with regard to the formation of such a company'.[8] He then informed his associates that 'the thing is off for the present' but that he would renew his efforts later when 'I will do my level best to get all to come in.'[9] What had gone wrong? D'Arcy was drawn into a maelstrom of conflicting interests and financial pressures which impeded his efforts to raise funds and embittered his relations with some of his associates, particularly Wolff, who disposed of some of his interest. D'Arcy obtained counsel's opinion on 8 November 1901, Sir F.B. Palmer declaring that D'Arcy had no right to transfer the Concession without the consent of the Persian Government, but that it was permissible for him to form a company which, by contract with him, would obtain the benefit without any transfer and D'Arcy remain the concessionaire.[10]

Kitabgi arrived in London on 21 November 1901 from Tehrān, confirmed as Imperial Commissioner and authorised to let D'Arcy form a syndicate.[11] During his visit Kitabgi made it plain that he expected 'to keep in hand the direction of all things Persian, with the end in view that the English occupy themselves solely with the exploitation'.[12] He had already counselled Reynolds in Tehrān that 'it is often for trifles that the best enterprises have been destroyed in Persia' and advised him not to let the Persians get the impression that 'you go there to take their caps off their heads'.[13] In London he condemned Reynolds for his lack of generosity, 'avarice' as he termed it, and requested that he be accompanied by the adviser he proposed, Shaykh al-Mulk.[14] Encouraged by Redwood's optimistic report, which Reynolds had disclosed to him, and confident of his own position in Persia, Kitabgi was well prepared for the syndicate discussions, 'to see under what conditions Mr. D'Arcy means to share his eventual profits with others'.[15] D'Arcy appeared satisfied with the discussions, thanking Kitabgi on 5 December for his 'kind and invaluable assistance', but he warned that 'what we all must do is to think of the *success* of the concern, and not the profit, as if we make it succeed, the profit will follow for certain'.[16] On 18 January 1902 D'Arcy informed him that he was working hard 'to get the Parent Syndicate formed'.[17]

Less than a month later, on 15 February, D'Arcy was requested by Kitabgi for an advance of £25 000 on the Concession 'which has troubled me a great deal as I do not see how it is to be managed'.[18] D'Arcy was not ready for such an emergency for he had engaged himself only to pay after two years or on the formation of the first exploitation company and it was on this basis that he 'undertook to form a Parent Syndicate with sufficient money for the Boring only... The Position is very serious as if this money must be found, it is no use my going on with the formation of the Parent Syndicate...so the concern must be at a standstill and I am very much afraid that your Requirements may be the means of ruining the Business entirely.' The demand was dropped. On 24 March 1902 Kitabgi officially approved of the formation of a syndicate and staked out his claim, which it would have been difficult to disregard, 'of assisting at all the deliberations of the administration of the said syndicate and will be consulted in all questions relative to the Imperial Government of Persia, and to those of the country in general. The statutes of the syndicate must naturally be submitted to and approved by me.'[19] On 27 March 1902 D'Arcy informed Kitabgi that the members of the Syndicate, apart from himself, were Evelyn Ashley, Lord Burton, Sir Arthur Ellis, Mr Lynch, Lord Ramsay, Sir Horace Rumbold and Wolff, prominent diplomats, courtiers and men of business.[20] He consented to the various appointments of Kitabgi's sons, Paul as a representative in Tehrān, Vincent in London and Edouard as an assistant to Reynolds. By 15 May, Kitabgi, who was living then in Geneva, was informed that 'the syndicate business is now virtually settled', and given a copy of the Articles, which it was hoped to have signed in June 'when everybody will be in London'.[21]

Once again D'Arcy's optimism was premature. Kitabgi assumed that 'the statutes of the Parent Syndicate Ltd., just as they are written, no longer consider the simple creation of the claimants to fill up the gap of the concession but they constitute the formation of the first society for the exploitation of the concession'.[22] He may have been inadequately informed by Wolff.[23] D'Arcy attempted to correct the misunderstanding for it was a prerequisite that 'the borings be finished and the petrol discovered with proofs of its existence in sufficient quantities'.[24] D'Arcy was being cautious and pragmatic but Wolff alleged to Vincent Kitabgi that 'Mr. D'Arcy loves to earn money and does not want to make others profit by it.'[25] Wolff accused D'Arcy of promoting the Syndicate to evade financial responsibility. D'Arcy told Vincent Kitabgi that 'Sir Henry does not understand business very well; he is an excellent diplomat but not a business man.'[26] Distrust had appeared even before drilling operations had commenced.

Kitabgi travelled to London again in mid-July 1902 from Geneva at D'Arcy's invitation and expense, conferred with Wolff and rejected the recommendations for the Syndicate. Kitabgi professed to believe that the Parent Syndicate represented the first exploitation company mentioned in the Concession but D'Arcy was adamant that it had only the more limited objective of financing the preliminary operations. D'Arcy, who had accepted the initial risks at his expense, resented the pretensions of his associates, who were endangering the long-term prospects of the Concession, but Kitabgi and Wolff were apprehensive about surrendering long-term expectations for immediate financial coverage. Kitabgi made counter-proposals[27] but he overplayed his hand[28] and D'Arcy decided to continue alone until he had made other arrangements.[29]

Perhaps, even at this early stage, it was proving difficult to find a common wavelength on which to communicate with sufficient clarity between Persian and British interests. Yet D'Arcy, in spite of his disappointment, maintained friendly relations with Kitabgi, writing to him that 'the whole of the expenditure is now on my shoulders and I am doing all I can to control that expenditure to things which are absolutely necessary ... the expenses are a great tax on my resources'.[30] Kitabgi, however, replied that the real problem was not about finding oil or raising money, but, 'if there be any danger, it is in the familiarising of the Persian element to European contact'.[31] Nevertheless, when Kitabgi suddenly died of pneumonia in Italy on 20 December, D'Arcy, in extending his sympathy to the family, wrote that, 'I know I have lost a kind and sincere friend and a valuable and able colleague.'[32] Kitabgi had been indispensable in delivering the Concession, but had he survived he might have crippled it in its infancy.

By the end of 1902, D'Arcy's problem was that he had not succeeded in getting the agreement of his associates to set up a syndicate to guarantee the financial backing for the Concession, so he did not have the funding for a company to exploit the Concession. At one time he envisaged seeking an extension of the concessionary period in which to register a company by drafting a Supplemental Concession, but rejected the idea on account of its probable cost[33] and the opposition of Wolff, who was being obstructive and threatening as his own financial position worsened, thereby causing further expenditure without a corresponding monetary liability. An effort to interest Sir Ernest Cassel, international banker and friend of Edward VII, apparently failed and D'Arcy acknowledged in mid-April to Jenkin that he had no option but to form a company. So 'until we find oil...will carry on the work we are now doing. When oil is found it will be different. The Company will go on its way and I shall then continue the work we are now doing.'[34] D'Arcy wanted to launch the ship, he did not want to navigate it. By the middle of March, Reynolds had drilled some 900 feet, which encouraged D'Arcy to hope that the news 'may soon be followed by another wire saying oil in quantities is really found'.[35] There were many more such mirages in D'Arcy's desert.

Early in May 1903, D'Arcy took advice from a specialist in company law, E.T. Hargraves, and consulted Sir Howard Elphinstone about syndicates and forming a company. On 21 May the First Exploitation Company was registered containing the following main provisions.[36]

(1) The Company was to have the right, within one year, to select anywhere within the Concession area, blocks of land not exceeding in the aggregate one square mile, the Concessionnaire transferring to the Company all rights and privileges vested in him under his Concession in relation to such blocks of land.

(2) In consideration of the grant of these rights, the Concessionnaire was to receive 350 000 shares of £1 each issued as fully paid.

(3) The Company was to pay the Persian Government 16 per cent of its annual net profits, and, in exercising its rights under the Agreement, was to conform to all requirements of the Concession, and to indemnify the Concessionnaire against all liabilities in respect of any action that it might take.

The purpose of the company caused confusion and aroused the suspicions of Wolff and Vincent Kitabgi, who thought that, not only their rights were being jeopardised, but that obligations to the Persian government were being disregarded. Their concern was justified, so was D'Arcy's anxiety. D'Arcy was forming an exploitation company, not the concessionary company for he was in no position to do that, and, since he was not able to do so, he could not predict its composition nor forecast its policy, except in so far as it would be obliged to honour his commitments and those of his associates. He did not know who would provide the finance.[37] Ironically, the longer D'Arcy was prevented from raising finance, the more difficult it became to interest a financier and the more likely it was that his conditions would ultimately be more onerous. Even Wolff accepted that he was entitled to form the First Exploitation Company. He had complied with the concessionary requirements in forming a company. He had discharged his official obligations of £20 000 and 20 000 £1 shares to the Persian Government and his personal debts of honour of £19 000 and 30 000 £1 shares to those who had been involved in securing the Concession.[38] Vincent Kitabgi had made all the necessary arrangements in Tehrān with the assistance of his brother Paul. The Persian Government was informed that the terms of the Concession had been observed in these respects by Vincent Kitabgi, who had succeeded his father as Imperial Commissioner.[39] Whilst these legal and financial arrangements were being completed in London, the first practical steps to exploit the Concession were being taken in Persia.

(ii) Preparations in Persia

George Bernard Reynolds, who was engaged by D'Arcy as his first engineer, was a taciturn, energetic, self-reliant person. He had graduated from the Royal Indian Engineering College, served in the Indian Public Works Department and had worked in the oil fields of Sumatra. He was a competent, mostly self-taught geologist, a practical engineer, a passable linguist and a competent horseman. Remarkably self-reliant and adaptable, Reynolds was a 'loner', contemptuous of office 'wallahs' but generous to those who shared with him the discomforts of the scorching sun, the freezing nights and the barren landscapes. Without being impressive in appearance, apart from his bushy black moustache, he was physically tough and mentally alert, able to withstand and understand the rigours of the Persian countryside. Reynolds reached Tehrān on 10 September 1901. He was immediately taken in hand for a fortnight[40] by General Kitabgi, who had his own ideas about where and how to commence operations, irrespective of Dr Redwood's instructions. Kitabgi stressed to Reynolds his own knowledge and experience, pointedly inquiring that 'Now you begin to penetrate into the grammar of Persian affairs, tell me if it is possible to manage a like enterprise in Persia with the experience acquired in London?'[41] Reynolds was impressed and grateful but not intimidated, informing D'Arcy that 'I have been able to converse with him and learn far more of the human methods in vogue in Persia, than I could possibly have done had I hurried away.'[42]

The funding and finding of oil 1901-8

G.B. Reynolds, Crush and Willans c.1909

Kitabgi, however, was deeply disappointed in not being able to persuade Reynolds to go to Shushtar, where oil was plentiful.[43] On the basis of the geological survey undertaken by H.T. Burls during the spring of 1901, whilst the concessionary negotiations were being carried on in Tehrān, Redwood recommended examining the area around Zuhāb in the Qaṣr-i Shīrīn district. Burls arrived back in London early in July, confirming the observations of de Morgan on the prospects for oil but he did draw attention to the lack of water at Qaṣr-i Shīrīn, scarcity of timber, desolation of the countryside, dearth of fuel, difficulty of communications, shortage of labour and most important, transportation problems and tribal unrest.[44] He also visited Qaleh Dārābī in the vicinity of Ahwāz and briefly mentioned in his report, Shushtar and Masjid i-Suleimān. Redwood was enthusiastic about the reports of Burls that 'the territory as a whole is one of rich promise'.[45] Reynolds was requested to make arrangements for carrying the plant from Basra through Baghdad and over the Persian-Turkish frontier to the drilling sites. He left Tehrān on 21 September for Kīrmanshāh, which he reached on 10 October, having forfeited the initial 'favourable impression'[46] with which he had been received by Kitabgi, who later seemed determined to undermine his authority and impose his own direction on affairs in Persia.

Why was Kitabgi so insistent on Shushtar to the exclusion of the Qaṣr-i Shīrīn area in July, even before Reynolds arrived in Tehrān?[47] The reason is more associated with political and religious affairs than geological observations. Throughout the Qājār period, the religious authorities, the *ulemā*, were powerful, and at this time playing a very influential role in Persian political life, as the movement for constitutional reform was gathering pace. Kitabgi had close relations with Āqā Sayyid 'Alā al-Dīn, the principal Mujtahid, religious leader, of Shushtar, who was also well-known to Amīn al-Sultān. Kitabgi visited him in Tehrān on 8 July to seek his cooperation, suggesting that oil gained by Persia would be a loss to Turkey. When the Mujtahid returned the visit three days later, he pledged his friendly assistance to mutual advantage and agreed to write a commendatory letter to the principal Mujtahid at the holy Shī'īte city of Najaf, now in Iraq.[48] Kitabgi promised to 'persuade Mr. D'Arcy to put him in a position to satisfy all his friends there', who owned and worked some existing seepages.[49] Kitabgi introduced the Mujtahid to Sir Arthur Hardinge and to Reynolds on his arrival, whom he assured 'of the existence in abundance of oil and the certainty that a cordial reception would be given to them at Shushter'.[50] Reynolds politely indicated his interest, but was not prepared to change his plans. It is quite remarkable that at this stage there was little evidence of religious animosity, partly attributable to Kitabgi's deference to and consideration of religious susceptibilities. When it appeared later it was not spontaneous, but the result of personal intrigue against Reynolds by a protégé of Kitabgi, Shaykh al-Mulk, sent with him in order to smooth out 'the number of small difficulties inevitable in all beginnings', but which he exacerbated.[51]

Reynolds had cleared his fences in Tehrān. He moved on to new ground near Qasr-i Shīrīn where he visited the oil indications and met with much hostility.[52] A fortnight later, in mid-November, he was in Baghdad and later unloading *The Afrikander* at Basra which brought the first plant and machinery, valued at £1250.[53] In December some drillers arrived too early, and had to be returned. The slow trek to the mountainous valleys across the Mesopotamian plains with the cumbersome equipment began with a shortage of mules, makeshift waggons and obstruction from Turkish officials. Gradually Reynolds gained the confidence of the local tribal leaders, firstly Azīz Khān and then Muhammad Karīm Khān, who owned the seepages at Sar i-Pul, where the geological indications were favourable. There was, however, no prospect of drilling without local bargaining for 'the authority of the Shah was held in low esteem by our host',[54] and the landowners had 'no idea of the mineral rights of the owner of the ground being nil' but required payment 'over and above that laid down in the Concession'.[55] Starting operations was an exhausting, disheartening and troubled period for Reynolds among unfamiliar surroundings and people, improvising with machinery often broken and

The funding and finding of oil 1901-8

Chiāh Surkh no. 1 well 1903

with parts missing, keeping the peace between squabbling tribal leaders, managing his labourers unused to regular employment and industrial practices, nursing his relations with the local population and tolerating his Kitabgi-appointed assistants, whose counsels, if not always misguided, were frequently irrelevant. D'Arcy was worried at the lack of progress and telegraphed Reynolds on 15 April 1902, 'when probably commence drilling - delay serious - pray expedite'.[56] Reynolds replied that it was 'not possible to estimate' but that 'no exertion on my part shall be wanting'.[57]

Drilling commenced in November 1902, some six months later, the site perched on a small plateau in mountainous undulating country with a stream nearby and tents spread around. The party was composed of half a dozen Polish and Canadian drillers, three or four work shop machinists and a couple of blacksmiths from Central Europe, a number of rigmen, including some who had been employed at Baku from Āzarbāyjān, an Indian doctor, a Turkish surveyor, two English assistants, many Kurdish and Persian guards and a motley of camp followers, cooks and firemen. Surrounded by tribes perpetually at odds with each other, survival depended on strength of character and force of personality rather than on the precarious protection of ministerial decrees obtained in Tehrān[58] or the exhortations of indifferent and weak local governors. The water was foul for body and boiler, the attentions of insects unremitting, but work proceeded indefatigably at a slow pace with constant interruptions from the climate, mechanical failure, sickness and a variety of religious festivals. Throughout this period the attitude of Reynolds was practical, conciliatory but firm and, in spite of the intemperate accusations of Kitabgi that 'he has known how to make himself detested', he was well regarded.[59]

A perceptive pen picture of him appears in a report of Mr (later Sir) Henry Dobbs, Indian Civil Service, who passed through Chiāh Surkh in February 1903. Dobbs refers to his 'generosity and kindliness', his familiarity with tribal affairs and the respect in which he was held.[60] He alluded to the intrigues of the Shaykh al-Mulk, whom Kitabgi had foisted upon Reynolds, who 'tried to get all the payments of gift, salaries etc. into his own hands with the obvious desire of enriching his friends and acquaintances', claiming that 'Reynolds was exciting hostility in the neighbourhood by not employing Persians exclusively and by not dispensing money with sufficient liberality', charges also repeatedly expressed by Kitabgi. Dobbs sensibly cautioned that 'Apart from the question of the existence of oil, the undertaking will certainly fail, if the Concessionaires at home refuse to trust the man on the spot, and undermine his authority by listening to the tittle-tattle of interested persons like the Sheikh ul-Mulk.' Reynolds lived to see his management ultimately vindicated by the discovery of oil. If his Persian grammar was not always correct his vocabulary was well understood.

By the time of his return to England in early April 1902, the first well was over 900 feet deep and a pipeline route from Zuhāb to Muhammara had been surveyed. Reynolds had accomplished the exacting task of setting up camp with all its drilling paraphernalia, not excluding beer, sunhats, waterproofs and calendars. No exertion had been wanting for he was well aware of D'Arcy's anxiety already in August 1902 that

our time is getting short, and I cannot get one day's extension from the Shah. So this means that either you must find oil in quantity soon enough to enable me to form and float a subsidiary company before May next, or I must either pay the Shah the amount due under the concession out of my pocket or abandon the whole thing.[61]

At the same time as D'Arcy was pressing Reynolds to find oil, he was contemplating sending out another geologist, W.H. Dalton, partly to reassure himself and provide more geological backing for the Parent Syndicate which he was expecting to form, and partly, in all probability, to persuade Kitabgi that he was not neglecting the case for Shushtar. He recognised that without such a report it would be impossible to get people here to buy land or 'to take shares in any company that might be formed for working it'.[62] Redwood was not convinced of the need to go elsewhere in Persia.[63] Dalton, with assistance from Kitabgi, completed his survey both in the west and south at a cost of £2202[64] and reported on 15 May, before the deadline for the formation of the first company for exploitation had elapsed. His general conclusions were blandly imprecise, 'continuous recurrence of accumulations of oil the commercial value of which can be determined only by test drilling at judiciously selected points'.[65]

(c) 'Every purse has a limit' May 1903 – July 1904

(i) Searching for finance

In July 1903, taking a cure at Carlsbad, D'Arcy was pondering on the implications of Dalton's survey and Reynold's estimates for drilling in the south. He had delayed a decision pending 'some assistance towards the cost from those interested in the Concession, but at the same time, I have decided to do it myself even if this assistance is not forthcoming'.[66] He confessed to Jenkin, 'I want to be certain of all this as every purse has its limit and I can see the limit of my own and I want first to know what sum Mr. Reynolds thinks he can get oil for and then whether that money can be supplied.'[67]

There was no easy solution for D'Arcy, as he was so far committed that withdrawal would have involved considerable loss, for his concessional assets were only an indeterminable financial liability. He did not possess a single substantial asset of a proved oil well, let alone a field, to use as collateral to float a company. It was almost financial checkmate, whichever move he made. He had little alternative but to accept the advice of Hargraves, his business adviser, who warned him that approaching a financier then would give the impression that 'he is letting some one out and will try and make hard terms against you' and that he would do better to wait and 'see if you get oil'.[68] D'Arcy was hesitating over drilling at Shushtar in case 'Fisher's friends...decided one way or other.'[69] Admiral Sir John Fisher, Second Sea Lord, 1902, and First Sea Lord a year later, a leading advocate of the use of fuel oil in naval vessels, was also at Carlsbad at the same time as D'Arcy and was very impressed by his enthusiasm for his new venture, joking that 'I am thinking of going to Persia instead of Portsmouth'.[70] Limited experimental work was undertaken in 1902 with relatively little enthusiasm by naval engineers. The first trials of a coal-fired marine engine convertible to oil on a battle ship, *H.M.S. Hannibal*, took place at Portsmouth harbour on 26 June 1903.[71] It became a technical disaster, when the ship was enveloped in a pall of black smoke as a result of faulty burners, rather than the oil, which had been supplied by Sir Marcus Samuel, Chairman of Shell. As a result of this fiasco it was doubtless

The funding and finding of oil 1901-8

inevitable that no definite proposals then emerged from 'Fisher's friends', but later in July the Admiralty first inquired about the possibilities of the Burmah Oil Company supplying fuel oil for the Royal Navy.[72]

After D'Arcy received news of a show of oil at Chiāh Surkh in October 1903, it seems that he applied through E.G. Pretyman, then parliamentary secretary to the Admiralty, for a loan. Pretyman advised D'Arcy to forward a letter stating the position and the amount of money required to put the concession on a firm basis and that Lord Selborne, First Lord of the Admiralty, 1900-5, would then consider the matter and take the appropriate action.[73] Selborne had already appointed a small fuel oil committee to advise him. D'Arcy followed the advice, but the answer was negative, the Government was not interested. Nevertheless the Foreign Secretary, Lord Lansdowne, was worried about the international implications of foreign control over the Concession. Writing to Lord Curzon, Viceroy in India, and Sir Arthur Hardinge, on 7 December 1903, he reported that D'Arcy had already spent £160 000, needed another £120 000 for drilling in the south of Persia and that he was 'not sanguine of receiving support by British capitalists'. So concluded Lansdowne, 'As British Government are unable grant any assistance to a scheme of this nature, it is represented to me that there is danger of whole petroleum concession in Persia falling thus under Russian control', on which he invited comment.[74]

Curzon, who had been a director in the Persian Bank Mining Rights Corporation, was sceptical, not believing in the 'likelihood of Persian oil deposits being worked at profit and should not fear the sale of concession to anybody else', except that in Russian hands it might be used to spread their influence.[75] Hardinge initially expressed the same opinion as Curzon, that if the Russians obtained the Concesssion 'it would be most dangerous to British interests in Southern Persia'.[76] Later, however, after visiting Chiāh Surkh in January 1904, he felt that the pessimism of Curzon was unjustified and that it would be a pity to allow the Concession to pass into foreign ownership before it had been exhaustively tested. Agreeing that its financing was beyond a single individual capitalist, he advocated that, at the least, an effort should be made to prevent its acquisition by Russian interests who might construct a pipeline to the Gulf.[77]

D'Arcy was becoming desperate, it was cash not advice he needed. An attempt was made to raise a loan from Joseph Lyons and Co. as 'It is all I can do to keep the bank quiet and something *must* be done', but to no avail. He placed more of his Mount Morgan Gold Mining Company shares with the bank as security for his overdraft. On 25 November 1903 D'Arcy hired a suite at the Coburg Hotel in Grosvenor Square to inform his associates that he had come to the end of his financial tether and that he would be obliged to seek 'outside' capital if the Concession was to survive. Beyond concern, nothing substantial resulted from this meeting.[78]

He was greatly reassured by his friend, Major-General Sir Arthur Ellis, Equerry to the King, on 16 December of Rothschild interest. A fortnight later Ellis wrote optimistically to D'Arcy that he had seen and explained everything to Baron Rothschild who would get in touch with his cousin, Alphonse, in Paris to send a representative to London, adding that 'on the whole I feel sanguine that there is a fair prospect of success with their cooperation'.[79] D'Arcy was relieved but worried for, as he confided to Manisty, his solicitor, on 1 January 1904, 'the greatest difficulty in the matter is Wolff - as usual - as they hate him and do not want him in'.[80] A thorn in D'Arcy's flesh he had become a blight on the Concession. Vincent Kitabgi at this time too informed D'Arcy that he reserved his position as inheritor of his father's estate.[81]

D'Arcy's bankers, Lloyds, became more restless at the size of his overdraft, which stood on 31 December 1903 at £176 548 14s 3d, of which £4158 19s 5d was interest.[82] For this reason, after he had met M. Aron, the Rothschild representative on 29 January 1904, he urged his counsel, Mr Fletcher Moulton KC (later Lord Justice Moulton), to get a proposition prepared as soon as possible, as 'I am very anxious to get this matter pushed on, not only on account of the Concession, but also on account of the bank, as they will have to be reckoned with before long.'[83] D'Arcy was being squeezed, but he was still hopeful that his Persian affairs 'will be brought into Port within the next six months'.[84] Following further interviews which Ellis had with Baron Rothschild on 8 and 9 February, D'Arcy with Fletcher Moulton visited Alphonse Rothschild in Cannes towards the end of February.[85] His wife in an imaginative phrase looked forward to hearing 'they have struck the lake of oil',[86] but no bargain was struck and negotiations with the Rothschilds were suspended as the arrangements which they had concluded on 2 July 1903 with Royal Dutch and Shell offered them a more attractive prospect. It seems that at some stage the fuel oil committee was again informed of D'Arcy's difficulties, probably informally through Redwood who was on the committee.

As Pretyman explained later in 1919 in a letter to Sir Charles Greenway, who was then Chairman of the Company, he had

ascertained that Mr. D'Arcy was, at that moment, in the Riviera negotiating for a transfer of his concession to the French Rothschilds. I therefore wrote to Mr. D'Arcy explaining the Admiralty's interest in petroleum development and asking him, before parting with his concessions to any foreign interests, to give the Admiralty an opportunity, of endeavouring to arrange for its acquisition by a British Syndicate.[87]

D'Arcy accepted Pretyman's invitation to discuss the position with him. No commitments were made. D'Arcy seems to have approached Lord Lansdowne again, who telegraphed to Hardinge about D'Arcy's current financial plight and asked whether any assistance could be expected from the Government of India,[88] but there was no sign of urgency.[89]

D'Arcy redoubled his efforts as his bank became more demanding and requested the Concession itself as security for the overdraft, which by the end of April 1904 had increased to £186 366 9s 5d. This was an unacceptable condition for it would prevent further finance being raised on the Concession, as D'Arcy knew from the interest shown by the Standard Oil Company in early April, which thought of buying it outright, provided it was not encumbered in any way.[90] As he mentioned to Manisty, 'It would be a pity to give the security for at all events a few weeks as the American Group are still after the thing, and Sir E. Cassel is taking a few days to consider whether he will take the business up or not.'[91] At the end of the month he temporised unsuccessfully with the bank because he expected an offer from the American group but 'all the thanks I get is the enclosed letter demanding the custody of the Concession itself.[92] In June, Standard oil offered no definite proposals, Cassel rejected the proposition submitted to him and the Rothschilds declined to accept the terms drawn up by Fletcher Moulton at the end of the month. Wolff 'more troublesome than ever' was suggesting that the Concession would be forfeited by its lack of development.[93] In Persia too the oil strike in the second well on 14 January, which was, for D'Arcy, 'the glorious news from Persia and is the greatest relief to me',[94] had dwindled to a trickle and had therefore not, as Rosenplaenter, the engineer, hoped 'removed all anxiety from your mind regarding the ultimate success of our drilling operations in this field'.[95] The limits of the purse had been reached.

(ii) Drilling for oil

Reynolds was succeeded as engineer at Chiāh Surkh, when he returned home after his first contract expired, by C.B. Rosenplaenter, who took charge of operations in March 1903. Rosenplaenter, who had drilling experience in Assam and Baku, where it appeared he 'has worked pleasantly with Eastern people and has had Persians under his control',[96] was technically proficient and adaptable. Less robust and abrasive than Reynolds, he was just as determined and fully trusted by Redwood, for whom he had elsewhere shown his capacity for overcoming obstacles.[97] Rosenplaenter, like Reynolds, was more than the resident engineer, he was effectively the administrative manager of operations attending to all technical problems, the welfare of his staff, the provision of guards and

C.B. Rosenplaenter 1903

security, negotiations with landlords and officials, the supply of water and fuel, the organisation of transportation, the receipt and despatch of equipment, the supervision of building quarters and camp discipline and the arbiter of local disputes. Rosenplaenter too was respected for his compe-

The funding and finding of oil 1901-8

tence, authority and care. Sir Arthur Hardinge, who visited the camp, 6-11 January 1904, commended his behaviour, 'for one of the greatest difficulties attendant on Mr. D'Arcy's enterprise lies in the lawless character of the region in which he has to work...the real Rulers of the country are the tribal chiefs, great and small, who are constantly engaged in petty feuds and warfare with one another'.[98] Reynolds and Rosenplaenter had succeeded 'by conduct at once straightforward and tactful to remain on good terms with the turbulent and constantly warring native elements...no single untoward incident of any importance has troubled their relations with them'.

There was a multiplicity of technical difficulties, and Rosenplaenter displayed a talent for improvisation. Steel cables frayed and broke, cases split, boiler tubes cracked, tools dropped into the wells and were retrieved with intricate fishing skill, drilling bits splintered, well sides caved in, water corroded metal parts, timber was in short supply, equipment did not always fit and was bent, buckled or missing on arrival. It was arduous and occasionally dangerous work for on one occasion 'a pole broke on the upward stroke close to the top and when the tools dropped, another near the bottom broke. We fished fifteen poles out of the hole that were turned into corkscrews.'[99] There were worries about 'the increasing quantity of perfectly odourless inflammable gas', because the glass in the safety lamps had been broken and replacement fittings turned out to be the wrong size.[100] Optimistically Rosenplaenter tried to introduce some technological improvements by changing from the traditional method of percussion pole-type drilling which hammered the bit into the ground, to the newer method of cable drilling which was more flexible.

Progress, however, was slow and only the Canadian drillers, McNaughton and Buchanan, showed any expertise at all whilst 'our Baku men do not take kindly to the cable drilling as they think their services will not be required any longer'.[101] The experiment had later to be abandoned because the wire was too frail, the Polish drillers too inexperienced and the situation too uncertain, with a Russian vice-consul recently arrived at Kīrmanshāh, to provoke the Baku drillers.[102] One innovation was successful; the labourers 'have taken most kindly to wheelbarrows and while they are doing at least three times the amount of work they did before, they get no end of fun out of it'.[103] When the oil was first struck there was an immediate benefit, for its utilisation in the boilers brought about a rapid reduction in the price of wood which was offered at 2/5 of its former price and pilferage declined as it had been 'impossible to prevent the nightly wood thefts as the guards are probably the greatest offenders in this line'.[104]

The climate was extreme. In the low thick-walled stone houses that were constructed for the drillers the temperature rose to 120°F 'so as the nights are hot the men get very little rest and still less sleep'.[105] A week later on 5 August it was reported that progress was slow because of 'the infernal heat',[106] but when the rains came 'the water came down in torrents'.[107] In January the traditional mud covered reed roofs of the stables collapsed and the mules had to be driven to Qaṣr-i Shīrīn as no corrugated tin remained for repairs.[108] These natural events were disturbing, but more unpredictable were the human elements. They were not necessarily all surprising. Thus the Governor of Kīrmānshāh, Prince Farmān Farmānfar, the Imām Jum'a, the principal local religious dignatory, officials and religious leaders enjoyed visits to the site and they 'seemed very keen on receiving a substantial present from us, especially in the shape of some shares of our Company'.[109] So popular was their reception that Rosenplaenter was obliged 'to run a separate Mohamedan Kitchen for such native chiefs and Prominent Persians'.[110] The medical treatment provided for staff and public alike was highly appreciated. References by Rosenplaenter to contemporary affairs are few, but one was interesting in the light of subsequent events of the constitutional struggle: 'the Mullahs in the North are exciting the population as much as they can against the foreigners...the real fight is now between the Shah and the Mullahs for the control of the public affairs'.[111]

Serious and frequent tribal skirmishes across disputed tribal borders, whilst they did not directly impinge on the operations, disrupted food and fuel supplies. On 26 June 1903, for example, Rosenplaenter reported raiding by a Turkish tribe and retaliation so that 'for the last week the whole country north-east of the camp has been on fire'.[112] In August he was unable to complete a land survey on some property as 'the Ahmadawandi have been raiding there for the last two months'.[113] More threateningly in January 1904 two local tribes, with lands in the vicinity of the oil wells, massed for a clash with many people taking refuge in the camp with their children, flocks and chattels in cold and wet weather.[114] By admirable impartiality or the magical impression caused by the sudden show of oil at that moment, the tribes were reconciled and in the presence of Rosenplaenter swore eternal peace and friendship.[115]

The oil strike, auspicious for tribal peace, occurred in the second well drilled at 756 feet on 14 January 1904, and flowed at a rate of 600 barrels (a barrel containing 35 gallons) in twenty-four hours accompanied by brine.[116] The rains had washed away the collecting dams, oil oozed everywhere and pandemonium broke out when women swarmed over the camp to collect the salt water, oblivious of the blows of the guards.[117] Rosenplaenter restored order and allowed access to the brine on a regular basis. Unfortunately the oil failed to flow regularly in sufficient quantity to justify its early promise. Neither well showed more than occasional

The funding and finding of oil 1901-8

Azīz Khān and Karim Khān, with followers 1903

traces of oil. No. 1 had reached 2315 feet when it was discontinued on 6 May and No. 2 had reached 1348 feet on 23 June[118] when all operations were suspended at Chiāh Surkh by A.W.B. Holland, then in charge, who had been an assistant to Reynolds and had worked in charge of transport at Chiāh Surkh. Rosenplaenter himself left in the middle of May. Though frequently ill he had shown great fortitude, skill, endurance and patience.

Whilst Rosenplaenter was drilling at Chiāh Surkh, Reynolds had returned to Persia at the end of October 1903. D'Arcy contemplated drilling in the south and in September the instructions to Reynolds were to select at least six promising sites in the south-west on the basis of Dalton's report and negotiate suitable terms under which drilling could be undertaken with the agreement of the landowners.[119] D'Arcy did not have sufficient funds to drill in more than one place at a time. On 28 November, in Kuwait, Reynolds met the Viceroy, Lord Curzon, who was on a tour of the Persian Gulf, but it was little more than a social visit. Arriving in Shīrāz in January 1904, Reynolds was hospitably entertained by the consul, R.G. (later Sir Robert) Graham to whom he was indebted for much useful local knowledge and advice and they became good friends.[120] He reached Behbehān on 16 February,[121] journeying towards Ram Hormuz, which he reached at the beginning of March and a fortnight later, joined by Holland, arrived in Shushtar.[122] Travelling was dangerous because of the tribal feuding between the Sagwands and the Daraghwands[123] and the Dehlurān area to the north-west was much disturbed.

After arriving in Shushtar, Reynolds arranged to visit the seepages owned by the Sayyids, in charge of a religious endowment, to see the Bakhtiari Khans and survey the region for suitable sites. In a telegram he mentioned Masjid i-Suleimān for the first time on 31 March, 'Oil found in Gypsiferous rocks. The rocks here are saturated with oil as at Mandali. The property is a very valuable one.'[124] Dalton, however, preferred the prospects at Shardīn as being 'by far the best' and placed Masjid i-Suleimān as 'the next best'.[125] At a meeting on 1 April the Khans demanded 'practically 10 per cent of net profits of working the oil in their country'. They were indifferent to the terms of the Concession and the authority of the Shah, and they were not interested in the distinction between surface and sub-surface rights.[126] Reynolds was only authorised to offer 2 per cent. D'Arcy replied that he could 'only agree to give 10 per cent of profits if Persian Government will reduce royalty on this property by this extent', but Reynolds was not to enter into any binding contract.[127] When the conditions of the Khans were reported to the Persian Government by the Minister in Tehrān 'suggesting the reasonableness of reducing in such cases the royalty due to the Central Government', it refused to make any exceptions.[128] No firm agreement was reached with the Sayyids of Shushtar, who demanded, annually, eleven tons of crude oil, eleven tons of bitumen and £100 for the duration of the Concession. Reynolds was disposed to agree straightaway, 'In view of religious fanaticism...otherwise their rights are likely to cause considerable trouble.'[129] Though the terms were acceptable it was decided to settle only after oil had been obtained in commercial quantity.[130] At a time when the financial negotiations in London were in the balance, D'Arcy was not prepared to commit himself further. On 19 May, whilst he was waiting for fresh instructions in Baghdad, Reynolds was ordered not to make any fresh contracts and on 8 June summoned home.[131]

(d) The Burmah connection

By mid-1904 it must have seemed to D'Arcy that the dice were loaded against him, but a new player joined the game, the Burmah Oil Company, introduced by Pretyman. Burmah, registered in Edinburgh in 1886 and reconstituted in 1902 with a capital of £1 500 000, was founded by a group of Scotsmen led by David S. Cargill. It was a pioneering British company in overseas oil interests linked technically to the East Midlothian shale oil industry. Burmah transformed the primitive village-based oil gathering undertakings of Burma into an industry with a refinery at Rangoon and

The funding and finding of oil 1901-8

markets in India supplied by agents. The oil was of fine quality, the operations simple and the profits good. Production rose five-fold between 1900 and 1914, when it reached 1 000 000 tons. The development of marine engines for burning fuel oil in naval vessels had already been undertaken in the Russian and Italian navies[132] and was under active consideration by the Admiralty.[133] Surety and security were the prerequisites of supply, as the Admiralty informed the Secretary of State for India on 4 May 1904:

> they desire to obtain as far as possible in any concessions to prospect or drill in any oil fields situated in British Territory, the right of pre-emption of suitable residual oils for Naval use, and to secure a supply of such residual oils by requiring that the refining of the crude oil should be carried out in British Territory.[134]

The year before the Admiralty had inquired about the Burmah Oil Company supplying fuel oil and whether it would be prepared to provide a gallon sample, 'free of expense to the Crown'.[135]

The Burmah response on 2 November 1903 was positive and confident. Regretting that they were then 'not in a position, without adopting a new modus operandi, to offer supplies of fuel oil in anything like large quantities' they were, nevertheless, sure that, 'at no distant date, we shall be in a very different position and that large supplies of oil fuel may be available'.[136] Details of the oil to be supplied were forwarded but more important than the technical competence displayed was the determined assertion of dependability for 'we regard with the greatest confidence, the future of this Company and its expansion far beyond its present limits'.

These were the vigorous formative years of Burmah.[137] At the Annual General Meeting in 1905 its success was explained 'in a large measure due to the policy of expansion and extension which your Directors have been pursuing during the last two or three years'. As the deputy chairman C.W. Wallace a founder partner in the firm of managing agents, Shaw, Wallace & Co. Ltd, touchingly remarked, 'Now that we have emerged from the "baby" stage they have apparently resolved to compete with us.'[138] Defiantly, Burmah increased its capital by £500 000, enlarged its refining storage and transport facilities and persuaded the Indian Government to reject requests for Indian concessions by Standard Oil but increase their own concessionary area. As was said of David Cargill, who died early in 1904, a man of 'great courage with great caution',[139] these were the years of courage, when its affairs were administered 'with prudence and energy', according to Redwood, their technical adviser, who championed their case with the fuel oil committee.[140]

By February 1904, enough correspondence had been exchanged for the Admiralty to be satisfied that a trustworthy supply of fuel existed in a British possession[141] and for John T. Cargill, as chairman, to propose direct discussions.[142] The first of these took place on 15 March,[143] with Cargill, Wallace, Pretyman and Gordon Miller, Director of Contracts at the Admiralty, present. Negotiations proceeded satisfactorily, Cargill feeling able to meet the Admiralty's requirements of 50 000 tons a year from the Company's own resources, though not without a premonition that later 'we may hereafter be called up to extend – and perhaps largely extend – our operations in the Oil Fields of Burmah should other suitable sources of supply not present themselves meantime'.[144] On 2 July, the Admiralty announced that the oil sample had passed the test and was 'considered to be a very suitable fuel oil for service use', equal to the best quality Texas oil.[145] Cargill's strategy seemed to be to take advantage of Pretyman's views with sympathetic Admiralty support that British oil investment should be assisted and not allowed to fall into foreign hands. He was, therefore, prepared to seek preferential treatment from the Indian Government over increased concessionary areas and restrictive duty on foreign oil importation, in return for the increased outlay on refining and pipelines which would be required to provide fuel oil for the Admiralty. There was no room for patriotic complacency.

These factors were part of the background to the important meeting of 20 July 1904, which was not only a significant stage in reaching agreement for a fuel oil supply contract with the Admiralty, but was also the preliminary point of contact over Persia. Pretyman must have stressed the mutuality of interests between D'Arcy and Burmah and their likely impact on Admiralty fuel oil supplies but Burmah was under no delusion, declaring candidly in 1927 that,

It may be, and very often is, the case that private and Imperial interests are served by the same action, but it was primarily the protection of its Indian investments that took the Burmah Oil Company Ltd. into Persia, and it was its past conservation in finance that made possible not alone the initial venture but also the carriage of the burden of its disappointment and expense which for many years were met with.[146]

It was realism, not sentiment, which induced Wallace and John Cargill from the beginning to meet D'Arcy on 10 August. Thereafter Persia became a principal strand in their policy. What actual protection did Persia represent for Burmah? It was an insurance against exploration failure. Cargill had become worried about the lack of new exploration success in Burma as he confided to Redwood in October 1904, 'for a considerable time past we have been devoting much of our energies and a very large amount of Capital, in prospecting work over a large extent of territory, with a view to endeavouring to prove fresh deposits of Oil, but unfortunately up till now with no success'.[147] Meanwhile uncertainties over the Government of India's unwillingness to grant further licences for

The funding and finding of oil 1901-8

exploration were affecting their confidence in their ability to supply the Admiralty with fuel oil. Because of the bargaining and the doubts, a further year elapsed before the Admiralty supply contract was signed in November 1905.[148] An inter-company arrangement with Shell was concluded on 27 October[149] and an agreement with D'Arcy for the formation of the Oil Concessions Ltd on 5 May. 1905 was a decisive year.

What of D'Arcy as he contemplated the attractions of this financial association? He was encouraged because 'the Burmah people think well of it and Lord S (Strathcona) has consented to join them. I am to meet them tomorrow, and discuss terms. They are prepared to agree to £500,000 for capital...and £150,000 towards my outlay and half shares of the company', which he considered 'quite satisfactory to me'.[150] Lord Strathcona of Mount Royal, founder of the Canadian Pacific Railway and the Bank of Montreal, and Canadian High Commissioner in London, was a respected figure in financial circles. Cargill and Wallace were provided with documentation,[151] Redwood was consulted,[152] and Reynolds and Rosenplaenter warned to be available for 'the oftener and more they can contrive to see Messrs Cargill and Wallace and talk to them about the concession the better'.[153] The call of the moors was stronger[154] and it was not till early October 1904 that the two engineers were seen separately by Cargill[155] and D'Arcy was able to feel that 'the Burmah business looks promising'.[156] November was busy, for at the beginning of the month it was clear that Burmah and Strathcona had agreed 'to go into the Persian Business' and it was 'only a matter of terms'.[157] D'Arcy was offered £25 000 for the right to drill in the south with Burmah putting up £70 000 for drilling, some half of the expenditure thought necessary. If drilling was successful, D'Arcy would recoup his expenditure out of £1 000 000 working capital and divide the remaining £2 000 000 capital with Burmah, though he had hoped to get £1 250 000 in shares.[158] With Fletcher Moulton acting for D'Arcy, an agreement was reached on 27 November, but it was not settled till 25 January 1905 and confirmed by the Board of Burmah on 3 February.[159] D'Arcy was relieved,[160] and Fletcher Moulton, referring to 'endless negotiations and grievous delays', was satisfied that the terms he had reached 'with a body of very practical businessmen are as good as we could get and that the men are in earnest'.[161] Burmah formally assured themselves of the validity of the Concession and the protection which could be granted to British subjects by the Government.[162] The main terms were:

(1) The Concessions Syndicate was to pay D'Arcy £25 000 on account of his total expenditure (£225 000) in connection with the Concession.

(2) The Syndicate undertook, within three years, to spend at least £50 000 in proving the oil-bearing character of the Southern territory of

the Concession. If necessary, a further sum or sums amounting to £20 000 (making £70 000 in all) was to be spent. Any additional expenditure was to be at the option of the Syndicate.

(3) D'Arcy was, whilst the Agreement was in force, to hold the Concessions and all the property, plant and rights in Persia, Turkey or elsewhere in trust for himself and the Syndicate.

(4) The Syndicate was henceforward to pay all expenses of the Concession and FEC, and D'Arcy was to arrange for (a) the transfer from himself to the Syndicate of 300 001 shares in the FEC, and (b) for the resignation of a majority of the then Directors of the FEC and the election of nominees of the Syndicate in their place.

(5) If oil was not found in sufficient quantities, the Agreement was to be determined and D'Arcy was to repay the Syndicate the £25 000.

(6) If oil was discovered in sufficient quantities to justify the formation of a company, such a company was to be formed with a capital of £2 000 000 in ordinary shares.

(7) This company was to acquire the Concession and all rights from the Syndicate and D'Arcy, and was to issue to them, as consideration therefor, 800 000 and 1 200 000 ordinary shares respectively.

(8) The Company was to issue debenture stock to the value of at least £800 000 and, if necessary, up to £1 000 000 in all, in order to provide funds for: (i) Meeting the expenses connected with the formation of the Company. (ii) Repaying D'Arcy £200 000, being the balance of the sums expended by him on the Concession. (iii) Reimbursing the Syndicate for its expenditure. (iv) Developing the Concession by drilling wells, etc.

(9) D'Arcy undertook to take up and pay for £200 000 of the debenture stock or, alternatively, to take up and pay for the balance of that amount of Debenture stock not subscribed for by the public.[163]

It all seemed plain sailing for D'Arcy, but there were reefs ahead in the objections of his earlier associates. D'Arcy had kept them informed of the negotiations with Burmah, which had 'taken much longer than I ever expected',[164] but he did not anticipate difficulties, especially after receiving congratulations from Vincent Kitabgi, who was hoping for 'a great success in the future'.[165] This praise was the prelude before the storm which broke a week later on 6 February 1905, when Vincent Kitabgi disputed the agreement with Burmah.[166] He was joined by Wolff, who objected to D'Arcy being relieved entirely of the responsibilities as the concessionaire, being reimbursed for expenses already incurred and freed of 'all possible losses whilst he pocketed nine tenths of the benefices'.[167] Although the other associates, Wolff included, accepted the eventual terms on 3 May, Vincent Kitabgi maintained his attitude till the last moment. D'Arcy was greatly irritated in April with Vincent Kitabgi's contentions, Burmah's delays[168] and his own continuing financial outlay, all of which he claimed in an outburst against Fletcher Moulton 'is costing me £300 per week or £50 per day...money I shall never see again'.[169] By 14 April it appeared all was in order to form the syndicate which, as D'Arcy always maintained, was not a company 'formed for working the Concession within the meaning of Article IX' but only to prove the existence of oil.[170]

Vincent Kitabgi, who had maintained that he was entitled not only to 7 per cent of the original as well as any subsequent issues of capital, or, at least 7 per cent of the total net working profits of the Concession, consulted counsel, R. Younger K.C. (later Lord Blanesburgh) and J.T. Prior. They, whilst supporting his claim, pointed out 'as a practical matter that an advantageous disposal of the Concession is more likely to be secured by cooperation than by dissent between the co-owners. Indeed it would appear that the concession may become valueless to all the parties interested in it if Mr. D'Arcy's active interest in turning it to account be not retained.'[171] So Vincent Kitabgi agreed to reduce his claim to 7 per cent of all the benefits pertaining to the share benefits accruing from the agreement with Burmah.[172]

Acting on this, D'Arcy completed the final arrangements with Burmah, 'better than I could have obtained from any other company'.[173] On 5 May 1905 the Concessions Syndicate Ltd was incorporated with a capital of 100 000 in £1 shares, Lord Strathcona taking up 5000, all the rest being subscribed by Burmah. On 13 May D'Arcy received a telegram from Vincent Kitabgi repudiating his earlier acceptance and imposing new conditions. D'Arcy was outraged and threatened 'to tell the Burmah Co. that I will not complete'.[174] Kitabgi relented. It had been a frustrating search for finance, hardly the image of glorious imperial prescience mirrored in many commentaries.

2 THE CONCESSIONS SYNDICATE LTD 1905-9

(a) Introduction

With the financial backing of the Burmah Oil Company assured and the interest shown by the Admiralty, it might have been assumed that D'Arcy's worries were ended. Such optimism would have been presumptuous. The fate of the Concession remained in suspense till the bit of the drill struck the oil-bearing rock. It was not only that the situation in Persia was unpredictable. As Hardinge remarked when leaving Tehrān, at the end of 1905,

The funding and finding of oil 1901-8

It is as yet too early to hazard an opinion as to whether this oil enterprise will be crowned with success. The promoters are very sanguine, but they have perhaps inadequately appreciated the difficulties attending all commercial undertakings in a country possessing no regular or efficient administration, where authorities' one idea in relation to commerce is to levy blackmail on it for their own personal and immediate profit.[175]

The new element was political instability generated by the rivalry of those promoting and opposing constitutional reform, in which monarchical absolutism was to be replaced by a democratic assembly, Majlis, responsible for representative government. The ailing Muzaffar al-Dīn Shāh acceded to the demands for a Majlis on 5 August 1906 and the Fundamental Law completing the Constitution was passed on 7 October 1907 in spite of the opposition of Muhammad 'Alī Shāh, whose relations with the constitutionalists deteriorated so desperately that he was deposed in favour of his young son, Ahmed, in July 1909. The inability of the Government to enforce law and order in the provinces during the drilling operations in south-west Persia in the lands of the Bakhtiaris, the most important single tribal confederacy, which had its own political ambitions and internal struggles for power, was a significant element in the internal situation of Persia in this period.[176] Anglo-Russian diplomatic competition had reached a stalemate, which resulted in the Anglo-Russian Convention of 1907, affecting not only Persia, but also Afghanistan and Tibet. Serious German interest in Persia also became evident at this time.[177]

No less important than the Persian dimension was the relationship of D'Arcy to his new collaborators and the manner in which they managed the operations and subscribed to the funds. Reynolds was often sarcastic in his comments, but there is no doubt that the Burmah directors seriously, and almost fatally, underestimated the administrative and technical problems inseparable from operations in Persia. Tetchy, touchy and frequently petulant with his superiors as he was, Reynolds persevered and laid the foundations for the Iranian oil industry. He was patient in dealing with the Bakhtiari Khans and persuasive in handling his staff of different nationalities, sustaining their endeavours during the rains and throughout the heat. His engineering expertise was accompanied by a flair for adaptation when material was lost or damaged. He supervised the drilling through the complicated geological strata, he encouraged the construction gangs when their roads were washed away by swollen rivers and he inspired those depressed by lack of success, homesickness and local vexations with his sure authority and determination to strike oil. He was the rudder and anchor of the enterprise, keeping it on course and off the rocks.

The funding and finding of oil 1901-8

(b) The Bakhtiari Agreement: Khans and guards

The fate of the Concession depended upon discovering oil in as short a time as possible in the south-west of Persia where the Bakhtiaris exercised their own virtual autonomous authority over their lands. Without their agreement, operations were impossible. Local arrangements were indispensable. An inevitable, if unsatisfactory, consequence was that local British consular representatives became involved. British official concern in the contemporary situation was less than might then have been expected, given the absence of a properly institutionalised Persian government presence and the lack of adequate political experience and knowledge available to the Concessions Syndicate, apart from that proferred by members of the Kitabgi family, whose impartiality was not always evident.[178] It would be unrealistic to ignore this handicap, the difficulties it caused and the prejudices it aroused, for Reynolds and his later successors certainly suffered from too close an assumed identification of the Company's interests with those of the British and not the Persian Government.

The dilemma was apparent from the beginning of negotiations with the Bakhtiari Khans. Reynolds had left England on 2 May 1905 after a final conference in mid-April, when a site at Shardīn was chosen for the first well and it was decided that preparations for drilling at Masjid i-Suleimān should be started once agreement had been reached with the Khans.[179] In the meantime he was to moth-ball the plant and equipment at Chiāh Surkh in July and arrange for its safe keeping. It so happened that J.R. Preece, who was Consul-General in Isfahān and had wide knowledge of Persia extending over many years, was home on leave. He was persuaded on 14 June, at the request of D'Arcy and with the permission of the Foreign Office, to assist in the negotiations with the Khans on his return to Persia in October.[180] The delay thus caused was extremely irksome to Reynolds, not so much because of the involvement of Preece, but because he was prevented from using the best working months for surveys, road building and delivery of plant and equipment before the rains came, as he had been requested not to disclose his real intentions in advance of the negotiations with the Khans.[181] The delay was not only psychologically exasperating but practically it was disastrous, exacerbated by the subsequent failure to recruit a surveyor who would have complemented Reynold's efforts elsewhere. Reynolds realised the urgency of the situation and suggested approaching the Government of India for the loan of an assistant engineer to help in surveying.[182] D'Arcy too appreciated what was at stake and apologised for the 'extreme urgency and importance' of his request to Sir Thomas Sanderson, permanent under-secretary to the Foreign Office, for

The funding and finding of oil 1901-8

an engineer to enable the work to be completed soon and with as little expenditure as possible.[183]

The Indian Government had no objections but showed no enthusiasm and provided no engineer, Lord Curzon remarking that 'we are not hopeful as to prospects of the D'Arcy Concession'.[184] Meanwhile, whilst waiting for the arrival of Preece, Reynolds busied himself in Baghdad with plans for drillers' quarters and a dispensary,[185] modifications to transport equipment,[186] the hiring of mules, designing carts,[187] cladding for derricks, the engagement of a Turkish surveyor,[188] drawing up accounting procedures,[189] and arranging for the reception of goods and men at Muhammara and Ahwāz with the local agent of Lynch Brothers. Letters he despatched to the office of the Concessions Syndicate Ltd (CSL) where they were dealt with by James Hamilton, general manager and director of the Burmah Oil Company, an unimaginative self-opinionated man whose inability to understand Reynolds and appreciate the problems of Persia was a terrible failure in an undistinguished career. Leaving his assistant, Bertie, in charge at Muhammara, Reynolds left for Ahwāz on 26 September[190] going north-east to Shalamzār, in the foothills of the Zagros mountains west of Isfahān, the residence of the Il Khanī, Samsam al-Saltana, on 13 October, where he was joined by Preece three days later.

Bakhtiari Khans with Sardār Assad centre c. 1905

Negotiations with the four leading Bakhtiari Khans took place on 16 and 19 October 1905, and, as Reynolds describes it,

in all of which the Sirdar Assad, Hadji Ali Kuli Khan took, I may say the entire role as spokesmen of the Chiefs, no other Chief having it seemed a word to say in his presence...He, I should say, was masterful and has seen more of the world than most Khans, and has a greater flow of language, so it may have been a pre-arranged affair that he should hold the platform.[191]

On 20 October Sardār Assad moved to his own residence at Junaghān, where on the following day he was adamant in refusing to lease land. He demanded 5 per cent of the share capital issued by each working company, to which Reynolds and Preece had no option but to agree, though it was in excess of their negotiating position. Reynolds left the next day to telegraph the terms from Isfahān and receive instructions. When he returned on 10 November with an authorisation to settle, he discovered that Preece had persuaded the Khans to accept 3 per cent of all shares issued with no limit, but that no agreement had been reached on the guarding arrangements, for which £2000 p.a. had been offered irrespective of the number of drilling camps, later verbally restricted to four.[192] Following the insistence of Samsam al-Saltana and Shahāb al-Saltana, Il-Khānī and Il-Begī respectively, the highest tribal dignatories, Sardār Assad signed too. The fourth signatory was Sārum al-Mulk, Sardār Jang. The general terms agreed to on 15 November 1905 were as follows:[193]

(1) The Agreement was to remain in force for five years, during which period the Company had the right to search for oil, make roads, pipelines, build houses, etc. All arable or irrigated land required was to be handed over by the Khans 'at the fair price of the day'. Non-arable land was to be free.

(2) The Company was to pay the Khans £2000 per annum in quarterly instalments, in return for the guards furnished by the latter. The first instalment (£500) was to be paid after signature of the Agreement; in return the Khans were to assume responsibility for any robbery and for any damage to the Company's property in Bakhtiari territory. 'The Agent of the Company must keep cash in an iron box so that it is further from danger.' Before the finding of oil, the Khans were to furnish two bodies of guards to protect the two places where drilling was to be done. After the finding of oil, the Khans were to furnish as many bodies of guards as would be required to protect the various spots where drilling would be carried out.

(3) In the event of sufficient oil being found in Bakhtiari territory, the terms of the Agreement were to remain binding as long as the D'Arcy Concession continued in force.

(4) On the pipeline being constructed, the Company was to increase the guarding subsidy to £3000 per annum.

(5) After the formation of one or more companies to work oil in the Bakhtiari country, and after oil had been passed through the pipeline, the Company was to grant the Khans 3 per cent of all the ordinary shares

The funding and finding of oil 1901-8

issued by such company or companies, the said shares were to be fully paid.

(6) Should the employees of the Khans fail in their duties, the Company would have the right to ask for compensation for any loss.

(7) On the expiration of the D'Arcy Concession, all buildings that belonged to the Company were to become the property of the Khans. D'Arcy was both apprehensive and elated on hearing the news, admitting to Jenkin that 'Between ourselves I anticipate a good deal of trouble with Mr. Cargill over it...there is one thing certain if we can *now* get this matter settled the success of the Business is assured.'[194] A couple of weeks later he was 'delighted that Burmah agree, I was so afraid they would try for still further concessions...I think really now we can look on Persia as a success.'[195] As so often D'Arcy resembled an inexperienced climber who having ascended one ridge is surprised to find another beyond. There was no doubt that the assistance of Preece facilitated the negotiations with the Khans, as he was known and trusted by them,[196] but neither Preece nor Sardār Assad remained in close touch. When they left the scene, diverging pressures were already exerting themselves without their restraining presence. The guarding payments were of immediate advantage to the Khans, not like shareholdings future returns, but as the responsibility filtered down the rewards were in inverse proportion to the work actually undertaken.

This was the heart of the guarding controversy, which festered like an abscess on the operations among the Bakhtiaris. It was unpopular because the guards gained least themselves, but it was also a means by which the Concessions Syndicate could be coerced into granting better terms. It was at the mercy of conflicting family factions, to which the Bakhtiaris were prone, who promised or withdrew their services accordingly. Indeed, whilst returning to Ahwāz, Reynolds was attacked[197] and his surveyor molested on the way. He regretted that 'we did not reserve to ourselves the right to pay these Guards...The spark of discontent is there, and only needs fanning by our well-wishers to cause trouble.'[198]

Indeed the validity of the Agreement itself was doubtful. At the beginning of January 1906, the Persian Government declined to 'recognise arrangement made by His Majesty's Consul at Isfahān with the Bakhtiari Chiefs stating that the latter had no right to make it' and that 'D'Arcy should first have referred matter to them, and that they are only bound by terms of concession'.[199] The Government had been informed and the Shah had approved of the drilling which had been proposed.[200] It was also being challenged on national grounds by the disgruntled adherents of the Kitabgi family. Just after the conclusion of the Agreement in November Sardār Assad received an anonymous letter from Tehrān urging him for patriotic and religious reasons to 'prevent the Foreigner interfering in his country', particularly as far as the British were concerned, whose oil concession was being used to advance their political and commercial interests 'by intrigue, if they cannot gain their ends direct in the former, they do it thro the latter'.[201] Referred to apparent experience at Chiāh Surkh, Sardār Assad was warned against the appropriation of fuel by the operators for their own use without payment, the employment of non-Persians and the behaviour of Mr Reynolds, who had 'a natural enmity with Persians'. The handwriting resembled that of Nasr'ullāh Khān, father-in-law of the Shaykh al-Mulk, who had also been employed at Chiāh Surkh.

It was probably no coincidence that the employment of the Shaykh and Edouard Kitabgi had been terminated when the Concessions Syndicate took over and that Vincent Kitabgi had just been recalled as Imperial Commissioner by the Persian Government. It was no surprise that, after Sardār Assad himself denounced the Agreement in May 1906, D'Arcy received from the Shaykh al-Mulk a letter to this effect.[202] It was, however, not the existence of the Agreement which was at fault, but the necessity for it imposed by those who were among the first to criticise it, the Khans themselves. Thereafter it was tossed about like a shuttlecock among the players, none of whom wanted to keep it in play, none of whom wanted to hit it out of the political court and most of whom did not even enjoy the game and were always changing the rules. The existence of the Agreement was deeply resented by successive Persian governments till it was denounced by Rizā Khān in 1924, but the Company had little option but to accept some agreement imposed by the Bakhtiari Khans.

(c) Payment is the crux of the matter 1906

It was not till mid-November 1905 that Reynolds was able to visit Shardīn for the first time, when returning from Shalamzār to Ahwāz, have a plan of the site made, select a route by which plant, machinery and supplies might be carried and choose a suitable place for a depot. The first caravan loaded with heavy material for buildings moved off on 23 December. It rained, the nights were cold and water froze in the tents. Some local obstruction was overcome 'by the exercise of patience and a little tact and firmness'.[203] With the ground a quagmire and the carting heavy, progress was slow until the firmer going in the spring. In January 1906 alone, some 1000 tons were unloaded at Muhammara for haulage to the sites over slippery mud and soft sand by the simplest of mule-drawn carts. It was not until 22 August 1906 that drilling commenced at Shardīn, even before all the workshops and stores were erected.[204] Three weeks later a depth of 120 feet was reached hindered by problems over water and fuel.[205] A month

The funding and finding of oil 1901-8

later, Reynolds was reporting 'terribly slow business...Further I have not native labour fit to let me work at night.'[206] In the autumn it was still a hard slog with progress delayed by sickness, caused by contaminated drinking water 'best described as water with dung in suspension',[207] want of fuel and the wet weather which caused the sides of the well to cave in.

Reynolds was spartan in his habits but concerned for the welfare of his staff whom he felt should be in a fit state on arrival as 'the materials afforded for food here are rather trying for any digestion, so that teeth natural or false, are essential if a man is to retain his health'.[208] Such bantering was not appreciated by Hamilton, who later appeared hectoring in his homily that when staff 'are kept in good condition you will be able to get the maximum of work out of them'.[209] Reynolds was not sympathetic to indolence. He criticised Driller Harris, who complained of being short of 'grub...having only had cold boiled eggs and dry bread', when he inquired 'where the tins, some ½ dozen of Army and Navy Rations were which I had given him for use in an emergency, he said he was sitting on the box containing them and had not opened one'. 'He should have brought his mother out', was Reynold's verdict, 'the men have very little to growl at and if they would look after themselves a little and their own interests instead of sitting down and growling they would do better'.[210] Reynolds was a disciplinarian from the outset with a simple code of conduct for retaining the goodwill of the people among whom they lived. It was essential that 'our men behave themselves as reasonable beings not as drunken beasts...the women of the country must not be touched by our men...there must be no striking of them if they do wrong, and I cannot too strongly emphasis this as it is necessary and we can get what we want without it'.[211] He was not afraid to dismiss refractory staff, but it only occurred twice.

As the goods started rolling towards Shardīn there were changes in the Bakhtiari hierarchy as a result of family feuding, which was almost endemic, and Samsam al-Saltana was deposed in favour of Sardār Assad, and Sālār i-Arfā, nephew of Sardār Assad, became the new Il-Begī in mid-January 1906. Reynolds had no intention of interrupting his work even if it meant engaging guards himself,[212] but he was surprised when Sālār i-Arfā, in response to his allegations of disturbances along the route to Shardīn, blandly replied that in our country 'never is it necessary to have any Guard for anything at all'.[213] In mid-February, Reynolds was ready 'to take my Plant and men to the site of our work' and consulted Captain D. Lorimer, the consul at Ahwāz, on the best course of action. He recommended that Lorimer and himself should see Sālār i-Arfā and agree a plan 'as should it ever become necessary for our men to be withdrawn, owing to disturbances among the Tribesmen and insufficient guards, the

79

The funding and finding of oil 1901-8

results would be disastrous to the enterprise'.[214] Lorimer was cooperative and, riding separately, joined Reynolds in talks at the tribal encampment at Ram Hormuz on 23 February. Sālār i-Arfā was friendly but forthright that unless the guarding money was 'paid to the credit of His Excellency the Sirdar Assad, he - the Salar Arfa - had instructions to provide no guard and that our work must stop', irrespective of the provisions of the Agreement that a receipt for the payment of money had to be signed by all the signatory Khans.[215] The reason was blatantly political, for Sardār Assad was buying his way into power in Tehrān.[216] A compromise was reached whereby the second instalment of the guarding money was paid to Sardār Assad in the circumstances that he would refund it if the arrangement was unacceptable to the other Khans. Reynolds informed the Concessions Syndicate that he had no alternative to prevent the stoppage of work, but his initiative with the consul was deprecated in Glasgow.[217]

The action then moved to Tehrān where the Khans, briefly united again, were attempting to repudiate the Agreement to the chargé d'affaires, Grant Duff on 15 May 1906, at the instigation of Sardār Assad, who pleaded that they were 'men who were unacquainted with business matters' and had only concluded the Agreement out of regard for Preece 'without realizing what they were undertaking'.[218] He listed six objections which concerned the kind of buildings to be erected on their land, the insufficiency of the guarding payments, and the hearing of disputes between the Syndicate employees and Persians to be held by the local judiciary. Grant Duff disclaimed any authority in the matter, passed on the information and thought it incredible that '£2,000 a year should not cover the cost of maintaining eighty tribesmen'. It was Preece who advised D'Arcy and the Concessions Syndicate, having retired from the Foreign Office, and been appointed as political agent in respect of Persian affairs on 11 June.[219] D'Arcy was again apprehensive of Burmah's reaction 'as it will make them doubt the validity of all contracts made with Persians' and he advised prolonging 'the thing as much as possible and if it could be prolonged for some months, results may be obtained in Persia which could simplify matters considerably'.[220] In the event there was no crisis and the reply of Preece was clear in rejecting the proposals, which amounted to cancelling the Agreement.[221] Discontent rumbled on in Tehrān, but inaction prevailed as the Bakhtiari Khans played tug of war amongst themselves and with the Shah. Then in mid-September Samsam al-Saltana, restored again as the Il-Khānī, refused to sanction guards for work planned as Masjid i-Suleimān 'until a settlement is arrived at with respect to points they have raised with British Minister in Teheran'.[222]

Reynolds disapproved of Grant Duff, the chargé d'affaires, having taken the demands of Sardār Assad seriously, for by no calculation were the Khans being underpaid for the guarding services on which their maximum annual outlay could have been no more than £272.[223] The Khans were dissatisfied and as Preece admitted to the Foreign Secretary, Sir Edward Grey, it was 'the payment of Guards which apparently is the real crux of the matter',[224] as it had been from the beginning. By a fortunate coincidence both the Concessions Syndicate and the Minister, Sir Cecil Spring-Rice, agreed in returning the matter to Reynolds, thus vindicating his earlier stance, to settle with the assistance of Captain Lorimer.[225] Meanwhile Lorimer, whilst helping some of the Khans, Samsam al-Saltana, Mu'īn Humāyūn, Shahāb al-Saltana and Sārum al-Mulk to compose their differences with each other, persuaded them to settle their claims for an extra payment of £500 for the preservation of friendly relations.[226] Reynolds agreed and within a couple of days on 2 November confirmation was received.[227] Apart from a last minute flurry of concern over fluctuating rates of exchange the year ended peacefully.

(d) 'The unsettled state of south Persia and danger to the Persian business' 1907

D'Arcy, who had by no means left the stage, expressing himself with a characteristic blend of optimism and anxiety, confided to Preece on New Year's day,

> I can see no cause for alarm, as unreliable as the Bakhtiaris are, they are not such fools as to attempt to kill the goose that lays the golden egg, and the increased amount that they have agreed to take and are presumably satisfied with, will, let us hope cause them to continue in this frame of mind until Reynolds gets oil – and I do not think this is very far off... You must not think when I say I am attending to other things that I ever neglect this Persian business, as that always comes first, as apart from my large money interest in it I am, for my own sake, most anxious that it shall succeed. I am aware that the finances are running short and, of course, they will have to find more money. They will not like this, I fear, and I cannot think why, instead of finding more, they do not at once form the Big Company and go to work thoroughly. I am gently suggesting this to Hamilton on every favourable opportunity.[228]

Discussions took place between D'Arcy and Burmah directors during January and February 1907. On 27 February, the Burmah Board unanimously resolved that only on the cancellation of their obligation to subscribe £800 000 in the company to be formed to work the Concession would they be 'prepared to go on with the testing operations in the South and spend up to a further £30 000 on the same', making £100 000 in all, less than D'Arcy had reckoned three years previously.[229] D'Arcy was dismayed that they blamed the 'Persian unrest' for their reluctance to proceed and was worried about raising more money and the task – 'this

The funding and finding of oil 1901-8

really makes me shudder' - of getting his associates into line again.[230] He opted for the lesser of the evils,[231] but Manisty advised him otherwise, for the new proposals might have precluded him from recovering his initial outlay and would have involved him in disposing of more than one eighth of the interest of his associates.[232] The Burmah directors after considerable discussion agreed to guarantee £200 000, which at least safeguarded D'Arcy's original expenses. If this final offer was declined 'the Concessions Syndicate would abandon their testing operations'.[233] The Concession would then be up for auction again. D'Arcy was depressed. He thanked Manisty profusely 'for all you have done and are doing for me in this terrible business' and toyed with the idea of seeking finance from the Harmsworth-Newnes Group, but to no purpose.[234] Eventually, on 15 July, agreement was reached and signed a fortnight later. As D'Arcy informed Vincent Kitabgi, who remained very suspicious, 'it is a question of either getting the money from them or stopping all work and virtually abandoning the concession'.[235] G.T. Powell, a lawyer acting for Wolff, came to much the same conclusion in advising his client.[236] Wolff, grumbling terribly in May, was actually advocating 'the desirability of those concerned in the Concession joining German interests in concessions along the Turkish-Persian frontier'.

Why were the majority of the Burmah directors, apart from Wallace and Hamilton so reluctant to renew their commitments with D'Arcy? It was not because of an adverse financial position for, at the Annual General Meeting on 26 April 1907, it was reported that 1906 was 'a prosperous year', enabling them to write down the book value of unprofitable investments, including Persia, by £60 000, place £100 000 in the General Reserve, which was thereby increased to £340 000, and commission a new pipeline in Burma.[237] The failure of the Admiralty fuel oil contract to materialise, so laboriously negotiated, may have reduced their crude oil requirements, which could now be provided from their own improved production and exploration prospects in Burma. There was a change of emphasis at the Admiralty not only because of the Liberal Party's landslide electoral triumph in January 1906 but because 'the professional engineers at the Admiralty are advising the head not to commit themselves too deeply to Fuel Oil, as in their opinion the next few years will probably see a development in internal combustion engines worked by coal gas'.[238] On the other hand Burmah always adopted a cautious balance between supply and demand, for 'this Company's crude oil resources', affirmed R.I. Watson, a Burmah director in 1916, 'directly and indirectly produced by it, have never been for any length of time materially in advance of a more profitable market for them' and 'this arrangement with the Admiralty has never had and has not now any attractions' apart from its patriotic

The funding and finding of oil 1901-8

interest.[239] Redwood, perpetually ebullient, declared publicly that Burmah had large reserves of oil-bearing territory available, but he may not have been so convinced in private.[240] Was the Persian insurance policy now superfluous? Was the period of 'great courage' over and was 'great caution' the order of the day? Was it just effortless self-satisfaction basking in 'the blessings of peace in the oil trade of India?'. Persia probably appeared a worsening liability in comparison with the growing profitability of the controlled eastern markets in which Burmah was entrenched. The Persian commitments were cut to a minimum to retain a covering interest, and no more.

In Persia, Reynolds complained that the extra guarding payment had not improved the guarding arrangements to prevent loss and pilfering.[241] Lorimer, in his Spring meeting with the Khans, Samsam al-Saltana and Shahāb al-Saltana, on 3 March, remonstrated with them about compensation but they disowned all responsibility. They were only concerned 'to secure the whole £2,500 and not spend a penny...no cash payment is ever made. Payments are merely effected by remission of taxation.'[242] Lorimer regretted the weakness previously displayed towards them which was only encouraging further demands and evasion of responsibility and was determined not to give way. Eventually during his visit Samsam al-Saltana and Shahāb al-Saltana quarrelled and the latter secretly promised to be more accommodating.[243] Lorimer sensing that the family balance was tilting in favour of Shahāb al-Saltana accepted his good faith. His foresight was confirmed when Shahāb al-Saltana became Il-Khanī and Sārum al-Mulk, Il-Begī, the two principal tribal offices. In the south a particularly bad robbery was perpetrated by a well-known trouble maker, 'Alī Murād Khān, but the property was returned due to the exertions of the two Khans,[244] who certainly exercised more control till they too lost their positions when Samsam al-Saltana ousted them in June. Reynolds' comment on Samsam al-Saltana's brother was appropriate to most of the Khans, 'a man as full of intrigue as the egg of a nightingale is pregnant with music'.[245] Sardār Assad and Sālār i-Arfā returned from their European journey. Amīn al-Sultān was murdered in August after returning from Europe – 'a sad blow' for the Concession[246] – and D'Arcy's earlier troubled advice 'to sit tight and do nothing...we must put up with a certain amount of temporary inconvenience and let Reynolds go on. Of course Baksheesh is at the root of it all and that with my consent they will never get', was becoming less feasible.[247] Not only was there a deterioration in the guarding position, but there was rising impatience about the existence of oil.

At the end of May, Reynolds acknowledged that 'the question "When do you expect to strike oil?" is on the lips of all those interested in the

The funding and finding of oil 1901-8

'Alī Murād Khān 1907

success of this undertaking, but it is one I find exceedingly difficult to answer'.[248] Reynolds at this time had been discouraged by a letter from Redwood to which he replied that 'I cannot do for the Company any better than I am doing now and have been doing'.[249] E.H. Cunningham Craig,

The funding and finding of oil 1901-8

geologist to Burmah, later in November 1907, on his visit to the scene of the operations, agreed, writing of Reynolds 'without whose guidance and knowledge of the country I should have found it quite impossible to have worked out the many geological problems presented in so short a time, and whose constant courtesy and kindness will always make me his debtor'.[250] At the beginning of May the first well had been drilled to 925 feet,[251] but had encountered over 100 feet of hard cap rock, which perturbed Reynolds, and the second well had reached 738 feet. Because of the pressure of work and insecurity he was unable to correlate his findings with observations elsewhere, but he was pessimistic and by September was convinced that further drilling at Marmatain, a nearby site, and Shardīn was hopeless.[252]

Redwood and Dalton disagreed but Cunningham Craig supported Reynolds and in early January 1908 drilling ceased at Shardīn after the wells had reached 2172 feet and 1942 feet respectively. Mid-1907 was a crucial period, for with lack of success at Shardīn it became all the more vital to get the road to Masjid i-Suleimān finished and supplies in before the autumnal rains wrecked their chances. It was a scorching summer with tempers running short. 'Alī Murād called his villagers away without notice[253] and at the end of June, in a fracas at Baitwand, Driller Harris was stoned and injured.[254] Short of staff, striving to press on with drilling and opening up Masjid i-Suleimān, Reynolds, dependent on Lorimer, 'were you not at the back of me, I fear I should be soon "in extremis" ', was not in favour of any retaliatory action.[255] Inadequate protection was better than no protection. At the end of September, 'Alī Murād again threatened the drillers, who feared for their safety.[256]

Lorimer may have been exaggerating when he reported the situation in a serious light and anticipated danger to European life and property,[257] but it was a risk D'Arcy could not disregard, because 'the unsettled state of S. Persia is a Danger to our Business'.[258] Preece, whilst not sharing Lorimer's pessimism, agreed that it would be disastrous if all the plant was looted and the boring destroyed.[259] D'Arcy spoke to Sir Charles Hardinge, permanent secretary to the Foreign Office, who was concerned.[260] Action was taken but the arrival of the gunboat *Comet* was ludicrous because it failed to float over the shallows below Ahwāz and lay like a stranded whale against the bank. The appearance of the reinforcements of two officers, Lieutenants Ranking and Arnold (later Sir) Wilson, and twenty men for the consular guard, was welcome. As the Foreign Office informed Preece, 'it has been decided upon as a temporary measure with the object of affording some assistance and protection to the employees and property of the Oil Syndicate in view of the importance attached by His Majesty's Government to the maintenance of British enterprise in South West

The funding and finding of oil 1901-8

Persia'.[261] It did not replace the services of the Bakhtiaris, which, in fact, improved.

(e) The discovery of oil at Masjid i-Suleimān in May 1908

Masjid i-Suleimān was the last throw of the concessionary dice. At the beginning of 1906 Reynolds was enthusiastic about drilling there. 'I do not think,' he wrote to the Concessions Syndicate, 'justice would be done to the place if you did not decide to drill there. To the best of my judgement it is the better property of the two... You have incurred the cost of the plant and the extra cost of drilling there will be a trifle in comparison to the expenditure incurred already.'[262] It was a shrewd assessment, but overlooked the problem of the road. Reynolds pointed out that it was hard for those 'who have never set foot in these parts to realise that it is impossible to get a native whom one can put in charge of a gang of men to do earth work or any such work there may be to do'.[263] The work was not 'all beer and skittles'.[264] It was not till August 1906 that the road was under way, making 'fair progress' given difficult conditions and a shortage of explosives, with two teams working until the beginning of December,[265] when Bradshaw, in charge of road works, reported that the River Kārūn, 'a raging torrent' after the rains, had completely demolished everything

Working on the road to Masjid i-Suleimān 1907

The funding and finding of oil 1901-8

that had been done.²⁶⁶ Reynolds drafted all available staff on to the road to make up for lost time vowing to 'get into Maidan ba-Naphtun all right' so that 'when we have success nothing will give me greater pleasure than to learn that more of the Directors of Messrs. the C.S.L. have been there to judge for themselves'.²⁶⁷ Reynolds generously praised two of his assistants, Holland and Walters, without whom 'working at a time when no one in this country works if he can help it we should not have had the plant up at site'.²⁶⁸

In spite of these exceptional efforts, drilling at the first well at Masjid i-Suleimān, located by Reynolds, did not start till 23 January 1908 at 4.30 p.m.²⁶⁹ One of his last difficulties was caused by damage to the screwed casing, about which he had complained two years previously and which he had advised protecting with wooden blocks.²⁷⁰ The instructions he received in January were to close down work at Shardīn, 'Push ahead with two selected sites Masjid i-Suleiman' and return redundant drillers.²⁷¹ Reynolds retained all the drillers in order to press on with preparation for the second well, the site of which was still being levelled in mid-February and not started till March.²⁷² At the end of February Reynolds confidently asserted that 'a definite result will be obtained one way or the other, before it becomes necessary to pay the 15th May instalment to the Khans'.²⁷³ He was just ten days out. With staff leaving on the expiry of their contracts, which were not all being renewed, or merely prolonged on a temporary basis, Reynolds did well to sustain morale in the last trying months when sulphurous water was corroding wire ropes and gas was dangerous. In April, Reynolds was assured by Cunningham Craig and Redwood that oil would be struck at a moderate depth.²⁷⁴

The geologists may have been optimistic but the Burmah directors were again being cautious as the Agreement of 1907 was coming to an end and finance was becoming short as D'Arcy remarked to Preece on 1 April.²⁷⁵ A few days later another session of concessionary poker opened when Hamilton informed D'Arcy that 'their money is exhausted...unless I find half of the expenditure in future, the work must stop...of course, I cannot find £20 000 or anything, and what to do I know not'.²⁷⁶ He took some comfort from the comment of Thompson, Cargill's cousin, 'for their own protection, having either to prove Persia a success or no good to anyone else'. In fact both D'Arcy and Burmah were locked into the same position, with Burmah having the stronger hold. Burmah was confident on geological advice that by 1500 feet in depth it would be known whether oil was present or not.

Drilling was easier and by April it only required 500 feet more in the first well and 1000 feet in the second. Hamilton mentioned £40 000 to D'Arcy but he felt that 'in my opinion £10/15,000 should see the experiment

The funding and finding of oil 1901-8

through, seeing we were only spending at the rate of £3,500/4,000 per month'.[277] D'Arcy prevaricated on paying anything, perhaps on purpose. On 15 April the Board of Burmah requested D'Arcy to pay half of any expenditure up to £20 000 but that if he declined by the end of the month 'the Board would then consider whether they would not at once abandon the operations in Persia entirely'.[278] To emphasise the point they announced at the Sixth Annual General Meeting, two days later, that 'unless satisfactory results are shortly obtained this enterprise will be abandoned'.[279] On 19 May, a week before oil was struck, D'Arcy signed a further agreement with Burmah whereby it guaranteed a further expenditure up to £40 000 till 20 May 1909 to prove the existence of oil in return for recovering all their expenditure if and when a company was formed to exploit the oil discovered. They had little to loose and not long to wait.

At the beginning of May the wells had reached 933 and 563 feet respectively. Unexpectedly the drilling bit came unscrewed and lost in the hole for ten days while they fished for it with the temperature 110°F in the shade.[280] Then suddenly on 26 May 1908 about 4 a.m. at a depth of 1180 feet oil was struck.[281] On a testing flow the next day an estimated 297 barrels was recorded. Reynolds cabled the news, but it was a wire from Lieutenant Wilson, which arrived first in biblical code, 'See Psalm 104 verse 15 third sentence and Psalm 114 verse 8 second sentence', which being translated, 'That he may bring out of the earth oil to make a cheerful countenance'; 'the flint stone into a springing well'.[282] Reynolds, remembering his men, inquired what action he should take over rewards and returned to Ahwāz to bring his accounts up to date for his contract too was lapsing. On his way back in mid-June he received a letter of 14 May from the Concessions Syndicate, 'We would like if possible to put the two wells at Musjid-i-Sulaiman down to 1,500/1,600 feet and if no oil is found at this depth, to abandon operations, close down, and bring as much of the plant as is possible down to Mohammerah.'[283] Reynolds must have smiled wryly. No riposte was required. It just remained for the Company to operate the Concession acquired by D'Arcy.

3
THE FORMATION OF THE ANGLO-PERSIAN OIL COMPANY 1909

I INTRODUCTION

The striking of oil at Masjid i-Suleimān on 26 May 1908 was more than the culmination of years of intrepid exploratory endeavour or the possibility of commercial success. It could not have been foreseen, but it eventually signalled the emergence of the first oil-producing area in the Middle East, with all the economic and political consequences which this meant. It coincided, moreover, with a political crisis in Persia when Muhammad 'Alī Shāh intervened to suppress the parliamentary assembly, the Majlis, culminating in the bombardment of its premises and the dispersal, arrest and murder of some of its members by the Russian-officered Cossack brigade on 23 June 1908, under the Shah's orders. The two events were quite unconnected with each other, but subsequent economic and political developments remained closely intertwined in Persia. The injection of a measure of industrialisation into Persian society, in which there was political instability and social tension, did eventually produce economic growth, but it also exacerbated conflict within it. The interaction of these elements was dramatic and in some respects immediate for in Persia there had been no prolonged period of industrial apprenticeship, that familiarity with materials and technology which tempers ambition, recognises skill and values the importance of the practical application of knowledge. At the time of the formation of the Company, there was little industry in Persia.

The Constitutional Movement was accompanied by patriotic euphoria but it lacked real accomplishment. The splendid appearance of a national revival and independence contrasted with foreign influenced despotism and did represent a strength of emotion and a force of conviction which could not be ignored. In spite of the troubled conditions of the country, this political revivalism was accentuated with the Bakhtiaris under Samsam al-Saltana and Sardār Assad marching on Isfahān and Tehrān in the cause of the reforming movement, the insurrection and defence of Tabrīz by the Constitutionalists against earlier Russian intervention, the ignominious deposition of Muhammad ʿAlī Shāh and the accession of Ahmed Shāh, all occurring in 1909.

Thus, whatever the diplomatic justification for the Anglo-Russian Convention of 31 August 1907, conceived in terms of *realpolitik* and its ultimate success in preventing what the British militarily would have been unable to stop, Persia becoming a dependency of the Russian Empire,[1] it was, as Sir Cecil Spring-Rice, Minister in Tehrān, anticipated, regrettable in its implications for Persia. Partly because he was not consulted and partly because he was perfectly aware of the Persian political predicament, the Minister was apprehensive, and with less than the usual deference to a Foreign Secretary he warned him that 'a great impetus will at once be given to the already existing anti-foreign sentiment',[2] and some antagonism towards British interests.

The actions of the British Government towards Persia were seldom without their influence on oil affairs. Indeed, in July 1908, soon after Reynolds' return from Persia, C.M. Marling, chargé d'affaires at the Legation in Tehrān, was anxiously stating that in the oilfield, 'In order to avoid confusion, delay and waste of money, a competent and sufficiently numerous European staff is most necessary at the present moment, when the actual and expected developments of the oil field appear likely to involve negotiations for a refinery, telephones, pipelines etc.'[3] When the matter was referred to Preece, he rather lamely replied that it was under consideration.[4] The general impression of the oil strike was favourable; as Sir Charles Hardinge observed, it was 'excellent news for our interests in south-western Persia',[5] and would 'greatly increase our interest in south-western Persia'.[6] The Government, however, was careful to refer to general interest and not specific concern. Yet, notwithstanding some official caution, there was an understandable tendency on the part of some zealous local consular representatives to emphasise the useful political and commercial advantages which an extension of British interests in their areas would achieve. Thus Lorimer, who had been so helpful to Reynolds, remarked emphatically over the question of a British presence in south-west Persia that 'the greater the aggregation of our interests in this quarter, the more possible it is for us to exert pressures on the Persian Government'.[7]

Yet, however admirable an analysis of national interest, it does not necessarily follow that there will be a corresponding commercial benefit. Political response to economic opportunism varies from country to country, decade to decade. It is, therefore, of particular importance in understanding the relationship of the Company to the government of the day to ascertain at any given moment the factors which affected it. Thus, though Lorimer may have envisaged that the presence of a British oil company in south-west Persia would contribute towards tribal stability, improve the transportation system, expand trade, strengthen security and counter foreign enterprise in an area of British influence, such considerations, although the concern of the Company, were not the object of its operations.

Louis Mallet at the Foreign Office remarked, in forwarding the recommendations of Lorimer in September, that,

> I think these papers will be of use to the Syndicate in deciding how such an enterprise should be carried out if they decide to undertake it and I need hardly add that it is most desirable from the point of view of British interests, both political and commercial, that it should be taken by them since if it is not, there is every likelihood that the business will be secured and worked by subjects of a foreign Power.[8]

This may have been obvious to the officials of the Foreign Office and they may have been rightly anxious about German involvement in Persia and that the German Legation would be on the watch for opportunities to play the part of friend and adviser to Persia to the detriment of nearer neighbours. In particular they were concerned about the German penetration of trade in south-west Persia, as evidenced in the despatches of Herr Edward Mygind, correspondent of the *Berliner Tageblatt*,[9] but this was not the preoccupation of Preece and his colleagues who accepted the risk that all the concessionary eggs were in the Bakhtiari basket. Given that funds were limited, Preece asked, 'To get to the present point very large sums of money have been expended, is it worth while to expend in a purely tentative measure further large sums in addition?'[10] Lorimer was not only perturbed by the unreliability of the Bakhtiari Khans[11] but also by the prospect of Canadian drillers being replaced by those from America. This was not on technical grounds but because of 'the presence of persons over whom His Majesty's Government would have no power of jurisdiction, and over whose conduct, however unruly, they would exercise no control'.[12] The interests of the bureaucrat and the concessionaire were not always identical. The formation of the Company was to bring this out in the open.

Lorimer's concern was not entirely gratuitous, for neither he nor Arnold Wilson had been impressed with the management of the Concessions Syndicate Ltd, apart from Reynolds, and were sceptical of the commitment of the directors to exploit the Concession. In April 1908, the rumour in Tehrān, according to G.P. Churchill, the Oriental Secretary, was that 'the Syndicate is going to throw up the sponge';[13] Wilson was sarcastic over 'faint-hearted merchants, masquerading in top hats as pioneers of Empire', 'Scottish employers, whose short-sighted parsimony had so nearly wrecked a great enterprise'.[14] There were thus doubts about

The formation of the Anglo-Persian Oil Company

the determination of the Burmah Oil Company to develop the Concession which only the formation of a company would allay.

2 ACTION AFTER THE DISCOVERY OF OIL JUNE–NOVEMBER 1908

D'Arcy was delighted at the discovery, receiving the news appropriately at a dinner party. A month later, holidaying on Hayling Island, he asked Preece 'to look at the Concession and see if we have to give any notice on anything on finding oil as it is important that all the conditions in the Concession shall now be complied with'.[15] It was D'Arcy who took the initiative. He regretted the lack of an immediate response from the Burmah directors and chided them for wanting to drill more wells 'for why I do not know as if they all failed it could not affect existing facts. I suppose when they have made Musjid like the top of a Pepper Pot they will be happy.'[16] His relations with his partners in the Concessions Syndicate were tense. He was apprehensive, even over-anxious, and criticised their decision to recall Reynolds at the crucial moment of success, leaving Bradshaw behind in charge, but, he asked Preece, 'what can I do unless I give formal notice and a quarrel. I think we had better wait and see what Reynolds says.'[17] Preece had become his confidant. The situation in Persia depressed him and he observed tersely that 'Things at Teheran look bad and will not I should imagine be better until the Shah is bombed or dethroned.'[18]

D'Arcy's concern coincided with the arrival of the new Imperial Commissioner, Sādigh al-Saltana, Mut'amin Huzour, for the first time in June. He had succeeded Vincent Kitabgi on two occasions, in March 1905 before being replaced in May 1907 and then again appointed in September 1907. Already in January 1907 Sādigh al-Saltana had been inquiring about the Concessions Syndicate.[19] Indeed the Concession had been the subject of discussion in the Consultative Assembly when Sa'ad al-Dawla, who had been Persian Minister in Belgium and was an opponent of the Shah, commented that D'Arcy 'had engaged to employ natives and to observe certain other conditions' and that the Commissioner was not aware of the nature of his responsibilities.[20] On 20 January 1907 Sa'ad al-Dawla, briefed by Shaykh al-Mulk with the backing of Edouard Kitabgi, again criticised the lack of Persians employed in the oil operations. In reply it was said on evidence from the local authorities that 'apart from the managing staff and engineers, the whole of the employés were Persians',[21] The Minister for Mines, Muhandes al-Mamalek, and Sādigh al-Saltana were present at this meeting of the Majlis.

As a result of this questioning in the assembly it was thought wise to appoint Paul Kitabgi as agent of the Syndicate in Tehrān, particularly as

The formation of the Anglo-Persian Oil Company

the question of the Bakhtiari Agreement was also provoking much discussion at this time. Edouard Kitabgi had also advocated creating 'an influence favourable to Mr. D'Arcy's interests'.[22] In reality the Kitabgi family was quite dependent upon the patronage of the Amīn al-Sultān who had been assassinated in mid-1906, so the appointment of Paul Kitabgi was not renewed after the first year because his services had no practical benefit. As for relations with the Bakhtiari Khans, the advice on 20 May 1907 of Mr (later Sir) Percy Loraine, First Secretary at the Legation, that Lorimer should be the sole intermediary between the Legation, the Concessions Syndicate and the Khans, was accepted.[23]

Sādigh al-Saltana first communicated with Preece on 19 August 1908, apologising for sickness since his arrival and requesting a meeting with D'Arcy, 'as there are many matters regarding the oil concession about which I shall have to talk' and inquiring 'what is being at present done both in Persia and here regarding the oil concession'.[24] Having been informed on 24 June that oil had been found, it was natural that he wanted 'to know what steps you are taking to exploit the oil and to work the concession in a satisfactory manner', so that he could fulfill his obligations towards his Government. He raised again the nature of D'Arcy's agreement with Burmah and the outstanding rental which the Government believed was due to it under Article 4 from the seepages at Qasr-i Shīrīn, Shushtar and Dālakī.[25]

Preece overreacted in his comments to D'Arcy, thinking that Sadigh's letter was 'distinctly aggressive' and that it might have been written in collusion with German interests as 'if they can annul the Concession for any cause they may get a lump sum from the Germans'.[26] He wrote to Hamilton even more strongly, 'My reply is a fighting one and is intended to put him in his place.'[27] D'Arcy was disturbed and immediately asked Preece 'to send the short *non* fighting reply'. He was determined not only to prevent any unnecessary offence being given, observing that 'This matter *has more to do with me* than with Hamilton and I strongly urge you to do this',[28] but believed that it was highly important that 'the Concession or its Rights must not be jeopardised'. He was resolved to 'finish up - if we can - the position Regarding the Concession and the Rights of the Persian Government for once and for all', on his return from holiday in Scotland.[29] The intention was admirable, its realisation unlikely. D'Arcy saw the Commissioner in mid-September. He appeared to satisfy him about his agreement with Burmah and the progress of operations in Persia, and promised to keep him informed about the formation of the Company. At the beginning of November, Sādigh al-Saltana, pleased at the news that a third well had come in as a producer, was nevertheless impatient about 'the return to town for the winter of people and financiers when you would let me know definitely as to the date of the formation of a Company'.[30] He naturally wished to be able to inform his Government 'definitely as to this'.

Thus by November the Imperial Commissioner and D'Arcy were both anxious that the formation of the Company should not be delayed. Sadigh al-Saltana had already complained to Preece that 'it is nearly eight years since the Concession was granted and nothing of a practical nature has yet been done'.[31] It was reasonable for Sadigh al-Saltana to suggest that 'the Imperial Government have naturally been hoping to have derived some benefit', but unrealistic to claim that it should have been 'long since'. D'Arcy, with his habitual and premature optimism, thought early in September that 'all certainly looks as if we were not far from the initiation of the Co'.[32] He may have gained this impression from C.W. Wallace, at whose insistence he wrote to Charles Greenway politely requesting a meeting and apologising for 'troubling you without a proper introduction but probably Wallace has mentioned me and the oil Business to you'.[33]

This seems to have been D'Arcy's first acquaintance with Greenway, the first occasion on which Greenway was directly concerned in the enterprise with which he later became so closely identified. They soon established a mutual and sympathetic understanding and had similar social interests. Greenway was more at ease in the home counties than in the highlands. He was, in a sense, a protégé of Wallace, in whose firm of Indian managing agents, Shaw, Wallace and Co, he was a senior partner, and was experienced in the oil trade. Greenway had been involved in 1905-6 in the intricate negotiations between Burmah and Shell which eventually resulted in their joint marketing agreement over Indian markets. Thereafter he spent two years managing the distribution of Burmah petroleum products in India, during which time sales expanded and profits increased. He thus possessed not only a practical knowledge of petroleum affairs, but also marketing expertise and shrewd determination. 'Champagne Charlie' as he was depicted in later life, with monocle, spats and cigar, was a resilient, formidable and tenacious businessman, decorous, even fastidious, but who could trade punch for punch with his commercial competitors. His loyalty to Wallace was reciprocated by the older man's confidence in him.

D'Arcy was doubtless relieved at the prospect of dealing with someone other than Hamilton. Hamilton, corresponding with Cargill in July over the D'Arcy interest in an oil concession for Mesopotamia, had referred to 'friction with D'Arcy and Manisty, which, as we all know is strong at present'.[34] The animosity persisted in September with D'Arcy unable to 'understand Hamilton being sick at not seeing me',[35] and continued with differences of opinion over Reynolds. Greenway acknowledged D'Arcy's

The formation of the Anglo-Persian Oil Company

letter on 15 September and within a few days D'Arcy was thanking him for his 'very kind letter' and accepting Greenway's advice over some shares in spite of the fact that he 'did not intend going into anything further until this Persian Business of mine was settled, but I should so like to be associated with you on what appears to be a very good thing'.[36] This preliminary exchange set the cooperative and cordial tone of their relationship. On Greenway's suggestion, D'Arcy wrote to Hamilton at the end of September drawing his attention to the recent show of oil in No. 3 well and the need to form the company, as 'I am desirous that the matter should not be delayed longer than is absolutely necessary as I am being continually worried by those interested. There is of course also to be considered my position with Persian Government.'[37] Little sense of urgency was noticeable from the Burmah directors and D'Arcy found Hamilton's reply unsatisfactory. D'Arcy complained to Greenway and regretted having 'to trouble you so often about the Persian matter and the importance of it must be my excuse'.

Greenway assured D'Arcy that Wallace shared his views and it seems likely that Wallace took the initiative in pressing the Burmah directors to come to a definite decision. Although D'Arcy was not officially informed till after the Burmah Board Meeting on 28 October that 'Oil had been found in sufficient quantity to justify the formation of the big company',[38] he was already sufficiently and rightly confident to write to Manisty and also Vincent Kitabgi that 'nothing will stop the Burmah Oil Co from forming that great Company we have been wanting for so long.'[39] On 9 November D'Arcy had an important meeting with Wallace and Hamilton to discuss a basis for forming the company, all the more urgent as Cargill was leaving for a four month visit to India and Burma towards the end of November.[40] The decisive meeting occurred a week later on 17 November when a general measure of agreement was reached between D'Arcy, Cargill and Wallace.[41] Cargill made Wallace responsible for Persian affairs in his absence and Greenway was instructed to assist him.

These arrangements, quite fortuitous, were nevertheless to have significant repercussions. Wallace, under whose guidance the Anglo-Persian Oil Company was formed, had a talent for negotiation, an ability to conciliate and a flair for business. Within four months he had persuaded or charmed many men into dropping their differences and working more energetically than they were accustomed. It was a remarkable display of nerve, efficiency and amiability. His orchestration of the proceedings was impressive and his achievement probably tilted the balance of directorial responsibility towards London and away from Glasgow, with incalculable consequences for the Company, which thereby escaped some of the consequences of narrow-minded parochialism. As the principal assistant to Wallace, Greenway was not beholden to the Burmah directors for his position and regarded the Company, for whose formation he was partly responsible, more independently. He had no inhibitions, no prior obligations to divide his loyalty, which he totally reserved for the Anglo-Persian Oil Company.

There was, therefore, no reason to delay forming the company to develop the Concession. In the meantime Reynolds had been asked to return to Persia. The Burmah directors had shown little disposition to see Reynolds just after his arrival on leave, which surprised D'Arcy, but he was twice seen by Hamilton at the beginning of September in a rather perfunctory manner. Hamilton completely misjudged Reynolds and paid little attention to his advice, knowledge or experience. D'Arcy was perturbed, informing Greenway that,

I think he is a man who would be most useful for the new Company, as he knows the country, is liked and trusted by the British Authorities, and gets on well with the natives...He is a man who will never by a stupid action imperil the Concession, and if it is thought advisable to engage him, and the yea or nea is only a question of terms, I am quite confident that if *you* or *Wallace and I* saw him that these could easily be arranged.[42]

Hamilton was not convinced, and complained sarcastically that Reynolds 'had opened his mouth considerably wider than I bargained for'[43] and finally remarked to Cargill before Reynolds left in November that 'the type machine could not reproduce the words I would like to say about this man'[44]

Reynolds pointedly suggested to Hamilton on 24 October, 'I would be glad, before leaving, to hear what your programme may be for future work in Persia, as such were better discussed personally than by letter when I am there.'[45] The programme agreed for Reynolds on 19 November was prepared primarily for the appeal of the prospectus to potential investors. So at Masjid i-Suleimān he was to 'put down as many wells as possible – as far apart as can be conveniently arranged so as to define the field as much as possible – stopping the drill on the hard surface which we know covers the oil sand'.[46] A rig was to be erected at Shardīn and reports were expected on the possibilities of outlying fields. Every assistance was to be offered to B.F.N. Macrorie, a geologist, who, on Redwood's recommendation, was going to Persia to compile 'sufficient reliable data to form a report for insertion in a prospectus'. Results, not window dressing, were required for the successful flotation of the Company.

The formation of the Anglo-Persian Oil Company

3 THE INCORPORATION OF THE COMPANY
NOVEMBER 1908 - APRIL 1909

(a) Negotiations between D'Arcy and Burmah

By the beginning of December a memorandum existed, drafted by Greenway with amendments proposed by D'Arcy. The capital of the new company was to be £3 000 000 of which £2 000 000 was in ordinary shares and the remainder in preference shares. The ordinary shares were for the vendors as the purchase price of the Concession, while the proceeds of the preference shares and an issue of 5 per cent debentures were to be used for (1) repaying the actual expenses already incurred, (2) the cost of pipelines, a refinery and other facilities and (3) working capital.[47]

A Board of Directors was tentatively agreed, consisting of D'Arcy himself, Cargill, Wallace, Hamilton of Burmah, and Greenway. Others for possible selection included Lord Burton and Lord Orford, friends of D'Arcy, already financially interested in the Concession, E.G. Pretyman, J.R. Preece, Sir Hugh Barnes, Lt-Governor of Burma 1903-5 and member of the Government of India Council, 1905-13, and Mr Ailwyn Fellowes. D'Arcy at first hoped that Lord Cromer, who in April 1907 resigned after 24 years 'eminent services' in Egypt, or Lord Milner, colonial administrator and High Commissioner for South Africa, 1897-1906, would agree to be chairman. D'Arcy approached Sir Charles Hardinge to ask Lord Lansdowne to persuade Milner to accept but after an embarrassing wait of a month, Milner, apologising for the delay in replying, intimated at the end of January 1909 that he did not think 'he could possibly add duties so onerous as this Chairmanship would entail to the considerable amount of City work which he already has on his hands'.[48] D'Arcy was sorry, Wallace relieved and Greenway expressed it succinctly, 'It is a pity about Milner but I am not sure that Strathcona will not suit us better if he is obtainable.' He was and Wallace obtained his acceptance at a meeting in the first week of February.[49] They soon established a close understanding. Wallace benefited from the experience and knowledge of his new chairman, who trusted Wallace and was soon busily concerning himself with directors, accountants, bankers, brokers, underwriters, the Press and so forth. It was an effective working relationship of distinction and realism.

During December and early January, D'Arcy, Wallace, Greenway and Hamilton were almost continually engaged in drafting or commenting on the Articles of Association and the prospectus between themselves and with their advisers. In the midst of such activity, Wallace found their imposed confidentiality 'an absurd attitude of mystery and secrecy' and suggested that 'there should be removed from D'Arcy and from me the continual necessity for prevaricating and being mysterious in regard to matters which are really common knowledge'.[50] It was a positive sign of confidence for, as D'Arcy indicated to Preece on 9 January, 'I have been kept constantly going with all this Persian Business',[51] and to Manisty that he expected the company to be formed in the course of February.[52] A few days later he explained to Vincent Kitabgi that,

> I have been able to arrange something better for us than the Company contemplated, viz the 2 000 000 ordinary shares, and the whole property mortgaged for £1 000 000 or more to debenture holders. I propose to keep the 2 000 000 shares as before, but to get the working capital half in debenture and half in preference shares, which latter will get no dividend until the Company pays a profit.[53]

The one person not satisfied was Mrs D'Arcy who, with commendable marital pride, wrote to Manisty on 11 January about the prospectus, 'disappointed to see they had left my husband's name out of it absolutely. This, I think, a great mistake as far and wide his name is associated with this Persian business. He will not do anything of course, I have talked for months, but quite uselessly. So I am making a last bid for fame to you.'[54] Set against the multiplicity of issues at stake, this simple domestic vignette has a delicate feminine charm.

In November, the interests of the Persian Government were again discussed. D'Arcy had previously suggested that the Imperial Commissioner should retain lawyers to act on his behalf and confer with Manisty on how far he was entitled to be consulted and supplied with reports.[55] On 24 November Manisty had a long meeting with Mr Lumley, the solicitor, who had agreed to act for Sādigh al-Saltana, who stressed his desire to assist 'in every matter with the Concession, coupled on the Commissioner's side with an anxiety that he should be able to justify himself in his position with the Persian Government'.[56] Lumley accepted Manisty's opinion that D'Arcy's Agreement with Burmah was outside the provisions of the Concession and resembled a private 'arrangement you might make with your Bankers', the details of which need not be disclosed. He was, however, less convinced that steps had been taken under Article 11 of the Concession to consult adequately with the Commissioner. Manisty argued that it was dependent upon a company being formed and limited to 'protecting the Imperial Government in obtaining 16 per cent of the profits, exactly as in all colliery agreements clauses were inserted to protect the Colliery owner with regard to his royalties'. 'No doubt,' he explained, 'there would be a clause entitling the representative of the Commissioner to supervise, to ascertain the output of the oil and the disposition of it.'

Lumley reserved his position and maintained that such an interpretation was applicable from the granting of the Concession and that it should be covered by a written agreement, although he recognised that it would not be easy to define. Manisty rejected the idea as 'an impossibility until a Company was formed for the working of the Concession'. It was a contentious subject, for there is no doubt that in practice any suggestion of undue interference deemed to have taken place on the part of the Persian authorities over the details of the operation in Persia or the raising of finance in London would have had a detrimental, if not fatal, effect on the money markets.

In the middle of December, D'Arcy, Wallace, Preece and Manisty met Sādigh al-Saltana to report the progress on forming the company. D'Arcy referred to it as a 'horrible' occasion. The Commissioner protested firstly about the non-payment of the rental for the oil seepages, to which D'Arcy replied that as they were not being worked no rental was due, and secondly about the deduction of money from his salary to pay the Persian Legation in London, for which the Persian Foreign Ministry in Tehrān, not D'Arcy, was responsible. He also complained of a lack of consultation.[57] By the end of December the salary problem had been temporarily settled[58] and D'Arcy was striving to pacify the pride of the Commissioner by requesting Jenkin to address him as '*His Excellency* and His Excellency then all Round as it pleases them and does not hurt us'.[59] D'Arcy remained very concerned, and impressed upon Greenway at the beginning of January that with the good progress being made in the formation of the company 'we *must* consult the Commissioner very soon as his solicitors will have to advise him on every clause in the Memo of Association'.[60] Although progress was slower than anticipated, a month later D'Arcy, not disposed to ignore the Commissioner, requested Sādigh al-Saltana to be 'handy between now and the middle of March so that he can be consulted about the formation of the Company'.[61]

There were, moreover, two important concessionary matters upon which legal opinion was required, firstly whether there was any objection to the proposed company acquiring and operating the Concession and secondly the applicability of the 16 per cent royalty provision to more than one company involved in concessionary activities. In late January, Sir Frank Crisp, senior partner in Ashurst, Crisp and Morris, who had been appointed solicitors early in December, consulted Mr Robert (later Lord Justice) Younger KC, who advised that the proposed company could take over all D'Arcy's rights and liabilities as concessionaire and be directly responsible to the Government for the royalties on profits earned from working the Concession, whether by itself or by any other subsidiaries formed for that purpose.[62]

More serious, however, was the possibility of double royalty payments. It was Manisty, who had earlier been involved in the drafting of the original concessionary terms, who, after seeing a preliminary prospectus

The formation of the Anglo-Persian Oil Company

for the formation of the Bakhtiari Oil Company, raised the question, presuming 'it has all been thought out'.[63] It had not and D'Arcy sincerely hoped that 'he has only found a Mare's nest'.[64] Wallace was troubled and not for the first time, revealing to Adamson, a fellow Burmah director that, 'It occurred to me last October' but that he had brushed it aside and then forgotten about it.[65] Adamson and Hamilton were logical in their analysis but impractical in their proposals. They contended that the meaning of Article 10 'was to secure to the Government 16 per cent only, on the total net profits of all Companies operating under the Concession and it would be inequitable to demand a further 16 per cent on any portion of such profits merely because they had passed to the Parent Company instead of being distributed to individual shareholders'.[66] Besides 'if there were no Subsidiary Companies, and the Parent Company undertook the whole work, Government would only get their 16 per cent once'. Hence, apart from the First Exploitation Company, which had already been formed, 'there is no absolute necessity to float any other Companies beyond the P.O. Coy.'

Adamson and Hamilton proposed approaching the Persian Legation, but Wallace answered tersely that such action was tantamount to admitting that the problem was incapable of solution without 'interminable delay, a mission to Teheran and incalculable baksheesh'.[67] Wallace was in a dilemma for he recognised that the share capital required was large, 'the share capital of the working Companies must be at least £4,000,000'.[68] This was a formidable sum of money to be raised, the possibility of which would be seriously impaired if there was a chance of paying double royalty to the Persian Government under Article 10 of the Concession. Wallace proposed the suggestion of Sir Frank Crisp, 'the formation of what is known in the American financial world as the holding company'[69] but the Burmah legal advisers, Boyds, Miller and Thompson pointed out that it would be costly, with stamp duty, companies' capital duty and registration expenses, and that it suffered from the disadvantage that profits were payable in good years, but losses were not deductible from royalties in bad years.[70]

Crisp and Manisty were convinced that no court of law would decide that the Persian Government was entitled to 16 per cent of the profits of every company even if they included profits already taxed.[71] For further advice, Younger was again consulted and it was his opinion that 'the various Companies have not got to pay 16 per cent of the annual nett profits of every Company, but the Company is to pay 16 per cent of the annual nett profits of every Company'.[72] There was thus no objection to forming the contemplated Bakhtiari Oil Company or others for, as Wallace informed Manisty, there 'is only an obligation on one Company to pay a royalty of 16 per cent as the net profits of all or any Companies'.[73] It was not the first nor the last occasion on which the imprecision of the wording of the Concession caused difficulties of interpretation.

Just as the uncertainty over the 16 per cent royalty appeared to be resolved and Wallace was turning his attention towards the prospectus, he learnt at the end of January that D'Arcy wanted underwritten a further £200 000 on his behalf in addition to the £400 000 already agreed in November. 'This upsets everything,' he commented, 'for if a proposal less attractive than the November one is to be made to the underwriters, well I have been living in a fools' paradise since November, and I see no chance of success.'[74] D'Arcy seemed to have got cold feet, but, claimed Wallace, 'even if the thing were an absolute frost, and we none of us believe that for a moment, you would not in regard to this issue have to find another penny piece'. Wallace, feeling the pressures of the timetable, was momentarily caught off balance, but, on regaining his composure, questioned the whole underwriting procedure. The intention was 'to offer the public £1 200 000 of which £800 000 we (i.e. D'Arcy and BOC our shareholders and friends) underwrite half' with the underwriters taking the other half, £400 000.[75] Even if, however, D'Arcy's proposal was acceptable for underwriting the whole £1 200 000, its cost was prohibitive, for Mr Andrew Haes of Messrs Andrew Haes and Sons informed Wallace that 'no underwriters will come in for less than 5 per cent clear and there will also be an over-riding commission (for the intermediaries) of 1 per cent', making £24 000 in all.[76]

Strathcona objected to these terms and Wallace began to reflect on alternatives. Within a week he had discussed an absolutely new proposal with D'Arcy and Greenway and was on his way to Glasgow to discuss with his fellow Burmah directors 'an arrangement whereby the Anglo-Persian Oil Co might avoid the objectionable underwriting of Shares and Debentures'.[77] He spent an arduous week between Board meetings on 21 February and 1 March in persuading the Burmah directors to accept his ideas, which they completely rejected at first at a seven-hour session.[78] D'Arcy did not conceal his sentiments from Greenway that 'I always doubted if these Scotch men had the pluck',[79] but, undeterred, Wallace finally convinced his colleagues that his proposals were in their ultimate interests and that an immediate decision was necessary which could not be deferred till the return of Cargill. Returning to London on 2 March Wallace moved quickly. By the next evening he had seen D'Arcy several times, discussed the question with Manisty and finally in conference with Mr Fletcher Moulton KC, 'the business was accepted and put through'.[80] In brief, D'Arcy was to sell to Burmah all his interests in the Persian Concession and rights in Turkey in return for 170 000 Burmah ordinary shares.[81] It was a simple solution but depended on the Burmah Board undertaking almost all the investment in the ordinary share capital of the new company. It eliminated the need for underwriting.

(b) The Agreement

Wallace responded to the challenge, fully realising that 'I have now to remodel a great many things with scant time to do it in if we are to get the public issue made before we get into Budget troubles at the beginning of April.'[82] He badgered his colleagues and advisers, confessing that I did not lose an hour after the D'Arcy Agreement was adjusted, and I have not allowed anybody with whom I have been in contact to lose an hour if I could help it.'[83] He had little sympathy with the dilatory behaviour of lawyers and impressed his urgency upon Adamson 'to try to make up as much as possible for lost time'.[84] He received the approval of Strathcona, who was 'delighted with the change that our recent arrangements have enabled us to effect in the constitution of the Company' and was willing to take up his proportionate shareholding.[85]

Whilst Wallace was engaged in the legal details, the information for the prospectus and the settling of terms for the issue of shares, D'Arcy, a little apprehensively, had to satisfy his own associates that their interests had been safeguarded. It was no easy task, as he had admitted earlier to Wallace,

Each one of those interested with me have to be consulted at every point and the Imp. Com. as well on some points. My people have most of them Solicitors Employed and you know what that means. I have always found that if I consulted them when or before things are agreed upon and *before they are done*, they are much easier to handle.[86]

It was at Burmah's insistence in 1905 that he had been obliged to obtain 'the express sanction of the people interested with him to the Primary Agreement', the effect of which was to deprive D'Arcy 'of his previously existing free control of their interests'.[87] Now that the arrangements were being altered again, Manisty maintained that the associates had the opportunity of suing D'Arcy for damages if the new scheme was put through without previous sanction.

Sir Frank Crisp suggested an indemnity for D'Arcy against such claims but Wallace was reluctant to seek permission from his Burmah directors for such an authority. He suggested that D'Arcy should inform his associates that a more beneficial settlement had been reached, their acceptance of which was to be presumed unless he was notified to the contrary. The benefit was that instead of a company with 'a two million Ordinary Share Capital and the whole of its property mortgaged to the purveyor of

The formation of the Anglo-Persian Oil Company

working Capital', it would be one with that amount of ordinary capital but 'with only half the working capital provided by Debenture holders – the remainder by Preference holders, which latter will get no dividend or interest till the Co. is earning profits'.[88] D'Arcy was not enthusiastic but Wallace told his colleagues that 'I think that we shall hear no more of the matter – except perhaps in the way of growls.'[89]

On 9 March D'Arcy informed Adamson that he was satisfied with the new agreement, subject to consulting his associates which he was 'proceeding to do as quickly as possible'.[90] Wallace then was worried that 'we are making very slow progress' and that 'if this matter is not settled within a couple of days there is *no* chance of making an issue before Easter',[91] regarded by the brokers as an important consideration. There was no particular cause for alarm. On 12 March Sir F.B. Palmer KC gave his opinions on three essential issues which had been put to him.[92] He advised that only the approval of Vincent Kitabgi and Cotte was required before the new Agreement could be signed, that D'Arcy could only assign his Concession to a company or companies for working that concession and no other and that D'Arcy could agree with a person or company to have the full benefit of his rights for working the Concession, which would not be construed as a transfer but as an agreement to be carried out. This established the concessionary status of the Anglo-Persian Oil Company.

The opportune arrival of Vincent Kitabgi in London on 17 March enabled him to be acquainted with the new arrangements and give his consent the following day. He was given 11 900 Burmah shares, from D'Arcy's allocation and signed his agreement on 23 March. On receiving his shares he effusively congratulated D'Arcy on 19 May for terminating 'a business that has undoubtedly required a great amount of worry and care for so many years...Please accept my thanks for all you have done in my interests'.[93] Cotte signed on 21 March. Two days later D'Arcy himself signed. All pretence aside and greatly relieved he admitted to Wallace, 'I feel like signing away a child.'[94] Cargill, just returned from his Far Eastern tour, signed for Burmah on 25 March. His old friend and adviser, Lord Justice Moulton, aptly remarked to Manisty, 'My heartiest congratulations on the day's work. Things look very different for our friend from what they did two or three years ago!'[95]

The main points of the Agreement[96] included:

(1) D'Arcy would sell to the Burmah Group the D'Arcy Concession, property and rights (subject to the rights of the FEC under its Agreement of 4 June 1903 with D'Arcy), all his privileges under the Agreement with the Burmah Group of 20 May 1905, and the Bakhtiari Agreement, and all the shares in the FEC owned or controlled by him, to the extent to which

The formation of the Anglo-Persian Oil Company

the Concession, rights, powers, privileges and shares had not become the property of, and were held in trust for, the Concessions Syndicate.

(2) D'Arcy undertook to assign the Concession, property, rights and privileges and FEC shares, when required, 'to the Oil Company or to its nominees being a Company or Companies to be formed in terms of Article Nine of the said Concession subject always to the said rights of the Exploitation Company'.

(3) D'Arcy further agreed 'to indemnify and hold harmless the Oil Company from and against all and any claims by any person...Company or Companies...rightfully claiming by or through under or in trust for him'.

(4) The Burmah Oil Co. undertook to assume all D'Arcy's engagements and responsibilities under the Concession and his liabilities under the various Agreements.

(5) In carrying out the Principal Agreement...of 20 May 1905, and the Supplementary Agreements and Bakhtiari Agreement it was agreed that they could be varied in such way as the Oil Company and the Syndicate thought fit.

(6) The consideration for the sale of D'Arcy's concessionary rights, privileges, etc., was to be £203 067 19s. 6d. in cash (consisting of (a) the £200 000 unpaid balance of his expenditure on the Concession and (b) £3 067 19s. 6d. expended by him thereon after the signature of the 1905 Agreement with the Burmah Group), and 170 000 fully paid ordinary shares in the Burmah Oil Company.

4 THE ISSUE 'A GREAT SUCCESS'

Towards the end of March the major problems had been surmounted. It was agreed that the Company should be formed on 14 April and that the issue should be made two days later before the Budget and the Burmah Annual General Meeting. Bankers were appointed. At first it was hoped that the Bank of England would accept but in spite of Strathcona's endeavours it was unable to accept its name being put on an industrial prospectus.[97] The Bank of Scotland was an immediate choice. Cargill insisted on the Imperial Bank of Persia. The Bank of Montreal was proposed and D'Arcy suggested his own bankers, Parrs. The National Provincial was the third choice, then regarded 'by a long way the best Bank after the Bank of England'.[98] S.M. Penney and McGeorge in Scotland and J. and A. Scrimgeour in London, recommended by Strathcona, were chosen as brokers and their fees fixed. Brown, Flemming and Mur-

The formation of the Anglo-Persian Oil Company

ray were appointed as auditors. The first office in Winchester House, Old Broad Street, was leased and a telegraphic address, 'Anglopers', registered.

As all agreements, no matter how remotely connected with the proposed Company's business, had to be mentioned in the prospectus, the lawyers were heavily involved on behalf of their various clients.[99] The final proofs were ready for a preliminary directors' meeting on 5 April.[100] The Imperial Commissioner and his legal advisers were kept informed and consulted. As Wallace mentioned to Cargill, 'I have been a good deal occupied with D'Arcy and the Imperial Commissioner's Solicitors, Lumley's.'[101] All points were settled between Lumley's and Sir Frank Crisp[102] except that Sādigh al-Saltana felt that the Shah should have been given shares in the Bakhtiari and Anglo-Persian Oil Companies. Lumley's wanted their name on the prospectus but it was too late. It was, however, included in the newspaper announcements.

There was thus no attempt to conceal the activities associated with the formation of the Company from the Imperial Commissioner, who was again being embarrassed because his salary had been once more assigned in Tehrān to the Ministry of Foreign Affairs.[103] He had received all the relevant documentation according to D'Arcy, who saw him early in April, when he said that 'he had handed the "Statutes" over to his Dol [doulat = state], that there was no difficulty and that he imagined that the matter would be settled'.[104] His intentions may have been good but there was negligence and as a result the Persian Government was not kept informed and asserted that their rights were 'prejudiced by the illegal action of the concessionaire and will not ratify the statutes of the New Company which they cannot recognise'.[105] Preece had to explain that the Government was mistaken.[106] Sādigh al-Saltana seems to have been satisfied and good relations were kept with him.[107]

Towards the end of March there was an unexpected protest by the Admiralty to references to it in the prospectus. Redwood, the ubiquitous petroleum plenipotentiary, who was responsible as technical consultant for the geological information, reported to Wallace that the Admiralty 'strongly object to our making public that the Admiralty suggested our developing Persia, and on my remarking that the statement is absolutely true, Redwood tells me that the Admiralty would go so far as to deny the statement'.[108] Although Wallace realistically observed that 'as the Admiralty is our prospective good customer, we cannot afford to stamp on their corns',[109] there was no disguising the grievance which Burmah had felt towards the Admiralty since its abortive supply agreement of 1905 and the Persian involvement of the same year. The Admiralty had not assisted Burmah in its application for further exploration licences in Burma and, as

Wallace observed, 'the sacrifices that we had made in the interests of the Admiralty would be indefinitely expanded'.[110]

This dissatisfaction with the Admiralty probably also explains the Burmah desire publicly to associate the Admiralty with the formation of the Anglo-Persian Oil Company, not only to impart some official authority to the issue but also to emphasise the possibilities of sales of fuel oil for naval purposes, which might more favourably influence investors. It was commercial opportunism, not patriotic altruism, which influenced the Burmah Board, as can be understood from a long and significant letter from Wallace to Cargill of 2 November 1908.

Redwood has put before Pretyman your view that the *BOC* did *not* consider itself indebted to the Admiralty for putting them into this scheme, and a long argument had ensued between Pretyman and Redwood. I asked him when he next saw Pretyman to add to his arguments that even if the Admiralty persisted in believing that they had done BOC a good turn not to forget that the Admiralty had certainly not done that good turn for the sake of the BOC's blue eyes and that in the meantime, the party that had pulled the chestnuts out of the fire was the BOC and not the Admiralty. In other words that it would be quite time enough for the Admiralty to urge their claim for consideration when the Persian Oil Company began to eat the chestnuts, i.e. when the Persian Oil Company is paying good dividends to its shareholders. Supposing that the Admiralty did not wish to wait for Fuel Oil until that happy eventuality, then, obviously, they must pay the Persian Oil Company the price for its Fuel Oil equivalent to what the Persian Oil Company could get for its Petroleum manufactured into the most paying products, or arrive at some other means (by guaranteeing interest, or something of that kind) of compensating the Persian Oil Company for making Fuel Oil.[111]

Burmah was not indulging in imperial give-aways, then or later, for unless, according to Cargill in April 1909, the Admiralty was prepared to pay realistic prices for fuel oil, 'I do not see how we are ever going to make contracts with them which can possibly be of a paying character.'[112]

Nevertheless the prospectus contained a baited reference that 'the development of these fields is therefore calculated to be of immense benefit to the British Navy, and substantial contracts for Fuel Oil may be confidently looked for from the Admiralty'.[113] Redwood forecast for the prospectus that 'the proposed Company will enter into possession of productive oil-fields constituting the basis of an established industry'.[114] It is very probable that this opinion 'taking an even liberal discount off his constitutional optimism',[115] greatly sustained morale during the complicated and exhausting negotiations preceeding the formation of the Company. Expanding marketing opportunities were foreseen in the prospectus for Persian oil in the Middle and Far East, 'With the low cost at which this Company will be able to bring oil to these markets' not to mention 'an

The formation of the Anglo-Persian Oil Company

almost limitless market will be found for Fuel Oil' with its advantages over coal for marine purposes.

The Anglo-Persian Oil Company was incorporated on 14 April 1909, with an authorised capital of £2 000 000; £1 000 000 ordinary shares of £1 each were allotted as fully paid as 570 000 to the Burmah Oil Company, 400 000 to the Concessions Syndicate Limited and 30 000 to Lord Strathcona and £1 000 000 in 6 per cent preference shares. It was to be the third largest British oil company by capitalisation after Shell, £3.5 million and Burmah, £2.5 million. There were no real surprises among the directors appointed, who were Lord Strathcona, chairman, C.W. Wallace, vice-chairman, Sir Hugh Barnes, John T. Cargill, W.K. D'Arcy, William Garson, C. Greenway, James Hamilton and HSH Prince Francis of Teck, the only member of the Board ever to have a royal association. Strathcona had proposed both Garson, his legal adviser and the Prince, referred to in correspondence as 'The Detective', who had caused a spasm of alarm at the last moment by suggesting it was beneath his dignity for his name to appear on the prospectus.

The issue on 19 April was for 600 000 cumulative 6 per cent participating preference shares (out of an authorised total of one million) of £1 nominal value at par. A further £600 000 was raised by the issue of 600 000 5 per cent first debenture stock at par on the same day.[116]

In fact £791 500 was available, £600 000 for the purchase of assets and £191 500 for working capital, after deduction to the vendors, preliminary expenses and brokerage. It may be wondered if this estimated expenditure was assessed on any rational basis of what would be required, or whether it represented just a shot in the dark, bearing in mind the financial difficulties with which D'Arcy had already been faced. Redwood had initially forecast an expenditure of £10 000 to drill two wells in Persia, but in four years D'Arcy had spent some £200 000 all told and in three years the Concession Syndicate had spent some £130 000. There was, thus, some experience on which to base reasonable calculations of cost for working capital.

However, unlike D'Arcy, Burmah had consultant engineers, Andrew Gillespie and Sons, to advise them, who had already been concerned in the construction of a refinery in Rangoon, a pipeline from the fields to the port and tank storage. The cost of pipeline, weighing 8000 tons for example, supplied by Jacobs and Davies, of New York was £83 000, the freightage charged by F.C. Strick and Co. from New York to Ābādān was 21s 3d per ton, including discharging. The equipment for the pumping station at Tembi supplied by Messrs G. and J. Weir amounted to £17 395. The pipeline construction presented no special technical problems and was completed competently on time. The uncertainties concerned the refinery, originally designed by J. Gillespie for 2 000 000 gallons monthly (about

The formation of the Anglo-Persian Oil Company

Lord Strathcona

C. W. Wallace

J. Hamilton

C. Greenway

Prince Francis of Teck

W. M. Garson

The Directors of the Anglo-Persian Oil Company 1909

The formation of the Anglo-Persian Oil Company

W. K. D'Arcy

Sir Hugh Barnes

John T. Cargill

The Directors of the Anglo-Persian Oil Company 1909 (continued)

The formation of the Anglo-Persian Oil Company

7500 tons), according to his understanding of Burma oil and its yield of products, which did not correspond to that of Persian oil with its corrosive sulphur content. There was also little provision made for port facilities and a reception area for the off-loading of goods, nor for the provision of adequate transportation, whilst there was no attention to distribution and marketing requirements. It was a very tight schedule, pared to the essentials with little allowance for contingencies, but if the capital commitments were not irresponsibly underestimated, it was realised within a year that the return on capital expected was obviously rashly optimistic. The justification for the programme was that by September 1908 three wells had been brought in as producers of which one had flowed at 11 600 gallons a day and another at 108 000 gallons. Within the first year, six wells had been drilled capable of sustaining sufficient commercial production. The whole of the issued capital was not called up at once.

Initial calls, £1 on debentures and 5s on preference shares, yielded £750 000, leaving £341 500 after the settlement of immediate claims, of which some was placed with the Glasgow Corporation at 2¼ per cent for three months. Further capital was not called till October 1911 when a further £300 000 was issued in preference shares. The public responded enthusiastically to the issue. Cargill remarked that the Bank of Scotland was overwhelmed, 'nothing like the rush of applications yesterday has ever been known in Glasgow before, it being impossible at times to get inside the Bank at all, and all day long the public were standing five to ten deep at the counter with their applications'.[117] He conceded that the Bank had 'made a nice mess over the question of the closing of the List', and that in consequence 'we have managed to irritate quite a number of people'.[118] Nevertheless, Cargill was able to report to his Board, 'this issue had been a great success'.[119] The preference shares were oversubscribed some fifteen times whilst applications for debenture stock exceeded that offered by over half again.

What were the factors which contributed to such a surprising success? It was certainly not taken for granted. Wallace had been allocated some £3000 for public relations activities including newspaper advertisements to attract potential oil investors whom he believed, 'except for BOC shareholders...speaking generally and with comparatively few exceptions, cannot be very much in love with their oil investments',[120] classed by most brokers as purely speculative. Signs of unease on the part of the brokers were evident a week before the issue when they wanted to insert a commendatory slip into the prospectus. Wallace objected as it appeared 'a somewhat "loud" hint to the intending investors that the Debentures are not in themselves attractive', and he just hoped that they 'will succeed in placing at all events the bulk of the Debentures'.[121]

This Prospectus has been filed with the Registrar of Joint Stock Companies.

The List will be opened on the 19th April, 1909, and will be closed on or before the 21st April, 1909.

Anglo-Persian Oil Company, Limited

(Incorporated under the Companies (Consolidation) Act, 1908).

CAPITAL - - - £2,000,000,

DIVIDED INTO

1,000,000 Cumulative 6 per Cent. PARTICIPATING PREFERENCE SHARES of £1 each,

AND

1,000,000 ORDINARY SHARES of £1 each.

ISSUE OF

600,000 Cumulative 6 per Cent. PARTICIPATING PREFERENCE SHARES of £1 each at par,

PAYABLE

2s. 6d. per Share on Application.
2s. 6d. " " Allotment.

And the balance, as and when required, in Calls not exceeding 5s. each, at intervals of not less than two months.

The Preference Shares are entitled to a Preferential and Cumulative Dividend at the rate of 6 per cent. per annum on the amounts paid thereon, such Dividends for the first five years being guaranteed as hereinafter mentioned by The Burmah Oil Company, Limited.

After payment of the Cumulative Preference Dividend and payment of a Dividend on the Ordinary Shares for the year at the rate of 6 per cent. per annum, the profits in each year will be applied in payment of a further Non-Cumulative Dividend on the amounts paid on the Preference Shares at the rate of 2 per cent. per annum, and subject thereto a sum will be carried to a Special Reserve Fund out of the profits of each year, which fund will be applied only (a) in making up any deficit on the 6 per cent. Preference Dividend, and (b) in payment of the Capital paid up on the Preference Shares and the premium of 10 per cent. payable in respect thereof, but such Reserve may be used as part of the Working Capital of the Company.

Subject as aforesaid, the balance of the profits available for Dividend will belong to the holders of the Ordinary Shares.

On a winding-up the Preference Shares will be entitled to the preferential payment of an amount equal to 110 per cent. of the amounts paid thereon. The remainder of the surplus assets available for distribution will belong to the holders of the Ordinary Shares.

AND

£600,000 5 per Cent. FIRST DEBENTURE STOCK at par,

PAYABLE

£25 per cent. on Application.
£75 " " Allotment.

The Debenture Stock will be secured by a First Floating Charge on the whole of the Company's undertaking, and assets in favour of the Trustees named below, and will be redeemable at the Company's option at 5 per cent. premium, either in whole or in part, on the 31st December, 1920, or on any subsequent 31st December, on not less than six months' notice, and will be redeemed at the like rate on the Company going into voluntary liquidation for the purpose of re-construction or amalgamation. Commencing with the year 1920 the Company will redeem Debenture Stock to the amount of £20,000 annually, either by purchasing it in the open market, if obtainable under 5 per cent. premium, or by drawings in the usual way at 5 per cent. premium. The Company has the right to issue further Debenture Stock ranking *pari passu* with the above Stock up to a total Debenture issue equal to half the amount of the issued Share Capital for the time being.

Interest on the Debenture Stock will be payable half-yearly on 30th June and 31st December, the first payment being calculated on the instalments from the respective dates of payment. The Stock will only be transferable in multiples of £1.

Applications have already been received for 200,000 Preference Shares, and for £200,000 of Debenture Stock at par, and these Shares and Debenture Stock will be allotted to the applicants in full upon the terms of this Prospectus. Accordingly only 400,000 Preference Shares and £400,000 of Debenture Stock will be available for allotment otherwise.

The Directors will go to allotment only on subscription of the full amount of 600,000 Preference Shares and £600,000 of Debenture Stock.

No part of these issues has been underwritten.

Trustees for the Debenture Stockholders.

HIS GRACE THE DUKE OF SUTHERLAND, K.G., Stafford House, St. James's, London, S.W.
THE RIGHT HON. THE EARL OF LICHFIELD, 38, Great Cumberland Place, London, W.

Solicitors for the Trustees to the Debenture Stockholders.

FRESHFIELDS, 31, Old Jewry, London, E.C.

Board of Directors.

Chairman.

THE RIGHT HON. LORD STRATHCONA AND MOUNT ROYAL, G.C.M.G., G.C.V.O., 28, Grosvenor Square, London, W.

Vice-Chairman.

C. W. WALLACE, Director The Burmah Oil Company, Limited, Winchester House, Old Broad Street, London, E.C.

Directors.

SIR HUGH S. BARNES, K.C.S.I., K.C.V.O. (late Lieutenant-Governor of Burma), East India United Service Club, St. James's Square, London, S.W.
JOHN T. CARGILL, Chairman The Burmah Oil Company, Limited, 175, West George Street, Glasgow.
W. K. D'ARCY, Chairman London Board Mount Morgan Gold Mining Company, Limited, 42, Grosvenor Square, London, W.
WILLIAM GARSON, Writer to the Signet, 5, Albyn Place, Edinburgh.
C. GREENWAY, Merchant (R. G. Shaw & Co.), Winchester House, London, E.C.
JAMES HAMILTON, Director The Burmah Oil Company, Limited, 175, West George Street, Glasgow.
H.S.H. PRINCE FRANCIS OF TECK, K.C.V.O., D.S.O., 36, Welbeck Street, London, W.

Bankers.

NATIONAL PROVINCIAL BANK OF ENGLAND, LIMITED, Head Office, 112, Bishopsgate Street Within, London, E.C., and Branches.
BANK OF SCOTLAND, Edinburgh (Head Office); Glasgow; London.
THE IMPERIAL BANK OF PERSIA, 25, Abchurch Lane, London, E.C.

Solicitors for the Company.

ASHURST, MORRIS, CRISP & CO., 17, Throgmorton Avenue, London, E.C.

Solicitors for the Vendors.

For THE BURMAH OIL COMPANY, LIMITED, and THE CONCESSIONS SYNDICATE, LIMITED—BOYDS, MILLER & THOMPSON, Glasgow.
For LORD STRATHCONA—SKENE, EDWARDS & GARSON, W.S., Edinburgh.

Brokers.

J. & A. SCRIMGEOUR, 37, Threadneedle Street, London, E.C.
S. M. PENNEY & MACGEORGE, 24, George Square, Glasgow.

Auditors.

BROWN, FLEMING & MURRAY, C.A., 175, West George Street, Glasgow.

Secretary.

S. ARTHUR SMITH.

Offices.

WINCHESTER HOUSE, OLD BROAD STREET, LONDON, E.C.

The Prospectus of the Anglo-Persian Oil Company 1909

The formation of the Anglo-Persian Oil Company

Indeed the precautions taken over the issue suggest that there was apprehension, that the market was misread and that insufficient attention was paid to Scottish interest. Thus although it was decided not to underwrite the issue, a common practice in oil issues, £200 000 of the preference shares and £200 000 of the debentures were placed with clients of Scrimgeours and Penney and McGeorge prior to the general issue, the majority of which were taken up in Glasgow, not London.[122] Burmah shareholders were allotted 250 000 out of the 400 000 preference shares available, which only left 110 000 for the general public. As Burmah between 1907 and 1909 was paying a 30 per cent dividend, its reputation was high in investing circles, due to 'a policy matured by care and foresight by men of wide experience'.[123] As Burmah was guaranteeing the preference shares for five years, this was a crucial factor in their success, making the terms attractive to investors, who otherwise would not have received dividends till the Company was earning, which was the original intention of Wallace in January. The yields of 6 per cent and 5 per cent on preference shares and debentures respectively were normal for oil company stocks between 1890 and 1914. In April 1909, brokers George Whitehead and Chown were quoting 3¼-4½ per cent on high class investments and 4½ per cent and above on second class stock.[124]

At first an ordinary share capital of £2 000 000 had been proposed, then reduced to £1 000 000, which might have indicated terms too favourable to the vendors, an accusation subsequently made by the *Petroleum Review*.[125] In fact for the vendors the ordinary shares were the fruits of their endeavours. The ordinary capital did not contribute to the cash available for development, that was subscribed by the public for fixed interest rates on favourable terms in expectation of commercial success. *The Daily Chronicle* moderately described the issue as 'an attractive investment, although they have, of course, an element of speculation'.[126] *The Morning Post* was more critical about the unfavourable moment 'for launching a Persian venture' and thought that 'something more modest would have done for a start in that unexploited region of the world'.[127] Only *The Daily Express* referred to a connection between the Admiralty interest in fuel oil and the formation of the Company.[128]

For D'Arcy the 'Big Company' was now constituted and though he may have felt that he might have obtained a better deal in view of the public's response to the issue,[129] he had recouped his outlay and made a 'profit' of 170 000 Burmah shares [some £895 000 in value] for his associates and himself. Like his search for oil, the financial hunt was over. D'Arcy had not quite retired from the scene for, as he wrote to Preece at the beginning of May,

The formation of the Anglo-Persian Oil Company

'You are quite wrong in thinking that I now do not care very much about these things as I am just as keen as ever - *and even more* so - as I should not like to see the Co. or the Concession get into a tangle or a mess after the years you and I have spent on it to get it right and this is independent of the considerable interest I still have in the Concession as a shareholder of the BOC. So please remember that I am always glad to help and have promised the Burmah people that I would.'[130]

He concluded with the familiar anguish of the financier, a comment on Lloyd George's celebrated and contentious Budget of 29 April, with its Supertax and Land Values, putting it into his own personal perspective, 'the Budget is awful and will end in driving all capital out of the country'. It was ironical in spite of all D'Arcy's earlier efforts and the fortitude of Reynolds in discovering the oil, that it was the British Government which was eventually in 1914 to provide a sufficiently strong financial base on which the Company with its concession could really establish itself. In the intervening years the Company struggled to organise itself and equip itself with the productive and refinery facilities required to market its petroleum products.

4
PROGRESS IN PERSIA
1908-14

I INTRODUCTION

The discovery of oil at Masjid i-Suleimān on 26 May 1908 also changed both the scope and scale of operations in Persia. Reynolds had managed with half a dozen drillers, a few blacksmiths and mechanics, an accountant, a transport overseer, a doctor, an assistant and a number of local muleteers. For the building of roads, levelling of sites and the manhandling of plant and equipment he employed a local workforce on a seasonal basis generally recruited from the local tribesmen. Every effort had been concentrated on finding oil, but once that was achieved, however arduous and severe the conditions, the next stages of bringing the oil from the wellhead to the market place were just as demanding. A pipeline had to be laid to bring the oil from the field to a port. A refinery had to be built to transform the crude oil into saleable products. Jetties with landing and

Masjid i-Suleimān 1908

loading facilities had to be constructed to take the plant and equipment needed and despatch the oil by tankers.

The work in itself was daunting but in a region devoid of industrial resources, lacking skilled manpower and whose terrain and climate were hardly favourable, the undertaking was vastly complex. There was no telephone spanning the thousands of miles between London and Muhammara. If the endeavours and understanding of those involved faltered at times, if their bickering became bitter and soured their personal relations, if their frustrations over the delays in the arrival of machinery, or the inadequacies of their workers or if the brittleness of their nerves made them despair of success, it was hardly surprising. Set against the background of their difficulties and their unfamiliarity with their environment, towers the immensity of their achievement, the foundations of the first oil industry in the Middle East.

The optimism of the prospectus and the euphoria following the oversubscription for shares contrasted with the more sober assessment of Arnold Wilson in Ahwāz, who believed the optimism 'to be scarcely justified by the results of the past year'.[1] He maintained that such oil as had been discovered was confined to the area around Masjid i-Suleimān and doubted 'whether oil would be found at other places where indications of its existence were expected'. Moreover he thought that the cost of the pipeline had been greatly underestimated and he was sceptical of the ability of the Company to manage its affairs properly. The formulation of Company policy and its implications for the local Persian scene was, and persisted in many respects, the Achilles heel of the Company, the balancing out of commercial objectives and political constraints. By the end of 1910, nearly 2500 people were being employed by the Company, which had acquired its own distinguishable identity, no longer just a small exploration party. Its presence impinged on the national scene in its negotiations with almost autonomous rulers such as Shaykh Khaz'al of Muhammara and the Bakhtiari Khans for land and way leaves.

It was unfortunate that its early years coincided with a loss of Persian political authority, as exercised by rapidly succeeding governments, often weakened by personal differences and political opinions. Weakened for years by provincial separatism, royal inertia, military incompetence, administrative inefficiency and British and Russian interference to varying degrees, governments were fragmented amongst competing groups contending for personal supremacy, but lacking reasonable constraints. There had been no concerted attempt for years by the successive governments to control what happened beyond Tehrān and as a result negotiations with Shaykh Khaz'al and the Bakhtiari Khans were regarded later, in the mid 1920s, by Persians as an infringement of national sovereignty, almost the imposition of a veiled protectorate by the Company. This provoked an undesirable, if understandable, sense of resentment in later administrations who, ignoring the earlier circumstances, continued to suspect the motives of the Company. Furthermore, because of the absence of the Persian Government's authority in the provinces, the Company felt less obliged to pay the attention to it which it merited, even if it had not earned it, and to rely unduly on the British Legation and southern consulates. As Sir George Barclay, the Minister in Tehrān, commented in his *Annual Report* for 1910, 'During the year under review the work done by His Majesty's Legation and His Majesty's consular officers on the Persian Gulf in connection with the Anglo-Persian Oil Company's affairs has greatly increased. The necessity for a Tehran representative of the Company has been felt more than ever.'[2]

This representational role remained a problem. It was exercised during this period by Dr Young, in charge of political liaison in the south, who had first appeared in charge of the medical services for Reynolds in 1907, and had won a sympathetic reputation amongst the population for his common sense no less than for his professional care. In fact, from the beginning the Company endeavoured to minimise its relations with the Persian Government, tending to restrict them only to concessionary commitments. It had no wish to become involved in governmental intricacies and intrigues, preferring to be apolitical and concentrate on its industrial and commercial ability to compete in the international oil market. This was its business imperative, the success or failure of which was vital for its commercial survival, but it was also to make for the tension in its relations with the Persian Government.

Not long after the formation of the Company, D'Arcy had received advice from the Foreign Office which, Greenway informed Cargill, 'accentuates the necessity for getting the Persian firm established at the earliest possible moment'.[3] What kind of a firm? A provisional managerial arrangement was drafted on 3 May by Wallace. It was soon confirmed at a Board meeting on 25 May to appoint a firm 'to take charge of work in Persia and to represent the Company' and that 'the firm of Lloyd Scott and Co. Mohammerah be appointed the agents of this Company in Persia with full power to deal with the Company's affairs and interests in Persia subject to the direction of the Board'.[4] At the same time, another major decision was taken to open 'a Glasgow office of the Company under the supervision of Messrs Cargill and Hamilton for the purpose of (a) Buying stores, Plant etc. and for (b) Keeping the Company's Books of Account'. Concessionary affairs and coordination were the responsibility of the London office under Wallace, as managing director, assisted by Greenway. On 31 January 1910 Wallace resigned and Greenway succeeded him.

Progress in Persia

These arrangements reflected the realities of the situation, with the predominant Burmah shareholding and experience, a compromise rather than the rationalisation of managerial expertise or administrative structure. Hamilton, the general manager for Burmah in Glasgow, was made responsible for technical and accounting matters as he had been during the days of the Concessions Syndicate. He drew up the preliminary requirements for plant and equipment and prepared the estimates and orders. As the Company had no trained staff of its own, it seemed obvious to utilise the services of Burmah chemists, engineers, accountants and consultants, whose knowledge gained in Burmah and Rangoon would, it was presumed, be sufficient to deal with developments in Persia. Persian oil, however, was far from similar in its composition to that of Burma, which was practically free from sulphur, required little refining treatment and yielded sweet-smelling benzine and kerosine fractions. This was of fundamental importance not only for the early direction in which the Company was forced to grow, but also in the manner by which it gradually established its increasing independence from its parent.

The allocation of responsibilities between the Company and Burmah was thus important, but more significant was the decision over the manner in which the Company's affairs in Persia were to be managed. D'Arcy had not been an entrepreneur. He was primarily an investor reluctantly but resolutely drawn into playing an active part in ensuring a return on his investment. He was not a manufacturer, a trader or an inventor like a Bell, Courtauld, du Pont, Lever, Philips or Selfridge. He had no factory, no organisation, no staff apart from his secretary. His name did not become the trademark of a business, the hallmark of its products. There was no personal basis of accomplishment on which to found a company, just a concession to be exploited in accordance with the technical and administrative means then available. The Company was different to the Standard Oil Company, Shell or Gulf which coalesced around a recognisable personality, John D. Rockefeller, Sir Marcus Samuel or the Mellon family.

The Anglo-Persian Oil Company had to create its own identity and in its early days suffered from serious schizophrenia. The system of managing agents that was chosen was familiar to Wallace, Greenway, Cargill and Hamilton, for Burmah operated in Burma through Messrs Finlay, Fleming and Co., and in India through Shaw, Wallace and Co. The managing agency was the heritage of the European trading companies in the east. On their demise in the nineteenth century it evolved as a trading partnership, combining the purchases and sales of products and goods from various parts of the world in a complementary commercial relationship between different firms whose interests it represented and for whom it traded. It provided an indispensable and profitable service for merchants and to some extent managed local staple industries like tea-planting and rubber-tapping.[5]

This form of agency developed certain recognised traits, for those engaged in it were 'gentlemen' rather than 'players'. Advancement was a gradual progression of increasing responsibility from writer to partner. The characteristic atmosphere was hierarchical but paternal, dignified, deferential and trusting in which social life was focussed on the club, not the pub. Leisure centred on the horse, polo abroad, hunting at home. It fostered the dedicated service and intense independence of a small intimate group of respected like-minded business associates of similar interests. Confidence and collaboration rather than ambition were its qualities, but, as the nineteenth century was closing amid signs of growing American and Continental competition challenging the British dominance of maritime trade, the virtues of the managing agents turned to defects. Most failed to adopt more adventurous methods of trading. The initiative and dependability of the pre-telegraphic age were insufficient by themselves to cope with the rapid expansion of communications and transportation, a broadening of the range of products and commodities flowing in increasing volume between a greater number of countries at widely fluctuating prices. Within the Persian context the managing agency was tinged with Indian associations and distorted by an image of the Raj, the impression of an alien culture, which was never quite dispelled and remained to bedevil relations between the Company and its Persian employees even after the system of managing agents was formally terminated in 1923.

Its principal disadvantage, however, was that it had already become an anachronism as an organisation for managing an oil company in 1909. It interposed an intermediate layer of managerial responsibility between those working on the site in Persia and the Board in London, not even belonging to the same company, so that sometimes their respective interests did not even coincide. Besides this unfortunate aspect there was a signal failure to realise the overriding importance of technical knowledge and expertise which was needed for the Company's operations, as a result of which the staff of the managing agency, with few exceptions, lacked comprehension and competence in technical matters to such an extent that respect was lacking for them as mere office 'wallahs' and discipline suffered. Expected to manage, the managing agents were ignorant of the processes and practices being carried out, a frustrating and inefficient experience which nearly crippled the Company.

Progress in Persia

2 G.B. REYNOLDS: FIELDS GENERAL MANAGER, NOVEMBER 1908 – JUNE 1909

(a) Preliminary preparations

Reynolds, on his return to Persia in November 1908 from England, was apprehensive about the direction which operations would take as instructions seemed to him imprecise, for while 'you will be in charge of the Fields generally, you will be under the authority of the Company directly and possibly that of the Agents or office staff wherever it may be situated'.[6] This, he correctly anticipated, 'may be productive of trouble and might cause me to be placed in a position I would not wish to find myself in and some more clear definition of the authority under whom I work is desirable'. This lack of a clear definition of authority was an obstacle to managerial organisation throughout the period of the managing agency and Reynolds was the first to suffer, exposing the limitations of the system and the incompetence of its executives. He was severely criticised during this period by Hamilton, but replied and justified himself in his own sardonic style. 'You have no knowledge of the circumstances obtaining here, or you never would act, as you do, independently of this office', he wrote to Hamilton, which renders 'nugatory the work of your man here who, even were he backed up, would have no easy work in dealing with the people he has to come in contact with'.[7] It was his perception of the need for 'bringing about more satisfactory relations with the natives of all classes'[8] which enabled him to foresee the possibility of Dr Young, the Company's medical doctor in Persia, playing such a role.[9] Reynolds realised that 'Personality counts for more than you, at home, would credit, in dealing with these people in this country.'[10] It was for this reason that people had to be prepared to act on their own initiative but in a gentlemanly spirit.[11]

In spite of the shortness of his return to Persia on this occasion and the conflicting advice he received, Reynolds accomplished much, as the managing agency did not really begin to function till he was about to go on leave in June. He assisted over the preliminary negotiations over the acquisition of land for the refinery at Ābādān (see pp. 122–4). He made proposals for a telephone along the route of the pipeline.[12] He stressed again the need for a surveyor, which resulted in G.B. Scott from India being engaged to do the first accurate survey of the Fields area.[13] He helped B.N. Macrorie in his report on the oilfields, earning his 'admiration of the wide topographical and structural knowledge of the country in general, as well as notice of interesting particular features, which Mr. Reynolds has acquired', and his gratitude 'for his excellent arrangements for my

Progress in Persia

Masjid i-Suleimān 1909

journeys and camping'.[14] He investigated the possibility of electric drilling.[15] He initiated the first discussions on crude oil sales with the principal Persian merchant of the region, Muʿīn al-Tujjār.[16] He settled new guarding arrangements with the Bakhtiari Khans (see p. 128). He outlined transportation plans for employing the Company's barges on the River Kārūn.[17] He suggested the direct off-loading of equipment on the riverbanks at Ābādān to eliminate lightering while the jetty was being constructed.[18] He surveyed part of a possible pipeline route.[19] He considered the use of traction engines in place of mules for drawing the carts that carried the pipe.[20] He ordered further storage facilities for containing the oil which could not be capped or burnt off. Three further wells were drilled, the sixth carelessly piercing the cap rock in spite of Reynolds' implicit instructions to his assistant, Willans.[21]

Wallace recognised these services and granted Reynolds, with the approval of Cargill and Hamilton, an honorarium of £100.[22] Reynolds was grateful 'for this recognition of my interest in the business, and you may rest assured of its continuance in the future as strong as it has been in the past'.[23] Reynolds continued offering practical advice about the need for pipes to be cut in lengths for mules to carry,[24] the shortage of wood[25] and the lack of adequate accommodation for management and staff.[26] The nomadic pioneering days were over and recreational amenities would be needed so he ordered novels,[27] bowls[28] and gardening seeds.[29] He advised that the only suitable drinking water would have to be obtained from the River Kārūn, 14 miles distant from Masjid i-Suleimān.[30] In general this was a creative period. Indeed most of the measures contemplated by Reynolds were implemented later in the Company's development.

(b) Negotiations

(i) Shaykh Khaz'al

The discovery of oil not only made relations with the Bakhtiari Khans more important but brought another notable personality into prominence, Shaykh Khaz'al of Muhammara, an independent-minded local Arab ruler whose tribal confederacy exercised considerable autonomy in the area around the head of the Shatt-al-'Arab from the latter part of the reign of Nasīr al-Dīn Shāh and was only nominally subject to the Persian Government. The Persian army was in no state to enforce the authority of the Persian Government, where it was defied. Moreover in 1903 Muzaffar al-Dīn Shāh had confirmed his rights. In 1902 and 1903, Sir Arthur Hardinge had given him assurances of protection on behalf of the British Government in return for pledges of friendship and commercial privileges.[31] In January 1908, however, Shaykh Khaz'al requested from Major P.Z. Cox, Political Resident in the Gulf, the renewal and extension of these assurances because he regarded 'the near future with the greatest apprehension' because of 'the advent of the "Majlis" and the so-called constitutional government', which 'under the pretext of reform would attempt to clip his wings'.[32] This had already happened in 1902 to some extent with the collection of customs organised by the Belgian agents in the employ of the Persian Government. Shortly afterwards, in February 1908, Lorimer heard from the Bakhtiari Khans, Salār i-Arfā and Shahāb al-Saltana, similar misgivings that 'they found themselves so dissatisfied with the present state of the Persian Government that they were contemplating throwing off allegiance to it'.[33] Indeed, caught between the devil and the deep blue sea, they aimed 'to attain the position of quasi-independent protectorates, of which they cited Muscat and Kuwait as examples and with this end in view they were prepared to accept our sovereignty, paying their revenues to us and putting their population at our disposal for military training'. They expected to reach an agreement with Shaykh Khaz'al to further these aims, but this remained a temporary expression of friendship rather than a permanent alliance.[34]

These overtures from the south, adding to the constitutional events which were taking place in Tehrān, embarrassed Charles Marling, chargé d'affaires at the Legation, who felt 'we can scarcely make any reply such as would encourage the Bakhtiari Khans and Sheikh Khaz'al to believe that we favour any agreement between them aimed at their eventual independence. Such a step would scarcely be in accordance with the spirit of our recent undertaking to respect the integrity of Persia.'[35] The Foreign Secretary, concerned to preserve the status quo and not increase British commitments, favoured repeating the assurances to the Shaykh, as he was 'in a position to hinder and even to prevent the prosecution of any foreign enterprise in the country watered by the Karun'.[36] The Bakhtiaris were offered no encouragement as 'their recent behaviour towards British enterprises in their country such as those of the Oil Concession Syndicate, and of other companies, was not satisfactory'. They had commercial agreements with Lynch Bros.

Such was the state of play when Andrew Campbell, the general manager of the Burmah refinery at Rangoon, made his choice for a refinery site on the mud flats of the island of Ābādān, south of Muhammara, in December 1908. Reynolds had already referred to the possibility of acquiring ground there in mid-1908 before he left Persia on leave,[37] and it was he who was instructed in December to take up the question again on his return.[38] It was hoped to purchase land and do it anonymously to prevent extortionate valuations being set, but this was

The mud flats of Ābādān 1909

neither feasible nor acceptable.[39] It was anticipated that Major Cox would assist. By mid-February 1909 Reynolds had not received any firm instructions and in spite of objections from Hamilton sought the advice of Lorimer who got in touch with Cox.[40] As Cox was ultimately involved in successful negotiations with the Shaykh, his early observations are particularly relevant. He deplored the anonymous approach, remarking that the Shaykh 'would be quick enough to discern the body of an ostrich however deeply the bird's head was buried'.[41] Negotiations with the Shaykh had to be frank, with the Company relying on 'their representative's adroitness and our diplomatic assistance when the time comes, to secure terms as near market rates as possible', provided there was a right to sell the land. The Government was asked by Preece on 23 February to let Cox participate in the discussions. Three weeks later the Foreign Office agreed.[42] About the same time Sir Hugh Barnes wrote personally to Cox presaging a more aggressive attitude towards the provisions of the Concession with regard to land, for if it was not only uncultivated but uncultivable such land was free of all cost. He did recognise that 'it may be necessary to pay him something to ensure his cordial co-operation' but 'certainly not more than the ordinary market value'.[43]

Reynolds finally received his instructions in April but he was sceptical about the valuation placed upon the land.[44] He recognised that with modern methods of irrigation using pumps driven by oil engines land values would rise. Moreover, he suggested that it was 'Arab apathy which renders the ground waste, it will be Arab avarice which will prevent you getting it at the price you quote'.[45] Otherwise the alternative was to site the refinery outside his land or even elsewhere, in India, for example. The negotiations fell into three phases. Firstly on 23 April Reynolds had a friendly interview with Ḥājjī Ra'īs, the Shaykh's principal adviser, who 'can make or mar our negotiations with the Sheikh, being at the present time the strongest man in Arabistan'.[46] He was aware of the advantages of the proposals and to obtain his good offices he quite unashamedly asked for 1000 shares on the understanding that they were of a value of £1 each. Later that day Reynolds saw the Shaykh, who was only interested in renting not selling land, for which, in place of the £1200 offered by Reynolds, he suggested £2000 for an area of 140 acres, the cost of guarding to be paid by the Company. Reynolds reported that £1500 would probably be accepted and stressed the urgency of settling before a further increase was demanded as a result of the formation of the Company.[47]

In London, Reynolds' remarks provoked a flurry of activity in contrast with the preceding leisurely pace. There were consultations between the Foreign Office and the Company, the result of which, as Wallace wrote, was a 'desire to deal with this Chief fairly and liberally on reasonable

Shaykh Khaz'al centre with Hājjī Ra'īs on his left 1909

business principles' and an offer of an advance of £5000–£6000.[48] Reynolds was confused at the unexpected addition of a loan to the negotiating brief. He had already drawn up a draft agreement which he forwarded to Cox,[49] who gratefully remarked 'It is excellent having your Draft Agreement, as I can work on these lines.'[50] No further instructions arriving before the Shaykh left Muhammara for Ahwāz on 4 May, Reynolds returned to Masjid i-Suleimān to complete his arrangements for work to proceed during his absence on leave and took no further part in the negotiations with the Shaykh. Cox had indicated that his presence at the next round of talks was undesirable for 'what I had to do was to direct influence upon the Sheikh personally to give the Company suitable terms...It was no part of my business on the present occasion to go into any details of the arrangements to be arrived at.'[51]

On 15 May, Cox met the Shaykh and reached a satisfactory basis for a detailed and formal agreement.[52] The Shaykh was prepared to meet the requirements of the Company either by a simple yearly rental of £1000 or a yearly rental of £650 for ten years paid in advance. Amongst his conditions were that (1) all the Company's plant, machinery and workshops should revert to him on the lapse of the Concession, (2) a guarantee that no tribesmen be engaged without his permission, (3) he was to receive all treasure trove found on his properties and (4) in the event of the prolongation of the Concession he reserved the right to conclude new terms for further leases. The first condition conflicted with the terms of the Concession, but the others were reasonable. The Shaykh needed money, he was encouraging irrigation works and he was at odds again with the Bakhtiaris, so he had every inducement to be cooperative for his own benefit. Furthermore, Cox admitted impressing upon him 'the duty of behaving handsomely to the first extensive British enterprise in his territory in return for the support and favours he has so often received from us'. At any rate the prospects for a settlement looked promising and Cox was asked to accompany J.B. Lloyd (later Sir John),[53] who had just arrived in Muhammara in June to set up the managing agency, as the Company's representative in the negotiations, with 'power to effect a settlement on the spot'.[54] Wilson and W. McDouall, the consul at Muhammara, were also present.

The final negotiations, however, which began on 11 July 1909, were not easy, and understandably so. The presence of the Company threatened to disturb a traditional way of life and upset a political balance to which the population had become accustomed. Cox himself pertinently observed that, as it was 'the first important agreement which the Sheikh had ever entered into with a European company, it was not surprising that he should feel that he was breaking new ground in which innumerable pitfalls might be awaiting him. He was consequently extremely nervous and apprehensive, with the result that every petty detail of the agreement had to be dissected and discussed, and re-discussed *ad nauseam*. It was owing to this fact that it had to be entirely altered in form.'[55] Suspicious or just superstitious, he 'wanted the articles kept down to 20 for luck'. Prosperity might be advanced but he feared 'the development of our undertaking, the size of which will finally attract the attention of the Persian Government, who will take it over, to his detriment and to possible loss of his powers. He is disturbed at the magnitude of this Company's operations in his territory as it is.'[56] In the changing political climate of Persia the Shaykh felt vulnerable and strove to safeguard not only his own independence during his life-time, but that of his heirs also, so he procrastinated in order to secure the most favourable political guarantees from the British Government as possible, whom he had over a commercial barrel. Certain xenophobic and religious circles were passionately demanding the rejection of contaminating foreign interference and the Shaykh was later reviled in the Basra paper, *Al-Bussarah-al-Fayha,* of 9 April 1911 for the evil consequences of his encouragement of infidels: 'Oh people! the foreigner, and especially the English, if they enter your country they will corrupt and debase your honour. Oh, people! if the foreigners interfere in your affairs they will slaughter your children and shame your women.'[57] The dilemma of the Shaykh was unenviable.

By 15 July two apparently irreconcilable points remained. Firstly the Company insisted that any agreement must be coterminous with the Concession and secondly the Shaykh wanted the words 'sons and lineal descendants' for 'heirs and successors'.[58] The Company could not infringe the Concession and risk the objections of the Persian Government by compromising on the first point. The British Government could not indirectly concede an extension of its guarantees to the Shaykh, by inclining to commercial backdoor pressure to include his family. The economic aspects were not an insuperable problem. It was unfortunate that the Shaykh believed that only British diplomacy could secure the position to which he aspired, it was shrewd of him to take advantage of the fact that he was regarded by the British as a counter-weight to foreign presence in the Gulf.

Thus in the final analysis it was not so much the advantages of modern industry being attracted to his port which mattered to the Shaykh but the political leverage which he could exert to protect his independence vis à vis the central government in Tehrān and the neighbouring Bakhtiaris. In these circumstances it was political pressure which prevailed when Cox advised the Shaykh that it was 'intended that the agreement should be put through without fail at the present meeting and that they would be extremely displeased if I had to report that the Sheikh had proved unreasonable'. Without his British protective clothing, the Shaykh's weakness was exposed. Hājji Ra'īs, the Shaykh's confidant and adviser, seconded the efforts of Cox, for he was concerned less with family pride than with trading opportunities and would have regretted it if another site had been chosen for the refinery or the question referred to Tehrān. The Company achieved a favourable settlement. The refinery greatly increased the trade of Muhammara to the benefit of the Shaykh's revenues. British presence in the Persian Gulf was indirectly strengthened.

(ii) The Bakhtiari Khans

It will be recalled that, during 1907, relations between the Syndicate and the Bakhtiari Khans were far from friendly, though Lorimer maintained that there was 'not a trace of hostility in the attitude of the inhabitants of the country either towards the Syndicate or ourselves'. His opinion of the Khans was less favourable and he felt that since 'the arrival in the country of the Indian guard, a quite phenomenal state of tranquillity has supervened, which I hope will continue to obtain as long as the Indian guard remains here, and the policy of boldly resisting the Devil is persisted

Progress in Persia

in'.[59] Lorimer was opposed to further concessions to the Khans, which would only 'act as an incitement to constant and progressive blackmailing'.[60] Lorimer's attitude was resented by some of the Khans, and Sardār Assad, when he was in London in June 1908, attempted to complain about him to Sir Charles Hardinge. Hardinge, however, returned the ball back to the Bakhtiari court, suggesting that it was strange that the British Government, who 'were the friends of the Bakhtiaris, should be obliged to bring guards from India in order to protect British subjects from their tribe'.[61]

Nevertheless it was an anomalous situation, and towards the end of 1908 the retention of the Indian guard was being questioned. Lorimer preferred to retain it because 'it was not on account of any active goodwill on the part of the Khans that quiet has been maintained at the oil works'.[62] Wilson agreed.[63] Yet, at the beginning of December, Hardinge wrote to D'Arcy presuming that 'in view of the tranquillity prevailing in the district, the presence of the guard was no longer necessary', and that its recall should be the occasion of some quid pro quo.[64] If the presence of the guard continued to be desirable then, Hardinge cautioned, 'the expense involved cannot properly be further charged to public funds, and that it should accordingly be defrayed by your Board'. D'Arcy's reply was a masterly example of belling the imperial cat or, in more practical terms, trying to get something for nothing. Referring to the delays and losses which he had suffered because of the interruptions to his operations, he hoped that the sacrifices would not have been in vain for

we...are endeavouring to develop and have already met with marked success in laying the foundations of this new industry, an industry to be worked entirely by British initiative, in British hands, and by British capital, and one which we have every reason to believe should be looked upon with favour, if not indulgence by the British Government, since it may in the near future become a source of valuable fuel oil for our navy.[65]

The monthly cost of the guard at £174 8s was in fact a cheap insurance premium against disorder and was paid until the end of July 1909.

The improvement in relations with the Bakhtiari Khans which facilitated the recall of the Indian guard was as unexpected as it was fortunate. When Dr Young was suddenly summoned to attend the sick son of Shahāb al-Saltana, whom he cured, he encountered a Khan who was not only deeply grateful for the recovery of his son but one who was anxious to be cooperative. Dr Young realised, as had Reynolds, that their troubles with the Khans 'can be summed up in six letters - Guards'.[66] He was convinced that 'as long as this pawn remains on their chess-board, so long will the Khans continue the game'. He therefore suggested revising the Bakhtiari guarding arrangements by making definite proposals over the number required, registering their names, appointing a headman, settling the salary, and defining the duties. Shahāb al-Saltana admitted that it was a change of policy, 'a most difficult matter as you desired a concession which we continually refused and would not entertain', and that it was 'really only our esteem for Dr Young, which has prompted us'.[67] Lorimer, who was unable to be present at the negotiations between Reynolds and Dr Young, and Shahāb al-Saltana and Sardār Bahādur, son of Sardār Assad, at Malamīr, between 12 and 17 March 1909, doubted 'the ultimate sincerity of the Khans, who seem to be temporarily desirous of British goodwill...and whether the Syndicate will be able to undertake the management of the guard'.[68] Lorimer reminded Reynolds and Young that 'no arrangement can be considered final or technically valid until assented to by all the four original signatories', particularly Sardār Assad.

On 15 March a supplementary guarding agreement was signed for the guards to be paid directly through the head guard, for an allowance of £600 to be deducted from the previous yearly cost and for the arrears of £2500 to be paid. Reynolds, who had never been impressed with the earlier guarding arrangements, hoped that 'a new departure in our relations had been started',[69] and generously praised Dr Young: 'my thanks are due to him for his assistance and loyalty, the credit being his'.[70] No wonder Reynolds was annoyed with Hamilton, who was dragging his feet over renewing Young's contract on better terms, for if he left 'all that I have tried to impress on him as to his duties outside that of his profession will be thrown away and his successor will have to start anew'.[71] The later services of Dr Young to the Company completely vindicated the attitude of Reynolds.

As for Sardār Assad, Reynolds correctly anticipated that he was more embarrassed by the presence of the Indian guard than in revising the agreement, so he sweetened the pill of his acceptance by promising to have the guard withdrawn providing there was proper compliance with the new arrangements. As Reynolds surmised before meeting Sardār Assad, on 25 March, 'it struck me that we might mutually accommodate one another, and if the agreement were allowed by him to stand and have a trial of 2 or 3 months, on it being found to work satisfactorily the removal of the Guard from India might be allowed'.[72] Sardār Assad approved. It was an admirable compromise enabling face to be saved on all sides. It was a major achievement by Reynolds but it seems to have rankled with the consular officials, for in the Annual Report for 1909 it is stated that it was the Khans who approached Lorimer and there is no reference to Young who initiated the negotiations or Reynolds who conducted them.[73] Perhaps Reynolds was beginning to realise that Lorimer's antagonism towards the Khans was having an adverse effect on the Company's affairs.[74] The relations of the consular officials and the representatives of the Company ebbed and flowed.

3 MANAGING AGENTS

(a) Lloyd, Scott and Co. Ltd; preparations for production, pipeline and refinery 1909-10

Following the formation of the Company, little time was lost in arranging for a managing agency. On 3 May 1909 Greenway sent Cargill drafts of Articles of Association and an agency agreement, though it was not till 21 January 1910 that the firm was incorporated as Lloyd, Scott and Co.[75] and 21 March 1910 before the agreement was signed.[76] The agents were to manage the Company's business in Persia and the East generally, and receive a commission on direct sales of 5 per cent and 2½ per cent through sub-agents, with allowance for general and administrative expenses until the refinery products were themselves generating sufficient commission. The range of activities was not confined to the oil business but included authorisation to act as merchants, bankers, traders, commission, commercial and general agents, shipowners, carriers and dealers in all kinds of commodities. The right was given to establish, acquire and carry on branches, trading stations, factories, stores, depots, docks and ships, take over or enter into partnership with any business or person carrying on business of a similar nature.

It was clearly envisaged that the new firm should be a substantial trading house within the Persian Gulf area and the composition of its directors drawn as they were from the London Shaw Wallace associates and the Glasgow Finlay Fleming group reflected a series of interlocking directorships by which the firms respectively would complement their activities.[77] Greenway was the managing director. Lord Strathcona's lawyer, William Garson, was obviously wary of the implications of 'inside dealings' and proposed that two directors of the firm should reside in Persia, an interesting but unaccepted suggestion.[78] Shaw Wallace were requested to release J.B. Lloyd, a senior partner in Calcutta, and C.A. Walpole, of their Karachi office, to inaugurate the firm in Muhammara. They left Karachi on 15 May 1909 with cabled instructions and arrived in Persia just in time to see Reynolds briefly before he left for leave on 3 June.

The hand-over period was regrettably short. It was not surprising that in the months that followed problems abounded. Indeed, writing to Hamilton, Greenway acknowledged that 'in working in a new country under such conditions as we are, and with no local precedents or established custom to guide us, it is quite impossible to foresee all eventualities, and consequently there is certain to be a good deal of uncertainty and many references backwards and forwards, before we get settled down into proper working order' and that patience was required.[79] Expense became an increasingly important factor and in mid-February 1910 Greenway mentioned to Hamilton that 'Estimates are only Estimates you will say, but all the same we must look ahead and try and get as near as we can to the figures we forecasted, or be prepared for a devil of a slating from the shareholders when we begin to show our working results.'[80] Whilst Lloyd was in charge, authority functions were reasonably balanced, but on his departure, through illness, in April 1910 and his replacement by John Black, not only was there a change in personalities but also in the working tempo. Stresses and strains, to some extent inherent in the system, almost wrecked the enterprise as the laying of the pipeline and the construction of the refinery commenced, emphasising the clash of technical, administrative and personal interests, which Black was temperamentally quite unsuited to reconcile. A matter of major concern was the status and duties of N.C. Ramsay, the first refinery works manager, who sadly died early and C. Ritchie, at first in charge of pipeline construction and later manager in Ahwāz, who strenuously resisted the system.

Greenway saw the question as one of *'principle'*, when he opposed Hamilton over a special status for Ramsay in April 1910. 'There can only be,' he argued, 'one "boss" in Persia' and that 'can only be the *Managing Agents*, who are responsible to the Company for the proper and economical administration of *all* their business. To give the Refinery Manager independent authority during the period of construction, or at any other time, would in my opinion be a very serious mistake and make L.S. and Co.'s position an impossible one.'[81] In mid-July, Greenway was complaining that Charles Ritchie had joined the band of disputers and requesting Hamilton 'for the sake of discipline and dignity of our firm in Persia, I think you should make it clear that the Managing Agents in Persia must have supreme control in all local matters'.[82] Cargill, however, who had close personal ties with G. and J. Weir, the employers of Ritchie at that time, protested that 'instead of Lloyd Scott doing everything in their power to assist Ritchie...they are throwing quite unnecessary difficulties in his way',[83] and Lloyd warned Black that Ritchie 'must have absolute freedom as regards all technical questions, and you must be absolutely sure of your ground before interfering with him on any other questions'.[84]

Nevertheless, in spite of the failures of the system, work progressed on the pipeline, at the refinery and in the fields. Ritchie, who had worked on the pipelines in Burma, was asked in May 1909 to make a survey for the

Progress in Persia

ss *Anatolia*, first vessel alongside Ābādān 1909

Sternwheeler on the River Kārūn 1910

pipeline. Orders were placed with Jacobs and Davies, New York for 60 miles of 5 inch and 80 miles of 8 inch pipe in lengths of between 16 feet and 22 feet.

The first cargo of 23 000 6 inch pipes was delivered on 1 December 1909, and on 31 January 1910 the second consignment, including plant for the pumping stations along the pipeline, arrived. The pipes were off-loaded at a temporary floating landing stage of local craft lashed together and connected to the riverbank by improvised gangways of steel rails and timber. They were then stacked into barges going upstream on the River Kārūn, either dumped along the banks at intervals or carried as far as Ahwāz before being conveyed overland along a tramway for three miles and then by sternwheelers on the upper river beyond the rapids to the Company depot at Dar i-Khazineh for onward transportation. It was a laborious task and especially dangerous on the precipitous gradients of the hills.

The pipeline route was 138 miles long from Masjid i-Suleimān to Ābādān, crossing two ranges of hills, the Imām Rizā and Tūl i-Khayyāt at a maximum elevation of 1400 feet before dropping onto the flat desert plains 130 feet above sea level. It then mostly followed the course of the River Kārūn before spanning the Bahmashīr River by Ābādān. Ritchie returned to Persia in January 1910 to lay the pipeline, accompanied by some British engineers and Canadian foremen. Some 37 European and 1000 local labourers were employed on the undertaking which was completed eighteen months later in July 1911.[85] Gangs of fifty men under an overseer carried out the work on various sections, cleaning and greasing

Transporting pipe by jimms 1910

Laying the pipeline 1910

the pipes before screwing them together using six pairs of tongs with six men on each. Whilst the pipeline was technically a relatively simple operation, though the conditions were hazardous, the commissioning of the refinery was desperately difficult. Andrew Campbell, Burmah works manager at Rangoon,[86] submitted three alternative proposals to London for the refining of Persian crude oil,[87] on his arrival in Rangoon, in January 1909, from his visit to Persia to select a site for the refinery at Ābādān. On 11 May it was decided that efforts were to be concentrated on just two products, a 'water white' first grade burning oil for lamps and a lesser grade corresponding to a Burmah product known as 'Victoria', based on the processing of 2 000 000 gallons a month of crude oil for the two grades of kerosine.[88] Less than a year later ideas changed and Greenway was recommending in February 1910 producing a limited quantity of fuel oil as well as the kerosine.[89] Hamilton was agreeable, provided it did not involve expensive refrigeration plant to remove the wax from the residual fuel oil.[90]

In March 1910, Campbell examined samples of Persian crude oil in Burma[91] but without apparently realising the problems that would arise with smell and sulphur revised his earlier refinery scheme so as to double the amount of crude oil to be refined and also produce fuel oil.[92] Hamilton handled the ordering of plant[93] and equipment in association with the Burmah consulting engineers, A. Gillespie and Son.[94] The design of the refinery was fairly rudimentary with two main benches for crude oil distillation made up of eight individual stills 7 inches in diameter, 19 inches long, two other benches for redistillation and two groups of washers for acid and soda treatment.[95] This latter plant for kerosine treatment followed the common practice of refineries in using acid treatment as a cure for almost all refinery problems, rather than a recommendation based on detailed experiments with Persian distillates.

In a modern refinery, crude oil is pumped through coils of pipe inside a furnace where it is heated to a predetermined temperature and vaporised, the vapours then passing into a tall fractionating column where, as they ascend, they pass through a succession of perforated 'trays' or platforms and are brought into intimate contact with condensed liquid trickling downwards from higher up the column. By tapping off liquid from appropriate trays up the column, closely cut fractions, of gasoline, kerosine, gas oil, etc, can then be collected. In 1910, however, crude oil distillation was rather more a matter of separation by evaporation than fractionation. The original stills for distillation of crude petroleum were little more than scaled-up versions of the traditional retort, like a cast-iron pot from the lid of which a metal pipe curved over to connect with a condenser consisting of a coil of pipe passing through a tank of running water. When as much distillate as possible had been collected, the fire was let out, the residue discarded, and the still recharged. By the 1870s, the same principle, on a larger scale, was being employed, the still now being made from sheets of boiler plate in the form of a horizontal cylinder with a capacity of several hundred barrels. This was supported on a brick structure and heated from underneath by flue gases from a furnace at one end. In 1883, Norman M. Henderson, manager of the Broxburn Oil Company Limited, in Scotland, took this system a stage further by adapting it to operate on oil supplied in a continuous stream, rather than batch by batch. His process was intended for the distillation of shale oil, but by 1889 it had been adopted by the petroleum industry.

In brief, the Henderson system comprised a battery of horizontal cylindrical stills, each separately heated and provided with its own condenser system. These cylinders were connected in series and were heated so that each successive cylinder was at a higher temperature than the previous one. The connections were arranged so that oil could pass successively along the line of stills, from the coolest to the hottest cylinder, and by locating each cylinder a few inches below the level of the previous one this flow was achieved by gravity. Thus, at the coolest still, the most volatile fraction (and of lowest specific gravity) was evaporated off, condensed and collected, and the residue from this still flowed to the next hotter cylinder, where a distillate of higher specific gravity was collected, and so on, to the last still, from which a residual product (e.g. fuel oil) was withdrawn. This system became very popular among British refiners and was used by the Burmah Oil Company in its refinery at Rangoon. Its adoption also for Ābādān was therefore not surprising.[96]

The processing problem which arose was not unprecedented for it had already been encountered in the sour crude oils of Indiana and California in the United States, where much effort and research had been undertaken, but it was new to the Burmah chemists and engineers, who were initially quite unprepared for dealing with it. It took many years to analyse scientifically the chemical constituents and physical properties of Persian crude oil. It was the despairing work of a couple of hectic years during which the Company was nearly wrecked before a suitable refining process to produce a sufficient volume of a limited range of satisfactory products to ensure the Company's survival was devised. The difficulties were as unexpected as they were disastrous, given the limited technical knowledge and experience of those involved.

Preliminary work for the construction of the refinery at Ābādān began in October 1909, when R.R. Davidson, an engineer seconded by G. and J. Weir, arrived. He was joined in May 1910 by N.C. Ramsay, works manager, R. Pitkethly, assistant works manager, J.H.M. Young, superintending engineer and D.R. Porteous, storekeeper, all of whom were on the staff of Burmah. Plant and machinery began to arrive during summer 1910, but discharging was difficult in the absence of a jetty and the use of lighters caused delays and damage. Early in 1911 the first jetty was completed and the installation of a light railway system at the same time greatly improved the haulage of materials.[97] Unfortunately, although progress was made with brick-making and the importation of stone, the arrival of supplies and equipment was chaotic and the schedule for completion slipped. Nevertheless, when Greenway visited Persia at the beginning of 1910, he was enthusiastic about the progress of the pipeline and refinery, remarking of the former that it was '*most* satisfactory, and that Mr. Ritchie is entitled to great praise for the speed and thoroughness of his work in every direction'.[98] As for the refinery it too was 'in every way satisfactory ...The staff at the Refinery, from Mr. Ramsay downwards, are a very capable and energetic set of men, and an admirable spirit of enthusiasm and zeal appears to prevail among them...The Refinery should be completed and in running order by about the end of the year.' As Greenway left there was hardly a cloud on the horizon.

When Reynolds returned to Persia, after his leave towards the end of 1910 as fields manager, the circumstances had greatly changed. He was no longer the sole managing authority in Persia, as he had virtually been for over eight years, but an unfamiliar employee of a firm of managing agents who had little experience and much ignorance of local conditions. Dr

John Black (standing), C.A. Walpole, N.C. Ramsay and T.L. Jacks 1910

Young's terms had been finally accepted and he had gone on extended leave to improve his knowledge of tropical medicine. So Reynolds was deprived of the sympathy and companionship of a man he admired and respected. Reynolds had accepted the necessity for the administrative changes, but had not expected the deterioration in human relations. John Black, also from Shaw Wallace, who succeeded Lloyd, was a disastrous appointment. Lacking technical knowledge he was nonetheless predisposed to meddle in matters outside his competence. He asserted his own status by denigrating the position of others. Imposingly self-righteous, he was both indifferent to and intolerant of the sensibilities of others. His concept of loyalty was confined to himself. Reynolds cautioned him that 'if you could see your way to cease your cavilling and harassing with vexatious objections, you would be doing the Company better service and allow others to do the same'.[99] Lloyd warned him 'to see that all correspondence is conducted in an amicable spirit so that all friction may be avoided'.[100]

Black's attitude and sense of superiority gave rise to disputes, such as over the customs, which 'have given the Legation a great deal of trouble, and the local agents of the Company at Mohammerah have not made the Legation's task any easier'.[101] Cox was even more explicit to Black, condemning him for 'a somewhat markedly high-handed tone in your business correspondence, which I cannot think is in your real interests or likely to have the effect expected, but is rather calculated to alienate the sympathy of those with whom you are thrown in your everyday work'.[102] Greenway demanded that 'in future this style of correspondence will not in any circumstances be permitted'.[103] In August, Arnold Wilson, as vice-consul for Muhammara, expressed his grave concern over questions of the Company's policy, personnel and evidence of racial prejudice among 'rough engineers'.[104] An 'openly offensive attitude' was taken by Willans who, as Reynolds bitterly remarked, 'last met natives on the Zambesi'. Black offered to resign, but Greenway refused to accept,[105] though he continued to feel uneasy generally[106] and criticised Black for being dilatory, not exercising control over staff, lacking judgement and merely acting as a 'letter box'.[107] In November, Greenway contemplated sending out Lloyd but on the advice of Wallace and Barnes decided to make a visit himself, 'in view of the many questions to be arranged'.[108]

Confidence in Reynolds diminished from September.[109] He defended himself by claiming that 'the situation brought about by no act of mine, is calculated to bring discredit on those connected with it'.[110] He had not been idle, but he did observe the letter rather than the spirit of his engagement, taking no action until it was demonstrably and explicitly clear what his instructions were and what materials and labour were to hand. He took no initiative over delays caused by lack of transport, keeping within his own sphere of responsibility. Greenway and Hamilton allowed themselves to be persuaded that his alleged neglect was 'an attempt on the part of Mr. Reynolds to delay the Company's operations

Progress in Persia

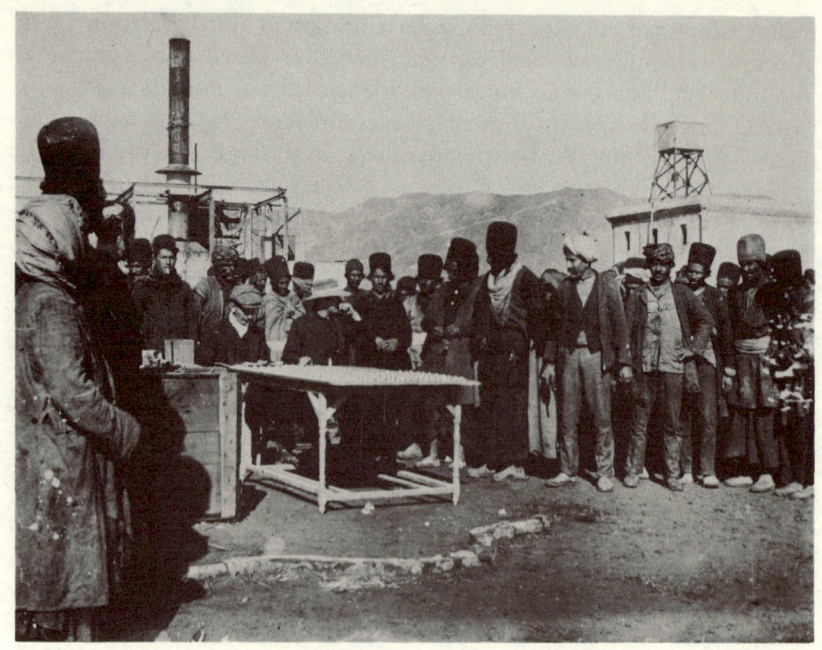

Payday at Masjid i-Suleimān 1910

Taking tank sections to Masjid i-Suleimān 1910

Progress in Persia

with a view to placing the Company in difficulties whereby he hoped eventually to secure the position of General Manager'.[111] This seems inconsistent with the character and actions of Reynolds, though it is not improbable that he was prepared to let Black stew in his own juice. Ritchie's accusation in October 1910 that 'he intends to break the Company as he seems to think he has been treated very badly' was badly biased[112] and he appreciated too late, in the light of his own experience, that 'It was not pleasant for Mr. G.B.R. to play second fiddle to your late Mohammerah Agent.'[113]

In the controversy over Reynolds and his replacement it was questioned whether he should be 'a good administrative engineer' or 'a good Office Man'.[114] Greenway, with Hamilton's approval, wrote that 'it has been suggested that the next head of the Field shall not be a technical man such as Reynolds but a good office man, who would have under him all the necessary technical men'. Reynolds was criticised, amongst other faults, for lacking 'the administrative ability necessary for successful management'.[115] It was a case of the kettle calling the pot black. Throughout the period of the managing agency a suitable form of management structure never existed, except in terms of personal improvisation and example.[116]

When Reynolds was summoned to London in December 1910 to explain his conduct, he left Masjid i-Suleimān prepared for production with storage tanks ready for oil and water and sufficient accommodation for staff. Eight wells had struck oil. There were no doubts about the oilfield he had discovered nor, as Wallace acknowledged, about his 'excellent work in the most trying circumstances during all the years prior to the formation of the Company', but he could not accept the new administrative arrangements or the incompetency of Black, so Greenway and Hamilton on their visit to Persia insisted on his being dismissed.[117] He received £1000 in compensation.[118] Pertinacious to the end, after proving oil in Persia, Reynolds made major discoveries in Venezuela – a peripatetic oil pioneer par excellence.

It was perhaps unfortunate that the first serious negotiations of Reynolds with the Bakhtiari Khans over land required for the construction of buildings at Masjid i-Suleimān and along the route of the pipeline were inconclusive. The Khans, after their successful participation in the Constitutional Movement and march on Tehrān, were more confident when they visited Masjid i-Suleimān on 13 March for talks. According to Lt Ranking, who had succeeded Lorimer as consul at Ahwāz, after being shown the various plants and informed of the various schemes, 'their ideas went up leaps and bounds'.[119] The Khans rejected Reynolds' offer of £10 000 for the land required and, as he had no further authority to agree to the £40 000 they proposed, they became impatient and threatened to close down the operations unless they were immediately compensated. Thus, under some duress on 17 March and rather hurriedly, Reynolds agreed to return to renegotiate within a month with new instructions provided that work was not interrupted. Somewhat pathetically he reminded Luft 'Alī Khān, Amīr Mufakhkham, Amīr Mujtahid and Yūsuf Khān that he had 'worked in contact with some members of your family for the last six years I suppose, and do not let any hasty act, such as you suggest, break our friendship'.[120]

Ranking severely censured Reynolds but Lloyd recognised that he was caught in a cleft stick as 'his hand was forced by the Khans' threat to stop the work, which, if carried out, would not only have considerably delayed progress, but would have damaged our prestige'.[121] At meetings held in Ahwāz on 22 and 23 March between Lloyd, Reynolds, Black and Ranking it was agreed that Lloyd and Ranking should return to the Khans. Greenway thought the demands so excessive as to preclude working on a remunerative basis.[122] As there was little room or inclination for genuine compromise during the 'protracted and difficult' negotiations which lasted over eleven days with four breakdowns, an interim settlement was reached whereby the Khans received an advance on account of lands to be taken up by the Company before the coming February, when the issue would be looked at afresh.[123]

(b) Strick, Scott and Co. Ltd 1911-13

(i) The visit of Charles Greenway to Persia

The dismissal of Reynolds and the failure of Black precipitated a re-appraisal of the managerial structure in Persia. As a result of proposals which seem to have emanated from Glasgow, Hamilton had discussions with G. and J. Weir about the possibility of Ritchie, then having completed half the pipeline, joining the Company.[124] There were no objections and it was proposed that after the completion of the pipeline he should remain in Persia for a few years in charge of all technical matters and the entire organisation of the oilfields, transport arrangements, pipeline and station work as 'General Manager of the Oilfields'.[125] It was suggested that there should be 'four chief officials of the APOC Company in Persia', W.S. Lamb in charge of commercial management, Dr Young concerned with medical and political affairs, Ramsay overseeing the refinery and Ritchie managing Fields, as the area was called, in which the oil wells around Masjid i-Suleimān were situated. Greenway was critical of these designations as they implied that Young, Ramsay and Ritchie were 'entirely independent of the Managing Agents'. He reminded Hamilton that Ritchie must work with the managing agents, looking to them as the representatives of the Company in Persia 'through whom all communications must pass'.[126] Greenway welcomed the idea that Ritchie be made a nominal member of the staff of the managing agents. The representation of the managing agents was strengthened by replacing Black with W.S. Lamb from R.G. Shaw and Co., another firm of managing agents operating in India associated with Shaw, Wallace and Co.

At this time too the range of interests and authority of Lloyd, Scott and Co. Ltd was augmented by a ten-year arrangement with F.C. Strick and Co. Ltd on 31 December 1910.[127] This firm acted as shipowners, shipbrokers, agents and traders from their office in London. They had business in the Persian Gulf where they leased the red oxide mines on the island of Hormuz, purchased grain, dates and other produce around Basra, acted as local merchants and general traders from the Gulf ports to Europe and along the west coast of India. They had arranged the first shipment of pipes from New York to Persia in 1909, were consulted over landing facilities for Ābādān and earlier had assisted Reynolds. The firm, therefore, brought benefits to Lloyd, Scott and Co.[128] It is less clear what the corresponding advantages were for F.C. Strick and Co. Ltd, but it appears that British trading interests in the Persian Gulf area were experiencing increasing German and other foreign competition. Lynch Brothers, for many years a leading British trading house, complained of falling trade, but showed little initiative in reviving it.[129] F.C. Strick and

Office of Strick, Scott and Co. Ltd., Muhammara 1912

Progress in Persia

Co. Ltd, with more enterprise, had made a cooperative agreement with the Ellerman Line in 1909[130] and they doubtless expected increased business in an extended association which would include an exclusive agency for the Company on a broad range of commodities, freight handling, and sales contracts. So Strick, Scott and Co. Ltd was constituted with its general business under C. Darby, assisted by C. Knight at Basra, and a Muhammara office under W. S. Lamb, assisted by C. A. Walpole and W. E. C. Greenwood.[131]

Whilst these developments were taking place the directors were becoming very worried at the state of affairs in Persia. At a Board meeting, on 28 November, Greenway wondered whether it would not be appropriate for Hamilton and himself to 'take a short trip to Persia to reorganise the working arrangements of the Company, and get acquainted with the actual conditions prevailing there'.[132] Although Greenway was reluctant to go, it was agreed on 19 December that they should both visit the operations in Persia 'with powers to settle on the spot any question that exists or may arise as to local matters'.[133] Leaving England a few days later they arrived in Muhammara on 12 January 1911. They were deeply

Charles Greenway in Persia 1911

disappointed at the situation in Fields, where, on the evidence submitted to them, which was not entirely impartial, they decided that Reynolds had been deliberately retarding the Company's operations. This conclusion was all the more regrettable 'because their visit made them realise more than ever the magnificent work that he did in the pioneering stages of the operations carried on by Mr. D'Arcy and by the Concessions Syndicate, and it is only due to him to say that the difficulties which he then overcame - physical, climatic, transport, and political - were such as entitled him to the highest praise'.[134] This was a generous tribute, but Reynolds was sacrificed for the principle of the managing agents.

Amongst other measures taken, Ritchie was appointed to be in charge of a new office of the managing agents to be opened at Fields. Willans was made assistant fields manager and Dr Young designated as 'Independent Political Adviser' for the Bakhtiari area and the country north of Ahwāz under the Muhammara office of the managing agents. It was fortunate that Greenway was in Persia to supervise these arrangements as Ranking, having learnt the rumour that Ritchie was succeeding Reynolds, objected strongly, because of his volatile temperament and unpredictable behaviour.[135] These observations were received in London with dismay on 2 February. Cargill despaired.[136] D'Arcy demanded that 'Ritchie should be recalled at once', and objected to the manner in which he was appointed.[137] Wallace, in spite of the dispiriting advice he was receiving from his colleagues, trusted Greenway to resolve the issue. He was not disappointed.[138] A fortnight later Wallace learnt that Greenway had satisfied Cox and the consular officials that the responsibilities of Ritchie were confined to technical and practical duties and that Young would look after political relations. It seemed a sensible solution, but it underestimated the tenacity of Ritchie's character.

Greenway and Hamilton inspected the laying of the pipeline and visited the site of the refinery at Ābādān, where they proposed that instead of 'costly iron framework buildings of European style...houses of the country style of building should be adopted generally, for the Refinery and the Field, these being far cheaper and more suitable'.[139] This decision to merge with rather than obtrude on the environment was wise. Greenway talked with a great number of the staff and felt reassured that 'work will now go ahead in a perfectly satisfactory way'.[140] He was informed about the land negotiations with the Bakhtiaris and the revised negotiating terms. He was appraised of the latest situation over the possibilities of drilling at Ahwāz and he agreed to postpone further action for the moment, as it threatened to become a contentious issue. There had been some unease about all the drilling prospects being in the single Bakhtiari basket. Macrorie, in his report of 18 March 1909, indicated that 'If operations are undertaken at

White Oil Springs, and are successful, developments in the Ahwāz range are not unlikely to open up some paying fields.'[141] Negotiations with Shaykh Khaz'al over the Ābādān site had encouraged the idea of drilling on his land at Ahwāz.

On 13 July 1910 the Company had mentioned to Wilson, acting-consul at Muhammara, that it was their intention to drill at Ahwāz, but because their existing concessionary rights 'did not propose to make any lease or agreement at all with the Sheikh of Mohammerah'.[142] Moreover, in keeping with their more assertive line, the Company was prepared to appeal to the Persian Government if any difficulties arose. Ranking advised caution and Lloyd responded by accepting the need to be conciliatory, but not on the basis of the Bakhtiari terms with a 3 per cent shareholding. Lloyd suggested a 3 per cent share of profits, though he had doubts about a satisfactory definition of profits in such a case. He was not convinced the Company would accept this suggestion, but felt that it might 'abandon altogether the idea of working at Ahwaz'.[143] Nevertheless the Board decided in November to go ahead with drilling without any specific promises to the Shaykh of Muhammara.[144] Wilson criticised the Company's attitude, advised that he would 'be unable to support you in the course you now propose' and placed upon the Company the sole responsibility for its action.[145] Cox was forthright that 'British interests might be found to lie in the opposite direction to the interests of the company in the particular project under consideration'.[146] He sympathised with the Company's predicament in 'having paid their price to the Central Government for their concession' they found themselves paying twice for the same privileges. The real point, however, he warned, was not 'abstract truths, but with the actual conditions represented by an impotent central Government and an Arab sheikh enjoying a large measure of administrative independence'. This being so, irrespective of any rights acquired, 'the Company's best interests would suffer, and our national interests as well, if they are to pursue their enterprise through the Persian Government in spite of the sheikh'. Such action would have been prejudicial to the Shaykh.[147] Cox, therefore, counselled the Company to be moderate in dealing with the person with whom 'they will presumably be in the closest direct intercourse, a policy of dignified conciliation, within reasonable limits, will serve the permanent interests of the Anglo-Persian Oil Company, as well as our national interests, present and future, far better than one of a contrary character'.[148] It was an eloquent appeal, firmly placing the operations of the Company within the context of the British position. Greenway during his visit had little option but to accept his advice. The attempt of the Company to stand firm on the terms of the Concession had failed. In July 1913, S. Lister James and H.T. Mayo, geologists seconded to Persia by Burmah, in the course of mapping possible oil prospects beyond the Masjid i-Suleimān area, recommended that Ahwāz 'is certainly worthy of exploration with the drill in view of its geological structure and horizon, and its geographical position'.[149]

(ii) Agents and managers

Charles Ritchie was one of the most controversial and extrovert figures of the early management in Persia. Dynamic, skilled and practical in his work he was demanding, ambitious and egotistical in character. One of his own comments makes an appropriate motto, 'We don't coddle idleness, and we have no room on the payroll for well-meant incompetence.'[150] In almost any environment he would have been formidable, in Persia he was indispensable but embarrassing. Tired of inspecting the pipeline on horseback, in 1911 he imported the first aeroplane into Persia, a Bleriot monoplane, to the surprise of his colleagues and the anguish of the Persian Government, who thought that 'it would be highly undesirable that it should be used in Persia, where the natives were ignorant and prejudiced and the Mullahs might make trouble'.[151] His impetuosity was more impressive than his piloting, and he crash-landed one day without injury. Even before Greenway had left Persia, Ritchie was observing to Lamb that, 'my experience of handling men and knowledge of human nature teaches me that it is impossible to expect wholehearted cooperation with a system such as you propose to introduce'.[152] The directors were dismayed, the Foreign Office suspicious. Wallace was adamant that Ritchie should not be appointed fields manager without the approval of the Foreign Office as 'our very existence in Persia depends upon the support of our Government and of the local officials' and that nothing must be done to jeopardise that 'support and goodwill'.[153] Greenway reminded his colleagues that there was no question of Ritchie being appointed fields manager and that he would remain under the control of the managing agents and that he should have 'sense enough to appreciate the very great length to which we are going in order to save his amour propre'.[154] Ritchie, who seems to have had an obsessional complex about his own self-importance, imagined that his stance had been vindicated and called upon Lamb to 'give me your confidence and that we work together as partners'.[155] An uncertain truce intervened whilst Ritchie, ably assisted by two other engineers from G. and J. Weir, J. Jameson and M. McIntyre, completed the pipeline and its pumping stations.

Whilst the pipeline was being completed it became imperative to settle the problem of land compensation with the Bakhtiari Khans, which had been pending since the interim settlement of Reynolds and Lloyd the year before. Dr Young, accompanied by Ranking, negotiated with Sardār Muhtesham and Sardār Bahādur at Masjid i-Suleimān between 17-28 April 1911. The Khans opened the bidding by placing no restrictions on the amount of land that could be acquired and valuating it at 50 tumans (£1 0s 10d) a jarib (a third of an acre) for cultivated land and 5 tumans for hill tracts and the like. This was an increase on the previous year, 20 tumans a jarib more. When negotiations were discontinued on 23 April, the Khans had halved their opening price on cultivable land, but this still amounted to £38 000 in all, whereas Young's negotiating maximum was £18 000. As the Khans were preparing to leave, Ranking persuaded Sardār Muhtesham to defer their departure and consider a price of 23 tumans a jarib. Whilst visiting the impressive pumping station at Tembi they agreed to reconsider their offer and submitted their lowest demand, £24 000. Dr Young was prepared to foreclose on £22 000 on his own authority, which the Khans accepted, taking £2000 as negotiators and two instalments of £10 000 and £5000 which, with the £5000 advance of the previous year, made up the agreed sum.

The Company had acquired 9.58 square miles at Fields and Tembi and a strip of land 17 miles long and 1 foot wide for the pipeline from Masjid i-Suleimān to the Bakhtiar limits, with the right to drill, erect machinery and build houses etc. on the land. The rate was not to be applicable to other land transactions which would have to be negotiated separately. Ranking considered it 'a bargain, the value of which will be recognised in future years'.[156] He believed that Dr Young had 'rendered the Company a signal service and was unstinted in his praise of the Khans', for 'during these negotiations they behaved themselves like gentlemen'. Greenway, greatly relieved that such a vital transaction had been settled, nevertheless remarked that his directors thought that the price of the land was excessive but 'in the circumstances they feel that the arrangement arrived at was the best that was practical'.[157] After six years of intermittent talks, the main issues with the Bakhtiari Khans had been virtually settled.

Once the pipeline was completed, in July 1911, Ritchie grew restless again. His achievements contrasted favourably with the dilatory progress of the refinery and the lack of drive displayed by Lamb, whom Ritchie treated with contempt. Although Ritchie's personal behaviour was objectionable, he was correct in doubting whether 'the relations between the present Fields Agent and your Mohammerah Agency will ever be harmonious with the present arrangements, altho' their anxiety to please the directorate will keep them from each other's throats'.[158] In this interesting letter to Greenway in October, Ritchie proposed a reorganisation of the responsibilities, based on the concept of a defined line-management administrative structure. This was the first serious analysis of the managerial structure appropriate for the operations in Persia. Ritchie did not claim any originality, stating that such a system was already operating in the Rand Mines in South Africa but believed that it 'settles all questions of precedence, and defines each man's duties without any objectionable criticism, interference or overlapping'.[159] He considered that it was the failure to differentiate responsibilities properly and to place a management that was technically ignorant in charge of technical matters that had caused the friction between Black and Reynolds and was imperilling the cooperation between himself and Lamb.

These differences were reflected in disagreements between Greenway and Cargill and Hamilton, who took a more pragmatic view. Greenway was not prepared to impair the primacy of the managing agents to appease Ritchie's pride. He accepted, in December 1911, 'the desirability of retaining Ritchie on the Fields until we have got everything there in proper working order, *if we can do so without sacrifice to the larger interests of the Company*', but 'his idea of being made the general "boss" of the APOC in Persia is not entertainable for a moment'.[160] Greenway, in the midst of marketing plans and talks with the Admiralty, was perturbed about the refinery complications and 'our present position of uncertainty as to what the percentages and qualities of our products will be'.[161] He realised that Lamb too had failed but he was trying to prevent any further fragmentation of managerial authority.

Towards the end of 1911 the pace began to tell on Ritchie and he began to suffer from mental and physical fatigue. As Greenway commented, 'His spartan methods of life, though magnificent, do not do for the East.'[162] Ritchie was resilient, he recovered and it was Lamb who left.[163] Nothing was solved. As Greenway knew, there was no one fully qualified to take Ritchie's place, but he was not prepared to give him the executive power which he wanted and for want of which he fretted and complained, taking 'no pleasure in the performance of my duties during the past two or three years, on the contrary, it has been distinctly distasteful to work under, what I consider, incompetent youths at Mohammerah'.[164] He scoffed at Lamb's successor, Walpole, who was not qualified 'for a better position than chief correspondence clerk'. Greenway, already in early 1913, anticipating a possible Admiralty fuel oil contract, had been considering changes in refinery processing and the augmentation of the pipeline and knew that Ritchie's services would be urgently required. Ritchie had replied that he was not 'putting a pistol at your head by leaving at an awkward moment, but he was not staying to play second fiddle'.[165]

Eventually, to keep the peace, as an Admiralty Commission, whose report would be crucial to the Company's existence, was about to visit Persia, a compromise was effected by which Ritchie was offered the special post of manager of the producing companies, the First Exploitation Company and the Bakhtiari Oil Company with discretion to correspond directly with London or Glasgow as appropriate.[166] Ritchie accepted. The Admiralty Commission came and went in late 1913. At the beginning of March 1914, Ritchie died of smallpox. The special post lapsed. The mediocrity of the managing agents reasserted itself. Ironically it was J. Jameson who became a director of the Company in 1939, one of Ritchie's assistants, who later revived his legacy by introducing a proper line-management structure on the demise of the managing agency in 1923. Ritchie had a controversial personality but his 'great energy and ability'[167] made its own distinctive contribution to the early progress of the Company in Persia.

(iii) The refinery on the rocks

The optimism expressed by Greenway about the refinery was short-lived. Construction had slipped behind schedule because of delays over labour supplies, equipment and materials. In May 1911, Ramsay died and Pitkethly, a competent chemist, but no industrial manager, succeeded him. The commissioning of the refinery was a protracted struggle to match design, process and product to the unknown nature of Persian crude oil. The refinery should have been on stream at the end of 1911. It was nearly eighteen months later before barely marketable products began to emerge to a barrage of complaints and general embarrassment. It was a traumatic period for the directors, a desperate experience for those at the refinery. The confusion was aggravated by management without technical understanding, and technical personnel without managerial expertise. The failures at the refinery nearly wrecked the Company and substantially modified its initial marketing strategy. The difficulties encountered by Greenway during this depressing period and his determined effort to find solutions marked the magnitude of his achievement, his strength of purpose and his increasing command of the direction of the Company.

Some sense of urgency over the refinery is apparent from mid-July 1911 when Lamb was cabled, 'In view of early completion pipeline is it not possible expedite completion refinery and tanks before January? You must exert every possible effort.'[168] Towards the end of the year, with the construction of the refinery reasonably advanced, increasing attention was being paid to the range of products marketable, and instead of two grades of kerosine it was felt that benzine, motor spirit, and fuel oil for river steamers should also be produced. R.G. Neilson, who succeeded Campbell as works manager at Rangoon and was assisting him with research into a cracking process at the laboratory of the New Oil Refining Process (Ltd) at Silvertown in London, was requested to treat Persian crude oil 'in the manner as provided for by the plant that we have sent to Persia' to see what yields he could obtain.[169] Greenway increasingly consulted Neilson directly without going through Glasgow.[170] Ābādān too was asked to cooperate, for without information on yields no marketing policy could be formulated. It was 'very urgent', cabled London to Ābādān in November 1911.[171]

At this stage a terrible lack of coordination was evident for, in addition to Neilson's work, Pitkethly was experimenting at Ābādān. Campbell back in Rangoon in January 1912 produced another scheme to distill crude oil, 4 million gallons a month, to give a 50 per cent yield of distillate, which, after chemical treatment would be redistilled to give a benzine (motor spirit) yield of some 20 per cent on the crude oil.[172] This modification of the original scheme by Campbell was acceptable and in line with the researches of Neilson and Pitkethly. It also coincided with the appearance of Greenway and Strathcona on 29 December 1911 before an Admiralty Committee considering 'whether or not it would be practical to largely or entirely replace Coal by Fuel Oil'.[173] It was the opening shot in a long campaign. Fortunately Campbell's new proposals, as laid down on 13 March, did not pose constructional problems at the refinery, only alterations to pipework. Unfortunately they did not solve the problems of odour or sulphur removal, which necessitated the installation of a bauxite filtration plant, which was designed and assembled at Rangoon, and sulphuric acid treatment.[174]

These unsuspected problems bedevilled the refinery programme. The end of the year had passed, the target of March was missed, April was contemplated after 'unforeseen delays and difficulties'.[175] Remedial action was not speeding the production of marketable products. More calls on the shares had to be made to finance the crisis for, as Cargill and Greenway feared, 'even after the Refinery is ready it will be some months before it can be working regularly at anything approaching a full throughput'.[176] The refinery was becoming a drag on the Company, but Greenway was having difficulty in getting from Hamilton reliable estimates of expenditure and potential revenue.[177] During 1911 and the beginning of 1912 much information had been obtained on consumption patterns and probable customers, care had been taken to design and register trademarks and thought given to the need for tins, cases, tanks, barges and all the paraphernalia of distribution so that marketing agencies could be set up with the collaboration of Strick, Scott and Co.

By March 1912, Greenway, forced to change his strategy, was urging a crude oil contract with the Asiatic Petroleum Company, the distributing company of the Royal Dutch-Shell group, for 'we should not miss this opportunity as it will be so much "found money" for us coming in at a time when it will be badly needed'.[178] A provisional contract was agreed on 23 April 1912 and the first crude oil delivered aboard the tanker *Sultan van Koetei* on 23 May 1912. Experiments were continued at Silvertown by Neilson, joined in June by another chemist, E. Lawson Lomax, who had worked in Mexico for the Mexican Eagle Company, on treating sulphur by sodium plumbite (Na_2PbO_2), a material made by dissolving lead oxide in caustic soda solution.[179] This appeared to be successful and Neilson prepared a report on its practical application in the refinery.[180] Greenway was encouraged to 'hope that our sulphur and odour difficulties in kerosine and benzine would be finally overcome in a very satisfactory and economical way'.[181] For many years it remained a tantalising mirage in a commercial desert. Marketing independence was not feasible on technical and financial grounds and on, 15 October 1912, after tortuous negotiations, Greenway concluded a ten-year contract for deliveries of crude oil, kerosine and benzine with R. Waley Cohen, a director of the Asiatic Petroleum Company.

In Ābādān the problems were acute. In March 1912 Greenway decided that Walpole should be put in charge of a separate refinery and commercial department which he took over at the beginning of July.[182] Shortly

Early bench of stills, Ābādān 1913

afterwards some oil was actually processed for the first time and Walpole appeared relieved, remarking to Darby in Basra that 'although the *Refinery is now actually running*, it is not yet properly tuned up, and every day brings to light some small hitch which has to be put right. This is, I suppose, only to be expected for the first week or two.'[183] Pipes leaked and the fire bricks failed to bond properly. By the end of the month he was lamenting to Darby, 'If you knew what a worry the blessed place is to me, I don't think you could consider I was deserving of anything but sympathy.'[184] He had anticipated making deliveries down the Gulf but in July[185] only a million gallons had been put through the refinery although the capacity was rated at 4 million gallons; in August it dropped to 635 000 gallons and in September it was 279 000 gallons. Moreover the yields fluctuated and the quality was unsatisfactory. Monthly expenses, however, which were estimated in March about £3000 a month had doubled by July to about £7400. Walpole, exasperated by the delays, harried the unfortunate Pitkethly in September, upbraiding him that 'you do not appear fully to realise the gravity of the present situation', criticising him for not having 'so far produced a single tin of finished oil' and warning him that 'Every day's delay in producing oil is costing the Company a large sum of money and unless matters can be satisfactorily explained there will be serious trouble.'[186] The tin plant too was not functioning satisfactorily. Walpole, indulging in some self-pity, confided to J. L. Wright, in charge of drilling a third well at Chiāh Surkh which was begun on 20 July 1912, that 'We are still turning out oil at an absurdly slow rate, about 100 cases a day is our latest record. It's simply maddening and I wish an earthquake would swallow the whole place up.'[187]

Worse was to come. The year had been pitted with problems over reaching the right specifications for benzine and kerosine.[188] December was no exception, although there was some improvement in refinery production and quality of kerosine as a result of Neilson's arrival there from London on temporary assignment before going to Burma. As a result of the agreements with the Asiatic Petroleum Company, the s.s. *Tangistan* was expected to take the first shipment of 135 000 cases valued at £37 000 from Ābādān in December. Greenway had not been enthusiastic about the profit on kerosine and benzine deliveries to the Asiatic Petroleum Company but he was realistic enough to appreciate that it was 'much more than we could expect to receive for some time to come were we to attempt to establish an independent marketing organisation in competition with the Asiatic'.[189] It was certainly necessary to be economical in expenditure, using 'the pruning knife in the matter of unnecessary luxuries',[190] but it was orders, contracts and quality that brought in the revenue.

Progress in Persia

Moreover, whilst a loan of £150 000 was being negotiated with Strathcona and D'Arcy, the opening moves on the Mesopotamian oil concessionary board were being taken by the Foreign Office and the Royal Commission on Fuel Oil and Engines was being chaired by Admiral Fisher. It was not the time for the existence of the Company to be at stake. On 11 December Greenway informed Hamilton that he was 'very uneasy about our financial position' and that 'owing to the delay in getting on to full production, our receipts appear to be a long way off balancing expenditure'.[191] A few days later news arrived that serious leakages in the refinery acid washers were interfering with production so that 'our financial position will be a very difficult one unless some means can be found of speedily bringing the Refinery up to its full producing capacity'.[192] Not long afterwards a barge sank whilst lightering the Asiatic Petroleum Company's tanker, *Murex*. When the s.s. *Tangistan* arrived towards the end of the month, only 19 500 cases of kerosine were ready for shipment. It was a humiliating and expensive disaster.[193] Affairs at the refinery were really 'in a very chaotic and serious condition'.[194]

Greenway had to confess in January 1913 that 'it is quite impossible for us at the moment to give a reliable estimate of the quantities of Benzine and Kerosene that we shall be able to declare during the next few months'.[195] A month later he foresaw no improvement in the financial situation before November when full production might be reached and there was 'no chance of showing any decent profits even in our Accounts for the year ending March 1914 when the BOC guarantee on the Preference Shares will expire'.[196] Kerosine continued to have a yellow tinge and benzine an unpleasant smell, but Neilson's efforts at the refinery were beneficial both in quality and output, which reached 1 313 300 gallons in March, 1 623 300 in April, 2 686 600 in May and almost 3 500 000 in July.[197] The storm had been weathered though there were frequent squalls over the kerosine and benzine contracts throughout 1913 and shareholders became rather importunate about the disappointing results of the refinery.[198]

In mid-1913, Pitkethly was invalided to England and did not return to Ābādān so it was decided in September to make some managerial changes. Much of the driving force behind them came from Sir Campbell Kirkman Finlay, a director of Burmah, who had become a director of the Company in June 1912. He had extensive experience of the oil industry in Burma where his firm, Finlay, Fleming & Co., acted as agents for Burmah and he made a realistic and blunt appraisal of the issues facing the Company. He was much respected by Greenway. In his diagnosis of the refinery staff problems, Finlay remarked in September that, 'they are lacking in experience, so much so that we all here, now, hesitate to accept anything they say. Everything seems to be done slackly...There is no cohesion and no go about any of them. They don't seem to know enough to look ahead...It is all tail and no head and the tail is trying to wag the dog.' He was scathing about Walpole, who 'does not seem able to handle other men and he has contributed as much to the tail-wagging position as anyone else...When things are going wrong and are permanently wrong, anyone who is a man at all would wade in and do his best.'[199]

He persuaded, with Greenway's agreement, Cargill and Hamilton to send Andrew Gillespie, one of their consulting engineers, from Rangoon to Ābādān and appoint Neilson as a temporary works manager. Walpole, who had been appointed general manager of Strick, Scott & Co. in July, was virtually superseded in charge of refinery affairs, as had previously happened when Ritchie was confirmed in charge over Fields in 1912, but desperate measures even at the expense of principles were necessary. The refinery, Finlay told Gillespie, 'has never run full. Its results in every direction are most unsatisfactory...I look entirely to results and the results are that so far no benzine which is marketable has been produced...Their kerosene has been objected to by the buyers as it films on the lamp chimneys...Their case-making is *not* a success...It has been one chapter of misfortunes after another since the Refinery tried first to start...There is no cohesion and no go about any of them.' Finlay would 'accept no excuses or explanations from anyone', only results, otherwise 'the company will be in very shoal and rocky ground soon if a remedy is not found'.[200] It took time to understand Persian crude oil, severely test the existing chemical knowledge and refining technology, but Neilson, who proved a capable works manager, set the refinery on the road to recovery and guided it for the next seven years after Gillespie left six months later.

4 WORKERS, CUSTOMS, BARGES AND TELEPHONES

It was probably inevitable that, in the course of the actual work of constructing the pipeline, the refinery and the ancillary facilities, difficulties would arise in the interpretation of the provisions of the Concession. One of these concerned the nationality of the workforce (Article 10), an issue of crucial importance throughout the whole concessionary period, and first raised by Sadigh al-Saltana in April 1909. The staff at that time, according to Wallace, consisted of five Austrian mechanics, five Canadian drillers, and six British whose posts were general fields manager, assistant fields manager, office assistant, surveyor, transport officer and doctor.[201] No returns on local staff were then available but a tentative attempt was made early in 1910 to provide them. Arnold Wilson was consulted and in a report of 21 May 1910 explained the local labour situation. He stressed the mixed population of the

Shatt-al-'Arab delta area with its ethnic Arab rather than Persian character, he mentioned the small employment of Persians in the Customs and on shipping compared to Arabs and Turks, and thought that 'No local resentment is therefore likely to be caused by your importing foreign labour to fill vacancies which, it is universally accepted, cannot be filled locally.'[202]

Yet, in spite of this impartial and reassuring local assessment, Greenway was apprehensive as a result of the Imperial Commissioner's objections to the employment of Ottoman subjects. In August he wrote to the managing agents that, 'I am afraid there will be serious difficulties unless you can satisfactorily justify the employment of so many aliens' and he called for the relevant statistical information.[203] The managing agents were not convinced of the necessity for accounting for the workforce and referred to the general inadequacy of Persian labourers, but Greenway dismissed such comments on the incompetency of the Persian workmen and suggested that comparisons with other employment would be more suitable. On 13 January 1911 the first detailed survey of the workforce (Table 4.1), with no distinction between local Persians and Arabs, was issued showing:[204]

Table 4.1 *Anglo-Persian Oil Company staff and labour in Persia 1911*

	Europeans	Indians	Persians	etc.	Total
Fields	17	66	457	1	541
Ahwāz	3	1	67	12	83
Ābādān	8	218	590	70	886
Pipeline	26	49	770	105	950
	54	334	1 884	188	2 460

With the expansion of operations in Persia from mid-1909, the growth in material imports and the increase in the number of staff, with their need for more personal effects and better amenities, difficulties arose over the classification of goods with the Customs authorities under Article 7 of the Concession. The Company at first claimed immunity for all items used in connection with the work and those employed, but this was naturally contested. In March 1910, agreement was reached that the head of Customs and the British Minister, Sir George Barclay, should determine what goods were liable for duty and reach a settlement on the assessments. This involved long and detailed discussions between the Customs, the Legation and the Company officials, which gave 'the Legation a great deal of trouble, and the local agents of the Company at Mohammerah have not made the Legation's task any easier'.[205] By the end of 1910, the Foreign Office ruled that provisions and clothes were not exempt from duty[206] and were determined to keep parity of treatment with other foreign enterprises in Persia.[207] Anomalies remained, and Greenway, whilst in Tehrān, was surprised to discover that tin plates imported for making oil tins, though not available locally, were liable for duty. Greenway recommended a change, for otherwise 'the burden of this would be so great that it would be very doubtful indeed if we could work to a profit'. He was anxious that a precedent should not be established as it would entail the payment of duty on 'all the stores and material required for refining and packing our products'.[208]

One dispute which might have had serious repercussions concerned the use of a launch and barges on the upper reaches of the River Kārūn. When in 1888 Nasīr al-Dīn Shāh opened the River Kārūn to international shipping, he excluded foreigners from the upper reaches and granted a monopoly to the Persian Company, Nasīrī, in which a leading Persian merchant, Mu'īn al-Tujjār, had a majority interest. The Shah stipulated that it must maintain an adequate service. As supplies poured in towards the end of 1909, it was perfectly obvious that the existing transportation would not be able to cope. At the beginning of 1910, after representation from the Company, the Foreign Secretary inquired of Barclay whether the 'Persian Government was likely to object to the placing of a launch and barges on the river for the transportation of oil field material'.[209] Through this intervention the Company received a limited clearance, but it was in a quandary. The Persian Company was unable and unwilling to augment its fleet, but the Concession, according to the Minister, was 'irrelevant to the point at issue'.[210] The Company was astonished, for it assumed that once a concession had been properly granted, no unnecessary obstacles would be allowed to prevent its fulfilment. It was simply unrealistic to suppose that the hundreds of tons of material could be carried from Ahwāz to the well sites and the route of the pipeline by mule. The pipes were not like sacks of grain to be slung on either side of a saddle. The cost would have been prohibitive if the material was not moved in bulk.

There was little Persian appreciation of the needs of an industrial age of which the Company was in many respects the harbinger. On the River Kārūn Mu'īn al-Tujjār would not allow his monopoly to be infringed, but would not cater for new demands, so, whilst the Government, preoccupied with political affairs, prevaricated, the pipes piled up. The Company found it incomprehensible that the general spirit if not the letter of the Concession should not be interpreted as giving permission 'to take any and all steps that may be necessary for carrying out the objects thereof in the speediest and most economical manner', not least because, as Greenway

Progress in Persia

said, 'by delaying the completion of the line, they will be depriving themselves during the period of the delay of the revenue to be derived by them from the operations of the Company'.[211] Barclay, in March 1910, edged his way towards a compromise by suggesting the granting of a permit for a launch, which had already arrived, for a year, but it was recognised that this was grossly inadequate.[212] In June three barges arrived for the Company. Muʻīn al-Tujjār had withdrawn his shipping. In July the Persian Government withdrew its permission for the launch.[213] It was an official impasse, but Arnold Wilson, negotiating locally, was satisfied that 'local opinion is entirely indifferent on the question, and no opposition is likely to be aroused here'.[214] So with the public refusal but private acceptance local officials allowed the barges to operate, though the Government persevered in its opposition.[215] It was not the first time that Tehrān and the provinces were out of step. Thousands of tons of material were carried in the Company's barges without which the operation would have been delayed for years and losses estimated at £500 a day would have been incurred. When Greenway challenged the Persian Ministers on his visit to Tehrān that such activity was not contrary to the Concession, they raised no objections. It was an expensive storm in a concessionary tea cup. It seemed as if the objectives of the Company and the Persian Government did not coincide.

Much the same kind of problem arose over the need for telephone communications along the pipeline in case of an emergency. The Company thought it was entitled to operate a line 'for use only in the ordinary

Barges on the River Kārūn 1910

course of their business'.[216] Although the Minister for Foreign Affairs 'admitted that a telephone line was indispensable for the proper working of the pipeline', he maintained, a little illogically, that the matter should be embodied in a separate concession.[217] By the time of Greenway's visit, the line from Masjid i-Suleimān to Ahwāz had been completed. Throughout the concessionary period the application and interpretation of the provisions of the Concession to new problems was part of the fascination, the exasperation and the satisfaction which arose in the relations between the Company and the Persian Government.

By 1913 it had taken a dozen years of unremitting effort to transform a concessionary document into the reality of an industrial enterprise. D'Arcy's speculative undertaking had grown into an industry through the efforts of many individuals. These included Kitabgi's initiative, Drummond Wolff's mediation, Reynolds' tenacity, Redwood's advice, Hardinge's discretion, Hamilton's dourness, Dr Young's ministrations, the bargaining of the Bakhtiari Khans, Pretyman's advocacy, Greenway's determination, Ritchie's drive, Walpole's indecision, the engineering skills of a handful of European staff and the labouring services of many Persians. They had contributed to the discovery of oil, the construction of a pipeline, the building of a refinery, the manufacture of products from Persian crude oil and the formation of a Company responsible for these activities. The pioneering had been completed. The Company was in business. Yet, just as D'Arcy's purse had almost been emptied to its limit, so was the Company facing a financial crisis in 1913. Just as D'Arcy found a partner in the Burmah Oil Company, so did the Company find a partner in the British Government.

5
FUEL OIL AND THE ADMIRALTY 1912-14

I INTRODUCTION

At the Admiralty on 29 December 1911, Captain Pakenham, Fourth Sea Lord, was presiding over a secret oil committee, at which Greenway and Strathcona were about to give evidence. 'The question at issue,' declared Pakenham, 'is as to whether it is advisable to increase the consumption of oil fuel in the British Navy at the present time, whether it would be advisable and to what extent, to substitute oil fuel for coal; and we are looking round as far as we can to gain information on all sources of supply either in British territory or elsewhere.'[1] The substitution of oil for coal was not a new issue in itself, for it had already been examined by the Selborne Committee in 1904-5, but the growth in marine engine technology and the emergence of a German naval power gave it an increased urgency.

The intention of the Government to convert the Navy from coal burning to oil fired propulsion was not of immediate importance to the Company, except in so far as it represented a possible market for the Company's products. Within a very short time, however, actual naval demands for fuel oil supplies had become a crucial factor in the Company's struggle for independent survival.

For the Company it was both a logical development from the earlier Burmah naval supply contract of 1905 and a fortunate coincidence at a time when it was beginning to experience terrible problems with its marketing plans due to refinery difficulties in Ābādān in producing satisfactory products of kerosine and benzine. This early failure to master the particular chemical complexities of Persian crude oil not only blighted the initial hopes of an independent marketing strategy and forced the Company into a partial collaboration with the Royal Dutch-Shell group on disadvantageous terms, but also precipitated a serious financial crisis. As a result, the survival of the Company was threatened by possible amalgamation with the Royal Dutch-Shell group. Yet it might be ensured by a substantial naval supply contract for fuel oil, which could be easily produced from

158

Fuel oil and the Admiralty 1912-14

Persian crude oil and was a product for which demand was rising. These were then the available options, but for Greenway there was no alternative to independence. Its preservation was his achievement for the price of the Government's shareholding.

From the appearance of Strathcona and Greenway before the oil committee two themes emerged which were to become prominent in all of the subsequent negotiations, the identification of the Company with national interests and the threat of absorption by the Royal Dutch-Shell group. As Strathcona explained his commitment to the Company, 'It was not as a mercantile company that I looked upon it, but really from an Imperial point of view',[2] and he described his visit to the First Lord of the Admiralty, McKenna, before accepting the chairmanship. Greenway reminded the members of the previous experience of Burmah, which as a result of its fuel oil supply contract with the Admiralty had invested in special plant, but had only been called on to deliver 36 000 tons over five years. Thus he expected some preferential consideration. The crux of the matter, however, was the limited availability of markets and the certainty of strong opposition from the Standard Oil and Royal Dutch-Shell groups. 'In fact,' declared Greenway, 'the Royal Dutch have already made overtures of one kind and another to us, and in connection with these have indicated that if we do invade these markets they are going for us and will do their best to smash us.'[3]

Some commentators have presumed that this competitive element was merely special pleading by Greenway, but this underestimates the commercial rivalry of the period. Greenway had taken a leading part in the Burmah—Shell negotiations of 1905 over Indian markets, which had left an indelible impression on his memory.[4] In mid-1911 he had expressed his concern to Cargill about the intentions of Robert Waley Cohen, a director of Shell,[5] who, delighted with the acquisition in the same year of the Dordtsche Petroleum Industrie, which had consolidated Royal Dutch interest in the East Indies after a struggle with Standard Oil,[6] professed himself interested in acquiring shares in the Company. 'He is very "cock-a-hoop" just now,' wrote Greenway, 'and goes so far as to say that no Petroleum Co. in a non-protected country can possibly hope to work successfully without an alliance with either their group or the Standard.'[7] Mischievious, malicious or merely amusing, Greenway was prepared to take it seriously.

It was not only in its marketing ambitions that the Company crossed the path of Royal Dutch-Shell interests but also in two other related fields. Firstly, Sir Marcus Samuel, founder of Shell Transport and Trading Company, had for many years been closely involved in promoting the use of fuel oil for naval purposes.[8] Secondly, because of D'Arcy's early interests in a Mesopotamian oil concession, Marriott having been sent to Constantinople in September 1901,[9] the Company maintained that it had prior rights in the area and opposed the formation of the Turkish Petroleum Company in 1912 in which the National Bank of Turkey, Deutsche Bank and Shell were associated.[10] Without some appreciation of the hostile environment in which many of the negotiations took place much of the bitterness and antagonism is unbelievable.

2 PROCESSES, PRODUCTS AND MARKETS

Greenway's immediate objective when he became managing director in January 1910 was 'to build up an absolutely, self-contained organisation'. He aimed at a company producing, refining, transporting and distributing products directly to customers, 'wherever there may be a profitable outlet for them without the intervention of any third parties'.[11] His determination to create what has become known as an integrated oil company engaged in all the activities of the business was his original commercial policy and his marketing strategy. There was an unmistakable sense of optimism in mid-1911 in anticipation of the commissioning of the refinery at Ābādān at the end of the year. Consideration was given to marketing in New Zealand, Australia, Ceylon, South Africa, East Africa, Zanzibar, Mauritius, Suez, Aden, almost an imperial roll call, and Japan, China, Korea, the Philippines, Malaya and Siam.[12] Trade marks such as 'Camel' and 'Cannon' for export markets and 'Palm Tree' and 'Lion and Sun' for internal Persian markets were devised. The merchant in Greenway was clearly stimulated and to a sceptical Hamilton he suggested in December 1911 that the Company should coin a special generic advertising name for its oil products, as its own was 'too big and there were lots of Anglos this and that. We want a short catchy word and one which is not too difficult to find...What about "Angloil", "Persoil", "Emproil", "APOC", "Motoil"?'[13] Orders for packing cases and the design of tins were drafted.

Agents were briefed, such as A. Besse, the principal trader of Aden, at the end of December, who was informed that 'We fully understand that we shall have to face the competition of the Standard Oil Co. and this we are quite prepared to do. Particular care and attention is being given to the "get up" of the cases and we feel confident you will be quite satisfied with the appearance and quality of the first shipment.'[14] Greenway asked R.G. Shaw and Co. to make discrete inquiries 'as we do not want our competitors to obtain any prior knowledge as to our marketing plans'.[15] Whereas, at the beginning of October, Waley Cohen had suggested that he might take a cargo of crude oil and Greenway was non-committal,[16] by the end of the month it had been agreed by Cargill, Hamilton and Greenway that

Fuel oil and the Admiralty 1912-14

all negotiations for selling crude to APC [Asiatic Petroleum Company] should be dropped.[17]

With preparations for getting the refinery on stream at Ābādān stalled because of processing difficulties, the realities of the refinery situation became so depressing that Greenway was obliged to reconsider his marketing strategy. When Waley Cohen in March 1912 again offered to contract for crude oil deliveries, Greenway was more receptive as the financial position had deteriorated.[18] To a hesitant Hamilton, Greenway justified his changed attitude as providing a breathing space for,

> while we are delivering this Crude to APC we can go ahead developing our trade in the Refined Products as much as possible. If and when the time comes that our trade in Refined Products overtakes the capacity of our present Refinery there will be nothing to prevent our extending it and *while we are extending it* we shall be getting an income from the Crude delivered to APC.[19]

It was not only the processing problems that were such a technical and financial embarrassment, but also the lack of installations and transportation facilities at a time when freight costs were rising throughout the world.[20] The Company acquired a small 1500 dwt steamer, s.s. *Ferrara*, its first vessel, for £6930, at the beginning of April,[21] but, as Greenway admitted to Barnes, one of the attractions of the crude oil sales was that 'the Asiatic undertake to provide the necessary Tankers (of sufficiently light draught to permit of crossing the Bar) which gets us out of one of our difficulties - viz that of securing tonnage at anything like a reasonable freight'.[22] The difficulties of the sand banks and keeping the navigational channels of the Shatt-al-'Arab dredged later became problems in the 1920s. Nevertheless, Greenway acknowledged to Hamilton, 'I am quite with you as to the desirability of our not getting ourselves tied up with APC.'[23]

This was the problem, especially as Greenway realised that, because the Company lacked its own independent marketing organisation only the Asiatic Petroleum Company could immediately provide sufficient outlets to take the expected refinery production of kerosine and benzine.[24] It was a two-edged attraction, financially beneficial to the Company, but at the time Waley Cohen was 'trying hard to make the Crude, Kerosene and Benzine transactions all dependent one on the other and to introduce restrictive conditions of one kind and another'.[25] An agreement in principle for a contract for crude oil and kerosine was agreed at a board meeting on 27 April 1912.[26] The subsequent negotiations, which lasted till October, before the final agreement was concluded, were protracted and frequently controversial. Waley Cohen naturally was exerting the maximum commercial leverage on Greenway by refusing to accept any references to the brand names of the Company[27] and insisting that Indian trade be included within the scope of the contracts.[28] The intention, claimed Greenway, was to make the Company bound by the provisions of the Burmah—Shell Agreement of 1905.

Greenway was to some extent hampered early in his negotiations by Cargill's belief that 'we cannot expect at first to find an outlet for any large amount of Fuel Oil'[29] and later by his timidity over not upsetting Waley Cohen, which indirectly weakened Greenway's negotiating position.[30] It was imperative to produce kerosine and benzine up to the specification of the contracts for if there were any deficiencies, realised Greenway, then 'it will probably necessitate an alteration in the whole of our marketing programme, as our sales to the APC, and our marketing arrangements with them, have so far been based on the assumption that we *shall* be able to produce a quality approximately equal to "Snowflake"'.[31]

The fiasco over supplies for the s.s. *Tangistan* in December 1912, the adverse filming defects of kerosine on lamps which were only gradually eliminated in 1913, the low yield of benzine and its persistent unpleasant odour which ruined its marketability, and proved impossible to remove in the existing state of refining knowledge, severely strained Greenway's temporary strategy and forced a reappraisal of the Company's marketing policy in the light of opportunities for fuel oil. By a curious coincidence, on 1 May 1912 Greenway was having a particularly vehement session with Waley Cohen on some marketing restriction, which he was seeking to resist and which was threatening to disrupt the proceedings completely, when a formal request was received from the Admiralty for information 'on the suitability of Persian Gulf Oil for use as a Fuel'.[32] This request was not entirely unexpected, for the Company prospectus had indicated just such a possibility of supplying fuel oil to the Admiralty and Greenway in his evidence to the oil committee in December 1911 had reaffirmed the willingness of the Company to supply fuel oil. Furthermore, Neilson had reported that the fuel oil would probably be up to the specifications for the Navy.[33] The Admiralty's inquiry provided a positive impetus for Greenway's favourable view of fuel oil prospects in spite of Cargill's pessimism.

It was Lloyd at the end of 1909 who first mentioned the possibility of fuel oil sales. Greenway then argued that

We should not shelve this question of the possibilities in connection with Fuel Oil without very careful consideration. If a market *can* be found for a fair quantity of fuel oil...it unquestionably is not one to be disregarded, if we can see our way to purchasing the necessary plant, particularly in view of the difficulties that will be in our way in finding a large outlet for Oil at remunerative rates.[34]

It is important to recognise Greenway's early interest in fuel oil lest it be assumed too readily that the initiative for the production of fuel oil was sponsored by the Admiralty or that it merely arose as a consequence of the

Fuel oil and the Admiralty 1912-14

problems of producing other products. It was certainly not part of the original conception of the refinery and there was little enthusiasm for it from the Burmah directors. It was Greenway who perceived its possibilities and read the market right. It will be recalled that it was initially planned for the refinery to produce kerosine in accordance with standard Burmah practice. The advice of the Burmah Agents, Finlay, Fleming and Co., was that it would not be remunerative to make fuel oil if suitable kerosine could be produced from the crude oil. The best course would be to get the refinery producing kerosine first and then if it was found that 'you have a huge margin of crude it will be time enough to begin talking about putting up a fuel oil plant'.[35] Such was the blinkered advice of an eastern trading house in 1909. In fact within a decade demand for fuel oil for the new marine engine technology, for example, by the Admiralty increased enormously, 1200 tons in 1902 to 277 850 in 1912. The availability of crude oil in Persia exceeded expectations. Problems over refinery processes made the production of fuel oil more profitable for the Company in relation to the estimates of revenue from sales of kerosine.

Already in February 1910 Greenway was questioning Hamilton on the costs and returns from the refinery proposals of Campbell. Greenway was one of the first in the Company to relate figures to yields and sales in a rational manner before the consequences of earlier misjudgements made them obvious. He estimated the net annual profit at £16 800 after depreciation, management costs, debenture interest and Persian Government royalty had been charged compared with Campbell's forecast of £75 800 and the assessment in the prospectus of £142 800.[36] So Greenway suggested that if the plans proposed did not offer a better return, they should be modified accordingly. Hamilton appeared resentful at Greenway's persistence and replied that he had no objections to supplying fuel oil if it was possible from the plant approved, as the 'scheme we are adopting is the cheapest', but cautioned rather fatalistically that 'laboratory work cannot always be relied upon'.[37] It seemed as if fuel oil was merely incidental, not essential in marketing programmes. Greenway's views prevailed and he was able in March to inform Black in Muhammara that he had been pressing the fuel oil question and as a result

the proposed Refinery (owing to the superior quality of Crude) will, it is expected, be able to deal with 3 000 000 gallons crude instead of the 2 000 000 originally anticipated, and that we shall be able to produce a part as Fuel Oil without refrigerating (owing to the small percentage of Wax) i.e. practically the whole of the products of the 3 000 000 gallons will be marketable, and that instead of burning a portion as Refinery Fuel (as contemplated in Campbell's original scheme) we shall use Crude as fuel. This is better.[38]

There were later adjustments, but by early 1912 Neilson was satisfied about the yield of kerosine and the acceptability of fuel oil 'for ordinary commercial use'.

At the beginning of 1912, Greenway began to press more urgently the claims for fuel oil, informing Campbell and Neilson that he wanted as large a yield of white kerosine as possible and assumed that 'we may be able to find a market for a considerable quantity of fuel oil'.[39] The supply was available, it was a case of the demand and Greenway hoped that the Admiralty would be interested. Barnes suggested the Indian railways.[40] Redwood was asked to assist in identifying fuel prospects, though, in the absence of production, concern was rather theoretical, if not speculative. By July, Greenway was committed to an active fuel oil marketing policy in spite of the doubts of some of his fellow directors. He realised that it was a way out of the continuing refinery troubles, which were still plaguing the production of kerosine and benzine, it offered relief from too close a collaboration with the Royal Dutch-Shell group and it promised a source of revenue for a product for which demand, to some extent, was rising to stimulate a developing technology.

It was an ace in hand but, with tricks being steadily lost, time was running out for playing it. Arguing with Cargill in June, Greenway maintained that 'If we are to work on the APC lines and confine ourselves to ordinary trade demands it will, of course, take a long time to work up any appreciable amount of trade in India', so he made efforts, not successful in the short term, to work up a trade in fuel oil for the Indian railways. There were two main advantages: firstly it concerned very large outlets where the Company would have the edge on price for bulk deliveries and secondly it was a market in which the Asiatic Petroleum Company was not involved, 'being unwilling to give the necessary guarantees as to continuity of supplies and permanency of price'.[41] He was also bidding for the fuel oil requirements of the Hamburg-Amerika Line which was operating to the Persian Gulf, offering a contract for a term of years so as to ensure 'a constant and adequate supply at a fixed price'.[42]

Greenway, obliged by financial pressures to seek an accommodation with the Asiatic Petroleum Company over markets and contracts for crude oil, kerosine and benzine, declined to sacrifice the advantages of fuel oil for a similar accommodation over trade in that commodity. In July he wrote to A.S. Debenham, an Asiatic director, that it was important to encourage the use of fuel oil but not 'wise for either of us to bind ourselves, at this stage of trade, to a hard and fast price...There is a large outlet for Fuel Oil in India *at a price* and having both of us plenty of this Oil to dispose of it should be our policy to create the trade first, and see about prices after we have made it.'[43] Greenway was not unreasonable but firm, having 'no desire or intention to work behind your backs in any way', and determined to exploit a market where the cost of coal was high enough for it to be replaced by fuel oil.[44] In the continuing acrimonious negotiations over the contracts between Greenway and Waley Cohen, Greenway became more than ever convinced that Waley Cohen 'by still further clipping our wings in this direction...thinks he will make it all the more difficult for us ever to break loose from the bondage - and for that reason we should have as much freedom as possible'. So 'I am strongly of opinion that we should at this point stick firmly to our guns.'[45] Moreover, Greenway was not pleased by Waley Cohen's casual remark that APC would be prepared 'to take up 250/500 000 in Preference and/or Ordinary shares, preferably the latter' if the Company needed to raise more capital.[46] Though not quite a shot-gun romance, the courting of the rival petroleum company was getting a little violent. The Admiralty had become a very desirable alternative suitor to be encouraged. In May 1912, Greenway had replied immediately and confidently to F.W. Black, Director of Naval Contracts, that the Company would soon be able to deliver 30 000 tons of no. 1 quality and 15 000 tons of no. 2 fuel oil.[47] Hamilton urged caution, but although Greenway agreed not to 'commit the Company to any large engagements without discussion', he advocated attracting the attention of the Admiralty by offering to contract for 200/300 000 tons a year, 'given sufficient inducement', so laying his cards on the table.[48]

3 FUEL OIL AND DIPLOMACY

In mid-1912 there was a coincidence of events which was ultimately to have a profound influence on the destiny of the Company. On 11 June Churchill asked Admiral Fisher, who had retired as First Sea Lord in 1910, to preside over the Royal Commission on Oil Supply, exhorting him that 'This liquid fuel problem has got to be solved and the national, inherent, unavoidable difficulties are such that they require the drive and enthusiasm of a big man...You have got to find the oil; to show how it can be stored cheaply; how it can be purchased regularly and cheaply in peace; and with absolute certainty in war.'[49] Early in August, the Foreign Office learnt from the embassy in Constantinople that a consortium had been formed and was composed of the National Bank of Turkey, and the Deutsche Bank to explore and exploit petroleum deposits throughout Turkey. It had been registered in London on 31 January 1911, as the African and Eastern Concessions Ltd. It was reconstituted on 25 September 1912 with the participation of Royal Dutch-Shell as the Turkish Petroleum Company Ltd.[50] It was an unexpected development and marked a definite revival of concessionary rivalry over the prospects for Mesopotamian oil.

Fuel oil and the Admiralty 1912-14

D'Arcy, as well as German and American representatives, had attempted unsuccessfully to have their claims accepted by the Turkish authorities. The Foreign Office, well aware of D'Arcy's involvement from 1903, wrote to Greenway towards the end of August inquiring whether there would be any welcome for an association with the newly-formed group, and, though the Foreign Secretary could not promise its feasibility, it might be possible to offer diplomatic support 'in the event of British interests being adequately represented in the Syndicate'.[51] The Balkans was a troublesome area for British diplomacy and, at a time when the British Government was endeavouring to strengthen the triple alliance of France, Russia and the United Kingdom, it was attempting to eliminate as many points of friction in the area, particularly as they affected Turkey, which touched the concern of all three partners to the alliance.

This Foreign Office questioning provided the cue for Greenway's entry on to the stage of oil diplomacy as much as the Admiralty's inquiry was to prompt his lines. For the next two years Greenway held the stage, an exasperating and brilliant performance of pertinacity, obstinacy and persuasion which, in many respects complemented Churchill's more important role as Neptune of the Admiralty. Often intemperate, occasionally unscrupulous and always aggressive they forced acceptance of their respective policies by the determination of their advocacy. Greenway's initial reaction was low-key, for he suggested to Cargill that such 'an amalgamation would doubtless mean the early exploitation of the Mesopotamian Oil fields which would not suit our interests at all'.[52] Still, by showing an interest it might be possible to postpone development for a considerable time, but if circumstances forced the pace and 'necessitate our taking up the concession sooner or later there will be no difficulty in forming a syndicate for the purpose or in finding for it any portion of the Capital which BOC/APOC are unable, or do not desire to provide'.[53] In the last resort it was better to be associated with rather than in competition against the new consortium.

Greenway recognised that the Foreign Office would of course like to see an amalgamation of interests as it would enable them to discharge their responsibilities towards D'Arcy, and encourage the National Bank of Turkey in which there was a predominant British shareholding, a satisfactory diplomatic solution. Cargill, however, who had never been favourably disposed towards the continuing interest in the Mesopotamian concession was strongly hostile 'to our Group attempting to take up this concession on its own'. He reminded Greenway that the Company had no money and that 'Before long they will be considerably in debt, as far as I am concerned the BOC will certainly not guarantee interest on any more APOC Preference Shares to develop a concession which under the most favourable circumstances would not be Revenue let alone Profit earning for a very considerable period.'[54] He totally discounted any fear that possible Mesopotamian production might influence negotiations with the Royal Dutch-Shell group and maintained that 'it would not have the slightest effect on the Company's oil fuel trade'. He would not recommend putting any capital into such an enterprise.

As he pondered the implications, Greenway became more convinced that a unique opportunity had presented itself for making the Company's position more prominent, even indispensable, in national policy. Undismayed by Cargill's strictures, he remonstrated that to abandon the field altogether was incomprehensible and that the only feasible alternative was to take up the running again independently. Greenway replied very positively to Sir Louis Mallet, assistant under-secretary at the Foreign Office, both in person and by letter on 2 September, particularly emphasising three points, which became the principal *leitmotifs* of the later negotiations.[55] Firstly he demonstrated the importance to the Company of the Mesopotamian concession, not only for its own intrinsic value but because it was closely related to the Company's interests in Persia which he suggested had been acquired under the auspices of the Admiralty. Secondly he referred to the growing significance of reliable fuel oil supplies for naval purposes, which the Company would be able to provide. Thirdly he raised the danger of foreign domination over oil supplies, which might not only threaten the existence of the Company but might well imperil British naval supremacy in time of war. This was the preliminary skirmishing in a shrewd campaign of resourceful sallies and the skilful undermining of entrenched positions. Mallet was impressed and, now opposed to the amalgamation with TPC, informed the Admiralty on 13 September 1912 of what had transpired between him and Greenway and asked for their comments.[56] Attempts then and later to mediate between Greenway and Sir Henry Babington Smith, President of the National Bank of Turkey, failed, for Greenway would not be satisfied with less than a 50 per cent shareholding in TPC and Babington Smith would offer no more than 25 per cent.[57] On 28 September Babington Smith was told by the Foreign Office that the British Government could not support the TPC by itself.[58]

During this time Greenway had several interviews at the Admiralty and Foreign Office, where he elaborated his position, over which he had become so confident that he formulated a policy for Board approval on 19 September.[59] He believed that the Admiralty was 'evidently very anxious to preserve Persia for all time as a source of Fuel Oil for the British Navy in order (1) that the Shell may not secure a monopoly and thus be in a position to demand their own price, and (2) that they might not run the risk of supplies being cut off in time of war'. He also felt that they were upset because the Foreign Office appeared to have excluded naval considerations in their earlier attitude to the Mesopotamian concession. By the end of September the Admiralty had declared that it was 'undesirable that foreign interests should receive any encouragement from the British Government' and that 'the maintenance of the Persian oil fields in the hands of a British Company' was important.[60] Greenway, though, required more than statements of support for British interests, he needed action for, 'unless the Government can come to some arrangement with his company to assist not only in the matter of contracts for supplies, but also some form of subsidy to aid development and active support in respect of applications for concessions in Mesopotamia, it will probably be impossible for the Anglo-Persian Oil Company to preserve its independence'.[61] This was the rub. This was the context in which Greenway's first proposals for Government aid were made. Without it the Company's position in Persia would be prejudiced and the opportunity for acquiring a concession in Mesopotamia lessened. It was Company necessity, not national policy, which caused their presentation in the first place.

Greenway proposed:

(1) *British Government &/or Indian Government* to give us a subsidy of £100 000 per annum, on which we could raise £2 000 000 additional Capital with which to lay additional Pipe Lines, develop further fields, extend Refinery, and also, if necessary, build tankers.

(2) The Indian Government to grant exemption from Import duty on all Persian Oil.

(3) The Admiralty (for the Navy) and the Indian Government (for Railways) to enter into a contract with us to purchase all the Fuel Oil we can produce up to 500 000 tons per annum @ 30/- per ton f.o.b., from which 5/- per ton would be deducted, to such extent as may be necessary, in repayment of the subsidy.

(4) The Government to use their utmost influence to secure for the A.P.O.C., or some allied group or Company, the Mesopotamian Concession.

(5) The Government have the right to nominate one or two representatives on the board of the A.P.O.C. and of any subsidiary or allied Companies that may be formed.[62]

The response was encouraging to Greenway. D'Arcy, Barnes, Finlay and Redwood were enthusiastic over 'a unique opportunity for effecting a great "coup".'[63] Cargill, more restrained, approved getting a Government subsidy 'sufficient to guarantee 5% on all the capital to be raised', otherwise the scheme would be impractical.[64] Wallace welcomed the idea as being 'quite ideal' for the Company but one which 'the Government could not contemplate for there was no precedent', adding ironically that, 'although a policy that has no precedent is almost essential to a successful progressive business, it is anathema nowadays in the eyes of British Governments'.[65] On 11 October Greenway submitted his proposals to the

Admiralty,[66] assured, as he wrote to D'Arcy, 'that the whole question has been thoroughly discussed between the Foreign Office and the Admiralty...and that they are unanimously agreed that it is absolutely essential to maintain British control over the Persian Oilfields and that to ensure this British control must be secured over the Mesopotamian Oilfields'.[67] He detailed for the Admiralty the Company's productive and refinery capacity, the measures and cost of increasing supplies which would 'ensure for all time British control over the Oil produced from the Persian Oilfields. . . [and] that supplies from this important Oilfield, probably the largest by far in any British or British controlled country, would not in time of war be subject to the restraints which might occur were this Company forced into a commercial alliance with a foreign Combine'.[68]

It was at this time that the issue of the 'foreign Combine' became acute again. It was Greenway's previous experience with the Shell group which determined his opposition to associating with them in the TPC. Then and later he played upon the 'foreign' character of Royal Dutch to make his point that Royal Dutch-Shell as constituted in 1907 was not British, though the minority Shell Transport and Trading founded by Samuel certainly was. After months of aggravating negotiations the crude oil, benzine and kerosine contracts with the Asiatic Petroleum Company were almost ready for signature. Waley Cohen was anxious to conclude.[69] He was also pressing very strongly on 'the subject of a Fuel Oil arrangement and is very insistent that something should be done *at once*'.[70] This peremptory manner annoyed Greenway and his carefully angled correspondence was to make Waley Cohen appear uncompromising and domineering.[71] Encouraged by the prospect of an Admiralty contract and Government support, Greenway was in no mood to temporise, but asserted his independence. Waley Cohen persevered in demanding 'some comprehensive mutual arrangement for dealing with your Liquid Fuel',[72] but Greenway replied defiantly that 'we must have an "absolutely free hand" for dealing with all Government, Admiralty, and/or Railway business', and he rejected the condition that the company should not, while proposals are under discussion, quote for any Government business 'without consultation and agreement of rates with you'.[73] Waley Cohen appealed over Greenway's head to the Burmah Board by maintaining that the Company was its subsidiary and bound by its commitments, so that it had to decide 'whether they desire to market their Liquid Fuel in competition with us or in association with us'.[74]

This attempt to divide the Board was a clumsy manoeuvre and left Cargill, who regretted the whole incident and was not necessarily sympathetic to Greenway's posturing, with no option but to back his stance on this issue.[75] Greenway successfully exploited the correspondence to prejudice attitudes towards Shell so that Mallet, not the most gullible of diplomats, minuted on 6 November that

It is clear from the printed correspondence [circulated internally in the Foreign Office from copies supplied by Greenway] between the Asiatic Petroleum Company and the Anglo-Persian Oil Company that the Shell group are aiming at the extinction of the latter as a competitor. One of their objects being to control the price of liquid fuel for the British Navy. The correspondence is interesting. It shows that the conclusion of a working agreement between the two groups broke down on the refusal of the Anglo-Persian Oil Company to include Liquid Fuel for Government in its scope.[76]

Shell, he had been convinced by Greenway, wanted 'to control the supply to the Admiralty...which would be of most serious import to this country'. So concluded Mallet, 'I think that we should go to every length in supporting the independence of the Anglo-Persian Oil Company and subsidise them if necessary, as well as supporting their Mesopotamian concession claims.'[77] The Foreign Secretary did not dissent from these opinions, confirming that 'Evidently what we must do is to secure under British control a sufficient oil field for the British Navy.'[78] There appeared to be an almost passive acceptance of Greenway's exposition. It was an impressive performance after only a couple of months playing on the diplomatic stage, but the audience was more critical for the rest of the run.

4 THE COMPANY IN DEEP WATER

It was not, however, all plain sailing for, when least expected, there appeared warning lights ahead. Greenway, both presumptuous and anxious, pressed on. Churchill was approached through Lady St Helier, a great aunt of Clementine Churchill and an acquaintance of D'Arcy.[79] A meeting was arranged between Sir Francis Hopwood (later Lord Southborough), Additional Civil Lord, and Black to see D'Arcy and Greenway on 12 November 1912.[80] It was an inconclusive, disappointing interview, at which it was intimated that 'there would be parliamentary objections to the scheme which had been proposed' and that it would be more advisable to sound out the Indian Government for a contract.[81] This had already been done unsuccessfully by Greenway. The following day he met Mallet and reported discouragingly about the lack of enthusiasm for even a supply contract and his increasing difficulties over the Royal Dutch-Shell activity 'in holding out substantial inducements and exercising considerable pressure' which was weakening 'the resistance of certain directors on Imperial Grounds'.[82] The Foreign Secretary in 'some perplexity' asked for 'the Admiralty's views in a final authoritative form as soon as possible', and suggested an inter-departmental meeting to discuss the question.[83] The officials at the Admiralty were not going to be rushed into a decision. The question of naval re-armament and a naval war staff were absorbing their attention, besides, they already possessed a capable contracts department and the reliability of proven supplies of Welsh steam coal was an asset not lightly to be disregarded. Churchill was aware of the existing conservatism and his differences with the permanent staff and the Admirals were doubtless reflected in his establishment of the Royal Commission on Oil Supply which began its deliberations in September.[84]

It was to this Commission that Greenway gave evidence on 19 November.[85] He had already been advised in late September by a member of the Cabinet that 'it would be better for me to explain the advantages to be derived from a Fuel Oil arrangement with the APOC to the Royal Commission'.[86] Greenway felt elated on leaving it, as 'All the *members* were most sympathetic and Lord Fisher after it was over kept me talking in Pall Mall for a considerable time. He is most emphatic that *something* must be done *at once*, both to secure Mesopotamia and to maintain British control over APOC.'[87] It was a gruelling session covering a wide range of topics including Mesopotamia, India, freight rates, apart from the position of the Company itself, and Greenway was closely questioned by members of the Committee, particularly Sir Thomas Holland, head of the Indian Geological Survey, Redwood and F.W. Black (later Sir Frederick). He submitted a memorandum on the Persian oilfields and the dangers of foreign control, themes which he developed at length. He placed the onus on the Admiralty for the survival of the Company, in view of its earlier intervention over the D'Arcy Concession, asserting that 'we have got to make up our minds whether we are to attach ourselves to the Admiralty, or rather whether the Admiralty are to exercise the control that we thought they would desire to exercise, or whether we should join hands with the Shell Company', whom he accused of 'working by every possible means in the direction of securing a monopoly of Oil Fuel in the whole world'.[88] Only the Company had substantial independent supplies of fuel oil. On its own it could not withstand a price war whereas 'by an alliance with the Shell Company we should be enabled to share in the full benefits of the commercial part of the business'.

He referred regretfully to his earlier interview when Hopwood had informed him that 'the Admiralty were not under an obligation at all to assist' the Company, that it 'must be treated on the same level as any other company' and that 'this suggestion of mine was quite impractical'. The members of the Commission were not disposed to accept Greenway's arguments on trust and Holland shrewdly queried why a subsidy was necessary if a supply contract was concluded, in which case 'do you not think you could raise your capital on mortgage?'. Greenway's reply was a stark reminder of the Company's financial predicament, a recurrence of the financial crises of the concessionary days for 'we have gone through three years of that already without paying any dividends and if we went through another three or five years without paying a dividend I do not know what would happen'. His candour reflected the reality. It was his intention to get the best of both worlds for 'We want to carry out our obligations to the State, provided that we can do so without detriment to the interests of our shareholders.'[89]

Greenway was unduly optimistic in assuming that 'it looks as if the Government have practically made up their minds to agree more or less to our proposals'.[90] The vehemence of his denunciation of Shell and his appeal over the heads of the Admiralty officials was bound to provoke a reaction, but for the moment, satisfied in his illusions, he attempted to press home his advantage. After giving his evidence to the Commission he was asked on the afternoon of the same day to set out his case for the benefit of the Foreign Office for an inter-departmental meeting the following day. He recapitulated his need to raise £2 000 000 if he was to supply the Admiralty with more than 75 000 tons a year of fuel oil which was the existing capacity of the refinery, by way of a government subsidy or annual payment.[91] The burden of the argument was the same, for if 'a Government subsidy and preferential rights in Mesopotamia were not secured to the Anglo-Persian Oil Company, then the financial inducements to come to an alliance with the Shell Transport Company would be so overwhelming that the directors, in duty to their shareholders, would have no alternative', and the policy promoted by Greenway would collapse, principally through lack of support from Cargill and the Burmah directors. This was no idle threat, for writing to Cargill in 1915 about the animosity between Waley Cohen and himself over negotiations then, Greenway remarked that when he 'has failed in his object of trying to squeeze the last drop of blood out of APOC by a direct attack on the Executive here, he has tried the effect of a flank movement in the hope that this would achieve the desired result by means of "dividing our house against itself"'.[92] 'That,' expostulated Greenway, 'is the history of the negotiations which took place with such unfortunate results in 1911-1912', and 'has again been repeated now'. Greenway outlined two methods of raising the money: (1) a government guarantee on the capital interest of 4 per cent a year, an estimated annual expenditure of £80 000 for 30-35 years, (2) a straight annual payment of £100 000 which would, in effect, disguise the subsidy element.[93]

To the consternation of the Foreign Office, the Admiralty, on naval and commercial grounds, refused to consider Greenway's proposals and was indifferent to the fate of the Company or the diplomatic implications of 'some risk of the oil fields in Mesopotamia and the whole of Persia being under foreign and largely German control'.[94] To prevent just such an eventuality the Foreign Office inquired 'are His Majesty's Government justified in seeking to maintain the independence of the Anglo-Persian Oil Company which consists largely of men such as Lord Strathcona of undoubted patriotism, by making them an annual payment and assisting them in acquiring the Mesopotamian oil fields'.[95] This was the question, the crux of the matter. Only the Admiralty could provide the answer, for it was clear in the view of the Foreign Office on 28 November 1912 that 'diplomatic assistance alone will be useless in preserving the independence of the Anglo-Persian Oil Company. It is pecuniary assistance in some form that they require: whether this should be given depends upon considerations that the Foreign Office cannot decide, but upon the decision that is given must depend the action of the Foreign Office.'[96] It was hoped that it would be given as soon as possible.

While waiting for the Admiralty reply, the Foreign Office instructed Sir Gerard Lowther, ambassador in Constantinople, that it attached great importance to the Mesopotamian concession being granted to D'Arcy.[97] In an effort to encourage the India Office to take a more active interest, the Foreign Office suggested that in the Persian Gulf 'our political position is largely the result of our commercial predominance' but that it would be seriously jeopardised 'if the Anglo-Persian Oil Company is allowed to pass under foreign control by absorption in the Shell Company'.[98] The India Office was not impressed and replied that because coal was very cheap and plentiful in most parts of India no locomotives had been fitted to burn oil.[99] As Alwyn Parker at the Foreign Office commented, it was shortsighted not to consider 'the question from the political point of view'.[100]

It was the Earl of Crewe, Secretary of State at the India Office, who first publicly questioned the assumption that 'the absorption of the Company by the interests represented by the Shell Company will be the inevitable result of the refusal of His Majesty's Government to accord the former, diplomatic or even financial support'.[101] His Lordship admitted that the price of oil and foreign interest in the Persian Gulf area might increase, but doubted whether it would affect the British position in Persia. Parker considered it 'an evasive answer'[102] but Mallet was a little disturbed, observing that the distinction was important and sought a further interview with Greenway,[103] who reiterated his fears of absorption and later stressed 'the pacifying influence' of the Company where it was operating in Persia.[104] Greenway knew that the financial situation was deteriorating, the refinery was not improving, the first kerosine supplies for APC were a dismal failure, 'political objections' to his proposals were increasing in spite of lobbying and the Admiralty remained unconvinced, a position which it made transparently clear in its communication to the Foreign Office on 28 December 1912.[105] Acknowledging the Company's rights in Persia and over Mesopotamia, the Admiralty would only commit itself 'to give as favourable consideration as practicable to tenders from the Anglo-Persian Oil Company, consistently with due consideration of supplies from other available sources', by no means the preferential treatment that had been expected.

So, indeed, Greenway's proposals were quite unacceptable to the Admiralty, which would not recommend either itself or the Indian Government 'finding £2 000 000 of capital for a British Company operating in territory which, although presumably largely subject to British influence is, nevertheless, foreign territory'. There could be no guarantee that subsidies or advances would be repaid because 'it would depend upon the success of the Company both in finding its supplies and in maintaining its markets against powerful commercial rivals whether the money would be repaid, and the Government would be obliged to appoint representatives to sit upon the board of a commercial company engaged in a business subject to much speculative risk'. It was therefore doubtful 'whether such a policy could be recommended to Parliament on naval grounds'. Moreover, the Admiralty rejected the foreign policy implications in such a contract as 'there are other oil-fields in which the arguments for similar action might prove to be equally, or even more urgent'. It wished to avoid becoming embroiled in commercial competition and observed that if an agreement between the Company and the Shell group was 'ultimately unavoidable, contracts with the Admiralty on ordinary terms might possibly be arranged...outside of any such arrangement'.

Whilst the Admiralty recognised that the Foreign Office might be able to 'justify more exceptional measures', it did not desire to set a precedent, certainly in a case which it believed had no exceptional merit. It would regret 'a greater monopoly in the oil fuel market' but such a development was beyond its responsibility. Its primary concern was 'whether Admiralty interests would be so jeopardised as to necessitate the consideration of a larger question of subsidising commercial companies', a policy which they have hitherto declined to entertain in other cases, and which, if once begun, would probably have to be extended. Indeed the only other example, which was hardly applicable, was the subsidy paid to the Cunard Line in 1903.[106] The outlook was bleak.

Mallet was greatly irritated at the contents of the Admiralty letter feeling that Greenway was responsible for having led him up the garden path and minuted angrily that,

Fuel oil and the Admiralty 1912-14

I do not like the attitude of the Anglo-Persian Oil Company, who have hitherto posed as being ultra-Imperialistic. Mr. Greenway first comes to me and hints that if the Shell obtain the Mesopotamian fields, it will be difficult then for the Persian Company to resist coming to an agreement with them, unless the Admiralty can give them a contract... Mr. Greenway now threatens complete absorption with the Shell unless the Admiralty give him a contract and the question of the Mesopotamian fields seems to have dropped out entirely.[107]

In Mallet's opinion, Greenway was now saying that 'unless the Admiralty make a contract with him, he will with the Shell'.[108] At a ruffled meeting on 9 January 1913,[109] Mallet informed Greenway of the Admiralty's response, to which he answered that an amalgamation was now inevitable even if the Company acquired the Mesopotamian concession.[110] Mallet questioned this logic, and, nettled by the turn of events, said that in such circumstances there was little point in pursuing the Mesopotamian concession and that an amalgamation with Shell would be surprising 'when it appeared that a marketing arrangement i.e. one for the sale of oil at a certain price, would amply suffice to meet the case'. That was precisely the attitude of Waley Cohen, but begged the question of the Company's independence in the light of its precarious financial position, for the Company not only required increased revenue but, what was more difficult to admit, more capital. Greenway pledged to Mallet his own opposition to a merger. In the meantime the India Office had reaffirmed its attitude on 4 January and side-stepped the issue of British interests in Persia, which, it was pointed out, was the responsibility of the Foreign Office.[111]

It seemed as if the Foreign Office was back on the defensive. It had initiated discussions on a controversial subject as a result of a review of Turkish affairs, but the point had been reached when it could only support a proposal to subsidise the Anglo-Persian Oil Company 'if Lord Crewe and the Lords Commissioners were able to show good grounds for doing so. Short of such a demonstration, Sir E. Grey has done all in his power to preserve the British character of the enterprise.'[112] To the Company, Grey remarked that the Government had supported it on the understanding that it preserved its British identity but that if this was compromised by combining with the Shell Group it 'could not of course hope to get from His Majesty's Government the same support as in the past'. This veiled threat was a very real sanction. Diplomacy could do no more. Fuel oil remained the key.

5 BACK ON COURSE

There was little more that Greenway could do. Cargill was away on a tour in the East and no important decisions would be taken until his return. It is highly probable that, although personal representations had not been successful,[113] Greenway and his colleagues were appraised of what was happening behind the scenes. Churchill's programme was gathering pace, the 15 inch guns, the fast cruiser division and the use of oil to ensure longer ranges and greater speed were being planned.[114] The battle of the naval estimates was beginning. The Admiralty would not, could not, announce any major measures until its policy had been decided and the early months of 1913 were crucial in this respect. On 29 January the Company tendered for oil supplies over a five-year period rising from 30 000 tons in the first year to 500 000 tons in the fifth year at the same price of 30s per ton f.o.b. as submitted in October,[115] which compared favourably with the rising prices of 37s 6d to 77s 6d a ton between 1911 and 1912. Over a week later Greenway informed the Admiralty that the Company had been asked to quote for fuel oil supplies for the German navy.[116]

A couple of weeks later the Admiralty stated that the contract tender was receiving careful consideration and that no other transactions should interfere with the offer made to the Admiralty.[117] Greenway reassured the Foreign Office that his colleagues were desirous 'by some practical means of maintaining the purely British character of the oil company' and sought to efface the impression of blackmail which Mallet seemed to have gained, by explaining the urgency of the matter caused by pressure from the Royal Dutch-Shell group and 'the exigences of our position'.[118] He was not seeking £2 000 000 of capital but only the amount paid in advance for deliveries of oil, and felt it not unreasonable that India should make some contribution to the 'Imperial Navy', a sentiment similar to Churchill's attempts to persuade the Canadian Government to pay for some warships in 1912-13.[119] At all events Greenway was prepared to discuss alternative proposals 'in a manner that would neither be onerous to the Government nor be open to political objections'.[120]

The idea of a conference was acceptable to the Foreign Office but the India Office remained reserved and cautious about any ideas of 'a subsidy to a speculative commercial undertaking' but did not oppose being represented at a meeting.[121] More positively, on 26 February, the Admiralty informed the Foreign Office that a single contract had been concluded with the Company for the supply of 30 000 tons of fuel oil for 1913-14 and that, as it was considering a proposal from the Company for a long-term contract for larger quantities, they preferred to defer the meeting unless it was of exceptional urgency.[122] There seemed to be a break in the clouds, because, when Greenway was informed that his contract proposals were receiving careful attention, it was suggested that better progress would be made if he was to call personally upon the Director of Navy Contracts.[123] The log jam was loosening. Greenway was told confidentially by Redwood towards the end of the month '"to sit tight" in regard to the Admiralty contract, because present indications seem to show that we shall get everything we want as the Admiralty are beginning to realise that it would be very unsafe for them to rely on Mexico as a source of supply'.[124] Mallet had already previously questioned Greenway about the political turmoil in Mexico, particularly in the period 1911-14 when four dictators rose and fell.[125] There was turbulence too in the Admiralty boardroom where the Fourth Civil Lord, George Lambert, who had served since 1905, was not in favour of having 'the light cruisers of this year's programme being designed for all fuel oil' because 'before we discard coal we should be certain of an adequate supply of oil for times of peace and emergency, a certainty as to which at present I confess to considerable doubts'.[126]

Even before Churchill explained on 26 March 1913, in his important speech in the House of Commons on the navy estimates, the interrelation between his new naval strategy and its dependence on oil, Greenway was convinced during the important week of 16-23 March that, despite the doubts that remained, the decision had been taken and that his cause was won. He informed Adamson in Glasgow optimistically

> that all the heads of the Admiralty, the responsible members of the Cabinet and the Members of the Royal Oil Fuel Commission, have now agreed to withdraw from their previous attitude and have decided that they must give us any financial assistance that may be *necessary*, inasmuch as now that they are committed irretrievably to the adoption of fuel oil, they must maintain a hold over the APOC supply as this is the only part of the world under British control from which they can rely, with any confidence, on sufficient supplies to meet their requirements.[127]

Greenway modified his earlier Admiralty proposals on 10 March by suggesting that advance payments for supplies be covered by deductions of 5s per ton from the contract price and offering the credit of the Company as security for the advances.[128]

Greenway repeated his idea of an Indian Government guarantee. He understood that parliamentary sanction could be obtained 'by means of a short "secret" bill which will be passed without particulars being divulged to the House of Commons'. He expected that the first advance could be payable on 1 July 1914 which would enable dividends to be paid then. After attending a meeting at the Admiralty on 13 March at which Churchill was present, Greenway was able to reassure Strathcona that 'negotiations are satisfactorily progressing in the way that we all desire'.[129] The first Admiralty memorandum with all the relevant information was drawn up on 18 March in which it was recognised that the Company's proposals, assessed by commercial criteria, 'might be acceptable and

Fuel oil and the Admiralty 1912-14

possibly highly advantageous', but 'a Government contract had to be viewed differently'.[130] Nevertheless it was conceded that 'the circumstances are so exceptional, however, that some measure of risk even in a Government contract is probably inevitable'.

On 26 March 1913 Churchill nailed his oil colours to the mast. 'There is no disputing,' he proclaimed, 'the immense advantages which the case of oil confers on ship design and many other aspects of naval warfare', but, he admitted, 'they are almost matched by dangers and difficulties of the most serious character'.[131] Amongst those he mentioned 'the absence of any fresh supply of liquid fuel indigenous to these islands and the scarcity of any such supplies in view throughout the British Empire', 'price movements...part of an attempt on a gigantic scale to corner the market and to control the output' and a shortage of tankers. In this connection forward contracts would be advisable, which he confessed, 'must necessarily open up a number of difficult commercial and administrative questions'. With a view to disarming criticism he explained that 'although oil is required in large quantities for the flotillas and small vessels, coal must remain the main motive power of the British line of battle'. Yet, whatever the problems, he asserted his 'confidence in liquid fuel for war purposes and that the difficulties which now confront us will ultimately be overcome'. As Churchill had told Lloyd George, 'he may have been prepared to take the whole responsibility of the present and prospective naval expenditure upon himself',[132] but he had to convince and could not afford to ignore, his colleagues, no matter how carefully he supervised the presentation of the case.

As far as oil was concerned it was clear that up to the end of May 'the Admiralty was uncommitted to any definite line of action on oil supplies' but prepared to take whatever initiative was necessary in its own interests after examining cautiously all the issues involved.[133] It recognised that rising fuel oil prices had made 'the Persia supply relatively more important than was originally anticipated, without altering the Admiralty view that too much reliance should not be placed on any one source of supply'.[134] It was naval strategy that determined the priorities. It was administrative convenience that influenced their implementation. It was realised that contractual arrangements were the best method of obtaining supplies, 'limiting Governmental interference with the concerns of private companies to the minimum necessary to secure supplies'. There was no desire to become involved in corporate affairs but it had to be admitted that 'if the Government were to proceed generally by way of guarantees or special legislation, conditions might have to be insisted upon for share in profits and management if risks of commercial enterprise are to be shared', though it was not contemplated that the necessity had yet arisen and as far as the Company was concerned 'the Admiralty will take no share in management'.

There had been exhaustive comment among Admiralty officials, whose general conclusion was that 'the proposed "contract" is very exceptional in character but so are the circumstances'. The elements of the case were simple and were introduced as 'The question of Oil Supply for the Navy' to the Cabinet on 19 June. It was submitted that

> as an act of Governmental executive responsibility this contract be entered into and that such risks as may attach to the proposed contract advances on the security offered, be assumed as a necessary administrative act to provide supplies which are essential as a consequence of the policy already adopted of fitting certain of His Majesty's ships to burn oil fuel for tactical and strategic advantages.[135]

As Asquith informed the King, the issue was much discussed, though no definite conclusion was reached except that the Admiralty should secure its oil supplies from the widest and most numerous sources possible.[136] The cabinet would agonise over many more meetings on naval affairs, which threatened to split the Liberal party until the outbreak of war made it seem like the Mad Hatter's tea party.

The principles, once accepted, were easily understandable. It was the administrative act which caused the difficulties and the first overtures to the Treasury were not received favourably. The Admiralty justified their case not on strategic or political, but financial considerations. Fuel oil prices were rising so that forward planning and contracting was advisable to offset the insecurity of supply and the rise in prices, which doubled between 1910 and 1912.[137] The Royal Dutch-Shell group was unwilling to offer more than a two-year contract for supplies.[138] The policy, however, was inclusive not exclusive as it was essential for the Admiralty to keep in contact with all the important available home and foreign sources of supply. The Company's price was competitive, the Admiralty expecting a benefit of from 10s to 20s a ton, or £4 000 000 to £8 000 000 net advantage over twenty years. At an average price of £1 10s f.o.b. Ābādān and freight it could be delivered to the United Kingdom for £2 17s 6d a ton which compared well with Texas and Romanian supplies of between £2 10s and £2 12s a ton f.o.b. Scottish oil produced from East Lothian shale mines was of good quality but cost between £4 10s and £5 10s a ton. The Company was expected to supply some 40 per cent of Admiralty fuel oil requirements. Therefore, bearing in mind all the circumstances, in mid-June the Admiralty regarded the Persian contract as 'an essential and indispensable part of the general arrangement' and the Government 'should be asked to assume the responsibility of authorising this contract with the approval of the Treasury'.[139]

Fuel oil and the Admiralty 1912-14

The Treasury did not approve and found it immediately
most objectionable and I cannot think that the difficulties connected with use of fuel oil are such as to drive us to an expedient unbusinesslike and so unsound...An arrangement of this character, even for a very limited term of years would be dangerous enough, but the risk is greatly increased by the proposal to bind the Government for 20 years to so speculative a business.[140]

Ten days later the permanent secretary, Sir Robert Chalmers, was equally dismissive, stating that 'I do not see any justification for a contract on these terms for so long a period as 20 years...My own feeling would therefore be to refuse to sanction the proposed contract.'[141] In his opinion 'it is sounder to pay for what you want as and when you want it'.

Chalmers had not moved with the times, for it was he who in 1904 had opposed Admiralty interest proposed by the Earl of Selborne, First Lord of the Admiralty, in the development of new oilfields, 'not to render direct financial assistance, but to guarantee to purchase at a reasonable price, as much of the annual production of residual oil of quality suitable for fuel as may be required'. The Admiralty were to indicate the minimum annual requirements in advance but not for more than three years.[142] The Treasury was agreeable to the naval policy of using oil up to 20 per cent instead of coal as fuel, at an extra cost of some £380 000, provided the supply was guaranteed, but Chalmers objected to certain tendencies observing that 'the Admiralty now foreshadow the possible acquisition of oil rights for themselves, presumably to be worked, - a step of dubious policy'.[143] The then Chancellor of the Exchequer, Austen Chamberlain, nevertheless accepted 'the proposal to contract for the purchase of fixed quantities of oil at a given price and for a term of years',[144] which resulted in the Burmah supply agreement with the Admiralty in 1905.

The Indian Government was showing itself not amenable to persuasion for, although in its communication of 26 December the Admiralty had not recommended a financial guarantee to the Company, from May it was pressing the advantages of such a course.[145] On 19 June the Admiralty requested a definite decision from the Indian Government, which prevaricated.[146] At another inconclusive meeting of the Cabinet on 9 July more proposals were put forward, 'for obtaining supplies of oil for the Navy from the Persian oilfields', but the suggestion that the Indian Government guarantee the interest on a fresh issue of capital was rejected.[147] The Admiralty would have to stand on its own and bear the total cost, which would strain its own estimates and patience.

The pace was quickening as Churchill resolved to settle the issue before the summer recess. He was deeply disappointed over the Indian Government's decision. As he wrote to Grey to solicit his support, the guarantee was the best solution as the supplies from Persia were indispensable but if

Fuel oil and the Admiralty 1912-14

not 'we must go forward alone by the more expensive and unsatisfactory method'.[148] He did not flinch from accepting that the Company 'will receive substantial financial aid in one form or another'.[149] At Churchill's instigation, a Cabinet committee was appointed which met the following day, 10 July 1913 attended by Greenway whose back was less up against the wall than it had been for some time. On Cargill's return from his eastern tour, the Burmah Board had decided in mid-May 'to continue financing the APOC in the meantime to any reasonable extent'.[150] The refinery at last was producing better kerosine but inferior benzine, although not very profitably or consistently. In June the refinery had just started the production of 70 per cent residue fuel oil, named 'Admiralty' in July.[151] This, in spite of some sulphur content, was marketable and by September its volume had already exceeded that of any other product and represented over 50 per cent of the total marketed products, which must have been gratifying to Greenway.[152]

Relations with Waley Cohen remained at a level of tolerable dislike apart from his contention, as Greenway told Cargill, that 'we have no right to charter tankers without his consent [which was] somewhat "colossal" even for him'.[153] When Greenway disputed this assumption, Waley Cohen insisted that 'APOC must only make freight arrangements with APC' and he 'gave vent to a lot of blustering talk about "unfriendliness" mixed up with threats of retaliation'.[154] Having chartered the *Soya Maru*, a Japanese ship, for eastern trade,[155] Greenway was less ruffled over this particular rumpus, especially as reports from New York indicating certain Royal Dutch-Shell action against Lord Cowdray's Mexican Eagle Company seemed to parallel and confirm the hostility that had been shown to the Company.[156]

It was during the course of discussions with members of the Cabinet on 10 July that the idea of a government shareholding began to emerge as the problem of justifying expenditure on the Company to party, Parliament and people began to be examined.[157] Black at the Admiralty asked Greenway whether the guarantee on the £2 000 000 required to meet the increased fuel oil production facilities could not be met 'by a bank or some other financial intermediary', which would be held covered by the Government. The Bank of England was suggested, but this financial cloak and dagger operation was impractical and Greenway advised the Government to face up to the position realistically 'by themselves taking up shares and/or Debentures to the amount of £2 000 000, giving a British Government guarantee on that amount of capital'. Conversations resumed in the evening when Wallace joined Greenway. The Chancellor of the Exchequer, Lloyd George, raised the question of a Burmah guarantee, but although Wallace was prepared to put it to the Board, 'he saw no reason at all why the Company would undertake such an obligation', and urged that 'the best course for the Government to follow was to provide themselves the £2 000 000...it would give Government a participation in the profits'.[158] Churchill took up the suggestion as 'the soundest course, from an economic point of view, for the Government to follow' even though 'there were, of course, obvious Parliamentary difficulties'. The Cabinet did not spare itself, for the following day it met again and was 'entirely occupied with various phases of the Oil question'. It finally agreed that the Chancellor should consult the Governor of the Bank of England, Walter Cunliffe, and sanctioned a rise in the estimates of £450 000 to increase the oil reserves to a six month level of consumption, as requested by Sir John Jellicoe, the Second Sea Lord. It accepted that 'it is desirable that the Government should acquire a controlling interest in a trustworthy source of supply, if possible both at home and abroad'.[159]

A few days later, on 17 July, Churchill spoke in the debate on the Navy estimates and warmed to his theme that the matter 'which holds first place in the public attention is the engaging topic of fuel oil'.[160] He described the stages of the oil programme, the advantages of fuel oil for naval design, performance and tactics and its indispensability for national survival because 'if we cannot get oil, we cannot get corn, we cannot get cotton and we cannot get a thousand and one commodities necessary for the preservation of the economic energies of Great Britain'. The problem was dependable supplies at reasonable prices because 'the open market is becoming an open mockery'. He envisaged that 'the Admiralty should become the independent owner and producer of its own supplies of liquid fuel; firstly, by building up an oil reserve in this country sufficient to make us safe in war and be able to override price fluctuations in peace; secondly, by acquiring the power to deal in crude oils as they come cheaply into the market'. There was no reason, he controversially asserted, why the Admiralty should not be able 'to retort, refine, top...or distil crude oil of various kinds until it reaches the quality required for naval use. This again leads us into having to dispose of the surplus products...I see no reason, nor do my advisers, why we should shrink from making this further extension of the vast and various business of the Admiralty.' In a powerful appeal for his policy Churchill proclaimed 'on no one quality, on no one process, on no one country, on no one route and on no one field must we be dependent. Safety and certainty in oil lie in variety and variety alone.' The public was stimulated, the press congratulatory, with *The Times* complementing Churchill on an authoritative statement of the national interest in oil[161] and *The Financial Times* referring to the seal of approval for oil.[162] It was an impressive and imaginative performance but the provision of finance for the Company was not yet assured.

6 BECALMED

Churchill had mapped his course and cleared his decks. Lloyd George was not satisfied with the refusal of Burmah to guarantee the contract. Cargill was adamant that he would commit no more finance. The storm burst at a second meeting with the Cabinet committee on 28 July 1913 which was attended by Greenway, Cargill, Finlay and Wallace, who reported that 'the Government suddenly veered round from the line which we all understood at a previous interview was still in existence'.[163] Greenway had understood from Black ten days previously that the Government would 'either agree to give a guarantee on the £2 000 000 or take up the Capital themselves and whichever is decided upon to bring in as soon as possible an Enabling Bill',[164] which, however, could not be passed before April. He confidently advised the Company to order the equipment needed. According to Wallace this latest proposal posed a 'heads I win, tails you lose' dilemma for the directors.[165] The Government would provide the money subject to Burmah guaranteeing the interest and ultimate repayment, with the Government having the option at any time of converting its advance into shares or debentures sufficient to ensure 'a substantial amount of control of the Company'. It was the Governor of the Bank of England who insisted upon a 'Burmah guarantee' and was responsible for the change of front. As this was unacceptable, the discussion terminated.

Churchill, who was persevering in his approach, decided to send out an independent Admiralty commission as a stalking horse, 'to push on matters as quickly as possible',[166] and to neutralise the opposition of Admiral Sir Charles (later Lord) Beresford, former Channel Commander-in-Chief, 1907-9 and bitter critic of Fisher, who had remarked in the parliamentary debates that 'the Government should not contract with any company without having their own geological expert to report on the locality'.[167] The commission was chaired by Sir Edmond Slade, a former Director of Naval Intelligence, Commander-in-Chief in the East and a noted protagonist of oil developments, with John Cadman, colonial adviser on oil affairs and Professor of Mining at Birmingham University and two geologists, E.R. Blundstone, who fell ill and was not able to travel, and E.H. Pascoe of the Geological Survey of India.

There is no doubt of the collective gloom which dispirited the directors, but it was Wallace again who rallied them, playing a conciliatory and constructive role. He encouraged Strathcona that 'I do not think we have heard the last word from the Government'[168] and cautioned Cargill about exaggerating the dangers to the Company.[169]

Discretion was needed so as not to 'write a word that would make this object more difficult to obtain'. It was to the indispensable and well-informed Redwood that Wallace turned as a confidential intermediary to inform the Government that another alternative was not precluded from consideration.[170] There were not many cards left in the pack but he too emphasised that 'I should dearly like to see the matter settled at once, for there are, as you know, strong influences working in favour of the undoubtedly profitable alliance between the Anglo-Persian and one of the other two Oil groups.'[171] Furthermore, regrettable though it was, 'If the Government have not now the necessary spirit to seize the opportunity at once and to develop it as quickly as possible – well then the next best thing is to tie the thing up securely by an option until further knowledge emboldens the present Ministers or enables their successors to begin later what might have begun this year.'[172]

Redwood met Wallace at short notice and, though 'patient, painstaking and sympathetic',[173] he doubted whether the Admiralty would be able to accept as a temporary solution buying fuel oil at Ābādān, as they would not be able to transport it and freighting would be too expensive, but he promised to plead the Company's cause. Unable to see Churchill, Redwood talked to Black who, since his first scepticism over the contract proposals, had become a firm advocate. He assured Redwood that the ending of the last Cabinet committee was 'in no sense a termination or break in the negotiations, but a termination of the particular way of bringing them to an issue proposed by the Govt. and declined by us'.[174] He returned the letter from Wallace as he expected that an Admiralty letter would be sent 'which would go far towards granting all that we had previously asked'.[175] To Greenway and Wallace, who saw him later, he confided that it was 'the idea of the Government to try and keep the matter open until receipt of the Report of the Commission', probably in November. In the meantime there was no chance of an interim solution, as there was no oil storage capacity available.[176]

This news was greeted with mixed feelings; relief that the Admiralty was not reneging on its promises, concern to receive 'at least some satisfactory assurances that in the event of the Report being favourable they will be prepared to complete the big Contract on the basis of one or other of the proposals we have put forward'[177] and frustration. Cargill, naturally worried about the continuing financial implications for Burmah, just hoped that 'the Refinery will get into thorough working order very shortly and that we will be able to keep our heads above water' until the Commission reported and a satisfactory fuel oil contract was negotiated.[178] On 3 September, with the announcement of the Commission, the Secretary of the Admiralty reported that discussions were temporarily suspended.[179] Wallace replied that the Company could not be expected to wait indefinitely 'to keep their hands free, lest in the interim circumstances arise which would cause the Company to fall between two stools',[180] but would assist the Commission to its utmost.[181] The Admiralty would not guarantee in advance the terms and conditions of any proposed contract but expected a final decision before the end of January 1914.[182]

Greenway, in further exchanges of correspondence, regretted the lack of progress and was prepared to reopen negotiations at any time.[183] In an informal letter to Black on 17 October he reminded him that it was over a year since they had discussed a relationship closer than that 'of temporary independent buyers and sellers', but that a point was being reached when

events are forcing our hands...it is now essential that fresh financial arrangements of one kind or another should be made in order to meet the further outlay connected with the cost of completing the equipment of our Refineries, and of providing the transport and other facilities necessary for developing our business on a scale commensurate with the extent of our supplies of crude...The whole of the Capital raised by us was exhausted about 9 months ago.[184]

Appeals to imperial pride provided no capital or revenue, especially when the Asiatic Petroleum Company had just taken a cargo of fuel oil from the Company at 25s f.o.b. Ābādān.[185] The threads in the very complicated pattern of negotiations were still being shuttled from side to side. Progress with the design was not being made.

Reference has been frequently made to the deteriorating financial position. It might be presumed that Greenway was crying 'wolf'. This was far from the case. The situation was much more serious than he publicly admitted and was the principal reason why Cargill was not prepared for Burmah to extend guaranteeing to the Company more than the 6 per cent preference shares, though it did not prevent him from making some cash available in the form of loans. Greenway was not exaggerating when he declared in October 1913 that the whole of the initial capital was exhausted the previous January. Table 5.1 summarises the consolidated sources and applications of funds from the formation of the Company to 31 March 1913, which indicates, perhaps for the first time, how desperate the financial position of the Company was before the Government took up its shareholding.

By 31 March 1913 the Company had not yet begun trading and hence no funds had been internally generated. The public had subscribed £900 000 for preference shares and £600 000 for debentures. The £1 000 000 ordinary shares were issued fully paid in part payment for the Concession. The £1 500 000 raised by the sale of preference shares and debentures had financed an investment of £1 038 263 in fixed assets, on the refinery, pipelines, launches, tanks, buildings and drilling plant, as well as an expenditure of £288 912 on office rent, salaries, travel, and sundry other

Fuel oil and the Admiralty 1912-14

Table 5.1. *Statement of source and application of funds of the Anglo-Persian Oil Company group 1909-13*

	£	£	£
Source of funds			
Sources outside the Company			
Capital subscribed			
Ordinary shares			1 000 000
Preference shares			900 000
Non-current liabilities			
Debentures			600 000
			2 500 000
Application of funds			
Purchase price of Concession			1 229 329
General expenditure			288 912
Increase in fixed assets			
Installations, etc., at cost			1 038 263
Increase in current assets			
Stock crude and products		80 138	
Current investments		9 419	
Debtors		68 003	
Cash		33 841	
		191 401	
Less increase in current liabilities			
Creditors	97 439		
Loans	150 466		
		247 905	
Increase in net current assets			(56 504)
			2 500 000

Source: BP consolidated balance sheets (see Appendix 3.1(e))

'preliminary expenses' and operating costs. The remainder went either to the Concession vendors in cash or to provide working capital.

The day to day survival of any company depends upon its ability to meet calls for immediate payment of current liabilities by cash. The liquidity position of the Company over the years 1910-15 is depicted in Table 5.2. Some deterioration in the net current asset balance of a company which is establishing itself and is yet to start trading, is to be expected since it is obliged to draw on cash balances, which can only be replenished by further capital issues. The net current asset balance of the Company, however, not only declined but by 1913 current liabilities actually exceeded current

Date	Consolidated current assets		Consolidated current liabilities		Consolidated net current assets	Increase in net current assets on previous year	Current[a] ratio	Liquidity[b] ratio
1910 31 March	Cash and balances Debtors Current investments Stocks	121 264 21 308 — — 142 572	Creditors Loans	42 491 — 42 491	100 081	100 081	3.35	3.35
1911 31 March	Cash and balances Debtors Current investments Stocks	100 528 17 475 15 384 — 133 387	Creditors Loans	43 248 — 43 248	90 139	(9 942)	3.08	3.08
1912 31 March	Cash and balances Debtors Current investments Stocks	37 647 84 452 7 849 23 099 153 047	Creditors Loans	93 140 — 93 140	59 907	(30 232)	1.64	1.39
1913 31 March	Cash and balances Debtors Current investments Stocks	33 841 68 003 9 419 80 138 191 401	Creditors Loans	97 439 150 466 247 905	(56 504)	(116 411)	0.77	0.45
1914 31 March	Cash and balances Debtors Current investments Stocks	26 731 83 903 8 743 147 415 266 792	Creditors Loans	225 895 258 062 483 957	(217 165)	(160 661)	0.55	0.25
1915 31 March	Cash and balances Debtors Current investments Stocks	131 494 345 553 — 126 629 603 676	Creditors Loans	350 017 — 350 017	253 659	470 825	1.72	1.36

Notes: [a] Current ratio — ratio of consolidated current assets to consolidated current liabilities
[b] Liquidity ratio — ratio of consolidated liquid assets (current assets less stocks) to consolidated current liabilities
Source: BP consolidated balance sheets (see Appendix 3.1(e))

Fuel oil and the Admiralty 1912-14

assets. This was an alarming state of affairs because, if creditors had pressed for payment, the Company would have been unable to meet short term claims out of its liquid assets and could have been put into liquidation by the creditors. The current ratio, that is the ratio of current assets to current liabilities, summarises a company's liquidity position. A ratio of less than one means that current assets are insufficient to meet current liabilities. In 1913 the current ratio based on the consolidated balance sheets was 0.77. In 1914 it fell to 0.55. By any impartial assessment the Company was on the brink of financial ruin, dependent entirely upon the continued confidence of its creditors. In fact, the true liquidity position was even worse. Consolidated current assets are generally calculated with the inclusion of stocks of the commodity being traded. An objection to the

Table 5.3. *Statement of source and application of funds of the Anglo-Persian Oil Company group for the year ended 31 March 1913*

	£	£	£
Source of funds			
Sources outside the Company			
Capital subscribed			
Ordinary shares			—
Preference shares			90 670
			90 670
Application of funds			
General expenditure		46 893	
Increase in fixed assets			
Installations, etc.			160 188
Increase in current assets			
Stock		57 039	
Current investments		1 570	
Debtors		(16 449)	
Cash		(3 806)	
		38 354	
Less increase in current liabilities			
Creditors	4 299		
Loans	150 466		
		154 765	
Increase in net current assets			(116 411)
			90 670

Source: BP consolidated balance sheets (see Appendix 3.1(e))

Fuel oil and the Admiralty 1912-14

inclusion of such stock as a liquid asset of the Company in the years 1913 and 1914 is that it would have been exceedingly difficult to have disposed of the stock for any cash value. If the value of this questionable asset is ignored, the position of the Company appears even more precarious. The liquid ratio, that is the ratio of liquid assets (current assets less stock) to

Table 5.4. *Statement of source and application of funds of the Anglo-Persian Oil Company group for the year ended 31 March 1914*

	£	£	£
Source of funds			
Sources outside the Company			
Capital subscribed			
Ordinary shares			
Preference shares			—
Sources within the Company			
Increase in retained profits			
Profit for the year		5 017	
add back, depreciation, fixed assets, stores etc.			
Write down of capitalised general expenditure			265 980
			270 997
Application of funds			
Purchase price of Concession			—
Preliminary expenses			43 263
Increase in fixed assets			
Installations		243 111	
Stores		145 284	
			388 395
Less increase in liabilities			
Stock		67 277	
Current investments		(676)	
Debtors		15 900	
Cash		(7 110)	
		75 391	
Increase in liabilities			
Loans	128 456		
Creditors	107 596		
		236 052	
Increase in net current assets			(160 661)
			270 997

Source: BP consolidated balance sheets (see Appendix 3.1(e))

Fuel oil and the Admiralty 1912-14

current liabilities, was 0.44 for 1913 and 0.25 for 1914. If a quarter of the creditors had insisted upon immediate payment in 1914, the Company would have been unable to produce the cash.

The APOC turned to friends and creditors for funds during 1913 and 1914. The consolidated source and application of funds tables for 1913 and 1914, Tables 5.3 and 5.4, show that only £90 670, money outstanding on already issued preference shares, came in as capital. In 1913 the Company kept in business (1) by borrowing £150 466 from two directors, D'Arcy and Strathcona; (2) by increasing the money owed to creditors by £4299 and (3) by running down debts outstanding and cash balances by £16 449 and £3806 respectively. Financing development by the employment of current funds is a doubtful and dangerous practice and the deterioration of the current ratio serves as a forceful reminder of this. In 1914, despite the commencement of trading which furnished the first internally generated funds, the Company resorted again to the expedient of current funding. Additional loans of £128 456 were contracted, principally from the Burmah Oil Company, while credit increased by £107 596 and cash balances declined by £7110 to a low point of £26 731. The Company could not continue for long on this financial basis. Trading had commenced but it was not until 1915 that a trading profit was made and not until 1917 that the Company paid a dividend on the ordinary shares or even assumed the full burden of paying the dividend on the preference shares. The contingent liability to Burmah on account of its guarantee to pay the 6 per cent preference share dividend has so far been entirely ignored in the calculations of liabilities. By 1914 it amounted to £165 785 though it would only become payable after provision for depreciation and reserve and the payment of 8 per cent on the preference shares and 6 per cent on the ordinary shares, healthy financial conditions which did not prevail until 1918.

Why did the Company find itself in such a dangerous financial position? Because both the costs of developing the Concession and the time it took before operations could commence were underestimated. The estimates of initial expenditure and potential earnings indicated in the Company's prospectus are shown in Table 5.5.

Actual costs as revealed by the consolidated balance sheet for 31 March 1914, the first year in which the Company presented a profit and loss account, were roughly double the estimate of £1 200 000 development expenditure in the prospectus. Capital investment in installations cost £1 426 658, more than twice the estimate of £600 000. Preliminary expenses and the cost of the Concession also outstripped their estimates and amounted to £43 263 and £694 464 respectively. In 1914 current liabilities actually exceeded current assets, but if it is assumed that the figure of £191 500 shown in the prospectus for working capital was a reasonable

Fuel oil and the Admiralty 1912-14

minimum allowance then the total funds applied to 31 March 1914 would have been £2 355 885, £1 155 855 more than the £1 200 000 shown in the prospectus. Moreover, far from generating a trading profit of £142 800 as anticipated, there was a loss of £17 915 in 1914. The £1 500 000 raised from the public was insufficient to complete the work undertaken but the Company was not prepared to return to the market before trading was underway. The Board preferred the expedient of current financing to the risk of undermining public confidence whilst negotiations were being carried on with the Admiralty.

It is in the light of the Company's acute cash problems of 1913 and 1914 that the financial importance of the agreement with the Government on 20 May 1914 should be seen. The financial effects are illustrated in Table 5.6, the source and application of funds statement for 1914-15.

The payment of a 7s 6d call on the 2 million shares issued to HMG produced £750 000 in 1914. In addition the Government took up 1000

Table 5.5. *Estimated expenditure and profit in the prospectus 1909*

Repaying vendors their expenditure to date connected with acquiring, the Concession, exploring, drilling, &c., including interest			say £	381 250
Preliminary expenses				11 500
Brokerage				15 750
Cost of pipelines, pumping stations, field tanks, &c.				300 000
Cost of refinery, tanks, &c.				200 000
Further drilling and other field work				100 000
				£1 008 500
Surplus available for working capital and interest on debentures during construction				191 500
				£1 200 000
With the above first instalment of plant it is estimated that the Company will be in a position to earn approximately:				
Working profits			say	£ 270 000
Less Depreciation on plant	say	£50 000		
Cost of management and all contingencies in United Kingdom	say	£20 000		
Debenture interest	say	£30 000		
				(100 000)
				£170 000
16 per cent royalty to Persian Government				(27 200)
				£142 800

Source: BP APOC prospectus 1909

Table 5.6. *Statement of source and application of funds of the Anglo-Persian Oil Company group for the year ended 31 March 1915*

	£	£	£
Source of funds			
Sources outside the Company			
Capital subscribed			
Ordinary shares		750 000	
Preference shares		100 000	
			850 000
Sources within the Company			
Increase in retained profits			
Profit for the year	62 258		
Tax paid to HMG	(142)		
		62 116	
add back depreciation, fixed assets stores, etc.		40 000	
		—	
			102 116
			952 116
Application of funds			
Purchase price of Concession			11 983
Preliminary expenses			6 207
Increase in fixed assets			
Installations		402 341	
Stores, etc.		42 582	
			444 923
Increase in long-term investments			
Due from Persian Government (compensation for cutting of pipeline)			18 178
Increase in current assets			
Stock		(20 785)	
Current investments		(8 743)	
Debtors		261 650	
Cash		104 763	
		336 885	
Less increase in liabilities			
Loans	(258 062)		
Creditors	124 122		
		133 940	
Increase in net current assets			470 825
			952 116

Source: BP consolidated balance sheets (see Appendix 3.1(e))

preference shares at par and the Burmah Oil Company 99 000, resulting in the injection of a further £100 000. It was this outside capital, not internally generated profits, which funded most of the year's capital expenditure of £444 923 and the increase in working capital of £470 825. The marked improvement in the current ratio, which moved from 0.55 in 1914 to 1.72 in 1915, was the result of paying off current loans totalling £258 062 and increasing cash deposits by £104 703 while the increase in creditors was more than offset by the increase of debtors. Taken together capital expenditures of £444 923, loan repayments of £258 062 and an increased cash balance of £104 763 totalled £807 748. In the absence of the £850 000 from outside funds it is difficult to imagine that the Company could have survived independently for long. If the £750 000 from the Government is deducted as a source of capital, but the £99 000 from Burmah and the actual retained profits are allowed as sources of funds (the most favourable case) and it is assumed that no capital expenditure took place, the current ratio would have still been no higher than 0.7. The Government's equity participation in the Company had the further beneficial effect of creating confidence in creditors. The option facing the Company was simple, Royal Dutch-Shell or the Government. Greenway made his choice of partner, but acceptance was agonisingly slow in coming, almost too late.

Black responded to Greenway's letter of 17 October by persuading his colleagues to explore certain possibilities, such as a contract with provision for advance payments, a contract with guaranteed interest and a contract with government share participation, which could be considered with Greenway.[186] This would enable detailed examination of the alternatives to be made, so that a decision could be taken once it was possible to do so. As the negotiations had been in the doldrums since July, even a partial resumption was preferable to waiting. On the Turkish front, too, there was little perceptible progress though H. Stock of Messrs Stock and Mountain had been appointed agent for the D'Arcy group in March.[187] The Turkish Petroleum Company did not seem confident of its ability to obtain a concession because of doubts over German rights, and further attempts at an association foundered.[188] The Board of Trade became involved in April, apprehensive that amalgamation might not be in the Company's best interests but uncertain of what to recommend.[189] The Foreign Office, however, was becoming impatient, and in May, June and July made strenuous efforts at a reconciliation between the groups.[190] Greenway and Cargill were content that 'the Concession will go to neither, at any rate for some time to come, which is just what we want'.[191] Greenway informed the Foreign Secretary of the dangerous consequences to the Company of the Royal Dutch-Shell group's acquiring a new source of supply closer to the major European markets, which would lead to a

Fuel oil and the Admiralty 1912-14

war of rates advantageous to them, so forcing the Company and Burmah into an amalgamation with them.[192] Nevertheless the Foreign Office persisted in trying to reach a solution.

7 IN PORT

In November there was a great boost to morale. Greenway received notice from Walpole that Slade appeared satisfied with the production potential of the oilfield and the operation of the refinery, but was concerned about the possibility of political trouble.[193] When he met Black ten days later he learnt officially of Slade's preliminary assessment that 'the Company will be able to carry out proposed contract'.[194]

A sense of reality was imparted to the discussions. Churchill authorised the preparation of a general bill to be submitted to the cabinet.[195] Hopwood advised some 'machinery in the contract which will enable us to check the expenditure of capital in whole and in part...and ensure the most satisfactory yield of oil fuel as to quality and cost'.[196] There was no question of giving the Company a *carte blanche*. He accepted that a good deal could be done 'by having a Director or two on the Board, but in addition we want safeguards in the Contract'.[197] This became a rather

Members of the Admiralty Commission in Persia 1913, left to right: Captain Noyes (in command of escort), E.H. Pascoe, Professor J. Cadman, Admiral Sir E. Slade and S. Lister James (in attendance)

contentious issue, ultimately settled through Sir John Bradbury, Joint Permanent Secretary of the Treasury, by a reasonable compromise between governmental responsibility and commercial accountability.

During serious discussions on 28 November, 4 and 15 December, 1913 alternative methods of raising the finance required were considered.[198] As higher interest rates were now applying in the money markets, advance payments were no longer feasible, so four options were suggested: firstly, scheme (A), government subscription for first 5 per cent debentures, £650 000, and second 5 per cent debentures, £1 350 000, with a free allotment of £500 000 fully paid ordinary shares, but this was unsatisfactory because of the high capitalisation and large amount of debenture debt; secondly, scheme (B), favoured by the directors, government subscription for first 5 per cent debentures, £900 000, 6 per cent cumulative preference shares, £600 000, and ordinary shares, £500 000, which was preferable because of a smaller capitalisation, smaller debenture debt, large proportion of first debentures to be secured by the Government, larger share of profits attachable to preference shares than debentures and more equitable to present shareholders; thirdly, scheme (C), least attractive to the directors, a 4 per cent government guaranteed bond for twenty years on an issue of debentures with a sufficient sum to yield after the deduction of expenses, £2 000 000, which would necessarily become public knowledge; and fourthly an arrangement in which the capital was loaned and gradually returned.[199]

By the end of 1913 on the basis of Slade's preliminary report Churchill caused a memorandum to be drawn up for submission to the Cabinet on points of principle.[200] Slade had privately informed Churchill that 'It seems to be a thoroughly sound concession, which may be developed to a gigantic extent with a large expenditure of capital. It would put us into a perfectly safe position as regards the supply of oil for naval purposes *if we had the control of the company* and at very reasonable cost.'[201] Churchill had no political inhibitions about a major shareholding in the Company, but his officials were more circumspect and the Treasury positively suspicious. The memorandum stipulated some budgetary control, the protection of the British identity of the Company and the nomination of two directors, among other provisions which were eventually incorporated in the final agreement. It proposed 'a contract for oil and an agreement for financial assistance subject to the Commission's final report'. It justified it because of 'the probable trend of events in oil production and prices and of engineering developments likely to affect oil consumption in the next few years'. It sought to achieve a financial balance by not crippling the company with debt in the short term with increased facilities, whilst avoiding in the long term the Government 'having borne a large part of the financial burden at the critical time...then leaving private capitalists to reap the profit if the affairs of the Company take a highly prosperous turn'.

Slade emphasised in his influential report of 26 January 1914 that,

the risk taken by the State in advancing at the outset the capital necessary to obtain control is in reality less than that which it would assume if it adopts the first method of financing the Company [scheme A], because it will have as an asset a proportionate share in the concession, which is in our opinion, an extremely valuable one, and will have the power to control the output so as to ensure the prudent development of the field in accordance with the requirements of His Majesty's Service.[202]

So concluded the Commission 'we strongly recommend that control of the Company should be secured by the Admiralty' and 'that it would be a national disaster if the concession were allowed to pass into foreign hands, and that all possible steps should be taken to maintain the Company as an independent British undertaking'. Admirals Fisher and Slade had served Churchill well. They provided the ammunition, he fired the guns but it was Greenway who supplied the powder. It was appropriately ironical at this time that Samuel, greeting Greenway effusively at the opening of the new Shell premises in London, should have indicated that 'he was very pleased to see me there as there was no doubt that our relations in the future must be of a much closer character', while Henri Deterding, general managing director of Royal Dutch-Shell, 'equally gushingly...took the opportunity of saying (with a twinkle in his eye) that though the new offices were now nearly filled up there was "still room left" for us and that he hoped we would bear this in mind'.[203] Such was the blend of the serious and the frivolous in the relations between the two companies.

Although the broad outlines of an agreement had been contained in Churchill's memorandum of 26 December, nearly two months passed before a case was submitted to the Cabinet. In the meantime, Churchill's naval programme was under fire, preventing a final decision being taken on the Admiralty contract. In retrospect the contemporary opposition may appear incredible but it was influential and articulate, as Margot Asquith's appeal to Lloyd George reveals, on 17 November 1913, 'Don't let Winston have too much money - it will hurt our party in every way - Labour and even Liberals. If we can't be a little economical when all foreign countries are peaceful I don't know *when* we can.'[204] At Cabinet meetings on 8 and 16 December there was no approval of the naval estimates.[205] On 1 January Lloyd George publicly disavowed them.

Hopwood, Churchill's close but uncertain colleague, gossiped to the King's private secretary, Lord Stamfordham, about the Cabinet being sick of the First Lord's 'perpetually undermining and exploiting its policy',[206] and his own desire for none 'of my Admiralty colleagues to get unnecessarily involved in what may easily become a disastrous conflict'.[207] Churchill on 12 January 1914 drew the attention of the King to the dangers facing the country and received a favourable answer.[208] Resignations were threatened. At further cabinet meetings on 29 January and 1 February at which a split was narrowly averted the naval estimates were passed.[209] Churchill could return to the contract. A week later the Cabinet 'after considerable discussions' agreed that 'a contract should be entered into with the Anglo-Persian Oil Company, whereby the Government would acquire for about £2 000 000 a controlling interest in that undertaking'.[210] It accepted that parliamentary sanction would be required and authorised the Admiralty to take the necessary action after 'careful consideration'. It was full sail ahead. Three weeks later, the general principles approved, a committee was appointed by the Cabinet to settle the details and prepare the parliamentary procedures.[211]

It was a curious coincidence, but at nearly the same time on 19 March, an agreement was signed which settled the question of the participation of the Deutsche Bank, the Royal Dutch-Shell group and the D'Arcy group, as the Company was referred to in this connection by the Foreign Office, in the Turkish Petroleum Company, from which the National Bank of Turkey had withdrawn.[212] The Foreign Office, in cooperation with the German Government, had virtually decided to impose a settlement, which facilitated, if it did not encourage, a rapprochement between the Deutsche Bank and the Company. At a meeting with the Foreign Office on 27 November, it was made clear that no better terms could be procured than ensured for the Company a 50 per cent shareholding in TPC, so that, as Greenway remarked, 'if these were not acceptable to us the Government could do no more on our behalf and would have to see if some other British Group could not be found to take our place, as the Government attached great importance to securing this additional British interest in Mesopotamia'.[213] Greenway had useful talks with Herr Stauss, oil adviser to the Deutsche Bank and managing director of the British Petroleum Company (the British subsidiary of the Deutsche Bank-controlled European Petroleum Union), in December and reached an understanding.[214] This was hastened by reports of Standard Oil, Russian, local Turkish interests and suspected Royal Dutch-Shell activity for an oil concession.[215]

Cargill was still a little sceptical about progress over reaching an agreement with the Government, but was reassured by Greenway and Slade that the negotiations had gone beyond individuals 'too far for there to be any possibility of our negotiations breaking down no matter what change may take place in the Government'.[216] Inseparable from such an important

Fuel oil and the Admiralty 1912-14

decision were the inter-departmental conferences, consultations, drafting and legal scrutinising in which the Admiralty and Treasury were principally involved. As had been previously noted, it was imperative for the Company to preserve its British identity and that 'development shall proceed on suitable lines to fulfil naval requirements without prejudice to the general commercial interests of the Company'.[217] Sir John Bradbury, who had succeeded Sir Robert Chalmers at the Treasury, was well-informed, pragmatic in his approach with a clear ascendency over his colleagues. He proposed that, as the transaction was essentially a speculative investment of public funds, it was right that the Treasury, bearing the risk, should take the dividends, thereby asserting an influential role in the affair.[218] It was in this respect that Bradbury argued that the two directors should be appointees of the Treasury in consultation with the Admiralty, for he disapproved of the possibility of the Admiralty acting directly in defence of its own interests if it dissented from the policy of the Company. In matters of dispute he believed that 'the points most likely to be involved in such appeals are (1) is a long view or a short view to be taken of the commercial interests of the Company and (2) whether the commercial interests of the Company are to be frankly subordinated to considerations of Admiralty policy?'[219]

The problem of the relationship between commercial opportunism and bureaucratic control, the imposition of a government veto, was a subject which Bradbury made his own and which virtually determined the relationship of the Company to the Government. He recognised as a potential danger that the Company, intent on maximising early returns, might embark on an improvident scheme of development which would be prejudicial 'not only to Admiralty interests but also to the ultimate interests of the shareholders and here we can hope to have the veto exercised with some success'.[220] It was in this respect limited to matters which did not involve an Admiralty interest that a veto might be applicable, but only with Treasury authorisation in consultation with the Admiralty. In other respects he contended 'so long as nearly half the capital of the undertaking is in private hands you cannot expect to have it explicitly recognised that the undertaking is not primarily a profit-making concern'. In his exposition he regarded it as important that there should be no 'hampering or interfering with the ordinary conduct of the Company's business from the purely commercial point of view' but he acknowledged that the Foreign Office should have 'a power of veto when questions of foreign policy arise, just as the Admiralty are to have in regard to questions of naval policy'. These reservations, which regulated the use of the Government veto and the conduct of the Government's directors, were formally explained in an accompanying Treasury letter, signed by Bradbury, to the

Fuel oil and the Admiralty 1912-14

contract and agreement and released for public knowledge in the House of Commons in 1929.

Greenway and Crisp, who drew up the original draft contract, were principally engaged on the Company's side throughout the protracted and complicated negotiations, which were often irksome. Slade, commiserating with Greenway on the delays, commented that 'Lawyers are proverbially dilatory folk and certainly Treasury lawyers seem to be peculiarly bad specimens of their class in that way.'[221] His colleagues were congratulatory about the way Greenway handled the negotiations. D'Arcy thought it was 'wonderfully carried thro'.[222] Wallace appreciating that 'the results that you have obtained are most remarkably successful' felt, probably truly, that 'no other one of us could have done for the Coy what you have done'.[223] Strathcona, whose imperial vision had sustained Greenway, was silent. He had died in January in his ninety-fourth year, an anchor of confidence in the troubled early times of the Company.[224]

On 11 May the Board of the Admiralty signalled their assent, the Cabinet approved on 13 May and a week later the agreement was signed.[225] The parliamentary debate took place on 17 June, conspicuous for emotion rather than reason.[226] Churchill, playing the champion and chauvinist, was rhetorically challenging and defiantly unscrupulous. His own comment, when questioned by Greenway after the result of the debate, in which 254 members voted with the Government and 18 against, 'how did you manage to carry the House with you so successfully?' was that 'it was his attack on monopolies and trusts that did it'.[227] Indeed he had traduced and unfairly impugned the integrity of Samuel, who had done much to pioneer the adoption of fuel oil for marine purposes.[228] It is a sobering and almost incredible fact that the product on which so much depended, the fuel oil produced, refined and supplied by the Company and which had been tested by the Admiralty, was below specification. Less than a week after the agreements had been signed, Campbell reported on a conference at the Admiralty, with Black, Slade and Mr Phillips (Admiralty chemist) attending, that 'It was stated at the outset that all Persian cargoes of Fuel Oil were unsatisfactory', except the first delivered by the *Soya Maru* in November 1913. The viscosity was too high for the oil, 'which was practically set at 32°F.'[229] Campbell had suggested blowing hot air through it, but this was more like a mediaeval recipe for thinning thick treacle. There was no difficulty in warmer climates and with agitation the oil liquidized readily, but in more temperate waters without heating it was a problem. Greenway disclosed to Hamilton in October 1914 that 'Slade has been in today...he says that the Admiralty are now being put to considerable difficulties in the North Sea in consequence of

Fuel oil and the Admiralty 1912-14

the unsatisfactory viscosity of our Oil'.[230] It was improved later during the war.[231]

Such technicalities were absent from the speeches of the members of Parliament, who were more concerned about the defensibility of the oilfield and pipeline in the turbulence of Persia and fears that the Russians would be provoked into annexing the northern provinces so that Persia would be irretrievably partitioned and lose its independence. Some criticised the Government for failing to disclose the details of the contract, amounting to charges of sharp practice. Others disapproved of Govern-

Evening News cartoon 18 June 1914

ment participation in private industry, or doubted the security of supply under war conditions or objected to Churchill's display of personal animosity. In the end Parliament and the leader in *The Times* seemed to agree that 'the most business-like course is to give the Admiralty the financial authority to act on it to a reasonable extent should the opportunity present itself, without being unduly tied down by the technicalities of Parliamentary procedure'.[232] On second thoughts *The Times*, which was in a particularly persophile period, visualised the real issue as a change in British Middle Eastern policy which 'may in the end lead them into responsibilities of a character which Ministers still seem unable to comprehend' and put that policy 'in the melting pot'.[233] *The Times* disliked 'the apparently reckless way in which this new enterprise has been initiated' and cautioned that 'We fear the country may come to regret an impetuous and careless undertaking.'[234] It was left, rather unexpectedly, to Professor E.G. Browne, the distinguished doyen of Persian studies and arch-critic of British policy towards Persia, in a letter to *The Times*, to put it in a more perceptive Persian perspective. 'Since,' he supposed, 'Great Britain can no longer remain indifferent to her fate, she may now use her influence strongly in this direction. Should this be the result of the Anglo-Persian oil contract it may, for all its dangerous potentialities, prove after all, to be a blessing in disguise.'[235] It was a pertinent reminder that the Concession was rooted in Persia, not Whitehall, irrespective of the preoccupation with fuel oil. In the period between 1914 and 1918, however, it was the uncertain attitude of the British Government and the obvious success of the operations in Persia in coping with the increasing war-time demands for fuel oil which principally effected the development of the Company.

6
THE GOVERNMENT AND THE COMPANY: THE EARLY YEARS 1914-19

I INTRODUCTION

The 'mariage de convenance' between the Anglo-Persian Oil Company and His Majesty's Government, which was witnessed at the Parliamentary Registry Office on 17 June 1914, was a mixed blessing.[1]

The early years were dominated by the First World War. The possibilities of the combustion engine became the realities of the bomber and the tank, dependent upon oil for their power. Thus the expeditionary force that went to France in 1914 had only 827 motor cars, 15 motor bicycles, and a horse for every three men, but at the Armistice there were 56 000 lorries, 23 000 motor cars and 34 000 motor bicycles, besides many tanks and aeroplanes.[2] The armies of the allies may have, according to Curzon, floated to victory on a wave of oil,[3] but, the supply of oil in 1917 was predominantly American. Oil had become a decisive strategic resource on a scale inconceivable when the Government acquired its shareholding in the Company. The circumstances under which this transformation took place, the widening range of interests which resulted and the international implications which followed, could not then have been imagined. It was, perhaps, the reality of practical objectives rather than any hypothetical justification which enabled the mutual relationship of Company and Government to adapt to a changing environment.

It is undeniable that the government shareholding in the Company changed the spirit of the D'Arcy Concession and had a profound impact on its standing within the context of international relations. The Company, however much it proclaimed its independence, was considered to be no longer just a private organisation, but a national enterprise for a national purpose. Most governments, consciously or not, believed that the hidden hand of the British Government was to be detected behind most, if not all, of the activities of the Company. On occasions, then, business differences resembled, indeed developed into, international crises and commercial transactions became politically complicated. Undesirable though it may have been, it was impossible to ignore this diplomatic dimension even

The Government and the Company: The early years

when the concessionary activities of the Company were confined to Persia.

The British Government was not oblivious of the possible external repercussions which might follow its acquisition of the major shareholding in the Company, but it was not over-concerned. A leader in *The Times* of 27 May 1914 had already brought to public notice the possible effect on Anglo-Russian relations,[4] which Churchill and Grey had not entirely ignored.[5] Still, the First Lord of the Admiralty was over-optimistic if not mistaken in assuming that 'we need not regard the Government interests in the Anglo-Persian as differing in character from a legitimate private British commercial interest'.[6] The initial Admiralty response to Russian reaction was to maintain that 'the sooner the Bill is through the House of Commons the better' and to propose the formation of a joint subsidiary company with Russian participation to work northern parts of the concessionary area in Persia, which would ensure that all possible Russian rights and interests were properly protected.[7] The provisions of the Anglo-Russian Agreement of 1907 relating to Persia had not been fully observed by the Russians in their activities in the northern provinces, but Grey was patient and conciliatory, reminding the Russian Foreign Minister, Serghei Sazanov, in 1914, of the independence and integrity of Persia. He regretted 'a general tendency for Russian political influence to extend into the neutral sphere'.[8]

Thus controversy with Russia was the first indication of the diplomatic element which would require attention in the Government's attitude towards the Company. Sazanov had informed Sir George Buchanan, the British ambassador in St Petersburg, that 'the action taken by His Majesty's Government had changed the whole character of concession ... he must ask us to state publicly that we would not avail ourselves of all the rights conferred on D'Arcy by the concession'.[9] There had, it was true, been Russian protests in 1901, and a decade later attitudes towards Persia had become the touchstone of Anglo-Russian relations. Although the diplomatic exchanges remained moderate in tone, the shrill comments of *Novoe Vremya* on 23 June were vehemently hostile, because 'nothing remains of the 1907 agreement beyond a piece of waste paper' and 'on account of the buying up of the Anglo-Persian Company, the neutral zone is abolished, and the region of exclusive British influence is advanced right up to the Kermanshah–Ispahan–Yezd line'.[10] Aggression had deprived Persia of her resources and as a result the integrity of Persia was jeopardised. The repetition of these accusations became a constant refrain in Russian propaganda directed at Persia and helped to perpetuate that feeling of insecurity which the Persian Government experienced in its dealings with the Company.

The Government and the Company: The early years

The question is, did successive British governments manipulate the activities of the Company for political purposes to pursue a predetermined and consistent national oil policy? Did the acquisition of the shareholding in the Company by the Government significantly change its oil perspective and contribute directly to fresh policies based on this new situation, for which, it must be remembered, the Government was only partially, and for a time reluctantly, responsible? Are Marian Kent's comments near the truth when she says in her study, *Oil and Empire*, that 'The development and pursuit of oil policies in the first two decades of the century laid clear lines for government and diplomacy'?[11]

Is Elizabeth Monroe closer to the mark in her account of Britain's moments of importance and impotence in the Middle East from 1914-56 when she writes that 'the purchase accounts for a world-wide impression of British Government interference in the trade. But in practice it produced no such thing ... The chief outcome of the arrangement was not a government venture in trade, but a highly profitable investment of public funds'? She concludes that 'all told British Government action in pursuit of Middle Eastern oil has been taken less often, and over much shorter periods, than is popularly imagined'.[12] Whatever the intention of the Government, the impression is more of improvisation in response to short-term considerations than anticipation of future considerations accompanied by positive pre-emptive action.[13]

It was not only that the British Government's response to a possible oil policy was ambiguous, but its attitude towards the Company itself was unpredictable in this period. This was particularly remarkable in the attempt to displace Greenway as Chairman. In November 1916, the exact date remains uncertain, Greenway was invited by F.C. Tiarks, an adviser to the Board of Trade and a partner in Schroders, the merchant bankers, to a dinner with Admiral Slade 'for the purpose of talking oil', as it was phrased.[14] Rather ironically as it was described by Greenway, it was intimated to him that

> the Board of Trade has expressed the view that it might be advisable to strengthen the Board in order to show a stronger front vis à vis the Shell Company and that in this connection it had been suggested that in view of the supposed 'personal antagonism' between myself and the Shell people - which antagonism it was admitted was solely due to the fact that the Shell people had always found me an obstacle to their schemes for securing control of the Anglo-Persian Company, and more particularly for having been responsible for inducing the Government to acquire an interest in that Company - it might be advisable for me to retire from the Chairmanship whilst at the same time continuing to give to it the benefit of my services by assisting the new Chairman in guiding the policy and administration of the Company.

The Government and the Company: The early years

It was an extraordinary suggestion. Greenway must have felt that he had been punched below the belt. His obstinacy was his self-defence. Preserving his dignity, Greenway replied that his only concern was 'the welfare of the Company' and that he might agree, subject to two conditions. Firstly, on personal grounds, he stipulated that the retirement should be effected so that it 'would remove the possibility of the change being regarded as a reflection upon my administration of the Company'. Secondly he required being 'satisfied that the change proposed would be in the best interests of the Company and of the Nation'.

It was disclosed that Slade was the nominee for chairman and that three new board members were to be appointed, 'men of standing in the City, one of them being a financier, another a shipping man, and a third a general business man', with the retirement of a similar number of present members. The proceedings had all the trappings of a *fait accompli*, but the conspirators lacked the spirit. Greenway recovered his nerve and retorted that 'it would be a serious mistake and utterly opposed to the interests of the shareholders whom I now represent were I to withdraw from the Company in this sudden way', particularly in view of the fact that none of the proposed new directors 'is acquainted with the present organisation and workings of the Company or has had any previous knowledge or experience of oil business'. Slade suggested an impractical compromise whereby Greenway should assist him 'as a general adviser on all the Company's affairs'.

It was a strange affair but the passage of time has effaced most of the details. It was curious that Slade should have been agreeable to replacing Greenway with whom he had and continued to have cordial and close relations and who shared all of Greenway's opposition to Royal Dutch-Shell. Inchcape apparently disapproved of the idea and stated at a board meeting on 15 December that 'it would not be to the interest of the Company that Mr Greenway should at the present stage withdraw from active association with the administration of the Company'.[15] Greenway was asked to retain his position for two more years. Slade was appointed vice-chairman. Tiarks and F. W. Lund, a shipping specialist, two of the proposed Board of Trade nominees for the Board, became directors of the Company in January 1917, contributing to its financial and shipping expertise. Greenway's position was restored subject to confirmation in 1918. The Board had been strengthened. It had been an anxious moment at a critical time, a bizarre incident. Within a month Greenway was successfully negotiating for the acquisition of the British Petroleum Co. Ltd, the key to the Company's marketing future. (See pp. 217-19)

In a different but important manner, the government shareholding influenced the relationship of Burmah to the Company, for Burmah's

The Government and the Company: The early years

predominant 97 per cent control of shares was reduced to 32.3 per cent. Greenway was no longer tied to the apron strings of Burmah. It is clear that once Greenway succeeded Wallace as managing director at the beginning of 1911 he took the decisive role in Company affairs. His direction of commercial activities and his handling of the negotiations with the Government gave him a prestige and experience which was reflected in increasing assertiveness and confidence. Unlike Wallace, who had been vice-chairman of Burmah, Greenway had never been on the Burmah Board. He had taken an independent line, frequently disagreeing with his Burmah directors, notably over the contracts with the Asiatic Petroleum Company during his negotiations with Waley Cohen, and his encouragement of fuel oil sales. This fundamental difference of attitude, far from narrowing over the years, diverged even more.

Greenway never disguised his determination to maintain the independence of the Company on a fully integrated basis with its own refineries, transportation system and marketing outlets. Cargill and his colleague, R.I. Watson, who, for all practical purposes, administered Burmah affairs in London from 1914 and liaised closely with Waley Cohen on Burmah–Shell relations, were less committed to such a policy and more prepared to compromise with their competitors on principles for the sake of market stability. It was not till the end of 1916 that the administration of the Company was centralised in London, in premises at Great Winchester Street, which became in all respects the Head Office. It was there that Greenway managed the Company, loyally assisted by Duncan Garrow, who had been transferred by Burmah on 27 July 1914 to become a director, and H.E. Nichols on 31 May 1915, who had once been an assistant secretary to D'Arcy. These three people constituted the general managing directorate during the first part of the war and, though their responsibilities overlapped, Garrow was mainly in charge of technical affairs and Nichols looked after administrative matters. During this period Greenway emerged as a chairman of immense energy, stamina, determination and occasional exasperation, who moulded the Company after his own image. It was a magisterial performance spanning over a decade during a formative time in the growth of the oil industry, not without its mistakes but always vigorous and clear in expression. Yet on that one occasion when the fate of the British Petroleum Company was in the balance, with Greenway striving to form an 'All-British' Company in which it would have been included, and opposing Royal Dutch-Shell attempts to acquire it, he almost became a commercial sacrifice on the government altar of political expediency.

What was the response of the British Government to the Company and how did it exercise its authority? The government shareholding was not a

The Government and the Company: The early years

gratuitous act of public altruism, but a deliberate investment of public funds because 'it was important and essential in Naval interests to secure [that] at least one large British Oil Company shall be maintained, having independent control of considerable supplies of natural petroleum, and bound to the Government by financial and contractual obligations'.[16] The emphasis was on the provision of fuel oil supplies to the Navy, not on the growth of the Company, nor on either the development of a domestic oil industry or on the formation of a comprehensive and concerted national oil policy. The expectation was that the action taken would 'ultimately prove to have contributed greatly to the *security of important naval supplies* and to a *very large economy of expenditure* in providing for a fuel which will without doubt became an absolute necessity in order to secure the *full efficiency* of *His Majesty's naval service*'[17] (italics mine). The objectives were limited and obvious. It was the responsibility of the government directors to ensure that they were attained without impairing the commercial viability of the Company or interfering with its managerial judgement. Herein lay the rub. The Company as it existed in 1914 was extremely weak in terms of resources, facilities and finance. The fulfilment of the Admiralty contract constituted a major part of its activities. It could not, however, remain a static entity, a mere procurement agency for a government department. Such a passive role had never been Greenway's intention. If, therefore, the Company developed and its activities expanded, there was at least the possibility, if not necessarily the inevitability, of a clash of interests.

It was to prevent this situation arising that the role and responsibilities of the government directors were defined in a letter of understanding drafted by Sir John Bradbury, permanent secretary to the Treasury, in May 1914 and publicly released in March 1929 (for complete text see Appendix 6.1). It still constitutes the basic terms of reference for government participation in the Company. Its main provisions are as follows:[18]

An ex officio director shall have the right to negative any resolution which may be proposed at a board or committee meeting, but that the other directors, or a majority of them, shall have the right to appeal therefrom to His Majesty's Government, which, for the purpose of the Article, is defined as meaning the Treasury and the Admiralty. His Majesty's Government are of the opinion that it would not be prudent or, indeed, practicable, to qualify the generality of the right to veto. On the other hand, it is felt that the ordinary directors (meaning by that expression the directors other than the ex officio directors), and incidentally the members of the company should have some safeguard in the matter. It is thought that the right which is to be given by the new Article to the ordinary directors of appealing to the two Departments will afford the requisite safeguard. The ordinary directors will, by appealing to the Departments, be in a position to ensure in regard

The Government and the Company: The early years

Lord Inchcape

Admiral Sir Edmond Slade

W. St. D. Jenkins

Sir Frederick Black

Government directors of the Anglo-Persian Oil Company 1914-32.

The Government and the Company: The early years

Sir Edward Packe

Lord Bradbury

Sir George Barstow

Government directors of the Anglo-Persian Oil Company 1914-32 (continued)

The Government and the Company: The early years

to any particular question that the right to veto is not exercised until the question has been considered and adjudicated upon by the Departments.

I am to add that His Majesty's Government do not propose to make use of the right of veto except in regard to matters of general policy, such as -

(1) The supervision of the activities of the company as they may affect questions of foreign naval or military policy;

(2) Any proposed sale of the company's undertaking or proposed change of the company's status;

(3) The control of new exploitation, sites of wells etc.;

(4) Sales of crude or fuel oil to foreigners, or such exceptional sales to other persons on long contracts as might endanger the due fulfilment of current Admiralty contracts:

and that their interference (if any) in the ordinary administration of the company as a commercial concern will be strictly limited to the minimum necessary to secure these objects. Further, in the case of any such interference, due regard will be paid to the financial interests of the company in which, under the proposed arrangement, the Government have themselves so large a stake.

Such were the guidelines under which the first government appointees, Admiral Sir Edward Slade and Lord Inchcape, who was a notable shipping entrepreneur and government adviser, acted. They received no further formal instructions and their respective interpretations of their responsibilities were much conditioned by their own inclinations, experience and perception of the welfare of the nation. Resembling at times a compass and at other times a shock absorber, the government directors were always a two way communications link between the Company and the Government, a pivot on which was balanced not only the priorities of government reached after a compromise between party political pressure and national preoccupations but also the requirements of a commercial enterprise in a competitive environment. It was notable, if accidental, that party political preoccupations during the war played little part in the relations between the Company and the Government.

Such then were some of the most important factors and issues which were to influence the evolving relationship of Company and Government in the early years. How fair is the comment of Sir John Cadman early in 1922, before he was appointed to the Board of the Company that, 'The operations of the Company have been very successful, but these have been achieved not because of, but in spite of the Government holding'?[19]

2 FINANCIAL OBJECTIVES AND OBJECTIONS

(a) The early calls on Government capital

The initial government investment of £2 001 000 was based on the estimated cost of improving the production facilities in Persia so as to carry

The Government and the Company: The early years

out the contract with the Admiralty for increasing fuel oil supplies. It was a simple contractual obligation, limited to a specific programme with no provision for any further commitment to guarantee the development of the Company. However Churchill may have extolled the attractions of a government sponsored oil industry during the parliamentary debates,[20] there was little enthusiasm in the Treasury for speculative enterprise. The outbreak of war in 1914 resulted in two contradictory trends. On the one hand it enabled the Treasury cautiously to delay calls on its existing investment obligations and defer requests for further capital issues; on the other hand it provided the Company with an opportunity to claim that the exigences of the war and rising costs necessitated increased oil investment in the national interest.

By the end of 1914 the Government had answered calls totalling 29 751 000, £38 000 on 19 August, £462 250 a day later and £250 750 on 30 November.[21] Four months later, because of rising expenditure and accelerating purchases to anticipate shortages of materials, the Company made another call, making 10s in the £1 in all. The Treasury demurred and suggested that 'for the time being the Company should borrow such sums as are immediately necessary and that when the sum actually borrowed amounts to say £125 000 the Government would be willing to meet a call for the amount borrowed, interest on the amount so borrowed to be paid by the Government'.[22] The Company had no option but to agree, especially as they did not incur any extra financial liability. Inchcape made arrangements with the Provincial Bank for an overdraft of up to £250 000, interest being paid on the amount outstanding at 3½ per cent. On 15 July 1915, however, the Treasury paid the fifth call, £250 000, £1 000 000 in all, half of the sum due, on the understanding that the Company would refrain from making any further calls for six months.

Indeed it was a year before the Company made another call of 2s 6d in the £ and Greenway was able to claim with self-congratulation that 'it will be seen that everything in our power has been done to meet the wishes of the Lords Commissioners to defer calls as far as possible'.[23] He showed that £1 279 416 had so far been spent and argued that further capital payments were due and that the overdraft facilities had been utilised to their fullest extent. Inchcape and Slade supported the Company's case.[24] The Treasury answered the sixth call on 11 September 1916, though regretting that 'this further call should have become necessary and they hope that during the period of the war every endeavour will be made to reduce capital expenditure to the lowest possible figure'.[25] Bradbury exhorted the government directors to ensure that the Company complied with this request.[26]

The Government and the Company: The early years

So on 2 October 1916 at a board meeting Inchcape tabled a letter 'to see that the Company does not commit itself to any fresh capital expenditure during the remainder of the war'.[27] Greenway reacted as if a gauntlet had been thrown down. A week later he replied to Inchcape referring to the capital expenditure estimate of £2 777 000 and detailing the outstanding commitments of £933 000 which almost matched the unpaid government liabilities of £949 000. He remarked on the 'much higher costs of materials and wages, higher freights and to extra time occupied, in carrying out the work owing to the disturbance and Military operations in Persia, and to our staff being largely employed on Government work'.[28] Bradbury was alarmed fearing that the Treasury 'will be open to serious criticism if it does not do its best *to curtail the development activities of this Company* in which it is directly interested'[29] (italics mine). He was even prepared to propose that 'if any new contracts are being placed for works or materials, I think we ought to interfere unless it can be shown that the expenditure is absolutely necessary to enable the Company to meet Admiralty requirements during the war'. There was no justification for capital expenditure for potential postwar requirements, at any rate at government expense. Greenway challenged Bradbury's assertion in a letter to Inchcape on 20 October stressing that the envisaged expenditure represented 'commitment for Plant under actual contracts already placed, and freight, insurance, labour and other expenses connected with the erection and completion of same'.[30] Slade supported Greenway and uncompromisingly declared that 'the expenditure was absolutely necessary to enable the Company to meet Admiralty requirements *during the war*'.[31]

The last months of 1916 were particularly difficult for Greenway. The position in Persia was unstable, with the general insecurity of the southern area due to German intrigue, tribal unrest and the weak administration of the managing agents at Muhammara no less than the pressures of military demands upon supplies and the use of the Company's facilities. The jockeying between the Company and the Royal Dutch-Shell group continued. The German submarine menace was beginning to be effective, forcing the Government into measures for controlling oil supplies. A decision on the construction of a refinery at Swansea was awaited. Negotiations over the Company's possible acquisition of the erstwhile German-controlled subsidiary of the European Petroleum Union, the British Petroleum Company, had reached a critical stage with Greenway campaigning vociferously to have it included in the 'All-British' Company.

There was also some embarrassment at this time for the Treasury, which was liable to be criticised for conniving with the Company to avoid implementing tight war-time financial controls. It appealed to the

The Government and the Company: The early years

Admiralty for guidance.[32] The Admiralty stated that whilst fuel oil demand under the contract of 20 May 1914 was estimated to be 12 500 tons a month during June 1916–June 1917, supplies were actually running at 30 000 tons and were expected to be 40 000 tons from January 1917. It therefore contended that it was important that the Persian output should be developed to diminish purchases from, and dependence upon, the United States.[33] Persian production of fuel oil represented a fifth of naval needs. As long as that supply was not in jeopardy, the Treasury was not concerned with other issues. Greenway supplied more financial data which showed that provided the Government honoured its outstanding obligations of £949 000 and Company expenditure could be reduced to £845 000, total outgoings could be covered by the £1 206 000 estimated to be available by 30 March 1918.[34] The Treasury was satisfied that there was no immediate danger of the Company not meeting its current commitments. With the acquiescence of Inchcape, Bradbury therefore wrote that 'In the circumstances I think that the Company should be informed, as you suggest, that they must not rely on obtaining money by this means, i.e. a further call on the Government'.[35] As Inchcape made clear to the Board, this effectively precluded any further government funding while the war lasted.[36]

Greenway was not disposed to accept the consequences of this virtual financial veto. Mentioning at the annual general meeting on 8 January 1917 that the financial results were satisfactory he argued that 'they would have been vastly more favourable had we been in a position to transport and market our Benzine and Kerosene products ourselves'. Having raised capital from the Government in 1914 to ensure the Company's survival, it would have been ironic a couple of years later if his hopes for growth and independence were blighted by government financial timidity, if not default on its obligations. The Treasury was more concerned to limit its cash commitments than promote its investment opportunities. Greenway then attempted to sugar the financial pill by suggesting, on 2 January 1917, that the Treasury paid up the outstanding balance due on ordinary shares, £750 000, and the £199 000 on debenture stock, to which they had committed themselves in 1914. The Company would then simultaneously take up stock in the new war loan or long dated Treasury bills for a corresponding amount. The credit of the Company would thereby be enhanced and the Government books would balance, to the benefit of both parties. During the war the Company came to hold a substantial amount of war loan stock. It purchased £76 827 during 1916-17, £890 225 in 1917-18 and £1 136 666 in 1918-19. These investments in war loan stock may be contrasted with the amounts paid on calls on the ordinary shares by the Treasury, £250 000 in 1916-17. During 1917-18 and 1918-19, the Com-

The Government and the Company: The early years

pany lent substantially more to the Government than it received in subscriptions of funds from it.

Furthermore, Greenway raised the point that if the Company suffered losses through the Government defaulting on its payments, the directors might be held personally responsible 'should any cantankerous Preference shareholder at some future time choose to take proceedings against us'.[37] Moreover, he later intimated, 'it would be more harmful for the Government to appear as being unable to meet its liability at all which would be the case, and be disclosed in our Annual Accounts and doubtless be commented upon in the Press'.[38] The Treasury was almost indifferent, mislaying the correspondence and taking five weeks to reply negatively to the war loan suggestion.[39] Greenway protested to the Treasury that 'the usual rate in the case of outstanding calls is to charge the shareholder interest at the rate of 10% per annum', but all to no purpose.[40]

(b) Interference and the refinery

Amongst the items for which Greenway was seeking finance was the construction of a refinery at Swansea. 'This urgent matter will not be left outstanding any longer', he remarked in the middle of February 1917.[41] The problem was complicated, he complained to Inchcape, because in spite of the Company's desire 'to meet the views of all Departments of the Government - particularly in these difficult times' there was a divergence of departmental views so that the Company was often 'drawn into discussion which may put us into quite a false position'.[42] The idea of a refinery in England had first been discussed at a board meeting on 30 November 1914, when a sub-committee was appointed including Greenway, Inchcape, Slade and three other directors. It submitted its first progress report on 25 January 1915, when it was agreed that the problems over the viscosity of the fuel oil on its arrival from Persia were best solved by refrigeration treatment which could be more efficiently and conveniently undertaken in this country. Various possible sites were inspected and the right type of plant selected. The Director of Naval Contracts continued to criticise the quality of Persian fuel oil, which was jelling in cold temperatures. The Admiralty, therefore, on 23 December 1916 advocated the rapid construction of a suitable plant and that 'with this end in view the Admiralty has made arrangements for the proposed refinery at Swansea to be treated as urgent war work and all possible assistance will be given you in the provision of material and labour'.[43] Whatever the prompting that may have occurred from the wings by Slade, the Board interpreted these remarks as a green light and on 9 January 1917 made preparations to proceed with the project and register a private company for the purpose, subject to Inchcape's concurrence on behalf of the Treasury.[44]

The Company had attempted to beat the gun but they were brought back under starter's orders. The Treasury did not contest the recommendations of the Admiralty but it was suspicious of the motives of the Company. Barstow, Bradbury's deputy, implied that 'The Swansea scheme has been hatching for some little time and there would appear to have been some lack of frankness in communicating to us the intentions of the Admiralty and the Company. Admiral Slade appears to be one of its most energetic supporters.'[45] Barstow suggested that Bradbury played a waiting game. The Treasury could question but not ignore the opinion of the Admiralty, which if it upheld the refinery project on the grounds of naval importance meant either an immediate payment of the outstanding calls or gradually as required.

Barstow too was not averse to acting with 'some lack of frankness', asking Bradbury 'Is there anything we could say which would draw from the Admiralty a reply different from their letter?'[46] As the Admiralty letter was unsigned he suggested it merely represented 'Admiralty observations'. Inferring, without evidence, that the Company might change its plans, he indicated to the Admiralty that it 'should defer writing to us officially until the actual proposal had been received'.[47] His letter to the Ministry of Munitions was also loaded with its implications of 'the heavy requirements of both labour and material which will be entailed upon the Company if the undertaking is proceeded with'.[48] A month later the Board had received no official communication from the Treasury, though Inchcape mentioned their reluctance to authorise any further payments.[49] A further financial memorandum[50] was prepared on the lines of that submitted on 2 December 1916. Net income to 31 March was estimated at £974 000, capital expenditure exclusive of the refinery £698 000, leaving a potential balance of £279 000. The refinery case was based on the difference between a refrigeration plant at Ābādān costing £200 000 or a new refinery at Swansea costing £800 000 which would bring in an estimated profit of £300 000 and for which the Treasury would have to answer further calls for £600 000 out of the £949 000 it owed, which seemed not unreasonable.

With the resignation of Slade as a government director in March 1917, when he came off the active strength of the Navy, and his appointment as vice-chairman, Inchcape became the king-pin of Government–Company relations. He had to reconcile the restrictive impact on the Company's financial position of the Treasury's stand, with the stringencies of wartime credit. He was both Treasury watchdog and successful businessman. He hoped to settle the refinery question by having it examined by impartial independent experts, who would determine the advantage or disadvantage of setting up a refinery in the UK. Even Barstow agreed that an early decision should be reached and that 'The governing factor of the situation seems to be the Admiralty requirement ... a technical question and should be decided by technical experts. We may suspect that the real object of the proposal is to get round the Shell Agreement but without technical support we certainly could not resist the Admiralty proposal.'[51]

Barstow's minute reveals his perplexity, 'not at all clear what is the proper way in which to approach the problem'. He realised that it was 'not easy for the Treasury to interfere further in the Company's policy on grounds of objection to capital expenditure, if the Admiralty on their side are pressing them to proceed'. If naval policy required rapid action 'I do not think we are justified on grounds of finance to play for delay especially if there was the serious danger of our having to buy very large quantities of American oil at an inflated price if we put the Persian oil out of action.' Whilst Barstow ruminated, Bradbury temporised, complaining of a lack of instructions, which merely masked his indecision. It is high time, he wrote to Inchcape, 'something was settled but, as far as the Treasury is concerned, there is no proposition before us'.[52]

It was Inchcape, after extensive consultation, who produced the compromise acceptable to both parties. He decided that 'it would probably be more in the interests of the Company to erect the refinery at Swansea than at Abadan', for which 'the Company out of its surplus profits should be able to meet the bulk of the expenditure, and it should have no difficulty in financing any balance without calling up fresh capital'.[53] Barstow fell in to line, supposing that no 'more favourable result than Lord Inchcape's compromise can be reached'.[54] Bradbury agreed, with warnings about liability for excess profits tax.[55] In an effort to prevent a repetition of Greenway's earlier manoeuvres, he expected Inchcape 'to secure that the total capital commitment entered into (including what is temporarily financed from surplus profits) shall not involve any excess on the present authorised capital of the Company without the Treasury being consulted and approving beforehand'. The fat was in the fire. The Company felt that an unfair advantage was being taken of it to impose unacceptable conditions on its - commercial freedom, an objection which came to a head over Treasury objections to the registration of the National Oil Refineries Ltd, the company for the refinery at Swansea. Inchcape does not appear to have questioned the propriety of the Company's action notified to him by Greenway on 13 March[56] and communicated by him without comment to the Treasury the following day.[57] The Treasury felt that they had been deceived and remonstrated with Inchcape.[58] Greenway was no less upset,

The Government and the Company: The early years

feeling that 'an entirely new question of principle had been introduced which was quite unacceptable to the Company'.[59]

In brief it was Greenway's belief that 'His Majesty's Government does not lay down that the Board has to obtain Treasury sanction for anything it may wish to do', but that the Government has 'the right of negativing any resolution which may be proposed at any meeting'. It was the first occasion that the issue of government interference in the affairs of the Company had arisen. Inchcape passed on without comment Greenway's view about the 'Government being barred from any interference with their commercial policy',[60] but he did express regret to Greenway that 'we seem to have got into rather a mess in regard to the National Oil Company' and felt it should not have been registered 'without the official sanction of the Treasury'.[61] It was unfortunate that the refinery, the cause of so much controversy, was not commissioned by the time its priority rating was withdrawn on 7 January 1918.[62] Indeed its construction had hardly begun. Its need had been demonstrated even if its position in the war-time priority scale had slipped.

The whole episode had not been a very creditable affair and it left a bitter taste. Bradbury might have hoped in April 1917 that 'Mr. Greenway will recognise that it is not the desire of the Treasury to interfere with the commercial policy of the Company' but he could not refrain from remarking that

the entering by the Company into new capital commitments is clearly a matter in which during the war at any rate the Treasury is bound to interest itself while the question whether any particular transaction is consistent with the contractual obligations of the Company might easily raise questions extending outside commercial policy into commercial ethics and lead to questions in Parliament.[63]

Greenway was not prepared to let such an implied moral reprimand pass unnoticed. 'There is not,' he declared with unmistakable indignation,

nor ever has been, the slightest intention on the part of the Board of the Anglo-Persian Co. to disregard any of their contractual obligations, and that inasmuch as the Board is composed of a number of ex-officials, Bankers, Shipowners and Merchants of the highest standing, including a representative of their own, any questions of commercial ethics can safely be left to them without the Treasury bothering themselves about matters which come within the scope of 'the ordinary administration of the Company as a commercial concern' on which it was laid down that the Government should not interfere.[64]

(c) The acquisition of the British Petroleum Company Ltd and the financial dilemma

It was a curious coincidence that about the same time as the negotiations over the refinery became tense in March and April 1917 another crucial decision in respect of the Company was agitating the Treasury. The British Petroleum Company Ltd (BP Company) was formed in London on 21 November 1906, a subsidiary marketing organisation of the Europaische Petroleum Union (EPU) of Bremen. By 1914 it had a secure position in the British oil trade distributing Shell products, having over 850 depots and employing nearly 3000 people. Only the Anglo-American Oil Company, the English subsidiary of Standard Oil (NJ) till 1911, had a larger share of the market. In May 1914 BP Company declared a dividend of 14 per cent, £69 200, on its ordinary share capital of £494 300,[65] but suddenly, on the outbreak of the war, it and its associated companies, the Petroleum Steamship Company Ltd and the Homelight Oil Company Ltd, were classed as enemy concerns because of their German connections. Throughout much of 1915 and 1916, Greenway was involved in various negotiations over its future disposal (see Chapter 7). Finally on 25 January 1917 Greenway amongst others was asked by the Board of Trade if he was interested in acquiring the three companies which had been placed under the Public Trustee on 2 August 1916.[66] On 19 March Greenway opened negotiations with the Public Trustee, C.J. Stewart,[67] and board sanction for the terms proposed was given on 2 April.[68] Greenway justified his offer on the grounds that the Company would acquire a ready made marketing organisation which would otherwise take many years to establish and that, conversely, this would deprive the Royal Dutch-Shell group of the opportunity to extend its monopoly and control of the oil trade of this country.[69]

The final obstacle to be overcome was the attitude of the Treasury to the proposals and on 31 March 1917 Inchcape wrote to Bradbury asking 'whether there is any objection to it from the Treasury point of view'.[70] Inchcape himself was favourably impressed for 'commercially it seems sound', but he was not prepared for a settlement with the Public Trustee without Treasury agreement. A minute from Barstow to Bradbury illustrates the three main factors influencing the Treasury decision.[71] Satisfied with Inchcape's approval, Barstow felt that although 'it may not be necessary for the Treasury to consider the matter in its commercial aspect', it was firstly essential to answer the question, 'Is it desirable that the Anglo-Persian Oil Co. in which Government credit is so largely involved should acquire an interest outside the Persian Oil fields?' Barstow presumed that 'it was certainly to the national interest that a British Government-controlled Co. rather than either Standard Oil, Shell or other leading oil interests should acquire the assets in question'. Yet even if that was so, Barstow had to admit that it was not 'what was intended when the Government went into Persian Oil. The object was to secure navy supplies. Might not Parliament object that they did not grant funds to the

The Government and the Company: The early years

Crown to enable it to invest in a Company dealing with other oil interests?' He advised consulting the Admiralty. Secondly, the Foreign Office might have a view on the policy of a government controlled-company dealing in oilfields in neutral countries.

Thirdly, there was the fundamental problem of the government shareholding if more capital had to be subscribed, for, in that case, declared Barstow, 'We should always be in the dilemma that if more capital is wanted and subscribed by the public, the Government control is weakened and if Government are to go on providing the capital we are plunging deeper and deeper into business in oil for which we have no special qualifications.' It was a very real dilemma and upon its ultimate resolution depended the fate of the Company. Was it to be bureaucratic or commercial at heart? Bradbury was in no doubt when he replied to Inchcape that 'the finance of the purchase will be self-contained, but it should be understood that the Treasury will not be called upon now or hereafter to find further capital (or alternatively to agree to an appeal to the public for further capital) beyond the authorised capital of the Company by reason of the purchase'.[72] He therefore advised that 'subject to this reservation, the Treasury would not offer any objection to the Company bidding for the property'. Inchcape reported this condition to Greenway on 10 April.[73] He emphasised that the commitments for the refinery were already 'pretty heavy' and that Greenway had to be absolutely sure of his financing arrangements. Greenway was confident of being 'quite easily able to finance' the purchase without diverting capital resources from Persian developments and without calling upon 'the Treasury for any assistance beyond the authorised Capital'.[74]

Greenway though relieved, was very concerned at the implications of Bradbury's restrictions on the raising of future capital because

obviously the Anglo-Persian Board cannot say today what developments or what extensions of the businesses of the three companies in question may become advisable in the future, and if such developments were likely to be of great advantage to the Government investment in the Anglo-Persian Company, it is not, I suppose, in the least probable that the Treasury would in ordinary peace times wish to take up a non-possumus attitude and say 'we will neither provide additional Capital ourselves, nor let you obtain it from the public'.

It was more important than just wishful thinking. It was central to Greenway's strategy for an integrated company. In a very real sense the BP Company and its associated subsidiaries represented the missing link, marketing, in the Company's chain connecting the oil well to the customer, without which its expansion in the post-war period would have been very limited. It became the nucleus around which the Company's distribution activities centred in the early 1920s. (See Chapters 7 and 11.)

The Government and the Company: The early years

(d) Funds for investment

By mid-1917 the outstanding calls due from the Government still amounted to £949 000. Once again the Company resorted to the short-term expedient of financing its rising expenditure by increasing its current liabilities. By 31 March 1917, total current liabilities amounted to £953 824 comprising bank loans, £161 000, and creditors, £792 824. This exceeded current assets of £727 600 by £226 224. In spite, however, of Bradbury's warning, demands for further capital were undiminished and in July Greenway made out a case for an additional £2 000 000 which he suggested raising by 6 per cent preference shares, participating up to 8 per cent, which would not affect voting rights. He justified these terms by the need to give 'the public a greater interest in the welfare and prosperity of the Company than they now have ... felt by the Board to be a matter of great importance - both politically and commercially - particularly now that the Company is entering into the Petroleum distributing business of the United Kingdom'.[75] Interestingly he earmarked 200 000 shares for gradual allocation to employees under a bonus and provident fund scheme with profit sharing, which was being considered. Greenway estimated expenditure of £2 350 000 in the near future, returning gross profits of £1 185 000, representing a yield of some 40 per cent on the ordinary share capital. If, he informed Inchcape, the Government had paid its calls on time, profits would have been higher, but only half the Company's programme had been completed. Moreover as shortages of oil from the United States were threatened and materials and labour were scarce, adequate financial provision was required immediately. He hoped the Capital Issues Committee would favour the authorisation 'in view of the great national importance of the work for which it is required and the Government's large financial interest in the Company'. A further reason for more finance, as Greenway admitted, was the necessity of keeping pace with the developments of other oil companies, especially the Shell and Royal Dutch Companies, which were much more heavily capitalised. He could not tolerate the Company being at a competitive disadvantage in comparison with its rivals.

The cost was too great for Inchcape and his reaction was petulant and very unfavourable, declaring to Bradbury that 'the issue of what are practically ordinary shares is uncommonly bad finance for the present ordinary shareholders'.[76] He later stated that 'the issue was being engineered for the benefit of Greenway, Tiarks and Company'. He alleged that 'Greenway and Slade are trying to rush this through in my absence',[77] accusations that were quite unsubstantiated. From his home in Scotland, while on holiday, he ridiculed the idea of public interest or brand loyalty,

The Government and the Company: The early years

for it was nonsense that 'the Company's business will benefit by the public holding the shares'. 'The public,' he affirmed, 'will buy their petrol in the cheapest market whether they are shareholders or not.' The idea was all 'humbug'[78] and he was not going to interrupt his holiday. He tersely advised that 'the smaller you can keep your ordinary capital, the better for the ordinary shareholder'[79] and advised the Treasury 'to pay up your calls if you conveniently can and let the Company borrow for their expansion'.[80] Inchcape seems to have misunderstood, assuming that Grenway had implied ordinary shares where he had only mentioned preference shares, which had been available to the public since 1909.

The Treasury was less flustered in its response on this occasion and more constructive in its approach. It recognised that there were two aspects of the contemplated issue, the justification of the large capital expenditure envisaged and the most expedient manner of raising the capital. It realised that the Company could not be deterred indefinitely from raising capital from the public, but could not accept that the proportion of the Government's ordinary capital would be reduced. It therefore seemed that 'it will really be better business for the Treasury to pay up its liability on the uncalled shares'.[81] Thus an appeal to the public would be postponed and the Company's sense of discrimination removed. Bradbury, whilst not rejecting the analysis, was not convinced that 'the additional capital is actually required for developments necessary to meet immediate naval requirements apart from the general developments of the Company's business after the war, which latter purpose is not a valid reason for a capital issue during the war'.[82] So he intended to reassure himself by consulting the Admiralty.

At a meeting of the Inter-Departmental Committee on Petroleum Products, which had been created as a war-time measure in February 1917, held on 18 September 1917 with Pretyman as chairman and Sir Boverton Redwood present as adviser,[83] Slade presented the case for the Company.[84] It was an important moment. There was no longer any pretence about basing the argument only on war-time supplies of naval fuel oil. The Company wanted to make certain of its capability to withstand the competitive post-war pressures. It possessed large productive resources, but lacked adequate facilities. Slade made five principal points. Firstly the existing throughput of the pipeline from Fields to Ābādān, 1 500 000 tons a year, was inadequate in view of possible increased commitments and needed to be doubled by the installation of auxiliary pumping stations. Secondly, the refinery capacity at Ābādān of 768 000 tons needed augmenting to process 1 200 000 tons a year to yield some 720 000 tons of fuel oil. Thirdly, the increasing offtake was already straining the jetty, loading, pumping and lighterage facilities, which needed improving

The Government and the Company: The early years

besides dredging to deepen the navigational channels. Fourthly, provision was needed for bunkering stations along the main maritime routes. Lastly, more tankers were required to transport the rising production of petroleum products, whose consumption was increasing. It was an ambitious, not a modest programme, which would involve a minimum expenditure of some £1 845 000. The committee was sympathetic, but was only empowered to deal with matters relevant to the war effort. It was informed that Admiralty requirements would rise from 30 000 tons monthly to 45 000 tons and was prepared to sanction raising £1 000 000 of fresh capital. Other items which could be defined as being concerned with reconstruction were referred to Dr Addison, the Minister of Reconstruction, formerly Minister of Munitions.

The outcome was not unsatisfactory to the Company. A senior government committee had been impressed by the presentation of their case. Treasury approval followed quickly and on 29 September the Government paid its final call of 7s 6d, £750 000 and £199 000 in respect of the 5 per cent debenture stock, £949 000 in all. Some six weeks later the Board was advised that Treasury sanction had been obtained for an issue of £1 000 000 preference (non-voting) shares ranking with those already issued and that the authority of the Capital Issues Committee had been received. On 19 November it was formally resolved by the Board to increase the issued capital by the creation of 1 000 000 additional preference shares.[85] The shares were issued *pari passu* with the preference share issue of 1909 bearing a dividend of 6 per cent participating to 8 per cent when the ordinary share dividends reached 6 per cent. They commanded a premium of 2s 6d which thus raised an additional £125 000 for the Company. Not long afterwards at a board meeting on 24 January, at which Inchcape was again present, it was agreed to create further debenture stock £1 800 000 issued as £199 000 to the Government, £201 000 to Burmah and £1 400 000 to the British Tanker Company.[86] This was the last financial operation during the war. It seemed that the operations of the Company were no longer to be confined to Persia. Not by Government intention but by the persistence of Greenway did the Company acquire a financial base from which to launch itself into the markets of the post-war era.

As for the Company's financial performance in the five years following the vital increase in the Company's equity by the creation of the Government's shareholding, the sources of funds drawn upon by the Company were principally internal. The commencement of trading in 1914 produced normal profits which were retained to finance the Company's growth. No dividend was paid until 1916–17. However, the reliance upon internal funds was not so much a declaration of independence from outside finance as a result of war-time restrictions upon the operation of the capital market and the Government's reluctance to take up further ordinary shares. As controls relaxed after the war the Company once again sought funds from the public.

The sources and applications of funds of the Company in the period 1914-19 are shown in Table 6.1. External sources provided £3 625 000 out of the £9 900 000 increase in funds. The composition of these funds is shown in Table 6.2, which shows the issues of shares and debentures by the Company. Ordinary shares increased by £2 000 000, the amount of the Government's shareholding under the agreement of May 1914. The Government's investment produced a flow of funds to the Company of £750 000 in 1914-15, £250 000 in 1915-16, £250 000 in 1916-17, and £750 000 in 1917-18, as the calls were met. The sale of preference shares produced £100 000 from the Government in 1914 and £1 125 000 from the public in 1917. The issue of the 1 000 000 preference shares, subscribed at a premium of 12.5 per cent (2s 6d) by the public in December 1917, was the main exercise in raising external finance. It was urgently required by the Company to keep development going during the war.

The £1 800 000 increase in debentures in 1918, shown in Table 6.2, was more a book-keeping exercise than a substantive source of new funds. According to the Company's Annual Report of 1918, 'further 5 per cent debenture Stock to the amount of £1 800 000 was issued for the purpose of providing additional Capital for the Company's subsidiary concerns'. The actual inflow of funds into the Company was, however, only £400 000, £199 000 being taken up by the Government and £210 000 by Burmah, the amount shown as a flow of funds from debentures in Table 6.1. The remaining 1 400 000 debentures were acquired by the British Tanker Company, a wholly owned subsidiary of the Company, an action which did nothing to increase the funds available to the Company. The issue of these debentures was a move to provide the necessary collateral for what amounted to a loan by the Public Trustee for Enemy Property to facilitate the acquisition of the BP Company by the Company which had been already agreed in 1917. The debentures were lodged with the Public Trustee as security for five annual payments of £280 000 in respect of the balance of the £2 000 000 purchase price of the BP Company.

The substantial growth in internally generated funds is evidence of the improvement in the Company's financial position after the financial crisis of 1914. Reserves grew from a deficit of £17 915 in 1914 to a surplus of £4 207 571 in 1919. Accumulated allocation for depreciation, an unknown but certainly negligible amount in 1914, rose to more than £2 million. The total increase in internally generated funds of some £6.4 million is approx-

The Government and the Company: The early years

Table 6.1 *Statement of source and application of funds of the Anglo-Persian Oil Company group 1914-19*

Source of funds	£	£	£
Sources outside the Company			
Increase in capital subscribed			
Ordinary shares		2 000 000	
Preference shares		1 100 000	
			3 100 000
Increase in share premium account			125 000
Increase in long-term liabilities			
Debentures			400 000
Sources within the Company			
Increase in retained profits		4 100 486	
add back, depreciation, fixed assets		2 051 995	
stores etc.		25 000	
			6 177 481
Increase in premium upon acquisition			107 254
			9 909 735
Application of funds			
Increase in purchase price of Concession			49 640
Increase in preliminary expenses			(37 238)
Increase in fixed assets			
Installations		5 125 326	
Stores etc.		1 184 927	
			6 310 253
Goodwill arising on acquisitions			1 005 964
Increase in long-term investments			
Due from Persian Government		697 978	
Investments		340 206	
			1 038 184
Increase in current assets			
Stock		557 520	
Current investments		2 145 049	
Debtors		1 140 012	
Cash		242 710	
		4 085 291	
Less increase in current liabilities			
Creditors	2 470 778		
Loans	71 581		
		2 542 359	
Increase in net current assets			1 542 932
			9 909 735

Source: BP consolidated balance sheets (see Appendix 3.1(e))

Table 6.2. *Issues of shares and debentures by the Anglo-Persian Oil Company group 1909-23*

Date		Ordinary shares nominal issue	Amount raised £	Preference shares nominal issue	Amount raised £	Debentures nominal issue	Amount raised £	6½ per cent notes	Gearing[a] per cent
1909	April	1 000 000	1 000 000	—	—	—	—	—	—
1909	October	—	—	600 000	600 000	600 000	600 000	—	120
1911	October	—	—	300 000	300 000	—	—	—	150
1914	May	2 000 000	2 000 000	100 000	100 000	—	—	—	53
1917	December	—	—	1 000 000	1 125 000	—	—	—	86
1918	December	—	—	—	—	1 800 000	1 800 000	—	146
1919	December	4 500 000	4 500 000	3 000 000	3 450 000	2 600 000	2 210 000	—	133
1921	March	—	—	3 500 000	3 500 000	—	—	—	180
1922	January	600 000	1 950 000	2 000 000	2 100 000	—	—	—	191
1923	January	850 000	3 187 500	—	—	—	—	—	173
1923	January	—	—	—	—	—	—	2 000 000	195

Debenture issues by Subsidiaries

1921	Britannic Estates	990 000
1922	Britannic Estates	335 000
1923	Britannic Estates	163 000
1924	Société Générale des Huiles de Pétrole	12 279

Note: [a] ratio of preference shares and debentures to ordinary shares, per cent
Source: BP consolidated balance sheets from file series 4P 6001 to 4P 7086

The Government and the Company: The early years

imately equivalent to the Company's capital expenditure upon fixed assets over the period.

Capital investment in the expansion of fixed assets absorbed the major part of the funds raised. The growth of accumulated fixed assets, at historic cost, is shown in Table 6.3. The years 1914-15 to 1916-17 witnessed a moderate expansion of the Company's installations and an increase in the value of the Company's fixed assets by about £600 000 in 1915-16 and the same again in 1916-17. In 1917-18 there was a marked acceleration in the rate of fixed asset formation which grew three and a half times to £2 126 563. The factors behind this are revealed in Table 6.4, which shows

Table 6.3. *Fixed assets and depreciation of the Anglo-Persian Oil Company group 1914-19*

	Accumulated fixed assets £	Increase in fixed assets for the year £	Accumulated depreciation £	Depreciation for the year £	Annual rate of provision for depreciation[a] per cent
1914–15	1 683 715	362 341	40 000	40 000	2.3
1915–16	2 332 653	638 938	311 500	271 500	11.6
1916–17	2 975 285	642 632	588 653	277 153	9.3
1917–18	5 101 848	2 126 563	1 463 694	875 041	17.2
1918–19	6 406 700	1 304 852	2 051 995	588 301	9.1

Note: [a] Ratio of depreciation for the year to accumulated fixed assets, per cent
Source: BP consolidated balance sheets (see Appendix 3.1(e))

Table 6.4. *Increase in fixed assets of the Anglo-Persian Oil Company group 1914-19* (£ increase in value, fixed assets at historic cost per annum)

	1914–15	1915–16	1916–17	1917–18	1918–19
Fields	na	na	63 311	98 923	143 924
Refineries	na	na	231 288	149 286	257 560
Pipelines	na	na	157 542	16 226	(12 495)
Tankers	na	na	222 063	1 145 827	380 775
Distribution[a]	na	na	—	729 442	537 521
Bunkering	na	na	—	—	—
Administration, etc.	na	na	(31 572)	(13 141)	(2 433)
Total	362 341	638 938	642 632	2 126 563	1 304 852

Notes: na not available
[a] Persian distribution facilities included with refineries
Source: BP consolidated balance sheets (see Appendix 3.1(e))

Table 6.5. *Distribution of fixed assets by activity of the Anglo-Persian Oil Company group 1909–19*

(£ fixed assets at historic cost)

	1909–10	1910–11	1911–12	1912–13	1913–14	1914–15	1915–16	%	1916–17	%	1917–18	%	1918–19	%
Fields	na	na	na	na	na	na	498 156	22	561 467	19	660 390	13	804 314	13
Refineries	na	na	na	na	na	na	940 871	40	1 172 159	39	1 321 445	26	1 579 005	25
Pipelines	na	na	na	na	na	na	585 868	25	743 409	25	759 635	15	747 140	11
Tankers	na	na	na	na	na	na	255 838	11	477 901	16	1 623 729	32	2 004 504	31
Distribution	na	na	na	na	na	na	—	—	—	—	729 442	14	1 266 963	20
Bunkering	na	na	na	na	na	na	—	—	—	—	—	—	—	—
Administration	na	na	na	na	na	na	51 920	2	20 348	1	7 207	—	4 774	—
Total	333 262	575 627	878 075	1 038 263	1 281 374 ⋆	1 643 715	2 332 653		2 975 284		5 101 848		6 406 700	

Notes: ⋆ less depreciation
na not available

Source: BP consolidated balance sheets (see Appendix 3.1(e))

The Government and the Company: The early years

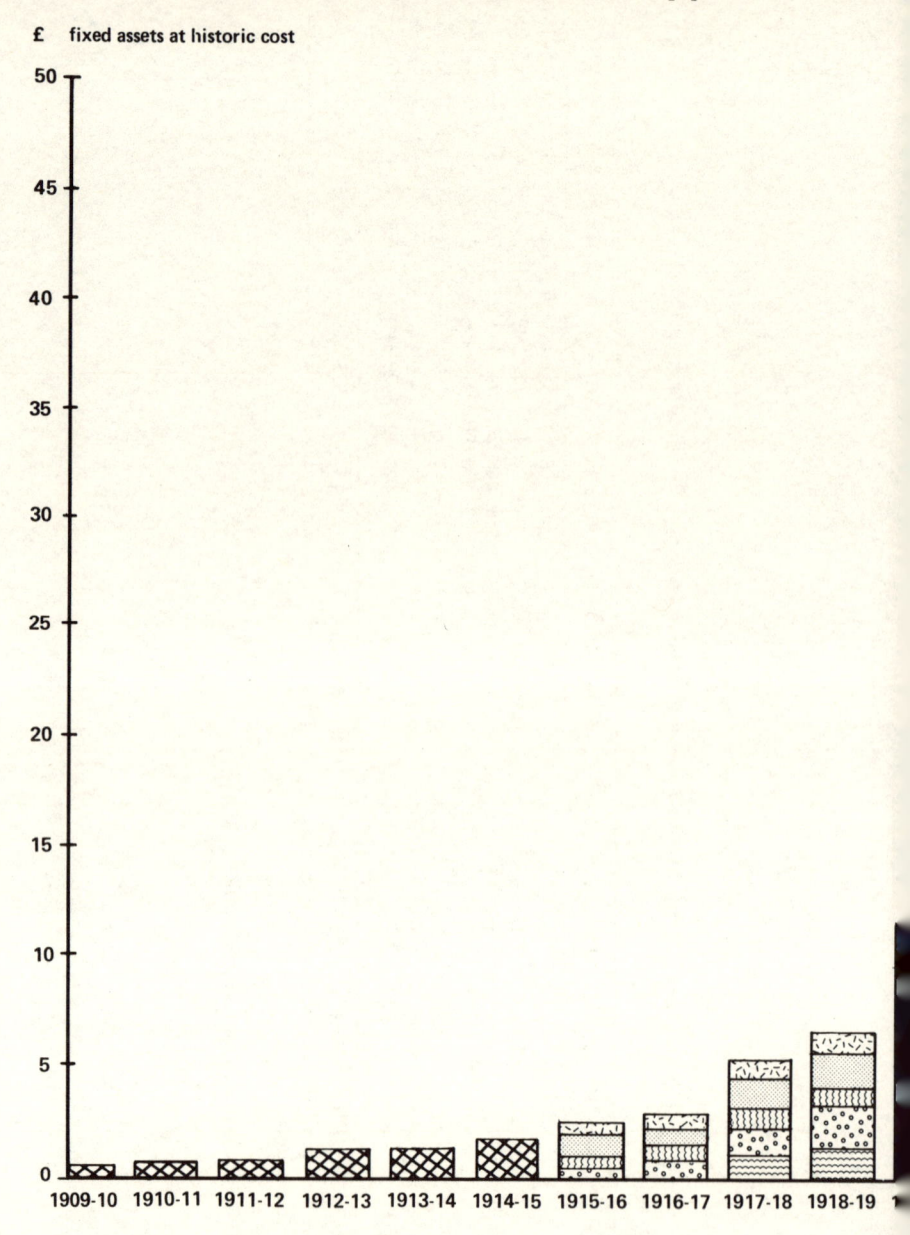

£ fixed assets at historic cost

The Government and the Company: The early years

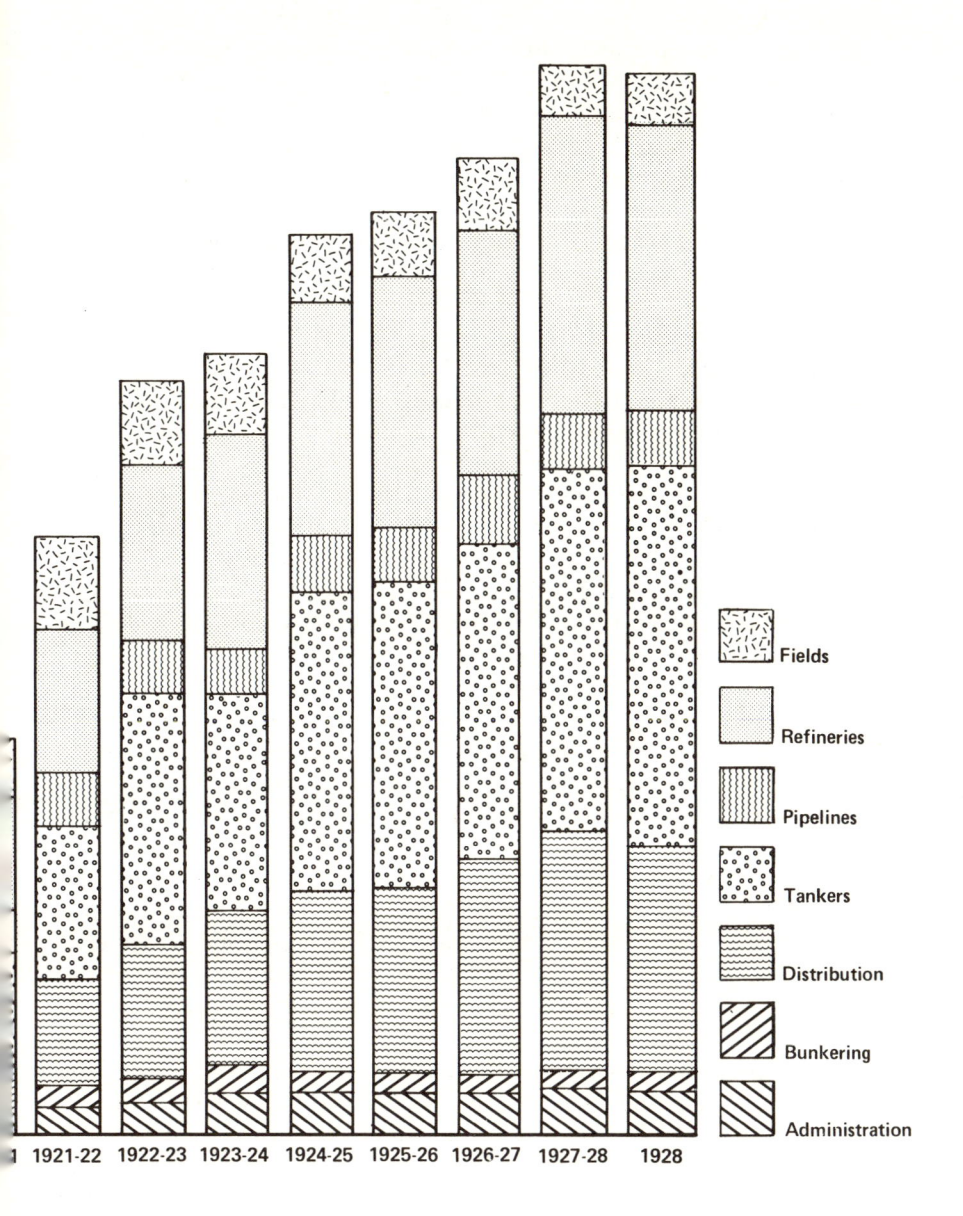

Figure 6.1 Growth of fixed assets of the Anglo-Persian Oil Company group 1909-28
Source: BP consolidated balance sheets (see Appendix 3.1(e))

the annual increase in the value of fixed assets in the different areas of the Company's activities. Heavy investment of £1 145 827 in tankers and £729 442 in distribution facilities accounted for most of the increase. The rise in the fixed asset value of the Company's tankers resulted from the addition of fourteen vessels to the fleet, two by purchase, six by order, and six upon the acquisition of the Petroleum Steamship Company, the tanker subsidiary of the Company, from the Public Trustee of Enemy Property in 1917. For further details see Chapter 7. It was the purchase of this latter company which provided the group with its first marketing outlets and accounts for the appearance of distribution assets in Table 6.4 for the first time in 1917–18.

The changing pattern of the Company's fixed assets is presented in Table 6.5 and illustrated in Figure 6.1, from details derived from the schedules to the accounts of the Company and its subsidiaries, which are only available from 1915–16 onwards. In the period 1909–10 to 1914–15, although the exact proportions are uncertain, virtually all the fixed assets were in Persia, in the oilfields and pipelines and at Ābādān. The pattern changed a little in the succeeding years 1915–16 and 1916–17 as the Company began to build up a tanker fleet, but still more than 80 per cent of fixed assets were located in Persia. During 1917–18 the Company was making the transition from a substantial producer of crude and products to a vertically integrated oil company. The pattern of the distribution of assets shifted in 1917–18 to approximately 50 per cent in Persia and 50 per cent outside, a balance which was roughly maintained to the mid-1920s.

The growth in the Company's fixed assets in the years 1914–15 to 1918–19 was, as already explained, financed largely from internally generated funds. This was possible because of the rapid improvement in the group's trading position in these years. The group's financial performance, based on consolidated accounts, is shown in Table 6.6. In 1914–15, 1915–16 and 1916–17 the group recorded a modest profit for the year before tax and dividends but after allowances had been made for depreciation, debenture and preference share interest, preliminary expenses and royalty. Expressed as a proportion of average net tangible assets the profit for the year constituted a return on investment of 1.8 per cent, 1.3 per cent and 10.3 per cent respectively. In 1916–17 the Company paid a dividend on the ordinary shares for the first time. A 6 per cent dividend on the ordinary capital was declared. Dividend payments of £128 219 consumed rather more than a quarter of the profit for the year. Nevertheless, the improvement in the Company's financial performance was such as to allow a six-fold rise in the increase in retained profit, from £43 313 in 1915–16 to £292 915 in 1916–17, which was used to help finance the growth of operations.

Table 6.6. *Anglo-Persian Oil Company group financial performance 1914-19*

Year	Profit for the year before tax and dividends[a] £	Tax paid to British Government[b] £	Dividends £	Retained profit £	Average net tangible assets for the year[c] £	Return on investment per cent[d]	Dividend rate per cent
1914–15	62 258	143	—	62 115	3 403 277	1.8	—
1915–16	55 085	11 772	—	43 313	4 005 991	1.3	—
1916–17	457 555	36 421	128 219	292 915	4 424 105	10.3	6
1917–18	2 112 620	182 954	204 986	1 724 680	6 256 006	33.8	8
1918–19	2 651 931	374 468	300 000	1 977 463	8 795 225	30.1	10

Notes: [a] Profit after deduction of debenture and preference share interest, preliminary expenses, overhead charges and royalty
[b] Income tax, corporate tax, excess profits duty
[c] Average of consolidated assets, except for intangibles (goodwill), *less* current liabilities, at start and end of year
[d] Ratio of profit for the year to average net tangible assets

Source: BP consolidated balance sheets (see Appendix 3.1(e))

The Government and the Company: The early years

The year 1917-18 marks a transformation in the Company's financial position. The profit for the year increased four-fold from £457 555 in 1916-17 to £2 112 620 in 1917-18 representing a leap in the rate return on investment from 10.3 per cent to 33.8 per cent. Moreover, this profit figure was arrived at after greater deductions for depreciation than had been hitherto allocated. Provision for depreciation increased three-fold between 1916-17 and 1917-18, from £277 153 to £875 041 (Table 6.3), a rise in the rate of annual provision as a proportion of accumulated fixed assets from 9.3 per cent to 17.2 per cent, the highest rate achieved in any year to the mid-1920s. Ordinary shareholders benefited from the Company's improved performance by an increase in the rate of dividend of a third, from 6 per cent to 8 per cent. Ordinary share dividend payments increased from £128 219 in 1916-17 to £204 986 in 1917-18. Ordinary shareholders received 10 per cent of the profits for the year; the remaining 90 per cent, £1 724 680, was allocated to reserves and employed to finance the expanding capital expenditure programme.

The following year, 1918-19 saw a further increase in the dividend rate of 2 per cent taking the total to 10 per cent. Again, the £300 000 distributed to ordinary shares took only a small part of the group profit for the year of £2 651 931. The bulk of the profit, 89 per cent, was retained and used to fund the growth of fixed assets and an improvement in the Company's current liability position. Group profitability was maintained at a high rate and the return on investment of 30.1 per cent was only a little below the previous year's level.

The explanation for the improvement in the group's financial performance during 1917-18 and 1918-19 lies in the rising profitability of both the parent company and its subsidiaries. Income to the trading account of the Company is shown in Table 6.7. Dividends paid to the parent by subsidiaries rose between 1916-17 to 1917-18 from £220 651 to £758 564. The Company's 'profit from trading in Persia' also rose substantially from £440 208 to £1 050 436. This increase is largely attributable to the rise in the sheer volume of product sales which, as shown in Table 6.8, grew 74 per cent from 416 000 to 725 000 tons. A small increase of 12 per cent in the average price per ton of product sales by the Company, from £2 8s 10d to £2 15s, assisted the rise in profit from the Persian operations.

In the following year, 1918-19, the volume of sales again rose substantially, 39 per cent, from 725 279 tons to 1 010 568 tons and once more accounted for a large part of the increase in gross profits from £1 999 973 to £3 902 684. An increase in the average price per ton, from £2 15s to £3 16s 3d, 38 per cent, also made an important contribution. These increases in profits more than compensated for the decline in dividends from subsidiaries from £758 569 to £632 170.

Table 6.7. Anglo-Persian Oil Company – sources of income 1915-28

(£)

	1915–16	1916–17	1917–18	1918–19	1919–20	1920–21	1921–22	1922–23	1923–24	1924–25	1925–26	1926–27	1927–28	1928 9 months
Trading profit	85 663	440 208	1 050 437	2 206 751	2 563 031	4 142 915	3 615 063	3 174 349	2 444 399	4 229 587	5 408 497	7 336 386	2 738 939	2 527 324
Dividends from subsidiary companies	154 482	220 651	758 565	632 170	1 897 132	2 672 697	1 237 781*	853 947*	1 265 665*	1 844 662*	2 125 294*	2 314 887*	2 826 256*	2 380 950
Interest from subsidiary companies	—	—	—	—	—	—	—	324 603	492 627	592 128	335 441	250 672	127 335	200 813
Dividends from outside companies	—	—	—	—	—	—	—	—	—	—	30 479	24 462	123 094	61 469
Sales of shares	—	—	—	—	—	469	25 869	14 317	60 458	—	—	—	—	—
Changes in reserve against valuation of stocks	—	—	—	—	—	—	—	—	—	(59 576)	4 559	(388 522)	252 844	119 741
Other income	11 578	3 384	8 096	2 470	428	592 751	6 959	27 631	38 052	2 666	2 162	6 374	455 353	15 024
Total incomes	251 723	664 243	1 817 098	2 841 391	4 460 591	7 408 832	4 885 672	4 394 847	4 301 201	6 609 467	7 906 432	9 544 259	6 523 821	5 305 321

Notes: * less payments to Khans as guard fees
Source: BP schedules to the profit and loss accounts of the Anglo-Persian Oil Company from file series 4P 6001 to 4P 6029

Table 6.8. *Anglo-Persian Oil Company trading account – income from sales, volume of sales and profits on sales and services 1916-28*

	1916–17	1917–18	1918–19	1919–20	1920–21	1921–22	1922–23	1923–24	1924–25	1925–26	1926–27	1927–28	1928 9 months
Income from sales (£)													
Refined products	1 035 597	1 999 973	3 902 684	4 597 183	7 219 366	6 148 523	5 660 085	5 115 242	7 024 353	18 211 031	20 379 937	16 732 256	13 819 845
Crude oil	3	18	38	24 739	146 189	639 662	1 117 431	990 308	1 636 010	340 002	501 278	824 200	669 197
Enriched crude	—	—	—	—	—	—	55 933	471 617	122 335	195 114	188 423	45 027	57 935
	1 035 600	1 999 991	3 902 722	4 621 922	7 365 555	6 788 185	6 833 449	6 577 167	8 782 698	18 746 147	21 069 638	17 601 483	14 546 977
Volume of sales (tons)													
Refined products	416 386	725 275	1 010 553	1 066 134	1 228 775	1 577 917	1 717 363	1 793 768	2 353 776	3 727 530	4 107 442	4 127 617	3 264 742
Crude oil	4	4	15	48 235	156 337	540 214	939 641	1 204 423	1 323 096	193 608	258 866	408 480	323 140
Enriched crude	—	—	—	—	—	—	23 631	94 872	56 396	62 596	62 807	16 018	18 146
	416 390	725 279	1 010 568	1 114 369	1 385 112	2 118 131	2 680 635	3 093 063	3 733 268	3 983 734	4 429 115	4 552 115	3 606 028
Profit on sales and services (£)													
Refined products	389 561	1 050 223	2 174 506	2 545 233	4 303 863	3 694 561	2 957 383	2 312 492	3 275 503	4 362 881	6 143 361	1 588 041	1 492 474
Crude and enriched crude	—	—	—	—	—	(28 513)	205 003	(226 034)	390 629	274 745	387 710	229 112	252 829
Pipeline	48 564	31 562	56 156	70 164	(58 693)	71 176	254 489	503 215	672 267	775 428	816 799	921 786	782 019
	438 125	1 081 785	2 230 662	2 615 397	4 245 170	3 737 224	3 416 875	2 589 673	4 338 399	5 413 054	7 347 870	2 738 939	2 527 322

Source: BP schedules to the profit and loss accounts of the Anglo-Persian Oil Company from file series 4P 6001 to 4P 6029

The Government and the Company: The early years

The improvement in the group's financial performance during 1917-18 as well as providing funds for capital expenditure and dividends for the ordinary shareholders restored a healthy current asset balance. The Company's liquidity position during the years 1913-14 to 1918-19 is shown in Table 6.9. The calamitous cash position of 1913-14 was turned around in the succeeding year, 1914-15, principally by the injection of equity capital by the Government. During 1915-16, however, current assets fell while current liabilities mounted. Cash and debtors were run down while an overdraft facility of £112 000 from the National Provincial Bank increased the Company's indebtedness.

Current liabilities at the end of the same financial year exceeded current assets by £67 899. The deterioration continued in the following year 1916-17. The current ratio, that is the ratio of current assets to current liabilities, fell from 0.85 to 0.76 while the liquidity ratio, that is the ratio of current assets less stocks to current liabilities, remained at less than 0.6. Although cash balances, debtors and holdings of government stocks all grew they were outstripped by the large increase in the amount owed to creditors, which rose from £340 475 to £792 824.

In these years, as in 1912-14, creditors were an important source of funds for the Company. While resort to such financial expedients can never be a satisfactory solution to a shortage of funds, the exercise was probably less hazardous in the years 1915-16 and 1916-17 than it had been in 1912-13 and 1913-14. The Government's shareholding had given the Company a blue chip rating amongst investors. It may also have inspired a confidence among creditors that in the last resort the public purse would pay their bills. In 1917-18 net current assets moved into a more positive balance. The current ratio of 1.36 in 1917-18, followed by a ratio of 1.44 in the following year, suggested that the financial corner had been turned.

3 THE GOVERNMENT, THE COMPANY AND AN OIL POLICY

(a) Introduction

At the outbreak of war in August 1914 the problem of oil supplies was not an immediate issue for the British Government. As a Board of Trade memorandum later revealed, the oil situation in 1915 excited little sense of urgency, for 'the full importance of petroleum and its products for war purposes and the vital necessity for maintaining adequate stocks and supplies does not seem to have been fully appreciated until the latter half of 1916 when steps were taken to restrict the use of petrol'.[87] It was not until early in 1916 that any attempts were made to assess the importance of the oil dimension in national affairs and place in some perspective the different

Table 6.9. *Liquidity position of the Anglo-Persian Oil Company group 1914–19*

Date	Consolidated current assets		Consolidated current liabilities		Consolidated net current assets	Increase in net current assets on previous year	Current ratio[a]	Liquidity ratio[b]
		£		£	£	£		
1914 31 March	Cash and balances Debtors Current investments Stocks	26 731 83 903 8 743 147 415 266 792	Creditors Loans	225 895 258 062 483 957	(217 165)	(160 661)	0.55	0.25
1915 31 March	Cash and balances Debtors Current investments Stocks	131 494 345 553 — 126 629 603 676	Creditors Loans	350 017 — 350 017	253 659	470 825	1.72	1.36
1916 31 March	Cash and balances Debtors Current investments Stocks	35 835 199 422 — 149 319 384 576	Creditors Loans	340 475 112 000 452 475	(67 899)	(321 558)	0.85	0.52
1917 31 March	Cash and balances Debtors Current investments Stocks	164 348 329 113 76 827 157 312 727 600	Creditors Loans	792 824 161 000 953 824	(226 224)	(158 325)	0.76	0.59
1918 31 March	Cash and balances Debtors Current investments Stocks	277 069 1 049 865 967 082 481 955 2 775 971	Creditors Loans	1 757 653 285 344 2 042 997	732 974	959 198	1.36	1.12
1919 31 March	Cash and balances Debtors Current investments Stocks	269 441 1 223 915 2 153 792 704 935 4 352 083	Creditors Loans	2 696 673 329 643 3 026 316	1 325 767	542 729	1.44	1.2

Notes: [a] Current ratio — ratio of consolidated assets to consolidated current liabilities
[b] Liquidity ratio — ratio of consolidated liquid assets (current assets less stocks) to consolidated current liabilities

Source: BP consolidated balance sheets (see Appendix 3.1(e))

The Government and the Company: The early years

aspects of governmental requirements. The Foreign Office was primarily concerned with keeping its options open in the post-war period. The Admiralty, with its strategic responsibilities, argued for the importance of regular oil supplies. The Board of Trade was concerned to reconcile differing attitudes and took the initiative in comprehensively considering the national oil supply situation as a specific problem and proposing a particular solution.

The Board of Trade's attempt to achieve a combination of British oil interests in association with the Shell side of Royal Dutch-Shell under British executive and financial control failed in 1916, but it certainly succeeded in raising the basic elements in the formulation of policy which was to permeate all subsequent thought on the subject.[88] Only when the definite responsibility for oil affairs was entrusted to a supra-departmental organisation, the Petroleum Executive, was it feasible to promote a policy with any hope of success. Yet, whatever the political desirability, expediency or necessity for a Government oil policy, it had to be related to existing commercial realities and to the exigencies of war conditions. Policy was not imposed, it emerged as a compromise *modus operandi* resulting from the interaction of government priorities, international events, commercial responses and personal influences.

It is perhaps ironical that even when the Harcourt Committee, which was set up under the direction of the Petroleum Executive (see below pp. 252–60), reported later in similar terms to those of the Board of Trade, its recommendations were never implemented. The ending of the war lessened the sense of urgency, the preoccupations of making peace diverted the attentions of the politicians and the resumption of competitive trading concentrated the minds of the businessmen on the opportunities of the market. The British Government already had the advantages of a 'mixed' solution for it was associated with an oil company. It encouraged the supplying of British markets through the competition of oil companies. Though the attainment of a comprehensive government oil policy during the war proved abortive, the airing of the issues involved ultimately enhanced both the understanding of the importance of oil in national and international contexts and the involvement of the companies which traded in it. The triangular relationship of the Government, the Company and Royal Dutch-Shell had been central to the efforts to establish a common approach to the oil question.

(b) Amalgamation – a commercial proposition

It was unfortunate that the crucial importance of the naval supply contract and the declaration of war left little time for the conciliation of the

The Government and the Company: The early years

conflicting interests of the Government, the Company and Royal Dutch-Shell. It was regrettable, but probably unavoidable that Samuel was left to smart under his sense of injustice at the accusations with which he had been taunted.[89] Too much of a patriot, despite assertions to the contrary, and too much of a businessman to prejudice national supplies or his company's sales, he was, nevertheless, alarmed and reacted bitterly to the news of the Government's shareholding in the Company. He raised serious objections to it and criticised the 'grave harm' which it would cause his company. So did Henri (later Sir Henri) Deterding, who, as the Managing Director of Royal Dutch, which controlled 60 per cent of the combined Royal Dutch and Shell interests from 1906, was the most powerful person in the group.

Samuel had expected his marketing contracts with the Company to be regarded 'as practically a permanent arrangement', by means of which he expected virtually to control Persian oil production and, by entering into contracts with the Admiralty, to stabilise the Admiralty's fuel oil requirements from Persian sources.[90] He hoped to be in a position to supply the incremental demand so as to prevent the swamping of the market, the possible cutting of prices and the potential danger to which his business might be exposed, a proposal which Churchill unceremoniously characterised as 'an agreement with the Shell to keep prices up to the present blackmailing levels'.[91] Government participation in industry was an anathema to Samuel, who was quite opposed to 'the grave damages that must necessarily attach to the policy of the Government directly associating themselves with a company which must inevitably compete with commercial organisation in selling products'.[92] It must have seemed to Samuel and his directors that the Company would have fallen like a ripe plum into his basket of associated companies spread across the world, which declared dividends of 41 per cent in 1912, 48 per cent in 1913 and 49 per cent in 1914 (for comparable oil company dividends see Appendix 6.4).

The contribution of the Royal Dutch-Shell group to the war effort was acknowledged and in time Samuel's resentment mellowed and he was able to address his shareholders proudly and pointedly at the annual general meeting on 12 July 1916. 'We have no subvention,' he emphasised, 'or subsidy of any sort or kind from the British Government or from any other Government... But while we do not ask, or suggest, that we should have any subvention or subsidy, we do claim that we should be frankly recognised and supported as a great British Company. I cannot say that we have always had that support and help which is now, and at long last, recognised as our due.'[93] Yet the rivalry between his company and the Company remained fierce, and, as before, no opportunity was neglected

The Government and the Company: The early years

to score points off each other. Not until Greenway and Samuel took their last professional curtain calls in the mid-twenties did their antagonism cease to be one of the most intriguing performances of the commercial drama of the period.

Royal Dutch-Shell sought to redress the balance, which seemed to have tilted unfavourably against it, and seized the opportunity presented by the increased national war-time need for explosives, especially toluol, a constituent of oils for making TNT, in mid-1915 to propose an amalgamation with Burmah. It is likely that Watson of Burmah and Waley Cohen for Shell were in favour of more collaboration between their respective companies. Cargill, himself, was cautious, perhaps apprehensive of a closer association and preferred to keep his distance. There is, however, no doubt that at this time relations between Cargill and Greenway were strained. On 15 November 1915 there were acrimonious discussions between them, when Greenway accused Cargill of supporting Royal Dutch-Shell and causing 'the difficult situation which has been created in our camp by this continued advocacy of APC arguments and support of their outrageous claims'.[94] He offered 'to relinquish my position and let the Government nominate another Chairman'. The Admiralty rightly believed that the amalgamation was proposed because of 'the impossibility of disposing of the increased output of inferior Borneo Kerosene other than through a close working agreement with the Burmah Company'.[95] Sir Graham Greene, Secretary to the Admiralty, was sceptical and thought it indicated, 'the anxiety of the Shell interest to absorb the Burmah Company and secure control of the Indian market'. It was a pretext for 'putting forward an amalgamation scheme which otherwise stood no chance of receiving the attention of the Home or Indian Governments'.

The Admiralty opposed this amalgamation proposal because it supported the independence of Burmah and 'still more because of the strong interest which the Admiralty has in the development of the hitherto closely allied Company - the Anglo-Persian'.[96] The Admiralty took a broad view and recognised the usefulness of the 'Shell' companies as good contractors. It was 'desirous of treating them in an equitable manner', but not at the expense of undermining the Government's interests in the Company. Referring to the Company's interests in Mesopotamia, which had to be safeguarded, and the importance of preserving a 'valuable competitive element', the Admiralty had 'no hesitation in recommending that strong efforts be made to maintain the present independent status of the Burmah Oil Company'. The Foreign Office, as Grey expressed it then, was 'in entire accord'.[97] The Viceroy of India, Sir Charles Hardinge, was unambiguous, 'the amalgamation of Burmah Oil Company with Shell

The Government and the Company: The early years

group, [should] if possible, be prevented', and he was prepared to refuse further exploration licences to ensure this.[98]

In November, when Royal Dutch-Shell was approached again to increase supplies of toluol, to which it responded admirably, Waley Cohen repeated the amalgamation proposals, adding the alternative possibilities of government purchases of Borneo crude oil, which was especially rich in toluol, for treatment at Rangoon or a scheme for treating it at Shell's Suez Refinery.[99] Once again the Admiralty saw no reason to change its mind and the Foreign Office declared that 'it would be extremely undesirable if such an amalgamation were permitted'. It was preferable 'to limit as far as possible the expansion of the large oil trusts and to encourage the formation of independent groups of British shareholders' in order to stimulate competitive forces.[100]

The Company at first took little direct part in this controversy over the amalgamation proposals, though Slade was active behind the scenes in discouraging the idea. Greenway concentrated on the monopoly issue and the importance of independent British oil interests. In October 1915, replying to approaches from minority shareholders in the BP Company, Greenway acknowledged the weakness of the Company, which 'was not at the moment in a position to enter into the petroleum distributing trade of the United Kingdom' nor could it 'lend them any assistance, or appear as a possible purchaser of a concern which might become a powerful rival of the Shell and Standard groups'.[101] The Company had not yet declared a dividend. Its pipeline in Persia had been damaged in February. Greenway was not, however, a passive spectator, for at the suggestion of the Admiralty he had been negotiating in October 1915 with Lord Cowdray, Chairman of the Pearson group of companies, civil engineers with world-wide interests including oil properties in Mexico,[102] for 'the foundation of an "All-British" Company for the distribution of the petroleum products of the Anglo-Persian and Mexican Eagle Oil Companies – and possibly also those of the Burmah and of any other purely British companies which might be disposed to join the scheme'.[103] Such a company would have a capital of £6 000 000 and an annual oil production of not less than 4 000 000 tons, surpassing the Royal Dutch-Shell group in both capital and production. Lord Cowdray insisted on overall control but agreed to 'Government Directors with certain powers of veto outside of the commercial administration of the Company'.

Although collaboration with Lord Cowdray failed to materialise, the idea of a national oil company remained a conspicuous feature of Greenway's strategy to defend the Company's interests during 1916–17. Greenway estimated that the Company, by its dependence on the marketing contracts with Shell, lost 60–70 per cent, between £1 000 000 and

The Government and the Company: The early years

£1 500 000 annually on its products. Independence was profitable and explains why the future of the BP Company was eventually vital in countering the amalgamation proposals. It was Sir George Barnes, Joint Secretary of the Board of Trade, who first informed Greenway on 15 October that it was for sale and mentioned that Mr W. Runciman, President of the Board of Trade, had enquired 'whether this would not be a good opportunity for establishing a British controlled agency for the distribution of petroleum in the United Kingdom to counteract the foreign monopoly now existing'.[104]

Greenway, in a long effusive letter to Barnes extolling the virtues of an 'all-British Company', which was unashamedly and probably unwisely personal, claimed credit for his efforts extending over fifteen years to prevent the absorption of Burmah and the Company by the Shell group which had resulted in 'a death blow to the schemes of Sir Marcus and his associates for securing a world-wide monopoly of the oil trade'.[105] It was still his intention to prevent 'by every means in my power the growth and consolidation of a Monopoly which apart from being inimical to the Anglo-Persian Company, I have always regarded as a grave National danger ... a National calamity, both monetarily and politically'. So committed was he to this objective that he was prepared to describe the Company as 'virtually a *Government department* desirous of doing its best for the Nation'. This was strong meat and it was not surprising that the Board of Trade found it indigestible. Indeed, during the first half of 1916 there was much inter-departmental discussion on the oil situation arising out of the amalgamation scheme with Burmah proposed by Samuel and Waley Cohen, who repeated the contention that the government shareholding in the Company 'would lead to a conflict of interest with other Powers, which is not in the interests of the State' at conferences with government officials in January 1916.[106]

Greenway, deliberately or inadvertently, in February precipitated a review of the situation by raising another critical and relevant matter. He requested confirmation from the Foreign Office of the letter of 15 November 1915, which had declared that the Company would be given the complete oil rights over any portion of the Turkish Empire which came under British influence.[107] The Foreign Office refused to give that assurance, probably under the prompting of Alwyn Parker, who had become its oil expert. Early in March, Grey suggested that an early decision on oil questions was desirable. He favoured examining 'whether the Royal Dutch-Shell Group cannot be brought under British control, by an amalgamation with the Burmah and Anglo-Persian Companies, or otherwise'.[108] There were implications for foreign policy after the war because of the growing importance of the Mesopotamian issue.[109] Grey

The Government and the Company: The early years

was apprehensive that 'Neither the Burmah Oil Company nor the Anglo-Persian Oil Company appear to dispose of the economic independence, the areas of supply, or the commercial ability to enable them to fulfil the necessary conditions.' Later in March, Parker, in an intemperate memorandum, made a bitter, almost slanderous, indictment of the Company, accusing its management of incompetence and Slade of being 'unable to see anything but perfection in that Company'. He suspected that 'a full and frank investigation by an independent committee under a strong chairman is being burked, and that we are laying up for ourselves a large harvest of bad management, expense, litigation, and diplomatic friction'.[110] He rejected the continuing validity of the March 1914 agreement over Mesopotamian oil rights in favour of the Company.

The Foreign Office seems to have changed its attitude towards the Company, because it wished to have a free hand in post-war negotiations over Mesopotamia, but the Admiralty persisted in its support because 'oil fuel is of such vital importance to the British Navy'.[111] The Admiralty was not prepared 'to trust entirely to the goodwill and self-interest of commercial companies (whose interests are not necessarily those of their shareholders) for the necessary exploitation on which supplies depend', and it doubted whether any concessions which the Royal Dutch–Shell group could make 'would be in the slightest degree commensurate with the giving over to them of a privileged position and rights of immense commercial value in India, Persia and Mesopotamia'. The Foreign Office failed to succeed in summoning an inter-departmental conference and the Board of Trade in early May disputed successfully any linkage between the amalgamation proposals and the problems of Mesopotamian oil.[112]

The future of Mesopotamia became a contentious issue between the British and French Governments at this time. It was thought to have been settled by the Sykes–Picot Agreement, in which strategic rather than oil interests were uppermost, a view which was approved by the Indian Government.[113] It was not till two years later, in August 1918, that Maurice Hankey, Secretary to the War Cabinet, successfully drew the attention of the Cabinet to the oil potentialities of Mesopotamia, by briefing Balfour, then Foreign Secretary.[114] In the meantime the Admiralty accepted that no settlement of the important Mesopotamian oil problem for the Company could be effected 'until the political situation in that region is more defined',[115] a message which had already been conveyed by the Foreign Office to the Company on 17 May 1916.[116] The position of the Company was becoming less sure. In October the Foreign Office was explicit. It no longer acknowledged the validity of the November 1914 agreement on Mesopotamian rights.

The Government and the Company: The early years
(c) The future of oil supplies - a departmental initiative

The Board of Trade was not content to leave oil affairs so undecided between the rival attractions of the Royal Dutch-Shell inspired proposal of 'amalgamation' and the Company sponsored 'All-British' solution. So in August 1916 it drew up a memorandum for the consideration of the Cabinet entitled, 'The Future of Oil Supplies'.[117] It is an important document for it recognised for the first time the importance of the national oil supply situation. Firstly, it acknowledged that 'the war has made clear that it is imperatively necessary for His Majesty's Government to take immediate and effective action to safeguard the future oil supplies of the British Empire'. Secondly, it declared that 'the problem of supply is, therefore, no longer merely a commercial question it is an Imperial question of the first magnitude'. Two steps had to be immediately taken, firstly 'to bring the British sources of supply under British control, so that their development may not be restricted by foreign concerns in the interest of their oil fields outside the Empire' and, secondly, 'to obtain control of as large foreign sources of supply as possible'. That being so, the establishment of an 'All-British' Company or combination for these purposes would be inadequate to meet the case as supplies from Mexico were unstable and insufficient from Burma and Persia. Finally, 'the Board of Trade came to the conclusion that any combination to secure the oil supplies of the British Empire which did not include the Royal Dutch-Shell Group would be ineffective, and that the only practicable course was to endeavour to bring about a combination in which British interests should have the control'.

There was much ingenuity observable in the analysis for it was acknowledged (1) that there should be effective British control both as regards capital and in the actual management of the undertaking; (2) that there should be complete security against any transfer of this control to non-British interests; and (3) that as the Company or combination would be quasi-monopolistic, the interests of the consumers should be safeguarded. It was then, as later, realised that 'To obtain for British interests the control of the Royal Dutch Company ... is entirely out of the question.' What was at stake was really the Samuel interests, the original Shell Transport Company which held 40 per cent of the group capital, which would be brought under 'permanent and effective British control'. These Shell interests alone were inadequate. So the amalgamation proposals were revived, it being 'an essential condition of such a scheme ... that the Burmah Oil Company should be brought into the new combination' to guarantee a preponderance of British interests. Such a combination would involve no government expenditure, no tariff

The Government and the Company: The early years

protection and no change in the government shareholding in the Company. Such a new company, for example 'The Imperial Oil Company', would have a British shareholding of at least 51 per cent, a directorate composed of three nominees from the Royal Dutch-Shell and two from Burmah. The Board of Trade pressed the Cabinet for an early decision, because despite all the 'long and difficult negotiations' the Shell representatives, Samuel and Waley Cohen, would not be able to persuade their Dutch colleagues to improve on the offer. Lewis Harcourt, at the Board of Trade was recommending more than a temporary war-time expedient. The Government had to decide whether the scheme presented 'greater advantages than the alternative policy of declining to make any arrangement with all the consequences that would be likely to flow from such a decision after the war'.

Greenway was well aware of what was happening and on 8 July he had already protested desperately to the Board of Trade that an 'All British Company' with the Company as its nucleus was a 'National necessity' and that this 'unique opportunity' for 'securing the foundation for a national centre of the oil trade of the Empire' must not be missed.[118] It was a curious reversal of accepted laissez-faire business attitudes, with the Government being implored to take a directly interventionist interest in private enterprise. Yet, the circumstances were exceptional. Greenway was not peddling philosophical panaceas, but struggling very energetically, with a mixture of commercial revivalism and practical politics, to preserve the independence of the Company lest 'British control of the Oil business of the United Kingdom be lost, and the grip of the Monopolists on the Oil trade of the country will become stronger than ever'. Information about the alleged war-time activities of Scandinavian subsidiaries of the Royal Dutch-Shell group was leaked, insinuating that they were trading with the enemy. Lobbying was encouraged to discredit their motives.[119]

The Company was in the doldrums, and in financial straits again — its supply of oil having been cut off in Persia for five months in 1915 through sabotage to its pipeline. Though Greenway had failed to persuade the Board of Trade not to put forward its 'Combination' proposals, Slade, taking conspicuous, almost unscrupulous, advantage of his official position spiritedly defended the Company, when he might have been expected to have been at least impartial. On 24 August 1916 in three trenchantly expressed memoranda, which, though repetitive in content, showed careful preparation, he denounced the Board of Trade scheme. In his 'Observations on the Board of Trade Memorandum on Oil'[120] he corrected mistakes and made critical remarks, objecting that: (1) there was no protection against a trade monopoly; (2) it amounted to actual foreign

The Government and the Company: The early years

domination in place of nominal British control; (3) it abandoned to foreign interests British sources of and commercial trade in petroleum products; (4) the monopolists' position was strengthened; (5) it meant rising prices; (6) it increased the insecurity of oil products in national emergencies; (7) revenue would be lost to the Exchequer; and lastly it would disturb the government shareholding in the Company. He had little trust in formal guarantees, paper provisions were ineffectual. He suspected that Royal Dutch-Shell influence would become paramount, 'a very extreme case of the tail being made to wag the dog'. He was convinced that the proposed 'combination' would be disastrous for the Company, which could never 'hope to obtain for its products anything more than a proportion of their actual value'.

Slade proposed a further solution based on Greenway's original idea of the 'All-British' company, which he elaborated in a secret memorandum entitled 'Petroleum Supplies and Distribution,' a 'National Oil Company', composed exclusively of British participation.[121] Slade pressed for a more radical strategy resembling Churchill's ambitious programme in the July 1913 Commons debate, when he opened up vistas of a national oil industry, like the naval dockyards, under Admiralty control. Slade, however, more realistic though no less visionary, looked forward to the time when 'the Nation would secure an independent position in oil as it now holds in coal'. He proposed that 'in order to exclude Foreign influence and to prevent an Oil Monopoly it is essential that H.M. Government should become a predominating factor in Oil *Production* and secure a controlling influence in the Distribution business of the Empire'. He envisaged an enlarged Company strengthened by Burmah and a revitalised BP Company not only in producing crude oil but also 'as the Distributing Agents in the British Empire for Oil Products'. Slade contended, rather deceptively, that in the Board of Trade scheme 'the Shell group in effect absorbs the British companies', but that in his proposal 'The British Companies would absorb the Shell.'

In another memorandum on 'The Strategic Importance of the Control of Petroleum' the prolific Admiral further expanded his proposals, proclaiming that no foreign interests for commercial or political reasons should 'have any power of hampering either the development of our own resources or shall control in anyway the distribution of the oil'.[122] Using for the first time in this connection the word 'policy', Slade defined it for the Government as consisting of: (1) retaining the effective control of British petroleum resources as far as possible entirely in its own hands; (2) the early construction of refineries in the United Kingdom to produce all the petroleum products required; (3) the establishment of marine installations at principal ports 'for the supply of oil fuel on commercial terms to the shipping trade'; and (4) the encouragement of oil exploration throughout the Empire and in countries under British control.

Meantime, in contrast with Slade's vehemence, official Admiralty reaction was muted. A. J. Balfour, who had replaced Churchill as First Lord of the Admiralty in May 1916, circulated on 18 August 'some stray reflections' prior to the first Cabinet committee meeting on the issue.[123] In a practical assessment he foresaw no difficulty for the Admiralty obtaining supplies in peace or war, provided it could carry and pay for them, for the current shortages were caused by shipping losses due to the first German U-boat offensive. He recognised that the Board of Trade scheme in the long term 'would apparently interfere with our complete control of the Persian oil field', but he seemed to be more concerned over prices. 'If,' he asked, 'there was no Government responsibility will the public be content to see the Government as merely a sleeping partner in a great monopoly, which is making what they will deem to be excessive profits out of their customers?' He was clearly apprehensive about the competence of Government 'to be responsible for the policy of a huge combine dealing with a prime necessity of modern life. Can we afford to *seem* responsible if in fact we are powerless?' It was a very pertinent political question.

After many discussions, Balfour in mid-October claimed that there appeared to be agreement: (1) that the contracts between Shell and the Company should be modified; (2) on a comprehensive arrangement between the new proposed company and the Company in respect of eastern bunkering business; (3) that Burmah shares in the Company were to be vested in trustees; and (4) that the BP Company was to be reconstructed to give the Company control.[124] It was a compromise designed to be helpful to everybody while favouring none. The Board of Trade took exception to the last condition alleging that 'this would entail the Government taking part in the purely commercial business of the distribution of oil products and that it would be unwise for them to do so', an extraordinary statement in view of the Company's acquisition of the BP Company a few months later.[125] Perhaps Balfour unconsciously refuted the objection, when he declared that 'the Anglo-Persian Oil Company can therefore perfectly well stand alone, and they may hope in time to become one of the largest oil companies in the world'. Balfour was clearly disposed to support the Company, and suggested that the capital invested by the Government in the Company was best protected by '(1) no foreign internal arrangement, (2) the provision of suitable refineries, (3) the provision of adequate transport arrangements, (4) an organisation at their free disposal for the distribution and sale of such of their products as are not taken by the Government'. His rather impractical suggestion of vesting the Burmah

The Government and the Company: The early years

shareholding in the Company in the hands of trustees was presumably meant to minimise the element of controversy.

Balfour maintained that 'nothing less than the free and unfettered use of the organisation of the British Company will be acceptable ... There would be such a large amount of by-products consequent on the amount of fuel required by the Admiralty, that it is essential to the commercial success of the Anglo-Persian Company that they should be placed on the market under the most favourable conditions.' This appreciation by the Admiralty of the commercial factor of the Company's business was a new dimension in the understanding of the importance of the Company. Nevertheless, safeguarding the business of the Company hardly amounted to a national oil policy. Yet, the Cabinet committee was authorised on 1 November to persevere in its efforts to reach agreement. The Board of Trade had done little more than propose an unrealistic scheme for the benefit of some commercial interests rather than all national requirements. Their behaviour resembled a disappointed Pandarus trying to entice reluctant suitors into a loveless union, the Company with Burmah or Shell with Burmah. There was an element of unreality in the proceedings, for, in a forthright letter to Greenway, Cargill remarked that

I cannot for one moment imagine the Shell group agreeing to the proposals put forward therein, nor do I think would the BOC ever consider an amalgamation with the Shell group under the scheme proposed which it seems to me would be bound to end in a fight in the West between the Shell-Burmah and the APOC Government organisation. As for a BOC/APOC amalgamation the APOC would have to show some years of great prosperity before the BOC shareholders could be got to look at that. The record of the APOC so far has inspired anything but confidence or satisfaction among them in the meantime.[126]

(d) The Petroleum Executive: The Harcourt Committee - a Government policy

It was not only the future of oil supplies that was unresolved on a national basis. A more pressing problem was the need for the organisation of war-time supplies which became belatedly first apparent early in 1916.[127] Imports of petrol had been about on average 40 000 tons a month in 1915, a little above the figure for 1914.[128] On 20 April 1916 the Board of Trade appointed the Petrol Control Committee, the first of the committees to deal with petroleum products during the war, 'to control the supply and distribution of Petrol and to consider what measures are necessary in the National Interest'.[129] By the time the Committee reported for the second time on 19 December it recommended that the oil question in all its aspects 'should be controlled by one Committee'.[130] By the end of 1916 there was no shortage of committees but there was a lack of coordination. At a

The Government and the Company: The early years

conference held at the Admiralty on 15 February 1917 an attempt to regulate a confused situation was made at the suggestion of the Minister for Munitions, by setting up a central inter-departmental petroleum committee which would 'exercise a general supervision as to policy', though the sense of direction and organisation were lacking.[131] There soon developed a fundamental difference of opinion between the Board of Trade, who believed the committee's function to be simply advisory on immediate problems, and the chairman, Pretyman, who was convinced that its work 'could not possibly be limited to war-time questions', but that 'one of its chief concerns would be possible future sources of supply'. The committee met in early March for the first time,[132] but within a few months its effectiveness had been diminished because 'Departmental jealousies and claims can only be effectively dealt with by an independent Committee...who have no interests to serve but those of the country and of the Government.'[133]

Walter Long, an able administrator, then Minister at the Colonial Office, was specially charged in May by the Prime Minister, Lloyd George, to 'undertake full responsibility for the supplies of oil products'.[134] Long had to settle the 'contradictory references and spheres of action that overlap and the lack of any authority to decide between the committees and departments'.[135] On 13 June the War Cabinet approved the proposals of Long and his petroleum adviser, John Cadman, who was Professor of Mining at Birmingham University and had served on the Admiralty Commission to Persia in 1913.[136] A Petroleum Committee was established, a compromise solution based on a 'controlling authority whose decision will be final subject to reference to the War Cabinet if the fighting forces are affected' but 'Executive action must be left to departments of state.' Though preoccupied by the pressing short-term requirement to allocate and distribute supplies for both military and civilian use while German submarine attacks on shipping mounted, Cadman looked ahead to technical improvements in transportation, better economic routing of shipping, increased exploitation of national resources and the investigation of petroleum substitutes.

In spite of the notable improvements brought about by the Petroleum Committee, responsibility for oil was still fragmented and it was felt desirable by Long and Cadman to have a more independent organisation to assert its control over petroleum subjects. As Long remarked in the House of Commons in October 1917 in connection with legislation on oil exploration in the United Kingdom, 'oil is probably more important at this moment than anything else; You may have men, munitions and money, but if you have not got oil, which is today the greatest motive power that you use, all your other advantages would be of comparatively

The Government and the Company: The early years

little value'.[137] The experience of 1917 with its crisis in oil supplies had revived the necessity for a proper oil policy and in November 1917 Long felt sufficiently confident to persuade the Prime Minister to set up a Petroleum Executive 'which will deal with all matters of policy in connection with the petroleum products in which His Majesty's Government is interested'.[138] It had taken a long time for such an executive organisation to emerge from the conflicting departmental interests, less from conviction over its inherent desirability than from a response to a desperate supply position. In the same year a Pool Board was formed composed mostly of executives from the oil companies to apportion out the available supplies of petroleum in relation to existing market shares.

The Petroleum Executive had hardly been set up with Cadman in charge, when Greenway, who welcomed its formation, nevertheless trailed his coat and with a shrewd sense of timing, suggested at the annual general meeting of the Company on 3 December, that

> what is wanted is an extension of the policy initiated when the Government secured a controlling interest in this Company, and the formation of an 'all British' Company, similarly controlled and free from foreign taint of any kind to deal with the development of oil fields outside the British Isles. This Company might absorb all the existing British oil-producing companies and at the same time undertake the examination and exploration, so far as concessions are obtainable of all the known oil territories of the world not already taken up by either these or other companies, but directing its attention more particularly to the British colonies and dependencies and to countries whose friendship can be relied upon.[139]

It was an urgent matter in view of the alarms over the possible decline in American production causing 'grave doubts as to whether she will be able to maintain her export trade for many years longer'.

It was a provocative speech. The President of the Board of Trade, Sir Albert Stanley, answering questions in Parliament, replied that 'The whole question is under careful consideration.'[140] *The Financial News* was enthusiastic, remarking that 'the Company was destined to be the biggest individual oil company in the world' and advocating a 'sound scheme ... to strengthen the control of the British Government over the Empire's supplies of this essential commodity' which should receive widespread support.[141] *The Times* agreed about 'a carefully planned scheme for ensuring, as far as is possible, that the supply of oil shall be sufficient to meet the vital needs of the Empire'.[142] Greenway had upstaged Samuel, who wrote an indignant letter to Cadman warning about the 'obvious disadvantages of the British Government associating themselves with a petroleum company entering into trading competition with other companies throughout the world'.[143] It was preferable to leave oil affairs to 'private companies, no matter what their nationality' than 'involve Governments in any strife

The Government and the Company: The early years

over such a bone of contention as to lead to international complications'. He advised that the position of his group 'might become so intolerable that they would withdraw the administration of their business from London' and that the City might no longer remain 'the headquarters of the Petroleum business'. The Government should desist from 'the mistaken course they have pursued of associating themselves directly with the Oil Trade and with one particular Group in it', advised Samuel. He was, however, prepared to accept a government director on the Shell Board, but this was unacceptable, as Cadman explained, because of the foreign control of Royal Dutch-Shell.

The Government was once again caught in the crossfire of the rival companies and Cadman, who had not long been appointed Head of the Petroleum Executive, was extremely annoyed, exasperated that the chickens in his new coop were pecking at each others' feathers and bitterly blamed Greenway.[144] He reprimanded him for having 'engineered' the reference to the 'all-British' company, forgetting that it had been a plank in Greenway's oil platform for over a couple of years and complained that it was very wrong at the present time.[145] Samuel's protests were taken seriously by Cadman, who cautioned against antagonising the Royal Dutch-Shell and Standard Oil Companies as they were supplying 'the greater part of our oil supplies'. Cadman proposed informing the Press that 'the formation of an all-British Oil Company was not under consideration at all at the present time'.

Sir Albert Stanley, President of the Board of Trade, felt that such a disavowal was like taking a sledge-hammer to crack a nut,[146] but Long disagreed, maintaining very strongly that 'if we do not speak out very plainly and definitely we shall estrange the Shell and perhaps even drive them away and this means disaster'.[147] Parker, at the Foreign Office, wrote to Cadman, with undisguised contempt for Greenway, that he was 'a very unreliable person, and that he runs the Anglo-Persian, with the support of Admiral Slade, who follows all Mr. Greenway recommends'.[148] He considered that 'a complaint should be made as to his indiscretion to the Government Directors ... in future all such utterances should be submitted in draft to HMG for their approval'.

The Admiralty, whilst rejecting 'the general tenor' of Samuel's letter, felt it was understandable in the light of Greenway's 'ill-advised' remarks.[149] It recognised the difficulties of the Company, being 'a Government controlled company' operating in areas 'outside the British dominions or definite spheres of interest', but acknowledged that without government backing it was unlikely that the Company, 'if left to itself, would be strong enough to maintain its position in the face of other great existing oil trusts and combines'. Therefore, it believed the lesser of two

Sir John Cadman 1918

evils was to continue government involvement in the Company, which necessitated 'much tact and judgement in the conduct of the affairs of the Company'. It ominously added that 'some change may shortly be

The Government and the Company: The early years

desirable in the personnel of the Board'. The sheet anchor of the Company was holding firm but was under considerable strain.

The result of this rumpus, according to Cadman, was the establishment of a committee 'in order to define what the policy of the Government was'.[150] The reason for the committee, known as the Harcourt Committee, after its chairman, Lewis Harcourt, formerly of the Board of Trade, was described by Long, on the advice of Cadman, as follows:

> It has become apparent to me that the time has arrived when it is necessary to formulate a policy by which His Majesty's Government shall be guided in all matters relating to the advancement and direction of petroleum industries. Up to the present time each department concerned has formulated its own policy and there has consequently been an absence of co-ordination which has frequently proved to be embarrassing while difficulty has been experienced in reconciling divergent interests. It is, therefore, my intention to entrust to a small Committee the important work of elaborating a general policy which shall be applicable in all cases and shall form a basis which will enable His Majesty's Government to deal uniformly with all questions relating to the industry whether departmental or commercial which may arise for decision and settlement in the future.[151]

It was certainly obvious that inter-departmental rivalry had thwarted attempts to appraise national oil problems comprehensively. It was equally true that discussions had more or less been confined to the single expedient of putting a British snaffle on the Royal Dutch-Shell group. This expedient, however speciously expressed, remained the principal intention. This was the fatal flaw in the approach to the problem of an oil policy proposed by the Harcourt Committee. An interesting aspect of the composition of the committee was Cadman's recommendation that it 'should consist of several businessmen of high standing who are not in anyway connected with oil companies, but who have had experience in dealing with large undertakings', as well as representatives of the major departments especially concerned with oil.[152] In this respect the appointment of Inchcape, proposed by Stanley Baldwin, Financial Secretary at the Treasury, was contested, but Andrew Bonar Law, Chancellor of the Exchequer, prevailed over Long's opposition, because he felt that it was 'essential that the Treasury representative should be a man of practical business experience'.[153] (For a list of the members of the committee see Appendix 6.2.)

The committee held its first meeting on 29 May 1918 at which an introductory tendentious memorandum by Cadman was presented, stating that 'the present war has demonstrated the numerous purposes for which the British Empire is dependent on petroleum and its products' of which 80 per cent of its supply came from the United States.[154] Advised that 'the industrial supremacy of the British Empire has been built upon

The Government and the Company: The early years

vast coal resources', the committee was asked 'to consider what steps should be taken to secure control of as much as possible of the world supply of natural petroleum'. The committee was reminded that the future of the Empire depended on a satisfactory solution of its oil problems and that 'Opportunities for strengthening the position exist now which may not recur, and no time should be lost in deciding on the policy which will ensure to the British Empire adequate supplies of petroleum products.' In practice the deliberations were mostly concerned with the question of the continuing government shareholding in the Company and the desirability of bringing the Royal Dutch-Shell group under British control. The proceedings of the committee fell into three main parts, firstly from May till the summer recess in mid-July, secondly from 19 September till Armistice Day, 11 November, comprising twelve sessions in all, principally concerned with the first stage of discussions on the Royal Dutch-Shell group. The third part lasted from the thirteenth meeting held on 14 November till the twenty-first and last meeting on 7 February 1919, when final proposals over the Royal Dutch-Shell group were formulated.

The committee at first concentrated on the possible control of Royal Dutch-Shell in the context of 'the general policy of the country as regards oil' and the directly interventionist attitude of Cadman in the matter. It was decided to 'hold out some definite offer to the Shell group in return for their making the whole group British and under a British group'.[155] It was easier to suggest the general objective than define the details of a proposal. Some members of the committee, Harcourt, Cadman, MacGowan and Lancelot Smith, held an exploratory meeting with Deterding and Samuel on 4 July, which the chairman optimistically described as 'very satisfactory, more so than he had expected'. Deterding did not reject 'a constitution which would mean British Control in some form or another over the Royal Dutch-Shell Combine', but believed that 'the Royal Dutch shareholders would agree to a British control of the whole combine if they were given additional capital that might be created ad hoc in the Anglo-Persian - say 2 million out of a total of 6 million - and he would be prepared to pay for this in cash, provided he had "an advisory seat" on the Board'.

Samuel offered safeguards on the transfer of his family shares which constituted almost half the voting power in Shell Transport and Trading Ltd. Deterding made no secret of his intention 'to utilise' to the greatest possible extent the exceedingly favourable geographical position of the different oilfields and installations then possessed by his group. He stressed the aspects of supply and demand and that the British market could not be insulated from market forces. Thus, in principle Deterding would accept some form of British control provided that it did not circumscribe

The Government and the Company: The early years

his commercial operations and on condition that he participated with a significant shareholding and voice in the Company.

At a later hearing in the autumn, Deterding was more emphatic, less compromising, declaring that, 'British control meant control by the public and not control by the Government', and that all proposals had to be assessed on commercial criteria. He was not impressed by phoney patriotism. The elimination of the government shareholding in the Company had now become a pre-requisite and he offered to buy the shares at par because he did not accept that 'any government ought to be a shareholder in any trading concern'. These conditions of Deterding were not substantially modified in subsequent discussions, except to become more stringent. Thus Deterding was only prepared to consider Shell interests in a deal that would have excluded those of Royal Dutch with its properties in the United States and Venezuela. On these terms the negotiations failed.

It proved impossible to provide the legal safeguards to ensure an effective enforceable control over the interests of Royal Dutch-Shell which were to have been transferred to a new company. The legal advisers, Mr A.C. Clausen, K.C., who believed that 'there did not seem any way of enforcing the undertakings or of imposing any penalty for non-fulfilment of measures to ensure British control', and Harold Brown of Messrs Linklaters, who remarked that 'the real difficulty was the question of Government interference in the commercial business of the Company if you wanted real control', finally had no practical solution to offer. Deterding was not perturbed at the breakdown in negotiations, which was reported on Armistice Day, for he 'would not be sorry if nothing happened' but Samuel was 'angry at the upshot of it' and relations between the two men became, again, somewhat soured. Samuel was much more emotionally committed to a 'British' solution than Deterding, who relied more on his business instincts for taking decisions.

It had early become obvious that the terms for any British control over Royal Dutch-Shell would have to take account of the Company and its government shareholding. Cadman was initially disposed to minimise the issue of the government shareholding, nonchalantly remarking that 'whether the money was Government money or private money it was all British capital', so 'we should endeavour to develop a scheme by which we could still maintain *British* control of a concern without necessarily having any Government money in it'. This was precisely the problem. Could proper British control be exercised without government money or intervention in one form or another? Could effective government control be maintained in a foreign-owned company? Who was paying the fiddler to play the tune he wanted?

The Government and the Company: The early years

Sir Robert Horne MP, a barrister with a commercial practice and successively Minister of Labour (1919), President of the Board of Trade (1920) and Chancellor of the Exchequer (1921), early realised that it was impossible to isolate the Company from the discussions, not only because the existing government shareholding could not be ignored, but because the government presence was an anathema to Deterding and Samuel. He warned realistically that 'we should not succeed with the Shell Company so long as the British Government held the majority of the shares in the Anglo-Persian'. Pretyman was in general agreement, reluctant to see any weakening of the government position in the Company 'without showing something very secure in the way of British control' instead of it.

This was the dilemma. Was effective British control of Royal Dutch-Shell feasible and if so could it only be achieved at the expense of the Company? Was Pretyman right that 'the Anglo-Persian was the creation of the British Government, and to leave it out in the cold, while fathering another company would be an impossible position'? What were the consequences for the Company if Harcourt was correct in surmising that, when approached, Deterding might reply that 'he would like to take the Anglo-Persian into the Combine, and that if we were not able to tell him that the Government shareholding was going to cease, our conversation would be more difficult'? The Company's position was clear, as Greenway expressed it in September to the committee. He pleaded for the Company to be allowed 'to proceed quietly with its development on ordinary business lines...as the nucleus of a real "All-British" Government-controlled Company'. He admitted with some bitterness and inconsistency, due to attempts then being made to curb the Company's activities, that 'the Government control of the Anglo-Persian Company was of no advantage to them' and that he would prefer 'to be free of Government holding of shares and of Government control altogether'. Greenway, who had received earlier reports on the equivocal position of the Company in the preliminary discussions of the committee, suspected the motives of Royal Dutch-Shell and their influence upon Cadman. He shared Inchcape's scepticism about the wisdom of an approach to Royal Dutch-Shell, because he bluntly believed that 'the great object of the Samuels and of Mr Deterding was really to eliminate the competition of the Anglo-Persian, and to secure supplies in the future'.

Reacting to these suspicions, Greenway and Slade lost no time in defending the Company and attacking its rivals. It had previously been agreed between the Treasury and the Petroleum Executive that 'the activities of the Anglo-Persian Oil Company in countries other than Persia may suitably be discussed by the committee'.[156] Greenway had already in a memorandum sent to Long on 12 March given details of all the

Company's activities outside Persia.[157] Yet on 16 May Cadman had suggested to the Secretary of the Treasury that 'pending the consideration by Lord Harcourt's Committee of the Anglo-Persian Company's operation and of its future relations with His Majesty's Government he is of the opinion that the company should be instructed that no undertakings should be entered upon in any country outside Persia without express sanction'.[158] The Treasury agreed.[159] The government directors, Inchcape and W. St D. Jenkins, a former Admiralty official in the contracts department, who had been appointed on 4 April 1916, knew of what amounted to an embargo on the Company's activities outside Persia. The Company was not informed of this until 4 July, when the immediate reaction was one of annoyance and it made a request for its views to be communicated to the committee.[160] The Company complained on 2 August to the Treasury of a 'restriction of the Company's business', a change of official attitudes and that

it would be impossible to carry on the Anglo-Persian Company either as an independent Company or to the best advantage of its shareholders unless, like other important Oil Companies, it is permitted to work on ordinary business lines and is free to carry on all its operations in any part of the world as it had been doing for some years past.[161]

Slade told Cadman that the Company was receiving unfair treatment from the committee and wrote a memorandum on 25 July 1918 on 'The Petroleum Situation in the British Empire',[162] which he had placed before the Cabinet with favourable comment through his friends in the Admiralty, particularly Admiral Sir Reginald Hall, Director of Naval Intelligence, and Maurice Hankey, Secretary to the War Cabinet.[163] This was a blistering attack on 'foreigners', who were using every means at their disposal, honestly or dishonestly, openly or secretly, to hamper the development of British interests. He contended that 'the power that controls the oil lands of Persia and Mesopotamia will control the source of supply of the majority of the liquid fuel of the future'. So he reasoned, 'we must therefore at all costs retain our hold on the Persian and Mesopotamian oil fields', and others within the Empire to prevent 'the intrusion in any form of foreign interests, however much disguised they may be'. In case there was any doubt as to the identity of 'the interest that is most inimical to British control at the present time' it was 'the Royal Dutch Company'.

No doubt Slade knew, as Pretyman did, about Samuel's attempt in December 1917 'to induce the Government to terminate their financial interest in the Company'. He penned a further polemic a month later on 'the Threatened Foreign Oil Monopoly'.[164] Cadman disclaimed any unfavourable bias against the Company on the part of the Petroleum Executive, or a desire to curb its operations,[165] but he reported to the Treasury

The Government and the Company: The early years

that, because of the government shareholding, it was 'reasonable and desirable that it should have an opportunity of criticising any new enterprises which the latter may have in view and which may involve not only commercial but political considerations of some importance'.[166] In an internal memorandum he was even more explicit that 'the Anglo-Persian must eventually either be even more a Government controlled company than at present or that the Government interest should be disposed of altogether'.[167] This did not seem to augur well for the Company's relations with the Government, but within a couple of months the omens were more favourable for the Company, but less auspicious for a government oil policy.

The Company could not be disregarded and even Harcourt, who was not particularly partial towards it, doubted whether 'we should part with our control of the Anglo-Persian in order to get a control which we could never say was an effective control'.[168] Inchcape, with reservations about Government involvement in private trade, maintained that 'the Anglo-Persian is going ahead and had tremendous possibilities' and that 'it would be a mistake for the British Government to be mixed up in another concern'. Even Cadman's enthusiasm for the accommodation with Royal Dutch-Shell was waning as he felt that Deterding was attempting 'to get a big combine which would be capable of holding up against American interests', but was convinced that 'we could not afford to antagonise American interests in any action we might take'. Cadman as a result of his experience on the Inter-Allied Petroleum Council was taking a less parochial view of national oil affairs.

Cargill who, as the Chairman of Burmah and a director of the Company, was intimately concerned in the outcome of the deliberations of the Committee, gave it moderate and sensible advice and injected a note of commercial realism into its rather abstract deliberations. He emphasised the practical contribution which the Company could make to a properly directed government oil policy. He criticised the attempted government embargo on the Company's activities outside Persia and, referring to his own experience, he affirmed that

no oil company can live by crude oil production alone and remain an asset of sure benefit to the Empire. It must or should do its own refining and distribution, and have the material, means and organisation to do this, since, failing this, it must sell its products to and through those more adequately organised...it must be in a position to ensure that the fight cannot *be* localised.

He was adamant that 'the Anglo-Persian's development outside of Persia - in and without the Empire should not be obstructed'. Cargill tried to be impartial on the proposals for controlling Royal Dutch-Shell, but cautioned that 'financial control merely secures a possible but never a

The Government and the Company: The early years

positive addition to the Empire oil reserves'. He was not interested in 'a purely financial transaction', it had to be 'an effective control', but this did not necessarily exclude working market arrangements between competing companies.

The committee concluded that there was no point in withdrawing the government shareholding from the Company and no possibility of enforcing effective British control over Royal Dutch-Shell and that there was insufficient compatability of objectives to produce a lasting agreement on the terms proposed. The wheel appeared to have come full circle. It was Cadman who revived the committee by introducing a new element that 'the French were trying very definitely to create a Government oil policy and to get a footing in oil, just as we had in Persia'. With this purpose in mind they were negotiating with Calouste Gulbenkian, the representative of Royal Dutch-Shell in Paris, who had been one of the principal intermediaries in negotiations over the Mesopotamian Concession on their behalf. The issue of the future of Mesopotamia had already figured prominently in Anglo-French diplomatic exchanges. Cadman proposed that since it had been decided that 'the Anglo-Persian should not be the bait' for control of the Royal Dutch-Shell group, the Deutsche Bank's shareholding in the Turkish Petroleum Company (TPC) should be offered instead as a bargaining counter.

There was, however, no disagreement in principle to offering the Royal Dutch-Shell group a larger share in the TPC 'provided they made themselves permanently British' and if the Foreign Office was prepared to modify its views over the validity of the 1914 Agreement. Some progress was made towards the end of December when Baldwin authorised the purchase of the Deutsche Bank shares in TPC following a memorandum by the Board of Trade pointing out the close connection with the Royal Dutch-Shell negotiations, 'the importance of which it is difficult to exaggerate'.[169] The diplomatic outlook was also confused by the aftermath of the war and the emergence of independent Arab states in territories formerly administered by the Turkish authorities.[170] The French were very active in pursuing an oil policy and their claims in the Middle East. Members of the committee differed strongly in their attitude towards a French presence in possible Mesopotamian oilfields. Pretyman and Black favoured excluding them, but Cadman thought that 'it might be in the interests of the Anglo-Persian Oil Company and the Royal Dutch-Shell group to have the French associated with them'.[171]

In mid-January 1919 the log jam suddenly began to break: Deterding wrote that he was 'quite ready therefore to discuss with the Government what are the practical steps so as to ensure such British control, as long as this is not a Government control'. He offered to include a neutral body to

The Government and the Company: The early years

ensure an effective British commercial control. It was a surprising change of mind and probably resulted more from Deterding's disappointing discussions in Paris than a change of heart. Perhaps he also realised that it was ultimately in his interests to play a larger rather than a smaller part in TPC if it was going to have a future. As he admitted to Cadman in January 1919 'the question as to the management of Mesopotamian fields by one of the Shell companies' was 'the main thing which induced [him] to all other considerations.' Deterding was a realist, an opportunist, who saw the increased importance that Mesopotamian oil might have in supplying Europe and the determination of the French to have a share in it. Besides, increasing American interest in foreign concessions and competition from their European subsidiaries were making their impact in the international oil trade.[172] The new situation was mentioned at a meeting of the Committee on 20 January, but the response of the committee was muted, if not hostile, to French participation. Black and Pretyman saw little connection between Deterding's offer and French claims. It was Cadman who put the negotiations into perspective, proposing a British controlled Royal Dutch-Shell group having an equal holding with the Company in the Mesopotamian Concession. Deterding had been negotiating with French interests, so the inclusion of the French could be arranged by them being given an equal proportion of shares from both companies and negotiations would be greatly facilitated.

Within a couple of days the general conditions for an acceptable agreement had been drawn up in a memorandum by Harold Brown in conjunction with Cadman, Black and Lancelot Smith. The main provisions in the anticipated new Shell organisation included: (l) three quarters of the directors to be British-born; (2) no change in the Articles of Association without the assent of the Governor of the Bank of England; (3) the majority vote in Shell to be permanently English; (4) the Royal Dutch British operating companies to be transferred to Shell; and (5) no new director to be elected without the consent of the Bank of England. This was speedily considered by the committee on 23 January, though much detailed negotiation remained. Pretyman and Black, who thought that 'the main profit of the Mesopotamian undertaking had been given away to the Dutch' opposed the agreement, but other committee members were in no mood to delay further.[173] They believed they had solved, not shelved, the problem and that the status of Shell had been guaranteed as a British enterprise. Moreover the role of the committee had been overtaken in the events surrounding the Peace Conference and some agreement was essential if the Government's negotiating position was not to be prejudiced.

As Cadman explained it, 'The Americans had been to the French to put in for the oil rights in Mesopotamia, and had pointed out that if they got

The Government and the Company: The early years

the concessions there they could find the capital to work them, no doubt through the Standard Oil Company.' This had rather alarmed the Foreign Office, the India Office and the Board of Trade, and the whole subject had been discussed at a meeting in Paris. The view of that meeting generally was that the Policy Committee's scheme was a sound one, and that 'negotiations with the French should proceed as soon as HM Government had agreed to the proposals of this Committee, in order to get the French on our side and so prevent the oil question coming up before the Peace Conference at all'.[174] They succeeded in this in spite of Clemenceau's belief on 30 January 1919 that 'La question des pétroles s'annonce comme devant être l'une des questions économiques les plus importantes la Conference de la Paix.'[175]

The proceedings of the committee did not fulfil its terms of reference and did not result in the formulation of a national oil policy. The results were hardly, as Long described them, 'most admirable'.[176] The simple solution of an amalgamation of British companies with the British interests in the Royal Dutch-Shell group proved impractical. Although the Cabinet approved the agreement on 5 May 1919, it was never implemented. The Government lacked the political will. There was insufficient common self-interest between the companies concerned for it to survive in the form proposed, for they had outdistanced the objectives, which they had once considered indispensable. In an expanding oil world they had more opportunities than they expected, so their growth was less restricted than they anticipated. Companies and governments came to terms in their own respective ways. The committee may have held the ring briefly for the international competitors to measure up to each other, but no more. It could not provide guaranteed supplies to the Empire on a permanent basis throughout the world. Ultimately without a positive and consistent government commitment to the overriding priority of an oil policy and its effective implementation there was little more that the committee could have accomplished. The agreement was never given effect, a victim of the conflicting international claims which emerged at the ending of the war, the uncertainties of British foreign policy and the inability to reconcile political principles with practical commercialism.

The Government shareholding was a response to a specific question of naval strategy. It hardly appears to have been an act of national oil policy. Indeed subsequently it seems to have been diplomatically embarrassing and commercially awkward. Only the Admiralty showed any semblance of consistency in its support for the Company. It was a paradoxical situation that Greenway and Slade were defending the Company against a closer association with Royal Dutch-Shell, whilst some government departments were promoting it. The interplay of personalities was par-

The Government and the Company: The early years

ticularly powerful in the presentations of and the opposition to the amalgamation proposals. The independent survival of the Company certainly hinged upon the government's shareholding but Cadman was right that its operations had been successful, not because of, but in spite of it.

7
PERSIA - THE SCENE OF OPERATIONS 1914-18

I INTRODUCTION

Whilst the British Government was debating its policy in London, the Company was producing oil in Persia. In assessing the performance of the Company during this period it will be recalled that, of the total government investment sanctioned in mid-1914, some 7 per cent was provided for the liquidation of earlier debts, 30 per cent for refinery extensions and improvements, 20 per cent for an additional 10 in. pipeline and 5 per cent for the 'geological examination and testing of new fields'.[1] The remainder was earmarked for field development, transport and communications. The maximum capacity of the original pipeline laid between January 1910 and June 1911 was about some 440 000 tons a year.[2] The plant ordered for the refinery, on the basis of a scheme by Andrew Campbell, was designed to handle 180 000 tons a year but by mid-1914, as a result of process changes to produce more fuel oil, throughput had been increased (without additional plant) to approximately 320 000 tons a year.[3]

As a result of the new supply agreement for naval fuel oil, Greenway believed that the Company would eventually be required to supply 500 000 tons of fuel oil annually to the Admiralty, for which some 720 000 tons of crude oil would need to be processed by the refinery. The increased rate of production depended on the additional 10 in. pipeline, which was not completed till January 1917, when production in that month was 84 000 tons. This tremendous progress can be gauged from the tenfold increase in production from 1912 to 1918, 80 800 tons to 897 402 tons. The programme set by Greenway was completed in spite of wartime uncertainties, shortages of materials, financial difficulties, losses at sea, insecurity, insufficient numbers of skilled engineers and the lack of a trained labour force. Improvisation characterised the work achieved and self-reliance marked the majority of those who managed the affairs of the Company in Persia.

Greenway never lost sight of his ultimate objective, his determination to create an integrated oil company engaged in all the activities of the business. As he admitted in 1925, he had wanted 'to build up an absolutely self-contained organisation', which would sell customers products to 'wherever there may be a profitable outlet for them without the intervention of any third parties'.[4] This was the dominant strategy of the Company, even though it was circumscribed by restrictions relating to the Shell contracts of 1912, reluctantly accepted because of financial and refinery problems. In a very real sense the Company grew rapidly because of the military needs of the war and the resultant technological developments associated with it, which caused an increasing demand for oil. Its productive success with high yield wells stimulated, after the end of the war, the quest for markets, which it felt were best assured by having its own distributing organisation, the British Petroleum Company Limited (BP Company), which in turn was supplied through its own tanker organisation, the British Tanker Company. Its technical expertise was reinforced by the establishment of its own research organisation.

Gradually as more exploration was carried out within the concessionary area in Persia improved scientific methods increased the effectiveness of the Company's activities and greater knowledge was acquired of the oil-bearing formations. It was not till 1918, however, with the careful observations of S.J. Shand, a South African geologist, who had served with the expeditionary force in Mesopotamia and had been seconded for a short while to the Company, that a tentative hypothesis was proposed for locating the reservoir rock in limestone rather than in sandstone, which had been the earlier view. Thereafter it became no longer a question of following seepages and surface indications, but of discovering the conditions in which oil could accumulate and measuring all the factors, temperatures, gas pressures, depths, etc., to develop the most economical methods of production and conservation. This expanding range of activities, skills and investments, in addition to those involved in refining, imposed severe strains upon the administrative capacity of the Company, whose technical operations took place at a vast distance from its head office and whose communications and supplies were liable to frequent interruption in the course of the war.

2 ADMINISTRATION

Charles Greenway was the mainspring of the Company from 1910 to 1927. With his mastery of detail, his stamina, his self-confidence and the loyal support, which he received from Garrow and Nichols, general managers and fellow directors during the war, he directed the Company aggressively, yet protectively. The government directors, Inchcape and

Persia - The scene of operations

Slade were active. Inchcape was closely involved in the business of the Company particularly on the financial side and, well trusted by government officials and ministers, his influence and caution were pervasive. Perhaps less than completely confident in Greenway and occasionally critical, Inchcape never withdrew his support. Slade intended taking a close interest in the administrative affairs of the Company. He early suggested taking over some of the functions exercised by the Burmah management for 'we shall arrange for all discussions on questions of policy - such as quantity and type of all plant and material ordered - to take place in London'.[5] He requested that 'a monthly statement of the expenditure incurred under each account shall be sent here three days before the date of each Directors' Meeting'. Throughout his term as government director, and later as vice-chairman, Slade was actively concerned in organisational issues. He recognised, probably on the prompting of Greenway, that the inefficient triangular relationship between London, Glasgow and Muhammara was unsatisfactory. Once war broke out, Slade became immersed in Admiralty affairs and the opportunity for strengthening the London office was momentarily lost. Greenway recognised the administrative shortcomings of divided responsibilities. Later, in a private letter to Walpole he informed him that it was his intention, 'which has only been retarded by the fact that Admiral Slade has been engaged night and day in war work ... to reform the whole system of administration of the APOC', regretting that 'this cannot be done in the meantime'.[6] Nevertheless, by the end of 1916 all the Company's administration was centralised in London and the Glasgow office was closed.

What seemed appropriate in Persia in 1909, when only Burmah staff had the experience and the expertise, was no longer so by 1914. In Persia the administrative situation was undeniably difficult and remained so throughout the period of the war. The managing agents were located in Muhammara with Walpole as general manager assisted by T.L. Jacks and W.E.C. Greenwood, clerks and accountants. Fields was administered from Ahwāz by Andrew Gillespie, formerly consulting engineer to Burmah. Also based in Ahwāz were J. Jameson, pipeline and transport superintendent, who had been Ritche's assistant in the construction of the pipeline and Dr Young who continued to be responsible for both medical and political affairs. At Masjid i-Suleimān, the fields manager was R.R. Thompson, assisted by C.E. Capito. At Ābādān, Neilson was works manager. Unfortunately the weakest spot in the whole organisation, the hub of the administrative wheel, was Walpole himself, who neither by training nor temperament possessed the appropriate understanding of what his responsibilities required nor sufficient personal authority. As a

Persia - The scene of operations

result the three main centres of operations lacked cohesion, though not individual initiative or effort.

Management coordination was missing. Correspondence was more recriminatory than explanatory. There was a tendency to find fault rather than offer support. Little personal camaraderie existed between the different members of the organisation, each part preserving its own individual identity. It would be unjust to suggest that the lack of collaboration was solely due to Walpole, for he was clearly overburdened with work, particularly once the construction of tank storage, river craft repairs and gunboat assembly for the armed services began. Yet Walpole was in charge, as he was constantly reminded: 'the work is wholly in your hands and the staff entirely under your orders'. Whilst London sympathised over 'the many difficulties to be overcome with mixed workmen, unskilled labour, congestion of shipments, ill-found facilities amidst Cholera, Enteric and official restrictions', Walpole had no option but to make the best of it.[7]

The real issue concerning the Persian administration was not only its inadequacy, but its incapability. The early difficulties of the managing agents might be ascribed to the complexity of the technical problems encountered, which delayed the commissioning schedule of the refinery. The conclusion was, however, inescapable that technical operations would predominate and that the earlier commercial ambitions were unrealisable. Greenway's early faith in Walpole, that 'it is all a question of tact and given this you should be able to come through the next year or two satisfactorily and establish your position indisputably',[8] was misplaced. Greenway was convinced that Strick, Scott & Co. would become the leading trading company in the area, a Gulf version of Jardine, Matheson & Co. He exhorted Walpole: 'no effort will be spared by you to secure for them the position which they are entitled to expect viz: that of "premier firm" in the Persian Gulf'.[9] Walpole, more at home in the traditional role of the managing agents and less at ease in the business of oil, frequently found his dual activities clashing. Walpole was required not only to be a commission agent, a merchant in the import–export trade, but also knowledgeable about the technical operations involved in the oil business and to manage them. He had to be reminded by Greenway that the commission that was earned 'is intended to cover *all* services rendered by them in connection with the APOC business and they are, of course, not entitled to make any indirect trading profits on any transactions they may carry out on behalf of that Company'.[10] There were allegations about profiteering, hiring out of Company craft, exchange dealings, etc., and Greenway warned that the consequences would be serious, especially if such activities 'came to the notice of the Directors, particularly those

Persia - The scene of operations

The staff of Strick, Scott and Co. Ltd., Muhammara 1917

representing the Government'. It was a very sensitive issue, as Greenway acknowledged, for 'both you and I are in an extremely delicate position ... representing as both of us do dual interests ... when there is any conflict of interests, err in favour of APOC'.[11]

Greenway was particularly critical of extravagance, the apparent absence of strict accounting control and indiscipline, instructing Walpole, 'please drive it into the heads of everybody that it is a *Commercial* Company and must be run on *strictly commercial lines*'.[12] 'Experience has shown us', he informed Young, 'that no man is indispensable as Fields and Pipeline Superintendent, or any other position, therefore we must henceforth give absolutely the first place to discipline.'[13] A new situation had arisen, even if it was the old problem in a more acute form: 'as a Government concern the Company must henceforth be worked on proper business lines and the intrigues and jealousies which have hitherto caused us so much trouble cannot and will not any longer be allowed to prevail'. Not only were the managing agents in charge, but they must be seen to be in charge, for 'as Managing Agents in Persia, it is the duty of Strick Scott and Co's. head office to conduct and superintend all the business of the Company in Persia'.[14] Walpole was the ultimate authority in commercial, financial, administrative and technical affairs, so it was 'to the *Managing Agents*, and not the technical staff that the Board looked in the matter of keeping down

266

expenditure' as 'the Managing Agents are just as well able to form an opinion as the technical men'.[15] This, unfortunately, was the trouble, for the incompetence of the Muhammara staff to handle the technical indents and check plant and material as it arrived not only disrupted the technical operations, but exacerbated relations with the technical staff.

Greenway reluctantly recognised in May 1916 the weakness of the organisation, 'they have not the time to properly consider various details essential for the proper and economical running of all business concerns'.[16] Their control over operations had become nominal and he admitted that the managing agents 'are *not* performing the services for which they are paid ... and that either we must put our house in order, or to own up to APOC that we are not justifying our existence and must either resign the Agency or work it on reduced terms'. Belatedly Greenway realised that 'none of the technical staff pay any attention' to the managing agents. Walpole had failed to take the reins into his own hands and 'secure the control of the Company's business necessary to justify our position as "Managing Agents"'. Was it just a personal failure, the result of Walpole's 'misdirected personal zeal' or something more fundamental? E. A. Chettle, a partner in Shaw, Wallace & Co. and on the Board of Strick, Scott & Co., advised Walpole to delegate, to divide his office into three departments with relevant subsections so as to 'place one man in charge of each Department and give him full responsibility even to the signing of the letters'. It was sound advice, indispensable for a manager who 'should reduce his own part of the detail work to a minimum so that he may keep his mind free for the hundred and one questions which are continually arising'.[17]

Chettle, moreover, was particularly percipient in his observations on 'two staffs with different masters', and was the first to appreciate the impossibility of achieving the objectives of the Company by its existing administrative infrastructure with divided responsibilities between the staffs of the Company and those of the managing agents. It meant, as Chettle explained, 'two sets of employees in the same office, two different scales of pay, two different forms of agreement, conflicting interest, different points of view' and clashes of loyalty. He thought that 'it would make for good and would benefit the APOC in the long run if we had one standard of salaries, one agreement and one set of employers or Board of Directors', for 'the staff would then all be in the same boat, their interests identical, the competition amongst members of the staff would be for position and pay and therefore of a healthy nature, and you "Walpole" would be in undisputed authority as the figure head or mouthpiece of a Board calculated to back you up in all things'. Chettle was right but with some diffidence thought that it was 'all in the nature of a dream, which will

Persia - The scene of operations

probably not come true'. He was wrong, it did, but six years later. The system of managing agents as applied to nineteenth century commercial practice was becoming most inappropriate for the administration of a twentieth-century industrial undertaking.

It would be an exaggeration to assert that the European staff, either those employed in the Fields area, eighteen at the outbreak of war and thirty-two when it finished, or the forty-eight in Ābādān at the beginning of 1915, suffered great hardships during this period. It is, nevertheless, unrealistic to pretend that conditions were easy. The successes and failures of the Mesopotamian expeditionary force[18] influenced morale. The cutting of the pipeline in February 1915 by dissident tribesmen was a traumatic event.[19] The unstable political situation of Persia was worrying even if relations with the Bakhtiari Khans were generally friendly. Some members of the staff were frustrated at not serving in the armed forces, and the absence of leave and the lack of amenities caused some tempers to fray. Accommodation was always short with much overcrowding particularly at Ābādān, and dormitory conditions which seemed satisfactory in London were unacceptable abroad. Thompson wrily observed, 'we find it very difficult to get more than two men to live amicably together, we have had cases where five men, living together in one bungalow, were running three distinct messes because the men could not agree'.[20] The Indian staff mostly had tents whilst the Persian labourers 'have their families, friends and relations round the Field and are very disinclined to leave them'.[21] Mules were the usual beasts of burden, horses the general means of travelling till the first Ford Model T was ordered in April 1917 to replace the elegant, but uncomfortable buggy.[22]

Conditions in Persia were simple and it took time for the medical services to be fully developed, as the rather extreme case on 15 October 1914 indicates, when the doctor reported, 'I had no instruments better than a carpenter's brace and saw: but I am thankful to say that up to now post-mortems have not been required, and I trust will not.'[23] The Fields hospital was not inaugurated till 1916. Drink was more a problem of high spirits than drunken brawling, but it was a health hazard in a hot climate and offensive to Moslem susceptibilities.[24] Sexual privation was generally alleviated by a visit to the 'dentist' at Basra, for feminine company was sparse, apart from the nursing staff, and married quarters rare. Clubs and sports facilities began to be provided both at the Company's expense and on local initiative, but, as elsewhere throughout the world, expatriate communities had to come to terms with themselves. It was not always amusing as E.B. Soane, brilliant linguist and mordant character, in charge of Chiāh Surkh in 1914, drily observed of Gillespie's presbyterian hospitality which 'always rather put one in mind of trying to excite a quite dead

Persia - The scene of operations

Fording the River Tembi early-1920

Mr Bradshaw in his 'buggy' near Masjid i-Suleimān 1908

Persia - The scene of operations

pig, and a day in his house is rather less gay than a prayer meeting in a mausoleum'.[25]

3 TECHNICAL OPERATIONS

(a) Production and exploration

Like a harbinger of good fortune, one of the wells, F7, which had come into production in August 1911 with an estimated initial modest flow of about 130 tons a day, suddenly on 24 March 1912 increased its output to an extraordinary 1600 tons a day, the equivalent of some 600 000 tons a year. With great difficulty the well was brought under control and throttled back through its inadequate cast iron fittings to approximately 1000 tons a day at a well head pressure of 320 p.s.i. As this well and another prolific producer B8(M8) shared a common flowline, their joint production totalled 1300 tons daily, and this quantity, combined with that from other wells which could not be shut in, exceeded the capacity of the pipeline (1100 tons a day) by about 400 tons a day. The surplus had to be burnt off until the additional 10 in. pipeline was completed in January 1917. Then the production of F7 was allowed to increase to about 475 000 tons a year,

The mudding off of F7, Masjid i-Suleimān 1926 left to right: J.M. Pattinson, H.Y.V. Jackson, J.L. Wright and J. Jameson

Persia - The scene of operations

at which level it remained till it was shut in for reasons of safety in 1926, after having contributed some 55 per cent of the total crude oil production to that time. It was a phenomenal record compared with the national average in America of 240 tons a year per well in 1919.

By the middle of 1914 thirty wells were producing or capable of production, so there was no shortage of oil. Indeed, throughout the concessionary period in Persia, the Company had a far greater productive than offtake capacity. The increased utilisation of the pipeline may be appreciated by comparing the average monthly production in mid-1913 at 27 000 tons of crude oil with the average in early 1916, 37 300 tons, or late 1916, 63 400. The complete commissioning of the new 10 in. pipeline in January 1917 with a capacity of 1 300 000 tons a year enabled production to rise to 70 900 tons monthly at first and reach an average of 82 000 tons monthly by the end of the year, matching the refinery capacity, as shown in Table 7.1.

Table 7.1. *Anglo-Persian Oil Company production of crude oil and drilling activity 1911–19*

(long tons)

Year[a]	Production		Year[b]	Feet drilled
1911–12	43 000	(7 months)	1911	9 161
1912–13	80 000		1912	10 111
1913–14	274 000		1913	3 623
1914–15	376 000		1914	1 997
1915–16	459 000		1915	2 670
1916–17	644 000		1916	5 778
1917–18	897 000		1917	7 645
1918–19	1 106 415		1918	8 554
1919–20	1 385 301		1919	8 523

Note: [a] Year end 31 March
Source: BP
Note: [b] Annual Year
Source: BP H16/111

In these favourable circumstances and because of the lack of equipment and shortage of trained drillers it was not surprising that drilling was not very actively pursued in the early war years. Table 7.1 also indicates drilling activity, 1911-19. It must not be supposed, however, that there was a lessening of activities. On the contrary, if the pace seemed less hectic than in the period following the discovery well, attention was being directed to some of the problems which would become the great issues of the post-war period. Some of the technical staff like Capito, Thompson,

Persia - The scene of operations

Jameson and M.C. Seamark, the first English driller to be recruited and sent to Persia in 1914, were adding to their experience and coming to terms with the production of Persian crude oil with its deeper wells and higher pressures than elsewhere. Oil production in many fields throughout the world was sustained by pumping, the nodding donkeys being such a conspicuous feature of the American oil scene, and the possibility of having to install such equipment troubled the early management. Thompson admitted that 'we have not at present available any data to enable us to predict in which part or parts of the Field the gas pressure will fall first'.[26] Gillespie had estimated that there would be an eventual need to pump no less than 1000 wells, a formidable undertaking in the conditions of southern Persia and involving an enormous expenditure.[27] Such statements indicate not only the early worries and ignorance, but also highlight the remarkable progress, which was subsequently achieved in ascertaining the physical characteristics of the oil reservoir, its behaviour and its ultimate control by efficient methods of production. In the decade from 1914 this experience was gradually accumulated, but not without trial, some error and one disaster.

It was not till mid-1916 that the question of greater production was seriously considered again with a proposed programme of 'two wells drilling continuously and two wells being put into shape'.[28] The objective was to determine the productive area of the field by drilling outwards from the producing wells so as not to exhaust 'the gas pressures in one particular area too rapidly, as otherwise flowing production would fail prematurely'. This was the haunting fear, as if the gas bubbles would burst and the oil would go flat. Six months later in a more ambitious drilling strategy, Garrow emphasised that 'our object must be so to develop the field that gas pressure is maintained over the longest possible period'.[29] There was however, more to drilling than worrying about falling gas pressures. The ideal in London did not always correspond with the reality in Persia and Thompson protested that 'with the existing method of drilling and our inadequate water supply, more than nine drillers cannot be usefully employed throughout the year'.[30] He argued that nothing should be undertaken 'until the water supply and transport question had been solved satisfactorily' and that 'the proposed increased drilling programme should not be started until either the Electrical Scheme has been completed or an increased water supply obtained'. The sourness of the water with its high content of mineral salts caused awful corrosion in boiler tubes and well casing, as Reynolds had earlier experienced. Transportation was unsatisfactory, for the winter rains ruined tracks and the carriage of heavy industrial equipment drawn by mules took time and much damage was caused to plant.

Persia - The scene of operations

To reduce the effects of corrosion in boilers it had been suggested in 1912 that electrical drilling be undertaken, but it was not till spring 1915 that a well, B6, was drilled from the surface to 417 feet by electrical power laid on from the workshops 'without the slightest difficulty or trouble in so doing'.[31] It was not, however, till 1917 that C. Dalley, the Company engineer in London, produced a plan for drilling by electricity. The lack of technical coordination and the incompetent forwarding of materials delayed the introduction of the scheme and it was not implemented till 1919.[32] Capito had proposed early in 1917 a solution to the water problem by constructing a mobile pumping house on the River Kārūn, which would rise and fall with the level of the current, but that too was bedevilled by indecision and delays, due to a lack of proper technical appreciation, and, of course, in the midst of a war, shortage of materials that were already in demand by the armed forces.[33] In mid-1917 Slade elaborated a development programme for production on a definite quantifiable basis, related to the expansion programme that had been presented to the Inter-Departmental Petroleum Committee, when the case for raising more capital had been outlined as related in Chapter 6.[34] He proposed a production of 900 000 tons in 1917 with nine wells drilled, 1 300 000 tons in 1918 and fifteen wells, and 1 700 000 tons in 1919 and twenty wells. He advocated that 'future development should therefore proceed on systematic lines with a view to conserving the gas pressure in the oil sands and to keeping the cost of production as low as possible', locating the wells at intervals of 1000 feet chosen by the geologists and driven by electricity. It was a splendid plan on paper. Within a couple of months Thompson warned about sending any more drillers as there was practically no work for them.[35] They had no casing with which to line the wells. Standardisation of equipment had also been considered but in vain.[36] Many orders for plant remained incomplete.

It was not just that the inefficiency of the managing agents impeded the development of the oilfield, but also that a basic lack of inter-disciplinary cooperation and understanding prevented practical collaborative efforts. The engineer, the chemist and the geologist were not technically related in their work. Thompson, by no means blinkered in his approach, initially rejected the idea of a chemist being appointed to assist him as 'a permanent man would be only another mouth to feed and as he would frequently be idle would do his best to find company'.[37] He was no more receptive at first to the idea of a geological office in Masjid i-Suleimān and hardly thought that 'we can keep a bungalow open for geologists if they are only going to stop here for about three weeks in the year'.[38] Later he was to change his opinion and state that 'the Fields Manager, and he alone, is responsible for the production of the Field and he has to see that this

Persia - The scene of operations

production is kept up, and without a Geologist resident on the Field, who follows continually exploration work, a good deal must be left to the manager's initiative'.[39] Little had changed since the complaints of Reynolds about the curtailment of his authority.

One horrible incident threw into relief the hazards and dangers to which the staff were exposed. On 9 July 1917 an oil valve split in the Tembi pumping station at a pressure of 700 lbs p.s.i. A great gush of oil spurted out, through which rushed Lindsay, the superintendent, to turn off the oil supply to the boilers but the oil ignited, enveloping him fatally in the flames. His assistant managed to switch off most of the pumps before the fire burnt the electrical connections. Their bravery prevented the fire from completely destroying the pump station. An accident on such a scale was exceptional, but the element of danger was always present.[40]

(b) The Ābādān refinery and the war effort

By mid-1913 the refinery at Ābādān had practically reached its designed throughput, 3.5 million gallons against 4 million gallons a month, though the quality of the products was poor and its efficiency low. Pitkethly had been invalided home with typhoid and his temporary successor as works manager, G. Thomson, struggled ineffectually to make improvements. Neilson arrived, as works manager, to take charge in mid-October. Nevertheless, in spite of all Neilson's efforts the refining of benzine, using a plumbite treatment apparently successful on a laboratory scale, proved quite unsatisfactory and no other possible alternative treatment with bauxite or redistillation made any appreciable difference. Neilson was in a technical cul de sac, there was no way forward with the process at his disposal and it was not till much later in 1921 that an entirely different approach solved this difficult problem.[41] The quality of the kerosine was better, but little more than adequate for the local markets. The production of fuel oil for possible Admiralty requirements commenced in June 1913, but, though refining was easier, its high viscosity in colder climates was a problem. It was, of course, possible to reduce the viscosity, the consistency of the oil, by incorporating the lighter boiling fractions, but this had to be balanced against too low a flashpoint, which would have made the oil easier to ignite and, thus, more dangerous to use.

Such was the position of the refinery towards the middle of 1914, when it was proving impossible to produce benzine in accordance with the Asiatic contract. It was agreed that an untreated distillate should be substituted instead for delivery to the Royal Dutch-Shell refinery at Suez, where expectations of sufficient quantities of Egyptian oil for refining had not materialised. Both parties to the original contract were relieved for different reasons. Indeed, it was a positive advantage to the Company, because it needed the capacity of the distillation units installed for benzine for its growing production of fuel oil. The volume of kerosine refined remained roughly proportionate to throughput.

During the war, the refinery at Ābādān settled down to producing fuel oil for the Admiralty as its principal product, some 65 per cent of total output. There were no significant developments at Ābādān other than the very real problems of keeping the refinery going and increasing its throughput in the midst of many other war-time cares. The area rented was doubled on 7 December 1914 when 695 more acres were leased from Shaykh Khaz'al on the previous terms, for 9 payments of £7200 for ten years rental of 720 *jaribs* (180 acres) in advance.[42] A third rental agreement was concluded on 3 September 1918 when a further 1091 acres were acquired, totalling 2413 acres in all. There had been little time for consolidation. Some waste was unavoidable, maintenance and safety were constant worries with the work-force. Persians were unused to regular industrial practices and discipline, and Indians were frequently restless and suffered from some cultural claustrophobia in an alien and not always sympathetic environment. The British staff were relatively few and almost irreplaceable in the context of war-time employment. In 1916 there were 1137 Persians, 1202 Indians, 50 other nationalities and a European staff of 53 employed at Ābādān, a four fold increase since 1910. In all the Company employed some 4000 people in its Persian operations in 1916: for the details of their numbers and distribution, 1910–16, see Table 7.2. All staff suffered from overcrowding.

By 1915 Neilson, by much improvisation and reallocation of plant, had managed to increase the refining capacity to 27 000 tons a month. In 1916 the construction began of four additional benches, part of the expansion planned in 1914 for increased government fuel oil supplies. Two benches were commissioned in July 1916 augmenting production to 38 000 tons a month. The construction of more units and the conversion and adaptation of other plant enabled the capacity to be increased to 61 000 tons a month for the first time in March 1917 and in July 1917 to some 88 000 tons a month, approximately commensurate with the volume of production.[43]

The additions to the refinery, sanctioned in March 1916 for the production of more fuel oil, were extensive and demanding on resources and manpower in the midst of work already being undertaken for the Government.[44] Neilson's reaction was emphatic, 'the proposed extra extensions involve a very large amount of additional work and I wish to state clearly that we will find great difficulty in tackling them at all efficiently and satisfactorily if we have anything like the amount of work at present on hand to undertake'.[45] It was a major undertaking involving the

Persia - The scene of operations

Table 7.2. *Anglo-Persian Oil Company staff and labour in Persia 1910–16*

(a) All centres

Year	Persians	Indians	Others	Europeans	Total
1910	1 362	158	146	40	1 706
1911	1 801	379	127	56	2 363
1912	2 449	553	97	43	3 142
1913	2 899	917	175	44	4 035
1914	2 744	1 074	395	64	4 277
1915	2 203	979	187	80	3 449.
1916	2 335	1 366	104	120	3 925

(b) Ābādān

Year	Persians	Indians	Others	Europeans	Total
1910	471	80	76	5	632
1911	587	277	56	12	932
1912	1 396	508	75	16	1 995
1913	1 827	865	111	22	2 825
1914	1 809	1 028	135	37	3 009
1915	1 290	895	67	47	2 299
1916	1 137	1 202	50	53	2 442

(c) Fields

Year	Persians	Indians	Others	Europeans	Total
1910	452	52	1	18	523
1911	564	72	2	26	664
1912	749	32	9	22	812
1913	970	47	64	20	1 101
1914	832	33	70	20	955
1915	842	51	28	26	947
1916	830	58	50	27	965

(d) Ahwāz and pipeline

Year	Persians	Indians	Others	Europeans	Total
1910	439	26	69	17	551
1911	650	30	69	18	767
1912	304	13	13	5	335
1913	102	5	—	2	109
1914	103	13	190	7	313
1915	71	33	92	7	203
1916	368	106	4	40	518

Source: BP reports to Imperial Commissioner

Persia - The scene of operations

construction of new stills, benches, warehouses, store-rooms, wax, pitch and lubricating plants, packing sheds, extra power, water and lighting supplies, more accommodation and amenities and more harbour facilities, apart from further staff and labour needs. The work would take two years and require Neilson's individual attention when his own 'time and energies are becoming less available every day to the legitimate work of carrying on the present refinery'. In June 1916 Neilson had been advised that the Admiralty demand was expected to rise to 40 000 tons a month, 480 000 tons a year, for which a crude oil refinery throughput of at least 720 000 tons was required as fuel oil represented over two thirds of the total output, as is indicated in Table 7.3.[46] This rate of refining was achieved for the first time in July 1917. Neilson had succeeded in bringing order out of chaos and had increased the capacity of the refinery five-fold in as many years.

About this time too the idea of the Company having its own research establishment arose. Andrew Campbell had retired from Burmah, but was acting as their consultant chemist, having set up a small laboratory in May 1915 at Putney, where, amongst other work, a study of Persian distillates was undertaken. Simultaneously close consideration was being given by the Admiralty and Redwood to the viscosity problems of fuel oil. Redwood sought the help of A.E. Dunstan, head of the chemical depart-

The research laboratory, Sunbury 1918 with Dr A.E. Dunstan and Dr F.B. Thole

Table 7.3. Ābādān Refinery output of products 1912–19

(long tons)

	Benzine	%	Kerosine	%	Fuel oil	%	Distillate	%	Total
1912–13	5 000	15	8 000	24	20 000	61	—	—	33 000
1913–14	14 000	11	24 000	19	75 000	61	11 000	9	124 000
1914–15	24 000	9	33 000	13	178 000	70	20 000	8	255 000
1915–16	26 000	11	18 000	8	164 000	72	20 000	9	228 000
1916–17	108 000	23	38 000	8	330 000	69	—	—	476 000
1917–18	147 000	18	86 000	11	582 000	71	—	—	815 000
1918–19	161 000	17	118 000	13	644 000	70	—	—	923 000

(refinery losses of an average of 7.4 per cent)
Source: BP AC 21

Persia - The scene of operations

ment at the East Ham Technical College, who, with a colleague, F.B. Thole, had already successfully studied some aspects of viscosity.[47] Greenway engaged Dunstan and Thole for the research in June 1915. It took many years to devise a practical refinery process to solve the problem, but the preliminary studies enabled certain principles to be formulated and knowledge was gradually accumulated on the properties and characteristics of Persian crude oil, indispensable for later research into products and process improvements. Greenway, well-satisfied with the services of Dunstan, sent him to Persia in November 1916 to study water requirements and resources.[48] On that visit, Dunstan also experimented at the refinery and was able to assess more accurately the possibilities of Persian oil.

On his return in May 1917 Dunstan expressed the view that 'the Company possessed a crude oil of vast potentialities but nobody knew anything at all of its actual composition and especially of the substances that made it difficult to refine'.[49] With considerable confidence and prescience Greenway and Slade agreed to set up a Company research organisation, and appoint Dunstan as 'Research Chemist'.[50] It is perhaps another indication of the gradual but definite desire of the Company to lessen its technical dependence on Burmah that it decided not to base its research activities on Campbell's existing laboratory at Putney. Dunstan fully recognised his debt to the friendship of Campbell, 'from whom I learned more than the mere rudiments of my new trade', in his own work. Dunstan and Thole found suitable, but dilapidated, premises in a Georgian mansion, named 'Meadhurst' at Sunbury on Thames with 2½ acres, which was purchased for £950 on 25 September 1917, and became the nucleus of the Company's research activities.[51] The first research was into viscosity, toluene production and the refining of benzine and kerosine.[52] Operational requirements were to determine the pattern of the Company's research.

What were the activities which were in danger of distracting Neilson's time and energy? War was declared against Turkey on 5 November 1914 and almost immediately afterwards an expeditionary force of the Indian army landed in Turkish territory at the head of the Persian Gulf. This had been preceded by some activity in which German inspired sabotage plans to block the Shatt-al-'Arab by scuttling certain vessels and to attack Ābādān, had been detected. A naval sloop, HMS *Odin*, patrolled the river estuary. It was joined in late September by another sloop, HMS *Espiégle*, which engaged Turkish forces opposite Ābādān on 6 November.[53] Two days later British forces were landed above Ābādān, repulsing a Turkish attack on 11 November before capturing Basra on 21 November. The immediate danger to Ābādān had been averted, a blow to Turkish prestige had been inflicted, encouragement given to local Persians and

Persia - The scene of operations

Arabs to rally to British support, and the safety ensured of local rulers loyal to British interests, such as the Emir of Kuwait and the Shaykh of Muhammara. Thereafter Basra became the bridge-head for the supply and provisioning of the expeditionary force in Mesopotamia. The Viceroy of India, Lord Hardinge of Penshurst, formerly Sir Charles Hardinge, called at Ābādān during his Persian Gulf visit in early February 1915.[54] Commending the staff for their services the Viceroy praised them for their contribution to the war effort.[55]

After the early engagements an apparent lull followed, but almost coinciding with the visit of the Viceroy the Turks incited, with the assistance of German agents particularly Herr Wassmuss, who was acquainted with the area before the war, some members of the Bawi tribe to damage the pipeline near Qaraneh, 4½ miles north-east of Ahwāz, loot stores and cut the telephone wires. It could have had disastrous consequences and the Company in London was extremely concerned, cabling H.W. Maclean, who was looking after its interests in Tehrān, 'Position very critical. Request Persian Government instruct Bakhtiari Khans provide immediately sufficient force guard to Wais and also to send strong force gendarmerie to Ahwaz to ensure protection Company's property in accordance with Clause 14 Concession.'[56] It was a perfectly proper request but impractical for although the Persian Government expected the allegiance of its tribes it was unable to command it. Both the Company and the Government were powerless to prevent the incident. After delays due to military operations, indecision, and discussions, the line was readily repaired once security was restored. Oil flowed to Ābādān again on 13 June, but the psychological harm done to the relations between the Company and the Persian Government never really healed and caused mutual recrimination when compensation was claimed by the Company and refused by the Persian Government.

Throughout the crucial months of 1915 and 1916 the presence of the expeditionary forces guaranteed the safety of Ābādān, but it was the self-interest and friendship of the majority of the Bakhtiari Khans which maintained security in the oil region around Masjid i-Suleimān. It was the attentions of Dr Young and the authority of Percy Cox, who had returned to the Persian Gulf as chief political officer to the expeditionary force, which helped to prevent disturbances.[57] While the Bakhtiaris kept to their agreements and the Shaykh of Muhammara was well-treated, the risk of serious disturbances in the midst of the oil operations was unlikely in spite of German agents and some local unrest. It was of little importance whether brigades or platoons were stationed to defend the Company's installations, a matter over which much agonised debate was spent, to no particular purpose, as sufficient troops were not available. The last alarm

Persia - The scene of operations

sounded with the collapse of the Russian army on the outbreak of the Revolution in October 1917 when Greenway expressed 'very gravest concern'. He feared that the Russian troops had become 'quite uncontrolled and uncontrollable', and that, instead of defending Persia against Turkish forces, were 'withdrawing looting along the way', so 'opening the road for a Turco-German occupation of the country'.[58] Greenway considered that there were insufficient forces to defend the oilfield. The danger, however, was minimal whilst the opposing Persian factions remained divided.

Meanwhile in Ābādān, as a result of a request from the Admiralty in February 1915, the Company had begun assisting in the assembly of 12 river gunboats which Messrs Yarrow were fabricating and sending out in sections. The India Office also asked for help in constructing barges, repairing river craft and providing tank storage facilities for the expeditionary force.[59] By May, Neilson had drawn attention to the fact that 'Government proposed work has now reached considerable proportions', and, whilst recognising that 'most of the Government work will be supervised by their own officials', he was certainly right in believing that 'we will in all probability have to give the time - or part at least - of some of our European engineers to help on the different work'.[60] Neilson did not shirk his responsibilities, though he was keen to have them acknowledged,

An aerial view of Ābādān 1918

Persia - The scene of operations

but he did carry a very considerable extra burden throughout the war, when 'the resources of my staff and myself will presently tend to become overstrained'. Greenway might complain that Company labour and supervision was being used for gunboat construction but it was inevitable in the circumstances, irrespective of the expenditure or the authority involved.[61] A year later further demands for the construction of 6 paddle steamers, 16 tugs and 55 larger barges were made, as well as a lighthouse depot and a telegraph station.[62] Ābādān's contribution to the war effort was impressive. The staff had done their duty.

(c) Geological aspects

After Reynolds had drilled in the discovery well on 26 May 1908 and a further six producing wells had been brought in a year later by May 1909, the Company felt no immediate need for further exploration, at least until the completion of the pipeline in 1911. Lorimer had already suggested in July 1908 further exploration to lessen dependence on the Bakhtiari Khans and Reynolds had attempted, unsuccessfully, to interest the Company in prospects in the Pusht-i-Kuh area and a resumption of drilling at Marmatain.[63] Further drilling commenced on 20 July 1912 at Chiāh Surkh, which Greenway had visited in early 1911. Drilling was eventually suspended there in April 1913 after the bit had dropped in the well. The casing was badly damaged in trying to retrieve it.[64] At the end of 1912 the idea of testing at Ahwāz was revived. S. Lister James, one of Redwood's roving geologists, who had learnt his skills from Dalton and Cunningham-Craig, both of whom had visited Persia, as recounted in Chapter 2, was sent to Persia and selected a site.[65] He was joined shortly afterwards in early 1913 by H.T. Mayo, a Burmah geologist and in 1914 by H.G. Busk. The well, however, after being spudded in in August 1913, was abandoned after encountering difficult formations in September 1915 at 3317 feet, a deep well for its time. Lister James also located a site at Naft Safid for a test well, but that also was unsuccessful. With encouragement from the Admiralty Commission, which he accompanied, Lister James recommended a site for a shallow well on Qishm Island, down the Persian Gulf near the Straits of Hormuz, in November 1914. Here too no oil was struck. An attack mounted on the camp in June 1915 by the local populace, was resisted by the manager, J.L. Wright and his staff.[66]

In 1915 an attempt was made to coordinate and advance the geological work. Macrorie, who had visited Persia in late 1908, became the nominal head of the Company's geological branch. On his visit to Persia in 1915 Macrorie did not visit Masjid i-Suleimān but confined himself to correlating the mapping being done in Balūchistān, along the Makrān coast and up

Persia - The scene of operations

Unloading a boiler at Qishm Island 1914

B.F.N. Macrorie, middle centre, with his wife to his right and H.G. Busk in front 1915

Persia - The scene of operations

as far as Bushire. If time had allowed he envisaged making sections of the Masjid i-Suleimān area and recording the strata but he had to be satisfied with collating all the information that was available and interpreting it in a systematic manner for the first time. It was also at this time that Thompson was asking, 'will the Geologists tell us definitely the chances of striking the main zone in depth and at what depth, in the wells under discussions - that is all we want to know?'[67] Uncertainties over the oil-bearing strata increased the risks of blow-outs. The first simple methods of preventing oil getting out of control by clamping a hydraulic jack to the casing were then being tested.[68] It was beginning to be recognised that a resident geologist on an oilfield had an important part to play in production control.

Macrorie's reconnaissance was followed in the subsequent winter season of 1916-17, when the security situation had improved, by tremendous geological activity and the recruitment of three more geologists, W.R.A. Weatherhead, G.W. Halse and J. Chapman-Brown. A systematic topographical survey of the Khūzistān province of south-west Persia and initiated on a 1 in. to 1 mile basis, which took three seasons. Later Company geologists described this mapping success in glowing terms as being 'of outstanding importance. Not only was their mapping of very high quality but the stratigraphical and structural information gathered and so clearly presented in map and report, formed the foundation on which was built all subsequent work on post-Asmari sedimentation and tectonics ... major contributions to both exploration and development progress in Iran.'[69] Most geological work hitherto had been concentrated on visible indications of oil seepages, but Macrorie advised the necessity for a more fundamental geological appreciation of the terrain and its formations. This was important, directing attention to the possible structural conditions in which oil could accumulate.

Mayo and Busk presented a paper in late 1918 to the Institute of Petroleum Technologists, which in many respects summed up the Company's geological achievements in Persia and some of the problems encountered.[70] A phase had ended. Information had been amassed and it needed analysis. Mayo and Busk were rightly concerned to identify the reservoir rock. However they did not recognise the Asmari limestone as the oil source. Instead they saw it to be what they termed 'the reservoir detrital limestones'. Such an interpretation was an advance on Cunningham Craig's earlier assumption of a sandstone origin, but Mayo and Busk were mistakenly confident that the search would be, after careful survey, 'a comparatively straight-forward matter'. By 1918, then, much of the ground in the concessionary area in south-west Persia had been covered by detailed topographical observations and much data obtained, but drilling

Persia - The scene of operations

success was still confined to the single known field, whose known production area had been significantly extended.

4 MARKETING

During this period the distribution and marketing of all products took place from Persia. As has been mentioned previously the delays in refinery construction, the difficulties in commissioning and the problems over the processes played havoc with the early production of benzine and kerosine and changed an independent marketing strategy into one of reliance on contracts with the Asiatic Petroleum Company. The supply agreement with the Admiralty enabled the Company to make regular bulk sales of a single product, fuel oil, to one customer at a definite price, obviating the need for a network of installations which could not be afforded. This forced alternative strategy for survival must not be allowed to obscure the primary objective of the Company to develop and supply the market itself, a policy which Greenway pursued with a pertinacity and obstinacy, remarkable in the circumstances. A failure to appreciate the keen competitive instinct of Greenway's mind is to miss the tense drama between two of the leading personalities of the commercial play of the day, Greenway and Samuel. The Company was in a quandary, its marketing prospects were insignificant in comparison to its production potential, but to become merely a wholesaler in partly refined products, which other companies would retail with their superior resources at a higher profitability, was a confession of ultimate defeat, which Greenway was never disposed to admit.

The quality of products was generally poor,[71] but during 1913 and 1914 as regular production improved Walpole and his colleagues built up a network of outlets and agents within the Persian Gulf and Mesopotamia. The early commercial policy was based on combatting the existing trade of Standard Oil in the area, as is evidenced, for example, in the instructions to Wallahdas Umerse, sub-agent at Muscat, to 'inform your clients beforehand that you intend always to sell at a cheaper rate than the Standard Oil Company'[72] for 'we wish you to monopolise the oil business in your markets, and you are therefore at liberty to underquote competitors at all times rather than let SOC obtain any business'.[73] Agents were appointed at Basra, Baghdad, Bushire, Bandar 'Abbās, Lingeh, Muscat, Bahrain, Muhammara and Isfahān as the main depots, receiving oils on a consignment basis for which they received 2½ per cent commission and were allowed to fix their own price levels, so long as they were cheaper than those of Standard Oil. Supplies of kerosine and benzine were packed in two gallon tins and distributed by the s.s. *Ferrara*.

Persia - The scene of operations

Fuel oil was supplied for the local river steamers, the first contract for which was with Lynch Bros for 100 tons a month at £1 17s 4d, per ton in December 1912. Further contracts were made in 1914 for regular supplies to the Euphrates and Tigris Steam Navigation Company, the Hamburg-Amerika Line for an annual minimum quantity of 1000 tons and in February 1916 for ten years with the British India Steam Navigation Company, which operated to and from India and the Persian Gulf.[74] Accompanied by activities in the Indian sub-continent, these were the modest beginnings of the Company's bunkering trade which became such a prominent aspect of its commercial policy. It was indeed inevitable that the Company should look to India as a market, once the Ābādān refinery became operational. F. Macindoe, the Company secretary, observed that 'given facilities in India, the potentialities of the trade to be secured are enormous'.[75] The possibilities of supplying the Indian railways with fuel oil had already been unsuccessfully explored in conversation with the Admiralty over the government shareholding (see Chapter 5). As early as 2 September 1912 the Company requested Strick, Scott & Co. to ship some fuel oil to Karachi, Bombay, Madras, Calcutta and Colombo, but Messrs Finlay Fleming & Co., the managing agents for Burmah, cautiously advised that 'while it is possible, with guaranteed supplies over a period of years at a rate that will tempt people to go in for Diesel Engines', sufficient immediate sales were unlikely, unless to railways, and even in their case it would take them a long time to convert from coal to oil.[76] Yet efforts were directed at the railways in November 1913, when the Indian North Western Railways carried out successful trials with fuel oil which compared favourably with coal-fired engines. Yet, in spite of lobbying from Slade when he was in Delhi in 1914 after the Admiralty Commission's visit to Persia, the Indian Government was not prepared to encourage the railways to experiment with fuel oil or exempt the Company from excise duty on Persian oil to enable them to become more competitive with cheap Indian coal.

The matter lapsed till August 1915 when Sir Trevredyn Wynne, a very distinguished railway engineer in India and retiring managing director of the Bengal—Nagpur Railway, joined the Company's Board, bringing with him a wealth of experience and contacts. Wynne journeyed to India in early 1916, to press the Company's case concerning 'the largely increased quantities of fuel oil that we shall shortly have available for sale and the consequent urgent necessity for opening new outlets for the same'.[77] The Company stressed that the adoption of fuel oil for railways 'should be considered not solely from the point of view of price, but also from that of the Imperial interests involved'. Wynne did his best 'to push the use of Anglo-Persian fuel oil on the Indian railways', but it was not until 1917 that the Railways Board resolved to substitute oil for coal on the North-Western and Great Indian Peninsular Railways, and indicated a desire for a contract up to 1934.[78] Deliveries actually commenced in June 1917 and 18 500 tons of fuel oil were delivered to the end of the year, but it was not until 31 January 1921 that a formal contract was signed, applicable from 1 January 1917. The Indian Government displayed a dog-in-the-manger attitude, commenting in 1917 that they 'deprecated our going on with the scheme as the Admiralty was doubtful whether either the oil or its transport can be counted on', and that before proceeding with the conversion of engines they 'would be glad to know if the Admiralty and other Government Directors on your Board have assented to the guarantee'.[79] Transport was a problem especially during the latter part of the war when shipping was so strictly controlled, but the Company managed to maintain its supplies.

Other fuel oil arrangements were concluded with Burmah, who provided storage and selling facilities at a charge of 5 per cent interest and 5 per cent depreciation on their capital cost with expenses, for disposing of fuel oil at their installations in India, with Messrs Shaw, Wallace & Co. acting as the agents. The Company was already interested in bunkering sites at Cochin, Marmagao, Tuticorin, Ernakulam and Colombo in 1913, though it was appreciated that while it had to make a start in the market 'we shall, I am afraid, have to face very slow sales'.[80] The Asiatic Petroleum Company also distributed Persian fuel oil in India, by an agreement reached in December 1912 on commercial contracts for 25 000 tons, but not in respect of government sales. There were frequent arguments over the compliance with the terms and the level of prices. The Company ran into difficulty in trying to extend its bunkering operations to Colombo where local indifference and Asiatic opposition prevented a favourable decision being taken till July 1917.[81] In mid-1917 an important site was acquired at Aden, which was later in the early 1920s to become a hub of Company activity along the Suez Canal trade routes and voyages across the Indian Ocean and up the Persian Gulf.[82] This was part of a deliberate policy which Greenway explained to Black in 1916: 'we are coming within sight of the completion of our extensions at Ābādān, and it is therefore essential that we should in the meantime open up every possible outlet for our products in the East'.[83]

The Company trade in Mesopotamia was ended abruptly in October 1914 when the Turkish authorities seized all the stocks at Baghdad and Basra, and there were no direct sales to the civilian population till Baghdad was captured in March 1917. Baghdad was, according to Walpole, 'by far the largest market for oil in the Persian Gulf sphere', and during some periods sales of kerosine were averaging 1000 cases a day.[84] The arrival of the expeditionary force in November 1914 and the general shortage of shipping and tin plate supplies caused the Company great difficulties in supplying the various sub-agencies particularly after it had just acquired the bulk of the kerosine trade of the Persian Gulf, displaced the Standard Oil Company there and raised prices to more profitable levels. By 1917 the Company was unable to maintain regular supplies of its products to its customers and complained to the British military administration that 'our trade down the Gulf is suffering to the advantage of our competitors'.[85] With the s.s. *Ferrara* fully engaged in towing barges out to Admiralty tankers for lightering at the bar of the Shatt-al-'Arab, opportunities for freighting were severely curtailed. So supplies to the markets were dwindling, prices were rising and much hardship was experienced throughout the cold winter because of the shortage of kerosine in outlying areas. Gradually the military authorities were persuaded in late 1917 to release certain stocks of kerosine and more tin plate was made available under Government licence. The situation improved, though arguments continued on the buy-back price from the Army and the retail price to be charged, on which there was no general agreement until September 1918. Controversy continued amid accusations of profiteering against Strick, Scott & Co. and allegations of racketeering against certain officials of the military administration.

Inevitably the armed services took most of the Company's production of kerosine and benzine, as well as much fuel oil for its river transport craft and gunboats. They monopolised the output of the Ābādān tin plant and requisitioned nearly all the available means of transportation. The importance of government requirements within the context of the Company's production can be imagined by comparing Greenway's estimates of supplies with the calculations of refinery throughput. In July 1917 Greenway suggested that the Company would be supplying the Government on an annual basis with fuel oil for the Navy amounting to 550 000 tons, 150 000 tons motor spirit for the needs of the allied forces, and about 80 000 tons of fuel oil, petrol and kerosine for expeditionary forces in Mesopotamia, some 780 000 tons in all.[86] This, in fact, was over-optimistic. Table 7.4 shows the actual amounts of products supplied to the Admiralty and the Mesopotamian forces. The remainder of product output was for local sales within the Persian Gulf and India and for the contracts with the Asiatic Petroleum Company.[87]

During the war years His Majesty's Government was the Company's most important customer. The ever growing demand for petroleum products by British armed services kept abreast of the rapidly rising refinery output. From 1915 to 1919 the Admiralty alone took two thirds of fuel oil output, itself 65 per cent of Ābādān's product output, and

Table 7.4. *Supplies of products to Admiralty and Mesopotamian forces 1914–20*

(long tons)

	Fuel oil supplied to Navy	Per cent of total refinery production of fuel oil taken on by Admiralty	Volume contracted by Admiralty	Excess supply over contract maximum	Products supplied to Mesopotamian forces
1914–15	73 000	41	50 000 – 70 000	3 000	—
1915–16	109 000	66	90 000 – 120 000	—	—
1916–17	226 000	68	100 000 – 150 000	76 000	3 000
1917–18	399 000	69	300 000 – 350 000	49 000	39 000
1918–19	424 000	66	300 000 – 350 000	74 000	148 000
1919–20	394 000	53	300 000 – 350 000	44 000	64 000

Source: PRO ADM 116 2318C and BP

Persia - The scene of operations

substantially more than contracted volumes. The sharp increases in profits in 1916-17 and 1917-18 as the volume of sales grew (see Chapter 6) underline the crucial importance of the Admiralty contract. Without the security of the Admiralty contract it is almost inconceivable that the Company would have preserved its independent existence.[88] The Admiralty contract[89] stipulated that from 1 July 1914 a quantity of 6 000 000 tons of fuel oil was to be delivered over a 20 year period. The aggregate was not to exceed 500 000 tons a year except in the event of war when the Admiralty had first option on all production. The price was 30s a ton f.o.b. Ābādān, subject to rebates when the Company profits exceeded 10 per cent on the ordinary shares, after all repayment of advances, payments of dividends on preference shares, interest on debenture stock, etc. Within the first year demand of some 10 000 tons a month was double the estimated requirements, within three years it had exceeded the maximum estimates. It is undeniable that the prodigious demand for petroleum products occasioned by the war was completely responsible for the unexpected volume of production which was required from the Company, so ensuring its financial stability and survival to be a commercial force in the post-war world.

One unexpected result of the volume of government demand for petroleum products as a result of the war and the enhanced profitability of the Company was its lessening dependence upon the Asiatic Petroleum Company contracts for the disposal of its products and the earning of its revenue during the war. Cargill had acknowledged to Greenway in the troubled situation that was already developing in March 1912, when Waley Cohen was making overtures about purchasing kerosine and benzine, that 'I have always felt that he would make a very strong effort to prevent APOC competing with him in kerosine, benzine and petrol, and it remains to be seen how far he will go in trying to achieve this object.'[90] Waley Cohen succeeded and, with considerable success after much controversy and argument, concluded crude oil, benzine and kerosine contracts for ten years on 15 October 1912 (see Chapter 4).[91] The Asiatic agreed to take crude oil deliveries of up to 60 000 tons annually at 15s 9½d a ton and kerosine, up to half the refinery output at 45s 9½d a ton subject to certain specifications over quality. Benzine deliveries were to be not more than 18 000 tons in each six month period, also at 45s 9½d a ton with similar provisions over quality. The Company accepted certain restrictions on its potential marketing areas and the volumes it could supply to those markets. Some modifications on disputed points were made on 1 January 1915. It was the benzine contract that caused the greatest difficulty because of the failure of the refinery process. The earlier deliveries were unacceptable and the Asiatic claimed a 12s 9d rebate for further treatment to make the benzine marketable, which was greatly in excess of the allowable refinery cost of 5s. Eventually 30 000 tons of once-run distillate were, for two years, substituted for benzine at a lower price for refining at Shell's Suez refinery.[92]

It was in the context of the Company's rivalry with the Royal Dutch-Shell group that the fate of the BP Company was so important (see Chapter 6). As early as the summer of 1915 Greenway had submitted a memorandum on the future of that company and its subsidiaries making the point that Shell did not have its own marketing organisation but distributed through the BP Company which Shell was possibly interested in purchasing. According to Greenway this would mean that 'all the tangible assets of the Companies of any value would be acquired by the Shell at "knock-out" prices, that the valuable goodwill of these concerns would be completely sacrificed and that the unique opportunity of securing a ready-made organisation (which it would take any new Company many years to build up)' would be lost.[93] Greenway strove to prevent this happening, at first in conjunction with other interests, like Cowdray, and later on his own by a campaign of proclaiming the attractions of an 'all British' Company and denigrating the activities of his competitors.

Eventually, after long negotiations with the Public Trustee Greenway agreed at the end of May 1917 to purchase, for £2 650 000[94] (some £900 000 more than had been agreed at a board meeting on 28 March), the BP Company and its subsidiaries. Included were 7 tankers, 15 ocean installations including tankage with a capacity of 185 000 tons, 520 inland depots, 535 railway tank wagons, 1102 road vehicles and motors, 4 barges and 650 horses. The purchase price of £2 650 000 included accrued dividends owing of £650 000 which effectively reduced the cost to £2 000 000. The purchase terms were for a cash down-payment of £600 000 and five annual instalments, from 1918 to 1922, of £280 000. The initial £600 000 in cash was raised by borrowing £420 000 from the BP Company itself and £180 000 from the vendor, the Public Trustee. Debentures to the value of £1 400 000 of the Company were issued and lodged with the Public Trustee as security for the outstanding instalments.

The Company anticipated no difficulty in meeting the annual instalments of £280 000 out of profits. The Public Trustee reserved the right to demand that outstanding instalments should be paid off upon the cessation of hostilities but the Company was confident that it would be able to raise sufficient funds either from the public or out of profits to cope with such a demand. It had acquired its own marketing organisation, and, though the institution of the Pool Board prevented much activity during the war, it was ready for service in the post-war markets under W.D. Braithwaite, a

Persia - The scene of operations

former member of the Shaw, Wallace and Co. staff. He was released from the forces early to take charge.[95]

One of the contentious issues was the freedom of the Company to distribute petroleum products in the United Kingdom because of the 1912 contracts with the Asiatic. Greenway, who had been so intimately involved in the negotiations, refuted the idea that the Company could in no circumstances sell any kerosine or benzine directly or indirectly to its own customers. In this interpretation he was supported by Sir Frank Crisp, the Company's legal adviser, who wrote to him in early April that 'the Agreements with the Asiatic Company do not cover anything but the production of the Anglo-Persian in Persia ... There would appear to be no reason why the Anglo-Persian should not acquire the British Petroleum Company as far as the Asiatic Agreements are concerned.'[96] The Company was fully integrated, the last piece had fallen into place.

Though only indirectly concerned with the operations in Persia, the formation of the British Tanker Company Ltd on 3 April 1915, with an initial capital of £100 000, was an extremely important event, not only in the development of the Company, but more particularly because of its significance in the evolving marketing strategy of self-reliance. In the memorandum which accompanied the estimates of probable expenditure submitted to the Admiralty in February 1914, Greenway included an item for £200 000, a tenth of the total, for shares in a tanker company to be formed. He justified this expenditure on the grounds that 'some tankers will be necessary in connection with the general trade of the Company, in order that it may be independent of the Anglo-Saxon Company who largely control the market', because he recognised that 'the construction by the Company of its own tankers would necessitate a large capital outlay.'[97] A proposal had earlier been made for the Company to participate in a tanker company, which would build and supply tankers as required at an appropriate return on capital without the Company incurring further capital costs. Negotiations involving Inchcape, Sir John Ellerman, F.C. Strick and the Company, in July 1914, for the proposed Imperial Tanker Company Ltd, with a capital of £900 000 of 400 000 £1 ordinary shares and 500 000 £1 preference shares, were, however, not successful.[98]

The Company already owned some shipping. The s.s. *Ferrara*, 1650 dwt was bought in April 1912 for distributing products in the Persian Gulf, and though an unsightly ship, described by one of the engineers in 1917 as 'the most terrible thing on God's earth', she had held together for 43 years when scrapped in 1923.[99] The next ship, no less an oddity than the first was a 1500 ton barge, named the *Friesland* which was 'something in the nature of a ship with the essential parts left out'.[100] The third ship was the 94 foot ocean-going tug, *Sirdar-i-Napht*, bought in 1914 for lightering purposes,

Persia - The scene of operations

but requisitioned during the war and armed with a three pounder gun. This hardly constituted a fleet, but in early 1915 orders were placed for five tankers with Messrs Armstrong, Whitworth Ltd on the Tyne, two of 5796 dwt and three over 10 000 dwt, and for two over 10 000 dwt with Messrs Swan Hunter also on the Tyne.[101]

All these ships and later additions to the fleet had their names distinctively prefixed with 'British'. They were delivered during 1917, apart from the *British Emperor*, which was delivered a year earlier and was employed out of Ābādān to Bombay, Karachi, Madras, Calcutta and other ports east of Suez at which the Company had agencies. In the later stages of the war they sailed under the direction of the Ministry of Shipping.

Greenway was criticised in some quarters of the press and parliament for these orders, but defended with confidence what he anticipated rightly would prove 'a most remunerative investment'. He justified his decision on the grounds that 'it must be apparent to everyone acquainted with the Oil Trade how dangerous it would be for a Company situated as ours is and requiring so much tonnage as we shall do after our Extensions are completed, to rely upon the chances of securing freight at reasonable rates in a market so restricted as that for Oil Tankers'. Early in 1916 the capital of the British Tanker Company was doubled. A very important development which accompanied the purchase of the BP Company in 1917 was the acquisition at the same time of its shipping associate, the Petroleum

The *British Emperor*, delivered in 1916

Persia - The scene of operations

Steamship Company. This possessed eleven tankers of which seven passed into the ownership of the Company, thus providing a useful nucleus for a tanker fleet and trained personnel. The British Tanker Company, whose capital had been raised to £3 000 000 in November 1917 by the creation of 2 800 000 £1 shares, all of which were allotted as fully paid, by the end of the war was participating in the running of tankers for the Royal Fleet Auxiliary Service on behalf of the Admiralty.

Greenway's judgement was vindicated by events, especially in the post-war period when shipping was freed from government war-time restrictions and the Company was able to take its place in the international oil industry. The productive capacity of the field at Masjid i-Suleimān had been amply sustained without any drop in pressure, the pipeline throughput had been satisfactorily increased and the refinery processing had been improved to provide a regular flow of reasonable products. After the experience gained and the progress made in the operations in Persia there was no reason for not expecting further expansion of production and refining activities. The Company possessed a shipping fleet and organisation which would enable it to transport crude or products at its own cost and in its own time. It had established a sufficiently strong base from which to take advantage of the facilities, assets and staff which it had acquired with the BP Company, and to assert its independence in the market place.

8
MANAGEMENT AND FINANCE 1918-28

I INTRODUCTION

The Company emerged from the war incomparably, almost unrecognisably, stronger. In mid-1914 oil produced by the Company barely averaged 750 tons a day drawn from just two wells from a single field in Persia. In Fields there was a staff of 20 Europeans and 832 Persians, and 103 Arabs and Indians. It operated an inefficient and unreliable refinery processing some 75 000 tons of unsatisfactory fuel oil, 14 000 tons of inferior benzine and 24 000 tons of indifferent kerosine a year. It owned no distributing installations, no fleet of tankers for transportation and relied upon marketing contracts with Royal Dutch-Shell and a supply agreement with the Admiralty for its sales. Its capital, including debentures, was £2 599 000. It had paid no dividends, it was operating at a loss. Its financial situation was parlous, its prospects unpromising, its assets derisory in comparison with its competitors. By the end of 1918 the position had improved and oil production averaged 2460 tons a day from five wells. At the end of 1918 there were 44 European staff and 3173 Persians and 128 others in Fields. It was refining to a better quality 644 000 tons of fuel oil, 161 000 tons of benzine, and 118 000 tons of kerosine. It had formed a tanker company in 1915, created a research centre and acquired a distribution organisation in 1917. Its capital had increased to £7 000 000, it made a trading profit of £415 827 5s 10d in 1917 and it was able to declare its first dividend.

In considering the Company at various stages in its growth, a sense of proportion has to be observed in the scale of its operations in order to appreciate the response of its management to policy needs and structural requirements. In many respects the war, whilst stimulating the activities of the Company, distracted it from the administrative reorganisation which should have kept pace with its growth. Furthermore, the respective interests of Burmah, the Government and the Company did not always coincide and the *modus vivendi* that in practice was established was the result of the reconciliation of different and at times divergent interests.

Management and finance

During this post-war period until he was succeeded in 1927 by Cadman, Greenway remained the man at the helm.[1] He did not have the prestige of a proprietor nor the panache of an entrepreneur. He was no hired hand offering his labour. He was a transitional figure in the managerial evolution, resembling more the image of a professional man, from the law, accounting or banking, but possessing the shrewdness of a successful merchant and some of the opportunism of the politician. His one failure was his difficulty in appreciating that the managing agency, a form of organisation which had functioned admirably for the trader in eastern markets throughout the nineteenth century, was inappropriate for the supervision of an enterprise based on modern industrial technology. He succeeded in steering the Company between the Scylla and Charybdis of its relations with Burmah and the Government. He recognised that the style of management, which he had exercised with the help of his two close colleagues, Garrow and Nichols, was unsatisfactory for the growing diversity of the Company's activities. It took time to produce the management and administration which reflected the needs of the Company. It was a painful and occasionally exasperating period of trial and error in which the alchemy of differing personalities was an inevitable part of the process.[2]

It has to be remembered that until 1913 there was virtually no trading by the Company and that its activity was primarily concerned with constructing the pipeline and refinery and recruiting staff for the purpose. Shaw, Wallace & Co. and R.G. Shaw, firms in which Wallace and Greenway were partners, helped with the arrangements to set up Lloyd, Scott and Co., later Strick, Scott & Co, the managing agents, who attended to the administration of affairs in Persia. All the technical matters were the responsibility of Hamilton in Glasgow. As has been previously noticed (see Chapter 7), Greenway early became dissatisfied with the handling of technical problems and staff relations. He himself was concerned with the marketing and concessionary aspects of the Company's policy. Pretyman in April 1914 had thought Greenway the natural successor to Strathcona. As for the chairmanship, he felt 'the strongest objection to seeing it hawked about... There is certainly the danger of the Government trying to nominate one of their own persuasion'.[3]

Pretyman may have considered it dangerous but this is what happened, according to Greenway, who noted later in 1925 that

between February 1914 and July 1914 the Chairmanship was successively - always at the instance of the Government - offered to Austen Chamberlain, Lord Scarborough, Lord Mount Stephen and Lord Selborne.[4] In each case the names were of course submitted to Cargill for approval before the offer was made. In the end - at the instance of the Government, who were anxious to get the post filled before the share purchase came before Parliament, and because we had then exhausted the list of what were thought to be suitable men of the "figure-head" type, I was asked if I could accept the post, and after submission of this proposal to Cargill the election was made.[5]

Wallace was also concerned, but the person most responsible for Greenway's appointment was Hopwood, who submitted his name 'to the Cabinet Committee dealing with the question of the purchase of the shares and was agreed to by them, subject to the consent of the Burmah Oil Company'. It was exceptional for Greenway to be both chairman and managing director at the same time. It was a crucial appointment giving Greenway unexpected scope and authority to pursue his own strategy with the consent of his Board but without deference to a separate chairman. It also led to the establishment of a tradition which has generally prevailed that the chairman is the senior managing director and that the Government is consulted.

The responsibilities of the government directors had been outlined in Bradbury's explanatory letter of 20 May 1914 and embodied in Article 91A of the Articles of Association (see Chapter 6), but the qualifications for these directors and their instructions were less well-defined. The Admiralty felt that they should have 'some knowledge of oil matters and clear conception as to the policy to be followed and results desired by the Government'[6] and that 'it will obviously be necessary that the two ex-officio directors shall work together in pursuance of the definite aims and interests of H.M. Government in this matter'.[7] This was the problem. What constituted government policy? Its desirability was one thing, its formulation, let alone its implementation, quite another matter. The Company sometimes suffered from political expediency masquerading as government policy or departmental compromise, which, as Greenway remarked to Inchcape in January 1917, puts 'us into quite a false position'.[8] Admiral Slade and Lord Inchcape were the first two appointed government directors, who doubtless received informal briefings about their duties but apparently no formal instructions about their responsibilities.[9]

Their influence was measured more by the persuasiveness of their personalities than the clarity of their purpose. It could hardly have been otherwise in the absence of a coherent policy in ever changing war-time circumstances. Certainly the preoccupations of the two directors closely mirrored their own respective expertise and opinions; national strategy and security for Slade and financial and commercial aspects for Inchcape. Just as the Company's assessment of its commercial potential in the market place changed according to its competitive position, so did the relationship of the Company to the government directors evolve over the years. The guiding principle, however, remained constant as Sir Hamar Greenwood, Secretary to the Department of Overseas Trade in the Board of Trade, confirmed for the first time publicly in answer to a parliamentary question on 18 March 1920, in the House of Commons: 'The Government does not interfere with the commercial arrangements of the Company, and will not, unless, which of course will never happen, they are antagonistic to the interests of the British Empire.'[10]

2 POST-WAR DEVELOPMENTS

(a) Administration in London

Greenway's position as chairman was reaffirmed at a board meeting held on 24 January 1918, when it was resolved that 'Mr Greenway shall continue to hold the position of Chairman for an indefinite period, and to fulfil the duties of Managing Director until such time as satisfactory arrangements can be made for relieving him of those duties.'[11] There was no loss of confidence in him. The episode involving him in 1916 mentioned in Chapter 6 had left no lasting marks. Slade, though retaining the title of vice-chairman, reverted to being an ordinary director 'without being responsible for, or taking any active part, in the administrative work of the Company'. The brunt of the administrative work continued to fall on Garrow and Nichols, who were again awarded special remuneration. In spring 1918 Greenway suffered a serious illness, from which he fully recovered, but his absence emphasised the precarious administrative basis of the Company.

Greenway appreciated that he had practically become a one-man band. He had 'during the war - with the very able assistance of Messrs. Nichols and Garrow - been "carrying on" this work to the best of my ability pending the practicability of making better arrangements, but have been conscious all the time that it is far more than any one man can tackle and that a much larger managing staff and decentralisation of the work are absolute essentials for the efficient working of the business'.[12] He concentrated on finding a replacement for himself, so that he could be relieved of the managing directorship and discharge the traditional role of the chairman. Yet he had to admit in January 1919 that

none of us has been able to find the outstanding 'big' man that it was agreed we should look out for, and I very much doubt if such a man - possessing all the necessary qualifications i.e. a more or less practical knowledge of (1) Geology, (2) Field Work, (3) Engineering, (4) Refining, (5) Shipowning, (6) Distributing Trade, (7) Accounts and Finance and (8) Company and Companising procedure - is to be found, and certainly not one of British nationality.

This was a frank admission that the management needed to be restructured to reflect the increasingly technical nature of the business and the impossibility of finding one man – 'to properly supervise and direct all the various branches of the Company's business'. Such a practice was no longer feasible for in 'none of the other big oil concerns is the responsibility for the management of these various branches left to a single individual'. Greenway knew that Royal Dutch-Shell had individual companies attached to the main company responsible for the different aspects of the business and that Standard Oil divided up 'the administration of the various branches of their business among a number of very highly paid men in positions equivalent to that of Managing Director'.[13] This was the type of organisation preferred by Greenway for he was conscious that, with the anticipated growth of the Company, control of the operations could no longer be centred on him. A new design was needed. It says much for Greenway's honesty and sense of purpose that he acknowledged that 'we have been altogether on the wrong track in trying to find a single man to take over the duties hitherto performed much too perfunctorily, latterly, owing to the enormous expansion of our operations' by himself.

The solution, therefore, was 'to appoint several Joint Managing Directors each having special knowledge of the Branch of the business for which he will be responsible, these Directors sitting as a Committee daily, or 2/3 times a week (as may be found most convenient) to discuss all important questions connected with their respective branches...The Chairman would, as a rule, also attend these meetings in order to direct the policy, but would not take any part in the executive work'. A precedent for such an organisation already existed in the BP Company, where the system, introduced by the Deutsche Bank, existed, of administering the business by means of a 'Management Committee' composed of the managing director and two other directors possessing practical knowledge of the distributing trade and receiving special remuneration beyond the ordinary directors' fees.

Accordingly Greenway proposed a form of administrative hybrid, a cross between American and German examples, by proposing a 'Management Committee' composed of the five heads of the separate but inter-related activities of (1) fields, pipeline and refinery, (2) commerce, engineering and general administration, (3) shipping, (4) finance, accounts and company affairs and (5) government liaison and concessionary matters. Garrow and Nichols were suggested for (1) and (2) respectively, J.D. Stewart, a partner in the Glasgow shipping firm of Gardiner and Co., was appointed for (3) and became a director on 23 February 1920. J.B. Lloyd, who had originally established the office of the managing agents in Muhammara and had recently retired as a senior partner in India of Shaw,

Management and finance

Duncan Garrow

H.E. Nichols

J.B. Lloyd

J.D. Stewart

Managing Directors of the Anglo-Persian Oil Company 1919-32

Management and finance

Sir John Cadman

W. Fraser

H.B. Heath-Eves

A.C. Hearn

Managing Directors of the Anglo-Persian Oil Company 1919-32 (continued)

Management and finance

Wallace & Co, was entrusted with finance and corporate affairs, becoming a director on 28 April 1919. A suitable person was not found to deal with government and concessionary matters. Greenway suggested that the posts, in the first instance, for five years from 1 January 1919, should carry a salary of £4000 a year with a 1 per cent commission on profits to be divided equally. Greenway expected to resign as managing director 'as soon as the new team has been properly established, and thereafter to retain the position of Chairman'.

Greenway's ideas were accepted at a board meeting on 27 January 1919[14] after earlier consultations with Cargill and R.I. Watson, a lean, spare, hard-working Scot, a director of Burmah, who became a director of the Company on 25 February 1918 and remained on the Board for nearly thirty years till his resignation on 23 December 1947. The principle of a management committee was eminently acceptable but the skill of direction was in the matching of people to posts, balancing the power of personalities so as to create an administration in which the parts related to the whole to produce a policy responsive to individual requirements and comprehensive enough for corporate objectives. Greenway's initiative set the management ball rolling but it took almost a decade of adaptation, or, more accurately, trial and error, before the Company achieved a satisfactory equilibrium between its strategic policy and its administrative structure.

The first management committee meeting was held on 26 February 1919,[15] at which Garrow, Nichols, Lloyd, Stewart and Sir Frederick Black, formerly Director of Contracts at the Admiralty, were present. Black succeeded, as government director, on 4 February W. St D. Jenkins, another Admiralty official, who had been a director for ten months after replacing Slade. On 30 June Black resigned as a government director and became a managing director, in effect the fifth member of the management committee envisaged by Greenway. The tentative nature of the new approach to management was recognised by Greenway himself. It was impossible 'to draw a hard and fast line as to what their respective duties would be and they would have to settle between themselves with due regard to efficiency and mutual convenience'.[16] It was a familiar chicken and egg predicament, for while 'each member of the Committee would be independent in his Branch of the business the desire was that no member of the Committee should decide upon any important vital question without general consultation'. The delegation of authority was limited and there was an obligation to consult together. The rudimentary beginnings of a management career structure are observable in the suggestion that 'each member should have an understudy who would also be available for future promotion in Persia, London or elsewhere'. By 17 September four

Management and finance

assistants had been recruited.[17] Not only was it considered right that the management committee should meet regularly on a formal basis, but also that they should frequently meet informally, and just as it was held necessary to have regular committee meetings so it was agreed that meetings of all the subsidiary companies should be held at stated intervals.[18]

During 1919 the committee bedded itself in so that in September Greenway felt able to resign as managing director,[19] though he was requested to continue taking part in the meetings and 'otherwise assist in the management of the Company - particularly in regard to new undertakings and general questions of finance and policy'.[20] He agreed to do this, involving himself more than was customary for chairmen, because of his 'strong desire to give every possible assistance to the Company until it has been firmly established on an independent basis in all Branches of its business'. His tutelage was still necessary and he had to remind the management committee in January 1921 that they were acting like a forum, not behaving as a committee. He did not expect the managing directors, as the members of the management committee had now all become, 'to sit *as a body* and vote upon every proposition which came before the Company...so far as it was practicable it was desirable that each Managing Director should regard himself as a separate entity in the business, responsible only to the Chairman or Deputy Chairman'.[21] Stewart acted as deputy to the chairman from 1921, but it was Cadman who was the first appointed deputy chairman in 1925.

Greenway had attached the greatest importance to the Company having a strong shipping connection and so he was also looking at the same time for 'a first class shipping man acquainted with the business from A to Z, viz. ship-building, working, chartering, insurance, repairs and claims - to supervise the whole business of our fleet, which will probably in 3-4 years number 60-80 vessels...we badly need a "Managing Director" to deal with all the big questions connected with the Company's shipping business'.[22] On 13 February 1919, Stewart was appointed. It was the start of a short and controversial career of a strident canny personality who left his mark on many pages of the early Company history, especially in connection with the Tanker Company. Time has faded many of the impressions he made and dimmed his importance: he remains something of an enigma. There may be doubts over his capabilities, suggestions of improper practices and his parsimony may have amounted to more than meanness, but without a doubt he was the first master of the Tanker Company, when shipping was beginning to play a large part in the Company's marketing strategy. W.D. Braithwaite, who had been appointed managing director of the BP Company, recognised, in response to a French inquiry on a

Management and finance

possible association with the Company, that 'we have a strong lever in the matter of participation in foreign companies in that we own steamers and they do not',[23] a vindication of Greenway's earlier decision in 1915 to set up the Tanker Company.

Britannic House nearing completion 1924

Management and finance

At this time too, early steps were being taken, following the disbanding of the Pool Board on 31 January 1918, which was set up in 1917 to control the war-time distribution of petroleum products, to distribute in the United Kingdom by broadening the activities of the BP Company and constructing the long-delayed refinery near Swansea. It was decided also to strengthen the marketing base overseas by setting up a chain of bunkering stations, which would be able to supply fuel oil, as naval demands were anticipated to fall in the post-war period.[24] It was agreed to enter European markets against the day when the ten-year contracts with Royal Dutch-Shell expired at the end of 1922 which, it was agreed on 15 December 1920, would not be renewed.[25] So, in association with Belgian interests, the first European subsidiary, L'Alliance, was formed in May 1919. This expansion of marketing activities placed pressure on the BP Company, for Nichols complained towards the end of 1919 to Braithwaite that 'your Department wants waking up or alternatively, it is under-staffed, and you might let me know where the trouble lies'.[26] The action taken was salutary for in February 1920 'The Board was advised that the British Petroleum Company Limited are establishing a foreign department· to thoroughly investigate the prospects and ramifications of the trade on the Continent', preliminary investigations having already taken place 'with a view of finding suitable outlets for all surplus production, particularly of petrol, after 1922'.[27]

Further administrative changes occurred in May 1921 when W.T. Watts was moved to the Company from BP Company, to take over 'Braithwaite's work in connection with Foreign Countries'.[28] Shortly afterwards shareholdings in subsidiary companies were transferred to the Company from BP Company in order to assert a more centralised control over foreign operations. A further stage was taken in mid-1921 when H.B. (later Sir Hubert) Heath Eves, who had managed the distribution of Burmah products in India for Shaw, Wallace & Co., was brought in to manage marketing, becoming a director, in January 1924, a position he held for thirty years till his retirement in 1953 as deputy chairman.[29] Towards the end of 1921 the technical side of the business was strengthened by the appointment of Cadman as technical adviser on the initiative of Greenway. As a result of expanding developments, office accommodation became inadequate, so that towards the end of 1920 any increase in the number of staff was impossible.[30] In December 1920 a site was acquired in Finsbury Circus for £570 000. Sir Edwin Lutyens designed the building, which, as Britannic House, remained the head office till 1967.[31]

By mid-1921 the administration under the overall direction of the Board appeared to be functioning reasonably well so that consideration of a successor to Greenway could not long be deferred. On 23 June 1921 the

Management and finance

question was fully discussed in Glasgow between Greenway, Cargill and Watson and it emerged that 'actually though not ostensibly to the outside public etc., Mr Douglas Stewart should be regarded as and should act in all respects as Deputy to Sir Charles Greenway'.[32] Stewart's role as 'Deputy' to Greenway was made possible by the appointment of his younger less competent brother, W.A. Stewart, to run the shipping department.[33] It was a curious choice, fraternal rather than suitable in character and unfortunate in its consequences, in that it lessened respect for the elder brother. As the committee of management was informed, Stewart was to be 'the final arbiter...on all questions, Departmental or otherwise, requiring decisions'. He was to free himself from departmental duties and 'set about the reorganisation and defining of the duties and responsibilities and spheres – departmentally – of each of the Managing Directors' so that 'each undertaking of the Company is definitely and clearly put under the charge of a Managing Director'.[34]

To approve the authorisation of capital or other expenditure an ad hoc body, the reference committee, was formed, which was obliged to submit proposals to Greenway or Stewart to improve financial coordination. In some respects the appointment of Stewart was retrogressive, detracting from the responsibilities of the managing directors and Greenway had to assure them that none of the decisions 'must be considered as in any way reflecting on any of the managing directors', and that the objective remained the same, 'to secure better organisation, greater control and the clearer definition of Departmental spheres'.[35] It is hard, however, to avoid the suspicion that Greenway compromised with the Caledonian connection in accepting the promotion of Stewart over his colleagues. It was Black who had mostly chaired the committees when Greenway was absent. Garrow and Nichols had kept going during the war, but it was Stewart who was preferred. The Board signified its agreement on 25 July.[36] No urgency was imparted to the proceedings and it was not till 22 November that the reference committee met for the first time and the new allocation of responsibilities was made. (See 1921 organigram, Appendix 8.1.) The succession seemed assured.

(b) The managing agents in Persia

In the immediate post-war period the administration of the managing agents was faltering and fumbling and it was severely criticised within the Company. It was ironical therefore, that it was the dissatisfaction of Lt. Col. Arnold Wilson, as he had become during the war, over their pricing policy for oil products in Mesopotamia, which came under his scrutiny as civil commissioner, that precipitated an examination of their role.[37] The managing agency was criticised as being 'faulty in principle', since the Company's local interests and oil distribution were undertaken by those who were 'also merchants and carry on a variety of activities'.[38] The issue came to a head on 8 April 1919 at an inter-departmental conference held at the India Office when Wilson was visiting London. Certain proposals were made to the Company,[39] to which Nichols replied, claiming that any price set should 'return to the Company a reasonable percentage of profit' but this was not specified.[40] Cadman, taking a practical attitude on behalf of the Petroleum Executive, suggested that the Company's trade 'has now developed to an extent which makes it desirable for them to undertake the direct management both as regards production and marketing'.[41] The Admiralty too agreed that 'with the great extension of the Anglo-Persian Company's trade there would be a distinct gain in efficiency and economy if the Company were to assume direct control' over all its activities in Persia.[42]

The Treasury, respecting the agreement that the Government did not become involved in matters of commercial concern, nevertheless wrote to Inchcape that 'in view of the great development of the Company's business the Company should undertake the direct management both of production and marketing as the delegation to a firm can no longer be necessary on grounds of economy of administration'.[43] Inchcape referred the question to Greenway, who responded firstly by challenging the right of the Government to interfere.[44] Secondly he disputed the argument for changing the system, 'one that very few business men with knowledge of commercial conditions in tropical countries would accept'. He believed the successful example of Burmah's use of managing agents compared favourably with the experience of Royal Dutch-Shell and Standard Oil whose 'selling organisations' he maintained 'are a long way behind those of Burmah in every way'.

Inchcape was inclined to agree with Greenway that 'it is not a bad thing to have a business firm attending to the sales and leaving the technical staff to attend to the getting of oil and to the work of refining'.[45] Greenway was delighted that Inchcape had 'put the position so clearly', but anxious that the Treasury understood that Strick, Scott & Co. Ltd, 'are *Managing Agents* in Persia and the East...also responsible for the technical part of the business as well as the selling, and for this purpose they keep a technical staff to direct the technical operations'.[46] The Treasury was not prepared to press the matter further,[47] but the seeds of doubt had been sown in the official mind, and Greenway was more optimistic over the outcome than he should have been. The situation could not remain unchanged.

In the Company Garrow had already, early in 1919, criticised Walpole for indulging in private correspondence and failing to do his parish

Management and finance

rounds, pointing out that 'you should have made yourself acquainted with the conditions on the spot by periodical visits'.[48] Walpole was admonished over the pumping additions to the pipeline to 'do everything to push this work forward'.[49] He was blamed for allowing matters to drift, for tolerating 'gross mismanagement from the top to bottom' and for offering unacceptable excuses.[50] This lamentable state of affairs, wrote Nichols, 'is due to absence of control and system'.[51] Organisation had not kept pace with development. Walpole shuffled the papers; he did not solve the problems. Moreover, the social atmosphere had changed. The person who had come out as a writer in the offices of the managing agents before the war was replaced by a man whose experiences in the armed forces had given him a different attitude to life. As Neilson expressed it, 'we have now got some men imbued with the modern ultra democratic spirit and there is an element of restlessness amongst them. It is up to us to do everything we can to make conditions as pleasant as possible - in fact to put the matter plainly, the attitude is "that the Company can well afford to be generous in granting all facilities for social entertainment."'[52]

Technical and social problems were the weak spots in the administration of the managing agents, as Garrow and Nichols discovered in their visits to Persia in 1919 and 1920 respectively. Garrow was appalled at the lack of cooperation between the different members of technical management, many of whom had not even met each other.[53] There was very little administrative coordination or responsible functional delegation of duties. On 7 December 1920 Nichols arrived in Ābādān and immediately impressed upon the managing agents 'the necessity of recognising the changed conditions and temper of labour everywhere'.[54] He devised a grading system for staff applicable to the some 15 000 people employed. He stressed the need for consolidation as 'we have always had to aim at the maximum throughput, let us now organise, and whilst still maintaining that throughput, aim at economy of running and so on, as the time will come when the cost of refining per gallon is far more important than it is at present'. He criticised the lack of proper scrutiny, the 'inefficient storage, bad packing and general rough handling' of materials, the goods that 'are just lying there rusting and rotting away', but he was optimistic over the future. He noted that 'we now have new blood in charge and this is sure to be to the Company's advantage. The staff is alright and all that is wanted is material and organisation.' The refrain was the same, both in London and Persia.

By mid-1920 Greenway too had recognised the vulnerability of the managing agents. He did not yet acknowledge that they had become an administrative anachronism, but believed that by strengthening them with better staff and increased finance, their administrative efficiency could be improved. He therefore proposed at a board meeting of Strick, Scott and Co. Ltd on 22 June that 'Arnold Wilson be engaged on a salary of about £5000', but the Board temporised on the appointment of such a controversial person at such a crucial time on such a salary.[55] Two months later he recommended that 'to increase Strick Scott's prestige a new company be formed with a capital of say £500 000', which was later approved with a capital augmented to £1 000 000.[56] Walpole fell sick and towards the end of 1920 accepted an appointment to take charge of the newly opened Paris office for a French associated company which was being formed; a consolation for meritorious but not distinguished service.[57] Greenway prevailed over the appointment of Wilson as resident director and a draft agreement on terms and conditions was reached on 29 January 1921.[58] Greenway advised him that 'you may rest assured that we shall, when the time comes for your retirement to this country, recommend your election to the Board', subject only to his satisfactory performance in discharging his duties.[59]

Greenway, instructing Wilson on his responsibilities, endeavoured to rectify the failures of the Walpole period.[60] Not only was Wilson requested to extend the scope and importance of the business, improve its efficiency, organisation and corporate spirit, but also to appoint properly qualified staff 'by technical knowledge and temperament to act as liaison officers between the Managing Agents and the Fields, Pipeline and Refinery Manager', and supervise 'a closer co-ordination and cohesion of the branches so that they work more intimately together and incidentally follow up each other's development'. The brief for Wilson's duties was an early exercise in job description and Greenway appeared apologetic, even embarrassed over it, because 'it has been rather difficult to define these on paper as in English business concerns they are usually more or less taken for granted, each man knowing from experience or precedent what powers he is entitled to exercise and the nature of his responsibilities without reference to his Board or senior partners as the case may be'. In France, he observed, 'as I have recently unfortunately experienced, it was different, a job being laid down in black and white'.[61] In London and Persia a new species was emerging: the manager with a precisely defined post, graded for remuneration in his particular function with a carefully determined contract for a fixed period of time. The Company was early acquainted with Organisation Man.

(c) Finance

The functioning of the administration in London and the performance of the managing agents in Persia had been adjusted to ensure that the organisation of the Company was responding to the challenge of the market place and the technical opportunities that were becoming available. It was also necessary to make financial provision to preserve and enhance the Company's competitive position. The Company had to resolve a very real dilemma for it was committed to a policy of commercial expansion, whereas the Government's perception of its involvement with the Company was much more limited. In an attempt to reach a satisfactory solution a meeting was held in May 1919 at the Treasury attended by Bradbury and Barstow of the Treasury, Cadman and J.C. Clarke of the Petroleum Executive and Black as a government director and Greenway and Lloyd. Bradbury defined the issue as being that 'so long as the policy of His Majesty's Government was to retain control of the Anglo-Persian Company the Treasury's main duty was to see that this was carried out and that operations were not initiated which might force HMG to increase their investment in order to maintain control'.[62] This meant submitting the case for Company expenditure to an arbitrary governmental calculation of its cash availability rather than determining it by the pressures of the market. Bradbury drew attention to 'the pledge given in the House of Commons in 1914 that the funds voted should not be expended outside Persia'. For Barstow had previously wondered if it was desirable that the Company should 'acquire an interest outside the Persian Oil fields'.[63]

Replying to Bradbury's inquiry whether the Company would need more funds from the Government in the near future, Greenway rather unexpectedly did not anticipate that this would be the case, although the contemplated capital expenditure amounted to some £22 000 000. He undertook that the Company 'would not without explicit sanction from the Treasury engage in operations which might directly or indirectly commit the Government to finding fresh capital' or which 'would reduce the controlling interest'.[64] With some inconsistency Greenway was writing to Inchcape less than three months later on 24 July about raising more capital, 'as the time has now come for arranging some of the finance required in connection with our various developments'.[65] He declared that 'the first step to take is to increase our ordinary share capital, as thereby we extend our financing power in other directions, - and at the same time secure a Market valuation for our shares - an advantage which may be of very great advantage to the Government and to the Burmah Oil Company at some future time'. He proposed issuing 500 000 non voting ordinary shares to the public which could be underwritten at a premium of £9 per share.

Inchcape was not impressed.[66] He told Greenway that 'the really proper and fair course is for the Company, if it wants additional working capital, to issue it to the present shareholders at par', believing that 'those who took the risks should reap the benefits'.[67] His home-spun advice was to be frugal not prodigal, 'to keep your dividends down to a modest amount and apply your surplus revenue in your business till such time as your developments have reached a point when no more capital expenditure is required'. The Treasury was opposed to increasing the ordinary capital.[68] Inchcape informed Greenway that 'it would seriously prejudice the Government if new capital were issued in which they did not share'.[69] It can be imagined that Greenway felt that the growth of the Company would be endangered if new capital was not raised.

On 29 September 1919 a sub-committee of the Board was formed to consider 'the urgent necessity for providing additional capital at an early date'.[70] Inchcape played a leading part in persuading the Treasury to accept his point of view.[71] An extraordinary general meeting on 1 December 1919 approved the issuing of 4 500 000 ordinary shares as well as 3 000 000 preference shares and £2 000 000 5 per cent debenture stock.[72] The issuing of the ordinary shares was the breaching of a tacit financial barrier behind which the Treasury had sheltered. It was not to be regarded as a precedent. It must not be supposed, however, that the Government's continued involvement in the Company went unchallenged. Even the Admiralty, once such a staunch supporter of the Company, was moved to question whether 'A large Government holding in a Company of this kind though entirely justified when as in 1913 it was necessary to avoid the risk of so valuable a concession falling into foreign hands, maybe found somewhat embarrassing both politically and commercially', and doubted whether further government money was necessary.[73] In the parliamentary debates on 11 and 12 December 1919 to authorise the bill on government expenditure introduced by Stanley Baldwin, Financial Secretary to the Treasury, members questioned 'the Government entering into a private enterprise'[74] or being compelled 'as the Company expands its capital, to acquire a larger amount in order to keep our balance of control'.[75] Yet another was worried lest the instability of Persia 'let us in for liabilities, military and political, which at present we should avoid at all costs'.[76] The Company could not take its relationship with the Government for granted nor depend upon it for finance.

Within a couple of months the Board was seeking to raise more finance and at the end of January it was agreed to issue £3 500 000 2nd preference shares, in accordance with Treasury views, carrying a fixed cumulative dividend of 9 per cent per annum with a voting right of one for every five shares.[77] Allotment was made on 21 March 1921 among the applications for 4 928 059 shares that had been received.[78] During the year 1921-22 expenditure rose rapidly as the production and refining facilities were

Management and finance

augmented in Persia and provision was made to market the Company's own products directly to the customer by increasing the size of the tanker fleet and acquiring distributing outlets in Europe and elsewhere along the main maritime routes, as well as in Australia. It was a massive programme needing enormous investment.

3 YEARS OF CRISIS 1921-23

(a) Management and succession

The expansion of activities that was taking place was not only straining the financial resources of the Company, it was intensifying pressure on the administration and calling into question its competence and the quality of its leadership. The reference committee met formally on Wednesdays, but failed to meet informally during the rest of the week.[79] Meetings became more routine than executive under Stewart's increasing influence, which was further strengthened at a board meeting on 31 July 1922 when he was 'empowered to give decisions on all matters, subject only to reference to the Chairman of the Company on matters of importance and without such reference in cases of urgency'.[80] Though conclusive evidence is lacking, Greenway may not have been pleased with these developments.

The question of the succession was unsettling the Board and the apparent rapprochement between Burmah and Royal Dutch-Shell in their attitudes to the government shareholding in the Company was bedevilling the Company's policy (see Chapter 9). It came to a head over the future of Cadman. In Autumn 1922 he was the centre of a boardroom storm when Sir Philip Lloyd-Greame, Secretary to the Board of Trade, wrote to J.C. Clarke, who had succeeded Cadman at the Petroleum Executive, that Baldwin, then President of the Board of Trade, should write to Greenway proposing Cadman as deputy chairman. Clarke realised that 'the subject is rather a delicate one' and that Baldwin would be better advised 'to take one step at a time, as I am inclined to think that such a suggestion might only cause irritation, as another man has already been designated for that post'.[81] Baldwin did write to Greenway privately 'with my own fair hand' at the end of August and officially on 7 September.[82] Admitting his diffidence for he had 'never been an advocate of Government interference', he urged tactfully, but with unmistakable clarity, that 'the position of your company in the near future would be strengthened by the appointment of Sir John Cadman as a Managing Director' because of his unique knowledge, experience and government service.[83] Greenway was not surprised and remarked to Cargill that 'I would much rather that the first move had come from our side, in the manner recently suggested by me,

Management and finance

than that the request should have come from the Government, as this would have *led* to greater co-operation and harmony amongst the Managing Directors.'[84] Watson disagreed and was ready to resist, but Greenway was prepared to relent, realistically recognising that it was better 'to give in gracefully than to have Cadman forced upon us in the face of our opposition with possibly future developments in the same direction if Cadman finds himself in a hostile camp'.

The Burmah directors rejected Greenway's advice and Cargill pressed for Baldwin to be informed that they 'were opposed to the suggestion on the grounds that it was in the nature of Government interference with the commercial administration of the Company'.[85] Greenway tried to temporise, writing to Baldwin on 27 September of the 'very strong opposition which the proposal had encountered', recognising Cadman's qualifications, which were already available in his capacity as technical adviser and inquiring 'exactly what you had in mind in this connection?'.[86] Sir Edward Packe, an Admiralty official, who had succeeded Sir Frederick Black as a government director on 12 December 1919, serving assiduously for nearly twenty-five years, reported to Baldwin that 'the opposition was of quite a heated nature' and that Greenway had been unable to calm the proceedings by implying that Baldwin's recommendation was simply a private opinion.[87] If Baldwin accepted such an approach, Greenway, argued Packe, 'could get a majority of the votes of the Board but it would be a near thing, as there is obviously great jealousy'. It is a measure of Greenway's achievement over the years in moulding the Company to his image and insisting on its independence from other groups or the Government, that his Board was no mere rubber stamp. The Burmah directors had their own interests to protect and though Cargill may have been prematurely lapsing into the role of an ineffectual elder statesman, Watson had a shrewd character. Burmah had assets locked up in the Company, but unless the government control was lessened, these were hard to realise and to invest elsewhere. Cadman, the Burmah directors correctly surmised, would be less sympathetic towards them. The rise of Cadman presaged a decline in the influence of Burmah and so it proved.

Clarke was aware of the nature of the struggle, in which Cadman's merits were incidental. He realised that

> Stewart really represents the Burmah interests, and the latter are as keen as ever in the amalgamation scheme [with the Royal Dutch-Shell] and will put it forward again at the first opportunity. If the Anglo-Persian comes in next time as a supporter of the scheme (as the Burmah will do their best to secure) it will be harder for HMG to resist. It, therefore, seems important to strengthen the element in the APOC which is not committed to the amalgamation scheme and which will at least take a wider and longer view.[88]

It was a strange reversal of roles when a government department was advocating steps to safe-guard the independence of the Company from government action.

Baldwin, aware of the delicacy of the situation, replied to Greenway in a letter 'polite, but firm in its character', conciliatory not hectoring in tone. The Government could not be precluded 'in its capacity as majority shareholder from making suggestions which appear to it to be in the interests of the Company'.[89] Indeed, 'no general support would be obtained for the view that, where so large a sum of public money is involved we are entitled to take no interest whatever in the constitution of the Board of the Company, and cannot even make a friendly proposal for strengthening it'. The hint was sufficient, Baldwin was informed by Greenway on 8 November that 'the intentions of the Board are in the direction of your suggestions'[90] and on the same day Stewart was empowered to invite Cadman to join the Board within a year,[91] though Greenway privately reassured Baldwin that it would happen within six months. It did actually occur in March 1923. At a later meeting with Cargill and Stewart, Cadman attempted to smooth the ruffled feathers by disclaiming doing 'anything that will cause dissension amongst the Managing Directors with whom I desire to work in the most harmonious manner in the best interest of the Company'.[92] It was affable and artful, but there was no love lost between the two contenders for the throne.

It could not have been predicted with certainty which of them would become chairman, but Stewart still appeared to have the best chance, though he was not necessarily Greenway's choice. Packe advised Barstow towards the end of November of Greenway's idea that when Slade retired from the vice-chair the successor designate 'should be appointed in his place', Greenway agreeing that 'such an appointment would rest with the Treasury'.[93] In the event whatever the horse trading over the promotional stakes, it was overshadowed by the worrying performance of the Company. Packe confessed to Sir Oswyn Murray, Permanent Secretary to the Admiralty, in May 1923 that 'Ever since the beginning of December last I seem to have been perpetually at Anglo-Persian business. It was then that I began to think that our financial position was not as good as it should be and I began to sit up and take notice.'[94]

Packe's forebodings were confirmed on 27 February 1923 when a disclosure was made to the Board that the bank balances and cash assets of all the companies showed a deficit of £2 143 076.[95] A month later Slade wrote to Greenway, after talks with his colleagues on the Board, believing 'it essential that there should be a full discussion at the Board, so that its members may clearly understand the exact situation...very little is known as to the financial position of the Subsidiary Companies, their profits and losses, the value of their assets, and how far each in turn is likely to make further demands on the purse of the Anglo-Persian, or to do anything to reduce indebtedness already incurred'.[96] 'It may be,' he worried, 'that very drastic steps ought to be taken to curtail the capital expenditure...but upon this it is obviously impossible to express any intelligent opinion until a diagnosis of the whole position is prepared and laid upon the table,' which he requested be done for the board meeting of 24 April. The turmoil in the Company's accounts was matched by the weakness of its administrative arrangements. So on 24 April a sub-committee of the board consisting of Southborough, Slade, Packe and Lund was formed to provide 'information regarding the operations and financial position of the Company as they may require and to discuss any questions of management'.[97]

A month later the Committee reported[98] with more of a whisper than a roar, requesting that better information be made available with reports from departments, more frequent board meetings, more extensive circulation of minutes and a review of the composition of all boards. It may be that these rather innocuous recommendations betrayed problems of a more controversial character, which a more authoritative committee needed to examine in greater detail. The opportunity was taken to appoint another committee composed of Greenway, Slade, Inchcape, Packe, Southborough, Cargill, Barnes, Wynne, Lund, Tiarks and Watson, all the non-executive directors but none of the managing directors, 'to consider and determine questions of management, (past and prospective) in view of the near expiry of the Managing Directors' Agreements'. The committee met on 7, 14 and 21 June. Stewart was interviewed at the first meeting. He was not receptive to collective responsibility, but advocated the appointment of a single managing director over departmental managers, being of the opinion that 'no administrative officer of the company should be on the board'.[99] It was an autocratic concept. Cadman proposed a settled annual programme linked to a budgeted expenditure, a general direction exercised through several executive heads with fully defined administrative powers in relation to departmental responsibilities and a finance committee to oversee and coordinate expenditure. Cadman wanted a clearer understanding of objectives, a better matching of resources and procedures, a system of delegation not subordination, based on collaborative participation in the executive process not separation from it.[100] Above all there was the need, which he had previously mentioned, for a more harmonious working amongst those in control of the management. The Company, poised for a rapid take-off, required a trained crew not a single pilot at the controls.

Slade too submitted an interesting and perceptive memorandum on the 'Organisation of APOC' on 19 June 1923.[101] He believed that 'the general organisation of the business is the same now in all essential particulars as it was when the Government first became shareholders', so that the various measures taken to administer the expansion of the Company's activities had led 'to lack of co-ordination and control', and that 'the growth of the business has in some direction, outstripped the organisation'. Slade proposed basing the structure of the Company on a series of functional subsidiary companies, with the main company acting as a holding company. He summarised his main recommendations '(1) Complete Control of All Finance by the Board, (2) the Division of Business into closely defined Departments, each with its Manager responsible to the Board of the APOC for the efficient conduct of his Department.'

The Board sub-committee proposed a compromise that 'the management shall be vested in a "Management Committee" working departmentally...with Mr J.D. Stewart as Chairman', which was to submit as soon as possible 'a scheme for the working of the Company by departments'.[102] Stewart made a major tactical mistake. He refused to chair the committee or help in the preparation of the scheme. He wanted a court; Cadman wanted a cabinet. Stewart may have been over-confident, but it was Cadman who got the credit for the work of the committee, when it was accepted by the Board on 26 July.[103] It was agreed in principle that 'whilst each Head of Department will be entirely responsible for the working of his Department, within any limitations that may be laid down by the Board, all matters of importance, as defined hereafter, shall be referred to a Management Committee, in whom the management of the Company, subject to the Board, shall be solely vested'.[104] Stewart as chairman was expected to 'direct and co-ordinate the work of the Departments'. One major reform for which Cadman was responsible and which was quickly implemented was the establishment of a finance committee which met for the first time on 30 July 1923 to introduce 'a settled annual programme linked to a budget of estimated expenditure'. In this form the administration of the Company continued for over a year when signs of friction reappeared and members of the committee were warned that they were 'individually directly and solely answerable to the Chairman and to the Board of Directors for the departmental administrative conduct of such policy'.[105] Cadman remained opposed to certain of the changes suggested and not all the firm decisions had been taken by the end of 1924.[106]

(b) The demise of the managing agents

The appointment of Arnold Wilson as resident director and the careful definition of his duties was expected to revive the flagging fortunes of the

Management and finance

managing agents and keep the system going beyond the expiry of its first contract in 1923. He arrived in Muhammara on 29 September 1921. A little over a year later, as he was beginning to play himself in,[107] the rules of the game were changed. Nichols informed him on 30 November of the new arrangements which were to replace the role of the managing agents and impressed upon him that 'above all we want you *to manage*, referring only to us questions of policy and expenditure and matters upon which we should be consulted'.[108] There was to be a single shared executive authority with T.L. Jacks as joint general manager with Wilson specialising in looking after the technical aspects of the Company's operations. Nichols was not suggesting 'a hard and fast division of the toil, quite the contrary in fact. We want to see the fullest consultation on all points in respect to all branches of the operations, so that when one is away from Muhammara the other can deal with all matters that arise.' He emphasised the main principle, 'the whole of the staff in Persia is under one control'. The task was not easy, since breaking the artificial barriers which had been allowed to grow up in the past required an 'interchange of staff and a closer relation between the rest while separate staffs will do much to establish that unified effort'. It was all one Company with a direct relationship between London and Persia with Muhammara as its junction box and control post. An office had been opened under W.C. Fairley in Tehrān in June 1921, but it was subordinate to Muhammara and little more than a sounding board.[109]

What had caused this change of mind, this removal of the managing agents? No confession of failure exists and the reason must be deduced from circumstantial rather than direct evidence. It seems likely that some of the earlier criticism by Arnold Wilson in April 1919 of excessive earnings of commission by the management agents was justified. Greenway himself admitted on 31 January 1921 that 'the commissions now being earned by the Managing Agents were much in excess of the amount anticipated at the time the agreement was entered into' and that there was a case for modifying it, 'subject to a settlement of the terms for the renewal period'.[110] The existing agreement ended on 31 December 1923 with provision for a further prolongation of ten years. In 1919 Strick, Scott & Co. Ltd earned £70 000 of which commission on sales of the Company's products was £33 000, 47.1 per cent of the total, in 1920 the comparable figures were £90 000, £57 000 and 63.3 per cent and in 1921, £1 300 000, £900 000 and 69.2 per cent. A sub-committee of the Board was set up which reported on 22 March that it had been agreed to reconsider the terms of the management agreement,[111] but progress was decidedly slow in spite of intermittent discussions.[112] On 22 February 1922 the Company showed signs of impatience over 'the question of the revision of the agency agreement', and in May 1922 Stewart referred for the first time to 'consideration of terms on which it may be advantageous to cancel the contract'.[113] An enlarged committee supported the proposal, and advised by auditors that 'it is difficult to conceive, in view of the probable expansion of the company's operations...that...the Anglo-Persian Company would not be involved in payments very substantially higher than under the terms for cancellation' which had been proposed.[114]

It was almost the end of the road for the managing agents. The committee felt that the cancellation would result in a large saving to the Company, as well as other advantages such as greater freedom of action in the conduct of its business, more effective control by being in direct touch with employees and customers, and disassociation from any other operations commercial or political. The last act was played out on 31 October 1922 when the Board approved the committee's recommendation that the managing agents' agreement be cancelled as at 31 December 1922 on the payment to Strick, Scott & Co. Ltd of £300 000 in compensation and £1 000 000 being the accepted value of all buildings, land and other assets, etc., and honouring all agreements with the oil staff who were willing to be transferred.[115] Strick, Scott & Co. Ltd went into voluntary liquidation.

Greenway and his associates had been slow to read the writing on the wall. The concept of a single organisation dealing directly in merchandising over a wide range of commodities and being combined with a supervisory technical function was no longer practical in the context of the oil industry.[116] Once the high proportion of oil commission earnings to other business had become so unbalanced, it was difficult to justify the existence of the managing agents, particularly once the Company had acquired its own marketing expertise. If Strick, Scott & Co. Ltd had developed its other activities it might have survived as a separate entity without its Company obligations, but the tide was running both economically and politically in the area against such agency arrangements. Its roots were not deep enough to withstand the competition from earlier established firms and it was allowed to wither away, an 'oil' firm without any oil business.

Meanwhile in Persia the joint general managers were struggling to assert their authority. 'We do not propose that there should be any drastic change in the management', Nichols had assured them,[117] but when Lloyd visited Persia in Spring 1923 he found many shortcomings.[118] He particularly criticised the state of Ābādān with its 'lack of organisation and responsibility', its management concerned with signing letters and answering telephone calls and the atmosphere 'saturated with the old ideas of autocracy'. He was impressed with the management of Fields under

Management and finance

Jameson, he praised the medical department, but was disappointed in the geological, shipping and accounting departments. He recommended increased use of budgeting procedures and stressed, as frequently voiced before him, the 'interchange of staff between Muhammara and other centres seems most desirable with a view to promoting harmony of working and the acquisition of all round knowledge of the business'. An important pointer to the malaise which existed in Persia was staff wastage. In a year, 1923-24, it amounted to 240 persons, some 16.5 per cent of the staff, at a cost of £58 764. Unsatisfactory liaison between the staff departments in London and Muhammara was a contributory cause effecting selection and recruiting procedures, which had been based on insufficient information about conditions of service, health, climate, marriage, accommodation etc.[119] The same defects noticeable in London were also afflicting Persia, arising from excessive departmentalism, and a fundamental failure to correct it. Collaboration and coordination were mumbled like incantations to invoke the power of the supernatural instead of remedying the faults that were visible. The management in Persia still lacked a technical cutting edge and until that was supplied it remained a blunt instrument to control an operation that was primarily technical.

(c) Finance for 'a gigantic business'

The Government had reluctantly agreed to the ordinary share issue of 12 December 1919, but the Treasury had only sanctioned an immediate call of 1s, leaving 19s for later calls. The real problem was the scale of the operations, which required a tremendous investment just when credit was tight and economic conditions highly unfavourable. In May 1921 Lord Inchcape was asked to arrange with the Treasury for the calling up of the balance remaining unpaid without which other fund-raising activities would be prejudiced.[120] A month later a memorandum on the Company's financial position was forwarded to Inchcape indicating an estimated excess of expenditure over revenue up to 31 March 1922 of some £10 500 000.[121] Set against this was a proposed preference share issue of £3 500 000, anticipated economies and postponed expenditure which would leave a shortfall of some £5 500 000. The main item was for tankers. Inchcape passed on the request to the Treasury with little comment, asking 'whether it is convenient for the Government to pay up £950 000 within the next few months'.[122] The Treasury replied that 'It would be most inconvenient'.[123] There were no statutory powers to issue the £950 000 or to borrow for the purpose, and, although the passing of supplementary estimates or a bill to raise the money was possible, the Treasury considered it 'most undesirable in the existing state of British opinion about expenditure and of American public opinion about the British Government's oil interests to embark on either of these two courses'.

Political concern was more persuasive than economic criteria. In short, as Inchcape informed Greenway, 'I see no prospect whatever of the Treasury agreeing in the present financial condition of the country to the call being made.'[124] It was not a new predicament for the Company, but Cargill was incensed, complaining that the refusal of the Treasury was 'childish in the extreme'.[125] He denounced the Government for spending money generously 'for electoral advantage on which they get *no return* at all except a hope' but 'when they draw the line at putting the country's money into a magnificent investment which holds out every hope of giving them a large and increasing annual return it is too absurd for words'. He wondered what were 'the real advantages we get from having the Government as shareholders in the APOC against the serious disadvantages there undoubtedly are'.

Inchcape was in no hurry to press the Company's case[126] and it was not till the latter part of November that Greenway was able to meet him and discuss the financial situation of the Company.[127] The response of Inchcape was unenthusiastic, gloomy and distinctly depressing. Writing to the Treasury on 12 December 1921 he claimed that the Company had 'been launching out into all sorts of schemes which have wiped out their profits'.[128] In an extraordinary attack, he remarked that the Company 'hold a letter from the Treasury in regard to the Government Directors, which precludes the latter from interfering with the commercial side of their enterprises. This practically means that we, the Government Directors have no control over what they may do.' This was inconsistent with his earlier observations and it has to be noticed that at this time he was less than constant in his attendance at board meetings, being much more absorbed in proclaiming the virtues of financial discipline at meetings of the Geddes Expenditure Committee set up by the Chancellor of the Exchequer, Sir Robert Horne, in August 1921. In the same month he had declared to Lord Lansdowne that 'the whole country is rapidly approaching insolvency owing to the reckless expenditure of the Government and their mad vote-catching schemes'.[129] His anxiety was justified for in the aftermath of the war the short sharp spectacular boom of 1919–20 occurred, followed by a depression in 1921.

It was in this respect that he was impatient with the Company going 'into all sorts of enterprises outside of Persia where they started, Tankers costing £40 a ton, Scottish Oil Shale, prospecting in Europe and all over the world, distributing arrangements in France and elsewhere. Everything may turn out all right but it is a gigantic business and we are powerless to

Management and finance

interfere with their activities.'[130] Inchcape was becoming the Company's commercial Cassandra. It was not just disapproval of the Company's policy which irked him but a growing political concern, for 'I must candidly confess I don't like the Government being mixed up in the concern as it now exists. My conviction is that if the Government can get out of its association with this Company at a profit, we ought to do so.' For this reason he suggested agreeing to the issuing of ordinary shares at £3 each so that 'when these came to be dealt in on the market, the Government might gradually get out of their shares, selling them quickly at a good price'. Inchcape appeared to be doing the right thing for the wrong reason, but the Treasury was finally prepared to accept his logic and the Company's pressing need.[131] The Chancellor of the Exchequer authorised the issue on 28 December 1921.[132] The issue was a resounding success.[133] There were 12 292 838 applications for the 600 000 ordinary shares on offer out of the authorised 1 000 000 at £3 5s 0d, of which 3 553 124 came from public investors, and 22 669 680 applications for the 2 000 000 8 per cent cumulative first preference shares of which 8 701 661 came from the public, a massive indication of confidence in the Company. The Board accepted Inchcape's condition that 'before any subsequent issue of Ordinary shares is made to the public to an extent to disturb the Government control, a special resolution shall be submitted giving the Government shares an increased voting power to safeguard us should we desire it'.

The calling in of the Government's outstanding liability of 19s in the ordinary share issue of 1919 continued to drag on. Lloyd, who makes his first appearance in these financial matters in January 1922 suggested to Inchcape that the Government should utilise its rebate on fuel oil purchases to pay its call.[134] This was unacceptable: 'entirely outside the bounds of constitutional rules and practice'.[135] The Treasury, nevertheless, was embarrassed and admitted that the position 'in respect of this uncalled capital is not a satisfactory one. Even if the accusation is unjustified, it is certain that the Company will continue with some show of justification to accuse HMG of obstructing its development.' Sir Basil Blackett, the Treasury accountant agreed that 'in these circumstances, I think the time has come when HMG should make arrangements to pay up' and felt that 'even if the idea of selling HMG's interests matures, we shall probably get a better price for our holdings if no liability attaches'.

Barstow, for the Treasury, was prepared to obtain the requisite authority by means of an Act of Parliament modelled on the procedure of 1919, which would 'not affect our Budget position, but only our general Ways and Means position'.[136] Lloyd hoped that the question could be treated with urgency by the beginning of the Company's financial year on 1 April

Management and finance

1922.[137] In a brief prepared for the Financial Secretary, he recalled that the Company had voluntarily agreed in 1919 not to make a further call without the consent of the Treasury, but stated that in the circumstances he did not think that 'the Government Directors could have vetoed the call, as the resolution by the Board would have been a financial matter to which the veto by the Government Directors would not have been applicable'.[138] It was gnawing the same old bone of contention, the exercise of the government veto, the question of interference, on which comments were freely made in the parliamentary debates of 10 and 14 March and 5 July, when the third reading was passed.[139] It had taken the Company fifteen months from May 1921 to 15 August 1922 to have the calls paid up on an issue to which the Government had subscribed in December 1919.

The delays in raising finance at a time of rising expenditure were precipitating cash crises, the most serious of which occurred towards the end of 1922 and the first part of 1923. On 26 September 1922, Lloyd presented a memorandum to the Board outlining different methods of financing the Company's cash requirements.[140] A few days later a case was presented to Inchcape for raising a further £6 000 000, of which £2 500 000 to £3 000 000 was to be borrowed from banks or finance houses, the 400 000 unissued ordinary shares from the earlier public issue of February 1922, further ordinary shares, debentures, preference shares and short-term notes.[141] The Company was anxious to issue more ordinary shares as those already issued, 8 100 000, were disproportionate to the number of preference shares issued, 10 500 000. Inchcape, about to visit India on a business trip, suggested that a decision should be deferred till his return.[142]

Barstow accepted Inchcape's advice, but nevertheless felt that he should inform the Company that 'the Treasury would offer no objections of principle to their raising additional capital up to £6 000 000 if necessary and if you approve'.[143] He counted upon Inchcape's assistance and hoped that the Company would be prepared to wait as Inchcape had requested.[144] The Company would not wait. By a unanimous and confident decision of the Board, including Packe, the other government director, it refused to delay because 'the Company would be incurring a financial risk which might lead to very serious consequences'.[145] The influence of Packe was growing. He became closely involved in the Company, for he held no other official appointment and had no competing business interests. He did not regard his appointment as a sinecure and devoted much time and attention to a very practical concern with the policy and administration of the Company, ever using his judgement impartially. It was probably no coincidence that the Treasury agreed at this time to the increase of fees to

Management and finance

directors from £500 to £1000.[146] He bluntly informed Barstow that he was 'quite in the dark as to Lord Inchcape's reasons for advising the Treasury that the new Issue could wait' and asked 'perhaps you would very kindly enlighten me.'[147]

It was a decisive intervention and marked the end of Inchcape's ascendancy as a government director and more particularly his role as the financial broker between the Company and the Government. He had acted sensibly, honestly and prudently since his appointment as one of the first two government directors. He had been forthright in opinion and laconic in expression, priding himself on putting his 'foot down always, with Treasury approval, where it was necessary to guard the Government interests'.[148] He was independent, critical of official busybodies, as he told Barstow in 1919 over the rumpus about the pricing policy of Strick, Scott and Co. Ltd, in Mesopotamia, 'I don't know what it is all about, I have never hesitated to express an opinion on the commercial policy when invited to do so, as has frequently been the case, but many steps have been taken and enterprises embarked upon without any particular reference to me.'[149] In the last decade of his life, however, Inchcape found that his opinions were running counter to the spirit of the age. The discipline and austerity of his beliefs, which had brought such success to the shipping enterprise which he had founded were no longer accorded the same respect. Inchcape felt disillusioned.

The affairs of the nation were desperate. There was political confusion as Lloyd George's Coalition Government broke apart with his resignation on 23 October 1922. *The Economist* described 1921 as 'one of the worst years of depression since the industrial revolution'. It was not surprising that Inchcape felt dejected. In earlier days his practical experience of and support for the commercial element in the relationship between the Company and the Government cannot be understated. Indeed it would not be exaggerating to state that without his appreciation of the Company's business opportunities and his backing of Greenway, the Company's growth might well have been stunted and its operations confined to Persia. Greenway provided the propulsion, Inchcape the stabilisers through the turbulent seas of the Government's relations with the Company.

The political events of the autumn, the general election called for 19 November and the return of a Conservative Government under Bonar Law with Baldwin as Chancellor of the Exchequer, delayed government business at this time.[150] By the end of November Packe had conferred urgently with Barstow and with the agreement of Baldwin the Company was allowed to make a public issue of ordinary shares up to £850 000, leaving 'unimpaired the Government voting majority' and the Treasury was to be consulted on the terms of the offer.[151] The outcome was an agreement with the underwriters for £3 15s 0d a share, which Packe acknowledged was 'better than I expected and to my own mind quite high enough'.[152] The issue, a success, was heavily oversubscribed on 16 January with applications being made for 9 926 853 shares. The Company had weathered the financial storms during a critical time in its growth, as the payments of dividends of 20 per cent in 1920, 1921 and 1922 indicated. It enjoyed the confidence of the investing public during a trough of financial despondency. Throughout the rest of this period it managed to fund its expenditure from loans and retained earnings and had no need to involve the Government in ordinary share issues, which might have possibly threatened the extent of its majority shareholding, which had actually dropped from 66.67 per cent in 1914 to 55.87 per cent in 1923 at which figure it remained till 1956. It had been a vital transitional period of some five years of almost frantic Company activity tempered by Treasury financial caution.

The sources and applications of funds over the years 1919-24 are summarised in Table 8.1. The statement's most notable features are the reliance of outside sources for funds and the large expenditure upon fixed assets. Out of a total increase in funds of £37 053 594, £28 444 641, that is 77 per cent, came from outside sources whereas between 1914-19 retained profit had been the principal source of funds, as shown in Chapter 6. The proportion of the increase in funds applied to fixed asset formation rose from 62 per cent in the years 1914-19 to 82 per cent during 1919-24. Both the pattern of funding and the uses to which the money was put merit closer examination. The outside funds shown in Table 8.1 were made available to the Company either as subscriptions to new equity, or as investments in fixed interest securities offered by the Company, or by virtue of minority shareholdings in subsidiaries included in the consolidated balance sheets. Money raised by the issue of further ordinary shares, including most of the share premium account, amounted to a third of the increase in funds from outside sources.

The ordinary shareholding was increased by the three issues of shares in December 1919, 4 500 000, January 1922, 600 000, and January 1923, 850 000. The large issue of December 1919 was subscribed pro rata by the only three ordinary shareholders, Burmah, which took up 1 425 000 shares, the Strathcona interest, which took up 75 000, and the Government, which took up 3 000 000, thereby maintaining their portions of the equity at the existing levels of 31.67 per cent, 1.67 per cent and 66.67 per cent respectively. The changing pattern of ownership of the ordinary shares of the Anglo-Persian Oil Company over the period 1909 to 1924 is shown in Table 8.2. In 1922, for the first time, ordinary shares were

Management and finance

Table 8.1. *Statement of source and application of funds of the Anglo-Persian Oil Company group 1919–24*

Source of funds	£	£	£
Sources outside the Company			
Increase in capital subscribed			
Ordinary shares		5 950 000	
Preference shares		8 500 000	
			14 450 000
Increase in share premium account			3 538 129
Increase in long-term liabilities			
Debentures		4 150 279	
Six and a half per cent notes		2 000 000	
			6 150 279
Increase in minority interest			4 306 234
Sources within the Company			
Increase in retained profits		1 486 248	
add back, depreciation, fixed assets		5 707 959	
stores etc.		(25 000)	
			7 169 207
Increase in premium upon acquisitions			349 934
Increase in pension fund			1 089 811
			37 053 594
Application of funds			
Increase in purchase price of Concession			886 621
Increase in preliminary expenses			219 300
Increase in fixed assets			
Installations		29 301 786	
Stores, etc.		1 014 805	
			30 316 591
Goodwill arising on acquisitions			1 067 669
Increase in long-term investments			
Due from Persian Government		(340 206)	
Investments		3 181 626	
			2 841 420
Increase in current assets			
Stock		2 949 979	
Current investments		(1 936 482)	
Debtors		3 159 973	
Cash		1 556 330	
		5 729 800	
Less increase in current liabilities			
Creditors	4 173 797		
Loans	(165 990)		
		4 007 807	
Increase in net current assets			1 721 993
			37 053 594

Source: BP consolidated balance sheets (see Appendix 3.1. (e))

Table 8.2 *Ownership of ordinary shares of the Anglo-Persian Oil Company group 1909–23*

	Total ordinary shares	Burmah Oil Company	%	Strathcona	%	HMG	%	Public	%
1909	1 000 000	970 000	97	30 000	3	—	—	—	—
1914	3 000 000	970 000	32.33	30 000	1	2 000 000	66.67	—	—
1915	3 000 000	950 000	31.67	50 000	1.67	2 000 000	66.67	—	—
1920	7 500 000	2 375 000	31.67	125 000	1.67	5 000 000	66.67	—	—
1922	8 100 000	2 375 000	29.32	125 000	1.54	5 000 000	61.73	600 000	7.41
1923	8 950 000	2 375 000	26.53	—	—	5 000 000	55.87	1 575 340 (125 340)	17.60

Source: BP: There is an anomaly of 340 shares.

Table 8.3. *Anglo-Persian Oil Company group financial performance 1919–24*

Year	Profit for the year before tax and dividends[a] £	Tax paid to British Government[b] £	Dividends £	Retained profit £	Average net tangible assets for the year[c] £	Return on investment per cent[d]	Dividend rate per cent
1919–20	3 042 945	783 654	627 863	1 631 428	16 242 244	18.7	20
1920–21	4 785 229	1 671 818	1 215 000	1 898 411	25 156 934	19.0	20
1921–22	1 150 151	235 753	1 245 000	(330 602)	31 447 367	3.6	20
1922–23	740 872	906 684	777 764	(943 576)	36 352 191	2.0	10
1923–24	863 624	738 037	895 000	(769 413)	38 744 993	2.2	10

Note: [a] Profit after deduction of debenture and preference share interest, preliminary expenses, overhead charges and royalty
[b] Income tax, corporate tax, excess profits duty
[c] Average of consolidated assets, except for intangibles (goodwill), *less* current liabilities, at start and end of year
[d] Ratio of profit for the year to average net tangible assets
Source: BP consolidated balance sheets (see Appendix 3.1.(e))

Management and finance

offered to the public. The sale of 600 000 shares of £1 nominal value at a premium of £3 5s raised £1 950 000, the balance of which, £1 350 000, is shown in the funds statement as an increase in the share premium account. The further sale to the public a year later of 850 000 shares of £1 nominal value at a price of £3 15s raised £3 187 500 and increased the share premium account by a further £2 337 500. The public's holding of the Company's equity grew from 7.41 per cent in 1922 to 17.6 per cent in 1923 while the holdings of the other shareholders fell proportionately.

The issue of shares and securities bearing a fixed rate of interest, preference shares, debentures, and 6½ per cent notes, brought in the major part of the funds raised from outside sources. Preference share issues by the Company totalling 8 500 000 shares in December 1917, at a premium of 12.5 per cent (2s 6d), December 1919, at a premium of 12.5 per cent (2s 6d), March 1921 at par, and January 1922, at a premium of 5 per cent (1s), raised £9 050 000 from the public. Sales of the Company's 5 per cent debenture stock raised £4 010 000 in 1918 and 1919 and the sale of notes bearing 6½ per cent interest in 1923 a further £2 000 000. Company funds provided by the sale of debentures to the public (see Table 6.2), were diminished by repurchases but augmented firstly by the issue of 1 488 000 debentures at par by a wholly owned subsidiary, Britannic Estates Limited, which was formed to administer the newly acquired Head Office site in Finsbury Circus, and secondly by sales of debentures worth £12 279 by the Société Générale des Huiles de Pétrole (the Company's French subsidiary).

The minority interest shown in the funds statement arose on account of the growth of subsidiaries after 1919 in which, although the Company was the majority shareholder, there were substantial minority holdings. These subsidiaries were joint ventures with local interests formed to operate in continental markets as outlets for the Company's products. Between 1919-20 and 1923-24 the value of the minority interest in such subsidiaries grew to £4 306 234. Internally generated funds were rather less important as a source of funds than might have been expected compared to the experience of 1914 to 1919.

Retained profits increased by a mere £1 486 248, though a further £5 682 959 was available to the group from allocations to depreciation. Annual figures for gross profit for the year, dividend, tax and retained profits are given in Table 8.3. Profit for the year 1919-20 was £3 042 945, slightly down on the previous year, but in 1920-21 it rose to £4 785 229. On return on investment, the ratio of profit for the year to average net tangible assets was 18.7 per cent in 1919-20 and 19.0 per cent in 1920-21 and, while less than the remarkable years 1917-18 and 1918-19, it justified the payment of a 20 per cent dividend on the ordinary shares. In the following three years, however, profits slumped dramatically, falling to £1 150 151, 1921-22, and to £740 872, 1922-23. The decline was halted in 1923-24 but a profit of £863 624 scarcely constituted a recovery to acceptable profitability. Return on investment in 1921-22 was just 3.6 per cent, the lowest rate for 5 years, while in 1922-23 and 1923-24 it declined to 2 per cent and 2.2 per cent respectively. The small increase in retained profits is hardly surprising in the light of these financial results. Although additions to the reserves were made in 1919-20 of £1 631 428 and 1920-21 of £1 898 411, in 1921-22, 1922-23 and 1923-24 reserves were run down by a total of £2 043 591 which was the reason for the modest increase in retained profits over the period as a whole.

The deterioration of the Company's financial performance in the years 1921-22, 1922-23 and 1923-24 was the result of the policy of forcing the pace of development adopted by Greenway. The sharp fall in profitability was the price paid for the pursuit of otherwise incompatible objectives in an increasingly difficult commercial environment. The Company endeavoured simultaneously to pay big dividends, to pursue an ambitious capital expenditure programme and to prospect for oil throughout the world. Profits net of exploration costs and dividends proved insufficient to fund the investment programme and hence recourse was made to the capital market. Pressure on profits came not only from competing requirements for funds but from generally worsening trading conditions in the oil industry as product prices declined in the early 1920s.

The investment programme of 1919-24 produced a five-fold increase in the historic cost value of fixed assets from £6 406 700 on 31 March 1919 to £35 708 486 on 31 March 1924, as shown in Table 8.4. Investment in fixed assets rose from £4.9 millions in 1919-20 to £9.2 millions in 1921-22, fell back to £7.5 millions in 1922-23 prior to a severe curtailment of the capital

Table 8.4. *Fixed assets and depreciation of the Anglo-Persian Oil Company group 1919-24*

	Accumulated fixed assets £	Increase in fixed assets for the year £	Accumulated depreciation £	Depreciation for the year £	Annual rate of provision for depreciation[a] per cent
1919-20	11 394 412	4 987 712	2 897 701	845 706	7.4
1920-21	17 941 682	6 547 270	3 856 976	959 275	5.3
1921-22	27 210 542	9 268 859	5 521 892	1 664 916	6.1
1922-23	34 801 048	7 590 506	6 905 491	1 383 599	3.9
1923-24	35 708 486	907 438	7 759 954	854 463	2.4

Note: [a] Ratio of depreciation for the year to accumulated fixed assets, per cent
Source: BP consolidated balance sheets (see Appendix 3.1.(e))

Table 8.5. *Distribution of fixed assets by activity of the Anglo-Persian Oil Company group 1919–24*

(£ fixed assets at historic cost)

	1919–20	%	1920–21	%	1921–22	%	1922–23	%	1923–24	%
Fields	1 370 267	12	1 981 683	11	3 333 298	12	3 568 823	10	3 314 781	9
Refineries	3 600 655	31	5 513 146	31	7 070 708	26	8 325 050	24	9 908 606	28
Pipelines	1 089 394	10	1 385 693	8	1 969 202	7	2 286 968	6	2 314 591	6
Tankers	3 991 623	35	5 684 955	32	7 686 134	28	11 719 098	34	10 207 260	29
Distribution	1 239 846	11	2 797 856	15	5 072 186	19	6 440 226	19	7 115 310	20
Bunkering	61 121	1	555 434	3	1 040 409	4	1 082 097	3	1 047 597	3
Administration	41 506	—	22 915	—	1 038 604	4	1 378 785	4	1 800 341	5
Total	11 394 412		17 941 682		27 210 541		34 801 047		35 708 486	

Source: BP consolidated balance sheets (see Appendix 3.1.(e))

Management and finance

programme in 1923-24, when expenditure totalled only £907 438. Allocation to depreciation followed a similar pattern during these years, peaking in 1921-22, which suggests the persistence of a substantial discretionary element in the provision for depreciation.

The pattern of the distribution of fixed assets among the Company's various activities is shown in Figure 6.1 (pp.228-9) and Table 8.5. Table

Table 8.6. *Increase in fixed assets of the Anglo-Persian Oil Company group 1919–24* (£ increase in value, fixed assets at historic cost per annum)

	1919–20	1920–21	1921–22	1922–23	1923–24
Fields	565 953	611 416	1 351 615	235 525	(254 042)
Refineries	2 021 650	1 912 491	1 557 562	1 254 342	1 583 556
Pipelines	342 254	296 299	583 509	317 766	27 622
Tankers	1 987 119	1 693 332	2 001 179	4 032 964	(1 511 838)
Distribution	(27 117)	1 558 010	2 274 330	1 368 040	675 084
Bunkering	61 121	494 313	484 975	41 688	(34 500)
Administration, etc.	36 732	(18 591)	1 015 683	340 181	421 556
Total	4 987 712	6 547 270	9 268 853	7 590 506	907 438

Source: BP consolidated balance sheets (see Appendix 3.1.(e))

8.6 shows the annual expenditure upon fixed assets each year from 1919 to 1924. The heaviest expenditures, £8 329 601 and £8 202 756 respectively, were on refineries, notably extensions at Ābābān and the construction of Llandarcy, and the growth of the tanker fleet. The proportion of the Company's fixed assets accounted for by these activities fluctuated over the period though it may be summarised as approximately rather more than a quarter for refineries and slightly less than a third for tankers. The investment of £5 848 347 in distribution facilities led to an increase in the proportion of the Company's capital devoted to distribution to a fifth of the total. Installations at fields, pipelines, bunkering stations and office buildings, notably in London, comprised the remainder of the Company's fixed assets. Expenditure on distribution, bunkering and administration together rose from 12 per cent in 1919-20 to 28 per cent in 1923-24. An important development which began earlier but accelerated in the early 1920s was the decline in the proportion of fixed assets located in Persia. In 1915-16 the value of investments in the Ābādān refinery, Persian pipelines and plant at fields constituted 87 per cent of the total but by 1923-24 they represented little more than 30 per cent of the Company's fixed assets.

Retained profits proved insufficient to finance even one twentieth of the capital investment programme. The availability of internally generated funds to be ploughed back into the business during the years 1919-24 was restricted by substantial expenditure on exploration, amounting to £862 915 on that outside Persia for the period 1919-24, and by generous dividend payments.

Payments of tax and allocations to ordinary share dividends further reduced the profit available for retention. The fluctuating, but regularly increasing, tax bill was largely beyond the Company's influence but the amount to be paid in dividends was decided by the Board. The rate of dividend and the amount paid each year from 1919 to 1924 to ordinary shareholders is shown in Table 8.3. Payments of £627 863 in 1919-20 and £1 215 000 in 1920-21 consumed 28 per cent and 39 per cent respectively of profits after tax. In the following year, 1921-22, the payment to ordinary shareholders grew to £1 245 000, an amount which actually exceeded the profit for the year after tax by £330 602, a difference which was made up by drawing on reserves. Doubtless the Directors hoped that the poor results were just temporary and that soon trading conditions would improve and their investments would correspondingly show a better return. The decision to maintain the 20 per cent dividend, despite the sharp fall in profitability, was taken with an eye to the Company's recently achieved stockmarket quotation since further sales of equity to the public were contemplated and a reduction in the rate of dividend would have reduced the premium at which the issues could be made.

The motives for selling ordinary shares to the public were both strategic and financial. Greenway, who had canvassed the idea prior to 1922, provoking only scepticism from Inchcape (see Chapter 6), hoped that a public interest would counterbalance the Company's dependence on the Government. There was also a purely financial argument in favour of expanding the equity funding of the Company. The Company's gearing, that is the ratio of ordinary shares to securities carrying a fixed interest charge or dividend, the debentures and preference shares, had been continuously rising, as can be seen in Table 6.2. The effect of this pattern of funding was to increase the Company's interest obligations to a level higher than necessary and perhaps higher than desirable. Since the Government was unlikely to consent to take up any further ordinary shares, being engaged at the time in reducing national expenditure, the Company turned to the public to increase equity funding.

Ordinary share dividends of 20 per cent, declared at the Ordinary General Meetings of 21 December 1921 and 11 December 1922, formed the backdrop to the offers to the public in January 1922 and January 1923 of £1 shares at the satisfactory premiums of £3 5s and £3 15s. The 20 per cent dividend declared for 1921-22 yielded a return of 6.15 per cent on the investments in the 1922 issue, rather less than the rate of interest borne by the 6½ per cent notes issued not long after. In the following year, 1922-23, the dividend was cut from 20 per cent to 10 per cent, a not ungenerous rate in view of the Company's real return on investment, though, as *The Times* commented, 'So drastic a cut in the dividend must create disappointment.'[153] Yield on the 1922 issue fell to 3.08 per cent while those shareholders, who only a few months earlier had subscribed to the second public sale at the higher premium, earned only 2.67 per cent.

Dividend payments to ordinary shareholders in 1922-23 and 1923-24 totalled £777 764. In 1921-22, for the first time, profit for the year proved insufficient to meet both tax demands and dividend. In 1922-23 the position was even worse and the dividend paid was not merely topped up by a reduction in reserves but paid in its entirety from funds derived from this source. The directors' report for the financial year to 31 March 1923 referred to the unexpectedly low level of output of the Ābādān refinery due to technical problems and the fire of November 1922, which seriously damaged the washeries for cleaning benzine and disrupted the operations of the whole plant. (See Chapter 11). Contemporary comment in the financial press mentioned the unexpectedly heavy expenses encountered in the establishment of a distribution agency in Britain, costly exploration operations outside Persia, which had proved 'the reverse of satisfactory' (see Chapter 11), and falling prices for petroleum products which affected every oil Company.[154]

In the light of the circumstances it was generally agreed by financial correspondents that the Company's performance was satisfactory. Yet, the directors, who adopted a confident stance in public, expressed fears and frustrations about the financial position in private (see p.314-15). A contributory factor to the complex financial problems of 1922 and 1923 was inadequate financial control over costs resulting from the Company's rapid expansion. Without consolidated accounts or adequate financial monitoring of the growing number of subsidiaries the Company was insufficiently aware of its overall financial position. The shock of the results of 1922-23 led to measures to redress these shortcomings including the establishment of a finance committee in 1923, tighter controls over budgets and expenditure authorisation and eventually to the standardised accounting procedures which were inaugurated in 1928.

An easing of the Company's financial problems is suggested by several indicators for the year 1923-24. A small profit for the year after tax contributed to the payment of £895 000 in a 10 per cent dividend. The deterioration in the rate of return on capital was arrested and, although the profit of the parent company earned by trading in Persia fell, dividends from subsidiaries and interest payments by subsidiaries increased. The liquidity position of the Company, which reached a low point in 1922-23, also improved in 1923-24.

Management and finance

The liquidity position of the Company on a consolidated basis over the years 1920 to 1924 is shown in Table 8.7. The large sums raised from outside sources by the sales of ordinary shares, preference shares and debentures during 1919-20 led to a sharp increase in current assets from £4 352 083 in 1918-19 to £13 720 684. In this year outstanding loans of £329 643 were paid off and, despite a rise in the amount to creditors, the net current asset balance soared to £8 322 252 and the current ratio reached 2.54. Although the net current asset balance remained in credit during the subsequent three years, it declined to a mere £968 648 by 31 March 1923. The current ratio was a slender 1.12, while the liquidity ratio dipped into deficit. The improved performance of the subsequent year, 1923-24, restored a reasonable balance, as indicated by the current ratio of 1.43.

4 THE YEARS OF IMPROVEMENT 1924-28

(a) The administration of Cadman

Considering the administrative uncertainties and changes of the early twenties it might be presumed that the performance of the Company suffered seriously. The growth in the post-war period was impressive as the Company began trading world-wide at a time of increasing demand for petroleum products. Yet, the administration was insecure. The individual parts were sound, but the design was inferior to the materials. The foundations were strong, but there was a limit to the size attainable by an ageing chairman, an inadequate deputy and a Board puzzling over the succession. Then, in the middle of June 1924, Stewart suffered from ill-health, the executive's complaint of duodenal ulcers, and was obliged to relinquish his duties,[155] to which he never returned. As a temporary measure the management committee decided that Nichols should chair its meetings.[156] This lasted longer than was tolerable and a year later it was recognised that 'the present arrangements are quite inadequate and dangerous'.[157]

It seems incredible that this unsatisfactory state of affairs lasted for so long, but Stewart still had strong support. Indeed it was not suggested that he be replaced, but that pending his return to his responsibilities a person 'should be at once appointed to act protem for Mr Stewart and to take over all his duties and responsibilities'. Greenway discussed the question with Cadman at the end of July 1925, who recommended Nichols, particularly as the concessionary negotiations with Iraq over the Turkish Petroleum Company were drawing to a close (see Chapter 11), and he would, therefore, be more able to accept further responsibilities.[158] There was an

Table 8.7 Liquidity position of the Anglo-Persian Oil Company group 1920-24

Date	Consolidated current assets		Consolidated current liabilities		Consolidated net current assets	Increase in net current assets on previous year	Current ratio[a]	Liquidity ratio[b]
		£		£	£	£		
1920 31 March	Cash and balances	2 064 171	Creditors	5 398 432				
	Debtors	4 466 281	Loans	—				
	Current investments	5 489 516						
	Stocks	1 700 716						
		13 720 684		5 398 432	8 322 252	7 046 529	2.54	2.23
1921 31 March	Cash and balances	2 688 221	Creditors	7 038 398				
	Debtors	5 395 452	Loans	—				
	Current investments	2 080 963						
	Stocks	1 423 721						
		11 588 357		7 038 398	4 549 959	(3 772 293)	1.65	1.44
1922 31 March	Cash and balances	3 073 941	Creditors	5 573 754				
	Debtors	4 017 160	Loans	816 224				
	Current investments	1 117 470						
	Stocks	2 239 060						
		10 447 631		6 389 978	4 057 653	(492 306)	1.63	1.28

Table 8.7. (cont.)

Date		Consolidated current assets		Consolidated current liabilities		Consolidated net current assets	Increase in net current assets on previous year	Current ratio[a]	Liquidity ratio[b]
1923 31 March	Cash and balances	3 596 084	Creditors	5 305 698					
	Debtors	3 497 506	Loans	2 829 000					
	Current investments	910 787							
	Stocks	1 098 969							
		9 103 346		8 134 698		968 648	(3 088 805)	1.12	0.98
1924 31 March	Cash and balances	3 654 914	Creditors	6 870 470					
	Debtors	4 383 888	Loans	163 653					
	Current investments	217 310							
	Stocks	1 825 771							
		10 081 883		7 034 123		3 047 760	2 079 112	1.43	1.17

Notes: [a] Current ratio — ratio of consolidated current assets to consolidated current liabilities
[b] Liquidity ratio — ratio of consolidated liquid assets (current assets less stocks) to consolidated current liabilities
Source: BP consolidated balance sheets (see Appendix 3.1(e))

extremely close rapport between Nichols, Lloyd and Cadman. It was a tragedy that Nichols suddenly died from pneumonia in Persia in January 1927. Unassuming and enlightened he grew in authority in the post-war years with an astonishing command of the complexity of industrial operations and administration and patience in negotiations, which made him a notable but modest member of the Board and a conciliatory influence.

The tide, however, was turning in Cadman's favour. Greenway decided that he must settle the succession issue and announce his retirement. He began to strengthen Cadman's position for on 28 July the Board appointed Cadman as a member of the influential finance committee,[159] which he had been instrumental in establishing. Early in August Greenway discussed the subject of his successor with Churchill, who had been appointed Chancellor of the Exchequer in Baldwin's Conservative Government on 6 November 1924. Churchill informed Packe on 11 August that 'in the view of the Government there can be no doubt that Sir John Cadman ought to be selected to fill the Chairmanship when it falls vacant, and that it would be highly desirable that until that event occurs he should be appointed to a position such as Deputy Chairman which would enable him to understudy the Chairman and would also invest him with adequate authority in the absence of the latter'.[160] He recommended that Packe and Bradbury, who had become a government director on 1 February 1925 on the retirement of Inchcape, should raise the question at a board meeting. At the same time Churchill wrote to Cargill to the same purpose hoping that 'in view of Cadman's eminent qualifications for the post the Government will be able to count upon your cordial and loyal co-operation in this policy'.[161] Cargill was upset. Whilst recognising Cadman's merits he must have been disappointed by Stewart's declining health, which was leaving the way open to Cadman. He bridled at the implications of Churchill's letter, which he expressed forcibly when he met him in mid August. Churchill responded towards the end of August by explaining that 'the Government do not claim a right to decide upon the Chairmanship of the Company, but only to express through their representatives on the Board, the wishes and conclusions which they have formed', and he agreed to see that 'the argument of principle which you set forth is fully weighed and balanced'.[162] Cargill was satisfied with this interpretation.[163]

At the next board meeting on 29 September,[164] the deed was done, when it was reported that Stewart had resigned on 26 September. It was moved by Slade that 'the Board learns with much regret of the contemplated retirement of Sir Charles Greenway at some not very distant date, and hereby resolves that Sir John Cadman be appointed to fill the vacancy to the Chair as and when it occurs'. Cadman's firm imprint upon the Company manifested itself with his preliminary recommendations on management, which he drafted early in October[165] and were accepted by the Board on 24 November 1925.[166] With only minor modifications due to changing circumstances, it remained his manual of principles and procedures throughout his chairmanship, the lodestar of his administrative structure and practice.

What is now required [he stated] is to determine, for each successively important stage in the control of the Company's affairs, how that control can in future be most effectively exercised and co-ordinated, where co-ordination is needed, up to the final stage where actual Board control is involved. The Unit for the purpose of this note is the executive Branch (or Department), - the personnel of which may be large or small, - each under the direction of a Manager or other experienced and responsible employee of the Company. Various units, dealing with different but related phases of the Company's operations, are grouped together to form Directorates, each of which is under a member of the Board, who is personally responsible to the Board itself for the proper executive control of his Directorate.

This was the basic structure composed of well-defined individual units, with a specific function controlled by a manager with definite responsibilities, assembled together in a rational and related manner to form a consistent coordinated operational grouping under the single executive authority of a managing director.

Cadman, however, was not just concerned about the construction, the bricks and mortar of the organisation. An important aspect of his conception of management was an idea he frequently expressed, 'harmony'. He believed, 'As it is necessary for each Management Director to ensure that his various Branches work in harmony and in pursuance of a common plan, so it is equally essential to ensure that this principle is safeguarded in the relationship between the several directorates. Individual contact between the various Managers and their responsible assistants is the first step.' He acknowledged that this had been 'enormously facilitated by assembling the several Directorates under a common roof'. The creation of a corporate *esprit* was fostered by a proper acknowledgement of individual qualities and responsibilities within recognisable executive parameters, a system of line management derived from military models and American administrative experience. So counselled Cadman, 'Interdepartmental questions requiring collective consideration, or investigation from different angles, may be dealt with by correspondence, by ad hoc meetings, or by small committees between responsible representatives of the Directors concerned.' Directors had to ensure 'subordinate collaboration is properly directed, economical of time, and does not degenerate into sterile debate or the convenient shelving of executive responsibility'. There had to be a gradual delegation of authority linked along the lines of management at different levels, a carefully differentiated system of vertical functioning, but it had also to be applied horizontally in a constant cooperative and coordinated effort of liaison 'where absolute continuity of touch is essential'.

The attitude of the management directors was crucial, their role being navigational, determining the direction from the bridge rather than the engine room. Their working relationship to each other was collaboration based on a normal pattern of personal contact and conversation from day to day, a mark of the Company's informal senior management methods, which became a permanent and distinctive feature of the small closely knit 'open door' association of the executive directors. Cadman appreciated, in formulating a comprehensive management policy, 'the necessity, imposed on the Company by the constant expansion of its activities, of periodically overhauling its system of management in order to keep its perspective up to date and maintain a timely adjustment of means to ends. Otherwise figuratively speaking - the progressive organisation of today may be in danger of becoming stationary tomorrow, and retrograde thereafter.' Such were the general principles of Cadman's vision of a dynamic, adaptable management policy with the parts adjusted and polished to the scale and size required according to their position and responsibilities, meshing and running together smoothly, requiring only fine tuning by the directors.

Cadman proposed four main directorates: (1) technical operations of discovery and production and refining; (2) distribution and the marketing of refined products; (3) finance in all its aspects; and (4) general services. He placed great emphasis on having 'throughout the Company's service, a general uniformity of practice' in staff matters. He felt 'It is equally necessary to ensure that entries, promotion, dismissals etc., and staff establishments are in general conformity with the actual needs of the various directorates, whilst not exceeding what is strictly necessary for the proper conduct of the Company's business.' Standardisation in the supply function 'over the whole range of the Company's operations in order to ensure uniformity of practice, and purchase to the best advantage, in all spheres of the Company's activities' was also essential to good management, particularly since between 1923-24 and 1925-26 purchases through head office totalled £3 200 000.

Over the question of the centralisation or decentralisation of general services, Cadman preferred a centralised relationship as being 'more effective and certainly more economical'.[167] He outlined a classic staff policy,

to harmonise the ideal of each Director having administrative control of his own staff with unification of system in the treatment and remuneration of the staff as a whole – both on entry and during their service with the Company. Staff will be entered on the requisition of the several responsible directors, and it will be an important duty of the Branch to draw Director's attention to the possibility, whenever it exists, of meeting one's departments' needs by promotion from another rather than by introducing new personnel into the higher posts.

Cadman cannot necessarily in all respects be credited with complete originality. His achievement was to coordinate the parts, incorporating particular improvements harmoniously, which enhanced the style and effect of the whole performance. The recruitment of graduate engineers and geologists had been initiated in 1922 when J.M. Pattinson and H.S. Gibson were appointed after coming down from Cambridge. Both later had distinguished careers, the former as deputy chairman of the Company and the latter as chairman of the Iraq Petroleum Company. Attention to administrative detail was disclosed by the appointment in January 1923 of a Mr C. Taylor Brading 'to reorganise and control the filing systems'.[168] Publicity and advertising had already been used, of which the most spectacular example was the Company's participation in the Wembley Exhibition of 1924. Information activities had included the launching of a house magazine, *The Naft*, in 1924. Attention was paid to the compilation of statistics and regular management reports to the Board were issued, also from 1924. Medical services, which had existed from the D'Arcy concessionary days,[169] were improved when Cadman appointed Dr Young to coordinate them on a comprehensive company scale.

The same administrative malaise that was afflicting the head office, excessive departmentalism and lack of coordination, was producing similar effects in Persia. Cadman's management objective was to look at 'matters of advantage or disadvantage to the Company as a whole, irrespective of departmental boundary lines and directorial responsibilities'. Cadman learnt at first hand during a visit to Persia in October–November 1924 what this meant in the technical operations, commenting on 'the need for much closer general contact between Persia and London than has taken place in the past'.[170] As others before him, he was impressed with Fields, 'here far more than anywhere else in Persia are evidenced the results of sound management and foresight', but these qualities were missing in Ābādān, which lacked 'any settled form of policy'. He deplored the failure to plan on the 'broad outlines of refinery policy of the future ahead of actual mechanical and scientific development'. Cadman's visit was a scientific blitzkrieg exposing weakness after weakness in plant, equipment and personnel. He was much concerned about what he termed 'the mechanical chain for the application of engineering principles'. He noted that 'the technical organisation of the Company has hitherto left much to be desired. The engineer has not been given his proper responsibility in the operation of the works.' Cadman

Management and finance

placed the technical function in the centre of the Company's activities, thereby making a decisive contribution to the efficiency and economy of the Company's operations, which enabled it to withstand the competition of its rivals, who may have had more extensive marketing success but no better production record.

Cadman introduced a major administrative innovation with the application of budgetary control to the Company's operations, 'a system of estimates of proposed annual expenditure and of endeavouring to work to these estimates'. This corresponded to the principle enshrined in the formation of the financial committee established in July 1923, of 'a settled annual programme linked to a budget of estimated expenditure'. In November 1925 Cadman strengthened the role of the finance committee which rationalised accountability and enforced control over financial affairs throughout the Company on a comparative and determined basis and to which the subsidiaries conformed from 1927-28. Cadman 'was convinced that it formed the only basis on which a business of this magnitude could be conducted efficiently'. Budgetary control provided 'the vital function of providing quick and adequate information to enable the Works Management to keep properly in touch with expenditure and so ensure a full application of business principles to the purely technical control'. It was this lack of technical control which caused the failures of the managing agents.

For Cadman there was a very close correlation between business principles and technical efficiency which could only be achieved by responsible and responsive management. In his report on his Persian visit he regretted that 'we have still a long way to go before we can rest assured that standards of prudent business management apply generally to all phases of the Company's operations, whether in Persia or at home'.[171] He attributed this delay to three main causes: (1) inadequacy of machinery for giving the technical management a full sense of responsibility in reference to financial aspects; (2) defective understanding between London and Persia on questions of operations, aims and policy being out of step; and (3) an absence of definite policy and long-range programmes, in which the confidence and cooperation of the Persian management should be involved. It was a mirror image of his views on London management with its deficiency in 'directive collaboration' for, he proclaimed, 'if we require the best team work in our staffs, we must first set the example'.

Cadman's management motto might have been 'Harmony and Efficiency', when he became chairman on Greenway's retirement on 27 March 1927. He approved of the principle *primus inter pares* and, referring in 1928 to the functions of the management committee, mentioned them as 'deliberative, consultative and advisory, and nothing in

Management and finance

its constitution shall impair *the direct responsibility of individual Management Directors to the Board*'[172] (italics mine). Management was the fulfilment of individual authority in association with corporate responsibility. A year later in May 1929, reviewing progress for the Board, he informed its members that 'almost daily close touch is now maintained between individual Management Directors, and the benefit of full co-ordination of view and exchange of opinion, without impairing direct responsibility to the Board of individual Management Directors is secured under the authority of the Chairman, or in his absence, his Deputy. In practice, recourse to the more formal machinery of Management Committee meetings is proving unnecessary.'[173] Six months later he was pleased about 'the admirable manner in which the administration was functioning'.[174] There was no need for the formal consultative machinery of the management committee. There was harmony over policy and efficiency in operation. Cadman had four managing directors. Hearn was in charge of concessionary and general affairs. Fraser was responsible for production, refining and United Kingdom distribution matters. Lloyd was the finance director and Heath Eves looked after world-wide distribution and shipping. (See Appendix 8.2 for 1930 organigram of these functions. Appendix 8.3 illustrates the number of associated companies, their relationship to the main functions and the Company's shareholding in them. Appendix 8.4 gives the directors of the Company 1909-32.)

(b) A better financial footing

The years of the mid 1920s saw the establishment of the Company on a much sounder financial basis than had been the case during the earlier period of the construction of the pipeline, the refinery and the ancilliary facilities, no less than the general requirements for the commencement of trading. The post war expansion programme had imposed severe financial strains upon the Company culminating in the 1923 crisis. The years 1924 to 1928 showed an increase in funds of £23.8 million (see Table 8.7). External sources contributed a mere 9 per cent to funds, most of which is accounted for by the £4 million debenture issue of December 1925 by the British Tanker Company. The amount of £2 154 227 for the increase in long term indebtedness shown in the source and application statement (see Table 8.8) reflects the repayment of other outstanding loans, notes and debentures. Retained profits made up the greatest part of the increase in funds, testimony to the improvement in the Company's trading position and the declared policy of Greenway. The remainder of the increase, the £4 475 000 in ordinary shares, did not represent an injection of additional capital but the capitalisation of the outstanding Share Premium Account of

Management and finance

Table 8.8. *Statement of source and application of funds of the Anglo-Persian Oil Company group 1924-28*

Source of funds	£	£	£
Sources outside the Company			
Increase in capital subscribed			
Ordinary shares		4 475 000	
Preference shares		—	
			4 475 000
Decrease in share premium account			(3 663 128)
Increase in long term liabilities			
Debentures and loans			2 154 227
Decrease in minority interest			(1 342 927)
Sources within the Company			
Increase in retained profits		8 246 681	
add back, depreciation		13 984 183	
			22 230 864
			23 854 036
Application of funds			
Increase in purchase price of Concession			676 051
Increase in fixed assets			
Installations		12 465 591	
Stores etc.		(592 598)	
			11 872 993
Goodwill arising on acquisitions			1 060 054
Increase in long term investments			2 293 787
Increase in current assets			
Stock		3 206 593	
Debtors		3 287 584	
Cash		3 278 705	
		9 772 882	
Less increase in current liabilities			
Creditors and loans		1 821 731	
Increase in net current assets			7 951 151
			23 854 036

Source: BP consolidated balance sheets (see Appendix 3.1(e))

Management and finance

£3 663 128 plus additional reserves. This took the form of a bonus issue to ordinary shareholders in the proportion of one new fully paid share for each two ordinary shares held on 20th November 1926.

The largest part of the growth in funds, a little more than half, was applied to the expansion of the Company's fixed assets, which increased in value by £12 465 591 between 1924 and 1928. The purposes to which this investment were put are shown in Table 8.9. The most important item of

Table 8.9. *Increase in fixed assets of the Anglo-Persian Oil Company group 1924-28* (£ increase in value, fixed assets at historic cost per annum)

	1924–25	1925–26	1926–27	1927–28	1928 (9 months)
Fields	(359 678)	133 042	(1 064 831)	514 301	(417 612)
Refineries	835 738	782 401	411 115	1 365 331	(148 613)
Pipelines	14 936	106 035	534 970	(384 726)	5 144
Tankers	3 340 607	432 724	767 092	1 725 602	711 421
Distribution	779 531	735 072	1 476 546	835 466	(821 205)
Bunkering	(291 598)	(25 033)	6 839	(1 582)	235 192
Administration	4 272	39 391	59 623	48 866	79 212
Total	4 323 808	2 203 632	2 191 354	4 103 258	(356 461)

Source: BP consolidated balance sheets (see Appendix 3.1(e))

capital expenditure over the whole period was the tanker fleet, which accounted for about half of the total growth in fixed assets. Between March 1925 and December 1928 the proportion of the Company's fixed assets constituted by the tanker fleet increased from 34 per cent to 36 per cent, as shown in Table 8.10. Investment in refineries and distribution facilities constituted around 25 per cent each of the growth of fixed assets over the years 1924-28, amounts sufficient to sustain the same proportion of the Company's fixed assets in refineries over the period and to result in an overall increase in investment in distribution from 20 per cent of fixed assets to 21 per cent. The proportions of fixed assets constituted by fields and pipelines declined from 1924 to 1928, continuing a trend apparent in the early 1920s. By the mid 1920s, however, the shift in the distribution of assets from upstream to downstream activities had stabilised at approximately 35 per cent in shipping, 25 per cent in refining, 25 per cent in distribution, 10 per cent in production and 5 per cent in administration.

Some 15 per cent of the growth in fixed assets represented increases in holdings of other companies shares and government securities, the acquisition of new concessions and the growth of balance sheet goodwill upon the acquisition of new continental marketing subsidiaries and

Table 8.10. Distribution of fixed assets by activity of the Anglo-Persian Oil Company group 1924-28

(£ fixed assets at historic cost)

	1924–25	%	1925–26	%	1926–27	%	1927–28	%	1928 (9 months)	%
Fields	2 955 103	7	3 088 145	7	2 023 314	5	2 537 615	5	2 120 003	4
Refineries	10 744 344	27	11 526 745	27	11 937 860	27	13 303 191	27	13 154 578	27
Pipelines	2 329 527	6	2 435 562	6	2 970 532	6	2 585 806	5	2 590 950	5
Tankers	13 547 867	34	13 980 591	33	14 747 683	33	16 473 285	34	17 184 706	36
Distribution	7 894 841	20	8 629 913	21	10 106 459	23	10 941 925	23	10 120 720	21
Bunkering	755 999	2	730 966	2	737 805	2	736 223	2	971 415	2
Administration	1 804 613	4	1 844 004	4	1 903 627	4	1 952 493	4	2 031 705	5
Total	40 032 294		42 235 926		44 427 280		48 530 538		48 174 077	

Source: BP consolidated balance sheets (see Appendix 3.1(e))

Table 8.11 *Liquidity position of the Anglo-Persian Oil Company group 1924-28*

Date	Consolidated current assets		Consolidated current liabilities		Consolidated net current assets	Increase in net current assets on last year[a]	Current ratio[a]	Liquidity ratio[b]
		£		£	£	£		
1925 31 March	Cash and balances Debtors Stocks	1 281 090 4 824 772 4 600 091	Creditors	7 170 654				
		10 705 953		7 170 654	3 535 299	487 539	1.49	0.85
1926 31 March	Cash and balances Debtors Stocks	4 320 639 6 395 331 5 726 898	Creditors	6 719 541				
		16 442 868		6 719 541	9 723 327	6 188 028	2.45	1.59
1927 31 March	Cash and balances Debtors Stocks	5 752 778 6 184 041 6 505 476	Creditors	8 994 626				
		18 442 295		8 994 626	9 447 669	(275 658)	2.05	1.32
1928 31 March	Cash and balances Debtors Stocks	4 008 503 7 123 753 6 198 598	Creditors	8 771 801				
		17 330 854		8 771 801	8 559 053	(888 616)	1.98	1.27
1928 31 December	Cash and balances Debtors Stocks	5 104 476 7 888 782 6 861 507	Creditors	8 855 854				
		19 854 765		8 855 854	10 998 911	2 439 858	2.24	1.47

Notes: [a] Current ratio — ratio of consolidated current assets to consolidated current liabilities.
[b] Liquidity ratio — ratio of consolidated liquid assets (current assets less stocks) to consolidated current liabilities.
Source: BP consolidated balance sheets (see Appendix 3.1(e))

Management and finance

bunkering facilities.[175] The remainder of the increase in the Company's funds was applied to the improvement of the cash position. The Company's liquidity position at the end of each financial year is shown in Table 8.11. The dramatic increase of net current assets in 1925-26 of £6 188 028 was largely the consequence of the growth of holdings of cash over the previous year from the £4 million debenture issue. The respective movements of money owed to the Company by its clients (debtors), which increased from £4 824 772 in 1925-26 to £6 395 331 in 1926-27, and money owed by the Company to suppliers (creditors), which declined from £7 170 654 to £6 719 541, further boosted the growth of net current assets for the year. The improvement in the current ratio from 1.49 in 1924-25 to 2.45 in 1925-26 epitomises the effect of these developments and the resulting improvement of the Company's cash position.

In the two following years the current ratio fell back to about 2 as creditors increased in 1926-27 and as cash balances were run down in 1927-28 for the redemption of outstanding debentures. The ratio improved by December 1928 to 2.24. Stocks, debtors and creditors increased gradually, as might have been expected, matching the growth of turnover.

The proportionate return on investment shown in Table 8.12 reflects the overall financial performance. Following the difficult financial years of 1922-23 and 1923-24, during which the return on investment was a mere 2 per cent, the rate rose to 9.3 per cent in 1924-25 after a dramatic improvement in profit for the year from £863 624 in 1923-24 to £3 654 907 in 1924-25. The rate of return remained 5-10 per cent in the succeeding four years, an acceptable though not spectacular performance.

The rate of dividend paid to ordinary shareholders improved in 1924-25, rising from 10 per cent in the preceding year to 12½ per cent, a level which was maintained in 1925-26, when profit for the year rose by £602 071. In the following two years, however, it fell to 7½ per cent, reflecting the drop in the level of profit for the year from £4 256 978 in 1925-26 to £2 139 133 in 1926-27 and £2 430 651 in 1927-28. For dividends 1913-32, (see Appendix 8.5). Retained profits were depressed in 1927-28 as a result of the high level of tax paid to the British Government in settlement of the long disputed liability to Excess Profits Duty incurred for 1920-21. Cadman presented the fall off in profit in the most favourable light when he told shareholders in November 1928 that in the light of the prevailing low prices for oil products 'the fact that, serious though it is, the effect on the profits is not greater, affords remarkable proof of the Company's inherent strength and of the success of the measures taken to bring about permanent economies'.[176] The rate of return on investment fell to 4.7 per cent in 1926-27 and 5.2 per cent in 1927-28. In 1928, for the 9 months prior to the accounting year being changed to a calendar-year

Table 8.12. *Anglo-Persian Oil Company group financial performance 1924-28*

Year	Profit for the year before tax and dividends[a] £	Tax paid to British Government[b] £	Dividends £	Retained profit £	Average net tangible assets for the year[c] £	Return on investment per cent[d]	Dividend rate per cent
1924–25	3 654 907	222 755	1 118 750	2 313 402	39 428 570	9.3	12½
1925–26	4 256 978	232 182	1 118 750	2 906 046	42 147 527	10.1	12½
1926–27	2 139 133	323 550	1 006 875	808 708	45 611 366	4.7	7½
1927–28	2 430 651	930 969	1 006 875	492 807	45 913 068	5.3	7½
1928 (9 months)	3 646 088	661 776	1 258 594	1 725 718	47 440 323	7.7	12½

Notes: [a] Profit after deduction of debenture and preference share interest, preliminary expenses, overhead charges and royalty
[b] Income tax, corporate tax, excess profits duty
[c] Average of consolidated assets, except for intangibles (goodwill), *less* current liabilities, at start and end of year
[d] Ratio of profit for the year to average net tangible assets

Source: consolidated balance sheets (see Appendix 3.1(e))

basis, the rate of dividend rose to 12½ per cent, reflecting an improvement in the trading position and an increase in profit for the year of £1 215 437.

By the beginning of 1929, the year which marked the beginning of the Depression, the Company had sustained a reasonably consistent and respectable performance for five years. Firstly, there was a recovery in the rate of return on capital employed after the crisis in 1922 and 1923. Secondly, the rate of growth of assets in the previous decade compared favourably with other oil companies, particularly as it was established later than its major competitors (see Table 12.1). In a particularly capital-intensive industry the Company had adequately established its capital base and was financing investment prudently and conservatively from its own internal generation of funds. This approach clearly stated in 1923 by Greenway and confirmed by him in 1925 in the face of criticism from some shareholders remained the hallmark of its financial policy for the next twenty five years.[177]

5 CONCLUSION

The clashes of temperament and differences of opinion which were associated with the development of the Company and its evolving relationship with the Government were its growing pains, its adolescent problems. Under Cadman the Company settled down to a career of solid achievement. Cadman was professional in outlook as befitted his scientific background. The Company prospered under his tutorship. He combined an instinctive rational approach, knowledgeable technical expertise and judgement with a flair for personal relations, sensible administrative understanding and an astute appreciation of the political environment. His time in university and government service provided him with admirable experience and expertise to act as chairman of the Company, which was so dependent upon modern technology and involved in government relations of many kinds. Greenway had been the brilliant virtuoso, Cadman the more measured performer.

The management of the Company in this period was of a scale and complexity that was unimaginable at its formation. The expansion of operations extending throughout the world, the developments in technology, the volume of production, the growth in the workforce, the demands for funds, the difficulties in concessionary and governmental relations stretched the capacity of management almost to breaking point. The pressure on the funding of investment in a period of tremendous expansion was particularly intense. The reconciling of resources to objectives was sometimes erratic. The clash of interests between the Company and the Government was often distracting. The disagreements

Management and finance

of the Board were disturbing, but Greenway kept his hand on the tiller until he handed over to Cadman. Cadman not only improved the technical and administrative efficiency of the Company, but he welded the Board into a more effective instrument of policy. As well as imparting a better feeling of individual responsibility throughout the Company, he established a greater sense of corporate identity.

9
GOVERNMENT AND CONCESSIONARY RELATIONS 1919-26

I INTRODUCTION

The Armistice of 1918 terminated the hostilities of war, but did not solve the problems of peace. The principles of Woodrow Wilson, the consequences of the Russian Revolution and the collapse of the Ottoman Empire changed more than the maps of the world and the minds of the politicians. They helped stimulate a sharper sense of national consciousness and thereby bring about the emergence of a new series of international relationships. Whilst this was most obviously true of the Balkans it was also relevant in the heartland of the Middle East where Arab, Turkish, Egyptian and Persian national sentiments unmistakably expressed themselves in an area of continuing concern to British interests.[1] This assertiveness, matching the stirring of nationalism in the Indian sub-continent and South-East Asia, was followed by a gradual contraction of colonial influence. The cost of the war in lives and resources, the penurious state of the post-war economy and the blurring of the imperial vision, forced successive British governments into reappraisals of national and international policies. If this had resulted in careful conclusions and concerted action it would have been beneficial, but, unfortunately and frequently, the lack of decision which was displayed caused more confusion and even greater uncertainty. There was no lack of anxiety over the state of Ireland, the mandates for Iraq and Transjordan, the future of the League of Nations, the relevance of the gold standard, and other issues. There seemed to be no shortage of advice from commentators, experts and officials. Politicians were profuse with their panaceas, but the immediate post-war decade was hardly notable for positive success in real achievements.

This observation is equally applicable to the failure of the British Government to propound a policy for oil.[2] It was not surprising in the midst of war, as has been seen (Chapter 6), that expediency took the place of policy, but there was less excuse in peace for the continuing uncertainty over intentions. Once the immediate danger of the lack of supplies had receded,

Government and concessionary relations

there was little inclination to take any strong initiative in the matter. The recommendations of the Harcourt Committee were lost in the prolonged and unseemly Anglo-French bickering over their respective positions in the Middle East[3] and Lloyd George's conviction that state rather than private enterprise should be allowed the concessionary rights in Mesopotamia. The Petroleum Executive was effectively, if not obviously, reduced in status and transferred to the control of the Board of Trade. An Admiralty proposal for the systematic storage of a year's reserve stock of naval fuel oil by the Government was accepted, but never implemented[4] for financial reasons. It was suggested that colonial oil leasing arrangements should be brought up to date and harmonised, but nothing was done.[5] Different departments of government continued to have differing views on oil affairs, but there was little coordination or consultation where interests overlapped or diverged. Government attitudes to the Company remain schizophrenic till 1925, when it was finally conceded that the Government had no intention of selling its shareholding in the Company.

The British Government was concerned about the Company's position, staff and assets in Persia, particularly while the power of Shaykh Khaz'al and the Bakhtiari Khans was crumbling, as a result of the determined efforts of Riza Khan (Minister·of War 1921, Prime Minister 1923 and crowned Shah 1926) to diminish their provincial autonomy.[6] It was feared that a breakdown of local authority might endanger lives and property, but there was little real agreement on what measures were to be taken in such an eventuality. On the whole there was a gradual disengagement from too close an association with the Company's affairs in Persia, especially once Cadman was designated as successor to Greenway.

For Persia these years were especially momentous. The collapse of Russia in 1917 seemed to some to presage the end of Russian intervention in Persian affairs, while the defeat of Germany was to others a grave disappointment. Yet others welcomed the opportunity of closer ties with the United Kingdom held out by the Anglo-Persian Treaty which was signed on 9 August 1919, after being negotiated by Sir Percy Cox at the personal direction of Curzon,[7] or encouraged American interest in their country. Some Persians under Kūchik Khān were fighting as an independence movement in the forested countryside of Gīlān in northern Persia. Other local rebellious groups were asserting themselves separately in Āzarbāyjān, Khurāsān, and the region around Hamadān.[8] Then, as British troops were evacuating Persia after attempts to contain a Turkish invasion and support anti-Bolshevik forces in Baku, an unexpectedly successful coup d'état was mounted on 21 February 1921 by a journalist, Sayyid Ziyā al-Dīn Tabatābāī, who had been a student in Paris before the

Government and concessionary relations

First World War, with the assistance of a colonel in the Russian sponsored Cossack Brigade, Riżā Khān.[9]

Within a short time negotiations, which had begun earlier in Moscow, were concluded (on 26 February 1921), whereby the Russian Government renounced all Tsarist treaties and concessions with Persia and waived all Persian debts to Russia. The Anglo-Persian Treaty of 1919, never ratified by the Majlis, was repudiated.[10] It seemed as if Persia had exorcised her foreign demons. A few months later Sayyid Ziyā al-Dīn was forced to flee as the rise to power of Riżā Khān began, which resulted in a new dynasty, the Pahlavī, occupying the throne of Persia.[11] By asserting his strong personal authority, Riżā Shāh succeeded in reviving Persia after the weakness of the Qājār period and in instituting many measures of modernisation and social reform. There was a fundamental difference for the Company between the provincial behaviour of the Bakhtiari Khans (see Chapter 2) and the autocratic centralising domination of Riżā Shāh. This had profound consequences for the conduct of its operations. The Company faced a new political situation in Persia, forcing it to adapt accordingly.

2 CLARIFYING THE ISSUES 1919-1920

(a) The letter and the spirit of the Treasury assurances

In September 1919 the relationship of the British Government to the Company was uncertain. Greenway reminded Inchcape that:

> The powers of veto asked for by the Government were a very much debated point at the time, the Burmah Oil Co. refusing at first to agree to them at all, and it was only after a good deal of discussion, and very ample and emphatic assurances given to both Cargill and myself that there was no intention whatever of interference in the commercial and financial administration of the Company, that the Burmah Oil Co. conceded the point on the understanding that a covering letter defining the scope of the powers should be given for future guidance and protection.[12]

It was not long before a profound misunderstanding occurred over the interpretation of the Treasury letter, which had been drafted by Bradbury. It concerned the proposal by the Company to issue non-voting ordinary shares to the Persian Government as part of its settlement of the outstanding compensation and royalties issues. The signing of the Anglo-Persian Treaty on 9 August 1919 seemed to augur well for Anglo-Persian relations, although oil was not then a consideration.[13] One of the Persian negotiators, Nusrat al-Dawla, Prince Fīrūz, the Persian Foreign Minister, arrived in Europe to attend the Peace Conference and to accompany Ahmed Shāh, the Persian monarch, on his European tour. He

Government and concessionary relations

was welcomed by the Foreign Office and the Company. The arrival of Fīrūz in England coincided with an issue of the Company's shares and he 'pointed out to Lord Curzon that it would be most deeply appreciated in Tehran if His Majesty's Government were to offer to the Persian Government some of their new shares, in view of the fact that the Oil Company's works are situated in Persia, and that the shares would not be procurable by any other means'.[14] Curzon was favourably disposed on political grounds to give the Persian Government a further financial interest in the Anglo-Persian Oil Company, but the matter was not pressed and no decision was taken.

After drawn-out negotiations with Fīrūz (see pp. 365-9), the Company proposed a settlement on 11 June, which included an optional offer of shares in the Company. The British Government was asked to authorise an issue of shares up to 130 000, which would not have affected the balance of voting rights. The offer had some analogy with the shares of the Persian Government in the First Exploitation Company and resembled the situation of the Bakhtiari Khans in the Bakhtiari Oil Company. Greenway was convinced that the terms of the agreement would remove 'once and for all the grounds for dispute between the Company and the Persian Government which have been the cause of so much trouble to all concerned during the past few years'.[15] Barstow, at first, in a note to the Chancellor, Austen Chamberlain, had commended the idea as 'a favourable bargain for the Co. and consequently for the Exchequer as shareholder. The F.O. have on political grounds pressed us to agree that the Persian Government might have an interest in the Co.'[16] Inchcape was amazed and condemned it as a potentially disastrous financial bargain which only valued the Company's shares at £5 when they were worth £20. He advised that it was 'infinitely better to settle for a cash payment of £650 000' and that 'I would be wanting in my duty as representing the Treasury on the Board if I failed to warn you against parting with any ordinary shares.'[17] Inchcape's views were unchallenged, because he requested, almost reprehensibly, that 'they were not to be communicated to my Admiralty colleague [Packe], who of course does not feel the same financial responsibility as I do'. Barstow complied, admitting that Inchcape had knocked 'the bottom out of this proposal in its financial aspect... I had too readily assumed that what they regarded a good bargain for the Co. must be a good bargain for the Government as the principal shareholders.'[18] The Chancellor, Austen Chamberlain, concurred, authorising Inchcape to use his veto if necessary and declining to offer any explanation for his decision to the Company.[19]

The Board was appalled and expressed its extreme surprise. Greenway, 'rather fierce',[20] calling on Barstow, protested that the Treasury had

Government and concessionary relations

violated the terms of the Treasury letter and ignored the 'non intervention by His Majesty's Government in the commercial and financial administration of the Company'.[21] Interference had become an anathema to Greenway; the integrity of the Company was suspect to Inchcape. Barstow attempted to pacify Greenway by stressing that the Treasury 'is exceedingly anxious to work amicably with the Company and has no wish to interfere with its commercial operations or to hamper its activities when these do not conflict with public policy'.[22] Sugaring the pill of disagreement with a coating of flattery, he declared that, 'with the prospects of the Company as favourable as, under your management we believe them to be, the Government is unwilling to reduce its interest by admitting new ordinary shareholders'. It was unctuous, but unacceptable.

Greenway insisted that 'a ruling may be obtained, once and for all, as to the extent of the powers of the Government under their contract with the Company in relation to financial and commercial matters'.[23] Only then would the Board 'be in a position to know when matters requiring prompt decisions arise, how far they can go without reference to the Government or to the Government Directors'. Inchcape had clearly seen the losses represented by the issuing of ordinary shares to the Persian Government in capital investment terms, but he had failed to appreciate the potential returns on Persian goodwill. It was a dilemma which the Company faced on other occasions. This, however, was not the end of the matter because, even before the notification of the Treasury's opinion, the Persian Government of Vusuq al-Dawla was falling and it was learnt that 'the Prince is now anxious to get all cash and no shares'.[24]

More than the Company's concession in Persia was at stake. Greenway informed Barstow that it was conceivable that some future Government might decide against the policy of investing public monies in 'private industrial concerns'. In such an event would the Treasury then, asked Greenway pertinently, have the right to act the part of the dog in the manger and say 'we won't subscribe ourselves and we won't allow you to issue any fresh Capital to the Public?'. Greenway, anxious for a decision favourable to the Company, and Barstow, desirous of avoiding a major public dispute, moved gingerly to a solution by referring the question to a conference of those concerned later in the year.[25] On 3 November 1920 this was convened, attended by Austen Chamberlain, Barstow, Inchcape, Packe and Cadman, and by Greenway, Lord Southborough, as Sir Francis Hopwood had become, Barnes, Cargill, Black and Slade for the Company.[26]

Greenway and Cargill were certain that commercial implied financial considerations also, when they had been negotiating in 1913–14. The Chancellor believed that on the 'issue of capital, the Government, both in the letter and spirit of the original agreement, had an absolute right of veto'. Into what was becoming a rather arid repetition of faded memories and legal hypotheses, Southborough brought some fresh air of sensible realism. Whilst justifying the original terms he pointed out that 'Since then conditions had absolutely changed and the Company was now contemplating extensions in many other countries ... a new condition of affairs had arisen, and if the activities of the Company were not to be unduly circumscribed, he thought it would be necessary to devise some new arrangements or draw up new instructions which would enable the Company to work and extend its operations under altered circumstances.' By this expansion of its activities the Company and the Government would benefit from increased profits and dividends.

Chamberlain was impressed by Southborough's statement of the position, but he was not prepared to renounce the right of the Government to exercise its discretion and even, if it was justifiable, to impose its ultimate sanction of the veto. He did not intend, however, 'to prevent the Company from issuing further capital merely on the grounds that the Government did not wish to put up their proportion', for each case had to be decided on its merits. He emphasised the advisability of earlier consultations with government directors and fewer direct approaches to the Treasury, allowing for more flexibility and understanding in discussions, a more cooperative and less autocratic relationship. It was a reasonable compromise, adjustable in the light of circumstances and based on a better recognition of the realities of the relationship and a practical appreciation of its implications for Government and Company. Indeed, in many respects, Bradbury's own recollections of the assurances he had formulated were confirmed, for he had accepted 'that the Company had a right to be safeguarded against perpetual interference by the Government in its day to day business transactions as a commercial firm'.[27] Moreover he recognised the proposition that 'the non-government directors of the Company were likely to deal with the production, refining and marketing of oil with better results from a business point of view the less they were interfered with by the nominees of the Government'. Responsibility and representation, but not interference, was the role of the government directors.

(b) Confusion over Mesopotamia

The lack of clarity in the Government's position on oil is exemplified in the muddled approach to matters affecting Mesopotamia. The Harcourt Committee, it will be recalled from Chapter 6, hoped to formulate a British oil policy by bringing the British interests of Royal Dutch-Shell together under a single British registered and controlled company. A

Government and concessionary relations

dominant British presence in Mesopotamia would then be managed by Royal Dutch-Shell. Greenway was contemptuous that the '"paper" control looks very much as if the Nation is selling its birthright for a mess of pottage'.[28] He need not have worried, because the triangular relationship between the British and French governments and Royal Dutch-Shell led to numerous misunderstandings which effectively aborted the recommendations of the Committee.

As early as 21 November 1918 the French and British representatives taking part in a meeting of the Inter-Allied Petroleum Conference were regaled at a dinner by a toast proposed by the principal French delegate, Sénateur Henri Bérenger, Président of le Comité Général du Pétrole, who raised his glass to 'la Politique interalliée du Pétrole réalisée par l'accord des gouvernements et des industries'.[29] It was an expression of allied euphoria, which followed the ending of the war. The sentiment was repeated on 17 December at a further meeting in Paris.[30] It was the French acting ambassador in London, F. A. de Fleuriau, who first formally communicated definite French proposals to the Foreign Office on 6 January 1919.[31] The hostile reaction of the Foreign Office was to maintain that 'The French claim that they should be given the whole share of the Deutsche Bank in the Turkish Petroleum Company is of course quite untenable.'[32] It was recognised that 'we are once more up against the Sykes–Picot agreement, which gives France control of the rich oil-bearing Mosul district and of the country through which any pipeline from the Mesopotamian or Persian oil-fields to the Mediterranean would have to pass'. It was thought better to defer a decision until the Peace Conference at Versailles had determined the fate of the area.

By the middle of 1918 the fate of Mesopotamia, with its supposed oil deposits, had become an important preoccupation of British Middle East policy, a key consideration in the attempt to formulate an oil policy.[33] Suddenly on 1 December 1918 Lloyd George, with Clémenceau in London, seemed to have struck a bargain, when he persuaded the French President to relinquish claims for Mosul in return for being guaranteed a share in Mesopotamian oil, if discovered, and for British support for a French mandate over Syria. Unfortunately, few officials were aware for some months of this private diplomacy, but it profoundly changed the British situation and angered many French officials.[34] It was one of many surprising developments, which characterised the changing diplomatic postures over Mesopotamia in the years which followed.

In spite of Foreign Office disagreement, an inter-departmental conference at the Admiralty on 15 January 1919 approved negotiating with the French and this was confirmed, to the consternation of the Foreign Office, by the British delegates at the Peace Conference in Paris on 1

February, with the agreement of the representatives from the Board of Trade and India Office.[35] Cadman, with the authority of Long, and in liaison with the Foreign Office Peace Conference delegation, negotiated with Bérenger and reached a provisional agreement on 6 March, but it was 13 March before it was forwarded to the Foreign Office for comment.[36] Curzon was annoyed both at the delay of the communication and its details.[37] Accepting that the agreement strengthened the case for the validity of the Mesopotamian concession and that French support was useful, Curzon dismissed the rest as 'a promise of facilities for two pipelines which we may never be in a position to construct through a district which the French may never be in a position to afford us the facilities promised'.[38] It appeared, however, that Curzon had failed to appreciate the point of the agreement, 'the whole object of which is to give the Royal Dutch-Shell Group a share in the Turkish Petroleum Company in return for British control of this hitherto Dutch controlled group'.[39] On 8 April 1919, in a spirit of 'cordial co-operation and reciprocity', Long and Bérenger signed the agreement for their respective governments.[40] In early May the Cabinet approved of the agreement, which had been initialled between Harcourt and Deterding on 31 January 1919.[41] On 16 May Curzon informed the French ambassador that the Long–Bérenger agreement had been approved. The pieces seemed to have fallen into place, but the cordiality was shattered on 21 May when Lloyd George, in a row with Clémenceau in Paris over Syria, repudiated the oil agreement.[42] It was confusion all round, 'a complete bombshell to the Foreign Office', leaving Curzon with no option but to annul the agreement formally on 22 July.[43]

Long and Cadman, aghast at the diplomatic shambles, tried to resuscitate the agreement, arguing in November the great overwhelming fact that oil is 'becoming every day more vital to our national life' and that there was little time left in which to stake a claim to the opportunities which had grown out of the war.[44] The French, too, realised their need to reach a settlement and on 21 December 1919 Sir Hamar Greenwood, Minister in charge of petroleum affairs, and Bérenger, concluded an agreement largely modelled on the previous one.[45] Once again Lloyd George, with the agreement of some Ministers, pulled the diplomatic rug from under his colleagues by declaring on 23 January 1920 that as a matter of principle 'the profits arising from the exploitation of the oilfields of Mesopotamia should accrue for the benefit of the State rather than for the benefit of Joint Stock Companies'.[46] This statement rendered difficult, if not impossible, to implement, not only the latest agreement with the French signed barely a month previously, but also the Long–Deterding agreement relating to the Royal Dutch-Shell arrange-

Government and concessionary relations

ments. It might have effectively destroyed the composition of the Turkish Petroleum Company and it was impractical. The exclusion of private interests as Mr F. Kellaway, who succeeded Sir Hamar Greenwood on 2 April, realised, revived French claims for a 50 per cent share and precipitated American opposition. 'The suggestion', he stated, 'that the oil fields should be operated by Government may seem attractive, but the disadvantages of such an enterprise are very considerable.'[47] Such an attitude was too absurd to last and Sir Robert Horne, President of the Board of Trade and formerly a member of the Harcourt Committee, persuasively argued in favour of securing control of Royal Dutch-Shell. He too felt that 'the proposal to develop these oilfields as Government property may have attractions to some but the Government does not possess the necessary organisation for so vast a business as the successful commercial exploitation of a large oilfield and the marketing of its products'.[48]

Once again reason prevailed, when it was realised what would be the cost of garrisoning troops to protect the operations, which Barstow imagined could amount to £10 000 000 a year.[49] The agreement, finally signed at San Remo on 24 April 1920 by Cadman and Philippe Berthelot of the French Ministry of Foreign Affairs, was again modelled on those signed earlier, but was more comprehensive and made provision for either state or private exploitation of the concession.[50] It was not long before the San Remo agreement was attacked by the Italians, who felt left out,[51] and the Americans, who believed they were deliberately ignored.[52] It was the beginning of the 'Open Door' controversy, which caused a torrent of newspaper comment and diplomatic despatches and eventually led to American participation, along with the French, in the Turkish Petroleum Company (see Chapter 12).

Clarity was not a conspicuous feature of immediate post-war British oil policy. It was neither creative nor innovatory; it reacted to events. It lacked conviction, for, in spite of all the well meant and serious efforts of Long and Cadman, the importance of the issues was not consistently appreciated by the Cabinet as a whole. Vacillation and confusion marked oil affairs, the effects of which adversely affected the national interest.

3 COMING TO TERMS WITH PERSIA

(a) Negotiations in Tehrān

The cutting of the pipeline in 1915 and the subsequent four months delay in effecting repairs blighted the early relations between the Company and

Government and concessionary relations

the Persian Government. The Persian Government had pledged itself under Article 14 of the Concession to be responsible for the protection of the Company's property and personnel. It never disclaimed that responsibility. It was, however, no more able to provide that protection in 1915 than in 1901 or 1908 or any other earlier year, for it had neither the authority nor the forces with which to do so.[53] With engaging frankness, Nāsir al-Mulk, a former Regent of Persia, suggested to Greenway, at a dinner at the Persian Legation in London on 18 June 1915, that because of the Persian inability 'in the present state of their finances' to check German intrigues and 'fulfil their duties as a Neutral Power', Greenway should represent the need to the British Government for a strong Persian military force financed 'by the Governments whose interests were at stake'.[54] At the beginning of 1916 the British Government did decide to act and formed the South Persia Rifles, whose successful activities were out of all proportion to their numbers. They were commanded by Brigadier (later Sir) Percy Sykes, who had served many years as a consul in Persia.[55] However, neither requests for financial assistance, nor the subsequent deployment of troops, could prevent what had already happened. Maclean, the Company's agent in Tehrān, discussed the claim for compensation with the Minister for Foreign Affairs, who fully acknowledged the responsibility of his Government and undertook to consult with the Ministers of the Interior and War how best to protect the Company's interests.[56]

At the same time the Company was requested to pay the expenses of the Persian Legation in London, some £4800, out of the royalties that were due to it. Greenway agreed to do this in the interests of friendly relations, though it had been his intention not to make 'any further payments at all of Royalties and Dividends until the whole of the amount of our claim, for the losses which we have suffered have been liquidated'. The Foreign office approved of Greenway's action.[57] In October 1915 when Muhtesham al-Saltana, the Foreign Minister, declared that 'in view of the fact that neighbouring powers have turned these districts into their battlefields a state of "force majeure" has arisen which causes the Government to be free from responsibility', it was clear that the two parties in dispute were on a collision course.[58] For Greenway the damage to the pipeline was 'not the *cause* but the *consequence* of the lawlessness of the Persians in question'.[59]

In June 1916, convinced of 'the undoubted liability of the Persian Government',[60] Greenway again paid the expenses of the Persian Legation in London on request,[61] which was appreciated by the British Minister in Tehrān, Sir Charles Marling,[62] the Persian Minister in London, Mehdī Khān 'Alā Saltana[63] and the Foreign Secretary. So far the Company and

359

Government and concessionary relations

the Persian Government reserved their positions. The Company was playing it long, hoping for a comprehensive settlement after the war, but at the beginning of 1917 the Persian Government proposed referring the dispute to arbitration and Sadigh al-Saltana, the Imperial Commissioner still in Tehrān, in mid-February so informed D. Brown of the Imperial Bank, who had replaced Maclean as representative of the Company in Tehrān.[64] Arbitration at that time was not very practical. Unless the grounds were precisely defined, Greenway was averse to such a proceeding.[65] In this he was supported by Mehdī Khān, who urged that 'the whole matter should be left over until after the conclusion of the War'.[66] At that point the Persian Government fell.

Greenway realised that an impasse existed. It was not advisable to defer a settlement of the issues raised until after the end of the war because of the Persian annoyance over the withholding of royalty payments.[67] It was better to reach a comprehensive agreement on all the outstanding points. On 7 November 1917 he drew up a draft set of proposals to this end.[68] Greenway recognised that the fundamental concessionary problem was the computation of the 16 per cent profits royalty figure. This issue was to poison relations between the Company and the Government for the next fifteen years. Whatever the faults on both sides, the suspicions or misunderstandings, it was very regrettable that a solution was not found early. The concessionary sore festered over the years till it was finally lanced by the cancellation of the Concession in 1932. There never seems to have been the right occasion on which to reach agreement or the right people to have done so. It was not for the want of trying to reach an agreement, but each solution seems to have been doomed to failure.

As the elements of the case hardly changed, Greenway's remarks may serve as an introduction. He believed that,

> the present basis of Royalty is likely to be productive of endless and yearly disputes in the future as to what sums are, or are not, legitimately chargeable for depreciation, amortisation, etc., etc., before the amount of 'annual net profits' can be ascertained, since it is not at all probable that the Persian Government will accept without question the allocations which the Directors may, in pursuance of ordinary business principles, decide to make from time to time in respect of such items.

He correctly observed that 'it is possible that the Persian Government might at some time be induced to question the prices at which we are selling our products to the British Government'.

Furthermore, Greenway considered that, with the anticipated growth of the Company, the Persian Government would be sharing in profits, never contemplated when the Concession was granted,

Government and concessionary relations

outside of the actual producing, refining and selling of oil produced in Persia, and as the Concession now stands the Persian Government are (through the British Petroleum Company and the British Tanker Company) participating in the profits derived from the selling and transport of oil produced in the United States, and may quite probably at some future time even be drawing a share of the profits derived from Oil produced in the United Kingdom and/or in Trinidad and/or other British Colonies.'

Under these circumstances, believed Greenway, 'The Persian Government has no right to expect to share in such profits.' Accordingly 'my Board are of opinion that a strong endeavour should be made to effect some rearrangement of the Royalty whereby the Persian Government shall only benefit from the profits on the Oil produced in Persia'. He also proposed that the Concession be prolonged till 1986, which was the duration of a concession in North Persia, belonging to Mr A. Khostaria, a Georgian of doubtful Persian nationality, for which Greenway was then negotiating.[69] In order 'to bring about such a settlement of all outstanding questions', indicated Greenway, 'we would be disposed to make a very liberal offer', consisting of:

(a) cancelling the claim amounting to £614 489 - in respect of the losses suffered through the cutting of the pipeline by the Persian tribesmen in 1915, and

(b) paying at once the royalties on all oil produced up to 31 March 1917 at the rate of 2s per ton - viz - £143 981 6s less the sum of £30 537 6s 8d which had already been paid on account.

Greenway believed this represented an attractive proposition, a major simplification of an ambiguous concession, which promised a better return to Persia. He estimated that the royalties payable up to 31 March 1917 on the 16 per cent profits basis amounted to £101 140 14s 5d whereas on a 2s tonnage basis they would be £143 981 6s 0d. The 2s per ton rate was the highest concessionary rate for oil produced in any of the British colonies and at an estimate of a maximum yearly production of 3 000 000 tons would yield the Persian Government £300 000 in revenue per annum. Greenway felt that the timing was right, because of 'the pressing financial needs of the Persian Government' and that 'a return of so much per ton is a much more valuable asset for the Persian Government than an uncertain one fluctuating with profits'.[70] That was a qualitative judgement on a matter which was fundamentally quantitative. The Persian Government would want cash in hand, not pie in the sky. It was an attitude that was to reappear later, the mistaken assumption that financial straits would lessen Persian demands. No Persian politician succumbed to the temptation. They believed that their silver lining was always just round the corner - and it usually turned out to be so.

Government and concessionary relations

On 23 November 1917 Greenway submitted his draft to the Foreign Office[71] hoping that the Government would give the proposals its strongest possible support, but the timing was awkward in the wake of the Russian Revolution and disturbances in Persia. Marling, pressed by the Persian Government to secure the royalties they were owed, and trying to rally Persian politicians favourable to the allied cause, strongly urged that 'until there is a reasonable prospect of useful negotiations being agreed, your Company should be careful not to disclose the terms which it is prepared to offer and that in no circumstances should communications to the Persian Government be made through the Minister in London'.[72] Greenway disagreed[73] and persuaded Lancelot Oliphant at the Foreign Office to recommend that his proposals be put to the Persian Government.[74] He also informed Mehdī Khān of them,[75] who was in turn criticised by the Persian authorities for commending them to their attention and was advised that the Company's action in retaining the royalties was contrary to the terms of the Concession.[76] Mehdī Khān was, furthermore, warned that any new proposals would be submitted to the Majlis for approval and that the Company should pay as soon as possible what was due to the Government, as its attitude was creating bad feeling against it.

A Turkish advance towards Tabrīz imposed a further strain on Persian politicians, who after three years of occupation and deprivation had split into competing factions for foreign favours. Oliphant was pessimistic, for 'at present none of our negotiations are very promising'.[77] In Tehrān, Marling thought that there was 'little prospect at present of early opportunity of useful negotiations on mining or oil projects unless His Majesty's Government consider them of sufficient urgency to form part of negotiations with Persian Government on larger questions of policy'.[78] There was no chance of this happening, however, because of the inadvisability 'of importing such matters into negotiations with the Persian Government on wider questions of policy'.[79]

During the middle of 1918 Greenway consistently expressed a desire to negotiate but this was thwarted by the difficulty of communications, by the lack of an authorised Company negotiator in Tehrān, by the rapid succession of Persian Governments[80] and by the deliberate prevarication of the Foreign Office.[81] In early August Vusuq al-Dawla was appointed Prime Minister in more stable political conditions. Cox replaced Marling as chargé d'affaires in Tehrān, arriving on 15 September, and in less than a year he had negotiated the Anglo-Persian Treaty, which was signed on 9 August 1919. The omens for settling the dispute between the Company and the Persian Government therefore seemed more auspicious. On 10 August 1918 the Persian Government renewed its demands for the pay-

Government and concessionary relations

ment of royalties,[82] but did not exclude the possibility of discussing new proposals, though it seemed unlikely that it would be able to do so immediately owing to the political opposition, which had previously manifested itself.[83] By November Cox was mildly reassuring about Vusuq al-Dawla's intentions, reporting that the

> extension of the concession to 1986 may not present much difficulty but that he is doubtful whether he is strong enough at present to carry out desired alteration through Cabinet as it would have to be submitted to investigation by experts and by Concession Committee ... He asked me to let matter stand over for a week or two when he hopes to be in a stronger position.[84]

This was a sign of Persian procrastination, which later became part of the negotiating process on many occasions, when delays were allowed to occur and decisions were allowed to emerge rather than be actively taken.

Greenway was impatient. It was a year since the Board had approved his new proposals and it was frustrating, as he contemplated the opportunities awaiting the Company, to have an uncertain concessionary base from which to operate. He had appreciated in April 1918 Marling's 'valuable suggestion as to the appointment of a "big" man to represent our various interests in Tehran'.[85] The problem, he reflected, was finding a suitable person 'of sufficient standing and personality, of the right age, and also possessing the necessary spirit of adventure to travel in Persia under prevailing conditions'. By September a 'big' man was available, a friend of Greenway with a resounding name, Colonel C. Willoughby Wallace,[86] who reached Tehrān towards the end of November, as a special envoy, to a friendly reception.

Advised by Mehdī Khān, Greenway believed it to be 'the psychological opportunity' for a settlement and hoped that all questions would be resolved within a week of Wallace's arrival. He was much too anxious for he was also suggesting to the Foreign Office that it would be a good idea if Qishm and the mudflats of Ābādān could be acquired by purchase or lease, but he received no favourable response. He had become rather tired of the Foreign Office.[87] Greenway informed Cox that Wallace would also negotiate later for mineral rights and railway concessions. The understandable impatience of Greenway led to the failure of Wallace, for Greenway's approach was a disaster. He made a major error of judgement. It was regrettable that he should have joined the compensation issue to the new proposals, rather than letting the proposals stand on their own merits, and more unfortunate that he should have mixed oil affairs with those for other concessionary requests. He offended those whom he might have persuaded to have been favourable. He provided the Persian Government with more than one pretext for avoiding a decision, which would inevitably have been contentious and challenged by its political opposition.

363

Government and concessionary relations

Cox did not give his consent to open negotiations till the end of January. Wallace had discretion to offer up to 3s a ton and the possibility of a loan to get the royalty established on a proper basis. At this rate and at production levels of 1 250 000 tons, 2 500 000 tons and 5 000 000 tons, the revenues would have been £187 500, £375 000 and £750 000 respectively.[88] Once again Greenway stressed to Oliphant 'the necessity for urgency' so that the negotiations would be completed in 3 to 4 weeks before the annual general meeting.[89] Negotiations began in February, but by 24 February a crisis was reached on the tonnage proposals, which the Prime Minister, Finance Minister and Justice Minister, generally in favour of a settlement, distrusted altogether. Wallace cabled that 'I am unable to make them alter their opinion. They have asked for guarantees from Company that amount based on 2s a ton will not be less than 16 per cent and if [it] is deficit must be made good.'[90] Wallace maintained that insisting on bringing pressure to bear would create unnecessary mistrust and that offering an increased loan might be advantageous. The reply to Wallace was uncompromising, 'Adjustment of Royalty is sine qua non and unless this can be effected all our monetary suggestions necessarily drop.'[91] This was the stumbling block, but it was also the *raison d'être* of Greenway's new approach.

The Persian negotiators were not convinced of the improvement in revenues being offered. They were playing, not unnaturally, for time, considering 'it essential that they should secure in their own way', according to Cox, 'the co-operation and concurrence of the rest of their colleagues and also of the Shah'[92] - memories of the negotiations in 1901. Cox was convinced that 'the three principal members of the Persian Cabinet had every intention of arriving at an understanding with the Company', but he was anxious lest the oil negotiations had adverse effects upon his own efforts to repair British–Persian relations, so deadlines were extended. The Persian negotiators were able to take advantage of the pressure on time, and their ability to link the diplomatic and oil negotiations, to improve their position. Cox had begun his treaty negotiations on 30 December and by mid-April the main issues had been settled, despite many difficulties.

On 4 March, Wallace was still hopeful,[93] but, in London, Cargill was not convinced that it had been conclusively proved to the Persian Government that 'the change from a percentage profit to a Royalty will be to their advantage'.[94] Nichols favoured giving Wallace more time 'to square everyone and everything'.[95] In Tehrān the Prime Minister fell sick[96] and the Shah was agitating to go to Europe.[97] The negotiations were again delayed. By the end of March no further progress had been made. With unconscious humour, Cox described the situation of the three principal

Government and concessionary relations

Persian negotiators, who realised that

in signing the documents presented to them they would be doing so in the name of the Persian Government, and became alarmed at the responsibility involved ... The Prime Minister, in spite of Colonel Wallace's utmost endeavours to persuade him, eventually expressed his regret that after careful consideration he felt unable to undertake the great responsibility of signing the proposed agreements on behalf of his Government without previously obtaining the consent of the Shah and the concurrence of his other colleagues.[98]

He was not being asked to do otherwise. Wallace remained in Tehrān till August, but to no purpose.[99] Once the Shah had left on his European visit, his agreement, even if he was disposed to grant it, was not available. Cox blamed the royalty issue, but the Company had no faith in personal assurances without signed guarantees.[100]

(b) The Armitage-Smith Agreement

There was a scene shift and when the curtain went up again on the negotiations it was not in Tehrān but in London. Ahmed Shāh left on his European tour in mid-1919 accompanied by Mīrzā Fīrūz, Nusrat al-Dawla, the Foreign Minister, leaving behind an empty treasury, a demoralised government and a divided country. Fīrūz took the opportunity in September to re-open negotiations and a preliminary meeting took place at the Foreign Office, which revealed the almost irreconcilable differences of approach.[101] Fīrūz maintained that 'the differences between the Company and the Persian Government must be settled and when that has been done it would be time enough to examine other questions'. Greenway believed that 'all difficulties could be avoided by making a new arrangement as to the royalties'. There was a mutual disposition, nevertheless, to reach a settlement. Fīrūz insisted that 'the Company should realise that the position in Persia had now quite changed', an appropriate reference to the chameleon-like quality of Persian politics, in which each political development appears to be unique.

In the more relaxed atmosphere which manifested itself, Greenway agreed to pay the arrears of royalties, subject to the findings of arbitration if it was necessary, and all agreed that the 'change in the royalty from 16 per cent to a tonnage basis should be examined and that if an agreement took place it would not be necessary to go to arbitration'.[102] This was a major break in the concessionary clouds. An impartial assessment of the comparability of the proposed tonnage basis with the calculations on the profit percentage should have been made earlier. Admittedly it had been considered, as Greenway informed the Foreign Office, at the time of the Wallace negotiations, but 'our auditors and legal advisers inform us that it would be difficult, if not impossible, to prepare a formula that would be likely to equally satisfy the Persian Government and ourselves'.[103]

It was now up to the experts to find a way clear. As a result of the death of Sir Frank Crisp in May, the Company had appointed new solicitors, Messrs Linklater & Co., and in mid-August Greenway had his first meeting with the senior partner, Mr Ralegh B. Philpotts, on Persian questions. The vital point was the interpretation of the status of subsidiary companies in the terms of the Concession. Philpotts stated that 'there are strong grounds for holding that the companies referred to mean strictly *local* companies with wells and works in the area'.[104] This reflected the advice previously given by Crisp, but, until the uncertainty was authoritatively clarified, the problem would exacerbate the concessionary relationship. It was not yet acute, but would become more exasperating as the number of new subsidiaries increased beyond the BP Company and the British Tanker Company.

Fīrūz, too, was taking advice and in October he invited Mr (later Sir) Sydney A. Armitage-Smith, a Treasury official, to become Financial Adviser to the Persian Government, a post envisaged under the Anglo-Persian Treaty. Armitage-Smith early recognised that any judgement on the comparison of the computation of royalties on a percentage or tonnage basis would necessitate obtaining 'the opinion of counsel on the proper interpretation of the concession (the drafting of which is not free from ambiguity)', and 'the technical advice of a professional accountant on the royalty statements'.[105] He suggested as accountant Mr (later Sir) William McLintock, 'one of the leading gentlemen in his profession', to whom he was not known personally, but had served with him on the Royal Commission of Income Tax, from April 1919 to March 1920.

Fīrūz appointed McLintock and on 28 November formally requested the Company to grant McLintock 'every facility in the carrying out of his mission'.[106] Greenway had drawn up a memorandum on the points at issue,[107] which he circulated to all concerned, including the Imperial Commissioner, Farīd al-Saltana, who had succeeded his brother, Sadigh al-Saltana, in August 1918.[108] McLintock acted swiftly on his brief[109] and within a month had made a preliminary assessment of the position,[110] followed by detailed discussions on matters concerning debenture interest, depreciation, excess profits tax and the position of subsidiary companies with Lloyd and the Company's auditor, R.A. Murray, of Brown, Fleming and Murray, who had acted in this professional capacity since the formation of the Company.[111] McLintock issued his report on 12 February 1920 and in the later view of Armitage-Smith, whose comments may be regarded as impartial, 'disclosed certain undoubted errors and irregularities of accounting, which had resulted in underpayment of royalty to the Imperial Government; it also brought into clear relief several questions of interpretation (some of which admitted of legitimate differences of opinion), which, in fact, all arise from the peculiar conditions under which the now world-wide activities of the Anglo-Persian Oil Company have developed'.[112] The report was less favourable to the Company than had been anticipated, clear evidence of McLintock's independence.

Some of his findings, however, dealt with certain aspects of accounting principles over which there was no explicit professional guidance and on which discretion was exercised according to individual judgement but in accordance with professional integrity. Thus some of his comments were directed not against the Company but its auditors, who were, in a sense, rival professional competitors, no less than fellow Scots. It is notable that, at a time when Scottish consultants were beginning to penetrate further into the growing market for accountancy advice in London's commercial circles, the Company's accountants Brown, Fleming and Murray and Thomas McLintock were among the most prominent. Perhaps McLintock's most unequivocal and unexpected recommendation was his dismissal of the Company's claims for compensation arising out of the cutting of the pipeline, 'having regard to the fact that the claims are mainly in respect of consequential loss for which the Persian Government does not appear to be responsible'. No less important in the long term was McLintock's contention, reported by Greenway, that the Persian Government was 'entitled to claim 16 per cent on the profits of all the subsidiary companies of the Anglo-Persian Company carrying on business outside of Persia', but this was, in Greenway's view, 'quite outside the scope of the Concession'. The Company's assumptions had been challenged. Greenway and Fīrūz had 'a long and very heated discussion' on 9 March, but at a meeting a week later between representatives of the Company, McLintock, and their respective advisers, some progress over reconciling differences was achieved.

Armitage-Smith had left for Tehrān on 27 February. Fīrūz, impatient and pessimistic about the chances of a mutually satisfactory outcome, proposed arbitration.[113] Cargill was depressed that 'the whole position is a most unfortunate one…It is much more complicated and difficult from the APOC's point of view than I had realised'.[114] The Company's advisers felt that an eventual solution to those issues mainly concerned with accountancy practice and procedures was attainable, but that it was conditional on receiving an authoritative opinion on whether 'the payment of 16 per cent on profits was to be limited to operations carried on in Persia'.[115] A brief was prepared for counsel, Sir John Simon KC and Alexander Neilson KC. Greenway maintained that the profits obtained from the carrying or sale of American oil or the exploitation of Scottish shale oil should be excluded from the calculation of profits from operations derived from Persian oil, but that if the profits from non-Persian oil were included 'the Company will have to take such steps as may be necessary to completely divorce its outside operations from those covered by the concession'.[116] 'This step', he acknowledged, 'is one to be avoided if possible in the interests of both parties, in the case of the Persian Government it would mean a largely reduced Revenue, in the case of the Anglo-Persian Company it would mean the disadvantage of not being able to carry on a world-wide business under one name.'

Such an eventuality did not arise, for on 30 March Simon and Neilson delivered their joint opinion, which included the statement that:

Nearly every Article of the Concession indicates that the scope of the enterprise is limited by the territory of Persia, and we do not think that the figure on which 16 per cent is to be calculated is intended to be increased by bringing in the profits of enterprises operating outside Persia, any more than it could be diminished by bringing in losses, which might be suffered in the course of trading by such outside enterprises.[117]

Relieved to have received such a positive opinion, Greenway immediately wrote to Fīrūz in Paris, before leaving for a holiday in Biarritz. He suggested that 'As the points in question are really legal ones on which no opinion of accountants can be conclusive', the next step was to bring the advisers together, 'before you and I take up the matter again'.[118] Fīrūz agreed,[119] but then refused and asked for arbitration.[120] Finally he invited Greenway to Paris, 'so that we have the opportunity of meeting often and talking over the matter fully'.[121] Lloyd was doubtful, surmising that 'the real means of settlement with the Prince is by a procedure in which neither you or I are adept and really do not know how to go about this method'.[122] Fīrūz had managed to make his presence in Paris indispensable for Persian foreign affairs and was enjoying himself immensely in the convivial company of Jean Cocteau, his protegé Raymond Radiguet, and other devotees of *Le Boeuf sur le Toit*.[123] An understanding was reached between Greenway and Fīrūz. A Treasury ruling on 13 May waived any objection to royalty being paid before excess profits tax had been deducted, so £192 000, the sum involved, was available for immediate payment.[124]

With both sides anxious to come to a settlement, Fīrūz being aware of the deteriorating state of Vusuq al-Dawla's Government, Greenway, Fīrūz, McLintock and Lloyd, reached a general agreement on 4 June. It provided that the Persian Government was entitled to 16 per cent of the profits arising from all operations directly associated with Persian oil, whether carried out in Persia or not, by the Company or its subsidiaries, but not otherwise. A schedule was to be prepared indicating exactly which

Government and concessionary relations

items were to be charged in calculating the net profits of the Company and its subsidiaries. In essence, this, subject to later slight modifications, was the basis of what came to be known as the Armitage-Smith Agreement. The Company, for its part, dropped its claims for compensation over the pipeline damage and deductions of the 3 per cent royalty paid to the Bakhtiari Khans from the royalties payable to the Persian Government, and agreed to pay either £500 000 in cash or issue 100 000 fully paid non-voting ordinary shares of the Company (see p.353) to the Persian Government in full settlement of all outstanding claims.[125] This was approved by the Board on 29 May[126] though not with the same degree of enthusiasm by all members, for Cargill was 'not at all happy' about 'the payments to these blackmailers'.[127]

Unfortunately the weakness of the internal Persian political situation intervened. The Government fell on 2 July and the negotiations were left in a state of suspended animation. Fīrūz lost his ministerial position and the payment put at his disposal[128] of £100 000 in cash or £50 000 in cash and 30 000 fully paid bearer non-voting Company shares, if the Persian Government accepted the agreement. It was the last occasion on which such an offer was made.[129] Thereafter there was confusion. Fīrūz claimed authority to continue negotiating, whereas Armitage-Smith intimated that the negotiations should be re-opened in Tehrān.[130]

Meanwhile the predicament of the Persian Government was increasingly desperate. Administration was breaking down as a result of separatist movements in a number of provinces, government expenditure was rising whilst revenue was declining, and central authority was becoming more fragmented in different districts. In these difficult conditions and conscious of the need to remedy the dreadful state of the finances, Armitage-Smith was requested by the new Prime Minister, Mushīr al-Dawla, to resume the interrupted negotiations. His instructions were drawn up on 29 August by the under-secretary at the Finance Ministry, 'Īsā Khān, who was subsequently appointed Imperial Commissioner on 23 December 1923.[131]

Although Armitage-Smith felt that a reasonable tonnage basis offered the best solution to the profits question, the Persian Government was not favourably inclined to this solution. The primary object of the negotiations, then, was to settle the basis on which the computation of the percentage profit was to be assessed.[132] Armitage-Smith arrived in England on 25 October 1920 and soon realised that his estimation of an acceptable basis of some 5s a ton was regarded as too high by the Company.[133] On a fixed basis it would have had to allow for fluctuations in market prices, but it was difficult to predict these. It was ironical that in the financial year in which the Armitage-Smith Agreement was signed, the royalty tonnage figure worked out at 6s 8d. The following year it came to 5s 1d and it was not till 1922–23 that it fell below 5s 0d a ton to 3s 7d, dipping with the decline in profitability of the Company. In the Iraq Concession of March 1925 the royalty was fixed at 4s per ton, though in 1928 the Shaykh of Kuwait was provisionally offered 5s 3d per ton by Frank Holmes and his Eastern and General Syndicate. (See Table 9.1 for royalty statistics 1918–25.) Greenway and Armitage-Smith agreed to concentrate on reaching agreement on what had already been achieved, rather than on breaking new ground.

Table 9.1. *Anglo-Persian Oil Company crude oil production and royalty statistics 1918–25*

Financial year ending 31 March	Crude production tons	Royalty £	Royalty per ton s d	Cumulative tonnage	Cumulative royalty £
1918	897 402	418 627	9 4	2 764 366	675 228
1919	1 106 415	650 324	11 9	3 870 781	1 325 552
1920	1 385 301	468 718	6 9	5 256 082	1 794 270
1921	1 743 557	585 290	6 9	6 999 639	2 379 560
1922	2 327 221	593 429	5 1	9 326 860	2 972 989
1923	2 959 028	533 251	3 7	12 285 888	3 506 240
1924	3 714 216	411 322	2 3	16 000 104	3 917 562
1925	4 333 933	830 754	3 10	20 334 037	4 748 316

Source: BP H16/23

Armitage-Smith too recognised that the key to the dispute lay in the interpretation of the 16 per cent profit basis and its applicability to subsidiary companies. He therefore decided to take a second opinion on the issue, consulting M.L. Romer KC and Mr W. Gordon Brown KC, who stated categorically on 1 December that 'the Persian Government has no right to be paid 16 per cent of the profits of such Companies as such whether derived from Persian oil or otherwise'.[134] 'We are of the opinion,' they added, 'that it would be legally possible for the Anglo-Persian Company to divest itself of all interest in the subsidiary companies, thereby leaving the Persian Government with an undisputed right to 16 per cent of the profits of the Anglo-Persian Company, but at the same time ensuring that such profits would consist merely of the profits (if any) realised on sales of the crude oil.' The negotiations took just under a month from mid-November till 9 December. McLintock, whose report had been so instrumental in taking a fresh look at the Company's concessionary position, considered that the agreement reached by Armitage-Smith was more favourable to the Persian Government than had been expected.[135]

Government and concessionary relations

Nevertheless tension had not been absent. After the first meeting Greenway exclaimed that 'we are farther apart than ever'.[136] The agreement, signed on 20 December, established that the Persian Government was (1) granted 16 per cent profits on all operations which involved Persian oil, (2) protected against artificial manipulation of freight charges and (3) guaranteed that acceptable deductions only were to be applied when assessing profits. It was agreed (4) that the Company was entitled to receive adequate interest on capital employed and a fair remuneration in respect of refining and distributing, (5) that the Company was to pay royalty after the annual general meeting of the year to which it applied and (6) that any differences arising out of the agreement should be referred for settlement to a chartered accountant, nominated by the Institute of Chartered Accountants.[137] (For the full text see Appendix 9.1.)

It had taken three years to resolve the differences between the Company and the Persian Government. The Armitage-Smith Agreement has been criticised by many commentators[138] and was repudiated in 1928 by a later Persian Government, not on the pretext that it had not been ratified by the Majlis but on the spurious contention that Armitage-Smith was not empowered to conclude an agreement, in spite of an official letter to that effect. Nevertheless the intervention of Armitage-Smith and the collaboration between himself and McLintock was decisive in its time. It attempted not only to qualify but quantify concessionary provisions which were not only imprecise but no longer appropriate. Greenway was right about changing the royalty basis, but wrong in his insistence on the linkage with compensation. In his impatience and determination to achieve a quick settlement, he misread, like others before and after him, the Iranian character and its preoccupation with politics. In Persia, decisions mature over time, they are rarely imposed at once. The Concession was no longer considered absolute; it was a question when it would become obsolete.

4 CHANGING GOVERNMENT RELATIONS

(a) Burmah rocks the boat

The failure of the engagement arranged between the Royal Dutch-Shell group and British interests had much to do with the indecision of the matchmaker, the British Government. As has already been noted, consistency was not the most conspicuous feature of post-war British policy. The ideal, however, of an amalgamation between British oil interests had not disappeared. In some respects the prevailing uncertainties

Government and concessionary relations

had stimulated renewed interest. The European companies were becoming anxious over the competition for continental markets posed by American oil companies, principally Standard Oil (NJ), but including Atlantic Refining Company, Texas Oil Company and Standard Oil (New York). Prospects for oil discoveries in the Middle East precipitated the clash of interests known as the 'Open Door' controversy. Royal Dutch-Shell and Standard Oil (NJ) were rivals for the affections of the French Government in oil affairs. In mid-1921 the Company engaged in discussions with Standard Oil (NJ).

Tossed about on these conflicting currents, Burmah felt insecure. In the scramble for new concessions and markets, Burmah was vulnerable, for it had relatively low reserves in a single production area, its Indian markets largely at the mercy of the continuation of the agreement signed in 1905 with the Asiatic Petroleum Company. Cargill lacked the combative entrepreneurial drive of Greenway. Young, when he succeeded his father as Chairman of Burmah in 1904, he had outlived his earlier colleagues on the Board and preferred to rest on his laurels and to savour his reputation for respectable sagacity rather than to imbue his company with vigour and vitality. Energy and enterprise were the contributions of his younger colleague, Robert I. Watson, who had gained practical experience in Burma and in the London office of Burmah, where he was closely involved in the commercial relations with Royal Dutch-Shell. He was the live wire, the positive lead to Cargill's earthy connections. An efficient administrator, Watson abhorred waste and the under-utilisation of resources, which both offended his principles and disturbed his Scottish conscience.

Watson, influenced by Waley Cohen, with whom he had been closely associated in business over the years, launched the new initiative towards an amalgamation of the Company and Royal Dutch-Shell interests on 29 July 1921. In outlining the advantages to Burmah, he was clear in analysis and cogent in argument. The amalgamation was attractive because

> it broadens the whole basis of their business and of their security in that it gives them an interest in World-wide oil fields and markets in place of their dependence on the oil fields of Burma, India and Persia, whose geographical position practically, if not entirely, limits their marketing powers to the East and, in a war of rates, largely isolates them there while their aggressors are compensating themselves in other parts of the world for the cost of their attacks in the East.[139]

It was indisputable that Burmah was vulnerable, but doubtful if the measures envisaged would eliminate the risks implied. Watson was virtually admitting that the continuing independence of Burmah was questionable. He was also expressing a lack of confidence in the Company and its management, but in a rather peculiar manner. There was a

Government and concessionary relations

considerable Burmah investment locked up and almost unrealisable in the Company, for Burmah was virtually precluded from disposing of it. It was obvious that the Company would have to incur a large expenditure if its ample supplies of Persian crude oil were to be delivered as petroleum products into the markets of the world, once its ten-year contracts with Royal Dutch-Shell terminated at the end of 1921. The Company certainly was dependent on a single oilfield, too narrow a base to play an international role. It was true that there were political problems in Persia, which were causing some concessional insecurity. Yet the responsibility and function of management is to remedy weakness and capitalise on strength, so it may, therefore, be asked whether the Burmah directors favoured the forward expansive policy which Greenway was effectively pursuing.

It is in this respect that the timing of Watson's initiative is interesting, for it coincides with the confirmation on 23 June of Stewart as the probable successor to Greenway as Chairman, whose appointment was likely to advance Burmah influence in the Company and set a more cautious pace of development. The Burmah opposition to Cadman's later appointment, first as director and then Chairman, revealed in Chapter 8, seems to confirm that at this time Burmah had come to regard the Company as getting out of control. Both Royal Dutch-Shell and Burmah, for different but complementary reasons, sought to curb the Company before it took the bit in its teeth and made off. So behind the plausibility, no less than the rationality, of Watson's proposal, lay the reality of a threat to the Company. It was also the occasion for the last comprehensive examination of amalgamation as a possible expression of government oil policy. Afterwards there was little incentive for the Government but to accept market forces and a special relationship of amicable indifference, perhaps diffidence, to the Company, which passed for policy in the absence of anything more positive in this period.

Watson's timing was also not irrelevant to the negotiations which had been taking place between the Company and Royal Dutch-Shell over the future of the ten-year contracts. At first the Company wanted to dispense with them and market independently, but problems in Persia, delays in the construction of the refinery near Swansea, and pressure from the Burmah directors, induced the Company to consider a 'Trading Arrangement for the Sale of Benzine in the United Kingdom and Ireland', proposed by Royal Dutch-Shell.[140] This was expected to reduce capital outlay and running costs and thereby place both companies in a better competitive position vis-à-vis Standard Oil (NJ) and be capable of extension to other petroleum products. Greenway, commending it to the Treasury, estimated the capital savings at £2 500 000, which at 6 per cent per annum represented £150 000 a year. It would enable both companies to take advantage of new developments in distribution technology in creating a complete network of kerb-side pumps for the delivery of petrol. Barstow did not feel entitled to question it on commercial grounds, but he had reservations about possible criticism that the Company was making 'an arrangement with a profiteering monopolistic Co. to fleece the consumer'.[141] Clarke at the Petroleum Executive shared Barstow's concern and advised that 'any alliance between the Shell and Anglo-Persian for the distribution of petrol is certain to provoke much criticism'.[142] Clarke remarked shrewdly that 'the Shell group is rather anxious to associate itself more closely with the Anglo-Persian, in which it sees a new and powerful competitor'.

Inchcape was cavalier, commenting that it was 'a very sensible arrangement' but that it would be even better 'to endeavour to arrange with the Standard to have one installation for the three Companies'.[143] With Shell actively engaged in exploration in South America — particularly in Venezuela and bringing in the discovery well at Signal Hill in Long Beach, California, on 25 June 1921 and about to acquire the properties of the Union Oil Company of Delaware in October — Royal Dutch-Shell was not likely to look favourably on such a conjectural alliance.[144] Barstow merely noted that Inchcape's view appeared 'to be based on business considerations only'. No government commitment was reached at an inter-departmental meeting on 27 July on the 'Trading Arrangement'. Baldwin, the President of the Board of Trade, was not very enthusiastic, remarking that even if it was commercially attractive the arrangement 'would be bitterly attacked in Parliament and by the public who had a prejudice against oil companies and combinations and did not recognise the big work which the oil companies had done.'[145] The suggestion withered to be replaced by a more limited contract between the Company and Royal Dutch-Shell for 'a quantity of Benzine of a minimum quantity of 15 000 tons per month to a maximum quantity of 30 000 tons per month for a period of five years'.[146]

Such was the background to the renewed courtship between some British oil interests and Royal Dutch-Shell. The case which Watson presented recapitulated many of the earlier arguments. He recognised that previous proposals involved only paper control over the British interests in Royal Dutch-Shell, but he was offering *an actual financial preponderating British share majority*'.[147] On his estimation, the share percentage was 53.18 per cent Royal Dutch and 46.82 per cent British, but if the government holding in the Company was included the share percentage became 50.17 per cent British and 49.38 per cent Royal Dutch. This, claimed Watson, was 'an actual if bare British majority holding which can be made completely effective within the combination for all commercial, financial and political

Government and concessionary relations

purposes', apart from the production and marketing from Dutch sovereign territories. Forestalling criticism, Watson argued that no monopoly would be created 'because apart from other independent organisations the Standard would always remain as a powerful competitor'.

No particular urgency seems to have been displayed over the memorandum. The Admiralty received a copy on 11 October 1921,[148] and believed that there was 'little doubt that the Shell Company are at the back of the present scheme', and that 'it would mean a radical change of Government policy, particularly in India, and further friction with the USA'.[149] It felt that no 'advantage whatever would accrue to the Admiralty'. At the instigation of Sir Philip Lloyd-Greame (later Earl of Swinton), an inter-departmental meeting was convened in his rooms at the Board of Trade, where he had responsibility for petroleum affairs, on 26 October, at which representatives of the Board of Trade, Treasury, Admiralty, India Office, Foreign Office and Petroleum Department (formerly Executive) were present.[150] The departments had not changed their spots. The Board of Trade agreed that 'the establishment of an effective British control over the Royal Dutch-Shell group was worth paying a substantial price for', but not at the expense of the consumer. Barstow for the Treasury welcomed 'any opportunity of going out of business undertakings, provided that they could do so on proper terms. Participation in business enterprises involved divided Government interests and led to diplomatic, industrial and financial difficulties'. The Foreign Office too was not enthusiastic about the government involvement in the Company, as it led to continued difficulties 'as every action of the Company was ascribed to direct Government inspiration'. The Admiralty made proposals of its own.[151]

Lloyd-Greame felt that the importance of the amalgamation proposals merited further consideration by a specially appointed ministerial committee and circulated an explanatory secret memorandum to this effect on 6 January 1922.[152] He reaffirmed the desirability that 'the Royal Dutch-Shell group should be brought under effective British control' and praised its management, 'markedly great enterprise, ability and success'. On the other hand he was dubious about the Company's future, presuming that it 'is at the beginning of its difficulties; that it will lose much money in forcing its distribution in keenly contested markets, and that in the immediate future its shares will depreciate in value'. Furthermore, he was not impressed that its 'whole revenue is at present derived from an area of a few square miles in Persia. Any interruption, either from natural causes or through hostile action, of the output of this small field would be disastrous, and the broadening of the basis of the Company's producing interests is, therefore, imperative.'

Government and concessionary relations

Noting Watson's conviction that the reduction in expenditure resulting from the pooling of resources would be passed on to the consumer, Lloyd-Greame admitted that the Government would be accused 'not merely of permitting, but of definitely approving the formation of a great trust', but pleaded that 'the commercial advantages of fusion, on which the consumer must eventually share, are too strong to be ignored, and that no monopoly is being created'. He was little concerned about the possible effects that such an amalgamation would have abroad, apart from the United States, where he thought it would be regarded 'as evidence of a determination to build up a British organisation strong enough to fight and beat the Standard Oil Company', so countering the attempts of the American company to make 'its influence felt to our detriment in various countries where it is by no means scrupulous as to the weapons it employs'. It was good pump priming oil chauvinism, but no longer an adequate response to the petroleum problems of the period.

His assumption that the new combination of companies would escape the same sort of fierce criticism that had been vented against Standard Oil was unimaginatively naive for a Conservative Minister. He believed that the risk involved was 'largely a commercial risk and it would be for the combine, by avoiding the unscrupulous methods of the Standard, to ensure that it is not hampered by similar ill-will'. The same misconception seems evident in his attitude to the government shareholding in the Company, to which he knew Royal Dutch-Shell took 'very strong exception'. It was the same rock on which previous endeavours had foundered, but he believed that Deterding would not 'reject the Government as a sleeping partner if this were insisted on' and that he 'would come to terms rather than let the amalgamation fall through'. With some inconsistency, he welcomed the possibility of the Company entering into closer relations with Standard Oil, 'sound and inevitable business and will, I think, be good policy as well', whilst believing that 'the likelihood of an American alliance might be attractive to the Royal Dutch-Shell'.

Indeed, although much of his reasoning was disputable, it was weakest on the American dimension. It was ironical that, whilst he was advising secrecy over the proceedings of the committee, because 'any publication of the provisional approval might well give rise to a situation in which H.M. Government would find it difficult, if not impossible, to carry out its intention', an alleged Government commitment to Royal Dutch-Shell was an open secret in the United States, causing considerable alarm in oil and government circles, irritating an already fractious situation. The Washington Conference on naval disarmament in November 1921, at which the Empire delegation was led by A.J. (later Earl) Balfour, had just steered clear of oil topics, but it had been touch and go.[153] Baldwin felt that

Government and concessionary relations

the success of the conference 'had exceeded our most sanguine expectations'.[154]

On 5 November *The Times* carried a long serious article on 'Oil Power', in which it reported that if the Government was not prepared to discuss oil issues 'the Conference is likely to break down'.[155] Not always accurate, the article was well-informed, stating that 'in the operations of certain oil companies there is a taint of British Government control', not only in respect of the Company but over Royal Dutch-Shell as well. It suggested that 'the British Government does not sell its national security if it sells its shares in the Anglo-Persian Oil Company and if it severs whatever may be its concession with the Shell Royal-Dutch group'. Finally *The Times* correspondent advocated the adoption of the 'Open Door' policy as the 'safest guarantee Great Britain can possess of obtaining sufficient oil supplies for British industries and for British ships'. The American Press was in full cry over the 'Open Door' controversy,[156] the decline of American oil reserves and the British Government's intervention in oil affairs.

These press reports stimulated much interest in government and other circles. The Petroleum Department favoured an understanding over the 'Open Door' issues.[157] Pretyman, who had been so closely involved in oil affairs since 1905, was very worried, objecting to an 'Open Door' policy as being 'a free area where the strong can worry the weak'. He feared the danger of the Royal Dutch-Shell absorbing the Company because 'the amalgamation of these two companies is now on the tapis'.[158] This, he thought, might be 'good business' but would probably result in the consumer being fleeced and the independence of the Company impaired. Having written to Lloyd George, he was assured by the Prime Minister that oil would not be on the agenda of the Washington Conference and that as Cadman was in the United States on Company business - in discussions with the directors of Standard Oil for the Company on a North Persia Oil Concession and Mesopotamia - 'You may therefore rest assured that we shall not be caught napping.'[159]

It was a much more anxious time than Lloyd-Greame had appreciated, the gravity of which was better expressed by the British ambassador in Washington, Sir Auckland Geddes, who had had frequent conversations with Cadman during his visit to the United States.[160] Geddes believed that American disquiet over oil affairs was primarily due to misunderstandings regarding the position and policy of the British Government with 'special reference to Government's holdings in Anglo Persian Oil Company and growth of power of Royal Dutch-Shell group'.[161] He felt that a dangerous situation was being created, aggravated by rumours, 'which are beginning to be heard in this country, that negotiations are in progress for the purpose of bringing Royal Dutch-Shell definitely under British control',

Government and concessionary relations

through the sale to it of the Government's shareholding in the Company. 'If such a sale were consummated or if rumours regarding it should gain credence', observed the ambassador, 'old jealousies would be actively revived and progress which has been made towards a better understanding very seriously retarded.' The Foreign Office was worried.[162]

On 24 February 1922 the Prime Minister agreed that a committee should be appointed to look into the amalgamation scheme, which was 'of great importance and considerable complexity'.[163] It was given terms of reference 'to consider the proposed amalgamation of the Royal Dutch-Shell, Burmah and Anglo-Persian Oil Companies, and the policy to be adopted in regard to the British Government's interests in the Anglo-Persian Oil Company'.[164] It was constituted with Baldwin, President of the Board of Trade, as chairman, on 6 March. The first meeting was held on 10 March.

(b) The Government makes up its mind

The second meeting of the committee took place on 13 March and was important for the attendance of Balfour, who spoke of his experiences in America, warning of the powerful Standard Oil (NJ) lobby and the absolute dependence of the United States on oil. He agreed with the ambassador about Royal Dutch-Shell and the government shareholding and thought that 'It would be better to co-operate with the Standard Oil Company.'[165] Lloyd-Greame recognised that the Government was in a dilemma. If cooperation with Standard Oil was sought, it would offend Royal Dutch-Shell and sacrifice the chance of bringing it under British control, but on the other hand if amalgamation was achieved it would greatly antagonise Standard Oil. The reconciliation and not the exacerbation of oil interests was the most desirable solution, particularly when the future of the Turkish Petroleum Company was at stake. The Admiralty was sceptical.[166] It was almost like a re-run of the Harcourt Committee, but taken from a different angle.

The following six meetings between 16 March and 5 April were addressed by representatives of the oil companies involved and the government directors. Greenway was not going to play second fiddle to any group. He rebuffed all charges of incompetence and, in asserting the independence and confidence of the Company, maintained that 'the Company would gain very little advantage by joining up with either the Standard or Royal Dutch Companies'. Watson differed in most respects from Greenway, for not only was he sympathetic towards the policies of Royal Dutch-Shell, but he was opposed to the Company's expansionist strategy, deprecating 'capital expenditure in order to enable the Anglo-Persian oil through a world-wide organisation if this could be avoided by some such scheme as the proposed merger made possible...the amalgamation by using existing organisations would reduce the speculative element of building up a distributing organisation based on one field'.

Taking a static rather than dynamic view of oil marketing prospects, Watson argued that 'If the Anglo-Persian Company are going to increase production there must either be a corresponding reduction by their competitors, or a corresponding increase in the oil trade', which he thought was unlikely. Deterding accepted the primacy of the law of supply and demand, urged collaborative economies in operations[167] and rejected the idea of the Government retaining its shares in the Company; 'any form of nationalisation should be avoided'. Waley Cohen and Captain Samuel, son of Marcus Samuel, attacked the Company and dismissed any possibility of an association with Standard Oil, alleging bitterly that it was its corrupt business methods that had caused the antagonism of the American Government. They were adamant that 'the amalgamation would not be acceptable in its present form unless the British Government sold their shareholding'.

Inchcape and Packe, the government directors, were optimistic and uncompromisingly on the side of the Company, which 'would stand to gain very little by associating with the Shell and Royal Dutch Companies'. Inchcape was concerned that if 'a combination was formed, the consumer was bound to go to the wall'. Inchcape may have been influenced by an earlier exchange of correspondence with Watson in February, which was illuminating on some of the motives which had prompted Watson to put up the amalgamation proposals. Watson, prematurely anticipating the sale of the government shareholding, claimed that Burmah was entitled to first refusal of the shares. Referring to the investment, which Burmah put into the Company, Watson argued, somewhat speciously, that the Burmah assets in the Company

> should not depend on the vacillations of political life or views and that, when we agreed to bring Government in as partners with a preponderating shareholding to secure *their* objects, it was never intended that this should be allowed to act as a boomerang on ourselves as it might were Government's shares to get into hands other than our own.[168]

Requesting that the situation 'be put on a more secure basis' for Burmah and the Government, he enclosed in his letter to Inchcape recommendations which amounted to a muzzling of the Company. Inchcape was not at all impressed and replied to Watson the next day that 'the possible sale of the Government shares in the Anglo-Persian...is not in perspective in any way at present'.[169] Not mincing his words he affirmed that, 'the British Government are under no obligation to give the first refusal to the Burmah Oil Company, and I cannot conceive that HM Government would have made any such unbusinesslike and absolutely unworkable agreement'. So, he concluded, 'there is no occasion to consider the question now'. Sir Robert Horne, last of the Coalition Government's three Chancellors of the Exchequer, accepted Inchcape's advice, but was lukewarm in so doing, noting that 'I do not think we should fail to consider any offer that can be made.'[170]

On 7 April it was the turn of the departments to voice their opinions.[171] Sir Louis Kershaw, under-secretary, India Office, did not favour amalgamation, nor did Admiral Boyle, Fourth Sea Lord, and other Admiralty officials, who insisted that 'direct control of the Anglo-Persian Company should be retained'. Sir Gilbert Grindle, assistant under-secretary, Colonial Office, faced in two directions, considering that the case for amalgalmation had not been proved' but 'he would prefer to see the Government sell their shares'. Sir James Stevenson, adviser on business questions to the Colonial Office, also faced in opposite, but different, directions, thinking that amalgamation should take place but that the Government should keep its shares. Weakley of the Foreign Office was diplomatically unsure in which direction to face. Barstow, reflecting current Treasury misgivings, stated that 'it would not be possible for the Treasury to continue to hold Anglo-Persian shares indefinitely, political pressure would become too great and they would be forced to sell'. He too had no objection 'to the Government selling their shares provided an adequate price could be obtained', but he did not consider that the Government could remain shareholders in a company in which the Royal Dutch and Shell were 'predominant partners'. Sir Hubert Llewellyn Smith, chief economic adviser, Board of Trade, left it for the Government to decide. Clarke, head of the Petroleum Department, was certain that 'there were overwhelming political objections, both foreign and domestic, to the proposed combine'.

It was a departmental patchwork pattern of contrasting colourful opinions and little evidence of design. To Lloyd-Greame it had been enlightening and his summing up was more judicious than his earlier comments might have supposed. 'Commercially,' he remarked, 'there was no argument against the combine', but that was not all, for 'the British Government however did not go into the Anglo-Persian Company to make money but to form an independent Company for national reasons'. National reasons should determine the issue and on these grounds he believed that 'the amalgamation should be refused'. The evidence of the Admiralty was important, that of Balfour conclusive. He agreed with Clarke, who was close to Cadman, that 'if the Government held their shares and went into the combine the position would be impossible from the domestic and foreign point of view'. He was not despondent about the

Government and concessionary relations

Company holding their own, either in competition with or in agreement with other companies. In spite of Lloyd-Greame's admonition to keep the proceedings confidential, the press, particularly *The Daily Dispatch*, which broke the news on 9 February, was kept informed.[172] Oliphant thought the leaks 'scandalous'[173] and Mr (later Sir) Robert Vansittart, under-secretary, Foreign office, admitted that 'Mr Bedford heard all about this discussion within a few days of its substance having been brought before the Cabinet.'[174]

In spite of the divergence of views expressed, the final report made it clear that the Government had to decide whether to participate in a great international trust, and/or sell its shareholding in the Company. After weighing the merits and disadvantages of amalgamation, the report concluded that no 'effective and permanent control, which would be exercised continuously in British national interests' could be expected from it. It was, therefore, recommended that 'His Majesty's Government should refuse permission to the Anglo-Persian Company to enter the proposed amalgamation' and that 'His Majesty's Government should retain the existing Government shareholding in the Anglo-Persian Oil Company for the present.'[175] It was not the enunciation of a new policy, but a declaration for the *status quo*, another exercise in departmental compromise. Once more the Government was let off the hook of having to take positive action. It was a relief for the Company, ignored in 1916 and neglected in 1918. Its nomination to the Establishment's oil see appeared to set the seal of approval and preclude the need for an alternative oil policy. In a decade the search for a government oil policy had almost come full circle, back to the Company.

It might have been presumed that the debate was ended. Yet, as there was much business logic in favour of a closer association between the companies, though not necessarily in the manner of the amalgamation suggested, and as the Company was indeed caught in the financial storm of developments as predicted by its opponents, there was every incentive for Burmah and Royal Dutch-Shell to press home their commercial advantages. Walter Long (Viscount Long as he had been honoured on his retirement from public life in May 1921), who had contributed so much to national oil affairs, was moved to write to Curzon, Foreign Secretary, on 27 February 1923 on the subject. He warned that 'if we relax our efforts to keep control of our one large British Company and to secure from it the largest supplies available we shall find ourselves in serious difficulties, not only in the event of war, but in peace time'.[176] He feared that, 'strong influences are at work to try to induce the Government to relinquish its interests in the Anglo-Persian'. The Company was passing through a difficult period (see Chapter 8).

Government and concessionary relations

The Foreign office was aware that Royal Dutch-Shell believed that 'the measures they have taken are such as will ensure absolute success when the question comes up again'.[177] Oliphant thought that relations with the Company 'are of the most harmonious nature',[178] and indeed their improvement is an interesting feature of this period. It seems to have been associated with progress in the negotiations for the participation of American interests in the Turkish Petroleum Company, in which the Company was taking the leading part, and which was an important aspect of current diplomatic exchanges. Curzon was, therefore, able to assure Long that he knew of 'no grounds for making any change in the existing financial arrangements between the Government and the Company'.[179]

The calm was not to remain for long, but the disturbance came from an unexpected quarter, Winston Churchill. In August 1923, if not before, he was definitely approached by Waley Cohen, on behalf of Royal Dutch-Shell and Burmah, to represent them and persuade the Government to accept the amalgamation proposals. The fee was £5000. Churchill's political career was in the doldrums. He had lost his parliamentary seat, Dundee East, in the general election, which toppled the Coalition Government in October 1922. He had recently purchased Chartwell. It was a regrettable turn of events when a First Lord of the Admiralty, who had taken the Navy into the Oil Age by an imaginative and almost unprecedented investment of public funds, became the paid hack of those interests which he had previously opposed. Baldwin, then Prime Minister, was also equivocal in his attitude when approached by Churchill on 14 August. Churchill found him, as he wrote to his wife,

> thoroughly in favour of the Oil settlement on the lines proposed. Indeed he might have been Waley Cohen from the way he talked. I am sure it will come off. The only thing I am puzzled about is my own affair. However, I am to see Cohen on Friday. It is a question of how to arrange it so as to leave no just ground of criticism.[180]

It is clear that Waley Cohen was the chief instigator, Churchill a willing accomplice and Baldwin a complacent partner. In terms of political philosophy, Baldwin's compliance is understandable, but on practical and personal grounds it is surprising, because it was at his suggestion that Cadman had been appointed a Company director against the wishes of Watson and Cargill, who feared Cadman's opposition to the amalgamation proposals, of which Baldwin was well aware.[181]

By 2 September Churchill had definitely accepted the brief. Baldwin facilitated his interviews with Lloyd-Greame at the Board of Trade and with L.S. Amery, First Lord, at the Admiralty. According to Churchill, Baldwin told him that he was 'on general grounds averse from the continued participation of the British Government in the oil business, and that

Government and concessionary relations

£20 000 000 would be a very good price for the Government to obtain for their shares'.[182] In view of Churchill's latent conversion to Conservatism and his subsequent unexpected appointment as Chancellor of the Exchequer in Baldwin's Government of 1924, these exchanges are more than of purely oil interest. The Conservative Ministers seem to have got out of step with their permanent officials, especially those of the Foreign Office and Treasury, who were reluctant to dredge the same controversial channels yet again. Churchill's opportunism was exposed on 13 November when Baldwin suddenly announced a General Election. Determined to make his parliamentary comeback, Churchill immediately dropped his oil commission. Politics was his metier, Parliament his milieu and the monopolists were left to fend for themselves, but the hare that he had started continued to run.

The first official intimation that a new initiative on the amalgamation proposals was being contemplated came in a letter from Mr (later Sir) Neville Chamberlain, Chancellor of the Exchequer, to Curzon on 17 October 1923, marked personal and secret, giving him 'some account of what is in the wind'.[183] It was proposed at the next Cabinet meeting 'to authorise Lord Inchcape as a Government Director to negotiate for the sale of the five million shares held by the British Government to a combination formed of the Burmah Oil and the Royal Dutch-Shell Companies'. With some candour Chamberlain admitted that the case 'hangs on the possibility of making an arrangement which will satisfy the Admiralty'. This was feasible and would protect their interests more than relying on 'the limited field operated by the Anglo-Persian Company', an adept, but familiar, thrust at the jugular vein of the Company. More questionable was his comment that 'the affairs of the Anglo-Persian do not seem to have been conducted with ordinary business prudence and skill for some time past'. According to Chamberlain, Lord Inchcape, whose recent remarks had oscillated between approval and opprobrium of the Company was 'strongly of the opinion that we should do well to take the chance which is offered us, provided that we can get the price I have named'. Lastly Chamberlain referred to the diplomatic 'suspicion and friction', which he alleged the Government's involvement in the Company caused.

The Foreign Office was surprised and Weakley in a long minute saw nothing new which was relevant to re-opening a case which had been closed eighteen months before.[184] Vansittart was curious that 'something far more important must be at stake to induce the veering of opinion among Ministers which the Chancellor's letter portends'.[185] Curzon was bewildered that 'Mr Baldwin has so completely changed his mind'.[186] The Admiralty was puzzled. Churchill had seen Amery on 29 September,[187] who noted that the reaction to 'Mr. Churchill's scheme' and his replies to questions 'are entirely unsatisfactory from the point of view of Naval interests'.[188] It was objected that 'The alleged safeguards and advantages offered by the proposed combine, on being probed, are all found to be of little or no value', and that 'the ultimate financial result of the deal might be far from satisfactory'.[189]

By this time information was percolating through to the Press. On 30 October *The Morning Post* referred to rumours that the Company was to be taken over by Royal Dutch-Shell, 'a transaction' it imagined, which, 'would represent one of the most remarkable events even for the history of the exploitation of the World's oilfields'.[190] *The Times* took up the story on 10 November, suggesting that on reversing its earlier policy the Government 'has doubtless been influenced by considerations of high policy as well as those of an ordinary business character'.[191] When the subject was first raised in the House of Commons on 15 November, Chamberlain blandly replied that no decision had been reached, but that in any event nothing would be done to jeopardise the supply of fuel oil for the navy and mercantile marine. However, he would not give an assurance that Parliament would be consulted before a decision was taken.[192] He fenced on further questions on 17 and 18 November 1923 and 21 January 1924. The Labour Party, on the threshold of their first parliamentary majority, was opposed to the sale of the Government's shareholding and its National Executive requested Ramsay MacDonald, its parliamentary leader, to inform Baldwin that 'the disposal of such shares would be contrary to public policy'.[193] Even the disapproval of the ordinary motorist was expressed, through the Motor Legislation Committee.[194]

It was a chastened Conservative minority Government at the opening of Parliament on 15 January 1924. Two days later at a Cabinet meeting, Amery, on behalf of the Admiralty, rejected the amalgamation proposals. He disapproved of much of the supporting case, but found quite unacceptable that 'in no circumstances would the Group bind itself by a long-term contract to supply at a fixed sum'.[195] By refusing to accept this condition, which had been the kernel of the 1914 agreement, Royal Dutch-Shell lost the opportunity of scooping the government pool for fuel oil. Once again for limited, but valid, commercial reasons, it lost the opportunity of hobbling the Company. Such a chance never occurred again. For Amery this was *decisive* and showed that 'our interests and those of the Group are not in harmony and cannot be harmonised'. It was not surprising that over the years the Admiralty had been so consistent, but it was notable that the Treasury had changed its mind and backed the Admiralty. The Cabinet had no option but to recognise that 'they would not be justified in taking a decision on so large a question without more exhaustive inquiry than was possible at the moment'.[196] The Government fell on a vote of

Government and concessionary relations

confidence on 21 January and the first Labour Government took office.

Philip Snowden, the new Chancellor of the Exchequer, on 26 January 1924 circulated to his Cabinet colleagues a memorandum from Barstow, who was as emphatic in his recommendations as Amery was. 'The conclusions of the Treasury', he wrote, 'on a careful review of all the arguments for and against the proposed transaction is that it is right to be *unhesitatingly rejected*, and the proposed purchasers should be told that on no account will His Majesty's Government part with the shares.'[197] It was, thus, the advice of officials, more than party political persuasion, which determined the fate of the amalgamation proposals. *The Times* probably voiced the opinion of the majority, when it declared on 30 January that, 'Be their motives what they may, however the Government's decision is in our opinion, a sound one.'[198] The Company, on this occasion, had taken little public part in the proceedings, over which indeed it had not been consulted.

Once again it might have been reasonably assumed that the muddied waters would have settled quietly, but on 1 February Cargill and Watson issued a press statement praising the proposals which the Government had rejected.[199] On 14 February the Chancellor stated in Parliament that the Government 'have no intention whatever of reconsidering their decision'.[200] With the return of a Conservative Government to power in November 1924, under Baldwin, interest revived and press reporting, probably inspired, renewed public interest. Greenway, appealing to the Government, claimed that the rumours were 'having a very unsettling effect on the staff of the Company' and emphasised that it was 'highly desirable that the Government should make some definite declaration of their policy in regard to this matter at the earliest possible moment'.[201] The Admiralty was sympathetic and Sir Oswyn Murray, the permanent secretary to the Board of Admiralty, 1917-36, hoped that the Government would state, 'once and for all that they do not intend to part with their shares'.[202] Finally Sir Warren Fisher, who succeeded Barstow as secretary to the Treasury informed Greenway, 'The Prime Minister desires me to inform you that His Majesty's Government have no intention of departing from the policy of retaining these shares.'[203]

It had been a tangled skein of discussions, personalities and motives. The Government had finally made up its mind about the Company but it had taken a decade to do so. What had begun as a provocative and opportunistic decision by the First Lord of the Admiralty, partly at the instigation of the Company and partly on naval grounds, had become a statement of government policy in the public interest by the Prime Minister.

Government and concessionary relations

5 THE CHANGING SITUATION IN PERSIA

(a) Introduction

Persia was changing. The Armitage-Smith Agreement may have seemed conclusive after a couple of years of wrangling, but this was deceptive. The latterly effete and ineffective Qājār dynasty was stumbling towards its collapse and abolition. Inertia and corruption characterised the central administration, which was disregarded where it was not defied. Persia was struggling to express a sense of national identity, which reflected its own cultural traditions but recognised contemporary social and economic developments elsewhere in the world. Rizā Khān, a colonel in the Cossack Regiment, emerged as the leader from a coup d'état in February 1921. He presented a modern Persian image, which he stamped upon his country during his reign, after he crowned himself Shah on 25 April 1926. A tall imposing figure, who came to dominate his generation, he admired the discipline of the soldier. He despised the pretence of the politician. A man of determination, he was nonetheless subject to introspection; self-confident, he was unreasonably suspicious. Simple in his style of living, he became unduly avaricious. His own master but nobody's friend, he swept away much of the fustian and frumpery of Persian society without, unfortunately, achieving a real fusion of the traditional and the modern. In his early days he moved both cautiously and impetuously, but gradually asserted increasing central authority by suppressing local rebellions. He bolstered national independence by an aggressive attitude to foreign relations. His impact upon Persia was unmistakable.

As the power of Rizā Khān strengthened, though not without challenge, so the relations between Persia and the United Kingdom were affected and the position of the Company became more prominent in Persian affairs, for both political and economic reasons. This process was already a feature of the period before Rizā Khān's coronation. The changing relationships can be marked by the fact that Rizā Khān was a party to the repudiation of the Anglo-Persian Treaty, which had so upset Curzon,[204] whose attitude had already been depicted by James Morier in his picturesque novel on Persia, *The Adventures of Hajji Baba of Ispahan*, first published in 1824. It is there observed that 'One of the most remarkable features in the character of our English guests was their extreme desire to do us good against our inclination... They felt a great deal more for us than we did for ourselves.'[205] This was a warning, which Sir Percy Loraine, British Ambassador to Persia 1921-26, early appreciated, for he remarked in a letter to Gertrude Bell, Oriental Secretary in Baghdad, that 'The Persians have got to learn for themselves, and if you want them to do that its no use

Sir Arnold Wilson and Sir Percy Loraine 1924

fiddling with them and their affairs, still less intervening and pretending you don't.'[206] It was a distinct change of emphasis and enabled him to appreciate impartially the accomplishments of Rizā Khān, to achieve an understanding with him and to improve British relations with Persia accordingly.

Loraine had accepted the basic premise, in May 1923, that 'Persia will never be really independent and orderly until the whole country is brought under a single and unquestioned authority, which must necessarily be that of the National Government, and until the civilian population has been disarmed, so that all physical power rests in the hands of the State.'[207] There were risks he admitted, but this 'policy, if carried out without unnecessary friction or disturbance, would relieve us of many responsibilities which we have hitherto borne, and would make Persia an altogether more comfortable neighbour'. 'The only two things' he acknowledged, 'we need be really anxious about are the safety of the oilfields and the special position of the Sheikh of Mohammerah'. These were issues even before Rizā Khān became Prime Minister. The Company became early aware that it would not escape the attentions of the Government in Tehrān. The Governor of Shushtar informed the British consul in Shīrāz, E.G.P. Peel, in March 1922, that the Persian Foreign Ministry had 'declared every agreement which the Anglo-Persian Oil Company may have made with local Khans or Chiefs of Tribes to be null and void, as constituting a violation' of the Concession.[208]

Dr Young, whose service in the Company began as a medical doctor to Reynolds and his staff and was later involved in negotiations with the Bakhtiari Khans and who was very conversant with the Persian character, wondered in mid-1922 about the future of the Company in Persia, in terms reminiscent of D'Arcy and later perplexed observers. He asked himself 'Why any step taken by us, or even contemplated to be taken in the direction of development and progress, out of which the Persian Government cannot make capital is at once misinterpreted as against the Concession, against the law, or against something or somebody?' Was the antagonism 'real or apparent?' he inquired. What 'would lead to a better understanding?' 'We have nothing to do with general politics', he continued,

and as far as possible wish to be kept out of it. What we wish the Persian Government to realise - as we have now got the Khans to realise - is that this is the goose that lays the golden egg, and the only laying goose that they have in the country, that the way to stimulate it to lay more eggs is not by holding on to its throat and strangling its progress, but by feeding and protecting it.

He hoped that a visit to Tehrān might provide the answers.[209]

(b) The imposition of central authority

It was not long before Young witnessed one of the problems himself, for, by a striking coincidence, his journey to Tehrān took him past the scene of an ambush of 400 government troops at Shāhīl, in Bakhtiari territory, south-west of Isfahān, on 30 July 1922. He foresaw immediately that 'this is an unfortunate affair which may lead to serious complications between the Persian Government and the Bakhtiari Khans, and, incidentally also, to unpleasantness to us, because we may find ourselves between the devil and the deep sea'.[210] He recognised that a struggle for supremacy would ensue, that Rizā Khān would avenge the defeat of his troops and that the Company would be blamed as a scapegoat. He knew the weakened state of the Khans.[211] The incident had come at an inopportune time, because Jacks and Wilson, who were running the managing agents at Muhammara, were both beginning to realise that the actions of the Persian Government 'may be of great benefit to our interests, and may not. It can be of benefit with a properly constituted central administration in Teherān.'[212] As Jacks stated, 'It is to the Persian Government that we have to look for protection under our Concession, and it has only been due to its impotence that either the Bakhtiaris or the Sheikh of Mohammerah have been able to achieve their present positions.'[213] Thus it was prior to, and not after, Rizā

Government and concessionary relations

Khān had asserted his authority over the Bakhtiari Khans and Shaykh Khazʿal that the Company's management in Persia had begun to adapt itself to the power the Minister of War was displaying, though nobody, particularly the Persians, knew how far he would be successful in asserting himself.

Young found the situation in Tehrān hostile and confused, 'so complex, so unstable ... and there is no one who cares to offer an opinion about the future'.[214] He reported that the Company was openly attacked for having instigated the raid on the troops at Shāhīl and the 'newspapers, bribed by the Bolshevists and the men like Prince Firooz, showed no sense of shame'. Accusations of direct interference in Persian internal affairs became a frequent complaint against the Company, often from contradictory directions. Young had drawn attention to two sources, continuing Russian antagonism towards British interests in Persia under a new ideological guise, and the disappointed ambitions of politicians, whose criticism of the Company enabled them to excuse personal failure and generate a feeling of xenophobia. As for Bolshevik influence, the First Congress of the Peoples of the East had been held in Baku in September 1920, at which the second largest delegation (192) was from Persia, where a communist party had been founded a few months earlier in June.[215] As early as 1918 Iran had figured prominently in Soviet communist strategy. In *Vostok i Revolutsia*, K. Troyanovsky had proclaimed, 'For the success of the oriental revolution Persia is the first nation that must be conquered by the Soviets ... Persia must be ours; Persia must belong to the revolution.'[216] Gregory Zinoviev, President of the Comintern, was chairman of the Congress and appealed for a 'true Holy War against the English and French robber capitalist'. The principal target for Soviet-inspired agitation was the alleged British colonial intervention in Persian affairs symbolised by the Anglo-Persian Treaty of 1919. After that had been revoked and the Persian–Russian Treaty of 26 February 1921 signed, attention was concentrated on the Company, which was described as a tool of the British Government. The opposition to the Company was gradually intensified and Riẓā Khān was attacked as he consolidated his hold on the country with the alleged connivance of the British Government and began taking a more independent line from Russian objectives on foreign policy. In 1927 at the Second Congress of the Persian Communist Party held in Urumīyeh (renamed Rezāʾīyeh in 1930), the confiscation of the Company's assets in Persia became a principal objective.

Fīrūz had initially suffered as a result of the *coup d'état*, having been imprisoned in Tehrān and accused of the betrayal of Persian rights. He appealed for protection to the British Minister, Herman Norman, who was not prepared to do more than intercede for fair treatment.[217] Fīrūz felt insulted and abandoned and never forgave the British authorities for the humiliation he had received at the hands of his own compatriots. The repercussions of Persian domestic political problems on external relations was felt particularly by the Company, which often suffered from the backlash of such interractions. Nevertheless, whatever disappointment Young may have felt about the anti-British atmosphere in Tehrān, he was impressed with Rizā Khān, for 'The Minister of War is the only outstanding figure to be admired in the present Cabinet ... He seemed to bear our interests well in mind, for he mentioned that before all else, he would take effective measures to protect our works and pipeline.'[218] When Young raised the question of the anti-British propaganda, Rizā Khān regretted it and referred to 'the difficulties in dealing with Persians, whom he characterised as bigoted and ignorant'. This seemed to presage what actually happened, the imposition of an autocratic rule. Young sympathised with Sir Percy Loraine, the British ambassador, 'in a most difficult and embarrassing situation. He has taken a broad view of the problems in Persia, and it is the only correct view to take.'

As a result of his visit and discussions in Tehrān, Young was more than ever convinced that

our salvation lies in a strong Central Government, and if we cannot support one ourselves, we should at least do nothing which might prejudice the formation of one in the natural struggle towards this end. To put it in a nutshell, we should begin to train men like the Bakhtiari Khans, The Sheikh, the Vali etc., that it is to our common interest to assist a proper Central Government, and gradually get rid, on the one hand, of the suspicion that we are out to partition Persia, and on the other, of the belief entertained by local elements that we should support them against any Central authority desirous of putting its house in order.

Young proposed to Nichols four objectives, namely; (1) 'support every action directed towards the ultimate formation of a powerful Central Government'; (2) lay 'all our tribal agreements before the Persian Government'; (3) 'bring our operations prominently before the Persian Government' and (4) 'diplomatic assistance should only be involved on important occasions'. He believed that by 'representing all matters through diplomatic channels at an early stage, we merely afford our representations political colour'.[219]

This was an important enunciation of the principles which were eventually to influence the Company's policy towards the Persian Government, but the management in London, especially Nichols—who was principally concerned with concessionary affairs—was slower to recognise the need for a revaluation of the existing relations. Nichols was inclined to sit on the fence and do nothing that would disturb the status quo. He recognised that developments might 'lead us to reconsider and perhaps modify our position in some respects' but 'I do not think it will be wise to in any way encourage Teheran to take a closer personal interest in our affairs at the fields.'[220] He advised, above all else, preserving the strictest neutrality in all Persian affairs, as the outcome of the power struggle developing was quite unpredictable.

Tehrān should be advised, suggested Nichols, repeating the metaphor that the Company 'is a unique bird that is laying unusually large golden eggs for them and that it will continue to do as long as it is not interfered with'.[221] Yet, it was unrealistic to assume, as Nichols did, that there would be no cause for Persian interference, any more than it was unreasonable to imagine that the British Government would not protect its legitimate interests, if it felt that the conduct of the Company was infringing them or acting contrary to them. This intention soon became obvious at a meeting, which Arnold Wilson had with Riza Khān at Bushire on 28 November 1922, on the occasion of Ahmed Shāh's return from Europe. Riza Khān informed Wilson that he looked forward to increasing royalties, hoped that 'we would press on our development work in Persia as fast as possible' and that he wished 'to see the Persian Government strengthened... by placing all tribal chiefs and leaders directly under the Minister of War so that they could be adequately controlled and prevented from going astray'.[222] The reaction of Nichols to this news was unenthusiastic. He was disturbed that 'if the Tribal Chiefs and Leaders in the South came directly under his control there *will* be trouble'.[223] Nichols was wrong. The Bakhtiari Khans were no match for Riza Khān, who played them off against each other, exacted taxation from them, deprived them of official positions and reduced them to minor local dignitaries, dependent upon his patronage with units of the Persian army stationed among them.

Whilst this was taking place, Loraine, in May 1923, informed Curzon that the time for decision had arrived, as 'the development of Persian military power and establishment of virtual dictatorship by Minister of War, the basis of the whole situation has changed since my arrival here. We have got to decide now, and without much delay, whether we are going to support or oppose extension of authority of Central Government throughout the entire country.'[224] Loraine had avoided taking sides.[225] He had acted in a conciliatory manner, but he did not think that 'we can afford any longer to remain neutral, for both dignity of His Majesty's Government and importance of British interests in Persia would eventually be compromised thereby'.[226] The collapse of Bakhtiari opposition, therefore, as Loraine correctly anticipated, coincided with, and directly contributed to, the growing power of Riza Khān, bringing him into conflict with the Shah and his circle of sycophantic courtiers.[227] Riza Khān contemplated bringing Shaykh Khaz'al under submission[228] and, contemptuous of his ministerial colleagues, was intriguing for his own further self-advancement. He indicated to Loraine at the end of May 1923 that the British Government 'would indeed find it in their interest to encourage internal security in Persia and to entrust the protection of British interests to the Imperial authorities'.[229]

Loraine recognised the War Minister's intentions and his determination to implement them, but cautioned him 'not to endanger British interests of which, by far the most important one, was the Anglo Persian Oil Company ... our next most important interest was in the Sheikh of Muhammera'.[230] The drama of the following year was marked by the subjugation of Shaykh Khaz'al without exposing the operations of the Company to danger. The British Government whilst acknowledging its association with the Shaykh had to extricate itself from the diplomatic tangles of his submission, without getting too embarrassed in the process. Loraine had to preserve his relations with Rizā Khān without necessarily approving all his actions. He had recognised in October 1923 that the War Minister 'thanks to his comparative singleness of thought and action has become the real and dominant power in Persia'.[231] The political maze was being penetrated. On 29 October Rizā Khān became Prime Minister. Shortly afterwards Ahmed Shāh left Tehrān for Europe, never to return. A new political situation was being created, for it was not long before the Qājār dynasty was deposed.

Rizā Khān deliberately, and because of the lack of strong enough alternatives, filled a political vacuum. The Majlis failed to act decisively, in Loraine's opinion,[232] and successive governments wasted time 'in futile discussions, futile measures and futile quarrels'.[233] Loraine regretted that 'the all too frequent changes of Government in this country have a most unsettling effect and render the transaction of business with the Persian Government even more difficult than it intrinsically is by reason of the Persian character'. He had no illusions about the government which Rizā Khān had formed, which, 'even if it is constitutional in form, is certainly dictatorial in character'. As Loraine later wrote, he was well aware 'of the abnormally close interconnection between foreign and domestic affairs which is so characteristic of the Persian body politic, and has been such a terrible trap in the past for foreign diplomatists accredited to this court'.[234]

The fate of Shaykh Khaz'al was an internal Persian matter, but had a bearing on the position of the Company, insofar as the security of the operations was involved. Loraine was hopeful of reaching a compromise with Rizā Khān.[235] On 21 September 1923, Rizā Khān, confident of his political position, sent a detachment of Persian troops south to set up a military post at Shushtar.[236] He declared that 'his action in Arabistan would not endanger the interests of the Anglo-Persian Oil Company or of

Government and concessionary relations

Riżā Khān with his entourage and Company officials at Dar-i-Khazineh 1925

Sheikh Khaz'al' and that he desired 'to take over the responsibility for the safety of the oil fields in Arabistan'.[237] On 8 October Loraine went south himself. He was impressed with the 'real magnitude' and 'exceptional interest' of the oil operations and 'the completeness and thoroughness of the Company's work and organisation'.[238] He impressed upon Shaykh Khaz'al the limitations of British support in the event of a rupture of his relations with the Persian Government. The Shaykh, however, felt that he was faced with a creeping paralysis of his power. The detachment at Shushtar was represented as a guard for the Governor-General. The posting of a Persian officer at Ahwāz was more likely to be a gaoler for the Shaykh. Still Loraine felt relieved on his return to Tehrān.[239]

Opinion in London was again agitated and divided. Nichols tartly remarked of Loraine that 'he is inclined to undue optimism, and we can only hope that we may be wrong'.[240] He disapproved of his visit to the south. Having established a military force in Shaykh Khaz'al's home ground, Riżā Khān waited for a favourable opportunity to settle scores with him. He occupied himself with government business in the capital, aided by the services of the American financial adviser, A.C. Millspaugh, who was appointed in autumn 1922.[241] Riżā Khān's administrative gifts were insufficient to manage the machinery and organisation of government. He was a man of action, not an organiser. He had not yet acquired

Government and concessionary relations

his impressario, his Minister of Court, Mīrzā Abdul Husayn Tīmurtash, and, beset by conflicting political and religious advice as to whether he should found another dynasty or became a president, he procrastinated and the lethargy of his Ministers persisted. Loraine was in despair for 'It is difficult to conceive of an institution more difficult to do business with than the Persian Ministry for Foreign Affairs...The slightest matter is subjected to the most vexatious delays, and the simplest questions cannot be regulated without the expenditure of time and energy quite disproportionate to the issue involved.'[242] Moreover the strains of his new position were inducing a certain manner of unpredictability in Rizā Khān. As Loraine had previously noticed, 'the danger of him is not wrongheadedness or cussedness, but a variable humour which sometimes suddenly starts him flying off full steam ahead at a quite unexpected tangent'.[243]

Then suddenly in mid-August, whilst both Loraine and Wilson were on leave from Tehrān and Muhammara respectively, the screw began to be tightened on Shaykh Khaz'al by the Persian Government. Nichols warned the Foreign Office that he viewed the recent trend of events in south-west Persia with anxiety and that action was being taken inconsistent with previous pledges, 'which threaten gravely to imperil vital British interests in that region'.[244] The Company was in the middle, straddled between the Shaykh and Rizā Khān, and alarmed about the security of its installations and the safety of its staff. The Shaykh played what he thought was his trump card, his British connections,[245] but that only exacerbated the impatience of the Prime Minister. No compromise appeared possible, but the problem was the extent of the support the Shaykh could muster and how effective and sharp the campaign of Rizā Khān would be.

The Foreign Office took a harder line against Shaykh Khaz'al than some of the consular officials from the Indian Government were disposed to take,[246] but Oliphant was relieved to hear from Young and Nichols that the Company agreed with its policy of mediation and 'biased neutrality'.[247] There was no question of sending military forces to defend the Company's installations or staff.[248] There was no longer the same respect for the Shaykh, who had become an anachronistic character. He was indifferent to the welfare of his people, taxing them unjustly and living in a make-believe world of his own independence and invincibility.[249] Loraine on his return to Persia went to Muhammara on 14 November 1924. He persuaded the Shaykh to desist from open rebellion, and, after some disappointments,[250] prevailed upon the Shaykh and Rizā Khān to meet him in Ahwāz 6-7 December.[251]

The immediate conflict was averted and an armed clash avoided.[252] Adopting 'an attitude of watchful inaction', Loraine waited. The Shaykh

Head of the military guard, Masjid-i-Suleimān 1924

refused to visit Tehrān at Rizā Khān's request, but Loraine hoped that he would be left to wither on the tree, from which he would drop in his own time. On 19 April 1925, however, Shaykh Khaz'al was captured rapidly at night and conveyed to Tehrān, where he was detained until his death.[253]

Government and concessionary relations

Loraine was personally disappointed and offended at the breach of trust which the Prime Minister's action implied. A number of questions were asked in the House of Commons about the treatment of the Shaykh. As for the Company, the arrest had been carried out so unexpectedly and efficiently that none of the terrible consequences anticipated arose, although London was worried.[254] In a sense it was an anti-climax, because local power was already being enforced by the military Governor-General for Khūzistān, as Arabistān had been renamed, General Fazullāh Zahedi, who has master-minded the arrest, the first of many exploits in the service of his country. Assured and capable, he started the practice of posting government representatives, police and military guards at the Company's installations.

As the Company's management in Persia realised, it was the calibre and capability of the local officials that was crucial to the success of the Company's relations.[255] In this sense the removal of Shaykh Khaz'al was ultimately irrelevant to the Company. General Zahedi established a very favourable precedent, a real improvement in relations, which Jacks candidly acclaimed as being, 'a steadily improving feeling in evidence towards our operations in the mind of the new régime and the idea at first prevalent that our work was influenced by political motives is steadily giving way to the opinion that our objects are directed only towards the work of the Company.'[256]

By 1925, therefore, the disturbances in governmental and concessionary affairs seemed to have subsided. Misunderstandings appeared to have been clarified. Relations generally improved, though little could be taken for granted in the interaction between politics and business, which had a kaleidoscopic quality of almost infinite changeability and permanent interest. The relations of the Company with the British Government had become more stable, while relations with the Persian Government were satisfactory on the surface.

10
TECHNICAL ACTIVITIES: YEARS OF ENDEAVOUR AND ACHIEVEMENT 1918-1932

I INTRODUCTION

Greenway, at the annual general meeting in 1924, referring to the progress of the Company since its formation, declared effusively that it was 'a record of development which, I am confident, has not been equalled in the same short space of time by any other concern in the commercial history of the World'.[1] It was a large claim and it certainly contrasted with the precarious financial circumstances of a decade earlier, when he was negotiating for the Admiralty supply contract and the Government shareholding. Success on such a scale was unexpected. Indeed not only was the pre-war work of the Company in Persia fraught with inexperience, particularly at Ābādān, but during the war, as revealed in Chapter 7, the unexpectedly large demand for products strained resources and staff in the most difficult conditions. Not only were production and refining facilities fully stretched, but assistance and supplies were provided for the expeditionary force in Mesopotamia. Production from the wells was maintained, but the fear of falling gas pressure, which would have necessitated pumping the oil worried the staff, who understood little about the behaviour of the oilfield on which they were working. There was little appreciation of the interrelationship of the different aspects of the technical operations. Because the plant frequently arrived with parts missing or broken and because there were no local suppliers, it was necessary for the Company to provide almost everything that was required itself from its own stores or workshop in Ābādān or the Fields. Obviously, the First World War stimulated advances in the technology and applications of oil. Consequently the consumption of petroleum products increased spectacularly.

Nevertheless, what was the particular reason for the Company's ability to supply its share of market demand at an economic cost? Naturally there were a number of contributory factors: managerial enterprise; the natural productiveness of its wells; the economies and flexibility of its own tanker fleet; but perhaps most important of all, the growing appreciation of the

Technical activities: Years of endeavour and achievement 1918-1932

technical aspects of its operations. The Company had learnt them the hard way. The early disasters of the refinery at Ābādān had nearly bankrupted it. Experience and practical hard work, the jackets-off manner of Scottish engineers, retrieved the situation and characterised the approach to technical problems. The lack of local industry and the absence of skilled labour in Persia meant that the Company was almost entirely dependent on its own facilities. These were equipped to service the mechanical, electrical and constructional activities in which it was engaged throughout its extensive operations. Plant was made and repaired in the workshops from the parts and machinery that were stocked in the stores. A sense of self-reliance arose for there was no alternative given the distance and the time it took to freight supplies along the sea lanes. There was little local linkage, few local contractors. The Company was obliged to create its own self-sufficiency, train its own employees and solve its own problems. It thus acquired a depth and width of oil industry expertise under exacting working conditions on which it could draw, a human reservoir of practical experience and knowledge. Research was directed to application not abstraction, to the accumulation of data for use, rather than theoretical formulation.

Yet, however important was human endeavour and ingenuity, it was the natural prolific productiveness of the Persian wells which was the principal economic advantage. The wells of Persia were the first to come on stream in the Middle East, the forerunners of the great productive oil fields of the region, which in 1980 contained 55.3 per cent of the world's "published proved" oil reserves, over three and a half times that of the total western hemisphere and nearly six times that of the Soviet Union. In the 1920s only in Persia were there wells like F7 and B17 capable of producing 586 000 and 880 200 tons (12 000 and 18 000 barrels a day) respectively a year. Yields elsewhere were minor in comparison. For example, in the United States they averaged less than 4000 tons a year. A remarkable phenomenon of the Persian wells was that, unlike those of many areas where a gusher might be capped but subsequently dwindle to a trickle, they tended to increase in productivity whilst flowing as oil was released from the limestone fissures and pores. The gas pressure was better conserved so no pumping was necessary. Thus when the bottomhole pressure at Masjid i-Suleimān was measured accurately for the first time in November 1923 at well Sh84 it was 478 p.s.i. By 1940 it had only dropped to 413 p.s.i. In the United States, however, production and pressure decreased considerably over years, so that, for example, the Glenn Pool in Oklahoma produced at a rate of 400 barrels a day (19 510 tons a year) but three years later production had fallen to 62.6 barrels a day (3050 tons a year). This favourable natural feature of the Persian wells and the mastery of production techniques that was attained contributed decisively to the competitiveness of the Company. The success of upstream performance more than compensated for any deficiencies in downstream operations.

The early wells were the result of tracing the seepages and the tell-tale geological anticlines, but the more profound knowledge of what constituted an 'oil field' depended upon the probing of the drill, the patient examination of temperatures, pressures and formations, the detailed analysis of oil, gas and water and that element of luck, which often favours the adventurous. In the years after the ending of the First World War the extent and natural characteristics of the oilfield of Masjid i-Suleimān were elucidated by a series of experimental scientific investigations of its physical properties, and its production was controlled on the basis of this information. In the laboratory the chemical elements of the crude oil were analysed and assessed to improve refinery processes and their suitability for an increasing range of products. Between the well-head and the customer was a vast number of intermediate stages including the production, the pipeline and the refinery operations before transportation and distribution to markets took place. All these stages had to be technically as well as administratively managed and maintained to appropriate standards and manning levels with the right degree of training and knowledge.

The outstanding contribution of Cadman to the Company's technical progress was his realisation of the overriding importance of an integrated scientific effort and the interrelationship of the various technical activities and functions. The engineer and the chemist had to collaborate with, not ignore, each other. Because of his early technical training and the administrative experience, which he had acquired as a mining inspector in government service, Cadman was ideally equipped to stimulate from the early twenties the scientific attitude of the Company, an outlook which permeated all levels of staff in Persia and elsewhere. He understood the principles and the practice and communicated easily and without condescension to the geologist, engineer and chemist no less than to his colleagues on the Board. He was concerned with what was industrially significant for the Company. A badly designed valve connection which prevented simple routine maintenance was, in its way, as important as establishing the hydraulic equilibrium of the porosity of oil-bearing rock strata. His technical expertise and experience were exceptional. His range of industrial understanding was immense. These qualities did not float to the top of experience or remain sediment at the bottom of his knowledge. They were held in suspended animation in his mind, just as the gas which provided the energy drive in production was naturally active in the oil.

Technical activities: Years of endeavour and achievement 1918-1932

Yet, vital as the contribution of Cadman was to the technical development of the Company, it was complemented by capable geologists, a notable production management and a sound research organisation. Under the overall responsibility of S. Lister James, who had first gone to Persia in 1913 on secondment from Burmah at the recommendation of Sir Boverton Redwood, and who had been appointed chief geologist in 1919, a number of geologists were working in Persia. Because of the relative independence of their activities, and the scale and diversity of the geological conditions, these geologists had plenty of opportunity of responding to the challenge posed to their professional abilities. They gradually accumulated an understanding and knowledge that was to provide the basis for a remarkable tradition of successful exploration, which was to ensure the Company's pre-eminent oil reserves position into the 1970s when the traditional concessionary system more or less ended. As for production, J. Jameson was primarily responsible for it from 1920 to 1928. He had gone to Persia as assistant to Charles Ritchie in 1909. A natural engineering genius with a practical flair and an affable personality of great organising ability, he became pipeline superintendent, assistant fields manager, fields manager, general manager in Persia and eventually a director of the Company.

Dr A.E. Dunstan was the founder, with Dr F.B. Thole, of the Company's research work at Sunbury. Though his initial investigations were into crude oil viscosity, all aspects of oil technology were grist to his intellectual mill. *The Science of Petroleum,*[2] of which he was principal editor, remains the *magnum opus* of its subject, a testimony to his width of oil knowledge. A jovial person, he was much appreciated by his staff and colleagues. Patient and capable, he recognised that

> it is inevitable, as the very nature of research, that a great number of ideas are tested experimentally and yield purely negative results. These are sometimes as important and as instructive as positive results, and although they are not conspicuous, the time and effort expended on them must not be regarded as wasted. In fact, a successful piece of work is often the ultimate result of many abortive experiments.[3]

It may not have represented a fundamental philosophy but it was a practical discipline.

In reviewing the nature and scope of the technical work undertaken in Persia and elsewhere or in exploration in North and South America, Africa, Europe and Australasia, it is important not to forget the human dimension of the Company's operations. From fewer than 117 European staff in Persia in 1919 and 3979 Persian and 2688 others, in 1930, the year of maximum employment in the period under review, the comparable figures were 1191, 20 095 and 9960. Table 10.1 shows the total overall

Technical activities: Years of endeavour and achievement 1918-1932

Table 10.1. *Anglo-Persian Oil Company staff and labour in Persia 1919–32*

Year	Persians	Indians	Others	Europeans	Total
1919	3 979	2 641	47	117	6 784
1920	8 447	3 616	35	244	12 342
1921	9 009	4 709	51	271	14 040
1922	18 441	4 285	2 940	490	26 156
1923	20 762	4 715	849	644	26 970
1924	18 384	4 731	648	738	24 501
1925	15 820	4 890	7 201	994	28 905
1926	15 843	3 588	6 042	1 020	26 493
1927	17 887	3 272	7 009	1 055	29 223
1928	16 382	3 050	5 365	1 000	25 797
1929	15 245	2 518	5 273	980	24 016
1930	20 095	2 411	7 549	1 191	31 246
1931	14 797	1 675	3 178	989	20 639
1932	10 343	1 420	2 346	744	14 853

Source: BP reports to Imperial Commissioner and BP 78/63/1–205

employment figures for all the centres of the Company's operations in Persia whilst Appendices 10.1-3 show comparative employment figures for the different centres. It required an immense administrative effort to manage, house and satisfy the social life of the expatriates in an alien environment in which practically all the facilities and amenities had to be

Bakhtiari tribesmen in the workshops at Masjid i-Suleimān 1914

Technical activities: Years of endeavour and achievement 1918-1932

provided by the Company itself. A few passages to Persia were provided in tankers, but many journeyed overland from Beirut to Baghdad by the enterprising Nairn transport convoys of cars and thence to Ābādān. Moreover the life of many of the tribesmen employed changed once they had accepted a settled sedentary, industrial occupation. Many of the predominantly Hindu Indian clerks, artisans, orderlies and cooks found the Persian ambience unsympathetic to their customs which contributed to their discontent in the early 1920s.

The period covered by this chapter leads on from the developments in Persia during the First World War, when production increased tenfold. Keeping refinery throughput up rather than economic processing had been the order of the day. The first four or five years were marked by endeavours to stabilise the situation in administrative and technical affairs. The remaining years of the D'Arcy Concession were distinguished by achievements as geological reconnaisance revealed promising sites, and a new oilfield, Haft Kel, was discovered. Data on oil reservoir conditions made possible a new concept of production, unitisation, the complete development of a single oilfield. Improved refinery processes led to better products and the dredging of the Shatt-al-'Arab eliminated inefficient lightering off Ābādān.

2 EXPLORATION AND PRODUCTION IN PERSIA: YEARS OF ENDEAVOUR 1918-1924

The primary objectives of the Company's exploratory effort at this time were firstly to determine the productive capacity of Masjid i-Suleimān and secondly to discover additional oilfields. Whilst the potential life of the Masjid i-Suleimān field remained unknown and the possibility existed of water encroachment into the oil zones, as was happening in Mexico, the Company could not rest easy with only a single proved field. These objectives seemed simple, but, in the absence of much verifiable data, there was much debate about the best methods of achieving success, particularly when it had not been definitely established that the oil reservoir was in the Asmari limestone.

Garrow, who was then the director in charge of technical affairs, on his visit to Persia in 1919 was greatly concerned about balancing market expectations with the productive capacity of the oilfield. He stated that anticipated crude oil demands represented 2 100 000 tons in the short term, 2 900 000 tons in the medium term and 3 070 000 to 4 120 000 tons in the long term (these figures were actually reached in 1922, 1923 and 1924-25 respectively). At the time of his visit there were 48 wells in sound producing condition which, he believed, 'in my humble opinion, is not nearly enough compared with our future crude commitments'.[4] While he regarded the producing area as extraordinary, he advocated as a precautionary measure against any unknown contingencies like 'a sudden drop in gas pressure' or a 'sudden influx of water from the flanks', a large increase in 'our reserves of drilled wells in the fields ready to be brought into immediate production in case of need'. He therefore recommended a crash five-year programme of drilling 15 wells annually to give a total of 123 producing wells.

In comparison with 1911-19, when the average footage drilled in a year was 6457 ft, the equivalent of five average wells, the effort required in terms of manpower and resources would have been extraordinary in the conditions then prevailing. It was an insurance policy on a grand scale and he was pessimistic about obtaining sufficiently accurate information to plan otherwise because, 'we have not seen and are unlikely to see for years any figures reliable and with any degree of accuracy representing the average decline in gas pressure per well over the whole field'. Garrow underestimated the progress of scientific investigation, for only three years later fifteen wells alone were producing over 2 000 000 tons.

By 1920 considerable geological research and observations were being done, 'the most important work yet undertaken by a geologist at Fields', according to Thompson, the fields manager, whose collaboration with geologists had become a distinguished feature of his time in Persia.[5] F.D.S. Richardson, a geologist, was preparing sections showing surface geological conditions, correlated in the same section with known underground evidence as revealed by drilling operations. In June 1920, Thompson issued his valedictory comments on the oilfield for which he had been responsible for five years.[6] Between 1912 and 1919 some 5 250 000 tons of oil had been produced. He believed that the conditions encountered were different from any other known oilfield, not necessarily unique, but arising from the fact that in 'no other proved oil bearing territory has the development been under the control of one management'. This was the real difference, the extraordinary opportunity for the Company, because elsewhere, suggested Thompson, 'the sole idea of the various interested Companies has been an anxiety to tap the oil horizon before their rivals, regardless of the damage done to the oil-bearing strata by faulty drilling to the detriment of the prolonged productive capacity of the field'. Figure 10.1 gives a diagramatic view of the careful manner in which the Masjid i-Suleimān oilfield was operated by 1930.

Thompson concluded that gas pressure was constant throughout the field which was itself continuous throughout its extent. He advised that it should not be overdrilled. He argued for a major change in drilling strategy, a new approach to petroleum engineering, believing that 'If, and

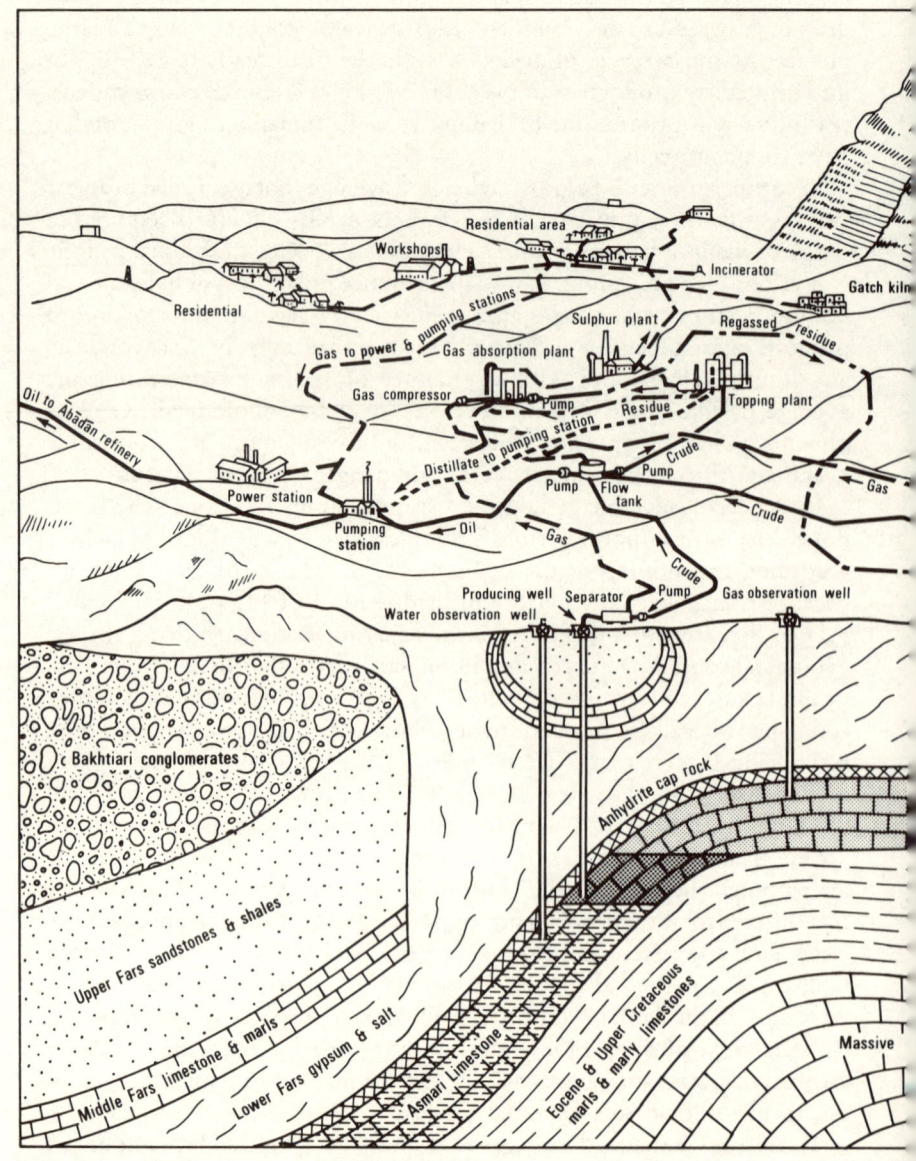

Technical activities: Years of endeavour and achievement 1918-1932

Figure 10.1 Oil production, Masjid i-Suleimaān
Source: BP

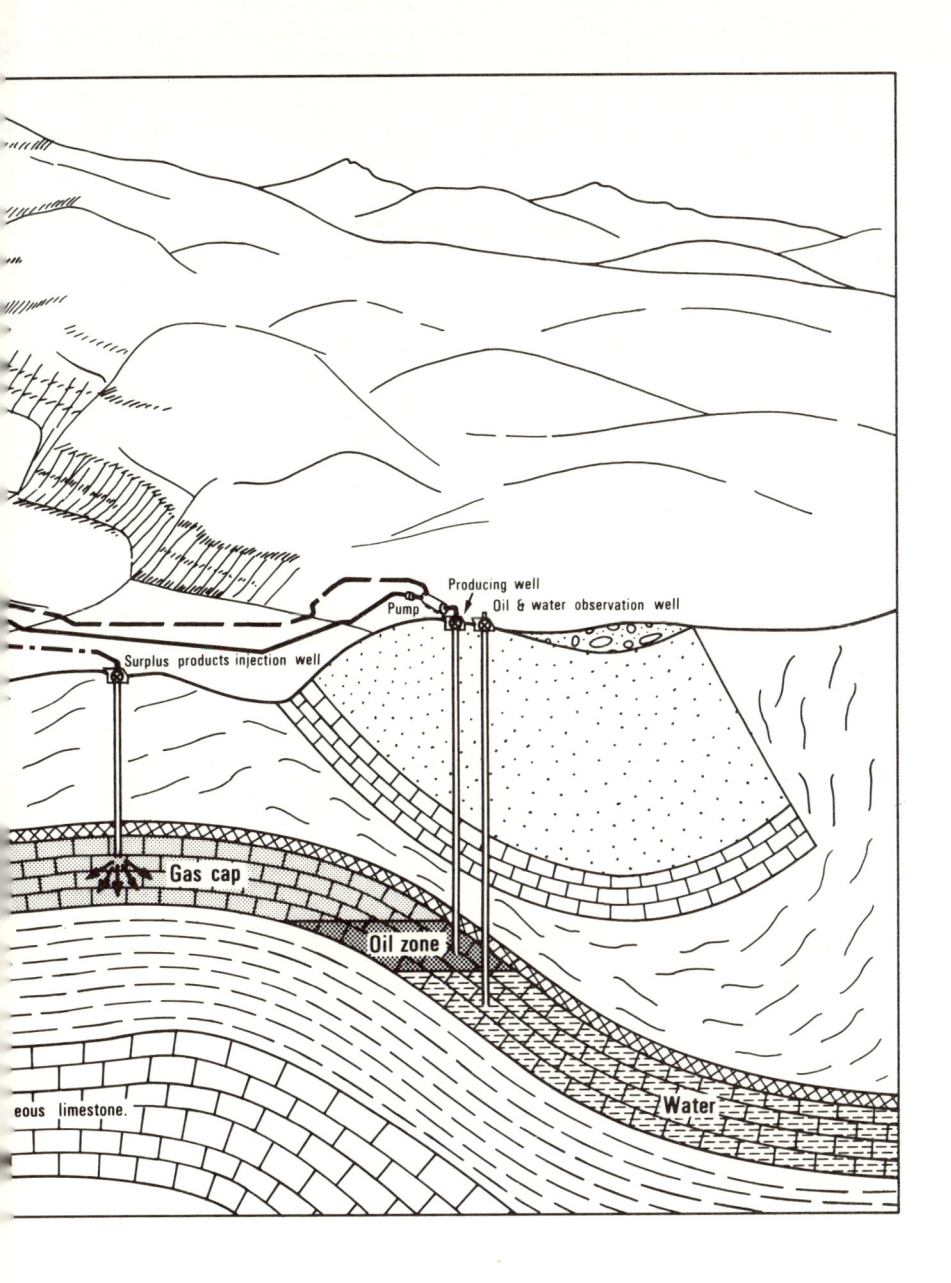

Technical activities: Years of endeavour and achievement 1918-1932

Technical activities: Years of endeavour and achievement 1918-1932

there does not seem any reason to doubt it, the central wells do draw their production from the whole of the oil producing rocks of the Field it would obviously be a waste of money and very possible waste of gas energy to drill any more wells *into* the oil reservoir ... until such time as the decrease in production necessitates the drilling of intermediate wells to assist the extraction of oil from its reservoir by pumping.' The implications of this advice were momentous for the Company. Development drilling was no longer to be a fairground lucky strike game, rows of steel derricks staking out chance sites, but the orderly spacing of rigs delineating the optimum production centres.

Thompson was the first in the Company to concern himself with 'flowhead pressure' and its correlation with that of 'the oil rock at the bottom of the well'. He had earlier stressed the necessity for a senior geologist being permanently attached to the field manager's staff for 'the Fields Manager and he alone is responsible for the production of the Field ... and without a geologist resident on the Field, who follows continually exploration work, a good deal must be left to the manager's initiative'.[7] Thompson was one of the earliest oil technologists to recognise the need for an integrated scientific appreciation of a technical problem that involved more than one discipline. It was the good fortune of the Company to have in its exclusive concessionary area, complete oilfields which it could develop without hindrance from competitors, in a scientific manner.

In many respects Thompson pointed the way forward for a closer examination of the local conditions, without which all was theoretical speculation. Between 1921 and 1923 Richardson finally solved the great exploration conundrum by convincingly proving the earlier hypothesis of Shand that 'the Main Limestone can be no other than the Asmari',[8] thus identifying the nature of the sub-surface limestone oil-bearing rock with the great visible limestone outcrops known as Asmari, a fact of fundamental significance for the Masjid i-Suleimān field. This confirmation was substantiated by detailed micro-palaeontological examination using thin sections of the various rock samples. Richardson made a collection of microscopic fossils, which were identified by Dr J. A. Douglas of Oxford University and subsequently the Company's palaeontological adviser for more than thirty years. It was an important activity within the exploration function in which the Company became pre-eminent.

Towards the end of 1922, in spite of Thompson's remarks, further thought was still being given to the drilling schedule, which had not been implemented on the scale envisaged by Garrow, because of the lack of trained staff, shortage of rigs, failure in electricity supplies, insufficiency of accommodation and the absence of coordinated management to undertake

Technical activities: Years of endeavour and achievement 1918-1932

An outcrop of the Asmari Limestone

such a comprehensive programme. Jameson, who had succeeded Thompson as fields manager, reflected early in 1923 that in spite of much progress there were still 'so many unknown factors ... as we are dealing with a Field which, as far as we know, has no parallel in the world'.[9] There was a danger of overdrilling with its consequent high expenditure, or underdrilling and so failing to produce the volume of oil required. The gas content of the reservoir was the key to the production potential and the siting of wells. Jameson proposed drilling down the flank, which although 'the most difficult and expensive seems the wiser to adopt from the point of view of conserving our natural resources'.

Jameson was suggesting a compromise between the 'Step Out' policy of siting rigs adjacent to each other and the 'Big Jump' proposals of placing them further apart according to the geological evidence. He was prepared to carry out the fifty rig programme propounded in London, but without

Technical activities: Years of endeavour and achievement 1918-1932

much enthusiasm. He believed his instructions to be out of proportion to the drilling hitherto actually achieved and inappropriate in comparison with the existing production drawn from fourteen wells. He did, however, recognise that all the oil eggs were in the one field basket for 'we have not so far a reserve Field' and there was no knowing 'what effect an annual rate of production of over 4 000 000 tons would have on the Masjid i-Suleimān field'. This was the crux of the production problem.

It is at this stage that Cadman's influence began to be felt. After a year familiarising himself with the Company's activities, its strengths and weaknesses and having established himself in the Company's management, Cadman was ready in spring 1923 to assert himself. He posed the question, 'where, in the present state of our geological knowledge, should existing drilling resources be principally concentrated, Maidan i-Naftun extensions, or outside areas?'[10] Problems could not be solved in isolation. Priorities had to be established and information assessed before decisions could be made. *Festinate lente* might have been Cadman's watchword, as he was convinced that 'no large new programme of outside testing can be submitted at this stage with reasonable confidence that the most promising areas are selected and that the possibilities are commensurate with the costs involved'.

So Cadman decided that new test drilling was to be concentrated on extending the productive capacity of Masjid i-Suleimān. This was not a policy of retrenchment, though its modest proportions may well have been partially determined by the financial crisis through which the Company was then passing as a result of the expansion of marketing activities in Europe and elsewhere (see Chapter 8). It was a tactic of mature consideration on which later to base a more forward policy. A better understanding of the behaviour of the oil reservoir was beginning to emerge as a result of some early investigations, which needed correlating and further examination. Firstly, the lack of success of outside testing had to be examined, and, secondly, an exploration policy formulated on the basis of assessing the failures of previous exploration and the opportunities for new initiatives. Cadman was certain that a detailed programme was essential, 'whereby the whole concession may be surveyed rapidly and effectively. After this has been done, and only then, will it be possible to settle upon a development programme calculated, in the period available, to make the most of all the potentialities of a concession of which so much still remains unknown.'

A useful view of the unimpressive state of the operations at this time to an outside observer is contained in a report compiled by three members of the staff of Standard Oil (NJ), Messrs Corwin, Seidel and Haynes, who visited Persia in mid-1924.[11] It contrasted with the enthusiastic later remarks of Greenway to the shareholders in the same year, for although they praised the extent of the Company's achievement they were less certain of its quality. They commented that drilling had been concentrated in the Masjid i-Suleimān area in 'connection with the exigencies of promoting the company and raising capital rather than to the wise and economical development of this field'. They were complimentary about the Fields staff by whom 'on the whole the undertaking is well and wisely managed' and 'carried on under adverse and severe desert and climatic conditions in an outlaying isolated region remote from any center of modern civilization'. The nature of the topography with its evident 'folding, faulting and non-conformity of the formations' was perplexing for the geologists, who were disappointed in their results. Their opinion of the refinery was bad, as it did 'not seem to have been very well planned and its present condition and arrangement is unsatisfactory'. The condition of the tankers they saw 'did not appear to be in the prime ship shape conditions one expects of a well managed, well handled fleet'. Fortune had favoured the Company, they believed, for it had been built 'on a far larger scale than production prospects might have appeared to warrant', with the result that they had sufficient 'facilities to warrant their present scale of operations'. It was Cadman's success within a few years to replace the element of chance with that of scientific control.

Meanwhile, by mid-1923, whilst Cadman was contemplating the issues, the boundaries of the unknown were steadily contracting. The oil reservoir code was being cracked, for on 8 June 1923 a notable draft was circulated on 'Gas Pressure Problems on Maidan i-Naftun Field with reference to the Conservation of Supplies and Future Drilling' by D. Comins, an engineer, and E.W. Scofield, a geologist.[12] Lister James in forwarding the report to Cadman described it as 'the most complete study of the producing field, which had yet been made from this point of view'. He believed that 'it should form a very sound basis for the collection of data of utmost importance to the Company in gauging the life and potentialities of the field which is at present the only developed source of supply in the Company's hands' and he generously attributed all the credit to the authors as the work was undertaken on their initiative. Cunningham Craig, more reserved as befitted the geological adviser, was no less complimentary, praising it as 'a great advance upon any work of this kind that I have seen attempted in other oilfields'.[13] It was of seminal importance and Cadman immediately recognised its significance as a basis towards 'a really adequate knowledge of the under ground conditions' and that it provided 'reasonable hypotheses on which to base further developments and investigation'.[14] He summarised its conclusions:

(a) The Maidan i-Naftun field is a single dynamic unit.

(b) Water pressure is apparently absent, and there appears at the moment to be no evidence of extraneous compensation for gas and oil extracted.

(c) Pressure measured at the surface appears to be dependent on the ground elevation and the character of the column of oil, gasified oil, or gas, in the well.

(d) The rate at which the oil will flow at the mouth of the well depends upon the relative elevation of the well and upon the porosity of the oil rock encountered by the well.

(e) There is a gradual fall in the oil level, which, 18 months previously, appeared to be something under 10 feet per 100 000 000 gallons of oil extracted.

The Asmari limestone oil reservoir was postulated to be a 'homogeneous hydrostatic unit, that is to say that there is free, if slow, communication between all oil'.[15] The implications of this for a controlled drilling schedule were immense in terms of manpower, resources and expenditure. The possibilities of improved technology for developing oilfields as separate self-contained units of production determined by their own individual characteristics were very advantageous in properly phased productive terms. The life cycle of a field could be determined, resulting in calculations of its reserves, flow rates, oil, water and gas levels and pressures. An idea of the typical relationship of the oil, water and gas levels to each other can be seen in Figure 10.2. In the following years more sophisticated measuring devices, more rigorous statistical analysis and more practical experience were deployed to establish with greater certitude the principles of 'unitisation', that is, scientifically controlled integrated oilfield development, which had been initially formulated through individual efforts encouraged by an enlightened local management, rather than by any consistent and coherent research team effort.

Exploration in general, however, beyond the only field which had been proved, Masjid i-Suleimān, was disappointing between 1919 and 1924, an unsuccessful procession from one site to another. At first in 1919 exploratory drilling was undertaken with tempered urgency, but as one dry hole followed another or difficulties occurred in drilling, it was replaced with undisguised anxiety. In 1918 one outside test well was being drilled, in 1919, 3, 1920, 4, 1921, 6, 1922, 11 and 1923, 17. In the same period the number of geologists employed rose to 7, 8, 10, 14, 18 and 26, the maximum employed in Persia. There was no single reason for failure, rather a number of factors.[16] They included differing and conflicting geological interpretations of the evidence, lack of management coordination, initial geological inexperience, inadequate practical appreciation of the conditions, accommodation difficulties and some security problems with surveys. Much competent topographical work was achieved on a

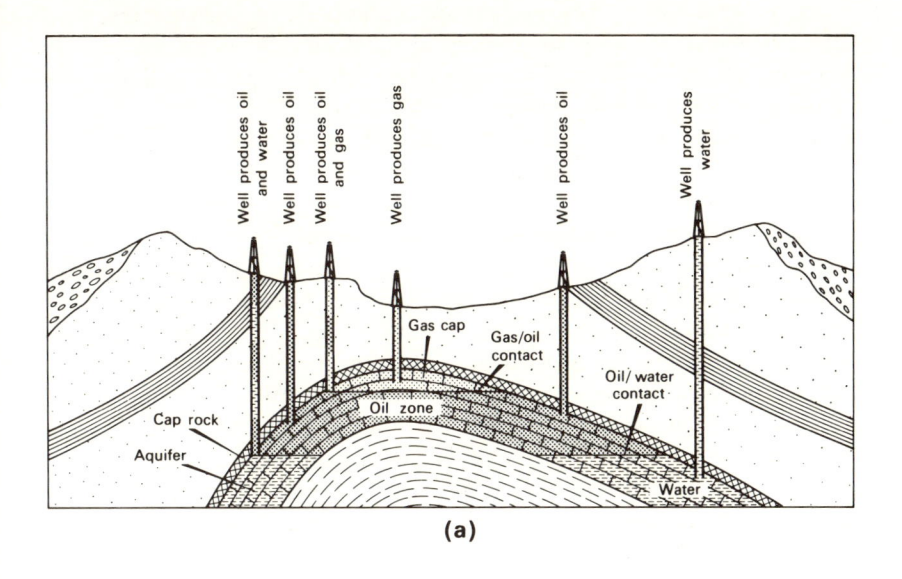

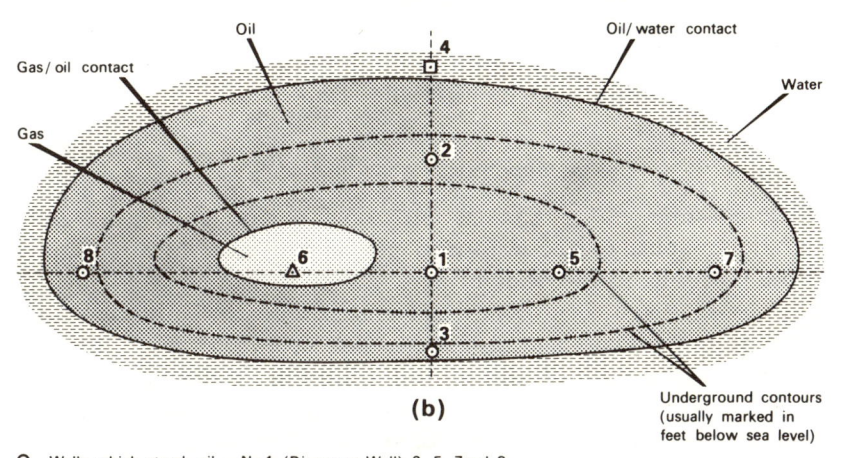

Technical activities: Years of endeavour and achievement 1918-1932

○ Wells which struck oil – No.1 (Discovery Well) 2, 5, 7and 8
   Well No.3 Struck oil and then passed into water.

△ Well No.6 Struck gas and then passed into oil.

□ Well No.4 Struck water.

Figure 10.2 Cross-section and contour map showing oil and gas levels
Source: *Our Industry Petroleum* (British Petroleum Company Ltd, 1977), p. 125

very detailed scale, giving a very positive aspect to an otherwise rather negative impression. Progress was not negligible, for patience rather than the spectacular characterises geological endeavour. There is certainly no doctrine of geological infallibility. Other oilfields were no guide to the geological conditions in Persia.

The gradual accumulation of more geological information through sustained observation contributed to a better understanding of the conditions in which oil might be found. To some extent the desirability of finding oil in places of administrative convenience, proximity to existing pipelines or accessibility to the refinery, had taken priority over other possible sites. Moreover, in discarding earlier theories and interpreting new data, the days of 'hit and miss' test drilling of individual prospects chosen on the criteria of seepages, local structures and other obvious surface indications, were giving way to more profound techniques for solving the exploratory puzzles. Amongst the sites drilled were Sar-i-Naftak in October 1919, Qundak in September 1920, Gach Khalaj in March 1921, Marmatain in September and November 1924, Bikarz in 1922, Dālparī in January 1923, Dehlurān in February 1923 and Chillingar in May 1923. Only in Naft Khana in the Transferred Territories between Persia and Iraq, where drilling began in February 1919, was oil discovered. The well caught fire and burnt for a week in May 1923.

3 YEARS OF ACCOMPLISHMENT 1924-32

(a) Improvements and innovation

The pioneering work of Comins and Scofield and other members of the technical staff had to be transformed into 'an actual working proposition and not an impractical vision of purely academic interest'.[17] So in 1924 Comins, assisted by L. A. Pym, was put in charge of the physical research department (drilling and production policy) with a brief covering experimental work on wells and the collection and interpretation of physical data related to reservoir conditions, which were supplied by the drilling, production, geological, geophysical and chemical sections. It was an inter-disciplinary approach. The object was 'to develop uniform and long-sighted drilling and production policy applicable to the total reservoir unit for which a precise knowledge of the subsurface and reservoir conditions was essential'.[18]

The Company was not the first, let alone the only organization to take an interest in the scientific development of oilfields, but in the United States comparable activity was hampered by legislation enshrining the law

Technical activities: Years of endeavour and achievement 1918-1932

of capture by which land owners who had sub-soil rights could drill to deprive neighbouring owners of oil in the field. As a result, according to H.S. (later Sir Stephen) Gibson, an early petroleum engineer with the Company and later Managing Director of the Iraq Petroleum Company, 'The guiding principle was to obtain as much oil as possible in the shortest space of time. Speed of drilling, therefore, became the greatest essential, and technical progress was for many years centred on this one operation, no attention whatever being given to the effect of such a policy on the ultimate amount of oil obtained.'[19] In effect, 'the driller was in sole charge of production methods'.

The objective of the policy of comprehensive production, unitisation, was to obtain the maximum ultimate recovery of oil from the reservoir and eliminate uncontrollable over-production. In this manner it was hoped to regulate supply, and achieve better estimates of recoverable crude oil reserves, obviating the need for the storage of large volumes of crude oil in tanks by utilising the reservoir as a vast underground tank. Fire risks, tankage cost and evaporation losses would all be reduced. Furthermore, other advantages would arise from confining drilling to only those wells essential to production requirements, thereby maximising the natural energy within the oil for bringing it to the surface and beyond. Other advantages were, less need for plant and equipment to withstand unexpectedly high production pressures, which could not otherwise have been predicted, the prevention of waste and the careful phasing of all demands for utilities, services and manpower.

There was also the benefit of operating to a definite production schedule, the prevention of avoidable production hazards such as blow-outs and the improvement of staff conditions following a better understanding of reservoir performance. It was upon such material, economic and social consequences of a well developed production programme that the Company was able to base its growth strategy in the most efficient and effective manner and in so doing offset some of the formidable advantages of its competitors, whose wells were closer to the centres of consumption, particularly in distribution and marketing. A proper programme of routine measurements was instituted in the fields area and new instrumentation was frequently designed and made or acquired to cope with the high pressures encountered.

New wells were drilled progressively down the south-west structure at Masjid i-Suleimān till, in 1924, one of them passed through the oil column and struck water. This was left as an observation well to establish the oil-water contact level, that is to say, whether it remained more or less constant between the two liquids. Fortunately little movement was detected, confirming the supposition that water, if present, was not freely connected to an external source, thus firmly refuting the strongly held opposite view of some of the Company's geologists. This was important because, in other limestone fields, water had been known to rise with great rapidity corresponding to a fall in pressure. It had been ascertained that the gas—oil level fell about 15 feet per each million tons of crude oil produced. The correlation of these factors led to a tentative calculation that the crude oil reserves were, in fact, considerable. By the end of 1926 further field delineation work had revealed the overall position of the edge water round the reservoir which showed conclusively that the pressure was constant overall.

Garrow, nevertheless, had continued to be apprehensive about the lack of wells drilled and pressed for an accelerated programme in mid-1924.[20] Jameson, whilst appreciative of the investigations being carried out, was still unsure about the oil—water level. So in the prevailing uncertainty he proposed that 'the drilling programme should be decided more by what the Company are prepared to spend as an insurance premium using scientific reasoning, more as the actuary with very little knowledge to work on'.[21] Drilling costs were not inconsiderable. With a throughput of some 4 500 000 tons a year, according to Jameson, the total drilling and revenue expenditure for a thirty-six well programme was roughly 4s 9d per ton (1s 11d direct expenditure on drilling and 2s 10d on all other services such as water, transport, electric power, maintenance and administration). Nevertheless production costs had generally been declining over the years as the efficiency of operations had increased, as Table 10.2 clearly demonstrates.

Drilling was certainly an important activity. At this time the 'standard' American cable tool type percussion rig was largely in use, as in Figure 10.3, steam operated and generally manned by American or central European drillers. In 1921 the Company decided to institute a programme to train young British staff as drillers on an apprenticeship basis because of the growing social problems and cost of American drillers. This scheme was modified a few years later as it was too specialised. At the same time it was decided to install proper power supplies in the fields area and a large central power station was erected by the Tembi river to supply a high tension electric grid system which enabled electric power to replace the steam driven rigs. This was more efficient, less costly and easier to maintain than the corroding boilers. The fields management staff were not easily convinced of the benefits of the rotary system of drilling, although Cadman commented favourably on the method after his visit to Argentina in 1923 in a letter to Jameson. The difficulties concerned the high pressures encountered in the Persian wells and the critical period when the overlaying cap rock, the dome of the oil reservoir, was pierced. Until the

Table 10.2. *Fields production costs per ton 1920–26*

	1920–21	1921–22	1922–23	1923–24	1924–25	1925–26
Throughput (tons)	1 743 557	2 327 221	2 559 028	3 648 634	4 308 500	4 522 922
Fields and general charges	8s 5.46d	6s 1.25d	5s 10.32d	5s 2.19d	4s 2.29d	3s 8.69d
Boring wells	*1s 2.39d	*1s 2.54d	*1s 6.48d	2s 11.69d	2s 1.84d	2s 1.77d
Pipeline charges	4s 2.34d	3s 10.94d	2s 8.64d	1s 8.35d	1s 3.99d	1s 0.41d
Depreciation	—	—	—	0s 6.91d	1s 8.89d	1s 9.22d
Total cost per ton	13s 10.19d	11s 2.73d	10s 1.44d	10s 5.14d	9s 5.01d	8s 8.09d

Note: ★ includes depreciation
Source: BP 4.c.6353
BP 4.c.6357
BP 4.c.6358

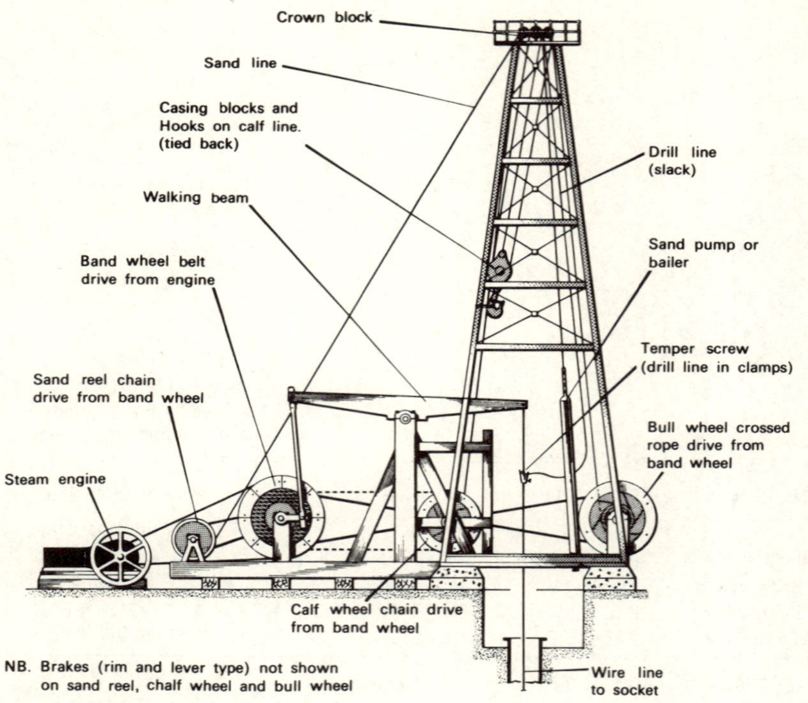

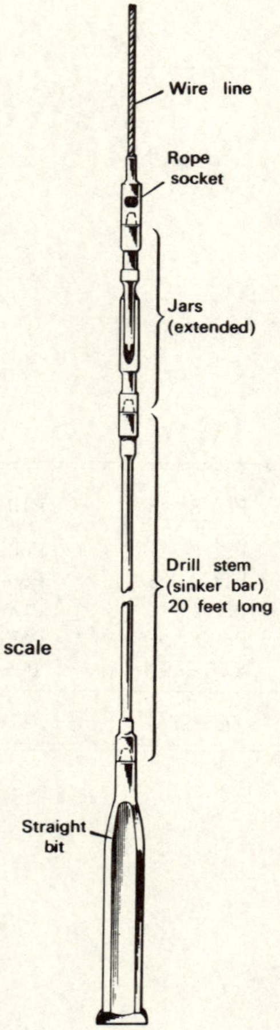

Labels on drilling rig diagram (top tool string):
- Wire line
- Rope socket
- Jars (extended)
- Drill stem (sinker bar) 20 feet long
- Straight bit

Diagrammatic and not to scale

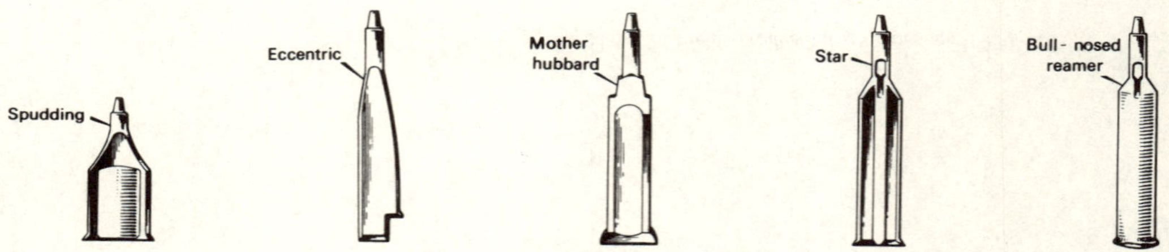

Labels on rig structure:
- Crown block
- Sand line
- Casing blocks and Hooks on calf line. (tied back)
- Walking beam
- Band wheel belt drive from engine
- Sand reel chain drive from band wheel
- Steam engine
- Drill line (slack)
- Sand pump or bailer
- Temper screw
- Bull wheel crossed rope drive from band wheel
- Calf wheel chain drive from band wheel
- Wire line to socket

NB. Brakes (rim and lever type) not shown on sand reel, chalf wheel and bull wheel

Cable Tool Bits used by BP (nb. shown enlarged):
- Spudding
- Eccentric
- Mother hubbard
- Star
- Bull-nosed reamer

Technical activities: Years of endeavour and achievement 1918-1932

The floor of a 'Standard' cable tool type percussion rig 1924

mud used in rotary drilling had become more specialised and reliable and the crews more skilled in its application a well was liable to blow out, as happened in the first Iraq well at Baba Gurgur in 1927. Jameson as late as 1926 was unenthusiastic about its prospects and worried about the safety aspects. Two such rigs had been imported in 1922 from the United States with their own crews, but although they could drill deeper more easily, the rapidly changing and often soft formations encountered necessitated frequent and laborious changes of bits. Gradually bits were improved, the drilling mud more reliable and blow out preventers utilised, and the rotary rigs were converted to motor-driven use. By 1926 the last of the American rotary drilling personnel had left Persia.

In March 1925, fifty-eight rigs were employed, but the number subsequently declined. In coping with the high pressures, 2500 p.s.i., and deep wells encountered in the drilling at Naft Khāna, rotary drilling was successful in 1927. As a result of this it was decided in 1928 to give rotary rigs a chance on the Haft Kel field in order that it could be put on production in as short a time as possible. The success was beyond expectations and cable tool rigs were soon replaced there, though utilised in outside tests. Rotary drilling had come to stay and in 1930 three motor driven rigs were ordered, the first of their kind, as well as electrically operated rigs, one of which actually drilled 8960 feet, a record in those

Technical activities: Years of endeavour and achievement 1918-1932

days. Well pressures increased beyond Masjid i-Suleimān, getting progressively higher at Haft Kel, Āghā Jārī and Pāzanun, so new techniques had to be devised to cope with these as well as problems such as mud control, fire risk and tool retrieval.

Within eighteen months, as a result of the studies and observations of Comins and his colleagues, Jameson was more confident, in a letter to Cadman on 12 January 1926, about the flowing life of the field.[22] He believed that 'a safe estimate of the time which will elapse before pumping has to be resorted to would now appear to be nearer fifteen years than ten'. In the event the Company never had to resort to pumping its wells in Persia. The reassurance was welcome for 'at the present time the drilling of wells on fields, purely for production is not warranted'. Indeed he was more certain that 'the outlook on fields is even brighter than it was a year ago'.[23] He was satisfied that there was already a safe productive capacity of 7 000 000 tons a year and that as a result of not having to embark on a new thirty-six well programme there would be a direct saving of at least £300 000 a year. This was a watershed in production policy. The theoretical claims of Comins had been vindicated, but he continued to widen the scope of the research, to analyse water samples, take bottom hole temperatures, investigate gas solubility, and assess limestone porosity and permeability.

A rotary type rig showing turntable and stem 1924

Technical activities: Years of endeavour and achievement 1918-1932

It was not all plain sailing. Although the discovery of a second field at Haft Kel in April 1927 had engendered a feeling of productive invulnerability, this complacency was shattered in August 1927, when well No. 56 on the Masjid i-Suleimān field began to produce salt water in some volume, although the bottom of the well was apparently some two hundred feet above the estimated oil—water levels. Tests soon showed that the phenomenon was very localised and explicable. Measures were taken to correct the gas—oil and oil—water levels and they responded to the appropriate attention.[24]

This rather frightening demonstration that the reservoir connection was not uniformly free throughout the oil reservoir, as had been assumed, and that partial barriers to oil migration within it were present, stimulated further efforts to determine a tighter application of reservoir control. These concentrated on maintaining a uniform pressure in all areas by carefully adjusting offtake as required, thus ensuring uniformity in the general oil—water level to prevent oil and water mixing. This could be achieved over time by a continuous process of monitoring the possible production variables so as to regulate normal production at its optimum rate. The quick diagnosis and immediate remedial action taken by the petroleum engineering department confirmed its indispensability as otherwise the field might have gone to water with calamitous consequences, if it had not been operated on a unit basis. During 1928 Haft

Masjid i-Suleimān from the main office 1926

Technical activities: Years of endeavour and achievement 1918-1932

Kel was planned methodically in a unit manner and in the same year Masjid i-Suleimān achieved its maximum rate of production, 5 358 000 tons in a single year.

Comins, addressing the American Petroleum Institute in Chicago, in 1928, was able to affirm that, as a result of a unit operation 'on our main field, it has been possible to collect, interpret and apply the data of the unit to the purposes of conserving capital instead of putting it in the ground, of conserving gas content and rock pressures, of estimating roughly the reserves, and of distributing the accorded allotted production of the unit in such a way that wells do not prematurely go to gas and do not go to water at all'.[25] The fears of a decade earlier had been finally dispelled. As an American geologist, Hugo Kamb, acknowledged in 1928 'The Masjid i-Suleimān field is probably the most efficiently developed oil pool in the world.'[26]

During the remainder of the D'Arcy Concession until 1932, there were further improvements in the techniques and apparatus used in petroleum engineering, important developments in the treatment of gas and a major innovation, the recycling of products surplus to immediate marketing requirements. Important aspects of this work received public acclamation in the papers delivered by members of the petroleum engineering staff to the First World Petroleum Congress held in London in July 1933.[27] Thus those who had seemed to be mad boffins, with their crazy schemes and Heath Robinson contraptions, had become recognised authorities, whose research, observations and application led to a totally automatic and enclosed oil production system with the oil invisible till its emergence as a specific product from the refinery ready for the customer. The advances in production technology were outstanding. The oilfield itself was massive by contemporary standards and perhaps nowhere else was there such a concentration of technical talent in such a self-contained community so exclusively engaged on such a large programme of work with so few distractions. The Fields Management under the encouragement of Jameson inspired by Cadman was practical and appreciative. A strong sense of purpose was present amongst those who lived and worked on site. The distinction between work and leisure was less noticeable than in a more usual office routine.

Gas had been a constant preoccupation in the Persian operations since the earliest days, when it was remarked that Masjid i-Suleimān 'all day and night smelt like a cataract of rotten eggs'.[28] By 1924 considerable improvements had been made in the recovery of gas, for Cadman stated that 12 000 tons of oil and 60 million cubic feet of gas were being extracted with practically no outward or visible sign of oil or smell of gas. This was the result of the flow system being operated in which

Technical activities: Years of endeavour and achievement 1918-1932

the producing wells are linked up from casing head to the receiving tanks at Tembi by a closed pipe system in which are incorporated high pressure gas separators on the field near the wells, and low pressure tank separators at Tembi. About one third volume of the total gas is led away from the high pressure separators by burning lines; the oil and residual gas passes on, under the influence of the reduced well-head pressures to two large separator tanks at Tembi.[29]

This flow system was then an improvement, but it was still wasteful and not particularly efficient. It was progressively improved from 1926 onwards with both high and low pressure separation systems. As Cadman realised 'the economic utilisation of fields gas is undoubtedly a very formidable problem, and its solution presents great difficulty'. W.L. Morgan, a gas expert from Standard Oil (NJ) who had gone out to Persia with Cadman in 1924 gave very useful advice. It was Gibson, however, who perfected the multi-stage gas separation plant, the first of which operated in 1929, as in Figure 10.4. The advantage was that the separation

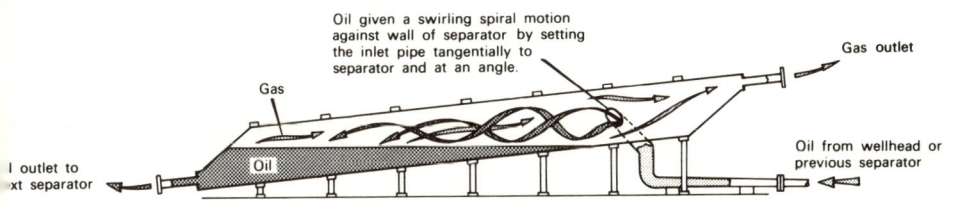

Figure 10.4 Inclined oil–gas separator 1930
Source: *Our Industry Petroleum* (British Petroleum Company Ltd, 1977), p. 138

and retention in successive stages of the volatile high fractions such as pentanes was as satisfactory as in conventional gasoline recovery plants, but far simpler in operation and more economic in capital and operating costs.[30] Further research by C.J. May and A. Laird indicated the optimum number of stages for various compositions of oil and the optimum pressure at which each stage should be controlled for the maximum recovery of some of the utilisable gases, resulting in the design of simple efficient horizontal cylindrical separators, particularly useful in high pressure oilfields[31].

The recycling of surplus products was a tremendous innovation, an admirable combination of practical requirements and theoretical considerations. The nature of Persian crude oil and the availability of better refining processes in 1928 meant that refining was out of balance with the market mix, leading to a surplus of fuel oil supplies in relation to rising benzine demand. There was therefore a dilemma for the Company of either reducing the price of fuel oil or storing it at a cost, in either case leading to a loss on sales, unless another solution could be found. About this time it began to be realised that although many of the technical staff believed cracks and fissures in the main limestone accounted for the largest volume, the porosity of the reservoir rock was not negligible.[32] In fact it was subsequently discovered in the mid-1930s that only some 10 per cent of the production of oil was from the cracks and fissures. Jameson, in particular, Gibson, and others, therefore argued that if the surplus fuel oil was pumped back to the field and injected through specially selected wells located high in the gas dome, it would make its way through the gas—oil level before being reabsorbed in the oil saturated limestone. In this way not only would the reservoir act as a storage but there would be the advantage of activating some of the lighter fractions of the crude oil.

In spite of some well-meaning but anxious opposition, fearful lest the pores and fissures be choked, the recycling of fuel oil was introduced in a carefully controlled manner in April 1929, initially at a rate not exceeding 400 000 tons a year. By 1931 the amount of fuel oil being recycled had doubled with its viscosity being reduced by gas treatment to facilitate its dispersal in the reservoir. Such an unprecedented practice was only possible in the light of the accumulated knowledge of all the characteristics of the reservoir. Its practical usefulness was very beneficial in the commercial circumstances of the Company. It was like a safety valve which bypassed unwanted fuel oil back to the reservoir, sensitive to market demands by regulating quantities accordingly, a very practical application of scientific data for industrial purposes. In 1930 a topping plant distillation unit for the removal of the volatile fractions from crude oil was built at Masjid i-Suleimān by which the fuel oil surplus to marketing requirements could be removed from the crude oil and directly injected into the reservoir, thus dispensing with the need to pump it back along the line from Ābādān. The recycling circuit was made tighter and more efficient. Between March and August 1931, 521 000 tons of fuel oil residue were recycled back to the oilfield. In May 1933 a comprehensive report concluded that recycling was extremely advantageous with no adverse side-effects on the productive functioning of the oilfields.[33]

An incidental but significant economic consequence of recycling was the enhanced value of the oil tonnage exported in relation to the royalties paid to the Persian Government, which were based on exportation not production. Since exports were mostly at this time in the form of refined products rather than crude oil, the return on sales of a higher valued product like motor spirit in comparison with fuel oil, was much greater, but the royalty payable was the same.

It is unnecessary to go into detail but it would be inexcusable to ignore the provision of the basic services upon which a great industrial

Technical activities: Years of endeavour and achievement 1918-1932

undertaking relies. The civil engineering activities of the Company were essential in the virtual absence of local contractors for anything but the simplest of operations. The erection of all kinds of buildings, the construction of bridges, jetties and railway tracks, the making of roads on a large scale were needed. Water supplies had always been a serious problem not only because of their scarcity but also because of their corrosive contents. A major achievement in 1926 was the siting of a pumping house on a sliding track by the River Kārūn at Godar Landar to allow for the differences on levels at various times of the year. This supplied good water throughout the fields area. Ābādān had its own supplies for cooling, steam and other purposes. Power supplies were developed on a massive basis, as none existed at all. The Company had to become self-sufficient because there was no provincial or national administration capable of providing the facilities at that time until the centralising measures and authority of Rizā Shāh in the late 1920s began to provide the rudiments of an industrial infrastructure on a limited scale.

'The Golden Stairs' road to Gach Sārān 1925

Technical activities: Years of endeavour and achievement 1918-1932

The water pumping station at Godar Landar 1926

Technical activities: Years of endeavour and achievement 1918-1932

Transport at Masjid i-Suleimān 1924

(b) Success in exploration

The years 1923-29 were vintage ones for exploration. In the previous five years the geological branch had grown in numbers and its activities had widened in scope, but it was indifferently administered, suffered from undue individualism and lacked professional cohesion. It had not been successful in finding new fields. From 1923 onwards, however, it was more coherently organised and had matured in experience. It had been difficult for the chief geologist, Lister James, to be engaged in field work and at the same time be responsible for planning exploration programmes in a number of countries (see Chapter 12), and cope with all the requirements of his staff. Cadman recognised the problem and, from his appointment in 1923 as the director for the fields, refineries and geological department, he was able to coordinate the technical activities of the Company from a central position. In mid-July H.T. Mayo was appointed principal geologist in Persia to coordinate all exploratory activities there.

Technical activities: Years of endeavour and achievement 1918-1932

Professor Hugo de Böckh (left) and G.M. Lees 1925

Yet the most important geological appointment was made earlier in 1923, that of the eminent Hungarian geologist, Professor Hugo de Böckh, formerly of the University of Budapest, as geological adviser. It was an inspired if controversial choice, which galvanised the geological function and gave it a confidence and direction which had been lacking. He did not

Technical activities: Years of endeavour and achievement 1918-1932

replace Lister James, with whom, though quite different in character, there was a warm personal relationship. De Böckh was a well-informed able field geologist of outstanding stamina, confidence and presence, who brought a new geological perspective to Persia. He encouraged the younger geologists by his commitment and knowledge. His surveys were grand progresses not furtive forays.

De Böckh's strength lay in personal example, in the spoken rather than the written word, for, although he was fluent in English, he was impatient in presenting his conclusions, which were not always logically or concisely expressed. His reports, therefore, tended to be a miscellany of observations and inferences, imperious in manner. Occasionally ideas were stated as facts, when they were only suggestions. His judgements were sometimes more sweeping than was geologically justifiable and he was wrong about Arabia and Iraq, but if style reflects the man there was no visible inconsistency. Thus his important report on his remarkable survey of 1924-25, which was his major contribution to the Company's exploratory programme in Persia, ended with the statement that 'if there is any larger oil field left in Persia, which we are fully entitled to believe, then it must be contained in the areas recommended and described above. It is a matter of chance how many of them may be proved to be really good fields.'[34]

His assertiveness was justified, as, out of his six 'immediate' recommendations, four proved ultimately to be major discoveries, but qualified by the fact that eight fields were later discovered in areas which he rated poor or ignored. De Böckh was aware of the value of geophysical aids to exploration and he had early experimented with them in Hungary. Though not employing such techniques in his two Persian surveys, probably because of the limited time at his disposal and the vast distances he covered, he encouraged their application by others. In 1923 the Company engaged its first geophysicist, W.R. MacDonald, who, with J.H. Jones and R. Davies, conducted the first geophysical survey in Persia near Ahwāz in 1924, applying the principles of physics to the study of sub-surface geology through measuring the variations in the magnetic and density properties of underground formation and so establish the existence of sedimentary basins where oil might have accumulated. By 1930 Jones, who had succeeded MacDonald as chief geophysicist, had undertaken his own seismic refraction parties using sonar techniques with geophones spaced out at equal intervals to establish the trends of buried anticlines, the first generally reliable method of detecting the Asmari limestone under irregularly folded strata rock.

In February 1923 Cadman had been reluctant to authorise a further programme of testing outside the main field at Masjid i-Suleimān until it

Technical activities: Years of endeavour and achievement 1918-1932

had been arranged 'to devote at least one, possibly two more seasons to intensive survey and to employ a much larger geological staff than is at present available in Persia'. This intensive survey was to be the responsibility of de Böckh. He made a preliminary reconnaissance on his first visit to Persia in the winter of 1923-24, on which was based his more comprehensive survey the following year. He returned with an impressive entourage including Lister James, Richardson and G.M. Lees, a geologist of great promise, who had recently joined the Company from Imperial College after a distinguished war service and a spell as a political officer in Kurdistān. In determining his priorities de Böckh had the advantage, not only of his own observations, but also of conferences with the geologists and the benefit of the knowledge contained in earlier reports. This was important as successful exploration is largely dependent on the accumulation of previous experience on which to base new findings. This gathering of information, topographical no less than the geological had been an important feature of the exploration function. Nearly all the geologists were at one time or another employed on mapping, allowing them together to compare and exchange ideas and information, so helping by their individual expertise and experience to solve the problems that confronted all those engaged in exploration and production activities in Persia. This spirit of professional cooperation in the Fields, (rather than an isolated kind of study mentality) was encouraged by de Böckh.

As a result of his survey, de Böckh was able to mention specifically some localities, to which he gave prospective ratings. Out of those recommended for immediate tests, Haft Kel, Āghā Jārī, Pāzanun, Gach Sārān, Zeloi and Gach Khalaj, only at the first locality was oil discovered while de Böckh remained with the Company, though it was K. Washington Gray and T.F. Williamson on Mayo's advice who actually chose the site before de Böckh had visited it. At Gach Sārān the first well was spudded (drilled) in on 19 April 1926 and oil struck with the third well in November 1928. Because of geological difficulties, the coming in of Haft Kel, and the effects of the Depression, further drilling was abandoned in October 1930, after five wells had been drilled. The first well was spudded in at Āghā Jārī on 6 November 1926 and later caught fire before being deepened to 6070 feet and abandoned. At Pāzanun a well was spudded in on 22 September 1926 before being suspended at 5320 feet in October 1930. Later these three areas were proved to be notable fields though Pāzanun was essentially a gas/light distillate field.

Near Zeloi three wells were drilled without success between 1925 and 1929, but the nearby field of Lālī was discovered when drilling was resumed in 1937 and the second well struck oil in July 1938, though it was not until June 1946 that it was proved commercially. No oil was dis-

Technical activities: Years of endeavour and achievement 1918-1932

covered at Gach Khalaj. At the least, as a result of de Böckh's efforts the Company was no longer dependent on a single field. The Company's exploratory activities in Persia 1901-32 had been expensive and intensive.[35] Some 400 000 square miles out of the total concessionary area of 480 000 square miles had been examined, some 150 000 square miles in detail, during 382 surveys in 141 different areas, 23 sites had been tested and 51 wells drilled, excluding Masjid i-Suleimān and Haft Kel. The footage drilled totalled 139 659 feet at a cost of some £3 000 000 (see Table 10.2). As seen from Appendix 10.2, costs at Masjid i-Suleimān and Haft Kel amounted to some £500 000.

In the long term the Company was sure that its concessionary area was potentially rich in oil resources and that it could plan its policy accordingly. The exploratory work undertaken in this period underpinned the growth of the Company in the decades that followed, till it lost its exclusive concessionary rights in Persia in 1951. It established the reputation of its geologists, whose professional abilities have been a prominent feature of the Company's success. It assured the foundations of the Persian oil industry.

4 THE ĀBĀDĀN REFINERY

The outstanding successes of exploration and production did not apply to the refinery at Ābādān. During the war it had functioned with difficulty and the demands of war service for the Mesopotamian expeditionary force had increased the already formidable burdens on the management, who just concentrated on keeping going. The expansion in output had been achieved at a cost, as Garrow noticed on his visit in 1919 when he commented that 'the Abadan area is unquestionably congested ... overloaded with refinery extension, barge and tanker work'.[36] He suggested freezing output 'until we have every department, including shipping and marketing, in thorough proportion all round, properly organized as there is, in my opinion, sufficient work ahead of Abadan in construction work to last them at least two years'. Nichols too on his visit in 1920 was aghast at 'the appalling condition in which some of the material had reached the site due to inefficient storage, bad packing and general rough handling'. For Nichols there was a different priority, 'we have always had to aim at the maximum throughput, let us now organise and organise, and whilst still maintaining that throughput, aim at economy of running and so on'.[37] It was, however, a large refinery with an industrial momentum of its own and required more than just exhortation to remedy its defects. It was still limited by the nature of its plant to

Technical activities: Years of endeavour and achievement 1918-1932

refining 65 per cent of its output as fuel oil and limited quantities of benzine and kerosine.

In the early twenties much attention was paid to providing better facilities, accommodation, workshops, jetties, the utilities of power and light, security, medical care, lighterage, etc. No comprehensive plan had been submitted for Ābādān's development. The productive capacity of Masjid i-Suleimān was uncertain and it was debatable whether it was right to rely exclusively on Persia, particularly if there were imponderable concessionary perils ahead and whilst exploration was being carried on elsewhere. In 1923 Lloyd was advocating that 'the obvious place for any extensions of the Refinery seems to me to be India. There you have the advantage of much cheaper labour and better facilities, and also a large existing trade in Fuel Oil'.[38] Indeed he went so far as to suggest that 'it certainly seems advisable that whenever possible all capital construction of a permanent nature should be constructed outside Persia, until an extension of the Concession has been obtained'. Technical and economic, not political reasons, ultimately decided the fate of Ābādān. The 'balance' of products had to be maintained in relation to market demand and productive proximity, though shipping, as at Ābādān, was expensive due to the narrow channels and the need for lightering.

Nevertheless, the state of the refinery was very unsatisfactory, caused by inadequate management struggling to bring new plans into operation, whilst coping with a backlog of imperfect maintenance. The managing agents' system had singularly failed to coordinate the different aspects of management. The role of the chemist was virtually neglected and so the performance of the refinery suffered in consequence. When Neilson was posted to London in 1921, two joint works managers were appointed, which really only increased confusion and uncertainty, until L.F. Bayne became the sole works manager in 1924. By the end of the war refinery throughput was about 1 000 000 tons a year. Within four years it had virtually doubled, but between 1922 and 1923 expectations were disappointed, falling in 1923 by about 700 000 tons and not realised till 1925. This shortfall reacted unfavourably on marketing prospects. (For refinery throughput and product yields see Table 10.3.) In late 1922 there was a disastrous fire, which meant that refinery throughput for 1922-23 hardly exceeded that of the previous year. The plant was suffering from extensive deterioration with an adverse affect on performance. Andrew Campbell, then manager of refineries branch, on a visit to Ābādān in late 1923, described the refinery as 'a crippled plant which will take some time yet before it is brought up to the same new standards as the Fields and Pipeline' and noted that its various units were out of balance.[39]

Table 10.3. Ābādān Refinery throughput and production 1919–32

(long tons 000s)

	Through-put	Benzine	%	Kerosine	%	Crude distillate	%	Fuel† gas oils	%	Other products	%	Loss	%
1919–20	1 167	203	17	140	12	—	—	742	64	—	—	82	7
1920–21	1 534	333	22	134	9	—	—	970	63	—	—	97	6
1921–22	1 780	394	22	163	9	—	—	1 138	64	—	—	85	5
1922–23	1 886	349	19	142	8	78	4	1 217	65	—	—	100	5
1923–24	2 138	*223	10	125	6	334	16	1 334	62	—	—	122	6
1924–25	2 890	310	11	181	6	326	11	1 920	66	—	—	153	5
1925–26	2 945	363	12	197	7	277	9	1 970	67	—	—	138	5
1926–27	3 125	409	13	192	6	331	11	2 060	66	—	—	133	4
1927–28	3 286	531	16	228	7	252	8	2 137	65	—	—	138	4
1928 (9 mo.)	2 938	694	24	289	10	1	—	1 876	64	—	—	78	3
1929	4 156	1 156	28	359	9	13	—	2 676	64	—	—	55	1
1930	4 547	1 131	25	456	10	20	—	2 902	64	—	—	38	1
1931	4 388	1 166	27	370	8	74	2	2 631	60	84	2	63	1
1932	4 979	1 066	21	380	8	—	—	2 429	49	1 054	21	50	1

Notes: na not available
  * refined benzine only, previous to 1923–24 figures include unrefined benzine
  † cracking stock + process oils

Source: BP AC 21

Technical activities: Years of endeavour and achievement 1918-1932

It was not only the state of the plant that was unsatisfactory at Ābādān. Labour relations too were suffering from neglect. The town itself, administered until 1924 by Shaykh Khaz'al, was cramped, unsanitary and lacking the facilities for a large and expanding population of differing nationalities and creeds whose customs were not always accorded the toleration which in such a society is requisite. To this artificial settlement which owed its existence to the presence of the refinery had been attracted a variety of local traders and unskilled labourers upon whom was superimposed a changing layer of Indian workers and artisans on contract, living in their own quarters, and a small European staff on three-year terms of service. War-time exigencies and the relative fewness of numbers kept discontent to a minimum, but conditions and the cost of living subsequently provoked protests from all sections of the workforce, particularly among the Indian employees amongst whom some semi-organised political agitation had broken out, as a consequence of the bitter resentment in India following the Amritsar riots of April 1919. On 9 December 1920, the Indian imported labour, some 3000 strong, went on strike and Nichols, who had only just arrived in Ābādān on a visit, was obliged to concede their demands for an 80 per cent increase in wages and other improvements. The following day Persian and Arab labourers also struck. Their demands too were accepted.

As a result of this experience, an overdue reconsideration of the terms and conditions of contracts for all the workforce was made. It is significant that the militancy was confined to Ābādān, for no such action took place elsewhere amongst the Company's operations in Persia. Nevertheless a comprehensive solution was required. With some modesty in view of the immensity of the task undertaken for the first time in the Company's administration in Persia, Nichols reported on his visit that

the wages, working and living conditions of every man jack in the Company's service have been investigated. They have all been classified according to their employment, and wages have been standardised everywhere. The general service has been immeasurably improved, and there is some sort of system now. When it is remembered that over 15 000 employees are concerned, and the various nature of this employment, it will be appreciated that this has been some task.

He had not solved all the problems for some, like accommodation, married quarters, medical services, leisure amenities, exchange rates and the sale of discharge certificates of Indian employees, needed more attention.

Eighteen months later in May 1922 another strike of Indian skilled labour broke out, but after a failure to reach a settlement with the leaders, the men were repatriated to India. It left the refinery seriously undermanned, but it provided an opportunity for Persians to fill the

Technical activities: Years of endeavour and achievement 1918-1932

Young Persian apprentices at Masjid i-Suleimān 1924

vacancies, as it was decided not to fill the positions with such labour from India, though Indian clerical staff, orderlies, process staff and cooks were still employed. Gradually more Persians were trained in technical trades and some were sent on university courses in the United Kingdom. A technical institute was built to provide a variety of skills. In 1924 yet another strike of Indian labour occurred, which the Company was better able to handle because of the success in training Persians. Gradually the number of Indians was reduced and that of Persians increased, a much more satisfactory state of affairs (see Table 10.1). The state of industrial relations, the pattern of Persian employment and the administrative organisation during the Company's concessionary period in Persia to 1951 will be more fully treated in a separate chapter in the next volume.

The expatriate community provided its own social life in a region where the countryside offered little to attract the European except mountaineering, riding or bird watching. So concert parties, amateur theatricals, sports and other forms of amusement and entertainment were organised voluntarily under the watchful eye and assistance of the Company. It was usually good natured, but occasionally the petty jealousies seemingly inseparable from such a life enlivened the tea parties and bars, but there was little real social discontent once the housing situation had improved, more married quarters became available and better medical facilities were provided.

Technical activities: Years of endeavour and achievement 1918-1932

A football match at Masjid i-Suleimān 1924

A regatta on the lake by the Tembi power station 1924

Technical activities: Years of endeavour and achievement 1918-1932

A fancy dress party at Ābādān 1924

Medical officers and hospital staff with Dr Young, centre left 1926

Technical activities: Years of endeavour and achievement 1918-1932

In the absence at that time of comparable Persian company, since few educated Persians were attracted by the opportunities available or the living conditions experienced in the humid climate of Ābādān, it was regrettable that aloofness rather than companionship came to characterise the social relations of the two peoples. Moreover that informality between the sexes which is publicly usual in European society did not then exist in Persia, a Moslem country. Later, when more educated Persians went to live in Khūzistān, there was resentment at what appeared to be the imperious manner in which they were treated, but nevertheless over the years many lasting friendships were made.

Difficulties continued over the refining of benzine and kerosine. In August 1921 the large-scale operation of the hypochlorite process for benzine began at the refinery. This too was dogged by misfortune over electricity supplies, failures of electrodes, impurities in supplies of brine and corrosion to the plant. In 1924 the troublesome electrolytic method of manufacturing hypochlorite solution was replaced by the simpler and cheaper method already in use at Llandarcy, on the advice of the research centre at Sunbury, of dissolving bleaching powder in water. The desulphurisation of kerosine by filtering through roasted bauxite was also attended by breakdowns in the plant, problems of handling and insufficient temperature in the furnaces. Indeed the demoralised management at Ābādān, according to Lloyd in 1923, 'seem to be agreed that it is impossible to satisfactorily desulphurise kerosene with bauxite'.[40] There were mistakes, but it required special training at Sunbury and Llandarcy for C.E. Spearing, the plant operator, before the process was working satisfactorily. Spearing had joined Sunbury in 1921 and much later became general manager of refineries department. Jameson, who had been appointed general manager, fields and refinery, expected early in 1924 that 'by the end of the year quite a different spirit will pervade the place and that the old departmental feeling will have been dispelled'.[41] This lack of effective coordination was acknowledged to be a serious defect at the senior management conference on the Persian operations held in Cairo in March 1924 summoned by Cadman. It was agreed that 'the course of past events, largely unavoidable, has brought about a position in which there is now a regrettable lack of balance and correlation between the refinery proper and its various auxiliary establishments'.[42]

The most penetrating comments on Ābādān were made after Cadman's visit there in November 1924. It was the first comprehensive technical appraisal of the refinery made by the Company and laid the foundations for most subsequent developments. Critically but reasonably, he reported that:

The Refinery is an impressive sight and occupies, with storage tanks, jetties, the

Technical activities: Years of endeavour and achievement 1918-1932

bungalow accommodation for European Staff and the village for native employees an area of about 3000 acres.

The total cost of the Company's property on the island is in the neighbourhood of six million sterling, and the monthly wage bill for the present staff of 366 Europeans and 9000 Natives is about £75 000.

As is well known, this refinery for a very long time after its inception was virtually a war centre. Its early growth therefore took place under circumstances which could not well have been more discouraging and confusing to those then responsible, and it is much to their credit that so much was done in the face of so many difficulties. With such an initial handicap, however, it is not surprising that it is still very far from being an effective unit in the general organisation, having regard to the magnitude of present-day throughput.

During the last 5 years adjustment under post-war conditions to any settled form of policy, has been lamentably slow, and the Refinery, as it exists today, is far from being stabilised on a sound profit-earning basis.

I must strongly emphasise the need - exemplified by all that can be seen at Abadan today - for planning the broad outlines of refinery policy of the future ahead of actual mechanical and scientific development. In the case of Abadan the monthly throughput has practically doubled as between 1920 and 1924 (34 000 000 gallons to nearly 65 000 000). It is doubtless the case the momentum of the war 'push' reinforced by the attractive market conditions of 1919 and 1920, led to bench construction being pushed far in advance of all the needed collateral equipment. Hence it is not strange that Abadan, as it exists today, is not a refinery in the proper sense of the word, but merely a gigantic topping or distillation plant, producing petrol, unrefined kerosine and fuel oil. In addition, the means by which these products are obtained still leave much room for technical improvement and working economies. The criterion of a first-class refinery is its capacity for reducing crude oil into terms of its most valuable constituents by the most economical processes, and hence we can obviously not yet regard Abadan with any degree of equanimity.[43]

Cadman was scathing about 'a state of chaos', caused by badly designed plant. He was scornful about the design of the bauxite plant, 'wondering if the designers are mentally defective'. Garrow on his visit in 1919, had been surprised that the managers of the refinery and fields and the pipeline superintendent had not met each other because 'the closer the intimacy between these heads of departments, the greater will be the cooperation, which will all be to the good of the work'. Cadman too was disappointed at the lack of liaison between London and Ābādān. He insisted on 'unification of engineering control, the fullest possible application of engineering principles to the Company's technical operations, and closer contact, particularly on all technical sides between London and Persia'. Thereafter Cadman instituted regular annual conferences involving technical management in London and Persia. Collaboration, not isolation was his managerial touchstone.

Technical activities: Years of endeavour and achievement 1918-1932

It was clear, nevertheless, that more was wrong than just the management, which had certainly improved after Jameson had been transferred from Fields and given overall responsibility for Ābādān. He was accompanied by H.Y.V. Jackson, the chief engineer in Fields, whose experience was broader than that limited to service in Burma which most managers had hitherto possessed. E.H.O. Elkington, who had served in the Indian army, after joining the Company had been posted to Fields, was put in charge of administration. Thus was new blood, new ideas and a renewed sense of purpose brought to Ābādān. The refinery was out of date, its equipment virtually obsolete. It was metaphorically little more than a gigantic pot for boiling up crude oil. Ten of its fifteen benches were old-fashioned stills with a combined throughput of 4800 tons a day, four others together had an output of 4100 tons a day, but a later unit to be commissioned, bench 30, had a capacity of 1500 tons a day. An idea of the earlier kind of benches used can be seen in Figure 10.5. None of them was preheated or able to achieve any precise degree of fractionation of distillate into regular narrow cuts, as was done in standard later practice of the kind shown in Figure 10.6. The first so-called 'fraction' to be separated from the crude oil was the same in 1924 as it had been since 1912, ORD, once-run distillate, a semi-refined benzine, which then had to be redistilled in a further bench in order to separate out the benzine and kerosine products. It was inefficient and uneconomic.

During 1925 there was much discussion about the need for reliably fractionated distillates in relation to the properties of Persian crude oil and the requirements of the market, the elimination of wasteful practices and the proper economics of scale appropriate for large throughputs.[44] An important result of the installation of proper fractionating columns, which were supplied by the American contractors, Badger & Co., at the crude oil benches of the refinery (the principle of which is illustrated in Figure 10.7), was that by September 1928 there was no further need for two distillations to take place. The Board was informed that this 'completed an important phase in the evolution of the Company's refinery and distribution policy'.[45] The change in the scale of the operations can be gauged by comparing the original complete refinery programme of two benches, which had a throughput of 260 tons a day with a single bench (no. 35) capacity of 3800 tons a day in 1928. In 1929 the first four thermal cracking units of the American Cross design, of which two had already been installed in Llandarcy in 1926, were ordered costing some £2 000 000, from M.W. Kellogg, the American contractors, for the processing of some 1 000 000 tons of fuel oil a year to yield 440 000 tons of benzine for improved quality motor spirit.[46] These were finally all commissioned by November 1931.[47]

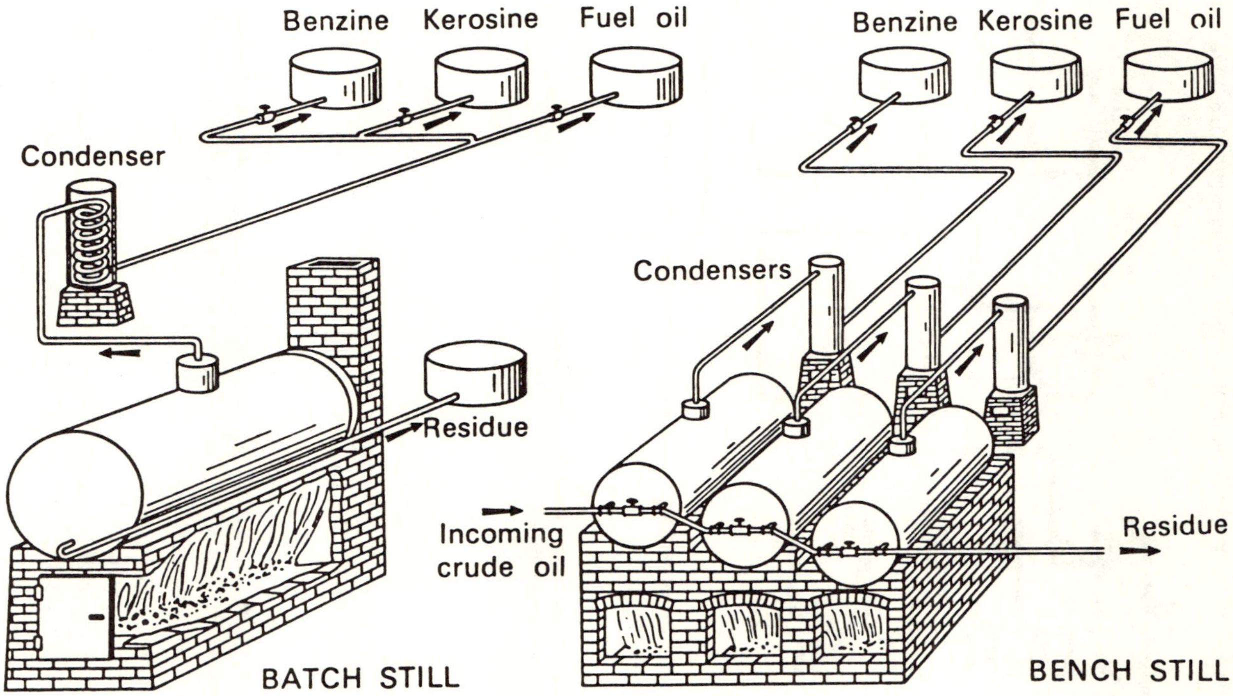

Figure 10.5 Batch and bench stills c. 1912
Source: After Kendall Beaton, *Enterprise in Oil. A History of Shell in the United States* (New York, 1957), p. 86

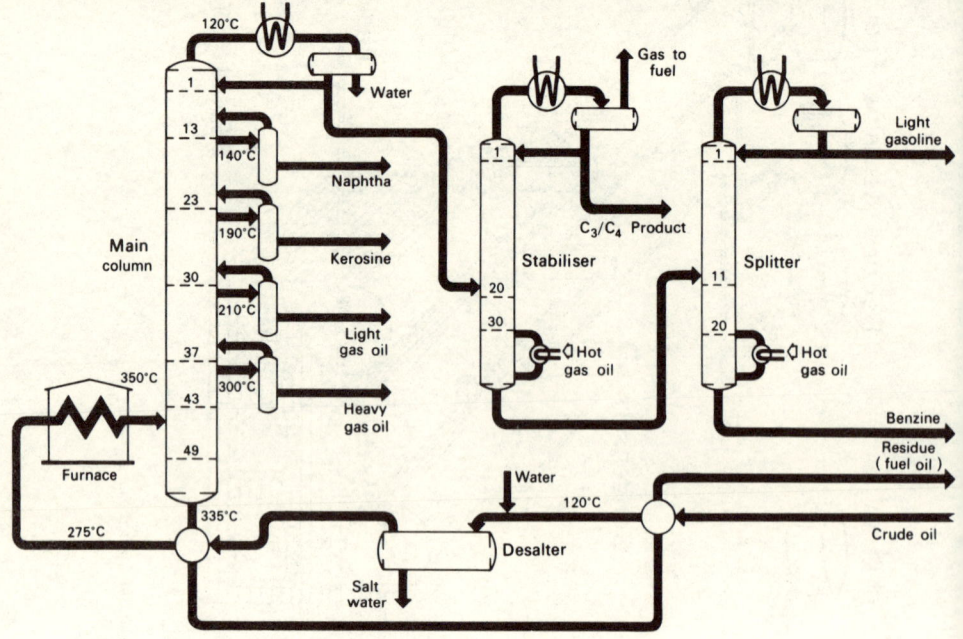

Technical activities: Years of endeavour and achievement 1918-1932

Figure 10.6 Crude oil distillation
Source: *Our Industry Petroleum* (British Petroleum Company Ltd, 1977), P. 231

When Cadman again visited Ābādān in January 1929 he was much impressed with it, 'so different from the condition I found on previous occasions'.[48] He generously praised H.Y.V. Jackson the works manager, a very talented engineer, who had died from smallpox a fortnight before Cadman's arrival, recording that 'much of the great improvement and development in Abadan Refinery stands as a tribute to his memory'. No longer apparently isolated from the main operations, Ābādān had become an integral part of the whole technical operation. Its inefficiency had improved over the years which was reflected in its lower operating costs, detailed in Table 10.4 along with comparable figures for the refineries at Llandarcy and Grangemouth. To some extent making valid assessments of such costs is difficult because of a lack of complete consistency in the items included in the data, but a good general idea is at the least possible.

By 1930 refinery throughput was more than double that of 1923-24, 4 550 000 tons a year. Ābādān yielded 1 130 000 tons of motor spirit, 456 000 tons of kerosine and 2 900 000 tons of fuel and diesel oil, (see Table 10.6 for detailed volumes and percentages). In the same year 635 tankers shipped 5 500 000 tons of crude oil and products. The improvements and the construction of new storage tanks, loading systems, extra

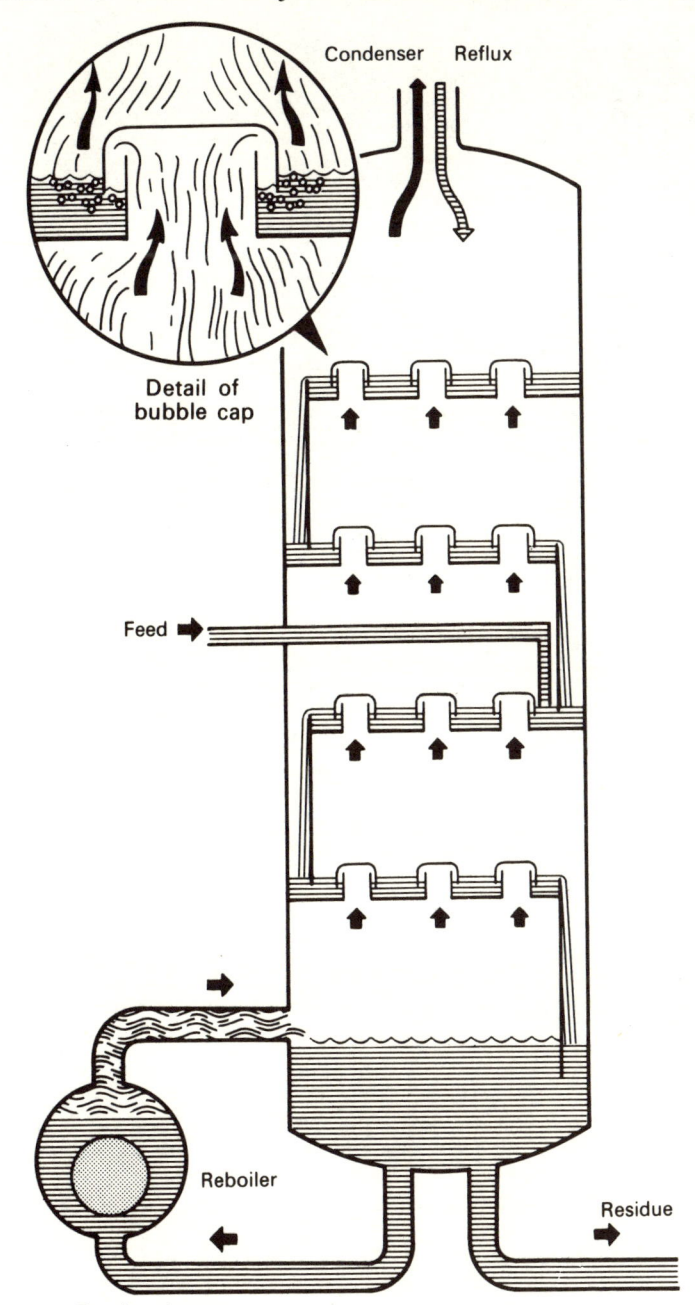

Technical activities: Years of endeavour and achievement 1918-1932

Figure 10.7 Fractionating tower
Source: *Our Industry Petroleum* (British Petroleum Company Ltd, 1977), p. 230

Table 10.4. *Anglo-Persian Oil Company group refinery costs per ton 1923-28*

(a) Ābādān

	1923–24	1924–25	1925–26	1926–27	1927–28	1928 (9 months)
Throughput (tons)	2 138 000	2 890 000	2 945 000	3 125 000	3 286 000	2 938 000
Distillation and finishing treatments	5s 2.38d	5s 1.11d	4s 7.35d	3s 9.96d	3s 5.06d	3s 4.15d
Finishing products, pumping, storing and transporting	0s 7.5 d	0s 3.33d	0s 2.54d	—	—	0s 1.11d
Indirect and general establishment charges	4s 10.66d	4s 3.30d	5s 0.39d	4s 6.37d	5s 0.69d	3s 5.19d
Total cost per ton	10s 8.61d	9s 7.74d	9s 10.28d	8s 4.33d	8s 5.75d	6s 10.45d

(b) Llandarcy

	1923–24	1924–25	1925–26	1926–27	1927–28
Throughput (tons)	910 757	1 165 876	1 080 252	1 111 430	1 199 300
Distillation charges	2s 8.76d	3s 4.91d	3s 10.48d	3s 9.04d	3s 2.34d
Chemical and finishing treatment	4s 9.31d	5s 2.92d	3s 10.34d	3s 8.52d	3s 5.9 d
Pumping and storage charges	0s 0.73d	0s 0.59d	0s 0.84d	0s 0.81d	0s 0.98d
General establishment and administration charges	4s 2.93d	3s 9.15d	3s 10.20d	3s 9.93d	3s 7.01d
Total cost per ton	11s 9.73d	9s 5.57d	11s 7.86d	10s 11.63d	10s 4.23d

Table 10.4. (cont.)

(c) Grangemouth	1923–24	1924–25	1925–26	1926–27	1927–28
Throughput (tons)	—	263 637	317 249	355 604	379 069
Distillation charges	—	1s 0.21d	0s 9.21d	0s 11.36d	0s 7.96d
Chemical and finishing treatments	—	2s 1.25d	1s 9.45d	1s 5.96d	1s 4.90d
Pumping and storage charges	—	0s 0.56d	—	—	—
General establishment and administrative charges	—	3s 1.80d	2s 5.54d	2s 3.33d	2s 0.41d
Total cost per ton	—	6s 3.82d	5s 0.20d	4s 8.59d	4s 1.27d

Sources: BP 4.c.6353
BP 4.c.6357
BP 4.c.6358

Technical activities: Years of endeavour and achievement 1918-1932

steam and power generation, water pumping, accommodation and amenities reached a peak in 1930 when 110 staff and 5500 workers were employed on them. The volume of construction materials reached 183 000 tons and the capital cost of refinery construction and improvement on hand was estimated at £2 000 000. A floating dock had been installed in 1928 and an aircraft landing strip was added in 1929 to what was already becoming one of the largest refineries in the world. After 1930 drastic economies were made as a result of the work already completed and the effects of the Depression. The labour force fell to 7500 in 1932. Imports of refinery equipment, with most planned construction work completed, dropped to 20 000 tons.

Ābādān, which was low, humid and hot, lacking the fresh climate and geographical interest of Fields, was never an easy place in which to work and live. The variety of people employed and the diversity of their occupations complicated social relations. It was a huge industrial enterprise of much complexity, remote from the main centres of national activity. So there grew up in it a fairly self-conscious alien community in an unrepresentative Persian environment living rather apart from the disparate Persian society present. The expatriate body, self-centred, and never deeply rooted, with its social distinctions and Company grades, had a sense of its

The ending of a shift, Ābādān 1926

Technical activities: Years of endeavour and achievement 1918-1932

Aerial view of Ābādān 1930

own self-importance, as it lived and worked and played together. By 1930 the refinery had been re-equipped and properly organised. It was no longer the weakest, but an indispensable and properly functioning link in the industrial chain of interconnected and interdependent activities from the well head to the petrol pump.

5 THE PIPELINE

As the Company was satisfying the demands of the market, production was increased and it became necessary to expand the capacity of the pipeline. At the end of the First World War the cost and scarcity of pipe made it preferable to install pumping plant rather than enlarge the pipeline.[49] So it was decided to erect three intermediate boosting stations between Tembi and Ābādān at 30 to 40 mile intervals located near the River Kārūn for boiler and water condensing supplies. Each station was originally planned to contain two pumping units, which would ensure adequate standby capacity for maintenance or breakdowns. The stations were situated near the small riverside villages of Mullāsānī, Kut 'Abdallāh and Dorquain and set up as self-contained small communities with brick houses, their own electricity supplies, power and water, clubs, medical dispensaries and sports amenities. The river steamers plying on the river made frequent calls and the desert tracks were passable for vehicles in the

Technical activities: Years of endeavour and achievement 1918-1932

The pipeline on the Imām Rizā slope c.1924

dry weather, but communications in the rainy season were liable to be cut off for weeks at a time.

An interesting and important innovation initiated by the Company's engineer was the use of large centrifugal pumps directly driven by condensing steam turbines. Normally for this kind of purpose reciprocating pumps had been used in the United States. So this was a major change in pumping technology, later to become general practice throughout the world in pipeline pumping stations.[50] The main advantage for operations in Persia was in the lower mechanical maintenance required, a major factor when skilled labour was scarce and continuous service required, so offsetting the admittedly lower hydraulic efficiency of centrifugal pumps and their higher fuel consumption. Tank storage for crude oil at the wells and the refinery was kept to a minimum by a careful adjustment of production to refinery requirements. Moreover, until the mid-1920s continuous operation was essential, as it was impossible to close in some of the larger older wells, because they had not been fitted with high pressure main valves to regulate the oil flow. Indeed some, like F7, had to be mudded off (shut-in) when their casing had become so corroded that there was a danger of their fittings not holding under pressure and blowing off, allowing the well to run wild.

Technical activities: Years of endeavour and achievement 1918-1932

The capacity of the pipeline was increased during 1920-23 to 5 000 000 tons yearly by 'looping', (that is adding pipe in the sections where throughput was restricted), because of growing demand. So in 1920 56 miles of 10 in. pipe was laid, in 1922 37 miles of 12 in. pipe, the first time such a diameter used in Persia, and in 1923 39 miles of 10 in. pipe. The use of mechanical transport had been developed for pipeline purposes including track vehicles with 10 ton trailers and six-wheeled 12 ton Scammel lorries. A 2 ft. 6 in. gauge railway from Dar-i-Khazineh to Tembi was also constructed during this period. A new pumping station was erected on the left bank of the Tembi River to separate it from the main power station for Fields on the opposite bank, to minimise fire risks. More pumping units were added to the boosting stations and the lay-out arranged to reduce fire hazards and facilitate operations and maintenance. By 1924 each of the four stations at Tembi, Mullāsānī, Kut 'Abdallāh and Dorquain were equipped with four identical pumping sets, which were mostly in service at the end of the concessionary period in 1951, so reliable did they prove.

In 1928 pipeline throughput was 5 700 000 tons, but with the discovery of oil at Haft Kel in 1927 plans were made to lay a line from the new field to join the pipeline at Kut 'Abdallāh. At first no pumping station was needed at Haft Kel itself, because well-head pressure was sufficient to force the oil to flow to tanks located at heights above the field elevated high enough for

Turbine-driven centrifugal pump, Tembi station 1926

Technical activities: Years of endeavour and achievement 1918-1932

the oil to flow by gravity down the line. 67 miles of 12 in. pipe were laid between Haft Kel and Kut ʿAbdallāh and two pumping units, twice the size of the existing units, were placed at Kut ᶜAbdallāh and Dorquain, during 1929 and 1930. In 1929 the pipeline was required to recycle the fuel oil surplus to marketing requirements from the refinery storage tanks back to the fields. No particular difficulty was experienced, except in cold weather when the viscosity of the oil had to be kept down by reheating in Ābādān and at Tul i-Khayyat. Recycling and the later improved practice of injecting separated gasoline from the gas separators on Fields into the crude for Ābādān, or even batches of 'fuel oil' in a 'plug', a set volume of oil to the refinery with a reduced content of lighter fractions, increased the need for vigilance.

The inclusion of volatile fractions in the crude necessitated special measures to prevent gas leaking from the suction glands of the pumps. The pipeline system, therefore, was more than usually elaborate to cope with the demands made upon it, including provision against corrosion from the natural elements and soil conditions, in both of which there were considerable variations and temperatures between below freezing point and 170°F. In the late twenties, welding was beginning to be used in maintenance but earlier all pipe joints were screwed couplings. Pipe corrosion occurred after only two or three years of being buried in the soil and in 1931 it was

River transport and offloading facilities at Dar-i-Khazineh 1926

Technical activities: Years of endeavour and achievement 1918-1932

Railway marshalling yards, Dar-i-Khazineh 1926

decided to lift all pipe and place it on sleepers, zig zagging it to counter the problems of expansion and contraction. Above the surface atmospheric corrosion was insignificant.

The pipeline organisation was called upon to operate the main lines of communication to the oilfields from the coast. It handled the transportation of material and personnel by river and road within its area. A fleet of river steamers and barges had to be maintained, roads surfaced, vehicles serviced, telephone and telegraphic lines operated. The headquarters was established in Ahwāz, the nerve centre, to ensure the security and safe operations of the pipeline. A company area was developed including warehouses and docks for the transportation of material, workshops, offices, a housing estate for all grades and nationalities, complete with amenities and facilities for clubs and hospitals. In 1930 employees engaged in pipeline activities numbered 3300 with some 100 British staff. These activities had become an essential function in the Company's operations in Persia.

6 THE DREDGING OF THE SHATT-AL-'ARAB

The lightering of tankers at the bar of the Shatt-al-'Arab below Ābādān was a time consuming and dangerous operation. It restricted shipping to low draughts, thereby greatly increasing costs.

Technical activities: Years of endeavour and achievement 1918-1932

The dredging of the Shatt-al-'Arab estuary was the subject of protracted negotiations between the Company and the British Government, an issue debated between government departments, a matter affecting different competing shipping concerns, a controversy concerning rival marine experts, a diplomatic focus of interest involving different governments and a maze of bureaucratic indecision for over two decades.[51] It was two German engineers who first suggested dredging the bars of the Shatt-al-'Arab in 1910 in connection with a possible extension of the Constantinople−Baghdad railway to Basra. In January 1911 the Company proposed to the British consul and the Turkish Governor at Basra the formation of an Anglo-Turkish Board for the purpose of dredging and maintaining the channel by levying dues on shipping using the waterway. In July the British Government suggested a riverain commission to the Turkish Government. The surveying of an Anglo-Russian Boundary Commission, 1913-14, delayed further action over the Shatt-al-'Arab.

At the beginning of 1914 Greenway informed the Foreign Office of the 'considerable difficulties and loss under the present conditions which necessitated lightering a large proportion of such cargo to moorings ... We are desirous of dredging being undertaken at the earliest possible date', because no laden vessels of more than 10 000 tons d.w.t. could approach or leave from the jetties.[52] The outbreak of the First World War, the entry of Turkey on the side of the Central Powers and the arrival of the British expeditionary force changed the situation. The military authorities appointed a port officer at Basra, who admitted that 'I have only a very slight idea as to what is the best way to go about dredging the Mohammerah Bar and outer bar' and so it proved by his choice of unsuitable dredgers. A competent report was prepared in 1916 by Sir George Buchanan, the first Director General of Port Administration and River Conservancy, but never implemented.[53]

So far it had been a saga of inactivity and in November 1917 the Company raised the subject officially again, which later resulted in a conference being convened on 9 April 1919 with officials of shipping interests, the Admiralty, the War Office and the Mesopotamian authorities but no agreement was reached on responsibilities and financial guarantees.[54] After more meetings it was decided in the absence of informal cooperation that it would be preferable to postpone the scheme until a port authority was in existence, which could enter into a more definite arrangement. This happened in 1922, with the formation of Basra Port Authority. During the winter of 1922-23 Mr F. Palmer of Rendel, Palmer and Tritton, consulting engineers, carried out a thorough survey of the Shatt-al-'Arab.[55] His recommendations were embodied in a report of June 1923. He advised dredging a new channel to a depth of 18 ft at low water

Technical activities: Years of endeavour and achievement 1918-1932

spring tides, by removing some 9 million tons of silt with two dredgers, the *Tigon* and the *Liger* and placing the operations under Col. John Ward of the Basra Port Directorate.

Work began early in 1925. On 11 March 1925 the Company entered into an agreement with the Iraq Government by which the Company loaned the Government £500 000, to be repaid by dredging dues from shipping. In return the Government undertook 'to continuously carry on the dredging of the Shatt-al-'Arab bar so as to provide a channel of not less than 300 ft wide and having a clear depth at its shallowest point of not less than 18 ft'.[56] By September 1925 Ward was dissatisfied with the alignment and set the dredgers in a different direction, which became known as the Rooka Channel. By April 1926 steady progress had been made and the channel was formally inaugurated by King Faysal on 29 April 1929.

The benefit to the Company's shipping operations was most marked. During the year March 1925 to 1926 453 tankers left the port carrying 3 690 000 tons of oil of which no less than 2 174 000 tons had been lightered. In the following twelve months with the Rooka Channel in use 4 112 300 tons were loaded at the Ābādān jetties. On 28 October 1926 the Company decided not to press for a broad two way channel but to request a depth of 19 ft subject to covering the extra expenditure and agreement with the Iraq authorities. By March 1928 a depth of 19 ft had been obtained throughout the channel. With production continuing to increase, further provision was thought necessary and discussions took place on widening the channel to 600 ft to minimise the risks of accidents blocking the channel. As it was anticipated that the largest offtake from Ābādān would not exceed 6 400 000 tons till 1931-32, a figure which was not actually reached till 1934, the further widening was not then regarded as urgent. Moreover an offtake of 8 000 000 tons was then possible and anything beyond that amount would have required an enlargement of the refinery beyond what had been contemplated and might have led to the development of a site at Khūr Mūsa, which was further downstream.[57] It was therefore agreed to keep the existing width of 300 ft but dredge to a depth of 20 ft. These improved conditions resulted in sixty-six ships being loaded and dispatched from Ābādān in one month, May 1930, a record that was not bettered till three and a half years later, in November 1933.

A new factor was introduced in 1930 with the proposals for a new international load line convention, that is decreased free-board for ships, which resulted in an additional permitted draught of one foot in the case of a 10 000 ton tanker, enabling it to be deeper laden. The convention came into effect in July 1932. To take fullest advantage of the new regulations the Company proposed that the channel width should be increased to 400 ft and its depth to 21 ft 6 in. As a result of extensive negotiations with the

Iraq Government a further and more comprehensive agreement was reached on 2 June 1932 embodying these new channel arrangements and superseding those concluded earlier.[58] As the greatest single user of the Shatt-al-'Arab the Company had most to gain or lose over the dredging. Until the Treaty of Sacdābād of 8 July 1937 between Persia, Iraq, Afghanistan and Turkey, and even later, the Company was, nevertheless, in the unenviable position of being criticised by Persia and Iraq for favouring one or the other because of its shipping interests in the Shatt-al-'Arab. The Persians objected to the jurisdiction exercised by the Basra Port Authority and both Persia and Iraq disputed the provisions of the 1913 Agreement on boundaries. Nevertheless, those shipping interests were indispensable to carrying supplies from Persia to the Company's markets. The dredging of the Shatt-al-'Arab greatly facilitated and reduced the costs of this transportation.

7 RESEARCH

The Company had early in 1917 realised the need for specialised research facilities and expertise to help solve its technical problems as they arose. During the first few years after 1917 research at Sunbury had concentrated on the problems of fuel oil gelling, thickening, toluene production and improvements in the refining of Persian distillates. With the end of the war there was renewed concentration on solving the distillation problems to increase product yield in both quantity and quality. Indeed research tended to be linked closely to dealing with problems rather than engaging in work of a more fundamental nature. Activities were essentially industrial rather than strictly academic in emphasis, practical rather than theoretical in application. Dunstan had hoped in his first annual report that 'it should be emphasised that one of the functions of the Research Department is to discover new components in the crude, new products therefrom and new applications for them. Just as the coal tar industry has flourished because of the utilisation of waste and by products, so in the case of petroleum it is desirable that the fullest use should be made of the wide range of chemical compounds existing therein.'[59] Occasionally during this period efforts were made to conduct more fundamental research, particularly after research advisers were appointed, but in general Sunbury was concerned with solutions rather than propositions.

Dunstan in 1916, before the establishment of Sunbury, attempted to treat benzine with an acidified solution of potassium permanganate. This worked well in the laboratory but had to be abandoned in 1917 because the quantities required in practice were so enormous. The upgrading of refining processes for benzine and kerosine remained an important priority in

Technical activities: Years of endeavour and achievement 1918-1932

Sunbury's programme of research. Another constant preoccupation in this period was dealing with the associated gas in the production of oil, which was not only dangerous but wasteful.

In 1918 Dunstan and Thole turned to the idea of using sodium hypochlorite to desulphurise Persian benzine and kerosene. It seemed an attractive possibility, having been first patented by Herman Frasch in the United States in 1894,[60] and required chemical constituents that could be manufactured easily by the electrolysis of brine in plant, which was already available and utilised in the bleaching industry. Dunstan and Thole successfully realised the necessity for keeping the sodium hypochlorite reagent in a slightly alkaline state to keep it stable. By the end of 1918 the process seemed promising, though it was recognised that after treatment the benzine developed an unseemly yellow colour which required filtration to remove it.[61] This was found to be possible through bauxite and much ingenuity was spent on the mechanics of such treatment through roasted bauxite granules. In his second annual research report Dunstan wrote that 'this discovery supported by independent analysis and by work, we may fairly claim to be of first importance, seeing that it is a step towards the elimination of chemical treatment'.[62]

Neither discovery was a guaranteed success in operation and a few years and much effort was required for results to be commensurate with expectations, but it was a significant achievement within the context of the research organization's resources and facilities, which were then simple pots, pans and bottles rather than sophisticated apparatus, which was not then available.[63] Indeed conditions were so primitive in the laboratory installed in the basement of the country house, Meadhurst, that passed for the research centre, that Nichols, visiting Dunstan after he had been taken seriously ill with pneumonia, was horrified at the conditions in 'that cellar' and the Board soon authorised the construction of a proper laboratory building on an additional 2.7 acre site.[64] It was completed in 1921 with workshops, a drawing office, boiler house, and outbuildings for plant experiments and chemical and engineering stores. It was a vast improvement.

A contemporary development of great importance for the Company and incidently for the research function had been the erection of a refinery called, imaginatively, Llandarcy, at Skewen near Swansea.[65] After delays during the war and the withdrawal of priority licences (see Chapter 6), work on the refinery did not begin again till February 1919, with Andrew Campbell in charge as Managing Director of National Oil Refineries. The first distillation operations commenced in July 1921. In some respects Llandarcy acted as a proving ground for Sunbury, but equally the refinery had its own laboratory and cooperation was close, unlike in Ābādān where

Technical activities: Years of endeavour and achievement 1918-1932

distance and local conditions were not conducive to easy collaboration. It was at Llandarcy that the sodium hypochlorite and bauxite treatment was first introduced. In the three years that followed operational problems were overcome. The actual treatment of benzine was satisfactory but the electrolysers were inadequate and their malfunctioning made the process initially more expensive than was estimated. A modification was introduced in 1922 with the availability of cheaper bulk supplies of liquid chlorine in favour of a chlorine/caustic soda solution. This resulted in the first sale of rights in a Company process to another firm. In 1923 the cost of treatment was further reduced by using calcium hypochlorite instead of sodium hypochlorite.[66]

Ābādān experienced many problems, not only with this process, but because of weak management, an insufficiency of competent chemists and the difficulties resulting from high ambient temperatures.[67] The sodium hypochlorite treatment was started in August 1921 and was eventually in 1923 proved satisfactory with calcium hypochlorite, as in Llandarcy.[68] The bauxite aspect proved more troublesome.[69] No less than 300 tons of bauxite were in continuous use, and 50 tons of raw bauxite had to be crushed and roasted each day to provide a daily make up of 30 tons.[70] Cadman in 1926 commented that 'subject to reservation as to the heavy cost of maintaining the mass of machinery involved, the process may now be said to be established'.[71] It had taken a long time of trial and error and it may well be wondered whether this experience did not colour the Board's thinking when it came to making a decision on the cracking plant to be ordered in 1925.

The physical process of cracking, the breaking up of hydrocarbon molecules by heat application, had been an early interest of Dunstan and Thole and other petroleum chemists. There were limits to distillation treatment, even when efficiently applied and effectively controlled. There was a need to change the nature of the crude oil so as to produce more lighter fractions of which motor spirit was composed, rather than heavy fuel oils, as the consumption of benzine, motor spirit, was increasing. The light crude oil found in Pennsylvania and Burma, for example, yielded good quality motor spirit in quantity, but Persian or Californian crude oil was heavy in character and yielded less quantity of motor spirit in proportion to fuel oil. The trick was to change the nature of the crude oil by cracking.[72]

By 1919 a number of cracking patents had been registered, but few were commercially viable, apart from the Burton process pioneered by the Standard Oil Company of Indiana in 1913.[73] A vapour phase cracking process invented by a Dr Ramage had been drawn to Cadman's attention whilst in the United States in 1921, but was disappointing. During 1922 a

Technical activities: Years of endeavour and achievement 1918-1932

'liquid-phase' approach was being investigated by Col. S.T.M. Auld, a senior member of the staff at Sunbury, which by the spring of 1923 had reached the pilot stage and was known as the 'A.D.H. Process', after the three scientists primarily involved, Auld, Dunstan and Holley.[74] A 50 ton proving unit was constructed at one of the Scottish shale oil plants, Uphall, and was ready in April 1925. The yield of benzine from Persian crude was quite insignificant for rising market demands from the existing refinery methods, so, rather than wait for the successful Sunbury developed process to be scaled up, the Company in 1925 decided to buy an 'off the shelf' package based on the Cross process first used commercially in 1920, from the American contractor, M.W. Kellogg & Co.[75] It was installed at Llandarcy in 1927.

While the Cross units were being installed, consideration was being given to a second cracking installation, the Dubbs process licensed by the American company, Universal Oil Products Ltd. This was particularly suitable for fuel oil as a charge stock and operated at a lower pressure. It was commissioned on 15 December 1927. The importance of motor spirit was not only related to the need for the cracking process, but also to the need for improved performance through additives. In 1924 the Board acknowledged that simple straight-run petrol was becoming unsatisfactory because of the growing number of high compression engines.[76] Later in 1926, for this purpose and in order to undertake controlled tests on a comparative basis, it was decided to form an engine research branch under the charge of L.J. Le Mesurier.[77] This branch functioned very efficiently and acquired a considerable reputation in engineering circles for its expertise and knowledge which was largely due to the dynamic personality of R. Stansfield, who was primarily responsible for the engine testing facilities, which were housed in a new building in 1930.

Another important aspect of early research done at Sunbury was the utilisation of gas.[78] Persian crude oil as it emerged from the well was not a simple liquid, but a froth. For every million gallons of crude oil produced, some 20-25 million cubic ft of gas was released, mostly methane and ethane, but as it bubbled out of the oil it flashed off light hydrocarbons like butane and pentane, of value for use in motor spirit. In the early days the toxic dangers from hydrogen sulphide were realised and measures taken to prevent its dangerous ill effects, but the positive qualities of the gas were ignored. Imagination, technology and finance were all lacking. Some early gas separators were ordered in 1917 from Messrs Trumble and Co. in the United States, but did not reach Fields till December 1919, by which time they were too small to be of any use. Garrow on his visit in 1919 reported that 'immediate action is imperative if the field is to remain inhabitable'. He arranged with Dunstan and the Engineering Department

Technical activities: Years of endeavour and achievement 1918-1932

that equipment should be designed to treat 1 000 000 ft of gas a day and that some of it should be used as boiler fuel, though it was 1922 before a boiler of the right kind was available. By the end of 1922 some progress had been achieved, but in relation to the extent of the problem it was a minor palliative.

Lloyd, in 1923 on his visit, put the problem into perspective, when he reported that 'the statement was made that there is enough gas in Fields to light the whole of London. It seems obvious that if all this gas which is now wasted could be converted and utilised in some commercial form at a profit, the Company would gain enormously. The problem is crying out for a solution ... the very best chemists available should be sent out to investigate, and as soon as possible.'[79] The fabulous orange and yellow coloured flickering flares were a perpetual reminder (and reproach) of the energy that was going up in flames for it was estimated in 1924 that some 75 000 000 cubic feet of gas were being burnt off. Jameson too felt that 'as every day adds to our responsibility for this colossal waste we consider that services of a fully qualified expert [should] be urgently procured'.[80]

A tentative start was made when Auld came to Persia early in 1923[81] and at the small Fields laboratory where a single Fields chemist, M.S. Mainland, began some experimental work on gas recovery.[82] In 1925 the chemical work at Fields was upgraded to a separate small research department under W.H. Cadman, brother of Sir John Cadman. The chemical staff tried to make carbon black for printers ink, but failed. Sulphur, however, was produced, though as it could not then be utilised, the commercial benefits were minimal.

Sulphur, however, was later used in 1931, in the refining of spirit produced from the cracking plants. Much effort was expended on passing gas through tubes at high temperature (pyrolysis) to produce liquids, but in spite of tremendous encouragement from Professor Thorpe little emerged because of the failure of the metal tubes employed to withstand the high temperatures required. 'The Fields Benzole Plant' became a technical white elephant. The time was too early, the technology too complicated, the demand in Persia too small for a solution to the problem of utilising the gas at the right cost apart from the extraction of a small percentage of light fractions for enriching benzine.

In Sunbury tests were carried out on uses for methane and ethane. At Ābādān attention was paid to practical steps for eliminating gas losses in the plant and the recovery of light fractions for motor spirit. It was not, however, till Cadman's visit to Persia in autumn 1924 that a real impetus was given to the problem, when he was accompanied by a gas expert from Standard Oil, W.L. Morgan. Cadman regretted the delay in using gas as fuel for boilers.[83] Morgan's proposals were accepted and H.Y.V. Jackson,

Technical activities: Years of endeavour and achievement 1918-1932

the chief engineer in Persia returned with Morgan to the United States on a further briefing for six weeks. Jackson's report was regarded as 'a suitable model for all who may be called upon to make enquiries' and his proposals were accepted and quickly implemented.

He recognised the technical advances made in the United States and 'decided therefore that advantage should be taken of past American experience and instead of treading the same torturous path, the design of the APOC plants should commence where American designers had left off'.[84] C.F. Braun and Co of Los Angeles provided the gas absorption units; the compressors were Swiss and the boilers, pumps and water coolers were purchased in the United Kingdom. Jackson's scheme provided for the substantial recovery of 100 000 gallons of gasoline a day from a crude oil throughput of 3 300 000 a day. The first units were operating in November 1926 and by January 1929 the volume of recovered gasoline injected into the pipeline amounted to nearly 2 per cent of the total volume of crude going to the refinery, a welcome addition to benzine supplies. The flaring of gas was a terrible waste of natural energy, in Persia and elsewhere. It has, however, to be set against the highly successful harnessing of the natural resources of the oil reservoir in the unitisation developments, which conserved the pressure and released them under control as productive energy.

Towards the end of 1924, Dunstan was transferred to London to become the Company's chief chemist in charge of all research and chemical affairs and to be close at hand to integrate such matters into the Company's management and so influence its policy in this respect. Thole took his place at Sunbury as chief research chemist. As Sunbury settled into its routine as a research establishment it may be observed that a sense of immediacy came to be lacking, a spark was missing. From a staff of two in 1917, by the end of 1924 the staff comprised forty-six people as can be seen from staff numbers in Table 10.4. Salaries and wages, which were £6031 in 1921-22, were £14 396 in 1923-24. Dunstan had controlled it all in the early days by himself with no assistance from committees, but by 1922 research had become so widespread that better administration was necessary at Sunbury no less than in other activities of the Company.

Cadman was concerned that intellectual stimulus should not be lacking and that the staff at Sunbury should be kept in touch with current academic research. So on 12 January 1923 he chaired the first meeting of the 'Research Advisory Committee' which included Dr J Thorpe (Royal College of Science), Professor F. Soddy (Oxford University), Professor R.V. Wheeler (University of Sheffield) and Dr Dunstan. On the subject of the Company's research work Cadman felt that 'the work should not necessarily have commercial aims in view specifically, and that certain purely scientific matters should be investigated which, at the outset, might not appear to have any commercial bearing. At the same time the solution of these problems might lead to better refining methods, more marketable products and the discovery of new processes, which would be patented, if necessary, by the Company.'[85]

The research advisers have always remained a feature of Sunbury's activities, but it is questionable if the original high hopes were realised as far as fundamental research was concerned. The contacts were beneficial, even indispensable in scientific terms, preventing research from becoming introspective or insipid. Yet the support of the advisers did not actually succeed in turning Dunstan's desire of laying before the Company 'the full chemical and physical history of their raw material' at least in the period under consideration. Nevertheless, the conferences of the Company's chemical staff, first held in 1926, were an opportunity to demonstrate that 'the Company's chemical problems are common to all the chemical staff and are not in any way parochial'.[86] These meetings helped to create a technical *espirit de corps* which permeated the Company.

After 1925 research work was concentrated primarily on product improvement with particular attention being paid to producing better kerosine for special purposes like long-time burning oil for use in railway lamps and for fuel in tractors and fishing boats. Motor spirit and possible anti-knock additives were subjected to exhaustive tests. It was the beginning of a real drive to improve motor spirit with all its benefits for the motorist and because of the increasing competition from other oil companies. A much closer liaison was kept with the distribution department on the reactions and requests of customers. Aviation spirit was prepared. In 1925 only about ten private aircraft were in use in the United Kingdom, but three years later there were 200 owners of private planes and some 23 flying clubs. Provision of supplies was guaranteed to the Imperial Airways on its eastern routes to Cairo and Karachi. Diesel oil was prepared for a market that was minute in 1930 with only 18 diesel engined vehicles on the road but with over 1300 two years later.

Much work was carried out on manufacturing lubricating oil. Limited production was carried out at Llandarcy from 1923. A decision was taken in 1925 to erect a plant there, but it was not till October 1927 that five grades were being produced at a rate of 1300 tons a month. Process improvements enabled this to be increased with a special distillation unit, engineered by the contractors, Foster Wheeler, to 3000 tons a month by late 1931. In France too, at the Company's refinery at Courchelettes, near Douai, a lubricating plant was successfully brought into operation in late 1927 and by March 1928 was producing 1325 tons a month. Thus the range and quality of products was greatly enhanced in these years with an eye to

Technical activities: Years of endeavour and achievement 1918-1932

the market. The gears of the Company's respective departments were meshing better.

In comparison with what had been attempted it may appear that the contribution of research to the Company's growth was less than that anticipated by Dr Dunstan and his colleagues. Yet in retrospect the research work which had from a dingy cellar laboratory spread out to the Company's operations throughout the world in a decade was sufficient to provide the basic expertise in most directions of petroleum technology and in some, associated with petroleum engineering, to make very significant progress. It is no disparagement to the efforts of the scientists to recognise the handicaps of the lack of accurate instrumentation, the absence of standardised testing procedures and the inadequacy of chemical engineering to permit the controlled degree of experimentation which was needed to substantiate the results achieved. These restrictions applied equally to scientists in other establishments such as Dr H.M. Stanley at the laboratories of Distillers Company at Epsom where in the early 1930s he was carrying out research into cracking techniques. It was often years before the pieces of research fell into place, like the alkylation process for making aviation spirit which was developed by Sunbury in the late 1930s. In the 1920s the foundations of research were well laid and its practical applications of growing importance to the Company's success.

Controversy surrounding concessionary relations has often tended to obscure operational achievements. The engineer or chemist is less in the popular limelight than the accountant or lawyer. Yet, the technical accomplishments of the Company in the decade 1920-30 were notable. The geological features of Persia became known in detail. Information on the behaviour of oil reservoirs was accumulated so that the totally new concept of unitisation was established and new methods of production practised. The nature of Persian oil was understood and better refinery processes devised. Techniques of drilling were adapted for Persian conditions. A vast network of supporting services was created, roads, electricity, water supplies, telephone lines, jetties, landing sites, transportation, accommodation, social amenities, education, security and so forth in a region devoid of the elements of an industrial base. The whole enterprise had to be administered not only in accordance with directions from London, but also to the satisfaction of the management and workforce in Persia with their multiplicity of jobs and variety of nationalities, the local population and the Persian Government. Moreover, the Company had to respond to the demands of the market, particularly in respect of motor spirit, to ensure that its products were acceptable to the customer. Its research staff needed to be aware of changing technologies and scientific advances so as to utilise them for the advantage of the Company. In the technical success

Technical activities: Years of endeavour and achievement 1918-1932

of the Company Cadman played a crucial role for he introduced a sense and application of scientific coordination, which had previously been lacking and which had a beneficial cross-pollination effect on all aspects of the Company's technical operations.

11
DOWNSTREAM ACTIVITIES 1919-28

I INTRODUCTION

'An absolutely self-contained organisation'. This was Greenway's vision of the Company, which cannot be sufficiently emphasised. This was his policy of supplying petroleum products directly to customers 'wherever there may be a profitable outlet for them without the intervention of any third parties'.[1] The Admiralty supply contract in 1914 was not a substitute for a marketing strategy, it was part of it. The contracts with the Royal Dutch-Shell in 1912 were not an admission of commercial defeat, they were a recognition of adverse commercial circumstances. Financial constraints and refinery inadequacies 1912-14, as indicated in Chapter 5, had prevented the earlier realisation of a more independent approach to the market. Once the war was over and restrictions on the sales of petroleum products had been lifted, and when the Pool Board had been disbanded at the end of 1919, the Company did not delay in taking the appropriate action. In December 1919 Greenway informed the annual general meeting that 'we are making extensive additions to both our coastal and inland depots throughout the UK with a view to establishing a selling organisation that will be second to none in this country; and thereby securing a position that will enable us to cater for a substantial share of the British trade in Petroleum products of all kinds'.[2]

There was, thus, no mistaking the intentions or minimising the effort involved. This was the justification for a distribution policy. The strategy depended on an economic–technical relationship between the different aspects of the oil business, the links in the chain of resource exploitation, exploration, production, refining, transportation and distribution. It was related to the particular nature of Persian oil and the petroleum products, which it was then possible to refine.[3] Crude oil is not a homogeneous substance. Different markets do not have identical demands. The skill of the distributor lies in optimising the availability of his particular supplies to the peculiarities of demand. The success with which this is achieved is one of the determinants of the profitability of the oil business. Thus for matching production to anticipated requirements, a knowledge, not only of productive capacity, but also of potential consumption patterns is necessary. A balance has to be kept between the respective operating functions, a managerial equipoise.

It is for this reason that the first five years after the ending of the war, 1918-23, may be characterised as a period of consolidating all available resources and establishing the Company on an integrated basis. There was little understanding of the characteristics of Persian oil. The extent or behaviour of the oilfield was unknown. The most appropriate refinery processes were still subjects for experimentation (see Chapter 10). The most effective system of management was undecided (see Chapter 8). The direction of new marketing initiatives was unclear. It was in these years that these issues were faced and settled, providing the foundations upon which later developments were possible. Greenway was determined not to be left behind in the post-war scramble for markets, but to take advantage of the acquisition of British Petroleum Company Ltd (BP Company) (see Chapters 6 and 7) and the suitability of Persian oil for fuel oil, a marketing strategy already defined in 1917, but which needed implementation.

Gradually once the productive capacity of the oilfield was better understood, the refinery processes improved, the marketing function established and management more organised, it became possible towards the end of 1923 to plan with more certainty. These years, to the middle of 1927, therefore, may be termed the period of expansion. At the annual general meeting towards the end of 1926, Greenway was able to assure the shareholders that 'our success in finding further outlets for our production encourages us to continue our policy of expansion'.[4] Two years before he had been confident of withstanding competition, irrespective of the rate wars being carried out to 'an insane extent, but we can await the result with perfect equanimity: since for every shilling that we lose our competitors must lose two or more'.[5] He advocated that for the Company 'the best form of protection against competition ... is to be established in as many markets as possible'. This provided the justification for further activities in Europe. In the earlier period, what were essentially supply arrangements were made by investing in local companies as in Norway, Denmark and France, but a more active role was presaged when the Company transformed its minority holding of 1921 in the French Company into a substantial majority holding in 1922. Thereafter, whilst leaving local management wide discretionary operational powers, direction and financial affairs were clearly controlled from London. Indeed in 1927 a continental manager was actually appointed with exclusive responsibilities for the European subsidiary companies and their accounting pro-

Downstream activities

cedures were standardised. A group consciousness was beginning to emerge.

As a result of the Company's enhanced production position in 1927 with its technical mastery of oilfield technology and the discovery of the second field at Haft Kel, its improved refinery expertise and its diverse markets in Europe and bunkering stations along the maritime routes, the Company became a real force in the international oil industry. The regard for Cadman in government and commercial circles symbolised a respect for a company, which once had been obliged to hold out the begging bowl to the British Government and had been in danger of being absorbed by Royal Dutch-Shell. Its standing on the international oil scene in company with Standard Oil (NJ) and Royal Dutch-Shell coincided with a bout of oversupply in the markets, a furious rate war between its major competitors, its common involvement with them in the Iraq Petroleum Company which had just discovered oil and its own resolve to increase its market share. An indication of the magnitude of the operations was that whereas in 1923 the disposal of a production of 4 000 000 tons was being contemplated, in 1927 a production of 6 000 000 tons was being planned for five years ahead.

However, by the beginning of 1928, the outlook was beginning to change: the situation was becoming more difficult with surpluses depressing prices as production rose in the United States and developed in South America. It was at this point that the Company and Royal Dutch-Shell finally came to terms over outlets in the east and Africa by forming the Consolidated Petroleum Company Ltd, in which they both participated equally, but which was managed by Royal Dutch-Shell. This had been preceded by a merger of Burmah and Royal Dutch-Shell Indian interests in a newly constituted company, Burmah-Shell Ltd in 1927. This rationalisation of the supply and market situation was carried further on an international scale at a meeting between Walter Teagle for Standard Oil (NJ), Deterding for Royal Dutch-Shell and Cadman for the Company, which took place at Achnacarry in Scotland in September 1928, when a tentative settlement was reached on market shares, known as the 'As Is' Agreement. This endeavour to find an acceptable formula, in which competition was to be effectively regulated on a limited basis, did not achieve immediate results owing to the complexity of reconciling the differing market shares in different countries and was overtaken by the onset of the Depression. It is, thus, more sensible to postpone consideration of these arrangements, and their effect on subsequent marketing policies from 1928, to the next volume. In this chapter an attempt is made to set the scene for the Company's downstream operations in the decade 1918-28, which may be described as three phases, consolidation, expansion and rationalisation.

Downstream activities

2 CONSOLIDATION

The progress achieved in the decade following the ending of the war can only be appreciated by understanding the position in 1918. Production was running at almost one million tons a year. The proved extent of the Masjid i-Suleimān field was 3½ square miles with forty five wells drilled capable of producing, although production was in fact maintained through only five wells for most of the time. It was anticipated by Garrow that the oilfield could actually produce 5 000 000 tons a year of crude oil.[6] The pipeline capacity was 1 132 000 tons a year. With the addition of three pumping stations in 1919, it was doubled to 2 700 000 tons annually. The existing refining capacity was 1 220 000 tons which yielded the following products annually:

Petrol (benzine)	156 750 tons	(310 gallons a ton)	13%
Kerosine	139 000 tons	(280 gallons a ton)	12%
Fuel oil	880 000 tons	(250 gallons a ton)	75%
	1 175 750 tons		

Garrow expected that when the refinery extensions then under construction were completed, making the capacity 1 750 000 tons a year, the following volume of products would be obtained in the same proportion:

Petrol	240 000 tons	14%
Kerosine	206 000 tons	12%
Fuel oil	1 305 000 tons	74%
	1 751 000 tons	

He reported at the end of December 1918 that aviation spirit and toluene could be made from benzine, and that from the fuel oil additional kerosine could be distilled. Gas oil, lubricants, petroleum jelly, wax and pitch could also be obtained. (See Appendices 11.1-4 for the actual tonnage of the main products sold in the markets 1920-32, Appendices 11.5-8 for volume and proportions of these products, and Appendices 11.9-11 for refinery throughputs of the same products.) There was thus capacity for development and possibilities for an increased range of products.

As has been pointed out in Chapter 6, the acquisition of the British Petroleum (BP) Company and its two subsidiary companies in 1917, no less than the formation of the British Tanker Company in 1915, was an integral part of Greenway's principal strategy. The BP Company which became the main instrument of marketing policy was 'an extensive ready-made organisation which it otherwise would take many years to build up,

Downstream activities

during which period it would be at a very great disadvantage as compared with the Shell and Standard',[7] who were the major competitors. The Company's objective was to ensure that it was 'permitted to work on ordinary business lines and is free to carry on its operations - whether producing, refining, transporting, or distribution to customers - in any part of the world'.[8]

When the Petroleum Executive and the Treasury tried to insist in March 1918 that, pending the recommendations of the Harcourt Committee, the activities of the Company should be restricted, Greenway reacted positively. He claimed, for example, that the nature of the bunkering trade needed contracts to be placed with shipowners for their total requirements spread across the maritime routes, which might lead to 'producing Oil in other countries to obviate competitive advantages accruing to the position of supplies available to other Companies'. The alternative was to dispose of products 'through one or the other of the two Companies which are carrying on their business without let or hindrance of any kind - in other words, it would lose its independence and a very large share of the profits it would otherwise earn'.[9] It was a real dilemma for the Company.[10] There was uncertainty but yet in 1918 the Imperial War Cabinet was favourably disposed towards the Company working in association with the Commonwealth Government in Australia.[11]

Greenway had no intention of letting the Company be hampered, as it was 'quietly pursuing a policy of development', and suggested to the Treasury that 'this policy should not only be maintained but be tacitly acquiesced in by the Government until the conclusion of the war, when the present objections to an open declaration of the Government's policy in Oil matters will no longer exist'.[12] The end of the war intervened before the Harcourt Committee had made up its mind and, even when it did, government procrastination over oil policy merely added confusion to indecision, as was pointed out in Chapter 9. Greenway, with characteristic optimism, revealed on 26 March 1919, at the annual general meeting, the favourable production potential that could be expected in Persia, for

> we anticipate no difficulty whatever in finding markets for this largely increased production. Our one and only difficulty is to provide Refining, Transport and Storage facilities fast enough to enable us to meet the demands upon us for our products. We have practically an unlimited supply of Crude Oil, and with the great increase in the demand for Oil Products of all kinds ... there is endless scope for us in the direction of the sale of our Products.[13]

The opportunities existed in the markets. The Company would have to create the facilities to supply its customers with the range and quality of the products which would satisfy them. This was the immediate objective of the post-war years when large expenditure was incurred for a vast amount of property all essential to the proper and economic working of our business, wells, pipelines, pumping stations, whole towns occupied by our employees, refineries, a railway, our tankers, and a large flotilla of smaller steamers, barges and other river and harbour craft, a vast amount of tank storage, ocean and inland bunkering and distributing installations, etc., in all parts of the world.[14]

Given the nature of Persian crude oil and the limitations of the refinery processes, it was then inevitable that little better could be expected in yield than 68 per cent fuel oil, the dominant product, 15 per cent benzine and 10 per cent kerosine with some 7 per cent losses. Hence the availability of products for the market was determined by the refinery processes, making the Company very vulnerable to any reduction in fuel oil offtake, which would inevitably reduce the volume of benzine and kerosine it could refine. However, in fact, purchases of products were made from other oil companies for a short time after the ending of the war and before Llandarcy came onstream in 1921, particularly in the United States, though less profitably for resale in the markets. The growth and volume percentages of the Company's main product sales are shown in Figures 11.1a and 11.1b respectively. Between 1920 and 1932 Company sales of benzine increased 7.3 times, from 262 000 tons to 1 925 000, kerosine 2.1 times, from 256 000 to 546 000 with peak sales in 1930 of 617 000 tons, and fuel oil and gas oil 3.9 times, from 944 215 to 3 722 342 tons. Admiralty demand of between 435 000 and 560 000 tons held up well for the rest of the period but a possible increase in its purchases to build up strategic oil stocks for the Royal Navy did not materialise (see Table 11.1a for tonnage of fuel oil delivered to the Admiralty). Supplies to the Indian railways, however, had increased as a result of the contracts negotiated in 1917, but were only settled in January 1921 with the supply of 150 000 tons a year with an option of a further 80 000 tons at a higher price.[15]

Great hopes were placed in the possibilities of the bunkering trade which had already begun in 1913 and was increased by the construction of sites in Madras and Aden. Some idea of the spread and importance of such outlets can be imagined from the number of installations either completed or being constructed in June 1919.[16] These included completed sites at Bombay, Calcutta, Cochin, Karachi, Tuticorin, Ābādān, Mombassa, London, Hull, Sunderland, Grangemouth, Avonmouth, Manchester and Belfast, with others contemplated or being erected at Swansea, Colombo, Marseilles, Port Said, Suez, Singapore, Durban, Freemantle, Melbourne, Southampton, Liverpool, Barrow, Tyne, Plymouth, Gibraltar, Malta and Dakar. Marine bunkering sales increased in India where Shaw, Wallace and Co. acted as agents. 37 823 tons were delivered there during 1923-24, rising to 86 861 in 1926-27. Delays had occurred because some of the Company tankers were derequisitioned more slowly than had been antici-

Downstream activities

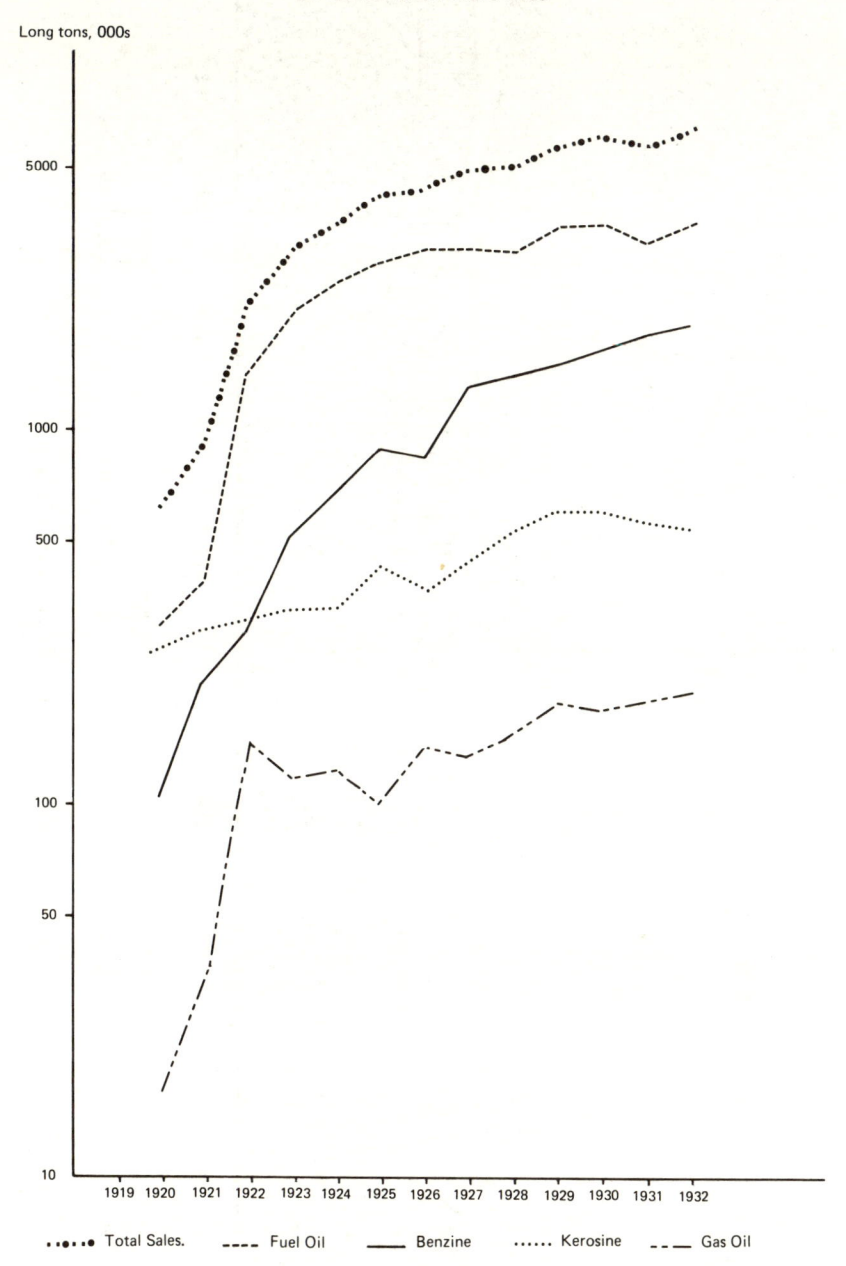

Figure 11.1a The growth of the Anglo-Persian Oil Company group sales of main products 1920–32

Source: BP 4K 7077

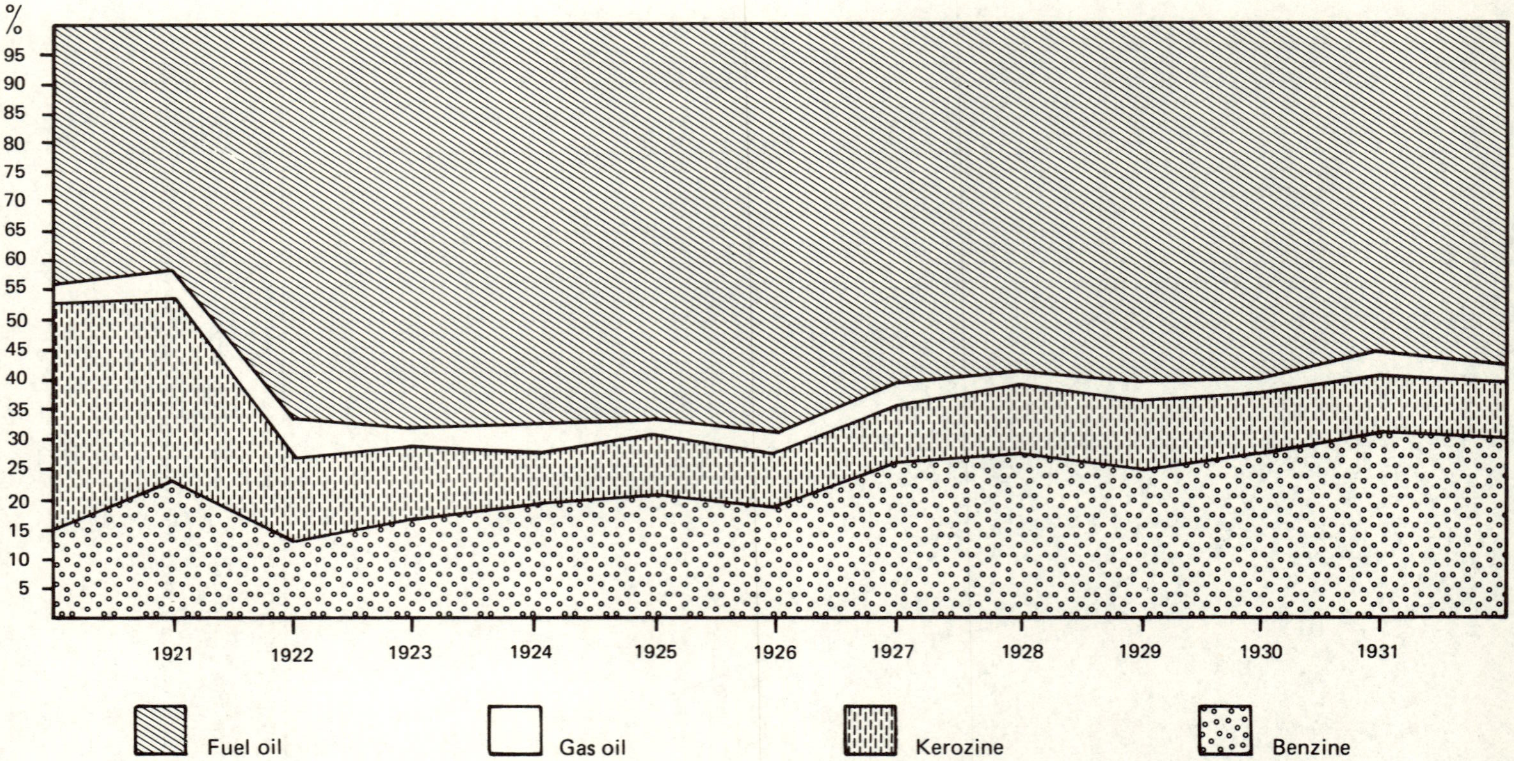

Figure 11.1b The volume of the Anglo-Persian Oil Company group sales of main products 1920-32
Source: BP 4K 7077

Downstream activities

pated and there was a shortage of steel with which to construct the tankage necessary, but it was an impressive programme.

In 1919 Greenway proposed the formation of a bunkering company in which the Company would have half the shareholding with the other half represented by various shipping interests in proportion to the tonnage owned by them.[17] The Board accepted the idea in April and Lloyd was requested to prepare a scheme. Greenway had discussions with Inchcape (P. and O.), Sir Owen Philips (the Royal Mail Steamship Company and the Union Castle Line) and Sir John Ellerman (the Ellerman Line) amongst others.[18] Such a bunkering company would have performed the dual function of guaranteeing supplies of good quality fuel oil to shipping concerns at a reasonable cost and assured the company of regular sales. The shipowners were initially agreeable and on 29 September the Board sanctioned the registration of the British Oil Bunkering Company.[19] As a result of a discussion on 2 July 1919 with Mr E.L. Doheny, the independent American oil marketer with interests in Mexico, who was about to form the British Mexican Company, it was agreed to market the products of the Mexican Petroleum Company of Delaware in Europe and so widen the scope of the enterprise into a 'World Bunkering Company'.[20]

Other interests were approached like the American Pierce Oil Corporation, which had supplied the BP Company with products, the Gulf Refining Company and William Cory and Sons, who were prominent in the coal bunkering trade. In some respects this ambitious approach outpaced reality. British Mexican fell by the wayside. On 5 March 1920 the British Oil Bunkering Co. Ltd was established, but little progress was made.[21] Supplies from Ābādān were insufficient. None came from Mexico. So the Company was chary of committing itself to specific contracts in view of priorities for deliveries to the Admiralty. Towards the end of the year, however, the Company found itself with excessive fuel oil stocks at Ābādān and made strenuous efforts through its agents to dispose of stocks and secure new business.[22]

During the early years of the twenties the competition between coal and fuel oil was considerable. Appendix 11.12 indicates the fluctuations in their prices from 1920, when prices were high with fuel oil at £10 18s 0d a ton and average coal exports at £3 19s 11d a ton. During the national coal strike in April 1921 fuel oil reached £14 10s a ton but afterwards dropped to £5 8s 9d a ton, with coal £1 14s 10d. In 1922 prices were lower; fuel oil was down to £3 10s 6d a ton and coal £1 2s 7d. Fuel oil prices held till 1929, but coal drifted lower. A trend was undeniable towards oil fuelled shipping according to information from Lloyds Register, which disclosed that the percentage of coal-fired shipping dropped from 96.6 per cent in 1914 to 55.9 per cent in 1932 whilst that fired by oil rose from 3.4 per cent in 1914 to 44.1 per cent in 1932 (see Appendix 11.13). This was also reflected in the increasing proportion of tankers under construction for the British merchant fleet rising from 6 per cent at the end of 1923 to 7.8 per cent in 1924, 15.1 per cent in 1925, 17.9 per cent in 1926, 21.5 per cent in 1927, falling to 14 per cent in 1928, before reaching 25.5 per cent and 42.8 per cent in 1929 and 1930 respectively (see Appendix 11.14).

The vagaries of market prices and the uncertainties over construction were reflected in the correspondence between Greenway and Ellerman about fuel oil tenders. Ellerman complained that Greenway's quotation of £10 0s a ton f.o.b. Ābādān in 1919 gave him no incentive to convert his shipping to fuel oil when he could obtain coal at Calcutta for 28s a ton.[23] Ellerman was not then tempted at £7 0s a ton. Caught in the general shipping depression of 1921, many British shipowners were reluctant to commission new tonnage but the Company, undeterred, continued to proceed with its new marine installations and the ordering of shipping to transport crude oil and deliver supplies of oil products.

Whilst some of the leading shipping concerns may have lacked confidence in the future, Greenway lost no time in emphasising to the shareholders in December 1920 that the provision of more fuel oil outlets was 'another necessary development of our business if it is to be carried on independently and our products be disposed of to the best advantage'. He warned that those 'who are first in the field for such oil as may be available will...have such enormous advantage over those who remain dependent upon coal that there are already very evident indications of a "scramble" for the existing supplies'.[24] This was certainly true in the short term for British imports of fuel oil rose from 1 391 000 tons in 1920 to 2 125 000 tons in 1921, but thereafter till 1928 they averaged 1 580 000 tons yearly (see Appendix 11.15). The Company's rising volume of sales of fuel oil in the market which increased eleven-fold in eleven years can be seen in Figure 11.1.

The crisis point for obtaining supplies was, however, certainly in the very early twenties and was a major reason for the association of Norwegian and Danish shipping and fishing interests with the Company, after the failure of the British Mexican Company to fulfil its contracts with them for fuel oil deliveries in 1920. Det Forenede Olie Kompagni A/S had an 86 per cent Company shareholding and 14 per cent Danish, but in Norsk Braendselolje A/S the shareholding was equally divided between the Company and Norwegian interests. Both Companies were formed on 21 May 1920 and were expected to have initial demands for fuel oil of 10 000 and 7000 tons a year respectively. In fact in Denmark fuel oil sales between 1923 and 1932 averaged 11 124 tons a year, tripled over the period, and totalled 111 242 tons, 17.9 per cent of total product sales of

Downstream activities

622 608 tons during this time. Benzine and kerosine sales also tripled in the same period. In 1923 benzine was 12 per cent of total sales, but rose in 1932 to 44 per cent; kerosine was 14 per cent and 32 per cent, but fuel oil fell from 50 per cent to 19 per cent. In Norway the figures were different for fuel oil sales actually averaged 37 371 tons a year between 1923 and 1932 and increased 6.2 times in the same years from 15 984 tons to 100 268 tons, constituting 53 per cent of total sales of 774 020 tons (1922–32). Benzine sales rose 15.3 times in the same period being 7 per cent of sales in 1923 and 15 per cent in 1932; kerosine sales rose 5 times but fell from 7 per cent to 5 per cent. Shipping and fishing vessels accounted for the greater part of fuel oil sales. (See Figures 11.2 for Danish sales in volume and 11.3 for Norwegian sales.) In France shipping and banking interests took the initiative over fuel oil supplies.

The bunkering company foundered. The shipping interests preferred the freedom of the market, placing contracts rather than taking up shares. The Company, better placed with a growing number of installations along the main maritime routes, was not so dependent on a captive but less profitable set of customers. More attractive was an agency agreement with Cory's, and on 22 November 1921 the managing directors agreed to abandon plans for the bunkering company and conclude an initial exclusive five-year agency agreement from 1 January 1922 with Cory's for the sale of marine oils other than directly by the Company, decisions confirmed by the Board a few days later.[25] It was the beginning of a close and very satisfactory business relationship for fifty years. Thus the chain of bunkering stations, envisaged during the war as replacing the coaling stations of the past with their economically strategic advantages on the shipping lanes of the World, emerged in the early 1920s as an essential aspect of the Company's marketing policy.[26] Fuel oil was an important commercial asset which had to be maximised, as it constituted some two thirds of the volume of the total sales of the Company.

From 1912 Ābādān supplied local markets in the Gulf area, but sales remained generally insignificant.[27] Burmah and Royal Dutch-Shell because of the agreement of 1905 virtually excluded the Company from India apart from fuel oil sales and batching oil for the looms of the manufacturers in Bombay and other towns. Burmah took deliveries of jute batching oil and fuel oil of 42 429 tons in 1922–23 and 101 860 tons in 1928 (see Table 11.1b). In July 1921 the Company and Burmah reached a 'mutual marketing understanding' whereby both companies resolved not to 'establish any organisation or compete in markets for spirit, kerosene, Jute Batching Oils and Lubricants, where the other may own or control a distributing organisation for these products. (By control we mean having a 75 per cent interest in an organisation)'.[28]

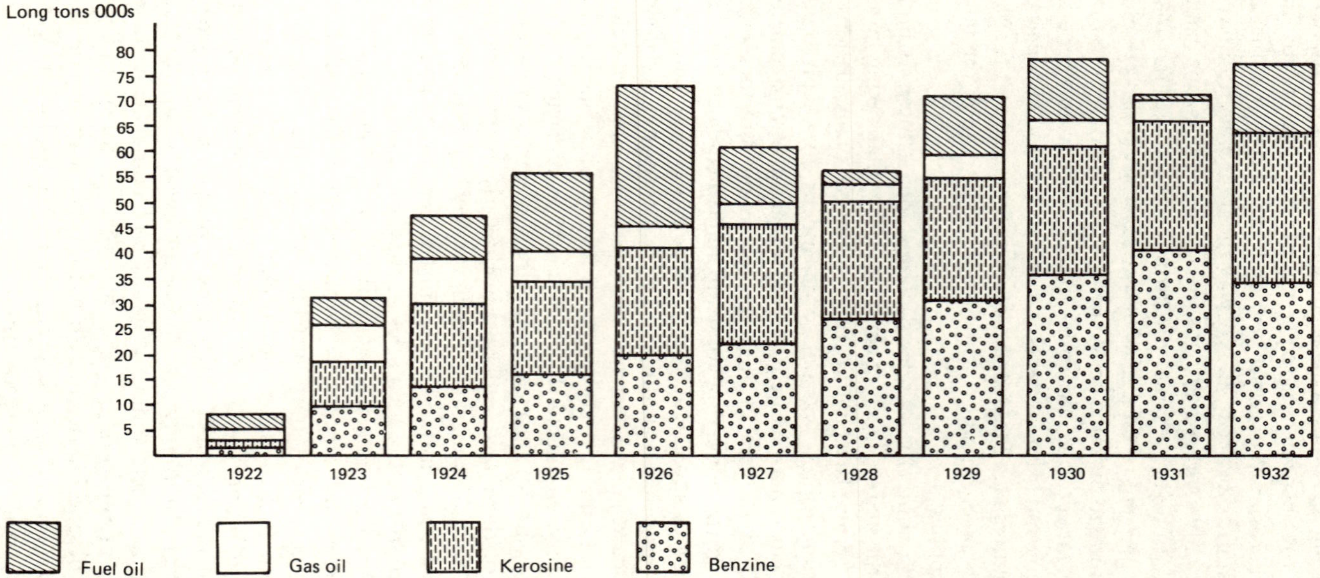

Figure 11.2 Sales – Det Forenede Olie Kompagni (Denmark) 1922–32
Source: BP 4K 7077

Figure 11.3 Sales – Norsk Braendselolje (Norway) 1922–32
Source: BP 4K 7077

Downstream activities

Table 11.1. *Anglo-Persian Oil Company fuel oil sales 1922–32*
(a) Admiralty contract (b) Burmah Oil Company
(long tons)

	Fuel oil	
	(a)	(b)
1922–23	434 493	42 429
1923–24	473 393	32 831
1924–25	509 817	40 353
1925–26	483 454	57 251
1926–27	492 235	59 333
1927–28	509 357	81 594
1928	512 804	101 860
1929	556 558	74 142
1930	621 118	56 960
1931	472 935	20 948
1932	559 819	14 034

Source: BP 77/124/18

This agreement and the contracts arranged with the Asiatic Petroleum Company in 1912 effectively precluded the Company from competing in Indian markets. In the early days of these contracts deliveries were small, 1555 tons of kerosine in 1913, 4883 tons in 1914 and 8335 tons in 1915. During 1912-22 Shell intended to take 631 000 tons of crude oil but only lifted 359 895 tons.[29] Once run distillate (ORD), a semi-refined benzine, had been accepted in 1914 by Shell, instead of the badly refined benzine from the refinery at Ābādān. The Company was not committed to renewing the contracts with Royal Dutch-Shell when they expired at the end of 1922. The managing directors on 15 December 1920 decided not to do so in accordance with Greenway's overall strategy of independence.[30] Continuing problems in Ābādān with processes, strikes, difficulties with the new subsidiary companies in Belgium, Norway, Denmark and France then upset Greenway's commercial time-table and he was obliged to keep his options open.

It would appear that early in 1917 Watson had proposed that the Company, Burmah and Royal Dutch-Shell should draw up a trading agreement, in respect of benzine, kerosine and fuel oil, other than sales to governments.[31] The markets concerned were to include India, Australasia, South Africa, the east coast of Africa and the Red Sea area. In return for the Company agreeing not to sell benzine or kerosine in the Dutch East Indies, the Philipines, Spice Islands, Celebes, Malaya, Siam, China or Japan, Royal Dutch-Shell would pledge itself not to compete in Persia, the

Downstream activities

Persian Gulf, Arabia or Mesopotamia. This was premature and unacceptable to the Company but these overtures pointed to other arrangements proposed intermittently in the 1920s and the one finally concluded a decade later in 1928.

At a meeting between A.C. Bedford, Chairman of Standard Oil (NJ), and Greenway towards the end of August 1921 trading arrangements between the two companies were discussed. This did not result in immediate market cooperation, but it did later facilitate longer term collaboration over Middle Eastern oil. Cadman followed up Bedford's discussions by visiting him in New York in December. This led to cooperation over a concession for North Persia in dispute between the two companies in 1922 and eventual association in the Iraq Petroleum Company, for which see Chapter 12.

Greenway in July 1922 consulted Watson before further discussions on possible marketing arrangements between the Company and Standard Oil.[32] Watson's advice indicated a general consistency of his view on the desirability of reaching marketing understandings between the major companies. His amalgamation proposals (see Chapter 8), which had been floated at this time would have prevented the expansion of the Company's marketing interests, for he was clearly attracted to closer collaboration with Royal Dutch-Shell. Nevertheless his opposition, as a Company director, to an expansionist policy and his preference for cooperative measures in the market between the major companies, ultimately influenced Company attitudes and contributed to the rapprochement with Royal Dutch-Shell at the beginning of 1928 and the informal commitments at Achnacarry a little later in the same year. It was in this spirit that he explained his conception of market logic to Greenway in view of the forthcoming talks with Walter C. Teagle, President, and Frederic D. Asche, Vice-President of Standard Oil (NJ). Professing that Burmah's interests alone must not prevent the realisation of the Company's objectives, Watson suggested that

> Because BOC and APOC are Eastern producers and the Royal Dutch-Shell are both Eastern and Western producers whereas the SOC are Western producers only, I feel that BOC/APOC commercial interests will, generally speaking, be better served by friendly relations with the Royal Dutch-Shell even at the expense of unfriendliness on the part of the SOC than by friendly relations with the SOC at the expense of unfriendly relations with the Royal Dutch-Shell.[33]

He was not prepared in any circumstances 'to give the Standard benzine in the East, where meantime they have no benzine trade'.

'The real solution', believed Watson, was 'an APOC/BOC/SOC/APC round table conference at which all parties put their cards on the table', though he was unsure whether the time was propitious for such an initiative. He was convinced, however, that 'events, sooner or later, are likely to force the issue and if a conference could "cut out" the otherwise resulting friction and possible losses it would be well worth the effort'. These talks did not lead to a closer marketing association between the Company and Standard Oil (NJ), but they improved relations. Meanwhile the earlier contractual arrangements with Royal Dutch-Shell had been superseded by a more limited contract for benzine signed on 16 February 1922, by which the Company undertook to supply a minimum of 15 000 tons a month and a maximum of 30 000 tons a month for five years.[34] The importance and convenience of this benzine contract to both sides is indicated by the fact that over the five years deliveries averaged 270 000 tons a year, a third of the Company's sales in benzine (see Appendix 11.1). Royal Dutch-Shell also purchased some supplies of kerosine, fuel oil and crude oil.

Watson's enthusiasm for a closer relationship between the Company and Royal Dutch-Shell was not, however, shared by all his colleagues on the Board. Indeed it had already been agreed in February 1920 that efforts should be taken to open up business opportunities in Europe, when

The Board was advised that the British Petroleum Company Limited are establishing a foreign department to thoroughly investigate the prospects and ramifications of the trade on the Continent, preliminary investigations in connection with which have been carried out by this Company, with a view of finding suitable outlets for all surplus production, particularly of petrol, after 1922.[35]

Greenway returned to this theme in May 1923 in the course of negotiations for acquiring an interest in the Europäische Petroleum Union (EPU). He remarked on the superior standard of the benzine which was required for delivery to Royal Dutch-Shell and the reduction in profit thereby incurred, which was greater 'than it would be were we to distribute it ourselves – or a total of £5 million and £10 million respectively for the full contract period of 5 years'.[36] 'It will,' therefore, observed Greenway, 'be enormously to our advantage to find our own outlets as soon as possible for the whole of the balance of benzine beyond the minimum of 180 000 tons per annum to which we are committed to the Asiatic.' Hence the advantage of 'the securing of a distributing outlet in Germany for our products whereby we should get the full benefit of the prices paid by consumers'. This was Greenway's marketing strategy of self-sufficiency. There were moments of accommodation to circumstances, but no compromise on the independence of the Company.

The first move into Europe had actually occurred on 14 July 1919 when the formation was officially announced of L'Alliance in the *Moniteur Belge* with equal shareholdings between the Company and the Belgian Société Anonyme des Pétroles de Grozny, although subsequently in March 1921

Downstream activities

the Company acquired the Belgian shareholding.[37] The connections were made through the assistance of M. Waterkeyn, the former Belgian director of the BP Company, who had been very helpful to Greenway in 1916-17 during his negotiations to acquire that company. The original purpose of the Belgian subsidiary was to act as 'the nucleus of a Continental distributing organisation'.[38] It was also related to moves prompted by the Foreign Office 'relative to trade between the British Empire and Belgium with a view to increase and develop that trade by every desirable means'.[39] Greenway was concerned to acquire a petroleum business with existing installations, works and storage facilities. There were complications over British exchange control regulations, negotiations with the Belgian sequestrator of enemy property, delays over land transactions and rising costs before the company was formed.[40]

It was also true that the Belgian group was very undercapitalised, and possessed no sure supply of products, in spite of its promises. In 1921 Waterkeyn was informed that 'it has been apparent to us for some time past that your group do not display the keen interest in this concern which we might have expected'.[41] As a consequence the Belgian shareholders were bought out. The acquisition of local management at the same time as the fixed assets had not been successful and the Company came to the conclusion that a majority shareholding was essential in subsequent acquisitions. This experience in Belgium was to some extent repeated in France. The growth of sales in Belgium was slow between 1923-32, 40 190 tons to 58 055 tons, representing an annual average growth rate of 4.2 per cent. It was benzine sales which increased most, 6.7 times from 1922 to 1932, 5769 tons to 38 847 tons, from 43 per cent of total sales to 67 per cent. Kerosine sales dropped in percentage from 26 per cent to 13 per cent of the total. Fuel oil sales fell even more, 23 per cent of the total to 4 per cent, with sales in 1932 at 2358 tons compared with those in 1922 at 3170 tons (for details of Belgian sales, see Figure 11.4).

The Company's most important continental marketing subsidiary of this period was formed in France on 12 January 1921, la Société Générale des Huiles de Pétrole.[42] Since 1919 French interest in associating with the Company had been shown, when late in that year M. Rosengart-Famel, who had served on the French Petroleum Committee, approached Braithwaite with proposals for bunker installations and oil-fired burners.[43] Braithwaite was not impressed with his suggestions or in purchasing Omnium International de Pétrole, which drew its supplies from Rumania. He did recognise, however, that 'there is evidently a considerable scramble for French business at present and I consider that we ought to send some representative who must be a fluent French linguist to France to study developments and if necessary open up negotiations'. At the end of

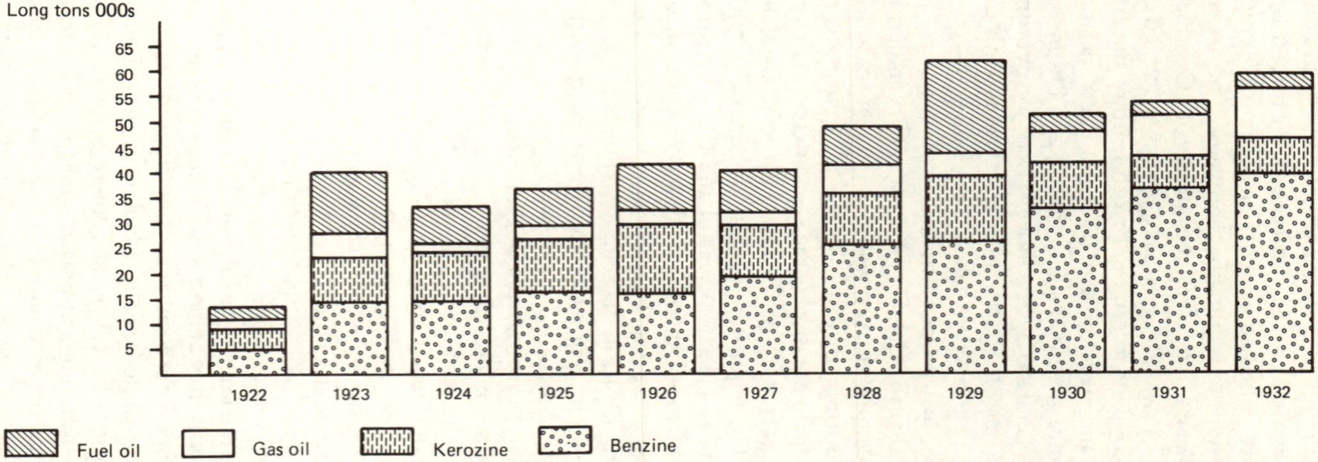

Figure 11.4 Sales – L'Alliance Société Anonyme (Belgium) 1922–32
Source: BP 4K 7077

Downstream activities

Directors of Société Générale des Huiles de Pétrole and members of the Board of the Anglo-Persian Oil Company at the Wembley Exhibition 1924

1919 Braithwaite, nevertheless, believed that 'the time is not ripe for anything more than the examination of possibilities at present, especially in view of the fact that immediate action is not essential to us'.[44]

Yet, earlier in 1919, at the suggestion of M. Brenier, the French agent of the P and O Line in Marseilles, the Company had begun to construct a bunkering installation there. When the French company was formed, Brenier became a director, an indication of his prominent role in the negotiations. Associated with the Société Navale de L'Ouest and the Banque de la Seine, for both of which Sir Basil Zaharoff acted representing certain French industrialists, were other French groups such as Paix et Cie, which had been active in the oil trade since 1863 and had a refinery at Courchelettes near Douai, George Lesieur et ses Fils with interests also in vegetable oils, Lille Bonnieres Colombes and Consommateurs de Pétrole. In spite of the predominance of French capital (55 per cent to 45 per cent), the French groups were unable to increase their investment to develop the company as rapidly as competition was requiring. So in 1922 the Company's shareholding was increased to 74 per cent. The French company possessed not only marketing outlets but also refining facilities and tankers. As in Belgium so in France sales of benzine increased, whilst those of kerosine decreased and fuel oil sales dropped in percentage terms to total sales. Between 1922 and 1932 benzine sales increased four times, rising from 35 per cent to 49 per cent of total sales, whereas kerosine fell from 22

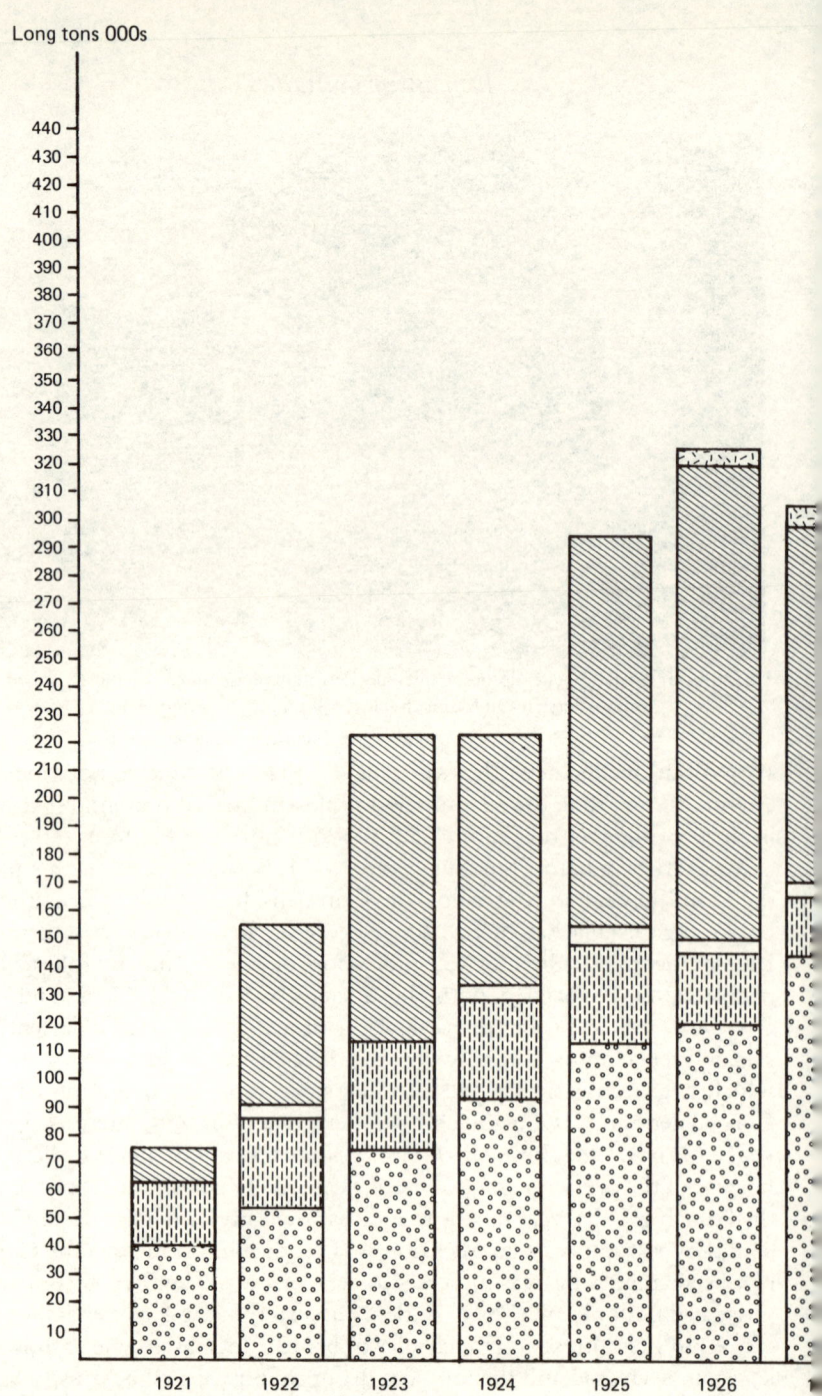

Figure 11.5   Sales – Société Générale des Huiles de Pétrole (France) 1921–32
Source: BP 4K 7077

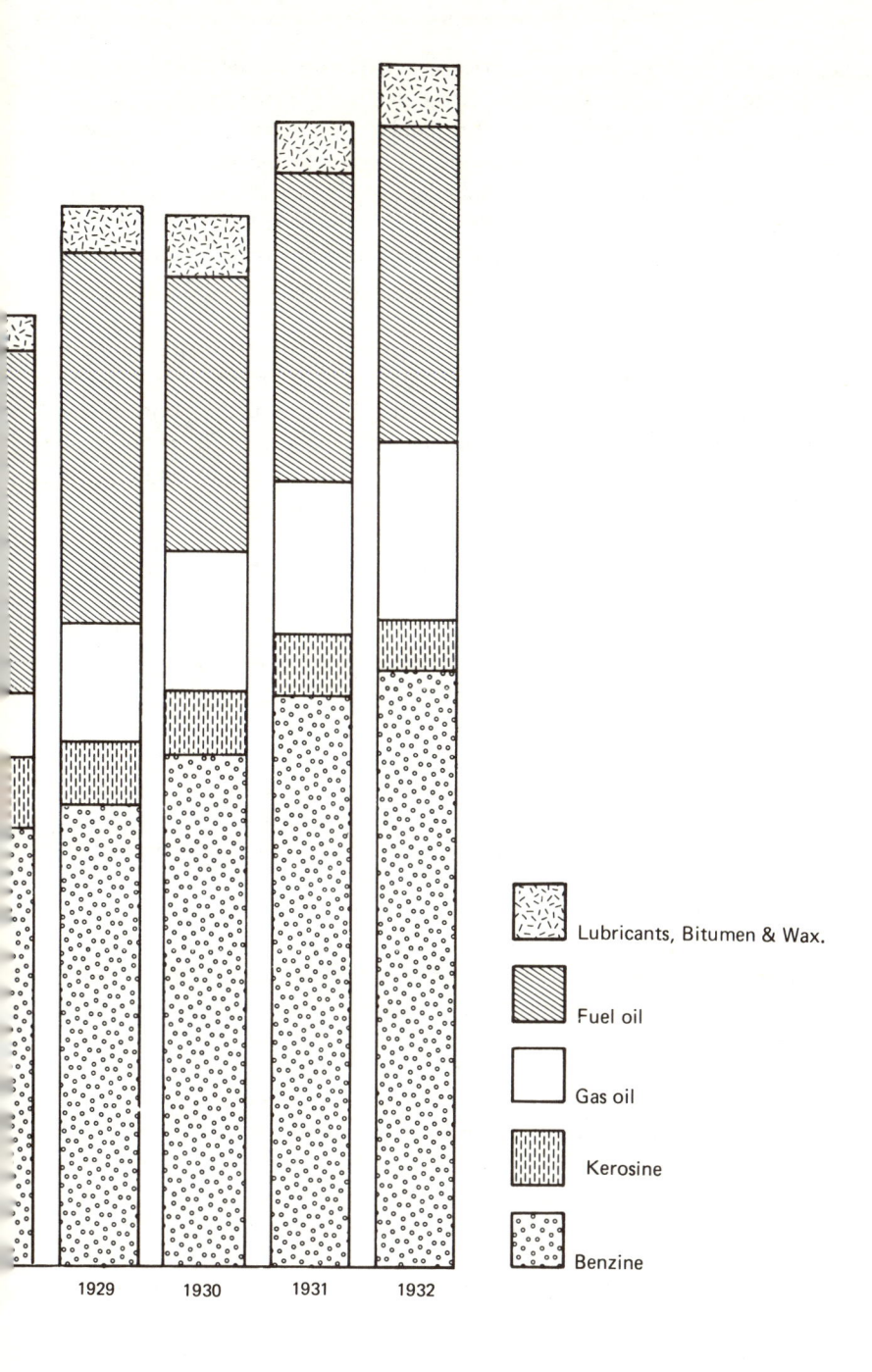

1929 1930 1931 1932

Lubricants, Bitumen & Wax.

Fuel oil

Gas oil

Kerosine

Benzine

Downstream activities

per cent to 5 per cent, from 33 200 tons to 19 100 tons. Fuel oil fell from 41 per cent to 26 per cent in the same period, dropping from its peak in 1926 of 172 204 tons to 114 848. On the other hand gas oil, lighter than fuel oil and used in diesel engines and smaller boilers, increased greatly from 2500 tons in 1922 to 66 000 tons in 1932. Total sales rose from 75 600 tons in 1921 to 438 400 tons in 1932. From 1924 the French refinery at Douai supplied up till 1928 about a third of the products sold, but from 1929 approximately half of them. (See Figure 11.5 for French sales and Appendix 11.15 for refinery throughput 1924-32.)

The early years were difficult in France not only in respect of creating a new organisation and networks, introducing new products and establishing sales and supply schedules, but also because of the political environment in which the new business was operating. As a result of marketing internationally, the Company was no longer immune from either competitive rivalry or political pressures. The pointed reaction of Stewart in March 1923 to unfavourable press comment, in his letter to F.G.C. Morris, who had been appointed the Company's Chief Representative in France in November 1921, is an early example of a clash of national and corporate interests in which the Company was to be increasingly involved. 'Our venture' wrote Stewart to Morris,

> into the French market has not so far resulted in anything but loss to the Anglo-Persian and the thanks we have got for making that loss is great abuse by a certain section, though an unimportant one, of the French press. The policy of the Company is not to oust other competitors from France or any other country, but to do a fair share of the country's requirements and this is to the advantage of your country or any other because it is better for France to be receiving supplies of oil from half a dozen sources rather than from one only, which might in certain circumstances either run short of oil or be cut off by reasons of international difficulties.[45]

The hub of the Company's marketing activities, however, remained centred in the United Kingdom on the BP Company. Already in April 1918 it was drawing up plans for an enlarged distributing organisation, designed 'to enable the company to be in a position to enter the Spirit and Fuel oil trade after the war'.[46] Some indication of the growth of the BP Company in the decade 1918-27 can be seen from the increase in its fixed assets, from £356 365 in fixed plant, installations, depots and premises to £3 275 340 and from £238 413 in wagons, lorries, cars, cans, cases, furniture, equipment, horses and their accoutrements and the like, to £2 093 205, in total £636 074 to £5 518 802, a nine-fold increase. There is a large rise in motor vehicles for distribution, motor lorries, for example, from £5643 to £1 051 652 and a large drop in horses £31 995 to £2330. (See Table 11.2 for a schedule of fixed assets 1918-27 at historic cost.)

Downstream activities

British Petroleum Company bulk delivery vehicles, Barton depot 1926

By early 1922 it was estimated that about 80 per cent of the programme had been completed and that the Company was in a position 'to distribute bulk spirit throughout any part of England and Wales'.[47] The sales pattern in the United Kingdom was not dissimilar to that in Belgium and France. Sales of benzine doubled from 158 600 tons in 1922-23, 26 per cent of the total, to 394 500 tons in 1931, 39 per cent. Kerosine sales fell from 188 500 tons in 1922, 31 per cent, to 173 100, 17 per cent, in 1931. Fuel oil sales almost doubled between 1922-23 and 1931, 242 800 tons to 408 600, peaking in 1926-27 at 587 900 tons. Gas oil sales did not change significantly, 22 761 tons in 1922-23 and 24 113 tons in 1931 peaking also in 1926-27 probably as a result of extra stocking in connection with the General Strike. Total sales were 612 700 in 1922-23 and reached 1 100 000 in 1926-27, a plateau from which there was little change in the five following years (see Figure 11.6). Competition from independent importers and quotas arranged by the main three distributing companies and a much lower rate of increase in consumption seemed to be mostly responsible.

An essential part of the strategy in the United Kingdom involved the refinery at Llandarcy, which was commissioned in 1921. Until 1922 most of the products sold by BP Company were obtained from the United States, but afterwards Llandarcy supplied most of the requirements, as can be seen from the yields in Appendix 11.16a. From 1924 these were augmented with supplies from Grangemouth refinery in Scotland. The Company's outlets and distribution facilities were increased by its acquisition of Scottish Oils Ltd, an amalgamation of the principal Scottish shale oil companies, on 3 September 1919, which strengthened its representation in Scotland. The minor refineries at Uphall, Pumpherstone and Grangemouth serving the shale oil industry were useful adjuncts to refinery capacity, whilst Grangemouth from 1924

Table 11.2. *British Petroleum Company fixed assets 1918–28 at historic cost*

(£ fixed assets at historic cost)

	1918	1919	1920	1921	1922	1923	1924	1925	1926	1927	1928 (9 months)
Land	41 296	52 938	56 149	120 661	124 599	126 353	129 688	129 606	147 687	150 257	154 136
Fixed plant											
Ocean installations	234 956	237 793	273 533	679 350	1 049 807	1 711 445	1 756 431	1 634 673	1 631 372	1 633 309	1 625 267
Sub-installations	—	130 832	144 301	216 364	361 268	481 678	570 609	559 948	563 855	607 373	616 472
Kerosene depots	—	977	65 945	254 385	360 476	134 657	136 489	103 108	98 859	90 735	84 016
Bulk spirit stores	121 409	—	—	82 862	281 818	378 608	360 622	302 891	270 580	256 694	230 906
Kero and spirit depots	—	—	—	—	334 685	394 250	466 337	541 092	664 180	721 676
Various premises	—	3 296	3 296	15 244	11 684	11 708	14 934	22 030	23 749	23 049	150 972
Total	356 365	372 898	487 075	1 248 205	2 065 053	3 052 781	3 233 335	3 088 987	3 129 507	3 275 340	3 429 309

Table 11.2. (*cont.*)

	1918	1919	1920	1921	1922	1923	1924	1925	1926	1927	1928 (9 months)
Rolling stock, loose plant, etc.											
Railway tank wagons	55 501	55 501	77 299	208 211	366 896	371 686	373 665	365 383	360 965	371 678	371 678
Motor lorries	5 643	14 612	161 177	564 985	754 055	921 957	939 407	894 527	946 639	1 051 652	1 014 431
Cars and vans	—	3 362	5 280	42 914	82 139	102 539	104 787	100 046	112 654	110 754	91 655
Cycles	3 698	3 753	5 321	6 568	6 196	6 091	4 845	2 878	2 864	2 285	3 028
Horse drawn tank wagons	49 000	48 286	62 780	67 262	60 201	53 034	44 618	17 081	13 922	9 860	8 077
Can racks	—	—	—	1 031	1 031	1 002	1 002	558	455	295	232
Cradle tanks	—	—	—	14 932	26 842	37 199	42 426	42 327	46 752	48 807	46 481
Barges and coasters	22 600	23 135	25 035	20 048	26 061	36 949	39 782	44 985	46 034	48 397	48 921
Steam wagons	—	—	—	9 347	24 281	30 671	30 659	30 675	42 704	42 497	37 163
Push cycles	—	—	—	775	640	579	583	435	399	394	371
Horses	31 995	32 951	33 289	26 445	18 807	13 575	9 491	5 022	3 666	2 330	672
Office furniture	21 224	20 406	23 847	35 510	43 244	59 242	62 664	58 502	54 561	57 336	61 765
Loose tools	14 546	16 433	15 626	9 348	12 040	14 865	16 418	9 233	9 736	8 426	8 737
Stable equipment	11 194	11 468	11 730	14 280	14 127	10 807	9 512	6 931	1 965	1 635	1 271
Kerbside pump tools	—	—	—	—	170	1 321	1 593	1 951	2 556	3 422	3 256
Steel barrels	22 919	32 499	64 526	72 157	75 658	75 439	75 329	70 092	74 141	77 712	80 291
Spirit cans	—	—	107 677	319 720	323 388	329 596	310 801	238 470	226 578	219 273	191 475
Spirit cases	—	—	15 322	15 381	15 372	13 700	13 426	11 150	10 390	8 772	7 605
Faucets	—	—	—	—	—	—	2 736	161	1 761	174	—
Handcarts	93	82	72	72	72	—	—	—	—	—	—
Depot equipment	—	—	—	—	—	—	—	28 573	17 245	17 815	19 451
Installation equipment	—	—	—	—	—	—	—	—	9 695	9 691	10 289
Total	238 413	262 488	608 981	1 428 986	1 851 220	2 080 252	2 082 744	1 928 980	1 985 682	2 093 205	2 006 849
Total	636 074	688 324	1 152 205	2 797 852	4 040 872	5 259 386	5 445 767	5 147 573	5 262 876	5 518 802	5 590 294

Source: BP British Petroleum Company financial schedules

Downstream activities

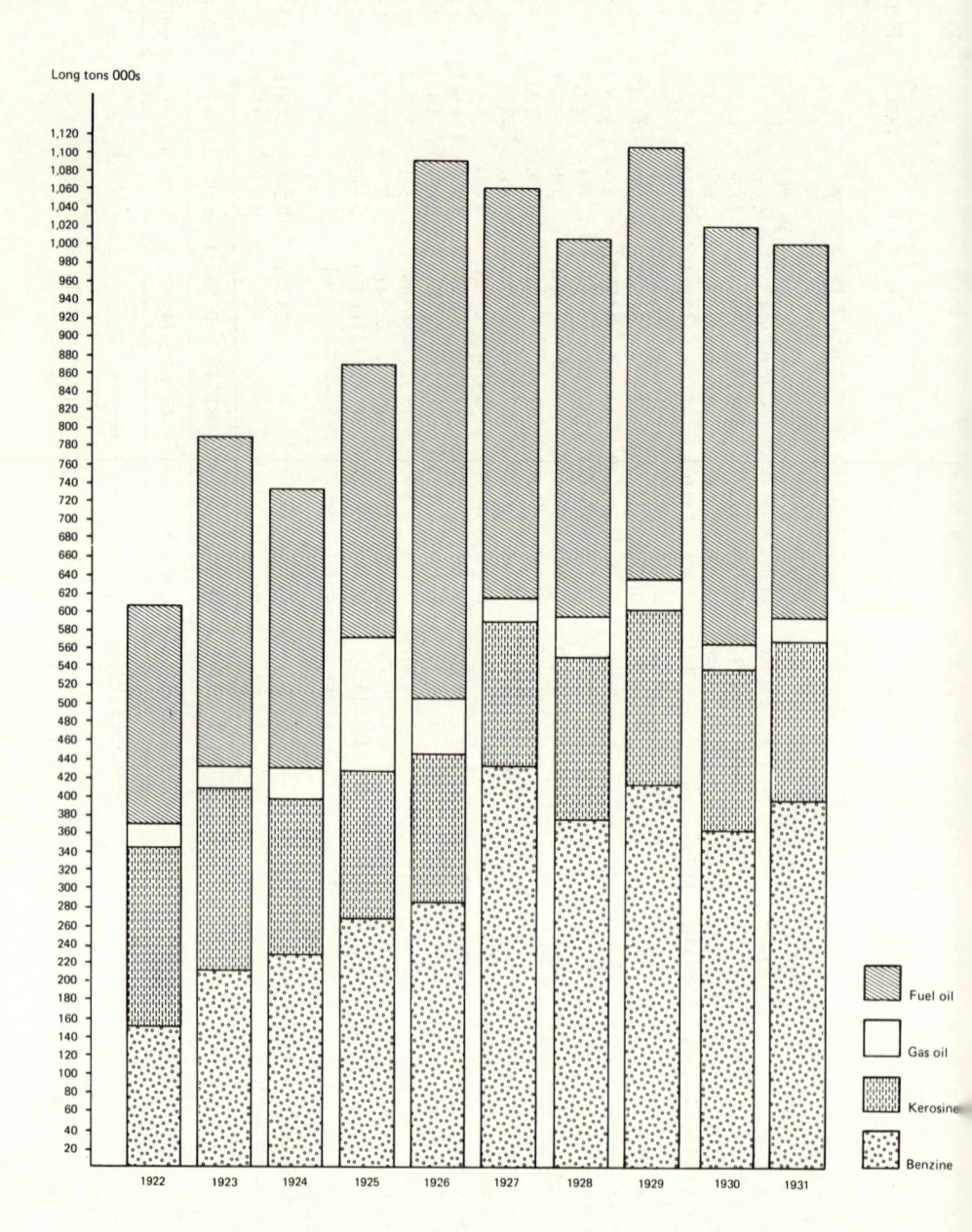

Figure 11.6 Sales – British Petroleum Company 1922–31
Source: BP 4K 7077

Downstream activities

played a significant role in furnishing products for distribution in Scotland (see Appendix 11.16b for its throughput).

The main competitive element in marketing concerned sales of benzine for the rapidly growing use of the internal combustion engine. The registration of cars increased from 187 000 in 1920 to 1 056 000 in 1930. The Company's total sales of benzine went from 261 750 tons in 1920-21 to 1 925 000 in 1932. Accompanying this tremendous rise in benzine consumption was a revolutionary change in distribution practices, the principal form of which had been by returnable two gallon cans. After the war the American system of pump deliveries, convenient to the motorist in his car or lorry from sites alongside the roads, reached Europe and gradually replaced the cumbersome method of delivering cans from filling and storage depots to garages. The new situation which faced the Company throughout its subsidiary companies can be illustrated from the experience of BP Company in the United Kingdom. It was estimated in July 1920 that the United Kingdom trade in motor spirit was some 700 000 tons, of which the Company had a little less than a tenth:

Anglo-American Oil Company	300 000 tons
Shell Marketing	250 000 tons
Anglo-Mexican Petroleum Co.	50 000 tons
Union Petroleum Products	25 000 tons
British Petroleum	60 000 tons
Scottish Oils Ltd.	10 000 tons
	total 695 000 tons

In March 1920 the Board learnt that the Anglo-American Oil Company, then not legally, but almost in practise, a Standard Oil (NJ) subsidiary, was introducing bulk storage to garages throughout the country and had to decide 'whether the installation of bulk storage plants should be encouraged or assisted by us pari passu with the extension of the Company's organisation or generally throughout the country without waiting for the readiness of the company's distribution system'. At the same time a long memorandum was being prepared on 'Supply Stations for Petrol' in view of the changing market techniques and practices being introduced in the United States.[48] The Company had to consider whether to follow this innovative challenge in promoting road petrol service stations. It was recommended to erect and to own

these stations rather than rely on individuals to do this. The latter method destroys to a great extent the value of one's brand of petrol etc. because the owner of the installation will buy from the most advantageous source of supply. The general idea is to have these depots placed at strategic points as regards motor traffic, erecting a small building of uniform type, with an enclosure in front and a carriage way through it, the precursor of the petrol service station.

Downstream activities

Still, however much the Company might wish to own and run its own service stations, garages as a whole and the Motor Trade Association in the United Kingdom formed in 1910 to represent and regulate the interests of the motoring trade did not favour the idea and, whilst accepting that it was possible to supply a commercial consumer in this way, obliged the companies not to supply directly to the public. Besides, the capital investment required did not then favour its wide-spread adoption. The Anglo-American, spending £6000 on a single site in the Harrow Road, was acting as the market leader.

The Company, with relatively few outlets and a large expenditure to develop its network throughout the country, nevertheless did not accept an Anglo-American proposal in April 1921 with others to 'form a Company ... to erect throughout the country petrol service stations to which each company would supply an agreed ration of spirit'.[49] The idea was attractive in that it would minimise capital expenditure on service stations, but neither this suggestion nor another from Royal Dutch-Shell at this time deflected the Company's resolve to increase, not stabilise, its market share as 'an arrangement on the lines suggested would necessarily involve a quota agreement and would not be in the interests of the Company seeing that they had yet to build up a spirit business, whereas the other two Companies were already extensively established'.

By the end of the year the Company had decided that it had no alternative but to make arrangements with the Bowser Company for their pumps and recommend 'that company's system of petrol storage and supply to garages throughout the country'.[50] The Company had to accept, not avoid, the kerbside pump challenge, because as 'every pump placed means an average of 500/1000 gallons weekly of spirit business, the pump question is most intimately concerned with the Company's expansion and it cannot afford to let the business go by without default', though the cost was high.[51]

By mid-May 1921 sixty-nine pumps had been installed by garages for delivering the BP Company's benzine without any financial commitment on its part, but as a result of increasing competition it was decided that the company should install them in garages upon payment. In mid-1922 a loss of £25 an installation was occurring, which was gradually reduced, although it was accepted that costs were likely to be incurred in this respect. By September 1923 some 7000 petrol pumps had been installed throughout the country by the oil companies which had led to problems for local authorities and the intervention of the Ministry of Transport in legal and safety measures. Two years later in July 1925 it was reported that the number of pumps installed had doubled, with Anglo-American having 6168, BP Company 6058 and Shell-Mex 4269. In 1925 it was estimated

Downstream activities

that BP Company had 20.5 per cent of the total UK motor spirit trade, 947 400 tons or 24.75 per cent of that of the main distributing companies, and for benzine the figures were 32 per cent, 409 300 tons and 39 per cent.

In view of the growing importance of motor spirit for the cars of an increasing number of motorists the provision of pump installations and the expenditure which this entailed was a matter of no little significance, particularly in France and Belgium, where the competitive position had been transformed by the introduction of pumps.[52] In reality there was little choice as was already obvious in 1924 when it was realised that 'further capital outlay will be inevitable, as continental trade tends towards this method of delivery'.[53] By 1926 in Germany, for example, Olex associated with the Company had 1226 pumps in service in 1086 filling stations and was planning the erection of a further 1000 pumps. Differing from United Kingdom practice, all the pumps were erected by the Company and owned by it.

By the end of 1923 the first phase of the Company's marketing was almost over. Greenway felt able to assure the shareholders that 'in regard to the distributing organisations both in the United Kingdom and abroad, the programme of developments is practically completed', and 'the capital expended on them is now, I am pleased to say, bearing fruit in the form of rapidly increasing sales of every one of our products'.[54] The foreign

Kerbside pump in France 1924

Pump installation in Germany 1926

subsidiaries were 'proving valuable auxiliaries to our distributing concerns in this country'.[55] Consolidation had been effected. The establishment of a marketing organisation had been achieved.

3 EXPANSION

Behind the enthusiasm of Greenway lay an unaccustomed caution. 'Negotiations,' he declared, 'are still proceeding for creating similar organisations in other European countries, but we are delaying final arrangements until we are ready to supply the quantity of our own products necessary to maintain these additional outlets.' The expansive energy of the Company was derived from matching its productive and refinery capacity to the opportunities of the markets. The success of its expansionary efforts was determined by its ability to compete. Getting right the equation of capacity equalling or just exceeding competition was the commercial problem for the Company. It was first expressed clearly in October 1923 by Heath Eves, who was to become director in charge of distribution in January 1924, when looking at the supply position for 1924 after taking account of crude oil availability, refinery make and market demand in an analysis of the supply situation. It probably represented the first Company attempt at such an exercise, the results of which are shown in Table 11.3. This revealed a deficit of 53 000 tons of kerosine and a surplus of 366 000 tons of fuel oil, which he was not disposed to sell ahead so as to preserve some elasticity in the refinery position. Otherwise it would be impossible 'to

Downstream activities

Table 11.3 *Anglo-Persian Oil Company group refinery availability of products 1924*

(long tons)

Refinery	Fuel oil	Kerosine	Benzine
Ābādān	1 800 000	—	220 000
Llandarcy	618 000	215 000	352 000
Grangemouth	138 000	20 000	35 500
Uphall	60 000	8 600	15 500
France	66 000	9 400	17 000
	2 682 000	253 000	640 000
Estimated requirements	2 316 000	306 000	592 000
Surplus:	366 000		48 000
Deficit:		53 000	

Source: BP H14/59

regulate the make of kerosene and benzine to follow possible swings of the market'.[56] Yet as he recognised 'with fuel oil representing some 63 per cent of throughput, it is essential that we sell ahead to a large extent in order to keep the way as clear as possible for the regular production of kerosene and benzine'. His calculations in detail, for estimated requirements for 1924, are in Table 11.4.

If his conclusions were valid for 1924, it was even more necessary to look further ahead and 'raise questions of policy regarding refinery make and distribution after the termination of the Asiatic Agreement on 31 December 1927 ... if we are to be prepared to handle all our make through our own organisation, after that date'. Assuming the applicability of existing refinery methods and a productive capability of 4 000 000 tons of crude oil a year, Heath Eves in mid-1925 expected forward estimates of refinery throughput and product demand to indicate on 1 January 1928 surpluses of 40 000 tons of kerosine and 15 000 tons of benzine. In that event, he asked, 'was the Company going to maintain productive capacity, strengthen selling organisations and/or establish new sales facilities in countries in which the Company was not yet represented?'

Was the Company going to expand or not? Greenway, who was still, probably, treading warily after the financial crisis of 1922-23 (see Chapter 8), did not advocate any extension of production capacity and, supposing that the existing sales organisation could cope with the demands placed upon it, did not imagine that further expenditure was necessary.[57] Lloyd,

Downstream activities

Table 11.4. *Anglo-Persian Oil Company group estimated products demand 1924*
(long tons)

	Fuel oil	Kerosine	Benzine
British Petroleum Co. Ltd. (fuel oil excluding bunkers)	156 000	200 000	240 000
Scottish Oils Ltd. (fuel oil excluding bunkers; excluding shale products)	42 000	8 000	20 000
Société Générale des Huiles de Pétrole	42 000	50 000	100 000
L'Alliance Société Anonyme	5 000	10 000	15 000
Det Forenede Olie Kompagni A/S	7 000	13 000	12 000
Norsk Braendselolje A/S	50 000	5 000	5 000
Trieste	7 000		
Ābādān (local)	120 000	20 000	10 000
Ābādān (refinery)	50 000	—	—
India (railway contract)	150 000	—	—
Fuel oil installations (internal)	200 000	—	—
Admiralty	500 000	—	—
Admiralty (shortage in 1923/4)	17 500	—	—
Burmah Oil Company	60 000	—	—
Bunkers:			
P. & O.	220 000	—	—
Other contracts	130 000	—	—
Ābādān tankers	260 000	—	—
Swansea tankers	100 000	—	—
Asiatic	—	—	190 000
For stock at Ābādān & Llandarcy	200 000	—	—
	2 316 500	306 000	592 000

Source: BP H14/59

the embodiment of financial prudence, wrote that 'we should not commit ourselves to any expenditure until the prospects of the oil industry are much brighter than they are at the moment'.[58] Garrow questioned the assumption that refinery technology would not change and predicted more advantageous yields of kerosine and benzine and less fuel oil.[59] In fact the growth of the market, improved sales, better refining processes and more assured production meant that within two years Heath Eves had a different marketing situation. For example, instead of forecasting a surplus of 151 000 tons of benzine on an availability of 721 000 tons for 1928, he expected that in 1930, even with an availability of 819 500 tons, 'we shall have to purchase in order to meet the requirements of our existing markets'.[60]

Confidence was restored. In April 1924 it was noted that estimates of the forward position showed that the availability of refined products 'will be in excess of the aggregate quantities of those products which will be

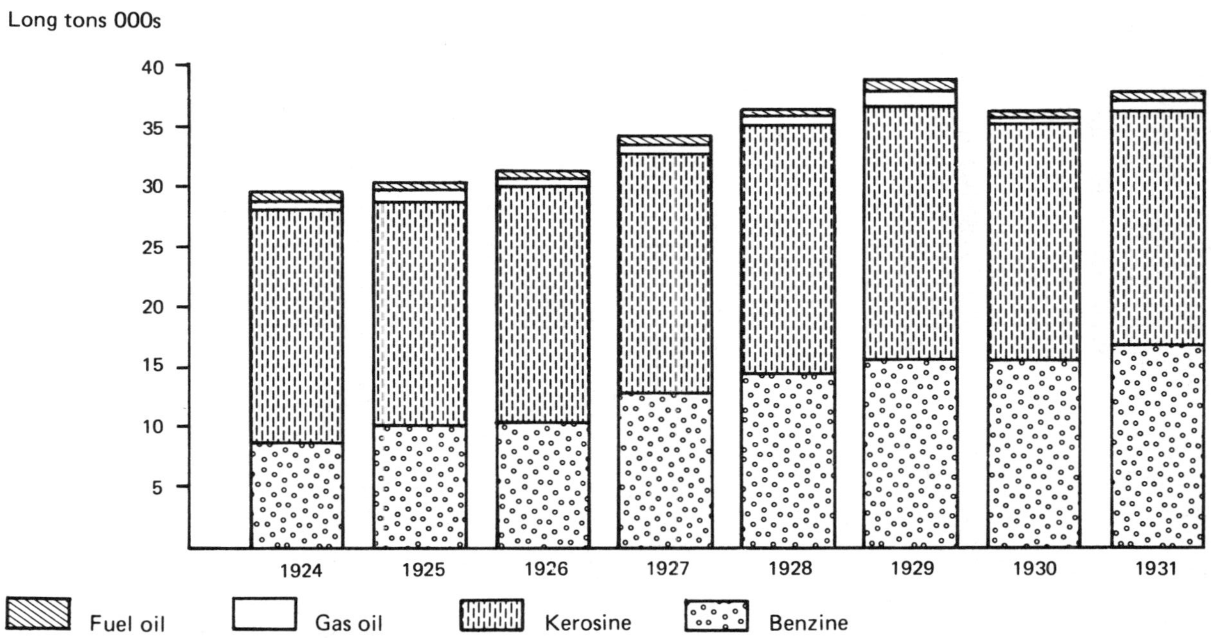

Figure 11.7 Sales – British Petroleum Company, Ireland, 1924–31
Source: BP 4K 7077

required to cover sales', though it was admitted that certain specialised products could not be produced.[61] Greenway in November 1924 reported to the shareholders that he had nothing but 'good news to give you' over production, that 'As regards our refineries the position is entirely satisfactory' and that in distribution 'we are making satisfactory progress in every direction ... we get more and more firmly established in all the markets into which we have so far made an entry, and new trade continues to show a steady increase'.[62] He deprecated market rate wars, but was not perturbed about the outcome for the Company, whose marketing outlets were increasing. It formed a company in Ireland on 12 October 1923, whose offtake remained small, 29 780 tons in 1924-25 and 37 580 in 1931. Sales of fuel oil were negligible, averaging 1 per cent of total sales, but kerosine provided most sales, averaging 60 per cent, some 20 500 tons yearly. Sales of benzine doubled in the same period to 16 800 tons, 45 per cent of the total. (See Figure 11.7 for sales tonnages.) Benzina Petroleum in Italy was incorporated on 12 January 1924, tripling sales from 21 700 tons in 1925-26 to 67 670 tons in 1929, of which fuel oil predominated, averaging 80 per cent, rising from 19 700 tons in 1925-26 to 53 600 tons in 1929, when it was 69 per cent of total sales. Benzine and kerosine sales increased moderately till 1929, reaching 6980 tons, 15 per cent and 5 890 tons, 13 per cent of total sales respectively. The improvements in sales 1930-32 mostly reflected deliveries in the Italian markets to the subsidiaries there of Royal Dutch-Shell and Standard Oil (NJ) made under a trading agreement concluded in April 1930 (see Figure 11.8 for sales tonnages).

Two former subsidiaries of EPU were acquired in 1924. Oestereichische Naphta Import Gesellschaft of Austria (Oenig) (see Figure 11.9 for sales tonnages) and Petroleum Produkte Aktiengesellschaft of Switzerland (PPAG), which in 1927 merged with The Deutsche Petroleum AG's subsidiary in Switzerland to form Benzin-und Petroleum Aktien Gesellschaft (BPAG) (see Figure 11.10 for sales tonnages). There were small sales in Austria, 1560 tons in 1924 and 2800 tons in 1932, mostly of fuel oil, followed by kerosine and benzine, though in 1929 gas oil sales were relatively high in comparison with other products. In Switzerland fuel oil sales were negligible, but benzine sales rose from 1770 tons, 65 per cent of the total in 1925 to 28 230, 61 per cent in 1932, averaging 68 per cent. Kerosine rose gently in volume in the same period from 874 tons to 4350, but declined from 32 per cent to 9 per cent of total sales. From 1927 gas oil sales became significant, 13 400 tons in 1932, 29 per cent of total sales, supplied mostly to railways.

On 7 June 1926, there was completed, after long negotiations stretching over some four years, the Company's acquisition of a 40 per cent shareholding in 'Olex' Deutsche Petroleum-Verkaufsgesellschaft in Germany,

Downstream activities

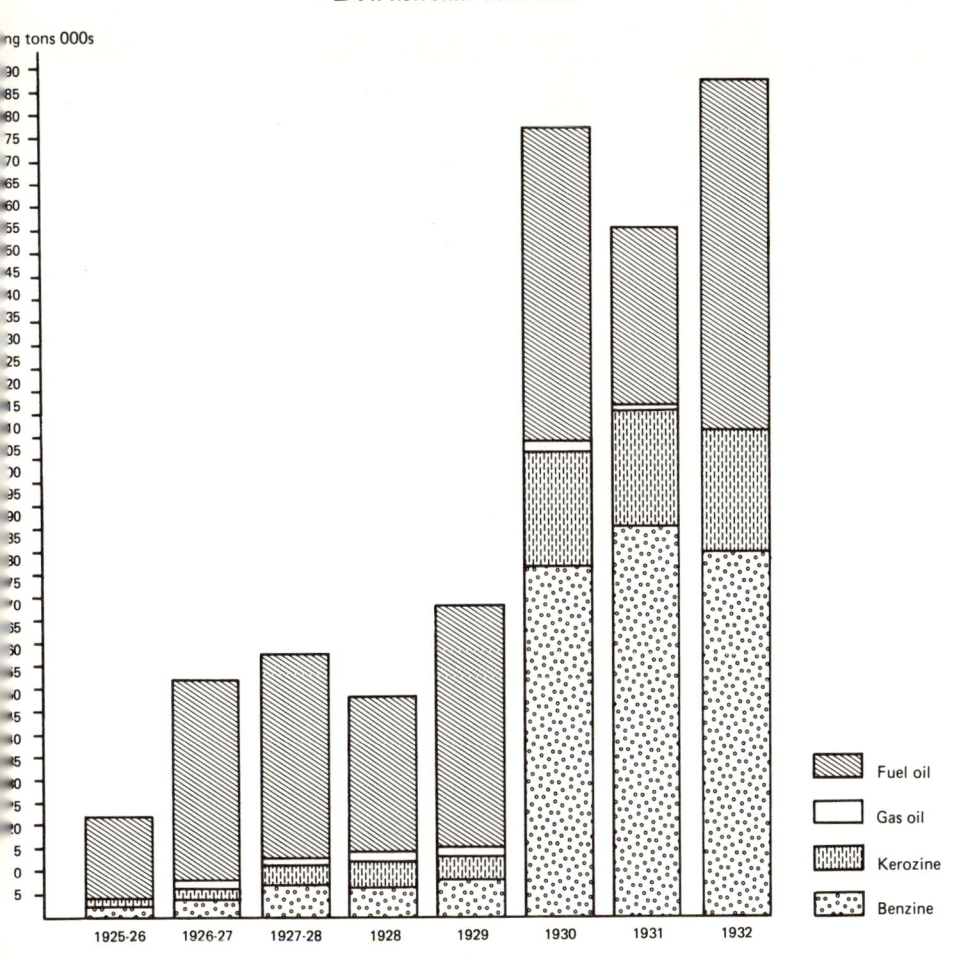

Figure 11.8 Sales — Benzina Petroleum (Italy) 1925—32
Source: BP 4K 7077

also of EPU parentage. Serious negotiations began in December 1924 for taking a 35 per cent interest in the German company for £125 000, but German interests offered a 40 per cent interest for a larger amount.[63] The Board was at first reluctant to get more deeply involved, but a further merger of other German oil groups enhanced the attractiveness of participating in a stronger broader based company, which was formed on 7 June 1926.[64] Five years later in April 1929, the Company raised its shareholding in 'Olex' to 75 per cent and two years later in July 1931 it obtained complete control and the Company became a wholly-owned subsidiary. Total sales quadrupled between 1926 and 1932, 52 000 tons to 208 000,

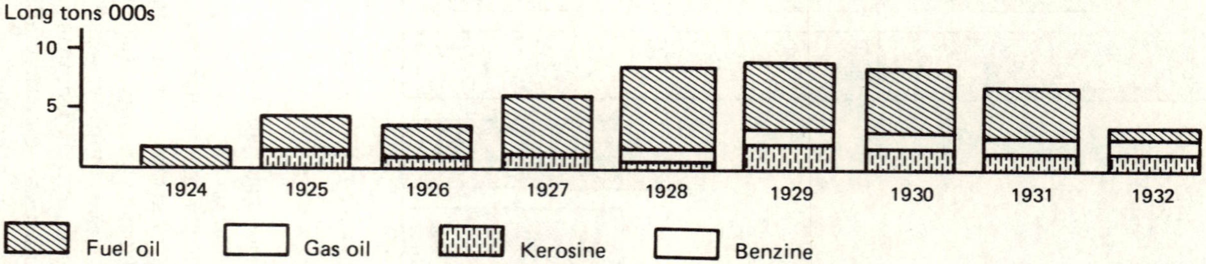

Figure 11.9 Sales – Oestereichische Naphta Import Gesellschaft (Austria) 1924–32
Source: BP 4K 7077

Downstream activities

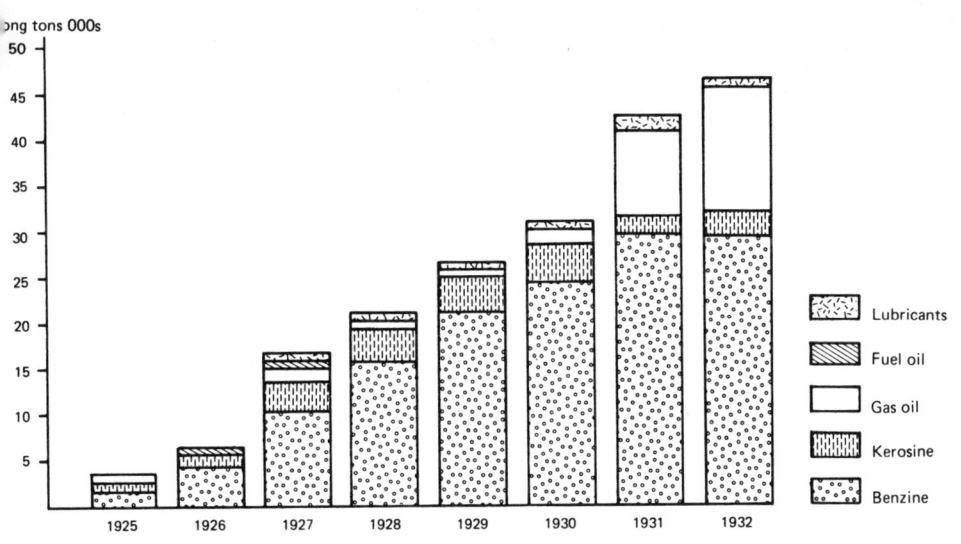

Figure 11.10 Sales — Benzin-und Petroleum Aktien Gesellschaft (Switzerland) 1925–32
Source: BP 4K 7077

making it the subsidiary with the third volume of sales after the BP Company and the French subsidiary, SGHP. Benzine sales dominated with a large rise, 48 times between 1926 and 1929, 3700 tons to 180 120. After a rise in kerosine sales between 1926-27 and 1929, 31 600 tons to 48 000, they dropped to 28 600 in 1929, 14 per cent of total sales. Fuel oil sales, apart from an exceptional year in 1928, were insignificant, but between 1927 and 1932 gas oil sales averaged 14.5 per cent of the total. (See Figure 11.11 for sales tonnages.) As a result of the German negotiations the Company took an interest in another EPU subsidiary, Petroleum Handels Maatschappij in Holland. Sales in Holland were practically confined to benzine and gas oil. The volume of sales decreased between 1927 and 1932, from 14 000 tons to 12 000. Kerosine sales averaged overall 56 per cent and those of gas oil 40 per cent. (See Figure 11.12 for its sales tonnages.)

This virtually rounded off the developments of continental subsidiaries, which had begun in 1919, with the exception of Svenska Bensin and Petroleum Aktiebolaget in Sweden which were incorporated on 14 December 1927, in which the Company held a 99 per cent shareholding. Another Swedish Company, Aktiebolaget Bensin and Oljekompaniet, was formed on 15 May 1928 with a Company shareholding of 74.33 per cent and Swedish interests of 25.66 per cent. Benzine sales were dominant (see Figure 11.13). A small company was also formed in Iceland in 1928, where there had been some sales since 1920.

497

Downstream activities

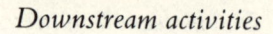

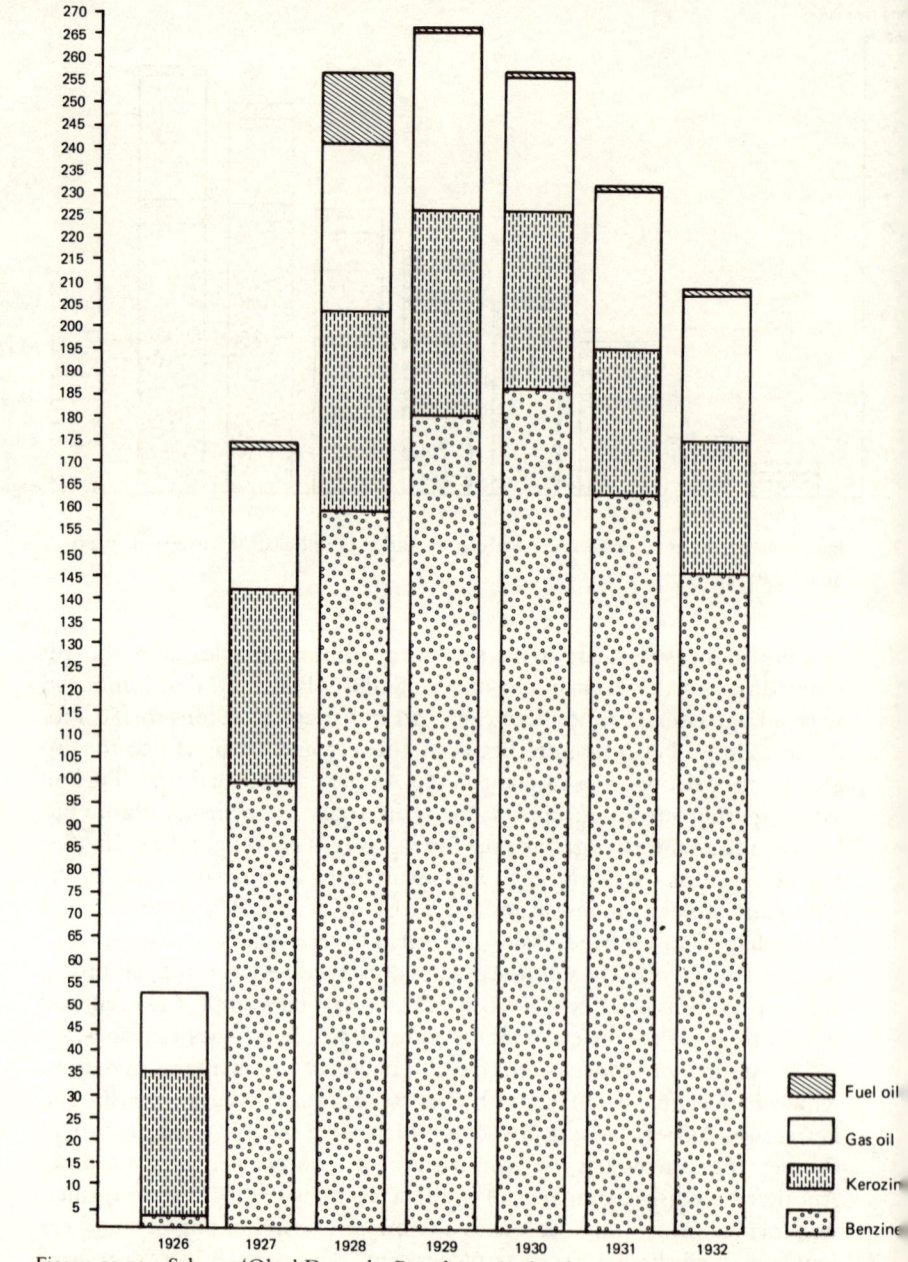

Figure 11.11 Sales – 'Olex' Deutsche Petroleum-Verkaufsgesellschaft MBH (Germany) 1926–32
Source: BP 4K 7077

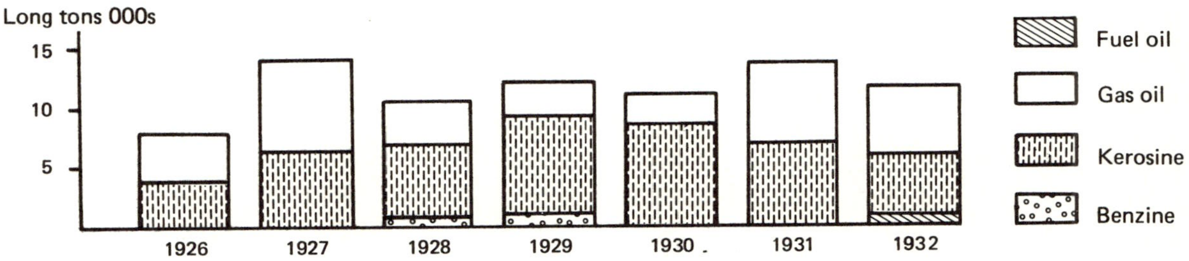

Figure 11.12 Sales – Benzine en Petroleum Handel Maatschapij N.V. (Holland) 1926–32
Source: BP 4K 7077

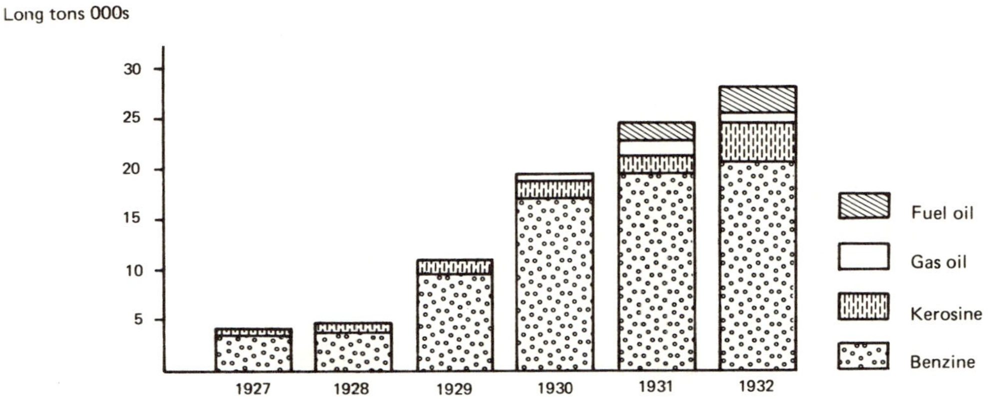

Figure 11.13 Sales – Svenska BP (Sweden) 1927–32
Source: BP 4K 7077

Downstream activities

In November 1926 Greenway remarked that 'our success in finding further outlets for our production encourages us to continue our policy of expansion'.[65] He was not at all apologetic about the aggressive marketing performance of the Company, recognising 'the pursuit of our policy of maintaining every inch of ground in this country, of neglecting no attractive opportunity of gaining a footing in Continental markets, of opening up at well-selected centres on the African Continent, of an active programme in Australia and finally of an intensive cultivation of the Iraq and Persian and other markets'.[66] Market success necessitated a strengthening of the administrative responsibilities of the marketing function. In April 1927 Heath Eves, whilst retaining overall charge of marketing, received three assistant directors: Morris, based in Paris, who was to look after the marketing of the continental subsidiary companies, Braithwaite, who attended to United Kingdom affairs and J.C. Clarke, who had joined the Company in 1925 from the Petroleum Department to oversee administration and supplies.[67] This was not defensive strategy, but the deployment of an active command structure to attack the markets.

The growth of kerbside pumps for the convenience of the motorist was accompanied by an imaginative advertising campaign[68] commissioning many of the prominent artists of the day such as Rex Whistler and E. McKnight Kauffer. The widespread use of the BP logo, designed for a competition in 1920 by an employee, and the house colours of green and yellow chosen by J.E.J. Taylor and Edmond Paix of the Paris office one spring day after a lunch in the country and adopted throughout the Company in 1925, were having a cumulative effect in establishing its public identity. Other French advertising initiatives at this time included the adoption of the term 'energol' and an early example of a publication for tourist information. The sponsorship of motor spirit at Brooklands and other tracks, with, for example, Sir Malcolm Campbell, and the provision of aviation spirit to record-breaking pilots, such as Sir Alan Cobham, widened the appeal of the Company's image. It was intended to stimulate the sales of products, and increase the awareness of its own brands. At this time too the Company became aware that not only did it have to provide better service for the motorist, who was becoming a more discriminating customer as a result of competition and engine improvements, but that he was also expecting a wider and improved range of products.

The Company had realised in 1925 that 'As we cannot beat our competitors in price we must rely on quality and publicity to secure and keep our market.'[69] Nevertheless, distribution costs, which had been estimated at 9d a gallon for motor spirit in 1922, were gradually reduced and between 1924 and 1928 dropped further to 3.6d a gallon as Table 11.5 shows. In October 1926 the Company recognised that it was necessary to

Downstream activities

She wants Easy Starting

and she gets it—
she always runs on

"BP"

The British Petrol

Do You?

British Petroleum Co. Ltd.
22, FENCHURCH ST, LONDON. E.C. 3
Distributing Organization
of the
ANGLO-PERSIAN
OIL CO.
LTD.

Fill up with "BP" these cold mornings and see how easily your engine starts.

Two BP adverts 1923

Downstream activities

He wants POWER

and he gets it—
he always runs on

"BP"

The British Petrol

Do You?

British Petroleum Co. Ltd
22. FENCHURCH ST. LONDON. E.C.3
Distributing Organization
of the
ANGLO PERSIAN
OIL CO.
LTD

Six records were broken on "BP" in the recent 200 miles Light Car Races at Brooklands.

Downstream activities

3 Miles a Minute
on
"BP"
The British Petrol

Captain Malcolm Campbell, driving his Napier-Campbell car "Bluebird" at Pendine Sands, Carmarthenshire, on Friday, February 4th, set up new world's speed records on "BP" as follows:

    Flying Kilometre - 174·883 m.p.h.
       ,,   Mile - - 174·224 m.p.h.

These are the mean speeds of two runs in opposite directions. The fastest speed in one direction over a mile was 179·158 m.p.h. Between the kilometre and the mile Captain Campbell's speed was timed to average 183·2 m.p.h.

(Subject to R.A.C. confirmation.)

For Acceleration, Speed and Power, use "BP," the British Petrol.

British Petroleum Co. Ltd. Britannic House, Moorgate. E.C.2
Distributing Organization of the
ANGLO - PERSIAN OIL CO. LTD.

BP advert using Malcolm Campbell 1927

Downstream activities

Table 11.5. *British Petroleum Company motor spirit distribution costs per gallon 1924–28*

	1924–25	1925–26	1926–27	1927–28	1928 (9 months)
Ordinary sales	6.6d	6.2d	5.9d	4.8d	4.5d
Total sales (incl. sales to affiliated companies and head office sales)	6.6d	6.2d	5.4d	3.8d	3.6d

Note: Distribution costs consisted of the following: landing charges, coastwise freights, carriage and freight, installation charges, packages, transportation charges, depot charges, delivery charges, leakage, advertising, bad debts, administration expenses and depreciation.
Source: BP, British Petroleum Company accounts compiled from file series 4P6001 to 4P7086

introduce a range of lubricating oils 'if only to protect their spirit position'.[70] It was agreed that the Company 'can no longer offer to the public a service from which such an important product is absent'.[71] It had to provide the whole range of products for the motorist. An indication of the range and volume of petroleum product imports into the United Kingdom market 1918-32 is given in Appendix 11.17 and the relative importance of lubricating oils in it. Some six months later lubricating oils were available in the United Kingdom and a year later they were being refined in France. From 1925 much research had been devoted to improving the quality of all products, particularly motor spirit. On 1 July 1926 the Company after hesitating for three years, made a mutual agreement with the National Benzole Company to be assured of its own supply of benzol from coal processing to add to petrol. Braithwaite had advocated in May 1923 'the necessity for the Company to follow the lead of its competitors and place on the market a Benzole mixture' otherwise it 'would be risking a serious check to their progress if they remained out of the movement'. He was disappointed. It took another couple of years before the Board really appreciated the problem and encouraged sufficient marketing and engine research to improve the quality of the Company's benzine. The Board as a whole lacked marketing interest or expertise. Only Greenway and Heath Eves had any entrepreneurial enthusiasm for the market.

In May 1927 Heath Eves surveyed the marketing position five years ahead and foresaw, in the light of anticipated expansion, the following demand (in tons) from existing markets detailed in Table 11.6.[72] Apart from the subsidiaries in Belgium, Denmark, Norway, France, Italy, Switzerland, Austria, Holland, Germany, Australia and the United Kingdom, he was contemplating entering the markets of South Africa,

Downstream activities

Table 11.6. *Anglo-Persian Oil Company group forward market position from May 1927 to 1932*

(long tons)

	Benzine	Kerosine	Fuel oil
1927–28	1 082 000	387 000	3 150 000
1928–29	1 143 000	391 000	3 250 000
1929–30	1 218 000	405 000	3 350 000
1930–31	1 301 000	415 000	3 450 000
1931–32	1 392 000	425 000	3 550 000

Source: BP H18/21

with an annual consumption of 70 000 tons benzine and 35 000 tons kerosine and Egypt, 31 000 tons benzine and 223 000 tons kerosine. Other potential markets included North Africa, Spain, Portugal, Greece, Portuguese South Africa, Madagascar and Ceylon, which together represented an annual consumption of 217 000 tons benzine and 122 000 tons kerosine. These figures pointed to a requirement of 6 000 000 tons of crude oil, which was the expected productive volume, pipeline throughput, refinery capacity and tanker offtake.[73] If, however, more production was to be expected, then 'those responsible for distribution should have in advance some indication of the quantities, which they will be required to handle'. Possible alternatives were posed, which were not necessarily mutually incompatible. Firstly Heath Eves proposed 'to provide our own distributing organisations', but admitted that it would involve 'heavy capital expenditure' and secondly 'we might consider a much wider arrangement with the Asiatic [Royal Dutch-Shell] (or the Standard)'.

Believing that the Company was now not only capable of holding its own, but taking an incremental increase of the market share, he acknowledged that there already existed a close working arrangement in the United Kingdom 'with the Shell and Anglo-American Oil Company. This may not go as far as we should like in its affect upon distribution costs, but it has had undoubted advantages.' Already in 1919 there were agreements by Shell-Mex, the UK marketing subsidiary of Royal Dutch-Shell, Anglo-American and BP Company to schedule prices.[74] On 20 February 1923 the Board of BP Company was informed of proposals to establish a zoning system in relation to Russian competition over prices in some parts of the United Kingdom, but declined to participate.[75] Russian petroleum imports, estimated at 40 000 tons a year, entering the British market were beginning to exert a considerable pressure on price stability, which the three main oil companies were trying to enforce. By 1924 'pirate' trading in general from both Russian and American sources was having a considerable undermining effect on the attempts to maintain price levels. Watson in 1923 had suggested that the three main distributing companies 'buy the Russian oil at the source'. W. Fraser, Chairman of Scottish Oils and a director of the Company, felt in 1924 that market palliatives and costly customer services were no substitute, for the real solution was that 'some arrangement should be arrived at between the three big companies whereby the excessive competition could be at least minimised'.[76]

In May 1927 Braithwaite characterised market strategies in the United Kingdom as being 'gallonage at any price' for Standard Oil, which would 'take almost any measures to secure big business and in any chance of business of appreciable volume tend to adopt a somewhat liberal interpretation of the inter-company conventions'.[77] Royal Dutch-Shell favoured the dealer and not the service station, believing that 'If you have got the public behind you, you are master of the situation', and increased the most expensive and unnecessary type of competition - namely that of quality. Braithwaite also preferred the dealer, relying on a great number of customers rather than a few large buyers. He admitted that though the sales of its motor spirit were least in volume, the Company was 'almost certainly the most popular of the big three, due to the fact that it has as a general rule a better class of representative than any other company'.

Gradually informal discussions between the main companies in the United Kingdom became more regularised, with particular committees dealing with certain subjects and a quota arrangement began to emerge. In February 1926 Cadman candidly revealed that 'Each of the interested companies were going into this matter in order to get something out of it, we were out to get one third of the trade and to reduce the costs of distribution.'[78] Yet a quota system was not a simple solution, for as Heath Eves knew 'it was important that the Company should within the next one or two years make a great effort to maintain its quota position fully'.[79] On the other hand, as in France in 1927, once having attained a position of selling in excess of its quota, should the French subsidiary, particularly in regard to the transition from package to bulk trade, endeavour to maintain that position or for financial reasons risk a fall to the position of undersellers?[80] On the Continent it was recognised 'speaking generally, in almost each market there is an arrangement of some kind in regard to prices', but it was admitted by Heath Eves that they were 'frequently of a very unsatisfactory nature, owing to (a) the difficulty of controlling foreign staffs and making them adhere to any agreed principles and (b) the fact that our control ceases before the oil reaches the consumer'.

These were the general considerations affecting the oil business of the Company in the mid-twenties, when it had embarked upon an expansionist marketing policy to the limits of its productive and refinery capacity.

4 RATIONALISATION

Heath Eves in May 1927, looking towards the future, felt that

> where new markets are opened up, we should establish distributing machinery under our direct control, but we should use every effort to bring about satisfactory trading arrangements with the Standard and the Asiatic, which will enable us to deliver our goods to the public in each market with the minimum expense. We should also endeavour to bring about close working with both the Standard and Shell groups to enable the three Companies to deliver oil as far as possible to the points of consumption nearest its source, and thereby secure the savings in freight which such a plan would bring about.[81]

This was not a policy of surrendering market advantage in areas of declining importance in order to participate in others of better prospects; it was a distributive balancing act. There was no sense of inferiority in his proposals for he had already rejected a bilateral solution of a closer arrangement with Royal Dutch-Shell 'of a nature so close that under them our products would have been sold through the established organisations of the Asiatic'.[82] This would obviously have made savings in capital expenditure, but he thought it 'exceedingly doubtful whether we could ever secure under such an arrangement a strong enough say in the affairs of the Asiatic, and through them on World oil questions, as would compensate us for the loss of "APOC" identity in the selling markets of the World'. If the Company contemplated further market penetration, through cooperative arrangements, it would not be with Royal Dutch-Shell only, but also with Standard Oil (NJ).

Heath Eves had formulated his policy as a result of intimate experience of negotiating with Royal Dutch-Shell and Waley Cohen in particular. Admittedly it was at a difficult time, when neither Waley Cohen nor Watson had renounced hopes of the Company actually being obliged, through Government action, to accept an enforced amalgamation with their respective companies. In July 1925 Heath Eves had raised the question of closer cooperation with Royal Dutch-Shell 'in markets which we have not yet entered, under a scheme whereby we would become, in the course of time, 50 per cent shareholders in the existing organisations of the Asiatic in those markets'.[83] In reporting to the Board in November he had little cause for optimism. Waley Cohen had declared that merely to deal with markets outside of those in which the Company owned distribution facilities offered too small a scope for an agreement. He considered it useless to continue with the conversations, unless the Company was prepared to include an amalgamation of its subsidiaries in those markets, where it was already established, with Royal Dutch-Shell.[84] Heath Eves, nevertheless, was authorised to continue negotiations', but by the following July he had to confess his failure to reach an acceptable agreement.[85] He was rebuffed. Waley Cohen insisted on capitulation not collaboration.

Heath Eves was convinced that there was no likelihood within a reasonable time of achieving 50 per cent holdings in new markets with the cooperation of Royal Dutch-Shell and 'thereby a real voice in their Distributing Companies'.[86] He was not interested in playing second fiddle. Moreover he was apprehensive over possible public opinion on 'the creation of a Trust and the establishment of an effective monopoly in oil distribution'. So it was decided that 'entering each new market should be dealt with on its merits as it arises, and that we should proceed on lines which will allow the Company to retain its independence as far as possible'. The Company was not willing to sacrifice its identity in the market place. There was no viable alternative. The Company was not prepared to accept Waley Cohen's proposals in 1925 or 1926 to 'confine itself to the markets in which it is already established', subject to incremental quota arrangements, and 'dispose of the balance of its products through the organisation of the Asiatic along the lines of the existing Benzine Contract'.[87] A prolongation of the benzine contract for a further three years was agreed in October 1927 as well as one for 100 000 tons of crude oil a year. The last marketing initiative in this period was disclosed in mid-1927 with the suggestion, which had been mulled over for a year, of entering Egypt with motor spirit and kerosine at a cost of £250 000.[88]

Within a year and a half the commercial scene was unrecognisable. In a period of remarkable activity Cadman, who had become Chairman in March 1927, had agreed with Deterding and Teagle a sketch of possible international cooperation. Cadman was doubly involved. On the one hand the Company had to safeguard its concessionary position in Persia, particularly after the discovery of Haft Kel had added to its productive capacity, by preparing for 'future outlets for Persian production, present and potential' especially as the duration of the Concession was limited. The Company had to secure as many marketing opportunities as possible. On the other hand with increasing production from South America, more accessible and closer to European consumption areas, Cadman believed that 'the boundaries of our markets for Persian production maybe expected to shrink or, at any rate to change'.[89] This was a challenging state of affairs. At the same time Cadman was apprehensive of the deteriorating relations between Royal Dutch-Shell and some American oil companies over the supplies of Russian kerosine which Standard Oil of New York

Downstream activities

began supplying to Indian markets in September 1927. These were the spurs to action, one involving the Company, the other of an international aspect, which caused Cadman to take the initiative. The Company had never been stronger and Cadman had everything going for him. He was at the plenitude of his powers. 1928 was his *annus mirabilis*, with the September Achnacarry Agreement between Deterding, Teagle and himself, his participation proposals to the Persian Government and his chairmanship of the Turkish Petroleum Company.

It would, however, be greatly exaggerating to assume that Cadman was original in the commercial overtures he was making from July 1927. Indeed it has been one of the constant themes of these pages to emphasise the mutual attractiveness and repulsion with which the Company and Royal Dutch-Shell fascinated and exasperated each other. Moreover the acceptance at this particular period in the commercial history of the Company of a rationalisation of the markets is not so surprising. From the early twenties in the United Kingdom, and later in Europe, working agreements in quotas had been accepted in varying degrees. Heath Eves, the proponent of the Company's expansionist policy under the guidance of Greenway, did not reject the advantages which they offered but opposed the restrictions associated with them.

Watson, who had frequently questioned the Company's expansive marketing strategy, preferred a closer association with Royal Dutch-Shell. Watson did not favour participating in subsidiary companies with local national interests. He later bitterly attacked an agreement reached between Cadman and Mussolini in 1928 because moves 'in the direction of "independent" marketing up to date have not been too happy. In France our "original" and "essential" nationals proved a broken reed. In Belgium we had to buy them out and I don't think we have lost any trade position by becoming 100 per cent Anglo-Persian there. In Germany the "essential" and "most" valuable national association promises to follow the history of our earlier French experience. In one of the Scandanavian countries at least, it has not been happy.'[90]

So concluded Watson, 'where direct marketing seems necessary for the Anglo-Persian, we should if and where possible, exhaust first the potentialities of co-operation with the real holders of power, i.e., one or other of the big producing groups, before tying ourselves up with the really essentially powerless Nationals, and ipso facto, antagonising such groups'. If the Company resisted such cooperation, Watson believed that it would only be caught in a 'possibly otherwise avoidable war of rates which leaves the market profitable to none and results in...having to delve into one's pockets even more to relieve one's National partner of the losses on the venture he has made'. Therefore it was best to be associated with

Downstream activities

producers who were also marketers, because they could either match consumption or restrict production.

It was an inadequate analysis because it left out of account national government policies, as was the case with France in 1928, with its oil legislation, and assumed an ability to regulate production, which proved quite illusory in the case of Russia and Rumania. It did, however, have a certain credibility in a period of overproduction and declining profitability, which was exacerbated by a chronic economic depression. Similarly, in other industries, such as textiles and chemicals, such regulatory trading agreements were regarded as a cure for commercial problems. As a director of both Burmah and the Company and a confidant of Waley Cohen, Watson, with his singleness of purpose, enjoyed for a time a disproportionate influence in the Company.

The rationalisation phase, which Cadman introduced, may be dated to a meeting in mid-July 1927, at which Cadman, Deterding and Watson were present. As Cadman reported to the Board on 26 July it was envisaged forming a company with Royal Dutch-Shell 'in order to introduce a general economy in capital and transport to operate east of Africa from Port Said to Cape Town and west coast of India and Ceylon, on a 50:50 basis both as regards capital and trade, indigenous products to have first call in the home market'.[91] It was approved in principle and Heath Eves was instructed to negotiate. Two months later Cadman informed the Board of his conversations with Deterding and Teagle which might involve 'protracted negotiations regarding distribution in the UK and...regarding Eastern Markets'.[92] Cadman had not started the ball rolling, but he had given it a direction. He persuaded W. Fraser, already on the Board, to leave Scotland to live permanently in England to assist in these affairs, the beginnings of their very close association. In his memorandum of 23 September, 'Distribution in the Middle East', Cadman justified the new company on the grounds of an increased offtake of an additional 44 000 tons of benzine and 107 000 tons of kerosine in an area where the Company sold only 12 300 tons of benzine and 4000 tons of kerosine. Moreover the Company would obtain 50 per cent of the profits from the existing distribution of 20 000 tons of benzine and 90 000 tons of kerosine, through participating in a holding company 'in connection with producing, prospecting, selling, refining and distribution'.[93]

In commending the idea Cadman referred to the imperative necessity of acquiring new outlets adjacent to production and refining facilities at the lowest possible cost. The Company was exerting itself, 'every possible opportunity for advance is anxiously sought and, if reasonably promising – firmly grasped'. He was not advocating a cutback in marketing activities, but it would be improvident to ignore 'the complicated and frequently unprofitable character of trading in many European countries today; and of the condition of stalemate to which insensate consumption and multiplication of facilities has brought the trade' in the United Kingdom. He warned that London was 30 days steaming from Ābādān, whereas Venezuela with its rising oil production was only 19½ days off. The Company had to establish its commercial equilibrium by tightening its grip 'upon all markets geographically so-placed as to constitute our own preserve'. Cadman realised that 'the quest for increased offtake in contiguous markets must be increasing'.

As a result of the apparently improved relations between the Company and Royal Dutch-Shell symbolised in the mutual respect which Cadman and Deterding had for each other, Burmah and Royal Dutch-Shell considered their own relationship in the light of the furious trade war which had broken out with Vacuum Oil Company and the Standard Oil Company of New York in the Indian markets.[94] They decided in November 1927 to set up a joint marketing company for India to avoid duplication of facilities, Burmah-Shell Oil Storage and Distributing Company. This news caused some consternation among the Company's management, Lloyd even suggesting that it removed the restrictions on the Company competing with Burmah in India, once its share of the market had dropped below 75 per cent.[95] By the end of the year it had been agreed that the Company could consign oil to Burmah by whom it would be marketed in India through the new Burmah-Shell company. This was approved at a Board Meeting on 5 January and confirmed by Watson the following day on behalf of Burmah.[96]

This agreement, which was finally concluded on 29 March 1928, but back-dated in its application to 1 January, clarified the situation in respect of India, recognising that the Company was anxious to maintain an interest in the fuel oil market of India and extending its interest in the markets there for other oils.[97] The Company had not been excluded from India; rather, a greater opportunity for increased offtake was probable than could just have been expected from their agents Shaw, Wallace and Co., whose agency was terminated in 1928. For Cadman it was a 'general extension of our markets'. India had previously been a market for the Company's fuel oil but, Cadman reminded the shareholders in 1928, 'without participating at all by way of capital, we have...arranged to consign to the new company...a substantial share and as the market grows an increasing amount of the import trade of that enterprise'.[98] In the first year 388 628 tons of Persian oil products were delivered to India, 307 903 tons of fuel oil and 80 725 tons of kerosine.

The agreement with Burmah over India was a positive contribution to the Company's distribution policy, not an apology for it. The same spirit

Downstream activities

animated the discussions between Deterding and Cadman, which were resumed in early January, resulting in a Heads of Agreement being initialled on 31 January.[99] The Government raised no objections in principle to the idea of the new Company[100] and after further detailed negotiations the Consolidated Petroleum Company Ltd was formed on 27 November 1928, comprising Egypt, Syria, Palestine, Red Sea Ports, East Africa and South Africa, Ceylon, Madagascar, Mauritius and Reunion and remained formally in existence till February 1981. Its *raison d'être* was claimed to be the economies in distribution which could be effected to the benefit of both consumers and companies by eliminating wasteful duplication of services.

In commenting upon these developments to the shareholders in November, Cadman stressed the principle of 'drawing upon these nearest sources of production'.[101] The Board was satisfied that 'nothing but good can come of this significant union of interests'. Whilst the new company was not concerned to eliminate competition in other markets, it did represent a significant burying of the commercial hatchet after years of animosity. Cadman did not visualise the new arrangement as impairing the Company's independence. On the contrary, he emphasised its 'basis of absolute equality', a comment which previously would have carried little conviction, but was then acceptable, so much had the relationship between the Company and Royal Dutch-Shell changed over the years.

Cadman was not just content to mend the relations between the Company and Royal Dutch-Shell. He had a vision of a better international relationship between the major oil companies, a blend of idealism and realism. It would seem that Cadman voiced his anxieties for the first time on 18 August 1927, when he met Teagle, who was on a visit to London. They had a number of discussions including lunch with Deterding on 31 August, till Teagle left on 1 September. They discussed the question of Russian oil supplies in European markets and abroad which had risen ten-fold in the United Kingdom between 1923 and 1928 and the abnormal state of affairs which existed in the distribution of petrol in the United Kingdom and other European countries, and particularly its high cost. According to Cadman, Teagle 'was at one with me that something should be done to cut down these expenses and he was prepared to use his influence in this direction and, if necessary, to discuss the matter with Powell [F.E. Powell, Chairman, Anglo-American Oil Company] Deterding and myself'.[102]

Cadman was concerned to break the log jam which had occurred between the companies as a result of the controversy over Russian supplies. This had existed since the 'London Memo' of July 1922, stipulating informally that until there had been a restitution or compensation for the oil properties expropriated by the Soviet authorities there would be no purchases of Russian oil supplies.[103] Deterding, although uncommitted to the idea of an embargo at first, later became a strong supporter. After several years of ineffectual and divided attempts to impose a boycott, which was thwarted by the strong bargaining position and commercial skill of the Soviet representatives, some of the companies broke ranks and ran for the substantial profits to be earned from trading in Russian oil products. In January 1927 negotiations for an overall agreement, to which Royal Dutch-Shell were to have been a party, between Standard Oil and Soviet negotiators collapsed. Teagle, who was not personally enthusiastic over the negotiations, seems to have been relieved at their failure. It was cold comfort to the Standard Oil of New York and Vacuum Oil companies, who were expecting an agreement so as to supply their eastern markets. Nevertheless they promptly shipped Russian kerosine to their Indian markets in mid-1927. This enraged Deterding, who countered with a fierce war of rates, reminiscent of earlier trading tactics in the same area.

On 22 February 1928 Cadman, having settled the new relationship with Deterding, between the Company and Royal Dutch-Shell over eastern markets, turned his attention again to the wider issues of oil diplomacy and suggested to Teagle the establishment of 'a small "clearing-house" for matters of the very highest policy' in which the Company, Royal Dutch-Shell and Standard Oil were involved.[104] He also wrote in March to C.F. Meyer, President of Standard Oil of New York, proposing a coordination of policy.[105] Without the cooperation of American oil interests, no measure of international agreement was possible. In November 1927 Cadman had commented to the shareholders on 'The abnormal situation created by excessive competitive production in the United States and the growing exports from Russia.' Overproduction meant not only 'very cheap products for the consumer' but also 'industrial disorganisation...and the dissipation of one of the world's most precious assets'. Appendix 11.18 gives an idea of petrol prices 1918-32.

Much of the responsibility, according to Cadman, lay in the United States for 'How to conserve that country's oil reserves without stinting the present generation is perhaps the greatest and most complicated economic problem the United States authorities have ever been called up to face.' Cadman was not seeking to escape from commercial reality in unexceptionable platitudes. He was concerned at the excessive and intolerable waste of a natural resource that was not replenishable, an asset that was irreplaceable. He respected not only the convenience of the consumer, but also the claims of the producer. Moderation, not profligacy, was his response. The United States had in 1922 absorbed its own production but in 1927 exported a quarter of it. In his address to the American Petroleum Institute on 6 December 1928, Cadman refused to denigrate oil as a com-

Downstream activities

mercial intoxicant or a political drug, referring to it as 'a store of energy to be conserved, released and applied as part of a concerted operation owing its inception to more than one nation, and therefore yielding its tribute to more than one treasury'.[106]

It would be a misunderstanding of Cadman's motives to assume he was imparting a spurious tone of moral or scientific respectability to the operations of the market place. He was imbued with a sense of responsibility, which transcended, but did not despise the profit motive. In an age not as yet so conscious of the environment, referring to the multiplication of selling agencies, pumps, lorries, tank-wagons, and other distributing facilities, he observed to shareholders in 1928 that 'there is at present an absolutely spend-thrift competition in this domain, a competition which, I regret to say, has done much to impair the amenities of our country-side'. In the preamble for the working agreement, which was prepared for the discussions at Achnacarry, to which Cadman had proposed to Teagle and Deterding, he was much concerned to dispel from the public mind the impression that 'the petroleum industry operates solely under a policy of greed and has itself initiated methods of wanton extravagance'.[107] Yet he was not wearing a commercial hair shirt, he was not an apologist for the capitalist ethic. Industry had to be prosperous Cadman warned, that 'is our first duty to the shareholders', but 'prosperity, however, does not mean a place in the sun only for a few world-wide operators. Every concern that can produce or operate competitively but efficiently must be able to share in it. Let me strongly emphasise the fact that in no sense is any creation of a trust aimed at.'

Such were Cadman's intentions, such was his response to the marketing conditions of 1927–28, with their rising production and falling prices. His policy was not inconsistent with the Company's marketing developments, its downstream activities, which had not been passive in character, but directed towards the growth of a fully integrated organisation operating on a world-wide basis, unconstrained by any possible limitations deriving from its Government shareholding. Its marketing ability can be measured by its phenomenal success between 1919 and 1928 in bringing Persian oil to the United Kingdom (see Figure 11.14). For overall United Kingdom consumption 1900–32 see Appendix 11.19.

5 OVERSEAS MARKETS

(a) Persia

Before the Company had begun to market in Europe after the war it had already begun selling petroleum products in Persia from Ābādān in 1913.

Downstream activities

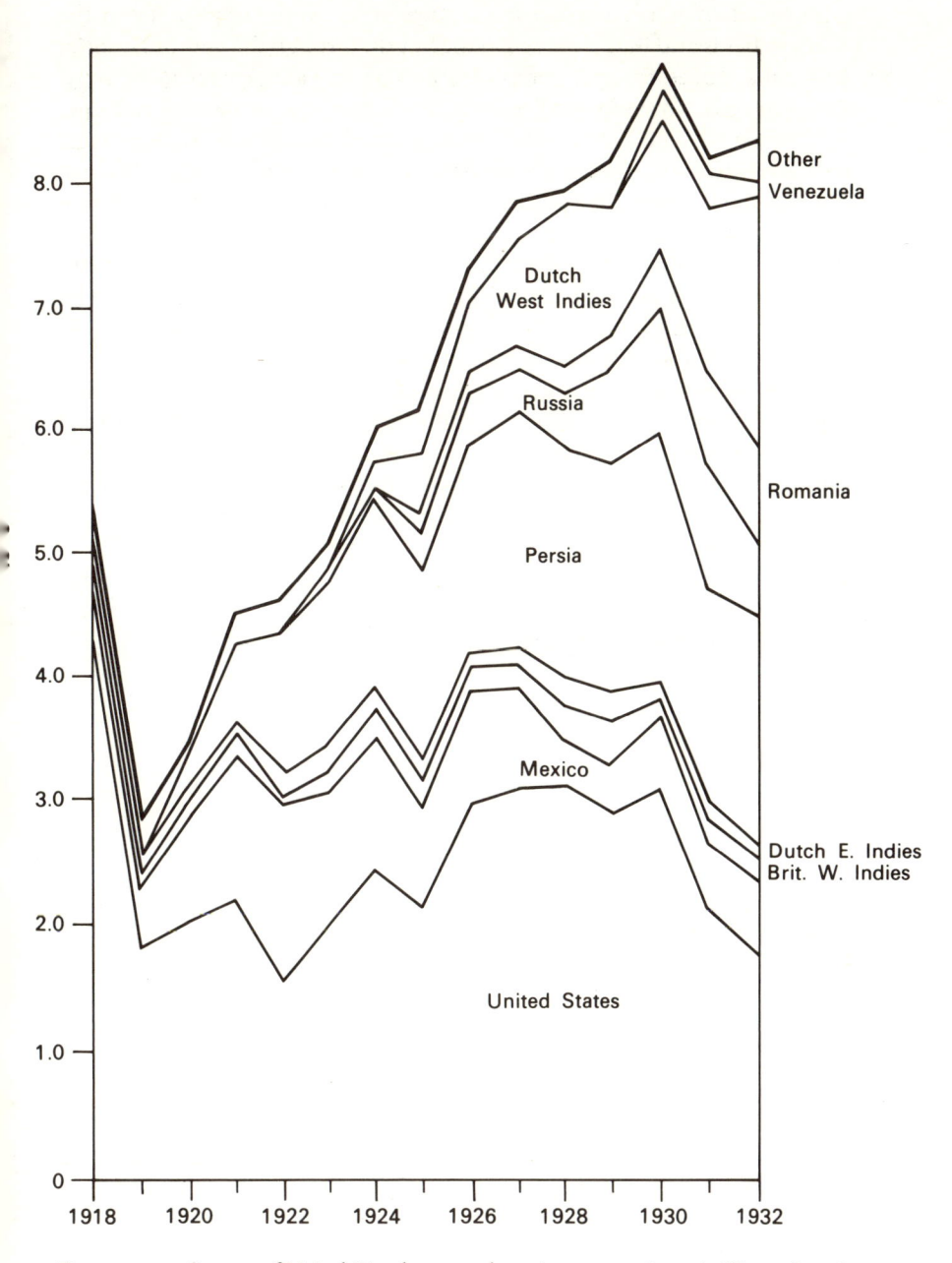

Figure 11.14 Sources of United Kingdom petroleum imports 1918–32 (millions of tons)
Source: Ministry of Fuel and Power, *Statistical Digest*, 1950

Downstream activities

Almost all of north Persian oil requirements were supplied from the Russian fields at Baku. Yet even in the South, through the port of Bushire, Russian supplies entered Persia, amounting in value to £2636 in 1903, £9644 in 1904, £6808 in 1905, £357 in 1906-07, £3298 in 1907-08 and £402 in 1908-09.[108] There were, therefore, justifiable economic reasons for a strong reaction to a new competitor in a market adjacent to Russian oilfields, no less than for a political response to possible British penetration of a Russian sphere of influence. Other oil imports came from the United States and Hungary. Once the refinery had been commissioned at Ābādān, supplies were available locally. Kerosine generally constituted the main product sold until 1925, constituting over 50 per cent of total sales, reaching its highest figure, 13 300 tons, in 1930, but actually dropping in volume from 1931, when it was exceeded by benzine sales for the first time. Benzine sales rose gradually till 1925, 701 tons, 6 per cent of total sales, with kerosine 4100 tons, 38 per cent, and fuel oil 6000, 56 per cent out of a total of 10 800 tons. Fuel oil sales fluctuated between 1490 tons in 1921 and, exceptionally, 12 000 in 1932, but averaged 3680 tons, 27 per cent of total sales, between 1921 and 1931. The major expansion of sales took place after 1927, doubling between then and 1929, when the Company began to supply central and northern Persia in competition with Russian distributors (see Figure 11.15).

In the dislocated conditions in the north after the Russian Revolution, oil supplies became short, so the Company attempted to make deliveries

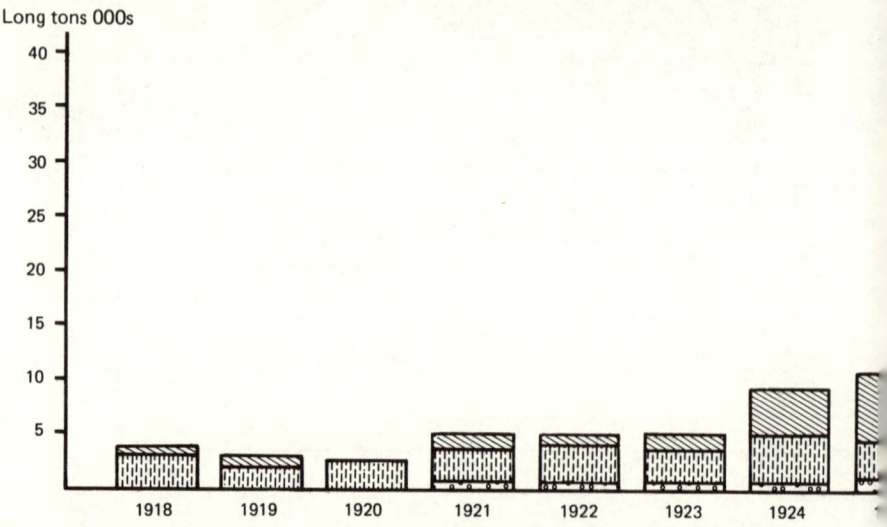

Figure 11.15   Sales – Anglo-Persian Oil Company in Persia 1918-32
Source: BP 4K 7077

Downstream activities

to northern centres, but transportation costs were excessive. Russian supplies resumed and there was criticism of the quality of the Company's products, though that can be partially discounted on account of adverse propaganda. By November 1923 Nichols admitted that 'The Tehran Agency as a distributor of oil is practically closed.'[109] It was clear that a year later the Russians were 'determined to drive APOC products from the Central, Western and Eastern Persian markets',[110] and they established an organisation, Persanaft, with 15 per cent participation of Persian commercial interests to do just that. The Company continued to concentrate on local markets in the south, the Persian Gulf and Iraq, where it achieved reasonable sales.

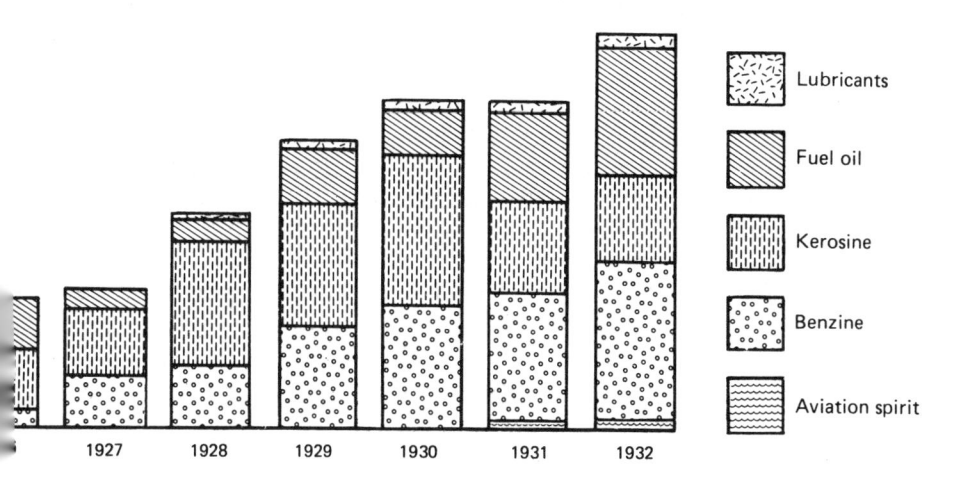

During the winter of 1925-26 there was a serious grain shortage as a result of a bad harvest in Persia. Relief operations on a large scale with motor transport were mounted by the Persian Alimentation Service under Colonel McCormack, one of the American assistant advisers associated with A.C. Millspaugh, the American financial adviser to the Persian Government. The emergency coincided with a dispute with the Russians over fishing rights in the Caspian Sea and the Russian Government imposed a trade embargo on exports including motor spirit. Fairley, the Company's representative in Tehrān was instructed to 'take immediate steps to assist [the] Persian Government', and provide motor spirit at a reasonable price.[111] The Company responded to the challenge[112] and the relief work was satisfactorily completed. Jacks was asked to prepare a 'scheme for definite and permanent organisation for North Persia sales'.[113] The Shah had been impressed and 'made it clear to Sir Percy Loraine that he wished to see the Anglo-Persian Oil Company market their products on a vaster scale'. As the acting Commercial Secretary reported, the Company

> have risen to the occasion and exploited this opportunity to attempt to break the Russian monopoly for oil products in the North, and, to a very large extent, further south, thereby demonstrating to the Persian Government and people that it is at last in a position to supply them with products which they would normally feel themselves entitled to have, namely, those of their own country.[114]

During Cadman's visit to Tehrān in April 1926, he attempted to consolidate on the goodwill that had been gained by the Company's assistance to the Persian Government. In some respects expectations were greater than achievements because the lines of communication to Ābādān were long and terrible till the completion of the Khuramabād road in 1927, and there was disagreement on prices, and problems over sites for depots.[115] Yet, gradually, a network was established, agents appointed, staff recruited, prices reduced and Russian competition defied.[116] In 1927 sales of motor spirit tripled over the previous year. If it was not commercially profitable, it was politically expedient. By 1928 the Company's distribution network had greatly expanded, with sales of kerosine for heating and illumination, fuel oil for irrigation pumps in 'rapidly expanding agricultural activities', and lubricating oils.[117] There were more trading difficulties as a result of disputes between the Persian and Russian governments in 1929 and the Company was approached to become the exclusive supplier for the Persian Government, but, to the disappointment of the Persians, declined to become a monopoly supplier and distributor. It did, however, further strengthen its organisation, including distribution activities, with pumps in Tehrān, and arranging with agents over most of the country for supplies of petroleum products.[118] In 1931 northern sales were put under the charge of Mustafa Fateh, a senior member of Persian staff, in the capital. By 1932 the market for oil products could 'be said to be roughly halved between the Anglo-Persian and Russian suppliers'.[119]

One interesting development on the Persian distribution scene was the proposed formation of a Persian distribution company. It had been first raised by Cadman as a possibility in late 1927. Cadman was looking for ways of encouraging Persians to show 'a good deal of national sympathy into our affairs, which we deserve and need'.[120] As the distribution of the Company's products in Persia was then being undertaken on a widespread basis, it was reasonable to assume that 'a Persian investment in and a connection with it might be of mutual advantage' in furthering 'the distribution of our Persian products throughout Persia'. There was therefore a political and an economic interest which were complementary. A preliminary case was prepared by H.R. Cooke, the Chief Accountant, in London, which was favourably received by the Management Committee. It was hoped that the new company 'would serve as an instrument for winning the sympathetic co-operation of influential Persians in our selling operations in Persia'.[121]

On 27 March the Board, subject to certain reservations about the inalienability of the Persian shareholding, approved.[122] Cadman justified the idea because it would provide 'a true conception of the problems affecting oil production and exploitation' through 'the participation of individual Persians, alike in the rewards and hazards of our enterprise there, and that in a form more intimate and personal than the basic royalty can afford'.[123] It was an imaginative idea, which would have been practical in application and directly appealing to pocket and pride. It could, however, 'proceed only upon the assurance of a substantial measure of support'. Such was the rationale for the South Oil Marketing Company Ltd, whose Board was to be composed of eight members, four Persians, including the Chairman, and four nominated by the Company and which 'would undertake the whole of the APOC's oil marketing in Persia'.

On this basis Jacks mentioned the scheme to Tīmurtāsh, Minister of Court, on 26 May 1928 and engaged a lawyer, Dr Hassan Khān Naficy, to advise him on the applicability of the Persian Commercial Act of 1925 to the proposed company. On 29 May, Jacks informed the Shah of the proposals, which were welcomed. Jacks, however, was cautious about possible Persian interest or the provision of Persian capital, but work proceeded on drafting the memorandum and articles, and settling administrative matters such as supply agreements. In September 1928, Braithwaite, who was deeply involved in London, remarked that 'we are anxious to see the Company registered without delay, and we trust that you will find it possible to do so'.[124] There was a clear commitment to the idea, it was not just a hobby-horse of the Chairman.

In December arrangements were still being discussed, but by then these had been overtaken by events, for in January 'further action with regard to the formation of the Company is at present suspended'.[125] In August, Cadman and Tīmurtāsh had met at Lausanne and enough common understanding appeared to have emerged to aim for a comprehensive settlement of all the concessionary problems by offering the Persian Government participation in the Company. This, on a grander scale, would have embodied all the objectives of the proposed distribution company. Detailed discussions were therefore adjourned pending agreement on the principle issues which were to be discussed in Tehrān early in 1929 (see

Downstream activities

Chapter 13). In retrospect it was an idea that ought to have met with success.

(b) Iraq

Mesopotamia had already become, in the couple of years following the commissioning of the refinery at Ābādān, an outlet for the Company's products. During the First World War large supplies were delivered to the expeditionary force there and the subsequent British civil administration. By 1922 conditions had returned to a commercial basis, but complaints were expressed early in that year about the cost of the Company's products. Cox, then High Commissioner, reported to the Colonial Office that the 'high price of Qalyan oil [kerosine] has caused universal discontent among cultivators' and suggested that the Company should 'consider in their own interests a considerable and immediate reduction'.[126] As kerosine then constituted about 30 per cent of the Company's sales in Iraq, mostly to individual small purchasers, it was important not to lose the sympathy of the market or the Government, so the price of kerosine was reduced. Arnold Wilson, informing London that 'all concerned are becoming keener than before to do business with us', warned that there would be 'a reduction of sales instead of expansion unless our prices drop'.[127] There was at this time a certain rigidity in London in setting local prices. Jacks complained later in November 1924 that this practice left no room for local discretion in the control of distribution,[128] which was true for both Iraq and Persia. It was a year before the distribution department in London allowed prices to be reduced.[129] The railways took regular supplies of fuel oil under contract and from 1922 aviation spirit was supplied to the Royal Air Force.[130]

A new development took place in November 1925 with the formation of the Khanaqin Oil Company (KOC). Between 1924-25 and 1932 total sales doubled from 67 700 tons to 125 600, as did fuel oil sales, 41 300 tons, 6 per cent of the total, to 92 600, 73 per cent. Kerosine sales, apart from an unusual drop in 1926-27, remained relatively constant around 20 000 tons annually, falling from a peak in 1927-28 and dropping from 29 per cent of total sales in 1924-25 to 15 per cent in 1932. Benzine sales, after rising gradually from 1924-25 to 1929 to 10 200 tons, were fairly steady till 1932, around 10 per cent of the total. Aviation spirit tonnage was boosted by sales to the Royal Air Force, averaging, between 1924-25 to 1932, 2300 tons a year, some 2.6 per cent of total sales. (See Figure 11.16 for sales in Iraq.)

After oil had been found in commercial quantities at Naft Khana in 1923, protracted negotiations ensued with the Iraqi authorities over the

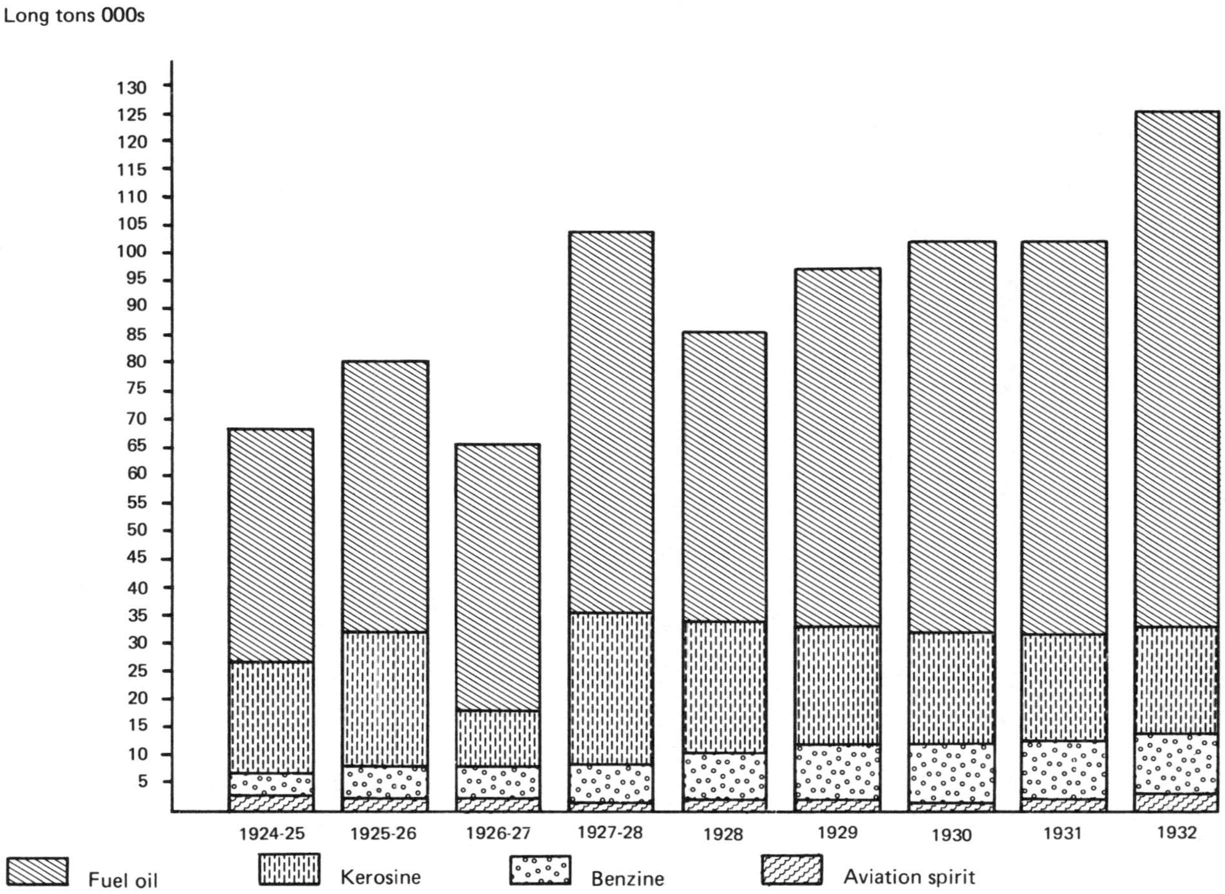

Figure 11.16 Sales – Anglo-Persian Oil Company in Iraq 1924–32, ex Ābādān and from Khanaqin Oil Company from February 1927

Source: BP 4K 7077

manner of exploiting this field.[131] Eventually agreement was reached and the Company undertook to construct a refinery at Khanaqin, the Alwand refinery, which came onstream in February 1927. By 1932 this had reached an annual throughput of 59 000 tons providing 70 per cent of the total product sales in Iraq (see Appendix 11.15b). In August 1928 an agreement was signed in respect of deliveries by APOC to KOC which regularised the position of KOC as the major supplier to the Iraqi markets.[132] The Company eventually agreed in 1932 in Iraq, what it refused to do in Italy, to act more or less as a monopoly distributing agency (with the cooperation of the Iraq Petroleum Company) under government protection.[133] It resisted similar efforts to impose upon it a comparable role in Persia, where the situation was more complicated by the considerable Russian presence in the Persian oil markets. The Company had no desire to become embroiled in domestic political issues. There was an added complication to distribution activities when concessionary or exploration factors were involved: the same commercial criteria did not always apply as elsewhere.

(c) Australia

A different kind of distribution experience is revealed in the case of Australia, involving a close government association. Discussions began early in 1918 with W.M. Hughes, the Commonwealth's Labour Party's Prime Minister, when he was in London for an Imperial War Cabinet meeting, on a comprehensive scheme for a production, refining and marketing company.[134] An agreement was later reached in 1919 between the British and Australian governments on a joint exploration programme in Papua with the Company undertaking the work.[135] Hughes, in London in January 1919 prior to attending to the Peace Conference in Paris, had further discussions with Greenway. By 20 May a firm proposal was made for the formation of a company 'with a view to the creation of an industry in the Commonwealth to produce, refine and market the products of mineral oils, a capital investment of £1 000 000 to be registered in Australia, with the Government having a 51 per cent shareholding and the Company 49 per cent'.[136]

There was little doubt that the main incentive for the Company lay in the expectations of oil being discovered in Australasia. During 1918 the proposal of the Company was being considered in Australia, as well as other propositions, including one from Royal Dutch-Shell.[137] It was the beginning of the Papuan oil mirage which has continued to this day. It was 'confidently anticipated that any refinery erected in the Commonwealth can operate as from an early date on indigenous oil'.[138] The association

Downstream activities

between the Company and the Commonwealth Government 'would be in the very best interests of Australia because at the present time the whole of the petroleum products consumed in the country are imported from foreign countries, whilst there is little doubt in our minds that Australia possess large mineral oil resources of its own'. There were big stakes involved as the Company desired 'the exclusive right to examine and develop all petroliferous areas within the Federal Commonwealth (including of course New Guinea and Papua)'.

In reality, as mentioned in Chapter 12, these exploration hopes did not materialise. The Company was saddled with the burden of carrying crude oil from Persia to Australia to a relatively small refinery of 200 000 tons per annum capacity at Laverton, Melbourne, for a total population that was not large, some six million people, scattered throughout the Commonwealth over vast distances against the well established opposition of Royal Dutch-Shell and the Vacuum Oil companies. The Bill authorising the Commonwealth Oil Refineries Limited (COR) was passed in May 1920.[139] The refinery was commissioned in 1924. As for the market share, it was optimistically expected in 1924 that 'the COR will be able to obtain a third of it within the first few years'.[140] By September 1925 it had achieved a 4 per cent share of the market and two years later it remained much the same.[141] Total sales increased ten times between 1924-25 and 1930, to 102 000 tons but declined in 1931 and 1932 to 83 500 tons. Benzine and fuel oil provided the main sources of sales. Benzine sales rose from 1800 tons, 18 per cent of total sales in 1924-25, to 45 700, 50 per cent, in 1932. Fuel oil sales increased from 8000 tons in 1924-25, 77 per cent of total sales, to a peak of 50 700 in 1930, but fell as a percentage of total sales to 50 per cent. Between 1926-27 and 1932, kerosine sales averaged 7 000 tons, 9 per cent of total sales (see Figure 11.17 for sales and Appendix 11.15c for refinery throughput).

Visions of imperial grandeur and special relationships, rather than the cold logic of the market place, had influenced decisions and no indigenous oil came to the rescue, for by 1930 hope had been abandoned.[142] Guidelines for a distribution policy included a rejection of a price cutting campaign, which could 'only lead to a war of rates which could have serious results financially'. It was more important that 'salesmen and distribution facilities generally, are, if possible, in efficiency ahead of others'.[143] Yet, the pattern of distribution which had evolved in Australia was not markedly similar to the European model. When Slade and Watts visited Australia in 1924 although they deplored the fact that the Company had to sell through agents on a commission basis outside Sydney and the state of Victoria, there was no satisfactory alternative to employing as agents the old established firm of Dalgety and Co., which 'with their

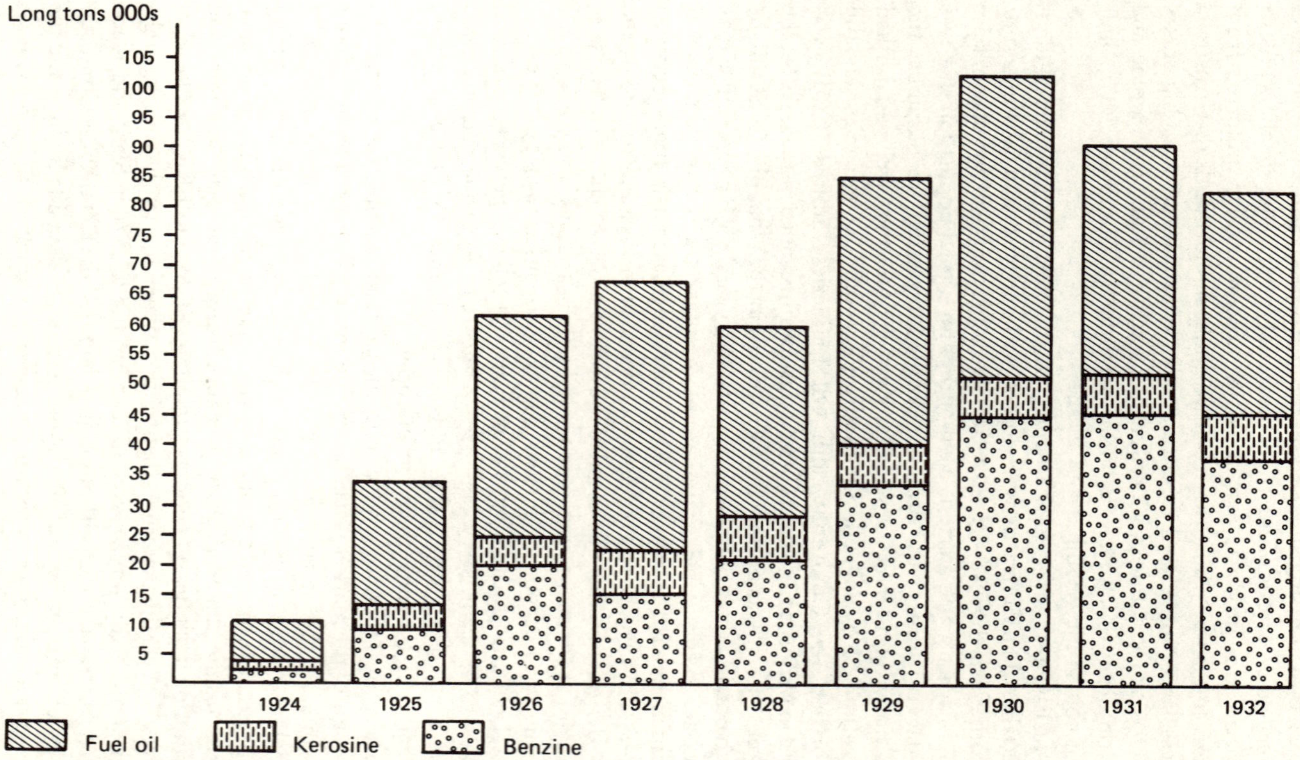

Figure 11.17 Sales – Commonwealth Oil Refineries 1924–32
Source: BP 4K 7077

Downstream activities

enormous organisation will effect sales more readily than any traveller COR could put in'.[144]

Competition was intense. The refinery production of kerosine was at first a drag on the market. A sufficiently good quality of benzine could not be early produced and the other companies were able to import cheaper products. COR was undercapitalised and subsisted from 1926 on appreciable rebates on crude oil and motor spirit supplies from the Company.[145] In 1925 COR was beginning to experience difficulties in keeping up with the installation of pumps by its rivals and appealed for more capital 'to provide for the wastage of the company's assets through carrying on operations at a substantial loss'.[146] The Commonwealth Government, however, refused to sanction any further increase of funds, though the Company provided an advance up to £195 000 for more refining and distribution facilities, to bring the market share up to 20 per cent to which they felt they were entitled.[147] The hopes of the Government and the Company had not been fulfilled. It was a decade of a disappointing relationship and in August 1930 Heath Eves was admitting that 'the best course would be for the Commonwealth Government to sell out to its partners'.[148] The association with the Commonwealth Government, originally conceived in terms analogous to the relations between the Company and the British Government, only served to show that such a compatability of interests was not necessarily identical in all cases. Indeed it was unique.

6 SHIPPING

The moving of large quantities of crude oil and products from Ābādān to refineries and markets in Europe, Australia, and along the bunkering routes of the world required a large scale transporting fleet of tankers. The increasing demand for the Company's products, its growing bunkering activities throughout the world and its construction of refineries meant a larger tanker fleet. The formation of the Company's shipping company, the British Tanker Company and its growth and activities during the war, has already been referred to in Chapter 7.

At the end of the war the Company purchased tankers from the shipping agents, Stephens Sutton and Stephens, some of which were German prize ships. The fleet which had been acquired through purchases and orders amounted, at the beginning of 1920, to 30 tankers with a total d.w. tonnage of just under 270 000 tons. The size and importance of the tanker company may be imagined by a comparison of its monthly salary cost with that of the Company as a whole, some 48 per cent of the total in February 1918.[149] This is a high percentage, even allowing for the distort-

Downstream activities

Table 11.7. *Cost of Anglo-Persian Oil Company group staffing 1918*

	£	£	£
Anglo-Persian Oil Company Limited			
London		1 400	
Persia	3 220		
plus 15 per cent	483	3 703	5 103
British Tanker Company Limited			
Administration		375	
Masters, Officers and Engineers (all steamers)		4 425	4 800
British Petroleum Company Limited			1 431
Homelight Oil Company Limited			340
D'Arcy Exploration Company Limited			208
			£11 882

Source: BP 77/49/8, staffing memorandum 1918

ing effect of war-time employment. Table 11.7 gives also an indication of the relative size of administration and seafaring staff. In January 1919, Greenway recognised that 'Our executive staff in the shipping department is quite good but we badly need a "Managing Director" to deal with all the big questions connected with the Company's shipping business.'[150] Garrow, who had attended to his shipping responsibilities ably in collaboration with Lund, could not continue to devote the necessary time to the tanker company. As the size of the fleet increased 'there is ample work for an "all-time" man'. J.D. Stewart was appointed to the post on 13 February. Stewart had learnt his business in the hard exacting commercial school of Glasgow tramp shipping. He was shrewd, forceful and well experienced in the trade. James Gardiner and Co., which had been established some forty years and with whom Stewart was a partner, operated a modest fleet of some fifteen ships between 3500 and 5200 tons and, taking advantage of the likely immediate post-war boom in shipping, had sold out at the end of the war.

As the boom burst, so was Stewart able to recruit a number of shipping personnel known to him personally, whom he brought south to staff the tanker company. Indeed many of those who joined the tanker company in those days later served it with distinction in senior managerial posts, such as J.R. Robertson, A.J. Richardson, R. Gillespie, J.H. Jackson, F. Fenton, the first company naval architect, among the most prominent.[151] There was no intention on the part of Greenway that the tanker company should

Downstream activities

play a minor part in the Company's business. On the contrary, Greenway was a strong protagonist of shipping interests, regarding a tanker fleet as indispensable so that the Company could market at its own discretion and not according to the freight rates and conditions exacted by others. He believed that the Tanker Company should cover 90 per cent of the Company's shipping requirements. If the Company was to exploit the production of distant Persia, it had to have its own transportation resources.

The worldwide supply patterns of the Company in this period were relatively simple. In 1921 48 per cent of the cargoes lifted were loaded at Ābādān, which was then the only source of Company-owned crude oil and Company-refined products, 855 000 tons out of 1 781 000 of crude oil and 351 000 tons against 1 431 000 tons of products were carried. Port Arthur was the main loading port in the Gulf of Mexico, where 33 per cent of all cargoes were lifted. The loadings in the United Kingdom were mostly in the coastal trade carrying products to different depots and installations. The United Kingdom received 66 per cent of the tonnage carried, 1 174 000 tons, followed by Indian destinations, 214 000 tons. Europe only received 21 000 tons. Some 70 per cent, 1 240 000 tons, was carried in the Company's own tankers and 30 per cent, 541 000, in managed vessels, including some for the Admiralty and on behalf of other owners. Cargo taken through the Suez Canal amounted to 574 000 tons, about a third of the total carried (see Tables 11.8a and Appendix 11.20).

In 1928 the pattern had not changed very drastically except in volume. The total cargoes carried amounted to 4 566 000 tons of which 3 685 000, 80 per cent, came from Ābādān, and 672 000 tons, 14 per cent, came from the Gulf of Mexico. The United Kingdom remained the main country of destination, 1 747 000 tons, half the lifting from Ābādān, 281 000 tons from the Gulf of Mexico, 2 044 000 tons in all, 45 per cent of total liftings, but cargoes discharged in Europe also increased to 595 000 tons, 13 per cent of the total. The loading in Ābādān to the United Kingdom and Europe consisted of 1 411 000 tons of crude oil, 63 per cent, and 825 000 of products, 2 236 000 in all (see Tables 11.8b and Appendix 11.21). The refineries at Swansea and Grangemouth absorbed most of the crude oil delivered to the United Kingdom. Ninety two per cent, 2 053 000 tons, of the trade from Ābādān to the United Kingdom and Europe was carried in the Company's own tankers and 8 per cent, 183 000 tons, in chartered vessels. The tanker fleet in 1928 consisted of 80 sea-going tankers, 5 coastal vessels and 4 government-owned steamers, with 13 sea-going tankers on time charter. Typical running costs for a serviceable representative 10 000 d.w. tanker operating in 1922 can be seen in Table 11.9, at a freightage rate of £1 17s 6d per ton. Port disbursements at £45 per day, fuel £39, insurance

(a) Trading pattern 1921 — main cargo routes
(cargo tons)

Table 11.8. *Shipping movements of the British Tanker Company*

Discharge areas \ Loading areas	Ābādān	Gulf of Mexico	United Kingdom	North America (East)	Far East	Eastern Mediterranean	Totals
United Kingdom	481 000	442 000	158 000	66 000	—	27 000	1 174 000
North-west Europe	—	10 000	6 000	5 000	—	—	21 000
Mediterranean	93 000	15 000	18 000	—	9 000	—	135 000
Aden and Red Sea	47 000	—	—	—	—	—	47 000
India, etc.	214 000	—	—	—	—	—	214 000
Australasia	8 000	—	—	—	—	—	8 000
East Africa	5 000	—	—	—	—	—	5 000
South Africa	7 000	—	—	—	—	—	7 000
Gulf of Mexico	—	62 000	—	50 000	—	—	112 000
North America (East)	—	53 000	—	5 000	—	—	58 000
Totals	855 000	582 000	182 000	126 000	9 000	27 000	1 781 000
						Via Suez Canal	574 000

Table 11.8. (cont.)

(b) Trading pattern 1928 — main cargo routes (excluding coastal voyages in Northern Europe)

Loading areas / Discharge areas	Persian Gulf	United Kingdom	Gulf of Mexico	Mediterranean	Far East	USA East Coast	South America	Totals
Scandinavia	27 000	—	8 000	6 000	—	—	9 000	50 000
North-west Europe	462 000	—	58 000	—	—	25 000	—	545 000
United Kingdom	1 747 000	—	281 000	16 000	—	—	—	2 044 000
Northern Europe	2 236 000	—	347 000	22 000	—	25 000	9 000	2 639 000
Mediterranean	285 000	81 000	26 000	17 000	—	—	—	409 000
Egypt	72 000	—	—	—	—	—	—	72 000
Aden	321 000	—	—	—	—	—	—	321 000
East Africa	35 000	—	—	—	—	—	—	35 000
South Africa	18 000	—	6 000	—	—	—	—	24 000
India and Burma	633 000	—	—	—	8 000	—	—	641 000
Far East	—	—	18 000	—	—	—	—	8 000
Australia	85 000	—	—	—	—	—	—	85 000
USA East Coast	—	—	136 000	—	—	—	10 000	146 000
South America	—	—	139 000	—	—	—	32 000	171 000
Gulf of Mexico	—	5 000	—	—	—	—	—	5 000
Totals	3 685 000	86 000	672 000	39 000	8 000	25 000	51 000	4 566 000
							Via Suez Canal	2 516 000

Source: British Tanker Company vessel movement books

Table 11.9. *Typical British Tanker Company running costs 1922*

British Councillor: 23 May 1922–27 January 1923
(10 925 summer deadweight tons – built 1922)

	23 May–12 August			13 August–29 October			30 October–27 January			Totals			Per day		
	£	s	d	£	s	d	£	s	d	£	s	d	£	s	d
Port disbursements	3 738	10	8	3 698	14	10	3 895	3	7	11 332	9	1	45	6	7
Insurance	2 433	13	4	1 919	9	–	1 443	13	9	5 796	16	1	23	3	9
Wages	1 517	12	11	1 273	7	9	1 447	4	3	4 238	4	11	16	19	–
Provisions	525	–	10	499	8	7	576	5	4	1 600	14	9	6	8	1
Stores (Deck)	139	14	2	132	17	10	153	6	9	425	18	9	1	14	1
(Engine)	108	5	4	102	19	9	118	16	8	330	1	9	1	6	5
Maintenance	190	7	5	181	1	7	208	18	10	580	7	10	2	6	5
Repairs	1 159	9	8	1 102	18	5	1 272	12	1	3 535	–	2	14	2	10
Galley coal	26	–	8	24	15	3	28	11	5	79	7	4	–	6	4
	9 838	15	–	8 935	13	–	9 144	12	8	27 919	–	8	111	13	6
Bunker fuel	3 736	11	3	2 922	18	–	3 185	2	–	9 844	11	3	39	7	7
Total expenses	13 575	6	3	11 858	11	–	12 329	14	8	37 763	11	11	151	1	1

Table 11.9. (*cont.*)

Freight earned															
Ābādān to Swansea	18 161	5	–	17 923	2	6	17 891	5	–)	56 169	8	5	224	13	7
Swansea to Antwerp							2 193	15	11)						
Lighterage at Ābādān							1 174	7	9	1 174	7	9	4	13	11
Passage monies	150	–	–	578	13	6	450	–	–	1 178	13	6	4	14	3
Total earnings	18 311	5	–	18 501	16	–	21 709	8	8	58 522	9	8	234	1	9
Profit	4 735	18	9	6 643	5	–	9 379	14	–	20 758	17	9	83	–	8
Days	82			78			90			250			1		
Ports of call	Sunderland			Swansea			Swansea								
	Swansea			Port Said			Antwerp								
	Port Said			Ābādān			Port Said								
	Ābādān			Port Said			Ābādān								
	Aden			Swansea			Port Said								
	Port Said						Swansea								
	Swansea														
Cargo tons															
Ābādān to Swansea	9 686			9 559			9 542								
Swansea to Antwerp							3 809								
Freight rates															
Ābādān to Swansea	£1.17.6			£1.17.6			£1.17.6								
Swansea to Antwerp							£–.11.6								
Cost of Suez Canal ballast passage (including disbursements)	£1 224			£1 224			£1 224								
Cost of Suez Canal loaded passage (including disbursements)	£1 758			£1 758			£1 753								

Downstream activities

£23, wages £17 and repairs £14 include the main items in a daily cost of £151. Revenue amounting to £234 left a gross profit of £83 a day.

Moreover, since it was Greenway's professed policy to supply continental markets, he needed tankers not only to ship the main products of fuel oil, benzine and kerosine, but also to carry crude oil to Llandarcy in 1922 and later for other Company refineries at Grangemouth, Courchelettes and Laverton. It was for this reason that he planned at the beginning of 1919 to have a fleet of '60-80 ships within 3-4 years'. By the time that the second building programme was completed in September 1925, the tanker fleet was composed of 61 ships totalling 500 000 tons d.w. Of the 39 ships of 385 000 tons in the whole programme, 32 were delivered between August 1921 and November 1923, a formidable rate of construction and commissioning, which was not to be exceeded till the massive post-war-building programmes of the 1950s. It required a greatly strengthened organisation. The successful implementation of the programme was a notable personal achievement of Stewart and his staff at a time which was not easy for such an arduous undertaking.

Greenway's enthusiasm for a large tanker fleet, as well as his expansionist marketing policy, was not necessarily shared by all his colleagues. Cargill and Watson were particularly phlegmatic in their approach. Thus early in 1918 Greenway, anticipating a rush for shipping construction after the ending of the war, suggested purchasing an interest in Palmers Shipbuilding Company of Jarrow principally in order to establish a direct interest in a shipbuilding concern and so ensure priority on the options for berths in a yard.[152] He believed also that the Admiralty might cause a tanker tonnage scarcity by retaining ships in service to build up a strategic oil reserve of some 5 000 000 tons. He foresaw a need for shipping by Burmah, of at least five ships. He estimated that the Company would need 'to build or purchase at least 25 additional boats between now and 1922, to enable them to carry their Products other than the Admiralty Fuel Oil: and unless we can get the call on some ships I do not see how this is to be done'.[153]

Inchcape held the same views as Greenway, but the Burmah directors were not convinced and the idea of a Company shareholding in Palmers Shipbuilding Company or any other shipbuilding company was never pursued again.[154] Instead a berth was reserved for ten years at Messrs Swan Hunter on a basis that 7 to 8 vessels could be built in five and a half years for nett cost plus 25 per cent to cover establishment charges and profit, which for 10 000 ton tankers was estimated at about £26 10s 0d per ton d.w., though actually costing £30 per ton d.w.[155] Seven 10 000 ton tankers and a small coaster of 2200 tons were delivered. The contract did not run for ten years but was terminated in July 1926 on payment of £12 000 compensa-

Downstream activities

tion. In the short term the Burmah directors were right because by the end of 1918 the Company had tankers surplus to requirements, but Greenway was able to charter 9 tankers to Royal Dutch-Shell at a freight of £22 6s 0d. 'This,' he wrote to Cargill, 'is very good business', as it implied a profit of some £500 000 over a full year on these terms.[156]

In the long run Greenway's shipping policy was justified. The Company decided to concentrate on 10 000 ton tankers, mainly because of the restrictions on draught imposed by the bars in the Shatt-al-'Arab. It was not because of building limitations, as Standard Oil (NJ) had ships of 22 000 tons coming into service. The basic design for the second programme of ships remained more or less unaltered till the mid-1930s, when it was superseded by the 12 250 ton class. The arrangements for tanks and pumping systems changed little. Quarters and accommodation were also hardly altered. The single shaft and propeller transmitted 3000 hp and gave an average speed of about 10 knots loaded. The Company was responsible in 1921 for a major marine innovation in tanker propulsion, for instead of installing the generally favoured well-tried triple expansion reciprocating engine, it began to substitute for it, in 25 ships of the second programme, the steam turbine engine. Although turbine engines with single reduction gears were already in use in warships and passenger vessels, the double reduction gears needed to reduce the high rotating speed of the turbines to the slow revolutions necessary in the propulsion of a 10 knot tanker was a major engineering achievement. Fuel oil consumption, which had averaged some 45 tons a day, dropped to 27 tons on a comparable basis.[157]

Already while ships for the second programme were being fitted with steam turbine engines, consideration was being given to the use of single marine (diesel) engines and four ships powered with this kind of engine were ordered for the last vessels of the second programme. In the early

Launching of the *British Aviator*, by Lady Greenway on 20 May 1924

days of the marine diesel it would seem that this was less on technical grounds, though it did represent another very large saving in fuel costs, down to a day's sailing on 10 tons, than because the Company was anxious to promote sales of its own product, diesel oil, by a practical demonstration of its suitability. Greenway, at the launch of the *British Aviator* in May 1924, the first diesel-engined tanker to be added to the fleet, declared that he was gratified that 'the Diesel type of engine is rapidly driving the steam engine off the seas; because this means not only greater demand for a Persian oil fuel for use in the form in which it gives the best economic results, but also a more effective conservation of the combined oil resources of the world'.[158]

In the third programme, 1926-31, 33 ships were ordered, of which 23 were fitted with diesel engines, and 25 were 10 000 tonners. In the application of marine engine technology to tankers the Company was a pioneering influence and it is remarkable that its essentially conservative-minded 'Safety First' Scottish ship management was technically so advanced. Even if the inspiration cannot be directly attributed to Stewart, there is no doubt that before his retirement in 1925 he had made the major contribution in encouraging if not initiating the innovatory practices. These can be seen in the comparison between the main tanker fleets in 1931 in Table 11.10.[159]

Table 11.10. *Numbers of steam turbine and motor driven ships, and steam reciprocating vessels in three of the principal oil company tanker fleets 1931*

	Steam turbine and motor driven	Steam reciprocating	Total
Royal Dutch-Shell	44	62	106
Standard Oil (NJ)	34	104	138
Anglo-Persian Oil Company	51	31	82

Source: Lloyd's Registry of Shipping, register books

One important difference between the second and third programmes concerned the cost of ships, for the Company was able to negotiate fixed prices of between £132 500 and £135 000 instead of between £180 000 and £430 000 for the average 10 000 ton tanker. The order books of the shipbuilders were not so full. Tanker building constituted an important part of the employment of the shipyards. As the *Yorkshire Post* commented at the time of the launching of the *British Colony* on 4 April 1927,

British shipbuilders, who have suffered so severely from the acute depression under which the industry has laboured during recent years have found a very

Downstream activities

important measure of relief in the orders for new oil tankers, mainly placed by the Anglo Persian Oil Company...when the new tankers now ordered are completed all of the eighty vessels will have been built in British yards, the majority in the last eight or ten years.'[160]

No less remarkable than the extent of the third building programme was its financing. On 11 December 1925 an extraordinary general meeting authorised increasing the share capital of the tanker company from £3 000 000 to £4 000 000, converting it to a public company and approving the issue of £4 000 000 Ten Year 5½ per cent First Debentures. The issue, priced at 97½, was oversubscribed. The *Financial Times* reported that 'The Public has yet another opportunity of subscribing for a sound and attractive investment.'[161] The value of the fleet was estimated at £9 000 000. It was the last occasion on which the public had the chance to invest in the tanker company, for all subsequent capital for shipbuilding was raised through various City and international institutions by differing methods, becoming more complex as costs escalated. The growth of the tanker fleet 1921-31 is shown in Table 11.11.

On 29 June 1925, Stewart retired. In February 1926 Heath Eves added shipping to his portfolio of Company affairs and in September Sir Basil Kemball-Cook became managing director with Robertson as manager of the tanker company. Kemball-Cook had a distinguished career as a civil servant with the Admiralty and more particularly during the war as a key member of the Ministry of Shipping as Director of Naval Sea Transport and in 1917 as Director of Admiralty Transports, which included control of all tanker operations. He was well known to Cadman. After the war he served on the Reparations Commission. With his Etonian and Cambridge background he was a contrast to the rougher Stewart and while he may have lacked some of his drive, he was a capable administrator, who was able to some extent to coast on the success of his predecessor. Kemball-Cook had a concern for the welfare of his staff and fleet personnel and he is remembered as a congenial, considerate and competent man, who was not particularly stretched in his responsibilities. There is no doubt that conditions for those sailors engaged on eastern service were trying, not so much for climatic reasons as for the long separations that were often endured from their families. Just as the tremendous expansion in Persia had caused severe personnel problems, so much the same had occurred in the shipping sphere. A common joke at the time was that the initials BTC meant 'Better times coming'. During 1926 certain issues arose with some urgency and Kemball-Cook managed to alleviate the worst of the issues over pay and conditions and to bring rates up to comparable conditions in the shipping industry. The administration which he established (see Appendix 11.22) remained much the same till the end of the Second World War.

Table 11.11. *Growth of the British Tanker Company fleet 1921–31 in terms of numbers of vessels and deadweight tons*

Class or d.w. tonnage	Fleet at 31 Dec. 1920 No.	Tonnage	Disposals 1921–25 No.	Tonnage	2nd building programme No.	Tonnage	Fleet at 31 Dec. 1925 No.	Tonnage	Disposals 1926–31 No.	Tonnage	3rd building programme No.	Tonnage	Fleet at 31 Dec. 1931 No.	Tonnage
ex Petroleum Steamship Co.	6	46 855	1	10 700	—	—	5	36 155	5	36 155	—	—	—	—
ex Prince Line	2	11 700	—	—	—	—	2	11 700	2	11 700	—	—	—	—
ex Stephens Sutton	2	8 898	1	3 800	—	—	1	5 098	1	5 098	—	—	—	—
ex 'War' Class RFA (Royal Fleet Auxiliary)	2	16 910	—	—	—	—	2	16 910	—	—	—	—	2	16 910
'Leafs'	6	55 920	1	11 000	—	—	5	44 920	5*	44 920*	—	—	—	—
5000/6000 Emperor	2	11 592	—	—	—	—	2	11 592	—	—	—	—	2	11 592
10 000/11 000 Empress	5	53 456	—	—	—	—	5	53 456	—	—	—	—	5	53 456
Small tanker	2	900	2	900	2	4 984	2	4 984	—	—	2	1 777	4	6 761
6000	—	—	—	—	3	18 267	3	18 267	—	—	5	34 278	8	52 545
9000	—	—	—	—	5	46 693	5	46 693	—	—	1	9 151	6	55 844
10 000/11 000	—	—	—	—	29	315 611	29	315 611	—	—	25	275 058	54	590 669
	27	206 231	5	26 400	39	385 555	61	565 386	13	97 873	33	320 264	81	787 777

Note: * Last 'Leaf' remained in service until December 1932
Source: BP British Tanker Company ship lists

Downstream activities

In 1917-18 the Company disposed of a production of 897 400 tons of which some 75 per cent was taken by a single customer, the British Government. A decade later the Company was marketing a production of 5 357 800 tons, a six-fold increase, of which the British Government's demand was some 10 per cent. In the same period the Company created its own transporting and distribution organisations. It was an ambitious programme not without its failures and which severely strained its financial resources in 1922 and 1923. It was hampered by the inferiority of its motor spirit as the age of the motor developed. Its marketing function does not appear to have enjoyed the kudos of its technical, exploratory or shipping staff, almost as if trade was unbecoming. Its principal competitors, Standard Oil (NJ) and Royal Dutch-Shell, had a headstart in the markets. The reluctance of some members of the Board to be actively engaged in the market place had an adverse effect on its marketing progress. Nevertheless the momentum given by Greenway towards the fullest integration of its activities was sufficiently sustained for the Company to achieve both marketing independence and growth.

12
THE EXPANSION OF INTERNATIONAL INTERESTS 1919-28

I INTRODUCTION

The Company's presence in Persia has inevitably overshadowed its other concessionary activities elsewhere in the world. These were not negligible; while they were not outstanding, they certainly cannot be disregarded. Failure no less than success reveals the nature of the Company and its place in the international oil industry.

In the House of Commons on 7 July 1914 Colonel Yate, member for Melton, asked for a 'distinct guarantee' that the Government's investment in the Company would be devoted by it 'wholly and solely to the development of the works in Persia, and not used for any other project in any other country whatsoever'. Churchill gave him the assurance that 'the money voted by Parliament shall be devoted exclusively in the Persian areas'.[1] At that time the answer was quite correct, for the installations in Persia were being greatly improved and an increasing flow of oil was about to be supplied to the Admiralty in fulfilment of the supply contract. Indeed, Greenway, who was consulted on the question, accepted the answer given, with that interpretation.[2] The request, however, highlighted a dilemma which the Company faced till the end of its concessionary period in Persia. Was it bound to remain exclusively committed to an interest in Persia? By the time of Riżā Shāh the Persian Government had become resentful of the Company's activities in other countries, which it believed competed with, if not deflected it from, its obligations towards Persia. This was not only an economic conflict of national and corporate interests, but also, as far as the Persians were concerned, in the case of Iraq, a bitter political issue. The important but neglected fact that D'Arcy had been simultaneously pursuing concessionary interests in both Persia and the Ottoman Empire meant that the Company had inherited a difficult situation, which it had not initiated.

There were no objections to Royal Dutch-Shell prospecting beyond the East Indies or Standard Oil operating outside the United States or the Nobels becoming involved in a web of outlets stretching across Europe

The expansion of international interests

and Asia or even to Burmah investing its Indian profits in Persia. The commercial logic accepted by the integrated oil companies made such developments inevitable and to disregard them was to relinquish the opportunities for profitable trading. The Company, however, was not only constrained by concessionary considerations. It was also in danger of being restricted by governmental limitations on its freedom to act in a commercial manner. There was, obviously, an impression amongst some Ministers and certain officials that the Company should be prevented from acquiring too much power and broadening its interests, other than to ensure supplies of fuel oil to the Admiralty. Indeed, in the preliminary stages of the Harcourt Committee's deliberations in spring 1918, an attempt was made by the Petroleum Executive through the Treasury to muzzle the Company, by insisting that 'no undertakings should be entered upon by the Company in any country outside Persia without express sanction' (see Chapter 6).

Greenway found such a restriction unacceptable and informed Inchcape that future success was 'dependent upon the maintenance of its present policy, to ensure that its business, like that of other producing, refining and distributing oil companies must necessarily be of a world-wide character'.[3] Jenkins, the other Government director at the time, thought it only referred 'to keeping the Treasury "posted up" in regard to any new undertakings and that it was not intended that there should be any prohibition', but as Greenway remarked to his colleagues on the Board, 'this is not what the letter says'.[4] The situation was clarified after further correspondence and meetings. Greenway was assured by the Treasury that his misgivings had 'no foundation in fact'.[5]

This clarification did not mean that the Company was immune from criticism. The evolution of the Company's relationship with the Government was controversial, as Chapters 6 and 8 demonstrate. So, it was not surprising that the Petroleum Executive should have remarked that 'we have encouraged the D'Arcy syndicate in Cyprus, Brunei and Jamaica, but are not going to put ourselves blindfold into their hands'.[6] The involved and protracted negotiations over the Mesopotamian oil concession exhibited some of the serpentine aspects of Government policies. The voices of officials representing the Foreign Office, the Admiralty, the Colonial Office, the Government of India and other Departments of State were seldom in unison and frequently out of tune. Particularly over the areas bordering upon Arabia, including Kuwait, Bahrain, Muscat and Qatar, there were marked differences of approach amongst the Political Agents themselves over the granting of oil concessions. There were conflicts of interest with those anxious about British presence in the area. These became more serious as the result of growing American interest in the oil

The expansion of international interests

prospects of the Middle East. Moreover there was an impression that the Company did not 'particularly want these concessions provided no-one else gets them' as a Colonial Office memorandum of 1924 expressed it.[7]

In other places such as in Africa the colonial administrations expected the Company to undertake exploratory work on little geological evidence in return for unattractive rights or licences for the sake of imperial objectives. In the aftermath of the war the Company was offered many concessionary opportunities on a speculative basis and, anxious to increase its concessionary chances, was tempted to dabble in them without sufficient control or satisfactory knowledge. It is really only towards the end of 1922, after Cadman had formed the fields, refinery and geological department, that exploration activities became more organised on a world-wide basis in relation to geological prospects and concessionary legislation, and better related to market opportunities. They came to be based upon the advice and expertise of its geological staff. A very active phase lasted till 1927, when the second oil field in Persia, Haft Kel, was discovered and Baba Gurgur became the first producing well in Iraq for the Turkish Petroleum Company (TPC). The Company was no longer dependent on a single oilfield upon which to base its world-wide activities. Yet, it still required a western source of production to balance its eastern production and improve its marketing position in competition with those oil companies who already had western production closer to the main areas of consumption in the United States and Europe. Hence the emphasis on exploration in South America, particularly Colombia and Venezuela.

Unfortunately its close association with the British Government precluded it from being granted concessions in those countries. It was, moreover, not only in South America that the association with the British Government was distrusted. It provided a convenient pretext for discrediting the Company in bidding for concessions, particularly over Bahrain. Thus in March 1924 the Political Resident in the Persian Gulf reported that

There is at present a very determined opposition to granting the concession to the Anglo-Persian Oil Company...At present any ill-wishers of the British or of the Anglo-Persian Oil Company never lose an opportunity of impressing upon their hearers that the Anglo-Persian Oil Company is a Government concern and that to grant a concession to this company is tantamount to giving it to the Government.[8]

Arnold Wilson, who was no stranger in the corridors of Whitehall, felt that certain officials had been less than impartial in dealing with the concessionary claims of the Company. This was confirmed in 1932 over Bahrain, when he was told 'What a pity the APOC did not get this concession, and what a crime Daly [the Political Agent] committed in getting it for so obvious a man of straw as Holmes.'[9] There was also a fear among Government Ministers that their integrity might be impaired if

The expansion of international interests

they were to show undue preference for the Company. Thus in 1923 the Colonial Secretary, the Duke of Devonshire, remarked to the Political Resident in the Persian Gulf that 'the position of His Majesty's Government as a principal shareholder in the Anglo-Persian Oil Company makes me anxious to avoid any line of action which might be represented as a championship of that Company based on motives of direct financial interest'.[10] Yet, a successor, Leopold Amery, just over a year later, had no inhibitions about applying some political pressure upon the Iraqi authorities to reach an agreement over the granting of a concession to the Turkish Petroleum Company (see below section 5).

Certain concessionary interests like those in Mesopotamia, north Persia or Australia fall outside the general pattern of activities, for, whilst most exploration was simply economic, in some cases it was tinged with political implications, or at any rate came to be treated as such. Besides, what has been assumed to be the political sensitivity or indifference of the Company has, in fact, often been due to genuine geological differences of opinion. Professor de Böckh, the Company's geological consultant, was convinced that the Arabian littoral was unpromising for oil deposits, a view that was influential in determining the Company's assessment of prospects in that area and shaping its policy. Whilst the Company did not encourage initiatives there, it did not exclude precautionary interest. Some of the Company's concessionary moves were defensive in purpose. Whilst it is true that in response to competitive bidding it reacted positively to protect its own interests, it would be a mistake to presume that it had no intention of developing alternative sources of oil to its Persian Concession. Garrow commented in 1921, 'We know what has happened in Mexico and although it is not considered likely that a similar influx of salt water will damage the Persian fields, it would be in the highest degree unwise to neglect any reasonable precautions we can make to ensure that we have a large margin of production' in Persia or elsewhere (see Chapter 10).[11]

Moreover as the Company expanded its concessionary interests it encountered in Latin America, no less than in the Middle East, the determination of American oil companies to exclude foreign competitors from areas which they were trying to reserve for their own privileged position in support of their own national objectives. The American fear of peacetime oil shortages after the vastly increased consumption of petroleum products during the war produced an acute attack of national jitters and distrust of erstwhile allies in the face of an alleged threat to national defence. As well as alarmist chauvinists some prominent experts expressed anxiety, like Dr Van H. Manning, Director of the United States Bureau of Mines, who predicted in October 1919 that 'within the next two to five years the oil fields of this country will face an ever-increasing decline.' The

The expansion of international interests

Director of the United States Geological Survey, Dr George Otis Smith, remarked in January 1920 that 'The position of the United States in regard to oil can best be characterised as precarious.' He advocated that 'The part our Government should take in planning to meet our future needs is to give moral support to every effort of American business to expand its circle of activity in oil production.' He accepted that 'this may mean world-wide exploration, development, and producing companies, financed by United States capital, guided by American engineering, and safeguarded in policy because protected by the United States Government.'

In the following three years a sense of national crisis persisted as reserves declined in relation to increasing consumption. Between 1919 and 1923, for instance, the registration of motor vehicles doubled in the United States to 15 000 000, so that 7 per cent of the world population owned 83 per cent of the 18 000 000 vehicles. Between 1914 and 1928 the number of registered vehicles increased fourteen fold from 2 to 28 million and the annual demand for motor spirit rose proportionately. As the production of Mexico, the largest exporter of oil in 1918, declined from 1921, it spurred exploration elsewhere in the western hemisphere and was replaced from 1923 by new fields in South America, where by 1929 60 per cent of all American oil investment overseas was concentrated, most of it in Venezuela and Colombia. Royal Dutch-Shell was also engaged in extensive exploration and particularly successful in Venezuela in this period. It is against these developments that the worldwide activities and growth of the Company in relation to its international competitors has to be placed. (See Table 12.1).

2 THIRD PARTIES

In May 1922 Cadman characterised the first phase of the Company's concessionary activities as having 'been primarily based on examination of territory which has been brought to the notice of APOC through third parties, and so conditions as regards terms of lease, royalty etc. have often had to be accepted as a "fait accompli"'.[12] As Greenway had explained in connection with a concession proffered by the British Equatorial Company in 1918, the procedure to be followed was to acquire concessions, examine them, test them if geologically favourable, and then float a working company if the tests were sufficiently promising.[13] This was a simple procedure which kept expenditure to a minimum. It did not involve any cash liability, other than the cost of geological examination, until the Company was satisfied with the geological evidence. At that point there would be the expense of testing operations, but it was expected

The expansion of international interests

Table 12.1. *Financial comparison of oil companies 1920 and 1927 in terms of total assets*

	1920		1927	
	$ (000)	£ (000)	$ (000)	£ (000)
Gulf	259 730	73 370	552 834	113 286
Standard Oil of California	245 755	69 422	579 308	118 711
Standard Oil of Indiana	237 635	67 129	462 606	94 796
Standard Oil of New York	299 593	84 631	678 089	138 953
Standard Oil of New Jersey	1 102 313	311 388	1 426 601	292 336
Texas Co.	333 434	94 190	324 806	66 559
Royal Dutch Shell*	320 000	90 395	480 000	98 360
APOC	109 533	28 303	247 826	50 784

Notes:
APOC figures are for the years April 1920–March 1921, and April 1927–March 1928
* estimated from separate accounts published by Royal Dutch and Shell Transport & Trading
Exchange rates 31–xii–1920 £1 = $3.54   31–xii–1927 £1 = $4.88
               31–xii–1920 £1 = fl 11.27   31–xii–1927 £1 = fl 12.07
               31–iii–1921 £1 = $3.87   31–iii–1928 £1 = $4.88
Sources: Gibb & Knowlton, *The Resurgent Years*, pp 674–5; APOC, Shell Transport & Trading, Royal Dutch, Standard Oil of New York Annual Reports and Accounts

that this expenditure would be met out of current revenue. Working capital for ultimate production would be contributed by the parties concerned in proportion to their interests, the Company taking fully paid ordinary shares as their payment consideration. It was ad hoc in application, rather than concerted in intention. The Company was a postbox in London, rather than a listening post abroad. Greenway's submission to Long of 12 March 1918 on the Company's concessionary interests outside Persia indicated precisely what these were, though none of them had been subjected to any test drilling by the Company.[14] They were comprehensive in scope rather than discerning in choice and included Mesopotamia, Kuwait, Colombia, Papua and Venezuela amongst those which had later importance. New Brunswick in Canada, the Gold Coast, Nigeria, Borneo, Egypt, New Zealand, Timor, Madagascar, Cyprus and the island of Zante in the eastern Mediterranean were also included, but in this period were either discarded early or proved to have no promising prospects.

Thus, even before the ending of the war, the Company was considering broadening its interests beyond Persia. Greenway was determined that the Company should so develop that it would be able to compete with Royal Dutch-Shell and Standard Oil (NJ). He did not want the Company to become dependent upon one or other or both for the distribution or supply of oil products. Moreover, whilst the security of the Persian concession was not then being directly threatened, the cutting of the pipeline in 1915,

The expansion of international interests

the subsequent controversy over responsibility for the incident and the complications over compensation had been unsettling experiences.

Just as Burmah had been apprehensive about the development of an alternative supply source near its markets in India, so was the Company vigilant about the possibilities of competing production centres close to its Persian oilfield. The profitable distribution of oil products was effected by the proximity of supply to market. This, Greenway informed the Treasury in August 1918, 'necessitates producing oil in other countries because Persian oil fuel could not be shipped to say a port on the Atlantic to compete with oil produced in say Mexico or Trinidad'.[15] The correlation between the exploratory and the marketing functions was principally economic, not political, in emphasis.

By the end of 1922, the extent of the Company's exploratory interests had become very widespread. It had spent £76 700 on abandoned investigations, £377 890 on prospects of continuing interest and £183 630 in connection with participation in concessionary syndicates, of which a third represented its involvement in the Turkish Petroleum Company, its single most important concessionary concern outside Persia. The Company had abandoned interest in Cyprus, Russia, Sicily, Brunei, Timor, Angola, Egypt, the Gold Coast, Guinea, Colombia, Ecuador, Peru, Madagascar and New Brunswick for a number of reasons. Generally it was unsatisfactory geological evidence leading to the rejection of propositions, but occasionally no further action was taken because the terms were unacceptable as in the cases of Sicily, Angola and Ecuador. In some areas before the end of 1922 the Company had more than one prospect, as in Angola, Ecuador and Peru which were in abeyance, as were those in British Colombia, Syria and the Hejaz in Arabia. Negotiations were continuing in Albania, Greece, Italy, Rumania, Spain and the Sudan.[16]

Actual exploratory work was being undertaken in Croatia, Hungary, North Borneo, Sinai, Nigeria, Nyasaland, Argentina, Honduras, New Brunswick, Newfoundland, Venezuela, Papua, and Queensland in Australia. The largest expenditure was being made in Egyptian administered Sinai, £150 000, and New Brunswick, £117 500, followed by Croatia, £90 000, Hungary, £42 500, and Nyasaland £33 334, none of which ultimately proved to be successful. This was recognised by Cadman, who wrote 'That little success has hitherto been attained, though unfortunate, can only be regarded as incidental to work of this character, where one success will pay for many failures.'[17]

It is difficult before 1922 to discern either much enthusiasm or consistency in the Company's concessional policy, which was administered by F.G. Watson, brother of R.I. Watson. It seems to have been more concerned with random opportunities brought to its attention rather than the

The expansion of international interests

pursuit of a clearly defined set of priorities. Mesopotamia, the littoral territories along the coast of Arabia and Papua were exceptions. The first two dated from D'Arcy's interest in the area, the third from arrangements agreed with the Commonwealth Government. With government assistance and because of the earlier D'Arcy concessionary interest, the Company had acquired in 1914 a half interest in the Turkish Petroleum Company (TPC). During the war the Government's commitment to the Company's interest in TPC wavered, but Greenway made sure that it was not disregarded. In February 1916, he expected the Government to ensure that the Company would 'in the event of any change in the Middle East favourable to British interests occurring, be given the complete oil rights over any portion of the Turkish Empire which may come under British influence'.[18] In May 1918 he repeated his request for acknowledgement of the Company's claims to a Mesopotamian concession, adding that the area under consideration be extended to include Kuwait and Bahrain, where 'in anticipation of obtaining the concession' the Company had already carried out some geological work.[19] The Company was confident that the Government would not obstruct their applications because in October 1913, at the time of the visit of the Admiralty Commission to Kuwait, Shaykh Mubarak al-Sabā had agreed never to give 'a concession in this matter to anyone except a person appointed from the British Government'.[20] The matter remained unresolved for some three years after 1918 whilst the Government struggled abortively to evolve some form of coherent oil policy.

The growing international importance of the Middle East, as a result of the war and the emergence of new Arab states, caused the British Government in January 1921 to review its representation in the area. The solution was a compromise in so far as it was recommended that the Arabian littoral of the Persian Gulf should remain

under the control of the Political Resident in the Persian Gulf; that this officer should be appointed as at present by the Government of India, but should be authorised to communicate directly with the Colonial Office on matters concerning the Arabian literal...and that the prior concurrence of the Colonial Office should be obtained by them to any measures of political significance.[21]

This meant that decisions were taken in London on advice influenced by the preconceptions of Indian Government officials. On 12 May 1921 the Company addressed the Foreign Office, as previously, on the subject of Arabian concessions. There was no inclination on the part of the Colonial Office or Petroleum Department to support the granting of 'blanket' licences by the Company. The Petroleum Department wrote to the Colonial Office on 20 August 1921 that 'it does not appear desirable that the Anglo-Persian Oil Company should be given an exclusive oil prospecting licence over the territories which they name on the Persian Gulf littoral'. The Minister in charge of petroleum affairs, Sir Philip Lloyd Greame, did not think that 'the claim that oil concessions in all these areas must necessarily be in the hands of a single company can in itself be sustained'.[22] It was clear that the Company could not expect, nor receive, any preferential treatment as a result of its association with the Government. After prompting, the Company was informed of the official attitude on 24 December 1921. The Colonial Office wrote that it was not practical for the Company to be granted a single exclusive licence over all the territories of the former Ottoman Empire, and that political conditions prevented licences from being given for Muscat, the Trucial states and Saudi Arabia, but negotiations were authorised with the Shaykhs of Kuwait and Bahrain under the aegis of the Political Resident.[23]

So only from the beginning of 1922 at the earliest, was it possible for the Company to undertake any concessionary negotiations with the Shaykhs of Kuwait and Bahrain, but not elsewhere in the area. Nichols replied to the Colonial Office within a fortnight accepting their comments but asking for concessions with the Shaykhs rather than just exploratory licences.[24] The Colonial Office at first insisted somewhat inconsistently that an exploration licence should cover the total area but that a separate mining lease would have to be negotiated for selected areas of drilling.[25] This may have been applicable for mineral prospecting, but was inappropriate for oil exploration, and these conditions were subsequently dropped. The Company objected to the limited duration of customs privileges for ten years. In a letter of 29 March 1922 to the Company from the Colonial Office it was stipulated that the granting of a concession was 'conditional upon the strictly British character of lessees', which would have to be confirmed.[26]

By 16 October the Colonial Office was prepared to authorise the Political Resident to assist the Company in negotiating agreements with the Shaykhs of Bahrain and Kuwait. Arnold Wilson, then joint general manager in Muhammara, and personally known to Shaykh Ahmad of Kuwait, on 2 February 1923 informed the Company that the Shaykh had indicated to him that he was prepared to accept arrangements proposed by the Company and approved by the British Government.[27] Although Wilson was ready at the beginning of November to negotiate with Shaykh Ahmad, more correspondence passed between Colonel A.P. Trevor, the Political Resident (1921–23), Major J.C. More, the Political Agent in Kuwait (1920–29), the Colonial Office and the Company, about the terms and conditions. In January the Political Agent, without the knowledge of the Company, disclosed to Shaykh Ahmad a preliminary draft of an agreement. The Shaykh was favourably disposed, although he submitted that the royalty should be based on '25 per cent royalty on net crude oil'.[28] In March the Company proposed a modified draft, which was still under discussion in May.[29] On 26 April the Shaykh of Bahrain invited the Company to make an agreement with him.[30] Negotiations were proceeding ponderously but hopefully.

Elsewhere exploration had not been conspicuously successful. There were great hopes that oil would be discovered in Papua. In 1918 the Company had tentative discussions with the Prime Minister, W.M. Hughes, of the Commonwealth Government of Australia over exploration in Papua and the establishment of a company in Australia to refine and distribute petroleum products.[31] In mid-November 1919 the Company agreed to examine the prospects for oil in Papua on behalf of the Commonwealth and British Governments, who each subscribed £50 000.[32] At the end of 1919, Lister James and five geologists left for Papua where in mid-July 1920 they reported progress with their surveys, but little hope of oil.[33] In 1921 the British Government withdrew and the Company paid for the continuance of the work in taking over the Government's share, until the Commonwealth took over the financing. The first well was drilled in 1922, but, after five wells had been unsuccessfully drilled in the difficult geological conditions, exploration was abandoned late in 1929 on the instructions of the Commonwealth Government.[34] The ambitious attempt to develop an indigenous Australian oil industry had failed. It was forty years later that earlier hopes were to be realised, not in Papua, but offshore in the Bass Strait, where substantial oil deposits were discovered.

3 A 'FORWARD POLICY'

(a) Introduction

Concessionary success had certainly not been commensurate with the efforts taken or the money spent. No alternative sources of supply to Persia had been discovered by 1923. In Persia, Cadman advocated extensive and well planned exploratory surveys to concentrate on the most favourable prospects under the coordination of de Böckh (see Chapter 10). Cadman wrote in May 1922 that elsewhere 'the adoption of a more forward policy designed as far as possible to eliminate the middleman from such transactions, is one of the objects to be arrived at. This involves a more active policy in the future on the part of the D'Arcy Company, working through its agents and geologists, and such a policy is considered to be advisable.'[35] In some respects it appeared that the policy had not changed, because there was the same wide geographical range of conces-

The expansion of international interests

sionary interests, but it was certain that assessments were made more quickly by the Company's geologists than previously. Moreover there was a clearly definable concentration of effort in specific areas. An indication of this is apparent from Table 12.2, which gives details of exploration expenditure of £2 500 000, 1918-28, of which that on Mesopotamia almost accounted for a half. In Europe, although the attention of the Company was drawn to possibilities for oil concessions in Austria, Greece, Yugoslavia, Poland, Portugal, Rumania and Spain between 1923 and 1926, it was only in Albania that the Company persevered.

(b) Albania and the Italian Government

Albania represented a particular concessionary problem for the Company. Early in January 1921, the Company, as a result of an introduction from Major Barnes of the British Italian Corporation, acquired a provisional concession from the Albanian Government.[36] This aroused strong Italian opposition, because of Italy's political and economic claims over Albania. By the end of 1922 the concession had not been ratified and competition for it followed. Standard Oil (NJ) even offered to fuse its interests with those of the Company, but this was declined.[37] On 22 January 1925, after a coup d'état, a Republic was proclaimed, but on 11 March the concession was confirmed to the Company. A day later the Italian State Railways also received one, after which negotiations began in Rome between Cadman and Heath Eves and the Italian authorities.[38] Cadman, as others at this time, seems to have been impressed with Mussolini, who for his part promised that 'the principles of mutual cooperation underlying our discussions will be applied in the future to all matters affecting your interests in relation to oil in Italy'.[39] The Company was offered a partnership in a company distributing Albanian oil once it had been produced[40] and requested its 'experience of oil affairs to be placed at the service of the company in the commercial and technical management'.[41] Cadman was duped by the Duce. A year later Mussolini founded a state oil company, Azienda Generale Italiana Petroleum (AGIP) whose activities contradicted the spirit of his assurances. Once again Cadman in October 1926 was reassured by the Italian dictator that the operations of the Company's Italian subsidiary, Benzina Petroleum, would be respected. Cadman was even tempted to supply oil products through the state company 'and give up our own branch of the business'.[42]

By the treaty of Tirana of 27 November 1926 and a defensive alliance between Italy and Albania, signed a year later on 22 November 1927, Albania was definitely included in the Italian sphere of influence and thereby influenced the Italian oil scene, with which it became intimately

The expansion of international interests

Table 12.2. *Anglo-Persian Oil Company group exploration expenditure in areas 1918-28*

North America	£	Far East	£
New Brunswick	161 468	Timor	3 387
British Columbia	6 944	Borneo	29 296
Newfoundland	4 793	New Zealand	4 103
	173 205		36 786

Central America	£	Europe	£
Guatemala	11 377	Albania	289 716
Honduras	23 464	UK (excl. Midlothian)	67
Mexico	5 945	Macedonia	14 438
Trinidad	23 661	Russia	270
Jamaica	234	Midlothian	53
	64 681	Hungary	51 000
		Société Française	7
		Italy	161
South America		Sicily	600
Ecuador	8 921	Portugal	1 733
Colombia	126 569	Spain	2 323
Venezuela	113 535		360 368
Peru	7 203		
Argentina	175 640	Other	
	431 868	GPA Syndicate	6 800
		Midian Oil	305
Middle East		Albert mines option	1 067
Turkish Petroleum Co.	1 062 578	Search Syndicate	900
North Persian Oils	104 648	Fanti consuls	244
Egypt	159 167	Unallocated exp.	45 318
Cyprus	1 140		54 634
Bahrain	75		
Syria	50		
Red Sea	475	Total expenditure	£2 499 830
Nejd	393		
Mersa Matruh	265		
	1 328 791		

Africa	£
Uganda	1 761
West Africa	1 456
Angola	150
Somaliland	6 935
South West Africa	2 056
Nigeria	1 290
Nyassaland	33 334
Sudan	2 265
Madagascar	250
	49 497

Source: D'Arcy Exploration Co. annual accounts 4P 6076

connected. In spite of the chequered history of the concession, geological advice was intermittently optimistic from the first surveys in 1923 to 1929. Nevertheless the structural features were complicated. Their interpretation was subject to considerable revision so that the geologist Wyllie's remark on Sicily is equally relevant for Albania, that 'the chaos of opinions regarding it is almost as great as the chaos of the structure itself'.[43] In 1923 it was believed that the prospects for obtaining one or more valuable oilfields in Albania appeared good.[44] In 1924 opinion was more guarded because 'though the petroleum prospects of Albania are worthy of serious consideration the high rate of optimism previously engendered is not supported by subsequent investigations'.[45] A year later there was an element of the valuer's caution in the comment that 'though Patos cannot be viewed with any considerable degree of optimism the chances of developing a field of small producers of heavy oil still remaining are sufficiently good to avert condemnation'.[46] Drilling began on the Patos structure in central Albania in March 1926 and ten wells and three years later a potential production of not more than 1 000 000 tons was revealed of poor quality oil of high sulphur content, which made the field unlikely to be commercially profitable. In another area, Ardenitza begun in October 1925, there were the same geological puzzles and unsuccessful drilling, but no oil at all.[47]

Whilst there were hopes of oil in Albania, there was a chance of an understanding between the Company and the Italian Government. Through the mediation of Sig. Piero Pirelli and Senator Ettore Conti, President of AGIP, leading Italian industrialists in the Confederazione Generale dell Industria Italiana and Associazione fra le Societ Italiane per Azioni and early supporters of Mussolini, Cadman visited Rome again. With the approval of Mussolini he agreed to prepare the marketing organisation contemplated in the agreement between the Italian Government and the Company,[48] by which, in effect, the Company's Italian subsidiary, Benzina Petroleum, would be merged with AGIP in return for assured supply contracts and outlets for Albanian production if it materialised. By May 1928 Heath Eves and Morris had drawn up a memorandum of agreement which was still being discussed in July, though it had virtually been accepted by the Italian Government subject to two reservations.[49] Firstly a relaxing of the terms of the supply contract was expected otherwise it would 'curtail the freedom of AGIP which has been created chiefly for the purpose of conquering some independence from the big oil trusts'.

Secondly according to Prince Caetani, Vice President of AGIP, it was hoped that 'a participation in the Turkish Petroleum Company thanks to the good offices of the APOC, would give to our association a more precise character of reciprocity and of partnership on equal footing both in

The expansion of international interests

Italy and abroad', no less than putting right an unjustified wrong which the Italians believed had been committed by their exclusion from the oil concession in Mesopotamia. This slight rankled deeply, and was not assuaged till the activities of Enrico Mattei in the 1950s restored a sense of pride to the Italian oil industry. Cadman, who looked upon the negotiations as more than just a commercial transaction, was relieved at their outcome, though embarrassed by the reference to the role he might play over the Turkish Petroleum Company. He believed that the agreement embodied 'an achievement upon which APOC is to be congratulated. It would be misleading to consider solely the return on fuel oil - offtake of total products of crude is one of the tests.'[50]

He might have added that one of the drawbacks in such negotiations with governments was relating exploration, refining and distribution to a single market in a monopolistic arrangement. Politically it seemed promising but commercially it was impractical, particularly when indigenous supplies of crude oil were lacking. National and corporate interests were different, if not often opposed. Within a couple of months, the Italian Government had virtually repudiated the agreements reached. The directors of AGIP, who had negotiated with the Company, were replaced and by December Mussolini had washed his hands of the affair. He had received no oil and no shareholding in the Turkish Petroleum Company. The Company was not prepared to subscribe to and take a financial interest in an organisation whose profits and financial stability were influenced by Government instructions dictated by political motives. By 1930 operations in Albania were suspended, and were abandoned in 1934.[51]

Composite concessionary arrangements worked in association with a government, as was the case of the March 1925 concession in Albania, were not suitable for the Company. A simpler, but still difficult situation, was the example of Australia, where in 1927 the Commonwealth Government because of its own financial limitations prevented additional capital investment in Commonwealth Oil Refineries (COR).[52] This resulted in freezing the share capital and stifling development. Nevertheless such experiences as in Italy were rare and only served to underline the good fortune which attended the Company over its Persian concession, which though politically disturbed was not really operationally interrupted.

(c) South America and the Government connection

It was a different form of government connection - that with the British Government - which was to influence the Company's concessionary aspirations in South America. The prize was great, for between 1920 and 1929 South American production rose enormously with a spectacular

The expansion of international interests

Table 12.3. *Oil production in South America 1920 and 1929* (in millions of tons per year)

Country	1920	1929
Peru	0.39	1.88
Argentina	0.23	1.32
Venezuela	0.07	19.38
Ecuador	0.01	0.19
Colombia	—	2.82
Bolivia	—	0.01
Total	0.70	25.60

Source: US Senate, Special Committee Investigating Petroleum Resources, *American Petroleum Interest in Foreign Countries,* 79th Cong. 1st sess. (1945), pp. 354–7.

increase in Venezuela, as Table 12.3 shows. Concessionary interest in South and Central America had already been shown in the first phase of the Company's concessionary activities, but only in Argentina can it be said to have resulted in any positive achievement. In the early twenties geological effort was expended in vain in Bolivia, Brazil, Chile, Ecuador, Guatemala, Honduras, Mexico, Nicaragua, Peru and on the island of Trinidad. Indeed these areas represented 20 per cent of exploratory expenditure 1914-28 of the D'Arcy Exploration Company. The yearly proportionate expenditure is shown in Figure 12.1.[53] Legislative conditions in most of the states of South America were quite different from Europe. State control was more pervasive and an understandable political animus was prevalent against any kind of neo-colonialism. The tendency towards dictatorial forms of government implied a more powerfully centralised, though arbitrary, system of administration. The Board had decided, therefore, by the end of 1923 to adopt a policy 'of direct Government negotiation and independent exploration'.[54] The petroleum legislation was carefully scrutinised to see if conditions were acceptable. Moreover, many parts of South America were relatively inaccessible for exploration or production, which meant expensive expeditions and long pipelines. Thus, in the case of Bolivia, if oil had been found, it would have involved its transportation to the Pacific Coast via the Andes, or to the River Plate, prodigious undertakings at that time.[55]

The geological evidence available to the Company did not favour Bolivia, Guatemala, Nicaragua or Peru, on which Wyllie noted about one part, 'With all solid rocks concealed, the Geologist is here confronted with a situation *almost* as awkward as that of a blind philosopher in a dark room, looking for a black cat which wasn't there.'[56] The real obstacle in Brazil,

552

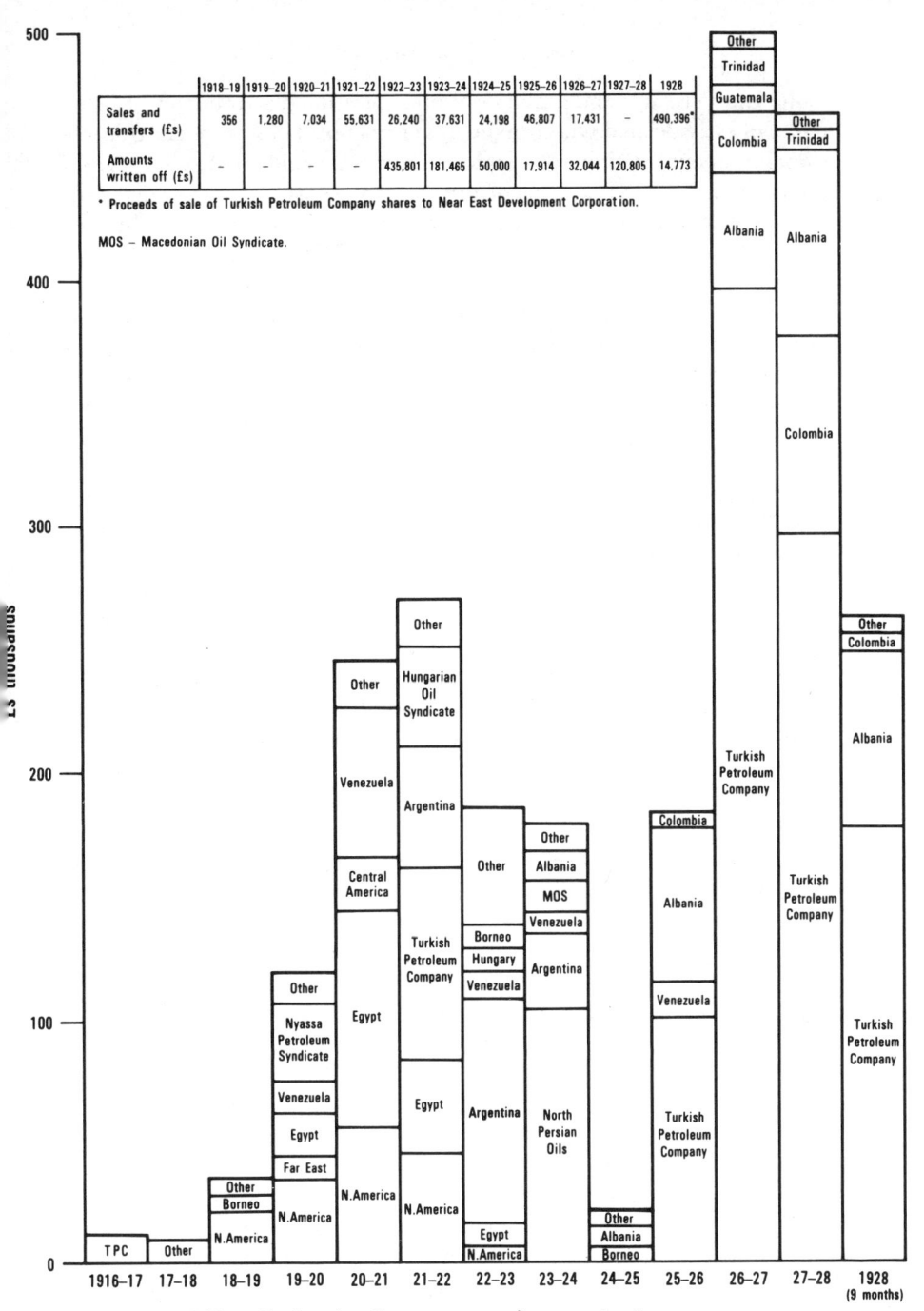

	1918–19	1919–20	1920–21	1921–22	1922–23	1923–24	1924–25	1925–26	1926–27	1927–28	1928
Sales and transfers (£s)	356	1,280	7,034	55,631	26,240	37,631	24,198	46,807	17,431	–	490,396*
Amounts written off (£s)	–	–	–	–	435,801	181,465	50,000	17,914	32,044	120,805	14,773

* Proceeds of sale of Turkish Petroleum Company shares to Near East Development Corporation.

MOS – Macedonian Oil Syndicate.

Figure 12.1 D'Arcy Exploration Company expenditure 1916–28
Source: BP 4P 6076, D'Arcy Exploration Company accounts 1916–28

The expansion of international interests

Chile and Peru was the problem of oil legislation discriminating against companies associated with foreign governments. Thus in Brazil 'Concessionaires of exploration or of exploitation cannot collaborate with foreign governments, nor with firms or private persons who are associated with them.'[57] In territories where the oil prospects were poor, the legal difficulties were only irritating, but in Venezuela and Colombia, where oil was already being produced and where the Company expected to find a western source of production, the legal restrictions were crippling. It proved impossible, moreover, to follow a consistent policy of only negotiating with governments, for, in the case of Venezuela, for example, the Company was involved in exploration activities with Central Mining and Investment Corporation Ltd and Trinidad Leaseholds Ltd, in the area of El Pozon since 1920 and drilling from 1924.[58] Many offers for concessions were made, including those in the Maracaibo Basin.[59] In 1925-26 unsuccessful negotiations took place between the Company and Pantepec Petroleum Company.[60] In 1926 the Company considered an offer from Nubar Gulbenkian, son of Calouste, to be involved in a proposal for the commercial development of the country's oil reserves in association with the Government, which was to receive 50 per cent of the profits.[61] In reality it was an attempt by President Gomez to redress the balance of Standard Oil (NJ) and Royal Dutch-Shell influence in the country.[62] The Company was not tempted, in spite of Gulbenkian's powerful advocacy that 'Venezuela will be an enormous producer of oil',[63] in view of 'the onerous terms that are likely to be insisted on by the Venezuelan Government'.[64] The risks were too high.

From July 1925, however, it was clear that the petroleum laws stipulated that no company in which a foreign government was a shareholder could work a concession in Venezuela,[65] though geologists of the Company remained at work within the country.[66] Nine months later, after negotiations, the Company's representative, Commander W.A. Thompson, proposed the registration of a company in Venezuela to which its concession would be transferred.[67] Vansittart at the Foreign Office advised the Company 'to use all caution and precaution'.[68] Another official was more explicit, warning that 'it would be the height of folly ... to spend a penny in Venezuela if there is the slightest doubt as to ... [the] legal position ... nor, can any reliance be placed on legal opinions or private assurances from temporary Ministers'.[69] Eminent Venezuelan lawyers were consulted, opinions of the Company's legal advisers sought and the Venezuelan Government approached.[70] A Board meeting on 27 July 1926 illustrated the dilemma. Nichols 'was most anxious to be able to start exploration work' but Lloyd pointed out 'the danger in consequence of H.M. Government interest'. It was decided that 'the necessary steps be taken to acquire

The expansion of international interests

interests in these circumstances, but no financial obligation to be incurred without further reference to the Board'.[71]

In spite of all the efforts nothing really changed and in April 1927, as a result of a special management meeting convened for the occasion to consider all aspects of the Venezuelan situation, it was proposed by Cadman that, having regard to the obscurity of the Company's legal position, 'it would be expedient to stay our hand in Venezuela, to retreat diplomatically from the advances made there, and definitely to await full consideration of the fruits of our policy in Colombia - in all its bearings on questions of production, of judicial issues and otherwise - before considering the resumption of active negotiations in Venezuela'.[72] It was perhaps ironical that the Company was experiencing such concessionary problems in Venezuela, for in 1912 a certain Mr R. Stirling had drawn the attention of the Company to an oil concession 'held by a small syndicate covering 3000 sq. miles near town of Maracaibo', which had been commented on favourably by none other than G.B. Reynolds, who was one of the first in the field in Venezuela, no less than in Persia.[73] By 1927 Venezuela had risen to 'a position of great prominence among the important oil producing areas of the world'.[74] From 1923 American oil interest in the country was considerable, including Standard Oil (NJ), Gulf Oil and the Atlantic Refinery Company, and concerned to eliminate British competition.[75]

Early in 1926, after Arnold Wilson succeeded F.G. Watson as managing director of the D'Arcy Exploration Company, he expressed some pessimism about oil possibilities in Africa and Asia. He believed only Albania was hopeful, but Arabia appeared 'to be devoid of all prospects'.[76] He concluded that, 'we shall be compelled in practice to concentrate our efforts to find a fresh oil field in Canada and South America'. Cadman, whilst contesting details of his analysis, was in general agreement that 'everything points to the necessity for our doing our best to obtain a standing in certain of the South American states. It is, of course, for this reason that we have recently been concentrating on Venezuela and Colombia, which, considered economically are best placed from our point of view.'[77] He advocated a policy of 'careful and deliberate expansion'. The importance of Colombia was not disputed a year later when A.C. Hearn, a former colleague of Cadman on the Inter-Allied Commission in 1918, with earlier service in the Admiralty, who had been appointed to the Board on 22 February 1927, remarked that 'Colombia is excellently situated as a complementary area for the concentration of Anglo-Persian efforts...Production from Colombia will not naturally compete with Persian oil, except in those western markets where owing to large haulage and canal dues, Persian oil is severely handicapped in competition with oil from nearer sources of supply.'[78] There was thus no lack of commitment to Colombia.

The expansion of international interests

It became a test case of the Company's ability to operate within the concessionary environment of South America.

The Company had not always been consistently attracted to Colombia. There was strong interest as early as January 1918 when Lister James carried out a survey and in November 1919 when it was proposed to take up concessionary opportunities, provided suitable facilities were obtainable from the Government.[79] Five years later disappointment temporarily caused a break in interest, when the Company acknowledged American opposition.[80] Later the Colombian authorities encouraged renewed interest by the Company,[81] but much the same kind of problems affected it in Colombia as had occurred in Venezuela,[82] for its position was apparently undermined by petroleum legislation similar to that in Venezuela. Exploration surveys were undertaken by the Company's geologist in 1925, 1926 and 1927. Nevertheless the Board confirmed its continuing interest in Colombia subject to financial limitations.

Early in 1926 Colonel Yates arrived in Bogota to represent the Company and settle the ambiguities over the application of the petroleum laws. After short negotiations with the Colombian Government he had reached a provisional conclusion in March 1926[83] to establish a local concession holding company and carry out exploration. In July it was acknowledged that 'our chief difficulty in starting operations in these countries is due to the risk incurred on account of the Government's holding'.[84] Yates returned to Colombia in October 1926, endeavouring to get options for concessions which could be legally operated by the D'Arcy Exploration Company.[85] After nearly nine months, Yates negotiated an agreement on national reserved oil lands which was signed in July but not ratified by the Colombian Congress, mostly because of American-backed opposition.[86] Still there was optimism, exploration permits were issued to investigate government lands and Lister James arrived to supervise the surveys.[87] The Foreign Office was helpful, feeling that 'the interest of such an experienced and important concern as the Anglo-Persian in oil exploitation in South America could only be welcome and that the Company could rely on all such support as we could properly give, should they get into difficulties', but it had to be discreet.[88]

There were different opinions about the desirability of preserving contacts in Colombia because the agreement had still not been passed by the Colombian Congress and geological reports on the government reserve lands at Uraba were pessimistic. Wilson in July 1928 was in favour of remaining in the country either in a technical capacity to assist the Government or marketing Colombian Government royalty oil.[89] By then some £120 000 had been spent. Hearn was unconvinced, doubting the value of the geological evidence and persuaded that 'whatever might be the future

The expansion of international interests

prospect of obtaining concessions in Colombia, we should no longer contemplate negotiations - either with the Government or with private owners - whilst the Petroleum Laws operate so decidedly to our disadvantage'.[90] Nevertheless the Board decided to make another effort and in September 1928 Arnold Wilson arrived for discussions with the Government and ran into a barrage of American criticism.[91] Certain amendments were accepted for the petroleum laws,[92] but no action followed. The Government decided in February 1929 to appoint international advisers to prepare new petroleum legislation after radical measures proposed in November 1927 and an emergency law of 1928 had not been passed.[93] It was hoped that it would improve the position of the Company. The text of the proposed petroleum bill had been received in September 1929, with some relief, but in reality, as T.M. Snow of the Foreign Office minuted, 'the Government in virtue of the law are to be in a position to control the administration of the companies and prevent them disposing of the oil'.[94] The conditions were apparently more favourable to the Company, but in reality as restrictive as before.[95] In spite of friendly overtures from President Mendez in 1930, the Company decided that the risks were too great.[96]

The real difficulty was that although the Company was legally capable of carrying out concessionary activities, it could not exploit them. This could only be done by a company without any government participation in it. From the middle of June 1926 all kinds of arrangements were examined but none proved acceptable. The promises of one government were not binding on another. There were no reasonable legal assurances on which the Company could depend and at the end of the day no changes in the wording altered the meaning of the Petroleum Law that 'a lease could not be held by a Company in which foreign Governments were admitted as partners'.[97] This was not discriminatory against British companies but arose from a law originally passed in 1825 and directed against a resurgence of Spanish domination. It was not, as Cadman had assumed, the result of American prompting 'either officially or unofficially at the time when the open door controversy was at its height'.[98] It was simply anti-colonial legislation. There might be arguments between Government Ministers, such as the Attorney-General and the Minister for Industry. It made no difference. By virtue of its government shareholding, the Company was excluded from Colombia and Venezuela, in which it was principally interested, and also from Brazil, Chile, Mexico and Peru.

Only in Argentina was there any appreciable Company presence on the South American oil scene. It was effected by two main factors; firstly the country was industrialising with an increasing demand for oil products, so the Government was encouraging exploration in the early 1920s. Secondly, by January 1924, a national oil corporation, Yacimientos Petroliferos Fiscales (YPF) had been established,[99] the first of its kind in South America, as part of a policy to prevent 'agents of neocolonial exploitation seeking to despoil the Latin American countries of one of their most essential raw materials and when necessary, intervening in politics to gain their ends'.[100] Such suspicion of foreign manipulation had a damaging affect on the Company's relations with the Argentinian Government.

It was early in 1915 when a concession in the Comodoro Rivadavia area in southern Argentine, where the first oil in the country was discovered in 1907, was offered to the Company. Greenway turned it down because he was unable to entertain any such proposition till the end of the war. If Standard Oil (NJ) wished to take it up, there was no alternative but to let them have it.[101] By 1920 only five oil companies were working in the region.[102] The Company's interest was revived early in 1920 when it was offered a 35 per cent share in a syndicate of the brothers Dodero and an association with a syndicate run by Sig. Sol in which the brothers were also interested, with various drilling and financial obligations.[103] W.R.A. Weatherhead, one of the Company geologists, commented favourably on the prospects by the end of 1920.[104] Garrow appears to have had reservations because 'the cost development of the Dodero concession would be extremely heavy'.[105] He doubted whether it could be profitably worked given its geographical position. A year later after a visit he was still pessimistic about exploration in Argentina as 'it is wild-catting in a high degree and requires a heavy purse'.[106] Nevertheless the Company took up its options and commenced drilling. Its associates, whose expertise was more financial than technical,[107] were in charge of local affairs. By mid-1923, in spite of apparently satisfactory progress reports, it had become clear that the conduct of the operations was bringing not only discredit upon the Company, whose local staff were regarded more as 'charlatans than respected businessmen', but causing it considerable loss.[108]

Cadman was sent out to investigate and arrived on 21 September 1923 in Buenos Aires to find a ghastly state of affairs of graft, extravagance, falsification, incompetence, embezzlement, ignorance, waste and a lack of any proper sense of money or moral values.[109] After examining the operations, he cut the wage bill by some 70 per cent by discharging those superfluous to requirements in a workforce of 214 including 31 drilling staff, 11 chauffeurs, 17 firemen, 24 mechanics, 15 cooks and waiters, 5 carpenters, 19 oddmen, etc. It was hardly surprising that the Argentinian Government looked with disfavour upon the Company and the tarnished reputation of its associates. Cadman attempted to place relations upon a better footing with the Government, for 'in view of the large amounts of

The expansion of international interests

money which we have already spent, it was imperative that I should know exactly where we stood'.[110] In the end neither cajolery nor flattery persuaded the Argentinian Government to grant the Company more exploratory permits on an acceptable basis.[111] Furthermore in the mining law introduced in January 1924 article 20 effectively isolated the Company, because 'corporations in which any foreign state is a shareholder are not eligible to acquire mines'.[112] Unless, therefore, the Company wished to abandon its existing holdings, it would have to come to some compromise arrangement of proving the presence of oil on its plots and entering into a marketing association with local interests.[113]

Oil was discovered in February 1924.[114] In the next two months some 364 tons were disposed of locally and by mid-November 28 000 tons had been produced and Greenway was hoping that 'we shall be able to produce sufficient oil in the Argentine to thoroughly justify our entry into that country'.[115] By mid-1924 deliveries to the Government had commenced, but within a few months the Government had declined to take further supplies and negotiations were taking place for alternative sales. At the same time not only was the Government refusing to extend the concessionary area to the Company and its associates, but it was drilling close to the Company's wells, so reducing its productive capability.[116] An unsuc-

Oil rigs of the Anglo-Persian Oil Company in the Comodoro Rivadavia area, Argentina 1924

The expansion of international interests

cessful visit by Greenway to Buenos Aires in 1925 failed to improve the situation and was regarded by the Argentinian authorities as an unwarranted interference in their affairs.[117] Even if the offsetting of wells within 50 yards was a dubious practice on commercial or technical grounds, the Mining Code set no limit to where wells could be located.

There was little prospect of the Company having any further exploratory opportunities, as Greenway admitted to the shareholders in November 1925.[118] In February 1926, however, Arnold Wilson, who was strongly in favour of the Company establishing a real presence in South America, advocated taking a risk in accepting another proposition in the Comodoro Rivadavia area.[119] Cadman was sympathetic 'as the development of this country in the future may be phenomenally rapid', but felt 'strongly that our policy must be one of hastening slowly' and like Garrow was not impressed with what had been offered.[120] The Company, therefore, decided to concentrate on maximising its return on the crude oil it was capable of producing — some 15 000–16 000 tons a month — and take up a half share in the Itaca Refining and Distribution Company, thus giving the Company a complete organisation in Argentina from the well to the consumer. A provisional agreement was reached with the Itaca Company in August 1926.[121] The Company had previously rejected a suggestion by Waley Cohen in February 1926 that Royal Dutch-Shell and the Company should cooperate in a refinery venture.[122]

The Itaca Company, according to Lloyd, who visited it in 1929, 'occupies a very humble position in the Argentine Oil Industry and one not worthy of the APOC'.[123] Political uncertainties were discouraging and, when another more restrictive petroleum bill was proposed in 1927, as a precaution 'in view of the ... legal dangers and reduced production prospects expenditure is being cut down to the minimum'.[124] The Company was hanging on in case conditions improved but its production declined.[125] Carl Solberg, a recent commentator on this period in Argentinia, has shown the internal struggle for supremacy was permeated with the emotive nationalistic economic issue of oil to 'gain and consolidate political power'.[126] The Company could not escape the consequences of the politically charged atmosphere of Argentina in which it was suspected of being a pretentious interloper which kept company with the British Government.

Given its early interest in areas where oil was subsequently discovered, the price paid by the Company for its lack of geographical coverage of oil resources in the Western Hemisphere in comparison with its competitors was high. Not until the Alaskan oil discoveries of the late 1960s was the Company able to redress the balance significantly.

The expansion of international interests

Concessions were also offered but not accepted in Afghanistan, Borneo, Siam and Timor.[127] Between 1927 and 1930 there was considerable interest in New Brunswick, British Columbia and the province of Alberta, Canada, including its Athabasca tar sands.[128] Yet Professor W.A. Nash of Birmingham University and the Company's geologists, Weatherhead and Richardson, faced with the complicated geological structures, did not then believe that oil could have accumulated in sufficient quantity to justify the construction of a pipeline some 750 miles long to the sea board from the Turner Valley region.[129] Concern was shown in Africa, but with little success. Thus the Colonial Office in 1926 suggested that the Government of Uganda would be interested in granting an exploration licence over some 10 000 square miles for two years.[130] In May 1928 the Company received a draft agreement. The negotiations were terminated after 2½ years because of the onerous conditions, especially those requiring output to be limited to 'the requirements of the inhabitants of the Protectorate or 50 000 whichever may be the less' and the construction of a refinery.[131] The geological indications were also unfavourable, as was the case with Kenya, the Gold Coast, Angola, North Africa, Nigeria, Ethiopia and Sudan.[132]

(d) Arabian concessions and Government provisions

It was one of the ironies of exploration that the area 'devoid of oil prospects', Arabia, became the pivotal point of world oil production in later years. As has been indicated earlier in this chapter, the Company had not ignored the Arabian littoral, particularly Kuwait and Bahrain, up to 1923. In May 1923, Major Frank Holmes burst upon the stage there with a splendid performance of concessional wizardry. Born in New Zealand, in 1874, he became a mining engineer of world-wide experience before serving in the British Army in the First World War in various areas, including the Middle East. In association with some of his pre-war mining friends and their financial backing, the Eastern and General Syndicate was formed in August 1920 for trading in the Middle East. In 1921 he was based in Aden, but moved to Bahrain in 1922, which became his base and where he was sympathetically received in Arab merchant circles. Within a few years Holmes had changed the concessionary position in Arabia and more than anybody else was responsible for ushering in its age of oil. Holmes was a powerful personality of impressive physique, gregarious in company and tenacious in business. A chum rather than a gent, Arabs found him approachable and understandable.

Holmes made his début at the Uqair Conference 22 November–2 December 1922, which was held to settle the boundaries between Iraq and

The expansion of international interests

Saudi Arabia and Kuwait and Saudi Arabia. Sir Percy Cox, Ibn Saud and Major J.C. Moore, who represented Shaykh Ahmad, were present. Holmes attended and made his first moves to seek an oil concession for the al-Hasa province from Ibn Saud. He concluded a provisional draft agreement for exclusive oil and mining rights. Though the Company had applied for a similar concession through the Colonial Office, as Cox knew, it would appear that Ibn Saud in the diplomatic circumstances of the time was reluctant to become entangled in an indirect concessionary relationship with the British Government.[133] An important consequence of the Uqair Conference was the disappointment of Shaykh Ahmad at the boundary settlement between himself and Ibn Saud. Colonel H.R.P. Dickson, who succeeded Major More as Political Agent in Kuwait in 1929, was present when Cox broke the news to Shaykh Ahmad of having granted to Ibn Saud some two thirds of the territory claimed by him. The Shaykh maintained that he had been 'robbed', and this coloured his attitude to the British Government.

Whilst these negotiations of Holmes were being carried on, the Company was informing the Colonial Office of seepages at Masira Bay in Oman, which it believed would attract concessionaires, so 'We desire to forestall such applications and we shall be greatly obliged if the Political Resident may be instructed by cable to support our application...for an exclusive prospecting licence.'[134] This was not granted, because the result might be that 'the Company, although unable themselves to investigate and exploit the whole territories covered by the licence, will prevent potential competition from doing so'.[135] A potential competitor had arrived in the area. On 6 May 1923 Ibn Saud granted Holmes the concession for al-Hasa, one of the provisions of which was 'an undertaking not to sell the whole or part of any concession' to the Company.[136] Holmes asked his principals in the Eastern and General Syndicate to make a quick down payment, earlier than was due, as 'it would assist me materially to secure a very strong hold over not only The Territory of Nejd other than the Hasa Concession Area, but also over the Kuwait territory and of Bahrein'.[137]

In his concessionary activities Holmes was greatly assisted by two Arab friends, who were personally known to each other, Muhammad Yatim, a member of a prominent merchant family in Bahrain, who became his personal assistant, and Mullah Saleh, who was Shaykh Ahmad's secretary and close adviser. Just after Ibn Saud had granted the al-Hasa concession, Holmes, in Bahrain on 9 May, cabled Shaykh Ahmad 'not to grant oil concessions to any other company without first seeing the terms offered by my company'.[138] At the same time Yatim informed Mullah Saleh of 'the liberal terms offered by the Company which has been successful with His Highness Ibn Saud'.[139] A week later Holmes arrived in Kuwait and

The expansion of international interests

offered the following terms for an oil concession: (1) 70 year duration; (2) annual protection sum of £3000; (3) downpayment of £2000 on the commencement of work; (4) equipment and machinery to revert to Shaykh after 35 years, to the Company before that time if operations cease; (5) settlement of disputes by arbitration in London; (6) 1 per cent export dues on oil exports; (7) import duties on provisions, but not plant; (8) Shaykh to receive 20 per cent of net profits and share option of up to 20 per cent of those issued and (9) salaries of Shaykh's officials in connection with the concession to be paid by the Company.[140]

These terms were more advantageous than those which were offered by the Company when Arnold Wilson visited Kuwait at the end of May and met the Shaykh on 2 June to discuss the draft concession of 8 March, which had been communicated to the Political Resident in the Persian Gulf.[141] The Company offered a downpayment of £750 with an annual minimum of £2000 and a royalty of Rs3.8 (5s 3d) a ton to be reviewed after 12 years. Shaykh Ahmad would not settle with Arnold Wilson then, nor would he promise to do so, other than to tell him that, 'I shall not enter into an agreement with any other company without your information.'[142] The British Government, however, was not prepared to be indulgent when APOC appeared to be dragging its feet. By April 1924, the Colonial Office felt that it had discharged its obligations to the Company. Support by the British Government had been misrepresented as 'being due to solicitude for our own pocket'. There was considerable sympathy for the Political Resident's view that the Company should be given a definite time limit after which Holmes should be 'unloosed'.[143] Indeed there was antipathy towards the Company from some Colonial Office officials, who felt that 'if the APO Coy really wanted to *work* these concessions they could very easily have found a means (with all their money bags) of overcoming local opposition and prejudices'.[144]

The Company had lost the initiative and Arnold Wilson, who seems not to have enjoyed a close relationship with Nichols, was unambiguous in explaining the reason. He wrote to Nichols on 17 August, that

> It will be clear to you from earlier correspondence that the Shaikh of Koweit up to the beginning of this year was willing and anxious to close with the company, subject only to a reconsideration of the amount of royalty per ton... Your instructions on the other hand (the latest of which was dated the 14 March) were that it was not desired that we should take active steps in the matter of the agreement, and we had no option but to comply.[145]

After the Colonial Office in October 1922 had agreed that the Political Resident could render assistance to the Company over a Kuwait concession, Arnold Wilson expressed a willingness in November to open negotiations, but was deterred owing to the Company's commitments elsewhere.

The expansion of international interests

The opportunity was lost and never regained. On 13 July Shaykh Ahmad informed the Political Resident, Colonel Knox, that the APOC terms were 'entirely unacceptable to himself and his people'.[146] He was probably still very resentful at what he believed to be the injustice of the Uqair settlement, and determined to assert himself against the British Government. He was also, doubtless, making his opening ploys in the concessionary game which he had begun to play.

Meanwhile the Company's standing in Bahrain was also being questioned, as 'Everybody regarded it as a Government concern with Government officials who brought political pressure to bear.'[147] No doubt Holmes and his backers were playing their cards carefully, but there was some underlying political discontent, which, in expressing itself, drew attention to the Company's relations with the Government. In October the Company wished to send a geological survey party to Bahrain, but the Shaykh refused his permission.[148]

The British Government was no longer dealing with a single contender for Arabian concessions, but two, who were both British and towards whom their impartiality was expected. Thus in the case of Bahrain, officials had already recognised that 'the greatest difficulty we have to face is that HMG are, and are known in the Persian Gulf to be, large shareholders in the APOC', that it would be difficult 'to persuade a senile and malignant Sheikh of the purity of our motives if we tell him that the only Company fit to hold an oil concession in Bahrein is one in which HMG is a major shareholder!' Nine months later those opposed to the Company claimed that 'the Anglo Persian Oil Company is a Government concern and that to grant a concession to this company is tantamount to giving it to the Government'.[149] In a letter from the Secretary of State for the Colonies to the Political Resident, there was an attempt to resolve the dilemma. The Duke of Devonshire outlined the undertakings given by the Shaykhs of Kuwait and Bahrain not to grant 'any concessions for the development of oil in their territories to any person, or persons, not approved ("appointed") by His Majesty's Government'. The object was to protect the Shaykhs against 'the pernicious activities of unscrupulous Concession hunters' and to prevent the infiltration of foreign influence in the Persian Gulf, which was regarded as politically undesirable.[150]

The Company believed that it had played by the rules drawn up by the Colonial Office in 1921, but, before any agreements had been concluded, Holmes 'avowedly and probably actually, in ignorance of the necessity for obtaining the prior permission of His Majesty's Government' had entered into direct relations with the Shaykhs and induced them to offer concessions. This was unacceptable behaviour, and in consequence 'the Eastern

The expansion of international interests

and General Syndicate was not a firm approved by His Majesty's Government', and priority was to be accorded to the Company, provided they matched the terms of their rivals. If however, the Company was not 'prepared to offer to the Sheikh terms which are as favourable in the opinion of the Sheikh himself and of His Majesty's Government as those offered' by Holmes, then the Government was 'prepared to withdraw their opposition to the grant of a concession to the latter'.[151] The Government would hold the ring, but the two companies would have to fight it out.

This is what the Shaykhs expected. The ensuing rivalry for concessions had three important results. Firstly, it encouraged the Shaykhs to play off the contenders for the highest stakes. The Political Resident at Bushire reported in June 1923, for instance, that 'in a perfectly open manner and with no suspicion of shame the Sheikhs are ... getting the two Companies to bid as high as possible against each other ... [The] present position is thus one damaging to British interests and the worst sufferer is legitimate business.'[152] Secondly, it obliged the Company to be interested in concessions to safeguard its own interests no less than geological prospects. Thirdly, it compelled the Colonial Office to change its original concern of preventing 'foreign commercial interests from penetrating into the Persian Gulf' into a decision as to which British horse it was going to back. The Colonial Office, caught in a dilemma, decided that 'so far as His Majesty's Government are aware, the Eastern and General Syndicate, although possessing neither the wide experience of oil production nor the efficient organisation and financial strength of the APOC, are a substantial and reputable firm'.[153]

Competitive offers were on the table. On 2 January 1924 the Political Agent in Kuwait asked the Shaykh when his decision on the Company's proposals could be expected, but he declined to commit himself for another six months. Holmes visited Kuwait in March and with the approval of the Colonial Office agreed a concession with Ibn Saud and Shaykh Ahmad for the Neutral Zone lying between their respective territories. This enhanced the prestige of Holmes, which was further advanced when his Swiss geologist, Dr Arnold Heim, and three geological assistants, arrived to survey Kuwait in April.

Yet Dr Heim's conclusions were anything but encouraging. He reported that; (1) *'Kuwait is a country of some possibility, but not of high promise'*; (2) In the Neutral Zone there was 'no reason to recommend this concession for oil'; (3) he had 'no reason to recommend the concession for El Hasa for drilling on oil'; and (4) drilling in Bahrain would be 'a pure gamble'. In short, *'the countries of Eastern Arabia thus rapidly traversed by the writer do not present any decided promise for drilling on oil'*.[154] On 27 May the Colonial

The expansion of international interests

Office made it clear that it would not allow the Company to postpone indefinitely a decision on the concessions in Bahrain and Kuwait. The Company would have to bring the Shaykhs to the negotiating table by 31 March 1925.[155] The Company made a bold bid to do so in July 1924, when Shaykh Ahmad was invited to visit the operations in Persia, where he was suitably impressed, but declined to reveal his intentions. Indeed the Shaykh was probably aware that the auction would commence in April 1925. He was not prepared to prejudice the bidding from which he expected to benefit.

There is no evidence that the Company was indifferent at this stage. In July 1924 a report to the management committee reflected concern for

Although the geological evidence we present at present does not indicate that there is much hope of finding oil in Bahrein or Kuwait, we are, I take it, all agreed that even if the chance be 100 to 1 we should pursue it, rather than let others come into the Persian Gulf and cause difficulties of one kind or another.[156]

In October 1924 Nichols asked Arnold Wilson to take all steps to acquire a concession in Bahrain.[157] Late in 1924 and early in 1925 the Company made strenuous efforts to persuade the Shaykhs to come to a favourable decision, even contemplating, but not actually proffering, monetary inducements and enlisting the support of local notables in their cause, but to no purpose.[158] The Colonial Office was asked in vain in February for a prolongation of priority rights, but the Political Resident was instructed to point out to the Shaykhs the desirability of the Company being granted concessions. The Company complained that the Political Agent in Bahrain, Major Daly, had been less than helpful.[159] Holmes maintained his presence by drilling water wells for the Ruler of Bahrain, Shaykh 'Abd Allāh.[160] Arnold Wilson in October suggested that the Company should do likewise, but Nichols turned down the idea.[161]

Rumours circulating in October that Holmes had received a concession for Bahrain were confirmed on 2 December.[162] Success over the Mesopotamian concession in March 1925 and a concession for Muscat granted in May kept alive the Company's concessionary hopes in the Middle East. In October, before any news of Holmes' application for the Bahrain concession seeped out, Nichols informed Cadman that 'The question of concessions for Kuwait and Bahrein remains in suspense.'[163] He regretted that the Colonial Office would not accept a provision for immunity from customs for Company goods beyond ten years, as it would have constituted a dangerous precedent elsewhere, and that it refused to allow direct negotiation with the Shaykhs. He was still not convinced that there was any urgency, alleging the poor geological prospects, local opposition from leading merchants 'who fear that with constant work available they will lose their present absolute economic power over the labour engaged in

566

The expansion of international interests

pearling', the failure of Holmes to begin drilling operations in Nejd and the lack of competition. Nichols was unenthusiastic and Cadman unimpressed, though he referred the question to the geologists.

After the Bahrain concession had been granted to Holmes, the Company renewed its interest in Kuwait and was permitted by Shaykh Ahmad to send a geological party there under Lees with Wyllie and Mayhew in January 1926. Once again the geological evidence baffled the experts. They reported on 13 February that 'it is very improbable that, in the total absence of direct geological evidence, a convincing case could ever be made out by this means for exploring the unknown depths of Koweit territory with the drill'. Thus 'The unfavourable view of prospects in Koweit that is deducible from Professor de Böckh's synthesis of all previous work, cannot be gainsaid.'[164] Ten days later The Eastern and General offered to sell to the Company their concessions in Bahrain, al-Hasa and the Neutral Zone in return for recouping their investment of some £52 000. A month later Lees reported unfavourably on oil prospects in Bahrain. The Eastern and General modified their terms on 11 March, to which Wilson in London practically agreed.[165] Cadman, in Muhammara before attending Rīza Shāh's coronation, declined in early April to accept them, doubtless after consulting Lees himself on the latest geological advice.[166]

Holmes failed to persuade any American companies to show any interest in his concessions during a visit to the United States in September and October, but T.E. Ward, who was the Syndicate's representative in New York, was requested to be on the alert for any likely offers.[167] Holmes drilled water holes in Kuwait during 1927, in one of which traces of oil occurred, which were kept confidential, but were enough to persuade Gulf Oil Corporation to take over the Eastern and General's concessions in November 1927. Gulf later renounced the Bahrain concession in favour of the Standard Oil Company of California. Gulf involvement in the Turkish Petroleum Company Ltd, which insisted on the participating companies accepting the undertaking (The Red Line Agreement 31 July 1928) not to compete with each other in the former territories of the Ottoman Empire and only to negotiate jointly through IPC, prevented it from retaining its Bahrain concession.

From early 1928 Holmes concentrated on Kuwait, ostensibly for Eastern and General but actually as agent for Gulf Oil. He visited Shaykh Ahmad in April and was warmly received. He indicated that he possessed American backing, which would enable him to work any concession that might be given as capably as any competitor. In June Holmes returned to Kuwait, and presented his draft concession on 3 July 1928,[168] but, to his astonishment, the Shaykh rejected his proposals in August requesting

The expansion of international interests

higher royalties and that the concession should be non-transferable. In June Arnold Wilson inquiring for whom Holmes was working from the Colonial Office, noted that it 'having persistently obstructed our own efforts to obtain a concession on Bahrein and Kuwait, as also in Hasa, can scarcely refuse to give us this information'.[169] At this point the Company adopted certain spoiling tactics by encouraging opposition to Holmes in Kuwait for, convinced on the geological evidence that the oil prospects were very slight, it nevertheless was reluctant to have a potential competitor in its Persian backyard, especially at a time when there was considerable overproduction of oil and measures were being concerted to limit its effect on prices. Besides, possible production in Kuwait might prove to be a concessionary embarrassment in Iraq and Persia, particularly as supply and demand were so unbalanced.

The Company welcomed, but cannot be said to have instigated, the insistence of the Colonial Office in late November 1928 on the inclusion of a British nationality clause in any concession granted by the Shaykhs of Kuwait or Bahrain which would have effectively precluded American participation in a concession.[170] It was not till 1930 that the British Government modified the regulations sufficiently for operations to commence in Bahrain, by accepting a Canadian registered company, the Bahrain Petroleum Company, a subsidiary of Standard Oil of California, as concessionaire. It was not till 9 April 1932 that the British Government, under strenuous American diplomatic pressure in late 1931 and early 1932, relaxed their provisions over nationality for Kuwait, which had been in force since 1922.

Shaykh Ahmad was doubly frustrated in 1931 because the nationality issue made it difficult for him to play off the parties against one another.[171] He was experiencing economic difficulties as a result of deteriorating relations between himself and Ibn Saud. His trade with the interior of Arabia, which had been intermittently blockaded since 1920, was more extensively disrupted and the pearl fishing had suffered several disastrous seasons and much competition from Japanese cultured pearls. The situation was delicate, with Holmes endeavouring to persuade the Shaykh to disregard the British nationality clause, whilst the Political Resident was reminding him of his obligations to the British Government. In the background the Company professed to have no interest in the proceedings. The Shaykh, realistically, if reluctantly, recognised the protection afforded to him by the British Government, especially over his problems with Ibn Saud. He accepted, as he mentioned to Holmes in July, that the British Government 'is my own sincere Government which is always devoting its care to the welfare of my country and the safeguard of my rights, we must not ignore what it considers to us and our country'.[172]

The expansion of international interests

Holmes was offering hypothetical commercial advantages, the British Government actual support. Earlier such reasoning would not have been persuasive, but circumstances had changed and the Shaykh was not prepared to antagonise the British Government. The Company did not disappear from the scene but kept a low profile. In October 1930 the Petroleum Department inquired of Cadman whether there was 'any prospect of British interests being disposed to assist in prospecting for oil in Kuwait' as 'we do not like to see any area which offers any promise going entirely into American hands'. Cadman replied recounting the Company's interest, but complaining that the Colonial Office 'acting in a kind of tutelary capacity' was unwilling to modify the royalty terms and customs duties which it was prepared to recommend to Shaykh Ahmad. He compared, rather unfairly, the Company's desire to develop a concession as contrasted with the intention of Eastern and General to traffic in them.[173]

Later in August 1931 the Company requested approval for sending another party of geologists to Kuwait.[174] According to Holmes, in November 1931, its agents had 'been very active and are still so, both with their money and propaganda'.[175] Increasingly the stakes were getting higher and the partisans of both sides were straying from the touchlines on to the pitch. P.T. Cox carried out a geological survey in Kuwait from 14 February to 13 April 1932 and reported 'the Territory of Kuwait as an oil proposition is definitely in the "wild cat" class'. Still, he believed that 'there was a reasonably good chance of finding oil at depth near one or other seepages' though it might be heavy in quality, the marketability of which would be a factor 'in deciding whether the gamble is worth taking'.[176] Once more the geological aspects were hardly encouraging and E.H.O Elkington, the general manager at Ābādān, on 13 April informed Shaykh Ahmad accordingly that the Company would not be justified 'in approaching Your Excellency at present with a view to acquiring a concession'.[177] The Shaykh was deeply disappointed, for he was still anxious to keep both the competitors in play, and vented his annoyance on Holmes, whom he believed, wrongly, had been responsible for alienating the British Government, which he assumed had ordered the Company to withdraw.

The Shaykh's disappointment was short-lived. The Company bounced back on hearing the news that the British nationality clause question had been settled to the satisfaction of Gulf Oil.[178] On 11 May 1932 the Shaykh was informed by the Political Agent that the Company wanted to reopen concessionary negotiations, to which he answered positively. Three days later his friendship with Holmes was restored and with it the competitive flattery at which he was so adept, telling Holmes shortly afterwards that

The expansion of international interests

'No matter what terms APOC offers I will not discuss them, nor will I upon any consideration grant to APOC the Kuwait concession. I have promised the Kuwait concession to you and shall stand by my word.' On 30 May the Company cabled to Ābādān, 'Consider it essential to use all methods in our power to prevent Sheikh giving concession to Syndicate.'[179] The competitors were on their blocks under starter's orders. The next day they were off. Oil had been struck in Bahrain. The concessionary race was on. Within a few years the Company and Gulf Oil were associated in a joint concession for Kuwait and on 29 May 1933 Standard Oil of California outbid the Iraq Petroleum Company for a concession in Saudi Arabia from Ibn Saud. It was another decade before it was fully realised that the balance of oil power was shifting from the United States to the Middle East.

4 THE NORTH PERSIAN CONCESSION

It will be recalled that D'Arcy had excluded the five northern provinces of Persia from his concession, Māzandārān, Khurāsān, Astarābād, Gīlān and Āzarbāyjān, in anticipation of Russian objections. Some oil rights in the area, which had been granted in 1896 to Sipahsālār 'Azam under a decree of Nasīr al-Dīn Shāh, were offered in 1906 to D'Arcy and again in 1909 to the Company, but rejected. It was felt 'inasmuch as oil found on the Persian shore of the Caspian Sea would be locked off by us from the Persian Gulf and would have to face Russian oil in the Caspian, there would be scant hope of working it profitably on a large scale'.[180] In January 1916 the concession was acquired by Akikie Khostaria in circumstances of which no record seems to remain, extended and registered at the Ministry for Foreign Affairs on 12 March 1916 and again on 17 January 1917.[181] The attention of the Legation in Tehrān was drawn to it in April. The Company was subsequently informed, but took no action. Towards the end of 1917 Persia cancelled all Russian-held concessions, but no public announcement was made. Khostaria did little to prove his concession, but his title was not questioned and he paid for a time the salary of an oil commissioner, as specified in the concession.

Early in 1918, Khostaria, through a London broker, attempted to interest the Company in his concession at an exhorbitant price, but to no avail. Col. Wallace was offered a controlling shareholding during his Persian visit in early 1919, but Greenway was unenthusiastic. The Legation was again approached in December 1919 to see if any British firms would take it up, but Cox, doubtful over its validity, was reluctant to recommend it.[182] Finally in London towards the end of December another representative of Khostaria succeeded in impressing the Company with its

The expansion of international interests

worth, perhaps by indicating that Royal Dutch-Shell might renew the interest in it which they had shown in 1916. By February the Company had informed the Foreign Office that it was convinced of its authenticity and had agreed to purchase it from Khostaria and his associated Rupento Company. On 20 May 1920 the North Persian Oils Limited (NPO) was formed with an authorised share capital of £3 000 000 in £1 shares, 25 per cent of which were allotted to Rupento Company and a block to Khostaria.[183]

The Legation was instructed 'to take all necessary steps to ensure the recognition by the Persian Government of the transfer' as the Foreign Office was prepared to support the Company in its application.[184] Fīrūz, then in London, was made aware by Greenway of these developments.[185] In Tehrān, Hermann Norman, the Minister, informed the Persian Government that the transfer 'has been legally carried out and documents exhibited appeared to substantiate the concessionaire's contention that concession is still valid'.[186] The Company's action was controversial, if not unwise; the reaction of the Persian Government was dubious but definite; the behaviour of Khostaria was devious and doubtful. The Company like the Foreign Office may have misunderstood the state of Persian affairs and underestimated opposition to the Anglo-Persian Convention of 1919.[187] It may have assumed a continuing weakness in the Russian position and may have been influenced by Georgians offering concessions, including some to the French and Italians.[188] It may have wished to forestall possible American competition, but it stirred up a hornet's nest of resentment and opposition, coinciding with the British military withdrawal from Persia, which seemed to express the impotence of British power.

The reappearance of Russia and the diplomatic offensive in Persia undertaken by its envoy, Theodore Rothstein, towards the end of 1920 and early in 1921, partially restored its earlier prominence in Persian affairs. Norman pessimistically described 'British unpopularity and Persian defencelessness', the result of which, he passionately forecast, 'will be complete anarchy gradually spreading over the whole country and probably followed by Bolshevik penetration, which will naturally fill void left by your enforced retirement'.[189] A year later in July, before Norman was summoned back by Curzon, he cautioned that 'It is essential to realise bitter and widespread feeling against everything British at the present time.'[190] Norman may have been exaggerating. The Anglo-Persian Convention may have become a convenient scapegoat, attacking which rallied the national forces and discredited the previous government. Persian politicians who had displayed a partiality for cooperation with British interests were repudiated by their suc-

The expansion of international interests

cessors. From these political turmoils, the Khostaria concession was not exempt.

Norman had realised in mid-1921 that it was 'most inopportune to raise the question of any concessions, and any mention of Khostaria Concession now would be a challenge to Russia, which no Persian Government would take up'. Moreover, by mid-1921 it was no longer possible to ignore American concern in the Middle East.[191] In 1920 Persian policy was deliberately intended to persuade American interests to invest in the country. Just as British capital had been earlier attracted to finance the modernising movement of the 1880s and 1890s, so were American funds, expertise and advice sought first in 1910 and then in the early 1920s. Morgan Shuster, formerly American financial adviser to Persia in 1910, and Husayn 'Alā, Persian Minister in Washington, worked hard in this direction. Curzon in 1920 had not been convinced that American commercial involvement in Persia would be in British interests,[192] but Norman, considerably more perceptive than his critics have admitted, appreciated that in May 1921 'the admission of American participation in oil enterprises in the northern provinces of Persia might be of advantage to British interests as a counterpoise to Russian pressure in those regions, while it would ensure British policy here against a recrudescence of that hostility on the part of the United States Legation from which it has suffered in recent years'.[193]

Diplomatic habits, like others, are difficult to change and the withdrawal symptoms are painful, as is revealed by a comment on Norman's despatch, 'Persia is to us very much what Mexico is to the US, a troublesome neighbour whom we cannot control as we should like, but whom we do not want to see any other controlling.'[194] At the same time G.P. Churchill at the Foreign Office, who had been in the legation in Tehrān before the war, was lamenting that 'the present Persian Government contemplate throwing Persia entirely into the hands of the Americans'.[195] Vansittart took a more pragmatic view minuting that 'I cannot bring myself to feel very concerned about this American menace ...I am inclined to think it would be to our advantage to have Americans interested in regions where a Russian menace exists or threatens.'[196]

The Company was being squeezed between two irresistible forces. On the one hand the difficulties over the Khostaria concession were still unsolved and, as Qavam al-Saltana, the Persian Prime Minister, remarked, 'however much the Persian Government might admit validity of concessions, Russian opposition would prevent British company from working them'.[197] Curzon might despair that there were 'almost as many Persian policies as there were Prime Ministers', but it did not make the acceptance of the Khostaria concession any more appealing.[198] On the other hand some American interest in Persia, though cautious and tentative, was being shown with priority being given to the oil sector, which would inevitably centre on the concessionary position of the northern provinces.[199]

The coup d'état which brought Rizā Khān to power in February 1921 did nothing to lessen the need for increased government revenue, indeed it increased it. On 15 August Major Saunders, the British military attaché in Tehrān, reported that Rizā Khān was determined 'to form a Persian army commanded and officered throughout by Persians only...his scheme involves an expenditure of money which his country can ill afford'.[200] Encouraged by the ambitious Fīrūz, who was released from the prison in which he had been placed in the early days of the coup, the Persian Government redoubled its efforts to attract American capital. Standard Oil and Bethlehem Steel were suggested for loans by Morgan Shuster, who was acting as Persian financial agent in the United States.[201] The State Department, requested by 'Alā to persuade American companies to take an interest in oil concessions, approached Standard Oil (NJ).[202] The Company, learning of these overtures, informed the Foreign Office. Curzon instructed Norman to enter 'an immediate official protest to the Persian Government against the granting of any fresh concession for oil in Northern Persia, basing yourself on the prior rights already acquired by the Anglo-Persian Oil Company'.[203] The French and Germans too were offered some interests.[204]

All speculation ended on 24 November, when it was learnt that an understanding had been reached between Standard Oil (NJ) and the Persian Government, which precluded 'the right of transferring concession to any foreign government or association'.[205] The French, Russians and British protested.[206] Curzon was unwilling to sanction any British loan to the Persian Government whilst it was 'actively carrying on a definitely anti-British policy and seeking to introduce foreign influence with the avowed object of supplanting us in Persia', not least by offering an oil concession already acquired by an English company to an American oil company.[207] The diplomatic impasse was regrettable, coming at a time when feelings were running high over the Mesopotamian concession (see section 5), when there were allegations in the American press that British oil companies were cornering the oil supplies of the world and when emotional appeals were continuing over the 'Open Door' controversy.[208]

In Tehrān, Loraine, newly arrived in the Persian capital, was not 'at all happy about our situation in regard to Khostaria concession...This question will poison discussion of many other questions at issue with Persian Government.'[209] It was for this reason that he advocated the 'Far best solution seen from this end would be an amicable agreement between

The expansion of international interests

The Key to the Future, New York American, 14 November 1921

Anglo-Persian Oil Company and Standard Oil Company.' In Washington, the British ambassador was recommending that 'nothing should be done to encourage Persian Government in their efforts to play off United States Government against His Majesty's Government'.[210] Sir Auckland Geddes was concerned about the state of Anglo-American relations and actively supported a rapprochement between the two companies. In fact this was already taking place. Bedford had met Greenway in London in mid-August to discuss a number of issues, including the North Persia concession, which they agreed to resolve together, for the Americans had not yet made any formal commitment to a definite concession.

It was a most fortunate and timely coincidence that Cadman, who had left on 14 November for the United States on a technical fact-finding visit,

The expansion of international interests

his first assignment for the Company, was able, on Greenway's instructions, to carry on discussions with Bedford. Cadman had a double task. In the first place he was concerned to negotiate a mutual agreement between the two companies to regulate their participation in a concession for northern Persia, and secondly he was to draw up an appropriate concessionary agreement.[211] Cadman had to maintain the validity of the Khostaria concession lest it should appear that both of the companies were condoning an illegal act by accepting the Persian Government's cancellation of the concession, but he had to respect the American refusal to get involved in political issues which predated their own interest. The negotiations fell into two parts, those dealing with the concessionary issues, which were confined to the two companies, and those concerned with the attached loan for the Persian Government, which involved more complicated diplomatic considerations. Cadman had his first meeting with some of the directors of Standard Oil (NJ) on 2 December 1921. On 5 December he delivered a major address to the American Institute of Petroleum, which was appealing and informative and well received. He spoke of international goodwill, industrial understanding, commercial integrity and the application of scientific principles to business matters. He talked informatively with many involved in oil issues and in the Hardinge administration on the need for a better and more open understanding of oil affairs.

In New York he had the first of a series of lengthy discussions with Bedford and his colleagues on 12 December. In Washington he was impressed with the cooperative attitude of the State Department and kept the ambassador briefed on what was happening. Geddes was particularly appreciative of the importance of the role Cadman was playing. It was not just a question of reaching an accommodation over the Khostaria concession; 'A consideration of even greater moment,' he declared to Curzon, 'is that the successful establishment of common interests and consequent friendly relations between the Anglo-Persian and Standard Oil Companies might well give a new aspect to the whole oil situation and remove one powerful factor from amongst the hostile influences to be reckoned with in the relations between the United States and the British Empire.'[212] He was right. This was the real prize.

Cadman, confident and encouraged by the improved atmosphere which he had noticed in his conversations, proposed to Greenway that it was an opportune moment to raise the issue of American participation in the Mesopotamian concession. Greenway responded affirmatively but carefully, sanctioning the initiative which was to change international oil relations and make possible the consortium of oil companies which would operate the Mesopotamian concession.[213] Cadman raised the subject for the first time on 22 December to Bedford, who gave it a cautious welcome. The remarks of Geddes were echoed by Herbert Hoover, then Secretary of Commerce, who told Cadman that 'if the Anglo-Persian and the Standard were able to co-operate and understand each other that would solve the whole difficulty and we were not likely to hear any more from the United States'.[214] Cadman's oil evangelising was a mission of successful conversion.

Back in New York Cadman resumed his negotiations after Bedford and his colleagues had consulted the State Department and the Persian representatives. In principle Standard Oil (NJ) was prepared 'to go the whole hog in supporting Anglo-Persian in getting Khostaria concession ratified and revised particularly providing the terms to Khostaria can be reduced'. Shuster accepted that the two companies 'were now only prepared to proceed if the Khostaria concession was ratified', and that the provision of a loan depended on Persian acceptance of this condition.[215] It was a predicament for the Persian Government, because the concession had become a rotten political plank on which nobody wished to walk. In London the Persian Legation disavowed its legality. Russian opposition to the announced Standard Oil (NJ) concession made it difficult to capitulate to Russian demands without losing diplomatic face as well as the chance of an American loan.

Bearing in mind the rumpus over the Khostaria concession, it was perhaps naive of the two companies to imagine they could ride into Persia together on the back of a revised concession waving a $1 000 000 loan. Shuster, 'crazy to get money for Persia', may have overreached his capacity to commit the Persian Government, notwithstanding his declaration that he would 'have no difficulty getting Persian Government to agree' to the proposed arrangements between the Company and Standard Oil, of which he approved.[216] The Foreign Office was not in favour of providing a loan to the Persian Government, until they had acknowledged their acceptance of the proposals, but Shuster pressed for immediate payment. Cadman too 'did not agree to the payment of a loan or part of a loan to the Persian Government until final agreement had been reached with Persian Government on new concession'.[217]

The loan was the stumbling block.[218] The Company was not a direct party to it, but indirectly it was concerned because of the collateral security required on the royalty payments, which were already pledged for the outstanding British loans to Persia, a matter between the Persian and British Governments. Bedford was uneasy and 'did not wish to be mixed up in any political affairs' and was prepared 'to tell Shuster that everything was off and that Standard now withdrew their offer'.[219] With the negotiations stalled over the conditions for a loan, Geddes advised Curzon that it

The expansion of international interests

would be unfortunate 'if these promised negotiations should be discontinued, or if they should fail in bringing about an identifying of interests in Persia between the two companies, and incidentally giving United States Government a practical stake in stable conditions in the Near East'.[220] Curzon replied that the problem was of making the Persians responsible for the debts they had already incurred rather than increasing them, so postponing their settlement.[221] He, however, was 'entirely in favour of close co-operation between British and American oil interests, including joint financing of the loan on the security of the oil royalties'.[222] It was an ingenious compromise.

Curiously, support for Curzon's contention that conditions should not be made too easy for the Persian Government came in January 1922 from Rizā Khān, who told Major Saunders that he applauded 'the policy of His Majesty's Government withholding funds' because he believed that 'when Persians realised their inability to get money for the asking they would be compelled to work themselves to put their house in order'.[223] Bedford, though realising that the Company was in no way involved in the imbroglio over the loan, nevertheless reaffirmed his 'determination to withdraw from negotiations rather than have Standard Oil Company involved in any political difficulties relating to Persia'. He felt that 'State Department had treated him unfairly in not informing him fully of position before suggesting that he should open negotiations with Persian Government'.[224] Indeed, as Shuster told Cadman, it was the Persian Minister who had gone to the State Department and said to them that the Persians were 'anxious to grant concessions, particularly oil, to Americans'.[225] It was the State Department that had put him directly in touch with Standard Oil.

The Company took up the Curzon's compromise, which was clarified on 24 January 1922,[226] for it was not wished that the loan should prevent a settlement.[227] Just as the international complications over the loan seemed to have been solved, a serious dispute arose between the two companies. Standard Oil (NJ) was prepared to settle, but only on condition that, if it was not satisfied within a year with the geological prospects, it would withdraw and leave the Company in full possession of all its rights in the joint concessionary company.[228] As Cadman admitted, it was 'ridiculous'.[229] The Company was being pulled in two directions at once. On the one hand, Standard Oil was having geological cold feet but was agreeable to purchasing the contested concessionary rights of Khostaria. On the other hand the Company was hanging on to Khostaria's rights, which could not be held indefinitely without a settlement. Cadman traded cash against geology, by agreeing to Standard Oil's one year condition in return for an increased cash payment to acquire the concession from Khostaria. 'This is the best I can do,' Cadman reported to Greenway, 'and

The expansion of international interests

if you do not agree afraid deal is entirely off.'[230] A day later he repeated his plea that 'The friendliness which has been created is such that it would be a national calamity if we should break off negotiations on such a point resulting in fresh campaign being commenced more bitter than before.'[231]

Cadman had done his best. He had helped to create a better general atmosphere and in particular had established improved relations between the Company and Standard Oil (NJ). His presence had been greatly appreciated, but he sensed early in February that he was likely to outstay his welcome unless there were positive results from his visit. He feared his motives might become suspect in American circles in spite of his impartiality. Greenway, more sensitive over Persian questions, must have been relieved over the understanding that Cadman had reached, but he must also have realised how disastrously Standard Oil had pulled the rug from under the concession by its geological reservations and its insistence on a one-year proving period. As Geddes surmised, the issue was no longer an arrangement between companies over a single concession, it had become a crisis of inter-governmental confidence. Greenway agreed, but warned that care should be taken to ensure that 'Alā and Shuster were properly empowered to settle as 'All loans have to be authorised and confirmed by Council of Ministers and Medjliss.'[232] On 3 February agreement was reached between Cadman and Bedford and agreed by Shuster for the newly established Perso-American Oil Corporation,[233] in which the two companies were to participate equally.[234]

The ink had hardly dried before objections were heard. 'Alā excused himself by claiming that his 'intervention at this stage is not only unnecessary but wholly uncalled for'.[235] Shuster became apprehensive that instead of 'the development and operation of petroleum resources "under" the managing control of the Standard Oil Company' it had been changed to 'a joint exploration of petroleum resources by the Anglo-Persian and Standard Oil Companies', which, rather belatedly and less than convincingly, he considered 'a very vital objection'.[236] On the loan there was also a misunderstanding, with Standard Oil's counsel, Guy Wellman, believing that, 'one of the conditions of this advance was that the Persian Minister would undertake with Mr Shuster to get the concession as it stood and was contemplated on Dec. 18 1921, through the Persian Parliament'. Shuster maintained that 'there were no conditions whatever attached'.

Shuster had accepted the loan on 16 February, on behalf of the Persian Government, which then did not ratify the concession, rejecting the action of its minister and agent on 27 February 1922 in a despatch to its Washington Legation.[237] It objected firstly to the possibility of Standard Oil withdrawing from the concession after a year. Whether it was a pretext or not, there was some justification for the Persian attitude, as such a condition was more suitable for a prospecting licence than a concession. The second objection was the reference to the Company. This could hardly be excluded, when it was a joint party to a concession which it believed it held legally. The Persians were trying to stifle possible Russian criticism. Bedford was surprised. He was not convinced by the special pleading of Shuster to reconsider the question, because he believed that 'the Persian Government could not now repudiate the arrangement for the Anglo-Persian and Standard partnership after having accepted the million dollar loan'. He was not going to welsh on his promise to the Company for 'any solution of the present complication must be acceptable to the Anglo-Persian'. Shuster, when asked, agreed that Persian acceptance 'would be preferable for Persia than having the deal fall'.[238]

Loraine in Tehrān worried over the damage to Anglo-Persian relations that was resulting from the controversy.[239] He had proposed 'the practicability of some fusion of Anglo-American oil interests in Persia, and my early impressions of the situation here speedily convinced me of its entire desirability'.[240] Indeed, in the widest sense, Anglo-American cooperation offered 'the best prospect in present circumstances of raising Persia out of the slough of despond into which she is sinking ever more deeply'. He deplored the possibility of the two countries being played off against each other.[241] He was, therefore, very much concerned to retrieve the situation by pressing for amendments to allay Persian suspicions.[242] In London, on 28 March, in a visit to the Foreign Office with Nichols, Bedford agreed to omit the preamble, which set out the context of the joint company agreement.[243] The attempt to change the face of the concession was simply cosmetic.[244]

The Persian Government was interested in a new suitor in mid-1922, the Sinclair Oil Corporation, controlled by Harry F. Sinclair, which was attracted by the same sort of enticements as Standard Oil (NJ) and was also eventually disappointed. The Majlis authorised a concession on 14 June 1923, which was signed between the Corporation and the Persian Government on 20 December 1923. This was also subject to a loan for $10 000 000 and a provision for non-transference of concessionary rights. Sinclair had difficulty in raising the loan and besides his relations with the Russian authorities deteriorated. It was the disastrous Teapot Dome scandal of bribery over the naval reserves field in Wyoming disclosed in January 1924 which finally ruined Sinclair. Sinclair prevaricated but was in no position to take up his commitments. The unfortunate murder of American vice-consul Robert Imbrie in 1924 whilst photographing a religious ceremony did not really account for Sinclair's withdrawal.[245]

The Company gained nothing from its association with Khostaria in Persia. It was ironical that he should later have again become so actively concerned with Rizā Shāh, Dāvar, Tīmurtāsh. Fīrūz and others in sponsoring a company, Kavir Kurin, for drilling in the Simnān district, east of Tehrān, with Russian assistance and offers of participation in 1923 to French financial interests.[246] The Company encountered great animosity in its attempts to substantiate its claims to the concession at a very unfavourable moment in Anglo-Persian relations. Though it did not initiate the discussions with Standard Oil (NJ), it welcomed their outcome except for the one year stipulation.[247] It was completely unrealistic to imagine that any Persian Government could have approved of the possibility of a single company holding a monopolistic position over all the country's oil resources. Whatever may have been the Company's legal position, its image was damaged by an apparent insensibility to Persian opinion, for which the misleading double talk of 'Alā and Shuster was partly responsible. Yet, the Company could not have disowned its agreement with Standard Oil (NJ) without wrecking its American relationship. It was a terrible dilemma, which resolved itself when the Sinclair Corporation fell under the Persian concessionary spell. Still, the participation with Standard Oil (NJ) in the abortive North Persian Oil Concession was largely instrumental in creating a better understanding between the two companies and their respective governments over oil affairs, not least over Mesopotamia. Perhaps the single most important beneficiary was Cadman, for whom the negotiations were a personal triumph and established his credentials as the leading British oil executive of his day, a reputation which could not be ignored in the succession to Greenway as Chairman.

5 MESOPOTAMIA

Interest in a Mesopotamian concession had appeared frequently in the pre-war activities of the Company through D'Arcy's earlier concern, intermittently during the war, and more particularly in 1918, when, primarily as a result of the persistence of Greenway and Slade, it became a matter of importance to the War Cabinet. (For details of negotiations and the circumstances in which the Company acquired its half shareholding in the Turkish Petroleum Company (TPC) in 1914 see Chapter 9). In May 1918 Greenway put forward a formal application to the Foreign Office for the concession 'in view of the probability that the time has now or will shortly come for dealing with this matter'.[248] Slade too had championed the Company's case on strategic grounds, arguing already in October 1916 for alternative sources of oil, 'of which there were indications in Mesopotamia, Kuwait and Bahrain and in Arabia. It is important to secure control of all the oil rights in these areas so that no other Power can exploit them for their benefit.'[249]

The expansion of international interests

In July 1918 Slade wrote again declaring that 'we must therefore at all costs retain our hold on the Persian and Mesopotamian oilfields, and any other fields which may exist in the British Empire, and we must not allow the intrusion in any form of any foreign interests, however much disguised they may be'.[250] He persuaded Maurice Hankey, secretary to the War Cabinet, of the importance of Mesopotamia, who reported to the Cabinet that 'if this information is correct, the retention of the oil-bearing regions in Mesopotamia and Southern Persia wherever they may be' was important.[251] The deliberations of the Harcourt Committee (see Chapter 6), and the subsequent temporary settlement based on reconciling the interests of the Company and Royal Dutch-Shell, as well as a French involvement in the Turkish Petroleum Company, kept Mesopotamia in the political forefront. The immediate post-war phase with all its diplomatic convulsions may be said to have terminated with the San Remo agreement in April 1920 (see Chapter 9).

The following period was marked by the seemingly growing Anglo-American hostility, as pictured in the press, over the scramble for the control of oil resources, exacerbated by the apparently declining oil reserves' position in the United States.[252] Whilst emotion cannot be ignored, its effects should not be exaggerated, for much of it was accompanied by prejudice, ignorance and personal ambition. Once wiser counsels prevailed, the misunderstandings were settled. Towards the end of 1921 some officials in the Foreign Office, Petroleum Department and Colonial Office were envisaging an American participation in TPC. Weakley at the Foreign Office wondered

whether the best and safest course would not be to invite the TPC to negotiate with American and Italian interests for the formation of a new Company, and that after the formation of such a Company, the new concern should approach the Iraq Government for the grant of a concession to develop *all the oil resources in Iraq* including those in Mosul and Baghdad.[253]

Clarke, at the Petroleum Department, in November argued that giving the Americans an interest in Mesopotamian oil would help to improve the relations between the two governments, but he preferred commercial negotiations between the companies concerned rather than diplomatic initiatives.[254] In view of the fact that Clarke was a friend of Cadman, whom he succeeded as head of the Petroleum Department, and later joined the Company, it may be presumed that the views he expressed, so similar to those propounded by Cadman to Bedford, had a common source, almost certainly Cadman. A further straw in the wind was Gulbenkian's visit to the Foreign Office in November, in which he indicated that he would prefer Standard Oil (NJ) in TPC rather than out of it, though in this respect he differed from Deterding.[255] Sir Eyre Crowe, permanent under-secretary, was impressed, noting that the Foreign Office was 'not at all adverse from letting the Americans into Mesopotamia'.[256] At the Colonial Office, Churchill believed that 'so long as the Americans are excluded from participation in Iraq oil, we shall never see the end of our difficulties in the Middle East'.[257] Another practical development at this time was the transfer of the registered office of TPC to the Company's premises on 6 December 1921 and the appointment of Nichols as Managing Director. As Nichols remarked to Arnold Wilson, TPC 'has been suffering from a mild attack of sleeping sickness, that it was nobody's child, whereas it should be actively sticking up for its *droits acquis*'.[258]

As has been mentioned, whilst Cadman was in the United States, December 1921–February 1922, negotiating with Standard Oil over the concession of North Persia, he had started the Mesopotamian ball rolling with Bedford. The responsibility was now on the State Department to protect the interests of American companies provided that it was assured that the concept of the 'Open Door' was being maintained. Much of the negotiating time on Mesopotamia from December 1921 to March 1925 consisted of reconciling the various interests of the participating companies and their Governments. The Company was concerned to protect the predominant position it had acquired in 1914. Royal Dutch-Shell attempted to retrieve the share which it considered it lost in 1914, to maintain the improved position it held as a result of the recommendations of the Harcourt Committee in 1919 and to ensure that it did not lose any competitive advantage in comparison with the Company. The American companies who associated themselves in the Near East Development Corporation wanted the same status of equality as the other shareholders and they were obliged to sustain the principles of the 'Open Door' in deference to the United States Government.[259] The French, regretting the 'surrender' of Mosul, viewed their shareholding as compensation rather than rights acquired.[260]

The British Government, anxious to solve its oil problems, honour its international obligations and support the interests of its own nationals, was divided by differing departmental attitudes. The course of the negotiations was a series of minor individual sacrifices in order to secure the maximum common agreement. Nichols displayed dexterity and patience as managing director in keeping his shareholders in line, whilst directing the movements of E.H. Keeling, the company's negotiator in Baghdad. The Iraq negotiators showed considerable skill in playing their hand, which was not remarkable for the strength of its suits. Indeed, whilst the ultimate settlement was not to everybody's satisfaction, its achievement at all was remarkable for the first major consortium of international oil companies working together for a single concession.

The expansion of international interests

There were three main issues; firstly, reaching agreement between the shareholders, secondly, the concessionary negotiations, which took place in Baghdad, and, thirdly, relations between TPC and the British Government.[261] It took almost two years to settle the outlines of the working agreement between the participants. In March 1923 Nichols made an important visit to talk with the American group.[262] There was much initial reluctance from Royal Dutch-Shell and the French Government to allow an American involvement, accepted at first as only being 20 per cent and subject to deduction to accommodate other interests if it became necessary, such as those from Turkey, Italy or Iraq. All the major participants eventually settled in 1928 for 23¾ per cent with Calouste Gulbenkian getting 5 per cent.[263] The principle of the Open Door was upheld by the provision of choosing 24 plots with sub-leases, though this palpable infringement of Iraq's sovereignty was disputed by the Iraq Government, which preferred a single concessionaire.

It was eventually acknowledged to be equitable by the other partners that the Company, because of giving up part of its former dominant shareholding, should be compensated by a 10 per cent overriding oil royalty. It was settled that the oil produced was to be sold to the participants at cost, that the company would be essentially non-profit-making, and that royalty payments to the Iraq Government would be based on crude oil produced. This suited Greenway who commented that 'the percentage on profits basis of Royalty had caused us endless trouble with Persia, I hope I may never have to experience similar difficulties again'.[264] It was agreed to dispense with a refinery though Royal Dutch-Shell was anxious to have one built in Iraq to provide oil products. The self-denying clause was accepted with less than eagerness, but recognised to be an essential part of the agreement.

The actual concession negotiations, though not continuous, extended over eighteen months. The main sessions were held in Baghdad, October–December 1923, February–March 1924, September–December 1924 and January–March 1925. The first Iraq team of negotiators was composed of Yasin Pasha, Minister of Communications and Works, Najī al-Suwaydī, Minister of Justice, Sasūn Husqual, Minister of Finance and some British advisers.[265] There was very little agreement at first on the duration of the concessionary period, inclusion of Basra, a definition of drilling commitments, Iraq share participation, royalty payments, sub-lessee rights, place of company registration, exclusion of bituminous deposits and free oil. The Iraq negotiators were unaware of the articles of the San Remo Treaty. The Iraq negotiating committee was not always the same. Thus in mid-November 1923 the cabinet resigned and a new committee was appointed, 'Alī al-Ayubi Jawdat, Minister of Interior,

The expansion of international interests

Hajj Muhsin al-Shalash, Minister of Finance and Suhib Beg, Minister of Works. On 27 March King Faysal opened the Constituent Assembly, which became so preoccupied with the ratification of the Anglo-Iraq Treaty, which it passed in June, and the Organic Law settling the Constitution, which was approved in July, to the exclusion of other subjects, that Keeling returned to London in May 1924. The political atmosphere was not favourable to taking decisions and on 4 August the government resigned. A new oil committee was established consisting of Yasin Pasha, Prime Minister, 'Abd ul-Muhsin Beg, Minister of Interior, Muzahim Beg, Minister of Communications and Works, and Sasūn.

On 22 July 1924, the first meeting was held in London, at which all the representatives of TPC were present, the French having settled the nature of the company that was to represent their interest, Companie Française des Pétroles, with a mixed shareholding of public and private capital.[266] General agreement was reached on the concessionary conditions, but a disturbing issue arose over the shareholding terms offered to Gulbenkian, which he rejected. There were also difficulties with the British Government over the extent of the concessionary area and the inclusion of Mosul, because the delimitation of the frontier between Iraq and Turkey had not been agreed by the League of Nations Boundary Commission. Nevertheless, by the end of August the Colonial Office was able to admit that 'we see no objection to terms of draft which appears eminently reasonable and fair'.[267]

At the beginning of September Keeling returned to Baghdad. Criticism by the Iraq negotiators concentrated on the inclusion of Basra, rejecting the royalty basis of 4s per ton in favour of a sliding scale, no prolongation of the duration beyond 60 years, the appointment of an Iraq director, increasing drilling obligations, minimum production levels, veto on sub-leasing, reversion rights of TPC property outside Iraq, gold standard for royalty payments, customs duties and registration of an Iraq based company. Most seriously of all, on 8 November, they raised the question of an Iraq shareholding as indicated in the San Remo agreement.

This became the most crucial and divisive aspect of the negotiations, the one which TPC was most reluctant to concede. All these points had to be referred back by Keeling, who was not given wide plenipotentiary powers. Nichols had to discuss them with his co-directors, who had to receive their instructions from their principals. The procedure was tedious, particularly as the British Government had to be kept informed of the developments, as it felt that TPC was not always observing either the spirit or the letter of San Remo and thereby causing diplomatic embarrassment to the Government as a signatory. The Foreign Office might sym-

The expansion of international interests

pathise with the desire to exclude an Iraq shareholding but it could not welcome it.

Thus, by the end of February 1925, agreement had been reached on all points apart from the Iraq shareholding issue.[268] Nichols at the end of February rather histrionically claimed this to be impossible, unless the whole fabric of the Turkish Petroleum Company was torn to pieces. The Colonial Office was inclined to agree, but the Foreign Office was sceptical. On 4 March Nichols was ready to repair the fabric and informed the Colonial Office that TPC had no alternative but to accept an Iraq shareholding in a side letter to the concession.[269] On the same day Keeling advised keeping the concessionary powder dry and to make no commitment on the subject. Dobbs, the High Commissioner, however, was giving contrary advice. King Faysal on 8 March authorised the signature of the concession, without the shareholding, subject to two minor modifications on the 24 plots to be selected and the discount for product prices. The Concession was signed on 14 March 1925. After oil had been struck at Baba Gurgur on 14 October 1927, the final arrangements between the companies were concluded on 31 July 1928 for the Iraq Petroleum Company, as it came to be called.

Why did Iraq not pursue its advantage? Perhaps there was no one overwhelming reason, though financially the situation in Iraq was depressing. It may have been presumed realistically that immediate benefits were better than later expectations. Politically there was increasing pressure from the British Government to settle as it did not wish to shoulder a financial burden any longer than was unavoidable, though not necessarily to prevent the shareholding. The uncertainty may have been having a disturbing effect on the internal Iraq political situation. Lastly, the Iraq Government may have believed that failure to agree would react adversely on the expected favourable settlement by the League of Nations Commission, which was investigating the position of the Mosul vilayet between Turkey and Iraq. It may have been felt that the British Government could influence its recommendations, if the concession was signed. The Commission, composed of Count Teleki, a former Prime Minister of Hungary, de Wirsen, Swedish Minister in Bucharest, and Colonel Paulis of the Belgian Army, arrived in Baghdad in January 1925.[270] There is certainly more than a gentle allusion to the Commission's disposition to support the development of the province, which the granting of the concession would ensure. Dobbs had also hinted at a possible connection, which the Foreign Office had disliked.[271]

Curzon had declared candidly at the end of 1923 that TPC 'must be made to realise that the value of their rights is entirely dependent on diplomatic and political support, and that this means that due weight must be attached to political objects connected with the concession quite apart from commercial advantages resulting from a satisfactory political settlement'.[272] The TPC concession was the political concession par excellence. It was conceived in response to a political problem. It never ceased to be influenced by its political upbringing. The difficulty lay in its adaptation to temporary political exigencies without impairing the commercial trust between the participants. This was not always easy, as for example, when the Foreign Office wanted to preserve an open negotiating position at Lausanne and so prevent TPC from reaching any agreement until the status of Mosul was settled. Dobbs and the Colonial Office contested the Foreign Office view at an interdepartmental conference held in May 1924, that 'we must continue to maintain the view that no agreement could be made pending the outcome of the Mosul negotiations'.[273]

The Colonial Office was more cooperative and under Amery from October 1924 much more assertive in its support for TPC. Nichols may have regretted to Teagle that 'the prominence now given to oil in diplomatic discussion was dangerous', but it was inescapable in October 1924, when it seemed that the negotiations had become becalmed.[274] Dobbs urged the Government to intervene on behalf of TPC as Major Holmes was making advances to King Faysal. At the Foreign Office, Morgan minuted 'if the Irak Government refuses to fall in with our views, I do not see how we can force them to grant a concession to the TPC'.[275] His colleague, Osborne, remarked that the Government was not 'in any way committed to the Company except as we owe them the usual support due to a British enterprise, we can press their claim to the point of arbitration but not beyond'.[276]

Nichols, somewhat inconsistently, but understandably in view of the slow progress over the negotiations, wrote to Keeling at the beginning of November 1924 informing him that he was 'straining every point to make our case the first subject submitted to the new Colonial Secretary'. On 13 November 1924 Dobbs was instructed to assist the TPC, but progress was still slow.[277] Towards the end of February Amery argued that the passing of the concession was in 'the substantial interest of Iraq' and persuaded the Cabinet to form a committee on the subject. There was general approval for more pressure to be applied, but Osborne persisted in opposing this because 'it involves a complete repudiation of our oft-repeated assertion that our policy towards Iraq has nothing to do with oil'.[278] The Government prevaricated, hoped for the best and appealed to the company to compromise over the shareholding. Its intervention had not been decisive enough to have determined the contemporary course of affairs, but just sufficient to have given the impression of having done more than it did in retrospect.

The expansion of international interests

The Company in the decade following the First World War had taken concessionary interests in many parts of the world with varying degrees of geological success, but with little actual increase of its potential productive capability or its reserves position, except in Iraq. There were few directions in which it could face without becoming involved with the British Government. The connection with the British Government certainly did not advance, but obstructed its interests in South America. Over Mesopotamia, successive governments blew hot and cold before assisting in the negotiations for a concessionary settlement which was satisfactory to the Company, the other participants in the Turkish Petroleum Company and their respective Governments. It is an oversimplification to suppose that the Company's concessionary position was the result of historical accident. Nowhere, however, even in the British colonies, was it possible for the Company to obtain a concession simply on its geological merits. This may have been applicable to mining concessions, seldom to oil concessions, which in South America particularly, in Italy and in Persia also, had become already in the mid-1920s issues not only of the national economy but of the national conscience. Gradually the day of the third parties was ending and direct concessionary negotiations between oil companies and governments would predominate. This development made little difference to the exploratory success rate, which was determined by the bit and not the pen, but it appealed to national pride. It was part of the complex relationship between the industrialised and the developing countries with which the international oil industry was intimately and increasingly involved from the 1920s.

13
THE IMPORTANCE OF THE PERSIAN DIMENSION 1926-32

I INTRODUCTION

'I do feel convinced,' wrote Loraine of Rizā Khān at the end of 1925, 'that he is the one man able to put the affairs of this country in order and set its feet in the path of real progress.'[1] A few months later, on 25 April 1926, in a bizarre ceremony of glittering splendour, the former officer of the Cossack Brigade, who had become the Prime Minister, crowned himself Rizā Shāh Pahlavī.[2] Cadman, Chairman designate, invited to Tehrān for the occasion, decided to direct his attention 'to the establishment of a more friendly spirit and to the creation of the necessary machinery whereby much closer contact could be maintained with the Persian Government than had hitherto been possible'.[3] He felt 'the need for direct negotiations in the future between the Persian Government and the Company'. Cadman was encouraged by his audience with the Shah who professed himself to be 'personally satisfied with the Company's progress and even if the Government were getting no revenue out of it, the work the Company was doing was all in the interest of Persia'.[4] The opportunity appeared propitious for a new approach to the concessionary relationship. Appearances were deceptive, for six years later after a series of negotiations the Shah cancelled the D'Arcy Concession.

Behind the outward allegations of bad faith which precipitated this action of the Shah lay serious but genuine misunderstandings, no less influential for often being unconscious. There existed certain assumptions of which both sides were either insufficiently aware or to which inadequate recognition was given. It would be superficial to exaggerate cultural differences, but it would be equally disingenuous to ignore them. Disagreements arose not just from cross purposes but from arguments pursued on parallel lines, which were incapable of ever converging. Persia was the *raison d'être* of the Company. The nature and context of the concessionary negotiations, which started so promisingly in 1928 and failed so abruptly in 1932, were central to its existence.

The Persian dimension

Loraine's optimism was qualified by his reservation that if the Shah 'retains his mental and physical energy and his moral equilibrium, we can, I think, look confidentially forward, not only to a more permanent improvement of Anglo-Persian relations and a closer collaboration between the two Governments, but also to the inestimable advantage of a stabilised and progressive Persia'.[5] He recognised the danger of exclusive reliance on the Shah alone. He informed the Foreign Secretary, Austen Chamberlain, that

the course of events, may, therefore, depend on the passing mood or caprice of a single individual, Riza Khan. Those who might offer him good counsel fear that their advice would not be welcome or are far too timorous of his possible displeasure to tender it. Those who give him bad advice, who perpetually flatter him to the top of his bent, for the furtherance of their personal interests and the satisfaction of their petty ambitions, are capable of urging him to any folly...If the wise men hold their peace, the council of knaves and time-servers may prevail.[6]

This Hogarthian description indicates that behind Loraine's tempered optimism lay a feeling of unease, which Harold Nicolson, who acted as chargé d'affaires for a brief period after Loraine's departure, did not disguise in his elegant cynicism.

'The logic of Persian events,' Nicolson informed the Foreign Secretary, six months after the Coronation, 'pursues a zig-zag course, turning back upon itself at moments, and at moments diverging on some sudden tangent.'[7] He did not share Loraine's enthusiasm for the Shah and doubted if he 'possesses the intellectual or moral calibre necessary for his high functions'. That was a rather superior social judgement, but he was more convincing about the economic pressures, the administrative chaos, tribal restlessness, military scandals, judicial malpractices and government corruption, believing that 'over the whole country broods a dark cloud of uncertainty, insecurity and despair'. He regretted the fragmentation which the Shah was causing in Persian society, which was beginning to lack its previous elasticity and its remarkable power of resistance. For Nicolson 'The old Persia was a loose-knit pyramid resting on its base. The new Persia is a pyramid almost equally loose, but resting on its apex; as such it is easier to overthrow.'

This impression of malaise did indeed coincide with a period of introspection and lack of confidence of the Shah as he puzzled whether to rule constitutionally or dictatorially and wondered about whom he could trust to serve him. The doubts were not confined to foreign observers, for 'Alī Akbar Dāvar, who had a radical vision of a Persian society untrammelled by social prejudices and religious traditions, and who subsequently served the Shah closely for a number of years, was extremely critical of the situation. He believed the underlying causes of discontent were economic and social. He candidly told Jacks in September 1926, that 'Persians had learnt to utilise the materials in general use by Europeans which they now regarded as necessities for their daily lives but they have not learnt to be as industrious as Europeans'.[8] He was disappointed that 'the wave of hope' stimulated by the Coronation had not been sustained, 'the hope of progress and of improvement in the earning power of the masses' had receded. He condemned the activities of unscrupulous clerical leaders and rapacious military officers.

In spite of his support for the Shah, Dāvar blamed him for being 'too vacillating', and being swayed in different directions by his many councillors. As a result of this indecision 'the Shah was making blunders and the people were losing confidence in him'. As Loraine had expressed it when the Qājār dynasty was deposed at the end of 1925, the people were unsure if 'they have not merely exchanged King Log for King Stork'.[9] There had been much religious opposition to the Shah when he contemplated instituting a secular presidency on the lines of Ataturk's reforms in Turkey. When later he began to impose changes like the abolition of the compulsory wearing of the veil for women in public, improvements in public health and the widening of educational opportunities, this opposition became more irate.

The strength of the opposition to the Shah has to be appreciated, for it is a mistake to imagine that the path to power of Rizā Shāh was like a magical comet heralding the glory to come. Far from belittling his achievements, such a realistic appraisal places his successes and failures in a more appropriate historical context. For all the charisma with which he has been credited or the faults for which he has been criticised, he did suffer from a sense of insecurity. His contribution to the modernisation of his country is acknowledged. Yet, he lacked not patriotism but the finesse to reconcile the conflicting elements in the country. The nationalism he stimulated with its mock Achaemenian revivalism was paraded as instant progress. It is arguable that the façade of imperial grandeur which was displayed by the two Pahlavî monarchs was ultimately misleading to the nation. It certainly rested on a base that was too fragile to support the weight that was increasingly thrust upon it.

Throughout the second half of 1926 the Shah was apparently indecisive. In the 14th session of the Majlis the members continued to play the traditional game of personal politics. According to Sir Robert Clive, who had just succeeded Loraine as Minister, 'Such a system naturally paralyses all negotiations or action and is largely responsible for the hesitations and evasions which form so trying a feature of all dealings with Persian Ministers.'[10] Even the Prime Minister's reaction in 1926 to a motion of no confidence was to remind those in office 'to set aside disputes, contentious

The Persian dimension

and personal attacks and occupy the whole of their precious time in working for the welfare and happiness of the people'.[11] By the end of the year the Shah had recovered his nerve, called the bluff of his opponents and regained the political initiative in deciding to rule rather than reign. Clive detected a stronger sense of purpose because 'certainly today nothing can be done without His Majesty's consent'. Indeed Clive regarded 'Persia's position as precarious, as it was entirely dependent upon the life of the Shah'. He reported that 'a serious campaign is on foot, instigated, I have every reason to believe, by the Shah himself, to recover tariff autonomy, abolish the capitulations, reduce foreign concessions and...remove the last vestige of extraneous privileges'.[12] The Shah had proposed a programme.

It was a positive programme which would transform Persia. Who were his associates in this campaign for national revival, perhaps the inspiration? Foremost was 'Abdul Husayn Tīmurtāsh, formerly a member of the Majlis, then Minister of Public Works and in 1926 appointed Minister of Court. An enigmatic but capable person, whose vivacity and charm, manners and politeness, quintessentially Persian, masked a capacity for work, a mastery of intrigue and a flair for opportunism which surprised and exasperated his contemporaries. He was, according to Clive,

> second only to the Shah...He attends all meetings of the Council of Ministers and no one so far as I hear dares to oppose him...To hope to achieve anything without his goodwill is futile. It may even be that his vitality, energy and ambition, qualities so rare among Persians, are the actual driving force and that it is really Teymourtache and not Reza Shah who is ruling the country.[13]

Later, the Prime Minister was to tell Godfrey Havard, who was Oriental Secretary, 1923-31, that 'Timurtache interfered in everything and he was powerless'.[14] It was a strong triumvirate, Tīmurtāsh, Dāvar Minister of Justice, and Fīrūz Minister of Finance, which actually and effectively ran the affairs of state, from February 1927 when a new government was formed to implement the new programme.[15] This was the setting and some of the cast for the dénouement of the D'Arcy Concession.

2 A NEW DIRECTION

(a) A resident director in Tehrān

Cadman, on his visit to Tehrān in April 1926 for the Coronation of the Shah, decided to upgrade the Company's representation there from a listening to a command post, with responsibility for direct contact with the Persian Government, which had previously been maintained by the British legation. He decided 'at the outset to direct my attention to the

591

The Persian dimension

establishment of a more friendly spirit and to the creation of the necessary machinery whereby much closer contact could be maintained with the Persian Government than had hitherto been possible'.[16] Cadman hoped that a better understanding would be achieved by associating the Company more closely with the Persian Government, so that the scope, significance and technicalities of the Company's operations would be more appreciated by the Persians 'who would come more and more to regard our own activities through Persian eyes and in terms of a Persian vocabulary'. In short, as he indicated to the Shah in audience, he wanted a new approach by which 'the Company was very anxious to establish itself in such a position that the Persian Government would realise and appreciate the progress and development in the Persian Petroleum Industry'.[17]

Cadman promised to increase educational opportunities for Persian employees of the Company, assist with the development of road communications, regularise the telephone system operated by the Company, and undertake further exploration. He agreed to provide improved supplies of petroleum products to the northern provinces to counter trade sanctions which were then being imposed on Persia in connection with Russian demands for preferential trade tariffs. He expected that the position of the recently proved oilfield at Naft Khana in the disputed Transferred Territories on the Iraq – Persian border could be settled to permit production.[18] He decided to appoint T.L. Jacks as resident director in Tehrān to coordinate the Company's activities in Persia and to act as its official representative. Jacks had joined Strick, Scott and Co. in Muhammara as a writer in 1912. Confident and competent, well groomed and an accomplished polo player, he emerged after the war as a strong personality. In 1922 he was joint general manager in Muhammara with Arnold Wilson and in 1925 had carried out major changes in the administration of the Company's operations. The Company had been represented in Tehrān since 1922 by W.C. Fairley, who had a Persian assistant, Mustafa Khān Fateh, later to have a distinguished career in the Company.

Before he settled permanently in the capital Jacks made a number of temporary visits. His first important assignment was in October 1926, on the question of Naft Khana. The Company wanted to drill on the Persian side of the frontier. There were no exploration obstacles, for the Shah had acquired large estates in the area, which had been appropriately renamed Naft-i-Shāh. Oil had been proved on the Iraq side since 1923 after a spectacular fire at the drilling rig and this had supplied a small refinery there at Alwand from 1928. The Company regarded an agreement as a test case of the Government's sincerity. Harold Nicolson and Millspaugh,

From left to right, A.W.M. Robertson, L. Lockhart, Mustafa Fateh and W.C. Fairley, Tehrān 1926

who was American financial adviser to the Persian Government, were both pessimistic. They warned Jacks that 'no matter what the nature of the Agreement concluded might be, it was bound sooner or later to form the subject of adverse criticism in the Majlis'.[19]

Nevertheless Jacks was able to conclude a satisfactory agreement in an exchange of letters with the Prime Minister on 9 November 1926. It provided for the oil produced in the Persian part of the oilfield to be refined at Alwand and allowed back into Persia free of duty for local sales, the light equipment used during the operations to pass backwards and forwards across the frontier without customs or hindrance and that royalties should be on tonnage rather than on a profits basis.[20] The Iraqis had given their consent. It seemed a simple business transaction, which would lead to the production of Persian oil in close proximity to major areas of population and considerably reduce dependence on Russian supplies. The agreement was not submitted to the Majlis but later by an indiscretion, deliberate or accidental, of the veteran Persian politician, Vusūq al-Dawla, a former Prime Minister, the Majlis was apprised and some of the factions within it immediately assailed the Government. Tīmurtāsh, negotiating in Moscow, disowned the agreement on his return to Tehrān.

The Government was reproached in the Press[21] 'with allowing foreigners to drain the country of her oil resources and of deliberately reducing the revenue of Persia by granting illegal and unnecessary exemption from customs duty'. Early in January 1927 a political pamphlet published in Tabrīz by an Āzarbāyjān political society favourable to the

The Persian dimension

Shah requested that 'Persian railways be constructed, oil wells exploited and the import of luxury articles forbidden'.[22] It seemed as if the Shah was asserting himself, putting pressure on the Government and enunciating his new programme of action. Mustaufi al-Mamālek, the Persian Prime Minister, became a victim of personal passions and not for the first or last occasion a Company agreement with a Persian government was caught up in rival political cross-currents. When Jacks returned to Tehrān again in April 1927 he noticed a change in the atmosphere. The rejection of the agreement was a symptom: 'The Shah, and not the Majlis appears to be all-powerful'.[23] He was informed that the new cabinet, which had been formed in February, was not expected 'to put up any real support of the letters exchanged on November last'.

Jacks realised that 'much remains to be done before we can hope to achieve the complete co-operation of the Persian Government'. Tīmurtāsh expected the Company to 'erect a refinery on Persian territory instead of drawing off the oil from the Persian side to a refinery in Iraq'.[24] Jacks failed to persuade him that it was not an economic proposition to put up another refinery in Persia. Jacks observed of Fīrūz, that he 'will at least do nothing calculated to assist the Company, and he will not hesitate to be definitely antagonistic provided he can do so without risk to his own interests'.[25] Iraq was the bugbear, the alleged agent of British imperialism to which Persia would not bow. Iraq was the object of certain Persian religious and national animosity because of the Shī'īte population around the holy cities of Najaf and Karbalā and Iraq claims to sovereignity over the Shatt-al-'Arab.[26]

As the impact of the new measures of reform began to be felt, protest increased from two sectors of the populace, who had little in common, but who posed an awkward threat to the Government and, incidentally, helped to put the Company in the political pillory. On the one hand in 1927 the communist party of Persia, at its second congress, decided 'to endeavour to prove to the toiling masses that as long as the despotic monarchy continues, British imperialism and the plundering of the country will also persist'.[27] On the other hand the new judicial reforms being instituted by Dāvar had aroused the religious opposition, who felt that their status in society was being undermined and that the religious basis of Persian society was threatened. Bazaars were closed and the new measures were denounced in the mosques. The ideological and religious opposition to the new secular corporate state lay at the heart of the political dilemma which faced the new Persian dynasty, the incompatability of modern concepts with the traditional, particularly when they were promoted by an unrepresentative autocratic government.

The Persian dimension

The Company became a double scapegoat. On ideological grounds it was caricatured as an imperialist bogey, a capitalist bloodsucker. In religious circles it was characterised as being a partner in an unholy alliance with the Government in overturning traditional values and introducing alien principles. As the largest industrial undertaking in the country it could not conceal its prominence. It became the victim of national resentment against the activities of foreign concessionaires associated with efforts to modernise the country. Turkey, nevertheless, had managed to accept foreign investment without crippling national independence or offending national culture. Still the Company suffered from its identification with the British Government in the diplomatic tussle for influence which took place officially and clandestinely.

The year 1927 was one of frantic activity with measures for reform in education, the promotion of local industry, the planning of the north–south trans-Persian railway and in mid-year the denunciation of foreign privileges, the Capitulations, animated by a 'spirit of nationalism', which Clive believed had 'outrun the ordinary dictates of reason and common sense'.[28] He had found it 'impossible to obtain any satisfaction on outstanding questions from the Persian Government'. F.C. Greenhouse, in charge of the Tehrān office after the departure of Fairley and before the arrival of Jacks, also complained about unsolved issues.[29] In January 1928, however, there seemed signs that the hectic activity of the previous year might be replaced by a more moderate pace. Clive was assured by the Shah that he was 'ready to come to a settlement of all outstanding questions, but he thought, in the first instance, that it would be best to discuss everything with the Minister of Court before lines of an agreement were submitted to Council of Ministers'.[30] The Shah was anxious about the position of the Company and declared that 'he had issued strict standing instructions that the best relations were to be maintained with the Company', but that if there was any cause for complaint, the representative was 'to call on the Minister of Court'. 'His Majesty,' continued Clive, 'then began to sing the praises of the Company in almost extravagant terms.'

As Jacks arrived in Tehrān in mid-January 1928 to take up his appointment, as resident director, the omens seemed more favourable. It was certainly clear that the star of Tīmurtāsh was in the ascendant. It was hoped that the direct access to him, which had been promised by the Shah, would eliminate the endless visits to officials, who were reluctant to take decisions for fear of having them countermanded or themselves reprimanded for acting outside their authority. The misfortune was that the lines to the Minister of Court were jammed by the press of callers and the delays were merely transferred from one office to another.

The Persian dimension

Jacks was determined to measure up to his new responsibilities and make the most of his opportunities. He was impressive in appearance and cut a dashing figure in the Persian capital with his attractive wife and his hospitality. He soon enjoyed a favourable social reputation among both the members of the foreign colony and Persians. If it turned his head, it can only have seemed to him a natural reflection of the position to which he was entitled, but it also made him susceptible to attentions, which he should have regarded with more reserve. It may be wondered whether his judgement was not impaired by his self-confidence and that he gave the impression of possessing more authority than he was able to justify. Cadman needed him and he certainly responded appropriately. During his consultations in London at the end of 1927 and his conversation with Cadman, and on his way back to Persia in early January 1928, Jacks was wondering about the new concessionary approach which was to be adopted. Not of an original mind, Jacks was quick to pick up straws in the wind. He was aware of Cadman's belief in a new concessionary approach.

He realised that Persians increasingly resented the Company's activities outside Persia, though they did not draw the conclusion that if conditions impeded the Company's development in their own country it was hardly to be expected that it would not look for opportunities elsewhere. Jacks thought that the Persian Government might regard all the interests of the Company in crude oil sources outside Persia as a threat to itself, so he reasoned that if 'any real and lasting benefit is to be attained, it would seem advisable to devise a means whereby Persia would not be dependent entirely on a Royalty derived from nett profits obtaining from Persian Crude'.[31] Moreover, he pertinently remarked that, in view of the increasing world-wide operations of the major companies, Persia would 'attempt to establish that in as much as the world-wide position of the Company has its origin in Persian oil, she is justified in demanding participation in the entire ramifications of the Company'.

It was a simple analysis by Jacks, an early appreciation of the concessionary dilemma facing a company which had more than one conflicting concessionary interest and which was obliged to reconcile its business objectives with national pressures, a commercial balancing act on a political tightrope of variable tension. Jacks realised the potential vulnerability of the Company to measures of taxation as 'evidence is by no means wanting that the Persian Government intends to have its pound of flesh...if not a little more'. To anticipate such an eventuality Jacks suggested that,

the only way to deal satisfactorily with the question of our future relations with Persia is to use every endeavour to seek a transfer from a Royalty on the nett profits arising from Persian oil to a Royalty or partnership in a holding company

The Persian dimension

embracing the entire ramifications of the Company within and without Persia, and to seek as a quid pro quo for such a revision complete exemption from all internal and external taxation together with a suitable extension to the expiry date of the D'Arcy's Concession.[32]

Cadman was sympathetic though he thought the idea premature, preferring to settle all outstanding questions at once at a round-table conference. The Foreign Office too in its disputes with the Persian Government had similarly tried for a general treaty to settle all differences at once. This, Cadman admitted warily, seemed 'to be the only line of policy in view of our failure in the past to arrive at any definite settlement with individual Ministers and Ministries on isolated questions'.[33] He was prepared to form a distribution company in Persia, with a name such as 'The South Oil Marketing Company Ltd', with opportunities for Persian capital and representation on the Board (see also Chapter 11). This was an interesting proposal in line with Cadman's idea of interesting Persians in the Company's affairs, but its appeal was limited and its possibilities were overtaken by later attempts to revise the Concession. Yet, however imaginative, it might not have been well received, appearing to reinforce rather than reduce the role of the Company in Persian commercial circles and implicating it in domestic political and personal rivalries.

On his arrival in Tehrān Jacks set about establishing good relations with Tīmurtāsh, 'the mouthpiece of the Shah', the executor of the Government's programme, for 'the entire negotiations are falling on the shoulders of Teymourtache and the amount of work he is handling is surprising everyone'.[34] In Persia, administrative responsibilities were personalised, not institutionalised, and there was a lack of political continuity, a natural consequence of the Persian character and historical tradition in which effective delegation was little practised and decision-making confined to the highest authority. Cadman approved of Jacks' direct approach, because he believed that, 'the more we can impress upon the Persian Government that we consider ourselves a commercial enterprise working in Persia in direct alliance with it, the better'.[35]

Tīmurtāsh, however, was an individual Minister, no matter how powerful, and the concessionary relationship was but one subject, important though it was, amongst the many in his portfolio. This soon became apparent as a result of a visit which Fīrūz made to Khūzistān to show the Persian flag and cock a snook at the Iraq authorities over pilotage in the Shatt-al-'Arab, during the course of which he demanded that all tankers required official Persian permission to be loaded.[36] This would have been an administrative nightmare, given the poor state of Persian organisation in the provinces, and was quietly dropped after a conversation between Jacks and Tīmurtāsh. Jacks was impressed with his successful démarche

The Persian dimension

and, writing to Cadman, effusively praised the Minister of Court whose 'great ability would make him an extremely difficult man to replace', rationally true perhaps, but politically irrelevant.[37] Within a month Jacks was reporting hostile comments about Tīmurtāsh, noting that 'where there is smoke there is generally fire, and it is well known that the Shah's policy is never to allow anyone to attain too much power'.[38] Rizā Shāh was not going to be upstaged.

Jacks presumed that the friendly attitude of Tīmurtāsh towards him was 'to no small extent, prompted by the Shah's very sincere regard for our operations'. Yet, realism not sincerity was his touchstone. Jacks was convinced, at an interesting audience with the Shah on 29 May 1928, that he had issued definite instructions that 'our work is to be assisted in every way'.[39] This was no doubt true, as the economic projects contemplated by the Shah called for an increased national revenue over and above that recoverable from customs, taxation and special duties on sugar and tea. It was unfortunate, even tragic, that the Shah's dependence on oil royalties was growing at a time when international oil marketing conditions were causing a relative reduction, even a decline, in the Company's growth and profits, quite beyond its control. For the moment, however, the Shah had great expectations. These, as Amīn Banani acknowledged in his study of Iranian modernisation, 'were of both economic consequence and deep social significance. His goal was not only to introduce mechanical industry but to substitute the cohesive force of the central state for the old corporative basis of society.' Yet amongst the problems were a lack of skilled manpower, a shortage of managerial ability and local capital, indifference to, if not some suspicion of, industrialisation and 'a lack of faith in any long range political stability and in the willingness or the ability of the government to protect private investments'.[40] Jacks looked to Tīmurtāsh for cooperation, who in turn was relying upon his association with Jacks to facilitate the negotiations, which he knew would eventually be required to establish a new concessionary relationship, which would underpin economic development.

The Shah claimed, at the same audience, that he had 'never hesitated to assist and support the Company in its legitimate occupations and shall continue to do so in the future'. Jacks referred to Cadman's desire 'to remodel the arrangements at present in force for the computation of Royalty', which, in spite of the Armitage-Smith Agreement, caused annual controversy. Tīmurtāsh, seeing his opportunity, advised the Shah that the Company 'have of late expressed their willingness to settle the differences between the Government and Company. Mr. Jacks has shown full sympathy towards reaching an understanding and revision of the Concession, and this matter will receive the Government's consideration.'

The Persian dimension

Jacks outlined the worsening contemporary oil situation to which the Shah replied that 'if this house of mine is damaged, I suffer, similarly, if anything goes wrong with the Company, Persia is damaged'. An admirable sentiment, but cold comfort if he did not actually understand the situation.

Finally the Shah commented significantly at this audience that his one objection to the Company was that 'the majority of its shares are held by the British Government; otherwise its work has been very good'. No Persian could ever neglect the linkage between the Company and the British Government, a connection which persistently influenced Persian opinion of the Company. Though Jacks might protest that the British Government 'exercises no control in the management of the commercial affairs of the Company', it was inconceivable to any Persian, who could only imagine that duplicity was being compounded with complicity. The Company's efforts to persuade Persians of their independence from the British Government were like a mirage of truth in the desert of incredulity. Indeed as Persian relations with the British Government deteriorated during this period over claims to Bahrain, landing rights for Imperial Airways, recognition of Iraq and unresolved financial claims, so were relations between the Persian Government and the Company adversely affected.

Tīmurtāsh actually admitted to Jacks on 24 June that enmity between Persia and Iraq was responsible for the failure to settle the issue of Naft-i Shāh.[41] By its intransigent policy towards the Company, the Persian Government hoped to induce it to transfer the major part of its operations to the Persian sector of the Transferred Territories. Cadman was apprehensive lest Jacks disclose too much of his hand and compromise the negotiating position. He was, however, pleased to learn that Tīmurtāsh was journeying to Europe and that the Minister of Court had acknowledged that 'both the Company and the Government recognised that such a revision was necessary to meet the developments and present day requirements'.[42] Cadman hoped that the visit 'may prove opportune and provide the occasion for dealing with all the questions between us and the Persian Government as one correlative issue and avoiding piecemeal discussions and settlements'.

(b) The possibility of partnership

Tīmurtāsh arrived in London on 27 July 1928.[43] He was determined to harness the resources of the Company to the modernisation of Persia and so bring off a personal spectacular political and economic coup which would impress the Shah. Tīmurtāsh would enhance his own position. He envisaged not just tinkering with the parts of the old model but bringing out a brand new design. Unfortunately, like Dr Musaddiq later in the early 1950s, he found himself eventually trapped in a winner-takes-all situation with little room for manoeuvre and little possibility for compromise, a victim of his own ambitions. A feeling of insecurity impelled Persian politicians to protect themselves by pressing policies to please the Shah, for which he would claim the credit in success, but for the failure of which they would pay the penalty with disgrace. Jacks remarked that 'The Shah has never allowed anyone either in the Army or in Government circles to assume a position approaching absolute control', so 'Teymourtache will have to work with the utmost caution if he is long to continue to retain his present position'.[44]

Cadman was under no such constraints. His influence upon the Company, the oil industry and the British Government was at its peak. Chairman not only of the Company but also of the early established Turkish Petroleum Company, to be called in June 1929 the Iraq Petroleum Company, he was greatly respected by his colleagues and competitors. He was prepared to set a precedent in accepting Persian participation in the Company, a radical departure in concessionary practise. At a meeting in London on 31 July enough common ground and determination was revealed, in spite of major differences, to move on to substantive negotiations later in Lausanne.[45] The Armitage-Smith Agreement, which the Persian Government, but not the Company, rejected as a dead letter,[46] was put into abeyance pending the outcome of the negotiations. Tīmurtāsh was uncompromising in claiming a percentage of the profits from all the Company's operations, not just those in Persia and the elimination of all allowances. Cadman's colleagues were not completely convinced of the wisdom of their Chairman's approach, Lloyd suggesting that 'it bristles with such difficulties that it becomes an impracticable proposition'.[47]

Arriving in Lausanne on 23 August 1928, Cadman was accompanied by Dr Young, as his Persian adviser. The following day he was presented with a set of ten proposals by Tīmurtāsh, which included the negotiating of a new concession lasting sixty years from signature to supersede the D'Arcy Concession and a programmed reduction in the concessionary area. The Persian Government was to receive a royalty of 2s per ton on all oil produced, 25 per cent of the ordinary shares of the Company free of charge, and a £500 000 settlement of all claims under the D'Arcy Concession. The Company was to be registered in Persia as well as in the United Kingdom.[48] Tīmurtāsh told Cadman that the Concession was 'antiquated and broadly speaking, inapplicable to present day methods and requirements'. He looked forward to the introduction of new conditions which 'would stimulate the Persian Government to take a deeper interest

The Persian dimension

in this great enterprise than it has been able to do in the past'. He felt that an industry had been developed in which Persians had no real share and no financial reward would dispel this feeling. 'Give the Persian Government,' he implored Cadman, 'a share in the business, let them feel that they are real partners to whose interest it is to further the Company's development and progress in the country and their whole attitude would change.'

Cadman was less idealistic, more pragmatic in his desire 'to be free to go ahead with our plans of expansion and with a feeling that we have everyone with us, especially the Persian Government'. Behind the rhetoric was the question of revenue to the Persian Government from the Company's operations. Was it to be based on a royalty per ton, a percentage of profits, dividends on shares or oil in kind? If participation was desirable, then, according to Cadman, it had to be accepted that 'they were all on one footing, the Persian Government would share in the Company's fortunate and unfortunate years like other shareholders, and there would be no cause for complaint'.

In the detailed talks on 25 August Tīmurtāsh expressed the urgency of reaching an agreement as 'he would not care to lose an opportunity that he considered favourable'. The existence of the Company might be politically embarrassing to Persia, but its profits were economically indispensable for its future prosperity. Tīmurtāsh was expecting a definite income from the Company 'which would be a little more than they were receiving at present, and with prospects of further increases from their shareholding', basing his demands on the starting line of the £1 400 000 received in royalties for 1927. (For Persian royalties see Table 13.1.) Such a

Table 13.1. *Anglo-Persian Oil Company crude production and royalty statistics 1925 to 1931*

Financial year ending	Crude production tons	Royalty £	Royalty per ton	Cumulative tonnage	Cumulative royalty
31 March 1925	4 333 933	830 754	3s 10d	20 334 037	4 748 316
31 March 1926	4 556 157	1 053 929	4s 8d	24 890 194	5 802 245
31 March 1927	4 831 800	1 400 269	5s 10d	29 721 994	7 302 514
31 March 1928	5 357 800	502 080	1s 10d	35 079 794	7 704 594
9 months 31 Dec. 1928	4 289 733	529 085	2s 6d	39 369 527	8 233 679
1 year 31 Dec. 1929	5 460 955	1 436 764	5s 3d	44 830 482	9 670 443
31 Dec. 1930	5 939 302	1 288 312	4s 4d	50 769 784	10 958 755
31 Dec. 1931	5 750 498	306 382	1s 1d	56 520 282	11 265 627

Source: BP H16/23

The Persian dimension

sum, argued Cadman, was exceptional, 'which they may not see again for a long time in view of over-production today and more to come'. Cadman was certainly right. In 1928 they plummetted to £502 000. Within a month Cadman would be discussing an agreement to rationalise production and distribution with Teagle and Deterding at Achnacarry in Scotland. He was well-informed.

Tīmurtāsh was quite unconvinced. Such considerations were irrelevant in the context of Persia's economic objectives, which determined the revenues required, as budgets were not trimmed to the resources available. The oil revenue contribution needed for the economy was £1 000 000. The only point at issue was not the possibility of raising it but the method of attaining it. On the calculations of Tīmurtāsh this could best be obtained by a royalty of 2s 6d a ton and receiving 3 000 000 shares on which an average dividend of 12½ per cent was payable. Without such a settlement, declared the Minister of Court, 'The Majlis would say that the Government had been hoodwinked' and 'they were worse off than before'. Cadman was surprised at the proposal, which was out of all proportion to what he had in mind. He emphasised that 'if Timurtash went on on these lines the chances of bringing these negotiations to a successful conclusion would be more remote than ever...unless the Persian Government reduced its terms, little or no progress would be made'.

H.E. Tīmurtāsh, Persian Minister of Court, seventh from left, being greeted by Sir John Cadman, far right, at Waterloo Station 27 July 1928

The Persian dimension

Tīmurtāsh was unmoved. He was playing for high stakes and disregarded, as simply minor details, questions of valuation and the British Government's shareholding. He maintained that 'if this had been a new Concession instead of an exchange or extension of the present D'Arcy Concession the Persian Government would have insisted, not on 25 per cent, but on a *50-50* basis' (italics mine). It seemed an impasse but, notwithstanding the complexities of the issues involved, the discussions were amicable and merited an imaginative response. Cadman committed himself to reaching a package deal in association with the Persian Government.

3 REVISING THE CONCESSION

(a) Setting up the pieces

Since Tīmurtāsh had outlined his position, it was necessary for Cadman to define the attitude of the Company. In the three months that followed the meeting in Lausanne, apart from taking his sick wife on convalescence and his conversations with Teagle and Deterding at Achnacarry, Cadman was deeply engaged in the preparations of a new concessionary basis for the Company's activities in Persia. The Company was now firmly established, talking in terms of equality with Standard Oil (NJ) and Royal Dutch-Shell. It was no longer dependent on a single source of oil in Persia after the discovery of the Haft Kel field in 1927 and it was a partner in the international consortium, the Turkish Petroleum Company, which had drilled its discovery well at Baba Gurgur, also in 1927. Further developments could not rest on insecure foundations. It was essential to settle the concessionary uncertainties.

The basic problem, as had already been realised by Greenway, was that with the expansion of the Company its operations were no longer confined to Persia.[49] It had become an integrated company in a manner not envisaged in the Concession, no longer selling its production at a Persian port to other companies, its profits limited to a return on a single activity. Moreover the Company had come to represent the one great Persian industry, but the size of the British Government's shareholding in the Company was not counterbalanced by any appropriate Persian presence. Cadman believed that the Company could only assure its concessionary future against the rising tide of economic nationalism which was swelling in Italy, Turkey, and South America, already associated with oil politics, by securing a corresponding Persian interest and involving it more closely in the fortunes of an industry, which owed its origins to the natural resources of the country.[50] He thought that it seemed 'only reasonable to assume that concessionaires can regard their future as safeguarded against the rising tide of economic nationalism in proportion to the extent to which the national interests and their own approach identify'.[51] This was the epitome of the concessionary dilemma that was to become more acute for the oil companies in the 1960s and 1970s.[52]

An opportunity to reach a comprehensive agreement had presented itself with the appearance on the scene of Tīmurtāsh, 'a man of great intelligence, of wide outlook and of exceptional knowledge of the principles underlying the present issue'.[53] A further and decisive advantage in the estimation of the Board, but a questionable assumption, was that the Minister's 'official and personal weight are sufficient to ensure the approval of both Shah and Majlis to any scheme of reconstruction which he himself is prepared to sponsor'. These were the preliminary considerations. The particular factors which affected the situation comprised: (1) the relative brevity of the concessionary period; (2) obsolescence of the concessionary instruments; (3) the absence of a suitable identity of interests; (4) vulnerability to political pressures; (5) complexity of the financial relationship; and (6) resentment towards the Company's activities elsewhere than in Persia.[54]

The Board was prepared to offer the Persian Government a participatory shareholding in the Company, board representation, limitation of the existing concessionary area and a monetary settlement of past issues. What was the procedure to be adopted to resolve the differences and ensure a new and lasting concessionary relationship of mutual confidence and balanced self-interest? A major problem concerned the Government's shareholding in the Company.[55] On 11 October 1928 talks were begun at the Treasury with senior officials, after the government directors had approved in principle the proposal and it was generally accepted that 'the proposal to give the Persian Government a shareholding was sound policy, subject to such shares being inalienable'.[56] The consent of the Chancellor of the Exchequer, Churchill, however, could not be taken for granted, as he 'was in so unaccountable a mood'.

At the Foreign Office, Sir Ronald Lindsay, permanent under-secretary, was 'generally in sympathy with the policy of closer co-operation' with the Persian Government.[57] Vansittart there did not believe that there would be any American objections, particularly 'as the concessionary area was being reduced'.[58] He too felt a successful outcome might be conducive to improved understanding, but did not minimise the risks which would be entailed for British–Persian relations if it failed, especially as there were still hopes of reaching a settlement based on a general treaty. He also believed that shareholding rights should be inalienable and that in principle 'the difficulties and risks do not appear to us to be insurmountable or to

The Persian dimension

outweigh the advantages of the proposed arrangement'.[59] Sir Warren Fisher, permanent under-secretary to the Treasury, who had succeeded Sir George Barstow, was in agreement, though he admitted that there 'appears to be no precedent for two Governments being brought into the relation which this implies in connection with a company trading for profit'.[60] It was an exceptional undertaking. On 22 November Churchill and Amery assured Cadman of their support.[61] On 23 November 1928 Cadman was informed that the Government had no objection to negotiations being opened on the subject, provided that the controlling position of the Government's shareholding was maintained and that any shares allotted to the Persian Government were inalienable.[62]

Whilst Cadman was experiencing very great difficulty in persuading his colleagues to give him the opportunity of making 'pretty drastic changes' in the nature of the Concession,[63] in Persia the winds were blowing hot and cold. Tīmūrtāsh was anxious. Informing Cadman from Tehrān that only the Shah and himself knew of the initiative, he stressed the Shah's interest and rather presumptuously implied his gratitude that so much had already been agreed, such as the 25 per cent shareholding, the tonnage basis for calculating royalties, back payments to the Government, reduction in the concessionary area, the rescinding of the exclusive pipeline rights, the formation of a special company for the oil of Naft-i Shāh, the prolongation of the concessionary period, 'enfin toutes les questions qui étaient soulevées entre nous'.[64] Cadman kept Tīmūrtāsh informed about the progress he was making in formulating his position and the difficulties he had to surmount in convincing others 'of the desirability of such a radical change'. He cautioned Tīmūrtāsh that they were not dealing with a sapling but with 'an established concern of 27 years standing'.[65]

Some indication of the problems that were likely to be experienced became evident as a result of the visit of the Shah and government ministers to Khūzistān in early November. Jacks, in deference to Cadman's wish to remove the suspicion surrounding the Company, had already taken two parties of prominent Persians, including journalists, to the scene of the Company's operations in December 1926 and April 1927.[66] The visit in November was notable as much for the temper displayed by the Shah against his own officials in the provincial administration and the delays in the railway construction programme. He showed apparent indifference to the Company in his visit to Ahwāz, where, because of the appallingly wet weather, he was obliged to rely upon Company transportation put at his disposal. Some commentators, following the journalist 'Alī Dashtī's remarks in *Shafagh-i Surkh*, chose to regard the Shah's conduct as deliberate defiance of the Company, who it

The Persian dimension

was claimed 'was treating the local population as badly as the East India Company was alleged to have treated the Indians two hundred years previously'.[67] The Shah was not ambiguous when he requested Mustafa Fateh at a meeting on 17 November to tell the Company that he had always assisted it, though 'the present relations between the Government and the Company are not what they should be. The present arrangement is an old one and out of date and must be very soon changed. This change must be brought about to suit the interests of Persia.'[68]

Tīmurtāsh was more outspoken, more strident than his master's voice. Publicly he praised the Company, in private he warned Jacks that if 'by next spring I find myself discouraged and disappointed, I shall turn against you and fight you when you will experience a definite volte-face on my part...I see that you people have provided a much better way of living for yourselves here in the midst of this desert...than exists for 99 per cent of the people of Teheran.'[69] This tour had highlighted resentment of foreign enterprise and what appeared to be discrimination. In Lausanne, Tīmurtāsh had confided to Cadman his predicament over the modernisation of Persia which, 'if she had the right men, she could probably work out her own salvation in half the time. They were working for the creation of institutions on Western lines, not with the right, but with the wrong generation. The present generation may have all the goodwill, all the fire and energy, but it lacked the training and experience.'[70] In this respect, for Rizā Shāh and Tīmurtāsh the construction of the railway was more than a matter of economics, it was a challenge to national pride. The revision of the Concession was more than a question of royalties, it was a test of national will.[71]

There was, moreover a clash of interests. On the one hand, Tīmurtāsh wanted successful negotiations 'with this one great Persian industry in order that a sense of security may thereby be created in the minds of foreign capitalists', but at the same time he appeared not to recognise that if the terms were unattractive and the conditions unacceptable because of restrictions on operational activities and too much entanglement in bureaucratic red tape, commercial enterprise would be discouraged. Tīmurtāsh was having his difficulties over industrial development, as he admitted to Jacks: 'for the past two years I have been endeavouring to formulate a plan to procure money and technical advice...I have begged the Germans to undertake the installation of electric works and the French to undertake other interests. I want foreign capital. I desire to help you in order to prove that foreign capital receives fair treatment in Persia.' Forcing the pace of modernisation was producing unaccustomed stresses and strains in society, not least because of taxation on tea and sugar to fund the construction of the railway. The frantic pressure to achieve rapid

The Persian dimension

success was stretching the capacity to make that success possible. Cash was the priority. Revenue from the Company was central to the political and economic strategy of Tīmurtāsh.

He did not disguise his objectives. Indeed, clearly alerted, the new Majlis, which was convened in December 1928, was told by the Prime Minister 'Abbās Mehdī Hidayat, on the instructions of Tīmurtāsh, that 'the old concessionaries might, if they wished to count on the full support of the Persian Government ... find it advisable to consider some revision of their concessions'.[72] Tīmurtāsh did not conceal from Clive his responsibilities for the tenor of the remarks 'in order to prepare the way for a revision of the concession in the future'. The newspapers were encouraged to portray the granting of the Concession as having been perpetrated by ignorant officials bribed to do so by unscrupulous foreign financiers.[73] The accusations published were a mélange of alleged imperial and capitalist activities. Cadman was perturbed, but not impressed. He expressed his displeasure to Tīmurtāsh about an orchestrated press campaign which, 'on the eve of our meeting, must, I fear, produce an erroneous and painful impression in the minds of many people whose interests in the Company are at stake'. 'The ship,' he suggested, 'can only be brought safely to port in calm waters in a calm atmosphere'.[74] Tīmurtāsh, though surprised at the extent of the oil installations was impatient and in turn gave Cadman this advice: 'Put into your pocket your power to accept our proposals, which are but moderate, and leave behind, as I said to you, your book of accounts in London, or at any rate on the frontier and come as a welcome guest.'[75] There was no disguising the strength of purpose behind the charm. Nothing was being left to chance.

(b) The opening gambit

Cadman arrived in Ābādān on 31 January 1929 and after a fortnight's visit to the operations he arrived in Tehrān on 18 February. He was courteously received by the Shah, on 20 February, who told him that it was 'entirely to our interest to help and assist the Company in every way, simply because of the income we derive from its operations'.[76] Cadman explained the current state of the world oil industry, his plans for the Company, the nature of the British Government's involvement in the Company and his views on British–Persian relations. By 6 March Cadman, who was accompanied by a strong team of advisers including lawyers and accountants, had submitted a draft in keeping with the preference of Tīmurtāsh 'to have a new agreement rather than one which revised and augmented the D'Arcy Concession'.[77] Tīmurtāsh on receiving it, said that 'it would not take him longer than 48 hours to prepare his notes and he

The Persian dimension

then would be ready to discuss it after which he would discuss it with the Shah, submit it to the Cabinet and refer it to the Majlis'.

Dr Young thought that the Minister of Court 'seemed hopeful and constructive', but by 15 March Cadman was requesting some action and Tīmurtāsh was pleading that consideration of the draft 'was a much bigger job' than he had anticipated.[78] Doubtless it was, but the main reason for delay may well have been the result of instructions from the Shah for Dāvar and Fīrūz to be associated with Tīmurtāsh in the negotiations. Thereafter it ceased to be a tête-à-tête with Cadman. The inclusion of his two colleagues was probably an indirect reflection on the Minister of Court. It limited his room for manoeuvre and diminished the possibility of his own exclusive responsibility for success.[79] The expectations, deliberately aroused, necessitated a hard line, which was justifiable to reach Persian objectives, but the presence of his colleagues probably induced Tīmurtāsh to be more uncompromising, to prevent himself from being outflanked in the Shah's estimation by them.

The first plenary session was held on 18 March and negotiations lasted almost continuously till 24 March. On 22 March Cadman summarised Persian demands as being:

(1) A quarter participation in the whole enterprise.
(2) A royalty of 2s per ton.
(3) Return of about three quarters of the concessionary area.
(4) Guarantee of minimum annual revenue.
(5) Payment of all taxes and duties.
(6) Persian retention of their share and interest in all of the Company's activities, even after the expiry of the concession.

In exchange the Persian Government was offering:

(1) A twenty year extension of the concession.
(2) Moral support.

Cadman would not make any promises. He stressed the advantages of 'a real partnership', 'a community of interest'.[80] Tīmurtāsh wanted precise commitments such as a minimum annual payment. Cadman could not favour one shareholder over others and felt that 'if the Persian Government had no belief in the ability of the Company to develop and progress so as to produce greater revenue, then there was an end to the discussion'.

At the meeting on 22 March Tīmurtāsh became 'very excited, exacting and impossible', but Cadman characterised the Persian terms as 'exorbitant – they are asking too much'. Tīmurtāsh claimed that they were irreducible 'if the Majlis was to accept them and he was to avert Bolshevik criticism'. Russian subversion was being uncovered at the time, much to the embarrassment of Tīmurtāsh. He was unmoved by Cadman's appeal

The Persian dimension

not to 'lose an opportunity of settling the matter on the basis of the powers he had'. The concepts of partnership differed. For Cadman it represented a marriage 'for better for worse, for richer for poorer, in sickness and in health', but for Tīmurtāsh the precise obligations and advantages had to be defined in advance of the nuptial contract. Tīmurtāsh expected the partnership to be permanent; Cadman expected it to be limited to the duration of the concession. Tīmurtāsh would not grant the Company exemption from taxes, which was understandable, but he would not agree that they should not be unreasonable.

Two very detailed sessions were held on 23 and 24 March to try to 'get a settlement of the wording and the framework of the draft only leaving the figures for final agreement', in which the text of Harold Brown of Linklater and Paines, the Company's solicitors, was extensively revised by the Persian negotiators. On 30 March 1929 Tīmurtāsh presented his final conditions which included the creation of 4 475 000 ordinary shares giving the Government a complete and permanent 25 per cent interest with all the accompanying rights in the Company.[81] The negotiations were adjourned in a friendly manner with the approval of the Shah for Cadman's further consideration in London. Cadman feared that the extent of Tīmurtāsh's demands would cause consternation in financial circles.[82]

It was unfortunate, even tragic, that an accommodation was not reached. The time was right; the people were right; the terms were wrong. Tīmurtāsh overplayed his hand and mistook Cadman's affability for acquiescence. It was a fatal miscalculation.[83] As Cadman regretted, it was an opportunity lost which might not occur again—and did not.

Within six months the New York Stock Exchange had collapsed.[84] Fīrūz was in disgrace on charges of complicity in a tribal uprising in Fars and communicating with the deposed Shah. Tīmurtāsh himself was under suspicion. Russian interference revealed itself in unrest in Khūzistān and among the tribes. The treaty negotiations between the British and Persian Governments were suspended amid bickering and mistrust. Economic problems became more intractable. Foreign advisers like Millspaugh and others were no substitute for proper measures of self-reliance. There was goodwill between Tīmurtāsh and Cadman, but the chance had been missed. The attractions of a new concessionary spirit were less relevant than cash in hand. Tīmurtāsh could not match Cadman's assurance and lacked the confidence to make the imaginative response, which might have procured a practical settlement on some of his terms if he had conceded others to Cadman.[85] Looking over his shoulder at Dāvar and Fīrūz and facing the Shah, Tīmurtash could not afford to risk his position before he was called to account for his actions. He could not afford to wait

The Persian dimension

for the success of participation to be demonstrated before coming to the end of his political tether. Loser loses all, and he had everything to lose. It was ironical that his failure hastened the day of his own downfall, brought about by a disappointed, doubting, disillusioned and, above all, suspicious Shah.

(c) Delayed moves

The action passed to London where the Company prepared a new draft by 7 May for the Imperial Commissioner and his advisers.[86] Tīmurtāsh expected all to be completed by the end of September, when he anticipated settling the terms of the Anglo-Persian Treaty with Clive.[87] The draft was ready by 13 September but, on receiving it, Tīmurtāsh requested a number of delays before being ready to re-open negotiations.[88] Meanwhile communist activities of subversion continued,[89] including a minor insurrection at Ābādān.[90] Tribal unrest, particularly in Fars and northern Persia, erupted, primarily caused by military officers with their exactions and their corrupt practices. Fīrūz was arrested on charges of seditious activities and embezzlement. The personal power struggle was unabated. Tīmurtāsh was attacked because of his association with Fīrūz. The Shah's suspicions were encouraged and the Minister of Court suffered a temporary eclipse, which, according to Clive, paralysed the Government in the autumn of 1929.[91] In the confusion rumours were rife and the Company and the British Government were accused alike by Tīmurtāsh of instigating the dissension in the country.[92] Yet Tīmurtāsh asked for Clive's help in restoring order[93] and Husayn 'Alā, Persian Minister in France, on the instructions of Tīmurtāsh visited the Foreign Secretary, Arthur Henderson, to persuade him to collaborate in eliminating the prevailing 'obstructionist attitude' against the Persian Government.[94] It seemed a strange request, only partly explicable in terms of the schizophrenia exhibited towards the British Government.

Early in 1930 Tīmurtāsh was back in the saddle again, riding the country on a tighter rein, but obviously bruised. As he confessed to Clive, the Shah's greatest fault was 'his suspicion of everybody and everyone. There was really nobody in the whole country whom His Majesty trusted and this was very much resented by those who had always stood faithfully by him.'[95] This was an aspect of the Shah's character which became more pronounced in the years which followed. Yet as Clive, who was an unsympathetic but not inexperienced observer, noted, it was not an exceptional characteristic. He remarked on 'the inherent distrustfulness and suspicions of every Persian not only of every other Persian but of every foreigner in Persian employment'.[96]

The Persian dimension

Economic issues were increasingly more important throughout 1930. In March Persia went on the gold standard. The balance of trade, excluding oil revenues, remained very unfavourable. Little improvement was effected by a trade monopoly law passed in April, which inaugurated a form of state trading, controlling by a system of permits and licences the whole import and export trade of the country, with the exception of the

Table 13.2. *Persian annual average exchange rates and parity 1900–31*

Year	Kran rate in pence	Parity in pence	Deviation from parity in pence	% deviation
1900	4.57	4.15	0.42	10
1901	4.53	4.00	0.53	13
1902	4.21	3.54	0.67	19
1903	4.28	3.64	0.64	18
1904	3.60	3.89	−0.29	− 7
1905	3.89	4.09	−0.20	− 5
1906	4.36	4.54	−0.18	− 4
1907	4.85	4.44	0.41	9
1908	4.57	3.58	0.99	28
1909	4.44	3.50	0.94	27
1910	4.40	3.62	0.78	21
1911	4.36	3.61	0.75	21
1912	4.30	4.12	0.18	4
1913	4.32	4.05	0.27	7
1914	3.82	3.72	0.10	3
1915	4.10	3.48	0.62	18
1916	6.18	4.60	1.58	34
1917	8.22	6.01	2.21	37
1918	8.66	7.00	1.66	34
1919	9.61	8.40	1.21	14
1920	7.06	9.04	−1.98	−22
1921	4.86	5.43	−0.57	−10
1922	4.32	5.05	−0.63	−12
1923	5.08	4.70	0.38	8
1924	5.71	4.99	0.72	14
1925	5.52	4.72	0.80	17
1926	4.93	4.22	0.71	17
1927	4.87	3.82	1.05	28
1928	4.99	3.93	1.06	27
1929	4.14	3.60	0.54	15
1930	3.78	2.60	1.18	43
1931	2.80	2.16	0.64	30

Note: Parity calculated by multiplying the silver content of the kran by the average sterling price of silver in London
Source: Yaganegi, E.B., *Recent Financial and Monetary History of Persia* (New York, 1934), p. 73; quoted in Julian Bharier, *Economic Development in Iran 1900–1970* (London, 1971), p. 122

The Persian dimension

Company's operations but without the administrative structure and trained personnel to ensure its successful implementation. The exchange rate fell (see Table 13.2), and inflation rose.[97] Many state affairs were becalmed during 1930. Cadman contacted Tīmurtāsh at the beginning of the year and on subsequent occasions.[98] Jacks raised the question of the resumption of negotiations with Tīmurtāsh in March and was assured that it was expected that they would be 'completed and submitted for the ratification of the Majlis before its dissolution in the Autumn'.[99]

No action took place, but much indignation was vented to keep the issue simmering. 'Alī Dashtī was inspired to write the editorial in *Shafagh-i Surkh* on the 'Revision of Concessions', which condemned concessions 'granted to foreigners by the absolute governments of the past before the advent of the Persian Constitutional Government, which are a heavy burden on the life of the nation'. 'In no way,' claimed Dashtī, 'are we mentally or morally bound to bear patiently the unlimited losses which have been left to us by the corrupt governments of the past.' So, 'if, therefore, a nation rises against its government and deposes it, then it will have the right to revise the past actions of such a government'.[100] It was a further revelation of the sense of injustice, justifiable or not, which lay beneath the surface of apparent cordiality.[101] Tīmurtāsh repeated this message in November to Jacks, who was about to go on leave and asked that 'Cadman reconsider his previous negotiations with me, so that a new basis may be found to meet the changed economic conditions in Persia'.[102] However, neither then, nor in January 1931, when Cadman visited him in Tehrān, did Tīmurtāsh table any possible modifications to his demands, except to request that the Persian Government be given 'a definite annual payment on which they could base their Budget'. The Shah hoped that Cadman would 'find some way of revising the concession to our mutual advantage and satisfaction and in a way which would replenish the Government's coffers',[103] but no counter-proposals were forthcoming nor a reply to the draft of 13 November 1929. The negotiations were stultified.

(d) The middle game

Meanwhile in London, the Imperial Commissioner, 'Īsa Khān, on 13 March 1931, raised again the vexed question of reaching an agreement on the royalties.[104] It was probably done at the prompting of Sayyid Hassan Khān Taqīzādeh, who had played a prominent part in the Constitutional Movement and had replaced Fīrūz as Finance Minister in August 1930. Discussions on this had been suspended when the Persians had repudiated the Armitage-Smith Agreement in 1928.[105] Cadman and Tīmurtāsh, at

The Persian dimension

Lausanne in August 1928, decided to leave the Agreement in abeyance pending a final settlement. Cadman called a management conference on 31 March 1931[106] to discuss all the outstanding Persian issues, which now included the payment of income tax, which had first been mentioned unofficially in April 1929 and was the subject of an income tax law prepared in March 1930 by Dr Schniewind, the German financial adviser. The Company did not dispute the liability for income tax but objected to the amount computed. A separate company to exploit the production from Naft-i Shāh was accepted. The Armitage-Smith Agreement, which was still recognised by the Company, had been referred to the respective financial advisers to settle.

The participation provisions remained the principle obstacle to the concessionary negotiations because Tīmurtāsh did not accept that due weight should be given to the value of the undivided equity which the Persian Government would receive in connection with such shares. He based his claim, 'both as regards percentage of shares and tonnage royalty, on a level designed to give them a standard of actual cash receipts every

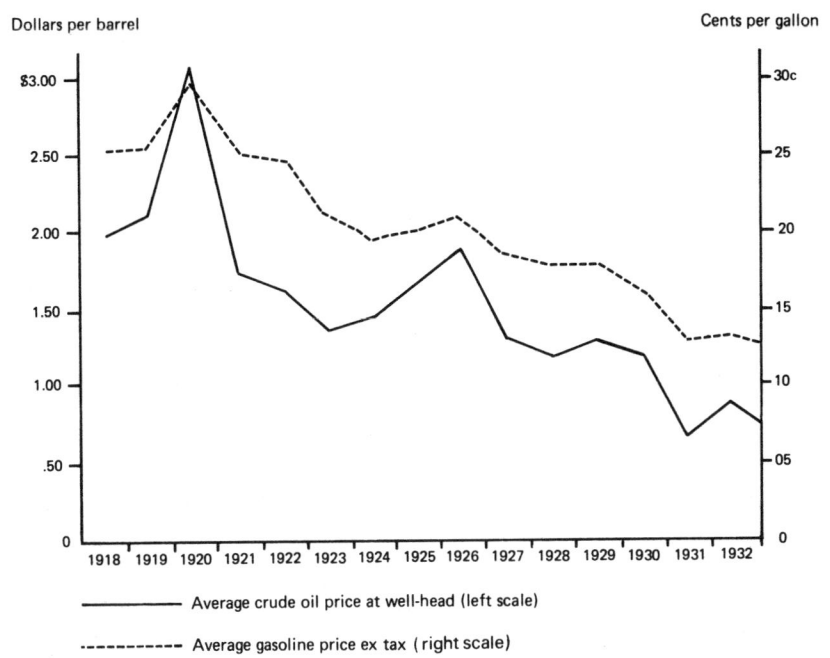

Figure 13.1 US average crude oil and gasoline prices 1918–32
Source: J.G. McLean and R.W. Haigh, *The Growth of Integrated Oil Companies* (Boston, 1954), p. 86

year which should be equal to practically the highest level of such payments which we had hitherto made'. Otherwise it was felt that agreement was close on the limits of the exploration area, extension of the concession, land acquisition procedures, refining and transportation rights, Persian Board representation and arbitration.[107] There was, however, a fundamental difference since the negotiations had taken place. The difficult trading conditions which had begun in 1927 had become worse as prices dropped a dollar a barrel at the well-head in the United States between 1926 and 1932, as is seen in Figure 13.1 on p.613.

As a result of this situation, a radical commercial change had taken place in the oil industry, for no longer did competitive advantage lie with companies which had a high production potential. The chief factor influencing profitability was the 'ability to find and maintain markets for refined products of crude at very highly competitive and ever falling prices'. There were, therefore, as Cadman remarked, 'very distinct limits to the burden which the Persian Oil industry could bear if it was to continue successfully to compete in World markets under the adverse conditions now prevailing'. By a curious coincidence, whilst the Company's management was debating the action it was going to take, Tīmurtāsh on the same day sent a set of fourteen proposals to London, believing that 'the difficulties which once existed in the way of arriving at such an understanding have disappeared', and optimistically suggested that 'approval of the new Concession would encounter no difficulties if his proposals were accepted'.[108] They represented very comprehensive and far reaching commitments, including some new submissions:

(1) The revision of the area which is at present included in the D'Arcy Concession.

(2) Cancellation of the exclusive pipeline right for Persian petroleum.

(3) The settlement of a method for paying Government royalty (with a fixed basis and subject to a sliding scale).

(4) A method for the participation of the Persian Government (as a shareholder) in the Company's operations, and settlement of the rights attaching to the shares.

(5) The solution necessary to assure to the Persian Government adequate revenues under the heading of Royalty and Dividends, which should not be less than £2 500 000 sterling annually under the existing conditions of production.

(6) A progressive increase in the production of Persian petroleum.

(7) The creation of refineries to deal with an 'important quantity' of Persian petroleum in Persia.

(8) The development of production of non-Persian petroleum under conditions which would avoid prejudicing Persian petroleum.

The Persian dimension

(9) The solution of the question of the taxes payable by the Company, in view of the fact that the British Government considers this to be a question to be settled between the Persian Government and the Company.

(10) A temporary settlement of the question of taxation by acceptance of the Note of the 25th January, handed to Sir John Cadman by H.E. Taqīzādeh, the Minister of Finance.

(11) The rapid settlement of previous disputes existing between the Government and the Company, having regard to the present need of the Government to increase the national gold reserve.

(12) The assurance of supplies of Persian petroleum to the Persian Government at cost prices.

(13) The supply of petroleum and its products, for internal consumption in Persia, at a reasonable price.

(14) The creation of an exploiting company for the district of Shah-Abad.

The likely future impact of Iraq oil on the international market was not absent from some of these proposals, which were certainly intended to protect both Persian production and government revenues from foreign competition. There was, thus, inevitably some inconsistency, albeit understandable in claiming a participatory share in the Company as a whole, whilst maintaining demands for preferential treatment. Indeed the crucial problem remained as before, the valuation, obligations and rights of the shareholding to be allotted to the Persian Government. There was still the strongest desire to reach a settlement, but in view of the world oil outlook some of the terms of Tīmurtāsh, under the entirely changed conditions which were then confronting the Company, looked unreasonable, though others were not unacceptable.

This was not appreciated by Tīmurtāsh, who merely imagined the caution to be a debating point, a negotiating ploy of no relevance to the Persian economic situation, which was actually suffering from the same problems. In fact if the demands of Tīmurtāsh had been met in full, they would have amounted to £2 700 000, which would only have left £17 700 for distribution to the shareholders in a year, when the dividend declared was only 5 per cent. Tīmurtāsh did not accept that 'in the changed outlook of the industry it was clearly impossible to meet many of the demands now made by the Persian Government in connection with an offer which, under the entirely changed conditions confronting the Company, if not already submitted could not have been made at this time'.[109] In Tehrān 'Alī Dashtī[110] continued his campaign of denigrating the D'Arcy Concession in *Shafagh-i Surkh*, alleging it to be the origin of Persian economic troubles.[111]

The Persian dimension

(e) Stalemate

Jacks returned to Tehrān on 28 June 1931 hoping to resume formal negotiations to find that relations between Tīmurtāsh and Taqīzādeh were strained. Clive detected a lessening of the Minister of Court's popularity and blamed him for economic measures 'forced on the country in defiance of the principles of sound finance and economics and contrary to expert advice'.[112] Three meetings between Jacks and Tīmurtāsh in early July made no further progress. Jacks became more aware of the desperation of Tīmurtāsh, who declared that 'the Government has embarked on certain financial programmes which, if failed in, will mean its ruin. Money to Persia today is a matter of life and death.' In short, he argued, the Government 'finds itself in a terrible state and the Company's assistance will be greatly appreciated' - but on what terms? Tīmurtāsh was demanding, not as previously just £1 000 000 as a minimum payment, but £2 500 000, for the country required 'every year £1 000 000 for its Gold Reserve, £1 000 000 for economic and public works, and £500 000 for military expenditure' (see Table 13.3 for government revenues). Moreover the Persian Government required £400 000 in respect of money due to the Italian Government for purchases of naval ships in the following year and further amounts for unspecified expenditure.

Jacks was aware of the economic situation[113] and sympathised with the needs of the country but stated that 'these could bear no relation to the profits of the Company and the amount of Royalty which his Government might expect'. It seemed to be putting the economic cart before the concessionary horse, but Tīmurtāsh was adamant that the Company had 'to give us either a production or a cash guarantee, the former up to 8 000 000-10 000 000 tons per annum, the latter by shares or a percentage of profits not less than £2 500 000 a year. (It was five years later, in 1936, before production reached 8 000 000 tons and royalties topped £2 500 000.) Tīmurtāsh still professed to be fearful that 'the exigencies of marketing and the strategic principles of distribution might eliminate Persian production altogether'. He was not concerned that his demand 'might seriously restrict the Company's activities in World markets' and so prove detrimental to Persia's interests. He would subordinate the Company to Persia's requirements by taking action against it 'as would ensure ... a proper control of the Company's expenditure'. He would 'prevent it from engaging itself in any outside activities which were prejudicial to Persia's interests'. He objected to the Company having built 'a huge world-wide organisation out of the profits derived from Persian oil'. He insisted that 'circumstances had changed and that his previous offer to Sir John Cadman was dead'.[114] 'What I mean you to understand,'

Table 13.3. *Persian Government revenues 1923–29*

	March 1923–March 1924 £	%	March 1925–March 1926 £	%	March 1926–March 1927 £	%	March 1927–March 1928 £	%	March 1928–March 1929 £	%
Customs	1 671 177	32.6	2 201 591	32.8	1 889 858	28.4	3 068 459	38.9	3 670 818	44.9
Direct taxation	1 387 977	27.1	1 389 887	20.7	1 267 255	19.0	954 675	12.1	1 037 670	12.7
APOC royalties	516 555	10.1	954 456	14.2	1 039 257	15.6	1 488 392	18.9	596 855	7.3
Indirect taxation	545 044	10.6	950 525	14.1	730 136	11.0	667 555	8.5	816 969	10.0
including — opium excise	246 288	4.8	376 807	5.6	323 929	4.9	270 446	3.4	348 844	4.3
tobacco excise	96 111	1.9	255 998	3.8	270 088	4.0	272 383	3.5	296 874	3.6
Posts and telegraphs	487 222	9.5	399 863	6.0	403 877	6.1	275 094	3.5	254 029	3.1
Crown domains	106 977	2.1	248 503	3.7	228 835	3.4	259 872	3.3	452 020	5.5
Road taxes	152 088	2.9	183 399	2.7	784 528	11.8	814 857	10.3	752 954	9.2
Other	260 760	5.1	392 793	5.8	310 922	4.7	353 118	4.5	595 509	7.3
Total revenue	5 127 800		6 721 017		6 654 668		7 882 022		8 176 824	

Note: Exchange rates used — 1923–24, 45 krans = £1; 1925–26, 43.5 krans = £1; 1926–27, 48.6 krans = £1; 1927–28, 49.25 krans = £1; 1928–29, 48.03 krans = £1

Sources: Dept of Overseas Trade, *Report on the Trade and Industry of Persia*, April 1925; *Report on the Finance and Commerce of Persia*, 1925–27, 1928; *Economic Conditions in Persia*, March 1930 (all these are available in the library of the Department of Trade)

he told Jacks, 'is that the worst of future years must not be less favourable than the best of past years.' It may have made political sense, but it lacked commercial logic.

Cadman was stunned at what he regarded the 'excessive difference' between their respective views on what was possible and equitable.[115] Writing to Tīmurtāsh he deplored the trading conditions of the oil industry, but he had to protect his Company's position and safeguard its existence.[116] Both Cadman and Tīmurtāsh had to defend their respective interests which was perfectly understandable. The difficulty for both of them was that these clashed and had to be reconciled to mutual satisfaction. Cadman suggested that the whole question 'can only be effectively discussed when times are more propitious and the present chaotic condition of the oil industry has disappeared'.[117] Cadman was disappointed that 'sane and sensible views' had not prevailed. This acknowledgement of a stalemate in the revision negotiations apparently seemed a relief to Tīmurtāsh, who could concentrate on settling past disputes, the concessionary bird in the hand being better than the hypothetical one in the future. He would 'not discuss questions further from the point of view of revision, but from the strict interpretation of the D'Arcy Concession'.[118] This raised again the vexed question of the Armitage-Smith Agreement.

In August Tīmurtāsh asked a commission of Taqīzādeh, 'Īsa Khān and Jacks to try to regularise the position on taxation and royalties.[119] This achieved little success, except to ventilate again all the disputed subjects. Tīmurtāsh seemed 'determined to talk no more, but to demand such guarantees as will ensure to us a proper development of our Oil Industry', as he informed Jacks at an important meeting on 31 August at which Dāvar, Taqīzādeh, 'Īsa Khān, M. Clavier, French director of Internal Revenue, Jacks and Fateh were present.[120] The Minister of Court appeared to have convinced himself of the bad faith of the Company, which, in his view, was about to transfer its future development activities elsewhere, but he did not pause to question either the logic or rationale for such an action in relation to the Company's existing investment in Persia.

Tīmurtāsh was annoyed with Cadman for 'after all these many years of mere words I now receive a letter from him which definitely closes the door to revision'. 'We have talked enough', he maintained about the theory of partnership, 'the door to which you have now closed'. It is almost as if Tīmurtāsh felt that he had come to the end of the road only to find it was a cul de sac, but he was being unrealistic, for all his undoubted abilities and determination to re-invigorate Persia. If he could not have all, he would have none. With a touch of the macabre he described the Concession to Jacks as resembling 'an old and sick father who cannot be got rid of. We have to wait until he dies', but he did assert that 'Its validity has never been questioned and never will be. It is a Law which cannot be altered, amended or repealed other than with the consent of both parties.' Tīmurtāsh was terribly frustrated, no less than Cadman, but for different reasons. In the end reconciliation not frustration would settle their problems.

(f) Another game

The visit of Tīmurtāsh to Europe in September 1931 to place the Crown Prince in a Swiss school provided the opportunity for Cadman to meet him again. This was arranged in Lausanne on 6 October. In the final analysis the priorities of national sovereignty were incompatible with the concessionary system, but for the moment neither the Persian Government nor the Company could do without each other. A balance had to be struck between national and commercial considerations. The Company could not neglect the rights of the Persian Government, but the Government 'cannot have it both ways, that is, they cannot pursue a policy designed to reduce the Company's profits to a minimum and, at the same time hope to induce the Company not to seek safeguards in other directions against unjust imposition'.[121] It was a crisis of confidence. Nevertheless, Tīmurtāsh and Cadman agreed to abandon the participation proposals and substitute another agreement for that reached by Armitage-Smith, disowned by the Persian Government in 1928, but regarded as valid by the Company, whose hand was strengthened by the opinion of Wilfred Greene KC and V.R. Idelson on 30 October that the Armitage-Smith Agreement was 'legally binding on the Persian Government'.[122]

The controversy over the Armitage-Smith Agreement had soured concessionary relations for a decade. It was ironical that 'Īsa Khān, who at the Ministry of Finance in 1920 had quite clearly authorised Armitage-Smith to act on behalf of the Persian Government, had begun to argue that in changed circumstances since 9 May 1928 the Financial Adviser had had no such authority and had exceeded his powers. In a note on the subject prepared by him in Tehrān on 6 September 1931, no doubt for Tīmurtāsh, he drew attention to the earlier opinion of M.D. Kerly K.C. and Rayner Goddard of 22 March 1921, obtained by the solicitors to the Imperial Commissioner, Messrs. Lumley and Lumley, as being more favourable to the interests of the Persian Government. He based his assumptions on a letter of Lumley and Lumley to the then Imperial Commissioner of 27 July 1921, in which it was suggested on evidence supplied by the Commissioner, that Armitage-Smith may not have been empowered to negotiate on the terms he did and that the Persian Government was not bound by the

The Persian dimension

Agreement. Armitage-Smith, however, strenuously denied that he had acted improperly. The congratulations which he received from Persian Ministers at the time he reached agreement with Greenway and the wording of his letter of appointment as negotiator 'to finally adjust all questions in dispute between the Anglo-Persian Oil Company and the Imperial Government of Persia,' seem to justify his position.[123]

It was very regrettable that legal interpretations over the Armitage-Smith Agreement, no less than professional differences over accounting practices, bedevilled the concessionary relationship, which became more obsessed with the letter rather than the spirit of the Law. That too was perhaps a reflection on the mutual lack of confidence which existed, despite protestations to the contrary.

The next stage in the negotiations with Tīmurtāsh was graphically described by Cadman,

he came to London, he wined and he dined and he spent days and nights in negotiating. Many interviews took place. He married his daughter, he put his boy to school [Harrow], he met the Secretary of State for Foreign Affairs, a change took place in our Government, and in the midst of all this maze of activities we reached a tentative agreement on the principles to be included in the new document, leaving certain figures and the lump sum to be settled at a later date.[124]

Cadman was determined to reach a settlement, beyond what seemed prudent to some of his Board. For Tīmurtāsh in London, without his government colleagues breathing down his neck, it offered a chance to break out of his political strait-jacket and in solving the issue achieve a personal triumph, turn the tables on his enemies, restore the confidence of the Shah in himself and render a real service to his country. His motives were recognisable but his methods were often arrogant and inconsistent. He had a mercurial temperament, fascinating, but exasperating. He had a slalom ability, sweeping through the gates by a hairsbreadth, the audacity of which seemed to make a fall at once unimaginable, but also inevitable. He was in a perpetual race against the clock; supremely confident, he was curiously vulnerable.

The first round of negotiations took place on 13 November[125] and the legal and accounting experts of both sides set about defining exactly all the terms used to describe the Company's activities in order to arrive at a mutually acceptable accuracy as to their meaning.[126] Cadman requested the experts to produce 'the necessary detailed agreement in the simplest possible form'. The comment was like the opening chorus of a Greek tragedy enunciating the fatal flaw in the tissue of human relations, because the more the experts struggled to cover all the eventualities precisely, the more they became enmeshed in the complications of their own phraseology. By 30 November Tīmurtāsh had provided a draft text of the

The Persian dimension

agreement.[127] It became apparent that the major problems which plagued the Armitage-Smith negotiations remained: the ascertaining of the annual net profits of the various companies comprising the Company's group and their assessment for allowances in the computation of profits. The drafts became more and more complicated as Tīmurtāsh and his advisers made them more and more detailed,[128] but finally on 23 December Cadman and Tīmurtāsh reached a provisional settlement,[129] with much mutual, premature congratulation. Tīmurtāsh mentioned that 'Our common efforts were exerted to arrive at a complete understanding and reconciliation of the interests of the two parties.' Whilst Cadman emphasised that 'The understanding we have reached will when completed prove a vital factor in the establishment of that friendly entente which you have always championed.'[130]

Negotiations were resumed in Paris on 7 January and on the following day, according to Cadman, 'We agreed the general principles of the document, which we decided to submit to our respective accountants and lawyers.' It was initialled. Only the date for agreeing the figures remained. The twelve main points which had been settled, included:

(1) The Company was to pay the Government 16 per cent by virtue of the D'Arcy Concession and 4 per cent by virtue of the new agreement - these percentages applying to its net profits from the winning, refining, transporting, storing and distributing of Persian oil as well as from all operations connected therewith, whether these operations had been carried out by the APOC itself or by a subsidiary and whether they had taken place inside or outside Persia.

(2) The trading profits from the Persian oil operations were to be, so far as possible, calculated separately for the APOC and for each of the subordinate companies, while the net profits, on which the 20 per cent royalty was to be paid, were to be the aggregate of the net profits.

(3) Elaborate provisions were made for the assessment of the profits of the various companies and of the sums which the Company would be allowed to deduct from its revenue in order to arrive at the net profits.

(4) Without prejudice to the D'Arcy Concession, the Government and the Company undertook to carry out the agreement both in its spirit and its letter and to collaborate as closely as possible in order to obtain the maximum benefits for each of them. The Company undertook to do its best to develop its concession in order to render service to Persian interests and also to increase the scope of its operation in Persia as soon as the conditions of the world oil market were favourable enough.

(5) The Company was to pay the Government in lieu of income tax 4 per cent of the net profits, thus raising the royalty from 16 per cent to 20 per cent. In return the Government agreed to free the Company and all its

The Persian dimension

subordinate companies up to the expiry of the D'Arcy Concession from any import tax or other duties on the capital, assets, revenue, turnover or profits ascribable to the operations of Company or of its subordinate companies.[131]

Suddenly Tīmurtāsh submitted a demand for payment to the Persian Government of £3 250 000, which he claimed it was owed, less a deduction of £750 000 making £2 500 000 in all, suspiciously like the sum mentioned to Jacks in Tehrān. Cadman was not amused and 'At this the fur flew. Teymour rushed out of the room in a rage, and I have never seen him since, or indeed ever again.'[132] It was a bizarre incident. The maximum the Company owed, according to exhaustive calculations, was £237 000, but even if the most doubtful amounts were included, it did not exceed £500 000, which Cadman, once the agreement had been finalised, was prepared to double once 'satisfied that the solution reached is one that will do more for the Company in the future than it is possible to gauge today, even although the cost is very high'. It was meant as a gesture of support for Tīmurtāsh. Cadman offered £1 000 000 in a lump sum settlement. Cadman perplexed and intent on a settlement afterwards tried to calm the muddied waters by flattering Tīmurtāsh and thanking him for his personal efforts.[133] Tīmurtāsh responded, but, again ignoring the realities of the world oil situation, complained that, if the present offer did not compare more favourably with the past 'by a figure more or less worthy of attention, the advantages of the new agreement would be of no effect'.[134]

It is difficult to account for the behaviour of Tīmurtāsh. He had a free negotiating hand, responsible only to the Shah.[135] He may have misjudged Cadman, assuming that he could bluff him at the end, so that he could retrieve the difficult economic position in Persia by a large injection of funds from his inflated demands for back payments. If so, that too was a gamble which failed. He may even have stalled at the moment of decision, reluctant to commit himself to a decision on his own, reluctant to have it repudiated by the Shah or rejected by his colleagues. He may, for one reason or another, really have needed the cash and tried to shock Cadman to ensure his acceptance of the already initialled agreement. Once again the opportunity for reaching a settlement was lost.

(g) Checkmate

Cadman made a real effort to keep the negotiations in play. As Tīmurtāsh was returning to Persia through Moscow, where he was lavishly entertained and praised, Cadman offered to backdate certain of the payments and include 1931 in the new royalty of 20 per cent,[136] but Tīmurtāsh was

The Persian dimension

not satisfied.[137] He needed an increased lump sum of a further £250 000. Cadman refused. The settlement, the result of weeks of intensive consideration by the experts for both parties was generous, 'certainly far more than I had contemplated at the beginning of our negotiations', commented Cadman.[138] On 6 February Jacks reported that the Shah seemed pleased at the outcome of the negotiations and Tīmurtāsh requested 'as personal favour' an increase of £50 000-60 000 'when subject to your agreement to increase immediate steps will be taken to ratify agreement'. Cadman agreed to interest on past claims being paid but no more. Tīmurtāsh, still feeling frustrated,[139] promised to submit the agreement that had been negotiated by them to the Cabinet 'as a disinterested person leaving it to them to decide'.[140] He had disregarded 'Īsa Khān's advice to settle[141] and persisted, unsuccessfully, in asking for more money,[142] but Cadman was not prepared to lay out any more.[143] Tīmurtāsh complained to Jacks of Cadman's 'lack of sympathetic support in the difficulties which were confronting him here'.[144] Nevertheless the Persian Cabinet approved the terms of the agreement. Jacks and the Imperial Commissioner were so informed on 13 February 1932[145] and an advance payment was made to the Persian Government of £100 000. It was Taqīzādeh who finally authorised 'Īsa Khān to conclude the negotiations on behalf of the Persian Government on 4 April.[146] It seemed as if a settlement was in sight, especially as Tīmurtāsh sent the agreement to Cadman, remarking that 'the will of His Imperial Majesty put aside all difficulties, and now that the Council of Ministers has approved the Agreement, you have nothing to do but sign it'. He begged Cadman to send him £50 000 to found a museum in Tehrān as a 'personal request'. On 22 May Jacks wrote that the lump sum of £1 000 000 'in settlement of all outstandings has been definitely allocated in toto to the Ministry of War for this year's Budget'. Agreement appeared to have been reached.

The Imperial Commissioner and his advisers made numerous minor amendments to safeguard the interests of the Persian Government, as a result of which the document became 'a very complicated and difficult one'.[147] The Company's accounting and legal advisers were worried. Hearn, who was responsible for the negotiations, exhorted the advisers 'Above all, the completion of the finally agreed document is a matter of urgency.'[148] Cadman also stressed the need to 'submit without delay the formal document'.[149] The Imperial Commissioner had given priority to plugging potential loopholes rather than reducing delays.[150] It seemed as if the draft was ready on 4 April.[151] Then Tīmurtāsh sent further amendments from Tehrān and became impatient at the time taken by 'Īsa Khān,[152] who excused himself.[153] This may have been prompted by his knowledge that Taqīzādeh was preparing an alternative draft with

The Persian dimension

the help of M. Clavier, the French financial adviser, and that the Ministry of War had outstanding debts of £1 500 000, which the Shah wanted paid as soon as possible.[154] Cadman and the Imperial Commissioner initialled the documentation on 12 May 1932.[155] 'Īsā Khān commended the final text to the Persian Government and glorified his part in protecting their interests.[156] Cadman had reluctantly conceded certain provisions which gave the Persian Government 'far more than I really consider equitable in order to facilitate speedy ratification'.[157] Again he was to be disappointed.

The text was received on 29 May in Tehrān with something less than enthusiasm.[158] Tīmurtāsh, complaining to Jacks of the length of the schedules, proposed redrafting it in a procedural tactic to facilitate its passing by the Majlis.[159] He also inquired of the estimated royalty payment for 1931 and was told the following day that it would be £306 870 on the old basis, the lowest since 1917 and that the ordinary dividend declared was 5 per cent.[160] Tīmurtāsh could hardly believe it, in spite of all the warnings he had been given about the state of the oil industry. Shortly afterwards he complained that 'the amended Agreement has been so complicated that he cannot make head or tail of it'.[161] On 6 June Jacks met Tīmurtāsh, Taqīzādeh and Dāvar and was told by Tīmurtāsh that 'Īsā Khān was 'responsible for the very involved phraseology of the draft and openly dubbed him as stupid and a fool'.[162] Tīmurtāsh objected to some of the definitions agreed by 'Īsā Khān and the advisers. He requested that the French translation be clarified. He seemed to be evading a decision again.

The reaction of Cadman was immediate, he would sign the draft of 8 January if Tīmurtāsh wished.[163] It was, however, clear that a new element had intervened, the disastrous level of royalties. In spite of his talks during his European visit from September to January with officials of the Treasury, the Bank of England and other foreign governments over exchange rates, the gold standard and the financial aspects of the Depression, Tīmurtāsh seems to have imagined that Persia would escape from its worst effects, possibly shielded by the oil royalties. He protested that the royalty was 'so small that even taking into consideration the reduction of prices and the general depression, its acceptance seems extraordinarily difficult'.[164] 'Īsā Khān, though unduly pernickety in checking the text of the agreement, had a better appreciation of the general situation and advised him that, 'to protest and criticise the Company is out of place since they have incurred a loss of £6 000 000 revenue in respect of oil for the past year compared with the two previous years...although the amount of oil sold is about equal to that for the two previous years'.[165] The appropriate comparisons between royalties and production are contained in Table 13.1.

The Persian dimension

Tīmurtāsh had no real excuse for his purported ignorance. The facile assumption that more money alone would stabilise the precarious condition of the Persian economy, with its burden of military expenditure running at some 40 per cent of revenue, its ambitious railway plans and necessary industrial programme, was quite an insufficient response to an obviously deteriorating financial situation. Unfortunately it characterised his reaction of preferring the superficially more acceptable political option to the more unpopular but positive economic action that was needed. Since Tīmurtāsh had associated himself so exclusively with the agreement, by its failure he became personally vulnerable to criticism. To protect his own position he had to disown the proceedings for which he was responsible and to lead their rejection so as to preserve his own popularity and his prestige with the Shah. It was a general misfortune that negotiations had been failing at the last moment and were then being re-opened later. It was like a sore which festered because it was being continually scratched. It was regrettable that Harold Brown, the Company's legal adviser, was unable to go to Tehrān in June and that Cadman was otherwise committed at that time.[166] A visit that summer might have tipped the scales. Equally it might have prolonged the wrangling. The pace was faltering and was never regained. In order to smooth the path Cadman offered an immediate advance of £100 000[167] on the settlement of past claims and was prepared to accept the French and binding translation of the Company's Persian legal adviser, Dr Naficy;[168] all to no avail.

The linkage between the low royalty payment for 1931 and the agreement became more explicit. 'I should not like,' Tīmurtāsh told Jacks, 'to see this unfavourable impression prevailing when the new Agreement is introduced into the Chamber.'[169] Taqīzādeh and Tīmurtāsh clashed, the former requesting the Company to put the royalty on a week's deposit pending a decision by the Ministers[170], and remarking to Jacks that the Minister of Court 'was not an accredited Minister of the Government',[171] but Tīmurtāsh at first declined to accept payment[172] and then asked for it to be put on six months deposit.[173] No wonder Cadman was confused by conflicting instructions resulting from apparently divided responsibility in Tehrān.[174] Enmity between Ministers and anxiety over the worsening economic troubles were aggravated by the unpredictable behaviour of the Shah, who was rumoured to have 'again been busy "cursing" the Cabinet, no doubt his irritability is not unconnected with the economic difficulties confronting the country'.[175] The avarice and anger of the Shah, wrote Jacks to Hearn, 'was affecting all sense of individual security. No one seems willing to incur the "Almighty's" wrath by a frank exposition of the position, the Press is muzzled, and his information generally is derived from the Military

The Persian dimension

and Police, both of which are concerned in covering up their own shortcomings.'[176]

Indeed Jacks warned that 'it should not be overlooked that we are dealing with H.I.M. the Shah, whose wrath has been aroused by finding that oil is not gold in these days at least, and as H.I.M. is pleased to believe that he is omnipotent, the play acting should not surprise us both more than the Royalty has surprised him'. At the end of June Tīmurtāsh initiated a series of press attacks on the Company, which Sir Reginal Hoare, who had succeeded Clive as Minister in 1931, characterised as 'absurd in its unanimity and unanimous in its absurdity'.[177] Editorials attacked the political aspect of the reduction in royalty payments as prejudicing the country's economy, especially when 'her need for foreign exchange and addition to the country's reserve is more than before'.[178] Articles complained, in spite of the annual scrutiny of the accounts by Sir William McLintock and the concerted advice of lawyers and accountants retained by the Imperial Commissioner, that 'the Government has little say in the accounts which such companies keep like secrets of freemasonry'.[179] With disregard for the economic realities of supply and demand the Company was condemned for not producing from all its wells as 'the Persian Fields could flood the World with Persian oil'.[180] With some inconsistency, 'Alī Dashtī, after accusing the Company of ignoring the interests of Iran, appeared to criticise the Government for not taking 'the trouble to appoint a careful expert like Armitage-Smith to clear and adjust the complicated and dark accounts of the Company'.[181] On 5 July *Pravda* championed Persian protests and raised the spectre of British Imperialism.

On 6 July Tīmurtāsh changed tack again, asking for 'a complete revision if Persian interests were protected'.[182] Cadman, though conciliatory and disappointed at the turn of events,[183] was unable to promise Tīmurtāsh that Persia would be insulated from the effects of the Depression[184] and believed that after all the time spent in negotiations for a better concessionary basis 'under the circumstances and in the present world condition of trade no other arrangement seems likely to be more advantageous'.[185] Similar advice was given by 'Īsa Khān.[186] Tīmurtāsh was offended, alleging to Jacks on 10 July that he had been offered a 'take it or leave it' threat, impugned Cadman's sincerity and doubted his efforts to achieve a settlement.[187] Clive too had experienced the remarkable talent of Tīmurtāsh for negative capability, his ability to give the impression of progress without actually making any advance, for no agreement had been reached on the Anglo-Persian Treaty talks, which had been going on intermittently since Loraine's arrival in 1921.

Tīmurtāsh had no scruples in simply rejecting the terms which had been so laboriously negotiated, the culmination of four years of almost ceaseless effort to improve the imprecise terms of the Concession and render its interpretation more definite. He was prepared to go back to the drawing board 'as the position warranted complete review'. He now professed, 'It was useless to expect that a Royalty based on a percentage of the net profits could ever be understood by the Persian people.' He blamed the Concession for 'all the misunderstanding and suspicion' but ignored the earlier attempts at revision. Tīmūrtāsh may well have felt that 'his great ambition had always been to revise the basis of the Company's relations with the Persian Government'. His patriotism was not in doubt, but his confidence was questionable that 'there was every indication that the atmosphere was now more favourable for revising the Concession'. Tīmūrtāsh resembled a concessionary Sisyphus rolling his proposals to the brow of the hill but failing to push them over for agreement before they tumbled down again. It was exhausting.

Within a few days Tīmūrtāsh suffered a heart attack.[188] The agreement was discarded because it 'would leave Persia's essential needs unsatisfied'.[189] Only the apparent insult of the royalty payment for 1931 was remembered, an affront to national dignity. Tīmūrtāsh survived his stroke and pressed for a revision like that attempted in 1929, but questions like 'Why did the Company sell Persian oil in unprofitable markets?'[190] did not inspire much confidence in London and the political temperature in Tehrān was not felt to be conducive to putting forward proposals, but rather to awaiting them. Once again, although his influence was waning as a result of a corruption scandal implicating a friend of his in the National Bank[191] and the dislike of his colleagues,[192] Tīmūrtāsh threatened to adopt more drastic action in dealing with both the British Government and the Company and intensifying the press campaign against them,[193] as he pondered new proposals. At this stage the Shah became more openly concerned, and increasingly impatient with his Ministers. Jacks thought that the Persian Government 'will have to adopt aggressive and forceful measures' and the Shah ordered Furūghī, the Foreign Minister, to insert condemnatory statements about the Company in foreign newspapers.[194]

Cadman was worried and informed the British Government of his concern on 17 October before leaving for an important visit to the United States. Cadman informed Jacks that he very much hoped the new Persian proposals 'will be based on a full sense of realities and of equity ... in which case Minister of Court may rest assured they will be given most careful considerations'.[195] On 29 October Tīmūrtāsh claimed that his proposals 'were almost complete',[196] as he did on 16 November.[197] At the beginning of November the Shah visited Khūzistān, and at Ahwāz greeted Jacks, who 'enjoyed the distinction of being the only person with whom His Majesty shook hands'.[198] He later inspected his new Italian-built-fleet, the

The Persian dimension

railway and other installations elsewhere. An editorial in *Iran* praised the Shah and his accomplishments for the nation and requested the Shah to bestow a gift on his country 'on his return from the South by cancelling the concession...Otherwise it would be impossible to secure our interests through negotiation, correspondence and protests.'[199]

Back in Tehrān, the Shah dismissed the Court accountant, a protégé of Tīmurtāsh.[200] It was a signal heralding the doom of Tīmurtāsh, which followed shortly afterwards with his arrest. Tired of the vacillation of his ministers, the Shah spotlighted his own performance in a *coup du théatre*. On 26 November to the surprise of his ministers, he cancelled the D'Arcy Concession at a Cabinet meeting. The ministers dealing with concessionary affairs had become puppets on the royal string. Political pressure prevailed over economic criteria. It was understandable that the Persians committed to modernising their country felt frustrated, not so much by the immensity of their undertaking or the short time they set themselves in which to accomplish it, but by the apparent indifference of others towards its realisation. It has been a Persian characteristic to embark on imposing projects with only the outlines, not the details, decided, trusting to confidence rather than practicability. There is no disputing the basic premises of Riẓā Shāh's modernisation programme in 1928, the plans of 1948, the initiatives of 1962 or the visions of 1973, but the scope and the time scale were out of phase. It almost seems as if pressure for rapid results was necessary more to galvanise activity for the prevention of political opposition rather than to anticipate the social strains and economic pressures which would be precipitated by the impact of change. Advice to moderate the pace incurred displeasure as implying Persian inability to sustain the effort or, even worse, an aspersion on that capability.

Oil was required for national progress, the major source of foreign exchange (see Table 13.4). Oil was a national resource, therefore if it was not being produced in sufficient quantities or sold at a high enough price to fund national development the fault, according to the Persian view, lay not with the Government but with the Company, which was obstructing national growth and keeping the country backward. The Company had not disputed the Persian argument but rejected the conclusion, maintaining that both parties were constrained by the commercial factors affecting international trade including the decline in prices for major commodities which accompanied the world depression. An acceptable compromise of mutual satisfaction was required. In 1932 Tīmurtāsh was on the brink of a settlement. In 1929 he had the best offer which any Persian Government received of a shareholding in the Company, which, even if it seemed to him unsatisfactory at the time, in retrospect was obviously highly advantageous. Indeed it could be argued that the Company escaped lightly from

The Persian dimension

Table 13.4. *Value of total Persian visible exports and oil exports 1913–32* (in millions of krans and £s, fob)

	Total exports krans	£	Oil exports krans	£	Oil exports as a percentage of total exports	Kran/£ rates of exchange
1913	456	8.2	18	0.3	4	55.56
1914	396	6.3	34	0.5	9	62.83
1915	377	6.4	22	0.4	6	58.54
1916	434	11.2	67	1.7	15	38.83
1917	339	11.6	107	3.7	32	29.20
1918	271	9.8	155	5.6	57	27.71
1919	368	14.7	181	7.2	49	24.97
1920	371	10.9	234	6.9	63	33.99
1921	502	10.2	323	6.5	64	49.38
1922	734	13.2	429	7.7	58	55.55
1923	768	16.3	383	8.1	50	47.24
1924	1 000	23.8	515	12.3	52	42.03
1925	1 059	24.4	545	12.5	51	43.48
1926	1 104	22.7	654	13.4	59	48.68
1927	1 060	21.5	597	12.1	56	49.28
1928	1 518	31.6	1 038	21.6	68	48.10
1929	1 575	27.2	1 087	18.8	69	57.97
1930	1 464	23.1	1 005	15.8	69	63.49
1931[a]	1 736	20.3	1 018	11.9	59	85.71
1932	1 675	17.5	1 143	11.9	68	95.93

Note: [a] 15 months
Source: Bharier, J., *Economic Development in Iran 1900–1970*, (London, 1971), pp. 111, 122

the possibility of a Persian shareholding, which might have curtailed its world-wide expansion and, by restricting its operations, hindered its growth and development.

The expectations of Cadman, however, that a commercial company could participate with a foreign sovereign government in a corporate association were, in reality, impractical. The centrifugal realities which kept them apart were stronger than the centripetal attractions which bound them together. The idea of Persian Government participation in the Company had been an imaginative attempt to solve the concessionary dilemma of conflicting interests, but like most such endeavours it required that 'willing suspension of disbelief for the moment' which would have made faith in it possible. The cultural contrast was too wide ever to be bridged. The respective political and economic priorities were too divided to be reconciled. Market realities did not always coincide with national aspirations. National pride resented foreign exploitation. Compromise was intrinsically difficult, requiring more than personal commitment, for

The Persian dimension

it depended on the properly constituted delegation of authority to act in accordance with well-defined instructions.

Both Cadman and Tīmurtāsh had the measure of each other. Both men were reaching beyond the limitations of their actual responsibilities. Cadman was seeking a brave new oil world of collaborative endeavour amongst industrialists and with governments. The consortium of oil interests represented in Iraq, the tentative cooperative arrangements between the oil companies over oil distribution, and the participation proposals with the Persian Government constituted his visionary attempt to prevent the excesses of competition and concessionary conflict, even before world trading conditions gave his proposals an urgency which may have obscured their earlier idealism. Cadman was deeply disappointed by his failure to persuade the Persians to share his hopes for participation. Tīmurtāsh, too, devoted his talents, like another great Persian reformer of the mid nineteenth century, Mīrzā Taqī Khān, to working for his country and monarch with a tenacity which did credit to his conscience, if not always to his intelligence. Imbued with a relentless determination to transform Persia into a modern state in as short a period as possible, he tried to achieve too much in too brief a time. His success and his ambitions were resented not only by those whom he offended, but also by the one whom he served most of all. The continuous pressure of his life and the overwhelming burden of his activities kept him upon a perpetual treadmill of action from which he was seldom able to escape to reflect upon the direction in which he was moving and the decisions he needed to take. His impatience contrasts with the calm of Cadman. Constantly vigilant, it was almost inconceivable that he could take Cadman at his word in the face of so much mistrust of foreigners and so little confidence in the approval of the Shah. Persian courts were the graveyards of discarded favourites and distrusted ministers, as Tīmurtāsh himself learnt only too well, but too late.

The positions and personalities of Cadman and Tīmurtāsh, the pride and prejudices affecting British–Persian relations were neither sufficiently compatible nor complementary. The participation of the Persian Government in the Company remained an unfulfilled pipe dream. The intentions were honourable, but it was ultimately inconceivable that the partnership could have endured. Cadman was expecting a permanent arrangement, but for Tīmurtāsh, despite his earlier enthusiasm, it came to represent an unacceptably inferior relationship. He might have contemplated a temporary alliance for a fixed term, but neither the Shah, nor he nor other Persian ministers, then or later, could have envisaged indefinitely compromising their sense of national sovereignty or disowning their heritage of natural resources for a provisional advantage of uncertain consequences

The Persian dimension

over which they would be powerless. In 1932 Persia did not have the capability of exerting control over its oil industry, but it had the will to preserve its freedom of action.

CONCLUSION

The growth of the Company in the two decades from 1909 to 1928 was a remarkable phenomenon. In 1908 a few wells had been proved by the drill. In 1928 production of over 5 000 000 tons had been exceeded. There was no dominant entrepreneurial founder who bestowed a succession of paternal legitimacy upon the business. The discovery of some new technical process did not occur to transform a competitive position, introduce a new product, effect a change in taste or provide a new form of social service. The Company was not a pioneer in the oil industry. Its formation was almost accidental, due more to circumstances than a single cause. D'Arcy's concession was a personal investment rather than a conscious decision to develop a national supply of oil.

Indeed the absence of a dominant founding personality who branded his mark upon the Company meant a greater sense of freedom, a chance to respond to opportunities rather than to follow in another's footsteps. There was a greater degree of adaptability, more reliance on practice, less on precedents. Thus in response to the financial crisis of 1913-14, even recourse to government participation was not excluded. Yet, having accepted a government shareholding, the Company preserved its independence and did not act like a government department. Its ethos remained commercial not bureaucratic. It achieved with some skill a balancing act between commercial realities and patriotic service.

There was no inevitability about the Company's success. On the contrary, all the evidence points to a series of challenges which became the experience of which maturity is the expression. Its early developing years included the technical disasters of the refinery in Ābādān; the frustrating failure of early marketing initiatives; the financial disaster which made Government intervention of one kind or another indispensable for survival; the demands for war-time supplies; the drive for integrated operations; the struggle to develop an international rather than a national strategy; the preservation of identity against competition; the complicated concessionary relationship with the Persian Government; the technological stimulus of the production from the Persian oilfields; the changing nature of exploration throughout the world; the appropriate form of management structure; the organisation of subsidiary companies within a group structure and so forth. All these situations confronted the Company with problems and decisions, which contributed to a particular form of corporate individuality resembling but also differing from its competitors. This is its history comprised.

It would be unrealistic to assume that the satisfactory relationship which ultimately came to be established between the Company and the Government represented a national oil policy. There is little indication of a consistent sense of direction and rather more evidence of much reaction to events and opportunism. The Government's attempts to 'capture' Royal Dutch-Shell and make it wear national instead of international colours, were doomed to failure for a lack of similarity of interests. Politically induced settlements were seldom successful. A realisation of the competitive position was more easily understood between companies. The animosity between the Company and Royal Dutch-Shell was a vital stimulus in the survival of the Company. Yet, eventually the Company and Royal Dutch-Shell reached an understanding in the commercial ring when it was clear that a verdict from the national judges could not be expected. Over the Mesopotamian concession the Company and Standard Oil (NJ) found more in common than was agreed by their respective national diplomats. Yet it is obvious that the power of the major oil companies to dominate aspects of the international oil industry through their integrated operations was resented by some as an early manifestation of the modern multinational phenomenon.

Its Persian origin left its mark upon the Company's development. On the one hand the Company discovered unexpectedly large oil resources which, because of the extent of the area granted in the concessionary agreement, were capable of the most comprehensive and scientific exploitation then possible. On the other hand the Company was identified with that image of the British Government which many Persians have tended to associate with their misfortunes over the last century. This may have been irrational, but it was certainly responsible for a lack of mutual confidence. Cultural differences, some intolerance and different attitudes to industrial development made for a measure of misunderstanding, which, nevertheless, given the scale of the operations and their impact on the economy and political scene in Persia, were less disruptive than might have been envisaged during a period of some political instability.

The stimulus imparted to industrial technology during the First World War enormously increased the postwar demand for petroleum products, called into question existing methods of exploration, production and refining and conferred a new economic and political prominence on the

Conclusion

possession of crude oil resources to which many countries aspired but few attained, so raising the national stakes even higher in the concessionary race. Fears of oil shortages in the United States in the early 1920s were replaced by an ever growing surplus in the mid-1920s from the newly discovered fields in California, Arkansas, Texas, Oklahoma and Louisiana culminating in the huge main East Texas field in 1930, thus strengthening the productive capacity of the American oil industry. The début of South America on the oil scene at the same time was astonishing.

The tendency, however, to exaggerate the importance at this time of the contribution of oil to the world energy supply must be resisted, or its later significance, even dominance, in the 1960s and 1970s, will not be sufficiently appreciated. Solid fuels supplied most of the energy consumed in 1925, 82.9 per cent, liquid fuels, 13.2 per cent, natural gas, 3.2 per cent and hydro electric power, 0.7 per cent. The United States had the highest consumption of oil, 19.2 per cent of total energy representing 48.3 per cent of world oil consumed. The country nearest to these figures was the United Kingdom, 3.8 per cent and 12.3 per cent respectively (see Appendix C.1 for details of selected countries in 1925). Coal, the fuel of the industrial revolution, was certainly still the principal source of energy in the mid 1920s. Nevertheless oil for lamps did give way to oil for engines, leading to an improved range of products of which the most significant was benzine, motor spirit, and new approaches to marketing strategy to gain the confidence and custom of the motorist. In the early twenties the Company was ill-prepared for this challenge, but responded to it by a better coordination of its technical activities, improved management control and an expanding distribution policy of marketing subsidiaries in different countries, based on its exploitation of an oilfield of great magnitude which it had learnt to operate scientifically and economically. It was a decade of remarkable transformation only marred by the failure to achieve a more realistic concessionary understanding with the Persian Government.

The vitality and determination of the Company owed much to the assertive personalities of Greenway and Cadman. Greenway's rugged and often obstinate defence of his Company, which offended some government officials, was complemented later by the diplomatic and administrative tact of Cadman, whose familiarity with the people in the corridors of power enabled him to persuade where Greenway had to convince. The drive for an integrated company which Greenway so relentlessly pursued, and in so doing distanced himself from the more complacent attitude of Burmah, matched the technical contribution of Cadman, which underpinned later developments.

Cadman's sponsorship of the discussion, at Achnacarry in 1928 with the participation of Deterding of Royal Dutch-Shell and Teagle of Standard

Conclusion

Oil (NJ), the formulation of the Group Agreement between the participants in the Iraq Petroleum Company, and the highest annual production of oil ever reached at Masjid i-Suleimān, made 1928 a memorable year which symbolised the progress and the recognition which the Company had gained in the international oil industry within two decades of its incorporation, its years of development.

APPENDICES

Appendices

Appendix 0.1. World crude oil production 1900–32

(thousands of tons)

	1900	1901	1902	1903	1904	1905	1906	1907	1908	1909	1910	1911	1912	1913	1914	1915	1916
Total production	20 018	22 475	24 404	26 158	29 255	28 871	28 626	35 430	38 294	40 095	43 995	46 223	47 308	51 724	54 704	57 991	61 409
USA	8 539	9 314	11 915	13 485	15 716	18 083	16 979	22 295	23 963	24 587	28 128	29 590	29 924	33 348	35 673	37 732	40 371
Canada	123	102	71	65	74	85	76	106	71	56	42	39	33	31	29	29	27
Mexico	—	1	5	10	17	34	67	135	528	364	488	1 685	2 223	3 449	3 521	4 418	5 442
Trinidad	—	—	—	—	—	—	—	—	—	8	19	38	59	68	86	101	125
Germany	48	42	48	60	85	75	78	102	135	137	139	136	138	115	105	94	88
Poland	315	436	556	703	798	774	734	1 135	1 693	2 004	1 701	1 412	1 146	1 049	864	718	884
Romania	219	225	276	371	483	593	856	1 090	1 108	1 252	1 305	1 491	1 742	1 819	1 722	1 615	1 201
Russia	10 171	11 432	10 811	10 146	10 542	7 377	7 906	8 302	8 347	8 855	9 441	8 884	9 130	8 434	8 996	9 201	8 834
Argentina	—	—	—	—	—	—	—	—	2	2	3	2	6	18	37	69	116
Columbia	—	—	—	—	—	—	—	—	—	—	—	—	—	—	—	—	—
Ecuador	—	—	—	—	—	—	—	—	—	—	—	—	—	—	—	—	—
Peru	37	37	38	37	39	50	71	101	127	189	169	197	235	278	247	346	348
Venezuela	—	—	—	—	—	—	—	—	—	—	—	—	—	—	—	—	—
British Borneo[a]	—	—	—	—	—	—	—	—	—	—	—	—	—	19	43	53	84
Burma	145	192	217	337	454	555	539	583	677	896	824	866	955	1 064	995	1 101	1 140
Japan (incl. Taiwan)	117	150	134	162	164	181	210	231	251	253	245	233	223	260	354	393	398
Netherlands India	302	539	326	774	874	1 054	1 098	1 340	1 380	1 482	1 481	1 634	1 456	1 500	1 533	1 600	1 684
Egypt	—	—	—	—	—	—	—	—	—	—	—	3	29	13	101	28	54
Persia	—	—	—	—	—	—	—	—	—	—	—	—	—	249	391	485	601
Other	2	5	7	8	9	10	12	10	12	10	10	13	9	10	7	8	12

638

Appendices

	1917	1918	1919	1920	1921	1922	1923	1924	1925	1926	1927	1928	1929	1930	1931	1932
Total production	67 502	67 586	74 614	92 468	102 819	115 288	136 340	136 150	143 481	147 225	169 474	177 822	199 445	189 267	184 232	175 796
USA	45 009	47 776	50 787	59 454	63 380	74 836	98 310	95 831	102 516	103 473	120 957	121 003	135 211	120 538	114 239	105 390
Canada	29	41	32	26	25	24	23	22	45	49	64	84	150	204	207	140
Mexico	7 422	8 568	11 688	21 083	25 959	24 467	20 079	18 749	15 505	12 137	8 607	6 732	5 998	5 306	4 435	4 403
Trinidad	215	279	247	280	316	328	409	545	589	667	722	1 031	1 170	1 264	1 308	1 359
Germany	86	36	36	33	37	43	46	54	73	88	89	85	94	159	216	216
Poland	836	810	818	753	694	702	725	759	800	784	717	737	670	658	626	552
Romania	499	1 172	888	998	1 123	1 321	1 458	1 794	2 235	3 129	3 539	4 131	4 666	5 587	6 594	7 223
Russia	8 466	3 647	4 262	3 413	3 889	4 792	5 256	6 099	7 052	8 657	10 397	11 466	13 509	17 095	22 225	21 073
Argentina	163	182	179	222	273	385	456	623	850	1 054	1 158	1 217	1 261	1 208	1 572	1 764
Columbia	—	—	—	—	9	43	57	60	135	865	2 015	2 671	2 723	2 731	2 448	2 203
Ecuador	8	8	8	8	8	8	12	13	21	29	72	145	185	208	236	214
Peru	346	339	353	378	496	713	765	1 125	1 239	1 445	1 359	1 611	1 802	1 671	1 354	1 329
Venezuela	16	45	57	61	192	295	564	1 214	2 643	4 954	8 474	14 194	18 453	18 345	15 653	15 643
British Borneo[a]	73	68	80	137	189	382	529	559	571	663	663	701	710	659	517	509
Burma	1 084	1 099	1 173	1 124	1 172	1 145	1 128	1 130	1 111	1 075	1 078	1 173	1 174	1 113	1 101	1 183
Japan (incl. Taiwan)	384	328	300	298	300	276	242	243	257	240	240	261	271	262	275	219
Netherlands India	1 769	1 715	2 082	2 353	2 276	2 291	2 667	2 748	2 875	2 851	3 686	4 311	5 272	5 601	4 770	5 235
Egypt	127	260	204	140	168	159	141	151	165	150	170	247	251	268	273	254
Persia	959	1 157	1 361	1 641	2 238	2 986	3 386	4 345	4 703	4 811	5 327	5 834	5 657	6 151	5 956	6 640
Other	11	56	59	66	75	92	87	86	96	104	140	188	218	239	227	247

Note: [a] Sarawak and Brunei
Source: Petroleum Almanac. Barrels converted to tons at the rate of 7.45 barrels = 1 ton

Appendices

Appendix 1.1. *The D'Arcy Concession 1901*

(Translation)

Between the Government of His Imperial Majesty the Shah of Persia of the one part and William Knox D'Arcy of independent means residing in London at No. 42 Grosvenor Square (hereinafter called "the Concessionaire") of the other part.
The following has by these presents been agreed on and arranged, viz.:

Article 1

The Government of His Imperial Majesty the Shah grants to the Concessionaire by these presents a special and exclusive privilege to search for, obtain, exploit, develop, render suitable for trade, carry away and sell natural gas, petroleum, asphalt and ozokerite throughout the whole extent of the Persian Empire for a term of 60 years as from the date of these presents.

Article 2

This privilege shall comprise the exclusive right of laying the pipelines necessary from the deposits where there may be found one or several of the said products up to the Persian Gulf, as also the necessary distributing branches. It shall also comprise the right of constructing and maintaining all and any wells, reservoirs, stations and pump services, accumulation services and distribution services, factories and other works and arrangements that may be deemed necessary.

Article 3

The Imperial Persian Government grants gratuitously to the Concessionaire all uncultivated lands belonging to the State which the Concessionaire's engineers may deem necessary for the construction of the whole or any part of the above-mentioned works. As for cultivated lands belonging to the State, the Concessionaire must purchase them at the fair and current price of the Province.

The Government also grants to the Concessionaire the right of acquiring all and any other lands or buildings necessary for the said purpose, with the consent of the proprietors, on such conditions as may be arranged between him and them without their being allowed to make demands of a nature to surcharge the prices ordinarily current for lands situate in their respective localities. Holy places with all their dependencies within a radius of 200 Persian archines are formally excluded.

Article 4

As three petroleum mines situate at Schouster Kassre-Chirine in the Province of Kermanschahan and Daleki near Bouchir are at present let to private persons and produce an annual revenue of two thousand tomans for the benefit of the Government, it has been agreed that the three aforesaid mines shall be comprised in the Deed of Concession in conformity with Article 1, on condition that over and above the 16 per cent mentioned in Article 10 the Concessionaire shall pay every year the fixed sum of 2,000 (two thousand) tomans to the Imperial Government.

Appendices

Article 5

The course of the pipelines shall be fixed by the Concessionaire and his engineers.

Article 6

Notwithstanding what is above set forth, the privilege granted by these presents shall not extend to the Provinces of Azerbadjan, Ghilan, Mazendaran, Asdrabad and Khorassan, but on the express condition that the Persian Imperial Government shall not grant to any other person the right of constructing a pipeline to the southern rivers or to the south coast of Persia.

Article 7

All lands granted by these presents to the Concessionaire or that may be acquired by him in the manner provided for in Articles 3 and 4 of these presents, as also all products exported shall be free of all imposts and taxes during the term of the present Concession. All material and apparatuses necessary for the exploration, working and development of the pipeline shall enter Persia free of all taxes and custom-house duties.

Article 8

The Concessionaire shall immediately send out to Persia and at his own cost one or several experts with a view to their exploring the region in which there exist, as he believes, the said products, and in the event of a satisfactory nature, the latter shall immediately send to Persia and at his own cost all the technical staff necessary with the working plant and machinery required for boring and sinking wells and ascertaining the value of the property.

Article 9

The Imperial Persian Government authorizes the Concessionaire to found one or several companies for the working of the Concession.

The names, "statutes" and capital of the said companies shall be fixed by the Concessionaire, and the directors shall be chosen by him on the express condition that on the formation of each company the Concessionaire shall give official notice of such formation to the Imperial Government through the medium of the Imperial Commissioner and shall forward the "statutes" with information as to the places at which such company is to operate. Such company or companies shall enjoy all the rights and privileges granted to the Concessionaire, but they must assume all his engagements and responsibilities.

Article 10

It shall be stipulated in the contract between the Concessionaire of the one part and the Company of the other part that the latter is within the term of one month as from the date of the formation of the first exploitation company to pay the Imperial Persian Government the sum of £20,000 sterling in cash and an additional sum of £20,000 sterling in paid-up shares of the first company founded by virtue of the foregoing Article. It shall also pay the said Government annually a sum equal to 16 per cent of the annual net profits of any company or companies that may be formed in accordance with the said Article.

Appendices

Article 11

The said Government shall be free to appoint an Imperial Commissioner who shall be consulted by the Concessionaire and the directors of the companies to be formed. He shall supply all and any useful information at his disposal and he shall inform them of the best course to be adopted in the interest of the undertaking. He shall establish by agreement with the Concessionaire such supervision as he may deem expedient to safeguard the interests of the Imperial Government.

The aforesaid powers of the Imperial Commissioner shall be set forth in the "statutes" of the companies to be created.

The Concessionaire shall pay the Commissioner thus appointed an annual sum of £1,000 sterling for his services as from the date of the formation of the first company.

Article 12

The workmen employed in the service of the Company shall be subjects of His Imperial Majesty the Shah, except the technical staff such as the managers, engineers, borers and foremen.

Article 13

At any place in which it may be proved that the inhabitants of the country now obtain petroleum for their own use, the Company must supply them gratuitously with the quantity of petroleum that they themselves got previously.

Such quantity shall be fixed according to their own declarations, subject to the supervision of the local authority.

Article 14

The Imperial Government binds itself to take all and any necessary measures to secure the safety and the carrying out of the object of this Concession, of the plant and of the apparatuses of which mention is made for the purpose of the undertaking of the Company and to protect the representatives, agents and servants of the Company. The Imperial Government having thus fulfilled its engagements, the Concessionaire and the companies created by him shall not have power under any pretext whatever to claim damages from the Persian Government.

Article 15

On the expiration of the term of the present Concession, all materials, buildings and apparatuses then used by the Company for the exploitation of its industry shall become the property of the said Government, and the Company shall have no right to any indemnity in this connection.

Article 16

If within the term of two years as from the present date the Concessionaire shall not have established the first of the said companies authorized by Article 9 of the present Agreement, the present Concession shall become null and void.

Appendices

Article 17

In the event of there arising between the parties to the present Concession any dispute or difference in respect of its interpretation or the rights or responsibilities of one or the other of the parties therefrom resulting, such dispute or difference shall be submitted to two arbitrators at Teheran, one of whom shall be named by each of the parties, and to an Umpire who shall be appointed by the arbitrators before they proceed to arbitrate. The decision of the arbitrators or, in the event of the latter disagreeing that of the umpire, shall be final.

Article 18

This Act of Concession made in duplicate is written in the French language and translated into Persian with the same meaning.

But in the event of there being any dispute in relation to such meaning, the French text shall alone prevail. Teheran Sefer 1319 of the Hegine, that is to say May 1901.

(Signed) WILLIAM KNOX D'ARCY,
By his Attorney,
(Signed) ALFRED L. MARRIOTT.

Certified that the above signatures were affixed in my presence at the British Consulate General at Gulaket near Teheran, on this 4th day of the month of June 1901 by Alfred Lyttelton Marriott, Attorney of William Knox D'Arcy, in accordance with the Notarial Act dated 21st March 1901, and seen by me.

(Signed) GEORGE GRAHAME,
Vice-Consul.

Thus far translation.
Here follows in English.

Certified that the writing in the Persian and French languages on this and the preceding seven pages were registered in the Archives (Register Book) of H.M.'s Legation, Tehran, on pages 117 to 124, on the 5th June 1901.

Dated at Gulaket near Tehran this 6th day of June 1901.

(Signed) GEORGE GRAHAME,
Vice-Consul.

Appendix 3.1. Definition of financial terms and an explanation of the basis of the consolidated accounts

(a) Ordinary Shares/Dividend

A company needing money can issue (sell) ordinary shares (stock) to investors in exchange for cash. An investor buying such shares takes an equity risk in the company's fortunes. Generally speaking, ordinary shares represent the most junior and permanent form of capital and the investor is unlikely to get much of his money back if the company runs into trouble. He can of course sell the shares in the market more or less at his own choosing. Owning ordinary shares gives the investor the right to vote at shareholders' meetings and therefore gives a limited say in the running of the company.

Income on ordinary shares arises when a company pays a dividend. In general dividends can only be paid to investors if the company has made a profit in a given year. The amount to be paid is decided at a shareholders' meeting on the recommendation of the Directors but is usually limited to the amount of after tax profit made. In practice it is often less than this, to allow profits to be reinvested in the company.

(b) Preference Shares/Cumulative Preference Shares
Similar to ordinary shares except that usually owners of preference shares have no right to vote at shareholders' meetings, as in the United States also, and therefore cannot affect the running of the company, but they are entitled to be paid the given percentage of profit before the ordinary shareholder can receive their dividends. Income is again in the form of dividends and the amount to be paid is a fixed percentage of the investment (e.g. 6%) but again can only be paid from profits. Investors in cumulative preference shares have added protection in that if losses are made, the dividends due are accumulated, and paid in full as soon as sufficient profits are available. Again there is frequently a market in such shares.

(c) Debenture Stock:
Companies can also issue or sell debenture stock (bonds) to raise money. The investor who buys debentures is lending the company money in the accepted sense of the word. This money will be repaid by the company after a period of as much as twenty-five years, often in instalments. In the meantime interest at a predetermined rate (e.g. 10%) is due to debenture owners (irrespective of whether the company is making profits). Debenture stock is frequently ranked in seniority as regards access to the company's funds, but is not secured by a mortgage on the property of the company, as in the United States.

The decision as to whether to issue shares or debentures, or borrow from banks is, in fact, a complex issue. Suffice it to say here that each type of "borrowing" has its advantages and disadvantages which must be considered at the time of making the decision.

(d) Calls:
When shares are issued, the company may not need or may consider it prudent not to require all the proceeds immediately. If so, only part of the price is paid by investors at the outset. Subsequently the company makes "calls" on the investors asking for more money, often at predetermined dates, until such time as the full issue price for the shares has been received.

(e) Consolidation of Accounts
The corporate structure of the Anglo-Persian Oil Company group of companies was that of the Anglo-Persian Oil Company Limited acting as a holding company, but also trading on its own, and a set of subsidiary companies, owned entirely by the parent, and associate companies, in which there was a minority outside interest. The subsidiaries and associates had a responsibility for particular executive functions, such, as for example, exploration, the D'Arcy Exploration Company, production, the Bakhtiari Oil Company, shipping, the British Tanker Company, refining and distribution, the National Oil Refining Company. Each company was a separate entity which published its own annual balance sheet and profit and loss account.

Consolidated accounts for a group of companies combine the assets and liabilities, earnings and disbursements, of all the interconnected companies into a single balance sheet and a single profit and loss account. This enables assessments to be made of the commercial performance and financial position of the group as a

Appendices

whole, about which conclusions cannot be drawn from the accounts of either the holding company or individual subsidiaries. Since no consolidated accounts were prepared for the Anglo-Persian Oil Company group prior to 1929, even for internal use, it was necessary to undertake the consolidation of the company's published accounts. It is this compilation which appears in the text and to which reference is made in the tables.

Standard consolidation procedures were followed for the elimination of intergroup balances and other adjustments. Financial information in far greater detail than appears in the published accounts was available from sets of schedules to the accounts which formed the basis for the contemporary preparation of the accounts. These are found in the file series BP 4P 6001-7086 with supplementary information from subsidiary and associated companies.

In the rare cases when the accounts of a subsidiary and the parent company did not match the figure given in the schedules of the Anglo-Persian Oil Company Limited, was accepted as authoritative. The details given in the text for the distribution of the company's fixed assets, its liquidity position, and the return on investment, are derived from these computed consolidated balance sheets and represent the activities of the Anglo-Persian Oil Company group as a whole.

Appendix 6.1. *The Bradbury letter 1914*

Treasury, Whitehall, S.W.
20th May, 1914

Gentlemen,

With reference to the Financial Agreement which has been duly settled on behalf of His Majesty's Government and sent to your company for signature, I am directed by the Lords Commissioners of His Majesty's Treasury to offer the following observations regarding the provisions of the amendments proposed to your Articles of Association:

1. By the new Article 91 A it is provided that an *ex officio* director shall have the right to negative any resolution which may be proposed at a board or committee meeting, but that the other directors, or a majority of them, shall have the right to appeal therefrom to His Majesty's Government, which, for the purpose of the Article, is defined as meaning the Treasury and the Admiralty. His Majesty's Government are of opinion that it would not be prudent, or, indeed, practicable, to qualify the generality of the right to veto. On the other hand, it is felt that the ordinary directors (meaning by that expression the directors other than the *ex officio* directors), and incidentally the members of the company, should have some safeguard in the matter. It is thought that the right which is to be given by the new Article to the Departments will afford the requisite safeguard. The ordinary directors will, by appealing to the Departments, be in a position to ensure in regard to any particular question that the right of veto is not exercised until the question has been considered and adjudicated by the Departments.

I am to add that His Majesty's Government do not propose to make use of the right of veto except in regard to matters of general policy, such as —

(1) The supervision of the activities of the company as they may affect questions of foreign naval or military policy;
(2) Any proposed sale of the company's undertaking or proposed change of the company's status;

Appendices

(3) The control of new exploitation, sites of wells, etc.;
(4) Sales of crude or fuel oil to foreigners, or such exceptional sales to other persons on long contracts as might endanger the due fulfilment of current Admiralty contracts;

and that their interference (if any) in the ordinary administration of the company as a commercial concern will be strictly limited to the minimum necessary to secure these objects. Further, in the case of any such interference, due regard will be paid to the financial interests of the company in which, under the proposed arrangement, the Government have themselves so large a stake.

While His Majesty's Government are not prepared to enter into any binding agreement in regard to the exercise of the veto, you are at liberty to treat the above as an assurance as to the general lines upon which they will act in the matter, not only in regard to the Anglo-Persian Company Limited, but also in regard to the subsidiary companies.

2. By the words added to Article 96 it is provided that the *ex officio* directors should always be present at committee meetings. Occasions may arise when it may be desirable that both the *ex officio* directors should be present, but as a general rule the presence of only one of them would be necessary. Indeed at some meetings it may not be necessary that either of them should be present.

3. You are at liberty to make such use of this letter as you may think fit at the proposed meetings of the shareholders.

I am, Gentlemen
Your obedient Servant,
(Signed) JOHN BRADBURY

Messrs. The Anglo-Persian Oil Company Limited,
Winchester House,
Old Broad Street,
London, E.C.

Appendix 6.2. *Members of the Harcourt Committee 1918*

Rt. Hon. Viscount Harcourt	(Chairman)
Rt. Hon. Viscount Inchcape	(Treasury)
Rt. Hon. E.G. Pretyman	(Civil Lord of Admiralty)
Sir Frederick Black	(Admiralty)
Prof. Sir John Cadman	(Director, Petroleum Executive)
Mr. Alwyn Parker	(Foreign Office)
Mr. Lancelot Smith	(Board of Trade)
Mr. B.A. Kemball Cook	(Ministry of Shipping)
Sir Harry MacGowan	(Managing Director, Nobil's Explosives Co. Ltd)
Sir John Ferguson	(London Manager, National Bank of Scotland)
Lt. Col. Sir Robert Horne	(Director, Department of Materials and Priority, Admiralty)
Col. R.S. Williamson	(Staffordshire colliery proprietor and mining engineer)
Mr. J.C. Clarke	(Deputy Director, Petroleum Executive)

Secretary: Captain A.S. Jelf

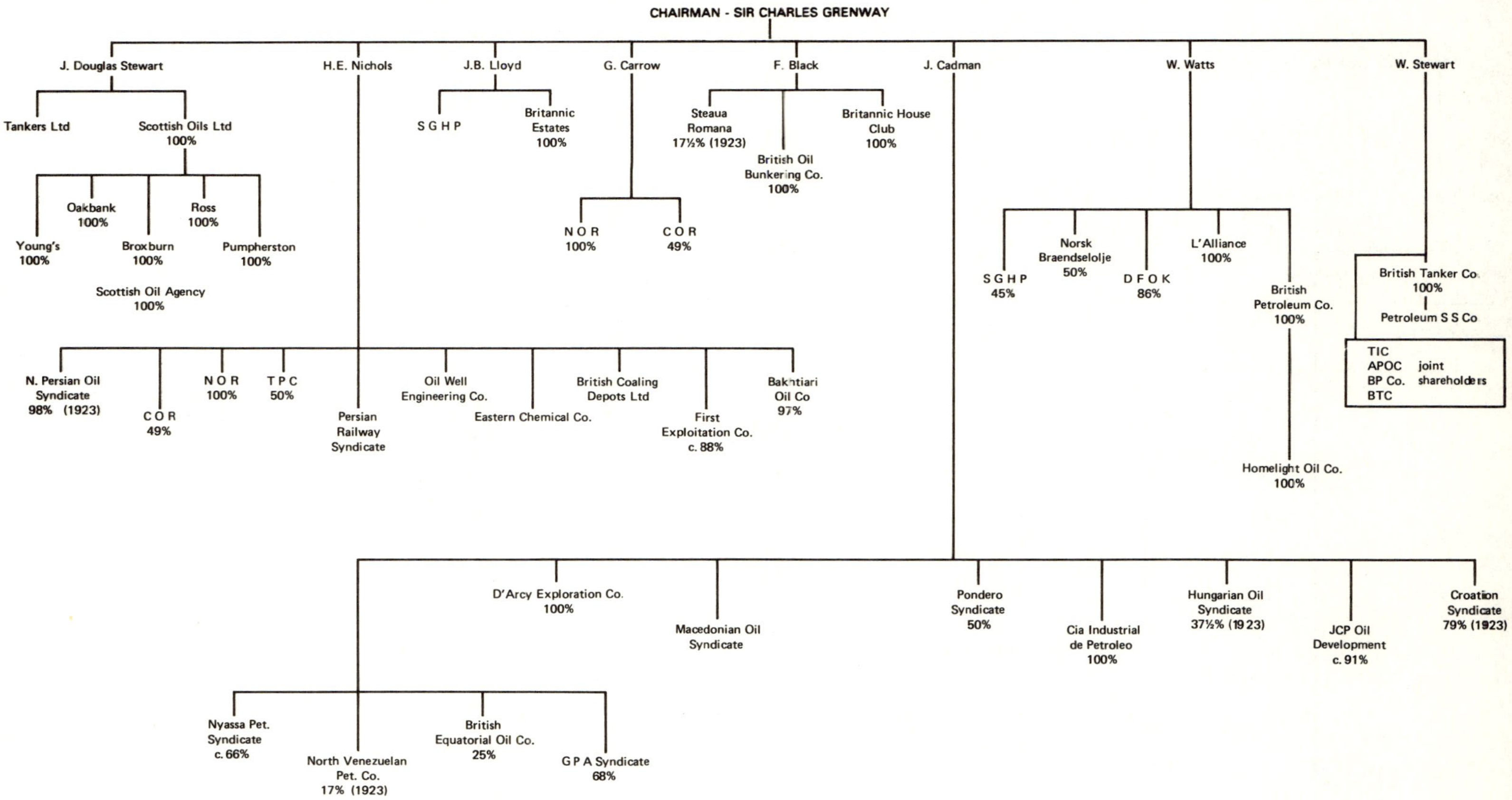

Appendix 8.1 The administration of the Anglo-Persian Oil Company November 1921
Source: BP H11/250

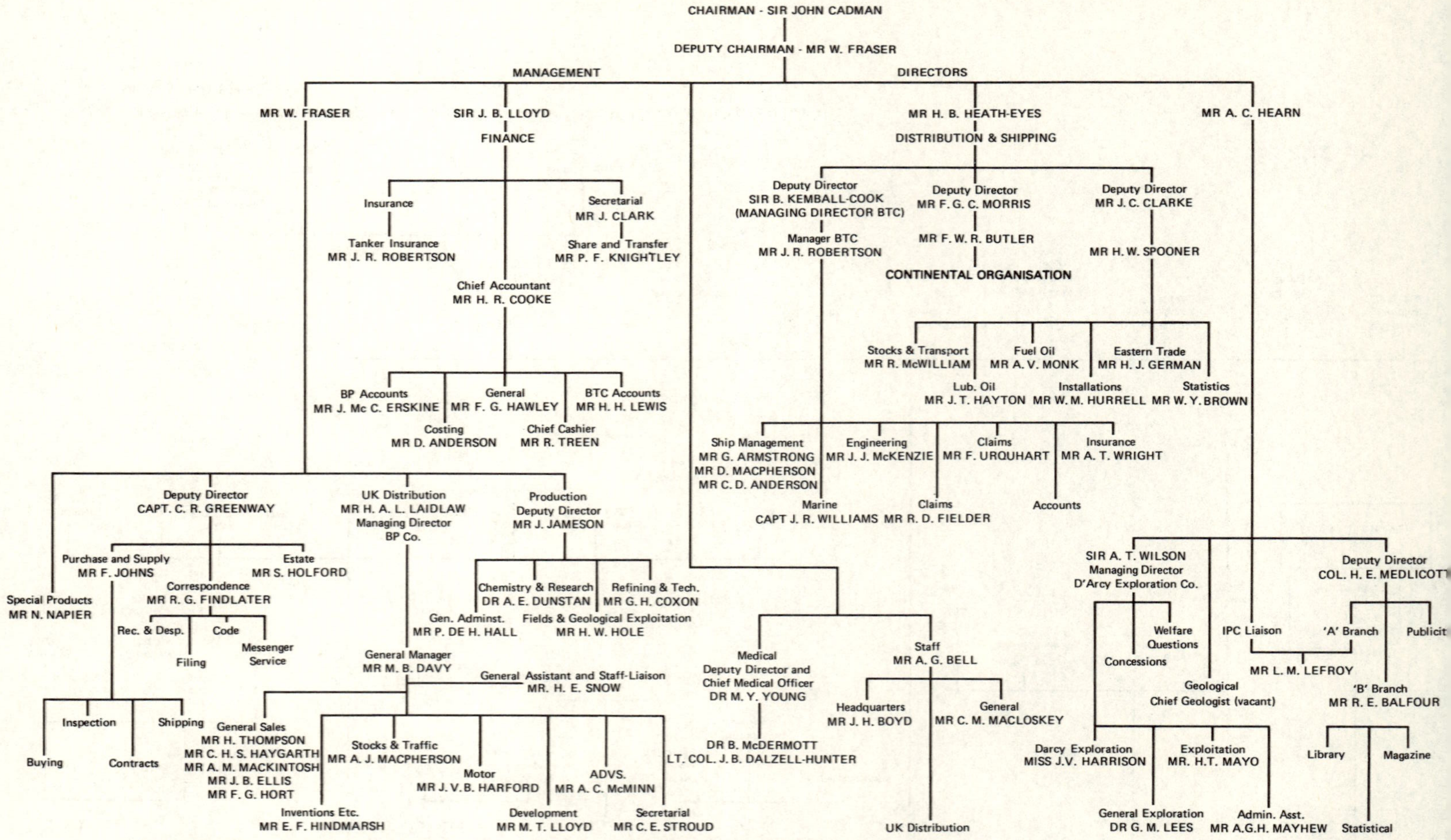

Appendix 8.2 The administration of the Anglo-Persian Oil Company December 1930

Source: BP H12/110

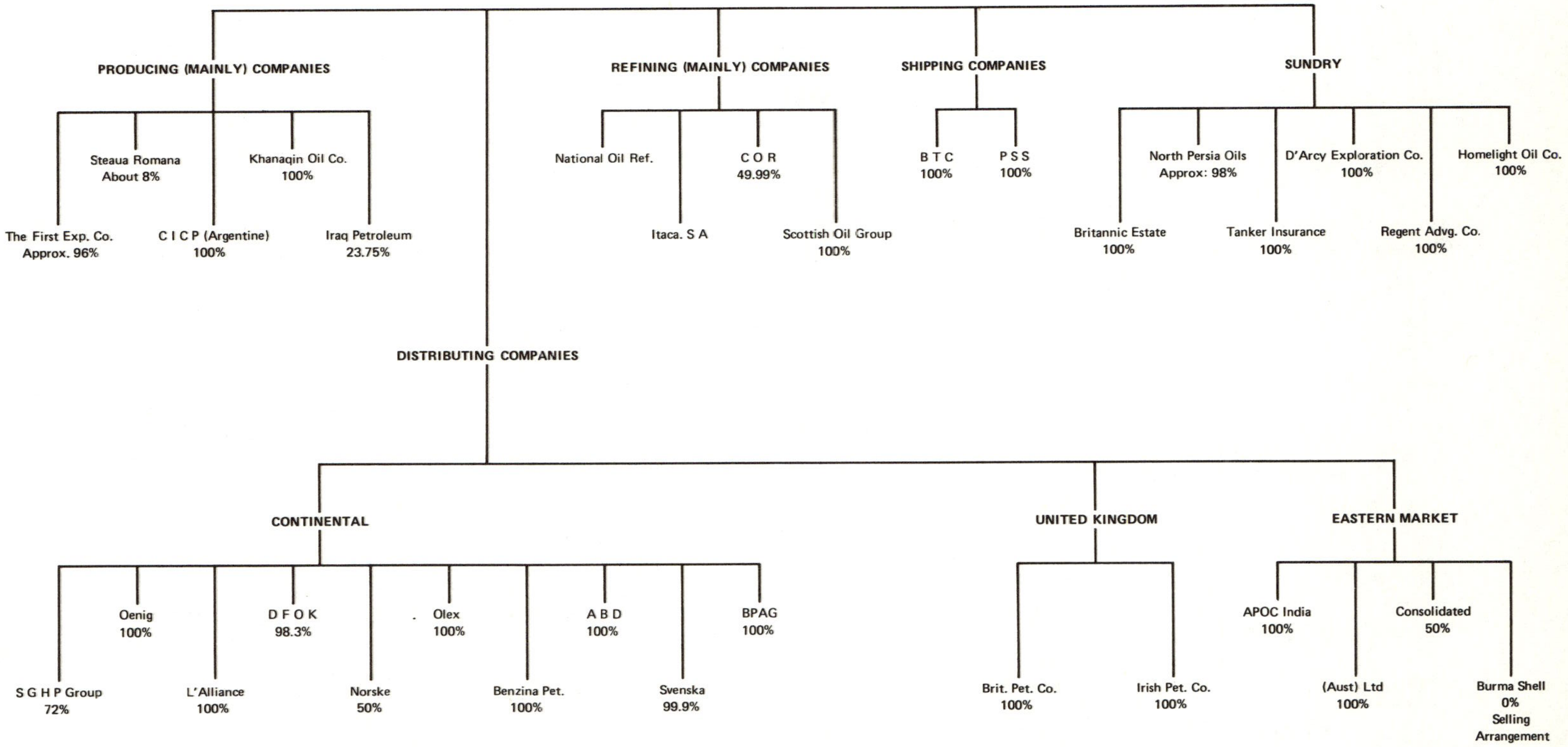

Appendix 8.3 Anglo-Persian Oil Company organisation 1930
Source: BP H11/250

Appendices

Appendix 8.4. Directors of the Anglo-Persian Oil Company 1909–32

	Appointed	Resigned	Died	Remarks
Lord Strathcona & Mount Royal, GCMG, GCVO	15 April 1909	—	21 January 1914	Chairman 15 April 1909–21 January 1914
†C.W. Wallace	15 April 1909	27 August 1915		Vice Chairman 15 April 1909
Sir Hugh S. Barnes, KCSI, KCVO	15 April 1909	—	15 February 1940	
†Sir John T. Cargill, Bt., DL, LLD	15 April 1909	31 May 1943		
W.K. D'Arcy	15 April 1909	—	1 May 1917	
William M. Garson	15 April 1909	24 July 1914		
Lord Greenway of Stanbridge Earls	15 April 1909	—	17 December 1934	Chairman 10 July 1914–27 March 1927. President 27 March 1927–
†James Hamilton	15 April 1909	23 February 1920		
HSH Prince Francis of Teck, KCVO, DSO	15 April 1909	22 October 1909		
†Sir Campbell K. Finlay	10 June 1912	1 January 1918		
*Viscount Inchcape of Strathnaver, GCSI, GCMG, KCIE	27 July 1914	31 January 1925		
*Admiral Sir Edmond J.W. Slade, KCIE, KCVO	27 July 1914	8 January 1917		Vice Chairman 15 December 1916
Duncan Garrow	8 January 1917 (as government director)		20 January 1928	
H.E. Nichols	27 July 1914	29 January 1924		
Sir Trevredyn R. Wynne, KCSI, KCIE	31 May 1915	—	25 January 1927	
	30 August 1915	—	28 June 1942	
F.W. Lund	29 January 1917	30 May 1950		
F.C. Tiarks	29 January 1917	31 May 1949		
†Robert I. Watson	25 February 1918	23 December 1947		
*W. St D. Jenkins, CBE	29 April 1918	14 February 1919		

650

Appendices

	Appointed	Resigned	Died	Remarks
Lord Southborough of Southborough, PC, GCB, GCMG, GCVO, KCSI	24 June 1918	6 November 1924		
*Sir Frederick W. Black, KCB	4 February 1919	30 June 1919 (as government director)		
	30 June 1919	27 March 1923		
Sir John B. Lloyd	28 April 1919	31 July 1946		
*Sir Edward H. Packe, KBE	12 December 1919	—	11 May 1946	
J. Douglas Stewart	23 February 1920	26 September 1925		
Lord Cadman of Silverdale, GCMG, FRS, LLD	1 April 1923	—	31 May 1941	Dep. Chairman 29 September 1925 Chairman 27 March 1927–31 May 1941
Lord Strathalmond of Pumpherstone, CBE, LLD	1 April 1923	31 March 1956		Dep. Chairman 21 January 1928 Chairman 24 June 1942–31 March 1956
Sir Hubert B. Heath-Eves	29 January 1924	30 April 1953		
*Lord Bradbury of Winsford, GCB	24 February 1925	27 July 1927		Dep. Chairman 28 October 1941–31 July 1950
†Gilbert G. Whigham	29 September 1925	31 December 1946		
T. L. Jacks, CBE	24 November 1926	8 May 1935		Rs. Director, Persia
A. C. Hearn	22 February 1927	31 December 1938		
*Sir George L. Barstow, KCB	27 September 1927	30 July 1946		

Note: *Government directors
†Directors from Burmah Oil Company.

Appendix 8.5. Oil company dividends on ordinary shares 1913-32

(per cent)

	1913	1914	1915	1916	1917	1918	1919	1920	1921	1922
Shell Transport (all free of tax)	35%	35%	35%	35%	35%	35%	35%	35%	27½%	22½%
Royal Dutch (paid in London by N.M. Rothschilds & Sons. Tax position unclear)	48	49	49	38	48	40	45	40	31	26½
APOC*	—	—	—	6(lt)	8(tf)	10(tf)	20(lt)	20(lt)	20(lt)	10(lt)
Burmah (dividends on ord. shares to June 1924 paid free of tax)	27½	27½	27½	30	32½	30[a]	50	30[b]	30	30

	1923	1924	1925	1926	1927	1928	1929	1930	1931	1932
Shell Transport	22½	22½	22½	25	25	25	25	17½	7½	7½
Royal Dutch	25	23	23	23½	24	24	24	17	6	6
APOC*	10(lt)	12½(lt)	17½(lt)	12½(lt)	7½(lt)	9⅜(lt) actual	20	15	5	7½
Burmah	30	35	35[d]	30	20	20	30	22½	17½	20

Note: [a] July 1918, bonus of 50% in fully paid ordinary shares.
[b] August 1920, bonus of 80% in fully paid ordinary shares.
[c] Plus bonus of 50% in fully paid ordinary shares.
[d] Plus bonus of 33⅓% in fully paid ordinary shares.

*APOC years ran from April to March until 1928. Thus APOC dividends, for example, in column for 1916 are for April 1916 to March 1917. The figure in the column for 1928 is for 9 months.
lt = less tax. tf = tax free.

Source: Walter E. Skinner, *Oil and Petroleum Yearbooks, 1913-32.*

Appendices

Appendix 9.1. *The Armitage-Smith Agreement 1920*

AGREEMENT dated December 22nd One thousand nine hundred and twenty between The Imperial Persian Government and The Anglo Persian Oil Company Limited with respect to determining the manner in which the annual sum or Royalty payable to the Persian Government under the D'Arcy Concession dated in May One thousand nine hundred and one shall as from the thirty first March One thousand nine hundred and nineteen be ascertained

Definitions.

In this Agreement unless the context otherwise requires "Persian Oil" shall be deemed to mean oil won pursuant to the said concession within the territory of the Persian Empire covered by the concession and any product of such oil.

'The Government' means the Imperial Persian Government.

'The Company' means the Anglo-Persian Oil Company Limited.

'Subsidiary Company' shall be deemed to mean (a) any Company of which 'the Company' owns whether directly or through some other subsidiary Company a number of shares sufficient to give to 'the Company' the control of more than fifty per cent of the total votes which can be cast at a general meeting of shareholders of such Company (b) any Company more than one half of the Directors of which are nominated or appointed by 'the Company' and/or by any subsidiary company and in addition in the case of shipping Companies (c) any Company which is managed by 'the Company' 'a controlling interest' is the interest of 'the Company' in a subsidiary Company.

Article 1. Subject to the conditions limitations and exceptions hereinafter mentioned the Imperial Persian Government (hereinafter referred to as 'the Government') is entitled to receive from the Anglo Persian Oil Company Limited (hereinafter referred to as 'the Company') the royalty of sixteen per cent of all the annual net profits arising from the winning refining and marketing of Persian Oil whether all the stages of the above processes be handled by the Company itself or through subsidiary companies or by means of pooling schemes or other arrangements and whether the refining and marketing takes place within the Persian Empire or not subject always to the single exception that the Government is not to receive royalty on the profits arising from the transporting of oil by means of ships but subject to the conditions and limitations hereafter mentioned the profits however arising from the employment of lighters and other small craft in the Persian Gulf will be subject to the above mentioned royalty.

Article 2. In ascertaining the net profits arising from Persian Oil freight costs will when the oil is carried in tankers of 'the Company' or of any subsidiary company be based upon the ordinary market time charter rates for tankers similar to those employed in carrying the oil irrespective of the freights actually paid such time charter rates to be fixed year by year on the first day of April for the ensuing twelve months at the rate current on that date.

For the purpose of computing such freight costs voyage rates shall be charged based on the time charter rates and full account shall be taken of all other freight earned by the ships during the voyage in question. If at any time during the months of January February and March in any year either of the parties hereto shall give notice in writing to the other that in the opinion of that party there is no free market in time charters for oil tankers then failing agreement between the parties that

Appendices

question and if it is decided in the affirmative also the question of what will be a fair and proper rate of freight to be charged as from the first day of April next following the giving of such notice against Persian Oil for the purposes of this Agreement shall be submitted to a single arbitrator whose decision shall be final. Such Arbitrator shall in default of agreement between the parties be nominated by the President for the time being of the Chamber of Shipping in London. As regards the Royalty accounts for the years ending thirty first March One thousand nine hundred and twenty and thirty first March One thousand nine hundred and twenty one the parties will as soon as possible after signature of this agreement agree rates or failing agreement within three months of the date hereof rates shall be settled by an arbitrator as above provided.

Article 3. The provisions of this and the next following Article of this agreement shall apply to subsidiary Companies refining distributing or dealing with Persian Oil outside Persia and to any other company refining distributing or dealing with Persian Oil outside Persia where 'the Company' is able to procure the necessary accounts to be prepared by such Company and the necessary facilities for inspection to be given by such Company to the Government. In the case of any Company to which this clause applies the following deductions shall be made from the net profits ascertained as hereafter provided on which Royalty is to be calculated before computing the amount of the royalty viz:—

(a) In the case of refining companies:—
A deduction of six shillings per ton in respect of the first three quarters of a million tons throughput of Persia Oil per annum a deduction of five shillings and six pence per ton on all throughput of Persian oil between three quarters of a million tons and one million tons per annum and a deduction of five shillings per ton on all throughput of Persian Oil in excess of one million tons per annum.

(b) In the case of distributing companies:—

Qualities	Quantities of Persian Oil distributed by a single Company in any year	Rate of deduction per gallon per pound or per ton of Persian Oil
Kerosene	150,000 tons	5/8d. per gallon
Spirit	200,000 ,,	1d. ,,
Liquid fuel	300,000 ,,	1/5d. ,,
Gas Oil	25,000 ,,	1/2d. ,,
Lubricants and all other oils not otherwise specified	20,000 ,,	1d. ,,
Wax and candles	4,000 ,,	1/8d. per lb.
Pitch	50,000 ,,	2s.6d. per ton
Medicinal oils	100 ,,	6d. per gallon

Appendices

In the event of the quantities of any quality distributed by any Company exceeding the quantities above stated by not more than fifty per cent then the rate of deduction on such excess for that quality shall be reduced by one eighth and in the event of the quantities of any quality distributed by any of the Companies exceeding the above quantities by more than fifty per cent then the rate of deduction on such excess over fifty per cent for that quality shall be reduced by one quarter.

(c) The above deductions shall be made from the total net profits of any company arising from Persian Oil before calculating the Royalty and if such deductions more than absorb the whole of the profit then any deficiency so caused shall not be carried forward to any subsequent year and any such deficiency in the case of one Company shall not be set against the net profit in the case of any other Company PROVIDED ALWAYS that such deductions shall not be made once for refining in respect of any quantity of oil and once for marketing distributing or dealing with any "quality".

Article 4. In cases where a refining or distributing Company to which this Article applies handles other oil or oil products in addition to Persian Oil the net profits on Persian Oil on which Royalty is to be paid shall be ascertained each year as follows:—

(a) In the case of refining companies:—
1. When the refining company does not buy the oil but refines the oil for payment then the cost of refining Persian Oil (including a proper proportion of overhead charges other than those which are not chargeable under this Agreement) shall be ascertained as nearly as possible from the books of the refining Company and the net profit attributable to Persian oil shall be obtained by deducting such cost from the charges made for refining such oil.
2. When the refining company purchases the oil then the actual price paid by the refining company for the Persian Oil refined during the year shall be ascertained from the books.

    The cost of refining the Persian Oil (including such overhead charges as aforesaid) will be ascertained as nearly as possible from the Books and added to the said price and the total will be deducted from the selling value of the products of such refining the balance being the Profit or loss on Persian oil for the purpose of ascertaining the selling value of the refined products from Persian oil the total quantities of the refined products from Persian and other oils shall be allocated between Persian and other oil on the basis of the respective outputs from the respective crude oils if refined separately. If Persian and other crude oils are mixed for refining purposes then the allocation shall be made on the basis of the quantities of each class so refined and the respective qualities as determined by chemical analysis. The selling value of refined products sold during the year shall be taken at the prices realised. Refined products not sold during the year shall be taken at the prices subsequently realised.

(b) In the case of distributing companies:—
The prices realised for Persian and other oil products distributed during any year shall be kept separately and there shall be deducted therefrom in

each case the price paid for such products by the distributing company in order to arrive at the respective gross profits on Persian and other oils.

The total net profit of the Distributing Company from the distribution of all classes of oil during the year shall be ascertained as hereinafter provided (Article 7) and shall be apportioned between Persian and other oil in proportion to the respective gross profits ascertained as aforesaid.

In cases where a Company both refines and distributes oil the accounts of such Company for the purposes of this Agreement shall be made out as if the two branches of the business were carried on by separate Companies.

'The Company' shall keep and shall procure that all Companies to which this and the preceding clause apply shall keep proper books of account and other records to enable the necessary calculations of cost and profits to be made for the purposes of this Agreement.

Article 5.
(a) In the case of any subsidiary Company in which the Company holds the whole of the share capital the total net profits arising from Persian oil (arrived at in accordance with this Agreement) shall be included in the Royalty Statement subject to and shewing the deductions provided for in Clause 3. In the case of any other subsidiary company or of any other company to which the provisions of Articles 3 and 4 apply the net profits arising from Persian Oil shall be determined in accordance with this Agreement but the Government shall only be entitled in respect of any year to royalty on a proportion of the net profits from Persian Oil for such year after making the deductions provided for in Clause 3 bearing the same relation to the whole of such profits as the proportion of the whole profits of such Company for such year which 'the Company' would receive in respect of its shareholding or otherwise if the whole profits were distributed bears to the whole of such profits. If 'the Company's' interest in any company has been increased or diminished during any year then an allowance shall be made in respect thereof having regard to all material circumstances.

(b) In the case of Companies in which 'the Company' is interested but to which Articles 3 and 4 do not apply 'the Company' shall include in the statement of net profits on which Royalty is to be calculated a fair commercial profit in respect of all Persian Oil sold to any such other Company having regard to the period of the contract the quantities and qualities of oil to be supplied and all other terms of any material agreement. Any difference as to what is a fair commercial profit shall be referred to arbitration as hereafter provided.

Article 6. All Directors Fees and Office Charges of 'the Company' shall be allocated fairly as between 'the Company' and all subsidiary companies as may be agreed by the parties or as may be settled by arbitration.

Article 7. The net profits of 'the Company' and of subsidiary companies or other companies to which Articles 3 and 4 hereof apply shall be taken for the purposes of this Agreement to be the net profits for each year as adjusted for Income Tax purposes subject to the following conditions viz:—
(i) Any adjustments made in respect of any period prior to thirty first March One thousand nine hundred and nineteen shall be excluded.

Appendices

(ii) Depreciation shall only be allowed to the extent to which it may be allowed for Income Tax purposes and shall not include any sums in respect of Depreciation carried forward from any period prior to thirty first March One thousand nine hundred and nineteen.

(iii) No deduction shall be made in respect of Excess Profits Duty Corporation Profits Tax Income Tax or any other taxation of a similar nature imposed by the British Government or by any Colonial or Foreign Government (other than the Persian Government).

(iv) No deductions shall be made from the profits for interest or dividends of any description paid and interest and dividends received shall be excluded from the profits on which royalty is payable.

(v) Where for the purposes of this Agreement it is necessary to determine the profits of any Company which is not liable to British taxation the profits of that Company shall be determined as nearly as may be in the same manner as they would be if the Company were liable to British Income Tax.

(vi) No deduction shall be allowed in respect of royalty payable under this Agreement by 'the Company' or any subsidiary company and no deduction shall be allowed in respect of payments relating to dividends guaranteed by the Company except in so far as such dividends are themselves brought into account as part of the receipts of some other company on which royalty is calculated.

(vii) No deduction shall be made in respect of the annual value of lands and buildings owned and occupied under schedule A.

(viii) The net profits and losses for each year ascertained as aforesaid (and subject to the provisions relating to deductions referred to in Article 3) shall be aggregated and royalty shall be payable on the balance (if any) of profit after deducting the losses but if in any year the aggregate losses exceed the aggregate profits the excess shall not be carried forward to a subsequent year except to the extent that such loss is due to depreciation allowed under sub clause (ii) of this clause.

Article 8. Royalty shall be deemed to have accrued due on thirty first March each year in respect of the twelve months ending on that day but such Royalty shall not become payable until the date of the holding of the General Meeting of 'the Company' for passing the accounts for such year. The Royalty shall carry interest at the rate of six per cent per annum free of tax from thirty first March on which it accrued due until payment 'the Company' will endeavour to secure that the accounts of all subsidiary and other Companies to which Articles 3 and 4 apply shall be made up to the thirty first March in each year but if in any cases this is not found practicable then for the purposes of this Agreement the net profits of such company for its financial year last preceding the thirty first March shall be substituted for the net profits to the thirty first March and any necessary adjustment shall be made.

Article 9. A statement of the royalty payable shall be prepared by 'the Company' each year and shall be submitted to a person to be designated in that behalf by the Government fourteen days before the date of the holding of the Annual Meeting of the Company. Such statement shall be deemed to be correct except as regards any items challenged by the Government within six calendar months of the delivery of

Appendices

the statement or any supplemental statement delivered in explanation or amplification thereof.

If the statement of royalty is in the opinion of the nominees of the Government not sufficient to enable him to judge whether the terms of the Concession and of this Agreement have been fulfilled then the Company undertakes to give the nominee of the Government access to all information which he may reasonably require for that purpose.

In the event of any dispute arising in connection with the said statement or the calculation of royalty hereunder or as to any apportionment or adjustment to be made hereunder or otherwise arising out of or under this Agreement the question or questions in dispute shall be submitted to a Chartered Accountant to be nominated by the President for the time being of the Institute of Chartered Accountants in England who shall be empowered to decide the dispute having regard to the terms of the Concession and of this Agreement and to the generally accepted view of what constitutes 'nett profits' where a percentage thereof is payable to another party. The decision of such arbitrator shall be final.

Article 10. THE Government undertakes to use its best endeavours to facilitate the work of 'the Company' and its subsidiary companies and the Company agrees that it will not enter into any fictitious or artificial transaction which would have the effect of reducing the amount of royalty payable.

As WITNESS the hands of the respective duly authorised representatives of the Government and the Company the day and year first above written.

SIGNED by Sydney Armitage Armitage-Smith
the Financial Adviser to the Imperial   (sgd)
Persian Government for and on behalf of The   SYDNEY ARMITAGE-SMITH
Imperial Persian Government in the presence
of

    (sgd) WILLIAM MCLINTOCK,
       Chartered Accountant,
        Bond Court House,
         Walbrook, London.

SIGNED by   For and on behalf of
for and on behalf of the Anglo
Persian Oil Company Limited in   the Anglo Persian Oil Company Ltd.
the presence of

    FRED. G. WATSON,   (sgd) C. GREENWAY
  23 Great Winchester Street,   Chairman.
      London, E.C.2.
       Solicitor.   F. MACINDOE
                                                       Secretary.

Appendices

Appendix 10.1. *Anglo-Persian Oil Company staff and labour in Persia 1919–27*

Year	Persians	Indians	Others	Europeans	Total
(a) Ābādān					
1919	806	2 499	38	36	3 379
1920	1 080	2 687	35	71	3 873
1921	1 608	3 313	51	99	5 071
1922	4 941	2 679	1 048	100	8 768
1923	7 336	2 654	379	220	10 589
1924	6 521	2 782	454	303	10 060
1925	6 862	3 001	4 405	402	14 670
1926	7 946	2 161	1 442	428	11 977
1927	10 171	2 062	1 273	527	14 033
(b) Fields					
1919	3 173	119	9	44	3 345
1920	2 788	323		81	3 192
1921	4 536	730		105	5 371
1922	7 632	807	212	218	8 869
1923	8 290	1 099	194	239	9 822
1924	8 617	1 155	117	282	10 171
1925	6 348	1 140	2 136	464	10 088
1926	6 033	842	2 727	431	10 033
1927	5 103	661	2 579	334	8 677
(c) Ahwāz and on the pipeline					
1919		23		37	60
1920	4 579	606		92	5 277
1921	2 865	666		67	3 598
1922	2 226	635	1 238	96	4 195
1923	2 472	682	27	90	3 271
1924	1 692	534	19	71	2 316
1925	1 647	494	191	73	2 405
1926	1 375	328	642	73	2 418
1927	1 522	281	1 120	70	2 993

Sources: Reports to Imperial Commissioner and BP 78/63/103–50.

Appendices

Appendix 10.2. *Schedule of test wells drilled in Persia 1901–32 (excluding drilling at Masjid-i-Suleimān and Haft Kel)*

Area (arranged from south to north)	Dates of drilling	No. of wells	Depths	Results	Estimated cost
1 Qishm	1916–24	2	3 305 ft & 1 661 ft	Oil obtained but not in commercial quantity.	£ 166 000
2 Kūh-i-Mund	1931–32	1	3 837 ft	Only very heavy oil obtained, and in small quantity.	95 000
3 Cheshmeh-i-Naft (Dasht-i-Oil)	1922–23	1	512 ft	Shallow well drilled near seepage. Oil obtained, but not in commercial quantity.	4 400
4 Sulabadār	1924	2	1 530 ft & 278 ft	First well obtained oil, but not in commercial quantity. Second well abandoned following results of first well.	
5 Chillingar	1923–25	2	2 360 ft & 2 484 ft	Oil obtained, but not in commercial quantity.	862 000
6 Gach-i-Garaghuli (Gach Sārān)	1926–30	5	959 ft to 4 521 ft	Oil obtained in one well, and anticipated that oil will be found in commercial quantity. Operations suspended 1930.	
7 Gach-i-Pokak	1930	1	954 ft	No oil obtained. Operations suspended 1930.	
8 Pāzanun	1926–30	1	5 320 ft	No oil obtained.	229 000
9 Āghā Jārī	1926–30	1	6 070 ft	No oil obtained.	
10 Marmatain	1907 1922–24 1930–31	8	787 ft to 2 876 ft	Oil obtained, but not in commercial quantity.	317 000
11 Kundak	1920–23	1	2 775 ft	No oil obtained.	24 000
12 Naft-i-Safid (White Oil Springs)	1914–19	2	2 095 ft & 2 195 ft	Oil obtained, but not in commercial quantity.	74 000

Appendices

Area (arranged from south to north)	Dates of drilling	No. of wells	Depths	Results	Estimated cost
13 Yamāhā	1926–28 1930–31	2	3 707 ft & 8 960 ft	No oil obtained. The second well is the deepest well drilled in Persia.	78 000
14 Sar-i-Naftak	1919–28	1	3 735 ft	No oil obtained.	121 000
15 Gach Khalaj	1921–23 1926–29	3	2 355 ft to 4 082 ft	No oil obtained.	
16 Pīrgāh	1927–29	1	4 266 ft	No oil obtained.	130 000
17 Zeloi	1926–29	3	3 297 ft to 5 655 ft	No oil obtained.	
18 Ahwāz	1913–15	1	3 317 ft	No oil obtained.	22 000
19 Dālparī	1923–24	2	1 085 ft & 1 152 ft	No oil obtained.	570 000
20 Dehlūran	1921–24	1	2 214 ft	No oil obtained.	
21 Naft Khana	1927–28	3	742 ft to 2 811 ft	One well obtained oil in commercial quantity. Operations suspended 1928 pending negotiations on unit operation of the field.	168 000
22 Naft-i-Shāh	1930–31	4	250 ft to 656 ft	Shallow wells drilled near seepages. Only traces of oil obtained.	17 000
23 Chiah Surkh	1903– 5 1912–13*	3	1 065 ft to 2 328 ft	Oil obtained, but not in commercial quantities.	125 000
TOTAL 23 Areas		51 Wells	(139 659 ft)		£3 002 400

Note: * During these periods the area was Persian territory. It was included under 'Transferred Territories' from 1914.
Source: BP H16/23.

Appendices

Appendix 10.3. *Sunbury research staff 1917–32*

Year	Technical*	Secretarial + administration**	Workshops and other supporting staff
1917	2	—	—
1918	2	—	NA***
1919 (End)	6	—	NA
1920 (End)	ca 9	1	NA
1924 (Mid)	ca 17	3	ca 21
1925 (Jan.)	20	3	23
1926 ,,	23	2	22
1927 ,,	31	2	19
1928 ,,	33	3	29
1929 ,,	32	3	32
1930 ,,	34	3	42
1931 ,,	48	4	45
1932 ,,	39	4	42
1932 (Dec.)	41	4	37

Notes: * Figures for Technical staff taken from 'Staff Returns' submitted by Sunbury to head office (From 1925 onwards.) The figures are indicative only, since Sunbury staff were commonly away at Refineries on Temporary Duty, and conversely, Abadan staff on leave in the UK were often posted to Sunbury for a short period.

** From June 1927, an 'Administrative Assistant' was appointed to Sunbury.

*** 'NA' denotes information not available.

Appendices

Appendix 11.1. Anglo-Persian Oil Company group sales 1920–32 – benzine

(long tons)

	1920–21	1921–22	1922–23	1923–24	1924–25	1925–26	1926–27	1927–28	1928	1929	1930	1931	1932
European sales													
Albania	—	—	—	—	—	—	—	—	—	515	22	—	—
Austria	—	—	—	—	98	476	370	363	323	294	251	77	51
Belgium	—	—	8 700	14 419	14 772	17 702	15 635	21 237	26 158	28 760	33 231	36 362	40 025
Denmark	—	—	2 225	11 880	14 678	16 323	21 325	26 932	27 174	30 725	36 748	40 611	34 126
France	—	40 026	55 483	83 358	94 662	121 406	128 478	143 361	159 349	186 850	200 680	213 554	252 388
Germany	—	—	—	—	—	—	9 026	130 143	153 904	180 123	185 172	163 202	146 228
Holland	—	—	—	—	—	—	—	—	436	921	—	—	736
Iceland	—	—	—	—	—	—	—	—	864	1 388	1 895	1 850	1 566
Ireland	—	—	—	na	8 827	10 079	10 453	12 947	14 603	15 911	15 482	16 886	—
Italy	—	—	—	—	—	1 262	2 916	6 439	6 113	6 980	76 326	85 333	77 603
Madeira	—	—	—	—	—	—	—	—	287	345	327	381	313
Norway	na	na	1 440	3 339	4 551	5 951	8 153	11 413	14 735	17 591	20 984	21 370	22 117
Saar[a]	—	—	—	—	—	—	—	373	2 009	2 752	3 254	3 221	3 088
SNOM[b]	—	—	—	—	—	—	—	—	16 104	5 729	—	—	—
Sweden	—	—	—	—	—	—	—	2 952	3 551	9 482	17 291	20 066	21 255
Switzerland	—	—	—	—	—	2 470	3 772	10 908	15 844	21 067	24 457	29 388	28 256
UK	91 593	166 729	214 616	256 021	277 042	314 704	352 505	612 141	556 539	629 988	611 896	654 238	764 131
Yugoslavia	—	—	—	—	—	—	—	—	190	428	326	—	—
Various bunkers	—	—	—	—	—	—	—	—	—	—	—	—	—
Total	91 593	206 755	282 464	369 017	414 630	490 373	552 633	979 209	998 853	1 139 849	1 228 342	1 286 559	1 391 883

663

Appendix 11.1. (cont.)

(long tons)

	1920–21	1921–22	1922–23	1923–24	1924–25	1925–26	1926–27	1927–28	1928	1929	1930	1931	1932
Extra-European sales													
Argentina	—	—	—	—	—	—	—	—	12 561	15 134	21 483	27 680	26 925
Australia	—	—	—	—	—	12 409	20 913	14 437	21 561	34 045	45 015	45 681	37 569
Burmah-Shell area	—	—	—	—	—	—	—	—	—	—	—	—	—
Consolidated area	—	—	—	—	—	—	—	—	2 990	75 519	81 334	75 519	74 790
Eastern installations	—	—	—	—	—	—	—	—	—	—	—	—	—
Iraq	11 235	7 790	8 251	6 295	6 785	8 468	7 914	8 956	10 547	12 007	12 117	12 975	14 837
Persia	—	—	—	—	1 178	1 699	3 679	4 006	5 652	8 931	11 867	13 428	16 158
Total	11 235	7 790	8 251	6 295	7 963	22 576	32 506	27 399	53 311	145 636	171 816	175 283	170 279
Other parties													
Admiralty	—	—	—	—	—	—	—	—	—	—	—	—	—
Asiatic Petroleum Co.	158 916*	124 622*	28 801*	150 406	259 702	376 786	251 453	305 468	343 411	203 196	246 658	358 926	362 577
Burmah Oil Co.	—	—	—	—	—	—	—	—	—	—	—	—	—
Total	158 916	124 622	28 801	150 406	259 702	376 786	251 453	305 468	343 411	203 196	246 658	358 926	362 577
Refineries													
Refinery bunkers	—	—	—	—	—	—	—	—	—	—	—	—	—
Works fuel	—	—	—	—	—	—	—	—	—	—	—	—	—
Total	—	—	—	—	—	—	—	—	—	—	—	—	—
Total sales	261 744	339 167	319 516	525 718	682 295	889 735	836 592	1 312 076	1 395 575	1 488 681	1 846 816	1 820 748	1 924 739

Notes: [a] Saarlandische 'Olex' Company
[b] Societa Nazionale Olii Mineralide Milano
* Estimated tonnage supplied

Source: BP 4K 7077

Appendix 11.2. Anglo-Persian Oil Company group sales 1920–32 – kerosine

(long tons)

	1920–21	1921–22	1922–23	1923–24	1924–25	1925–26	1926–27	1927–28	1928	1929	1930	1931	1932
European sales													
Albania	—	—	—	—	—	—	—	208	572	297	10	—	—
Austria	—	—	—	—	—	112	—	296	1 063	691	977	756	1 384
Belgium	—	—	6 264	8 716	8 438	12 909	11 787	10 457	10 818	10 806	10 120	8 018	7 316
Denmark	—	—	2 477	11 135	22 396	19 061	21 766	23 406	22 968	23 870	24 818	25 833	24 672
France	—	23 811	34 627	37 364	35 870	35 364	26 045	20 026	19 188	17 845	20 905	21 478	21 585
Germany	—	—	—	—	—	—	45 673	49 033	46 804	48 091	40 220	33 042	28 619
Holland	—	—	—	—	—	—	6 831	6 524	6 482	8 054	8 006	7 354	5 532
Iceland	—	—	—	—	—	—	—	628	2 498	2 083	1 999	1 666	1 441
Ireland	—	—	—	na	20 374	19 904	20 695	20 635	20 897	20 953	20 000	19 889	—
Italy	—	—	—	—	—	698	2 759	4 449	4 995	5 894	25 178	25 170	28 756
Madeira	na	—	—	—	—	—	—	82	73	93	107	158	145
Norway	—	na	1 472	4 121	5 124	6 628	7 339	8 106	8 196	8 305	8 385	8 182	7 428
Saar[a]	—	—	—	—	—	—	—	264	866	856	862	751	740
SNOM[b]	—	—	—	—	—	—	—	—	923	73	—	—	—
Sweden	—	—	—	—	—	—	—	298	313	673	1 229	2 195	3 664
Switzerland	—	—	—	—	—	1 140	2 759	3 554	4 089	4 179	3 908	3 942	4 355
UK	233 836	245 726	245 336	245 599	210 885	209 197	208 452	199 068	222 253	222 565	210 260	208 870	218 577
Yugoslavia	—	—	—	—	—	—	—	224	—	18	63	—	—
Various bunkers	—	—	—	—	—	—	—	—	—	—	—	—	—
Total	233 836	269 537	290 176	306 935	303 087	305 013	354 106	347 258	372 998	375 346	377 047	367 304	354 214

Appendix 11.2. (cont.)

(long tons)

	1920–21	1921–22	1922–23	1923–24	1924–25	1925–26	1926–27	1927–28	1928	1929	1930	1931	1932
Extra-European sales													
Argentina	—	—	—	—	—	—	—	7 579	9 027	12 850	12 390	8 808	7 644
Australia	—	—	—	—	—	4 224	5 881	8 322	7 238	6 220	6 479	7 022	7 978
Burmah-Shell area	—	—	—	—	—	—	—	—	80 725	90 926	79 353	47 798	36 528
Consolidated area	—	—	—	—	—	—	—	—	5 088	93 356	108 628	110 568	110 754
Eastern installations	—	—	—	—	—	—	—	—	—	—	—	—	—
Iraq	22 084	18 603	19 057	20 107	19 665	23 992	9 635	26 535	24 264	22 123	19 829	18 373	18 647
Persia	—	—	—	—	4 301	5 159	4 999	8 302	11 129	11 606	13 299	10 374	9 755
Total	22 084	18 603	19 057	20 107	23 966	33 375	20 515	50 738	137 471	237 081	239 978	202 943	191 306
Other parties													
Admiralty	—	—	—	—	—	—	—	—	—	—	—	—	—
Asiatic Petroleum Co.	—	—	—	—	—	94 398	—	52 030	29 941	—	—	—	—
Burmah Oil Co.	—	—	—	—	—	—	—	—	—	—	—	—	—
Total	—	—	—	—	—	94 398	—	52 030	29 941	—	—	—	—
Refineries													
Refinery bunkers	—	—	—	—	—	—	—	—	—	—	—	—	—
Works fuel	—	—	—	—	—	—	—	—	—	—	—	—	—
Total	—	—	—	—	—	—	—	—	—	—	—	—	—
Total sales	255 920	288 140	309 233	327 042	327 053	432 786	374 621	450 026	540 410	612 427	617 025	570 247	545 520

Notes: [a] Saarlandische 'Olex' Company
[b] Societa Nazionale Olii Mineralide Milano

Source: BP 4K 7077

Appendices

Appendix 11.3. *Anglo-Persian Oil Company group sales 1920–32 – fuel oil*

(long tons)

	1920–21	1921–22	1922–23	1923–24	1924–25	1925–26	1926–27	1927–28	1928	1929	1930	1931	1932
European sales													
Albania	—	—	—	—	—	—	—	—	—	—	—	—	—
Austria	—	—	—	—	2 797	4 224	4 171	4 573	5 238	5 462	6 044	3 952	473
Belgium	—	—	5 847	10 678	7 477	8 583	9 580	9 191	7 218	17 880	11 579	6 131	15 352
Denmark	—	—	5 471	4 743	7 608	17 218	27 716	16 792	3 736	15 514	16 552	1 416	24 023
France	—	11 760	85 461	90 639	92 082	151 952	172 417	125 875	123 925	153 271	197 775	193 039	223 994
Germany	—	—	—	—	—	—	—	3 170	21 985	5 898	6 418	4 829	5 105
Holland	—	—	—	—	—	—	—	—	—	—	—	—	—
Iceland	—	—	—	—	—	—	—	16	36	46	60	137	275
Ireland	—	—	—	na	359	369	430	526	699	522	475	661	—
Italy	—	—	—	—	9 040	19 672	44 810	45 997	35 178	53 611	69 300	38 372	76 087
Madeira	—	—	—	—	—	—	—	—	—	—	—	—	—
Norway	na	na	15 984	28 038	25 761	24 595	35 011	25 199	23 910	44 176	40 493	47 648	100 268
Saar[a]	—	—	—	—	—	—	—	—	—	—	—	—	—
SNOM[b]	—	—	—	—	—	—	—	—	—	—	—	—	—
Sweden	—	—	—	—	—	—	—	—	—	—	—	—	1 664
Switzerland	—	—	—	—	—	92	520	98	—	99	—	—	—
UK	128 027	279 867	288 797	406 355	357 188	456 769	672 644	521 671	493 651	552 122	520 757	462 366	448 117
Yugoslavia	—	—	—	9 357	—	—	—	—	—	—	—	—	—
Various bunkers	—	—	34 720	—	—	—	—	—	—	—	—	—	—
Total	128 027	291 627	436 280	549 810	502 312	683 474	967 299	753 108	715 576	848 601	869 451	758 551	895 358

Appendix 11.3. (*cont.*)

(long tons)

	1920–21	1921–22	1922–23	1923–24	1924–25	1925–26	1926–27	1927–28	1928	1929	1930	1931	1932
Extra-European sales													
Argentina	—	—	—	—	—	—	—	15 699	51 093	65 728	43 504	10 641	2 652
Australia	—	—	—	—	10 287	31 716	35 747	42 606	31 616	44 481	54 408	38 370	36 759
Burmah-Shell areas	—	—	—	—	—	—	—	114 010	307 903	260 547	244 364	237 644	247 012
Consolidated area	—	—	—	—	—	—	—	—	625 454	754 818	811 627	803 328	936 955
Eastern installations	—	—	419 482	593 372	681 770	767 559	967 764	887 348	31 127	37 980	37 292	33 987	24 633
Iraq	170 879	104 167	78 934	68 898	41 321	47 626	47 578	69 121	52 003	63 693	70 626	71 171	92 134
Persia	—	—	—	—	17 651	4 911	565	1 618	2 219	5 598	4 468	7 732	12 228
Total	170 879	104 167	498 416	662 270	751 029	851 812	1 051 654	1 130 402	1 101 415	1 232 845	1 266 289	1 202 873	1 352 373
Other parties													
Admiralty	*	*	434 493	473 393	509 817	483 454	492 235	509 357	512 804	556 558	621 118	472 935	559 819
Asiatic Petroleum Co.	*	*	*	—	38 411	54 835	13 431	15 073	54 689	160 467	132 957	7 868	31 009
Burmah Oil Co.	*	*	42 429	32 831	40 353	57 251	59 333	81 594	101 860	74 142	56 960	20 948	14 034
Total	—	—	476 922*	506 224*	588 581	595 540	564 999	606 024	669 353	791 167	811 035	501 751	604 862
Refineries													
Refinery bunkers	*	*	262 467	300 723	410 999	456 229	181 616	424 501	347 366	482 603	449 056	506 641	481 340
Works fuel	—	—	—	—	198 037	210 851	232 557	125 060	112 970	128 859	155 214	162 354	185 522
Total	627 826	806 735	262 467	300 723	609 036	667 080	414 173	549 561	460 336	611 462	604 270	668 995	666 862
Total sales	926 732	1 202 529	1 674 085	2 019 027*	2 450 958	2 797 906	2 998 125	3 039 095	2 946 680	3 484 075	3 551 045	3 132 170	3 519 455

Notes: ^a Saarlandische 'Olex' Company
^b Societa Nazionale Olii Mineralide Milano
* Allocation of supplies uncertain

Source: BP 4K 7077

Appendix 11.4. Anglo-Persian Oil Company group sales 1920–32 – gas oil

(long tons)

	1920–21	1921–22	1922–23	1923–24	1924–25	1925–26	1926–27	1927–28	1928	1929	1930	1931	1932
European sales													
Albania	—	—	—	—	—	—	—	—	—	—	—	—	—
Austria	—	—	—	—	—	—	—	—	—	249	1 580	1 231	894
Belgium	—	—	2 729	3 432	1 150	2 265	2 215	2 649	280	2 110	5 651	7 591	8 987
Denmark	—	—	3 574	8 294	8 744	4 311	3 472	3 723	78	5 030	4 313	3 567	4 287
France	—	—	2 404	303	3 914	6 682	9 485	15 795	4 414	3 940	47 473	52 673	59 727
Germany	—	—	—	—	—	—	23 247	34 576	3 743	40 115	31 803	36 717	32 916
Holland	—	—	—	—	—	—	7 748	5 835	23 981	36 504	3 369	6 193	5 943
Iceland	—	—	—	—	—	—	—	368	36 190	3 297	3 276	3 010	2 644
Ireland	—	—	—	na	227	257	220	189	4 142	2 378	487	151	—
Italy	—	—	—	—	—	—	813	595	1 502	793	770	225	—
Madeira									456	1 182			
Norway	na	na	2 329	6 958	12 365	13 794	15 259	15 408	811	16 408	19 365	19 647	21 113
Saar[a]	—	—	—	—	—	—	—	—	15 457	—	—	10	76
SNOM[b]	—	—	—	—	—	—	—	—	—	—	—	—	—
Sweden	—	—	—	—	—	—	—	—	—	164	606	2 202	1 094
Switzerland	—	—	—	—	—	—	—	1 960	29	1 600	3 166	8 416	13 415
UK	17 483	33 918	137 048	98 393	100 355	73 914	81 891	55 757	1 737	65 803	48 590	43 539	40 627
Yugoslavia	—	—	—	—	—	—	—	—	55 050	5	—	—	—
Various bunkers	—	—	—	—	—	—	—	—	—	—	—	—	—
Total	17 483	33 918	148 084	117 380	126 755	101 223	144 350	136 884	147 870	179 578	170 449	185 172	191 723

Appendix 11.4. (*cont.*)

(long tons)

	1920–21	1921–22	1922–23	1923–24	1924–25	1925–26	1926–27	1927–28	1928	1929	1930	1931	1932
Extra-European sales													
Argentina	—	—	—	—	—	—	—	1 381	5 997	7 771	8 910	7 823	4 496
Australia	—	—	—	—	—	—	—	—	—	—	—	—	—
Burmah-Shell area	—	—	—	—	—	—	—	—	—	—	—	—	6 600
Consolidated area	—	—	—	—	—	—	—	—	—	—	—	—	—
Eastern installation	—	—	—	—	—	—	—	—	—	—	—	—	8
Iraq	—	—	—	—	—	—	—	—	—	—	—	—	—
Persia	—	—	—	—	—	—	—	—	—	—	—	—	—
Total	—	—	—	—	—	—	—	1 381	5 997	7 771	8 910	7 823	11 104
Other parties													
Admiralty	—	—	—	—	—	—	—	—	—	—	—	—	—
Asiatic Petroleum Co.	—	—	—	—	—	—	—	—	—	—	—	—	—
Burmah Oil Co.	—	—	—	—	—	—	—	—	—	—	—	—	—
Total													
Refineries													
Refinery bunkers	—	—	—	—	—	—	—	—	—	—	—	—	—
Works fuel	—	—	—	—	—	—	—	—	—	—	—	—	—
Total													
Total sales	17 483	33 918	148 084	117 380	126 755	101 223	144 350	138 265	153 867	187 349	179 359	192 995	202 827

Notes: [a] Saarlandische 'Olex' Company
[b] Societa Nazionale Olii Mineralide Milano

Source: BP 4K 7077

Appendices

Appendix 11.5. *Anglo-Persian Oil Company group volume and proportions 1920–32 – benzine*

(long tons)

	Europe	%	Extra-European	%	Other parties	%	Refinery sales	%	Total
1920–21	91 593	35	11 235	4	158 916★	61	—	—	261 744★
1921–22	206 755	61	7 790	2	124 622★	37	—	—	339 167★
1922–23	282 464	88	8 251	3	28 801★	9	—	—	319 516★
1923–24	369 017	70	6 295	1	150 406	29	—	—	525 718
1924–25	414 630	61	7 963	1	259 702	38	—	—	682 295
1925–26	490 373	55	22 576	3	376 786	42	—	—	889 735
1926–27	552 633	66	32 506	4	251 453	30	—	—	836 592
1927–28	979 209	75	27 399	2	305 468	23	—	—	1 312 076
1928	998 853	72	53 311	4	343 411	24	—	—	1 395 575
1929	1 139 849	77	145 636	10	203 196	13	—	—	1 488 681
1930	1 228 842	75	171 816	10	246 658	15	—	—	1 646 816
1931	1 286 539	71	175 283	10	358 926	19	—	—	1 820 748
1932	1 391 883	72	170 279	9	362 577	19	—	—	1 924 739

Note: ★ missing data
Source: BP 4K 7077

Appendix 11.6. *Anglo-Persian Oil Company group volume and proportions 1920–32 – kerosine*

(long tons)

	Europe	%	Extra-European	%	Other parties	%	Refinery sales	%	Total
1920–21	233 836	91	22 084	9	—	—	—	—	255 920
1921–22	269 537	94	18 603	6	—	—	—	—	288 140
1922–23	290 176	94	19 057	6	—	—	—	—	309 233
1923–24	306 935	94	20 107	6	—	—	—	—	327 042
1924–25	303 087	93	23 966	7	—	—	—	—	327 053
1925–26	305 013	70	33 375	8	94 398	22	—	—	432 786
1926–27	354 106	95	20 515	5	—	—	—	—	374 621
1927–28	347 258	77	50 738	11	52 030	12	—	—	450 026
1928	372 998	69	137 471	25	29 941	6	—	—	540 410
1929	375 346	61	237 081	39	—	—	—	—	612 427
1930	377 047	61	239 978	39	—	—	—	—	617 025
1931	367 304	64	202 943	36	—	—	—	—	570 247
1932	354 214	65	191 306	35	—	—	—	—	545 520

Source: BP 4K 7077

Appendices

Appendix 11.7. Anglo-Persian Oil Company group volume and proportions 1920–32 – fuel oil

(long tons)

	Europe	%	Extra-European	%	Other parties	%	Refinery sales	%	Total
1920–21	128 027	14	170 879	18	★	—	627 826	68	926 732★
1921–22	291 627	24	104 167	9	★	—	806 735	67	1 202 529★
1922–23	436 280	26	498 416	30	476 922★	28	262 467	16	1 674 085★
1923–24	549 810	27	662 270	33	506 224★	25	300 723	15	2 019 027★
1924–25	502 312	20	751 029	31	588 581	24	609 036	25	2 450 958
1925–26	683 474	24	851 812	30	595 540	21	667 080	25	2 797 906
1926–27	967 299	32	1 051 654	35	564 999	19	414 173	14	2 998 125
1927–28	753 108	25	1 130 402	37	606 024	20	549 561	18	3 039 095
1928	715 576	24	1 101 415	37	669 353	23	460 336	16	2 946 680
1929	848 601	24	1 232 845	35	791 167	23	611 462	18	3 484 075
1930	869 451	24	1 266 289	36	811 035	23	604 270	17	3 551 045
1931	758 551	24	1 202 873	38	501 751	16	668 995	22	3 132 170
1932	895 358	25	1 352 373	38	604 862	17	666 862	20	3 519 455

Note: ★ missing data
Source: BP 4K 7077

Appendix 11.8. Anglo-Persian Oil Company group volume and proportions 1920–32 – gas oil

(long tons)

	Europe	%	Extra-European	%	Other parties	%	Refinery sales	%	Total
1920–21	17 483	100	—	—	—	—	—	—	17 483
1921–22	33 918	100	—	—	—	—	—	—	33 918
1922–23	148 084	100	—	—	—	—	—	—	148 084
1923–24	117 380	100	—	—	—	—	—	—	117 380
1924–25	126 755	100	—	—	—	—	—	—	126 755
1925–26	101 223	100	—	—	—	—	—	—	101 223
1926–27	144 350	100	—	—	—	—	—	—	144 350
1927–28	136 884	99	1 381	1	—	—	—	—	138 265
1928	147 870	96	5 997	4	—	—	—	—	153 867
1929	179 578	96	7 771	4	—	—	—	—	187 349
1930	170 449	95	8 910	5	—	—	—	—	179 359
1931	185 172	96	7 823	4	—	—	—	—	192 995
1932	191 723	95	11 104	5	—	—	—	—	202 827

Source: BP 4K 7077

Appendices

Appendix 11.9. *Anglo-Persian Oil Company group refinery throughputs 1920–32 – benzine* (long tons 000s)

	Ābādān	Llandarcy once-run distillate	Llandarcy crude	Uphall	Grangemouth	Laverton	Douai	Total throughputs
1920–21	333	—	—	—	—	—	—	333
1921–22	394	—	50	—	—	—	—	444
1922–23	349	—	108	—	—	—	—	457
1923–24	223	—	(147)[a]	—	—	—	—	(370)
1924–25	310	135	186	—	58	7	40	736
1925–26	363	152	184	17	69	13	46	844
1926–27	409	161	194	24	82	22	44	936
1927–28	531	184	199	32	83	13	35	1 077
1928	694	33	113	23	58	11	23	955
1929	1 053	—	140	33	88	18	38	1 370
1930	1 131	—	148	32	91	18	40	1 460
1931	1 166	—	128	26	107	17	45	1 489
1932	1 066	—	80	29	94	15	47	1 331

Note: [a] estimated figure: interpolated figure as substitute for missing data.
Source: BP 4K 7077

Appendix 11.10. *Anglo-Persian Oil Company group refinery throughputs 1920–32 – kerosine* (long tons 000s)

	Ābādān	Llandarcy once-run distillate	Llandarcy crude	Uphall	Grangemouth	Laverton	Douai	Total throughputs
1920–21	134	—	—	—	—	—	—	134
1921–22	163	—	21	—	—	—	—	184
1922–23	142	—	65	—	—	—	—	207
1923–24	125	—	(79)[a]	—	—	—	—	(204)
1924–25	181	108	93	—	31	3	22	438
1925–26	197	82	66	10	32	5	20	412
1926–27	192	75	73	11	33	8	22	414
1927–28	228	78	80	13	39	5	18	461
1928	289	97	72	11	36	5	16	526
1929	359	60	94	12	50	8	23	606
1930	456	—	89	12	41	7	27	632
1931	370	—	81	13	35	6	23	528
1932	380	—	72	10	30	5	21	518

Note: [a] estimated figure: interpolated figure as substitute for missing data
Source: BP 4K 7077

Appendices

Appendix 11.11. *Anglo-Persian Oil Company group refinery throughputs 1920–32 – gas oil and fuel oil*

(long tons 000s)

	Ābādān	Llandarcy once-run distillate	Llandarcy crude	Uphall	Grange-mouth	Laverton	Douai	Total through-puts
1920–21	970	—	—	—	—	—	—	970
1921–22	1 138	—	238	—	—	—	—	1 376
1922–23	1 217	—	451	—	—	—	—	1 668
1923–24	1 334	—	(532)[a]	na	—	—	—	(1 866)
1924–25	1 920	1	614	na	170	24	40	2 769
1925–26	1 970	1	557	51	210	37	41	2 867
1926–27	2 060	—	568	64	233	43	41	3 009
1927–28	2 137	3	587	81	251	38	64	3 161
1928	1 876	6	348	66	192	29	55	2 572
1929	2 676	4	423	91	260	38	89	3 581
1930	2 902	na	410	93	268	57	104	3 834
1931	2 631	—	240	63	223	36	108	3 301
1932	2 429	—	155	85	252	37	110	3 068

Note: [a] estimated figure: interpolated figure as substitute for missing data
Source: BP 4K 7077

Appendix 11.13. *World tonnage and proportion of coal and oil used in vessels 1914–32*

(100 tons and over)

	Coal tons gross	%	Oil tons gross	%
1914	43 859 381	96.6	1 544 496	3.4
1922	45 338 327	73.9	16 004 625	26.1
1923	44 876 570	71.9	17 458 803	28.1
1924	42 384 270	68.9	19 129 870	31.1
1925	41 862 181	67.1	20 578 195	32.9
1926	40 925 114	65.3	21 736 823	34.7
1927	40 514 719	64.0	22 752 582	36.0
1928	40 674 097	62.4	24 483 316	37.6
1924	40 358 396	60.8	26 048 997	39.2
1930	40 069 679	58.9	27 954 125	41.1
1931	39 289 061	57.2	29 423 740	42.8
1932	38 194 758	55.9	30 173 383	44.1

Source: Lloyds Register of Shipping, statistical tables and annual reports

Appendix 11.12. United Kingdom fuel oil and coal prices 1918–32

	Fuel oil		Average declared value at pits per ton (f.o.b.) of coal exported at certain ports			Average declared value per ton (f.o.b.) of coal exported	Average selling value per ton of coal raised at pit	Ascertained selling value per ton of coal at pits in S. Wales and Monmouthshire
	Domestic	Bunkers	A	B	C			
1918	280s	—	29s 7d	28s 2d	29s 11d	30s 3d	20s 11d	—
1919	154s	—	39s 11d	43s 1d	48s 4d	47s 3d	27s 4d	—
1920	218s	225s	77s 3d	83s 4d	82s 9d	79s 11d	34s 7d	—
1921	108s 9d	—	33s 7d	36s 6d	34s 3d	34s 10d	26s 2d	24s 9d
1922	70s 6d	64s 9d	23s 2d	23s 9d	21s	22s 7d	17s 8d	20s 4¾d
1923	70s	68s	25s 11d	26s 3d	24s 7d	25s 2d	18s 10d	21s 9¾d
1924	82s	82s	24s 10d	24s 9d	21s 11d	23s 5d	18s 10d	21s 2d
1925	81s 3d	75s	22s 1d	22s 6d	17s 1d	19s 10d	16s 4d	18s 11¾d
1926	77s 6d	72s 6d	19s 2d	19s 11d	15s 9d	18s 7d	19s 7d	16s 7¼d
1927	79s	79s	19s 6d	19s 7d	15s 7d	17s 10d	14s 7d	15s 8¼d
1928	71s	68s	16s 10d	16s 11d	13s 7d	15s 7d	12s 10d	14s 0¾d
1929	67s 6d	67s 6d	17s 1d	17s 6d	14s 2d	16s 2d	13s 5d	14s 11¾d
1930	67s 6d	67s 6d	17s 6d	18s	14s 8d	16s 8d	13s 7d	15s 6d
1931	62s 6d	67s 6d	17s 3d	17s 7d	13s 6d	16s 3d	13s 6d	15s 2¾d
1932	60s	—	17s 3d	17s 5d	13s 1d	16s 3d	13s 3d	15s 6¾d

A – Newport   B – Cardiff   C – Newcastle

The fuel oil prices given are average annual prices per ton on the London oil market; in bulk, ex-wharf or ex-ocean installation. For domestic delivery, up to 1928 add 10s and thereafter 7s 6d. Prices at Manchester were some 5s higher.

Source: *Petroleum Review*. Coal prices come from the *Colliery Year Book & Coal Trades Directory*, 1933 and 1962.

Appendices

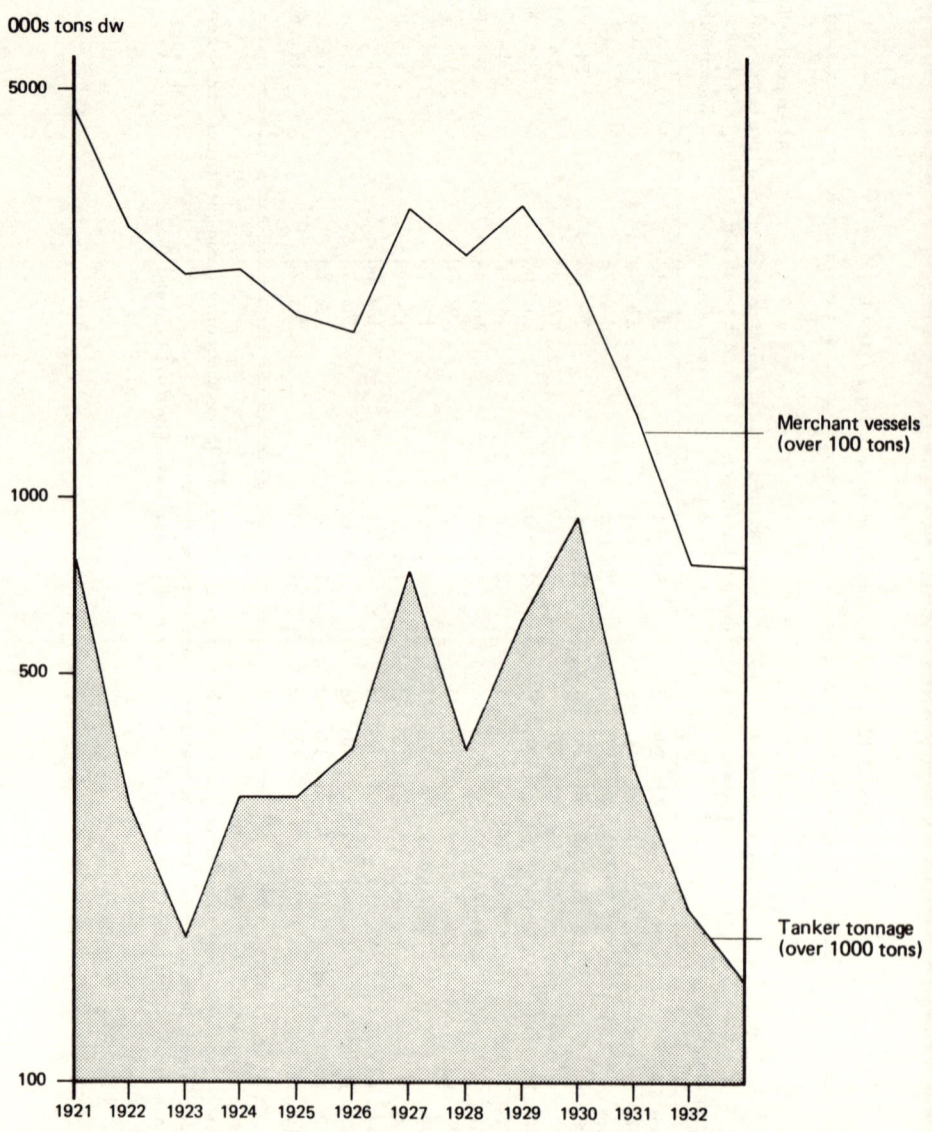

(a)

Appendix 11.14 Tanker tonnage (over 1000 tons) and merchant vessels (over 100 tons) under construction 1921–32 (a) World (b) United Kingdom

Source: *Petroleum Times*, 17 June 1949, p. 445 from the quarterly Lloyd's Register shipping returns

Appendices

(b)

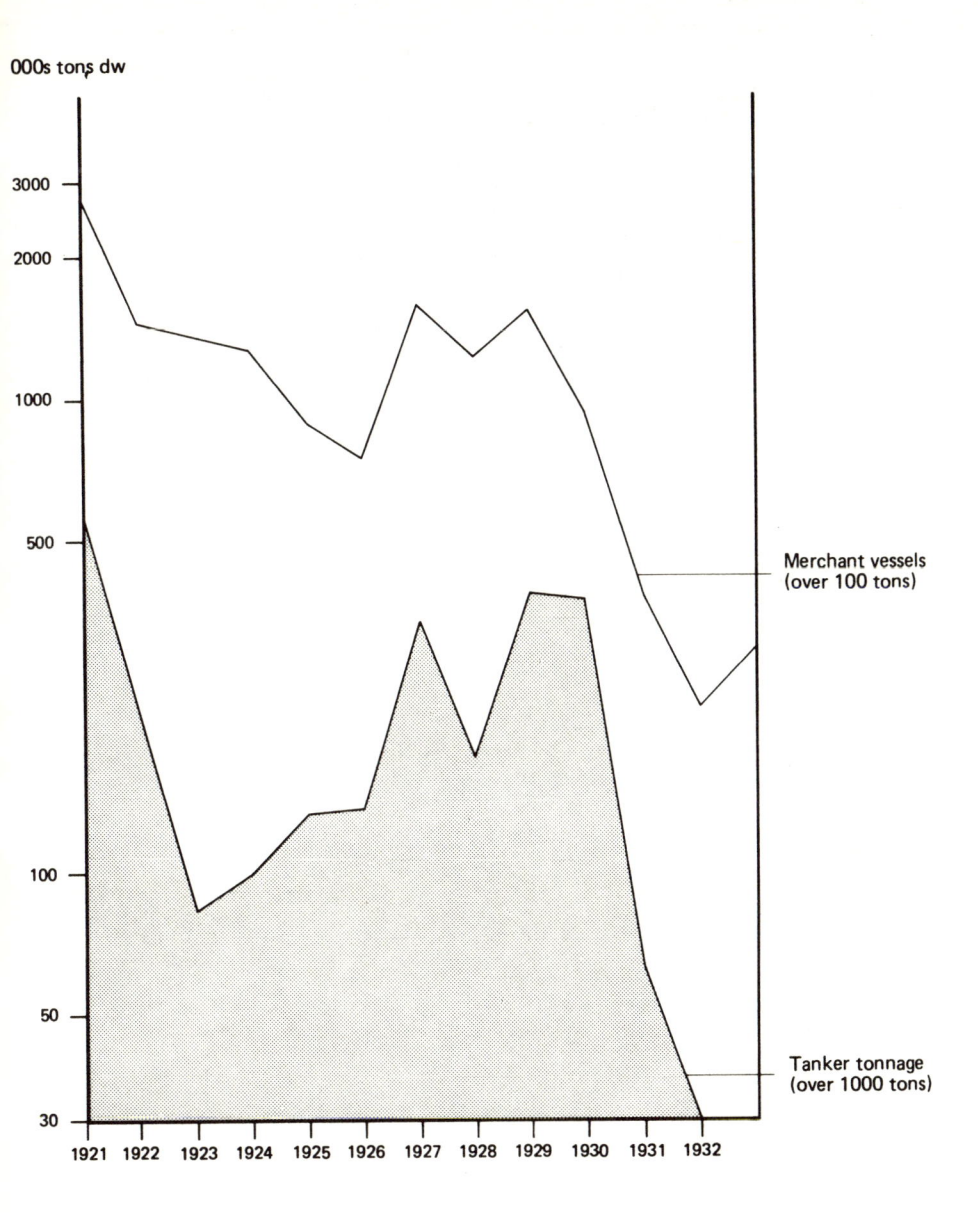

000s tons dw

- 3000
- 2000
- 1000
- 500
- 100
- 50
- 30

1921 1922 1923 1924 1925 1926 1927 1928 1929 1930 1931 1932

Merchant vessels (over 100 tons)

Tanker tonnage (over 1000 tons)

Appendices

Appendix 11.15. The Anglo-Persian Oil Company overseas refinery throughput 1924–32

(Long tons 000s)

	Through-put	Benzine	%	Kerosine	%	Fuel and gas oils	%	Other products	%	Loss + gas	%
(a) Courchelettes Refinery (Douai)											
1924–25	111	40	36	22	20	40	36	5	4	4	4
1925–26	112	46	41	20	18	41	36	1	1	4	4
1926–27	112	44	39	22	20	41	36	1	1	4	4
1927–28	132	35	27	18	14	64	48	8	6	7	5
1928	117	23	20	16	14	55	47	17	14	6	5
1929	179	38	21	23	13	89	50	20	11	9	5
1930	202	40	20	27	13	104	52	22	11	9	4
1931	205	45	22	23	11	108	53	23	11	6	3
1932	203	47	23	21	10	110	54	18	10	6	3

Source: BP AC 21

	Through-put	Production Benzine	%	Kerosine	%	Fuel oil	%	Semi-refined oils	%	Loss	%
(b) Alwand Refinery											
1927	*38	6	16	7	18	23	59	—	—	2	6
1928 (9 mo.)	68	11	16	12	18	40	59	2	3	3	4
1929	73	13	18	12	16	43	59	2	3	3	4
1930	78	13	16	14	18	46	59	2	3	3	4
1931	76	12	16	13	17	45	59	3	4	3	4
1932	89	11	12	15	17	55	62	5	6	3	3

Note: * June–December 1927
Source: BP 76/65/146–206

	Through-put	Benzine	%	Kerosine	%	Production Fuel oil	%	Loss	%	Refinery fuel	%
(c) Commonwealth Oil Refineries Laverton											
1924–25	37	7	19	3	8	24	65	2	5	*1	3
1925–26	57	13	22	5	9	37	65	2	4	—	—
1926–27	76	22	29	8	11	43	56	3	4	—	—
1927–28	58	13	22	5	9	38	66	2	3	—	—
1928	47	11	23	5	11	29	62	2	4	—	—
1929	67	18	27	8	12	38	57	3	4	—	—
1930	89	18	21	7	8	57	64	3	3	4	4
1931	65	17	26	6	9	36	55	2	3	4	6
1932	63	15	24	5	8	37	59	2	3	4	6

Note: * once-run distillate
Source: BP AC 21

Appendix 11.16. *The Anglo-Persian Oil Company United Kingdom refinery throughput 1921–32*

(long tons 000s)

	Throughput	Benzine	%	Kerosine	%	Fuel and gas oil	%	Other products	%	Gas	%	Loss	%
(a) Llandarcy refinery													
1921–22	383	50	13	21	5	238	62	*59	15	—	—	15	4
1922–23	730	108	15	65	9	451	62	*64	8	—	—	42	6
1923–24	865	na	—	na	—	na	—	na	—	—	—	na	—
1924–25	‡920	186	20	93	10	614	67	2	—	—	—	25	3
1925–26	835	184	22	66	8	557	67	5	—	—	—	23	3
1926–27	865	194	22	73	8	568	67	7	—	—	—	23	3
1927–28	916	199	22	80	9	587	64	19	2	—	—	31	3
1928	581	113	19	72	12	348	60	†32	6	—	—	16	3
1929	701	140	20	94	13	423	60	24	4	2	—	18	3
1930	693	148	21	89	13	410	59	28	4	2	—	16	3
1931	503	128	25	81	16	240	48	39	8	1	—	14	3
1932	375	80	21	72	19	155	42	52	14	1	—	15	4

Notes: * once-run distillate
† includes 'process oils' 11 694 tons, 2%
‡ production includes make ex stocks of 'process oils' as 4174 tons, 0.5%
na not available

679

Appendices

(b) Grangemouth refinery

	Throughput	Benzine	%	Kerosine	%	Fuel and gas oil	%	Loss	%
1924–25	265	58	22	31	12	170	64	6	2
1925–26	317	69	22	32	10	210	66	6	2
1926–27	355	82	23	33	9	233	66	7	2
1927–28	378	83	22	39	10	251	67	5	1
1928	290	58	20	36	13	192	66	4	1
1929	405	88	22	50	12	260	64	7	2
1930	406	91	22	41	10	268	66	6	2
1931	370	107	29	35	9	223	60	5	2
1932	381	94	25	30	8	252	66	5	1

Source: BP AC 21

Appendices

Appendix 11.17. *United Kingdom petroleum imports 1918–32*

(long tons, 000s)

	1918	1919	1920	1921
Crude oil	—	29.8	16.7	405.8
Motor spirit*	643.2	662.6	689.7	837.0
Other spirit	—	1.6	—	0.1
Kerosine	528.6	547.8	574.8	533.4
Gas oil	147.1	113.8	214.3	307.3
Fuel and diesel oil	3 554.5	1 119.9	1 391.1	2 125.1
Lubricating oil	410.7	264.4	423.7	203.9
Paraffin wax	—	—	87.6	39.2
Other	—	1.9	0.3	0.2
Total	5 284.1	2 741.8	3 398.2	4 452.0

	1922	1923	1924	1925
Crude oil	868.5	1 338.5	1 857.5	2 276.3
Motor spirit*	1 037.3	1 090.8	1 407.7	1 349.5
Other spirit	—	7.8	10.2	20.2
Kerosine	544.8	514.7	445.3	505.9
Gas oil	280.6	283.0	271.6	290.6
Fuel and diesel oil	1 570.5	1 454.9	1 542.3	1 338.0
Lubricating oil	277.8	328.9	407.0	337.4
Paraffin wax	48.5	57.3	68.3	62.0
Other	0.1	0.3	5.1	0.7
Total	4 628.1	5 076.2	6 015.0	6 180.6

	1926	1927	1928	1929
Crude oil	2 149.8	2 659.2	1 992.0	1 949.4
Motor spirit*	1 873.6	1 794.0	2 449.1	2 700.3
Other spirit	9.7	22.6	40.1	82.4
Kerosine	721.3	764.6	677.8	910.8
Gas oil	471.3	384.0	471.9	455.8
Fuel and diesel oil	1 594.8	1 757.7	1 803.5	1 622.4
Lubricating oil	367.3	366.4	421.7	392.1
Paraffin wax	63.9	76.4	78.6	75.0
Other	1.4	0.9	0.5	2.4
Total	7 253.1	7 825.8	7 935.2	8 190.6

	1930	1931	1932
Crude oil	1 843.9	1 377.5	1 474.0
Motor spirit*	3 182.0	3 017.3	3 237.2
Other spirit	61.0	60.4	49.7
Kerosine	877.8	967.7	774.0
Gas oil	523.3	340.2	388.5
Fuel and diesel oil	1 964.4	1 943.2	1 973.8
Lubricating oil	407.8	390.1	345.2
Paraffin wax	71.0	65.6	59.6
Other	0.9	0.8	2.6
Total	8 932.1	8 162.8	8 304.6

Note: * includes aviation spirit
Source: Ministry of Fuel and Power, Statistical Digest, 1950. Conversion factors for 1918 and 1919: crude, 253 imperial gallons per long ton; motor spirit, 300; kerosine, 280; other spirit, 300; gas oil, 264; fuel oil, 237; lubricating oil, 249.

Appendices

Appendix 11.18. *London petrol prices retail per gallon (first grade) 1918–32*

1918	1 May	3s 8½d	
	2 December	3s 6½d	
1919	1 January	3s 3d	
	19 May	3s 0½d	
1920	4 February	3s 8½d	
	30 August	4s 3½d	First ex-pump prices. Prices henceforth are ex-pumps
	11 October	4s 0½d	
1921	1 January	3s 5½d	'Consumers Tax' removed
	28 May	2s 11½d	
	18 August	2s 5½d	
1922	26 September	2s 0d	
1923	19 July	1s 8½d	
	25 September	1s 6½d	
1924	2 February	1s 11d	
	4 September	1s 7½d	
	16 September	1s 6½d	
1926	26 February	1s 7½d	
	1 November	1s 6d	
	20 December	1s 5½d	
1927	16 March	1s 3½d	
	4 April	1s 2½d	
	13 August	1s 1½d	
1928	1 April	1s 0½d	
	28 April	1s 4¾d	Duty of 4d/gal. imposed on light hydrocarbon oils
1929	1 March	1s 7d	
	1 November	1s 6½d	
1930	23 September	1s 4½d	
1931	3 March	1s 2½d	
	28 April	1s 4½d	Duty raised from 4d to 6d/gal.
	22 May	1s 3½d	
	18 July	1s 2½d	
	11 September	1s 4½d	Duty raised from 6d to 8d/gal. in 'Emergency Budget'
1932	14 September	1s 7½d	

Source: Institute of Petroleum: from *Petroleum Review* and *Petroleum Times*

Appendix 11.19. *United Kingdom inland consumption of petroleum products 1900–32*

(long tons)

Year	Motor aviation and industrial spirit	Kerosene (burning oil and vaporizing oil)	Derv fuel[a]	Gas/diesel and fuel oils[b] (Inland Trade)	Lubricating oils	Bitumen	Other products[c]	Total
1900	—	870 000	—	—	165 000	—	—	1 035 000
1910	190 000	615 000	—	356 000	239 000	—	1 000	1 401 000
1921	850 000	536 000	—	726 000	342 000	44 000	88 000	2 586 000
1922	1 040 000	539 000	—	805 000	346 000	67 000	91 000	2 888 000
1923	1 207 000	572 000	—	924 000	333 000	146 000	95 000	3 277 000
1924	1 563 000	558 000	—	941 000	395 000	194 000	97 000	3 748 000
1925	1 765 000	683 000	—	956 000	405 000	200 000	103 000	4 112 000
1926	2 070 000	684 000	—	1 844 000	385 000	238 000	106 000	5 327 000
1927	2 304 000	744 000	—	1 125 000	430 000	282 000	109 000	4 994 000
1928	2 702 000	691 000	—	1 122 000	455 000	335 000	115 000	5 420 000
1929	2 971 000	722 000	—	1 243 000	471 000	353 000	108 000	5 868 000
1930	3 324 000	676 000	—	1 266 000	472 000	372 000	107 000	6 217 000
1931	3 468 000	707 000	3 000	1 335 000	453 000	400 000	107 000	6 473 000
1932	3 586 000	722 000	10 000	1 441 000	412 000	396 000	104 000	6 671 000

Notes: [a] Derv fuel is fuel used for diesel-engined road vehicles. Derv fuel consumption for 1928, 1929 and 1930 was 100 tons, 100 tons and 600 tons, respectively
[b] Figures for gas, diesel and fuel oils include refinery consumption and an allowance for tar oils handled by the petroleum industry
[c] Other products include white spirit, liquid gases

Sources:
(a) 1900–1932 estimated
(b) A.L. King, 'Statistics relating to the Petroleum Industry, with particular reference to the UK register', in *Journal of the Royal Statistical Society*, Series A (General), vol. CXV, part IV, 1952

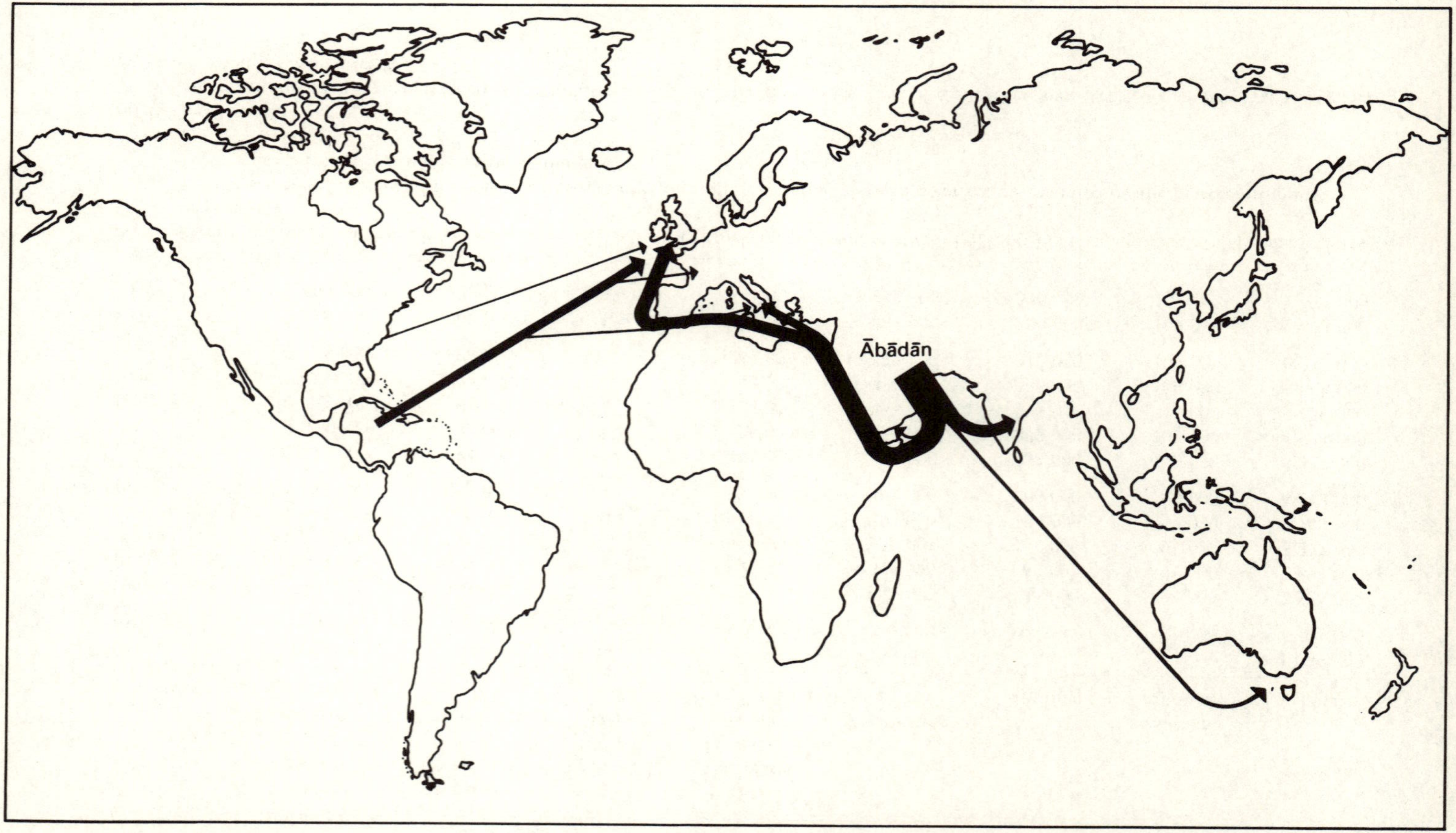

Appendix 11.20 British Tanker Company cargo movements in owned and period chartered tonnage 1921
Source: British Tanker Company vessel movement books.

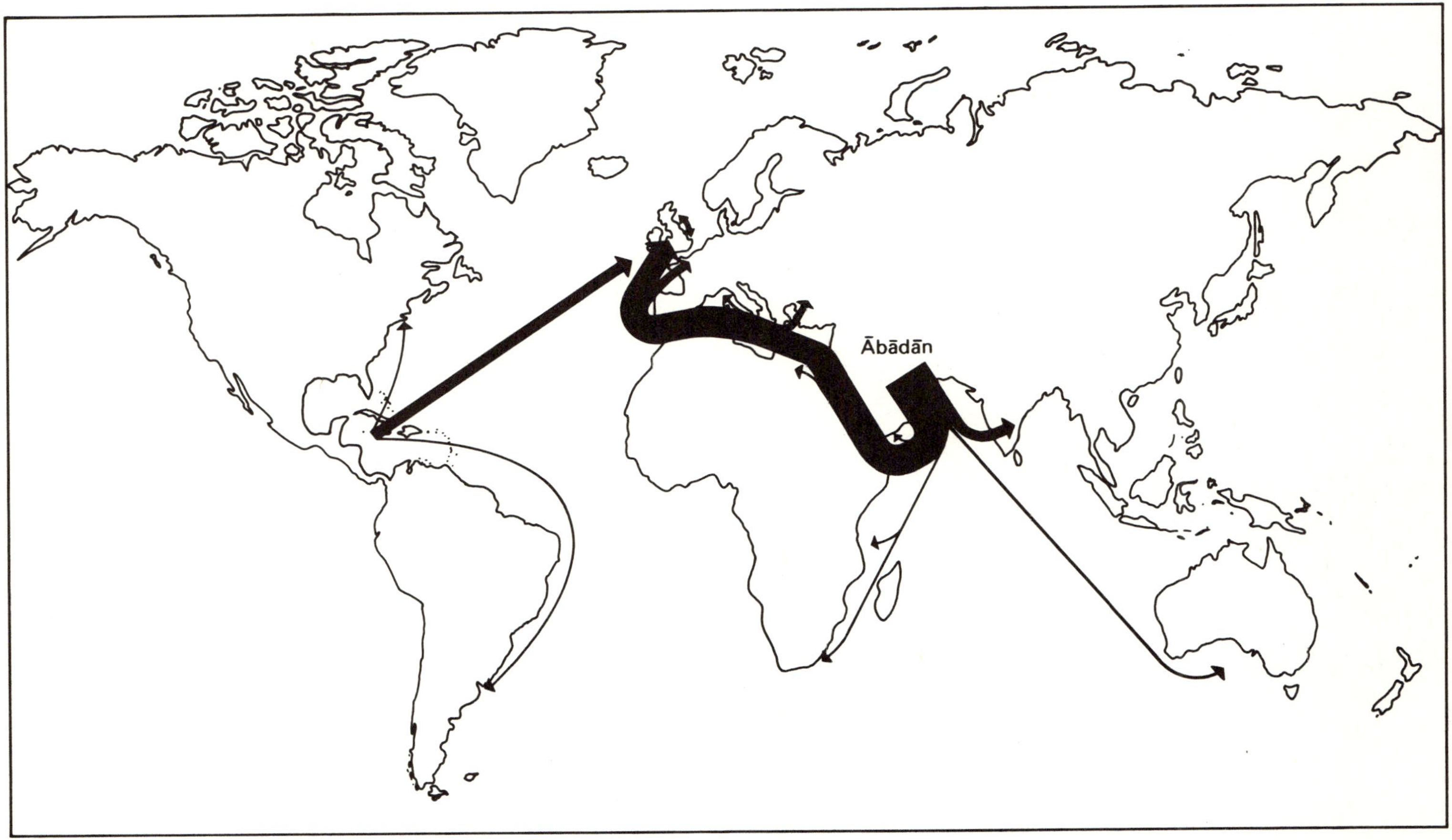

Appendix 11.21 British Tanker Company cargo movements in owned and period chartered tonnage 1928
Source: British Tanker Company vessel movement books

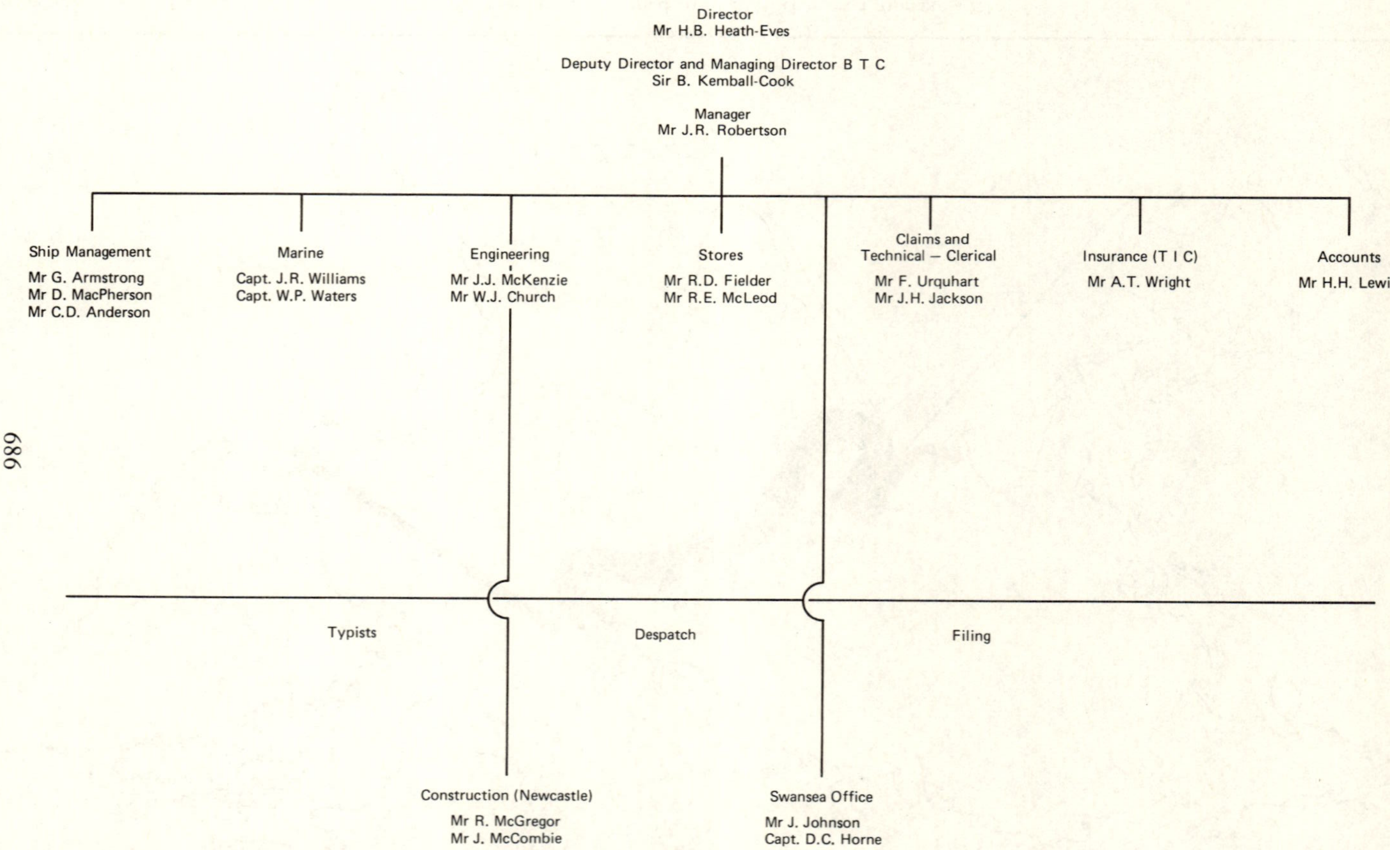

Appendices

Director
Mr H.B. Heath-Eves

Deputy Director and Managing Director B T C
Sir B. Kemball-Cook

Manager
Mr J.R. Robertson

Ship Management	Marine	Engineering	Stores	Claims and Technical – Clerical	Insurance (T I C)	Accounts
Mr G. Armstrong	Capt. J.R. Williams	Mr J.J. McKenzie	Mr R.D. Fielder	Mr F. Urquhart	Mr A.T. Wright	Mr H.H. Lewis
Mr D. MacPherson	Capt. W.P. Waters	Mr W.J. Church	Mr R.E. McLeod	Mr J.H. Jackson		
Mr C.D. Anderson						

Typists — Construction (Newcastle) — Despatch — Swansea Office — Filing

Construction (Newcastle)
Mr R. McGregor
Mr J. McCombie

Swansea Office
Mr J. Johnson
Capt. D.C. Horne

Appendix 11.22 Shipping administration of the British Tanker Company 1930
Source: BP H12/10

Appendices

Appendix C.1. *World energy consumption in selected countries, 1925*

(in 000s metric tons of coal equivalents)

	1 Total energy consumed	2 % of world total consumption	3 Consumption per capita (kgs)	4 Liquid fuel consumption (coal equivalents)	5 % of world total liquid fuel consumption	6 % of liquid fuel to total energy consumed (% of 4 to 1)
USA	717 714	48.3	6 196	137 615	70.0	19.2
UK	182 279	12.3	4 037	6 842	3.5	3.8
Germany	161 689	10.9	2 560	1 764	0.9	1.1
France	75 518	5.1	1 873	2 790	1.4	3.7
Japan	30 483	2.1	515	1 340	0.7	4.4
Canada	31 139	2.1	3 258	3 905	2.0	12.5
USSR	25 320	1.7	165	8 669	4.4	34.2
Poland	22 625	1.5	773	806	0.4	3.6
Czechoslovakia	22 263	1.5	1 645	306	0.1	1.4
India	19 036	1.3	57	2 814	1.4	14.8
Italy	12 944	0.9	336	1 190	0.6	9.2
Other	183 523	12.3	—	28 699	14.6	—
Total	1 484 533			196 740		

Source: based on Joel Darmstadter, et al, *Energy in the World Economy, A Statistical Review of Trends in Output, Trade and Consumption since 1925* (Baltimore and London, 1971) Table xi, p. 103

BIOGRAPHICAL DETAILS OF IMPORTANT PERSONALITIES

'Alā, Mīrzā Husayn Khān (1884–1964). Educated at Westminster School. Delegate to the Paris Peace Conference, 1919. Persian Minister in Washington, 1921–5. Minister of Public Works, May 1927. Persian Minister to Paris, 1929.

Amery, Rt. Hon. Leopold Stennett (1873–1955). Assistant secretary, War Cabinet and Imperial War Cabinet, 1917. First Lord of the Admiralty, 1922–24. Secretary of State for the Colonies, 1924–1929.

Amīn al-Sultān (d. 1907). Minister of Court and Chief of Customs, 1883. Prime Minister, 1885 and 1896. Left Persia, 1903 on world tour. Reappointed Prime Minister, 1907. Assassinated 1907.

Armitage-Smith, Sir Sydney (1876–1932). Private secretary to the Chancellor of the Exchequer, 1908. Represented HM Treasury at the Paris Peace Conference, 1919. Financial adviser to the Persian Government, 1920–21. Secretary General, Reparations Commission, 1924–30.

Asquith, Herbert Henry; 1st Earl of Oxford and Asquith (1852–1928). Chancellor of the Exchequer, 1905–08. Prime Minister, 1908–16.

Baldwin, Stanley; 1st Earl of Bewdley (1867–1947). Financial Secretary to the Treasury, 1917–21. President of the Board of Trade, 1921–22. Chancellor of the Exchequer, 1922–23. Prime Minister, 1923–24 and 1924–29.

Balfour, Arthur James; 1st Earl (1848–1930). Prime Minister, 1902–05. First Lord of the Treasury and Leader of the House of Commons, 1895–1906. First Lord of the Admiralty, 1915–16. Foreign Secretary, 1916–19. Head of British Mission to Washington Conference, 1921–22.

Barclay, Sir George (1862–1921). First Secretary, Tokyo, 1902–05. Councillor, Constantinople, 1905–06. British Minister, Tehrān, 1908–12.

Barnes, Sir Hugh (1853–1940). Lt Governor of Burmah, 1903–05. Council of India, 1905–13. Director, Imperial Bank of Persia; chairman, 1916–37. Director, APOC, 1909–40.

Barstow, Sir George Lewis (1874–1966). Controller of Supply Services, HM Treasury, 1919–27. Director, Prudential Assurance Company Ltd., 1928; chairman, 1941. Government director, APOC, 1927–46.

Bedford, A. Cotton (1862–1925). Director, Standard Oil Company, 1907–11. A vice-president, Standard Oil (NJ), 1911–16; chairman, 1917–25. Chairman, Petroleum Committee of National Defence, 1917.

Bérenger, Senator Henri (1867–1952). Président du Comité Général du Pétrole, 1917. Member, Inter-Allied Petroleum Committee, 1918. Commissaire-Général aux Essence et Combustibles, 1918–20.

Black, Sir Frederick (1863–1930). Director of Naval Stores, 1903–6. Director of Navy Contracts, 1906–14 and 1918–19. Director-General of Munitions

Biographical Details of Important Personalities

Supply, 1915–18. Acting chairman, British War Mission to USA, 1917–18. Government director, APOC, February–June 1919; director, 1919–23.

Bradbury, John Swanswick; 1st Baron of Winsford (1872–1950). Insurance Commissioner, 1911–13. Joint permanent secretary, H.M. Treasury, 1913–19. Delegate to Reparation Commission, Paris, 1919–25. Government director, APOC, 1925–27.

Braithwaite, W.D. (d. 1944). Shaw, Wallace and Co., India, 1902. Director, British Petroleum Co., 1917. Joint deputy-director of the distribution department, APOC, 1927–29.

Brown, Harold (1876–1949). Senior partner, Linklaters and Paines, solicitors to APOC, from 1919.

Burton, Michael Arthur Bass; 1st Viscount (1837–1909). Director, Bass and Co. Ltd, and South-Eastern Railway Co. Ltd. Friend and associate of W.K. D'Arcy.

Cadman, Sir John (1877–1941). Professor of Mining and Petroleum Technology, Birmingham University, 1908–20. Consulting petroleum adviser, Colonial Office. Member, Admiralty Commission to Persia, 1913–14. Director, Petroleum Executive, 1917–21. Member, Inter-Allied Petroleum Committee, 1918. Director, APOC, 1923; deputy Chairman, 1925; Chairman, 1927–41.

Campbell, Andrew (d. 1941). Linlithgow Oil Co., 1885. Refinery manager, BOC, Rangoon, from 1889. Advisory chemist and manager of the refineries department, APOC, and managing director, National Oil Refineries, 1913–25.

Cargill, Sir John T. (1867–1954). Director, BOC, 1902–43. Chairman, 1904–43. Chairman, Concessions Syndicate Ltd, 1905. Senior partner, Finlay, Fleming & Co., Rangoon. Director, APOC, 1909–43.

Cassel, Sir Ernest Joseph (1852–1921). Partner, finance house of Bischoffsheim and Goldschmidt, 1884. Involved in formation of the National Bank of Turkey, 1909. Friend of Edward VII.

Chalmers, Robert; 1st Baron of Northiam (1858–1938). Chairman, Board of Inland Revenue, 1907–11. Permanent secretary, HM Treasury, 1911–13. Governor of Ceylon, 1913–16. Joint secretary, HM Treasury, 1916–19.

Chamberlain, Rt. Hon. Sir Austen (1863–1937). Civil Lord of the Admiralty, 1895 and 1900. Chancellor of the Exchequer, 1903–06 and 1919–21. Secretary of State for India, 1915–17. Secretary of State for Foreign Affairs, 1924–29.

Churchill, Rt. Hon. Sir Winston (1874–1965). Under-Secretary of State for the Colonies, 1906–08. President, Board of Trade, 1908–10. Home Secretary, 1910–11. First Lord of the Admiralty, 1911–15. Secretary of State for War and Air, 1919–21. Colonial Secretary 1921–24. Chancellor of the Exchequer, 1924–29.

Clarke, J.C. (d. 1936). Admiralty Contract Department, 1904. Deputy-director, Petroleum Executive, 1917–18. Director of Petroleum Department, 1921–23. Joint deputy-director, distribution department, APOC, 1927–36.

Clémenceau, Georges (1841–1929). Minister of the Interior, March–October 1906. Prime Minister, 1906–09. Prime Minister and Minister of War, 1917–20.

Clive, Rt. Hon. Sir Robert Henry (1877–1948). 1st Secretary, Diplomatic Service, 1915. British Minister, Tehrān, 1926–31.

Cohen, Sir Robert Waley (1877–1952). Joined Shell Transport and Trading Co. Ltd, 1901. Assistant managing director, Asiatic Petroleum Co., 1903. Director, Shell and Asiatic, 1906. Petroleum adviser to the Army, 1914–18. Group managing director, Royal Dutch-Shell, 1921.

Biographical Details of Important Personalities

Cowdray, 1st Viscount of; Weetman Dickinson Pearson (1856–1927). Joined family firm of engineering contractors, S. Pearson & Son Ltd, 1872; partner, 1875. Acquired first oil concessions in Mexico, 1902. Director, Mexican Eagle Oil Co., 1908–1919. Director, Anglo-Mexican Petroleum Products Co. Ltd, 1912–19.

Cox, Major-General Sir Percy Zachariah (1864–1937). Political Resident, Persian Gulf, 1909. Secretary, foreign department, Government of India, 1914. Chief political officer, Indian Expeditionary Force "D", 1914–18. Acting Minister, Tehrān, 1918–20. High commissioner, Mesopotamia, 1920–23.

Crisp, Sir Frank (1843–1919). Senior partner, Morris Ashurst, Crisp & Co., solicitors to APOC, 1909–19.

Curzon, George Nathaniel; 1st Marquess of Kedleston (1859–1925). Viceroy and Governor-General of India, 1899–1905. Lord Privy Seal, 1915–16. Secretary of State for Foreign Affairs, 1919–24. Leader of the House of Lords, 1916–24.

D'Arcy, William Knox (1849–1917). Solicitor, born in Devon. Held principal interest in Mount Morgan gold-mine, Queensland, Australia. Granted oil concession by Persian Government, 28 May 1901. Formed First Exploration Co., 21 May 1903. Formed with BOC the Concessions Syndicate Ltd, 5 May 1905. Director, BOC, 1909–17. Director, APOC, 1909–17.

Dashtī, 'Alī (1887–1980). Editor of *Shafagh-i Surkh* from 1922. Prominent in the Republican movement, 1924.

Dāvar, 'Alī Akbar (1887–1934). Prosecutor General, 1911. Director of Public Education 1921. Deputy for Varāmīn, 1922. Formed the Radical Party, 1925. Minister of Public Works, 1925–26. Minister of Justice, 1927–33.

Deterding, Sir Henri Wilhelm (1866–1939). Representative of Netherlands Trading Society, East Indies. Royal Dutch Oil Co., 1896. Succeeded J.B.A. Kessler as general manager, 1900. Managing director, Asiatic Petroleum Co., 1903. Managing director, Royal Dutch-Shell, 1907–1936.

Dunstan, Dr A.E. (1878–1964). Chemistry lecturer, East Ham Technical College and researched into the viscosity of oil. Engaged by Admiralty to analyse naval fuel oil, 1915. Set up a research laboratory for APOC at Sunbury, 1917. Chief chemist, APOC, 1924–1947.

Eves, Sir Hubert Heath (1883–1961). General manager, Shaw, Wallace & Co., India. Head of the distribution department, APOC, 1921. Director, APOC 1924–50; deputy Chairman, 1941–50.

Farīd al-Saltana. Imperial Commissioner, August 1918—December 1923.

Finlay, Sir Campbell Kirkman (1875–1937). Senior partner, Finlay, Fleming & Co., Rangoon. Director, Strick, Scott & Co., 1912–16. Director, APOC, 1912–18. Director, BOC, 1914–18.

Fīrūz Mīrzā, Prince (Nusrat al-Dawla; 1888–1937). Minister of Justice, 1916 and 1918–19. Minister for Foreign Affairs, 1919. Governor of Fars, 1923–24. Minister of Justice, August—December 1925. Minister of Finance, 1927–29.

Fisher, Admiral John Arbuthnot; 1st Baron of Kilverstone (1841–1920). Second Sea Lord, 1902–03. First Sea Lord, 1904–10 and 1914–15. Chairman, Royal Commission on Oil Fuel and Engines, 1912–13.

Fisher, Sir Norman Fenwick Warren (1879–1948). Permanent Secretary, HM Treasury, 1919–39.

Furūghī, Mīrzā Muhammad 'Alī Khān (1873–1942). Minister of Justice in various Cabinets, 1911–15. Delegate to the Paris Peace Conference, 1919. Minister for

Biographical Details of Important Personalities

Foreign Affairs, 1923–24 and 1930–33. Minister of Finance, 1924–25. Acting Prime Minister, 1925. Minister of War, 1926–27. Persian delegate to the League of Nations, 1928.

Fraser, Sir William; Lord Strathalmond (1888–1970). Managing-director, Pumpherston Oil Co. Ltd, 1911. Managing-director, Scottish oils Ltd., 1919. Director, APOC, 1923–56; deputy-Chairman, 1928–41; Chairman, 1941–56.

Garrow, Duncan (d. 1931). Partner, Finlay, Fleming & Co., Rangoon. Director, APOC, 1914–24.

Garson, William (d. 1915). Legal adviser to Lord Strathcona. Director, APOC, 1909–14.

Geddes, Sir Auckland Campbell (1879–1954). Director of Recruiting at the War office, 1916–17. Minister of National Service, 1917–19. President of the Board of Trade, 1919–20. British Ambassador to the USA, 1920–24.

Greenway, Charles; 1st Baron of Stanbridge Earls (1857–1934). Joined Shaw, Wallace & Co., India, 1893; partner, 1897. Senior partner, R.G. Shaw & Co. Managing-director, Lloyd, Scott & Co., 1910. Director, APOC, 1909–34; managing director, 1910–19 and Chairman, 1914–27; president, 1927–34.

Greenwood, Hamar; 1st Viscount of Holbourne (1870–1948). Secretary, Overseas Trade Department, 1919–20.

Grey, Edward; 1st Viscount of Fallodon (1867–1953). Secretary of State for Foreign Affairs, 1905–16.

Griffin, Sir Lepel Henry (1840–1908). Chief Political Officer in Afghanistan, 1880. Chairman, Imperial Bank of Persia, 1889–1908. Chairman, Persian Bank Mining Rights Corporation, 1890–99.

Gulbenkian, Calouste (1869–1955). Son of Armenian merchant. Director, National Bank of Turkey, 1910. Director, Turkish Petroleum Co. 1912–29. Director Iraq Petroleum Co. 1929–33.

Hamilton, James (1860–1920). Director and general manager in Glasgow, BOC, 1906–20. Director, APOC, 1909–20. Director, Strick, Scott & Co., 1910–1920.

Hankey, Sir Maurice (1877–1963). Secretary, Committee of Imperial Defence, 1912–38. Secretary to the War Cabinet, 1916, the Imperial War Cabinet, 1917–18 and to the Cabinet, 1919–38.

Harcourt, Lewis; 1st Viscount (1863–1922). Secretary of State for the Colonies, 1910–15. Chairman, Petroleum Imperial Policy Committee, 1918.

Hardinge, Rt. Hon. Sir Arthur (1859–1933). Minister at Tehrān, 1900–05; Belgium 1906–11; Portugal 1911–13. Ambassador to Spain, 1913–19.

Hardinge, Charles; 1st Baron of Penshurst (1858–1944). Secretary, Persian Legation, 1896. Permanent Under-Secretary of State for Foreign Affairs, 1906–10 and 1916–20. Viceroy of India, 1910–16. Ambassador in Paris, 1920–23.

Hearn, A.C. (1877–1952). Assistant Director of Stores, Admiralty. Chairman, Anglo-French Commission to Romania, 1919–20. Joined APOC, 1920; deputy director, 1925; director, 1927–38.

Hidāyat, Mehdī Qulī. Minister of Justice, 1907. Minister of the Interior, 1918. Governor-General of Āzarbāyjān, 1920–22. Minister of Public Works, 1923 and 1926–27. Prime Minister, 1927.

Holland, Sir Thomas Henry (1868–1947). Director, Geological Survey of India, 1903–09. President, Burmah Oil Reserves Committee, 1908. Professor of Geology and Mineralogy, Manchester University, 1909–18.

Biographical Details of Important Personalities

Horne, Sir Robert (1871–1940). Director, department of Materials and Priority, Admiralty, 1917. Director, Admiralty labour department, 1918. Petroleum Imperial Policy Committee, 1918. Minister of Labour, 1919. President of the Board of Trade, 1920–21. Chancellor of the Exchequer, 1921–22.

Inchcape, Viscount; of Strathnaver (1852–1932). Legislative Council of the Viceroy of India, 1891–93. Council of India, 1897–1911. Member, National Economy (Geddes) Committee, 1921–22. Chairman, Indian Retrenchment Committee, 1922–23. Vice president, Suez Canal Co. Chairman, P & O, 1915–32. Chairman, British India Steam Navigation Co. Government director, APOC, 1914–25.

'Īsa Khān (1879–1933). Director of the Tehrān Financial Department, 1910. Assistant Secretary of Finance, 1918. Minister of Finance, 1921. Imperial Commissioner, December 1923–33.

Jacks, T.L. (1884–1966). Oil assistant, Strick, Scott & Co., Muhammara, 1909–13; assistant manager, 1917–20; joint general manager, 1921–22. Joint general manager, Muhammara, APOC, 1923–25; resident director, Tehrān, 1926–35.

Jameson, J. (1885–1961). Pipeline assistant, APOC, 1909–11. Pipeline superintendent, 1911–14. Pipeline and transport superintendent, 1914–20. Fields manager, 1921–23. General manager, fields and refineries, 1923–26. General manager, Persia, 1926–27. Deputy director and general manager of Production, 1927–39. Director, 1939–61.

Jenkins, Sir Walter St. David (1874–1951). Secretary, Admiralty Oil Committee, 1903–06. Secretary to the Admiralty Committee of the Royal Commission on Oil Fuel and Engines, 1912–13. Government director, APOC, 1918–19. Director of Navy contracts, 1919–36.

Khaz'al, Shaykh (1860–1936). Appointed Governor of Muhammara, Shatt-al-'Arab and Kārūn by Persian Government, 1898. Held great influence over tribes of 'Arabistān (later Khūzistān) and opposed the curtailment of his power by the Persian Government. Given assurances of protection from British Government, 1902–03. Arrested in Muhammara and detained in Tehrān from April 1925.

Kitabgi, General Antoine (d. 1902). Director of Persian Customs. Helped Baron Julius de Reuter with his concessions. Influential in promoting the interests of the D'Arcy Syndicate. Imperial Commissioner, 1901–02.

Kitabgi, Edouard. Youngest son of General Kitabgi. Assistant to G.B. Reynolds at Chiāh Surkh.

Kitabgi, Paul. Second son of General Kitabgi. Engaged as a representative of W.K. D'Arcy in Tehrān, 1902. Agent of the Concessions Syndicate Ltd., 1907.

Kitabgi, Vincent. Eldest son of General Kitabgi. Imperial Commissioner, 1902–05 and June—September, 1907.

Lambert, George (1866–1958). Civil Lord of the Admiralty, 1905–15. Member, Royal Commission on Oil Fuel and Engines, 1912–13.

Lansdowne, 5th Marquess of; Henry Charles Keith Petty-Fitzmaurice (1845–1927). Viceroy of India, 1888–93. Secretary of State for War, 1895–1900. Secretary of State for Foreign Affairs, 1900–05.

Law, Rt. Hon. Andrew Bonar (1858–1923). Secretary of State for the Colonies, 1915–16. Chancellor of the Exchequer, 1916–18. Prime Minister, 1922–23.

Lloyd, Sir John Buck (1874–1952). Senior partner, Shaw, Wallace & Co., India, 1904. Opened Muhammara office for Lloyd, Scott & Co., 1909. Director, Strick, Scott & Co., 1909–22. Director, APOC, 1919–46.

Biographical Details of Important Personalities

Lloyd George, David (1863–1945). Chancellor of the Exchequer, 1908–15. Minister of Munitions, 1915–16. Secretary of State for War, 1916. Prime Minister, 1916–22.

Lloyd-Greame, Philip; Lord Swinton (1884–1972). Parliamentary Secretary, Board of Trade, 1921–22. President, Board of Trade, 1922–23 and 1924–29.

Long, Walter Hume; 1st Viscount (1854–1924). Secretary of State for the Colonies, 1916–18. First Lord of the Admiralty, 1919–21.

Loraine, Rt. Hon. Sir Percy (1880–1962). Third Secretary, Tehrān, 1907. First Secretary, Madrid, 1916; Warsaw, 1919. British Minister, Tehrān, 1921–26; Greece, 1926–29. High commissioner for Egypt and the Sudan, 1929–33.

Lorimer, Lt. Col. David Lockhart (1876–1962). Vice-consul for 'Arabistān, 1903–09. Political Agent, Bahrain, 1911–12. Consul, Kirmān and Balūchistān and assistant to the Political Resident, Persian Gulf, 1912–14 and 1916–17.

Lund, Frederick William (1874–1965). Director, British Steamship Investment Trust. Director, APOC, 1917–50.

MacDonald, Rt. Hon. James Ramsay (1866–1937). Prime Minister and Secretary of State for Foreign Affairs, January—November 1924. Prime Minister, 1929–35.

McGowan, Sir Harry Duncan (1874–1961). Managing director, Nobel's Explosives Co. Ltd, 1918. Chairman and managing director, Explosives Trade Ltd, and Nobel Industries Ltd, 1918–26. President, ICI, 1926–30.

McKenna, Rt. Hon. Reginald (1863–1943). First Lord of the Admiralty, 1908–11. Home Secretary, 1911–15. Chancellor of the Exchequer, 1915–16.

McLintock, Sir William (1873–1947). Senior Partner, Thomson McLintock & Co., accountants.

Mallet, Rt. Hon. Sir Louis du Pan (1864–1936). Private secretary to Sir Edward Grey, 1905–07. Assistant Under-Secretary of State in charge of Near and Middle Eastern affairs, 1907–13. Ambassador to Turkey, 1913–14. Retired, 1920.

Marling, Sir Charles (1862–1933). Counsellor, British Embassy in Tehrān, 1906–09 and chargé d'affaires, 1910. British Minister, Tehrān, 1915–19; Copenhagen, 1919–21; the Hague, 1921–26.

Meftah, D'vud Khān (b. 1870). Head of the English section, Ministry for Foreign Affairs, 1909. Consul General, India, 1911–20. Persian Minister in London, 1920–25.

Mehdī Khān, 'Alā Saltana. Chargé d'affaires and Minister in London, 1908–19.

Milner, Alfred; 1st Viscount (1854–1925). War Cabinet, 1916–18. High Commissioner for South Africa, 1897–1905. Governor of the Transvaal and Orange River Colony, 1901–05. Secretary of State for War, 1918–19. Secretary of State for the Colonies, 1919–21.

Murray, Sir Oswyn (1873–1936). Director of Victualling, the Admiralty, 1905–11. Assistant secretary, 1911–17. Permanent Secretary, 1917–36.

Murray, R.A. (1862–1937). Senior Partner, Brown, Fleming & Murray, auditors to APOC from 1909.

Mushīr al-Dawla (1873–1935). Minister in St. Petersburg, 1902. Minister for Foreign Affairs, October 1907. Minister of Justice, 1908–9. Prime Minister, 1915. Minister for War, 1917–18. Prime Minister, 1920 and 1922–23.

Mussadiq, Dr Muhammad Khān (1885–1967). Studied Law in Switzerland. Governor-General of Fars, 1920. Minister of Finance, 1921. Governor-General of

Āzarbāyjān, 1922. Minister of Foreign Affairs, 1923. Opposed the change of régime in 1925.

Mustaufī al-Mamālek (1875–1932). Minister of Finance 1909. Premier of the Nationalist Cabinet, 1910. Minister of War, January 1913. Prime Minister and Minister of Interior 1915–16. Prime Minister, 1918, and 1923.

Neilson, R.G. (1876–1956). Works manager, BOC, Rangoon, 1910–1913. Works manager, APOC, Ābādān, 1913–21. Technical adviser and manager, refineries branch, 1922–27.

Nichols, H.E. (1874–1927). London staff, Mount Morgan Mining Co., 1895. Personal assistant to W.K. D'Arcy, 1901–09. Assistant to the managing director, APOC, 1909. Director, APOC, 1915–27.

Nicholson, Sir Harold (1886–1968). British delegation to the Peace Conference, 1919. HM Legation, Tehrān, 1925. HM Embassy, Berlin, 1927. Resigned from Diplomatic Service, 1929.

Norman, Herman Cameron (1872–1955). 1st Secretary, HM Diplomatic Service, 1907. Counsellor, 1914. Secretary of the British delegation to the Peace Conference, 1919. British Minister. Tehrān, 1920–21.

Oliphant, Sir Lancelot (1881–1965). British Legation at Tehrān, 1909–11. Assistant secretary, 1920. Counsellor, 1923. Assistant under-secretary, 1927.

Orford, 5th Earl of; Robert Horace Walpole (1854–1931). Friend and associate of W.K. D'Arcy.

Packe, Sir Edward Hussey (1878–1946). Private secretary to successive First Lords of the Admiralty, 1916–19. Government director, APOC, 1919–46.

Pakenham, Admiral Sir William Christopher (1861–1933). Captain, 1903. Chairman, Admiralty Oil Committee, 1911. Lord Commissioner of the Admiralty, 1911–13. Admiral, 1922.

Parker, Alwyn (1877–1951). Third secretary, Diplomatic Service, 1902. Assistant clerk, 1912. Head of the Contraband Department, 1914–17. Counsellor, 1919. Private secretary to Lord Hardinge of Penshurst. Resigned from the Diplomatic Service, 1919.

Pretyman, Rt. Hon. Ernest George (1860–1931). Civil Lord of the Admiralty, 1900–03 and 1916–19; secretary, 1903–06. President, Admiralty Oil Committee, 1903–06. Parliamentary secretary, Board of Trade, 1915–16.

Qavām al-Saltana (1873–1955). Minister of War, July–October 1910. Minister of Interior, 1911 and 1917–18. Minister of Finance, 1914. Governor general of Khurāsān, 1918–21. Prime Minister, 1921–22 and 1922–23.

Rahnamā, Zain al-'Ābidīn (b. 1887). Editor and proprietor of *Iran*. Under-Secretary of Public Works, 1926. Assistant to the Prime Minister, 1927.

Redwood, Sir Boverton (1846–1919). Petroleum adviser to HM Government. Adviser to W.K. D'Arcy, BOC, and APOC. Member, Royal Commission on Oil Fuel and Engines, 1912–13. Technical adviser, HM Petroleum Executive.

Reynolds, George Bernard (d. 1928). Graduate of the Royal Indian Engineering College. Employed in Sumatra oilfields. Engaged by W.K. D'Arcy in 1901 to drill for oil in Persia. Struck oil, 26 May 1908 at Masjid i-Suleimān. Fields general manager, 1908–09 and 1910. Left APOC, 1911. Subsequently explored for oil in Venezuela.

Ritchie, Charles (d. 1914). Supervised construction of first pipeline in Persia, 1909–11. Flew first aeroplane in Persia.

Riza Shāh (1878–1944). Riza Khān rose from ranks of Persian Cossack Brigade to become Colonel. Joint leader of coup d'état, February, 1921. Minister of War,

Biographical Details of Important Personalities

March 1921. Prime Minister, October 1923. Succeeded to Persian throne as Rizā Shāh, April, 1926. Abdicated, 1941.

Runciman, Walter; 1st Viscount of Doxford (1870–1949). Financial Secretary, HM Treasury, 1907–08. President, Board of Trade, 1914–16.

Sādigh al-Saltana (Mut'amin Huzour; 1800–1900). Imperial Commissioner, March, 1905—June 1907 and September 1907—August 1918.

Samsam al-Saltana (Najaf Qulī Khān; 1852–1930). Il-Khān and Il-Begī between 1903 and 1912. Governor of Isfahān, associated with Constitutionalists, 1908–10. Prime Minister, Minister of Interior, Minister of War, 1911. Prime Minister, 1911–13. Leading Bakhtiari Khan in Tehrān, 1915–30, and supporter of Rizā Shāh.

Samuel, Marcus; 1st Viscount Bearsted (1853–1927). In partnership with his brother, established Marcus Samuel & Co., in London, and Samuel Samuel & Co., in Japan, 1892. Formed Eastern Tank Syndicate to ship Russian oil to the East, 1892. Chairman, Shell Transport & Trading Co. Ltd, 1897–1921.

Sardār Assad (Hājjī Qulī Khān; 1856–1917). Influential Bakhtiari Khan, although not a titular tribal leader. Principal negotiator in the Bakhtiari Agreement with Reynolds, 1906. Active in Constitutional Movement, 1909. Minister of Interior, 1909 and 1910. Minister of War, 1910.

Selborne, 2nd Earl of (1858–1942). Under-Secretary of State for the Colonies, 1895–1900. First Lord of the Admiralty, 1900–05.

Shuster, Morgan (1877–1960). Served in the Philippines Customs. Financial adviser to Persia, 1911. Author of 'The Strangling of Persia', 1912. Adviser to Persian Government concerning North Persian oil concessions, 1920–24.

Simon, Sir John Allsebrook KC (1873–1954). Solicitor-General, 1910–13. Attorney General, 1913–15. Secretary of State for Home Affairs, 1915–16. Chairman, Indian Statutory Commission, 1927–30. Secretary of State for Foreign Affairs, 1931–35.

Slade, Admiral Sir Edmond (1859–1928). Director, Intelligence Division of the Admiralty, 1907–09. Commander-in-Chief, East Indies, 1909–13. Head of the Admiralty Commission to Persia, 1913–14. Government director, APOC, 1914–16; vice-Chairman, 1916–28.

Smith, Sir Henry Babington (1863–1923). British representative, Council of Administration of Ottoman Public Debt, 1900. President, National Bank of Turkey, 1909. Director, Turkish Petroleum Co., 1912–18.

Snowden, Philip; 1st Viscount of Ickanshaw (1864–1937). Chancellor of the Exchequer, 1924 and 1929–31.

Southborough, 1st Baron; Francis John Hopwood (1860–1947). Under-Secretary of State for the Colonies, 1907–11. Civil Lord of the Admiralty, 1912–17. Chairman, Grand Committee on War Trade. Director, APOC, 1918–24.

Spens, Ivan (1890–1964). A Senior partner, Brown, Fleming and Murray.

Stanley, Sir Albert (1874–1948). General manager, American Electric Railways, 1895–1907. Director general of Mechanical Transport, 1916. President, Board of Trade, 1916–19.

Stewart, J. Douglas (d. 1928). Partner, Gardiner & Co., Glasgow Shipping firm. Managing-director, British Tanker Company, February 1919. Director, APOC, 1920–25. Acting deputy to the Chairman, 1921–25.

Strathcona and Mount Royal, Lord (1820–1914). Resident Governor, Hudson Bay Company. Director, Canadian Pacific Railway Co. Ltd. President, Bank of

Biographical Details of Important Personalities

Montreal. High Commissioner for Canada in London, 1896–1911. Chairman, APOC, 1909–14.

Tabātabā'ī, Sayyid Ziyā al-Dīn (1891–1969). Editor of 'Ra'd', 1915–16. Persian representative, Āzarbāyjān, 1919. Carried out coup d'état with Rizā Khān, February 1921. Prime Minister, March—June 1921.

Taqīzādeh, Sayyid Hassan Khān (1877–1970). Prominent member Constitutional Movement and member First Majlis. Negotiated the Soviet-Persian Commercial Treaty of 1921. Minister of Foreign Affairs, 1926. Persian Minister in London, 1929–30. Minister of Finance, 1930–33.

Teagle, Walter Clark (1879–1962). A vice-president of a Standard Oil Company, 1901. Head of European marketing, SOC, 1908. A vice-president, Standard Oil (NJ), 1911–14; president, 1917–37; chairman, 1937–42.

Teck, HRH Prince Francis of (1870–1910). Served in the Army. Director, APOC, 15 April—22 October 1909.

Tiarks, Frank Cyril (1874–1952). Partner, J. Henry Schroder & Co., 1902. Director, Bank of England, 1912–45. Director, APOC, 1917–49.

Tīmurtāsh, 'Abdul Husayn Khān (1888–1932). Governor of Gīlān, 1918. Minister of Justice, 1922. Governor-General of Kirmān, 1923–24. Minister of Public Works, 1924. Minister of Court, 1925–32.

Vansittart, Robert Gilbert (1881–1957). 1st secretary, HM Diplomatic Service, 1919. Counsellor, 1920. Secretary to Curzon, 1920–24. Assistant under-secretary of State for Foreign Affairs and Principal Private Secretary to the Prime Minister, 1928–30. Permanent Secretary, 1930–38.

Vusūq, Mīrzā Hasan Khān (Vusūq al-Dawla; 1868–1930). Minister for Foreign Affairs 1911 and 1913–14. Prime Minister and Minister for Foreign Affairs, 1916–17, and 1918–20. Negotiated the Anglo-Persian Convention, 1919. Minister of Finance, 1926.

Wallace, C.W. (1855–1916). Senior partner, Shaw, Wallace & Co. Senior partner, R.G. Shaw & Co. Director, BOC, 1902–15. Managing director, APOC, 1909–10; director, 1909–15; deputy-Chairman, 1909–15.

Walpole, C.A. (Retired 1922). Shaw Wallace & Co., Karachi. Assistant manager, Strick Scott and Co., Muhammara, 1909–13; manager and general manager, 1913–20. General manager, Société Générale des Huiles de Pétrole, Paris, 1921–22.

Watson, Robert I. (1878–1948). Joined Finlay, Fleming & Co., Rangoon, 1902. Member, London board of BOC, from 1912. Director, BOC, 1918–48; managing director, 1919–48. Director, APOC, 1918–47.

Whigham, Gilbert G. (1877–1950). Joined Finlay, Fleming & Co., Rangoon, 1904. General manager in India, BOC, from 1911. Director, BOC, 1921–46; Director, APOC, 1925–46.

Wilson, Sir Arnold (1884–1940). Lieutenant, Indian Army detachment, Ahwāz, 1907–09. Acting consul, Muhammara, 1909–11. British Commissioner, Turco-Persian Frontier Commission, 1913–14. Assistant political officer, Basra, 1915–17; deputy chief political officer, 1917–18. Acting Civil Commissioner and Political Resident, Persian Gulf, 1918–20. Joint general manager Muhammara, Strick Scott & Co, 1921 and for APOC, 1923–24. Managing director, D'Arcy Exploration Company, 1926–32.

Wolff, Rt. Hon. Sir Henry Drummond (1830–1908). Clerk in Foreign Office, 1846. Minister at Tehrān, 1888. A founder member of the Primrose League.

Biographical Details of Important Personalities

Wynne, Sir Trevredyn Rashleigh (1853–1942). President, Railway Board of India, 1908–14. Imperial Legislative Council of India, 1908–14. Director, APOC, 1915–24.

Young, Dr M. Y. (d. 1950). Medical officer in Persia, 1907. Chief Medical Officer, Persia, 1909–26. Deputy director and Company Chief Medical Officer, 1926–36.

NOTES
Notes to pp. 15-17

1. The acquisition of the D'Arcy concession

1 On the pre-Islamic history of Iran see Arthur Christensen, *L'Iran sous les Sassanides* (Copenhagen, 1936); M.A.R. Colledge, *The Parthians* (London, 1967); Richard N. Frye, *The Heritage of Persia* (London, 1962); Roman Ghirshman, *Iran, Parthians and Sassanians* (London, 1962); Georgina Herrmann, *The Iranian Revival* (London, 1977); A.T. Olmstead, *History of the Persian Empire* (Chicago, 1948); Edith Porada, *Ancient Iran* (London, 1965). A general introductory history of Persia is Alessandro Bausani, *The Persians* (London, 1971) and a general cultural introduction is Roger Stevens, *The Land of the Great Sophy*, 3rd edn (London, 1979).
2 On Iranian history from A.D. 652 to 1502 see the relevant volumes of *The Cambridge History of Iran*: vol. 4, Richard N. Frye (ed.), *The Period from the Arab Invasion to the Saljuqs* (Cambridge, 1975) and vol. 5, J.A. Boyle (ed.), *The Saljuq and Mongol Periods* (Cambridge, 1968); Richard N. Frye, *The Golden Age of Persia* (London, 1975). A general introductory Iranian history in Islamic times is to be found in the relevant chapters of P.M. Holt, Ann K.S. Lambton, and Bernard Lewis (eds.), *The Cambridge History of Islam*, vol. 1, *The Central Islamic Lands* (London, 1970).
3 For the Safavid and Zand periods see L. Bellan, *Chah Abbas I*, (Paris, 1932); L. Lockhart, *Nadir Shah* (London, 1938) and *The Fall of the Safavi Dynasty and Afghan Occupation of Persia* (Cambridge, 1958); John R. Perry, *The Zands* (Chicago, 1979); Roger Savory *Iran under the Safavids* (Cambridge, 1980).
4 The early Qājār period 1794-1848 is inadequately covered. The second period 1848-1925 also lacks proper historical coverage, though individual studies are available, and are later cited as appropriate. P. Avery, *Modern Iran* (London, 1965), contains a general survey of the latter period. Economic affairs are well represented by Charles Issawi (ed.), *The Economic History of Iran 1800-1914* (Chicago, 1971), and religious aspects by Hamid Algar, *Religion and State in Iran, 1785-1906: The Role of the Ulama in the Qajar Period* (Berkeley, 1969).
5 Joseph M. Upton, *The History of Modern Iran, An Interpretation* (Harvard, 1965), p. 3.
6 Shaul Bakhash, *Iran: Monarchy, Bureaucracy and Reform under the Qajars: 1858-1896* (London, 1978).
7 Bausani, *The Persians*, p. 167.
8 Bakhash, *Iran*, pp. 77-120.
9 Hamid Algar, *Mīrzā Malkam Khān, a Biographical Study in Iranian Modernism* (Berkeley, 1973).

Notes to pp. 17-20

10 Ibid., p. 112, quoted from Malkam Khān, Uṣūl-i Tamaddun.
11 Bakhash, Iran, p. 47, quoted from Mīrzā Ḥusayn Khān to Foreign Minister, 5 August 1866.
12 Ibid., p. 165, quoted from the memoirs of Amīn al-Dawla, Khāterāt-i Siyāsī, p. 107.
13 Ann K.S. Lambton, 'The Tobacco Régie: Prelude to Revolution', Part I, Studia Islamica, 23 (1969), 119-57, Part II, idem 24 (1969), 71-90; N.R. Keddie, Religion and Rebellion in Iran. The Iranian Tobacco Protest of 1891-1892 (London, 1966). The effects of Persian currency problems and the silver standard are dealt with by P.W. Avery and J.B. Simmons, 'Persia on a Cross of Silver, 1880-1890', Middle Eastern Studies, 10 (1974).
14 Issawi, The Economic History of Iran, pp. 14-19.
15 Ann K.S. Lambton, 'Persian Trade under the Early Qajars' in D.S. Richards (ed.), Islam and the Trade of Asia (Oxford, 1970), pp. 225-6.
16 See Issawi, The Economic History of Iran, Chapter 6, Industry, sections: 1 Handicrafts, 1850s; 2 Crafts in Isfahan, 1870s and 3 Guild Organisation, Early Nineteenth Century.
17 Ibid., pp. 304-5.
18 Annette Destrée, Les Fonctionnaires Belges au Service de la Perse, 1898-1915 (Leiden, 1976).
19 The most complete geographical information on Iran is The Cambridge History of Iran, vol. 1, W.B. Fisher (ed.), The Land of Iran (Cambridge, 1968). On land tenure and administration see, Ann K.S. Lambton, Landlord and Peasant in Persia (London, 1953).
20 Julian Bharier, Economic Development in Iran 1900-1970 (London, 1971), p. 20.
21 Jenkinson, Anthony and other Englishmen, Early Voyages and Travels to Russia and Persia, E.D. Morgan and C.H. Coote (eds.), Hakluyt Society, First Series, nos. 72-73, 1885; T.S. Willan, The Early History of the Russia Company 1553-1603 (Manchester, 1956).
22 A.C. Wood, A History of the Levant Company (Oxford, 1935).
23 Boise Penrose, The Sherleian Odyssey (London, 1928); E.D. Ross, Sir Anthony Sherley and his Persian Adventures (London, 1933).
24 K.N. Chaudhuri, English East India Company: The Study of an Early Joint Stock Company 1600-1640 (London, 1965).
25 William Foster (ed.), Sir Thomas Roe, The Embassy to the Moghul (London, 1926), p. 335; Roe to Robbins 7 or 17 January 1616/17 and Pettus to Middleton 2 June 1617 quoted in R.W. Ferrier, 'An English View of Persian Trade in 1618', Journal of the Economic and Social History of the Orient, 19 (1976), 182-214. For later English trade with Persia see R.W. Ferrier, 'The Armenians and the East India Company in Persia in the Seventeenth and Early Eighteenth Century' Economic History Review, Second Series, 26 (1973), 38-62.
26 William Foster (ed.), Sir Thomas Herbert, Travels in Persia, 1627-29 (London, 1928).
27 Jonas Hanway, An Historical Account of British Trade over the Caspian Sea (4 vols., London, 1753). For British trade in the Persia Gulf in this period, see Abdul Amir Amin, British Interests in the Persian Gulf (Leiden, 1967).
28 R.M. Savory, 'British and French Diplomacy in Persia 1800-10', IRAN, 10 (1972), 31-55. On the Persian Gulf area see A.T. Wilson. The Persian Gulf

Notes to pp. 21-28

(London, 1928) and J.B. Kelly, *Britain and the Persian Gulf 1795-1880* (Oxford, 1968).

29 James Morier, *A Journey through Persia, Armenia and Asia Minor* (London, 1812).
30 Denis Wright, *The English Among the Persians* (London, 1977), p. 23, and Barbara English, *John Company's Last War* (London, 1971).
31 F.J. Goldsmid, *Telegraph and Travel* (London, 1874).
32 PRO FO 65/1202 quoted in Firuz Kazemzadeh, *Russia and Britain in Persia 1864-1914* (New Haven, 1968), p. 10.
33 PRO FO 60/506 India Office to Foreign Office, 22 May 1889, quoted in R.L. Greaves, *Persia and the Defence of India 1884-1892* (London, 1959), p. 25. On the Eastern Question see H.C. Rawlinson, *England and Russia in the East* (London, 1875).
34 Algar, *Malkam Khān*, pp. 168-84.
35 Salisbury to Lascelles, 6 October 1891, Salisbury Papers, quoted in Greaves, *Persia and the Defence of India*, p. 142.
36 PRO FO 60/507, Foreign Office to Treasury, 2 July 1889, quoted in Greaves, *Persia and the Defence of India*, p. 176.
37 Quoted in Greaves, *Persia and the Defence of India*, p. 139.
38 L. Lockhart, 'Histoire du Pétrole en Perse jusq 'au Début du XX Siecle', *La Revue Pétrolifère* (Paris, 1938).
39 W.K. Loftus, 'On the Geology of Portions of the Turco-Persian Frontier and of the Districts Adjoining', *Quarterly Journal of the Geological Society*, 40 (1854), pp. 464-9.
40 W.K. Loftus, *Travels and Researches in Chaldaea and Susiana* (London, 1857).
41 Samuel Green Wheeler Benjamin, *Persia and the Persians* (Boston, 1887), pp. 18-19.
42 George Nathaniel Curzon, *Persia and the Persian Question*, vol. 1 (London, 1892), p. 66.
43 Marvin L. Entner, *Russo-Persian Commercial Relations, 1828-1914* (Florida, 1965), p. 60.
44 PRO FO 60/511, Drummond Wolff to Salisbury, 30 June 1890.
45 PRO FO 60/576, Lepel Griffin to Rosebery, 6 August 1893.
46 PRO FO 60/576, Lepel Griffin to Rosebery, 6 December 1893.
47 PRO FO 60/576, Currie Minute, 28 October 1893.
48 Bushire imports 1885, PRO FO 60/483, Report on the Trade of the Persian Gulf for 1885, by Consul-General Miles; Tabrīz imports, PRO FO 60/483, Report on the Trade of Tabreez for 1885 by Consul-General Abbott.
49 Bushire imports 1888, PRO FO 60/505, Report on the Trade of South Persia and Persian Gulf for 1888 by Political Resident Ross; Report on Trade of Tabreez for 1888-89 by Consul-General Abbott.
50 H.W. MacLean, *Report on the Condition and Prospects of British Trade in Persia*, Cd: 2146, p. 70.
51 PRO FO 60/505, Report on the Trade of South Persia and Persian Gulf for 1888 by Consul-General Ross, p. 2.
52 Jacques de Morgan, 'Note sur les gîtes de Naphte de Kend-e-Chirin (Gouvernement de Ser-i-Paul)', *Annales des Mines*, February 1892, pp. 1-16.
53 Jacques de Morgan, *Mission Scientifique en Perse* (5 vols., Paris, 1894-1905).
54 De Morgan, *Mission Scientifique*, vol. 2, p. 87.
55 *Ibid.*, pp. 80-1.

Notes to pp. 28-40

56 *The Statist*, 24 March 1900.
57 PRO FO 60/660, Hardinge to Lansdowne, 1 February 1902.
58 BP H17/1, Memoirs of C.S. Gulbenkian, 16 September 1945.
59 Quoted in Issawi, *The Economic History of Iran*, p. 348, Souchard to A.E. Freycinet, Correspondence Commerciale, Tehrān, vol. 3, 14 July 1885.
60 Sir Henry Drummond Wolff, *Rambling Recollections*, vol. 2 (London, 1908), p. 329.
61 BP H12/35, Wolff to Kitabgi, 25 November 1900.
62 *Ibid.*
63 BP H17/96, Wolff memorandum c.1900.
64 Wolff, *Rambling Recollections*, vol. 1, Preface.
65 BP H12/35, Kitabgi to Wolff, 25 December 1900.
66 These terms were later modified with the approval of General Kitabgi's heirs in 1905 and a final settlement was agreed in 1909 prior to the formation of the Company.
67 BP H12/35, Contract, 1 March 1901, between D'Arcy, Kitabgi and Cotte.
68 BP H17/47, Marriott Journal.
69 BP H16/70, D'Arcy to Kitabgi, 7 March 1901.
70 PRO FO 248/733, Gosselin to Hardinge, 12 March 1901.
71 *Ibid.*, Hardinge to Sanderson, 10 April 1901.
72 BP H17/47.
73 *Ibid.*
74 *Ibid.*
75 PRO FO 60/731, Hardinge to Lansdowne, 26 April 1901.
76 BP H17/47.
77 *Ibid.*
78 *Ibid.*
79 PRO FO 60/640, Hardinge to Lansdowne, 12 May 1901.
80 BP H17/47.
81 *Ibid.*
82 Some 6 months later Hardinge was less optimistic and complaining of 'the surrender to Russia of some fresh political advantage', FO 60/660, Hardinge to Lansdowne, 29 January 1902.
83 PRO FO 60/731, Hardinge to Lansdowne, 30 May 1901.
84 BP H17/47.
85 *Ibid.*
86 *Ibid.*
87 *Ibid.*
88 *Ibid.*
89 *Ibid.*
90 *Ibid.*
91 *Ibid.*
92 *Ibid.*
93 *Ibid.*
94 *Ibid.*
95 Arthur H. Hardinge, *A Diplomatist in the East* (London, 1928), pp. 278-9.
96 PRO FO 60/731, Hardinge to Lansdowne, 30 May 1901.
97 BP H12/35, Kitabgi Dossier.
98 *Ibid.*

99 Quoted in Kazemzadeh, *Russia and Britain in Persia*, p. 356, from B.N. Anan'ich, 'Rossia i Kontsessiia d'Arsi', *Istoricheskie zapiski*, 66 (1960), p. 281.
100 BP H17/47.
101 *Ibid.*
102 *Ibid.*
103 *Ibid.*
104 *Ibid.*
105 PRO FO 60/731, Hardinge to Lansdowne, 30 May 1901.
106 H.W. MacLean report, Cd: 2146, p. 9.
107 PRO FO 881/8526, Memorandum on British Policy in Persia, 31 October 1905, quoting Lansdowne to Hardinge, 6 January 1902.
108 *Ibid.*
109 Lord Lansdowne; declaration, House of Lords Debate, 5 May 1903, quoted in B.C. Busch, *Britain and the Persian Gulf 1894-1914* (Berkeley, 1967), p. 256.
110 Text of D'Arcy Concession in J.C. Hurewitz, *The Middle East and North Africa in World Politics, a Documentary Record*, 2nd edn (New Haven and London, 1975), vol. 1, pp. 483-4; Draft Concession in BP H12/35.
111 BP H16/70, D'Arcy to Kitabgi, 14 July 1901.
112 BP H14/43, D'Arcy to Lansdowne, 27 June 1901.
113 PRO FO 248/739, Hardinge to Lansdowne, 30 May 1901.
114 PRO FO 248/733, D'Arcy to Lansdowne, 27 June 1901.
115 Quoted in Kazemzadeh, *Russia and Britain in Persia*, p. 356.
116 *Ibid.* p. 360.
117 Firuz Kazemzadeh, 'The Origin and Development of the Persian Cossack Brigade', *The American Slavic and Eastern European Review*, 15 (1956), 351-63.
118 Greaves, *Persia and the Defence of India*, p. 49, enclosure no. 2, Wolff to Salisbury, 1 October 1888.
119 PRO FO 60/661, Hardinge to Lansdowne, 6 November 1901.
120 Entner, *Russo-Persian Commercial Relations*, p.70.
121 *Ibid.*, p. 77.
122 *Ibid.*, p. 41, Lamsdorf's instruction to Russian Minister to Persia, 1904 from A. Popov, (ed.), Tsarskaia Rossiia i Persiia v epokhu russko-iaponskoi voiny', Krasnyi arkhiv, 4(53) (1932).
123 Issawi, *Economic History of Iran*, p. 312.
124 *Ibid.*, p. 334.
125 Quoted in Entner, *Russo-Persian Commercical Relations*, p. 54.
126 See William J. Kelly and Tsuneo Kano, 'Crude Oil Production in the Russian Empire: 1818-1919', *The Journal of European . Economic History*, 6 (1977) pp. 307-38.
127 Quoted in Issawi, *The Economic History of Iran*, p. 329.
128 Oil in Russia was generally measured by the 'pood', a unit of weight equivalent to 36.112 English pounds. Conversion factors are: 1 pood = 4.2 imperial gallons; 1 US barrel = 8.33 poods of crude oil or 8.00 poods of kerosene. In 1900, the exchange rate between the rouble and the pound was approximately 10 roubles to the £. Russian oil production peaked in 1901 at 706 million poods (84.7 million barrels). See Kelly and Kano, 'Crude oil production in the Russian Empire': S. and L. Pershke, *Russkaya neftyanaya promyshlennost*, Tiflis, 1913, pp. 66, 83, 85 and 86.
129 PRO FO 60/660, Memorandum for 'Abbās Kulī Khān in conversations with Amīn al-Sultān', 26 January 1902.

130 PRO FO 60/660, Hardinge to Lansdowne, 29 January 1902.
131 PRO FO 60/660, Hardinge to Lansdowne, 16 February 1902.
132 Kazemzadeh, *Russia and Britain in Persia*, p. 382, Argyropoulo to Lamsdorf, February 1902. See also PRO FO 60/660, Sir Charles Scott despatches to Foreign Secretary, 15 and 20 February 1902.
133 Kazemzadeh, *Russia and Britain in Persia*, pp. 56-8.
134 B.H. Sumner, *Tsardom and Imperialism in the Far East and Middle East, 1880-1914* (London, 1942), p. 21.
135 Quoted in Issawi, *The Economic History of Iran*, p. 334, Anan'ich, 'Rossiya i Kontsessiya d'Arsi', p. 290.
136 Kelly and Kano, 'Crude Oil Production in the Russian Empire', *The Journal of European Economic History*, 6 (1977), p. 322.
137 L.J. Lewery, 'Foreign Capital Investments in Russian Industries', Department of Commerce Miscellaneous Series, no. 124 (Washington, 1923), pp. 15-23.

2. The funding and finding of oil 1901-8

1 BP H16/153, Redwood to D'Arcy, 9 September 1901.
2 BP H16/2, D'Arcy to Jenkin, 24 September 1901.
3 BP H12/35 p. 73, Kitabgi to Wolff, November 1901.
4 L. Lockhart, 'The Record of the Anglo Iranian Oil Co. Ltd.', unpublished Company record, p. 12.
5 BP H16/153, Redwood to D'Arcy, 9 September 1901.
6 BP H10/25, D'Arcy to Reynolds, 6 July 1901.
7 BP H16/10, D'Arcy to Kitabgi, 13 August 1901.
8 BP H16/2, D'Arcy to Jenkin, 20 August 1902.
9 *Ibid.*, D'Arcy to Jenkin, 25 August 1902.
10 Lockhart, 'Record', p. 13.
11 BP H12/35 pp. 65 and 73, 16 September 1901.
12 *Ibid.*, p. 80, 3 December 1901.
13 *Ibid.*, p. 64, 12 September 1901.
14 *Ibid.*, pp. 75-7, 28 November 1901.
15 *Ibid.*, p. 62, 12 September 1901.
16 *Ibid.*, p. 80, D'Arcy to Kitabgi, 5 December 1901.
17 *Ibid.*, p. 82, D'Arcy to Kitabgi, 18 January 1902.
18 BP H16/70, D'Arcy to Kitabgi, 16 February 1902.
19 BP H12/35 pp. 87-8, Kitabgi to D'Arcy, 24 March 1902.
20 *Ibid.*, pp. 88-9, D'Arcy to Kitabgi, 27 March 1902.
21 *Ibid.*, p. 100, D'Arcy to Vincent Kitabgi, 15 May 1902.
22 *Ibid.*, p. 107, Kitabgi to Wolff, 6 June 1902.
23 *Ibid.*, pp. 114-15, D'Arcy to Vincent Kitabgi, 20 June 1902.
24 *Ibid.*, p. 113, D'Arcy to Kitabgi, 20 June 1902.
25 *Ibid.*, p. 122, Vincent Kitabgi to Kitabgi, 7 June 1902.
26 *Ibid.*, p. 124, Vincent Kitabgi to Kitabgi, 8 July 1902.
27 *Ibid.*, p. 130, Article XI, Draft Articles for Parent Syndicate, 17 June 1902.
28 *Ibid.*, pp. 134-5, notes of meeting, 22 July 1902.
29 *Ibid.*, p. 138, D'Arcy to Kitabgi, 11 August 1902.
30 BP H15/117 p. 152, D'Arcy to Kitabgi, 5 October 1902.
31 *Ibid.*, p. 154, Kitabgi to D'Arcy, 9 October 1902.

Notes to pp. 52-60

32 *Ibid.*, p. 166, D'Arcy to Vincent Kitabgi, 23 December 1902.
33 *Ibid.*, p. 170, Vincent Kitabgi to D'Arcy, 28 January 1903.
34 BP H16/2, D'Arcy to Jenkin, 15 April 1903.
35 *Ibid.*, D'Arcy to Jenkin, 24 March 1903.
36 BP H12/421, Articles of Association of the First Exploitation Company Ltd, 21 May 1903.
37 BP H15/117 pp. 184-5, D'Arcy to Vincent Kitabgi, 11 July 1903.
38 *Ibid.*, p. 185, Vincent Kitabgi receipt, 13 July 1903.
39 *Ibid.*, pp. 181-2, Vincent Kitabgi acknowledgement, 21 June 1903.
40 BP H12/35 p. 60, 10 September 1901.
41 *Ibid.*, p. 64, 12 September 1901.
42 *Ibid.*, p. 66, Reynolds to D'Arcy, 20 September 1901.
43 *Ibid.*, p. 74, 22 November 1901; see also PRO FO 60/731, Hardinge to Lansdowne, 16 September 1901.
44 BP H4/147, Burls to Redwood, reports of 13, 20 and 27 July 1901, pp. 1-6.
45 BP H17/96, Redwood, 'Report on the Petroliferous Territory of Persia', 30 July 1901, p. 11.
46 BP H12/35 p. 61, Kitabgi to D'Arcy, 10 September 1901.
47 *Ibid.*, pp. 48-50; pp. 50-3, 8 July 1901.
48 *Ibid.*, p. 59, 26 August 1901.
49 *Ibid.*, p. 58, August 1901.
50 *Ibid.*, p. 62, 12 September 1901.
51 *Ibid.*, p. 77, 26 November 1901.
52 *Ibid.*, pp. 69-72, Reynolds to Paul Kitabgi, 30 October 1901.
53 BP H12/24 p. 17, Reynolds to D'Arcy, November 1901.
54 BP H12/35 p. 86, Reynolds to D'Arcy, 22 March 1902.
55 BP H12/24 p. 140, Reynolds to D'Arcy, 24 March 1902.
56 *Ibid.*, p. 185, D'Arcy to Reynolds, 15 April 1902.
57 *Ibid.*, p. 208, Reynolds to D'Arcy, 25 April 1902.
58 BP H12/35 p. 65, 16 September 1901.
59 *Ibid.*, pp. 145-8, Kitabgi to D'Arcy, 29 September 1901.
60 PRO FO 60/731, Dobbs to Lawrence, 4 March 1903.
61 BP H12/35 p. 142, D'Arcy to Reynolds, 31 August 1902.
62 *Ibid.*, p. 143, D'Arcy to Kitabgi, 27 September 1902.
63 BP H16/153, Redwood to D'Arcy, 9 September 1902.
64 *Ibid.*, Redwood to D'Arcy, 20 May 1902.
65 BP H14/147, Dalton, 'Report on the Oilfields of South-Western Persia', 15 May 1903.
66 BP H16/2, D'Arcy to Jenkin, 28 July 1903.
67 *Ibid.*
68 BP H12/80 p. 80, Hargraves account with D'Arcy, 11 January 1903.
69 Lockhart, 'Record' p. 47, D'Arcy to Fletcher Moulton, 8 August 1903.
70 On Fisher's enthusiasm for fuel oil, see A.J. Marder, *From Dreadnought to Scapa Flow* vol. 1, (London 1961), pp. 45, 269-71 and ed. *'Fear God and Dread Nought', the Correspondence of Admiral of the Fleet Lord Fisher of Kilverstone*, 3 vols. (London 1952-59).
71 See Robert Henriques, *Marcus Samuel, First Lord Bearsted and Founder of the Shell Transport and Trading Co., 1853-1927* (London, 1960), pp. 400-2.
72 PRO ADM 116/3807, Admiralty to BOC, 24 July 1903.
73 Lockhart, 'Record', p. 47, D'Arcy to Manisty, n.d.

Notes to pp. 60-66

74 PRO FO 60/731, Lansdowne to Curzon, 7 December 1903.
75 *Ibid.*, Curzon to Lansdowne, 9 December 1903.
76 *Ibid.*, Hardinge to Lansdowne, 24 December 1903.
77 IO L/P&S/10/143, Hardinge to Lansdowne, 27 January 1904.
78 BP H12/80 p. 80, Coburg Hotel account, 25 November 1903.
79 Lockhart, 'Record', p. 48.
80 *Ibid.*, p. 49.
81 BP H15/117 p. 208, Vincent Kitabgi to D'Arcy, 30 January 1904.
82 BP H12/80 p. 85, Bell to Jenkin, 13 July 1904.
83 Lockhart, 'Record', p. 49.
84 BP H16/2, D'Arcy to Jenkin, 2 January 1904.
85 BP H12/27 p. 59, Jenkin to D'Arcy, 29 February 1904.
86 BP H16/2, Nina D'Arcy to Jenkin, 16 February 1904.
87 Quoted in Lockhart, 'Record', pp. 50-51.
88 IO L/P&S/10/143, Lansdowne to Hardinge, 12 March 1904.
89 PRO FO 371/2075, Gaston de Bernhardt, 'Report on Mr. W.K. D'Arcy's Oil Concession in Persia', 3 January 1913.
90 Lockhart, 'Record', p. 51.
91 *Ibid.*
92 *Ibid.*
93 *Ibid.*, p. 52.
94 BP H16/2, D'Arcy to Jenkin, 19 January 1904.
95 BP H17/89B, Rosenplaenter to Jenkin, 14 January 1904.
96 BP H12/35 p. 143, D'Arcy to Kitabgi, 27 September 1902.
97 BP H17/89A, Redwood to Rosenplaenter, 24 June 1903.
98 IO L/P&S/10/143, Hardinge to Lansdowne, 27 January 1904.
99 BP H17/89B, Rosenplaenter to Jenkin, 12 February 1904.
100 BP H17/89A, Rosenplaenter to Redwood, 12 June 1903.
101 *Ibid.*, Rosenplaenter to Jenkin, 19 June 1903.
102 *Ibid.*, Rosenplaenter to Jenkin, 7 November 1903.
103 *Ibid.*, Rosenplaenter to Jenkin, 1 September 1903.
104 *Ibid.*, Rosenplaenter to Jenkin, 27 December 1903.
105 *Ibid.*, Rosenplaenter to Redwood, 31 July 1903.
106 *Ibid.*, Rosenplaenter to Jenkin, 5 August 1903.
107 *Ibid.*, Rosenplaenter to Jenkin, 13 November 1903.
108 BP H17/89B, Rosenplaenter to Jenkin, 29 January 1904.
109 BP H17/89A, Shaykh al-Mulk to Rosenplaenter, 24 July 1903.
110 *Ibid.*, Rosenplaenter to Jenkin, 27 December 1903.
111 *Ibid.*, Rosenplaenter to Jenkin, 25 October 1903.
112 *Ibid.*, Rosenplaenter to Jenkin, 26 June 1903.
113 *Ibid.*, Rosenplaenter to Jenkin, 15 August 1903.
114 BP H17/89B, Rosenplaenter to Jenkin, 14 January 1904.
115 *Ibid.*, Rosenplaenter to Jenkin, 18 January 1904.
116 *Ibid.*, Rosenplaenter to Jenkin, 14 January 1904.
117 *Ibid.*, Rosenplaenter to Jenkin, 5 and 12 January 1904.
118 BP H12/27, Holland to Jenkin, 30 June 1904.
119 BP H17/89A, Jenkin to Reynolds, 4 December 1904.
120 BP H17/89B, Grahame to Reynolds, 23 June 1904 and 27 September 1904.
121 BP H12/27, Reynolds to Jenkin (two letters), 27 February 1904.

Notes to pp. 66-70

122 *Ibid.*, Reynolds to Jenkin, 31 March 1904.
123 Arnold Wilson describes the prevalent instability in A.T. Wilson, *S.W. Persia, Letters and Diary of a Young Political Officer, 1907-1914* (London, 1942), pp. 141-56.
124 BP H12/27, Reynolds to Jenkin, 31 March 1904.
125 Lockhart, 'Record', p. 46, Dalton to Redwood, 12 July 1904.
126 BP H12/27, Reynolds to Jenkin, 2 April 1904.
127 *Ibid.*, Jenkin to Reynolds, 25 April 1904.
128 BP H17/89B, Grahame to Reynolds, 23 June 1904.
129 *Ibid.*, Reynolds to Jenkin, 10 April 1904.
130 BP H12/27, Jenkin to Reynolds, 25 April 1904.
131 *Ibid.*, Jenkin to Reynolds, 19 May and 8 June 1904.
132 See J.E. King, 'The New Broad Arrow: Origins of British Oil Policy', *Mariners Mirror*, 189 (1953).
133 PRO ADM 1/7594C passim, e.g. no. 20554, Admiralty to FO August 1901; ADM 1/7676 and ADM 1/7824 passim.
134 PRO ADM 116/3807, Admiralty to Secretary of State for India, 4 May 1904.
135 *Ibid.*, Admiralty to BOC, 1 July 1903.
136 BP 77/49/18, BOC to Miller, 2 November 1903.
137 For details of the Burmah Oil Company's history, see T.A.B. Corley's forthcoming volume.
138 BP 77/49/18, BOC Board Minutes Book 2, 13 October 1902.
139 *Ibid.*, Tribute to D.S. Cargill 3rd AGM, 26 April 1905.
140 *Ibid.*, Redwood to Jenkin, 4 February 1904.
141 *Ibid.*, Miller to BOC, 15 February 1904.
142 *Ibid.*, Cargill to Miller, 25 February 1904.
143 *Ibid.*, Redwood to Pretyman, 15 March 1904.
144 *Ibid.*, Cargill to Miller, 26 April 1904.
145 *Ibid.*, Melrose report: 'Suitability of Burmah Oil as Liquid Fuel', 2 July 1904.
146 Statement from Chairman's speech BOC AGM, 1927.
147 PRO ADM 116/3807, Cargill to Redwood, 6 October 1904.
148 *Ibid.*, Admiralty to BOC, 28 October 1905.
149 For the history of oil affairs in India see B. Dasgupta, *The History of the Oil Industry in India* (London, 1971).
150 Lockhart, 'Record', p. 52.
151 BP H16/2 D'Arcy to Jenkin, 12 August 1904.
152 *Ibid.*, D'Arcy to Jenkin, 14 August 1904.
153 *Ibid.*, D'Arcy to Jenkin, 20 August 1904.
154 BP H12/27 Jenkin to Reynolds, 30 August 1904.
155 *Ibid.*, Jenkin to Reynolds, 29 September 1904.
156 BP H16/2 D'Arcy to Jenkin, 24 October 1904.
157 *Ibid.*, D'Arcy to Jenkin, 8 November 1905.
158 Lockhart, 'Record', p. 53.
159 BP 77/49/18, BOC Board meeting, 3 February 1905.
160 BP H16/71, D'Arcy to Jenkin, 26 January 1905.
161 Lockhart, 'Record', p. 54.
162 PRO FO 60/731, Boyds and Miller to Sanderson, 9 February 1905 and *ibid.*, Grahame draft letter, 24 February 1905 and BP H14/43 Gorst to Boyds and Miller, 24 February 1905.

163 BP 79/4/66, Persian Concession; D'Arcy's Agreement with BOC, 20 May 1905.
164 BP H15/117 p. 215, D'Arcy to Vincent Kitabgi, 21 January 1905.
165 Ibid., p. 216, Vincent Kitabgi to D'Arcy, 30 January 1905.
166 Lockhart, 'Record', pp. 58-9.
167 BP H15/117 p. 216, Wolff to Vincent Kitabgi, 23 February 1905.
168 Burmah were raising capital in connection with the Admiralty Supply Agreement and were reluctant to include the D'Arcy Concession arrangements in the prospectus issued in early April.
169 Lockhart, 'Record', p. 56.
170 Lockhart 'Record', p. 56, Boyds and Miller to Manisty, 14 April 1905.
171 BP H15/117 p. 233, Counsel's Opinion, 11 April 1905.
172 Ibid., p. 235, Vincent Kitabgi to D'Arcy, 19 April 1905 and ibid., p. 241, Norton to Vincent Kitabgi, 15 May 1905.
173 Ibid., p. 237, D'Arcy to Vincent Kitabgi, 10 May 1905.
174 Lockhart, 'Record', pp. 57-8.
175 PRO FO 416/26, Hardinge to Grey, 23 December 1905.
176 G.R. Garthwaite, 'The Bakhtiari Khans, the Government of Iran and the British 1846-1915'. *International Journal of Middle East Studies*, 3 (1972), 24-44.
177 On German interest in Persia at this time see B.G. Martin, *German-Persian Diplomatic Relations 1873-1912* ('s Gravenhage, 1959), pp. 80-158.
178 Wilson, *S.W. Persia*, p. 84, appreciated the issue, 'The position of a Company which is working under a Concession from one Government (Persian) but depends on the goodwill of a provincial administration (Arab and Bakhtiari) and the military and moral support of a third (British and Indian), with a head office in Glasgow, dealing with the Foreign Office (in London), and a Foreign Dept. (Simla) through local offices (in Persia) is not easy.' The life of Wilson, who frequently appears in this history, has been sympathetically written by John Marlowe, *Late Victorian* (London, 1967).
179 BP 77/49/11, Cargill (?) to Jenkin, 31 March 1905.
180 BP H16/71, D'Arcy to Nichols, 12 June 1905.
181 BP H17/89B, Reynolds to CSL, 9 August 1905.
182 Ibid., Reynolds to CSL, 14 August 1905.
183 BP H14/43, D'Arcy to Sanderson, 26 September 1905.
184 IO L/P&S/10/143, Curzon to FO, 1 November 1905.
185 BP H17/89B, Reynolds to CSL, 1 September 1905.
186 Ibid., Reynolds to CSL, 3 September 1905.
187 Ibid., Reynolds to CSL, 16 August 1905.
188 Ibid., Reynolds to CSL, 9 September 1905.
189 Ibid., Reynolds to CSL, 16 September 1905.
190 Ibid., Reynolds to CSL, 4 December 1905.
191 Ibid.
192 Ibid.
193 BP H9/107, Bakhtiari Agreement, 15 November 1905.
194 BP H16/71 D'Arcy to Jenkin, 28 October 1905.
195 Ibid., D'Arcy to Jenkin, 13 November 1905.
196 BP H17/89B, Reynolds to CSL, 4 December 1905.
197 Ibid., Reynolds to Samsam al-Saltana, 28 November 1905, ibid., Reynolds to CSL, 4 December 1905, ibid., Reynolds to Samsam al-Saltana, 7 December 1905.

Notes to pp. 77–82

198 BP 77/49/3 (1) Reynolds to CSL, 5 January 1906.
199 BP H13/86 Grant Duff to Grey, 12 January 1906.
200 Lockhart, 'Record', p. 71.
201 BP H17/89B, Reynolds to CSL, 4 December 1905.
202 BP H16/90, D'Arcy to Preece, 17 June 1906 and BP H17/52, Preece to CSL, 26 June 1906.
203 BP 77/49/3 (1), Reynolds to CSL, 4 January 1906.
204 BP 77/49/3 (2), Reynolds to CSL, 23 August 1906.
205 *Ibid.*, Reynolds to CSL, 10 September 1906.
206 *Ibid.*, Reynolds to CSL, 30 October 1906.
207 *Ibid.*
208 BP 77/49/3 (1), Reynolds to CSL, 17 January 1906.
209 BP 77/49/4 (1), Reynolds to Hamilton, 26 January 1907.
210 *Ibid.*, Reynolds to Hamilton, 26 January 1907.
211 BP 77/49/3 (1), Reynolds to Hoogenboezm, 31 January 1906.
212 *Ibid.*, Reynolds to Lorimer, 17 January 1906.
213 *Ibid.*, Reynolds to Sālār-i-Arfā, 8 January 1906 and *ibid.*, Sālār-i-Arfā to Reynolds, 13 February 1906.
214 BP 77/49/3 (1), Reynolds to Lorimer, 17 February 1906.
215 *Ibid.*, Reynolds to CSL, 28 February 1906.
216 BP 13/86, Grant Duff to FO, 26 January 1906.
217 BP 77/49/3 (1), Reynolds to CSL, 28 February 1906.
218 BP H13/86, Grant Duff to Grey, 18 May 1906.
219 BP H17/52, CSL to Preece, 11 June 1906.
220 BP H16/90, D'Arcy to Preece, 24 June 1906.
221 BP H13/86, Preece draft memo, n.d., sent 18 June 1906
222 *Ibid.*, Reynolds to CSL, 17 October 1906.
223 BP 77/49/3 (2), Reynolds to CSL, 10 October 1906.
224 BP H13/86, Preece to Grey, 26 October 1906.
225 *Ibid.*, Gorst to Preece, 29 October 1906, and *ibid.*, Preece to Hamilton, 30 October 1906.
226 BP 77/49/3 (2), Lorimer to Reynolds, 21 October 1906; See also BP H13/86, enclosure in Spring-Rice dispatch, received 7 December 1906.
227 BP 77/49/3 (2), Reynolds to CSL, 12 November 1906 and BP H13/86, Gorst to Preece, 2 November 1906.
228 BP H16/90, D'Arcy to Preece, 1 January 1907.
229 BP 77/49/18, BOC Board meeting, 27 February 1907.
230 Lockhart, 'Record', p. 85.
231 BP 77/49/18, BOC Board meeting, 6 March 1907.
232 Lockhart, 'Record', p. 86.
233 BP 77/49/18, BOC Board meeting, 20 March 1907.
234 Lockhart, 'Record', p. 86.
235 BP H15/117 p. 264, D'Arcy to Vincent Kitabgi, 8 August 1907.
236 Lockhart, 'Record', pp. 86–7.
237 BP 77/49/18, BOC Directors' Report, 17 April 1907.
238 BP 77/49/11, Wallace to Cargill, 17 September 1906.

Notes to pp. 83-88

239 BP H7/119, R.I. Watson, memorandum: The Burmah Oil Company Limited, p. 22, 10 February 1916.
240 BP 77/49/18, BOC 5th Annual General Meeting, 26 April 1907.
241 BP 77/49/4 (1), Reynolds to Lorimer, 20 February 1907.
242 *Ibid.*, Lorimer to Political Resident, 6 March 1907.
243 BP 77/49/4 (1), Lorimer to Legation, 25 March 1907.
244 BP 77/49/4 (2), Reynolds to Political Resident, 20 May 1907, *ibid.*, Lorimer to Reynolds, 24 May 1907.
245 *Ibid.*, Reynolds to CSL, 29 May 1907.
246 BP H17/52, Preece to Hamilton, 5 September 1907.
247 BP H16/90, D'Arcy to Preece, 12 June 1907.
248 BP 77/49/4 (2), Reynolds to CSL, 29 May 1907.
249 *Ibid.*, Reynolds to Redwood, 31 May 1907.
250 BP H4/147, Cunningham-Craig Report, 2 January 1908.
251 BP 77/49/4 (1), Reynolds to CSL, 26 February 1907; *ibid.*, Reynolds to CSL, 30 April 1907.
252 BP 77/49/4 (3), Reynolds to CSL, 22 September 1907.
253 BP 77/49/4 (2), Reynolds to CSL, 30 June 1907.
254 *Ibid.*, Bradshaw to Reynolds, 1 July 1907.
255 *Ibid.*, Reynolds to Lorimer, 14 August 1907.
256 BP 77/49/4 (3), Bertie to Reynolds, 27 September 1907.
257 BP H16/90, D'Arcy to Preece, 20 September, 1907.
258 BP H13/86, FO to Preece, 16 September 1907.
259 *Ibid.*, Preece to FO, 30 September 1907.
260 *Ibid.*, Hardinge to D'Arcy, 11 and 17 October 1907 and BP H16/90, D'Arcy to Preece, 5 October 1907.
261 BP H13/86, FO to Preece, 31 December 1907.
262 BP 77/49/3 (1), Reynolds to CSL, 17 January 1907.
263 BP 77/49/3 (2), Reynolds to CSL, 11 July 1906.
264 *Ibid.*, Reynolds to CSL, 6 August 1906.
265 *Ibid.*, Reynolds to CSL, 10 October and 14 November 1906.
266 *Ibid.*, Reynolds to CSL, 26 December 1906.
267 BP 77/49/4 (1), Reynolds to CSL, 18 February 1907.
268 BP 77/49/5 (1), Reynolds to CSL, 29 April, 1908.
269 *Ibid.*, Reynolds to CSL, Bradshaw to CSL, 3 February 1908.
270 BP H17/89B, Reynolds to CSL, 18 December 1905.
271 BP 77/49/5 (1), CSL to Reynolds, 18 January 1908.
272 *Ibid.*, Reynolds to CSL, 10 February and 25 March 1908.
273 *Ibid.*, Reynolds to CSL, 26 February 1908.
274 *Ibid.*, Reynolds to CSL, 11 April 1908.
275 Lockhart, 'Record', p. 99.
276 *Ibid.*
277 BP 77/49/12 (1), Hamilton to D'Arcy, 13 April 1908.
278 BP 77/49/18, BOC Board Meeting, 15 April 1908.
279 *Ibid.*, BOC 6th AGM Board Report, 17 April 1908.
280 BP 77/49/5 (1), Reynolds to CSL, 16 and 24 May 1908.
281 *Ibid.*, Reynolds to CSL, 26 May 1908.
282 Wilson, *S.W. Persia*, p. 42.
283 BP 77/49/5 (1), CSL to Reynolds, 14 May 1908.

Notes to pp. 90-95

3. The formation of the Anglo-Persian Oil Company

1. PRO FO 800/351, Nicolson Papers, O'Beirne to Nicolson, 2 November 1911, quoted in David Maclean, *Britain and her Buffer State*, Royal Historical Society Studies in History Series, no. 4 (London, 1979), p. 105.
2. PRO FO 416/32 no. 119, Spring-Rice to Grey, 11 April 1907.
3. PRO FO 416/37 no. 240, FO to Preece, 30 July 1908.
4. BP H14/43, Preece to FO, 2 August 1908.
5. PRO FO 371/497, Hardinge minute on Marling to Grey, 29 May 1908.
6. *Ibid.*, Hardinge minute on India Office to Foreign Office, 27 July 1908.
7. BP H14/43, Lorimer to Marling, 28 July 1908, enclosure in Mallet to D'Arcy, 12 September 1908
8. *Ibid.*, Mallet to D'Arcy, 12 September 1908.
9. PRO FO 881/9656, Annual Report Persia 1908, Barclay to Grey, 10 February 1910, p. 13.
10. BP H17/52, Preece to Hamilton, 25 September 1902, memorandum papers sent from FO to D'Arcy.
11. BP H14/43, Lorimer memorandum, 27 July 1908, enclosure in Mallet to D'Arcy, 12 September 1908
12. BP H14/43, Campbell to Preece, 2 October 1908.
13. BP H16/101, Churchill to Preece, 24 April 1908.
14. A.T. Wilson, *S.W. Persia, Letters and Diary of a Young Political Officer, 1907-1914* (London, 1942), pp. 41-2.
15. BP H16/89, D'Arcy to Preece, 23 June 1908.
16. *Ibid.*, D'Arcy to Preece, 19 June 1908.
17. *Ibid.*, D'Arcy to Preece, 9 August 1908.
18. *Ibid.*, D'Arcy to Preece, 19 June 1908.
19. BP H12/82, Sādigh al-Saltana to D'Arcy, 1 January 1907.
20. PRO FO 416/31 G.P. Churchill memorandum, 'Summary of Proceedings of Persian National Assembly', December 1906 to January 1907, enclosure in Spring-Rice to Grey, 3 January 1907.
21. PRO FO 416/31, G.P. Churchill memorandum, 'Summary of Proceedings of Persian National Assembly', 3 to 29 January 1907, enclosure in Spring-Rice to Grey, 30 January 1907.
22. PRO FO 416/31, 'Memorandum of Mr. Kitabgi on the Affairs of the D'Arcy Oil Company in Persia', enclosure in Spring-Rice to Grey, 22 March 1907.
23. PRO FO 416/31, Loraine to Spring-Rice, 20 May 1907.
24. BP H12/82, Sādigh al-Saltana to Preece, 19 August 1908.
25. *Ibid.*, Sādigh al-Saltana to D'Arcy, 1 January 1907.
26. *Ibid.*, Preece to D'Arcy, 23 August 1908.
27. *Ibid.*, Preece to Hamilton, 22 August 1908.
28. BP H16/89, D'Arcy to Preece, 24 August 1908.
29. *Ibid.*, D'Arcy to Preece, 27 August 1908.
30. BP H12/82, Sādigh al-Saltana to Preece, 4 November 1908.
31. *Ibid.*
32. BP H16/89, D'Arcy to Preece, 10 September 1908.
33. BP H14/43, D'Arcy to Greenway, 2 September 1908.
34. BP 77/49/15, BOC Letter Book No.9, Hamilton to Cargill, 15 July 1908.
35. BP H16/89, D'Arcy to Preece, 8 September 1908.
36. BP H14/43, D'Arcy to Greenway, 19 September 1908.

Notes to pp. 95–102

37 *Ibid.*, D'Arcy to Hamilton, 30 September 1908 and D'Arcy to Greenway, 2 October 1908.
38 BP 77/49/18, BOC Board Minutes, 28 October 1908; see also BP 77/49/12 (2), Wallace to Adamson, 28 December 1908.
39 Lockhart, 'The Record of the Anglo Iranian Oil Co. Ltd.', unpublished company record, p. 115.
40 BP H16/89, D'Arcy to Preece, 8 November 1908.
41 BP 77/49/12 (1), BOC to D'Arcy, 16 November 1908.
42 Lockhart, 'Record', pp. 105–6.
43 BP H14/43, Hamilton to D'Arcy, 1 October 1908.
44 BP 77/49/15, Hamilton to Cargill, 6 November 1908.
45 BP 77/49/12 (1), Reynolds to CSL, 24 October 1908.
46 *Ibid.*, (1), Secretaries to Reynolds, 19 November 1908.
47 Lockhart, 'Record', p. 115.
48 BP H12/112, Hardinge to D'Arcy, 27 January 1909.
49 *Ibid.*, Wallace to Adamson, 6 February 1909.
50 BP 77/49/12 (2), Wallace to Adamson, 28 December 1908.
51 BP H16/89, D'Arcy to Preece, 9 January 1909.
52 Lockhart, 'Record', p. 116.
53 *Ibid.*
54 *Ibid.*
55 BP H12/82, Sādigh al-Saltana to Preece, 8 November 1908.
56 *Ibid.*, Manisty to D'Arcy, 26 November 1908.
57 BP H16/89, D'Arcy to Preece, 14 December 1908.
58 BP H12/82, Sādigh al-Saltana to Preece, 22 December 1908.
59 *Ibid.*, D'Arcy to Jenkin, 25 December 1908.
60 BP H12/112, D'Arcy to Greenway, 2 January 1909.
61 BP H16/89, D'Arcy to Preece, 6 February 1909.
62 Lockhart, 'Record', p. 117, Opinion of Robert Younger KC, 8 February 1909.
63 BP H12/112, Manisty to D'Arcy, 15 January 1909.
64 *Ibid.*, D'Arcy to Wallace, 16 January 1909.
65 *Ibid.*, Adamson to Wallace, 21 January 1909.
66 *Ibid.*, Adamson to Wallace, 22 January 1909.
67 *Ibid.*, Wallace note, 25 January 1909.
68 *Ibid.*, Wallace minute, 25 January 1909.
69 *Ibid.*, Wallace to Adamson, 25 January 1909.
70 *Ibid.*, Thompson to Hamilton, 27 January 1909.
71 *Ibid.*, Wallace to Adamson, 28 January 1909.
72 *Ibid.*, Wallace to D'Arcy, 5 February 1909.
73 *Ibid.*, Wallace to Manisty, 10 February 1909.
74 *Ibid.*, Wallace to D'Arcy, 29 January 1909.
75 *Ibid.*, Wallace to Adamson, 2 February 1909.
76 *Ibid.*, Wallace to Strathcona, 15 February 1909.
77 *Ibid.*, Wallace to Strathcona, 3 March 1909.
78 *Ibid.*, D'Arcy to Greenway, 27 February 1909.
79 *Ibid.*
80 *Ibid.*, Wallace to Adamson, 3 March 1909.
81 *Ibid.*, Heads of Agreement enclosed in Wallace to Adamson, 3 March 1909.
82 *Ibid.*, Wallace to Adamson, 3 March 1909.

83 BP 77/49/12 (3), Wallace to Boyds, Miller and Thompson, 1 April 1909.
84 BP H12/112, Wallace to Adamson, 5 March 1909.
85 *Ibid.*, Wallace to Adamson, 4 March 1909.
86 *Ibid.*, D'Arcy to Wallace, 6 January 1909.
87 *Ibid.*, Wallace to Adamson, 13 January 1909.
88 *Ibid.*
89 *Ibid.*, Wallace to Adamson, 21 January 1909.
90 *Ibid.*, D'Arcy to Adamson, 9 March 1909.
91 *Ibid.*, Wallace to Adamson, 11 March 1909.
92 *Ibid.*, Opinion of Sir F.B. Palmer, 12 March 1909.
93 BP H15/17, Kitabgi to D'Arcy, 19 May 1909.
94 BP H12/112, D'Arcy to Wallace, 23 March 1909.
95 Lockhart, 'Record', p. 119.
96 Lockhart, 'Record', p. 120.
97 BP 77/49/12 (3), Wallace to McGeorge, 1 April 1909.
98 *Ibid.*, Wallace to Cargill, 31 March 1909.
99 *Ibid.*, Cargill to Strathcona, 27 March 1909.
100 *Ibid.*, Wallace to Barnes, 30 March 1909.
101 *Ibid.*, Wallace to Cargill, 7 April 1909.
102 *Ibid.*, Wallace to Cargill, 8 and 13 April 1909.
103 *Ibid.*, Mallet to Preece, 3 April 1909.
104 BP H16/89, D'Arcy to Preece, 14 and 26 April 1909, and BP H17/166, Wallace to Cargill, 12 April 1909.
105 BP H12/112, Campbell to Preece, 27 April 1909.
106 *Ibid.*, Preece to Under-Secretary FO, 29 April 1909.
107 BP H17/166, Wallace to Cargill, 18 May 1909.
108 BP H12/112, Wallace to Cargill, 29 March 1909.
109 *Ibid.*
110 BP 77/49/15, Wallace to Cargill, 2 November 1908.
111 *Ibid.*
112 BP H17/166, Wallace to Cargill, 26 April 1909.
113 APOC Prospectus, 16 April 1909.
114 *Ibid.*
115 BP H12/112, Wallace to Adamson, 6 February 1909.
116 APOC Prospectus, 16 April 1909.
117 BP H17/166, Cargill to Wallace, 20 April 1909.
118 *Ibid.*
119 BP 77/49/18, BOC Board Minutes, 23 April 1909.
120 BP 77/49/12 (3), Wallace to Cargill, 30 March 1909.
121 *Ibid.*, Wallace to McGeorge, 8 April 1909.
122 BP H17/166, Cargill to Wallace, 7 April 1909, and *ibid.*, wires to and from Glasgow, 20 April 1909.
123 *Petroleum Review*, 25 April 1908.
124 BP H17/166, 'Geo. Whitehead and Chown Memorandum', 17 April 1909.
125 *Petroleum Review*, 24 April 1909.
126 *The Daily Chronicle*, 17 April 1909.
127 *The Morning Post*, 17 April 1909.
128 *The Daily Express*, 17 April 1909.
129 BP H12/112, Greenway to Pratt, 28 April 1909.
130 BP H16/89, D'Arcy to Preece, 1 May 1909.

4. Progress in Persia

1. PRO FO 416/111, 'Annual Report Persia 1909', Barclay to Grey, 10 February 1910, p.34.
2. PRO FO 416/111, 'Annual Report Persia 1910', Barclay to Grey, 28 February 1911, p.32.
3. BP H17/166, Greenway to Cargill, 3 May 1909.
4. BP APOC Board Minutes, 25 May 1909.
5. For an idea of the history of the managing agency see Vera Anstey, *The Economic Development of India*, 3rd edn (London, 1942), and T.A.B. Corley, 'Communications, Entrepreneurship and the Managing Agency System: The Burmah Oil Co. 1886-1928', unpublished paper for business history seminar, Polytechnic of Central London, 4 May 1979.
6. BP 77/49/5 (2), Reynolds to CSL, 9 October 1908.
7. BP 77/49/6 (1), Reynolds to CSL, 4 May 1909.
8. BP 77/49/5 (2), Reynolds to CSL, 15 July 1908.
9. *Ibid.*
10. BP 77/49/6 (1), Reynolds to CSL, 4 May 1909.
11. BP 77/49/6 (2), Reynolds to CSL, 16 January 1909.
12. *Ibid.*, Reynolds to CSL, 5 January 1909.
13. *Ibid.*, Reynolds to Shaw Wallace and Co., Calcutta, 8 January 1909; PRO FO 416/43 no.55, APOC to FO, 12 January 1910 and no. 96 enclosure Govt of India to FO, 20 January 1910.
14. BP 77/49/6 (2), Macrorie to Hamilton, 25 January 1909 and Reynolds to CSL, 5 February 1909.
15. BP 77/49/6 (2), Reynolds to CSL, 21 February 1909.
16. *Ibid.*, Reynolds to Agent of Mu'in al-Tujjār, 21 January 1909.
17. *Ibid.*, Reynolds to CSL, 23 February and 1 March 1909.
18. BP 77/49/6 (1), Reynolds to CSL, 29 July 1909.
19. *Ibid.*, passim.
20. BP 77/49/6 (2), Reynolds to CSL, 4 January 1909.
21. BP 77/49/6 (1), Willans to Reynolds, 28 May 1909, enclosure in Reynolds to CSL, 30 May 1909.
22. BP 77/49/6 (1), Wallace to Reynolds, 26 July 1909.
23. *Ibid.*, Reynolds to Wallace, 27 July 1909.
24. *Ibid.*, Reynolds to Macindoe, 6 August 1909.
25. *Ibid.*, Reynolds to APOC, 28 August 1909.
26. *Ibid.*, Reynolds to CSL, 25 May 1909.
27. *Ibid.*, Reynolds to CSL, 16 April 1909.
28. *Ibid.*, Reynolds to CSL, 17 April 1909.
29. *Ibid.*, Reynolds to Macindoe, 31 August 1909.
30. *Ibid.*, Reynolds to APOC, 5 August 1909.
31. IO L/P&S/10/132, minute, original assurance given by Sir A. Hardinge to the Shaykh, 7 December 1902. On Shaykh Khaz'al see R.M. Burrell in *The Encyclopaedia of Islam*, E. Donzel, B. Lewis and Ch. Pellat (eds.), vol. *IV* (Leiden, 1973), pp. 1171-2.
32. IO L/P&S/132, enclosed in note, Cox to Butler, 22 March 1908.
33. IO L/P&S/132, Lorimer to Cox, 3 February 1908.
34. *Ibid.*, Marling to Grey, 21 May 1908.
35. *Ibid.*, Marling to Grey, 23 April 1908.
36. *Ibid.*, Mallett to Morley, 20 May 1908.

37 BP H15/129, Langley to Preece, 30 July 1908.
38 BP 77/49/12 (2), Wallace to Adamson, 16 February 1909.
39 BP H12/112, D'Arcy to Wallace, 1 January 1909, and BP H15/129, Hamilton to Greenway, 8 January 1909.
40 *Ibid.*, Reynolds to Cox, 1 April 1909.
41 *Ibid.*, Cox to Lorimer, 9 March 1909.
42 *Ibid.*, Mallet to Preece, 15 March 1909.
43 *Ibid.*, Barnes to Cox, 26 March 1909.
44 BP 77/49/6 (1), Reynolds to CSL, 8 April 1909.
45 BP H15/129, Reynolds to CSL, 17 April 1909.
46 BP 77/49/6 (1), Reynolds to CSL, 24 April 1909.
47 *Ibid.*
48 PRO FO 416/47 no. 309, Wallace to FO 28 April 1909, and no. 307, Grey to Barclay, 28 April 1909; BP H15/129, Letters from Wallace et al., 21-28 April 1909.
49 BP H15/129, Reynolds to Cox, 30 April 1909 and BP 77/49/6 (1), Reynolds to CSL, 1 May 1909.
50 BP 77/49/6 (1), Cox to Reynolds, 4 May 1909.
51 BP H15/129, Cox to Reynolds, 16 May 1909.
52 PRO FO 416/47 no. 476, Cox to Grey, 18 May 1909, and BP H15/129, Cox to Reynolds, 16 May 1909.
53 PRO FO 416/47 no. 635B, Cox to Barclay, 9 June 1909; *ibid.*, no. 646, Wallace to Mallett, 9 June 1909, and *ibid.*, no. 661, Grey to Barclay, 12 June 1909.
54 PRO FO 416/47 no. 665, Mallet to Cox, 12 June 1909; *ibid.*, no. 707, Wallace to FO, 18 June 1909, and *ibid.*, no. 753, Grey to Barclay, 24 June 1909.
55 PRO FO 881/9551 no. 428, Cox to Grey, 25 July 1909, with enclosures.
56 BP H17/78 (2), Black to APOC, London, 5 November 1910.
57 PRO FO 416/48 no. 228, APOC to FO, 18 May 1911, enclosure 1.
58 PRO FO 881/9551 no. 428, Cox to Grey, 25 July 1909.
59 BP H13/82, Lorimer to Cox, 22 January 1908.
60 *Ibid.*, Mallett to Preece, 19 May 1908.
61 *Ibid.*, Mallett to Marling, 10 June 1908.
62 PRO FO 416/38 no. 162, Barclay to Grey, 7 November 1908.
63 *Ibid.*, no. 215, IO to FO, 18 November 1908.
64 *Ibid.*, no. 290, Hardinge to D'Arcy, 1 December 1908.
65 *Ibid.*, no. 441, D'Arcy to Hardinge, 28 December 1908.
66 BP H13/82, Young memorandum, 28 February 1909.
67 *Ibid.*, Sardār Mutesham and Sardār Bahādur to Reynolds, 4 March 1909.
68 *Ibid.*, Mallett to Preece, 19 March 1909.
69 *Ibid.*, Reynolds to Lorimer, 27 March 1909.
70 *Ibid.*, Reynolds to CSL, 27 March 1909.
71 BP 77/49/6 (1), Reynolds to CSL, 4 May 1909.
72 BP H13/82, Reynolds to Lorimer, 27 March 1909.
73 PRO FO 416/111, 'Persia Annual Report 1909', p.32.
74 BP H13/82, Reynolds to Lorimer, 30 March 1909.
75 PRO Board of Trade (BT) 31 19192/107085, Articles of Association of Lloyd, Scott and Co.
76 BP 77/139/86, Agreement between APOC and Lloyd, Scott & Co. Ltd, 21 March 1910.

Notes to pp. 129-137

77 BP H7/24, E.A. Chettle memorandum for Strick, Scott & Co. Ltd Board, January 1920.
78 BP 78/63/30 p.138, Greenway to Cargill, 16 February 1910, 'I despair of ever getting the APOC Agency Agreement through as Garson is always bringing up new points.'
79 BP 78/63/30, Greenway to Hamilton, 4 February 1910.
80 BP 78/63/1, Greenway to Hamilton, 17 February 1910.
81 BP 78/63/30, Greenway to Hamilton, 21 April 1910.
82 BP 78/63/1, Greenway to Hamilton, 11 July 1910.
83 *Ibid.*, Cargill to Greenway, 29 July 1910.
84 *Ibid.*, Lloyd to Black, 27 July 1910.
85 For the early history of the pipeline, see A.C. Hartley, 'The Anglo-Persian Oil Co's Pipelines in Persia', *Transactions of the Institution of Engineers and Shipbuilders in Scotland 1934* paper no. 921, pp. 85-128.
86 BP 77/49/12(2), Wallace to Reynolds, 30 December 1908.
87 BP H15/117, Finlay Fleming and Co. to APOC, 9 May 1909.
88 *Ibid.*, BOC to Kirkman Finlay, 11 May 1909 and BP H2/125 Greenway to Black, 18 March 1910.
89 BP H2/125, Kirkman Finlay to Lloyd, 12 December 1909 and Greenway to Cargill, 25 January 1910.
90 *Ibid.*, Hamilton to Lloyd, 17 February 1910.
91 Campbell's tests on Persian crude samples in March 1910 are referred to in BP H9/37, Campbell to Finlay, 11 January 1912.
92 BP H2/125, Greenway to Black, 18 March 1910.
93 BP H9/37, *passim*.
94 *Ibid.*
95 *Ibid.*, Gillespie to Neilson, 23 January 1912.
96 For experience in the United States, see Harold F. Williamson and Arnold R. Daum, *The American Petroleum Industry, The Age of Illuminations 1859-1899* (Evanston, 1959), and Walter Miller and Harold G. Osborn, 'History and Development of some important phases of Petroleum Refinery in the United States', *The Science of Petroleum*, A.E. Dunstan, A.W. Nash, Benjamin T. Brooks and Henry Tizard (eds.)(London, 1938), Vol. *II* pp. 1466-77. For the technical developments in the Scottish shale oil industry, see E.M. Bailey 'The Oil Shales of the Lothians', *Mem. of the Geological Survey of Scotland*, 3rd Edition (1927), and D.R. Stewart, Oil Shale of the Lothians, *Mem. of the Geological Survey of Scotland* (1912), pp. 136-94.
97 George Thomson, 'Abadan in its Early Days', *Naft*, APOC Magazine, vol. 7 (1931), 14-18.
98 BP 77/91/148, Greenway and Hamilton, Report on Persia, 28 April 1911.
99 BP H17/78 (2), Reynolds to L.S. and Co., 5 December 1910.
100 BP 78/63/1, Lloyd to Black, 27 July 1910.
101 PRO FO 416/111, 'Annual Report Persia 1910', p.36.
102 L. Lockhart, 'The Record of the Anglo Iranian Oil Co. Ltd.,' unpublished Company record, Cox to Black, October 1910, p.148.
103 *Ibid.*, Greenway to Black, p. 148.
104 BP H17/78 (1), Wilson to Black, 6 August 1910, and BP H10/25, Black to Greenway, enclosure, 18 August 1910.
105 BP 78/63/1, Greenway to Hamilton, 6 September 1910.
106 *Ibid.*, Greenway to Hamilton, 21 October 1910.

Notes to pp. 137-144

107 BP H17/78 (2), Greenway to L.S. & Co., 23 September 1910.
108 BP 78/83/1, Greenway to Hamilton, 17 November 1910.
109 *Ibid.*, Greenway to Hamilton, 12 September 1910.
110 BP H17/78 (2), Reynolds to APOC, 5 December 1910.
111 BP 77/91/148, Greenway and Hamilton, 'Report on Persia', 28 April 1911.
112 BP H10/25, Ritchie to G. & J. Weir, 3 October 1910.
113 BP H16/103, Ritchie to Greenway, 13 October 1911.
114 BP 78/63/1, Greenway to Hamilton, 12 September 1910, and BP/H2/125, Greenway to Black, 18 March 1910.
115 BP 77/91/148, Greenway and Hamilton 'Report on Persia', 28 April 1911.
116 See R.W. Ferrier, 'The Early Management Organisation of British Petroleum and Sir John Cadman', *Management Strategy and Business Development*, Leslie Hannah (ed.) (London, 1976), pp. 130-47.
117 BP H10/25, Wallace to Reynolds draft, n.d.
118 *Ibid.*, Wallace to Greenway, 10 February 1911, *ibid.*, Reynolds to Wallace, 13 February 1911, and *ibid.*, Cargill to Wallace, 15 February 1911.
119 PRO FO 416/45 no. 69, Ranking to Marling, enclosure 1 in Marling to Grey, 24 June 1910.
120 *Ibid.*, no. 69, Reynolds to Amīr Mufakhkham and Amīr Mujtahid, 16 March 1910, enclosure 4 in Marling to Grey, 24 June 1910.
121 BP H11/203, Lloyd to Walpole, 23 March 1910.
122 PRO FO 416/43 no. 468, FO to Greenway, 31 March 1910, and PRO FO 416/45 no. 147, Greenway to Norman, 27 July 1910.
123 *Ibid.*, no. 69, Agreement between Lloyd and Amīr Mufakhkham and Amīr Mujtahid, 9 April 1910, enclosure 6 in Marling to Grey, 24 June 1910.
124 BP 78/63/1, Greenway to Hamilton, 17 November 1910.
125 BP H16/103, Weir to Ritchie, 16 November 1910.
126 BP 78/63/1, Greenway to Hamilton, 23 November 1910.
127 BP 77/139/105, Agreement between F.C. Strick & Co. Ltd and Lloyd, Scott & Co. Ltd, 31 December 1910.
128 BP 78/63/30, Greenway to APOC, Glasgow, 18 February 1910.
129 PRO FO 881/9551, Wilson, Muhammara Trade Report, 21 August 1909.
130 James Taylor, *Ellermans: A Wealth of Shipping* (London, 1976).
131 BP 78/63/1, Greenway to Hamilton, 13 December 1910.
132 BP APOC Board Minutes, 28 November 1910.
133 BP APOC Board Minutes, 19 December 1910.
134 BP 77/91/148, Greenway and Hamilton, 'Report on Persia', 28 April 1911.
135 PRO FO 416/47 no. 156, Mallet to APOC, 2 February 1911.
136 BP H16/103, Cargill to Wallace, 4 February 1911.
137 *Ibid.*, D'Arcy to Wallace, 5 February 1911.
138 *Ibid.*, Wallace to FO, 16 February 1911.
139 BP 77/91/148, Greenway and Hamilton, 'Report on Persia', 28 April 1911.
140 *Ibid.*
141 PRO ADM 116/3806, Macrorie, 'Report on Persian Oil-Fields', 18 March 1909.
142 PRO FO 416/111, 'Annual Report Persia 1910', Barclay to Grey, 28 February 1911, p. 32.
143 PRO FO 416/47 no. 7, Barclay to Grey, 18 December 1910, enclosure 5, extract from letter of 23 September 1910.
144 BP APOC Board Minutes, 28 November 1910.

Notes to pp. 144-151

145 PRO FO 416/47 no. 7, Barclay to Grey, 18 December 1910, enclosure 9, Wilson to L.S. & Co., 9 November 1910.
146 PRO FO 416/47 no. 7, Barclay to Grey, 18 December 1910, enclosure 6, Cox to Wilson, 6 November 1910.
147 PRO FO 416/44 no. 207, Marling to Grey, 28 April 1910.
148 PRO FO 416/47 no. 7, enclosure 6, Cox to Wilson, 6 November 1910.
149 BP H4/147, Lister James report, July 1913.
150 BP H16/103, Ritchie to Greenway, 28 October 1913.
151 BP 78/63/30, Macindoe to APOC Glasgow, 6 April 1911.
152 BP H16/103, Ritchie to Lamb, 26 February 1911.
153 BP 78/63/1, Greenway to Hamilton, 6 May 1911.
154 *Ibid.*, Greenway to Hamilton, 9 May 1911.
155 BP H16/103, Ritchie to Lamb, 15 May 1911.
156 PRO FO 416/49 no. 9, Ranking to Barclay, enclosure in Barclay to Grey, 9 June 1911.
157 PRO FO 416/49 no. 159, Greenway to FO, 24 July 1911.
158 BP H16/103, Ritchie to Greenway, 13 October 1911.
159 *Ibid.*
160 BP 78/63/2, Greenway to Hamilton, 28 December 1911.
161 *Ibid.*, Greenway to Hamilton, 24 November 1911.
162 *Ibid.*, Greenway to Cargill, 24 January 1912.
163 BP 78/63/3, APOC London to Lamb, 9 May 1912.
164 BP H16/103, Ritchie to Greenway, 5 May 1913.
165 *Ibid.*
166 *Ibid.*, Greenway to Ritchie, 13 August and 3 October 1913.
167 BP H17/34, Greenway to Greenwood, 6 March 1914.
168 BP 78/63/31, APOC London to S.S. & Co., 10 July 1911.
169 BP H9/37, Hamilton to Neilson, 23 November 1911.
170 By this time Neilson was working solely on problems relating to APOC crude and all his letters and reports were addressed to Greenway.
171 BP 78/63/31, APOC London to S.S. & Co., 24 November 1911.
172 BP H9/37, Campbell to Finlay, 11 January 1912 and Cargill to Greenway, 5 February 1912: 'Pitkethly is after all under the altered circumstances working upon the right lines in his experiments. Quite possibly he had heard from Campbell that it was necessary to alter the original scheme of refining in this way.'
173 BP 78/63/2, Greenway to Cargill, 30 December 1911.
174 BP 77/49/13, Finlay Fleming to Strick Scott, correspondence during February and March 1912.
175 BP 78/63/2, Greenway to Cargill, 23 February 1912.
176 *Ibid.*, Greenway to Cargill, 12 March 1912.
177 *Ibid.*, Greenway to Cargill, 14 March 1912.
178 *Ibid.*
179 'Mr. Greenway had heard...that our products would not be at all satisfactory without the aid of a proper desulphurising process, hence Lomax was brought in', BP H13/114, Neilson to Campbell, 14 November 1913.
180 BP H13/114, Neilson report, 16 July 1912.
181 *Ibid.*, Greenway to Neilson, 22 July 1912.
182 BP 78/63/2, Greenway to Cargill, 13 March 1912.
183 BP H7/32, Walpole to Darby, 5 July 1912.

717

184 *Ibid.*, Walpole to Darby, 31 July 1912.
185 *Ibid.*, Walpole to Darby, 3 July 1912.
186 *Ibid.*, Walpole to Pitkethly, 21 September 1912.
187 *Ibid.*, Walpole to Wright, 29 October 1912.
188 BP 78/63/3, Greenway to Cargill, 20 and 27 August 1912, and H7/32 Walpole to Pitkethly, 28 September 1912.
189 *Ibid.*, Greenway to Cargill, 11 June 1912.
190 *Ibid.*, Greenway to Cargill, 18 June 1912 and *ibid.*, Greenway to Hamilton, 24 June 1912.
191 *Ibid.*, Greenway to Hamilton, 11 December 1912.
192 *Ibid.*, Greenway to APOC Glasgow, 17 December 1912.
193 BP 78/63/32, Nichols to APOC Glasgow, 23 and 30 December 1912.
194 BP 78/63/32, Nichols to APOC Glasgow, 27 December 1912.
195 BP 78/63/3, Greenway to Hamilton, 30 January 1913.
196 *Ibid.*, Greenway to Hamilton, 4 February 1913.
197 BP 77/49/13(1) Finlay to Greenway, 26 September 1913.
198 BP 78/63/3, Greenway to Hamilton, 19 February 1913 and *ibid.*, Greenway to Cargill, 29 May 1913.
199 BP 77/49/13 (2), Finlay to A. Gillespie, 26 September 1913.
200 *Ibid.*
201 BP H14/23, Wallace to Sādigh al-Saltana, 3 June 1909.
202 Lockhart, 'Record', p.146; PRO FO 416/111, 'Annual Report Persia 1910', p. 36.
203 Lockhart, 'Record', p.146.
204 *Ibid.*, p.147.
205 PRO FO 416/111, 'Annual Report Persia 1910', p. 35.
206 *Ibid.*
207 PRO FO 416/45 no. 90, Grey to Marling, 14 July 1910.
208 BP 77/91/156, Greenway Report to APOC Board, 4 May 1911.
209 PRO FO 416/43 no. 258, Grey to Barclay, 22 February 1910.
210 *Ibid.*, no. 277, FO to Greenway, 25 February 1910.
211 *Ibid.*, no. 309, APOC to FO, 4 March 1910.
212 *Ibid.*, no. 363, Barclay to Grey, 14 March 1910.
213 PRO FO 416/45 no. 85, FO to APOC, 13 July 1910.
214 *Ibid.*, no. 443, Barclay to Grey 3 September 1910, and *ibid.* no. 447, Barclay to Grey, 6 September 1910, enclosure Wilson to Marling, 21 July 1910.
215 PRO FO 416/47 no. 49, Barclay to Grey, 24 December 1910.
216 *Ibid.*, no. 373, FO to Preece, 6 May 1909.
217 PRO FO 416/111, 'Annual Report Persia 1910', pp. 33-4.

5. Fuel oil and the Admiralty 1912-14

1 BP H16/68, President, Admiralty Committee, 29 December 1911.
2 *Ibid.*, minutes of evidence from Admiralty Committee on Oil Fuel, 29 December 1911.
3 *Ibid.*
4 See B. Dasgupta, *The Oil Industry in India* (London, 1971), pp. 20-4; F.C. Gerretson, *History of the Royal Dutch*, vol. 3 (4 vols. Leiden, 1958), pp. 211-16 and G.G. Jones, 'The State and Economic Development in India 1890-1947: The Case of oil', *Modern Asian Studies*, 13 (1979), 353-75.

Notes to pp. 159-164

5. On Sir Robert Waley Cohen see Robert Henriques, *Robert Waley Cohen* (London, 1966).
6. See Gerretson, *History of the Royal Dutch*, vol. 4, pp. 81-4 and Ralph W. Hidy and Muriel E. Hidy, *Pioneering in Big Business, 1882-1911* (New York, 1955), pp. 502-3.
7. BP 78/63/1, Greenway to Cargill, 14 June 1911.
8. See Robert Henriques, *Marcus Samuel First Viscount Bearsted and Founder of the 'Shell' Transport and Trading Company 1853-1927* (London, 1960), particularly pp. 400-3, 513-16 and 527-40.
9. Between 1901 and 1904, D'Arcy made several attempts to acquire a concession for Mesopotamia with Redwood involved on his behalf and Burls doing a short geological survey. Nichols made visits to Constantinople in 1903 and 1904.
10. On Mesopotamia see Marian Kent, *Oil and Empire: British Policy and Mesopotamian Oil 1900-1920* (London, 1976) and Stephen Hemsley Longrigg, *Oil in the Middle East: Its Discovery and Development*, 3rd edn. (London, 1968).
11. BP 78/87/1, Greenway's speech at the AGM, 10 November 1925.
12. BP 78/13/1, Greenway to Cargill, 17 August 1911 and BP 78/63/2, Greenway to Hamilton, 16 November 1911.
13. *Ibid.*, Greenway to Hamilton, 7 December 1911.
14. *Ibid.*, Greenway to Besse, 28 December 1911.
15. *Ibid.*, Greenway to R.G. Shaw and Co., 19 December 1911.
16. BP 78/63/1, Greenway to Hamilton, 3 October 1911.
17. BP 78/63/2, Greenway to Cargill, 25 October 1911.
18. *Ibid.*, Greenway to Cargill, 9 October 1911.
19. *Ibid.*, Greenway to Hamilton, 16 April 1912.
20. See for example figures in *Petroleum Review*, 5 October 1912, p. 233.
21. s.s. *Ferrara*, a two deck general cargo vessel, built in 1880 as a coaster in the North Sea trade.
22. BP 78/63/3, Greenway to Barnes, 27 April 1912.
23. BP 78/63/2, Greenway to Hamilton, 16 April 1912.
24. *Ibid.*, Greenway to Hamilton, 17 April 1912.
25. *Ibid.*, Greenway to Hamilton, 24 April 1912.
26. BP Board Minutes, 27 April 1912.
27. BP 78/63/3, Greenway to Cargill, 9 August 1912.
28. *Ibid.*, Greenway to Cargill, 12 August 1912.
29. BP 78/63/3, Cargill to Greenway, 1 February 1912.
30. *Ibid.*, Greenway to Cargill, 20 August 1912.
31. *Ibid.*, Greenway to Cargill, 25 June 1912.
32. *Ibid.*, Greenway to Redwood, 2 May 1912.
33. BP 78/63/2, Greenway to Cargill, 24 January 1912.
34. BP H2/125, Kirkman Finlay to Lloyd, 12 December 1909 and Greenway to Cargill, 25 January 1910.
35. *Ibid.*, Kirkman Finlay to Lloyd, 12 December 1909.
36. *Ibid.*, Greenway to Hamilton, 17 February 1910.
37. *Ibid.*, Hamilton to Greenway, 18 February 1910.
38. *Ibid.*, Greenway to Black, 18 March 1910.
39. BP 78/63/2, Greenway to Cargill, 5 February 1912 and *ibid.* Greenway to Cargill, 24 January 1912.
40. *Ibid.*, Greenway to Cargill, 4 March 1912.

Notes to pp. 164-170

41 BP 78/63/4, Greenway to Cargill, 18 June 1912.
42 BP 78/63/3, Greenway to D. Rittmeister, 9 July 1912.
43 *Ibid.*, Greenway to Debenham, 22 July 1912.
44 *Ibid.*, Greenway to Cargill, 19 July 1912.
45 *Ibid.*, Greenway to Cargill, 12 August 1912.
46 *Ibid.*, Greenway to Cargill, 9 August 1912.
47 *Ibid.*, Greenway to Black, 2 May 1912.
48 *Ibid.*, Greenway to Hamilton, 7 May 1912.
49 Churchill to Fisher, 11 June 1912, quoted in Randolph S. Churchill, *Winston S. Churchill Young Statesman 1901-14*, vol. 2 (London, 1967), pp. 608-9.
50 PRO FO 371/1486 no. 36674, Babington Smith to FO, 29 August 1912.
51 *Ibid.*, no. 35252, Mallet to Greenway, 23 August 1912.
52 BP 78/63/3, Greenway to Cargill, 26 August 1912.
53 *Ibid.*
54 BP 77/139/110, Cargill to Greenway, 28 August 1912.
55 PRO FO 371/1486 no. 37181, Greenway to Mallet, 2 September 1912.
56 *Ibid.*, no. 36674, FO to Admiralty, 13 September 1912.
57 Amongst the references to these discussions, see BP 77/139/110 and 77/139/116, Greenway to Cargill, 22 October 1912 and 7 November 1912; PRO FO 371/1486 no. 42763, Maxwell to Nicolson, 10 October 1912, and no. 47482, Greenway to Maxwell, 30 October 1912.
58 PRO FO 371/1486 no. 40516, Nicolson to Babington Smith, 28 September 1912.
59 BP H16/68, Greenway to Cargill, 19 September 1912.
60 PRO FO 371/1486 no. 40516, Admiralty to FO, 26 September 1912.
61 BP 77/139/110, Greenway to Cargill, 10 and 22 October 1912.
62 BP H16/68, Greenway to Admiralty, 11 October 1912.
63 *Ibid.*, Greenway to Cargill, 19 September 1912.
64 *Ibid.*, Cargill to Greenway, 20 September 1912.
65 *Ibid.*, Wallace to Greenway, 21 September 1912.
66 *Ibid.*, Greenway to Admiralty, 11 October 1912.
67 BP 78/63/3, Greenway to D'Arcy, 10 October 1912.
68 BP H16/68, Greenway to Admiralty, 11 October 1912.
69 Gerretson *History of Royal Dutch*, vol. 4, pp. 235-42.
70 BP 78/63/3, Greenway to Cargill, 21 September 1912.
71 PRO FO 371/1486 no. 47482, Greenway to Maxwell, 30 October 1912, enclosure Correspondence between Asiatic Petroleum Company and Anglo-Persian Company re Oil Fuel.
72 *Ibid.*, Waley Cohen to Greenway, 15 October 1912.
73 *Ibid.*, Greenway to Waley Cohen, 16 October 1912.
74 *Ibid.*, Waley Cohen to Greenway, 17 October 1912.
75 *Ibid.*, Cargill to Waley Cohen, 18 October 1912.
76 PRO FO 371/1486 no. 47466, Mallet minute, 6 November 1912.
77 *Ibid.*
78 PRO FO 371/1486 no. 46485, minutes by Grey, Nicolson and Mallet, 6-11 November 1912.
79 BP H16/68, Lady St Helier to D'Arcy, 5 November 1912 and Admiralty to D'Arcy, 8 November 1912.
80 *Ibid.*, Marsh to D'Arcy and Greenway, 8 November 1912 and D'Arcy to Greenway, 10 November 1912.

720

Notes to pp. 170-177

81 PRO FO 371/1486 no. 40516, FO to Admiralty, 15 November 1912.
82 *Ibid.*
83 *Ibid.*
84 Royal Commission on Fuel and Engines, under Admiral Fisher, started proceedings on 24 September 1912 and submitted fuel report on 27 February 1913; see ADM 116/1208/9.
85 BP H16/68, Greenway's evidence to Royal Commission, 19 November 1912.
86 BP 78/63/3, Greenway to Cargill, 19 October 1912.
87 BP 78/63/6, Greenway to D'Arcy, 19 November 1912.
88 PRO ADM 116/1208/9.
89 BP H16/68, Greenways evidence to Royal Commission, 19 November 1912.
90 BP 78/63/3, Greenway to D'Arcy, 19 November 1912.
91 PRO FO 371/1486 no. 49500, Parker memorandum, 19 November 1912.
92 BP 78/28/8, Greenway to Cargill, 15 November 1915.
93 PRO FO 371/1486 no. 49500, Parker memorandum.
94 *Ibid.*, no. 50815, Nicolson minute, 20 November 1912.
95 *Ibid.*
96 *Ibid.*, no. 49186, FO to Admiralty, 28 November 1912.
97 *Ibid.*, no. 51845, Grey to Lowther, 6 December 1912.
98 *Ibid.*, no. 51935, FO to India Office, 9 December 1912.
99 *Ibid.*, no. 53280, India Office to FO, 13 December 1912.
100 *Ibid.*, nos. 51935 and 53280, Parker minute, 6 and 16 December 1912.
101 *Ibid.*, no. 52580, India office to FO, 13 December 1912.
102 *Ibid.*, no. 53280, Parker minute, 16 December 1912.
103 *Ibid.*, no. 53280, Mallet minute, 16 December 1912.
104 *Ibid.*, no. 54317, Greenway to FO, 19 December 1912.
105 *Ibid.*, no. 55654, Admiralty to FO, 28 December 1912.
106 F.G. Hyde, *Cunard and the North Atlantic 1840-1973* (London, 1975), pp. 137-48.
107 PRO FO 371/1486 no. 55654, Mallet minute 31 December 1912.
108 *Ibid.*
109 PRO FO 371/1760 no. 2463, Mallet minute, 9 January 1913.
110 PRO FO 416/54 no. 217, FO to IO, 5 February 1913.
111 PRO FO 371/1760 no. 722, Admiralty to FO, 4 January 1913.
112 *Ibid.*, no. 218, Mallet to Greenway 5 February 1913.
113 BP H16/68, Fisher to Greenway, 23 January 1913 and D'Arcy to Greenway, 26 January 1913.
114 See Winston S. Churchill, *The World Crisis 1911-1914* (London, 1923), pp. 126-36.
115 BP H16/68, Greenway to Black, 20 January 1913.
116 *Ibid.*, Greenway to Admiralty, 26 January 1913.
117 *Ibid.*, Greene to APOC, 11 February 1913.
118 PRO FO 371/1760 no. 7026, Greenway to FO, 12 February 1913.
119 Churchill, *Winston S. Churchill*, vol. 2, p. 665.
120 PRO FO 371/1760 no. 7026, Greenway to FO, 12 February 1913.
121 *Ibid.*, no. 8390, India Office to FO, 20 February 1913.
122 *Ibid.*, no. 9375, Admiralty to FO, 26 February 1913.
123 BP H16/68 Greene to Greenway, 27 February 1913.
124 BP 78/63/3 Greenway to Wallace, 28 February 1913.

Notes to pp. 177-181

125 On Mexico at this time see Gerretson, *A History of the Royal Dutch*, vol. 4, pp. 253-68, and for the Pearson interests, Keith Middlemas, *The Master Builders* (London, 1963), pp. 209-30 and J. A. Spender, *Weetman Pearson, First Viscount Cowdray 1856-1927* (London, 1930).
126 PRO ADM 167/47, Lambert to Secretary Admiralty, 18 April 1913.
127 BP H16/68, Greenway to Adamson, 6 March 1913.
128 PRO FO 371/1760 no. 11238, Greenway to Admiralty, 6 March 1913.
129 BP H16/68, Greenway to Lord Strathcona, 17 March 1913.
130 PRO ADM 116/3806, 'Admiralty Memorandum in Regard to the Anglo-Persian Oil Company's Proposals for a Contract to Supply Fuel Oil', 18 March 1913, updated 24 May 1913.
131 Hansard, House of Commons, vol. 50, cols. 1771-73, 26 March 1913.
132 Quoted in Churchill, *Winston S. Churchill*, vol. 2, p. 607, Churchill to Lloyd George, 9 December 1912.
133 PRO ADM 116/3806 Admiralty memorandum, 24 May 1913.
134 A useful chart of fuel oil prices is contained in Marian Kent, *Oil and Empire* (London, 1976), p. 204.
135 PRO CAB 41/34, 19 June 1913.
136 This conclusion anticipated Churchill's policy statement on 17 July 1913 in the House of Commons in the debate on the naval estimates.
137 A very useful survey of the fuel oil issue is in G. Gareth Jones, 'The Oil-Fuel Market in Britain 1900-14. A Lost Cause Revisited', *Business History*, 20 (1978), 131-52.
138 PRO ADM 116/3806, Admiralty to Treasury, 19 June 1913 and PRO T1/11953/20174/1916 (2), Admiralty to Treasury, 19 June 1913.
139 Ibid.
140 PRO T 1/1195 3/20174/1916(2), Hawly minute, 21 June 1913.
141 Ibid., Chalmers minute, 30 June 1913.
142 PRO T 1/10131 B/13036, 15 March 1904.
143 Ibid., July 1904.
144 Ibid., Murray to Secretary, Admiralty, 2 August 1904.
145 BP 78/63/3, Greenway to Cargill, 15 May 1913; PRO FO 371/1761 no. 2213, Admiralty to FO, 13 May 1913 and enclosed letter Admiralty to India Office, n.d.
146 PRO FO 371/1761 no. 28100, Admiralty to India Office, 19 June 1913.
147 PRO CAB 41/34, 10 July 1913.
148 PRO FO 800/87 no. 439, Churchill to Grey, 9 July 1913.
149 Ibid.
150 BP 78/63/4, Greenway to Cargill, 15 May 1913.
151 BP H10/82, refinery cost chart, July 1913.
152 Ibid., refinery cost chart, September 1913.
153 BP 78/63/4, Greenway to Cargill, 16 June 1913.
154 Ibid., Greenway to Cargill, 20 June 1913.
155 The *Soya Maru* was chartered 1913-15, when she was returned at the request of her owners. In 1913 she only carried two cargos for APOC, being employed on sub-charters to the Admiralty and Asiatic Petroleum Company, making £4000 profit, BP 78/63/5, Greenway to Albino, 6 October 1914.
156 BP 78/63/4, Greenway to Cargill, 24 June 1913.
157 BP H16/68, Greenway memorandum of meeting with Cabinet Committee, 10 July 1913.

Notes to pp. 181-195

158 Ibid.
159 PRO CAB 41/34, 12 July 1913.
160 Hansard, House of Commons, vol. 55, col. 1465, 17 July 1913.
161 *The Times*, 18 July 1913.
162 *The Financial Times*, 19 July 1913.
163 BP H16/68, Wallace, Memorandum of Interview at H. of C., 28 July 1913.
164 Ibid., Greenway to Cargill, 23 July 1913.
165 Ibid., Wallace Memorandum.
166 BP H16/68, Greenway to Cargill, 23 July 1913.
167 Hansard, House of Commons, vol. 55, col 1622, 17 July 1913.
168 BP H16/68, Wallace to Strathcona, 30 July 1913.
169 Ibid., Wallace to Cargill, 1 August 1913.
170 Ibid., Wallace to Redwood, 6 August 1913.
171 Ibid.
172 Ibid.
173 BP H16/68, Wallace to Cargill, 7 August 1913.
174 Ibid., Wallace to Cargill, 9 August 1913.
175 Ibid.
176 Ibid., Greenway to Black, 12 August 1913 and Greenway to Cargill, 12 August 1913.
177 Ibid., Greenway to Cargill, 15 August 1913.
178 Ibid., Cargill to Greenway, 18 August 1913.
179 Ibid., Greene to Greenway, 3 September 1913.
180 Ibid., Wallace to Greene, 17 September 1913.
181 Ibid., Admiralty to APOC, 8 October 1913.
182 Ibid.
183 Ibid., Greenway to Admiralty, 17 October 1913.
184 Ibid., Greenway to Black, 17 October 1913.
185 Ibid., Cargill to Greenway, 16 October 1913 and Greenway to Cargill, 17 October 1913.
186 Ibid., Greenway to Cargill, 21 October 1913; PRO ADM 116/3806, Black memorandum, 21 October 1913 and *ibid*., Green to Greenway.
187 PRO FO 371/1760 no. 4977, Grey to Lowther, 31 January 1913, BP 77/139/110 Greenway to Stock, 21 February 1913.
188 BP 77/139/110, Stock to Nichols, 22 March 1913.
189 Ibid., and 77/139/116, H. Llewellyn Smith (Board of Trade), to FO, 16 May 1913.
190 BP 77/139/111 and 77/139/116, FO to Greenway, 22 May 1913.
191 Ibid., Greenway to Cargill, 11 June 1913.
192 Ibid., and 77/139/116, Greenway to Cargill, 18 June 1913.
193 BP H16/68, Walpole to Greenway, 11 November 1913.
194 PRO ADM 116/3806, Black minute, 28 November 1913.
195 PRO ADM 116/3486, Admiralty memorandum for the Cabinet, Anglo-Persian Oil Company, Proposed Agreement, December 1913.
196 PRO ADM 116/3806, Hopwood minute to Black submission, 28 November 1913.
197 Ibid.
198 PRO ADM 116/3486, 'Memorandum on proposed Admiralty Contract', 28 November, 4 and 15 December 1913.
199 Hyde, *Cunard*, p. 147.

Notes to pp. 195-200

200 PRO ADM 116/3486, Anglo Persian Oil Company Proposed Agreement, December 1913. On the Company's views of the proposals see BP H16/68, Greenway to Cargill, 10, 17 and 23 December 1913 and Cargill to Greenway, 22 December 1913.
201 PRO ADM 116/3486, Slade to Churchill, 8 November 1913, excerpt in Admiralty memorandum for the Cabinet, Anglo-Persian Oil Company, Proposed Agreement, December 1913.
202 PRO ADM 116/3806 Admiralty Commission Second Interim Report, 26 January 1914.
203 BP 78/63/4, Greenway to Cargill, 17 December 1913.
204 Quote in Churchill, *Winston S. Churchill*, vol. 2, pp. 655-6, Margot Asquith to Lloyd George, 17 November 1913.
205 *Ibid.*, pp. 656-65.
206 Quoted in *ibid.*, p. 667, Hopwood to Stamfordham, 5 January 1914.
207 Quoted in *ibid.*, p. 668, Hopwood to Stamfordham, 11 January 1914.
208 *Ibid.*, pp. 669-71.
209 *Ibid.*, pp. 675-82.
210 PRO CAB 41/35, 19 February 1914, see also PRO CAB 37/119, Churchill minutes, 16 February 1913.
211 PRO CAB 41/35, 12 March 1914.
212 PRO FO 371/2120 no. 12324, 19 March 1914. 'Arrangements for Fusion of the Interests in the Turkish Petroleum Concession of the D'Arcy Group and of the Turkish Petroleum Company'.
213 BP 77/139/116, Greenway's memorandum of interview at the Board of Trade on the 27 November 1913: See also PRO FO. 371/1761 no. 54729 Ashley to Parker, 5 December 1913.
214 BP 77/139/116, Greenway's memorandum of interview with Herr Stauss on 1 December 1913 and *ibid.*, Stauss to Greenway on 5 December 1913.
215 BP 77/139/113 Stock to Nichols, 22 and 27 September 1913, 11 and 13 March 1914 and *ibid.*, FO to APOC, 2 September 1913.
216 BP H16/107, Greenway to Cargill, 26 March 1914.
217 PRO T 1/11963/20174/1916 pt 2, Anglo Persian Oil Company Proposed Agreement, 19 February 1914.
218 *Ibid.*
219 PRO ADM 116/1687C, Bradbury to Black, 11 April 1914.
220 *Ibid.*
221 BP H16/150, Slade to Greenway, 7 May 1914.
222 *Ibid.*, D'Arcy to Greenway, 18 April 1914.
223 *Ibid.*, Wallace to Greenway, 19 April 1914.
224 *The Times*, 22 January 1914.
225 PRO ADM 116/1687c, APOC Dossier, 13 May 1914; PRO CAB 41/35, 14 May 1914; and PRO ADM 116/1687D, HMG–APOC Agreement, 20 May 1914.
226 Hansard, House of Commons, vol. 63, cols. 1131-1250, 17 July 1914.
227 BP 78/63/4, Greenway to Cargill, 19 June 1914.
228 On this see Henriques, *Marcus Samuel*, which, while not always impartial, gives another point of view.
229 BP H15/177, Campbell to APOC, 26 May 1914.
230 BP H9/38, Greenway to Hamilton, 19 October 1914.

231 It was in 1915 that Dr A.E. Dunstan and Dr F.B. Thole, at first under the aegis of Sir Boverton Redwood and then at the Company's Research Centre at Sunbury from 1917, worked on the viscosity problems of fuel oil from Persia crude oil.
232 *The Times*, 6 June 1914.
233 *Ibid.*, 18 June 1914.
234 *Ibid.*, 20 June 1914.
235 *Ibid.*, 30 June 1914.

6. The Government and the Company: the early years 1914-19

1 Hansard, House of Commons, vol. 63, cols. 1131-1252, 17 June 1914.
2 A.J.P. Taylor, *English History 1914-1945* (Oxford, 1965), pp. 8 and 122-3, note 4.
3 *The Times*, 22 November 1918, from speech of Curzon to members of the Inter-Allied Petroleum Conference Dinner, 21 November 1928.
4 *The Times*, 27 May 1914.
5 PRO FO 800/88, Churchill to Grey, 27 May 1914.
6 *Ibid.*, Churchill to Grey, 15 June 1914.
7 *Ibid.*, Admiralty memorandum, 20 July 1914.
8 PRO FO 416/60, enclosure, Grey memorandum to Russian ambassador, 10 June 1914.
9 PRO FO 416/61, Buchanan to Grey, 7 July 1914.
10 PRO FO 416/60, Buchanan to Grey, 20 June 1914.
11 Marian Kent, *Oil and Empire: British Policy and Mesopotamian Oil 1900-1920* (London, 1976) p. xi.
12 Elizabeth Monroe, *Britain's Moment in the Middle East, 1914-1956* (London, 1963), pp. 98-9.
13 It is fair to remark that many Persian commentators do not accept this conclusion. Thus Nasrollah Saifpour Fatemi, *Oil Diplomacy Powderkeg in Iran* (New York, 1954), p. 19, suggested that 'Cargill and his collaborators hoped that the Anglo Persian Oil Company might serve the British Empire in the same way that the East India Company helped to establish British rule over India', a comment which, in fact, he borrowed from 'Ali Dashti.
14 BP 81/55/3, Greenway memorandum, 'explanatory of proposals for reconstitution of the Board', n.d. (probably mid-November 1916).
15 BP APOC Board minutes, 15 December 1916.
16 PRO ADM 116/1687 D, Agreement with the Anglo-Persian Oil Company Ltd., 1914.
17 *Ibid.*
18 BP H11/52, Bradbury to APOC, 20 May 1914.
19 BP H11/127, Cadman speech, National Petroleum War Service Committee reunion, 7 January 1922.
20 Hansard, House of Commons, vol. 55, cols. 1466-1482, 17 July 1913 and vol. 63, cols. 1131-1153, 17 June 1914.
21 PRO T 1/12229/45465, 19 July 1916.
22 BP APOC Board Minutes, 29 March 1915.
23 PRO T 1/12229/45465, Greenway to Secretary, Treasury, 4 August 1916.
24 BP APOC Board Minutes, 12 and 23 August 1916.

25 PRO T 1/12229/45465, Bradbury to Company, 4 September 1916.
26 *Ibid.*, Bradbury to Inchcape and Slade, 4 September 1916.
27 BP APOC Board Minutes, 2 October 1916.
28 PRO T 1/12229/45465, Greenway to Inchcape, 9 September 1916.
29 *Ibid.*, Bradbury to Inchcape, 13 October 1916.
30 *Ibid.*, Greenway to Inchcape, 20 October 1916.
31 *Ibid.*
32 *Ibid.*, Barstow to Baddeley, Admiralty, 24 October 1916.
33 *Ibid.*, Director of Naval Contracts, minute, 3 November 1916.
34 *Ibid.*, Inchcape to Bradbury, 2 December 1916.
35 *Ibid.*, Bradbury to Inchcape, 7 December 1916.
36 *Ibid.*, Inchcape to Bradbury, 4 January 1917 and BP APOC Board Minutes, 9 January 1917.
37 PRO T 1/12229/46465, Greenway to Inchcape, 2 January 1917.
38 *Ibid.*, Greenway to Inchcape, 13 February 1917.
39 *Ibid.*, Bradbury to Inchcape, 12 February 1917.
40 *Ibid.*, Greenway to Inchcape, 15 February 1917.
41 *Ibid.*
42 *Ibid.*
43 *Ibid.*, Oliver, Admiralty to APOC, 23 December 1916
44 BP APOC Board Minutes, 9 January 1917.
45 PRO T 1/12229/46465, Barstow, minute to Bradbury, 17 January 1917.
46 *Ibid.*, Barstow, minute to Bradbury, 23 January 1917.
47 *Ibid.*, Barstow to Baddeley, Admiralty, 17 January 1917
48 *Ibid.*, Treasury to Ministry of Munitions, 23 January 1917.
49 *Ibid.*, Greenway to Inchcape, 15 February 1917.
50 *Ibid.*, Inchcape to Greenway, 16 February 1917 and Inchcape to Bradbury, 27 February 1917.
51 *Ibid.*, Barstow, minute to Bradbury, 19 February 1917.
52 *Ibid.*, Bradbury to Inchcape, 20 February 1917.
53 *Ibid.*, Inchcape to Bradbury, 2 March 1917.
54 *Ibid.*, Barstow minute to Bradbury, Chalmers and Baldwin, 5 March 1917.
55 *Ibid.*, Bradbury to Inchcape, 7 March 1917 and Greenway to Inchcape, 9 March 1917.
56 *Ibid.*, Greenway to Inchcape, 13 March 1917.
57 *Ibid.*, Inchcape to Bradbury, 14 March 1917.
58 *Ibid.*, Bradbury to Inchcape, 16 March 1917.
59 *Ibid.*, Greenway to Inchcape, 23 March 1917.
60 *Ibid.*, Greenway to Inchcape, 26 March 1917.
61 *Ibid.*, Inchcape to Greenway, 20 March 1917.
62 BP APOC Board Minutes, 24 January 1918.
63 PRO T 1/12229/45465, Bradbury to Inchcape, 26 March, 1917.
64 *Ibid.*, Greenway to Inchcape, 12 April 1917.
65 BP 77/139/118, Audit of Cash, Stone and Co. of British Petroleum for Public Trustee, 7 May 1917.
66 PRO T 1/12054/18743, Board of Trade memorandum, 'The British Petroleum Company Limited', 1 January 1917.
67 BP 79/91/14, Greenway to Stewart, 19 March 1917.
68 BP APOC Board Minutes, 2 April 1917.

Notes to pp. 218-240

69 PRO ADM 1 8537/240, Greenway memorandum re British Petroleum Company, 13 October 1915.
70 PRO T 1/12054/18743, Inchcape to Bradbury, 31 March 1917.
71 Ibid., Barstow minute to Bradbury, 7 April 1917.
72 Ibid., Bradbury to Inchcape, 4 April 1917.
73 BP 79/91/14, Inchcape to Greenway, 10 April 1917.
74 PRO T 1/12054/18743, Greenway to Inchcape, 11 April 1917.
75 PRO T 1/12229/45465, Greenway to Inchcape, 11 July 1917.
76 Ibid., Inchcape to Bradbury, 14 July 1917.
77 Ibid., Inchcape to Bradbury, 3 August 1917.
78 Ibid., Inchcape to Bradbury, 7 August 1917.
79 Ibid., Inchcape to Greenway, 2 August 1917.
80 Ibid., Inchcape to Bradbury, 3 August 1917.
81 Ibid., Barstow, minute to Bradbury, 25 July 1917.
82 Ibid., Bradbury to Inchcape, 31 July 1917.
83 Ibid., Thirty-Seventh Meeting of the Inter-Departmental Committee on Petroleum Products, 18 September 1917.
84 Ibid., Slade, memorandum, 'Anglo-Persian Oil Company's Proposed Increase of Capital', 6 September 1917.
85 BP APOC Board Minutes, 19 November 1917.
86 Ibid., 24 January 1918.
87 Quoted in Robert Henriques, *Sir Robert Waley Cohen* (London, 1966), pp. 213-24.
88 G. Gareth Jones 'The British Government and the Oil Companies 1912-1924: The search for an oil policy', *The Historical Journal*, 20, 3 (1977), 647-72, refers to it as an 'obsession', p. 671.
89 'We have no quarrel with the "Shell". We have always found them courteous, considerate, ready to oblige, anxious to serve the Admiralty and to promote the interests of the British Navy and the British Empire - at a price', Churchill, in the House of Commons, Hansard, vol. 63, col. 1151, 17 June 1914.
90 PRO CAB 37/120, Samuel to Hopwood, 29 May 1914.
91 Ibid., Churchill, Cabinet minute, 9 June 1914.
92 Ibid., Samuel to Hopwood, 29 May 1914.
93 Robert Henriques, *Marcus Samuel, First Viscount Bearsted, Founder of Shell Transport and Trading Company, 1853-1927* (London, 1960), p. 613.
94 BP 78/28/8, Greenway to Cargill, 15 November 1915.
95 PRO to 371/2426, Admiralty to Ministry of Munitions, 1 December 1915.
96 Ibid., Admiralty to Foreign Office, 28 July 1915.
97 Ibid., FO minutes by Oliphant and Parker, 29 July and 14 August 1915 and ibid., FO to IO, 6 August 1915.
98 Ibid., Viceroy to India Office, 9 September 1915.
99 Ibid., Admiralty to Ministry of Munitions, 1 December 1915. On the provision of toluol see Henriques, *Marcus Samuel*, pp. 597-605. On this and other oil matters during the war see *History of the Ministry of Munitions*, vol. 7. pt 1 (London, 1922), pp. 134-56.
100 PRO 371/2426, FO to Admiralty, 14 December 1915.
101 PRO ADM 1 8537/240, Greenway, memorandum re British Petroleum Company, 13 October 1915.
102 Ibid.

103 *Ibid.*, on Lord Cowdray see J.A. Spender, *Weetman Pearson, First Viscount Cowdray 1856-1927* (London, 1930). On his early oil interests see G. Gareth Jones, *The State and the Emergence of the British Oil Industry* (London, 1981), pp. 63-77, which is also informative on other oil developments in these years.
104 *Ibid.*, Greenway memorandum re British Petroleum Company, 13 October 1915.
105 *Ibid.*, Greenway to Barnes, 3 March 1916.
106 PRO FO 382/1096, Waley Cohen to Parker, 21 January 1916.
107 PRO FO 371/2721, Greenway to FO, 24 February 1916.
108 PRO T 1/11952/20174, FO to Treasury, 2 March 1916.
109 See V.H. Rothwell, 'Mesopotamia in British War Aims' 1914-1918, *The Historical Journal*, 13, 2 (1970) 273-94.
110 PRO FO 371/2721, Parker minute to O'Beirne, War Department, 17 March 1916.
111 *Ibid.*, Admiralty to FO, 15 April 1916.
112 *Ibid.*, Board of Trade to FO, 6 May 1916.
113 Hirtzel agreed with Sykes' opinion; see Cab 42/16, IO political department memorandum, 'The War with Turkey', 25 May 1916, and memorandum 'Germany, Turkey, England and Arabia', 31 October 1916.
114 PRO Cab 21/119, Hankey to Balfour, 1 and 11 August 1918; and Stephen Roskill, *Hankey: Man of Secrets, 1877-1918* (London, 1970), vol. 1, p. 586 on Hankey's lunch with Balfour on 3 August 1918; and *ibid.*, p. 583 'We ought to make it a first class war aim and peace aim to acquire oil fields in Persia and Mesopotamia', lunch with Slade, 29 July 1918. L.S. Amery agreed: 'An argument I have overlooked with regard to Mesopotamia is the all-important question of the control of oil,' Amery to Sir Henry Wilson, Chief of the Imperial General Staff, 1 August 1918, *The Leo Amery Diaries Volume 1: 1896-1929*, ed. John Barnes and David Nicholson (London, 1980), p. 230.
115 PRO FO 371/2721 no. 119250, Admiralty to FO, 20 June 1916.
116 *Ibid.*, no. 86698, FO to APOC, 17 May 1916.
117 PRO ADM 1 8537/240, Board of Trade memorandum, 'The Future Control of Oil Supplies', 12 August 1916.
118 *Ibid.*, Greenway memorandum, 8 July 1916.
119 *Ibid.*, Slade to Pretyman, 26 July 1916 and *ibid.*, Greenway to Sercold, 28 July 1916.
120 PRO CAB 37/154, Slade memorandum, 'Observations on the Board of Trade Memorandum on Oil', 24 August, 1916.
121 *Ibid.*, Slade memorandum, 'Petroleum Supplies and Distribution', 24 August 1916.
122 *Ibid.*, Slade memorandum, 'Strategic Importance of the Control of Petroleum', 24 August 1916.
123 *Ibid.*, Balfour Cabinet minute, 18 August 1916.
124 PRO ADM 1 8537/240, Balfour Cabinet minute, 'Progress of the Negotiations with regard to the Burmah–Shell Amalgamation', 19 October 1916.
125 PRO FO 370/287, Board of Trade memorandum, 'Petroleum Department', October 1916.
126 BP 77/139/116, Cargill to Greenway, 25 October 1916.
127 On 14 January 1916 *The Times* reported a 'dearth of petrol...to many people it will come as a surprise'. See *The Times*, 26 May 1916. See also *History of the*

Notes to pp. 247-252

Ministry of Munitions, pp. 138-49 and Jones, *op. cit.*, for figures of supply and the organisations of the war-time committees.
128 On 14 November 1915, *The Times* reported that 15 982 832 gallons of motor spirit were imported.
129 PRO POWE 33/1, preliminary report of the Petrol Control Committee, 12 May 1916.
130 *Ibid.*, second report of the Petrol Control Committee, 19 December 1916.
131 PRO FO 368/1864, minutes of meeting on 15 February 1917; *ibid.*, memorandum 'Petroleum Supplies', 15 February 1917; and *ibid.*, Admiralty to FO, 23 February 1917.
132 *Ibid.*, Admiralty to FO, 5 March 1917.
133 PRO POWE 33/1, minute to PM, 'Petrol Supplies', 15 May 1917.
134 Long described his own part in Walter Long, *Memories* (London, 1923), pp. 257-65, where he pays a generous tribute to Cadman's outstanding services, 'the success which happily attended our administration is entirely due to his great ability, wonderful industry and unsurpassed knowledge of oil questions', p. 258.
135 PRO POWE 33/1, Long, draft memorandum, n.d.; and *ibid.*, minutes of Petrol Supplies Conference, 24 May 1917; and *ibid.*, Bury to Long, 25 May 1917, minutes of Petrol Supplies Conference, 25 May 1917 and Pretyman to Long, 30 May 1917 and 1 June 1917.
136 *Ibid.*, War Cabinet minute 162, 13 June 1917; and *ibid.*, Long memorandum, 'Petrol and Petroleum Products', n.d.
137 Hansard, House of Commons, vol. 98, col. 37, 16 October 1917.
138 PRO FO 368/1864, Cadman to Parker, 27 December 1917.
139 *The Financial Times*, 4 December 1917.
140 Hansard, House of Commons vol. 100, col. 841, 10 December 1917.
141 *The Financial News*, 8 December 1917.
142 *The Times*, 14 December 1917 and see 5 December 1917.
143 PRO POWE 33/42, Samuel to Cadman, 6 December 1917, and later *ibid.*, Samuel to Long, 19 December 1917 and Cadman to Samuel, 20 December 1917.
144 *Ibid.*, Cadman, minute to Batterbee, 17 December 1917.
145 *Ibid.*, minutes of a Conference at the Colonial Office on the policy for the formation of an 'All-British' oil company, 21 December 1917. Cadman had deliberately, since the formation of the Petroleum Committee, sought to establish a better relationship with Royal Dutch-Shell, for government departments 'had been in the habit of treating the Shell group with a reserve which does not cultivate good feeling, I hope we shall be able to remove this state of affairs.' PRO POWE 33/3, Cadman to Batterbee, 24 July 1917. Slade went so far as to inform Hankey that he 'believed him to be too much in with the Dutch oil people', Roskill, *Hankey*, p. 586. Cadman and Deterding certainly had a mutual respect for each other.
146 *Ibid.*, Stanley to Long, 28 December 1917.
147 *Ibid.*, Long to Stanley, 29 December 1917.
148 *Ibid.*, Parker to Cadman, 21 December 1917.
149 *Ibid.*, Admiralty to Petroleum Executive, 28 February 1918.
150 PRO FO 368/2255, report and proceedings of the Petroleum Imperial Policy Committee (PIPCO) 29 May 1918 to 10 February 1919, p. 59.
151 PRO POWE 33/12, draft invitation by Long, 10 May 1918.

152 *Ibid.*, Cadman, minute to Batterbee, 4 March 1918.
153 *Ibid.*, Davidson to Cadman, 29 May 1918 and Long to Bonar Law, 4 June 1918.
154 PRO FO 368/2255, PIPCO; references in the text to the proceedings of the Harcourt Committee are derived from this source.
155 *Ibid.*
156 PRO POWE 33/40, Petroleum Executive to Treasury, 9 May 1918.
157 *Ibid.*, Greenway memorandum, 12 March 1918.
158 *Ibid.*, Petroleum Executive to Treasury, 16 May 1918.
159 *Ibid.*, Chalmers to Cadman, 24 June 1918.
160 BP APOC Board Minutes, 29 July 1918; a special sub-committee of the Board was appointed to deal with this specific issue.
161 PRO POWE 33/40, APOC to Treasury, 2 August 1918. The Company also wrote on 8 August 1918 about newspaper reports over possible government oil policy.
162 PRO ADM I 8537/240, Slade Memorandum, 'Petroleum Situation in the British Empire', 25 July 1918.
163 *Ibid.*, Hall minute, 30 July 1918 and Rawlin's minute, 16 September 1918. Hankey was impressed, 'I had a most important discussion with Ad. Wemyss [First Sea Lord 1917-19] about Slade's paper on oil in Mesopotamia...I have written to the P.M. and Balfour and seen Geddes about this. It is supremely important for our future to get this oil', Roskill, *Hankey*, p. 585.
164 *Ibid.*, Slade memorandum, 'The Threatened Foreign Oil Monopoly', 21 August 1918.
165 PRO POWE 33/40, Cadman, minute to Batterbee, 2 September 1918.
166 *Ibid.*, Cadman to Treasury, 4 September 1918.
167 PRO POWE 33/45, Petroleum Executive Memorandum, n.d.
168 PRO FO 368/2255, PIPCO.
169 PRO T 1/12442/54465, Stanley to Baldwin, 13 December 1918 and Foreign Office memorandum on the question of buying shares in the TPC held by the Deutsche Bank. Baldwin to Stanley, 21 December 1918; see also PRO FO 368/2255 PIPCO.
170 FO CP 11435, memorandum by the British Legation, Paris, on British Policy in the Middle East, 18 February 1919. See also, for a new look at politico-economic issues in relation to foreign policy, FO CP 11428, V. Wellesley memorandum on the reconstruction of the Foreign Office, 30 November 1918.
171 PRO FO 368/2255, PIPCO.
172 Deterding and Bérenger were on good terms since 1917 but in spite of all the efforts of Gulbenkian there was no certainty that Royal Dutch–Shell would play the decisive part in French oil policy that Deterding hoped. On the question of TPC, *Shell* Deterding to Cadman, 25 January 1919, quoted in Jones, *op. cit.*, p. 212. On American oil interests at the time see John A. de Novo, *American Interests and Policies in the Middle East, 1900-1939*, (Minnesota, 1963), especially Chapter 6; and *idem*, 'The Movement for an Aggressive American Oil Policy Abroad, 1918-1920', *American Historical Review*, 61 (July 1956) 854-76.
173 PRO FO 368/2255, PIPCO.
174 See also advice given to FO by Petroleum Executive, PRO FO 371/2237, Petroleum Executive to FO, 6 January 1919. On French policy see PRO FO

368/2095, Long memorandum on meeting with Bérenger, 17 December 1918 and *ibid.*, de Fleuriau to FO, 6 January 1919.
175 PRO FO 368/2242, Clemenceau to Bérenger, 30 January 1919.
176 PRO FO 368/2255, PIPCO, p. 20; see also PRO CAB 24/76, Petroleum Executive Memorandum for the War Cabinet, 22 February 1919 which also includes the Harcourt/Deterding Memorandum and PRO POWE 33/68, Long to Cadman, 21 February 1919. 'I congratulate you and all concerned.'

7. Persia — the scene of operations 1914-18

1 PRO ADM 116/1687, Greenway Memorandum, 'Rough Estimate of Probable Expenditure', 20 February 1914.
2 See A.C. Hartley, 'The Anglo-Persian Oil Company's Pipeline in Persia', *Transactions of the Institute of Engineers and Shipbuilders in Scotland*, 1934, p. 88.
3 BP Sunbury R1/10/1(D6244) Refining and Technical 'Throughput Book'.
4 BP 78/87/1, APOC AGM, 10 November 1925.
5 BP 78/63/4, Greenway to Hamilton, 3 July 1914.
6 BP H14/35, Greenway to Walpole, 9 February 1916.
7 BP H14/35, Chettle to Walpole, 6 July 1916.
8 BP H9/38, Greenway to Walpole, 24 March 1915.
9 *Ibid.*, Greenway to Walpole, 23 April 1915.
10 BP H14/22, Greenway to Walpole, 24 October 1915.
11 *Ibid.*, Greenway to Walpole, 30 December 1915.
12 *Ibid.*, Greenway to Walpole, 9 December 1915.
13 *Ibid.*, Greenway to Young, 17 June 1915.
14 *Ibid.*, Greenway to Gillespie, 1 October 1915.
15 BP H14/35, Greenway to Walpole, 8 February 1916.
16 *Ibid.*, Greenway to Walpole, 9 February 1916.
17 *Ibid.*, Chettle to Walpole, 25 May 1916.
18 The official history is F.J. Moberly, *The Campaign in Mesopotamia 1914-1918*, 4 vols. (London, 1923-27).
19 Incidental references to affairs in Persia during the war are in Arnold T. Wilson, *Loyalties. Mesopotamia 1914-1917* (Oxford, 1930) and Philip Graves, *The Life of Sir Percy Cox* (London, 1941), chapters 14-17. On German activities in Persia see Christopher Sykes, *Wassmus* (London, 1936).
20 BP H7/40 Pt 1, Thompson to Strick Scott, 27 September 1915.
21 BP H7/39 Pt 3, Capito to Strick Scott, 7 August 1914.
22 BP H7/41 Pt 1, Thompson to Strick Scott, 6 April 1917.
23 BP H7/39 Pt 3, medical report of Dr Moir, 19 October 1914.
24 *Ibid.*, Thompson to Strick Scott, 26 July 1915.
25 BP H7/23, Soane to Walpole, 3 December 1915. Soane, described by Arnold Wilson as 'an erratic genius', had a profound knowledge of Persia and Kurdistān, see E.B. Soane, *To Mesopotamia and Kurdistan in Disguise*, 2nd edition (London, 1926), first published 1912.
26 BP H7/40 Pt 1, Thompson to Gillespie, 13 September 1915.
27 *Ibid.*, Gillespie to Thompson, 24 June 1915.
28 BP 78/63/6, Garrow to Clarke, 30 September 1916.
29 BP H7/33 Pt 1, Garrow to APOC Glasgow, 18 December 1916 and 2 January, 1917.
30 BP H7/40 Pt 2, Thompson to Strick Scott, 26 February 1917.

31 BP H7/33 Pt 1, APOC, London, to Gillespie, 30 July 1912 and BP H7/18 Pt 1, Garrow to BOC, 25 May 1915.
32 BP H16/123, Dalley to APOC, 28 March 1919.
33 BP H7/41 Pt 1, Thompson to Strick Scott, 9 April 1917.
34 BP H16/123, Slade to Strick Scott, 5 July 1917.
35 BP H7/41 Pt 2, Thompson to Strick Scott, 29 October 1917.
36 *Ibid.*, Thompson to Strick Scott, 16 March 1918.
37 BP H7/33 Pt 2, Hamilton to Garrow, 14 November 1916.
38 BP H7/40 Pt 2, Thompson to Strick Scott, 8 January 1917.
39 BP H7/41 Pt 2, Thompson to Strick Scott, 7 May 1918.
40 Gas masks had been ordered, but never arrived, BP H7/41 Pt 2, Thompson to Strick Scott, 15 March 1918.
41 This was the treatment of the benzine with sodium hypochlorite begun at Ābādān in August 1921. BP Sunbury, Fifth Annual Report of the Research Department 1921.
42 BP H9/36, memorandum regarding Anglo-Persian Company's refinery at Ābādān, 20 January 1915. The *jarib*, a Persian land measurement, was of different dimensions until standardised by a law of 1926 and the introduction of the metric system in 1935, see A.K.S. Lambton, *Landlord and Peasant in Persia* (London, 1953) pp. 405-7.
43 BP R1/10/1(D6244), Refining and Technical 'Throughput Book'.
44 BP APOC Board Minutes, 27 March 1916.
45 BP H9/36, Neilson note, 2 June 1916.
46 *Ibid.*, Neilson note, 3 June 1916.
47 BP Sunbury, A.E. Dunstan, memoir 'Do You Remember', 1947.
48 *Ibid.*, See also BP Sunbury, A.E. Dunstan, reports from Persia, December 1916–March 1917.
49 BP Sunbury, Dunstan, memoir 'Do You Remember'.
50 *Ibid.*
51 BP Sunbury, First Annual Report of the Research Department, 1917.
52 *Ibid.*
53 BP H7/22, Neilson to Walpole, 9 November 1914.
54 BP H9/36, Instructions from Neilson concerning the visit of the Viceroy, 1 February 1915.
55 In spite of the Viceroy's comments, some staff remained anxious about their positions. See BP H9/36, Thorburn to staff, 22 February 1915 and Neilson to Walpole, 1 October 1915.
56 BP 78/63/20, APOC London to Maclean, 18 February 1915.
57 For instance see BP H12/29, Gillespie to Strick Scott, 7 June 1915; and BP 78/63/16, Greenway to Strick Scott, 8 July 1916.
58 BP H16/107, Greenway to FO, 26 July 1917.
59 BP H9/36, Greenway to Strick Scott, 11 November 1915.
60 *Ibid.*, Neilson to Walpole, 29 May 1915.
61 *Ibid.*, Greenway to Walpole, 21 January 1916.
62 BP H14/35, R.G. Shaw & Co. to Walpole, 5 February 1916.
63 PRO FO 416/36, Marling to Hardinge, 14 August 1908, Greenway wanted Reynolds to concentrate his efforts on Fields where 'there is so much to be done,' Greenway to Black, 10 March 1910, quoted in Lockhart, *Record*, p. 155. Cost was also a consideration as the managing agents were informed later about the Pusht-i-Kuh, 'out of the question...owing to the heavy cost of

Notes to pp. 282-291

linking up with their refinery,' APOC to Strick Scott and Co., 24 March 1910. *ibid*. These instructions were confirmed in May, 'keep your drilling staff entirely employed on boring fresh wells *for production purposes only*,' APOC to Strick Scott and Co., 13 May 1910, *ibid.*, p. 156, enclosure 2, Lorimer memorandum, 27 July 1908.

64 BP H11/203, contains details of the holding operation at Chiāh Surkh and its transfer to Turkish territory, see correspondence April to June 1914.
65 I owe this and other interesting information to Mr S. Lister James as a result of visits to him in 1976 and 1977.
66 BP H12/29 Walpole to Gillespie, 21 June 1915 and BP Board Minutes, 26 July 1915.
67 BP H7/41 Pt 2 Thompson to Strick Scott, 7 May 1918.
68 *Ibid.*, Thompson to Strick Scott, 5 November 1917.
69 S. Elder, A. Laird and T.C. Richards, 'Historical Review of Exploration and Oil-Field Development in South West Iran 1901 to 1951', UN Economic Commission for Asia and The Far East, 2nd Petroleum Symposium, Tehrān, 1-15 September 1962.
70 H.T. Mayo and H.G. Busk 'Some Notes on the Geology of the Persian Oilfields', *Journal of The Institute of Petroleum Technologists*, 5 (1918-19), 3-33.
71 BP 77/49/13 Pt 2, Sir C.K. Finlay to Gillespie, 26 September 1913.
72 BP H13/108, Strick Scott to W. Umerse, 12 July 1913.
73 BP H15/2, Strick Scott to W. Umerse, 16 August 1913.
74 BP H17/32, *passim*.
75 BP 78/63/31, F. Macindoe to APOC Glasgow, 26 April 1912.
76 BP 77/49/13 (iv), Finlay Fleming to Burmah Oil Co., Glasgow, 8 July 1912.
77 BP H5/49, Greenway to Sir Trevredyn Wynne, 11 October 1915.
78 BP APOC Board Minutes, 4 June 1917.
79 BP 77/49/7, Indian Railways Board to Heath Eves, 7 April 1917.
80 BP 78/63/4, APOC to Admiralty, 17 September 1913.
81 BP APOC Board Minutes, 2 July 1917.
82 *Ibid.*
83 BP 78/63/8, Greenway to Black, 16 February 1915.
84 BP H11/203, Walpole to C.M. Ross, 27 April 1914.
85 BP H5/69, Walpole to Lt Col. Howell, 27 October 1917.
86 BP H16/107 Greenway to FO, 28 July 1917. These estimates are not excessive.
87 The surviving archives give very little indication of the volume and distribution of local sales at this time.
88 For details of the Company's financial position in 1914 see Tables 5.4.
89 PRO ADM 116/1687D, the contract between APOC and the Admiralty, 20 May 1914.
90 BP H17/6, *passim*.
91 BP 82/1/1 Benzine, Kerosene and Fuel Oil Contracts with the Asiatic Petroleum Co., enclosed in R. Kennedy to APOC, 17 October 1912; BP H17/6, Correspondence between Asiatic Petroleum Company and APOC, 1912.
92 BP H17/34, Garrow to Muhammara, 1 May 1914 and 12 and 26 June 1914.
93 BP 77/139/116, Greenway memorandum, 'British Petroleum Company, Petroleum Steamship Company, Homelight Company', n.d. 1915.
94 BP 77/139/118 'APOC - Finance Arrangements for Purchase of British Petroleum Company etc.' n.d. probably 31 May 1917 and BP 77/139/11

733

'Memorandum re Purchase of British Petroleum Company and Allied Concerns', enclosed in Greenway to Inchcape, 1 June 1917.
95 Sir Harry Townend, *A History of Shaw Wallace and Co. Ltd.* (Calcutta, 1965), for private circulation.
96 BP 77/139/116, Crisp to Greenway, 4 April 1917
97 PRO ADM 116/1687, Greenway memorandum, 'Rough Estimate of Probable Expenditure', 20 February 1914.
98 BP 78/63/5, Greenway to Albino, 7 July 1914.
99 Interview with Mr J.W.S. Straughan, July 1977.
100 L. Lockhart, *The Record of the Anglo Iranian Oil Co. Ltd.*, (unpublished) p.233.
101 BP 78/63/5, Greenway to Cargill, 22 January 1915.

8. Management and finance 1918-28

1 There is no biography of Greenway, but *A History of Shaw Wallace & Co. and Shaw Wallace & Co. Ltd*, compiled by Sir Harry Townend (Calcutta, 1965) for private circulation covers Greenway's years in India and the obituary notice in *The Times*, 18 December 1934, is a general appreciation. On Cadman see John Rowland and Basil, Second Baron Cadman, *Ambassador for Oil, the Life of John, First Baron Cadman* (London, 1965).
2 On the changes in the Company's management in this period see R.W. Ferrier, 'The Early Management Organisation of British Petroleum and Sir John Cadman', ed. Leslie Hannah, *Management Strategy and Business Development* (London, 1976), pp. 130-47.
3 BP 81/55/2, Pretyman to Greenway, 16 April 1914.
4 Austen Chamberlain (1863-1937), had been Civil Lord of the Admiralty, 1895, 1900, Financial Secretary to Treasury, 1900-02, Postmaster-General, 1902-03 and Chancellor of the Exchequer, 1903-06. Lord Scarborough (1857-1945) served in the Army and gave long distinguished public service. Lord Mount Stephen (1829-1921) distinguished himself in Canadian business. Lord Selborne (1859-1942) had been Under-Secretary for the Colonies, 1895-1900, First Lord of the Admiralty, 1900-05 and High Commissioner for South Africa, 1905-10.
5 BP 77/49/8, Greenway record note, 16 September 1925.
6 PRO ADM 116/1687B, Director of Contracts minute, 5 March 1914 and *ibid.*, Bradbury to Secretary of Admiralty, 4 March 1914.
7 *Ibid.*, Admiralty to Treasury, 1 April 1914.
8 PRO T 1/12229/45465, Greenway to Inchcape, 2 January 1917.
9 PRO T 1/11953/20174/1916, Bonham Carter to Sir T. Heath, 24 June 1914, Bradbury to Bonham Carter, 8 July 1914 and Hopwood to Bradbury, 8 July 1914.
10 Hansard, House of Commons, vol. 126, cols. 2367-8, 18 March 1920.
11 BP APOC Board Minutes, 24 January 1918.
12 BP 77/49/8, Greenway, Managing Directorship Memorandum, 23 January 1919.
13 On the administration of Standard Oil see Ralph W. Hidy and Muriel E. Hidy, *Pioneering in Big Business 1862-1911* (New York, 1955), pp. 40-75; George S. Gibb and Evelyn H. Knowlton, *The Resurgent Years, 1911-1927* (New York, 1956); Alfred D. Chandler, *Strategy and Structure, Chapters in the History of the American Industrial Enterprise* (Cambridge, Mass, 1962), pp.

Notes to pp. 302-308

163-224 and *The Visible Hand, The Managerial Revolution in American Business* (Cambridge, Mass, 1977), pp. 320-6 and 418-24.
14 BP APOC Board Minutes, 27 January 1919.
15 BP 78/13/49, Minutes of Managing Directors' Meetings, 26 February 1919.
16 *Ibid.*, 4 April 1919.
17 *Ibid.*, 17 September 1919.
18 *Ibid.*, 15 May 1919.
19 *Ibid.*, 23 September 1919.
20 BP APOC Board Minutes, 29 September 1919.
21 BP 78/63/49, Minutes of Managing Directors' Meetings, 19 January 1921.
22 BP 77/49/8 Pt 2, Greenway, Managing Directorship Memorandum, 23 January 1919.
23 BP H14/9, Braithwaite to Greenway, 18 November 1919.
24 BP 78/63/49, Minutes of Managing Directors' Meetings, 5 January 1921.
25 *Ibid.*, 15 December 1921.
26 BP H14/8, Nichols to Braithwaite, 8 December 1919.
27 BP APOC Board Minutes, 23 February 1920.
28 BP 78/63/49, Minutes of Managing Directors' Meetings, 25 May 1921.
29 *Ibid.*, the question was first discussed on 30 July 1920.
30 *Ibid.*, 17 November 1920.
31 *Ibid.*, 15 December 1920.
32 BP H11/250, Greenway memorandum of meeting in Glasgow, 15 July 1921.
33 BP 78/63/50, Minutes of Managing Directors' Meetings, 27 July 1921.
34 *Ibid.*
35 *Ibid.*
36 BP APOC Board Minutes, 25 July 1921.
37 Correspondence covering a year from November 1917 to September 1918 on this question between Walpole of Strick, Scott & Co. and E.B. Howell, Deputy Commissioner, Basra is found *passim* in BP H5/69.
38 BP 77/72/16, conference at Indian Office, 8 April 1919.
39 PRO T 1/12544/18025, IO to APOC, 9 May 1919.
40 BP 77/72/16, Nichols to IO, 26 June 1919.
41 *Ibid.*, Cadman to IO, 24 July 1919.
42 PRO T 1/12544/18025, Admiralty to Treasury, 18 August 1919.
43 BP 77/13 9/86, Barstow to Inchcape, 22 August 1919. See also PRO TI 12544/18025, Barstow Minute, September 1919.
44 PRO T 1/12544/18025, Greenway to Inchcape, 9 September 1919.
45 *Ibid.*, Inchcape to Barstow, 8 October 1919.
46 BP 77/139/86, Greenway to Inchcape, 9 October 1919.
47 PRO T 1/12544/18025, Treasury to Petroleum Executive and Treasury to Admiralty, 14 October 1919; *ibid.*, Barstow to Packe, 11 February 1920.
48 BP H14/36, Garrow to Strick Scott, 13 March 1919.
49 BP H7/36, Nichols to Strick Scott, 24 July 1919.
50 BP H9/144, Nichols to Strick Scott, 27 March 1919. See Walpole's defence *ibid.*, Walpole to Greenway, 18 March 1919.
51 *Ibid.*, Nichols to Walpole, 5 May 1919. Walpole was not unacquainted with what was wrong, see *ibid.* Jacks to Walpole, 14 January 1919, but lacked the will to put it right, not only from personal inadequacy but probably also because of the mental fatigue from long exposure in a rather debilitating climate without leave.

52 *Ibid.*, Neilson to Greenwood, 21 April 1920.
53 BP H16/111, Garrow 'Notes on a Visit to Persia and Mesopotamia', 10 February 1920; see also BP H16/124 Pt 2, Garrow to Strick Scott, 22 July 1920, 12 and 19 August 1920.
54 BP H17/39, Nichols 'Notes on Visit to Persia, Mesopotamia and Egypt', 25 April 1921.
55 BP H7/24, Strick Scott Board Minutes, 22 June 1920.
56 *Ibid.*, 17 August 1920; see also *ibid.*, 19 October 1920, 16 November 1920 and 15 February 1921.
57 *Ibid.*, 18 January 1921.
58 BP 77/72/97, Wilson to Greenway, 29 January 1921.
59 *Ibid.*, Greenway to Wilson, 3 February 1921.
60 *Ibid.*, Greenway, 'Duties and Responsibilities of the Resident Director', 14 February 1921.
61 *Ibid.*, Greenway to Wilson, 14 February 1921.
62 PRO T 1/12366, meeting at Treasury, 6 May 1919.
63 PRO T 1/12054/18743, Barstow to Bradbury, 7 April 1917.
64 PRO T 1/12366, meeting at Treasury, 6 May 1919.
65 *Ibid.*, Greenway to Inchcape, 24 July 1919.
66 *Ibid.*, Inchcape to Bradbury, 28 July 1919.
67 *Ibid.*, Inchcape to Greenway, 28 July 1919.
68 *Ibid.*, Bradbury to Inchcape, 9 August 1919.
69 *Ibid.*, Inchcape to Greenway, 15 August 1919.
70 BP APOC Board Minutes, 29 September 1919.
71 *Ibid.*, 27 October 1919.
72 *Ibid.*, 24 November and 1 December 1919.
73 PRO T 1/12533/16661, Admiralty to Treasury, 19 January 1920.
74 Hansard, House of Commons, vol. 122, col. 1762, Sir F. Banbury's speech, 11 December 1919.
75 *Ibid.*, vol. 22, col. 1765, Mr A. Acland's speech, 11 December 1919.
76 *Ibid.*, vol. 22, cols. 1864-5, Lt Commander Kenworthy's speech, 12 December 1919.
77 APOC Board Minutes, 31 January 1921 and PRO TI 161/499/57678/1, Greenway to Inchcape, 1 February 1921.
78 BP APOC Board Minutes, 21 March 1921.
79 BP H11/250, Stewart to Hearn, 24 November 1921.
80 BP APOC Board Minutes, 31 July 1922.
81 PRO POWE 33/96, Clarke to Duff, 24 August 1922.
82 *Ibid.*, Baldwin to Lloyd-Greame, 28 August 1922.
83 *Ibid.*, Baldwin to Greenway, 7 September 1922.
84 *Ibid.*, Greenway to Cargill, 12 September 1922.
85 BP APOC Board Minutes, 27 September 1922.
86 PRO POWE 33/96, Greenway to Baldwin, 27 September 1922.
87 *Ibid.*, Packe to Baldwin, 27 September 1922.
88 PRO T 161/278/32301/02, Clarke to Barstow, 29 November 1922. Three days previously Packe had written in a similar vein to Barstow, see *ibid.*, Packe to Barstow, 26 November 1922.
89 PRO POWE 33/96, Baldwin to Greenway, 19 October 1922. The writing of this letter had been preceded by correspondence and meetings between Lloyd-Greame, Clarke and Greenway; see *ibid.*, Lloyd-Greame minute, 4

October 1922, Lloyd-Greame minute to Baldwin, 13 October 1922, Clarke to Lloyd Greame, 16 October 1922 and Clarke to Lloyd-Greame, 18 October 1922.
90 *Ibid.*, Greenway to Baldwin, 8 November 1922.
91 *Ibid.*, Stewart to Cadman, 8 November 1922.
92 BP 81/55/6, Cadman to Stewart, 5 November 1922.
93 PRO T 161/278 32301/02, Packe to Barstow, 16 November 1922.
94 *Ibid.*, Packe to Murray, 23 May 1923.
95 BP APOC Board Minutes, 27 February 1923.
96 BP 76/43/36, Slade to Greenway, 23 March 1923.
97 BP APOC Board Minutes, 24 April 1923.
98 *Ibid.*, 29 May 1923.
99 BP H11/250, committee meeting, 7 June 1923.
100 *Ibid.*, committee meeting, 21 June 1923.
101 *Ibid.*, Slade memorandum, 'Organisation of APOC', 19 June 1923.
102 *Ibid.*, Recommendation to the Board for Future Management, 28 June 1923.
103 *Ibid.*, Final Report on 'Arrangements for Future Management', 26 July 1923.
104 *Ibid.*, Management Committee Report, 16 July 1923.
105 *Ibid.*
106 Some idea of the continuing discussions is in BP H11/250, especially Management Committee Reports of 8 November and 19 December 1923.
107 Some of Wilson's early proposals are in BP 77/139/140.
108 BP 78/63/16, Nichols to Wilson, 30 November 1922.
109 *Ibid.*, Nichols to Strick Scott, 23 June 1921 and *ibid.*, Nichols to General Managers, 1 November 1923.
110 BP APOC Board Minutes, 31 January 1921.
111 BP 78/63/49, Minutes of Managing Directors' Meetings, 22 March 1922.
112 The delay in negotiations can be seen in BP 77/139/140 Strick Scott Board Minutes, particularly 21 June and 16 August 1921 and 21 February 1922.
113 BP APOC Board Minutes, 29 May 1922.
114 BP 5113/9 (Sec) Brown Fleming and Murray to Stewart, 28 September 1922.
115 BP APOC Board Minutes, 31 October 1922; see also BP 77/139/140, Strick Scott Board Minutes, 7 November 1922.
116 In fairness to Greenway, it has to be recognised that Shaw, Wallace & Company, formed in January 1886, survived as managing agents and became a public company on 25 July 1947, adapting themselves over time to new trading conditions. Jardine, Matheson and Company, once primarily traders and managing agents, formed on 1 July 1832, have also survived to become an important international company with widespread interests, see *Jardine, Matheson and Company, an historical sketch* (Hong Kong, 1960).
117 BP 78/63/16, Nichols to Wilson, 30 November 1922.
118 BP H8/100, Lloyd memorandum, Visit to Persia, 9 May 1923.
119 BP 78/63/16, Nichols to General Managers, 30 October 1924.
120 BP APOC Board Minutes, 30 May 1921.
121 PRO T 161/140/S12245, APOC Financial Memorandum to Inchcape, 24 June 1921.
122 *Ibid.*, Inchcape to Barstow, 28 June 1921.
123 *Ibid.*, Blackett to Barstow, 1 July 1921.
124 *Ibid.*, Inchcape to Greenway, 4 July 1921.
125 *Ibid.*, Greenway to Inchcape, 12 July 1921.

126 BP APOC Board Minutes, 31 October 1921.
127 BP APOC Board Minutes, 28 November 1921. At this time the Company advised the Board of Trade of the urgency of the problem, PRO T 161/499/S7678/1, Lloyd to Hilton Young, 5 December 1921.
128 PRO T 161/499/S7678/1, Inchcape to Barstow, 12 December 1921.
129 Quoted in Hector Bolitho, *James Lyle Mackay, First Earl of Inchcape* (London, 1936), pp. 166-7. It is remarkable that this, the first, and so far the only, biography of Inchcape, contains not a single reference to his role as one of the first two government directors of the Company. On the economic details see Derek H. Aldcroft, *From Versailles to Wall Street 1919-1929* (London, 1977), particularly chapters 3 and 5.
130 PRO T 161/499/S7678/1, Inchcape to Barstow, 12 December 1912.
131 BP APOC Board Minutes, 21 December 1921. As a result of the Board meeting, Greenway wrote to Inchcape, who characterised the letter as 'hysterical...urging as an imperative necessity the immediate issue of the fresh capital for the Anglo-Persian', PRO T 161/499/S7678/1, Inchcape to Barstow, 23 December 1921.
132 PRO T 161/499/S7678/1, Barstow to Inchcape, 28 December 1921.
133 *Ibid.*, Inchcape to Barstow, 5 January 1922 and BP APOC Board Minutes, 8 February 1922.
134 PRO T 161/140/S12245, Lloyd to Inchcape, 12 January 1922.
135 *Ibid.*, Blackett to Barstow, 26 January 1922.
136 *Ibid.*, Barstow to Inchcape, 28 January 1922.
137 *Ibid.*, Lloyd to Inchcape, 31 January 1922.
138 *Ibid.*, Lloyd to Hilton Young, 13 March 1922.
139 Hansard, House of Commons, vol. 151, cols. 1699-730, 10 March 1922., *ibid.*, vol. 151, cols. 2129-42, 14 March 1922 and *ibid.*, vol. 156, cols. 543-8, 5 July 1922.
140 BP APOC Board Minutes, 26 September 1922.
141 PRO T 161/499/S7678/1, Stewart to Inchcape, 3 October 1922.
142 *Ibid.*, Inchcape to Barstow, 6 October 1922.
143 *Ibid.*, Barstow to Inchcape, 16 October 1922.
144 *Ibid.*, Fiske to Greenway, 19 October 1922.
145 *Ibid.*, Greenway to Barstow, 2 November 1922 and BP APOC Board Minutes, 31 October 1922.
146 PRO T 161/278 3230/02, Packe to Barstow, 16 November 1922.
147 PRO T 161/499/S7678/1, Packe to Barstow, 12 November 1922.
148 PRO T 1/12544/18025, Inchcape to Barstow, 6 January 1920.
149 *Ibid.*
150 PRO T 161/499/S7678/1, Greenway to Barstow, 14 November 1922.
151 *Ibid.*, Barstow to Greenway, 29 November 1922 and Greenway to Barstow, 4 December 1922.
152 *Ibid.*, Packe to Barstow, 3 January 1923. Board sanction was obtained on 2 January 1923.
153 *The Times*, 28 November 1923.
154 *The Financial Times*, 28 November 1923.
155 BP APOC Board Minutes 24 June 1924; Greenway anticipated it would only be for two or three months.
156 BP 78/63/51, Management Committee Minutes, 25 June 1924.

157 BP H11/250, Greenway memorandum, 'Management Committee', 28 July 1925.
158 BP H11/250, Cadman to Greenway, 30 July 1925.
159 BP APOC Board Minutes, 28 July 1925.
160 BP 77/49/8 Churchill to Packe, 11 August 1925.
161 *Ibid.*, Churchill to Cargill, 11 August 1925.
162 *Ibid.*, Churchill to Cargill, 24 August 1925.
163 *Ibid.*, Cargill to Churchill, 26 August 1925.
164 BP APOC Board Minutes, 29 September 1925.
165 BP H11/250, Cadman draft on management n.d..
166 BP 76/43/36, Cadman memorandum 'Management Organisation', 24 November 1925; and BP APOC Board Minutes, 24 November 1925.
167 BP 76/43/36, Cadman draft 'General Department', 17 September 1926. Approved at Board Meeting, 28 September.
168 BP 78/63/41, Clarke to Taylor Brading, 16 January 1923.
169 For the early history of the Company's medical services see *The Naft*, vol. vii, July 1932, no. 4, pp. 6-13, *ibid.*, vol. viii, November 1932, no. 6, pp. 7-11 and vol. ix, January 1933, pp. 11-15.
170 BP 71/102/2, Cadman report, 'Visit to Persia, Autumn 1924'.
171 *Ibid.*
172 BP H11/250, Cadman draft memorandum 'Executive and Management Organisation', 24 September 1928.
173 BP APOC Board Minutes, 28 May 1929.
174 *Ibid.*, 28 January 1930.
175 The decline in the minority interest from 1925 to 1928 by £1 342 927 is the result of the omission from the consolidation of some declining outside shareholdings in continental marketing companies.
176 BP78/87/1, APOC AGM, 6 November 1928.
177 BP78/77/1, APOC AGM, 17 December 1923. 'No prudent businessman - be he merchant, manufacturer, or tradesman - takes all of his profits year by year out of his business, since in most cases, if he did so, it would quickly die of inanition, but retains some portion of them in the business for the purpose of endeavouring to maintain or expand his operations. This, gentlemen, is the policy we have been following'; *ibid.*, 10 November 1925, 'throughout *my* business career it has been my practice to put back each year into my various businesses a considerable portion of my profits, and I am quite sure that every businessman present here today will agree with me as to the wisdom of this policy, particularly in the case of an industrial concern with such wide ramifications, and so many vicissitudes as ours.'

9. Government and concessionary relations 1919-26

1 See Elizabeth Monroe, *Britain's Moment in the Middle East 1914-1956* (London, 1963 and 1981); Reader Bullard, *Britain and the Middle East: from the earliest times to 1950* (London, 1951); John Marlowe, *The Persian Gulf in the Twentieth Century* (London, 1962); Elie Kedourie, *Britain and the Middle East: the vital years: 1914-1921* (London, 1956).
2 'If Britain had a policy with regard to oil at all, it was, to say the least, a very vague and confused one...it was realised that British interests must somehow control the exploitation of oil in this area [Mesopotamia] but as to how this

was to be effected or what concrete plans should be made to secure these aims, all was undefined and obscure', C. Davies, 'British Oil Policy in the Middle East 1919-32' (Edinburgh, PhD thesis, 1973), p. 94.

3 See J. Nevakiki, *Britain, France and the Arab Middle East* (London, 1969).
4 For an account of the problems over fuel oil reserves and the Treasury constraints see Davies, 'British Oil Policy', pp. 55-71. The financial stringency was a result of the Cabinet 'Ten Year Rule' to the service departments that their estimates for 1920-21 should be based 'on the assumption that the British Empire would not be engaged in any great war during the next ten years', ADM 167/56, War Cabinet memo 616A, 15 August 1919, quoted in Stephen Roskill, *Naval Policy between the Wars*, vol. 1, *The Period of Anglo-American Antagonism 1919-1929* (London, 1968), p. 215.
5 PRO POWE 34/1, Petroleum Department memorandum, 'Oil Concessions in British Colonies and Protectorates British Control of Companies', n.d.
6 Nance F. Kittner, 'Issues in Anglo-Persian Diplomatic Relations, 1921-1933' (London, PhD thesis, 1980), has interesting comments and sources on the British Government's attitude to Persia in this period.
7 Philip Graves, *The Life of Sir Percy Cox* (London, 1941), pp. 248-64. For a contrary view of the treaty see J.H. Balfour, *Recent Happenings in Persia* (London, 1922).
8 Peter Avery, *Modern Iran* (London, 1965) and L.P. Elwell-Sutton, *Modern Iran* (London, 1941), provide introductions to the Persian politics of this period.
9 On British military operations L.C. Dunsterville, *The Adventures of Dunsterforce* (London, 1921); Lord Ironside (ed.), *High Road to Command. The Diaries of Major-General Sir Edmund Ironside 1920-22* (London, 1972). For the most recent account of the coup d'état see Denis Wright, *The English Amongst the Persians* (London, 1977), pp. 179-84.
10 George Lenczowski, *Russia and the West in Iran, 1918-1948* (New York, 1949), pp. 48-71.
11 A satisfactory impartial assessment of the reign of Rizā Shāh remains to be written, but see the biography, Donald N. Wilbur, *Riza Shah Pahlavi The Resurrection and Reconstruction of Iran 1878-1944* (Hicksville, 1975) and the miscellany, George Lenczowski (ed.), *Iran under the Pahlavis* (Stanford, 1978).
12 PRO T 1/12544/18025, Greenway to Inchcape, 9 September 1919.
13 PRO FO 416/65, No. 208 and No. 209, Cox to Curzon, 22 August 1919.
14 PRO POWE 33/67, FO to Treasury, 4 December 1919.
15 BP H12/54, Greenway draft letter to Barstow, 5 August 1920, and *ibid.*, Greenway to Barstow, 9 June 1920 (PRO T 161/2/S120 APOC to Treasury, 9 June 1920).
16 PRO T 161/2/S120, Barstow to Chancellor, 19 June 1920.
17 *Ibid.*, Inchcape to Barstow, 28 June 1920.
18 *Ibid.*, Barstow to Chancellor, 28 June 1920.
19 *Ibid.*, Chancellor to Barstow, 30 June 1920, *ibid.*, Barstow to Greenway, 5 July 1920.
20 *Ibid.*, Barstow to Inchcape, 11 August 1920.
21 *Ibid.*, Greenway to Barstow, 5 August 1920.
22 *Ibid.*, Barstow to Greenway, 12 August 1920.
23 *Ibid.*, Greenway to Barstow, 24 August 1920.
24 BP H12/54, Greenway to Packe, 30 June 1920.

Notes to pp. 354-357

25 *Ibid.*, Barstow to Inchcape, 25 August 1920; *ibid* Greenway to Barstow, 29 August 1920; *ibid.*, Barstow note, 2 September; PRO T 161/51/S3341, APOC to Treasury, 2 September 1920, and *ibid.*, Barstow to Chancellor, 19 October 1920.
26 PRO T 161/61/S3341, Conference notes, 3 November 1920.
27 *Ibid.*, Bradbury to Barstow, 8 September 1920.
28 BP 77/49/8, Greenway memorandum, Mesopotamian Oil Concession, 17 April 1919.
29 Quoted in André Nouschi, *Luttes Pétrolières au Proche-Orient* (Paris, 1970), p. 53. See also Henri Bérenger, *Le Petrole et la France* (Paris, 1920).
30 PRO FO 368/2095, Report of meeting of the Inter-Allied Petroleum Conference, 17 December 1918.
31 PRO FO 368/2095, de Fleuriau to Curzon, 6 January 1919.
32 *Ibid.*, Kidston minute, 6 January 1919.
33 'By 1918 the British official machine had become very oil conscious', V.H. Rothwell, 'Mesopotamia in British War Aims, 1914-1918', *The Historical Journal*, 13 (1970), p. 287.
34 PRO FO 368/2095, Percy to Clark, 5 June 1919 and Villiers minute, 12 June 1919. Bérenger's view that 'La France ne put pas plus vivre sans pétrole que sans charbon,' Bérenger to Cambon, 6 December 1918, Ministère des Affaircs Etrangères, AE. Y. International vol. 192, did not satisfy some officials of the Foreign Ministry, who were more concerned with the territorial rights of France in the Fertile Crescent; see *ibid.*, vol. 194, Pichon to London, 23 June 1919 and Paris note, 1 August 1919 for French reaction.
35 PRO 368/2095, Conference to discuss the French request for a common policy regarding oil, 15 January 1919; see also *ibid.*, Curzon to Balfour, 20 February 1919, on Foreign Office and Petroleum Executive views.
36 See FO CP 11435, memorandum by British delegation, Paris, on British policy in the Middle East, 18 February 1919 for the problems between the Paris delegation to the Peace Conference and the Foreign Office in London which effected negotiations involving oil affairs, see e.g. PRO FO 371/4209, Kidstone minute, 18 February 1919; PRO FO 608/231, Mallet and Balfour minute, 3 February 1919 and PRO FO 371/4209, minutes of meeting in Paris, 1 February 1919.
37 PRO FO 371/4209, Memorandum of Agreement between Senator Henry Bérenger and the Rt Hon. Walter Long, 6 March 1919; *ibid.*, Mallet to Curzon, 17 March 1919.
38 *Ibid.*, Curzon to Balfour, 2 April 1919.
39 PRO FO 608/231, Tufton minute, 9 April 1919.
40 PRO FO 368/2095, Tufton to Clark, 8 April 1919, enclosing copy of Memorandum of Agreement.
41 PRO CAB 24/76, Petroleum Executive Memorandum for the War Cabinet, 'The Acquisition of British Control over the Royal Dutch-Shell Group', 22 February 1919; PRO CAB 23/10, War Cabinet Minutes, 8 May 1919. PRO FO 368/2095, Curzon to Cambon, 16 May 1919.
42 PRO FO 368/2095, Lloyd George to Clémenceau, 21 May 1919, *ibid.*, Villiers minute, 11 June 1919 and *ibid.*, Davies to Curzon, 11 July 1919.
43 *Ibid.*, Curzon to Cambon, 27 July 1919.
44 *Ibid.*, Long memorandum, 'Oil Supplies', for Cabinet, 4 November 1919.
45 PRO POWE 33/89, Greenwood–Bérenger Agreement, 21 December 1919.

46 PRO FO 371/4231, minutes of a conference of ministers, 23 January 1920.
47 PRO CAB 24/104, Kellaway memorandum 'Mesopotamian oilfields' for Cabinet, 22 April 1920.
48 PRO CAB 24/103, Horne memorandum 'Mesopotamian oilfields' for Cabinet, 16 April 1920.
49 PRO T 172/1387, Barstow note, 21(?) April 1920.
50 PRO FO 371/5085, memorandum of agreement between Berthelot and Cadman, 24 April 1920.
51 *Ibid.*, Italian ambassador to FO, 20 August 1920.
52 See Parliamentary Papers, House of Commons (Cmd 1226), 'Correspondence between His Majesty's Government and the United States Ambassador respecting Economic Rights in Mandated Territory'; John A. De Novo, *American Interests and Policies in the Middle East 1900-1939* (Minneapolis, 1963), pp. 169-84.
53 For the state of the Persian army in the late Qājār period see R.M. Burrel, 'Aspects of the Reign of Muzaffar al-Dīn Shāh of Persia 1896-1907' (London, PhD thesis, 1979), Chapter 3, 'The Condition of the Army', pp. 52-96.
54 BP H16/107, Greenway to FO, 22 January 1915, enclosure, 'Memorandum of an Interview with H.E. Mehdī Khān', 21 January 1915.
55 See Floreeda Safiri, 'The South Persian Rifles' (Edinburgh, PhD thesis, 1976).
56 BP H16/156, Greenway to FO, 10 June 1915.
57 *Ibid.*, Crowe to Greenway, 1 June 1915 and *ibid.*, Macindoe to Mehdī Khān, 18 June 1915.
58 *Ibid.*, Muhtesham al-Saltana to Maclean, 29 September 1915.
59 *Ibid.*, Greenway to Brown, 11 November 1915.
60 *Ibid.*, Mehdī Khān to Greenway, 21 May 1916 and *ibid.*, FO to Greenway, 7 June 1916.
61 *Ibid.*, Greenway to FO, 28 June 1916.
62 *Ibid.*, de Bunsen to Greenway, 3 July 1916.
63 *Ibid.*, Mehdī Khān to Greenway, 6 July 1916.
64 *Ibid.*, Brown to Greenway, 15 February and 29 March 1917 and *ibid.*, Sādigh al-Saltana, 25 February 1917.
65 *Ibid.*, Greenway to FO and Greenway to Brown, 26 April 1917.
66 *Ibid.*, Greenway to FO, 18 May 1917.
67 *Ibid.*, 'Alā al-Saltana to Marling, 2 October 1917; *ibid.*, Graham to Macindoe, 10 October 1917 and *ibid.*, Sādigh al-Saltana, 18 December 1917.
68 *Ibid.*, Greenway memorandum to Board, 7 November 1917.
69 This was the origin of the controversial North Persian Concession, the subject of negotiations between the Company and Standard Oil (NJ) to develop it jointly and of the attempt by Sinclair Oil Corporation to acquire it.
70 BP H16/156, Greenway to Inchcape, 9 November 1917.
71 *Ibid.*, Greenway to FO, 23 November 1917 and *ibid.*, Graham to Greenway, 11 December 1917.
72 *Ibid.*, Graham to APOC, 27 December 1917.
73 *Ibid.*, Greenway to FO, 31 December 1917.
74 *Ibid.*, Greenway to Cargill, 8 January 1918.
75 *Ibid.*, Greenway to Mehdī Khān, 28 December 1918.
76 *Ibid.*, Mehdī Khān to Greenway, 30 January 1918.
77 PRO FO 371/3265, Oliphant minute, 12 February 1918.
78 *Ibid.*, Marling telegram, 9 February 1918.

79 *Ibid.*, India Office to FO, 23 February 1918.
80 BP H16/156, Greenway to Oliphant, 28 February 1918 and *ibid.*, Greenway to Wood, 21 March 1918; *ibid.*, Greenway to Sādigh al-Saltana, 9 May 1918; PRO FO 371/3265, FO to Marling, 26 July 1918.
81 *Ibid.*, Graham to Greenway, 28 May 1918; PRO FO 371/3265, Oliphant minute, 30 July 1918.
82 PRO FO 371/3265, Persian Government telegram to legation in London, 10 August 1918.
83 *Ibid.*, Wood to Greenway, 21 August 1918.
84 *Ibid.*, Cox to FO, 5 November 1918.
85 BP 78/28/8, Greenway to Marling, 2 April 1918.
86 PRO FO 371/3265, Oliphant to Cox, 21 September 1918.
87 BP 78/28/8, Greenway to Wood, 8 October 1918 and BP 77/49/8, Greenway to FO, 17 January 1919.
88 BP H16/161, Greenway memorandum, 30 January 1919.
89 *Ibid.*, Greenway to Oliphant, 31 January 1919.
90 *Ibid.*, Wallace to APOC, 24 February 1919.
91 *Ibid.*, APOC to Wallace, 28 February 1919.
92 *Ibid.*, FO to APOC, 1 March 1919.
93 *Ibid.*, Wallace to APOC, 4 March 1919.
94 *Ibid.*, Cargill to Greenway, 4 March 1919.
95 BP 78/69/22, Nichols to Greenway, 3 March 1919 and BP H16/161, Cargill to Greenway, 6 March 1919.
96 BP 78/63/22, Nichols to Cargill, 7 March 1919.
97 *Ibid.*, Nichols to Greenway, 22 March 1919.
98 BP H16/161, Spicer to APOC, 29 March 1919.
99 *Ibid.*, Nichols to FO, 4 April 1919.
100 *Ibid.*, Greenway to FO, 9 April 1919.
101 *Ibid.*, Minutes of meeting at FO, 22 September 1919.
102 *Ibid.*, Nichols to Wallace, 15 October 1919; BP APOC Board Minutes, 27 October 1919.
103 BP H16/161, Greenway to FO, 5 March 1919.
104 *Ibid.*, Philpotts to Greenway, 16 August 1919.
105 BP H15/183, Report of Armitage-Smith to Persian Government, 22 December 1920.
106 BP H16/161, Fîrûz to Farîd al-Saltana, 28 November 1919.
107 *Ibid.*, Greenway memorandum for Firūz, 27 November 1919.
108 *Ibid.*, Greenway to Farīd al-Saltana, 27 November 1919.
109 *Ibid.*, Farīd al-Saltana to APOC, 28 November 1919.
110 *Ibid.*, McLintock to APOC, 23 December 1919 On Sir William McLintock see Rex Winsbury, *Thomson McLintock the First Hundred Years*, (London, 1977), private publication, pp. 36-44; on R.A. Murray, Edgar Jones, *Accountancy and the British Economy 1840-1980*, (London, 1981) pp. 85-9.
111 *Ibid.*, McLintock to Lloyd, 15 January 1920.
112 BP H15/183, Report of Armitage-Smith to Persian Government, 22 December 1920.
113 BP H16/161, Fīrūz to APOC, 19 March 1920 and Greenway to Murray, 11 March 1920.
114 *Ibid.*, Cargill to Greenway, 26 March 1920.
115 *Ibid.*, Greenway supplemental memorandum, 29 March 1920.

116 *Ibid.*, Greenway memorandum, 26 March 1920.
117 *Ibid.*, Counsel's opinion, 30 March 1920.
118 *Ibid.*, Greenway to Firūz.
119 *Ibid.*, Lloyd to Greenway.
120 *Ibid.*, Firūz to Greenway, 6 April 1920 and Firūz to Lloyd, 7 April 1920.
121 *Ibid.*, Firūz to Greenway, 16 April 1920.
122 *Ibid.*, Lloyd to Greenway, 23 April 1920.
123 Francis Steegmuller, *Jean Cocteau* (London, 1970), pp. 243-4. See also Arthur Gold and Robert Fizdale, *Misia: The Life of Misia Sert* (London, 1980), p. 322. Firūz, Cocteau and Radiguet visited London together and a Paris party attended by Firūz was the inspiration for Radiguet's novel, *Comte d'Orgel* (Paris, 1924).
124 BP H16/161, Barstow to Greenway, 13 May 1920 and Greenway to Firūz, 13 May 1920.
125 *Ibid.*, Greenway to Firūz, 11 June 1920 and 16 June 1920.
126 *Ibid.*, Greenway to Packe, 9 June 1920.
127 *Ibid.*, Cargill to Greenway, 14 June 1920.
128 *Ibid.*, Lloyd to Greenway, 2 July 1920.
129 In fact Firūz, anticipating the fall of the Persian Government, was 'anxious to get all cash and no shares', BP H16/161, Greenway to Packe, 30 June 1920. Firūz felt very cheated over the affair and complained about it in 1926 to Cadman who refused to discuss it privately, but was prepared to raise it with Rizā Shāh, to which Firūz objected. He bore a grudge against the Company to the end of his life. He was also very bitter toward the British Government for failing to intervene and have him released when he was imprisoned in Tehrān after the coup d'état in 1921.
130 BP H16/161, Oliphant to Greenway, 27 July 1920; *ibid.*, Lloyd to Greenway, 29 July 1920 and *ibid.*, Greenway to Oliphant, 11 August 1920.
131 BP H15/183, Report of Armitage-Smith to Persian Government, 22 December 1920, Appendix III, 'Īsā Khān to Armitage-Smith, 29 August 1920.
132 *Ibid.*, Report of Armitage-Smith.
133 On the application and importance of the Armitage-Smith Agreement see forthcoming article, R.W. Ferrier and R.W. Roberts, 'Profits, Allowances and Oil Royalties; The Anglo Persian Oil Company and the Armitage-Smith Agreement', which will deal with the relevant issues in greater detail.
134 BP H15/183, Report of Armitage-Smith, Appendix VII, Counsel's Opinion, 1 December 1920.
135 *Ibid.*, Appendix XII, McLintock report, 22 December 1920.
136 BP H16/161, Greenway to Armitage-Smith, 16 November 1920.
137 The text of the Armitage-Smith Agreement is to be found in the International Court of Justice, *Pleadings, Arguments, Documents, Anglo-Iranian Oil Co. Cases* (The Hague, 1953), pp. 229-35 and Appendix 9.1.
138 M. Nakhai, *Le Petrole en Iran* (Brussels, 1938), p. 53, refers to 'le Caractére provisoire de l'accord', with which N.S. Fatemi agrees, *Oil Diplomacy Powderkeg in Iran* (New York, 1954), p. 155. Yet the instructions of Armitage-Smith were to 'finally adjust all questions in dispute between the Anglo-Persian Oil Company and the Imperial Government of Persia', The International Court of Justice, *op. cit.*, p. 228. The authenticity of the instructions has not been disputed.

Notes to pp. 372-379

139 PRO ADM 116/3452, Watson memorandum, 'Proposed Combination of the Royal Dutch-Shell, Burmah and Anglo-Persian Oil Companies', 29 July 1921.
140 PRO T 161/515/S20744, Greenway memorandum, proposed 'Trading Arrangement for the Sale of Benzine in the United Kingdom and Ireland', 6 July 1921.
141 Ibid., Barstow to Gregg, 13 July 1921.
142 Ibid., Clarke to Lloyd-Greame, 7 July 1921.
143 Ibid., Inchcape to Gregg, 14 July 1921. This view was similar to the opinions expressed by H. MacGowan to the Harcourt Committee at its second meeting, of making working arrangements between the Company and Royal Dutch-Shell 'as he believed there to be between the Standard Oil and Shell Companies', PRO FO 365/2255 PIPCO.
144 For the history of Royal Dutch-Shell interests in the United States, see Kendall Beaton, *Enterprise in Oil* (New York, 1954).
145 PRO T 161/515/S20744, Barstow to Gregg, 14 July 1921 and PRO POWE 33/92 Minutes of meeting held at Board of Trade, 27 July 1921.
146 BP APOC Board Minutes, 21 December 1921.
147 PRO ADM 116/3452, Watson memorandum, *op. cit.*
148 Ibid., Clarke to Jenkins, 11 October 1921.
149 Ibid., Jenkins minute to Fourth Sea Lord, 21 October 1921.
150 Ibid., Notes of meeting held in Lloyd-Greame's rooms, 26 October 1921.
151 Ibid., Jenkins memorandum on a contract for the combination of the Royal Dutch-Shell, Burmah and Anglo-Persian oil companies, 16 November 1921.
152 PRO FO 371/8288, Lloyd-Greame memorandum 'Proposed Amalgamation of the Royal Dutch-Shell, Burmah and Anglo-Persian Oil Companies', for Cabinet, 6 January 1922; subsequent references to Lloyd-Greame's comments on pp. 42-5 refer to this source.
153 Max Egremont, *Balfour* (London, 1980), pp. 317-19 and Blanche E.C. Dugdale, *Arthur James Balfour* (London, 1936), p. 333 quoting Balfour on the Conference, 'an absolute unmixed benefit to mankind'.
154 Quoted in Stephen Roskill, *Naval Policy between the Wars 1919-1929*, p. 405; for the Conference from a naval viewpoint, *ibid.*, pp. 300-30.
155 *The Times*, 5 November 1921.
156 For example, *Oil, Paint and Drug Reporter*, 9 November 1921; see also PRO POWE 33/93 Petroleum Department comment, 5 December 1921.
157 PRO POWE 33/93, Clarke to Lloyd-Greame, 9 November 1921.
158 Ibid., Pretyman to Lloyd George, 14 November 1921.
159 Ibid., Lloyd George to Pretyman, 25 November 1921. Pretyman was satisfied by the reply, *ibid.*, Pretyman to Lloyd-Greame, 2 December 1921.
160 BP H18/38, Cadman's diary of visit to US, 1921-2.
161 PRO FO 371/8288, Geddes to FO, 18 January 1922.
162 Ibid., Weakley minute, 14 February 1922.
163 Ibid., Lloyd-Greame to Cabinet, 6 January 1922.
164 Ibid., enclosure in Hill to Vansittart, 24 February 1922.
165 Ibid., second meeting of Baldwin Committee, 13 March 1922.
166 Ibid., statement of Admiralty position, 10 March 1922.
167 A tenet to which Deterding increasingly subscribed, see Sir Henry Deterding, *An International Oil Man* (London, 1934), p. 118, 'it will be on the

Notes to pp. 379-386

basis of more and more co-operation rather than on intensified competition, the commerce of the future will increasingly and almost entirely depend'.
168 PRO T 161/211/20734, Watson to Inchcape, 20 February 1922.
169 *Ibid.*, Inchcape to Watson, 21 February 1922.
170 *Ibid.*, Horne to Baldwin, 2 March 1922.
171 PRO FO 371/8288, ninth meeting, Baldwin Committee, 7 April 1922.
172 *Manchester Daily Despatch*, 9 February 1922 and later, 2 June 1922.
173 *Ibid.*, Oliphant minute, 12 June 1922.
174 *Ibid.*, Vansittart minute, 14 June 1922.
175 PRO FO 371/8288, Final Report of Committee, 12 June 1922.
176 PRO FO 371/9405, Long to Curzon, 27 February 1923.
177 *Ibid.*, Weakley minute, 2 March 1923.
178 *Ibid.*, Oliphant minute, 3 March 1923.
179 *Ibid.*, Curzon to Long, 21 March 1923.
180 Quoted in Martin Gilbert, *Winston S. Churchill 1922-39*, vol. 5 (London, 1976), p. 9.
181 It is unfortunate that the Baldwin papers deposited at the Cambridge University Library shed no light at all on the motives or details of this event.
182 Gilbert, *Winston S. Churchill*, vol. 5, p. 14.
183 PRO FO 371/9029, Chamberlain to Curzon, 17 October 1923.
184 *Ibid.*, Weakley minute, 19 October 1923.
185 *Ibid.*, Vansittart minute, 19 October 1923.
186 *Ibid.*, Curzon minute, 20 October 1923.
187 Gilbert, *Winston S. Churchill*, vol. 5, p. 14.
188 PRO ADM 1 8658/55, questions on Churchill's scheme, n.d.
189 *Ibid.*, minute to First Lord, 14 November 1923.
190 *The Morning Post*, 30 October 1923.
191 *The Times*, 10 November 1923.
192 *Hansard*, House of Commons, vol. 168, cols. 350-1, 15 November 1923.
193 *The Times*, 14 December 1923.
194 *The Times*, 15 December 1923.
195 PRO ADM 1/9799, Amery memorandum to Cabinet, 10 January 1924. See also *The Leo Amery Diaries Volume 1: 1896-1929*, ed. John Barnes and David Nicholson (London, 1980), p. 363, 11 January 1924, 'Saw Lord Bearsted who wanted to talk to me about the Anglo-Persian Shell combination, etc., on which I had to tell him that I had definitely decided against the merger.'
196 PRO ADM 1/9799, Jenkins note, 12 February 1924, referring to proceedings of Cabinet meeting, 17 January 1924.
197 PRO ADM 1/9799, Barstow memorandum, enclosure in Snowden to Cabinet, 26 January 1924.
198 *The Times*, 30 January 1924.
199 *The Times*, 2 February 1924.
200 *Hansard*, House of Commons, vol. 169, cols. 1038-9, 14 February 1924.
201 PRO ADM 1/9799, Greenway to Murray, 12 November 1924.
202 *Ibid.*, Murray minute, 14 November 1924.
203 *Ibid.*, Warren Fisher to Greenway, 17 November 1924.
204 PRO FO CP 11910, Curzon speech to House of Lords, 26 July 1921.
205 James Morier, *The Adventures of Hajji Baba of Ispahan* (London, 1824), The World's Classics edition, p. 442.

206 Quoted in G. Waterfield, *Professional Diplomat, Sir Percy Loraine* (London, 1973), p. 22.
207 PRO FO 416/72, Loraine to Curzon, 21 May 1923.
208 BP H16/18, Moayyed al-Dawla to Peel, 22 March 1922. Nichols, in London, thought it disquieting, BP 78/63/16, Nichols to Strick, Scott, 9 June 1922.
209 BP H16/18, Young to Nichols, 27 July 1922.
210 *Ibid.*, Young to Strick, Scott and Co., 5 and 12 August 1922.
211 BP H9/16, pt. 1 p. 8 extract, Young to Nichols, July 1922.
212 BP H16/18, Young to Jacks, 1 August 1922.
213 *Ibid.*, Jacks to Durie, 23 August 1922. See also G.R. Garthwaite, 'The Bakhtiari Khans, the Government of Iran and the British 1846-1915', *International Journal of Middle East Studies*, vol. 3, 1972, pp. 24-44 and R.M. Burrel, 'Shaykh Khaz'al', *The Encyclopaedia of Islam*, new edition (Leiden, 1978), vol. iv, pp. 1171-2.
214 BP H 16/18, Young to Strick, Scott and Co., 19 October 1922 and earlier *ibid.*, Young to Jacks, 19 August 1922, 'whilst the Bakhtiaris are principally blamed, we are also accused of having instigated them to cause this raid…it is evident that the gap between us and the Persian Government is becoming wider'.
215 See Sepehr Zabih, *The Communist Movement in Iran* (Berkeley, 1966), pp. 1-63.
216 Quoted in Lenczowski, *Russia and the West in Iran*, pp. 9-10.
217 PRO FO CP 11910, Norman to Curzon, 16 and 19 July 1921.
218 BP H16/18, Young to Jacks, 19 September 1922, and enclosure, Young note on interview with Minister of War, 28 August 1922.
219 *Ibid.*, Jacks to Nichols, 27 September 1922.
220 *Ibid.*, Nichols to Young, 6 September 1922.
221 *Ibid.*
222 *Ibid.*, Wilson to Nichols, 10 December 1922.
223 *Ibid.*, Nichols to Wilson, 8 January 1923.
224 PRO FO 416/72, Loraine to Curzon, 5 May 1923.
225 *Ibid.*, Loraine to Curzon, 19 April 1923.
226 *Ibid.*, Loraine to Curzon, 5 May 1923.
227 *Ibid.*, Loraine to Curzon, 15 April 1923.
228 *Ibid.*, Loraine to Curzon, 20 April 1923.
229 PRO FO 416/73, Loraine to Curzon, 28 May 1923.
230 *Ibid.*, and *ibid.*, Loraine to Curzon, 31 May 1923.
231 *Ibid.*, Loraine to Curzon, 30 October 1923.
232 *Ibid.*, Loraine to Curzon, 31 October 1923.
233 *Ibid.*, Loraine to Curzon, 30 October 1923.
234 PRO FO 416/77, Loraine to Chamberlain, 6 November 1925.
235 PRO FO 416/73, Loraine to Curzon, 30 October 1923.
236 *Ibid.*, Loraine to Curzon, 16 October 1923.
237 *Ibid.*, Saunders interview with Rīza Khān, 24 September 1923; Rīza Khān wrote Loraine a letter to this effect, *ibid.*, 7 October 1923.
238 *Ibid.*, Loraine to Curzon, 31 October 1923.
239 *Ibid.*, Loraine to Curzon, 14 November 1923.
240 BP 78/63/16, Nichols to General Managers, Muhammara, 8 November 1923, and *ibid.*, 21 November 1923.
241 See A.C. Millspaugh, *The American Task in Persia* (New York, 1926).

242 PRO FO 416/74, Loraine to MacDonald, 11 February 1924.
243 BP H16/18, Loraine to Wilson, 18 July 1923.
244 PRO FO 371/10134, Nichols to FO, 18 August 1924.
245 *Ibid.*, Jacks to APOC, 11 August 1924.
246 *Ibid.*, Mallet minute, 18 September 1924; the Legation was also firm in its attitude, PRO FO 416/74, Ovey to FO, 16 September 1924 and PRO FO 416/75, Ovey to MacDonald, 20 September 1924.
247 *Ibid.*, Oliphant minute, 19 September 1924.
248 PRO FO 416/74 MacDonald to Ovey, 9 October 1924 and PRO 416/75, MacDonald to Ovey, 23 September 1924.
249 BP 78/63/16, Nichols to General Managers, Muhammara, 6 August 1924, 10 and 18 September and 2 October 1924.
250 PRO FO 416/75, Loraine to Chamberlain, 25 November 1924.
251 *Ibid.*, Loraine to Chamberlain, 27 November 1924.
252 *Ibid.*, Loraine to Chamberlain, 6 December 1924.
253 PRO FO 416/76, Loraine to Chamberlain, 12 May 1925; and for Loraine's reaction to the incident see Waterfield, *Professional Diplomat*, pp. 99-108.
254 BP H9/124 London to Muhammara, 27 February 1925 and 4 March 1925.
255 *Ibid.*, Elkington note, 4 March 1925 and *ibid.*, Jacks to Nichols, 10 March 1925.
256 *Ibid.*, Jacks to Nichols, 16 March 1925.

10. Technical activities: years of endeavour and achievement 1918-32

1 APOC Annual General Meeting, 25 November 1924.
2 *The Science of Petroleum,* managing editor, A.E. Dunstan 4 vols. (Oxford 1938). Dunstan's own personal memoir 'Do You Remember', written in 1947 on the occasion of his retirement, is an interesting set of recollections on his Company service.
3 BP H7/83, Dunstan, Research Report, 1929-30.
4 BP H16/11, Garrow, Notes on a visit to Persia and Mesopotamia, November and December 1919.
5 BP H16/125 pt 1, Thompson to Strick Scott, Muhammara, 19 May 1920.
6 BP H17/23, Thompson to Strick Scott, Muhammara, 12 June 1920.
7 BP H17/41 pt 2, Thompson to Strick Scott, 7 May 1918.
8 See BP, W.J. Baker and M.M. Pennel, *Petroleum Engineering Compendium of the Iranian Oilfields*, 10 vols., 1952, Appendix 1, A. Laird, 'Historical Survey of Petroleum Engineering Progress in the Control of the Iranian Fissured Limestone Reservoirs', p. 2.
9 BP H17/23, Jameson to Muhammara, 13 February 1923.
10 BP H8/98, Cadman's note, Persia - drilling programme, 1 February 1923.
11 BP H5/187, enclosure in Cadman to Jameson, 11 September 1924.
12 BP H17/104, Comins and Scofield Report issued 23 July 1923 and BP H17/23, Lister James to Cadman, 15 June 1923.
13 BP H17/23, Cunningham Craig note on the hydrostatics of Maidan-i-Naftun, 26 June 1923.
14 BP H17/105, Cadman's note, Comins and Scofield Report, 26 July 1923.
15 BP H17/104, Comins and Scofield Report, 23 July 1923.
16 The author is indebted to the late P.T. Cox, who served the Company so ably as a geologist in Persia and elsewhere before becoming general manager in

Notes to pp. 412-437

Fields and managing director of the D'Arcy Exploration Company, for much of the exploration knowledge in this chapter and elsewhere in the volume.

17 Comins, 'Unit Operation of Oil Fields', *The Petroleum Times*, 16 February 1928, p. 307.
18 *Ibid.*
19 H.S. Gibson, 'Scientific Unit Control', *The Science of Petroleum*, vol. 1, p. 334.
20 BP H8/98, Garrow's memorandum on future drilling, 8 July 1924.
21 *Ibid.*, Jameson to Cadman, 19 August 1924.
22 BP H16/121, Jameson to Cadman, 12 January 1926.
23 *Ibid.*, Jameson to de Böckh, 11 January 1926.
24 see H.S. Gibson, 'The Production of Oil from the Fields of South Western Iran', *Journal of the Institute of Petroleum*, 34 (1948) 374-402.
25 Comins, 'Unit Operation of Oil Fields', *Petroleum Times*, 16 February 1928, p. 310.
26 Hugo R. Kamb, *American Association of Petroleum Geologists Bulletin*, 12:5 (1928), 562-4.
27 Amongst those papers were: H.W. Strong, 'The Significance of Underground Temperatures', *Proceedings*, vol. 1, pp. 124-8; C.A.P. Southwell, 'Scientific Unit Control', *ibid.*, pp. 304-9; M.C. Seamark, 'The Drilling and Control of High Pressure Wells', *ibid.*, pp. 354-60; L.A. Pym, 'The Measurement of Gas-Oil Ratios and Saturation Pressures and their Interpretation', *ibid.*, pp. 452-7 and D. Comins, 'Gas Saturation Pressure of Crude under Reservoir Conditions as a Factor on the efficient operation of oilfields', *ibid.*, pp. 458-66.
28 Henry Longhurst, *Adventure in Oil: The Story of British Petroleum* (London, 1959), p. 35.
29 BP H16/112, Cadman's report, Visit to Persia, Autumn 1924, pp. 10-12.
30 H.S. Gibson, 'The Production of Oil from the Fields of South Western Iran', *op. cit.*
31 For a recent account of oil production techniques see *Our Industry Petroleum*, 5th edn. 1977, pp. 134-40. This compendium of technical information, produced and published by British Petroleum Ltd., deals with many aspects of the petroleum industry.
32 BP, Baker and Pennel, *Petroleum Engineering Compendium*, Appendix 1, p. 11.
33 *Ibid.*, pp. 10-13.
34 BP H17/97, de Böckh report, 1924.
35 BP H16/23, memorandum, 'APOC Search for Oil in Persia 1901-32, excluding Masjid i-Suleiman and Haft Kel', 6 January 1933.
36 BP H16/111, Garrow, notes on a visit to Persia and Mesopotamia, November and December 1919.
37 BP H17/39, Nichols, notes on a visit to Persia, Mesopotamia and Egypt 1920.
38 BP H8/100, Lloyd memorandum, visit to Persia, 1923.
39 BP H11/13, Campbell to APOC London, 14 January 1924.
40 BP H8/100, Lloyd, memorandum on visit to Persia 1923.
41 BP H7/83, Jameson to APOC London, 25 February 1924.
42 BP H16/112, Conference at Cairo, 20-30 March 1924.
43 *Ibid.*, Cadman report, Visit to Persia, Autumn 1924.

Notes to pp. 438-454

44 Neilson, then general manager refineries branch, commented, 'in the first instance we would be wise to fit only one bench each at Llandarcy and Abadan' for crude fractionation and 'if results turn out as we expect, we can then plunge ahead with further developments'. BP H7/83, Neilson report, December 1925.
45 BP 78/63/159, Management Committee Report, September 1928.
46 On the various methods of cracking see *Science of Petroleum*, vol. 3 Section 31, B.T. Brooks, 'A Brief History of Petroleum Cracking'. BP H11/140, Coxon to Cadman, 24 February 1930.
47 Much information on Ābādān has been generously given by J.M. Pattinson, who as General Manager, Persia, 1939-46, has unique knowledge.
48 BP H18/42, Cadman Report, Persia and Iraq, 1929.
49 Much of the information on the pipeline is derived from A.C. Hartley, 'The Anglo-Persian Oil Company's Pipelines in Persia', *Trans: Institute of Engineers and Shipbuilders in Scotland*, 1914, no. 921, pp. 85-128.
50 Personal communication from J.M. Pattinson.
51 BP H18/199 and H8/11, *passim*.
52 BP H18/199, Greenway to FO, 24 February 1914.
53 *Ibid.*, Hamilton to Buchanan, 2 August 1915.
54 *Ibid.*, Buchanan to Garrow, 27 May 1916.
55 BP H11/103, report on The improvement of the channel across the bar of the Shatt-al-'Arab, June 1923.
56 BP H11/104, report on the Shatt-al-'Arab Bar dredging scheme, April 1926.
57 BP H18/11, Kemball-Cook memorandum, 18 May 1928.
58 *Ibid.*, draft of Shatt-al-'Arab dredging agreement, 9 May 1932, and Gass to Finance Minister Baghdad, 2 June 1932.
59 BP First Annual Report of Research Department, 1915-17.
60 See Harold F. Williamson and Arnold R. Daum, *The American Petroleum Industry, The Age of Illumination 1859-1899* (Evanston, 1959), pp. 616-19; Ralph W. Hidy and Muriel E. Hidy, *Pioneering in Big Business 1882-1911* (New York, 1955), pp. 158-65, 282-90, 437-43, show the early refining problems of Standard Oil with sour Lima-Indiana crude oil.
61 Dunstan's first patent on the hypochlorite process was taken out in 1918, British Patent No. 139223.
62 BP Second Annual Report of Research Department 1918.
63 Personal testimony of Dr Thole to the author.
64 BP, A.E. Dunstan, *Do You Remember*, personal memoir, 1947.
65 For the early history of the negotiations for a refinery in the United Kingdom, see BP 79/91/9.
66 On Llandarcy and the hypochlorite process see A.M. O'Brien 'National Oil Refineries Ltd., Skewen, South Wales, during 1923', *Journal Institute of Petroleum Technologists*, 1924, vol. 10; A.E. Dunstan and B.T. Brooks, 'Refining of Gasoline and Kerosine by Hypochlorites', *Journal of Independent Engineers and Chemists*, December 1922, vol. 14 no. 12 and A.E. Dunstan, F.B. Thole and F.G.P. Remfry, 'Bauxite as a Refining Agent for Petroleum Distillates', *Journal of the Society of the Chemical Industry*, 13 June 1924, vol. 43 no. 24. The *Journal of the Institute of Petroleum Technologists* and its other publications provide a valuable source of technical literature on developments in the oil industry.
67 See BP H9/31, H9/144 and H8/12.

68 At the end of 1923, the liquid chlorine consumption at the Llandarcy calcium chlorite plant was in the order of 15 tons per day.
69 'There seems to be a feeling against the use of Bauxite among the Abadan Chemical Staff', BP H11/13 Campbell report, 14 December 1924. Cadman had reservations in 1924 because 'we are endeavouring to apply a process of our own invention, at present only partially developed, and this fact is to some extent responsible for the incomplete state of our refining operations in Abadan - I will not say wrongly so - instead of applying refinery practice elsewhere'. BP H16/112, Cadman report, visit to Persia Autumn 1924. In his 'Secret Diary' he was less discreet, writing that 'There are so very many extraordinary things about the design of the bauxite plant and I am wondering if the designers are mentally defective', BP H10/141, Cadman Secret Diary of visit to Persia 1924.
70 BP H16/112, Cadman report, visit to Persia Autumn 1924.
71 BP H18/41, Cadman's report, visit to Persia and Iraq, Spring 1926.
72 *Science of Petroleum*, vol. 3, Section 36 Cracking, has articles dealing with the significant aspects of the theory and nature of cracking.
73 See George Sweet Gibb and Evelyn H Knowlton, *The Resurgent Years 1911-1927* (New York, 1958), pp. 113-22. In 1919 the total output of cracked spirit in the USA was 16 200 000 barrels of which the Burton process accounted for nearly 100 per cent, J.L. Enos *Petroleum Progress and Profits - a History of Process Innovation* (Cambridge, Mass., 1962).
74 Sunbury Technical Records, Q420.33; and S.J.M. Auld and A.E. Dunstan 'The Development of a Liquid-Phase Cracking Process', *Journal of Industrial and Chemical Engineering*, 18 (1926) 803-7.
75 BP 78/63/119, Management Committee to Board, March 1925.
76 BP 78/63/113, Management Committee Report to the Board, August 1924.
77 BP 78/63/40, Management Committee to Board, December 1926.
78 Following his visit to Persia in 1916-17 Dunstan had stressed the potential value of gas in his annual reports of 1918, 1919 and 1920, but in 1921 there was still no reliable means of measuring the volume of gas apart from one meter 'but either it is out of order, or no one can determine how it should be used', Auld report, 1923, BP Sunbury Technical Records, U.500.32. Garrow had pointed out in 1919 that, 'it has been said that the oil industry of America has been handled in a pioneer spirit of sheer unmitigated pillage (which is true), and if we wish this stigma effectively removed from our doorstep, we must at once take steps to collect this separated and valuable gas', BP H16/111, Garrow notes on a visit to Persia 1919.
79 BP H8/100 Lloyd memorandum, visit to Persia 1920.
80 BP Sunbury Technical Records U.500.1 Jameson report, May 1923.
81 BP Sunbury Technical Records, U.500.32 Auld Report 'Utilisation of Natural Gas - Burma and Persia Report No. 1', May 1923.
82 BP Sunbury Technical Records U.500.32a, W.H. Cadman report, 15 February 1925.
83 BP H16/112 Cadman report, visit to Persia 1924.
84 BP H16/113 H.Y.V. Jackson reports, Gasoline Recovery Persia, visit to America, 20 April 1925.
85 BP Minutes of 1st Meeting of Research Advisory Committee, 12 January 1923.
86 'Conference of Company's Chemists', *The Naft*, September 1926, p. 35.

11. Downstream activities 1919-28

1. BP 78/87/1 APOC AGM, 10 November 1925.
2. BP 78/87/1 APOC AGM, 8 December 1919.
3. See in particular Chapters 5, 7 and 10. This was a problem in different forms for most oil companies.
4. BP 78/87/1 APOC AGM, 2 November 1926.
5. BP 38/87/1 APOC AGM, 25 November 1924.
6. BP 77/49/8, Garrow, Maidan-i-Naftun Area, 30 December 1918.
7. BP 77/139/116, Greenway memorandum, 'British Petroleum Company, Petroleum Steamship Company, Homelight Company', n.d. 1915.
8. BP 77/49/7, Macindoe to Secretary, Treasury, 2 August 1918.
9. Ibid.
10. In his speech to the AGM on 20 December 1920, rebutting criticism against marketing in France, Greenway drew attention to the choice which faced the Company of either creating its own distributing organisation in overseas markets for its own products or 'to sell them to one or the other of the only two companies which are in a position to handle them, at such prices as they may be willing to pay' for if the Company was itself marketing all its own products, 'our profits would be double what they are today'.
11. BP B 45 (Sec) DEC Minutes Bk 2, 25 March 1918 and BP B 49 (Sec), 29 April 1918.
12. BP 77/49/7, Macindoe to Secretary, Treasury, 2 August 1918.
13. BP 78/87/1 APOC AGM, 26 March 1919.
14. BP 78/87/1 APOC AGM, 25 November 1924.
15. BP C227 (Sec), Memorandum of Agreement with Secretary of State for India, 16 June 1921.
16. BP 77/49/8, List of Anglo-Persian Oil Company's Liquid Fuel Bunkering installations, 10 June 1919.
17. BP 77/45/8, rough scheme, British Bunkering Co. Ltd, 10 June 1919.
18. BP 77/72/136, Miscellaneous Notes on Marketing, compiled by L. Lockhart.
19. BP Board Minutes, 29 September 1919.
20. BP 77/49/8, Memorandum of Meeting re Bunkering Company, 2 July 1919.
21. BP 78/63/49, Minutes of Managing Directors' Meetings, 5 March 1920.
22. Ibid., 25 August 1920.
23. BP H11/124, Sir John Ellerman to Greenway, 28 January 1921.
24. BP 78/87/1 APOC AGM, 20 December 1920.
25. BP 78/68/49, 22 November 1921. BP Board Minutes, 28 November 1921.
26. BP 00001830, F.G.C. Morris 'AIOC Supply and Distribution Past, Present and Future', April 1943.
27. BP H16/111, Garrow, Report on Visit to Persia and Iraq, November/December 1919; and BP H18/40, Appendix 4, Jacks memorandum, 'Marketing', November 1924.
28. BP 79/88/12, Lloyd to Burmah, 21 July 1921.
29. BP 78/28/9, APOC distribution department, Crude Oil shipments to APC, November 1912-April 1920.
30. BP 78/63/49, 15 December 1920.
31. BP 77/49/7, Draft Proposals for a Pool with APC 1917. About the same time Watson was drawing up a Trading Agreement between Burmah and the Company, see ibid., Trading Agreement, 1917.

32 These would seem to have come about as a result of the favourable impression created in Standard Oil circles by Cadman's earlier visit of December 1921 – February 1922 for talks on cooperation over the North Persian concession and Mesopotamia.
33 BP 77/139/119, Watson memorandum, 10 July 1922.
34 BP H5/140, APOC/APC agreement for benzine, 16 February 1922.
35 BP Board Minutes, 23 February 1920.
36 BP H10/163, Greenway, 'Memorandum explanatory of negotiations for acquiring an interest in the Europaische Petroleum Union', 11 May 1923.
37 The Board had earlier been informed on 26 May 1919 of the formation of L'Alliance.
38 BP 77/139/82, Draft Articles of Association, 17 October 1918.
39 *Ibid.*, Belgian Trade Committee, Terms of Reference, Kearney to Waterkeyn, 23 September 1919.
40 For these developments see BP 77/139/82, BP H17/2, and Board minutes *passim*.
41 Until M.E. Meganck became manager in 1920 the administration of L'Alliance was quite inadequate, see BP 77/22/136, Fuller to Lockhart, 19 November 1937.
42 For the history of the French Company see J. Huré, *Histoire de cinquante années de la naissance de la SGHP à SF BP d'aujourd'hui* (SFBP private publication, 1971), For French petroleum history see Charles Pomaret, *La Politique Française de combustibles liquides* (Paris, 1923), Guillaume de Labarriére, *Un Instrument de la politique economique nationale, la Compagnie française des Pétroles* (Brest, 1932), Edgar Faure, *La Politique française du Pétrole* (Paris, 1938) and Jean Rondot, *La Compagnie française des Pétroles* (Paris, 1962).
43 BP H14/9, Braithwaite to Greenway, enclosure, 18 November 1919.
44 BP 77/139/103, Braithwaite to Mitaranga, 8 December 1919.
45 BP 78/63/27, Stewart to Morris, 15 March 1923. On the appointment of Morris to Paris, see H16/107, Stewart to Morris, 3 November 1921.
46 BP B.29 (Sec) BP Company Minutes, 26 April 1918.
47 *Ibid.*, 25 April 1922.
48 For market shares see BP B.29 (Sec) BP Company Minutes, 21 July 1920; on the reaction to the Anglo-American's initiative over bulk storage installation, *ibid.*, 24 March 1920 and preliminary discussions over Bowser pumps, *ibid.*, 14 December 1920. For the legal position of Anglo-American in relation to Standard Oil (NJ) see Henrietta M. Larson, Evelyn M. Knowlton and Charles S. Popple, *History of Standard Oil Company (New Jersey) 1927-50: New Horizons* (New York, 1971), pp. 314-15. Whatever the exact legal position of the Anglo-American Oil Company, Greenway in public referred to Mr Powell as 'the head of...the English branch of the Standard', and that was the basis of their relationship, BP 78/87/1, APOC AGM 20 December 1920.
49 BP B.29 BP Company Minutes, 3 August 1921.
50 BP 78/14/11, Morris to Lloyd, memorandum, Roadside Pumps in France, 19 June 1924.
51 BP 78/63/111, APOC Management Committee Report, June 1924.
52 BP H14/8, memorandum 'Supply Stations for Petrol', 8 March 1920.
53 BP B.29 (Sec) BP Company Minutes, 19 April 1921.
54 BP APOC AGM, 17 December 1923.
55 BP APOC AGM, 11 December 1922.

56 BP H14/59, Heath Eves note on Next Year's Crude Position, refinery make and requirements, 26 October 1923.
57 BP H19/59, Greenway note, 2 November 1923.
58 *Ibid.*, Lloyd Note, 2 November 1923.
59 *Ibid.*, Garrow Note, 7 November 1923.
60 *Ibid.*, Heath Eves memorandum, APOC's Future Marketing Policy, 24 July 1925.
61 BP 78/63/109, APOC Management Committee Report, April 1924.
62 BP APOC 78/87/1 AGM, 25 November 1924.
63 For the history of BP's subsidiary in Germany and its antecedents see Fren Förster, *Geschichte der Deutschen BP 1904-1979* (Hamburg, 1979). The Company's interest in EPU dates to end of 1919, see BP 78/63/23, Black to Roney, 8 December 1919, with considerable discussions throughout 1922, see BP 78/63/26, *passim* and Board Minutes. See also BP H14/1, Report on EPU and subsidiaries by Brown, Fleming and Murray, 24 April 1922. There were more talks in 1923, see BP 78/63/27. For the initiative in 1924 see BP Board Minutes, 5 December 1924 and 27 January 1925. For an account of Dutch oil history, see the doctoral thesis for the University of Amsterdam, Adriaan Koelmans, *Van Pomp tot put in Honderd Jaar* (Amsterdam 1971).
64 BP Board Minutes 26 January 1926; see also H10/163 and H12/58 for Purchase Agreement.
65 BP 78/87/1 APOC AGM, 2 November 1926.
66 *Ibid.*
67 BP Board Minutes, 26 April 1927.
68 Information on the choice of the BP colours was given in personal discussions with Mr J.E.J. Taylor. On the competition for the logo, information came from Mr A.R.T. Saunders, who was the prize winner, BP Company, Board Minutes, 20 May 1925.
69 BP H14/159, Management Committee Papers, 27 January 1925. On the Company's sponsorship programme see in particular the coverage of national events in *The Naft*, 1924-32.
70 BP Monthly reports to Management Committee, 6 October 1926.
71 BP 78/63/52, Management Committee Minutes, 6 August 1926.
72 BP H18/21, Heath Eves note, Marketing Policy, May 1927.
73 BP H11/144, Jameson to Fraser, Fields, Pipeline and Refinery Capacities, 14 June 1927.
74 BP B.29 (Sec) BP Company Board Minutes, 29 July 1919. These agreements were the subject of informal meetings between the three main importing and distributing companies throughout the 1920s, as well as quota settlements, advertising restrictions and service station proposals.
75 BP B.29 (Sec) BP Company Board Minutes, 20 February 1923.
76 *Ibid.*, 24 April 1924.
77 BP H18/21, Braithwaite to Heath Eves, 17 May 1927, enclosure, Petrol Trade in the UK, 9 May 1927.
78 BP 78/63/52, Management Committee Minutes, 8 February 1926.
79 BP 78/63/53, Management Committee Minutes, 15 September 1926.
80 BP 78/63/54, Management Committee Minutes, 14 December 1927.
81 BP H18/21, Heath Eves note, Marketing Policy, May 1927.
82 BP Board Minutes, 27 July 1926; BP 81/55/8, Heath Eves memorandum, Future Marketing Policy, 26 July 1926.

83   BP Board Minutes, 28 July 1925.
84   *Ibid.*, 24 November 1925.
85   *Ibid.*, 27 July 1926.
86   *Ibid.*, 27 July 1926, BP 81/55/8, Heath Eves memorandum, Future Marketing Policy, 26 July 1926.
87   BP H14/159, Heath Eves, memorandum, APOC's Future Marketing Policy, 24 July 1925.
88   As early as September 1924 possible market outlets were under consideration in Egypt, South Africa and Aden 'when stocks of fully refined kerosene' were available, see BP Monthly reports to Management September 1924. In 1926 packed kerosine and petrol were shipped to East Africa, for marketing by agents Gibson and Co., *ibid.*, September 1927, in spite of the lack of bulk facilities, *ibid.*, April 1928. For Egypt see BP 78/63/53 Management Committee Minutes, 22 June 1927 and Board Minutes, 28 June 1927.
89   BP H16/31, Cadman memorandum, Distribution in the Middle East, 23 September 1927.
90   BP 81/55/9, Watson memorandum, 5 June 1928, see also BP H11/181.
91   BP Board Minutes, 26 July 1927.
92   *Ibid.*, 27 September 1927.
93   BP H16/31, Cadman memorandum, Distribution in the Middle East, 23 September 1923.
94   See B. Dasguta, *The Oil Industry in India* (London, 1971).
95   BP 77/72/122, Lloyd to Cadman, 11 November 1927.
96   BP Board Minutes, 5 January 1928.
97   BP H11/52, Committee of Imperial Defence Conference, evidence of Cadman, 16 February 1928.
98   BP 78/87/1 APOC AGM, 6 November 1928.
99   BP 79/88/12, Heads of Agreement, 31 January 1928.
100 PRO FO 371/12875, joint memorandum by Treasury and Admiralty, 'Scheme of Distribution in the Middle East', enclosure in Grigg to Gower, 13 February 1928.
101 BP 78/87/1 APOC AGM, 6 November 1928.
102 H14/155, Cadman memorandum 'Notes on a discussion with Mr. W. Teagle', 18 August 1927.
103 George Sweet Gibb and Evelyn H. Knowlton, *History of the Standard Oil Company (New Jersey) The Resurgent Years 1911–1927* (New York, 1956), p. 340. See also BP H8/127.
104 BP 81/55/7, Short Journal of Events, Cadman to Teagle, 22 February 1928.
105 *Ibid.*, Cadman to Meyer, 7 March 1928.
106 BP H13/132, Cadman's address to American Petroleum Institute, 6 December 1928.
107 BP C222 (Sec) W. Fraser "As is", 18 August 1928.
108 BP H2/125, Chick to Lloyd, 4 September 1909.
109 BP 77/139/87, Nichols to APOC Muhammara, 1 November 1923.
110 BP H5/17, Fairley to APOC Muhammara, 10 October 1924 and *Ibid.*, 6 October 1924.
111 BP H7/107, APOC London to Fairley, 17 February 1926.
112 *Ibid.*, Fairley to APOC London, 18 February 1926 and *ibid.*, APOC London to Jacks, 19 February 1926.

113 BP H7/107, Fairley to APOC London, 20 February 1926.
114 PRO FO 416/78, Acting Commercial Secretary, Tehrân, to Department of Overseas Trade, 25 March 1926.
115 H11/18, Jacks to Cadman, 13 October 1926.
116 BP H11/130, Greenhouse to Tîmurtâsh, 28 January 1931.
117 BP 78/63/80, Braithwaite and Heath Eves to Finance Committee, 12 June 1928.
118 BP H11/130, Braithwaite memorandum, 27 February 1928.
119 *The Naft*, May 1932, Oil Distribution in Persia.
120 BP H11/19, Cadman to Jacks, 4 January 1928.
121 BP H11/130, Cooke to Medlicott, 21 February 1928.
122 BP Board Minutes, 27 March 1928, and BP 78/63/54 Management Committee Minutes, 21 March 1928.
123 BP 78/63/80, Cadman memorandum, 20 March 1928.
124 BP H11/130, Jacks to Cadman, 5 May 1928; *ibid.*, Jacks to Gass, 15 May 1928; *ibid.*, Cadman to Jacks, 21 June 1928 and *ibid.*, Braithwaite memorandum, 31 September 1928.
125 For the sequence of events see BP H11/130, APOC London to APOC Tehrân, 11 December 1928; *ibid.*, Braithwaite to APOC, Abâdân, 28 December 1928 and Clarke to APOC Tehrân, 22 January 1929.
126 BP H17/58, Cox to Colonial Office, 2 March 1922.
127 BP [IPC File C22B], Wilson to Nichols, 1 February 1922.
128 BP H18/40, Jacks memorandum, Marketing, November 1924.
129 BP 78/63/53, Management Committee Minutes, 12 November 1925.
130 BP 78/63/45, Heath Eves to Secretary, Air Ministry, 28 April 1922.
131 BP 78/63/18, Nichols to Muhummara, 22 October and 12 November 1925.
132 BP 78/63/103, APOC-KOC Agreement, 31 October 1928.
133 BP H4/97, Hearn to Elkington, 20 August 1931; *ibid.*, Iraq Minister of Economy and Communications to IPC, 26 September 1932, 'the position of your Company and Government should be definitely defined in order to avoid confusion'; *ibid.*, Lefroy to Elkington, 23 October 1931; *ibid.*, Skliros to KOC, 8 December 1931 and *ibid.*, KOC to IPC, 2 December 1932.
134 BP Board Minutes, 25 March 1918.
135 BP H17/21, historical survey of exploration in Papua (New Guinea).
136 BP 77/49/8, Nichols to Hughes, 20 May 1919.
137 BP Board Minutes, 29 July 1918.
138 BP 77/49/8, Nichols to Hughes, 20 May 1919.
139 BP 76/54/11, Oil Agreement Bill, May 1920. See also Australian Hansard, First Session, 1920, p. 1703.
140 BP H14/13, Bird Memorandum, n.d. 1924.
141 BP COR Board Minutes, 18 September 1925 and BP 78/63/80, 1927.
142 BP H11/121, Heath Eves to Bird, 7 August 1930.
143 BP H13/123, Heath Eves to Bird, 9 April 1923.
144 BP H10/151, Slade report, Australia, 1 September 1924.
145 BP Board Minutes, 29 September 1925, 30 March 1926 and 1 June 1926.
146 BP COR Board Minutes, 28 September 1925.
147 BP H11/64, Cadman to Gibson, 1 August 1928 and *passim*.
148 BP H11/121, Heath Eves to Bird, 7 August 1930.
149 BP H18/25, Present monthly salaries of employees of Anglo Persian and associated companies, 5 February 1925.

Notes to pp. 526-541

150 BP 77/49/8, Greenway memorandum, Managing Directorship, 23 January 1919.
151 Personal testimony of R. Gillespie, J.H. Jackson and F. Fenton to Edward Platt.
152 BP 77/49/8, memorandum, Palmers Hebburn Company Ltd, 6 February 1918.
153 BP 77/49/8, Greenway to Cargill, 12 February 1918.
154 BP 77/49/8, Watson to Cargill, 13 February 1918.
155 BP 77/49/7, Greenway memorandum, Building of Tanker Tonnage, 23 October 1918.
156 BP H16/43, Greenway to Cargill, 19 December 1918.
157 For the technical information on the details of tankers, I am much indebted to Commander Edward Platt, formerly director of BP Tanker Co., for his advice and collaboration on the history of the tanker company; Keith Taggart, formerly manager of economics and estimating branch of BP Tanker Co., for his knowledge of the economic aspects of tanker operations; and G.B. King, formerly managing director of the BP Tanker Co., now the BP Shipping Co., for his continuing interest and encouragement.
158 *The Naft*, vol. 1, July 1924, no. 1 p. 8.
159 The general conservation of English shipowners towards diesel engines was not shared by their Scandinavian counterparts, especially the Danes who accepted the new form of propulsion more readily.
160 *Yorkshire Post*, 4 April 1927.
161 *Financial Times*, 12 December 1925.

12. The international dimension 1919-28

1 Hansard, House of Commons vol. 64 col. 1037, 7 July 1914.
2 BP 77/49/8, Note on interview at Treasury 6 May 1919. Greenway was consulted by the Admiralty and it was agreed that the answer given would not involve the Company in any other obligation than that the £2 000 000 subscribed by the Government should be spent solely in Persia, and that it would then leave them free to operate anywhere else. Also, that 'since more than £2 000 000 has since been spent on Persia, the Company is free so far as this obligation is concerned to operate elsewhere'.
3 BP 77/49/7, Macindoe to Inchcape and Jenkins, 10 July 1918.
4 BP 77/49/7, Greenway memorandum re Treasury Letter, 16 July 1918.
5 PRO POWE 30/40, Treasury to APOC, 10 October 1918.
6 PRO POWE 33/45, Petroleum Executive memorandum, 5 August 1918.
7 PRO CO 727/9 no. 29139, Clauson memorandum, 20 June 1924.
8 PRO CO 727/8 no. 18975, Political Resident to Colonial Office, 28 March 1924.
9 BP 3B3045, Agency Bahrain to Wilson, 4 June 1932; see also the Colonial Office 'having persistently obstructed our own efforts to obtain a concession in Bahrein and Kuwait, as also in Iraq', BP 3B3045, Wilson note on Kuwait - Bahrain, June 1932.
10 PRO CO 727/5 no. 40376, Duke of Devonshire to Political Resident, 13 October 1923.

Notes to pp. 541-548

11. BP H8/98, Garrow note on crude oil production, 14 November 1921. The comments of Dr Manning appeared in *National Petroleum News*, 29 October 1919; those of Dr Smith in *New York Times*, 5 January 1920 and *National Geographic Magazine*, February 1920. Details of vehicle registration and investment are from American Petroleum Interests in Foreign Countries, *Hearings before a Special Committee Investigating Petroleum Resources, United States Senate, 1945* (Washington, 1946) pp. 408-10 and 157-81 respectively and John G. McLean and Robert Wm. Haigh, *The Growth of Integrated Oil Companies* (Harvard, 1953).
12. BP 77/139/14, Cadman memorandum on D'Arcy Exploration Company, 15 May 1922.
13. BP 77/139/13, Greenway memorandum on APOC oil policy, 7 October 1920; and BP H10/44, Method of dealing with new propositions.
14. BP 77/49/7, Greenway to Long, APOC oil interests outside of the area covered by their Persian Concession, 12 March 1918.
15. BP 77/49/7, Macindoe to Treasury, 2 August 1918.
16. BP H16/44, principal investigations and tests carried out or in progress 1922.
17. BP 77/139/14, Cadman memorandum, 15 May 1922.
18. PRO FO 371/2721, Greenway to FO, 24 February 1916.
19. PRO FO 371/3402, Greenway to FO, 16 May 1918.
20. Exchange of letters, Cox and Shaykh Mubarak, 27 October 1913 in A.H.T. Chisholm, *The First Kuwait Concession* (London, 1975), note 6 p. 89. This volume, written and compiled by the Company's negotiator in Kuwait, 1932-34, contains much documentation on oil affairs in the Gulf 1911-34; hereafter cited as Chisholm, *Kuwait*.
21. P. Tuson, *The Records of the British Residency and Agencies in the Persian Gulf* (London, 1979), p. 29.
22. PRO CO 727/3 no. 42023, Petroleum Department to Colonial Office, 20 August 1921.
23. BP 3B3044, Colonial Office to APOC, 24 December 1921.
24. BP 3B3044, Nichols to Colonial Office, 6 January 1922.
25. Chisholm, *Kuwait*, pp. 5 and 91.
26. Chisholm, *Kuwait*, p. 90, Colonial Office to APOC, 29 March 1922.
27. BP 3B3044, Colonial Office to APOC, 16 October 1922; *ibid.*, Wilson to APOC, 2 February 1922 and APOC Muhammara to APOC London, 26 April 1923.
28. *Ibid.*, p. 91, Political Agent Kuwait to Shaykh Ahmad, January 1923 and *ibid.*, p. 5.
29. *Ibid.*, pp. 91-3.
30. BP 3B3044, APOC Muhammara to APOC London, 26 April 1923.
31. APOC Board Minutes, 24 January 1918 and 25 March 1918.
32. BP 77/91/30, Cmd. 1286, Oil in Papua; see also BP B49 (Sec), DEC Board Minutes, 17 November 1919.
33. BP 76/54/20, Summary of D'Arcy Investigations in Papua and New Guinea 1919-1937.
34. BP B49 (Sec), DEC Board Minutes, 30 September 1929.
35. BP 77/139/14, Cadman memorandum, 15 May 1922.
36. BP 79/91/8, Wallace to Barnes, 6 May 1921 and BP H10/172, A short history of APOC in Albania.

Notes to pp. 548-554

37 PRO FO 371/5728, Temperly memorandum 1922 on interview with Frasheri; *ibid.*, FO 371/7332.
38 BP B49 (Sec), DEC Board Minutes, 30 March 1925 and BP 77/139/16.
39 BP H11/181, Mussolini to APOC, 1925.
40 BP 77/139/16, Agreement between Italian Government and APOC, 20 March 1925.
41 The Company had been interested in exploring in Italy with a syndicate including de Böckh and one with other Italian interests, but to no result; see BP H11/187, Summary of negotiations for concessions in Italy, 28 February 1925 and BP H10/153, BP H11/187 and BP H14/74.
42 BP Board Minutes, 30 November 1926.
43 BP 72/223/1, Wyllie notes 'Oil prospects in various countries', 1930.
44 BP 77/139/16, Preliminary Survey, 1923, Mayo and Montgomery.
45 *Ibid.*, 1924 Surveys, Richardson, Montgomery, Wrathall, Newton and Herbage.
46 *Ibid.*, Surveys November 1924 - February 1925, Montgomery, Wrathall and Herbage
47 BP B49 (Sec), DEC Board Minutes, 23 November 1925 and 26 March 1926 and BP H10/172, Commercial Development.
48 BP H18/1, Italy, 28 October 1928, contains a survey of negotiations 1923-28. On Italian industrialists and facism see Roland Sarti, *Fascism and the Industrial Leadership in Italy 1919-40* (Berkeley, 1971).
49 BP H11/181, Heath Eves and Morris memorandum, 21 May 1928.
50 *Ibid.*
51 BP 77/139/20, Albania.
52 BP H11/64, *passim.*
53 BP H16/44, Principal Investigations and tests carried out or in progress 1922.
54 See BP H16/44, Cadman memorandum, 15 May 1922.
55 BP H9/103, Cadman memorandum, APOC and Bolivia, 13 October 1922.
56 BP 78/70/73, Wyllie report on Peru, 4 February 1925.
57 BP 78/70/15, Brazil notes on 1927 session of Congress and petroleum legislation.
58 BP Management Committee reports, 15 February 1924 and BP B 49 (Sec) *passim* 1920-7.
59 BP H5/7, Maracaibo Oil Exploration Company (MOEC) Agreement, November 1922 and also 78/70/176, 15 December 1922, BP 3A3097, Lister James to DEC, 2 December 1925, BP 77/12/122, Thompson to Cadman, 2 March 1926 and BP 78/70/123, Memorandum and Articles of Association of the British Equatorial Oil Company Ltd, 28 September 1920.
60 BP 79/91/8, Cadman memorandum, Pantapec Petroleum Company, 21 April 1925 and BP 78/70/120, Thompson to Watson, 21 May 1928 and *ibid.*, Cadman to Baker, 29 July 1928.
61 BP 78/70/161, Correspondence Gulbenkian - Wilson, August–September 1926 and BP 3A3097, Wilson's interview with Gulbenkian, 25 August 1926.
62 BP 3A3097, Thompson to Wilson, 26 August 1926.
63 *Ibid.*, Gulbenkian to Cadman, 6 September 1926.
64 *Ibid.*, DEC to Gulbenkian, 10 September 1926.
65 BP 77/139/121, Venezuelan Law on Hydrocarbons, 18 July 1925.
66 BP H16/44, Lister James to FRG Dept, 19 October 1925.

67 BP 77/139/121, Wilson's note for Management Committee and résumé of negotiations 1925-26, 20 March 1926.
68 PRO FO 371/10603, Vansittart minute, 5 January 1926 and BP 77/139/121, 10 March 1926, Vansittart considered it essential for the British Government to waive rights on having a government director on the Board of any Venezuelan company.
69 PRO FO 371/11110, Snow's minute, 12 April 1926.
70 BP 78/63/52, Management Committee Book 2, 22 April, 2 June, 23 June, 15 July and 28 July 1926.
71 BP APOC Board Minutes, 27 July 1926.
72 BP APOC Board Minutes, 11 April 1927.
73 BP H11/218, Stirling memorandum, 'Oil concession in Venezuela, 20 November 1912 and 5 December 1912.
74 PRO FO 372/12063, memorandum, 'Crude Oil Production in Venezuela', 27 July 1927. See also Edwin Lieuwen, *Petroleum in Venezuelan History* (Berkeley, 1954) and *Petroleum in Venezuela, a History* (New York, 1967) and Franklyn Tugwell, *The Politics of Oil in Venezuela* (Stanford, 1975).
75 See also US Federal Trade Commission, *Report on Foreign Ownership in the Petroleum Industry* (1923) and, for a polemical view, Ludwell Denny, *We Fight for Oil* (New York, 1928).
76 BP H16/44, Wilson memorandum, 2 February 1926.
77 *Ibid.*, Cadman to Wilson, 15 February 1926.
78 BP H15/137, Hearn memorandum on Colombian contract, 23 September 1927.
79 *Ibid.*, Cadman memorandum for Management Committee, 24 April 1925 and BP 78/70/771, 1918 Surveys in Colombia.
80 BP H15/137, Cadman memorandum, 24 April 1925; BP B49 (Sec) DEC Minutes, 3 November 1924.
81 BP APOC Board Minutes, 26 May 1925 'the veto against the Company endeavouring to obtain concessions in Colombia be removed, was discussed and approved'.
82 BP H9/91, memorandum on Colombian Oil legislation, 1873-1928, n.d. and BP H15/137, Hearn memorandum, Colombia, 30 July 1927.
83 BP 77/139/121, Wilson's report on Colombia, 15 April 1926.
84 *Ibid.*, Recommendation of APOC Management Committee to DEC, 15 July 1926 and BP 78/63/52, Management Committee Minutes, 22 April, 2 June, 23 June, 15 July, and 28 July 1926, give details of discussions on legal problems concerning Colombia; see also BP 78/70/771, Nichols memorandum, Colombia July 1926.
85 *Ibid.*, Hearn memorandum, Colombia, 12 January 1927.
86 BP 78/63/89, Agreement of 11 July 1927; H15/137, Linklaters and Paines to Wilson, 19 September 1927 and *ibid.*, Hearn memorandum on Colombian contract, 23 September 1927; *ibid.*, Hearn memorandum on Colombia, 30 July 1927.
87 BP B49 (Sec) DEC Minutes, 16 February and 17 May 1928.
88 PRO FO 371/11110, Craigie, record of conversation with Wilson, Yates, Thompson and D'Arcy Exploration Co. representative, 15 April 1926.
89 BP H5/137, Wilson report on Colombia, 12 July 1928.
90 *Ibid.*, Hearn report on Colombia, 17 July 1928.

Notes to pp. 557-560

91 BP B49 (Sec) DEC Minutes, 19 July 1928 and H9/91 Wilson visit to Colombia 1928; PRO FO 371/12753, Wilson report on US reaction to APOC activities in Colombia and BP 75/19/10 Wilson report on Colombia, 1928.
92 BP B49 (Sec) DEC Minutes, 17 October 1928.
93 *Ibid.*, 14 February 1929.
94 PRO FO 371/12753, Snow minute, 15 November 1928.
95 BP H17/129, Cadman minute 1929, 'I have never varied from the point that we should not consider any proposal until Colombia has done what we asked.'
96 BP H15/11, Managing directors reports, DEC, 25 October 1929, 12 February and 17 April 1930.
97 BP 78/28/46, Colombia Petroleum Laws 1919-31.
98 PRO FO 371/10603, Torr minute, 26 October 1925.
99 On the oil industry in Argentina see Carl E. Solberg, *Oil and Nationalism in Argentina* (Stanford, 1979).
100 *Ibid.*, p. 177.
101 BP 78/28/8, Greenway to Rechnitzer, 24 March 1915.
102 BP 71/137/1, Hunter report on Patagonian Oilfields, 20 April 1920.
103 BP 77/139/14, Watson memorandum 'Sol' Concession, 21 January 1920 and BP Z0365, Watson memorandum on Argentine interests, 5 January 1921.
104 BP 77/139/14, Weatherhead report on the oil prospects of Southern Argentina, 10 December 1920 and BP Z0365, Watson memorandum Argentina, 24 December 1920.
105 BP Z0365, Garrow report on Dodero Syndicate, 18 January 1921.
106 *Ibid.*, Garrow notes on a visit to Argentina, May 1922.
107 BP 71/137/1, Russel notes on operations, 16 January 1923. In June Russel had reported 'The Fuel Oil trade in the Argentine is apparently capable of great expansion. The organisation we now have is perfectly well able to handle a distributing trade and will place for securing business', *ibid.*, Russel notes on Argentina, June 1922.
108 BP B49 (Sec) DEC Board Minutes, 26 July 1923 and BP 78/63/87, Cadman report, APOC activities in Argentina, 19 November 1923.
109 BP 78/63/87, Cadman report 'In the affairs of the Dodero Syndicate I found similarly evidenced a lack of any proper sense of money values.' In his diary, BP H18/38, Cadman referred to the political repercussions of the activities of the Company's associates, 19 October 1923.
110 BP H18/38, Cadman diary, 19 October 1923.
111 BP 77/139/130, Cadman application for concessions, *pertenencias* 20 October 1923.
112 *Ibid.*, Reforms in the Mining Code, 1924.
113 *Ibid.*, Smellie report, 22 December 1924.
114 BP B49 (Sec) DEC Board Minutes, 19 June 1924.
115 APOC AGM, 25 November 1924.
116 BP B49 (Sec) DEC Board Minutes, 22 December 1924 and BP 77/139/130.
117 BP H15/168, *Financial News*, 6 April 1925; Solberg, *Oil and Nationalisation in Argentina* pp. 101-2.
118 BP AGM, 10 November 1925.
119 BP H16/44, Wilson note, 2 February 1926.
120 *Ibid.*, Cadman to Wilson, 15 February 1926 and *ibid.*, Garrow note 1 February 1926, 'APOC should concentrate on the land they already have.'

Notes to pp. 560-563

121 BP H15/122, memorandum on arrangements with Itaca Company for APOC crude oil, 1926; BP H17/201, Garrow memorandum, Anglo-Persian relations with Itaca Co., 6 July 1927; BP Board Minutes, 23 February 1926.
122 BP 77/139/136, Hearn interview with Waley Cohen, 26 February 1926.
123 BP 78/63/86, Lloyd report on Argentina visit, 31 October–16 November 1929.
124 BP 77/139/136, Management Committee report, 23 November 1927.
125 BP 78/70/12, Richardson reports on Comodoro Rivadavia, 11 September 1931 and 30 October 1931.
126 Solberg, *Oil and Nationalism in Argentina*, p. 117.
127 BP B49 (Sec) DEC Board Minutes, 29 June and 27 July 1925 and 15 September 1927; *ibid.*, 1918-27 passim; BP 76/54/15, Borneo Petroleum Syndicate Ltd, 1923-32, BP 78/63/41, APOC to directors, 10 January 1924; BP H10/59, 1922-26, Wilson memorandum, Oil Prospects in Siam, 18 January 1926; BP 76/54/24, History of Oil exploration in Timor, 1932.
128 BP B49 (Sec), DEC Board Minutes, 16 December 1926, 20 January, 17 March and 14 July 1927; BP 78/63/22, Nichols to Cargill, 20 June 1919 and BP 78/70/22, Wyllie to Wilson, 20 October 1930 on New Brunswick; BP 78/63/44, Nichols to Cadman, 25 June 1919.
129 BP 3B3022, Negotiations with Nordoy Company 1930 and BP H15/11, reports on British Dominions Land Settlement Corporation Ltd, May and September 1930.
130 BP 78/70/94, Nichols report, Petroleum in Uganda, 21 September 1926.
131 BP 78/70/95, Wilson to Crown Agents, 2 August 1929.
132 (a) BP 78/70/40, Harris Report on Kenya and Oil Concession, 29 September 1925.
(b) BP 78/63/44, Nichols to Dept Overseas Trade, 14 October 1919.
(c) BP H16/44, Cadman to Nichols, 15 February 1926.
(d) BP 72/223/1, Wyllie, Oil prospect in various countries, 1930.
(e) BP 78/70/4, Petroleum Dept report, Petroleum in Nigeria, Tanganyika and Kenya, November 1931.
(f) BP 78/70/1, Wyllie report, Abyssinia, 10 March 1925.
(g) BP H10/43, reports 12 October 1923–5 January 1924.
133 H.R.P. Dickson, *Kuwait and her Neighbours* (London, 1956), pp. 267-80; Cox's part in the negotiations of Holmes is indicated in PRO CO 727/5, Oil Concessions Nejd, report by J.B. Mackie, 24 May 1923 and *ibid.*, minute 26 July 1923.
134 PRO CO 727/4, APOC to Under-Secretary Colonial Office, 16 November 1922.
135 PRO CO 727/4, memorandum 13 January 1923.
136 Holmes to E and GS 13 May 1923, quoted in Chisholm, *Kuwait*, p. 98.
137 *Ibid.*
138 *Ibid.*, pp. 95-6.
139 Yatim to Mullah Saleh, 9 May 1923, quoted in Chisholm, *Kuwait*, p. 95.
140 Wilson to APOC London, 17 August 1923, quoted in Chisholm, *Kuwait*, p. 97.
141 Minute of meeting between Wilson and Shaykh Ahmad, 2 June 1923, quoted in Chisholm, *Kuwait*, pp. 96-7.
142 *Ibid.*
143 PRO CO 727/8, Clauson minute, 29 April 1924.

Notes to pp. 563-569

144 PRO CO 727/8, Hall minute, 30 April 1924.
145 Wilson to APOC London, 17 August 1923, quoted in Chisholm, *Kuwait*, pp. 97-8.
146 Colonial Office to Acting Resident on the Gulf, 6 September 1923 quoted in Chisholm, *Kuwait*, p. 100.
147 IO R15/2/96 Tel. 70C, 12 May 1923.
148 BP 3B 3044, Wilson to Knox, 6 October 1923, *ibid.*, Resident to APOC, 12 October 1923.
149 PRO CO 727/7 minute, 2 June 1923 and PRO CO 727/18, Political Resident, Persian Gulf to Colonial Office, 28 March 1924.
150 Colonial Office to Acting Resident in the Gulf, 6 September 1923, quoted in Chisholm, *Kuwait*, p. 99.
151 *Ibid.*, pp. 99 and 100.
152 PRO CO 727/6, Resident Bushire to Secretary of State for India, 2 June 1923.
153 Colonial Office to Acting Resident in the Gulf, 6 September 1923, quoted in Chisholm, *Kuwait*, p. 100.
154 Dr A. Heim, Geological Report, The Question of Petroleum in Eastern Arabia, 5 September 1924, quoted in Chisholm, *Kuwait*, pp. 108-9.
155 BP 3B 3044 Colonial Office to APOC, 27 May 1924.
156 *Ibid.*, note to Management Committee on Bahrain and Kuwait, 9 July 1924.
157 *Ibid.*, Nichols to Wilson, 9 October 1924.
158 *Ibid.*, Jacks to Daly, 18 December 1924, *ibid.*, Daly to Jacks, 7 January 1925 and *ibid.*, APOC Muhammara to APOC London, 28 January 1925.
159 *Ibid.*, Jacks to Hearn, 11 March 1925.
160 *Ibid.*, Jacks to APOC London, 23 December 1924.
161 *Ibid.*, Wilson to Nichols, 5 October 1925 and *ibid.*, Nichols to Wilson, 22 October 1925.
162 BP 3B3045, Nichols to APOC Muhammara, 3 November 1925.
163 Nichols to Cadman, 10 October 1925, quoted in Chisholm, *Kuwait*, p. 111.
164 APOC Geological Report, 13 February 1926 quoted in Chisholm, *Kuwait*, pp. 117-18.
165 On the exchange of correspondence between APOC and E and GS see Chisholm, *Kuwait*, pp. 118-20.
166 BP 3B3045, Cadman to APOC London, 2 April 1926.
167 T.E. Ward, *Negotiations for Oil Concessions in Bahrain, El Hasa (Saudi Arabia), The Neutral Zone, Qatar and Kuwait* New York, (private publication, 2nd edn, 1965).
168 Text of Holmes draft concession, July 1928, quoted in Chisholm, *Kuwait*, pp. 121-5.
169 BP 3B3045, Wilson note on Kuwait and Bahrain, 25 June 1928.
170 Terms of 'British Nationality' clause of 29 November 1928, quoted in Chisholm, *Kuwait*, pp. 16, 17 and 126.
171 *Ibid.*, p. 17. The Colonial Office wrote to Holmes on 31 January 1931 that 'the Sheikh of Kuwait has definitely refused to grant a concession to any concern that is not entirely British ... His Majesty's Government are not prepared to advise the Sheikh to reconsider his attitude in this matter.'
172 Sheykh Ahmad to Holmes, 2 July 1931, quoted in Chisholm, *Kuwait*, pp. 18 and 42.
173 Correspondence between Cadman and Cole, 18 and 21 October 1930, quoted in Chisholm, *Kuwait*, pp. 127-8.

174 Correspondence Hearn, Starling and Giffard, 20 January, 25 August and 26 August 1931, quoted in Chisholm, *Kuwait*, p. 128.
175 Holmes to E and ES and Gulf Oil, 1 November 1931, quoted in Chisholm, *Kuwait*, p. 20 and similarly Gulf Oil memorandum for State Department, 30 November 1931.
176 Cox, 'The Oil Prospects of Kuwait Territory', 12 May 1932, quoted in Chisholm, *Kuwait*, p. 154.
177 Elkington to Shaykh Ahmad, 13 April 1932 quoted in Chisholm, *Kuwait*, p. 155.
178 On this subject in general see Chisholm, *Kuwait*, pp. 17, 20-1 and Foreign Office and State Department correspondence, December 1931 – May 1932; *ibid.*, pp. 130-42.
179 Chisholm, *Kuwait*, p. 22, Holmes to Gulf Oil, 6 June 1932 and APOC London to Ābādān, 30 May 1932.
180 For an early account of this concession see BP H10/80.
181 *Ibid.*
182 BP H10/80, Memorandum on the North Persian Oil Concession, pp. 3-4. There was some British encouragement of Caucasian peoples at this time.
183 *Ibid.*, p. 4. For the Shell interest, *Shell*, Deterding to Schibaieff Co., 26 October 1916, quoted in Jones, *The State and the Emergence of the British Oil Industry*, (London, 1980), p. 154.
184 BP 78/63/44, Black to FO, 12 April 1920.
185 *Ibid.*, Greenway to Firūz, 27 April 1920.
186 PRO FO 371/4919, Norman to FO, 7 September 1920 and 18 August 1920.
187 This was especially true of the Foreign Secretary, Lord Curzon, who consistently disregarded the advice of the Minister in Tehrān, H. Norman. On the Anglo-Persian Convention see William J. Olson, 'The Genesis of the Anglo-Persian Convention of 1919' in Elie Kedourie and Sylvia G. Haim, eds., *Towards A Modern Iran: Studies in Thought, Politics and Society* (London, 1980) pp. 185-216.
188 BP 78/63/45, Greenway to Kandelaki, 3 September 1920; PRO FO 416/66, Derby to Curzon, 18 May 1920.
189 PRO 416/66, Norman to Curzon, 18 June 1920.
190 PRO 416/68, Norman to Curzon, 27 June 1920.
191 On American oil policy at this time see John A. de Novo, 'The Movement for an Aggressive American Oil Policy Abroad, 1918-1920', *American Historical Review*, vol. XL, no. 4, July 1956, and *idem*, *American Interests and Policies in the Middle East 1900-1939* (Minneapolis, 1968); George Lenczowski, *Oil and State in the Middle East* (New York, 1960); Benjamin Shwadran, *The Middle East, Oil and the Great Powers* (New York, 1973), which also has a full bibliography, and S.H. Longrigg, *Oil in the Middle East* (Oxford, 1968).
192 Curzon learning from Firūz about possible American oil interest in Persia commented that, 'I at once realised that he was referring to the American Standard Oil Company, and that that omnivorous organisation was endeavouring to secure a foothold on Persian soil ... I warned him strongly against any attempt to introduce the Standard Oil Company in Persia, assuring him that this would mean a competition which would be a source of certain trouble in the future and which the British Government could not be expected to regard with any favour', PRO FO 416/66, Curzon to Cox, 10 April 1920; see also *ibid.*, Derby to Curzon, 8 May 1920. A year later he was

Notes to pp. 572-576

less anxious, not afraid accordingly of the Americans 'unless they make themselves disagreeable or dangerous to us over the oil. After all they seem on our side against the Bolsheviks who are the real peril,' PRO FO 371/6448, Curzon minute, 29 July 1921.

193 PRO FO 371/6448, Norman to Curzon, 8 May 1921.
194 *Ibid.*, Sperling minute, 3 August 1921.
195 *Ibid.*, Churchill minute, 30 July 1921; Churchill's further comments are interesting in hindsight, 'They want to borrow a sufficient sum to pay off their debts to us not to use the balance to organise a National Bank under American guidance and to build railways. They also want to engage an American to reorganise their finances'.
196 *Ibid.*, Vansittart minute, 29 July 1921.
197 IO L/P and S 10/910, Norman to FO, 7 May 1921.
198 Hansard, House of Lord, 26 July 1921.
199 'The object most likely to attract American investors would be oil', PRO FO 371/6448, Bridgeman memorandum on conversation with C. van H. Engert, American chargé d'affaires, Tehrān, enclosure Norman to Curzon, 10 May 1921.
200 PRO FO 416/69, Saunders to FO, 21 August 1921; see also *ibid.*, Bridgeman to Curzon 30 November and 8 December 1921.
201 *Ibid.*, Norman to Curzon, 10 August 1921.
202 De Novo, *American Interests and Policies in the Middle East*, pp. 283-4.
203 PRO FO 416/69, Curzon to Norman, 29 August 1921.
204 The French chargé d'affaires, nevertheless, remarked that 'he would far sooner see concession in British than American hands, in view of Anglo-French arrangements, as the French right to share of oil produced in the Mosul field', *ibid.*, Bridgeman to Curzon, 25 November 1921; *ibid.*, Bridgeman to Curzon, 2 and 14 November 1921.
205 *Ibid.*, Bridgeman to Curzon, 24 and 29 November 1921.
206 *Ibid.*, Bridgeman to Curzon, 29 November 1921 on Russian protests.
207 *Ibid.*, Curzon to Bridgeman, 5 December 1921.
208 See de Novo, *American Interests and Politics in the Middle East* pp. 107-91.
209 PRO FO 416/69, Loraine to Crowe, 23 December 1921.
210 *Ibid.*, Geddes to Curzon, 23 December 1921.
211 BP H16/67 Cadman visit to American 1921-22.
212 PRO FO 416/70 Geddes to Curzon, 2 December 1921.
213 BP H16/67 Cadman to Greenway, 17 December 1921 and Greenway to Cadman, 21 December 1921.
214 BP H18/38, Cadman secret diary of visit to USA, 1921-22.
215 *Ibid.*
216 BP H16/67, Cadman to Greenway, 20 December 1921 and BP H12/44 Cadman to Greenway, 30 December 1921.
217 BP H16/67, Cadman to Greenway, 19 December 1921. The Persian Government was not disposed to recognise the validity of the Khostaria Concession, see BP H10/24, FO to APOC, 27 September, 28 November, 7 December and 13 December 1921, see also *The Times* 15 December 1921. For Firūz part in Standard Oil concession see PRO FO 416/70, Loraine to Curzon, 7 January 1922. On 21 December at the AGM Greenway deplored the 'confiscatory action', and wrote to Cadman 'once Persian Government handle any money it will be made more difficult to get them to agree

Notes to pp. 576-579

recognition of Khostaria concession', BP H16/67, Greenway to Cadman, 20 December 1921.

218 BP H16/67, Greenway to Cadman, 4 January 1922 and PRO FO 416/70 Loraine to Curzon, 6 January 1922.
219 *Ibid.*
220 PRO FO 416/70, Geddes to Curzon, 15 January 1922. Three weeks before, Geddes had suggested withholding the loan to apply pressure upon Persia so that 'the hopes of financial assistance from America which that Government now entertain will be very much weakened and they may be forced to abandon their unfriendly activities and intrigues', *ibid.*, Geddes to Curzon, 23 December 1921.
221 *Ibid.*, Curzon to Geddes, 18 January 1922.
222 *Ibid.*, Curzon to Geddes, 17 January 1922.
223 *Ibid.*, Loraine to Curzon, 20 January 1922.
224 *Ibid.*, Geddes to Curzon, 18 January 1922.
225 *Ibid.*, Geddes to Curzon, 23 January 1922.
226 PRO FO 416/70, Curzon to Geddes, 24 January 1922.
227 BP H16/67, Greenway reassured Cadman that he was not 'antagonistic to a loan' as such though he was reluctant to participate in one but 'we do not desire to do anything which is not agreeable to SOCNY [Standard Oil Company New York]'. Greenway to Cadman, 17 and 18 January 1922.
228 BP H12/44, SOCNY memorandum, 20 January 1922.
229 BP H16/67, Cadman to Greenway, 25 January 1922 and *ibid.*, Greenway to Cadman, 26 January 1922.
230 *Ibid.*, Cadman to Greenway, 26 January 1922.
231 *Ibid.*, Cadman to Greenway, 27 January 1922.
232 *Ibid.*, Greenway to Cadman, 2 February 1922.
233 BP H12/44, Persian Loan and Concession memorandum, 3 February 1922.
234 *Ibid.*, APOC - SOC Agreement, 6 February 1922.
235 *Ibid.*, 'Alā to Shuster, 7 February 1922.
236 *Ibid.*, Shuster memorandum to Wellman, 7 February 1922.
237 BP H10/80, Shuster's summary of Persian Government message to Washington Legation, 27 February 1922.
238 PRO FO 371/7815, Cadman to Sperling, 14 March 1922 with Welman memorandum re Persian matter, 1 March 1922.
239 On 26 February Loraine had been assured by Mushīr al-Dawla 'most positively that Anglo-American cooperation was in itself welcome, and they understood that it is essential from business point of view but ... Government and Medjliss would be profoundly grateful if, in order to avert complications with Russia, the matter could be put through without overt mention of British Company', PRO FO 416/70, Loraine to Curzon, 28 February 1922. Loraine was worried that without a peaceful resolution of the Khostaria Concession not only would it strain Anglo-Persian relations but 'would also leave the door open for American enterprise to enter this country in open rivalry, and even hostility to British interest, in the role of a saviour from a British tyranny', *ibid.*, Loraine to Curzon, 15 March 1922.
240 *Ibid.*
241 On the other hand 'Rizā Khān is in full sympathy with the idea of Anglo-American cooperation and appreciates its benefits', *ibid.*, Loraine to Curzon, 20 February 1922.

242 *Ibid.*, Loraine to Curzon, 15 March 1922. Oliphant was fatalistic about the advance believing that if the Companies 'think that by casting their bread upon the waters it will return to them, it is not for us to stop them', PRO FO 371/7815, Oliphant minute, 17 March 1922. Vansittart was indignant, 'The Persian contention is preposterous, if they take the advance they must surely be bound to complete the bargain and grant the concession', *ibid.*, Vansittart minute, 17 March 1922.

243 Oliphant questioned 'the desirability of this office having any personal and *oral* dealings with the Bedford', and regarded 'him as an oil magnate and as such should prefer to have his views in writing rather than merely recorded in conversation', *ibid.*, Oliphant minute 23 March. Vansittart was more phlegmatic, 'I don't think we need be afraid to let the Mr Bedford come to the FO provided we don't forget that who sups with the devil needs the devil of a long spoon', *ibid.*, Vansittart minute, 24 March. Both characters fit themselves for Spy caricatures.

244 *Ibid.*, Oliphant minute, 28 March 1922.

245 On the Sinclair concession, see de Novo, *American Interests and Policies in the Middle East*, pp. 285–6 and B. Shwadran, *The Middle East, Oil and the Big Powers* (London, 1956) pp. 76–8.

246 For French efforts to obtain oil concessions on the north of Persia from Gulbenkian's offer in September 1920, see Ministère des Affaires Etrangères, AE. Perse, 1918–29, vols. 49–51. On Khostaria's role in promoting French interests in particular see *ibid.*, vol. 50, Prevost to Poincaré, 1 February 1923, with a copy of the terms of the Khostaria concession of 1916 and *ibid.*, vol. 51 Ballerau to Foreign Minister, 2 December 1927.

247 BP H10/80, memorandum on North Persia Oil, January 1937.

248 BP 77/139/119, Greenway to FO, 16 May 1918.

249 PRO CAB 24/3, Slade memorandum, The Political Position in the Persian Gulf at the end of the War, 31 October 1916.

250 PRO ADM 1/8537/240, and FO 368/2255, Slade memorandum, The Petroleum Situation in the British Empire, 29 July 1918.

251 PRO CAB 21/119, Hankey to Geddes, 30 July 1918. See also, 'An argument I have overlooked with regard to Mesopotamia is the all-important question of the control of oil . . . We ought as a matter of safety to control sufficient ground in front of our vital oilfields to avoid the risk of having them rushed at the outset of the war,' Amery to Sir Henry Wilson, Chief of the Imperial General Staff, 1 August 1918, in *The Leo Amery Diaries Volume 1: 1896–1929*, John Barnes and David Nicholson (London, 1980), p. 232.

252 See amongst other secondary literature already quoted, *The International Petroleum Cartel*, Staff Report to Federal Trade Commission Washington, 1952 and *US Senate Report 1945*, 'American Petroleum Interests in Foreign Countries'; G. Sweet Gibb and E.H. Knowlton, *The Resurgent Years: 1911–27* (New York, 1956), especially Chapter 11, The Quest for Crude Oil in the Middle East, 1919–1928, pp. 278–317, for the need by Standard Oil (NJ) for crude oil outside the United States to supply foreign markets. For the British position see *Correspondence between His Majesty's Government and the United States Ambassador respecting Economic Rights in Mandated Territories* (Cmd 1236, 1921), and PRO FO 371/7278, Geddes to Curzon, 20 January 1922.

253 PRO FO 371/6364, Weakley minute, 13 December 1921.

254 PRO FO 371/6362, Weakley note of meeting with Clarke, 30 November 1921.
255 *Ibid.*, Tyrell memorandum on meeting with Gulbenkian, 24 November 1921; BP H17/1 Gulbenkian *Memoirs*; BP H5/85, Cadman to Tyrell, 11 November 1925.
256 *Ibid.*, Crow note on Tyrell memorandum, 25 November 1921.
257 PRO FO 371/7782, Churchill to Curzon, 1 February 1922.
258 H16/175, Nichols to Wilson, 6 December 1921.
259 Gibb and Knowlton, *Resurgent Years* pp. 292-3. The original companies interested were Standard Oil (NJ), Standard Oil of New York, Gulf Corporation, Atlantic Refining Company, Texas Petroleum Company and Sinclair Oil Corporation.
260 Ministère des Affaires Etrangères, AE 367 Y Internationale, vol. 194, Bérenger to Millerand, 15 March 1920.
261 On different views of the background and course of the negotiations within an Iraq context see Peter Sluglett, *Britain in Iraq 1914-1932* (London, 1976) and Helmut Mejcher, *Imperial Quest for Oil, Iraq 1910-1928* (London, 1976); E and E.P. Penrose, *Iraq International Relations and National Development* (London, 1978).
262 BP 79/91/6, Nichols Diary of my visit to New York, 23 April 1923.
263 Longrigg, *Oil in the Middle East*, p. 70.
264 BP 79/91/6, Greenway to Clarke, 1 September 1922.
265 BP 82/2/1. (IPC file), Keeling memorandum of discussion with Yasin Pasha, 1 November 1923, and *ibid.*, subsequent reports as meeting with Iraq Committee, 8 and 10 November 1923.
266 On negotiation with the French authorities see BP H3/40, BP 77/139/119, PRO FO 371/8995, and PRO FO 371/8996. Jean Rondot, *La Compagnie Française des Pétroles* (Paris, 1962), pp. 13-38, is a brief historical survey, and see Richard F. Kuisel, *Ernest Mercier, French Technocrat* (Berkley, 1967), pp. 21-44, for a biographical study of the founder of the French company.
267 PRO FO 371/10085, Secretary of State for Colonies to Acting High Commissioner, 27 August 1924.
268 PRO CAB 27/268, Committee on Petroleum Policy in Iraq, 27 February 1925.
269 PRO FO 371/10827 Nichols to Amery, 4 March 1925.
270 PRO FO 371/10080, see also S.H. Longrigg, *Iraq 1900 to 1950* (London, 1953), pp. 66-84 and Peter J. Beck, 'A Tedious and Perilous Controversy. Britain and the Settlement of the Mosul Dispute, 1918-1926', *Middle Eastern Studies*, vol. 17, no. 2, April 1981 pp. 256-76, especially pp. 266-73.
271 PRO FO 371/10827, Dobbs to Colonial Office, 2 March 1925 and *ibid.*, minutes by Morgan and Osborne, 6 March 1925.
272 PRO FO 371/7786, Curzon to FO, 1 December 1923.
273 PRO FO 10084, Morgan minute of interdepartmental meeting at Colonial Office, 12 May 1924.
274 BP 79/91/1, Nichols diary.
275 PRO FO 371/10086, Morgan minute, 21 October 1924.
276 *Ibid.*, Osborne minute, 21 October 1924.
277 PRO FO 371/10086, Amery to High Commissioner, 13 November 1924.
278 PRO FO 371/10827 Osborne minute, 24 February 1925.

Notes to pp. 588-596

13. The importance of the Persian dimension 1926-32

1. PRO FO 416/78, Loraine to A. Chamberlain, 31 December 1925.
2. Lady Loraine had offered her services for the occasion and her mother wrote an account of the ceremony, Violet Stuart-Wortley, *Life without Theory, an Autobiography* (London 1946), p. 95. Another description is in Vita Sackville-West, *Passenger to Tehran* (London 1926), pp. 138-54.
3. BP H18/41, Cadman to Loraine, 8 May 1926.
4. *Ibid.*, Cadman's secret diary, 6 May 1926.
5. PRO FO 416/78, Loraine to A. Chamberlain, 31 December 1925.
6. PRO FO 416/77, Loraine to A. Chamberlain, 22 October 1925.
7. PRO FO 416/79, Nicholson to A. Chamberlain, 30 September 1926. On Nicholson's short period in Tehrān see James Lees Milne, *Harold Nicholson*, vol. 1 1886-1929 (London, 1980), pp. 243-307.
8. BP H11/18, Jacks' diary, 9 October 1926.
9. FO 416/77, Loraine to A. Chamberlain, 6 November 1925.
10. PRO FO 416/80, Clive to A. Chamberlain, 13 January 1927.
11. *Ibid.*, Maustaufi's reply in Clive to A. Chamberlain, 11 February 1927.
12. PRO FO 248/1383, Clive to A. Chamberlain, 25 February 1927.
13. *Ibid.*, Clive draft to A. Chamberlain, 27 January 1927.
14. PRO FO 416/82, Clive to A. Chamberlain, 29 December 1927.
15. Joseph M. Upton, *The History of Modern Iran: An Interpretation* (Harvard, 1965), pp. 58-9.
16. BP H18/41, Cadman's secret diary, Cadman to Loraine, 8 May 1926; see also PRO FO 416/78, Loraine to Oliphant, 1 June 1926.
17. *Ibid.*, 6 May 1926.
18. BP H18/41 *passim*.
19. BP H11/18, Jacks to Cadman, 30 October 1926. Millspaugh, before his contract was not renewed by Rizā Shāh, wrote an account of his mission. See A.C. Millspaugh, *The American Task in Persia* (New York, 1926).
20. BP H11/18, Jacks to Cadman, 11 November 1926. For the letters exchanged see PRO FO 416/80, Clive to A. Chamberlain, 13 January 1927, enclosures 1 and 2.
21. For example see PRO FO 371/12282, Clive to A. Chamberlain, 17 June 1927 with enclosures.
22. PRO FO 248/1383, Proclamation of Āzarbāyjān Union, 12 January 1927.
23. BP H11/19, Jacks to Cadman, 26 April 1927.
24. PRO FO 371/12282, Clive to A. Chamberlain, 21 April 1927.
25. BP H11/19, Jacks to Cadman, 26 April 1927.
26. See Nance F. Kittner, 'Issues in Anglo-Persian Diplomatic Relations, 1921-1933' (unpublished PhD Thesis, University of London, 1980), Chapter VI, pp. 216-48.
27. Sepehr Zabih, *The Communist Movement in Iran* (Berkeley and Los Angeles, 1966), p. 58.
28. PRO FO 416/81, Clive to A. Chamberlain, 18 June 1927 and BP H11/19, Clive to Cadman, 12 April 1927.
29. PRO FO 416/81, Persian Economic Report of E.R. Lingemann, 7 October 1927.
30. PRO FO 416/82, Clive to A. Chamberlain, 1 January 1928.
31. BP H11/20, Jacks to Cadman, 9 January 1928.

Notes to pp. 597–605

32 *Ibid.*
33 *Ibid.*, Cadman to Jacks, 6 March 1928.
34 *Ibid.*, Jacks to Cadman, 19 April 1928.
35 *Ibid.*, Cadman to Jacks, 31 May 1928.
36 *Ibid.*, Jacks interview with Timurtāsh, 18 April 1928.
37 *Ibid.*, Jacks to Cadman, 17 May 1928.
38 *Ibid.*, Jacks to Cadman, 23 June 1928.
39 *Ibid.*, Jacks to Cadman, 1 June 1928.
40 Amin Banani, *The Modernisation of Iran, 1921-1941* (Stanford, 1961), p. 137.
41 BP H11/20, Jacks to Cadman, 25 June 1928; BP H11/21, Jacks to Cadman, 12 July 1928 and Cadman to Jacks, 24 July 1928.
42 BP H11/20, Jacks to Cadman, 25 June 1928.
43 BP H11/21, Jacks to Cadman, 26 July 1928.
44 *Ibid.*
45 BP H16/20, Cadman memorandum, interview with Timurtāsh, 31 July 1928.
46 For the official comments on this controversy see *League of Nations Official Journal*, Dispute between the United Kingdom and Persia in regard to the concession held by the Anglo-Persian Oil Company. December 1932, Annex 1419c pp. 2298-2305, Memorandum by his Majesty's Government in the United Kingdom submitted to the Council on 19 December 1932; *ibid.*, February 1933, Annex 1422b, pp. 289-95, Memorandum from the Imperial Government of Persia, 18 January 1933.
47 H16/20, Lloyd memorandum, 21 August 1928.
48 *Ibid.*, Young, a record of Lausanne discussions, 31 August 1928.
49 *Ibid.*, Secret note n.d. September 1928.
50 For the development of national oil policies elsewhere in this period see S.H. Longrigg, *Oil in the Middle East* (Oxford, 1968).
51 H16/20, Consideration of scheme under review n.d. September 1928.
52 See, for example J.E. Hartshorn, *Oil Companies and Governments: An Account of the International Oil Industry in its Political Environment* (London, 1962), Edith Penrose, *The Large International Firm in Developing Countries: The International Petroleum Industry* (London, 1968), Michael Tanzer, *The Political Economy of International Oil and the Underdeveloped Countries* (London, 1969), S. Cleland and I. Seymour (eds), *Continuity and Change in the World Oil Industry* (Beirut, 1970) and Louis Turner, *Oil Companies in the International System* (London, 1978). More particularly concerned with OPEC is Zuhayr Mikdashi, *The Community of Oil Exporting Countries: a Study in Governmental Co-operation* (London, 1972) and a more challenging view is expressed by J.B. Kelly, *Arabia, the Gulf and the West: a Critical View of the Arabs and their Oil Policy* (London, 1980).
53 BP H16/20, Young memorandum, 'Views expressed by Timurtash on visit to Lausanne', 23-25 August 1928.
54 *Ibid.*, Secret note n.d. September 1928.
55 *Ibid.*, memorandum, 'Our line of future policy with Persian Government', n.d. September 1928.
56 *Ibid.*, Cadman to Barstow, 11 October 1928.
57 PRO FO 371/13059, Fisher to Lindsay, 15 October 1928.
58 *Ibid.*, Vansittart to Cushenden, 15 November 1928.
59 *Ibid.*, Vansittart to Fisher, 19 October 1928.

60 Ibid., Fisher to Lindsay, 15 October 1928.
61 BP H16/22, Cadman to Barstow, 22 November 1928. See also *The Leo Amery Diaries Volume 1: 1896-1929* (London, 1980), ed. John Barnes and David Nicholson, p. 572, 20 November 1928; 'A small hush Cabinet meeting about the APOC', and 22 November 1928 'there were no serious difficulties involved.'
62 Ibid., Grigg to Barstow, 23 November 1928.
63 BP H16/20, Cadman to Timurtāsh, 30 September 1928.
64 Ibid., Timurtāsh to Cadman, 20 October 1928.
65 Ibid., Cadman to Timurtāsh, 15 November 1928.
66 The first visit is mentioned in BP H11/19, Jacks to Cadman, 20 January 1927.
67 Quoting 'Alī Dashtī in *Shafagh-i Surkh*, 5 December 1928.
68 H16/100, memorandum of audience of Shah to Fāteh, 19 November 1928.
69 Ibid., Jacks to Cadman, 15 November 1928.
70 H16/20, Views expressed by Timurtāsh n.d. August 1928.
71 PRO FO 416/83, Clive to A. Chamberlain, 29 December 1928.
72 Ibid., Clive to A. Chamberlain, 7 December 1928.
73 See for example *Setareh Iran*, 25 November 1928, 'Certain foreign capitalists have succeeded in swindling the weak and ignorant Persian Government of the period' (translation).
74 BP H16/20, Cadman to Timurtāsh, 3 January 1929.
75 BP H16/20, Timurtāsh to Cadman, 6 December 1928 and *ibid.*, Timurtāsh to Cadman, 12 December 1928.
76 BP H18/42, Cadman Diary, Persia and Iraq, 1929, 20 February 1929.
77 BP H12/31, Notes of discussions with Timurtāsh, 6 March 1929.
78 Ibid., Notes of discussions with Timurtāsh, 15 March 1929.
79 This opinion was confirmed in a personal interview with Mustafa Fāteh on 12 July 1977.
80 BP H18/42, Notes of discussions with Timurtāsh, 18 March 1929.
81 BP H16/21, Timurtāsh to Cadman, 30 March 1928.
82 BP H18/42, Cadman to Timurtāsh, 2 April 1929.
83 PRO 371/13794, Clive to Chamberlain, 28 March 1929.
84 On the impact and causes of the Depression see Charles P. Kindleberger, *The World in Depression 1929-1939* (London, 1973).
85 PRO FO 371/13794, Clive to A. Chamberlain, 28 March 1929.
86 BP H10/174, Cadman to 'Isā Khān, 7 May 1929.
87 Ibid., APOC Tehrān to APOC London, 14 August 1929.
88 Ibid., APOC Tehrān to APOC London, 23 September and 9 October 1929.
89 These activities were mentioned in the revelations of the former OGPU agent Agabekov in *Les Dernieres Nouvelles*, 22 October 1930, when he described his principal task, 'By destroying the oil base of English in the South of Persia, we would materially hinder deliveries of oil supplies to the British Navy.'
90 BP 75/8/1, Note on incidents leading up to May Day disturbances in Ābādān, 14 June 1929; PRO FO 416/184, Fletcher to Henderson, 2 June 1929.
91 PRO FO 416/85, Clive to Henderson, 4 September 1929.
92 BP 75/8/1, Timurtāsh to 'Alā, 8, 15, 18 July 1929.
93 Ibid., Clive to Henderson, 16 July 1929.
94 PRO FO 416/85, Henderson to Clive, 9 July 1929.
95 BP 75/8/1, Clive to Henderson, 19 March 1930.

96 PRO FO 416/89, Clive to Henderson, 26 July 1930; see also *ibid.*, Clive to Henderson, 4 July 1930.
97 BP 75/8/1, Notes on Lingemann's report on the exchange crisis, 18 March 1930.
98 BP H16/22, Cadman to Jacks, 8 January 1930; *ibid.*, Cadman to Timurtāsh, 13 June 1930 and BP H10/174, Jacks to Cadman, 10 January 1930.
99 BP H10/174, Jacks to Cadman, 23 March 1930.
100 BP H10/174, Jacks to Cadman, 17 March with enclosure, *Shafagh-i Surkh*, 16 March 1930.
101 Jacks averred that 'My own relations with Teymourtache have never been more cordial than they are now', BP H10/174, Jacks to Cadman, 29 March 1930.
102 BP H10/174, Jacks note of interview with Timurtāsh, 4 November 1930.
103 BP H9/72, Cadman Diary, 25 January 1931.
104 BP H12/3, Note of meeting, 13 March 1931.
105 BP H12/30 *passim*; and BP H16/20, Jacks interview with Timurtāsh, 31 July 1928.
106 BP H10/174, Persia outstanding questions aides-mémoires, 31 March 1931.
107 *Ibid.*
108 *Ibid.*, Greenhouse to Cadman, 7 April 1931, with enclosure of 14 points of Timurtāsh.
109 *Ibid.*, Jacks memorandum, negotiations pending to revise the D'Arcy Concession, 7 May 1931 and Persian outstanding questions, conference 13 and 14 May 1931.
110 PRO FO 416/88, Clive to Henderson 30 April 1931.
111 *Ibid.*, Parr to Henderson 16 March 1931, enclosures of *Shafagh-i Surkh*, 2, 4 and 8 March 1931.
112 PRO FO 416/89, Clive to Henderson, 26 June 1931. Clive had a bad impression of Timurtāsh, believing him at his last interview to be a person 'of complete insincerity and bad faith', PRO FO 416/89 Clive to Henderson, 5 July 1931.
113 Jacks had informed Cadman that 'the economic situation here daily becomes more difficult', Jacks to Cadman, BP H10/174, 22 July 1931. He noted resentment towards Iraq, *ibid.*, 12 July 1931.
114 For these three meetings see BP H10/174 Jacks notes of interviews with Timurtāsh, 1, 6 and 11 July 1931.
115 BP H10/174, Cadman to Jacks, 31 July 1931.
116 *Ibid.*, Cadman to Timurtāsh, 7 August 1931.
117 *Ibid.*, Cadman to Timurtāsh, 17 August 1931.
118 *Ibid.*, Jacks to Cadman, 27 August 1931 and Jacks to Cadman, cable, 29 August 1931.
119 *Ibid.*, Cadman to Jacks, 28 August 1931.
120 BP H12/3, note of conference held, 31 August 1931.
121 *Ibid.*, Aide mémoire for Cadman, Lausanne, 2 October 1931.
122 Hearn was in charge of compiling the material for the case on the Armitage-Smith Agreement, BP H12/3, Hearn to Jacks, 9 September and *passim*. On the opinion see BP H12/3, 30 October 1931.
123 BP H12/3, APOC Tehrān to APOC London, 5 September 1931 with enclosure, 'Īsā Khān, 'Extracts from legal opinion obtained in London respecting the alleged Armitage-Smith Agreement', Tehrān, 6 September

1931. On the opinion George W. Stocking, *Middle East Oil: A Study in Political and Economic Controversy* (London, 1971), p. 26 is wrong in assuming that Lumley and Lumley were actually retained by Rizā Shāh 'to examine the documents related to the Armitage-Smith Agreement.' They had acted for the Imperial Commissioner since 1909. The letter in French and English of 'Īsā Khān appointing Armitage-Smith on 29 August 1920, is in International Court of Justice, *Pleadings, Arguments, Documents, Anglo-Iranian Oil Company Case* (The Hague, 1952), pp. 228-9.

124 BP H10/175, Cadman to Jacks, 17 February 1932.
125 BP H14/169, Cadman's notes of 13 November 1931 given to Tīmurtāsh.
126 *Ibid.*, Draft for meeting of 13 November 1931.
127 *Ibid.*, Cadman to Jacks, 1 December 1931.
128 See BP H14/169, Hearn to Fraser, 4 December 1931; *ibid.*, Tīmurtāsh's note to Cadman, 9 December 1931; French original in BP H12/5; *ibid.*, note of discussions, 12 December 1931 and *ibid.*, note of discussions, 17 December 1931.
129 Hearn admitted the text was 'often clumsy - and will clearly need proper drafting', BP H12/5, Hearn's comments on French text, 23 December 1931.
130 BP H14/169, Tīmurtāsh to Cadman, 28 December 1931 and Cadman to Tīmurtāsh, 23 December 1931.
131 BP H16/6, Draft Agreement, Paris, 8 January 1932.
132 BP H10/175, Cadman to Jacks, 17 February 1932.
133 *Ibid.*, Cadman to Tīmurtāsh, 8 January 1932.
134 *Ibid.*, Tīmurtāsh to Cadman, 10 January 1932.
135 Jacks believed that Tīmurtāsh had kept the Shah informed but had not consulted the Persian Government. Clive in April 1931 had suggested that the Shah 'entirely depends on the advice of the Minister of Court in all matters other than the army and police' but that Tīmurtāsh was 'extremely unpopular', PRO FO 371/15337, Clive to FO 15 April 1931.
136 BP H10/175, Cadman to Tīmurtāsh, 12 January 1932.
137 *Ibid.*, Tīmurtāsh to 'Īsā Khān, 17 January 1932.
138 *Ibid.*, Cadman to Tīmurtāsh, 18 January 1932 and *ibid.*, Cadman to 'Īsā Khān, 18 January 1932.
139 *Ibid.*, Tīmurtāsh to 'Īsā Khān, 19 January 1932.
140 *Ibid.*, Jacks to Cadman, 7 February 1932.
141 *Ibid.*, 'Īsā Khān to Tīmurtāsh, 5 February 1932.
142 *Ibid.*, Jacks to Cadman, 6 February 1932.
143 *Ibid.*, Cadman to Jacks, 6 February 1932.
144 *Ibid.*, Jacks to Cadman, 9 February 1932.
145 *Ibid.*, Jacks to Cadman, 8 and 19 February 1932.
146 BP H16/50, Taqīzādeh to 'Īsā Khān, 4 April 1932.
147 BP H12/6, Brown to Hearn, 17 February 1932.
148 *Ibid.*, Hearn to Brown, 18 February 1932.
149 BP H10/175, Cadman to Messrs. Brown, Flemming and Murray, 19 February 1932.
150 BP H12/6, Spens to Cadman, 22 February and 17 March 1932.
151 *Ibid.*, Brown to Cadman, 5 April 1932.
152 BP H16/50, Tīmurtāsh to Cadman, 10 and 12 April 1932 and *ibid.*, Tīmurtāsh to 'Īsā Khān, 5 May 1932.
153 *Ibid.*, 'Īsā Khān to Tīmurtāsh, 8 May 1932.

154 BP H12/7, Jacks to Hearn, 7 May 1932 and *ibid.*, Jacks to Cadman, 17 May 1932.
155 BP H16/50, Cadman to Barstow, 13 May 1932.
156 *Ibid.*, 'Īsā Khān to Tīmurtāsh, 20 May 1932.
157 *Ibid.*, Cadman to Jacks, 13 May 1932.
158 BP H16/30, Jacks to Hearn, 30 May 1932.
159 BP H10/176, Jacks to Cadman, 2 June 1932.
160 *Ibid.*, Cadman to 'Īsā Khān, 2 June 1932 and *ibid.*, Jacks to Tīmurtāsh, 5 June 1932.
161 *Ibid.*, Jacks to Cadman, 4 June 1932.
162 *Ibid.*, Jacks to Cadman, 7 June 1932.
163 *Ibid.*, Cadman to Jacks, 9 June 1932.
164 BP H16/30, Tīmurtāsh to Jacks, 5 June 1932.
165 BP 75/8/1, 'Īsā Khān to Tīmurtāsh, 10 June 1932.
166 BP H16/30, Cadman to Jacks, 9 June 1932.
167 BP H16/30, Hearn to 'Īsā Khān, 10 June 1932.
168 The question of the text is controversial. It was difficult, but whether it was so complicated as to justify the complaint of Tīmurtāsh that 'even the Government is incapable of understanding its meaning', is doubtful. The French text had been translated by Leslie Burgin, 'who is absolutely bilingual and is a lawyer into the bargain', and it was likely that when translated into Persian it caused ambiguities of expression when the Persian and English versions were compared. It is in this context that Cadman's acceptance of Dr Naficy's text was an important concession. See BP H16/30, Jacks to Hearn, 9 June 1932, *ibid.*, Hearn to Jacks, 17 June 1932 and BP H10/176, Jacks to Cadman, 16 June 1932.
169 BP H16/30, Tīmurtāsh to Jacks, 4 July 1932 and *ibid.*, Tīmurtāsh to 'Īsā Khān, 5 July 1932.
170 *Ibid.*, Jacks to APOC London, 19 June 1932 and *ibid.*, Taqīzādeh to Jacks, 27 June 1932.
171 *Ibid.*, Jacks to APOC London, 30 June 1932.
172 *Ibid.*, Hearn to 'Īsā Khān, 20 July 1932.
173 *Ibid.*, Jacks to APOC London, 27 June 1932.
174 *Ibid.*, Cadman to Jacks, 1 July 1932.
175 *Ibid.*, Jacks to Hearn, 28 June 1932.
176 *Ibid.*, Jacks to Hearn, 9 July 1932. EI
177 PRO FO 416/91, Hoare to Simon, 16 July 1932.
178 BP H12/8, *Iran*, 27 June 1932.
179 *Ibid.*, *Iran*, 29 June 1932.
180 BP H12/18, *Itteläʿat*, 1 July 1932.
181 *Ibid.*, *Shafagh-i Surkh*, 28 June 1932.
182 BP H16/30, Jacks to Cadman, 7 July 1932; see also *ibid.*, Tīmurtāsh to 'Īsā Khān, 7 July 1932.
183 BP H10/176, Cadman to Jacks, 8 July 1932.
184 BP H16/30, Cadman to Jacks, 5 July 1932.
185 *Ibid.*, Cadman to Jacks, 13 July 1932.
186 *Ibid.*, 'Īsā Khān to Jacks, 12 July 1932.
187 *Ibid.*, Jacks to Cadman, 19 July 1932.
188 *Ibid.*, Jacks to Cadman, 23 July 1932.
189 *Ibid.*, Jacks to Cadman, 19 July 1932.

Notes to pp. 627-628

190 *Ibid.*, Hearn to Jacks, 29 July 1932.
191 Jacks was sure that the disclosures were harmful to Timurtāsh; 'As Teymourtache has really directed the Bank's affairs over the Head of the Minister of Finance [Taqīzādeh], it will not surprise you to learn that his name figures in current rumours. Not unnaturally, the opportunity of his illness is being taken advantage of by his enemies, and one wonders if, as is generally the case here, there is no smoke without fire, his influence may not as a result receive a set back', BP H16/30 Jacks to Hearn, 24 July 1932. He was also accused of being unduly pro-Russian, see Miron Rezun, 'Reza Shah's Court Minister: Teymourtash,' *International Journal Middle Eastern Studies* 12 (1980) 119-37 and *The Soviet Union and Iran: Soviet Policy in Iran from the Beginnings of the Pahlavi Dynasty until the Soviet Invasion in 1941* (Geneva, 1981).
192 It was clear, as Jacks remarked, that Taqīzādeh would 'not be adverse to taking a definite hand in the negotiations which he has evidenced are very much the concern of his Ministry'. On 11 August Jacks had the impression that Taqīzādeh would handle negotiations and 'not as hitherto by the Minister of Court', BP H16/30, Jacks to Hearn, 18 August 1932. Jacks thought that with this possible development 'the Government recognises that it has got to moderate its attitude', though Taqīzādeh made it clear he was opposed to the existing basis of computing royalties. The assumption of intense rivalry between Timurtāsh and Taqīzādeh has been confirmed to the author in a discussion between himself and the daughter of Timurtāsh, Iran, 27 June 1980.
193 BP H16/30, Jacks to Lloyd, 29 August 1932, 'the Government's determination at all cost to force the Company to re-open negotiations for complete revision' and *ibid.*, Jacks to Cadman, 4 September 1932, 'as neither the British Government nor the Company had shown any willingness to come to terms with the Persian Government, the latter was going to adopt more drastic action in dealing with both'.
194 *Ibid.*, Jacks to Hearn, 8 October 1932 and BP H10/176, Jacks to Cadman, 29 October 1932.
195 *Ibid.*, Cadman to Jacks, 25 October 1932.
196 BP H10/176, Jacks to Cadman, 15 November 1932.
197 *Ibid.*, Jacks to Cadman, 19 November 1932.
198 *Ibid.*, Jacks to Cadman, 15 November 1932. Jacks had been warned by Timurtāsh 'not to be surprised if both the Company and myself were completely ignored by His Majesty, whose present mood ... was uncertain'.
199 BP H10/176, Jacks to Cadman, 19 November 1932, enclosure *Iran* 16 November 1932.
200 Jacks commented that 'There is no room to doubt that Teymourtache's wings have been clipped' and that it was 'a direct blow' to his prestige, BP H10/176 Jacks to Cadman, 24 November 1932.

INDEX

A Diplomatist in the East, 39
Ābādān, refinery at, 8, 107, 143, 160, 215, 285, 290, 293, 308, 520; comments on, 339, 429-30, 436-8, 440; construction of, 135; design for, 133-5; demonstrations at, 432-3, 610; early problems at, 149-53, 158, 161, 274, 398, 474, 632; negotiations for site, 119, 122-6, 144; post-war conditions, 330, 422, 438, 440, 445, 448, 453-4, 469; war-time, 221, 264, 268, 275, 277, 279-82
Ābādān, site of, 107, 120, 131, 132-3, 141, 151, 179, 184-5, 216, 221, 230; post war, 318, 363, 397, 402, 423, 432-3, 436, 441-2, 444-5, 449, 451-2, 466, 470, 511, 518, 569-70, 607; sales from, 471, 514, 516, 527
ᶜAbbās Qūlī Khān, 40
ᶜAbdul Muhsin Beg, 584
Achnacarry, 403, 514, 602-3
Adamson R.W., 100, 102-3, 177
Addison, Dr C., 1st Viscount, 222
Aden, 160, 466, 561; site acquired, 287
Admiralty, 164, 264, 292, 313-14, 353, 532, 535; attitude to oil policy, 237-242, 245-52, 256, 260, 311, 356, 375, 382-5; BOC fuel oil contract with, 10, 60, 68-70, 82, 158-9; Commission of to Persia, 147, 184, 194-6; Company fuel oil contract with, 11, 13, 147, 162, 165, 213, 262, 274-5, 285, 288-90, 290, 351, 397, 461, 466, 469, 532, 538-9; concern for a home refinery, 214-17; intermediary between BOC and D'Arcy, 60-1, 72, 112; negotiations for fuel oil contract, 165-185, 196-200, 203, 207, 211; reaction to Company prospectus 105-6; war-time activities of Company for, 281-2; war-time relations with Company, 212-13, 281;
Admiralty Commision, 147, 196, 248, 282, 286, 545
Admiralty Oil Committee, 158-9, 165, 171-2, 177
Adventures of Hajji Baba of Ispahan, The, 386
Afghanistan, 73, 432; concessionary interest, 561
Africa, 14, 540, 555, 561
African and Eastern Concessions Ltd, 165
Afrikander, The, 56
Aghā Jārī, 8, 418, 428
Ahmed Shāh, 73, 90, 352, 364-5, 391-2
Ahwāz, 55, 75, 77-9, 85, 88, 115, 124, 130, 139, 145, 155, 157, 264, 280, 282, 393-4, 449, 605, 627
Ahwāz barrage concession, 46
Aktiebolaget Bensin & Oljekompaniet, 497
Aktiengesellschaft für Oesterreiche-Ungarische Petroleum Produkte, 3
ᶜAlā, Husayn, Minister in Washington, 572-3, 578, 580; minister in France, 610
Alaska, 560
Albania, concessionary interest, 544, 548, 550-1, 555
Albania, Government of, 548
Alberta, concessionary interest, 561
Al Bussarah-al-Fayha, 125
Alexander I, Czar, 20

776

Index

Al Hasa, concessionary interest, 562, 565, 567-8
Allahverdiantz, Mr, 26
Alwand, 522, 592-3
American Institute of Petroleum, 420, 513, 575
Amery, L.S.: attitude to Iraq concession, 541, 586; Persian participation in Company, 605; reaction to Churchill proposals for Government withdrawal from Company, 382-5
Amīn al-Dawla, 17
Amīn al-Sultān, Mīrza ᶜAlī Asghar Khān, Atabeg-i Aᶜzam, 28-9, 35-40, 44-6, 56, 83
Amīr Mufakhkham, 140
Amīr Mujtahid, 140
Ananich B.V., 46
ss *Anatolia*, 131
Andes, 552
Anglo-American Oil Company, 5, 218, 487-8, 505, 512
Anglo-Iraq Treaty, 584
Anglo-Mexican Petroleum Company, 487
Anglo-Persian Oil Company (1909) (Anglo-Iranian Oil Company (1935), British Petroleum Company Ltd (1955), referred to as the Company), 295, 538; acquisition of BP Company, 217-29, 291-4; Armitage-Smith negotiations, 160, 166-8, 174, 197, 369-71, 386; As-Is Agreement, 463, 509, 512-14; BOC post-war, 371-85; British Government war-time oil policy, 235, 237-42, 243-7; concessionary activity, (a) Persian Gulf area, 545-7, 561-70; (b) Albania, 548, 550-1; (c) South America, 551-2, 554; (d) Venezuela concession, 555; (e) Colombia concession, 555-7; (f) Argentina concession, 557-60; (g) North Persia concession, 570-80; (h) post-war Mesopotamian negotiations, 580-6; concessionary policy, 539-44, 547, 560-1, 587; downstream activities after the war, (a) integration strategy, 461-2, 476, 489-91, 500, 537; (b) bunkering, 466, 469-71, 479; (c) with Royal Dutch-Shell, 474, 476, 505-8, 510-11, 513; (d) with Standard Oil (NJ), 475, 505-8, 510-13; (e) European subsidiaries, 476-7, 482, 494-5, 497; (f) UK marketing, 482-3, 487-8; (g) advertising, 500; (h) motor spirit competition, 504; (i) Persian market, 514, 516-19; (j) Iraq market, 520, 522; (k) Australian market, 522-4; early marketing, 160-5, 185-8, 290; fall of Bakhtiari Khans, 388, 390; financial crisis 1912-14, 9-10, 166-7, 185-6, 188-91, 193; formation of, 89, 94-107, 110, 112-13; Government finance for, (a) 1914-18, 210-14, 220-3, 226, 230, 232, 235; (b) 1919-24, 310-12, 320-4, 327-8, 330-3; (c) 1924-28, 341, 343, 346, 348; Government negotiations (1912-14), 166-85, 194-9; Government restrictions on activities, 465, 538-9; Harcourt Committee, 249-58, 260-1, 355; Llandarcy (Swansea) refinery, war-time priority, 214-17; management, 12-14, 204-6, 295-7, 312-16, 336-41, 348-9; managing agents, 117-18, 129-30, 137, 139-48, 306-9, 316-19; marketing, 310; Mesopotamian negotiations, 11, 160, 166-8, 174, 197; possibility of Persian Government shareholding, 1919-20, 351-4; pre-war operations in Persia, 115-17, 120-1, 132, 145-6, 154-7; research, 277, 279, 452-9; rivalry with Royal Dutch-Shell, 158-9, 169-70, 193, 291; Rizā Shāh's attitude to, 386-91, 394, 396, 595, 598-9, 606; royalty negotiations with Firūz, 365-9; sabotage of pipeline, 280; shipping, 292-4, 525-7, 532-5; technical progress in post-war Persia, (a) general, 397-8; (b) exploration and production, 402-4, 406-10, 412-14, 417-23, 425-9; (c) refinery, 429-30, 432-4, 436-40, 444; (d) pipeline, 445-9; (e) dredging of

Index

Shatt-al-ʿArab, 449-52; war-time operations in Persia, 262-8, 270-75, 277, 280-2
Anglo-Persian Treaty (1919), 351-2, 366, 386, 389, 571
Anglo-Russian Boundary Commission, 450
Anglo-Russian Convention of 1907, 73, 90, 203
Angola, concessionary interest, 544, 561
Annales des Mines, 27
Arabia, concessionary interest, 545, 555, 561, 580
Ardenitza, 550
Argentina, 11, 414, 544, 552, 557-60
Argentina, Government of, 558-60
Argyropoulo, Kimon Manuilovich, 39-40, 46
Arkansas, 634
Armitage-Smith, S.A., (later Sir Sydney), 366-7, 369-71, 619-21, 626
Armitage-Smith Agreement: legal opinion on, 619-20; negotiations for, 365, 369-71, Persian antagonism towards, 598, 600, 613, 618; repudiation of 612
Armstrong, Whitworth Ltd, Messrs, 293
Aron, M., 61
Asche Frederic D., 475
Ashley, Evelyn, 51
Ashurst, Crisp and Morris, 99
Asia, 1, 46, 539, 555
Asiatic Petroleum Company, 4-5, 507, Company contracts with, 149, 151, 161-2, 164, 173, 181, 185, 239, 274, 285, 287-8, 290, 292, 372, 474, 476, 491, 505, 508
As-Is Agreement, 463
Asmari, limestone oil reservoir, 263, 402, 406, 410
Asquith, Margot, 196
Astarābād, 570
Astra-Romana, 5
Astatki, (refinery residue), 7
Atatürk, Mustafā Kemāl, 7, 590
Atlantic Refining Company, 13, 372, 555
Auld, Col. S.T.M., 455-6

Austria, 494, 504, 548
Australia, 14, 30; concessionary activity, 522-3, 541, 544; marketing interests, 160, 312, 474, 500, 504, 522-5
Aviation Spirit, 458, 464
Avonmouth, 466
Āzarbāijān, 16, 57, 351, 570, 593
Azienda Generale Italiana Petroleum, 548, 550-1
Azīz Khān, 56

Baba Gurgur, 417, 540, 585, 603
Babington-Smith, Sir Henry, 167
Badger and Company, 438
Baghdad, 55-6, 67, 75, 285, 287, 386, 402, 581-5
Bahmashīr River, 132
Baku, 1, 3, 7-8, 24-6, 28, 33, 35, 45, 47, 57, 62, 64, 351, 389, 516
Bahrain, 7, 285; concessionary interest, 540, 545-7, 561-2, 564, 566-7, 570, 580; Persian claims on, 599
Bahrain Petroleum Company, 568
Baitwand, 85
Bakhtiari Khans, 67; attitude to early Company operations in Persia, 115, 120-2, 126-8, 139-40, 143-4; land negotiations, 145-6; negotiations with Reynolds, 73-81, 83, 87, 91, 125-6, 157, 282; post-war, 351-3, 369; relations with Rizā Khān, 388-91; war-time, 268-80
Bakhtiari Oil Agreement, 76-8, 80
Bakhtiari Oil Company, 105, 148, 353
Baldwin, Stanley (later 1st Earl Baldwin of Bewdley): amalgamation proposals, 374; Chancellor of Exchequer, 323; Churchill proposals, 382-5; Financial Secretary, 252, 258, 311; management succession of Company, 312-14; Prime Minister, 336
Balfour, A.J., (later 1st Earl Balfour), 242, 246, 376-78, 380

778

Index

Balkans, The, 350
Balūchistān, 282
Banānī, Amīn, 598
Bandar ᶜAbbās, 20, 285
Bank of England, 194, 181-3, 624
Bank of Montreal, 104
Bank of Scotland, 104, 110
Banque de la Seine, 479
Barclay, Sir George, 116, 154, 156
Barnes Major, 548
Barnes, Sir George, 241
Barnes, Sir Hugh, 97, 107, 123, 137, 164, 168, 315, 354
Barrow, 466
Barstow, G.B., (later Sir George): amalgamation proposals 1921-24; 374-5, 380, 385; BP Company, 218-19; Company finance, 310-11, 321-23; Government director, 209; Persian Government shareholding, 353-4; refinery negotiations, 215-17; retirement from Treasury, 605
Basra, 55-6, 125, 141-2, 151, 268, 279-80, 285, 287, 450, 583-4
Basra Port Authority (later Basra Port Directorate), 450-2
Bass Strait, 547
Batum, 3
Bauxite, treatment, 453-4
Bawi, tribe of, 280
Bayne L.F., 430
Bedford, A.C., 381, 475; North Persia concession, 574-7, 579; interest in Mesopotamia, 581-2
Behbehān, 66
Beirut, 402
Belfast, 466
Belgium, 3, 474, 477, 479, 483, 489, 504, 509
Bell, Gertrude, 368
Benjamin, S.G.W., 25
Benzina Petroleum, 494, 548, 550
Benzine (Motor Spirit, Petrol): early and war-time sales of, 161-2, 169, 213, 290-1, 295, 474; early refining problems of, 148-52, 158, 164, 274-5, 290; post-war production problems and yields, 430, 436-8, 440, 464, 466; post-war sales of, 374, 471, 475-7, 479, 482-3, 487-9, 491-2, 494, 497, 500, 504-6, 508, 510, 516, 520, 523, 525, 532; reasearch into, 279, 452-5, 457-8
Benzin-und Petroleum Aktien Gesellschaft, 494
Bérenger, Sénateur Henri, 356-7
Beresford, Admiral Sir Charles (later Lord), 183
Berliner Tageblatt, 91
Berthelot, Phillippe, 358
Bertie, Mr, 75
Besse, A., 160
Bethlehem Steel Corporation, 573
Bharier, Julian, 19
Bikarz, 412
Birmingham University, 248, 561
Black, John, 130, 136-7, 139-41, 147, 163
Black, F.W. (later Sir Frederick), 165, 171, 287; director, 302, 354; Government director, 208, 258-9; negotiations with Company, 170, 181, 184-5, 193-4, 199
Black Sea, 3, 21
Blackett, Sir Basil, 321
Blundstone, E.R., 183
Board of Trade, 255, 358; concern with Company, 204-5, 218; control of Petroleum Executive, 351; interest in Turkish Petroleum Company, 193; management of Company, 312; petroleum policy, 235, 237, 241-8, 250, 252, 258-9, 298; post-war, 357, 374-5, 378, 380, 382
Böckh, Professor Hugo de, 541, 567; character, 426-7; Persian surveys, 428-9, 547
Bogota, 556
Bolivia, concessionary activity, 552
Bombay, 286, 293, 466, 471
Bonaparte, Napoleon, 20
Borneo, 3, 239-40; concessionary interest, 543-4, 561
Boucicault, Nina (2nd Mrs. W.K. D'Arcy), 31, 61, 98
Boyds, Miller and Thompson, 100
Boyle, Admiral Hon. Sir Algernon, 380
Bradbury, Sir John, (later Lord Bradbury of Winsford): acquisition

Index

of BP Company, 216, 219; Company finances, 211-13, 220, 310-11; Government shareholding, 195, 198-9, 207, 297, 352, 354; Swansea refinery dispute, 215-17
Bradshaw, Mr, 86, 92, 269
Braithwaite, W.D., 291, 303, 477, 479, 500, 506, 519
Braun C.F. & Company, 457
Brazil, concessionary interest, 552; oil legislation in, 554, 557
Brenier, Georges, 479
Britannic Estates, Ltd, 327
Britannic House, 304-5
British Aviator, The, 533-34
British Colombia, concessionary interest, 544, 561
British Colony, The, 534
British Emperor, The, 293
British Empire, 249, 252-3, 256-8, 575, 581
British Equatorial Company, 542
British India Steam Navigation Company, 286
British Italian Corporation, 548
British Mexican Company, 469-70
British Oil Bunkering Company Ltd, 469
British Petroleum Company Ltd, 5, 197, 299, 366; acquisition of by Company, 205, 206, 212, 217-19, 223, 240-1, 245-7, 291-4; sales of, 263, 294, 303, 305, 361, 462, 464, 476, 482-3, 487-9, 497, 505
British Tanker Company Ltd, 222-3, 263, 303-4, 341, 361, 366; formed, 292-4, 464, 525, 527, 535
Brooklands, 500
Brown, D., 360
Brown, W. Gordon, KC, 370
Brown, Fleming & Murray, chartered accountants, 104, 366
Brown, Harold advice to Harcourt Committee, 254; advises Cadman, 609, 625
Browne, Professor E.G., 201
Broxburn Oil Company Ltd, 134
Brunei, 539, 544
Buchanan, Sir George, Director-General of Port Administration and River Conservancy, Basra, 450
Buchanan, Sir George, Ambassador to Russia, 203
Buchanan, Mr, 64
Buenos Aires, 558, 560
Bukhārā, 22
Bunkering, 466; company for, 469-71
Burls, H.T., 33, 55
Burma, 3, 67, 82, 97, 105, 130, 133, 151, 243, 372, 454
Burmah Oil Company (BOC), 3-5, 12, 13, 113, 222, 257, 286, 305, 307, 310, 324, 539, 544; Admiralty fuel oil contract, 10, 60; amalgamation proposals with Company and Royal Dutch-Shell, 1921-24, 372-85; association with Royal Dutch-Shell, 11, 109, 172, 194, 239-47, 312, 463, 471, 510-11; connection with Company, 12, 13, 205-6, 264, 279, 296, 297, 302, 313, 510-11, 532-3; early Persian operations, 73, 75, 117, 133, 135, 145, 152-3, 163;'formation of Company, 92-6, 97-101, 102-7, 110, 112, 190; Government negotiations over Company, 169, 172, 181-4; Mesopotamia, 166, 194
Burmah-Shell Agreement, 1905, 162, 471
Burmah-Shell Ltd, 463
Burton, 1st Baron, Michael Arthur Bass, 51, 97
Bushire, 20, 24-5, 27, 285, 516, 565
Busk, H.G., 282-4

Cadman, J. (later Sir John, Baron Cadman of Silverdale), 210, 261, 380, 463, 535; Admiralty Oil Commission, 183; Chairman, 8, 12, 14, 296, 346, 348-9, 351, 634; Company management, 303, 305, 312-16, 333, 336, 337-41, 373, 382; concessionary activities, 542, 544, 547-8, 550-1, 555, 557-8, 560, 566-9; head of Petroleum Executive, 248-60, 307, 310, 354; in United States, 1921-22, 377, 475, 574-8, 580,

780

Index

582; marketing, 463, 506, 508, 510-14, 519; Persian negotiations: (a) London and Lausanne 1928, 596-8, 600-7; (b) Persia 1929, 607-9; (c) exchange of views, 612; (d) London and Paris 1931-32, 620-6; (e) expectations, 629-30; Persian visit 1926, 518, 588-9, 591-2; San Remo negotiations, 357-8; technical contribution, 399-400, 408-10, 414, 418, 420-1, 425-7, 436-7, 454, 456-7, 460, 540; TPC negotiations, 581-2
Cadman, W.H., 456
Caetani, Prince, 550
Cairo, 458
Calcutta, 286, 293, 466, 470
California, 1, 5, 139, 374, 634
Calles, President Plutarcho Elias, 7
Cambell, Andrew, 8, 133, 262; chooses Ābādān site, 122; consulting chemist at Putney, 275, 279; early refinery problems at Ābādān, 148-9, 163-4, 199; managing director National Oil Refineries, 453; manager refineries branch, 430
Campbell, M (later Sir Malcolm), 500
Canada, concessionary interest, 555, 561
Canadian Government, 176
Cannes, 61
Cape Town, 510
Capital Issues Committee, 220, 222
Capito, C.E., 264
Capitulations, 595
Cargill, David S., 3, 67-8
Cargill, J.T. (later Sir John): Company negotiations over Government shareholding, 168, 181, 183-4, 197, 354; attitude to early operations in Persia, 117, 120, 129-30, 143, 147, 149, 153, 175; attitude to Mesopotamian Concession, 166-7, 193-4; character, 372; management, 296-7, 302, 312-15, 320, 336; negotiations over Admiralty supply contract, 68-9, 77; part in formation of Company, 94-7, 101-7, 110, 116; Persian negotiations, 364, 367, 369, 372; response to BOC—Royal Dutch-Shell and Company amalgamation proposals, 239, 247, 257, 382, 385; shipping, 532-3; on Royal Dutch-Shell, 159-62, 164, 169, 172, 290
Carranza, President Venustiano, 7
Caspian Sea, 19, 27, 517, 570
Cassel, Sir Earnest, 53, 62
Celebes, 474
Central America, 552
Central Mining and Investment Corporation Ltd, 554
Ceylon, 160, 505, 510, 512
Chalmers, Sir Robert, 190, 198
Chamberlain, J.A. (later Sir Austen), 180, 296, 353-5, 589
Chamberlain, Neville (later Sir), on Churchill's proposals for withdrawal of Government from Company, 383-4
Chapman-Brown, J., 284
Chettle, E.A., 267
Chīāh Surkh, 58, 60, 62, 66, 74, 78, 151; during First World War, 268, 282
Chicago, 420
Chile, concessionary activity, 552; oil legislation in, 554, 557
Chillingar, 412
China, 28, 160, 474
Churchill, Clementine, 170
Churchill, G.P., 91, 572
Churchill, W.S. (later Sir Winston), 203, 238, 246; disposal of Government shareholding in Company, 10, 382-5; Government connections, 10, 12, 100-4, 194-201; management succession, 336; naval policy, 165-6, 170-1, 176; oil policy, 176-8, 211-2, 538; Persian participation in Company, 604-5; US interests in Mesopotamia, 582
Clarke, J.C., 310, 312-13, 374, 380, 500, 581
Clausen, A.C., KC, 254
Clavier, M., 618, 624
Clémenceau, Georges, President, 356-7
Clive, Sir Robert: negotiations for a treaty, 610; on Persian dependence on Rizā Shāh, 591; on Persian

781

'system', 590, 595; on Tīmurtāsh, 591, 607; succeeded as Minister, 626
Coal, 149, 158, 171, 245, 286-7, 469-70, 504, 634
Cobham, Sir Alan, 500
Cochin, 287, 466
Cocteau, Jean, 368
Colombia, 540, 542; concessionary interest, 543-4; Congress of, 556; oil legislation in, 554-7
Colombo, 286-7, 466
Colonial Office, 248, 380, 520, 539-40, 545-6, 561-6, 568-9; Mesopotamia, 581-2, 584-6
Comet, 85
Comins, Captain D., 409, 412, 418, 420
Commodoro Rivadavia, 558-9
Commonwealth Government of Australia, 465, 522-3, 525, 545, 547, 551
Commonwealth Oil Refineries Co., 523, 525, 551
Communism in Persia, 389; Persian Communist Party, 594
Companie Française des Pétroles, 584
Concessions Syndicate Ltd: Bakhtiari attitude towards, 122; BOC attitude towards, 81-2, 92, 107, 117; formation and terms of, 70-2; operations of, in Persia, 74-5, 77-81, 85-6, 88, 91, 126
Consolidated Petroleum Co. Ltd, 463, 512
Constantinople, 33, 165, 173
Constitutional Movement, 89, 139
Conti, Senator E., 550
Cooke, H.R., 519
William Cory and Son Ltd, 471
Cossack Brigade, 44-5, 89, 386
Cotte, Edouard, 29, 32-3, 39, 41, 103
Cotton, Sir Dodmore, 20, 21
Courchelettes Refinery, near Douai, 458, 479, 482
Cowdray, 1st Viscount, Weetman, Dickinson Pearson, 240, 291
Cox, P.T., 569
Cox, Major P.Z. (later Sir Percy), 121, 137, 143, 520; Khostaria concession, 570; negotiations with Shaykh Khaz'al, 123-6; post-war relations with Persia, 351, 362-5; Uqair conference, 562; war-time activities, 280
Cracking, 454-5; 'A.D.H.' process, 455; Burton process, 454; Cross process, 455; Dubb process, 455 Ramage process, 454
Crewe, 2nd Lord Haughton, 1st Marquis of, 173, 175
Crisp, Sir Frank, 99-100, 102, 199, 292, 366
Croatia, concessionary interest, 544
Cromer, 1st Earl of, Evelyn Baring, 97
Crowe, Sir Eyre, 581
Crush, Mr, 55
Cunard Line, 174
Cunningham Craig, E.H. 84-6, 282, 284, 409
Curzon, 1st Marquess of Kedleston, George Nathaniel: Baku, 25; Mesopotamia, 585; oil relations with US, 575-7; on amalgamation of BOC, Royal Dutch-Shell and Company, 381-3; Persian policy, 23, 351, 353, 386, 391, 571-3, 577; relations with French, 357; Viceroy of India, 60, 66, 75
Cyprus, 539, 544; concessionary interest, 543

Daily Chronicle, The, 112
Daily Express, The, 112
Dakar, 466
Dālakī, 25-6, 42, 93
Dalgety and Company, 523
Daly, Major C.K., 540, 566
Dalley, C., 273
Dalparī, 412
Dalton, W.H., 58-9, 67, 85, 282
Daraghwands, 67
Dār al-Funūn, 16
Darby, C., 142, 151
D'Arcy, William Knox, 5, 18, 42-4, 116-17, 206, 388, 632; BOC negotiations, 67, 69-71, 80-2, 87-8, 103-4, 157; Concessions Syndicate Ltd, 73-4, 77-8, 81, 83, 85, 87;

creation of a concessionary company, 50-4; early life, 30-1; formation of Company, 92-105, 107, 112-13; Government negotiations, 168-70, 173; loan for Company, 152, 190; Mesopotamia, 11, 159, 538, 545, 580; need for finance, 60-2; negotiations for Persian concession, 29-30, 32-4, 36, 38-41, 570; operations in Persia, 48, 50, 54, 57-60, 64, 66-7, 127, 143; Persian loan offer, 46-7; relations with associates, 71-2

D'Arcy Concession, 18, 24, 74, 402, 420, 430, 508, 570, 591; cancellation of, 7, 9, 11, 360, 588; Company responsibility for, 88, 96-104, 113, 144, 154-7, 171, 190, 202, 362, 371, 430; financing, 48, 50-4, 59-62, 69-72, 81; legal opinions on, 366-8, 370; negotiations for, 29-42, 48; revisionary negotiations, 600-3, 607-9, 612-16, 618-22; Russian objections to, 44-7, 60; terms of, 42-4, 56, 67, 76-7, 92, 98-100, 125-6, 144, 154-7, 280, 359, 362, 365-71

D'Arcy Exploration Company Ltd, 547, 552, 555-6

Dar-i-Khazineh, 132, 447-9

Dashtī, ᶜAlī, 605, 612, 615, 626

Dāvar, ᶜAlī Akbar: early opinion of Rizā Shāh, 589-90; hostility to his reforms, 594; Minister of Justice, 591; oil interests, 589; oil negotiations 608-9, 618, 624

Davidson, R.R., 135

Davies, R., 427

Debenham, A.S., 164

Dehlurān, 67, 412

Delhi, 286

Denmark, 462, 470, 474, 504

Depression, The, 348, 428, 444, 624, 626

Deterding, H.W.A. (later Sir Henri), 1; As-Is Agreement, 463, 508-14, 602-3, 634; BOC, Royal Dutch-Shell and Company amalgamation proposals, 376, 379; evidence to Harcourt Committee, 253-5, 257-9, 357; general manager, Royal Dutch Company, 1900, 4-5, 196, 238; Mesopotamia, 581

Det Forenede Olie Kompagin A/S, 470

Deutsche Bank, 4-5, 160, 165, 197, 258, 299, 356

Deutsche Petroleum AG, 494

Devonshire, 9th Duke of, V.C.W. Cavendish, 541

Dickson, Colonel H.R.P., 562

Diesel Oil, 458

Distillers Company Ltd, 459

Dobbs, Sir Henry, 58, 585-6

Dodero Concession, 558

Doheny E.L., 469

Dordtsche Petroleum Industrie, 159

Dorquain, 445, 447-8

Douglas, Dr J.A., 406

Drilling, 414, 417-8

Duff, E. Grant (later Sir Evelyn), 80

Dunstan, Dr A.E.: chief chemist, 457; responsible for research, 277, 279, 400, 452-5, 458-9;

Durban, 466

East Africa, 160, 474, 512

Eastern and General Syndicate, 370, 561-2, 564-5, 567-8

East Ham Technical College, 279

East India Company, 19-20, 606

East Indies, 3, 6, 43, 159, 474, 538

Economist, The, 323

Ecuador, concessionary interest, 544, 552

Egypt, 20, 23, 27, 97, 274, 508, 512; concessionary interest, 543-4

Elizabeth I, Queen, 19

Elkington, E.H.O., 438, 569

Ellerman, Sir John, 292, 469-70

Ellerman Line, The, 142

Ellis, Major-General, Sir Arthur, 51, 61

Elphinstone, Sir Howard, 53

El Pozon, 554

Entner, Marvin, 25, 44

Enzelī, 33

Ernakulam, 287

HMS *Espiégle,* 279

Ethiopia (formerly Abyssinia), concessionary interest, 561

Index

Euphrates and Tigris Steam Navigation Co., 286
Europäische Petroleum Union (EPU), 5, 197, 212, 218, 476, 494-5, 497
Europe, 3, 14, 26, 312, 320, 352, 391, 408, 462-3, 476, 509, 512, 514, 525, 527, 538, 540, 548, 552, 599, 619
Excess Profits Duty, 346, 368

Fairley, W.C., 317, 517, 592, 595
Farīd al-Saltana, appointed Imperial Commissioner, 366
Farmān Farmānfar, Prince, 65
Fars, 609-10
Fāteh, Mustafa Khān, 592, 618; audience with Rizā Shāh, 606
Fath ᶜAlī Shāh, 16, 20-1
Faysal, King, 451, 584-6
Fellowes, Ailwyn, 97
Fenton, F., 526
ss *Ferrara*, 161, 285, 288, 292
Fields, 119, 140, 143, 146-7, 153, 290; after the war, 318, 339, 397, 403, 406-7, 409, 420, 428, 430, 438, 444, 447-7, 455-6; war-time, 264, 268, 272-4
Financial News, The, 249
Financial Times, The, 182, 535
Finlay, Sir Cambell Kirkman, 152-3, 168, 183
Finlay, Fleming and Company, 117, 129, 152, 163, 286
First Exploitation Company, The, 53, 54, 71, 100, 103-4, 148, 353
First World Petroleum Congress, 420
Firūz (Prince) Mīrzā Nusrat al-Dawla: American capital, 573; attitude in Khūzistān, 597; attitude to Company, 389, 594; concessionary negotiations 1919-20, 365-9; disgrace, 610, 612; Europe visit, 352; in 1929 negotiations, 608-9; Khostaria concession, 571; negotiations for Persian Government shareholding, 353-4; oil interests, 580; service to Rizā Shāh, 591
Fisher, Admiral of the Fleet, Sir John Arbuthnot Fisher (later Baron Fisher of Kilverstone), 10, 59, 183; Chairman Royal Commission on Fuel and Engines, 152, 165, 171, 176
Fisher, Sir Warren: Persian participation in Company, 605; retention of Government shareholding, 385
Fleuriau, F.A. de, 356
Foster Wheeler Co., 458
France, 3, 14, 166, 202, 320, 606; Company activities in, 14, 320, 458, 462, 471, 474, 477, 479, 482-3, 489, 504, 506, 509
France, Government of, 29; Mesopotamia, 12, 242, 258-60, 582-4; Persia, 573
Francis of Teck, HSH Prince, 107
Frasch, Herman, 453
Fraser, W. (later Sir William, Baron Strathalmond of Pumpherston), 341, 506, 510
Freemantle, 466
Friesland, The, 292
Fuel Oil: Admiralty requirements, 12-13, 106, 147, 149, 158, 162, 167-72, 174, 176-82, 184-5, 199-201, 207, 466; Admiralty supplies of, 207, 211, 213, 262, 274-5, 285, 288, 290; BOC supplies of, 68-70, 82, 159; competition with coal, 7, 149, 469-70; markets for, 148, 162-4, 169, 286-7, 532; post-war, sales of, 470-1, 474, 477, 479, 482-3, 490-2, 494, 497, 505, 511, 516, 518, 520, 523; problems and research into, 277, 279, 452, 454; refinery yields, 430, 440, 464, 466
Furūghī, Mīrzā Muahmmad ᶜAlī Khān, 627

Gach Sārān, 8, 412, 428
Gardanne, General Claude, 20-1
Gardiner, James and Co., 299, 526
Garrow, Duncan: alternative concessions, 541, 558; management, 299, 302, 307; marketing, 492; production problems, 406, 414, 464; visit to Persia 1919, 308, 402-3, 429, 437; war-time service with Company, 206, 263, 272, 296, 298, 306

Index

Garson, William, 107, 129
Gas, 420, 421, 453; research on utilisation, 455-7
Gas Oil, 482-3, 494
Geddes, Sir Aukland, 377, 574-6, 578
General Asphalt Company, 5
General Strike, 483
Geneva, 51-2
Geophysical techniques, 427
George V, King, 196-7
Germany, 3; Company activities in, 476, 489, 494-5, 497, 504, 509, 606; interest in Persia, 73, 91, 173, 279-80, 351, 359, 573; post-war, 351
German Government, 197
Gibraltar, 466
Gibson, H.S. (later Sir Stephen): joins Company, 339, petroleum engineer, 413, multi-stage gas separation, 421; recycling, 422
Gīlān, 27, 351, 570
Gillespie, Andrew, 153, 264, 268, 272
Gillespie, Andrew and Sons, 197, 133
Gillespie, J., 1, 107
Gillespie, R., 526
Glasgow, 116-17, 129, 149, 177, 264, 296, 396, 526
Godar Landar, 424
Goddard, Rayner, 619
Gold Coast, concessionary interest, 543-4, 561
Golubev, 45
Gomez, President Juan Vicente, 554
Gorshakov, Prince Alexander Mikhailovich, 22
Gosselin, Sir Martin, 33
Graham, R.G. (later Sir Robert), 66
Grangemouth Refinery, 440, 483, 527, 532; Grangemouth, site of, 466
Greece, 505; concessionary interest, 544, 548
Greenway, C., (later Sir Charles, Baron Greenway of Stanbridge Earls), 12-13, 61, 323, 349, 351, 409; Ābādān refinery, 148-50, 152-3; acquisition of BP Company, 218-19, 291-2; Government oil policy, 239-41, 244, 247, 249-50; managing agents, 116-17, 129-30, 137, 139-41, 145-7, 154, 265-7, 307-9, 317-18;

BOC, 13, 206; Chairman, 12-14, 61, 204-5; character of, 94; concessionary activities, 542-5, 558-60, 575; evidence to Admiralty Committee, 158-9; finance and the Government, 211-14, 220-2, 310-11, 320, 328, 341, 348; formation of Company, 94-7, 101, 107; Government restrictions on Company, 352-4, 465, 539; Khostaria concession, 570-1, 574-5, 577-8; management, 296-9, 302-3, 305-6; management succession, 313-16, 333, 336; managing director, 116; marketing policy, 133, 150-1, 160-5, 285-8, 461-2, 464, 469-70, 474-6, 489-92, 500, 504, 509, 522, 532, 537; Mesopotamian concession, 166-8, 197, 580, 583; negotiations with Government 1911-14, 168-77, 181-5, 193, 196-99, 538; negotiations with Persian Government 1926-32, 359-63, 365-8, 370-1, 603; Persian operations, 262-4; Persian visit 1910-11, 135, 142-3, 155-7; post-war relationship with Royal Dutch-Shell, 356; research, 279; Russian action in Persia, 281; Shatt-al-ᶜArab negotiations, 450; shipping, 181, 292-4, 304, 526, 532-4; success of Company, 397, 634; view of Royal Dutch-Shell, 159, 172, 290; war-time relations with British Government, 207; Watson's initiative on amalgamation, 373, 378
Greene, Sir Graham, 239
Greene, Wilfred, KC, 619
Greenhouse, F.C., 595
Greenwood, Sir Hamar, 298, 357-8
Greenwood, W.E.C., 142, 264
Grey, Sir Edward, 81, 175, 180, 203, 241
Griffin, Sir Lepel, 26
Grindle, Sir Gilbert, 380
Grozny, 1
Grube, E.K., 44
Guatemala, concessionary activity, 552
Guinea, concessionary interest, 544
Gulbenkian, Calouste, 28, 258, 581, 583-4

785

Index

Gulbenkian, Nubar, 554
Gulf Oil Co., 13, 117, 555, 567, 569
Gulistān, Treaty of (1813), 21

Haes, Andrew and Sons, 101
Haft Kel, 8, 402, 417-20, 428, 447-8, 463, 508, 539, 603
Muhsin al-Shalash Hajj, 584
Hājj Raᶜis, 123-4, 126
Hall, Admiral Sir Reginald, 256
Halse, G.W., 284
Hamburg-Amerika Line, 164, 286
Hamilton, James: formation of Company, 93-5, 97, 100; in charge of Concessions Syndicate Ltd operations in Persia, 75, 79, 81-2, 87; role in Company's Persian operations, 96, 107, 116-17, 119-20, 123, 128-30, 133, 137, 139-43, 147, 149, 153, 157, 296; sales, 160-1, 163, 165; visit to Persia, 137, 139, 142-3
Hankey, Maurice, (later Sir), 242, 256, 581
HMS *Hannibal*, 59
Harcourt, Lewis, Viscount 252-3, 257, 357
Harcourt Committee, 237, 252-60, 351, 355, 358, 378, 465, 539, 581
Harding, President Warren, 575
Hardinge, Sir Arthur, 28, 33, 35-6, 39-41, 43-6, 56, 60, 62, 64, 72-3, 121, 157
Hardinge, Sir Charles, (later Lord Hardinge of Penshurst), 85, 90, 127, 239, 280
Hargraves, E.T., 53, 59
Harmsworth-Newnes Group, 82
Harris, Mr, 79, 85
Havard, Godfrey, 591
Hearn, A.C., 341, 555-6, 625
Heath Eves, H.B., (later Sir Hubert), 305, 341, 490-2, 500, 504-9, 525, 535, 548, 550
Heim, Dr Arnold, 565
Hejaz, concessionary interest, 544
Henderson, Arthur, 610
Henderson, Norman M., 134
Herāt, 21
Hidāyat ᶜAbbās Medhī, 607

Hoare, Sir Reginald, 626
Holland, 3, 497, 504
Holland, A.W.B., 66, 87
Holland, Sir Thomas, 171
Holley, A.E., 455
Holmes, Major Frank, 370, 540, 561-9, 586
Homelight Oil Company Ltd, 218
Honduras, concessionary interest, 544, 552
Hoover, Herbert, 576
Hopwood, Sir Francis (later Lord Southborough), 170-1, 196, 297, 354-5; Company director, 315
Hormuz, 24, 141, 282
Horne, Sir Robert, 255, 320, 358, 380
Hotz and Company, of Bushire, 24
House of Commons, The, 177, 203, 245, 248, 298, 310, 384, 396, 528
Hughes, W.M., 522, 547
Hull, 466
Hungary, 3, 427, 516; concessionary interest, 544

Iceland, 497
Idelson, V.R., 619
Il-Begī, 76, 79, 83
Il-Khānī, 76, 80, 83
Imām Jumᶜa, 65
Imām Rizā, 132
Imbrie, Robert, 579
Imperial Airways, The, 458, 599
Imperial Bank of Persia, The, 23-5, 29-30, 40, 42, 104, 360
Imperial Commissioner: Farīd al-Saltana (1918-23), 366, 619; General Antoine Kitabgi (1901-2), 42, 50; ᶜĪsā Khān (1923-32), 612, 623-4; Sādigh al-Saltana, Mutᶜamin Huzur (1905-07 and 1907-18), 92-4, 98-9 105, 366; Vincent Kitabgi (1902-05 and 1907), 54, 92
Imperial Defence Committee 1905, 41
Imperial Tanker Company Ltd, 292
Imperial War Cabinet, 465, 522
Inchcape, 1st Earl of, James Lyle Mackay: acquisition of BP Company, 218-19; bunkering, 469; BOC, Royal Dutch-Shell and

Index

Company amalgamation proposals 1921-24, 374, 379-80; finance and the Company, 211-13, 220-2, 264, 310-11, 319-23, 331; Government director, 9, 208, 210, 263, 297; Government restriction, 539; Harcourt Committee, 252, 255-7, 260; management, 315; managing agents, 307; Llandarcy refinery, 215-16; relationship with British Government, 352-4; resigns, 336; tankers, 532

India, 3, 12-13, 21-2, 28, 44, 68, 141, 159, 164, 171, 239, 242, 286-8, 299, 305, 372, 375, 474, 510-11, 544

India, Government of, 21, 62, 74-5, 168, 174, 176-7, 180, 242, 286-7, 380, 394, 539, 545

India Office, 173, 175, 260, 307, 375

Indiana, 1, 135

Indian Mutiny (1857), 21

Indian Ocean, 44-5, 287

Indian Public Works Department, 54

Indian Railways, 164, 286; Bengal-Nagpur, 286; Great India Peninsular, 287; Indian North Western, 286-7;

Indo-European Telegraph Company, 21

Institute of Petroleum Technologists (later Institute of Petroleum), 284

Inter-Allied Petroleum Conference, 356, 555

Inter-Departmental Petroleum Committee, 221, 273

Iraq (name adopted in 1920 vice Mesopotamia), 350, 508; concessionary negotiations, 333, 581, 582-7; dispute with Persia, 452, 538, 594, 597, 599; markets in, 500, 517, 520, 522; oil struck at Baba Gurgur, 417, 540; Transferred Territories, 412, 592; Uqair Conference, 561-2

Iraq Government, 451-2, 583, 585-6

Iraq Petroleum Company (1929) (earlier Turkish Petroleum Company), 339, 413, 463, 475, 522, 570, 603

Ireland, 350, 494

ʿĪsā Khān: Armitage-Smith Agreement, 619; Imperial Commissioner, 612; role in concessionary negotiations 1931-32, 623-4, 626; royalty and tax issues, 612, 618; under secretary, Finance Ministry, 369

Isfahān, 6, 19-20, 45, 74-7, 89, 203, 285, 388

Itaca Refining and Distribution Company, 560

Italy, 7, 587, 603; Company activities, 494, 504, 548, 550-1; concessionary interest, 544

Italian Government, 616; Mesopotamia, 358, 583

Jacks, T.L.: audience with Shah, 598-9; early days in Persia, 136, 264; distribution in Persia, 517-18, 520; joint manager Muhammara, 317, 388; negotiations over Naft Khana, 593-4; on Rizā Shāh, 625-6; Persian negotiations, 612-14, 616, 618, 623-4; relations with Tīmurtāsh, 597-8; 600, 606; resident director, 590, 592, 595-6; views on concessionary matters, 596

Jackson, J.H., 526

Jackson, H.Y.V., 438, 440, 456-7

Jacobs and Davies, New York, 107, 132

Jamaica, 539

Jameson, J.: early days in Persia, 145, 148, 264, 272; General Manager, Fields, 319; responsibility for production in Persia, 400, 407, 414, 417-18, 420, 422, 436, 438, 456

Japan, 160, 474

Jardine, Matheson & Company, 265

Jawdat, ʿAlī al-Ayubi, 583

Jellicoe, Admiral Sir John, (later 1st Earl), 182

Jenkin, John, 31, 48, 50, 53, 59, 77, 99

Jenkins, W. St. D., 208, 256, 302, 539

Jenkinson, Anthony, 19

Jones, Sir Harford, 21

Jones, J.H., 27

Joseph Lyons & Company, 60

Junaghān, 76

787

Index

Kamb, Hugo, 420
Karachi, 286, 293, 458, 466
Karbalā, 594
Kārūn, River, 23, 86, 120-2, 131, 155-6, 273, 423, 445
Kauffer, Macknight E., 500
Kavir Kurian Company, 580
Keeling, E.H., 582, 584-6
Kellaway, F., 358
Kellog, Co. M.W., 438, 455
Kemball-Cook, Sir Basil, 535
Kent, Marian, 204
Kenya, concessionary interest, 561
Kerosine: APC contracts for, 150-2, 161-2, 164, 169, 239, 290, 476; early markets for, 1, 3, 44, 133, 148, 161, 275, 287-8, 285; early refining problems with at Ābādān, 150-3, 158, 162-3, 173, 213, 274-5, 436-8, 474; post-war sales of, 470-1, 477, 479, 483, 490-2, 494, 497, 505, 508, 510-11, 516, 518, 520, 523, 525, 532; research into, 279, 452-3; yields, 430, 440, 464, 466
Kershaw, Sir Louis, 380
Khanaqin, 522
Khanaqin Oil Company (KOC), 520
Khīva, 22
Khostaria, Akikie, 27, 361, 570-1, 577, 579-80
Khostaria Concession, 570, 572-3, 575-6
Khuramābād, 518
Khurāsān, 351, 570
Khūzistān (formerly ʿArabistān), 284, 392-3, 597, 605, 627
Khūr Mūsa, 451
Kirkuk, 28
Kirmān, 20
Kīrmanshāh, 55, 64-5, 203
Kitabgi, General Antoine, 42-4; death of, 52-3; introduced to D'Arcy, 5, 29-33, 48, 157; negotiations in Tehrān, 33-6, 38-41; negotiations over concessionary company, 50-2; operations in Persia, 54-9
Kitabgi, Edouard, 51, 78, 92-3
Kitabgi, Paul, 51, 54, 92
Kitabgi, Vincent, 52-4, 61, 71-2, 74, 77-8, 82, 95, 98, 103

Knight, C., 142
Knox, Colonel S.G., 564
Korea, 160
Krasnovodsk, 22
Kūchik Khān, 351
Kurdistān, 27, 428
Kut ʿAbdallāh, 445, 447-8
Kuwait, 66, 121, 280, 370; concessionary interest, 539, 543, 545-6, 561-3, 565-70, 580

Laird, A., 421
Labour relations: replacement of Indians by Persians, 432-3; strikes, Indian labour, 432-4; terms and conditions, 432; training, 433
Lālī, 428
L'Alliance, 305, 476
Lamb, W.S., 140-2, 145-8
Lambert, George, 177
Lambton, Professor A.K.S., 18
Lamsdorf, Count Vladimir Nikolaiivich, 44, 46
Lansdowne, Henry Charles Keith Petty Fitzmaurice, 5th Marquis of, 33, 35-6, 42-3, 60, 62, 97, 320
Lausanne, Treaty of, 7
Lausanne, 519; negotiations at of Cadman and Tīmurtāsh, 600-3, 606, 612, 619
Laverton Refinery, 523, 532
Law, Bonar, 252, 323
League of Nations, 350, 584-5
League of Nations Boundary Commission, 584-5
Lees, G.M., 426, 428, 567
Le Mesurier, L.J., 455
Lesieur, Georges et Fils, 479
Liger, The, 451
Lille Bonnieres Colombes, 479
Lindsay, Mr, 274
Lindsay, Sir Ronald, 604
Lingeh, 285
Linklaters & Paines (from 1920), Messrs, 254, 366, 609
Lister-James, S.: chief geologist, 400, 409, 425, 428; early service in Persia, 144, 194, 282; in Papua, 547; in Colombia, 556

Index

Liverpool, 466
Llandarcy Refinery, at Skewen, near Swansea, 330, 430, 440, 453-5, 458, 466, 483, 532
Lloyd George, David (later 1st Earl Lloyd George of Dwyfor), 113, 323; Government negotiations, 178, 181, 183, 196; Mesopotamia, 351, 356-7; oil policy, 248-9, 377
Lloyd-Greame, Sir Philip (later 1st Earl of Swinton), 312, 546, 375-8, 380-2
Lloyd, J.B. (later Sir John): attitude to BOC, 511; bunkering, 469; Company finance, 321-2, 341, 392; concessionary interest, 554, 560; management, 299, 302, 336; managing agents, 125, 129-30, 137, 140, 144-5, 162; reaction to Firūz negotiations, 368; visit to Persia 1923, 318, 430, 456; wary on Cadman's Persian negotiations, 600
Lloyd Scott & Co., 116, 129-30, 135, 137, 141, 296
Lloyds Bank Ltd, 61-2
Lloyds Register, 469
Loan and Discount Bank (Russian), 44
Loftus, W.K., 24
London, 21, 32, 38, 40, 50-1, 54, 115-16, 118, 123, 129, 139, 148-9, 151, 165, 218, 262, 264-5, 268, 272-3, 302, 307-9, 317, 319, 330, 339-40, 364-5, 367, 372, 390, 396, 407, 420, 437, 456, 462, 466, 511, 519-20, 522, 543, 545, 563, 570, 574, 576, 579, 584, 600, 609-10, 612-13, 627
Long, Walter (later 1st Viscount Long), 248-9, 252, 357-8, 381-2, 543
Loraine, Sir Percy, 518; attitude to Shaykh Khaz⁽ᶜ⁾al, 393-4, 396; Khostaria Concession, 573, 579; relations with and view of Rizā Khān, 387, 390-2, 394-5, 588, 90; view of Persians, 386
Lorimer, Captain D., 79-81, 83, 85, 90-1, 121, 123, 126-8, 139, 282
Louisiana, 634
Lowther, Sir Gerard, 173
Lubricating oil, 458, 464, 471, 504, 518
Lumley & Lumley, 98, 105, 619
Lund, F.W., 205, 315

Lutfᶜ Alī Khān, 140
Lutyens, Sir Edwin, 305
Lynch Brothers, 75, 122, 141
Lynch, H.F.B., 51, 285

McCormack, Colonel, 517
McDouall, W., 125
McIntyre, M., 145
McKenna, Rt. Hon. Reginald, 159
McLintock, W. (later Sir William), 366, 626, 367-8, 370-1
McNaughton, D.M.G., 64
MacDonald, Ramsay, 384
MacDonald, W.R., 427
MacGowan, H.D. (later Sir Henry, 1st Baron), 253
MacIndoe, F., 286
MacLean, H.W., 41, 280
Macrorie, B.F.N., 96, 119, 143, 282-4
Madagascar: concessionary interest, 543-4; sales possibilities, 505, 512
Madras, 286, 293, 466
Maikop, 1, 471
Mainland, M.S., 456
Majlis (Persian Parliament), 7, 73, 89, 92, 121, 362; post-war, 352, 371, 392, 578-9, 590, 593-4, 602, 604, 607-8, 612, 624
Makrān, 282
Malamīr, 128
Malaya (Malāyer), 160, 474
Malcolm, Captain (later Sir) John, 20
Malkum Khān, Mīrzā Nāzim al-Dawla, 17, 22-3
Mallet, Rt. Hon. L. du Pan, (later Sir Louis), 91, 167, 170, 173-7
Malta, 466
Management Committee, 299, 302, 333
Manchester, 466
Manisty, Mr, 61-2, 82, 94-5, 98-103
Manning, Dr Van H., 541
Maracaibo Basin, 554-5
Marling, C.M. (later Sir Charles), 90, 121, 359, 362-3
Marmagao, 287
Marmatain, 85, 282, 412

789

Index

Marriott, Alfred W.L., 33, 35-6, 38-41
Marriott, G.W., 33
Marseilles, 466, 479
Marv, 22
Masira Bay, 562
Masjid i-Suleimān (formerly Maidan i-Naftûn), 8, 24, 55, 67, 74, 80, 85-8, 96, 114-115, 132, 138, 270, 425, 427-8, 430, 464; Company operations at, 121, 124, 139-40, 146, 157, 269; post-war activities at, 398-9, 402-6, 408-10, 413, 418-20; war-time operations at, 264, 273, 280, 282, 282, 294
Mattei, Enrico, 551
Mauritius, 160, 512
May, C.J., 421
Mayhew, A.G.H., 567
Mayo, H.T., 144, 282, 284, 425
Māzandarān, 27, 570
Meadhurst, Sunbury-on-Thames, Company research station, 279
Mehdī Khān ᶜAla-Saltana, 359-60, 362
Melbourne, 466, 523
Mendez, President Miguel Abadia, 557
Mesopotamia, 263; Company markets in, 285, 287-8, 306, 323, 479, 520; war-time activities in, 280, 288, 397
Mesopotamian Concession: Company concern for, 239, 241-2, 256, 258-9, 541, 543, 545, 548, 580-7; D'Arcy and, 94, 159-60, 166, 580; French interest, 12, 259, 551, 581-4; Government attitude towards, 355-8, 377, 580-7; Greenway negotiations for, 166-79, 193; TPC and, 12, 165, 167, 258-9, 566, 580-7; US interest in, 573-5, 581-3
Mexican Eagle Oil Company, 150, 181, 240
Mexican Petroleum Company (of Delaware), 469
Mexico, 7-8, 150, 177, 240, 243, 402, 469, 541, 572; concessionary activity, 544, 552; oil legislation, 557
Mexico, Gulf of, 527
Meyer, C.F., 513
Middle East, 12-14, 46-7, 89, 106, 115, 201, 258, 350-1, 356, 372, 398, 539, 541, 545, 561, 570, 572, 582

Miller, Gordon, 69
Millspaugh, A.C., 393, 517, 592, 609
Milner, Sir Alfred, 1st Viscount, 97
Ministry of Munitions, 215, 248
Mīrzā Husayn Khān, 17
Mīrzā Taqī Khān, 16, 630
Mombassa, 466
Moniteur Belge, 476
Monroe, Elizabeth, 204
More, Major J.C., 546, 562
Morgan, J., 586
Morgan, M. Jacques de, 27-30, 55
Morgan Brothers, Frederick, Edwin and Thomas, of Rockhampton, 31
Morgan, W.L., 421, 456-7
Morier, James, 386
Morning Post, The, 112, 384
Morris, F.G.C., 482, 500, 550
Moscow, 22, 352, 593, 622
Mosul, 356, 581-2, 584-6
Motor Trade Association, 488
Moulton, Fletcher (later Lord Justice Moulton), 61-2, 70, 72, 101, 103
Mount Morgan Mining Company, 31, 48, 60
Mountstephen, 1st Baron, George Stephen, 296
Muhammad ᶜAlī Shāh, 73, 89-90, 92
Muhammad Karīm Khān, 56
Muhammara (later Khurramshahr), 58, 75, 78, 88, 115-16, 121-2, 124-6, 129, 137, 141-7, 154, 212, 285, 299, 592; post-war, 317-19; Rizā Shāh period, 388, 546, 567; war-time, 264, 267
Muhandes al-Mamalek, 35-6, 38, 40
Muhtesham al-Saltana, 359
Muᶜīn al-Tujjār, 120, 155-6
Muᶜīn Humāyūn, 81
Mullāsānī, 445, 447
Murād Khān ᶜAlī, 83-5
ss *Murex,* 1, 152
Murray, Charles, 21
Murray, Sir Oswyn, 314, 385
Murray, R.A., 366
Musaddiq, Dr Muhammad, 600
Muscat, 121, 539; Company activities at, 285; concessionary interest, 546, 566
Mushīr al-Dawla, 36, 40, 369
Mussolini, B., 7, 509, 548, 550-1

Index

Mustauf ī al-Mamalek, 594
Muzaffar al-Dīn Shāh, 28, 35-6, 38-41, 45-6, 50, 73, 121
Muzahim Beg, 584
Mygind, Herr Edward, 91

Naficy, Dr Hassan, 519, 625
NAFT, 339
Naft Khana, 412, 417, 520, 592
Naft Safid (White Oil Springs), 144, 282
Naft-i-Shāh, 592, 599, 605, 613
Najaf, 56, 594
Najī al-Suwaydī, 583
Nash, Professor W.A., 561
Nāsir al-Dīn Shāh, 16, 23, 29, 121, 155, 570
Nāsir al-Mulk, 359
Nasīrī Company, 155
Nasrᶜullāh Khān, 78
National Bank (Bank Melli), 627
National Bank of Turkey, 160, 165, 167, 197
National Benzole Company, 504
National Oil Refineries, 453
National Provincial Bank, 104, 211, 235
Near East Development Corporation, 582
Neilson, Alexander, KC, 367-8
Neilson, R.G.: researches into refining problems, 148-52, 162, 164; return to London, 430; works manager, Ābādān, 153, 264, 274-5, 277, 279, 281, 308
Nejd, 562, 567
Neutral Zone, 565, 567
New Brunswick, concessionary interest, 543-4, 561
Newfoundland, concessionary interest, 544
New Oil Refining Process Ltd, 149
New York, State, 1
New York, City, 107, 141, 181, 475, 567, 575-6
New York Stock Exchange, 609
New Zealand, 160, 561; concessionary interest, 543

Nicaragua, concessionary activity, 552
Nicholl, Manisty and Company, 32
Nichols, E.H., 48; Company service in First World War, 206, 263, 296, 298, 306; concessionary interest, 546, 554, 563, 566-7, 579; distribution in Persia, 517; management, 302, 305, 307, 333, 336; managing agents, 317-18; Mesopotamian negotiations, 582-3, 585-6; Persian negotiations, 364; research, 453; Rizā Shāh's policy, 390-1, 393-4; visit to Persia 1920, 308, 429, 432
Nicolson, H.G. (later Sir Harold), 589, 592
Nigeria, concessionary interest, 543-4, 561
Nobel Brothers, petroleum industry interests, 1, 3-5, 538
Norman, Hermann, 389, 571-3
Norsk Braendselolje A/S, 470
North Africa, 505
North Persia Oil Concession, 27, 361; negotiations between Company and Standard Oil (NJ), 377, 475; negotiations on, 1918-24, 570-80, 582
North Persian Oils Limited (NPO), 571
Norway, Company activity, 462, 470-1, 474, 504
Novoe Vremya, 203
Nyasaland, concessionary interest, 544

HMS *Odin,* 279
Ohio, 1
Oklahoma, 398, 634
'Olex' Deutsche Petroleum-Verkaufsgesellschaft, 489, 494-5
Oliphant, L. (later Sir Lancelot), 362, 381-2, 394
Oman, 562
Omnium International de Pétroles, 477
'Open Door', 358, 372, 377, 573, 582-3
Orford, 5th Earl of, Robert Horace Walpole, 29, 97
Osborne, D.G., 586

Index

Oestereichische Naphta Import Gesellschaft of Austria (Oenig), 494
Ottoman Empire, 7, 19, 350, 538, 546, 567

Pacific Coast, 552
Pacific Ocean, 45
Packe, Sir Edward: amalgamation proposals, 379; Company finance, 322-4; Government director, 209; management, 315; management succession, 313-14, 336; Persian Government shareholding, 353-4
Paix et Cie, 479
Paix, Edmond, 500
Pakenham, Captain W.C. (later Admiral), 158
Palashovskii, S.E., 45
Palestine, 512
Palmer, F., 450
Palmer, Sir F.B., 50
Palmers Shipbuilding Company (Jarrow), 532
Pantepec Petroleum Company, 554
Papua, concessionary interest, 543-5, 547
Parent Syndicate, 51-2, 58
Paris, 29, 32-3, 61, 258-60, 309, 351, 368, 500, 522, 621
Parker, Alwyn, 173, 241-2, 250
Parliament, 181-2, 197, 199-201, 249, 297, 321-2, 374, 538
Parrs Bank, 104
Pascoe, E.H., 183
Pattinson, J.M., 339
Paulis, Count, 585
Pāzanun, 8, 418, 428
Peace Conference, 259-60, 356-7, 522
Peel, E.G.P., 387
Penney, S.M. and McGeorge, 104, 112
Pennsylvania, 1, 3, 28, 454
Persanaft, 517
Persia (Iran, official name changed 1936), 5, 9, 125, 243, 336, 350, 362, 365, 371-2, 523, 555, 587, 622, 631; Admiralty Commission visit to, 147; Cadman visits to (a) 1924, 340, 399, 436-7; (b) 1926, 591-2; (c) 1929, 440, 607-9; (d) 1931, 612; Company activities out of, 310, 320, 332, 538-9, 543-4; Company negotiations, 596-7, 600, 603; Company representation in, 592; Company research in, 456; Concessions Syndicate, 69, 71, 72-88; D'Arcy Concession, 29, 31, 33-41, 42-7, 271, 354, 361, 368, 508, 538, 583, 588; D'Arcy's operations, 48, 52, 54, 59-60, 62-7; distribution in, 514, 516-19, 527, 597; early concessions in, 24-8; economy of, 89, 599, 602, 606, 611, 615-16, 618, 622, 624-5, 630; exploration in, 144-5, 263, 282, 284-5, 400, 402-3, 406-10, 412-14, 417-22, 425-9, 459, 541; gas in, 455-7; Greenway's visit to, 135, 140-5; history of, 15-19, 386; management agents in, 129, 264-7, 296, 306-9, 317-19; management in, 339, 389, 396; marketing in, 285-6, 474, 514, 516-19, 527, 597; policy over Shatt-al-ᶜArab, 452; reaction to Company in Rizā Shāh period, 593, 599, 601, 604-5, 618, 627-8, 631; relations with Russia, 35, 39-40, 43-6, 73, 200, 203, 351-2, 389, 571, 579, 609; relations with UK, 9, 19-24, 35-7, 41-2, 73, 90-1, 167, 173, 175, 178, 180, 201, 203, 210, 212, 242, 258, 311, 351-2, 359, 387, 390, 392, 571, 573, 589; staff in, 400-2, 432-3, 436, 444-5, 449, 459; the Company in (a) pre-war, 6-7, 11-13, 96, 104, 114-8, 119-20, 122, 132-3, 148, 163, 173-4, 222, 230, 232, 244, 391, 398; (b) war-time, 256-7, 262-3, 268, 272-3, 281, 292, 294; (c) post-war, 302, 312, 323, 330-1, 352-3, 373, 375, 391, 400, 402-3, 406-10, 412-14, 417-23, 425-9, 430, 445-9, 540, 566; US interests in, 572-3, 576, 577-80
Persian Bank Mining Rights Corporation, 25-6, 28, 43, 60
Persian Commercial Act of 1925, 519
Persia (Iran, official name changed, 1936), Government of, 21; Armitage Smith negotiates for, 369-71, 619-20;

792

Index

attitude to Kostharia and other oil concessions, 370-80; Bakhtiari Khans, 67, 77-8; Cadman meeting with 1931, 612; Cadman negotiations with: (a) 1929, 607-9; (b) 1931-2, 620-5, 626, 7; D'Arcy Concession, 42-3, 46, 50-1, 53-4, 93-4, 98-100, 126, 163, 203, 359; de Morgan mission, 27; financial requirements, 616; internal relations with Bakhtiaris and Shayk Khaz͑al, 121, 125, 144, 280, 388, 391-5; Fīrūz negotiations on behalf of, 365-9; Naft Khana negotiations, 592-4; pipelines damage compensation talks, 358-62; relations with Company, 7, 9, 116, 145, 156-7, 387, 390-1, 396, 538, 591-2, 594-5, 596, 597-9, 606, 614-15, 619, 626, 628-30; relations with Russia, 45, 203, 572; relations with UK, 90, 392, 573, 576, 589, 610; Reuter concession, 25, 43; shareholding proposals for, 352-3, 599-605, 613, 615, 629-30; Wallace negotiations with, 363-5

Persian Gulf, 27, 42, 44-6, 66, 116, 126, 129, 141, 164, 173, 265, 279-80, 282, 285-8, 292, 471, 517, 540-1, 545, 562, 566, 570

Persian Legation, London, 99-100, 359, 576

Persian Mint, 42, 44

Persian Petroleum Exploration Syndicate, 50

Persian-Russian Treaty (1921), 389

Perso-American Oil Corporation, 578

Peru: concessionary interest, 544, 552, 554; oil legislation, 557

Petrol Control Committee, 247

Petroleum Aktiebolaget, 497

Petroleum Committee, 248

Petroleum Department (formerly Petroleum Executive), 375, 377, 380, 545, 581

Petroleum Executive, 14, 237, 247, 249-50, 255-6, 307, 310, 312, 351, 374-5, 465, 539

Petroleum Handels Maatschappij, 497

Petroleum Produkte Atkiengesellschaft, 494

Petroleum Review, The, 112

Petroleum Steamship Company Ltd, 218, 230, 294

Philipines, 160, 474

Philips, Sir Owen, 469

Phillips, Mr, 199

Philpotts, Ralegh B., 366

Pierce Oil Corporation, 469

Pipeline: Company's in Persia, 119, 200, 221; costruction of first, 130, 132-3, 145-6; post-war operations, 430, 445-9; Russian project through Persia, 44-7; sabotage of Company's in First World War, 240, 244, 280, 358-9, 361, 367, 543

Pirelli, Piero, 550

Pitkethly, R., 148-9, 151-2, 274

Plate, River, 552

Plymouth, 466

Poland, concessionary interest, 548

Pool Board, 249, 291, 305, 461

Port Arthur, 527

Port Said, 466, 510

Porteous, D.R., 135

Portugal, 505; concessionary interest, 548

Powell, F.E., 512

Powell, G.T., 82

Pravda, 626

Preece, J.R., 74-7, 80-1, 85, 87, 90-3, 97-9, 105, 112, 123

Pretyman, Rt. Hon. Ernest G., 97, 221, 296; BOC-Admiralty fuel oil negotiations, 68, 106; connection with BOC-D'Arcy negotiations, 60-2, 67, 157; on oil policy, 248, 255, 258-9, 377

Public Trustee, 218, 223, 230, 291

Pump installations, 487-9

Pumpherstone, 483

Pusht-i-Kūh, 28, 282

Pym, L.A., 412

Qaleh Dārābī, 55

Qaraneh, 280

Qasr-i-Shīrīn, 27, 42, 55-6, 65, 93

Qavām al-Saltana, 572

Qatar, 539

Index

Qazvīn, 19, 45
Qishm Island, 26, 282-3, 363
Queensland, 31; concessionary interest, 544
Qundak, 412

Rabino, Joseph, 23
Radiguet, Raymond, 368
Ram Hormuz, 26, 66, 80
Ramsay, Lord William Henry, 51
Ramsay, N.C., 130, 135-6, 140, 148
Rangoon: BOC refinery at, 67, 107, 122, 133, 135, 148-9; site of, 117, 153, 240
Ranking, Lt. J.G.L., 85, 139-40, 143-4, 146
Recycling, 421-2
Red Line Agreement, The, 567
Red Sea, 474
Redwood, Sir Boverton, 282, 400; adviser to BOC, 68-9, 83; adviser to Company, 8, 96, 105-7, 164, 168, 177, 184, 277; adviser to D'Arcy, 32-3, 48-9, 50, 54-5, 58, 62, 157; adviser to Concessions Syndicate, 70, 84-5, 87; Government adviser, 171, 221
Rendel, Palmer & Tritton, 450
Research, 398, 452-9
Réunion, 512
Reuter Concession, 18, 23-4, 29, 43
Reuter, Baron Julius de, 25, 42
Reynolds, George Bernard: character, 54, 73, 157; Company operations, 113-14, 116, 119-21, 128-9; first Persian visit, 48, 50-1, 53, 55-9, 62, 64; in Venezuela, 555; last Persian tour, 135-7, 139-40, 143, 145, 147, 274; negotiations with Bakhtiari Khans, 67, 74-6; negotiations with Shaykh Khaz ͨal, 123-4; operations in Persia for Concessions Syndicate Ltd, 70, 73-5, 77-81, 83-7, 90-2, 96, 272, 282, 388; second tour in Persia, 66
Rezā ͨiyeh (formerly Urumīyeh), 389
Richardson, A.J., 526
Richardson, F.D.S., 403, 406, 428

Ritchie, C., 130, 140-1, 143, 146-8, 157, 264, 400; character, 143
Rizā Shāh (earlier Rizā Khān): attitude to Company, 390-1, 538, 595, 598-9, 605-6, 609, 623; cancels Concession, 7, 628; character, 386, 390, 393-4, 588-90, 600, 610; coup d'état, 352, 386; dismisses Tīmurtāsh, 628; imposition of central authority, 6, 78, 351-2, 388-9, 391-5, 423; on Army, 573; on loans, 577; oil interests, 580; programme for Persia, 591, 594; relations with Cadman, 567, 592, 607; relations with Loraine, 387, 392; unpredictability, 625; visit to Ahwāz, 627-8
Robertson, J.R., 526, 535
Rockhampton, 30-1
Romania, 3, 5, 179, 510; concessionary interest, 544, 548
Romano-Americana (Romāno-Americana Societate Anonimā Spentru Industria Comerciul si Exportul Petrolului), 5
Rome, 548, 550
Romer, M.L., KC, 370
Rooka Channel, 451
Rosengart-Famel, M., 477
Rosenplaenter, C.B., 62-6, 70
Rothsdchilds, oil interests, 4-5, 61-2
Rothstein, Theodore, 571
Rotterdam, 1
Royal Air Force, 520
Royal Commission on Fuel Oil and Engines, 152
Royal Dutch Company, 1, 4, 13, 61, 159, 169, 220, 238, 243, 254
Royal Dutch-Shell Group, 4, 5, 181, 238, 240, 250, 299, 307, 506, 508, 522-3, 537-8, 543; amalgamation proposals, 237, 239, 243, 313, 371-84; Turkish Petroleum Company, 160, 165, 197; Consolidated Agreement with Company, 463; contracts with Company, 12, 295, 305, 431, 461, 474, 476; fuel oil supplier, 179; Government attitude to, 11, 170, 241-2, 250, 252-60, 356-7, 371; India agreement with BOC, 463; merger

794

Index

connection with BOC, 312-13, 471, 474-5; Mesopotamian interests, 356-7, 581, 583; reaction to Harcourt Committee, 253-60, 355-6, 357; reconciliation with Company, 463, 475, 494, 507-13, 533, 581, 603, 633-4; relations with Company, 8, 13, 158-60, 164, 167, 169-70, 176, 193, 196, 205, 212, 218, 241, 244-5, 251; South American interests, 254, 542, 554, 560
Royal Navy, 9, 60, 106, 158, 167, 170, 179-80, 207, 242, 288, 466
Royalty to Persian Government: Armitage-Smith, 369-71; Firūz negotiations 1919-20, 365-8; London and Paris negotiations on, 621; reaction to payment for 1931, 624, 626; Jacks on, 596; Wallace negotiations, 360-2, 364
Rumbold, Sir Horace, 51
Runciman, W., 1st Viscount of Doxford, 241
Rupento Company, 571
Russell, Lord John, 22
Russia, 166; attitude to D'Arcy Concession, 33, 38-40, 43-7, 60; objection to Government shareholding in Company, 203; production and marketing in, 1, 3-5, 16, 25, 27, 45, 47, 398, 510, 512-13; relations with Persia, 16, 21-4, 28, 35-6, 89-90, 200, 351-2, 389, 518
Russia, Government of, 28, 35, 38-9, 44, 518
Russian Ministry of Finance, 44
Russian-Persian Customs Treaty (1903), 45
Russian Revolution, 7, 281, 350, 362, 516

Saʿdābād, Treaty of 8 July 1937, 452
Saʿad al-Dawla, 92
Sādigh al-Saltana, Mutʿamin Huzur, 92-3; concern over formation of Company, 94, 98, 105; on workforce nationality, 153; relations with Company 1915-18, 360; resignation, 366
Sagwands, 67
St. Helier, Lady, 170
St. Petersburg, 40, 46
Sālār-i Arfā, 79-80, 83, 121
Saleh, Mullah, 562
Salisbury, 3rd Marquis of, 22-3, 26, 41
Samarqand, 22
Samsam al-Saltana, 75-6, 79-81, 83, 89
Samuel, Captain Walter, 2nd Viscount Bearsted, 379
Samuel, Marcus (later Sir and 1st Viscount Bearsted), 1, 117, 196; controversy over Government shareholding, 199, 238, 249, 253-6, 379; founds Shell Transport and Trading Company, 4-5; rivalry with Greenway, 239, 241, 249-50, 285
San Remo Treaty, 358, 581, 583, 583-4
Sardār Assad, Ḥājjī ʿAlī Qūlī Khān, negotiations for oil agreement 1906, 75-80, 89; 127-8
Sardār Bahādur, 128, 146
Sardār Jang, Sarum al-Mulk, 76, 81, 83
Sardār Muhtesham, 146
Sar-i-Naftak, 412
Sar-i-Pul, 56
Sasūn Husqual, 583-4
Sassoon, D. & Company, 25
Saʿud, King ʿAbd al-ʿAzīz ibn, 562, 565, 570
Saudi Arabia, concessionary interest, 546, 562, 570
Saunders, Major M., 573, 577
Sazanov, Serghei, 203
Scarborough, 10th Earl of, Aldred Frederick George Beresford Lumley, 296
Schniewind, Dr, 613
Schröder, J. Henry & Company, 25, 204
Schofield, E.W., 409, 412
Scotland, 14, 483, 487, 602
Scott, Sir Charles, 46
Scott, G.B., 119
Scottish Oils Ltd, 483, 487, 506
Scrimgeour, J. & A., 104, 112
Seamark, M.C., 272

795

Index

Selbourne, 2nd Earl of, William Waldegrave Palmer, 10, 60, 180, 296
Selbourne Committee 1904-05, 158
Shafagh-i Surkh, 605, 612, 615
Shāh ᶜAbbās, 15, 19-20
Shahāb al-Saltana, 76, 81, 83, 121, 127-8
Shāhīl, 388-9
Shalamzār, 75, 78
Shale Oil Industry in Scotland, 7, 179, 320, 368
Shand, S.J., 263, 406
Shardīn, 67, 74, 78-9, 85-6, 96
Shatt-al-ᶜArab, 121, 154, 161, 279, 288, 402, 533; dredging of, 499-52; Persian claims over, 594, 597
Shaw, R.G. & Company, 141, 160, 296
Shaw, Wallace & Company Ltd, 12-13, 68, 94, 117, 292, 302, 305; and the managing agents, 129, 137, 141, 296; marketing agency, 287, 466, 511
Shaykh ᶜAbdᶜallāh of Bahrain, 566
Shaykh Ahmad ibn Sabā of Kuwait, 546, 562-9
Shaykh al-Mulk, 51, 56, 58, 78, 92
Shaykh Khazᶜal, 115, 121-2; attitude during war, 280; land negotiations, 275; negotiations over Ābādān, 123-6, 144; post-war position, 351; relations with Rizā Khān, 387-96, 432
Shaykh Mubarak al-Sabā, 370, 549
Shell-Mex Company Ltd, 488, 505
Shell Transport and Trading Company (Shell), 1, 4, 13, 61, 70, 117, 206, 218, 220, 291, 487; amalgamation proposals, 239, 243, 247; Government policy, 170, 173-5, 218, 237, 239; Harcourt Committee, 253-60, 465; relations with Company, 158-60, 169-71, 172-5, 204, 240-1, 250, 465, 505
Shipping, 525-7, 532-5, 537
Shīrāz, 6, 66, 387
Shushtar, 25-6, 42, 55-6, 58-9, 66-7, 93; post coup d'état, 387, 392-3
Shuster, Morgan, 572-3, 576, 578-80
Siam, 160, 474; concessionary interest, 561
Sicily, concessionary interest, 544, 550
Silvertown, 149-50

Simnān, 26, 580
Simon, Sir John, KC, 367-8
Sinai, concessionary interest, 544
Sinclair, Harry F., 579
Sinclair Oil Corporation, 579-80
Singapore, 466
Sipahsālār Aᶜzam, 27, 570
Sirdar-i-Napht, 292
Slade, Admiral Sir Edward: attitude to BOC, Royal Dutch-Shell and Company amalgamation, 240, 242, 244-6, 250, 255-6, 260; Chairman Admiralty Oil Commission to Persia, 183, 194-6, 286; director of Company, 298, 314-15, 354, 523; Government director, 204-5, 208, 210-12, 214-15, 220-1, 263-4, 297; on Mesopotamia, 580-1; war-time service to Company, 273, 279
Smith, L. (later Sir Lancelot), 253
Smith, Dr George Otis, 542
Snow, T.M., 557
Snowden, Philip, 385
Soane, E.B., 268
Société Anonyme des Pétroles de Grozny, 476
Société Générale des Huiles de Pétrole, (SGHP), 327, 497
Société Navale de l'Ouest, 479
Soddy, Professor F., 457
Sol, Sig., 558
Solberg, Carl, 560
South Africa, 160, 474, 504-5, 512
South America, 11, 13-14, 374, 463, 508, 540, 542, 551-2, 555-8, 560, 587, 603, 634
Southampton, 466
South Oil Marketing Company Ltd, 519, 597
ss *Soya Maru*, 181, 199
Spain, 505; concessionary interest, 544, 548
Spearing, C.E., 436
Spring-Rice, Sir Cecil, 81, 90
Stamfordham, 1st Baron, Lt. Col. Rt. Hon. Arthur John Bigge, 196
Standard Oil Trust (Group), 1, 3-5, 13, 62, 68, 117, 159-60
Standard Oil of California, 567-8, 570

Index

Standard Oil Company of Indiana, 13, 454
Standard Oil Company (New Jersey), 13, 299, 307, 533, 538, 603; activities in UK, 218, 240, 250; association with Company, 376, 378-9; competition of, 285, 288, 372-3 465, 487, 537, 543; concessionary activities in South America, 548, 554-5, 557; interest in Mesopotamia, 197, 260, 581-2; involvement in Achnacarry discussion, 463, 475, 513; marketing association with Company, 475-6, 494, 505-7, 633-4; negotiations with Company on North Persia Oil Concession, 377, 573-80; negotiations with Russia, 513; technical appreciation of Company, 408-9, 421, 456
Standard Oil Company of New York (Vacuum Oil Company, later Mobil Oil Company), 13, 372, 508, 511, 513, 523
Stanley, Sir Albert, 249-50
Stansfield, R., 455
Stanley, Dr H.M., 459
Statist, The, 28
Stauss, Herr Emil, 197
Stephens, Sutton and Stephens, 525
Stevenson, Sir James, 380
Stewart, C.J., 218
Stewart, J.D.: BTC, 299, 303, 526, 532, 534-5; management, 302-3, 306, 312-16; managing agents, 318; probable chairman, 373; resignation, 333; subsidiary companies, 482
Stewart, W.A., 306
Stirling, R., 555
Stock & Mountain, Messrs., 193
Stock, H., 193
Strathcona and Mount Royal, 1st Baron of, Donald Alexander Smith, 70, 97, 101-2, 104, 107, 149, 152, 158-9, 173, 177, 183, 190, 199, 296
Strathcona estate, 324
Strick, F.C. & Company Ltd, 107, 141-2, 292
Strick, Scott & Company Ltd (managing agents): activities to First World War, 142, 149, 153, 296; early marketing, 286, 288, 323; liquidation of, 318; post-war situation, 306-9, 317; war-time service, 265-6
Sudan, concessionary interest, 544, 561
Suez, 160, 293, 466; refinery at, 240, 274, 291
Suez Canal, 1, 21, 287, 527
Suhib Beg, 584
ss *Sultan van Koetei*, 150
Sumatra, 1, 43, 54
Sunbury, 436, 452-3, 455-9
Sunderland, 466
Susa, 27
Svenska Bensin, 497
Swan Hunter, Messrs, 293, 532
Swansea, 212; Llandarcy refinery near, 214-17, 305, 373, 466, 527
Sweden, 497
Switzerland, 494, 504
Sykes, Brigadier (later Sir Percy), 359
Sydney, 523
Sykes-Picot Agreement, 242, 356
Syria, concessionary interest, 512, 544

Tabātabāī, Sayyid Ziyā al-Dīn, 351-2
Tabrīz, 6, 19, 27, 89-90, 593
Talbot, Major Gerald, 23
ss *Tangistan*, 151-2, 162
Taqīzādeh, Sayyid Hassan Khān, 612, 615; involved in oil negotiations, 623-4; relations with Timurtāsh, 616, 625
Tashkent, 22
Taylor, J.E.J., 500
Teagle, Walter C.: As-Is Agreement, 463, 508-10, 513-14, 602-3, 634; discussions with Company in 1922, 475, and 1927, 512; Mesopotamia, 586
Teapot dome scandal, 579
Tehrān, 6, 19, 21-4, 26, 28, 32-3, 35-6, 44, 50-1, 54-7, 67, 72, 77, 80, 89-92, 100, 105 115-16, 121, 126, 139, 155-6, 317, 353, 358-60, 362-5, 367, 369, 572; post coup d'état, 387-91, 393-5, 517-19, 570-1, 573, 579-80, 588, 591-5, 597, 605-7, 612, 615-16, 619, 622-5, 627

Index

Teleki, Count Paul, 585
Tembi: fire disaster at, 274; power station, 107, 146, 414, 434; pumping station at, 445, 447; separator tanks at, 421
Texas, 1, 5, 69, 179, 634
Texas Oil Company, 13, 372
Thole, Dr F.B., 279, 400, 453-4, 457
Tholozan, Dr, 46
Thompson, R.R., 264, 272, 273, 282, 403, 406-7
Thompson, Commander W.A., 554
Thomson, G., 274
Thorpe, Dr J., 456-7
Tiarks, F.C., 204, 220, 315
Tidewater Pipeline Company, 13
Tiflis, 33
Tigon, The, 451
Times, The, 182, 201, 203, 249, 332, 377, 384-5
Timor, concessionary interest, 543-4, 561
Tīmurtāsh, Mīrzā Abdul Husayn, 580; attitude to Company, 598-9, 605-6; Cadman on, 604; character, 620; concessionary proposals, 612-17, 619; heart attack, 627; instrument of Rizā Shāh's programme, 591, 595, 606-7; interest in Kavir Kurian Company, 580; Naft Khana negotiations, 593-4; negotiations in Europe 1931-32, 619-27; negotiations in Persia 1929, 607-10; Persian distribution, 519; relations with Jacks, 597-8; relations with Rizā Shāh, 610, 622; rivalry with Taqīzādeh, 616, 625; talks in London and Lausanne, 599-603
Tirana, Treaty of, 548
Tobacco Régie, 18, 29, 43
Torrence, D.W., 26
Transjordan, 350
Transferred Territories, 592, 599
Trebizond, 21
Trevor, Colonel A.P., 546
Trinidad, 5, 361; concessionary activity, 552
Trinidad Leaseholds Ltd, 554
Trumble & Company, Messrs, 455
Tūl-i Khayyāt, 132, 448

Turkey, 7, 23, 28, 56, 71, 590, 595, 603; oil concessions in Mesopotamia, 43, 101, 165-7, 583-5; war-time danger to Company, 279-80, 450, 452
Turkish Government, 450
Turkish Petroleum Company (later Iraq Petroleum Company, 1929), 12; Cadman, Chairman of, 509, 603; Company and, 166-9, 197, 544-5; formation 1911, 160, 165; French shareholding in, 258-60, 357-8, 581; Government negotiations over, 165, 193, 197, 357; Italian interest, 550-1; negotiations with Iraq Government, 333, 580-7; oil struck at Baba Gurgur, 540; reconstitution 1914, 197, 258; Red Line Agreement of, 567; US shareholding in, 378, 382, 581
Turkomānchay, Treaty of (1828), 16
Tuticorin, 287, 466
Tyne, The, 293, 466

Ulemâ (mullahs, religious dignatories), 56, 65
Umerse, Wallahdas, 285
Union Oil Company, Delaware, 374
Union Petroleum Products, 487
United Kingdom (Great Britain), 3, 166, 240-1, 361, 634; marketing in, 5, 13-14, 179, 220, 240-1, 245, 292, 305, 341, 461, 482-3, 487-9, 500, 504-6, 512, 514, 527, 634; oil legislation in, 248; plant and machinery from, 457; relations with Persia, 19-24, 28, 47, 386; university courses in, 433
United Kingdom (British) Government: amalgamation proposals, 371, 373, 374-85; attitude to D'Arcy Concession, 60, 85, 90-1; Cadman's anxiety over concessionary negotiations, 627; Company concessionary activity in Persian Gulf, 541, 545-6, 562-6, 568-9; Company management, 295-8, 307, 312-14; creation of Petroleum Executive, 248-9; effect of shareholding in Company, 7-12, 157, 159, 191, 201-4, 210, 235, 261,

798

312, 348, 396, 463, 540-1, 551, 554, 557, 587, 595, 599, 603-4, 632-3, 607; exploration in Papua, 547; finance for Company, 210-14, 218, 220-3, 235, 309-11, 319-24, 331, 346; Harcourt Committee, 252-60; Mesopotamian Concession, 167, 355-8, 539-40, 545, 580-6; North Persian concession, 570-80; oil for the Navy, 158; oil policy, 204, 206-7, 235, 237-42, 243-7, 249-51, 262, 297-8, 350-1, 355-6, 358, 371, 373; Persian Government shareholding in Company, 352-4, 604-5; refinery priority, 214-17; relations with Bakhtiari Khans, 126-7; relations with Persian Government, 35, 41, 90-1, 351-2, 359-60, 391-2, 589, 610, 615; relations with Shaykh Khazᶜal, 121-3, 125-6; response to purchase of BP Company, 217-19; responsibility for Company, 207-10, 266, 297-8, 352-5; restrictions on Company, 217-19, 256-7, 465, 539; shareholding negotiations, 113, 165-70, 170-5, 176-81, 181-85, 193-201; Shatt-al-ᶜArab, 450; view on non-Persian concessions, 538-41; war-time demands on Company, 275, 280-1, 288, 290;

Foreign Office, 353, 572; Arabian concessions, 545; assistance to D'Arcy, 33, 85, 91, 116; attitude to Company-BOC-Royal Dutch-Shell association, 237-8, 240-2, 245-6, 250, 252, 259, 371, 373-85; Company Persian negotiations, 353, 597, 604; concern over Persian management, 145; departmental disputes, 539; French Government, 356-7; Mesopotamia, 152, 165-9, 173, 193-4, 197, 580-2, 584-6; negotiations with Shaykh Khazᶜal, 123, 394; North Persian concession, 571, 573, 576, 579; Persian customs and telephones, 155, 157; Preece, official of, 74, 80; relations with Persia, 21-2, 26, 359, 362-3, 365, 572; support for Company, 170, 172-6; Venezuelan concession, 554;

Treasury, 45; Company-BOC-Royal Dutch-Shell amalgamation proposals, 373, 375, 380, 383, 375; Company finance, 211-14, 221-2, 310-11, 319-23; Harcourt Committee, 252, 255-6; home refinery, 216-17; managing agents, 307; Persian participation in Company, 604-5; restrictions on Company activities, 465, 539, 544; shareholding negotiation with Company, 179-80, 193, 195, 198-9, 207; visited by Tīmurtāsh, 624;

Ministry of Transport, 488 ·

United Kingdom Legation in Tehrān, 34, 36, 80, 90, 116-17, 154-5, 570, 572, 591

United States (America), 6, 254, 487, 538, 567; contractors, 438; drillers from, 91, 417; interest in North Persia Concession, 570, 572-6; interest in the Middle East, 539, 581; Mesopotamian interest, 259, 358, 581-3; oil in the Middle East, 539-40; oil prices, 613; oil reserves fears, 541-2; oil supplies from, 5, 144, 213, 216, 220, 252, 361, 368; Open Door controversy, 376-9; processes from, 453, 455, 457; production, 1, 3-4, 135, 271-2, 398, 412-13, 463, 513; pumps from, 466; royalty rate, 43

United States Government, 379, 542, 574, 577, 582

State Department, 12; Mesopotamian Concession, 582; North Persia Concession, 573, 576-7

United States Bureau of Mines, 541
United States Geological Survey, 542
Universal Oil Products Ltd, 455
Uphall, 455, 483
Uqair Conference, 561-2, 564
Uraba, 556

Vali of the Pusht-i-Kūh, 390
Vansittart, Robert (later Sir), 381, 383, 554, 572, 604

Index

Venezuela, 5, 254, 374, 511, 540, 552; concessionary interest, 543-4, 552; oil legislation in, 554-7
Victoria, 523
Vusūq al-Dawla, 354, 593; Prime Minister, 362-3, 368

Wais, 280
Waley-Cohen, R. (later Sir Robert), 10, 150; BOC, Royal Dutch-Shell and Company amalgamation 1915-18, 240-1, 290; 1921-5, 372, 379, 382; contract negotiations with, 150, 159-62, 165, 169, 172, 175, 181; co-operation with R.I. Watson, 206, 239, 372; marketing negotiations with Heath Eves, 507-8; South America concessions, 560
Wallace, C.W., 68-9, 82, 206, 296, 95, 108, 112, 116-17, 139; negotiations with British Government, 168, 181, 183-4; Persian operations, 120, 123, 137, 143, 145, 153; role in formation and management of Company, 94-7, 99-103, 105-7, 297
Wallace, Colonel C. Willoughby, 363-5, 570
Walpole, C.A.: early days in Persia, 129, 136, 142, 147, 157; in charge of refinery department, 150-1; in charge of managing agents, 153, 194; wartime service, 264-6, early marketing, 285; post-war service, 308; in France, 309
Walters, Mr, 87
War Cabinet, 580-1
War Office, 450
Ward, Col. John, 451
Ward, T.E., 557
Washington, 377, 572, 574-5, 578
Washington Conference, 376-7
Washington Gray, K., 428
Wassmuss, Herr, 280
Waterkeyn, M., 477
Watson, F.G., 544, 555
Watson, R.I., 82, 544; amalgamation advocacy, 372-6, 379, 382, 385, 476; BOC and Royal Dutch-Shell trading agreement, 474-5, 507, 509-11; co-operation with Waley-Cohen, 206, 239, 372; discussion with Standard Oil (NJ), 475-6; management of Company, 302, 306, 313-14; tankers, 532
Watts, W.T., 305, 523
Weakley, E., 380, 383, 581
Weatherhead, W.R.A., 284, 558, 561
Weir, Messrs G. & J., 107, 130, 135, 145
Wellman, Guy, 578
Wembley Exhibition, 339
Wheeler, Professor R.V., 457
Whistler, Rex, 500
Willans, C., 55, 120, 137, 143
Williamson, T.F., 428
Wilson, Lt. A.T. (later Sir Arnold): acting consul Muhummara, 144, 153, 156; High Commission in Mesopotamia, 306-7, 520, 582; joint manager, Muhammara, 309, 316-17, 387-8, 592; meeting with Rizā Khān, 391; Persian Gulf concessions, 540, 546, 563, 566-8; service with consular guard, 85, 91; South American concessions, 555-7, 560; vice-consul in Ahwāz, 115, 125, 137
Wilson, Woodrow, President, 350
Wirsen, Carl-Einar Thare de, 585
Witte, Count Sergei Juliivich de, 44, 46
Wolff, Sir Henry Drummond, 5, 22, 23, 26, 28, 30, 50-4; action whilst minister in Tehrān, 29; financing the Concession and relations with D'Arcy, 61-2, 71, 82; role in D'Arcy Concession, 31-3, 35, 41, 48, 157
World War One 1914-18, 12, 14, 397-8, 402, 445, 450, 520, 561, 487, 633
Wright, J.L., 151, 282
Wyllie, B.K.N., 550, 552, 567
Wynne, Sir Trevredyn, 286, 315

Yacimientos Petroliferos Fiscales, 558
Yarrow, Messrs, 281
Yasin Pasha, 583-4

Index

Yates, Colonel, 538, 556
Yatim Muhammad, 562
Yazd, 203
Yorkshire Post, The, 534
Young, Dr James, 7
Young, J.H.M., 135
Young, Dr M.V., 116, 119, 140, 143, 157; adviser to Cadman, 600-3, 608; in charge of Company medical service, 339; negotiations with Khans 1909-11, 127-8, 146; post coup d'état developments in Persia, 388-90, 394; war-time service in Persia, 264, 266, 280
Younger, Robert (later Lord Blanesburgh of Alloa), KC, 72, 99

Yugoslavia, concessionary interest, 548
Yusuf Khān, 140

Zaharoff, Sir Basil, 479
Zāhedī, General Fazullah, Governor-General of Khūzistān, 396
Zante, Island of, concessionary interest, 543
Zanzibar, 160
Zeloi, 428
Ziegler & Company, 18
Zinoviev, Gregory, 389
Zinoviev, Ivan Alekseiivich, 24
ss *Zoroaster,* 4
Zuhāb, 27, 55, 58